荔波县志

（1978-2008）

荔波县地方志编纂委员会　编

方志出版社
Publishing House of Local Records

图书在版编目（CIP）数据

荔波县志. 1978—2008 / 荔波县地方志编纂委员会编. -- 北京：方志出版社，2017.3

ISBN 978-7-5144-2380-8

Ⅰ. ①荔…. Ⅱ. ①荔… Ⅲ. ①荔波县—地方志—1978-2008 Ⅳ. ① K297.34

中国版本图书馆 CIP 数据核字（2017）第 054353 号

荔波县志（1978—2008）

编　　者：荔波县地方志编纂委员会
责任编辑：张　颢
出 版 人：冀祥德
出 版 者：方志出版社
地址　北京市朝阳区潘家园东里 9 号（国家方志馆 4 层）
邮编　100021
网址　http://www.fzph.org
发　　行：方志出版社发行中心
电话　（010）67110500
经　　销：各地新华书店
印　　刷：昆明鹰达印刷有限公司
开　　本：889 × 1194　　1/16
印　　张：64.25
字　　数：1630 千
版　　次：2017 年 3 月第 1 版　　2017 年 3 月第 1 次印刷
印　　数：0001 ~ 2300 册
ISBN　978-7-5144-2380-8　　　　定价：488.00 元

序

当前，在以习近平同志为核心的党中央的坚强领导下，全国各族人民正在全面建成小康社会的决胜阶段奋勇向前、阔步迈进。全面建成小康社会，最艰巨最繁重的任务是在革命老区、民族地区、边疆地区、贫困地区。消除贫困、改善民生、实现共同富裕，是中国特色社会主义的本质要求，是中国共产党的重要使命。为了全面实现小康，党中央高度重视扶贫开发工作，全力推进脱贫攻坚工程，实施精准扶贫、精准脱贫。习近平总书记明确提出，全面实现小康，一个民族也不能少，不能落下一个贫困家庭，丢下一个贫困群众。扶贫开发是个系统工程，发展是第一要务，只有发展，因地制宜找准路子，才能最终实现精准扶贫、精准脱贫。“治贫”必先“治愚”，在加强经济和基础设施建设、提高教育水平等方面的同时，扶贫开发还要注重文化扶贫，特别是通过挖掘革命老区、民族地区、边疆地区、贫困地区的文化内涵、历史底蕴、地情资源，让广大干部群众了解地情、了解历史、了解本地区的优势和劣势，在思想上脱贫，尤为关键。

赓续不断地编修地方志是我国独有的优秀文化传统，绵延千年而不断。党中央、国务院高度重视地方志工作，近几年来，习近平总书记、李克强总理、刘延东副总理作出了一系列的重要指示。2015 年 8 月，国务院办公厅印发《全国地方志事业发展规划纲要（2015—2020 年）》（以下简称《规划纲要》），明确要求到 2020 年必须全面完成第二轮修志规划任务，这是全国地方志工作在全面建成小康社会进程中的硬性任务，也是全国地方志系统为全面建成小康社会的献礼。届时，将同步实现省省有省志、市市有市志、县县有县志，这不仅在中国文化发展史上是绝无仅有的，在世界文化发展史上也是罕见的。从目前来看，要实现这一目标任务，还存在不少困难和问题，特别是民族地区与贫困地区，面临着缺乏人才、资金等诸多困难。实现到2020年必须全面完成第二轮修志规划任务，一个省、一个市、一个县都不能少。自 2015 年 8 月，经中国地方志指导小组批准，中国地方志指导小组办公室启动民族地区与贫困地区志书出版资助工程（以下简称“资助工程”），对经国务院扶贫开发领导小组办公室认定的国家级贫困县（区、旗、县级市），中西部地区、少数民族边疆地区、经济欠发达地区存在出版经费困难的省市县三级综合志书进行出版资助。截至目前，已经确定资助两批 20 多部志书。2016 年 4 月，该工程成功入选国家新闻出版广电总局实施的“十三五”国家重点图书、音像、电子出版物出版规划项目。当前正处于全面推进扶贫开发工程的攻坚阶段，深入推进资助工程，是全国地方志系统配合推进精准扶贫、精准脱贫的重要工作，必须引起高度重视。

资助工程是地方志系统的政治工程。革命老区、民族地区、边疆地区、贫困地区蕴含着极为丰富的文化内容，编纂出版志书，对于继承和发扬优秀传统文化、民族文化、革命文化，加强民族团结、促进当地经济社会建设意义重大。革命老区、民族地区、边疆地区、贫困地区的志书是充分展示在中国共产党领导下这些地区经济社会建设取得的巨大成就、各族人民生活幸福安定的历史依据。特别是边疆地区的志书，是历代王朝、社会主义新中国对该地区行使主权的文化宣示，是真实记录边疆地区与祖国一脉相承、荣辱与共的重要载体。《规划纲要》明确要求到2020年全面完成第二轮修志规划任务，是党中央、国务院对各级政府和地方志工作机构的政治要求，必须不打折扣坚决完成，革命老区、民族地区、边疆地区、贫困地区也不能例外。资助工程既是全国地方志系统的文化扶贫工程，又是确保到2020年全面完成第二轮修志规划任务的推进工程，具有重要的政治意义。

资助工程是促进民族地区与贫困地区文化建设的基础工程。地方志书是全面系统地记述本行政区域自然、政治、经济、文化和社会的历史与现状的资料性文献，记述内容包罗万象，记述对象丰富多彩，是对一个地方的文化普查和历史资料的全面梳理。一个地方的经济社会建设，离不开文化支持。发展是硬道理，只有真正实现全面、协调、可持续发展，才能最终实现小康。与此同时，发展也必须是有序的而不是盲目的，必须是实事求是的而不是凭空设想的，必须是因地制宜的而不是照搬照抄的。实践证明，脱离当地的自然条件、历史基础、文化传承、人文习俗等搞所谓的建设，要么是盲人摸象、坐井观天，要么是揠苗助长、掩耳盗铃，要么是削足适履、画蛇添足，最终会落得个水土不服、无疾而终。对于民族地区与贫困地区来说，立足本地的资源、市场、人文旅游等优势，因地制宜找准发展路子，是确保科学发展的首要任务。民族地区与贫困地区，尤其是那些自古以来还没有编修过志书的地区，开展志书编纂既是对当地自然、政治、经济、文化、社会、生态等方面的发展历史、发展脉络、发展规律的全面摸底和调查，又是总结历史经验、汲取历史教训、挖掘历史智慧的全面梳理和探求。通过学习、利用地方志书，让各级领导干部、广大人民群众了解当地的历史、了解实实在在的地情，从历史中汲取营养和智慧为现实提供借鉴和服务，是确保民族地区与贫困地区发展不走弯路、不走冤枉路的有效手段。

资助工程是全国地方志事业协调发展的促进工程。第五届中国地方志指导小组成立以来，一直把走基层、探实情作为一项重要任务，截至目前，已经到30个省（自治区、直辖市）开展了调研。通过座谈、实地考察等多种形式，充分了解了当前全国地方志事业发展面临的主要困难和问题。其中，区域发展不平衡，中西部地区特别是边疆少数民族地区地方志工作与东部地区相比还存在不少差距，是制约全国地方志事业实现全面、协调、可持续发展的瓶颈所在。有的地方甚至出现了花费了大量的人力、物力，经过十余年的艰辛努力编纂出志书，因为缺乏出版经费迟迟未能出版的状况。正是基于以上了解到的情况，中国地方志指导小组及其办公室才下定决心启动资助工程。到2020年全面建成小康社会时，地方志事业区域发展不平衡问题必须得到妥善解决，这也是深入贯彻《规划纲要》的应有之义。而作为主业的修志编鉴，到2020年全面完成第二轮修志规划任务、实现综合年鉴编纂全覆盖的“两全目标”，是中西部地区特别是边疆少数民族地区地方志工作发展的重中之重。从现实意义来说，资助工程对于实现全国地方志事业全面、协调、可持续发展具有重要的促进作用。

在党中央、国务院的高度重视下，全国地方志事业发展迎来重大战略机遇。越是发展的关键时期，越要有大局观，越要从全国一盘棋的角度考虑问题。《规划纲要》作为顶层设计，确定的各项目标任务都要落到实处，而作为“两全目标”之一的到2020年全面完成第二轮修志规划任务，实现省、市、县一个都不能少的目标，是关键中的关键。希望借助资助工程的深入推进，进一步引起全国地方志系统对实现“两全目标”的重视，确保按期保质完成，用志书客观而忠实地记述中国共产党人带领全国各族人民全面建成小康社会的光荣与曲折历程，为全面建成小康社会贡献“志”礼。

是为序。

中国社会科学院院长、党组书记
中国地方志指导小组组长　王伟光

2016年10月于北京

民族地区与贫困地区志书出版资助工程领导小组

组　　长：王伟光　中国社会科学院院长、中国地方志指导小组组长

常务副组长：李培林　中国社会科学院副院长、中国地方志指导小组常务副组长

副 组 长：冀祥德　中国地方志指导小组办公室主任

成　　员：刘玉宏　中国地方志指导小组办公室副主任

邱新立　中国地方志指导小组办公室副主任

民族地区与贫困地区志书出版资助工程领导小组办公室

主　任：冀祥德　中国地方志指导小组办公室主任

副主任：邱新立　中国地方志指导小组办公室副主任

成　员：于伟平　方志出版社总编辑

陈　旭　中国地方志指导小组办公室方志处处长

李　沛　方志出版社首席编辑、省志编辑部主任

徐　宏　方志出版社地方史编辑部副主任

王丹林　中国地方志指导小组办公室方志处副处长

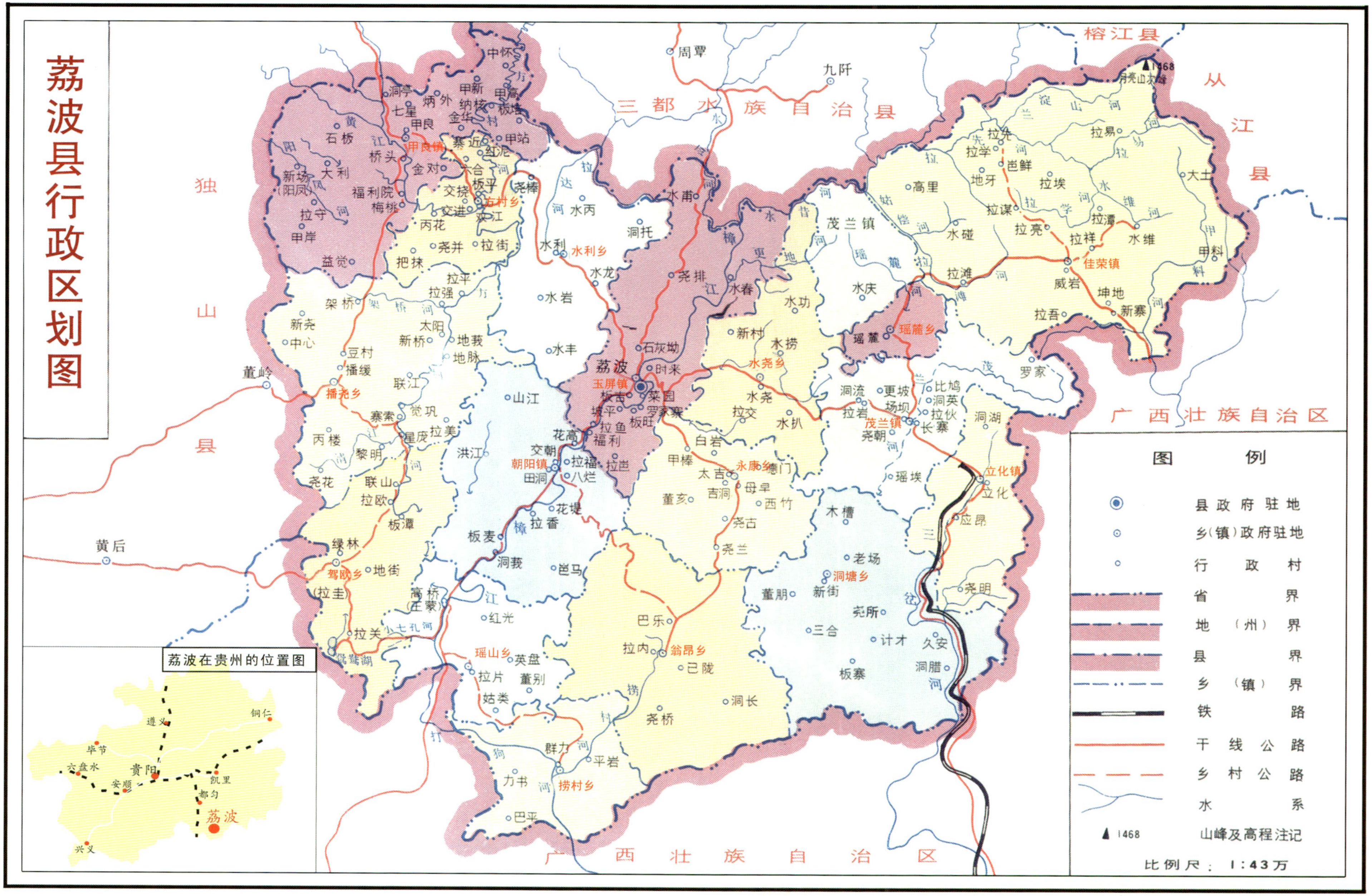

审图号黔S(2005)033

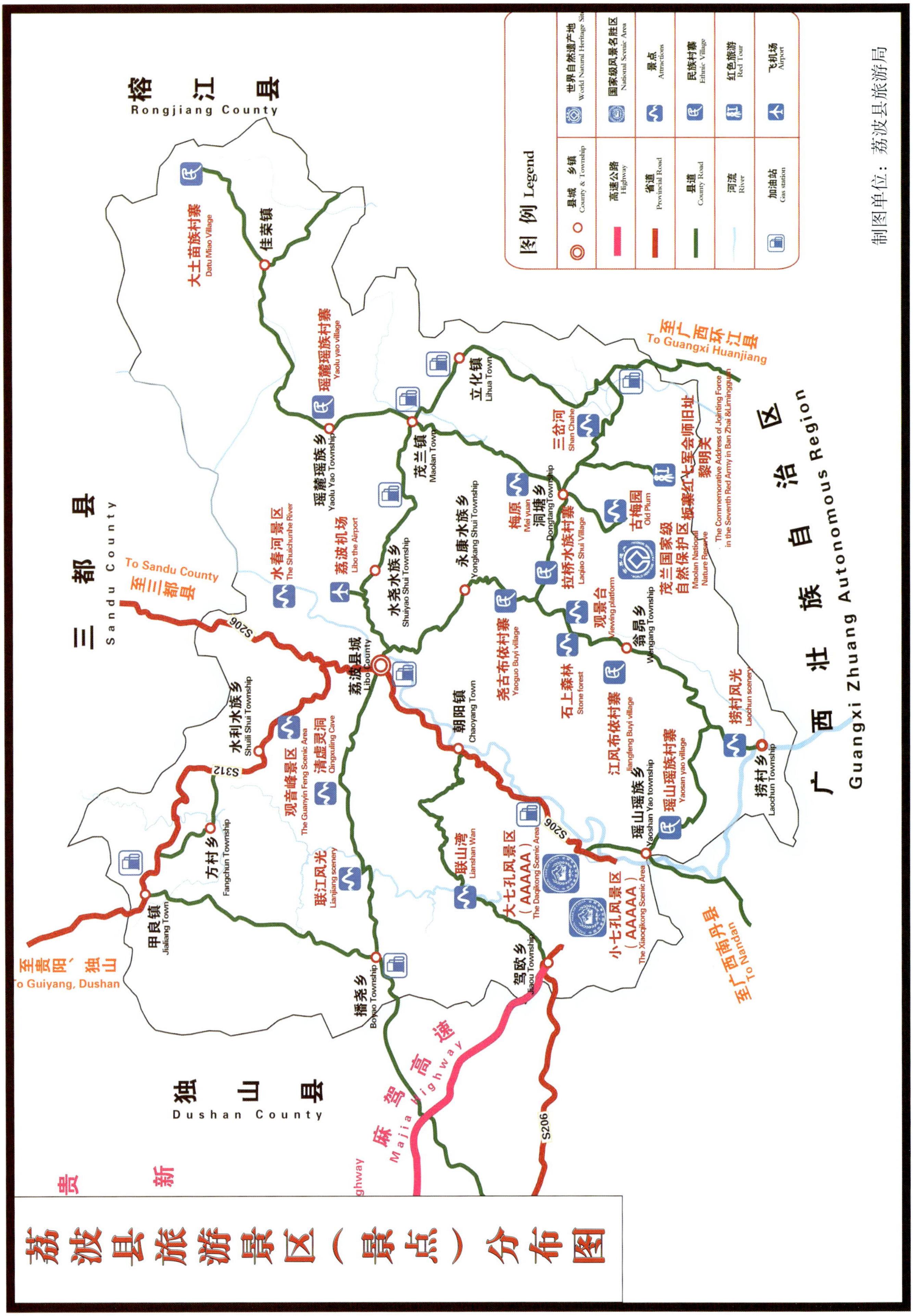

荔波县旅游景区（景点）分布图
图例 Legend
县城 乡镇 County & Township
高速公路 Highway
省道 Provincial Road
县道 County Road
河流 River
加油站 Gas station
世界自然遗产地 World Natural Heritage Site
国家级风景名胜区 National Scenic Area
景点 Attractions
民族村寨 Ethnic Village
红色旅游 Red Tour
飞机场 Airport
榕江县 Rongjiang County
三都县 Sandu County
独山县 Dushan County
广西壮族自治区 Guangxi Zhuang Autonomous Region
至三都县 To Sandu County
至贵阳、独山 To Guiyang, Dushan
至广西环江县 To Guangxi Huanjiang
至广西南丹县 To Nandan
荔波县城 Libo County
大土苗族村寨 Datu Miao Village
佳荣镇
瑶麓瑶族村寨 Yaolu yao village
瑶麓瑶族乡 Yaolu Yao Township
立化镇 Lihua Town
茂兰镇 Maolan Town
三岔河 Shan Chahe
水春河景区 The Shuichunhe River
荔波机场 Libo the Airport
水尧水族乡 Shuiyao Shui Township
永康水族乡 Yongkang Shui Township
梅原 Mei yuan
洞塘乡 Dongtang Township
拉桥水族村寨 Laqiao Shui Village
古梅园 Old Plum
茂兰国家级自然保护区 Maolan National Nature Reserve
板寨红七军会师旧址黎明关
尧古布依村寨 Yaoguo Buyi village
观景台 Viewing platform
翁昂乡 Wengang Township
石上森林 Stone forest
江风布依村寨 Jiangfeng Buyi village
瑶山瑶族村寨 Yaosan yao village
瑶山瑶族乡 Yaoshan Yao township
捞村风光 Laochun scenery
捞村乡 Laochun Township
水利水族乡 Shuili Shui Township
观音峰景区 The Guanyin Feng Scenic Area
清虚灵洞 Qingxuling Cave
朝阳镇 Chaoyang Town
联山湾 Lianshan Wan
大七孔风景区（AAAAA） The Daqikong Scenic Area
小七孔风景区（AAAAA） The Xiaoqikong Scenic Area
方村乡 Fangchun Township
联江风光 Lianjiang scenery
甲良镇 Jialiang Town
播尧乡 Boyao Township
驾欧乡 Jiaou Township
麻驾高速 Majia Highway
S206
S312
贵新

制图单位：荔波县旅游局

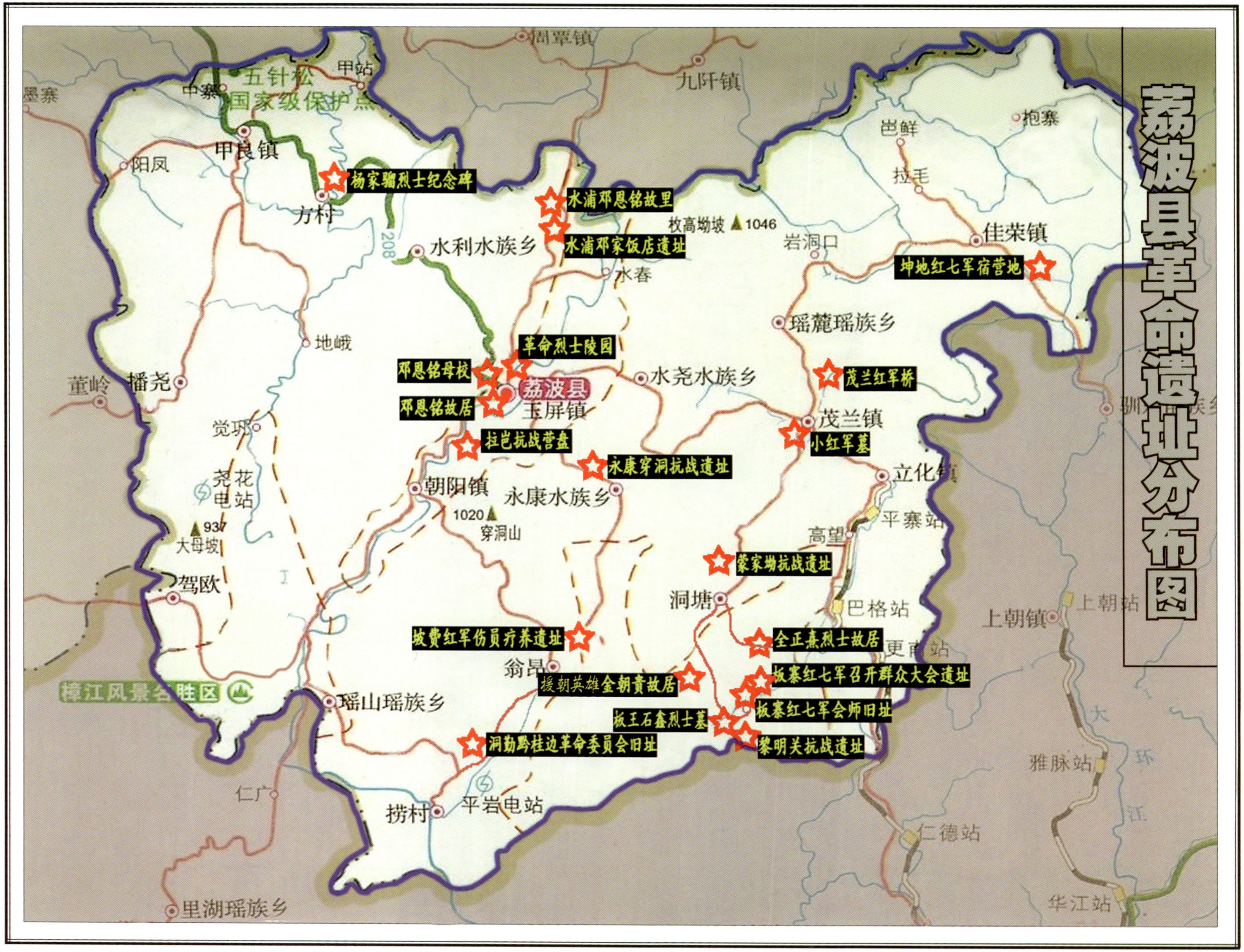
荔波县革命遗址分布图
杨家骝烈士纪念碑
水浦邓恩铭故里
水浦邓家饭店遗址
坤地红七军宿营地
革命烈士陵园
邓恩铭母校
邓恩铭故居
茂兰红军桥
小红军墓
拉岜抗战营盘
永康穿洞抗战遗址
蒙家坳抗战遗址
坡贵红军伤员疗养遗址
全正熹烈士故居
援朝英雄金朝贵故居
板寨红七军召开群众大会遗址
板寨红七军会师旧址
板王石鑫烈士墓
黎明关抗战遗址
洞勤黔桂边革命委员会旧址
荔波县
玉屏镇
甲良镇
方村
阳凤
中寨
甲站
五针松
国家级保护点
墨寨
周覃镇
九阡镇
岜鲜
抱寨
拉毛
佳荣镇
枚高坳坡 1046
岩洞口
水利水族乡
水春
瑶麓瑶族乡
地峨
水尧水族乡
播尧
董岭
觉巩
茂兰镇
立化镇
尧花电站
朝阳镇
永康水族乡
1020
穿洞山
937
大母坡
平寨站
高望
驾欧
洞塘
巴格站
上朝站
上朝镇
更甫站
翁昂
樟江风景名胜区
瑶山瑶族乡
仁广
捞村
平岩电站
雅脉站
大环江
仁德站
里湖瑶族乡
华江站
208

20 世纪 80 年代荔波县城全景

荔波县城夜景（2014 年 摄）

景观景点

小七孔古桥

六十八级瀑布

水上森林

鸳鸯湖

三岔河

拉关湿地

卧龙潭

拉雅瀑布

碧潭

翠谷瀑布

枫树湾香草园

大七孔天生桥

大七孔栈道

水春河峡谷漂流

青龙潭

佳荣七彩河河谷桫椤

茂兰喀斯特锥丛

观音峰

原始森林木质藤本

田园风光

捞村河谷

晨曦中的喀斯特

文物遗址

中共一大代表邓恩铭故居 （2012 年摄）

黔桂古驿道关隘——黎明关

板寨红七军会师旧址

荔波县城永济泉

产业发展

混凝土拌合站

安匀煤矿

下寨煤矿

荔波昌辉食业

大七孔水电站厂区一角

小七孔镇架桥村特种鱼养殖场

水利水族乡“无公害”畜牧养殖基地（2011 年摄）

黎明关水族乡军华肉牛养殖基地

瑶山瑶族乡血橙基地

朝阳镇枇杷园

玉屏镇拉岜蜜柚交易中心

甲良镇茶场

玉屏镇驼背树经果林基地

基础设施

县城邓恩铭广场（2012 年 摄）

县城红船广场 （2015 年 摄）

（1984 年 摄）

县城古榕街景（1998 年 摄）

（1986 年 摄）

樟江大桥 （2015 年 摄）

荔波古镇（2015 年 摄）

县城夜食街 （2015 年 摄）

荔波大剧院（2015 年 摄）

（1980 年 摄）

县城向阳路 （2015 年 摄）

县城迎宾大道 （2015 年 摄）

荔波机场（2015 年 摄）

麻驾高速小七孔收费站（2015 年 摄）

驾荔高速公路（2015 年 摄）

晨曦中的县乡道路（2000 年 摄）

小七孔大道 （2015 年 摄）

“一事一议”示范村——者吕 （2014 年 摄）

夜幕下的官塘大桥（2014 年 摄）

县城污水处理厂（2008 年 摄）

2012 年，新建的自来水厂

甲良镇鸟瞰图（2014 年 摄）

黎明关水族乡翁昂生态移民小区（2015 年 摄）

小七孔镇驾欧集市（2013 年 摄）

驾欧绿林移民新村（2008 年 摄）

佳荣镇全貌（2000 年 摄）

洞塘板寨瑶族移民新寨（2015 年 摄）

（2001 年 摄）

瑶山拉片村（2014 年 摄）

教育科技

荔波高级中学（2014 年 摄）

荔波第二中学（2014 年 摄）

荔波县中等职业学校（2011 年 摄）

荔波第一小学（2015 年 摄）

原荔波一小（1979 年 摄）

荔波县第二幼儿园一角（2015 年 摄）

2008 年 10 月，在邓恩铭广场举办百名少年现场书法大赛

2012 年，荔波高级中学首位考取清华大学学生姚茜

2013 年，荔波高级中学首位考取北京大学学生何昊

学校定期组织中小学生开展爱国主义教育活动

2007 年 11 月，在广州举办的第八届全国少数民族传统体育运动会上，荔波县代表队获陀螺比赛团体第一名

2010 年 4 月，荔波“矮人舞”走进中央电视台《芝麻开门》少儿节目

医疗卫生

2015 年新建的荔波人民医院

2005 年 12 月，引进的美国产 64 排 CT

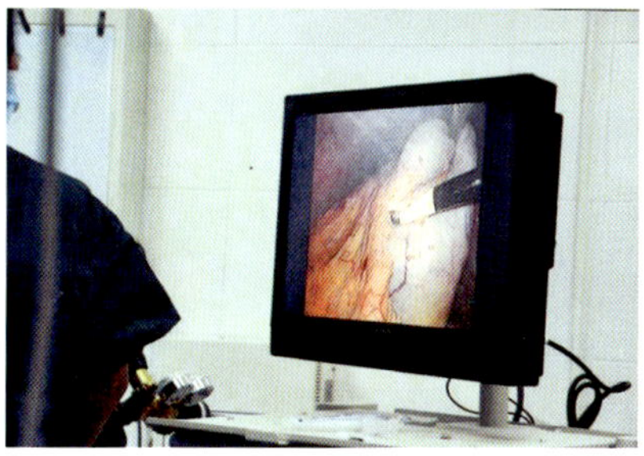
2013 年 3 月，引进的日本产奥林巴斯腹腔镜手术操作系统

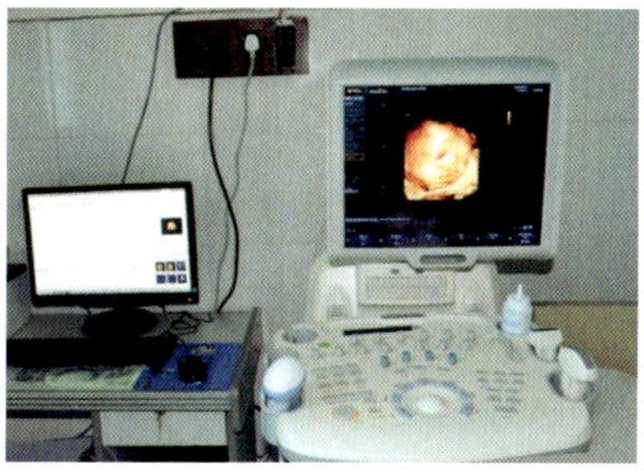
2012 年 12 月，引进的三星麦迪逊四维（实时三维）彩超 X8

2014 年新建的荔波县中医院

2014 年 9 月，开设的血透室

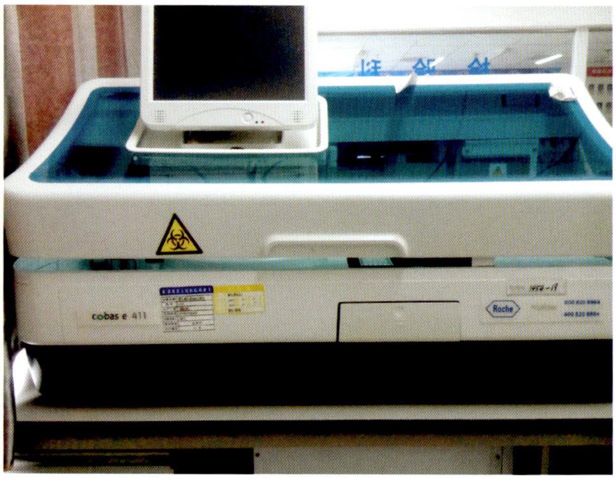

2014 年 10 月，启用德国罗氏电化发光分析仪

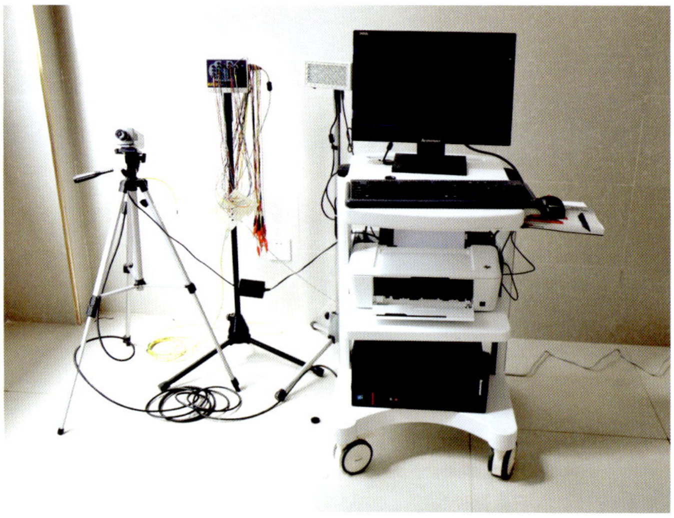

2014 年 9 月，启用神经电生理监测与分析系统（脑电图机）

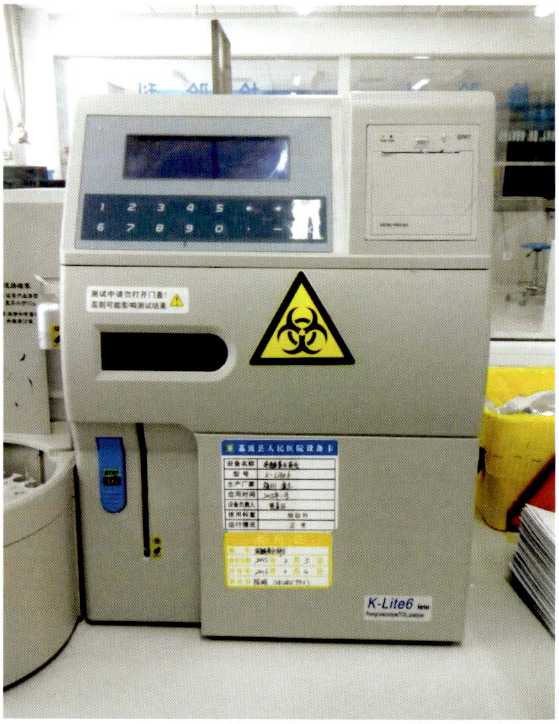

2015 年 1 月，启用电解质分析仪

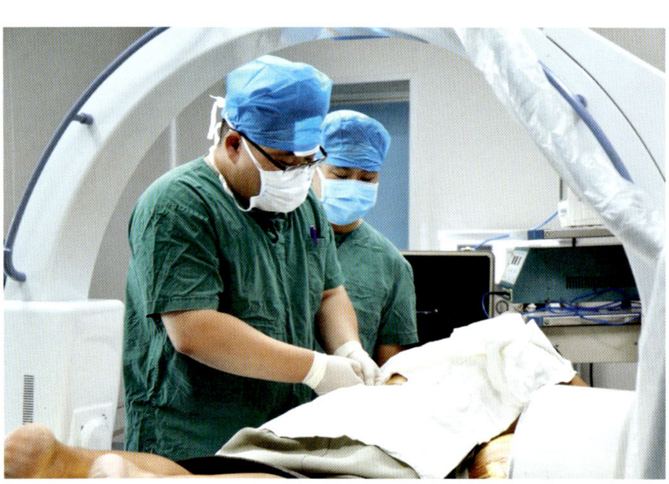

荔波县人民医院中医科成功实施首例椎间盘微创消融术

2015 年 7 月，新开设的重症医学科

旅游服务

中国·荔波樟江风景名胜区管理处
荔　波　县　旅　游　局

小七孔景区服务中心（2014 年 摄）

三力酒店 （2007 年 摄）

天泰酒店（2014 年 摄）

荔波樟江部落大酒店
（2014 年 摄）

瑶山瑶族乡拉柳“农家乐”山庄（2000 年 摄）

小七孔景区旅游观光车（2010 年 摄）

县城观光车（2012 年 摄）

民风民俗

瑶山瑶族迎宾或祭祀放排枪仪式

打陀螺

瑶山瑶族禾仓

瑶山瑶族铜鼓迎宾仪式

瑶山瑶族长席宴

瑶麓瑶族凿壁谈婚

“四月八”斗牛场景

布依族傩戏表演

“六月六”歌节

布依族祭祀活动中的“上刀山”“下火海”

水族卯节卯坡

水族迎亲对歌场景

水族卯节祭祖仪式

水族卯节开塘捉鱼习俗

水族马尾绣背带

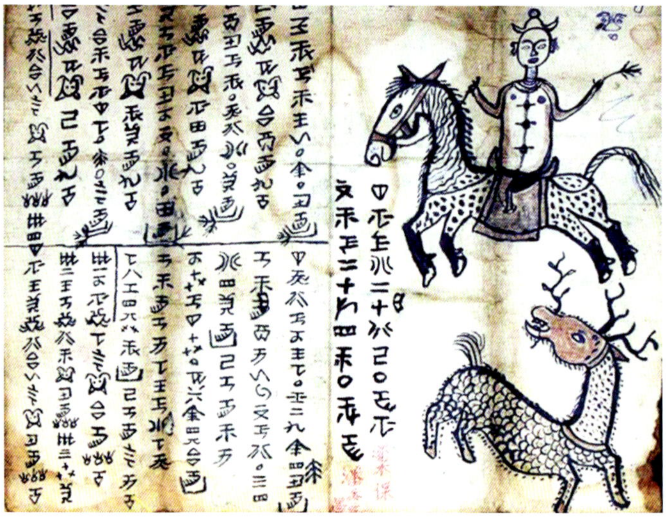

水书

水族图腾

苗族芦笙

苗族跳苗

苗族芦笙舞

民间艺人

欧海金 1943年7月出生，水族，贵州省荔波县水尧乡水捞村人。民间艺人、高级水书师，现为黔南州水书专家组成员，非物质文化遗产（水书习俗）传承人。

——欧海金收藏的水书

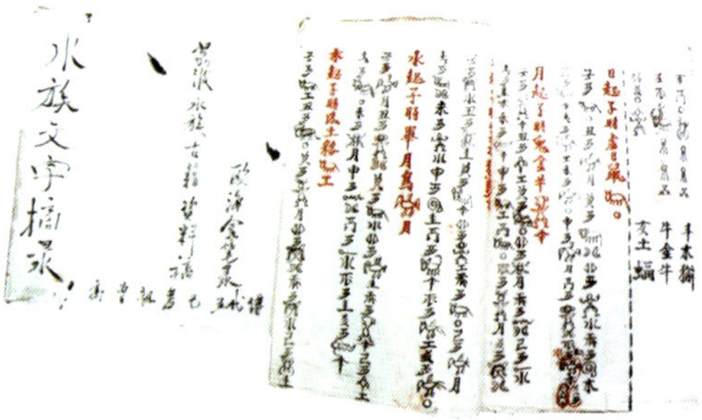

国家级非物质文化遗产传承人欧海金及其收藏作品

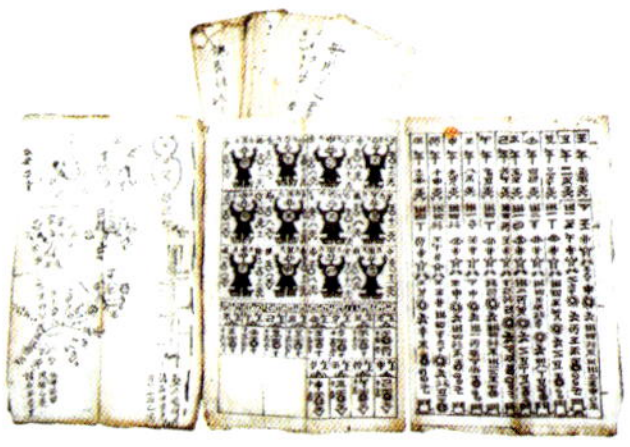

潘老平（左）1937年7月出生，水族，贵州省荔波县佳荣镇拉易村人。民间艺人、高级水书师，现为黔南州水书专家组成员，非物质文化遗产（水书习俗）传承人。

——潘老平收藏的部分水书

国家级非物质文化遗产传承人潘老平及其收藏作品

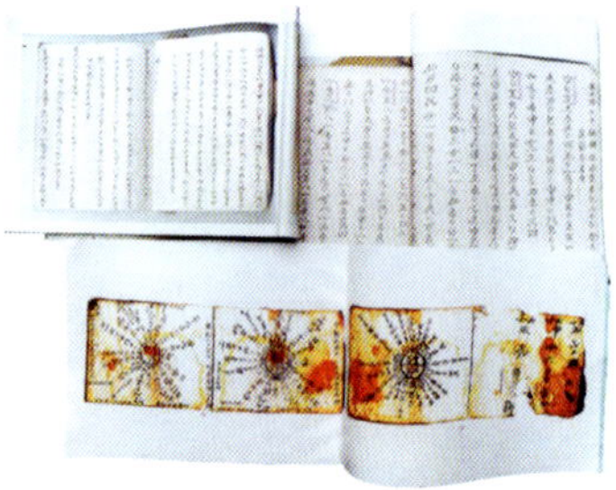

蒙熙能 1941年8月出生，水族，贵州省荔波县永康乡德门村人。民间艺人、高级水书师，现为黔南州水书专家组成员，非物质文化遗产（水书习俗）传承人。

——蒙熙能收藏和整理的部分水书

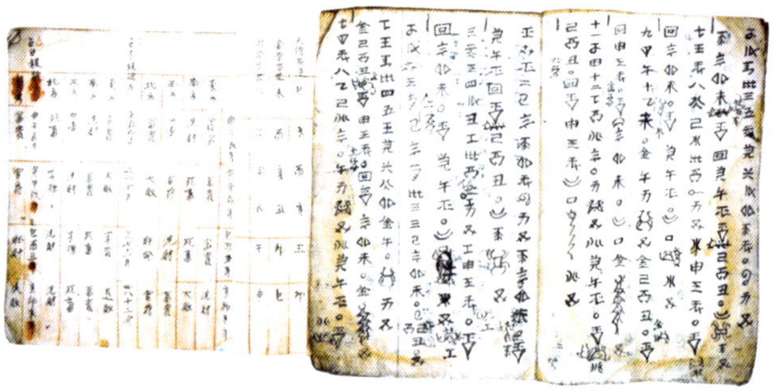

高级水书师蒙熙能及其收藏作品

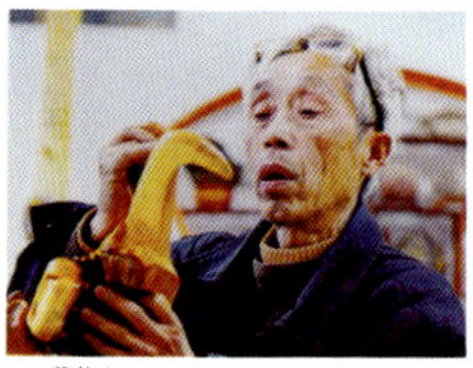

蒋荣生 1940年11月出生，贵州省荔波县玉屏镇人。民间艺人、高级工艺师。

——蒋荣生的根雕作品

高级工艺师蒋荣生及其作品

珍稀动植物

硬叶蔸兰（国家一级保护植物）

白花兜兰

红豆杉（国家一级保护植物）

小叶兰花（国家一级保护植物）

小叶兜兰

多花兰

掌叶木（国家一级保护植物）

中华秋沙鸭（国家一级保护动物）

红唇树蜥

荔波壁虎（荔波特有种）

猕猴（国家二级保护动物）

细痣疣螈（国家二级保护动物）

眼镜蛇

南方白甲鱼（荔波特有种）

长鳍光唇鱼（荔波特有种）

盲条鳅（荔波特有种）

红腹锦鸡（国家一级保护动物）

枯叶蝶（稀有种）

小七孔黔弱蛛（新种）

荔波特产

荔波银饰产品

荔波银酒具、银花瓶

荔波土花布

荔波竹凉席

荔波藤制工艺品

荔波青梅酒

荔波米片

荔波云耳、笋干、香菇

荔波蜜柚

荔波杨梅汤

荔波血桃

荔波风猪

荔波腌猪肉

荔波腊肉

重要活动

2001 年 11 月，著名歌唱家毛阿敏、蒋大为等在荔波邓恩铭广场“荔波旅游风光演唱会”演出

2004 年 9 月，徒步穿越喀斯特科考活动启动仪式

百家媒体、百位名家走进中国最美丽的地方荔波大型采风活动留影 2005.11.31

2006 年 1 月，荔波举办首届梅花节活动

2006 年 2 月，中央歌舞团到荔波演出

2007 年 6 月，荔波举办庆祝申遗成功联欢晚会

2007 年 6 月，荔波隆重召开申遗成功庆祝大会

2007 年 11 月，第二届贵州旅游产业发展大会在荔波召开

2007 年 11 月，第二届贵州旅游产业发展大会·晚会“荔波荡漾”实景

2008 年 4 月，中央电视台《乡村大世界》栏目走进荔波

2009 年 7 月，全国陀螺邀请赛在荔波举行

2009 年 8 月，中国南方喀斯特（荔波）与美国猛犸洞国家公园结为姊妹公园

2012 年 12 月，“中国绿手帕全球公益巡演”在荔波启航

2012 年 5 月，世界遗产与可持续发展论坛在荔波召开

2015 年 9 月，纪念抗日战争胜利 70 周年“荔波杯·最强中国梦”——第八届公益中国颁奖大典

2015 年 5 月，黔南州第七届旅游产业发展大会在荔波举行

2015 年 8 月，《跟着贝尔去冒险》的贝尔团队与县领导合影

抢险救灾

2000 年 6 月，荔波遭受百年不遇的洪涝灾害，樟江沿河大面积被洪水淹没，水位超警戒线 3.25 米，洪水冲毁了部分房屋、公路、桥梁等，造成直接经济损失 1.95 亿元

供电维修人员正在抢修因凝冻冰灾损坏的输电线路

2008 年，荔波遭受特大凝冻冰灾，图为倒伏的电线杆

专家考察

2002年1月，法国国家研究中心生态所所长、国际著名生态专家霍曼勒教授（右）在荔波考察

2006年8月，世界遗产评估专家、国际著名动物专家毕威廉先生在荔波考察

2006年9月，世界遗产评估专家桑塞尔（左二），世界遗产评估专家、国际著名自然保护学家王献溥教授（右二），中国著名世界遗产专家梁永宁教授（右一）在荔波考察

2006年9月，申遗期间，世界自然遗产保护联盟首席专家史密斯（右二）、威廉姆斯（右一）在荔波考察

2009年1月，中国联合国教科文组织秘书长田小刚（右二）在荔波考察

2009年5月，匈牙利Eotvos大学教授Miklos Kazmcr在荔波考察喀斯特地区土壤侵蚀速率和土壤发育与年尺度的变化规律

2010年5月，美国加州科学院博士Jim Shcvock到荔波考察苔鲜植物资源

2012年6月，世界遗产评估专家、世界自然保护联盟主席桑塞尔在荔波"世界遗产与可持续发展"国际论坛上作主题发言

2013年7月，英国生物多样性专家、肯特大学教授、东南亚生物多样性保护中心主任约翰·马敬能在生态文明贵阳国际论坛荔波分论坛上发言

2013年7月，非洲保护工作组联盟秘书长雷蒙德·卡特巴卡在生态文明贵阳国际论坛荔波分论坛上发言

2001 年 7 月，著名经济学家于光远（前右）到小七孔景区考察

2006 年 7 月，清华大学教授赵丽明（右）向荔波水书先生了解水族文字

2006 年 8 月，中国南方喀斯特研究院院长、著名世界遗产专家熊康宁教授（左二）在荔波考察

2011年4月，中国人与生物圈国家委员会主席、中国科学院院士许智宏在荔波考察

2013年7月，中国工程院院士、中国地质科学院水文地质研究院研究员卢耀如在生态文明贵阳国际论坛荔波分论坛上发言

北京林业大学副校长、国家著名梅花专家张启翔教授（右二）在荔波考察

中国人与生物圈国家委员会秘书长韩念勇教授（左）在荔波考察

2013年7月，中科院动物所博士解焱在生态文明贵阳国际论坛荔波分论坛上发言

中国工程院院士、著名林业专家唐守正教授（前）在荔波考察

北京大学世界遗产研究中心主任、国际著名世界遗产研究专家谢凝高教授（右）在荔波考察

名人荔波行

2006 年 1 月，中国作协副主席叶辛到荔波开展专题讲座

2006 年 1 月，棋圣聂卫平（前）在荔波梅园进行围棋车轮战

2007 年 8 月，著名导演张纪中（前左一）在荔波考察

2007 年，中国美术学院教授、硕士生导师胡寿荣（前）到荔波县瑶山乡采风

2010 年，香港著名书画家萧滋（左二）在荔波传授书法技艺

2011 年，著名画家、书法家、书画评论家梅墨生（右三）到荔波采风并题字

2011 年，著名油画家向光（右六）到荔波采风

2011 年，国家一级指挥、上海歌剧院首席指挥曹丁到荔波讲学观光考察

2013 年，贵州省书法家协会主席、著名书法家包俊宜（右二）到荔波考察并题字

2013 年，著名书法家程风子（右）到荔波采风并题字

中国著名经济学家、世界新经济研究院院长陈瑜（左），中国著名经济学家、世界新经济研究院常务副院长杨谨鸿（右）在荔波考察

2013 年 3 月，著名作曲家肖白（右二）到荔波县采风

著名旅游创新传播专家、德安杰环球顾问集团总裁贾云峰（前排左二）到荔波考察

荔波荣誉

世界遗产

WORLD HERITAGE · PATRIMOINE MONDIAL

中国 · 荔波

世界自然遗产地标志牌

全国旅游资源规划开发质量评定委员会

公　　告

（2015 年第 1 号）

依照中华人民共和国国家标准《旅游景区质量等级的划分与评定》与《旅游景区质量等级管理办法》，经有关省、自治区旅游景区质量等级评定机构推荐，全国旅游资源规划开发质量评定委员会组织评定，山西省晋中市平遥古城景区、辽宁省本溪市本溪水洞景区、吉林省长春市长影世纪城旅游区、黑龙江省漠河北极村旅游区、浙江省湖州市南浔古镇景区、福建省福州市三坊七巷景区、湖北省恩施州恩施大峡谷景区、湖南省郴州市东江湖旅游区、甘肃省敦煌鸣沙山月牙泉景区、海南省保亭县槟榔谷黎苗文化旅游区、四川省广元市剑门蜀道剑门关旅游区、贵州省黔南州荔波樟江景区、宁夏自治区银川市灵武水洞沟旅游区、江西省瑞金市共和国摇篮旅游区、新疆自治区喀什地区喀什噶尔老城景区等 15 家景区达到国家 5A 级旅游景区标准的要求，批准为国家 5A 级旅游景区。

现予公告。

全国旅游资源规划开发质量评定委员会

2015 年 7 月 13 日

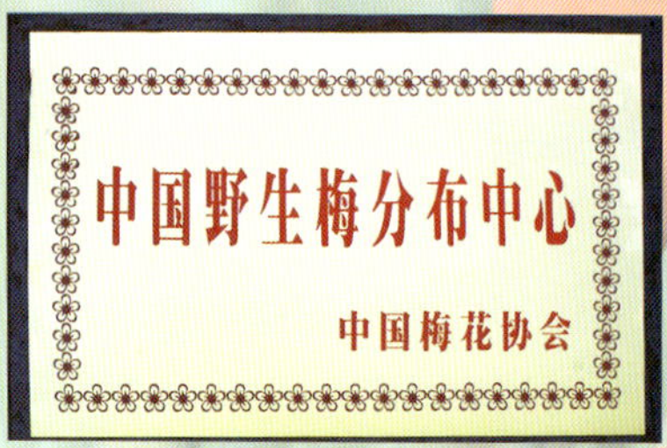

普及九年义务教育和扫除青壮年文盲县
中华人民共和国教育部
二〇〇一年

国家级非物质文化遗产
水书习俗
中华人民共和国国务院公布
中华人民共和国文化部颁发

国家级非物质文化遗产
瑶族猴鼓舞
中华人民共和国国务院公布
中华人民共和国文化部颁发
2008年6月

省级非物质文化遗产
瑶族打猎舞
贵州省人民政府公布
贵州省文化厅颁发
2005年12月

省级非物质文化遗产
布依族“雯当姆”
贵州省人民政府公布
贵州省文化厅颁发
2005年12月

省级非物质文化遗产
瑶族民间陀螺竞技
贵州省人民政府公布
贵州省文化厅颁发
2007年5月

省级非物质文化遗产
水族（九阡酒）酿酒技艺
贵州省人民政府公布
贵州省文化厅颁发
2009年9月

二〇〇〇年全省3000公里公路改造
组织实施奖
贵州省人民政府
二〇〇一年二月

普及九年义务教育 扫除青壮年文盲
合格单位
贵州省人民政府
二〇〇一年十二月

2003—2005年度
全省农业“三增”先进单位
一等奖
贵州省人民政府
二〇〇六年二月

授予荔波县一九九三年度发展乡镇企业
先进单位
中共贵州省委
贵州省人民政府
一九九四年九月

奖给
荔波县人民政府
林面积覆盖率蓄积量
同步增长成绩显着
贵州省人民政府

奖给
荔波县人民政府
保险先进县
贵州省人民政府
一九九二年十一月

奖状
荔波县荣获1995-1996年度
冬春农田水利建设先进单位

2015年11月，《荔波县志（1978—2008）》终审会在荔波召开

本志特约编审（前排左起）：江兴龙 冉孟华 姚锦超 蒙熙林 黄玉成 李德余 程志安 徐明镒 陈建军
本志编纂人员（后排左起）：卢崇果 胡 翀 黎少松 莫海希 邓贤海 何培逊 杨雪菲 覃明芬

荔波县党史县志编纂委员会（2001.8—2008.4）

顾　　问	逄焕华　潘朝显　陆兴华　黄玉成
主任委员	龙河云
副主任委员	高勇华　华廷龙　李　洪　姚锦超　王永波　杨志枰
委　　员	韦鸿敏　祁德祥　王声勇　周　灿　余祖刚　张显明
	蒙汉文　罗世槐　何羡坤　黎礼定　杨晓东　黎少松

荔波县史志编纂委员会（2008.5—2009.2）

名誉主任	王振金　陈稠彪　陆兴华　董豫黔
主任委员	李　洪
副主任委员	马应忠　韦鸿敏　高晓昀　潘永会　朱丽琼　李荣庆
委　　员	覃炳能　韦永达　莫壮权　莫如吉　罗　宏　罗孟群
	温　兵　龙　飞　覃洪耀　冯关芳　冉景丞　杨国军
	王大欢　蒋仕云　何云辉　岑义平　蒙永辉　张昌辉
	姚炳烈　蒙汉文　邓贤海　杨晓东　黎少松

荔波县史志编纂委员会（2009.3—2012.6）

名誉主任	闵路明　陈稠彪　陆兴华　董豫黔
主任委员	李　洪
副主任委员	马应忠　韦鸿敏　高晓昀　潘永会　朱丽琼　李荣庆
委　　员	覃炳能　韦永达　莫壮权　莫如吉　冯关芳　冉景丞 罗　宏　罗孟群　莫跃文　杨国军　温　兵　王大欢 蒋仕云　何云辉　岑义平　蒙永辉　姚炳烈　蒙汉文 邓贤海　杨晓东　黎少松

荔波县地方志编纂委员会（2012.7—2014.5）

名誉主任	闵路明　瓦标龙　李　洪　董豫黔
主任委员	高晓昀　马应忠
副主任委员	韦鸿敏　宋泽祥　潘永会　何云辉　龙　霜　朱丽琼
成　　员	韦永达　龙　怀　李学恩　廖明华　陈照林　何羡坤 冉景丞　龙　飞　杨　勇　莫万能　吴兴宇　蒋仕云 潘胜军　吴帮定　杨享禄　何　虎　姚炳烈　莫跃文 蒙汉文　邓贤海　罗遵建　莫海希　曹本健

荔波县地方志编纂委员会（2014.6—2016.5）

名誉主任	闵路明　叶　霖　李　洪　董豫黔
主任委员	覃　怡　黄桂林
副主任委员	韦鸿敏　宋泽祥　潘永会　何云辉　朱丽琼　杨国军
成　　员	姚正明　韦永达　龙　怀　莫万能　李学恩　廖明华 黎德盟　邓贤海　何　虎　杨享禄　何羡坤　龙　飞 杨　勇　蒋仕云　潘胜军　吴帮定　周　佶　姚炳烈 吴兴宇　罗遵建　莫海希　韦鸿伟　蒙汉文

荔波县地方志编纂委员会（2016.6—　）

名誉主任	尹德俊　叶　霖　李　洪　董豫黔
主任委员	覃　怡　罗仕凯
副主任委员	宋泽祥　何　虎　潘永会　胡小桃　莫治贵
成　　员	姚正明　吴化明　姚炳能　何彦超　梁建奎　王东静 廖　辉　蒙　隽　邓贤海　何羡坤　杨享禄　何凤均 梁志均　莫正来　潘兴发　莫正才　李学恩　龙帮科 韦永达　周　佶　姚炳烈　艾文革　蒙汉文　莫海希 何培逊

《荔波县志（1978—2008）》编辑部

顾　　问　周声浩　伍启林

主　　编　邓贤海

副 主 编　莫海希　何培逊　黎少松　陈建军　罗遵建

总　　纂　王素琴

分　　纂　陆兴和　陆春凡　白映泉

特约编审　黄玉成　李德余　蒙熙林　程志安　姚锦超
冉孟华　陈建军　徐明镒　黄吉林　廖其章
江兴龙

编　　辑　覃明芬　莫　令　杨雪菲　卢崇果　胡　翀
吴　倩

序

盛世修志，继往开来。旨在慰藉前人，激励当代，启迪后世，造福桑梓。

荔波，地灵矣！其自然资源得天独厚，著称世界。喀斯特地貌特征显著，锥状峰丛连绵起伏，形成水、山、林、洞、湖、瀑、峡的奇特景观，巧夺天工，赐予世界自然遗产地、国际人与生物圈保护区、国家AAAAA级重点樟江风景名胜区、地球绿宝石和世界最美喀斯特。这些山与水的结合，湖与瀑的交融，峡与壑的链接，造就了荔波生态的雄奇与壮丽，秀美与神秘。樟江环绕县城，自成太极，城中荔泉，清澈甘洌，为荔波增添了神奇与灵气。

荔波，人杰矣！其历史、人文资源厚重富集，享誉黔地。仅近现代以来，诞生了中国共产党的创始人之一邓恩铭，参加南昌起义将领蒙九龄，抗日殉国将领杨家骝，驾机与日军舰俱焚的空中英烈全正熹；邓小平创建的红七军一、二纵队在板寨战略会师，贵州抗战第一枪在黎明关打响；世居在这块土地上的22个少数民族和睦友好相处，犹如一个大家庭。他们用淳朴和善良传承着中华民族的优良传统，用勤劳和智慧，辛勤耕耘，演绎着开拓进取、团结奋进的故事。

“志为信史”。《荔波县志（1978—2008）》着意描绘了荔波地灵人杰，充分展示了改革开放30年政治、经济、文化和各项社会事业取得的成就。运用“述、记、志、传、图、表、录”之载体，取“篇、章、节”之架构，首为概述，次为大事记，后为专志，末为附录。全志以经济社会发展为主线，运用辩证唯物主义与历史唯物主义观点，把握历史发展的脉络，记述荔波翻天覆地的变化，凸现资源秉赋，彰显进取精神。既有宏观鸟瞰，一县概况尽收眼底；又有微观透视，沧桑变化了然志中。一卷在手，犹如县情在胸。执政者，可以之为镜，观兴废盛衰，知是非得失，把握未来发展方向；为民者，可以之为师，览家乡全貌，晓发展艰辛，珍惜今天幸福生活。其“存史、教化、资政”的意义和价值不可估量，是荔波县社会主义文化建设的又一重大成果。

欣悉，在《荔波县志（1978—2008）》编修期间，中央候补委员、中国社会科学院副院长、中国地方志指导小组常务副组长李培林莅临荔波关怀指导，给予肯定和点赞；省终审组在终审会上提出结合荔波全域旅游发展战略，把《荔波县志（1978—2008）》努力打造成为贵州一流的、面向世界的精品佳志。可喜可贺！县史志办领导班子和全体人员以“编史修志、资政育人”为已任，本着对历史、对人民负责的态度，历时数载，几易其稿，坚守寂寞，含辛茹苦，精益求精，为荔波文化建设和地方志事业默默奉献。其心可敬，其志可钦！

“治天下者以史为鉴，治郡县者以志为鉴”。荔波历史是荔波人民创造的。中共荔波县委、荔波县人民政府继续团结和带领全县各族人民奋力拼搏，跨越赶超，努力营造出宽松、便捷、舒畅、和谐的环境，与大家一起共享天更蓝、山更秀、水更清、乡愁更浓的欢乐生活。

中共荔波县委书记

荔波县人民政府县长 叶霖

2016年5月

凡　例

一、本志坚持马列主义毛泽东思想、邓小平理论、“三个代表”重要思想，坚持科学发展观为指导，深入贯彻习近平总书记系列重要讲话精神。遵循辩证唯物主义和历史唯物主义的观点，坚持实事求是原则，记述荔波县1978年改革开放以来的经济社会发展变化。

二、本志是1997年版《荔波县志》的续志，上限1978年，下限2008年。志中有关1978—1990年与前志重复的内容，作简单记述。人物部类中设有前志补遗。

三、本志为突出荔波县特色，专设“中国南方喀斯特荔波世界自然遗产地”“旅游业”“‘两瑶’扶贫与扶贫攻坚”篇，并将此三篇的有关资料下延至2015年，并在工业篇中突出对“煤炭工业”章的记述。

四、荔波世界自然遗产地主要由茂兰国家级自然保护区和荔波樟江国家级风景名胜区大、小七孔景区组成，一些相关内容分别在本志的第二篇和第十四篇中记述。

五、本志设“革命老区县——荔波”为特记，并在个别篇章中使用专记。

六、本志入志人物坚持“生不立传”原则，对断限内已故的有突出贡献、有影响的人物立传记述；对在世的有突出贡献、有影响的人物以人物简介记述。前志已记载的受省部级以上表彰的先进个人本志不再收录。

七、本志附录中收录限外资料“荔波县2009—2015年经济社会发展资料”。省、部级以上表彰的先进集体收入附录。

八、本志资料由县内各单位、乡（镇）提供，不注明出处。数据以统计局统计为准，未列入统计局统计的数据，以各单位提供的为准。

九、本志党委、政府工作机构分别集中记述，其他机构在相应部分记述。

十、本志行文规范，一律采用现代语体文记述，执行中国地方志指导小组制定的《地方志书质量规定》和《中华人民共和国国家通用语言文字法》（2001）、《出版物汉字使用管理规定》（1992）规定。标点符号、数字用法以国家标准《标点符号用法》（GB/T15834-2011）、《出版物上数字用法》（GB/T-2011）为准。

十一、本志机构名称、专用词较长的首次出现时用全称，之后用简称，在志末附机构及专用词全称与简称对照表。

十二、本志序言、总目录、概述及个别重要文献使用中英文对照。

十三、本志图片资料在编纂过程中制作，故不受时限限制，提供者、摄影者见后记。

目　录

TABLE OF CONTENTS

Part XVI Comprehensive Economic Management ······ (583)

概　述

一

荔波县境地理坐标介于北纬25° 07′～25° 39′，东经107° 37′～108° 18′之间。地处贵州省南部，黔南布依族苗族自治州南端。东北与黔东南苗族侗族自治州的从江县、榕江县接壤，东南同广西壮族自治区的环江毛南族自治县、南丹县毗邻，西面与独山县交界，北面同三都水族自治县相连。辖区东西最大距离67.3公里，南北最大距离58.5公里，总面积2431.8平方公里。

县境处于贵州高原南部斜坡向广西丘陵性盆地的过渡地带，地势南低北高。县城海拔高度为425米，最低的捞村河口为300米，最高的月亮山次峰为1468米，全县平均海拔758.8米。多数乡村在400～800米之间。

受地质构造控制，地形向斜成谷，背斜成山，形成山地与谷地由西而东相间排列，主要山脉和水系沿地质构造走向发育，组成全县山脉与河流谷地北偏东向长带状相嵌分布的格局。县境内沉积岩层广布，有新生代陆相碎屑岩，中生代海相碎屑岩和化学岩，古生代海相碎屑岩和泻湖相煤系，远古代浅变质海相碎屑岩和化学岩等。

荔波县属于中亚热带季风湿润气候区。由于地理纬度较低，境内山峦起伏，河谷深切，地形地貌复杂，气候类型多样，因而具有亚热带高原山地季风湿润气候特征。总的特点是：气候温热，四季分明，冬无严寒，夏无酷暑，夏长冬短，无霜期长，雨量充沛，雨热同季，灾害性天气少，对农业生产属于丰收型气候。在不同的地形、地势影响下，温度和地区差异显著，日照区别大，雨水时空分布不均，有明显的雨季和旱季。干旱、低温、洪涝及绵雨等主要的农业自然灾害天气时有出现。县内气候的垂直变化和地形小气候明显，各地四季的起止时间和持续时间也多不相同。一般来说，地形较高地区夏季较短，春季、秋季、冬季较长。

二

荔波县置县制始于明太祖洪武十七年（1384），时属广西庆远府。英宗正统十二年（1447）改属广西南丹州。宪宗成化十二年（1476）回属庆远府。孝宗弘治七年（1494）以后改土归流，置方村、蒙村、穿来村三巡检司，属广西承宣布政司庆远府河池州。武宗正德元年（1506）复建荔波县，属广西承宣布政司庆远府河池州。嘉靖年间（1522—1566），知县尹东袁建城。神宗万历元年（1573）后，设县城于穿来的喇轸村（今时来村旧县），建土城，设东西两门，属贵州都匀司。清顺治元年（1644）属贵州省，顺治十六年（1659）又改属广西庆远府，迁县治于方村里袄村（今方村乡街上）。雍正十年（1732）改属贵州都匀府。此后，荔波县建制属贵州省未变。1949年11月为荔波县人民自治委员会，1950年1月为荔波县解放委员会，1950年2月成立荔波县人民政府，1955年4月，县人民政府改称县人民委员会，1958年12月荔波县撤销，并入独山县，1961年8月恢复荔波县建制，1967年3月，县人民委员会改称为县革命委员会，1980年元月，县革命委员会改称县人民政府，1984年4月公社改称乡，全县辖4区1镇25乡（其中6个水族乡、2个瑶族乡），160个村，1187个村民小组。1991年，建镇并乡撤区后，全县辖5镇12乡170个村民委员会，4个居民委员会，1193个村民小组。2000年，撤销佳荣水族乡，建立佳荣镇，时辖6个镇11个乡。2004年，全县开展并村，辖6镇11乡，98个村（居）民委员会，1194个村民小组。至2008年，全县人口171427人，由22个民族组成。除汉族外，少数民族人口数为157750人，占全县总人口的92.02%，在少数民族人口中，布依族104884人，占总人口的61.18%；水族36639人，占总人口数21.37%；苗族8429人，占总人口的4.92%；瑶族5492人，占总人口的3.20%；壮族1356人，占总人口的0.79%；侗族526人，占总人口的0.31%；毛南族100人，占总人口的0.06%；其他14个少数民族人口为324人，占全县总人口的0.19%。

三

2008年，全县各类土地面积356.45万亩，人均占有土地21.6亩。林地190.10万亩，占土地总面积的53.33%；草地19.43万亩，占5.45%；城乡居民用地43709.9亩；工矿用地344.59亩；交通用地7814.4亩。2004—2005年，全县开展第三次森林资源调查，有林地面积12.67万公顷，活立木蓄积量595.45万立方米，疏林及零星树林蓄积量1.54万立方米，全县森林覆盖率56.1%，活立木总蓄量596.99万立方米。

境内主要矿产资源有煤炭、铁、铅、锌、碳酸钙、方解石、石灰石、白云石等，分为46个矿点。另有冰洲石、硅、铜、水晶以及贵重金属异常反应现象。煤炭是县内一大资源优势，全县总储量5.3亿吨，其中无烟煤3.1亿吨，烟煤2.2亿吨，已得到有效开发利用。

县境内河流落差大，水能资源丰富，河道累计落差6342米，水能理论蕴藏总量34.9万千瓦，可开发量24.43万千瓦，现已开发利用的14座水电站，装机43台，容量9.739万千瓦，占可开发量的39.86%。

荔波县境地理区位属典型的喀斯特地貌区，境内拥有集中连片的原生性喀斯特森林21285公顷，占全县总面积的20%，主要分布在茂兰国家级自然保护区和荔波樟江风景区，是迄今地球上残存分布集中，原生性强、相对稳定的喀斯特森林生态系统。植物区系处于贵州区系向广西区系过渡交错地带；动物区系属东洋界体中区西南山地亚区黔中山地丘陵地理省。有维管束植物154科514属1203种。其中种子植物144科493属1273种，属国家一级保护树种有南方红豆杉、喙核桃、鹅掌楸、杜仲等，省级保护树种18个，国家特有属15种，贵州新分布153个种类；脊椎动物400多种，其中鸟类16目43科122属200种，兽类24科42属16种，爬行类45种，两栖类26种，鱼类30种；苔藓类植物186种，大型真菌163种。其中国家一级重点保护野生植物8种，二级保护野生植物100种；国家一级重点保护野生动物4种，二级重点保护野生动物45种。此外，现有兰花植物34属87种，是中国兰花科植物保存最丰富的地区之一，其中白花兜兰为国家一级保护植物。丰富的自然资源，形成了独特的绿色喀斯特自然风光。

境内国家级茂兰喀斯特森林自然保护区，于1996年4月6日，联合国教科文组织正式批准纳入国际生物圈保护网络成员，总面积29万余亩。保护区内峰峦叠嶂，覆盖着密密的原始森林，形成壮丽的漏斗森林、谷地森林、洼地森林、槽谷森林四大景观。既有奇、幽、峻、秀、野、险、雄的自然美特色，又有浓郁的民族风情。景区内古树参天，植被繁茂，奇花异木，珍禽稀兽，青山绿水，鸟语花香，一望无垠的林海松涛，给人以无限的自然美感。景区内还有许多名贵的花、草、中药材、真菌、珍稀虫鱼和两栖爬行动物，是一座理想的天然实验室和科研基地，又是一座美丽的自然公园。

以樟江水系为主体的樟江风景名胜区共有代表性景点76处，其中一级景点17处，二级景点24处，三级景点35处，是一个融山、水、洞、林、湖、瀑、石多种景物景观于一体的景区，具有绿色锥状喀斯特独一无二的特殊景观。樟江风景名胜区总面积271.1平方公里，分为三大片：一为小七孔的涵碧潭、响水河、飞云瀑布、水上森林、翠谷、龟背山原始森林、野猪林、鸳鸯湖、天钟洞、蝙蝠洞、卧龙河、卧龙潭；二为大七孔的山神峡、天生桥、水神河、地峨峡、地峨宫、顶天杉、清水塘、万蛇塘、二层湖、笑天河、龙头山等连成一片，气势恢宏，美丽壮观。三为水春河峡谷景区。水春河峡谷从樟江而上，至水春15公里河道，经马尿滩、龙王洞、万鸟洞。峡谷两侧环境幽静，峭壁险峻，植被丰茂。谷中河水清澈，十三道浪相连，水天交相辉映，游人乘轻舟顺流而下，但觉云在水底飘，船在山上行，人在画中游之感。

借助县境拥有的世界上同一纬度仅存的喀斯特森林生态系统和樟江风景名胜区喀斯特原始森林及水文景观特色，2007年6月27日，荔波被第31届世界遗产大会全票通过，正式列为世界自然遗产地，获永久性保护。

四

中共十一届三中全会后，荔波县委、县人民政府在境内开展了一系列体制改革，为推动全县经济社会发展创造良好环境。

1979年起，全县推行定产到组、联产计酬生产责任制，后逐步完善为“家庭联产承包责任制”。1984年，明确农户土地承包期延长至2000年，农村基本经营制度进一步稳定和完善。1985年取消农产品统一派购制度，除对粮食等少数农产品实行合同收购外，其余均可进入市场交易，农产品购销体制由定购定销走向“双轨制”。1993年，实施粮食流通体制改革，取消粮食统购统销制度，放开粮食市场。1998年进行农村第二轮土地承包，延长责任地和荒山承包期，土地承包关系进一步稳定和完善。2004年取消烤烟特产税以外的农业特产税。2005年，执行国家免征农业税政策，对县内从事农业生产、有农业收入的单位和个人免征农业税。2008年，进行集体林权制度改革。改革开放30年来，荔波县农村、农业、农民三农问题发生了深刻变革，特别是对“两瑶”（瑶山、瑶麓）的扶贫开发，使瑶族人民逐步脱贫。

1980—1985年，境内国有工业企业实行厂长经理负责制，企业逐步实行利改税、利润包干办法。1986年后，企业实行经营承包责任制。同期对部分资不抵债的企业实行破产重组，并在部分企业进行股权转让尝试，未获成功。1998年后，对县内7户国有企业进行改革改制。岜合煤矿成为县内首家改制后股份制企业。1999年，继续对县联营水泥厂、县农机厂进行改革改制。县水泥厂实行产权、经营权转让改制后，推行效益目标管理责任制，实行聘任制及合同制。2001年，对县及乡（镇）企业供销公司进行破产清算，资产分离重组，职工改制安置。2007年，对樟江天然食品有限责任公司实行拍卖转让。至2008年，全县改制国有工业企业9户。

1983年后，随着非公有制商品经营的迅速发展，商品流通领域改革力度加大。是年，境内部分国有商业企业实行承包经营，至1985年，国有企业全面实行承包经营责任制。1989年起，推行企业经营自主权和经营责任制，企业自主经营，自负盈亏。1993年起，国有商业企业全面推行国有民营承包。1997年，在完善国有民营制度的同时，试行商业企业股份制改革，未获批准。2003年，启动新一轮国企业改革工作，县属5户商业企业列入改制范围，后因改制条件不成熟，未予批准。至2008年，商业所属5个企业仍为国有企业。

在推进系列改革的同时，不断优化开放发展环境，吸引外来投资入境开发。1995年成立招商引资机构，招商引资工作按照“一事一议”原则开展。1997年出台优惠政策，开展有组织招商，招商引资工作步入规范化。2001—2003年，先后制定并修订招商引资规定和奖励办法，启动招商引资“一站式”服务中心，组织各职能、执法部门入驻服务中心开设窗口，对外来投资商开展“一站式”服务。同期，利用节会和外出开展招商活动，招商引资取得明显成效。1995—2008年，全县共引进项目216个，引资到位资金14.0275亿元。

五

改革开放30年，通过全县上下共同努力，国民经济持续发展，经济总量快速增长。从1978年到2008年，生产总值由2323万元上升为113378万元，第一、二、三产业比由70.86∶16.83∶12.31调整到27.55∶34.63∶37.82，农业长期主体地位明显转变。人均生产总值由199元提高到16872元。财政总收入由127万元提高到18216万元，其中地方财政收入由127万元提升到8292万元。农民人均纯收入由143元提升到2618元。全社会固定资产投资总额1978年为103万元，1998年为16191万元，2008年为68357万元。金融机构存款余额1978年为335万元，其中城乡居民存款余额108万元，1998年金融存款余额20973万元，其中居民存款余额11669万元，2008年金融存款余额137305万元，其中居民存款余额79199万元。

农业经过30年发展，基础地位稳定提高，产业化经营逐步形成。1978年，全县农林牧渔业总产值3256万元。其中农业产值2154万元，林业产值311万元，牧业产值789万元。是年，粮食产量2.99万吨、油菜籽产量167吨，肉类产量0.06万吨，生猪存栏3.66万头。中共十一届三中全会后，以贯彻落实中央1号文件为契机，因地制宜，大力调整产业结构，促进了农业不断增效，农民持续增收。“畜牧、桑蚕、林果、蔬菜、茶叶、糖蔗”六大特色产业有序发展，基本形成“北部辣茶、中部果蔬、东南桑蚕”的特色产业发展格局。2008年，全县实现农林牧渔业总产值53625万元，其中，农业24661万元，占46%，牧业占32%，林业占9.8%。是年，粮食总产量5.99万吨，蔬菜产量3.73万吨，肉类总产量0.81万吨，大牲畜存栏6.08万头，生猪存栏7.52万头。有水果面积47000亩，桑园面积12640亩。

以煤炭产业为主的工业经济快速发展。改革开放以来，荔波煤炭产业经过从无序的私挖乱采到有序的规模开发，通过关闭整顿、整合技改、管理强矿三步战略的实施，至2008年各类煤矿32家，其中，整合煤矿10家，技改扩能扩界煤矿14家，维持生产现状煤矿2家，续建新建煤矿6家，总设计年生产能力为357万吨。年实际产销量保持在100万吨左右，是荔波经济的重要支柱产业。1978年，全县工业总产值289万元，1988年为37818万元，2008年增至135288万元。

旅游业迅速发展。确立“全县大景区”的发展理念，依托世界遗产品牌影响力，优化组合旅游精品线路，呈现出生态观光游、乡村体验游、民族风情游、红色文化游交相辉映的发展格局，带动了广大群众在旅游经营中直接受益。以“旅游搭台，经济唱戏”为旅游发展战略，全面加大旅游的对外宣传力度，荔波旅游业得到飞速发展，相继被评为中国最美的地方、国际旅游目的地等。以旅游为龙头及旅游产品加工和相关产业协调发展的经济体系逐步形成。2008年游客接待量首次突破200万人次大关。全县拥有各类宾馆、酒店102家，总床位达10000张，逐步形成了吃、住、行、游、购、娱等综合配套的接待能力。旅游业已成为全县国民经济的新兴支柱产业和增长点。

城乡商贸全面活跃。1978年，境内社会消费品零售总额894万元，其中批发零售贸易业825万元，占92.3%，住宿和饮食业33万元，占3.7%。第三产业产值286万元。之后，随着流通领域改革，商品经济日趋活跃，城乡市场繁荣发展，非公有制经济发展壮大，社会消费水平不断提高，社会消费品零售总额逐年攀升，1988年为2868万元，1998年为8656万元，当年第三产业产值过亿元，达1.15亿元，社会消费品零售总额突破亿元大关，2008年达3.2亿元。批发零售贸易业2.697亿元，占83.4%，住宿和饮食业4714万元，占16.6%。第三产业产值4.2883亿元，分别超过第一、第二产业产值。

非公有制经济发展壮大。改革开放后，实行多种经济成分并存，个体经营户逐年增多，1988年有个体工商户1405户，从业人员1785人。1979年始有私营企业。1998年后，落实加快非公有制经济发展政策，引进并鼓励社会资本投资非公经济，境内个体、私营、混合所有制经济在工业、农业、商业、交通运输、通信、城建等领域拓展。2008年，私营企业发展至122户，个体工商户2906户，从业人员3121人。

六

改革开放30年，县境基础设施建设投入不断加大，基础设施建设成果丰硕，城乡面貌日新月异。

1978年，荔波境内公路里程仅287公里，之后不断加大公路建设项目投入，修建和改建县、乡、村公路。到1990年，有县、区、乡公路20条（含简易公路）422.2公里，开通荔波至金城江、南丹、驯乐省际公路。4区1镇25个乡76个村通公路，另有村组公路及矿山公路100条，共429.5公里。1995年，全县通乡公路总里程741公里。至2008年，全境公路总里程1168.4公里，实现17个乡镇通油路，村村通公路。是年，麻驾高速公路列入开工计划，驾欧至县城、县城经榕江接厦蓉高速公路纳入省高速公路路网规划。县境已开通大客、中巴、长途快巴等多次班车直达都匀、贵阳、凯里、河池、南宁、广州等地。截至2008年年底，实现货物运输量179万吨/公里，货物周转量14120万吨/公里，旅客发送量172万人/公里，旅客周转量13015万人/公里，彻底解决了“货运难”“乘车难”的问题。2003年开工建设荔波机场，2007年正式通航，开创了黔南州通飞机的先河，并相继开通了荔波至深圳、荔波至广州、荔波至贵阳等航线，陆空立体交通优势成效明显。

境内邮电通信业务1994年前为邮政业和固定电话。1995年开通3000门程控电话。1996年开通126台、127台寻呼业务（BP机）。1997年开通模拟移动通信（90机大哥大）业务。1998年设电信公司，开设电信互联网，1999年设移动公司。2000年，建设开通无线接入方式电话通信系统，10月开通县城小灵通电话。是年，联通公司进驻荔波。至2008年，境内实现传输数字化、交换程控化，形成由多种通信手段和传输方式组成的覆盖全县的现代化网络。年末，开通19054门程控电话，开通小灵通4189户。移动联通移动通信实现村村通，移动用户32000户，宽带用户3054户。

1988年前，荔波城乡供电由境内小七孔一级至四级水电站供电。1999年9月，境内110千伏线路建成，从麻尾110千伏变电站降压运行输送国网电到荔波。至此，全县17个乡（镇）中，除佳荣、立化两镇部分村组由广西电网供电，甲良镇部分村组由独山供电局供电外，其余均由荔波供电局供电。2000年，境内启动农村电网改造工程，2004年年底全部结束，扩建和新建变电站4座；建设和改造10千伏线路1068公里。400伏线路283公里、220伏线路286公里；更换耗能变压器210台；完成配电台区改造762台。农网建设改造工程完成，乡（镇）、村通电率100%。2006年，境内有110千伏变电站2座，35千伏变电站5座。同年6月，因国家申报世界自然遗产工作需要，小七孔4座总装机5260千瓦发电站关闭撤除。

1990年前，荔波县城仅有繁荣路和向阳路两条主街道，次街道4条，除向阳中路为商业街外，其余为以路赶集，县城城区面积0.5平方公里。1991年始，分期对城区街道基础设施进行改造和扩建。2001年开始实施房地产开发，先后对沙梨园片区、板吉片区、苗圃片区、时来坝片区进行开发建设。至2008年，相继建成樟江大街、樟江北路、铜锣湾步行街、樟江园广场；新建绿化带、路灯、地下排水沟、供水管道、农贸市场、综合市场、三线入地等配套设施，按照“路网先行、拉开框架、优化布局”的格局，2001—2008年，实施城市建设攻坚战，老城区改造亮点呈现，新城区全面铺开。以实施时来路网中的江宾路、板我大道、官塘大道、阳光路、菜园路为重点，新区建设加快，城区面积由1978年的0.5平方公里扩大到3.8平方公里，城区道路总长23.6公里，城镇服务功能进一步增强，城镇化率达30.6%。在加快县城建设的同时，从20世纪90年代开始，把小城镇建设列入议程，作为推动和带动县城经济发展的重要事项，并结合旅游业的不断发展，把村镇规划建设与旅游发展结合起来。1996—2006年，先后完成甲良、茂兰、佳荣、立化、朝阳、翁昂、驾欧、方村、捞村、播尧、洞塘、王蒙、阳凤等乡（镇）小城镇建设。至2008年，荔波县先后荣获州级、省级“小城镇建设先进县”“园林绿化先进县”、省级“卫生城市”及国家级“卫生城市”称号。

七

在推动经济社会发展的同时，加快社会事业的发展步伐，各项社会事业取得丰硕成果。

教育事业：历届党委、政府高度重视教育工作，加大对教育事业的投入，重点发展基础教育和职业教育。先后组织实施了义务教育工程、农村寄宿制学校工程、义务教育薄弱学校改扩建工程和职校、高中扩招工程，教育基础设施和办学条件得到极大改善。2008年，全县有126个校点，其中独立高中1所，职业高中1所，初级中学8所，九年一贯制学校1所，小学105所，幼儿园10个；小学在校生17488人，初中在校生9115人，高中在校生4501人（其中职高生1942人），幼儿在园2947人；有教职工1993人，专任教师1797人。全县中小学校舍总面积175082平方米，小学生生均校舍6.4平方米，初中生生均校舍6.9平方米。2001年，经省政府评估验收，教育部认定，荔波县实现基本普及九年义务教育，成为贵州省国家级贫困县中第三个、黔南州第一个实现“普九”达标县。2008年，全县高考成绩名列黔南州第四位。同年，“两基教育”评估通过国家检查验收。

卫生事业：1978—2008年，境内城乡卫生医疗条件明显改善。30年中，卫生保健工作坚持预防为主、防治结合方针。各级医疗、防疫、保健机构健全。县设县人民医院、县中医院、卫生防疫站、妇幼保健站、皮肤病防治站、药品检验所；乡（镇）建卫生院、村设卫生室，形成点多面广的卫生防疫保健网。1991年建镇并乡撤区时，全县有县级医院两家，卫生防疫、妇幼保健、药品检验、皮肤病防治站各1家，区卫生院4个，乡卫生院26个，共有医务人员423人。1992年实施公费医疗管理改革，职工看病有定点医院。1997年实施医疗统筹，启动农村合作医疗试点。2000年全县乡村三级预防保健网络基本健全。2006年全面实施新型农村合作医疗。2008年，境内有县级医院2家，口腔病防治中心1家，乡（镇）、村三级医疗定点机构60所，新型农村农村合作医疗参合率94.75%。

文化事业：通过多渠道投入，群众文化、广播电视取得长足发展。县建有文化馆、图书馆、电视台，乡（镇）建中心文化站，建有农家书屋29个。新建乡（镇）地面卫星电视接收站11831座，电视人口覆盖率93%，广播人口覆盖率50.23%。县城数字电视有序推进。注重民族文化挖掘与保护，“水书”“瑶族猴鼓舞”被列入第二批国家级非物质文化遗产名录，县档案馆以水书古籍的珍贵价值被国务院列入“全国古籍重点保护单位”，成为全国唯一获此殊荣的县级档案馆。邓恩铭烈士故居被省政府命名为“全省爱国主义教育基地”。县城获得“全国文明城市”称号、“全国文明村镇”称号。极力打造“瑶山春晓、古榕夏阴、樟江秋月、梅园冬俏”等文化品牌，充分挖掘瑶族、水族、苗族及布依族等少数民族文化精品，逐步实现文化产业商业化。结合旅游打造民族文化品牌，成功推出“荔波荡漾”“瑶之韵”等民族文化系列活动，“土风计划”顺利推进。

社会保障：历届党委、县政府高度重视民生工作，按照“以民为本、为民解困、为民服务”的宗旨，不断加强社会保障工作，在救灾救济、农村低保、优抚安置、五保供养、改善贫困人口的住房条件等方面取得了可喜的成绩，切实做到灾难面前及时开展救灾救济，贫困人口应保尽保，实施茅危房改造工程和易地扶贫搬迁工程。2008年，全县共有8052户24000人纳入农村居民最低生活保障，881户1435人纳入城市居民最低生活保障。农村茅草房改造工程顺利完成，农村危房改造工程有序开展，基本解决贫困人口的“衣、食、住、行”困难。

在不断深化改革开放和经济建设进程中，荔波县面临新的发展机遇和新的挑战，全县各族人民在中共荔波县委、政府的领导下，高举建设中国社会主义的伟大旗帜，按照全面建设小康社会的要求，坚持科学发展观，加快经济结构调整，转变经济增长方式，增强自主创新能力，大力发展旅游产业，加快农业产业经营步伐，全面推进扶贫攻坚，使全县走上生态环境优美、经济社会和谐、人民生活富裕的发展之路，荔波的明天将会更加美好。

Overview

I

With the coordinates of 25° 07′ ~25° 39′ N and 107° 37′ ~108° 18′ E, Libo County is located in the south of Guizhou Province at the south end of Qiannan Buyi and Miao Autonomous Prefecture. It is bordered on Congjiang County and Rongjiang County of Qiandongnan Miao and Dong Autonomous Prefecture in the northeast, adjacent to Huanjiang Maonan Autonomous County and Nandan County of Guangxi Zhuang Autonomous Region in the southeast, bordered on Dushan County in the west and connected to Sandu Shui Autonomous County in the north. The area under its jurisdiction extends 67.3 kilometers from east and west and 58.5 kilometers from south to north, with the total area of 2,431.8 square kilometers.

The county is located in the transitional belt from the slope south of Guizhou Plateau to the hilly basin of Guangxi, with the topography lower in the south and higher in the north. The altitude of the county town is 425 meters. With the lowest altitude of 300 meters in Laocun River estuary and the highest altitude of 1,468 meters in the secondary peak of Moon Mountain, the average altitude of the county is 758.8 meters. Most villages have the altitude of 400 ~ 800 meters.

Controlled by geological structure, the landform constitutes valleys in syncline and hills in anticline, forming alternating arrangement of mountains and valleys from west to east. Main mountain ranges and water systems are developed along the strike of geological structure, forming the pattern of embedding arrangement of mountain ranges and river valleys in the shape of a belt in the direction of northeast in the whole county. Within the county sedimentary formation is extensively distributed, covering continental facies clastic rock of the Cenozoic Era, marine facies clastic rock and chemical rock of the Mesozoic Era, marine facies clastic rock and lagoonal facies coal formation of the Paleozoic Era as well as epimetamorphic marine facies clastic rock and chemical rock of the Proterozoic Era.

Libo County has the medium–subtropical monsoon humid climate. With low latitude, the county has rolling chain of mountains, deep river valleys, complicated landforms and diverse climate, with the characteristics of subtropical plateau mountain monsoon humid climate. The general characteristics are as follows: with warm and hot climate and obvious seasons, it is neither too cold in winter nor too hot in summer;

with long summer and short winter, long frost–free period and abundant rainfall, rain and heat are distributed in the same seasons; with less disastrous weather, it is beneficial for harvest of agricultural production. With the impact of different landforms and topography, it has significant difference in temperature, regions and sunshine. With uneven spatiotemporal distribution of rain, it has obvious rainy season and dry season. Such natural agricultural disastrous weather as draught, low temperature, flood and continuous rain appears from time to time. With significant vertical climatic change and contour microclimate in the county, the starting/ending time and duration of four seasons are different in most places. Generally speaking, the regions with relatively high topography have shorter summer and longer spring, autumn and winter.

II

Libo County was first established in the 17th Year of the Hongwu Period in the Ming Dynasty (1384), subordinate to Qingyuan State of Guangxi, then changed to Nandan Prefecture of Guangxi in the 12th Year of Emperor Zhengtong in the Ming Dynasty (1447) and subordinate to Qingyuan State once again in the 12th Year of Emperor Xianzong in the Ming Dynasty (1476). In the 7th Year of Emperor Xiaozong in the Ming Dynasty (1494), it pushed through a policy, which was later known as "Bureaucratization of Native Tusi Officers", with three inspection departments established in Fangcun Village, Mengcun Village and Jionglai Village, subordinate to Hechi Prefecture, Qingyuan State of Guangxi provincial administrative government. Libo County was reestablished in the First Year of Zhengde Period in the Ming Dynasty (1506), subordinate to Hechi Prefecture, Qingyuan State of Guangxi provincial administrative government. During the Period of Emperor Jiajing (1522 – 1566), the county magistrate Yin Dongyuan established city. County Town was established in Jionglai Lazhen Village (the former county town in Shilai Village today) after the First Year of the Wanli Period in the Ming Dynasty (1573), with Tucheng established, the east and west gate set, subordinate to Guizhou Duyun Department. It was subordinate to Guizhou Province in the First Year of the Shunzhi Period in the Qing Dynasty (1644) and to Qingyuan State of Guangxi in the 16th Year of the Shunzhi Period in the Qing Dynasty (1659) with the county town moved to Li' ao Village, Fangcun Village (Jieshang, Fangcun Township today). It was subordinate to Guizhou Duyun Department again in the Tenth Year of Emperor Yongzheng in the Qing Dynasty (1732). From then on, Libo County was subordinate to Guizhou Province until today. It was the People' s Autonomous Committee of Libo County in November 1949, the Liberation Committee of Libo County in January 1950, and the People' s Government of Libo County was established in February 1950. In April 1955, the People' s Government of Libo County was renamed as the People' s Committee of Libo and then the county was canceled in December 1958 and merged into Dushan County. The establishment of Libo County was resumed in August 1961. In March 1967, the People' s Committee of Libo County was renamed as the Revolutionary Committee of Libo County which was renamed as the People' s Government of Libo County in January 1980, and community was renamed as township in April 1984. The whole Libo County has jurisdiction over 4 districts, one town, 25 townships (including six Shui townships and two Yao townships), 160 villages and 1,187 villager groups. After establishment of town, merger of township and cancelation of district in 1991, the whole Libo County had jurisdiction over 5 towns, 12 townships, 170 villagers committees, 4 neighborhood committee and 1,193 villager groups. In 2000, Jiarong Shui Township was canceled, Jiarong Town was established and then the county had jurisdiction over 6 towns and 11 townships. In 2004 village merger was carried out in the whole county, and then the county had jurisdiction over 6 towns, 11 townships, 98 villagers (neighborhood) committees and 1,194 villager groups. By 2008, the county had the total population of 171,427 consisting of 22 ethnic groups. In addition to Han people, the county has the ethnic population of 157,750, accounting for 92.02% of the county' s total population. The ethnic population includes the Buyi population of 104,884 or 61.18%, the Shui population of 36,639 or 21.37%, the Miao population of 8,429 or 4.92%, the Yao population of 5,492 or 3.20%, the Zhuang population of 1,356 or 0.79%, the Dong population of 526 or 0.31%, the Maonan population of 100 or 0.06% and other 14 ethnic groups with the population of 324 or 0.19% of the county' s total population.

III

In 2008, the county has the land area of about 237,633.33 hectares, with the land possession of 1.44 hectares per capita, including the forest land of about 126,733.33 hectares or 53.33% of the total land area, the grassland of about 12, 953.33 hectares or 5.45%, the urban and rural residential land of about 2,913.99 hectares, the industrial and mining land of about 22.97 hectares and the transport land of 520.96 hectares. According to the third forest resource survey conducted in the whole county from 2004 to 2005, the county had the forest land of 126,700 hectares, with the stumpage of 5.9545 million cubic meters and the woodland and scattered forest stumpage of 15,400 cubic meters. The forest coverage of the whole county was 56.1% and the total stumpage was 5.9699 million cubic meters.

The main mineral resources in the county include coal, iron, lead, zinc, calcium carbonate, calcite, limestone and dolomite, distributed in 46 ore occurrences. In addition, the county has paradoxical reaction phenomena of iceland spar, silicon, copper, crystal and precious metal. Coal is a major resource advantage of the county, with the total reserve of 530 million tons, including 310 million tons of anthracite and 220 million tons of bituminous coal. The coal resource has been effectively developed and utilized in the county.

With large fall among rivers, the county has abundant hydropower resources, with the accumulative river fall of 6,342 meters, the theoretical total hydropower reserve of 349,000 kilowatts and the developable reserve of 244,300 kilowatts. Presently the county has 14 hydropower stations of development and utilization with 43 generators installed with the capacity of 97,390 kilowatts, accounting for 39.86% of the developable reserve.

Geographically, Libo County is located in the typical karst landform region. The county has concentrated large-piece primitive karst forest of 21,285 hectares, accounting for 20% of the total area of the whole county. The karst forest is mainly distributed in Maolan National Nature Reserve and Libo Zhangjiang Scenic Area, which is by so far the karst forest ecosystem with concentrated distribution, high primitivity and relative stability left on the earth. Located in the transitional alternating belt from Guizhou fauna to Guangxi fauna, the fauna belongs to the hilly geographic province of Middle Guizhou, Southwest Hilly Subregion, Indomalaya Ecozone Middle Region. It has 154 families, 514 genera and 1,203 species of vascular plants, including 144 families, 493 genera and 1,273 species of seed plants. National Grade I protected trees include Taxus chinensis

(Pilger) Rehd. var. mairei, Annamocarya sinensis, Liriodendron chinense and Eucommia ulmoides. It has 18 provincial protected tree species, 15 national particular genera and 153 species newly distributed in Guizhou. It has more than 400 species of vertebrate, including 16 orders, 43 families, 122 genera and 200 species of birds, 24 families, 42 genera and 16 species of beasts, 45 species of reptiles, 26 species of amphibians and 30 species of fish. In addition, it has 186 species of bryophyte and 163 species of large fungus. Among the plants there are eight species of national Grade I key protected wild plants and 100 species of Grade II protected wild plants; among the animals there are 4 national Grade I key protected wild animals and 45 species of Grade II protected wild animals. Besides, it now has 34 genera and 87 species of orchid. It is one of the regions with the most abundant orchid plants in China, with Paphiopedilum emersonii being national Grade I protected plant. The rich natural resources form the special green karst natural landscape here.

In Libo County, the Karst Forest in Maolan National Nature Reserve, with the total area of more than 19,333 hectares, was officially approved by the UNESCO as a member of the World Network of Biosphere Reserves on April 6, 1996. With lofty ridges and peaks, the Nature Reserve is covered with dense virgin forest, forming the four grand spectacles including funnel forest, bottomland forest, lowland forest and trough valley forest. In addition to the peculiar, serene, lofty, beautiful, wild, dangerous and grand natural landscape, it also has obvious folklores and folkways. In the scenic area, the ancient high trees, luxuriant vegetation, peculiar flowers and trees, precious and rare birds and bears, green mountains and waters, birds' singing, flower fragrance, vast forest and soughing of the wind in the pines give the people an infinite natural sense of beauty. With many precious flowers, grass, Chinese traditional medicinal crops, fungi, rare fish and amphibious reptiles, it is an ideal natural laboratory and research base as well as a beautiful natural park.

Zhangjiang Scenic Area led by Zhangjiang River System has 76 representative tourist attractions including 17 Grade I tourist attractions, 24 Grade II tourist attractions and 35 Grade III tourist attractions. With the unique green coniform karst view, it is a scenic area integrating hill, water, cave, forest, lake, waterfall and rock. With the total area of 271.1 square kilometers, Zhangjiang Scenic Area consists of three parts: one is Hanbi Pool, Xiangshui River, Feiyun Waterfalls, Water Forest, Green Valley, Guibei Mountain Virgin Forest, Wild Boar Forest, Yuanyang Lake, Tianzhong Cave, Bat Cave, Wolong Cave and Wolong Pool of Xiaoqikong; one is Shanshen Gorge, Tiansheng Bridge, Shuishen River, Di'e Gorge, Di'e Palace, Sky–Topping Fir, Qingshui Pond, Wanshe Pond, Erceng Lake, Xiaotian River and Longtou Mountain of Daqikong connected into one piece, grand and magnificent; and the other is Shuichun River Gorge Scenic Area. Shuichun River Valley goes upward from Zhangjiang River, with the river of 15 kilometers to Shuichun passing by Maniao Shoal, Longwang Cave and Wanniao Cave. On both sides of the gorge the environment is tranquil, the precipice is steep and the vegetation is luxuriant. In the gorge the water is clear with 13 waves connected, water and sky shining upon each other. Going downward in a boat, the tourists may have a feeling of cloud floating in water, boat running on the mountain and people going among a picture.

With the only karst forest ecosystem existing in the same latitude in the world as well as the karst virgin forest and hydrological landscape in Zhangjiang Scenic Area, Libo was passed by unanimous vote on the 31st World Heritage Conference on June 27, 2007 to be listed as a world natural heritage site for permanent protection.

IV

After the Third Plenary Session of the 11th Central Committee of the Communist Party of China, the CPC Committee of Libo County and the People' s Government of Libo County conducted a series of system reform in the county to create a sound environment for promoting the economic and social development of the whole county.

Starting from 1979, the whole county carried out the system of fixing output quotas to each group and production responsibility system linked to output, later gradually improved into the "household contract responsibility system with remuneration linked to output" . In 1984 it was specified that the farmers' land contracting period was extended to 2000, and the basic operating system in rural areas was further stabilized and perfected. The unified purchasing system of agricultural products was canceled in 1985, all the other agricultural products than a small number of agricultural products including cereals that were purchased based on contract may enter the market for trading, and the agricultural product purchase system transformed from fixed quotas for purchasing and marketing to "dual system" . In 1993, cereal circulation system reform was carried out, the unified cereal purchasing and marketing system was canceled and the cereal market was opened. The second round of land contracting was carried out in 1998 to extend the contract period of contracted land and barren hills, the land contracting relationship further stabilized and perfected. Other agricultural output taxes were canceled in 2004 than flue-cured tobacco tax. In 2005 the national agricultural tax-free policy was implemented, and agricultural tax was exempted for the organizations and individuals in the county engaged in agricultural production with agricultural income. Collective forest right system reform was carried out in 2008. In the past 30 years since the reform and opening up, great changes have taken place in the issues concerning "agriculture, farmers and rural areas" ; in particular, the poverty alleviation development for "Two Yao" (Yaoshan and Yaolu) has helped the Yao people lifted out of poverty.

From 1980 to 1985, the state-owned industrial enterprises in the county implemented factory director manager responsibility system, and the enterprises gradually implemented substitution of tax payment for profit delivery and profit contract. Enterprises implemented the contractual management responsibility system after 1986. In the same period, bankrupt reorganization was carried out for some insolvent enterprises and the attempt of equity transfer was made in some enterprises which finally failed. After 1998, seven state-owned enterprises in the county were reformed and transformed. Bahe Mine became the first joint-stock enterprise after transformation in the county. In 1999, reform and system transformation was continued to be carried out with the joint cement plant and agricultural machinery plant of the county. After implementing ownership and management right transfer system transformation, the county cement plant implemented efficiency goal management responsibility system, appointment system and contract system. In 2001, bankrupt liquidation, asset separation and reorganization and employee resettlement were carried out with the county and township (town) enterprise purchasing and marketing companies. In 2007, Zhangjiang Natural Food Co., Ltd. was transferred by auctioning. By 2008, nine state-owned industrial enterprises in the whole county were transformed.

After 1983, with the rapid development of nonpublic commodity marketing, the reform was intensified in the field of commodity circulation. In the same year, some state–owned commercial enterprises implemented contractual operation. By 1985, contractual management responsibility system was implemented in state–owned enterprises in all aspects. Starting from 1989, enterprise managerial autonomy and management responsibility system was carried out in enterprises where the enterprises operated autonomously and were responsible for their own profits or losses. State–owned commercial enterprises implemented state–owned and private contracting system in all aspects from 1993. In 1997, stock–right system reform was tried in commercial enterprises (not approved) while perfecting the state–owned and private–operated system. The new round of state–owned enterprise reform was started in 2003 and five commercial enterprises of the county were listed in the scope of reform. Later it was not approved due to immature conditions. By 2008, five commercial enterprises of the county were still state–owned enterprises.

While promoting the series of reform, the county continuously optimized the environment of opening up and development to attract foreign investment. In 1995 the business invitation and capital introduction department was established which worked based on the principle of "separate consideration of each matter". Preferential policies were launched in 1997 to carry out organized business invitation, and the business invitation and capital introduction work started to be standardized. From 2001 to 2003, the regulations and rewarding rules on business invitation and capital introduction were successively formulated and revised, "one–station" service center for business invitation and capital introduction was started, and various functional and execution departments were organized to settle in the service center to provide "one–station" service for external investors. In the same period, great effect was gained in business invitation and capital introduction through activities on festivals, events and activities in other places. From 1995 to 2008, the whole county totally introduced 216 projects, with the capital of RMB1,402.75 million paid in.

V

In the past 30 years since reform and opening up, the national economy has kept continuous development and economic aggregate kept rapid growth through joint efforts of the whole county. From 1978 to 2008, the gross production increased from RMB23.23 million to RMB1,133.78 million, the ratio of primary, secondary and tertiary industries was adjusted from 70.86:16.83:12.31 to 27.55:34.63:37.82 and the long dominant position of agriculture was significantly changed. The per capita GDP increased from RMB199 to RMB16,872, financial revenue increases from RMB1.27 million to RMB182.16 million (of which local financial revenue increased from RMB1.27 million to RMB8,292 million) and the per capital net income of farmers was improved from RMB143 to RMB2,618. The total volume of fixed asset investment of the whole society was RMB1.03 million in 1978, RMB161.91 million in 1998 and RMB683.57 million in 2008. The balance on deposits of financial institutions was RMB3.35 million in 1978 (of which the balance on deposits by urban and rural residents was RMB1.08 million), RMB209.73 million (of which the balance on deposits by urban and rural residents was RMB116.69 million) in 1998 and RMB1,373.05 million (of which the balance on deposits by urban and rural residents was RMB791.99 million) in 2008.

Through 30–year development, the position of agriculture as a foundation was stably improved and industrialized operation was gradually formed. In 1978 the gross production of agriculture, forestry, animal husbandry and fishery of the whole county was RMB32.56 million, including the agricultural production of RMB21.54 million, forestry production of RMB3.11 million and animal husbandry production of RMB7.89 million. In the same year, the cereal output was 29,900 tons, the rapeseed output was 167 tons and meat output was 600 tons, with 36,600 heads of live pigs in stock. After the Third Plenary Session of the 11th Central Committee of the Communist Party of China, with the opportunity of implementing the No. 1 Document of the Central Government, the county vigorously adjusted industrial structure based on the practical situation of the local area, promoting continuous efficiency improvement of agriculture and income improvement of farmers. Six characteristic industries including "animal husbandry, silkworm, forest fruit, vegetable, tea and sugarcane" were developed in order, basically forming the characteristic industrial development pattern of "red pepper and tea in the north, fruits and vegetables in the middle and silkworm in the southeast". In 2008 the whole county realized the gross production of RMB536.25 million in agriculture, forestry, animal husbandry and fishery, including the agricultural production of RMB246.61 million or 46%, the production of animal husbandry of 32% and the forestry production of 9.8%. In the same year, the cereal output was 59,900 tons, the vegetable output was 37,300 tons, and the meat output was 8,100 tons, with 60,800 heads of big domestic animals and 75,200 heads of pigs in stock. The fruit area was about 3,133.33 hectares and the mulberry field area was about 842.67 hectares.

The industrial economy led by coal industry was rapidly developed. Since the reform and opening up, coal industry in Libo has developed from unorderly mining to orderly development. Through implementation of the three-step strategy covering closing for rectification, integration for technical transformation and management to strengthen mining, the county had 32 mines of different types by 2008, of which ten mines were integrated, 14 underwent technical transformation, capacity and field expansion, 2 maintained the present production condition and 6 were renewed and constructed, with the design total annual production capacity of 3.57 million tons. With the actual annual production and sales volume kept at about one million tons, it is an important pillar industry of the economy in Libo. The gross industrial output value of the whole county was RMB2.89 million in 1978, RMB378.18 million in 1988 and was increased to RMB1,352.88 million in 2008.

Tourism was rapidly developed. The development idea of "county-wide great scenic area" was determined. Relying on the brand influence of world heritage, the selected tourist routes were optimally combined to present the development pattern of ecological sightseeing tour, countryside experience tour, folklore tour and red culture tour shining upon each other, directly benefiting the mass in tourism operation. With the tourism development strategy of "setting up stage with tourism and economy playing as the leading character", the county intensified the external publicity of tourism in all aspects. The tourism of Libo was rapidly developed, successively appraised as China's most beautiful place and international tourism destination. The economic system led by tourism was gradually formed with harmonious development of tourist product processing and relevant industries. In 2008 the number of tourists received exceeded 2 million person times for the first time. The whole county has 102 hotels of various types, totally with 10,000 beds, gradually forming the reception capacity supported with eating, living, traveling, touring, shopping and entertainment. Tourism has become the emerging pillar industry and growth pole of the whole county' s national economy.

Urban and rural trade was active in all aspects. In 1978 the total retail volume of social consumables was RMB8.94 million, of which the trade volume of wholesale and retail was RMB8.25 million accounting for 92.3%, the volume of accommodation and F&B industry was RMB330,000, accounting for 3.7%, and the output value of the tertiary industry was RMB2.86 million. Later, with reform in the field of circulation, commodity economy was increasingly active, urban and rural market was prosperously developed, nonpublic economy was developed and strengthened, the level of social consumption was continuously improved and the total retail volume of social consumables increased year by year, RMB28.68 million in 1988 and RMB86.56 million in 1998. The output value of the tertiary industry reached RMB115 million in the year and the total retail volume of social consumables exceeded RMB100 million, reaching RMB320 million in 2008. The volume of wholesale and retail trade was RMB269.7 million, accounting for 83.4%, and the volume of accommodation and F&B industry was RMB47.14 million, accounting for 16.6%. The output value of the tertiary industry was RMB428.83 million, exceeding the output value of the primary and secondary industries respectively.

Nonpublic economy was developed and strengthened. After the reform and opening up, multiple economic sectors coexisted and the number of privately-owned small businesses was improved year by year. In 1988 the county had 1,405 individual small businesses with 1,785 practitioners, and private enterprises started to appear in 1979. After 1998, the county implemented the policy of accelerating the development of nonpublic economy, guiding and encouraging social capital to be invested in nonpublic economy. In the county, individual economy, private economy and mixed-ownership economy were developed in such areas as industry, agriculture, business, transport, communication and city construction. In 2008, 122 private enterprises and 2,906 individual small businesses were developed, with 3,121 practitioners.

VI

In the past 30 years since the reform and opening up, the input in infrastructure construction of the county has been continuously improved with plentiful achievements gained in infrastructure construction and changes taking place with each passing day in the urban and rural image.

The highway mileage in Libo County was only 287 kilometers in 1978. Later the input in highway construction projects was continuously increased to build and rebuild county-, township- and village-level roads. By 1990, it had 20 roads (including hasty roads) of county, district and township level of 422.2 kilometers, with the interprovincial highways from Libo to Jinchengjiang, Nandan and Xunle open to traffic. Four districts, one town, 25 townships and 76 villages were accessible to highways. In addition, it had 100 village group roads and mine roads of 429.5 kilometers totally. In 1995 the total mileage of township accessible roads was 741 kilometers. By 2008, the total highway mileage of the county was 1,168.4 kilometers, with 17 townships accessible to tar-coated roads and each village accessible to roads. In the same year, the commencement of Mawei-Jia' ou Expressway was put on schedule, and the expressway from Jia' ou to the county town and the expressway of the county town connected to Xiamen-Chengdu Expressway via

Rongjiang was taken into the provincial expressway network planning. The county had several shifts of motor coach, medium-sized coach and long-distance express bus directly to Duyun, Guiyang, Kaili, Hechi, Nanning, Guangzhou and other places. By the end of 2008, the county realized the freight traffic volume of 1.79 million tons/kilometer, the freight mileage of 141.20 million tons/kilometer, the passenger distribution volume of 1.72 million persons/kilometer and the passenger turnover of 130.15 million persons/kilometer, thoroughly solving the difficulty in freight and vehicle taking. The construction of Libo Airport was commenced in 2003 and the airport was open to traffic in 2007, initiating the accessibility to airplane in Qiannan Prefecture. In addition, such flight routs were successively opened as the flight route from Libo to Shenzhen, from Libo to Guangzhou and from Libo to Guiyang, with significant effect gained in the advantage of three-dimensional land and air transport.

The post and telecommunication business in the county was postal service and fixed-line telephone before 1994, with 3,000 computerized telephones opened in 1995, and channel 126 and channel 127 paging business (beeper) opened in 1996. Analog mobile communication (90 cellular phone) business was opened in 1997. In 1998, telecommunication company was established and telecommunication internet was set, and mobile company was established in 1999. In 2000 wireless access telephone communication system was constructed and opened, and personal access phone system was opened in the county town in October. In the same year, Unicom was settled in Libo. By 2008, transmission digitalization and exchange computerization was realized in the county, with a modernized network covering the whole county developed consisting of multiple means of communication and transmission. By the end of the year, 19,054 computerized telephones were opened, and 4,189 users of personal access phone system were opened. Each village was accessible to mobile and Unicom communication, with 32,000 Mobile subscribers and 3,054 broad band subscribers.

Before 1988, electric power for urban and rural areas of Libo was supplied by Xiaoqikong Grade I through Grade IV hydropower stations in the county. In September 1999, the 110KV route was constructed in the county from Mawei 110KV Transformer Substation to Libo. All the places except for some villages and groups of Jiarong Town and Lihua Town with power supply from Guangxi Power Grid and some villages and groups of Jialiang Town with power supply from Dushan Power Supply Bureau were supplied with electric power by Libo Power Supply Bureau. In 2000, the rural power grid reconstruction project was commenced in the county which was completed at the end of 2004, with four transformer substations expanded and constructed and 1,068 kilometers of 10KV route constructed and reconstructed. In addition, 283 kilometers of 400V route and 286 milometers of 220V route were completed, 210 transformers of high energy consumption were replaced and reconstruction of 762 power distribution desks completed. The rural power grid reconstruction project was completed, with township (town) and village power accessibility rate reaching 100%. In 2006, the county had two 110KV transformer substations and five 35KV transformer substations. In June of the same year, four power stations of Xiaoqikong with the total installed capacity of 5,260KW were closed and removed as required for the work of world natural heritage application.

Before 1990, Libo County Town had only two main streets, namely, Fanrong Road and Xiangyang Road, and four secondary streets. Except for Middle Xiangyang Road which was a business street, all the other streets were used for fairs, and the area of the county town was 0.5 square kilometer. Starting from 1991, the neighborhood infrastructure of the urban area was reconstructed and expanded by phase. Real estate development was started in 2001, with development and construction carried out for Shaliyuan Subdistrict, Banji Subdistrict, Miaopu Subdistrict and Shilaiba Subdistrict. Zhangjiang Avenue, North Zhangjiang Road, Tongluowan Pedestrian Street and Zhangjiangyuan Square were successively constructed by 2008; and such supporting facilities were constructed as green belt, road lamp, subsoil drain, water supply pipeline, farm product market, general market and three–wire buried underground. According to the layout "led by road network, arranging framework and optimizing distribution", intensive urban construction was carried out from 2001 to 2008, with highlights presented in old urban area reconstruction and new urban area construction unfolded in all aspects. Focused on Binjiang Road, Ban'e Avenue, Guantang Avenue, Yangguang Road and Caiyuan Road in Shilai Road Network, new area construction was accelerated, the urban area was increased from 0.5 square kilometers in 1978 to 3.8 square kilometers, the total length of urban roads reached 23.6 kilometers, the urban service function was further improved and the urbanization rate reached 30.6%. While accelerating the construction of the county town, it listed small town construction into agenda from the 1990s as an important matter promoting and driving the economic development of the county town. In association with continuous development of tourism, rural planning and construction was combined with tourism development. From 1996 to 2006, it successively completed the construction of such townships (towns) as Jialiang, Maolan, Jiarong, Lihua, Chaoyang, Weng'ang, Jia'ou, Fangcun, Laocun, Boyao, Dongtang, Wangmeng and Yangfeng. By 2008, Libo County was successively entitled as prefectural and provincial "Advanced County for Small Town Construction", "Advanced County for Gardening Afforestation", Provincial "Health City" and National "Health City".

VII

While promoting the economic and social development, Libo County accelerated the development of social undertakings, with plentiful achievements gained in various social undertakings.

Educational undertakings: Each party committee and government of Libo County has emphasized educational work by improving input in educational undertakings with the focus on development of basic education and vocational education. The county has successively organized the compulsory education project, boarding school project in rural areas, reconstruction and expansion project for weak schools in compulsory education and enrollment increase project of senior high schools, significantly improving the educational infrastructure and school running conditions. In 2008, the county had 126 schools including one independent senior high school, one vocational senior high school, eight junior high schools, one nine–year system school, 105 primary schools and ten kindergartens. There were 17,488 primary school students, 9,115 junior high school students, 4,501 senior high school students (including 1,942 students of vocational senior high school) and 2,947 kindergarten students in school, with the teaching staff of 1,993 persons including 1,797 fulltime teachers. The total school building area of high and primary schools in the whole county was 175,082 square meters, with per capita area of 6.4 square meters for primary school students and 6.9 square meters for junior high school students. In 2001, based on assessment by the provincial government and recognition of the Ministry of Education, Libo County basically realized popularization of nine–year compulsory education, becoming the third among national poverty counties in Guizhou Province and the first in Qiannan Prefecture to meet the standard of "nine-year compulsory education popularization" . The county ranked the fourth place in Qiannan Prefecture in terms of the achievements in the college entrance examination in 2008. In the same year, "two-basic" education passed the national examination and acceptance.

Health undertakings: From 1978 to 2008, the urban and rural health and medical care conditions were significantly improved. In the 30 years, the guidelines of focusing on prevention and combining treatment with prevention were insisted in healthcare work. All the medical care, epidemic prevention and healthcare institutions of each level were sound. The on county level there were had county people' s hospital, county TCM hospital, sanitary and anti-epidemic station, health center for women and children, skin disease prevention and treatment station and drug inspection institute; on township (town) level there was health center and on village level there was clinic, with a health and anti-epidemic network formed with multiple points and extensive coverage. In the time of town establishment, township merger and district cancelation in 1991, the whole county had two county-level hospitals, one health and anti-epidemic station, one health center for women and children, one drug inspection station and one skin disease prevention and treatment station, four district-level health centers and 26 township-level health centers, with the total medical staff of 423 persons. Free medical care management reform was carried out in 1992 with fixed hospitals set for the employees to see a doctor. Overall medical care planning was carried out in 1997 and rural cooperative medical care pilot was started. In 2000 the rural three-level prevention and health care network of the whole county was basically sound. New rural cooperative medical system was implemented in all aspects in 2006. In 2008 the county had two county-level hospitals, one oral disease prevention and treatment center and 60 township (town) and village three-level fixed medical institutions, with the participation rate in new rural cooperative medical system reaching 94.75%.

Cultural undertakings: Mass culture and broadcast television were rapidly developed through multi-channel input. On the county level there were culture museum, library and TV station; on the township (town) level there was central culture station, with 29 rural studies established. The county newly constructed 11,831 township (town)-level ground satellite TV receiving stations, with the TV population coverage reaching 93% and broadcasting population coverage reaching 50.23%. Digital TV was promoted in sound order in the county town. The county emphasized ethnic culture excavation and protection, with "Shui calligraphy" and "Yao monkey drum dance" listed into the second list of national intangible cultural heritage. The archive of the county was appraised as "National Key Protection Unit for Ancient Books" by the State County with the great value of ancient Shui books, becoming the first county-level archive winning this honor. The former residence of Martyr Deng Enming was named by the provincial government as "Provincial Patriotic Education Base" . The county town was entitled as "National Civilized City" and "National Civilized Rural Area" . It was devoted to the development of such culture brands as "Yaoshan Chunxiao, Gurong Xiayin, Zhangjiang Qiuyue and Meiyuan Dongqiao" , fully excavating the cultural essence of such ethnic groups as Yao, Shui, Miao and Buyi, and gradually realizing cultural industry commercialization. The county developed ethnic culture brand in association with tourism, successfully launching such ethnic cultural activities as "Libo Dangyang" and "Charm of Yao" , with "Local Customs Plan" promoted successfully.

Social security: Each party committee and government of Libo County has attached great importance to the people' s livelihood work. According to the tenet of "people orientation, solving difficulty for the people and serving the people", the county has continuously enhanced the work of social security, with great achievements gained in such aspects as disaster relief, rural basic living allowances, five guarantees and housing condition improvement for the population in poverty. It practically realized timely relief in face of disasters and maximum guarantee for the population in poverty, implementing hut and dangerous house reconstruction project and poverty alleviation relocation project. In 2008, totally 8,052 households of 24,000 people in the whole county were taken into the scope of basic living allowances for rural residents and 881 households of 1,435 people were taken into the scope of basic living allowances for urban residents. The rural hut reconstruction project was successfully completed, the rural dangerous house reconstruction project was going on in sound order and the difficulty of the population in poverty was basically solved in terms of basic necessities including "food, clothing, housing and transportation".

In the progress of continuously deepening reform and opening up and economic construction, Libo County is faced with new development opportunities and challenges. Under leadership of the CPC Committee of Libo County and Libo County Government, all the people of Libo County, holding high the great flag of Chinese socialist construction and in accordance with the requirements for development of a mildly prosperous society in all aspects, insist the idea of scientific development, accelerate economic restructuring, transform the mode of economic growth and improve the autonomous innovation capacity. Meanwhile, the county vigorously develops tourism industry and accelerate the pace of industrial operation of agriculture, promote poverty alleviation in all aspects, thus to make the whole county take the development path of beautiful economic environment, economic and social harmony and well-off life of the people. Libo County will have a better future.

大 事 记

★ 1978年

2月24日—3月2日　召开全县科学种田大会，9个社镇、生产大队代表作科学种田经验交流发言。参加会议250余人。

9月16日　邓恩铭烈士故居列为省级文物保护单位。

11月　县城北郊的松林坡上建临时电视差转台试发电视信号，县广播站用16英寸黑白电视接收机收到广西电视台转播的中央电视台节目，这是县内第一次看到电视。

12月　根据省革命委员会关于政权派出机构和企事业单位不再设革命委员会的通知，撤销全县机关事业单位革命委员会和4个区革命委员会，恢复科、局、区公所名称。

是年　广西金城江至荔波茂兰矿区铁路建成通车，其中荔波境内27公里。除开通货运列车外，每天对开两班客货混合列车。这是境内唯一的铁路线。

★ 1979年

3月17—23日　全县1978年社会主义革命和社会主义建设群英大会和五级干部会议在县城召开，共1100余人参加。

3月20日起　中共荔波县委、县革委分开办公。

3月29日　首次引进广西65型人力水稻插秧机，在县内试用成功。

5月9日　县革委通知，撤销斗、批、改机构。撤销知识青年上山下乡领导小组及其办公室。

6月4日　县首次在时来、南门、茂兰6500亩水稻田中，安装235盏黑光灯，捕杀害虫。

6月15—30日　全县普降大暴雨，总降水量266.5毫米，比历年同期增一倍多，部分田土被水淹没，冲毁水电站2座，装机共24千瓦。

10月22日　将松林坡临时电视差转台移到城郊拉岜山，建成县内第一座电视差转台。

是年　在全县农村推行土地联产承包责任制。减免瑶山、瑶麓两个公社和全县138个贫困生产队的粮食定购任务。

是年　城关镇板吉大队党支部书记覃爱银被评为“全国三八红旗手”，受全国妇联表彰。

★ 1980年

1月14日 县革委为保护森林资源，制止乱砍滥伐，作出如下决定：1.坚持执行《中华人民共和国森林法（试行）》；2.坚决维护国家、集体的森林所有权；3.认真执行护林有功者奖，毁林者罚的政策。

2月12日起 对三类农副产品和完成派购任务的二类农副产品开展议价收购，议价销售。

3月17—23日 县第八届人民代表大会第一次会议在县城召开。出席会议代表255名、列席人员208名。会议审议县革委工作报告及县财政预决算安排、审议县法院、检察院的工作报告，通过《关于荔波县革命委员会改为荔波县人民政府的决定》。大会依法选举县第八届人大常委会主任1名、副主任5名、委员9名，柏文熙当选主任；选举县政府县长1名、副县长4名，吴洪铭当选县长；选举县法院院长、县检察院检察长；选举出席州第七届人大代表28名。从这次会议起县人民代表大会设立常务委员会。

4月12日 全县范围内发生风雹灾害，损毁房屋915间（其中全部倒塌53间），朝阳公社2座钢丝索桥被吹断，方村公社水电站被雷击坏发电机1台、变压器2台。全县小麦、油菜、玉米受重灾7065亩。

4月 各社、镇先后召开社员代表大会，宣布废止革委会，恢复镇人民政府、公社管理委员会，选举产生管理委员会成员。

6月 建成朝阳至瑶山、捞村公路的小七孔渡口。1989年王蒙大桥建成通车，渡口废。

7月18—23日 县三级干部会议召开，贯彻落实中央、省、州关于放宽农业政策精神，讨论具体措施。

8月 在坚持粮油统购统销、统一调拨的前提下，开展粮油议购议销。

10月5日 新华社记者杨锡玲采写的《贵州瑶山见闻》在内参发表，总书记胡耀邦作批语："少数特别落后地区，要派大员去用心研究，切实帮助那里的人民在两三年内翻过身来。"此后，省、州、县相继派干部到瑶山调研，帮助解决困难。

11月12日 县政府决定放宽林业政策，即：1.给社员划自留山，凡有宜林荒山的生产队，应就近划给每户社员自留山3～5亩。由各户自行植树造林，集体和个人对自留山收益，按1：9分成。2.国家、集体、个人所有林的权益都受法律保护，任何单位和个人都不得侵犯。3.国家对集体造林实行资助政策。

11月 州政府确定瑶麓、瑶山、岜鲜3所学校为民族小学。瑶山小学学生实行"三包"（包学杂费，包书本费，包穿、食、宿费），成为全州第一所寄宿制小学。对瑶山乡村级小学给予"两包"（包书本费、学杂费）照顾。

★ 1981年

1月18—23日	中共荔波县第四次代表大会在县城召开。到会代表264名，列席代表24名，特邀代表3名。大会审议并通过第三届委员会作的工作报告。大会选举产生第四届委员会委员25名、候补委员4名；选举县纪委委员7名。在第四届第一次全委会上，选举产生常务委员11名，王元当选书记。
2月17日	县委召开常委扩大会和三级干部会，学习贯彻中央、省、州关于“在经济上进一步调整，在政治上实现进一步安定”的方针。
4月28日	县委、县政府发出《对特殊困难的瑶山采取特殊照顾政策的决定》。
5月5日	全县开展讲文明、讲礼貌、讲卫生、讲秩序、讲道德、心灵美、语言美、行为美、环境美的“五讲四美”活动。
6月15日	全县旱情严重，县委作出《紧急动员起来，战胜干旱抗灾夺丰收的决定》。
8月1—5日	县城第八届人民代表大会第二次会议召开。
10月	全县开始计划免疫工作。
是年	全县开展林业“三定”（稳定山林权、划定自留山、落定林业生产责任制）工作，1198个生产队完成“三定”任务。

★ 1982年

2月23日	省政府公布第一批省级重点文物保护单位，荔波的邓恩铭烈士故居、水甫石棺墓群列入其中。
3月28—31日	县第八届人民代表大会第三次会议召开。
5月30日—6月2日	在荔波中学举办全县第一届少年田径运动会。
6月	城关区水尧公社联办煤厂发生瓦斯爆炸，死亡3人。
7月	第三次全国人口普查在县境开展。普查结果显示，全县有24327户、127489人。
11月7日	捞村公社板江渡口由于乘船人数超载，船上秩序紊乱，造成沉船伤亡事故，淹死5人。此为县内最大的一起沉船事故。
11月20日	岜鲜公社岜鲜大寨失火，烧毁民房55户，受灾280人，烧毁粮食50余吨。县政府及时拨救济款粮救济灾民，并发动群众献工献料、捐钱捐物，帮助灾民重建家园。
12月14日	县委四届三次全委会扩大会召开，讨论实现党风好转，全面开创荔波县社会主义建设新局面和工农业总产值翻两番的措施。

★ 1983年

3月1—17日	县第八届人代会第四次会议召开，会议听取和审议县人大、县政府和两院工作报告。
3月	县农业科学大会召开，县、区、社和有关部门负责人及科技工作者、农村科技户先进代表共459人参加大会。
4月4日	荔波县组建中国人民解放军昆明军区预备役第四师十二团三营后勤处，以及昆明军区后勤部预备汽车三团三连。次年缩编为中国人民解放军都匀预备役步兵师三团三营。
5月15日	广西环江县、贵州荔波县和五县联防办公室三方派代表，共同调查并协商解决荔波、环江两县边界纠纷问题。近年实行农业生产责任制后，荔波洞腊大队和环江河顿大队为交界的近万亩土地归属问题发生争议。
是日	县委决定在全县开展建设“文明村”和“文明单位”活动。
5月28日	县政府颁布《荔波县科学技术成果奖励暂行办法》。
6月	开展全县中草药资源普查，境内有药用植物700多种，产量较多的有60种。此外，药用动物（麝、熊、牛黄）及药用矿物（硫黄、雄黄）有少量出产。
7—10月	黔桂两省（区）对荔波煤矿开发问题进行会商，会商达成共识，形成贵州、广西两省（区）关于红茂矿务局在荔波境内开发煤田若干问题的会商纪要，明确煤田开发范围及照顾民族自治地方经济利益、环境污染和农田受损坏的赔偿、征用土地、招工等12个方面问题。
10月7日	在县城修建第一座冷库，面积149.6平方米，投资7万元。
12月	贵州省人民政府批复，县城关区改称玉屏区，城关镇改称玉屏镇，城关公社改称时来公社。1984年5月经黔南州人民政府批准，玉屏镇升格为区级镇，直属县辖，6月，建镇人民政府。
是月	机构改革中，经县八届人大常委会第22次会议通过，同意县长吴洪铭，副县长李德余、周志宏、蒙明儒的辞职请求，并决定蒙院芬代理县长，增补韦绍忠、袁希柳为副县长。
是年	县法院对全县在镇反、反右、“大跃进”“四清”“文化大革命”时期的案件进行复查，查出冤案1件、4人，宣布平反，恢复名誉，并做好善后工作。

★ 1984年

2月9日	全县地名普查工作结束，公布区、镇、公社、生产大队、街道居委会、街道、自然村寨的标准名称。从1984年2月20日起，一律以公布的称谓为准。

2月	县级机构改革开始，县政府工作部门保留21个。
2月28日	根据中央文件精神，县委作出延长责任田土承包期的决定，承包期自1980年起至2000年不变。
4月	将人民公社改为乡（镇），全县设4个区、1个镇、25个乡（其中水族乡6个、瑶族乡2个），166个村（居）、1190个村（居）民小组（其中居委会1个、居民小组4个）。
7月26—28日	全县民族团结先进集体、先进个人表彰大会召开，表彰先进集体30个和先进个人120人。评选出席省民族团结表彰大会的先进集体代表1人、先进个人2人，出席州先进集体代表10人、先进个人18人。
8月	国家卫生部确认荔波县已基本消灭丝虫病。
11月21—27日	政协荔波县第一届第一次会议在县城召开，出席会议政协委员87名。会议听取和审议县委统战部关于政协荔波县第一届第一次会议筹备工作报告，列席县第九届人大第一次会议。会议选举产生政协荔波县第一届委员会主席1名、副主席4名、秘书长1名、常委21名，蒙明儒当选主席。
11月22—28日	县第九届人民代表大会第一次会议在县城召开。到会代表155名、列席人员178名。会议听取、审议和通过“一府两院”、县人大常委会、计划、财政等6个工作报告。大会依法选举县第九届人大常委会主任1名、副主任4名、委员12名，吴洪铭当选主任；选举县政府县长1名、副县长4名，蒙院芬当选县长；选举县法院院长、县检察院检察长。

★ 1985年

1月24—26日	荔波县科学技术协会第二次代表大会在县城召开。
3月23—25日	县人大九届二次会议和政协荔波县一届二次会议在县城召开。
3月27日—4月1日	中共荔波县第五次代表大会在县城召开。大会到会代表196名，列席代表19名。大会听取和审议第四届委员会工作报告、县纪委工作报告，通过《关于中共荔波县第四届委员会工作报告的决议》《关于中共荔波县纪律检查委员会工作报告的决议》。大会选举产生第五届县委委员25名、候补委员4名；选举产生县纪委委员7名。在第五届第一次全委会上，选举产生常务委员8名，李秀振当选书记。
3月起	全县取消生猪派购，同时取消城镇居民肉票定量平价供应，实行市场调节价。
4月25日	县政府发布《荔波县征收农林特产税实施办法》。
4月	荔波县被省列为全省重点扶持的贫困县。
9月10日	第一个教师节庆祝大会在县城召开，县政府向全县外县籍任教15年、荔波籍任教20年以上的教师颁发荣誉证书，对有5人以上从教的家庭颁发“教师之家”

奖状，授予对教育工作有显著贡献的教师“辛勤园丁”称号。

11月2日 省政府公布第二批省级文物保护单位，瑶麓瑶族乡的瑶麓婚规碑列入其中。

12月 中共贵州省委书记胡锦涛到荔波考察工作。考察期间，到瑶山瑶族乡、立化乡实地调研。

★ 1986年

1—5月 省特等劳模、省农科院副院长、蔬菜专家李桂莲先后5次到荔波传授早熟蔬菜栽培技术，并重点培养6户种植示范户。

1月27—31日 县“两个文明建设”表彰大会在县城召开。

6月 茂佳公路上的瑶麓铜鼓坳隧洞开工。于1987年10月竣工通车，洞长96米，高6米，是县内唯一的公路隧洞。

是月 荔波县民族银饰厂生产的银饰品“四季手镯”在全省旅游工艺美术品、民族用品评比展销会上被评为民族优秀产品。

7月5日 荔波县科技扶贫服务团成立，成员11人。

10月 瑶山饮水工程动工兴建。用80毫米直径钢管从驾欧乡拉关村己定寨引甘泉水输送到瑶山乡所在地拉片村，全长7380米，解决瑶山乡政府机关、学校及村民共600多人，225头牲畜饮水困难和饮水卫生等问题，还灌田30余亩。

是月起 为期1年的全县工业普查工作展开，普查对象包括全民所有制、集体所有制工业。

11月22日 县委、县政府召开教育工作会议，讨论普及初等教育与任务。

11月 州政府确定，瑶庆小学为民族小学。县政府研究同意水利、水尧、永康、岜鲜4所小学办水族女生班优惠水族女生入学。

★ 1987年

2月25日 县1986年度“两个文明建设”表彰大会在县城召开。表彰先进集体30个，先进个人39名。

3月 全县开始颁发居民身份证。

4月8—11日 荔波县九届人大四次会议和县政协一届四次会议在县城举行。

4月 省政府批准茂兰保护区为省级自然保护区。

5月 县内第一艘机动旅游船在樟江投入运营，航线为县城—白岩—龙王洞—十三道浪河段往返运送游客。

6月12日 茂兰区立化乡六风井小煤窑发生瓦斯爆炸，死亡4人。

是月　动工修建播尧乡人畜饮水工程，从豆村提取溶洞水，用管道输送到乡政府所在地播尧场坝。1988年通水，解决2个村、11个村民小组、1092人、992头牲畜饮用水困难问题。

是月　县委、县政府对发展全县经济提出“依靠省州，面向两广，开发山区、兴县富民”的战略决策。

7月27日　县委、县政府作《关于计划生育的补充规定》，非农业人口，一对夫妇只能生一个孩子，农业人口继续提倡一对夫妇生一个孩子。

8月25—31日　政协荔波县第二届第一次会议在县城召开。会议听取和审议政协第二届委员会筹备工作报告和政协第一届常务委员会工作报告及提案审查委员会关于提案办理情况报告；列席县第十届人大第一次会议。会议选举产生政协荔波县第二届委员会主席1名、副主席4名、秘书长1名、常委23名，蒙明儒当选主席。

8月26—31日　县第十届人大第一次会议在县城召开。到会代表128名，列席人员148名。会议听取、审议和通过“一府两院”、县人大常委会、计划、财政等 6 个工作报告。大会依法选举县第十届人大常委会主任1名、副主任3名、委员11名，吴洪铭当选主任；选举县政府县长1名、副县长4名，韦绍忠当选县长；选举县法院院长、县检察院检察长。

9月　动工兴建瑶麓饮水工程，渠长10.86公里。工程于1990年6月28日竣工通水，解决全乡1300人和950头牲畜饮用水困难问题，同时灌溉部分农田。

10月20日　黔南州农村群众文化工作现场会在荔波县召开。

★ 1988年

1月11日　动工兴建永康水族乡吉洞村人畜饮水工程，1990年5月完工通水。解决了3个村民小组、95户、445人和300头牲畜饮水困难问题。

1月27日　黔南州政府决定由荔波、福泉、独山三县，代表中华人民共和国与联合国儿童基金会进行本周期的妇幼合作项目。4月落实荔波县合作项目，覆盖人口达全县总人口的50%，项目试点为4区1镇20个乡，84个村。12月9日，贵州省妇幼合作项目会议在贵阳召开，县合作项目领导小组组长黄玉成（副县长）代表荔波县在大会上作“开展妇幼合作项目，增进妇女儿童身体健康”的总结汇报。

是月　全县开展扫除“六害”（吸毒、贩毒、嫖娼、卖淫、黄色书刊、拐卖妇女儿童），同时严厉打击拐卖儿童妇女犯罪。

4月11日　县委、县政府表彰于4月7日扑灭时来乡上白岩组内江坡严重山林火灾的15个先进集体和92名先进个人。

同月 立化乡经验收合格，年底有瑶麓、朝阳、甲良、甲站4乡经验收合格，实现普及初等教育乡。全县在校少数民族小学生比例占在校生总数的92.4%，超过全县少数民族人口占总人口的比例。

5月9日 国务院发出《关于公布第二批国家级森林和野生动物类型自然保护区的通知》，茂兰自然保护区被列为国家级森林和野生动物类型自然保护区。

8月11日 县委、县政府作出《关于鼓励科技人员、干部职工到乡镇承办企业从事开发性生产的有关暂行规定》。

9月9—12日 中共荔波县第六次代表大会在县城召开。到会代表188名，列席代表15名。大会听取和审议第五届委员会工作报告、县纪委工作报告，并通过两个报告的决议。大会选举产生第六届县委委员27名，候补委员2名；选举县纪委委员11名。在第六届第一次全委会上，选举产生常务委员8名，李秀振当选书记。

10月6日 县委批转人大党组《关于在全县范围内进行执法大检查的意见报告》从11月开始用两个月时间，检查全县执法情况。

★ 1989年

1月6—8日 为开发小七孔旅游资源，州委、州政府在小七孔召开旅游资源开发工作会。

是月11日 县直机关单位建立支农联系点，县明确了各单位支农的乡（镇）。

2月11日 县委、县政府建立县直机关单位支农联系点制度，并确定各单位在乡（镇）的支农联系点。

3月7日 县1988年度“两个文明建设”表彰会在县城召开。表彰5个乡、9个文明村寨，56个先进集体、41名先进个人。

4月 邓恩铭烈士故居修葺完工，县委组织全县机关单位干部、职工及学校师生参观邓恩铭烈士故居，人数达4万人次。

10月 动工兴建茂兰场坝饮水工程，于1990年建成，解决茂兰区机关、学校、居民的饮用水问题。

11月23日 县委决定在全县开展打击、查禁、取缔卖淫嫖娼、制作贩卖传播淫秽物品、拐卖妇女儿童、偷种吸食贩卖毒品、聚众赌博和利用封建迷信骗财害命等社会丑恶现象和犯罪活动。

是年 县委、县政府组织干部群众开展创建省级卫生县城活动。

是年起 县国有商业按照政企分开、所有权与经营权适当分离的原则，落实企业经营自主权和经营责任制，企业自主经营、自负盈亏。

★ 1990年

1月10日　县委常委扩大会提出，1990—1991年全县要实现第二个翻番，经济工作重点要抓“粮、煤、林”三项。

2月14日　县委组织县党政机关下基层工作队，分别派到工业、煤炭、农业、教育等基层单位工作一年。

4月26日—5月2日　政协荔波县第三届第一次会议在县城召开。出席会议委员125名，列席人员25名。会议听取和审议第二届常务委员会工作报告及提案审查委员会关于提案办理情况报告；列席县第十一届人大第一次会议。会议选举产生第三届县政协主席1名、副主席4名、秘书长1名、常委20名，李德余当选主席。

4月26日—5月2日　县第十一届人民代表大会第一次会议在县城召开。出席会议代表143名，列席人员138名。会议听取、审议和通过“一府两院”、县人大常委会、计划、财政等6个工作报告。大会依法选举县第十一届人大常委会主任1名、副主任3名、委员11名，吴洪铭当选主任；选举县政府县长1名、副县长4名，韦绍忠当选县长；选举法院院长、检察院检察长。

4月　县政府决定兴建甲介、威桑等11个骨干煤井。有9个已先后出工程煤，有2个开始动工。

是月　建成甲站乡朋宾人饮工程，解决甲站村5个组，共897人、820头牲畜饮用水区，并灌田583亩。

7月1日　中共一大代表邓恩铭烈士故居开放暨塑像揭幕仪式在荔波举行。4日，县委发出《关于深入学习邓恩铭烈士事迹，弘扬烈士精神的意见》。

是月　第四次全国人口普查在境内开展。普查结果显示，全县有29071户、144086人。

8月　省政府批准荔波喀斯特森林风景名胜区经为省级风景名胜区。

9月18日　全县完成州分配的粮税任务，比1989年提前23天，荣获全州“四连冠”。县对提前和超额完成任务的区、乡评比奖励。

9月　县民族文工队参加在北京举行的“亚运会艺术节”表演。

11月23日　县委、县政府决定“七年消灭荒山，十年绿化荔波”。各区（镇）、乡主要负责人向县签订绿化承包责任状。

是年　兴建小七孔—麻尾、佳荣—广西驯乐公路。

★ 1991年

2月12日下午4时　境内遭受冰雹和大风袭击，时间10～15分钟，风力3～4级，冰雹直径0.3～2.5厘米。水尧、永康、翁昂、朝阳、时来等乡（镇）受灾，农作物受灾面积3500

亩，大风吹毁房屋350户。

7月12—14日 中国、日本、美国、德国、伊朗、泰国、英国、意大利、匈牙利等14个国家52名专家学者在茂兰保护区进行IGCP国际喀斯特地貌对比考察。

7—9月 按照省委、省政府《关于开展建镇并乡撤区工作的指示》精神，开展全县建镇并乡撤区工作。省政府批复撤销玉屏、朝阳、甲良、茂兰4个区，全县设5个镇、12个乡。

12月 县委成立县农村社会主义教育活动领导小组，从县直机关中抽调150名干部，组成第一批农村社会主义教育工作队，由宣传部组织集中培训后，分赴全县80个行政村进行宣讲。农村社会主义教育活动分思想教育、组织整顿、促进发展、考核验收4个阶段进行，为期4个月。

★ 1992年

1月14—17日 中共荔波县第七次代表大会在县城召开。到会代表179人，特邀代表10人，列席代表33人。大会听取和审议第六届委员会工作报告和县纪委工作报告。选举产生第七届县委委员33人、候补委员2人；选举产生县纪委委员13人；选举出席中共黔南州第六次党代会代表12人。在第七届第一次全委会上，选举产生常务委员11人，王化莹当选书记。

6月13日 省长王朝文到瑶山考察，要求加大扶贫开发和旅游带动致富力度。

6月 荔波喀斯特森林风景名胜区更名为荔波樟江风景名胜区。

7月16日 县委、县政府发出《关于建立旅游开发区的决定》，将小七孔、大七孔、水春河3个景区及其缓冲地带的生活服务区，玉屏镇服务中心、王蒙服务中心，以及拉片、水春、水扒、罗家寨4个民族村寨划为荔波樟江风景名胜区旅游经济开发区。

9月 在县城实施有线电视网络工程，传输电视节目12套，网络覆盖县城居民5000户。

12月10—12日 黔桂两省区八县市政协联谊协作会第一次年会在荔波县举行。

12月 县委从县机关单位抽调干部147人组成第二批农村社会主义教育工作队，分别到88个行政村开展社会主义教育活动。

是年 县内开始种植沙田柚。

★ 1993年

4月19—24日 政协荔波县第四届第一次会议在县城召开。出席会议委员135人，列席人员25人。会议听取和审议第三届常务委员会工作报告及提案审查委员会关于提案办理情况报告；列席县第十二届人大第一次会议。会议选举产生第四届县政协主席1名、副主席6名、秘书长1名、常委20名，黄玉成当选主席。

4月19—24日 县第十二届人民代表大会第一次会议在县城召开。到代表148名，列席人员118名。会议听取、审议和通过“一府两院”、县人大常委会、计划、财政等6个工作报告。大会依法选举县第十二届人大常委会主任1名、副主任4名、委员15名，覃顺芳当选主任；选举县政府县长1名、副县长5名，玉如敏当选县长；选举县法院院长、县检察院检察长。

8月23日 县委、县政府制定印发《关于减轻农民负担的实施意见》。

是年 县内进行飞机播种造林，共飞行22架次，用种20吨，飞播面积10.3万亩。

★ 1994年

1月10日 国务院发布第三批国家重点风景名胜区名单，荔波樟江风景名胜区被列为国家重点风景名胜区。

是月 省政府确定瑶山瑶族乡、瑶麓瑶族乡为重点扶持的“两山”（瑶山、麻山）特困乡。

4月 建立县“两瑶”（瑶山、瑶麓）扶贫开发试验区管委会，抽调11名干部分赴瑶山、瑶麓两乡协助乡党委、政府开展扶贫开发工作。

5月 在捞村、翁昂及广西边界一带，铲除罂粟4亩12210株。

5月6日 成都军区副司令员、中将马秉臣到荔波检查民兵预备役工作。

6月9日 中共中央政治局常委、全国人大常委会委员长乔石视察荔波瑶山。在荔波视察期间，参观了邓恩铭故居并题词：“弘扬烈士精神、开拓前进、振兴荔波”，为邓恩铭故居题写匾额。

9月28日 按照中央实行分税制的要求，全县税收分为国家税和地方税。

★ 1995年

3月 斯洛文尼亚洞穴探险考察队14人，到荔波进行为期半个月的喀斯特洞穴探险考察。

是月 县人大常委会审议通过，县政府颁布实施《荔波樟江风景名胜区管理暂行办法》。

6月25日 25日凌晨2时至26日中午12时，持续10个小时的特大暴风雨，降水量205毫米，樟江水位上涨6.88米，农作物受灾25770亩，房屋被淹78栋468间，倒塌房屋2栋26间，死亡牲畜18头，造成经济损失1977.25万元。

9月2日 县委、县政府颁布实施《关于招商引资的若干规定（试行）》《招商引资奖励办法（试行）》。

10月14日 在玉屏镇公路检查站截获海洛因500克，抓获犯罪嫌疑人3名。

10月26日 县委、县政府印发《关于贯彻〈中国教育改革和发展纲要〉的实施意见》。

是年 县政府下发《荔波县城镇国有土地使用权出让转让暨土地有偿使用暂行规定》。

是年 第三次工业普查展开，调查内容包括16个方面，普查对象为县境内的全部工业企业和附营工业单位。

是年 省委、省政府将邓恩铭烈士故居列为全省爱国主义教育基地。

★ 1996年

4月18日 县人武部收归军队建制。

是月 联合国教科文组织正式批准茂兰自然保护区为国际生物圈网络成员单位。

9月3日 举行水春河首次漂流仪式，国家有关部委，省、州、县有关部门，上海、广西等市（区）嘉宾300余人参加漂流仪式。

11月 税费征收推出栏杆政策，实行一次性收税。

12月17—19日 中共荔波县第八次代表大会在县城召开。到会代表220名，特邀代表26名，列席代表67名。大会听取、审议并通过第七届委员会工作报告和县纪委工作报告。选举产生第八届县委委员31名、候补委员4名；选举产生县纪委委员17名；选举出席中共黔南州第六次党代会代表12名。在第七届第一次全委会上，选举产生常务委员9名，张仕福当选书记。

是年 中共深圳市委、市政府确定深圳市商贸投资控股公司对口帮扶荔波县。

★ 1997年

3月5日 撤销瑶山、瑶麓原扶贫开发试验区管理委员会，组建瑶山扶贫攻坚工作队，时间3年。

是月 荔波县获林业部颁发“全国造林百佳县”称号。

6月7日 县委八届二次全委会议通过《关于进一步加强社会主义精神文明建设的决议》。

6月12日 全国人大民族委员会执法检查组到荔波检查贯彻实施《民族区域自治法》中关于教育、卫生、文化等方面规定的执法情况。

7月25日 县委、县政府印发《关于瑶山扶贫工作的实施意见》。

7月 县城开通模拟移动通信。

9月28日 县委、县政府颁布实施《关于招商引资奖励暂行办法》。

12月27日　荔波县获“省级卫生县城”称号。

★ 1998年

3月7—13日　政协荔波县第五届第一次会议在县城召开。出席会议委员135名。会议听取和审议第四届常务委员会工作报告及提案审查委员会关于提案办理情况报告；列席县第十三届人大第一次会议。会议选举产生政协荔波县第五届主席1名、副主席6名、秘书长1名、常委20名，黄玉成当选主席。

3月9—14日　县第十三届人民代表大会第一次会议在县城召开。出席代表158名，列席人员140名。会议听取、审议通过“一府两院”、县人大常委会、计划、财政等6个工作报告。大会依法选举县第十三届人大常委会主任1名、副主任6名，陆兴华当选主任；选举县政府县长1名、副县长5名，玉如敏当选县长；选举县法院院长、县检察院检察长。

4月11日　县委、县政府颁布实施《关于招商引资及争取县外无偿资金的奖励办法》。

4月16日11时13分　荔波发生4.9级地震，震中在荔波县捞村乡与广西南丹县木伦乡交界处，距荔波县城50公里。地震造成县内部分房屋不同程度开裂、歪斜、移位、倒塌，公路、桥梁、输电线路、矿山煤井、通信、水利设施等受损，受伤6人，造成直接经济损失6000万元。

5月　国务院批准茂兰保护区为茂兰国家级自然保护区。

10月1日　建立城市最低生活保障制度。

10月15日　国家环保总局批复将荔波列为第三批全国生态示范区建设试点地区之一。

11月　县委、县政府下发《关于稳定和完善农村土地承包关系的实施意见》及工作方案，明确农村土地除法律规定属国家所有的以外，属集体所有；实行“增人不增地，减人不减地”的政策将长期保持不变；全县从1994年1月1日起，耕地承包期再延长50年，非耕地资源开发的承包使用期再延长60年。至次年4月30日，全县颁发土地经营权证书32079份。

11月25日　荔波樟江柚果样参加全国第五次柚类科研评比，获“金杯奖”。

是年　建成水瑶移民新村，全村70户，330人。

★ 1999年

3月5日　县委、县政府发出《关于创建生态县、公园县的决定》。

11月1日　樟江柚在重庆参加全国柑橘品种结构调整战略研讨暨优新品种展示会，获特优产品推荐证书。

11月	县民族陀螺队代表贵州省参加全国第六届少数民族运动会，获男子团体第五名。
是年	县内暴发大面积穗颈稻瘟病，全县粮食减产20%。
是年	兴建成的110千伏输变电站并入国家电网，结束县内冬季经常停电的历史。
是年	县城开通互联网拨号上网业务，速率32KB。
是年	县委、县政府发出《关于创建科技先进县的决定》《关于创建文化先进县的决定》。

★ 2000年

3月	撤销佳荣水族乡，建立佳荣镇。
6月20—21日	境内连降大到暴雨，降水量达141.6毫米，樟江河水位高达22.25米，超警戒水位3.25米，超危急水位1.75米；导致多处山洪暴发，淹没农作物，冲垮房屋，损毁设施，公路垮塌，山体滑坡等灾害。造成农作物受灾面积108150亩，倒塌房屋1535间，损坏房屋5760间；受灾户数27653户，受灾人口124438人，直接经济损失19490.5万元。
7月10日	县委发出《关于荔波县保护母亲河行动方案的决定》。
7—9月	全县开展以讲学习、讲政治、讲正气为主要内容的“三讲”教育活动。
11月	第五次全国人口普查在境内开展。普查结果显示，全县总人口43625户，163500人。
是年	在县城沙梨园片区无偿划拨土地27亩，建教师新村以及征地规划建设乡镇小区。
是年	全县实现村村通电、村村通电视的目标。

★ 2001年

1月5日	中共贵州省委在荔波县城举行纪念中共一大代表邓恩铭烈士诞辰100周年活动。
2月22日	根据中央和省委、州委的部署，开始进行为期80天的“三个代表”（中国共产党始终代表着中国先进生产力的发展要求，代表着中国先进文化的前进方向，代表着中国最广大人民的根本利益）重要思想学习教育活动。全县106个县机关和17个乡（镇）干部职工4064人参加学习教育。
6月26—28日	中共荔波县第九次代表大会在县城召开。到会代表220名，另有特邀代表11名、列席代表83名。大会听取和审议并通第八届委员会工作报告、县纪委工作报告。大会选举产生中共荔波县第九届委员会委员31名；选举产生县纪委委员17名。在第九届第一次全委会上，选举产生常务委员10名，逄焕华当选书记。
8月24日	经省第九届人民代表大会常务委员会第二十三次会议批准，州人大会常委会公布施行《黔南布依族苗族自治州荔波樟江风景名胜区管理条例》。
9月30日	县委、县政府出台《荔波县投资兴业优惠政策》。

11月8日	上午，举行荔波机场开工庆典活动，国家有关部委领导，省、州党政军领导，省外有关单位负责人出席庆典活动，中央电视台、人民日报社及山东省、贵州省部分新闻媒体记者参加庆典活动。下午，在荔波樟江园文化广场举行大型文艺演出，著名歌唱家毛阿敏、蒋大为、刘秉义及歌手崔京浩等到场演唱。县城5万余群众观看演出。
11月	全县实现基本普及九年义务教育，成为贵州省国家级贫困县中第三个、黔南州第一个实现“普九”目标县。全县基本普及义务教育、基本扫除文盲达标工作通过省级评估验收。
是年	全县建成小水窖610口、沼气池694口，建设生态村寨5个，移民搬迁55户。

★ 2002年

8月5—10日	县委、县政府举办“全国卫视聚焦绿宝石荔波采风”活动，邀请北京电视台等19家国内新闻媒体参加，推介荔波生态绿色旅游。5日晚，举行文艺演出，向来宾展示荔波民族文化。
9月9日	县委、县政府发出《关于开展创建国家卫生县城活动的决定》。
9月	荔波县基本实现计划生育“村为主”工作目标。
11月6—11日	省邀请中国科学院地理科学与资源研究所、住房和城乡建设部风景名胜专家顾问研究员宋林华，国家著名喀斯特专家、南京大学教授俞锦标到荔波考察，正式确认荔波为世界遗产申报地。
12月24日	省委办公厅、省政府办公厅印发《关于划定荔波县为革命老区的通知》，划定荔波县为革命老区县。
是年	县城开通ADSL宽带，网速512KB。

★ 2003年

1月27日	荔波县被评为全省拥军优属先进单位，受省委、省政府、省军区表彰。
1月31日	第一次“盛世灯火映樟江”大型灯展活动开灯仪式在县城举行。
3月6日	板寨红七军第一、第二纵队会师旧址修葺工程、“八一”希望小学工程奠基仪式及祭奠革命烈士活动在荔波举行。
3月7—11日	政协荔波县第六届第一次会议在县城召开。出席会议委员149人，特邀人员29名，列席人员40名。会议听取和审议第五届常务委员会工作报告及提案审查委员会关于提案办理情况报告；列席县第十四届人大第一次会议。会议选举产生第六届委员会主席1名、副主席6名、秘书长1名、常委21名，田景胜当选主席。

3月8—12日 县第十四届人民代表大会第一次会议在县城召开。到会代表157名，列席人员125名。会议听取、审议和通过“一府两院”、县人大常委会、计划、财政等6个工作报告。大会依法选举县第十四届人大常委会主任1名、副主任6名、委员10名，陆兴华当选主任；选举县政府县长1名、副县长5名，潘朝显当选县长；选举县法院院长、县检察院检察长。

5月16日 县委、县政府下发《关于进一步加强人口与计划生育经费投入和严格执行“一票否决权”制度的实施办法》。

5月29日 县委、县政府颁布试行《关于招商引资的若干规定》《关于招商引资的奖励办法》，同时废止原《荔波县投资兴业优惠政策》《荔波县招商引资奖励办法》。

6月5日 县委、县政府发出《关于加快旅游业发展的决定》。

6月20日 县委、县政府下发《关于进一步加快新阶段扶贫开发与小康建设的决定》。

8月8—10日 贵州省旅游局、贵州电视台、贵州日报社、黔南州政府、荔波县政府在荔波县城共同举办“中国·荔波绿宝石之旅暨贵州少数民族服饰展演”活动。活动期间，签约项目66个，总投资47.3亿元，引进资金45.8亿元，吸引游客3万多人到荔波旅游观光。

10月9日 台湾三立电视台拍摄组到瑶山拍摄少数民族风情片。

12月13—17日 全县开展大规模打击非法盗采国家煤炭资源集中整治行动，炸封非法小煤井343口及各种采煤设备。

12月 县民族陀螺队代表贵州省参加全国第七届少数民族运动会，获男子团体第三名、男子单打第三名。

★ 2004年

1月1日 取消农业特产税（除烟叶外）。

6月9—11日 国际自然保护联盟（IUCN）专家、国际著名喀斯特学家、新西兰奥克兰大学教授威廉姆斯应邀考察荔波世界自然遗产提名地。

7月1日 红七军板寨会师旧址纪念馆开馆仪式暨板寨“八一”希望小学揭牌仪式在荔波举行。板寨“八一”希望小学由省军区拨款20万元、贵州省预备役师拨款10万元、中央危房改造经费20万元修建。

7月2—7日 《人民日报》、新华社、《光明日报》《经济日报》《中国文化报》《中国日报》《北京周报》《今日中国》、美国《彼岸》杂志、《解放军报》等10家媒体组成的中央媒体记者团到荔波进行为期6天的采访，对荔波申报世界自然遗产工作进行宣传。

8月13日 中国科学院地理科学与资源研究所研究员宋林华和贵州师范大学教授杨明德从贵阳乘车赴荔波考察申遗工作途中遭遇车祸，不幸罹难。

8月30日	举行贫困学生助学奖励资金颁奖大会，奖励救助高中生、初中生、小学生共1217人。
9月26日	全省“美德在农家”活动示范点授牌大会在县城举行，荔波县玉屏镇板旺村获“贵州省美德在农家活动示范点”称号。
9月29日—10月8日	举办徒步穿越茂兰喀斯特森林科考活动，省内外地质、生态、民俗界专家应邀参加，记者随3个科考分队作现场报道，科考活动在贵州电视台《贵州新闻联播》《发现贵州》栏目连续播出10天，央视国际频道、《贵州日报》《贵州都市报》等媒体作专题报道。
10月11日	中国科学技术协会批准荔波县为“全国科普示范县”。
11月	瑶山民族中学被省体育局、省民委、省教育厅确定为陀螺训练基地。
12月24日	荔波县获全国爱国卫生运动委员会命名的“国家级卫生县城”称号，成为全省第一个国家级卫生县城。
是年	各乡（镇）进行行政村合并，合并后全县有行政村98个。

★ 2005年

1月1日起	执行国家免征农业税政策。
1月22日	按照中央和省委、州委关于开展保持共产党员先进性教育活动部署，开始在全县开展保持共产党员先进性教育活动。整个教育活动分两批进行，至11月底结束。全县参加教育活动的党员覆盖面达99%。在教育活动中，为群众办好事、办实事1032件。
5月20日	首届全县中小学生信息技术创新与实践活动在荔波举办。
6月	荔波县通过省政府“两基”复查和“普实”验收。
是月	《“中国南方喀斯特”世界自然遗产提名地贵州荔波锥状喀斯特保护与管理规划》编制完成。
7月	为推进“中国南方喀斯特”申报世界自然遗产荔波预选地的申报进程，迎接国内外遗产专家的考察，县委、县政府制定《“中国南方喀斯特”申报世界遗产荔波提名地综合整治方案》，对荔波提名地环境进行综合整治。
7月	在国家地理杂志社举办的“中国最美的地方”评选活动中，荔波获得手机网络人气奖第二名和中国最美的森林奖项。
10月25日	县委、县政府发出《关于深入开展“四线百乡千村万名党员示范工程”创建活动加强建设社会主义新农村工作的决定》。
10月28—31日	县委、县政府举办“百位名家、百家媒体走进中国最美的地方——荔波”大型采风活动，文艺界、新闻界、旅游界125人应邀参加。

11月 国际喀斯特自然遗产管理专家、澳大利亚查尔斯特大学教授史密斯应邀到荔波提名地进行考察。

12月 荔波县开始实施新型农村合作医疗制度。

★ 2006年

1月12日—2月12日 首届“中国·荔波万亩梅花报春节暨原生态文化旅游月”活动在荔波举办。活动期间，获围棋“棋圣”称号的聂卫平与荔波围棋爱好者10人对弈、举行黔桂两省（区）猛牛争霸赛、民族民间特技表演、国际野生梅梅花研讨会、山地自行车大赛等活动。

1月 邓恩铭故居列为贵州省全民国防教育基地。

3月23日 荔波县被命名为第四批国家级生态示范区。

4月3日 县城举行申报世界自然遗产誓师大会及万人游行和签名活动，县委、县人大、县政府、县政协领导以及各乡镇、县直各部门、社会团体、非经济人士、学生和群众共2万多人参加大会。

4月29日 荔波县成立遗产管理办公室，为县政府直属正科级事业单位，承担全县国家遗产、世界遗产地的申报和管理的行政职能。

6月9—11日 IUCN专家、国际著名喀斯特学家、新西兰奥克兰大学教授威廉姆斯偕夫人应邀考察荔波提名地。

6月20日 黔南州政府在荔波主持召开会议，解决落实荔波申遗工作急需的环境整治资金和工作经费，在申请省开发银行贷款7000万元未到位的情况下，州政府先抽调2000万元，另外安排100万元工作经费。

7月29日 荔波县运动员覃建红代表贵州省参加中国第四届特殊奥林匹克运动会，夺得50米蛙泳金牌、100米蛙泳铜牌。

9月2—8日 国际洞穴协会原主席、澳大利亚悉尼大学教授朱丽娅应邀到荔波提名地进行考察。

9月2—10日 国际著名喀斯特学家、新西兰奥克兰大学教授威廉姆斯和国际喀斯特自然遗产管理专家、澳大利亚查尔斯特大学教授史密斯应邀到荔波提名地进行考察。

9月24—25日 全国政协副主席罗豪才率部分全国政协常委、委员视察荔波乡村公路。

10月23—25日 中共荔波县第十次代表大会在县城召开。大会到会代表243人，特邀代表27人，列席代表95人。大会听取和审议第九届委员会工作报告、县纪委工作报告。大会选举产生中共荔波县第十届委员会委员37名、候补委员7名；选举产生县纪委委员21名。在第十届第一次全委会上，选举产生常务委员9名，王振金当选书记。

是年 对小七孔景区86户村民进行移民搬迁，在驾欧拉主新建移民新村。

★ 2007年

1月2日	第二届“中国·荔波万亩梅花报春节暨2007年贵州赏花游首游式”活动在荔波举办，活动时间1个月。
1月5—8日	政协第七届荔波县委第一次会议在县城召开，出席会议委员155人，特邀人员29名，列席人员40名。会议听取和审议第六届常务委员会工作报告及提案审查委员会关于提案办理情况报告；列席县第十五届人大第一次会议。会议选举产生第七届委员会主席1名、副主席4名、秘书长1名、常委23名，董豫黔当选主席。
1月6—9日	县第十五届人民代表大会第一次会议在县城召开。到会代表147名，列席人员135名。会议听取、审议和通过“一府两院”、县人大常委会、计划、财政工作报告。大会依法选举产生县第十五届人大常委会主任1名、副主任4名、委员10名，陆兴华当选主任；选举县政府县长1名、副县长5名，陈稠彪当选县长；选举县法院院长、县检察院检察长。
1月10日	荔波县获省委、省政府、省军区授予“双拥模范县”称号。
1月17日	县委印发《关于在农村广泛开展“星级文明户”创建活动的决定》。
4月8—9日	中国外文局组织中国网、《北京周报》《今日中国》《人民画报》《人民中国》5家中央对外宣传媒体的外国专家及记者共13人赴荔波考察采访“中国南方喀斯特”世界自然遗产申报工作。
4月15日	成都军区政委、中将张海阳到荔波县考察指导。
4月26日	中国奥林匹克运动委员会副主席王宝良到荔波考察体育基础设施建设情况。
6月19日	第一架民航飞机降落荔波机场，荔波机场正式接受国家民航总局校飞中心为期7天的校飞检查。
6月27日	由贵州荔波、云南石林、重庆武隆捆绑申报的中国南方喀斯特世界自然遗产项目在新西兰召开的第31届世界遗产大会上全票通过，荔波成为贵州省第一个、中国第六个世界自然遗产地。是日晚，在县城樟江园广场举行盛大庆祝活动。
6月28日	在县城举行申报世界自然遗产成功庆祝大会及万人游行和签名活动，并在大七孔景区举行“世界遗产”标志牌揭牌仪式。
7月8日	芬兰、葡萄牙、沙特、巴基斯坦、冰岛等14国驻华大使到荔波，对荔波自然风光和传统民俗文化进行考察。
9月10—20日	县城客运机动三轮车进行清退，启动出租汽车客运经营。
9月16日	中国古籍保护中心研究馆专家周宗润一行到荔波对水书申报“世界记忆工程遗产名录”“世界人类口头与非物质文化遗产名录”工作进行调研。
10月18日	在樟江园广场举行50对老人金婚庆典活动，并为50对金婚老人颁发荣誉证书。

11月6日	第二届贵州省旅游产业发展大会在荔波召开。大会期间，举行“首届中国南方喀斯特文化旅游节”、文艺演出和黔南旅游考察、经贸招商、旅游招商推介及签约、中国南方喀斯特文化旅游座谈会等活动。
11月7日	荔波机场正式通航。
11月8—13日	东南亚地区暨中国生物圈保护区网络国际会议在荔波举行。东南亚12个国家和地区及国内68家自然保护区共120多名专家学者及代表围绕“文化多样性促进生物多样性保护和可持续发展”这一主题进行广泛交流和研讨，并签署《荔波共识》。
11月10—18日	县民族陀螺队在全国第八届少数民族传统体育运动会上，夺得男子团体第一名，男子单打第三名，女子单打第五名。
11月26—28日	2007年全国山地户外运动锦标赛在荔波举行，全国22支代表队参加越野跑、山地车、跑骑交替、漂流、定点穿越、登山、探险技能等项目的比赛。
是年	建立全县农村最低生活保障制度。

★ 2008年

1月22日	第三届“中国·荔波万亩梅花报春节暨2008年贵州赏花游”活动首游式在荔波举办。时间1个月。
1月中旬起	境内遭遇长达20多天有气象记录以来最严重的雨雪冰冻灾害。导致交通中断，输电线路、通信线路杆倒线断，停水、停电7天，生活物资供应困难。造成农作物受灾面积1.28万亩，倒塌房屋7间、损坏房屋1118间，死亡大牲畜2530头，经济林受灾面积1.35万亩；受灾户数34396户，受灾人口17.2万人；直接经济损失3296.5万元。
3月1日	国务院公布第一批国家珍贵古籍名录和第一批全国古籍重点保护单位名单，县内馆藏水书中的《庚甲》《泐金·纪日》《金银》列入国家珍贵古籍名录，县档案馆列为全国古籍重点保护单位。
4月5日	中央电视台《乡村大世界》走进世界自然遗产地栏目组在大七孔景区组织演出活动，县内布依族《矮人舞》《栏门酒》《摸八字》和瑶族《打陀螺》《凿壁谈婚》《掰柚子》等节目参加演出。
4月29日	佳荣镇拉易村一、二组发生特大火灾，烧毁房屋65栋245间，受灾78户。
5月12日	四川汶川发生8.0级地震，县委、县政府随即向全县人民发出《向四川地震灾区捐款倡议书》，全县党政机关、人民团体、社会各界向灾区捐赠款113.75万元。
6月7日	国务院公布第二批国家级非物质文化遗产名录中，荔波瑶族民间舞蹈《瑶族猴鼓舞》入选。

8月1日	深圳航空公司开通深圳—荔波往返航班。
11月2—7日	在浙江嘉兴举行的第二十一届聋奥会选拔赛暨2008年全国聋人锦标赛上，荔波籍运动员吴胜茂获羽毛球男子双打第二名，进入国家聋奥队。
11月11—12日	荔波县太极拳协会组队参加贵州省第四届健身气功交流展示大会，获集体项目三十二式太极拳、太极剑第一名。
12月9日	茂兰尧柳饮水安全工程开工建设，总投资740万元。
是年	中央文明委授予荔波县“全国文明城市”称号。
是年	经省人民政府评估验收，全县实现基本普及初等义务教育和基本扫除青壮年文盲目标。

特 记

革命老区县——荔波

一、荔波县有厚重的中国共产党武装斗争和革命活动的历史

（一）红七军在荔波的活动

1929年12月，由中共代表邓小平和张云逸、陈豪人等在广西百色策动广西省警备第四大队、教导总队和右江农军起义，成立了中国工农红军第七军和红七军党的前委，张云逸任军长，邓小平任政治委员和前委书记。红七军下辖三个纵队及特务营和教导队，全军约2800人。1930年2月，根据邓小平和中共广西特委的决定，广西省警备第五大队和左江工农赤卫队在龙州宣布起义，逐编为中国工农红军第八军，俞作豫任军长，邓小平兼任政治委员，下辖三个纵队，全军约2000人。同时，成立了红七军和红八军总指挥部，李明瑞任总指挥。

龙州起义后，总指挥部得知粤、桂军阀正在混战，南宁空虚，集中红七军和红八军21个连的兵力进攻南宁。国民党发现红七军的行动，速从贵县调来4个团的兵力，向龙州发起攻击，红八军大部受损，余部并入红七军。

1930年3月，红七军前委在凤山县盘阳（今属巴马县）召开会议，决定韦拔群率领第三纵队在东兰、凤山一带坚持与敌斗争，军长张云逸、总指挥李明瑞率领第一、第二纵队转到外线开展游击，以扩大政治影响，补充部队给养。两个纵队在黔桂边境开展游击。第二纵队在军长张云逸的率领下，历尽艰辛，途径东江、温平、水沅、川山和社村，翻越黎门关（现为黎明关），于4月16日进入荔波县瑶庆里的板寨（现属洞塘乡），分驻在板王、五圩、波格、拉美和板寨的上、中、下寨，军部驻板寨下寨（现为中寨）的姚顺廷家。同时，总指挥李明瑞率领的第一纵队，在思恩县城与敌边打边撤离后，艰苦跋涉，经大安、马口洞、宜北县城、洪山、驯乐等地，又分兵两路，一路经肯茶、更排进入荔波县瑶庆里的瑶柳、洞英、比鸠村寨；另一路经何家寨抵达荔波县巴容（现佳荣乡）的坤地，分驻在新寨、坡脚和坤地大寨等村寨，总部设在坤地大寨覃锡恩家。

红七军第一、第二纵队进入荔波县境在板寨胜利会师后，召开前委会议，作出奔袭榕江县重要决定，以打出军威和补充部队给养。在行军荔波和奔袭榕江途中，辗转于洞塘、茂兰、佳荣、水维、翁昂等乡的50多个村寨，不拿群众一针一线，买卖公平，广泛发动群众，号召各族青年参加工农红军。此间，佳荣乡坤地寨的青年妇女覃菊英，破除妇女不当兵的旧俗，毅然和男青年一起参加了红军，成为一名红军妇女战士。沿途书写标语，铲富济贫，惩办豪绅官吏，将中国共产党和红军的革命影响以及武装斗争的火种传播在荔波。至今，县境的威岩、坤地、坡费等地的墙壁上还保留

有当年红七军书写的“中国共产党万岁”“工农兵联合起来！建立工农兵自己的苏维埃政府”等革命标语。

（二）荔波县革命政权的建立及其活动

荔波县革命政权的建立，是由在广西东兰县坚持革命斗争的原红七军指战员，经过艰辛的活动而建立的，其后的革命斗争也是卓绝的。

原红七军第一、第二纵队北上江西后，第三纵队改编为二十一师，后改编为红军独立第三师。其六十三团三营营长韦汉超率领所部，频繁地在荔波与南丹的结合部活动。1933年2月，韦汉超抽选谭敏初、覃相国和韦英良等装扮为卖苦力的农夫，辗转于独山、都匀、榕江和荔波等县，寻找适合革命斗争的据点。他们在荔波县捞村乡群力村洞勤寨，得知何仕贤的父亲遭人陷害，身陷死牢，合计为其父排除了死难，何感激不尽，并结为至交。此后，韦汉超等经常对何灌输革命道理，其思想觉悟提高很快，表示积极拥护革命，永不变心。韦汉超找到了贴心人，便调来一些同志以卖苦工过活，开展革命活动，培养本地区的革命骨干。

1933年，在总指挥黄唤明的领导下，在南丹县拉索召开了有27人参加的组建“革命同盟会”会议，之后，由13人分为两个组分头开展工作。其中，有荔波籍捞村乡的何仕贤，翁昂乡的何凤楼、何凤清3人。不久，又在南丹县八圩拉池屯和荔波县佳荣乡平木村及捞村乡举行了“革命同盟会”会议，且平木同盟会规模较大。

荔波县革命同盟会的建立与发展，为组建革命委员会作了铺垫，加之韦汉超和何仕贤等人的积极活动，又创造了条件。因此，1934年5月，中共右江党组织派恩果中心县委书记陆浩仁到荔波，组建具有工农革命政府性质的“黔桂边区革命委员会”，选举韦汉超为主席，谭国联、何仕贤（荔波捞村人）为副主席，韦仕英、谭敏初为委员。黔桂边区革命委员会接受中共右江上游党组织和黔桂边革命委员会工农政府的领导。

荔波革命委员会的建立，把黔桂边的荔波、南丹、榕江、思恩、宜北、河池和东兰等县的革命政权组织连成了一片，使中共党员和革命积极分子活动范围更加广泛，区域逐渐扩大。1934年年底，韦仕英和韦汉超到瑶庆的瑶兰（今永康乡瑶兰村）以教书为掩护开展革命活动。1936年4月，韦仕英、谭国联、韦汉超到平寨（今立化乡平寨村）后又到巴辉（灰）（今朝阳镇）、寨马（今属瑶山乡）、黄（王）蒙（今瑶山乡王蒙村）、播缓（今播尧），覃桂芬到翁昂乡开展活动。1936年8月，韦仕英又到捞村乡群力村何仕贤、何素材处进行活动。活动的主要内容：一是与贫苦农民交朋友，讲解中共主张，发展革命同盟会组织；二是宣传右江上游革命委员会的有关文告；三是宣传中共的抗日民族统一战线的政策，把日寇赶出中国；四是反对国民党反动派不合理的征兵、派夫、征粮负担；五是发展中共组织，壮大党的力量。

1937年9月，右江上游革命委员会派黄唤明到南丹县拉索，召集在南丹、河池、思恩、天峨、宜北和荔波县边境活动的20多名骨干开会，组建“丹池边革命委员会”。会议选举韦汉超为主席，谭国联为副主席，韦仕英为组织委员，覃桂芬、韦寿昌为宣传委员，何仕贤（荔波县捞村乡人）、韦寿书为军事委员。委员会设在拉索，下辖荔波、宜北、思恩（今环江县）、榕江、天峨、南丹、河池、东兰的河东以及都安与河池交界的七百弄等地区，并将以上地区划为长老、荔波、南丹、天峨、思北等6个区，各区相应成立革命委员会，研究决定了各区负责人，何仕贤为荔波区主席。各区的主要任务是领导和组织该地区的群众开展抗日斗争。

（三）中国共产党组织在荔波建立及其活动

1935年5月，中共广西东兰县委员会在中共广西思恩中心县委员会的协助下，将中共东兰县委改建为中共东兰中心县委员会，黄举平任书记。东兰中心县委的领导范围是东兰、凤山、万冈、凌云、乐业、河池、南丹、天峨、都安及贵州省的荔波、贞丰、罗甸等县。是年，经中共东兰中心县委批准，中共荔波支部（称“荔十一支”）成立，韦汉超为支部书记。1936年9月，中共翁昂支部建立，谭耀机任支部书记。两个支部共有党员18人，隶属中共东兰中心县委。

中共支部建立后，韦汉超又集中原三营的部分骨干和荔波地方的骨干，开展反帝反封建的农民起义斗争和统战活动，其范围延伸至荔波及独山、榕江、南丹、思恩、宜北（今环江）等地，直到1937年7月7日抗日战争全面暴发。此后，斗争活动转入抗日宣传和统一战线工作。一是宣传共产党的抗日民族统一战线政策，反对国民党反动派不合理的征兵拉夫、征粮负担。受到广大群众的衷心拥护和热烈欢迎。二是宣传中共右江上游革命委员会有关文告。印发了敬告群众书、反对军阀抽丁传单等，号召民众觉醒起来。三是宣传边区革委在各地组织的抗日同盟会。号召民众参加这一组织，动员青年应征入伍，投身抗日。

1938年2月，中共贵阳女师支部派荔波籍女党员黄槐荫和贵阳籍女党员陈惠香到荔波女校，分别担任校长和教导主任，以此为掩护进行革命活动。她们每周以《新华日报》上登载的消息为内容，向师生进行形势教育，说明抗日民族统一战线的重要意义，宣传共产党的主张，教唱革命歌曲，利用赶场天搭台子向群众宣传抗日主张，揭露日寇的罪行，报告前线抗日消息，激发学校师生及广大群众的抗日情绪。

1942年8月，中共地下党员郑希侠（江苏省靖江县人），由石阡转移到荔波中学任校长。其间他联系延安，邮寄来《新华日报》《新生》等杂志进行学习和宣传，在教学中，教学生演话剧、唱革命抗日歌曲，宣传抗日。1943年5月，被国民党反动政府逮捕，次年在独山监狱牺牲。

（四）革命武装及武装斗争

1930年4月，红七军过荔波时，被国民党政府称为“土匪”的翁昂乡何光星的地方武装约有2000余人，盘于广西省的南丹县翁昂（现属荔波）、思恩县（现为环江县）的川山和贵州省荔波县的洞塘乡的结合部。经红七军有关人员的工作，与红七军结为友好，并做了许多有益于人民的事情。

改造后的何光星及其武装先后礼让红七军进驻板寨、为红七军伤病员治疗、保护红军掉队人员等。为此，国民党反动派惊恐和愤恨，想方设法施以谋害。1931年9月，国民党荔波县二区区长何峻峰以重金收买何逢春，在翁昂赌场枪杀了何光星。何的卫队也当场将何逢春击毙。

此外，红七军在荔波的革命活动，极大地激励着全县各族人民起来与反动派作殊死的武装斗争。一、何光星按照红七军的形象和斗争对象改造队伍，与红军着装一致。二、民众抗击日寇。1944年12月，日寇入侵荔波，县境各地抗击日寇的群体蓬勃兴起，较为突出的是九阡区石板寨（1956年划属三都县）水族群众，在十里长坡抗击日军，毙敌近百名，缴获枪支弹药战刀千余件。三、月亮山游击队。1948年8月，由邝先知等人组织的荔波县佳荣乡月亮山游击队70余人在佳荣地区活动，反对官府横征暴敛，打开潘老灵等3户地主家禾仓，把粮食分给群众，深得群众拥护，队伍发展到300余人。四、荔波县人民游击队。1949年12月，为迎接解放，由青年学生覃杰、潘文兴组织的人民游击队，在取得中国人民解放军一五一团和中共独山地委的同意后，一举解放了荔波县城。开创了单一的人民武装解放县城的先河。

二、革命老区申报

根据中共贵州省委办公厅、贵州省人民政府办公厅省办发〔1997〕31号文件精神，2000年，县委、县人民政府专门成立了县申报革命老区领导小组，下设办公室。随后，按照有关划定革命老区的标准和要求，组织力量赴广西河池、百色、南宁以及贵阳、重庆等地，对20世纪30年代中国共产党及其领导下的中国工农红军在县境的革命活动进行了深入的调查，搜集资料，核实史实。其间，先后走访老红军、老党员和知情者，到有关档案史志部门查阅文献材料、历史资料和报纸杂志，收集到了大量的文字资料和口碑材料。之后进行整理，形成了《关于要求划定荔波县为革命老区的调查报告》。《调查报告》以翔实的史料记述了1930—1936年红七军第一、第二纵队，右江独立师三营及右江党组织在荔波开展活动，广泛宣传中共的政治主张，开展武装斗争，惩办豪绅污吏，扩大中共和红军的政治影响。建立了中共荔波支部（荔十一支）、中共翁昂支部等党组织；组建了黔桂边（荔波）革命委员会等政权组织，使荔波成为中国共产党领导下的滇黔桂边区革命根据地的一部分，坚持革命斗争数年之久，其活动范围遍及全县17个乡镇（现行的行政区划）中的玉屏镇、朝阳镇、茂兰镇、立化镇、佳荣镇、翁昂乡、捞村乡、瑶山乡、播尧乡、永康乡、洞塘乡、瑶麓乡等12个乡（镇），超过县域50%以上。

2001年9月，中共黔南州委、黔南州人民政府向省委、省人民政府呈报荔波县申报革命老区的请示，并附荔波县申报老区的附件材料。省划定革命老区办公室（省委党史研究室），经对材料进行研究核实，并报省划定革命老区领导小组审核，认为荔波县符合省办发〔1997〕31号文件关于划定革命老区的标准，可以划定为革命老区县。

2002年12月24日，中共贵州省委办公厅、贵州省人民政府办公厅黔委厅字〔2002〕34号通知，经省委、省人民政府研究，同意划定荔波县为革命老区，辖革命老区乡镇12个。自此，荔波县成为全省34个、黔南3个老区县之一。

三、革命老区的建设与发展

2002年年底，荔波县划定为革命老区后，为改善老区乡镇的基础设施建设，2003年，省政府从中央划拨的革命老区转移支付资金中拨给荔波老区经费80万元。之后，每年按15%～20%递增。2008年起，县政府将革命老区经费分别拨划给12个老区乡（镇），作为乡村公路、移民建房、扶贫等基础项目建设资金。2008年，省政府拨给荔波县的革命老区经费增加到156万元。

经过长期的建设和发展，老区乡镇人均收入大幅提升，交通基础设施不断改善，通信基本覆盖，面貌大为改观。洞塘乡1997年人均收入为570元，至2008年提高到1980元，全乡通村公路达100%，电视覆盖率100%；朝阳镇1997年人均收入仅449元，至2008年提升到2675元；佳荣镇2008年12个行政村全通公路；瑶山瑶族乡6个村、46个村民组均实现村组通公路，境内1997年开通程控电话，到2008年，移动电话覆盖全乡。

在对老区乡（镇）开发建设的过程中，荔波县注重把境内特色的人文景观和红色资源结合起来，使游客在领略世界遗产地、地球绿宝石自然风光的同时，又潜移默化地感受到境内红色旅游文化的厚重。至2008年，已建成开放多处红色旅游景点。

1.中共一大代表邓恩铭烈士故居。1982年2月，省人民政府将邓恩铭烈士故居公布为第一批省级重点文物保护单位，1995年，公布为贵州省爱国主义教育基地，2006年10月，公布为贵州省全民国防教育基地。

2.板寨红七军会师旧址。距县城40公里，已修通油路。2006年，公布为省级文物保护单位。

3.黎明关。有“黔桂第一关”之称，是贵州打响抗日第一枪之地。为荔波红色旅游的重要景点之一。

4.民族抗日英雄全正熹故里。位于洞塘乡尧所村，距县城约40公里，已建成油路。

5.永康穿洞抗日遗址。2006年开辟为红色旅游景点。

此外，还有抗日英雄杨家骝将军墓及纪念亭、佳荣坤地红七军宿营地旧址等。荔波县已成为省内外红色精品旅游之地和重要的爱国主义教育基地。

第一篇
政区　地理

荔波县位于贵州省南部、黔南布依族苗族自治州南端，介于北纬25° 07′ ~25° 39′、东经107° 37′ ~108° 18′。东北与黔东南苗族侗族自治州的从江、榕江两县接壤，东南与广西壮族自治区的环江、南丹两县毗邻，西面与独山县交界，北与三都水族自治县相连。东西最长67.3公里，南北最宽58.5公里。全县总面积2431.8平方公里，占全省面积的1.38%。县政府驻地玉屏镇距省会贵阳334公里，距州府所在地都匀168公里。

境内东南面与广西环江县交界的有佳荣、茂兰、立化3个镇及洞塘、翁昂、捞村3个乡；西南面与广西南丹交界的有捞村、瑶山、驾欧3个乡；西面与独山县交界的有甲良、播尧、驾欧3个乡（镇）；北面与三都水族自治县交界的有佳荣、瑶麓、玉屏2个镇1个乡；东面、东北面与从江、榕江两县交界的有佳荣镇。

第一章 建置 区划

第一节 建置沿革

唐贞观年间（627—649），建婆览县，属江南黔州都督府东谢应州（按：治所在原荔波县属水婆，今三都恒丰）。

开元年间（713—741），建羁縻劳州、莪州（按：劳州即今荔波捞村；莪州即今时来乡板莪村，一说为莪蒲）。

宋开宝三年（970），建羁縻荔波州，属岭南西路广西庆远府（按：治所蒙石棒播远寨，即今玉屏镇播远寨）。

元世祖至元元年（1264），置羁縻荔波州，属广西行中书省庆远府南丹溪洞等处军民安抚司，后为蒙、皮、雷三姓土司割据。

明太祖洪武元年（1368），蒙、皮、雷三姓土司被征服，荔波并入思恩县。洪武十七年（1384）置荔波县，属广西庆远府。英宗正统十二年（1447）改属南丹州。宪宗成化十二年（1476）又属庆远府。孝宗弘治七年（1494）以后改土归流，置方村、蒙村、脊来村三巡检司，属广西承宣布政司庆远府河池州。武宗正德元年（1506）复建荔波县，属广西承宣布政司庆远府河池州。嘉靖年间（1522—1566），知县尹东表建城。神宗万历元年（1573）后，设县城于脊来之喇轸村（今时来村旧县），建土城，设东西两城门，属贵州都匀司。

清顺治元年（1644），荔波县属贵州省，顺治十六年（1659）又改属广西庆远府，迁县治于方村里袄村（今方村乡街上）。雍正十年（1732），改属贵州都匀府。乾隆二年（1737），移县治于蒙石里全亨村，改建石城，即今县治所在地。

民国元年（1912），荔波县属贵州省；民国2年（1913），属贵州巡按司黔中道；民国6年（1917）至民国15年（1926）属贵州省；民国24年（1935）属贵州省第十一行政督察专员公署（驻独山）；民国25年、民国26年（1936、1937）专员公署先后改编为第八和第二行政督察专员公署，仍辖荔波县至解放前夕。

中共一大代表邓恩铭的故乡——荔波

1949年12月，荔波解放后，由县人

民自治委员会（后改称解放委员会）行使政权。1950年2月4日成立荔波县人民政府。1955年4月县一届人民代表大会第四次会议以后，县人民政府改称县人民委员会，在此期间隶属独山地区专员公署（1952年改称都匀地区专员公署）。

1956年8月，撤销都匀地区专员公署，建黔南布依族苗族自治州，仍辖荔波县至今。

1958年12月，撤销荔波县建制，并入独山县。1961年8月恢复荔波县。

1967年3月15日，县人民委员会改为县革命委员会。1980年4月县革命委员会改为县人民政府。1984年4—6月公社改为乡人民政府，全县设4区1镇25乡（其中有6个水族乡，2个瑶族乡），164村，1187个村民小组。

第二节　行政区划

1978—1984年3月，县域设置城关（1982年改为玉屏）、朝阳、甲良、茂兰4个管理区，辖26个人民公社（镇）。

1984年4月，全县仍保留4区1镇（玉屏镇升格为区级镇），将25个人民公社改为乡（其中6个水族乡、2个瑶族乡），164个村，1187个村民小组。玉屏镇辖1个居民委员会，4个居民组，5个村民委员会，26个村民小组。玉屏区辖时来乡和永康、水尧、水利3个水族乡，共33个村、197个村民小组。朝阳区辖朝阳、王蒙、捞村、驾欧、翁昂5个乡和瑶山瑶族乡，共33个村、267个村民小组。甲良区辖甲良、方村、甲站、地莪、觉巩、播尧、阳凤7个乡，共50个村、371个村民小组。茂兰区辖茂兰、立化、佳荣、洞塘4个乡和水维、岜鲜、瑶庆3个水族乡及瑶麓瑶族乡，共46个村、325个村民小组。

1991年，开展建镇并乡撤区工作。7月，根据省政府的批复，撤销玉屏、朝阳、甲良、茂兰4个区；撤销玉屏镇、时来乡，合并建立玉屏镇，辖16个行政村、2个居民委员会，镇人民政府驻县城；撤销茂兰乡、瑶庆乡，合并建立茂兰镇，辖12个行政村，镇政府驻茂兰；将立化乡升格为立化镇，辖4个行政村，区划不变，镇政府驻立化；撤销佳荣乡、水维乡、岜鲜乡，合并建立佳荣水族乡，辖12个行政村，乡政府驻佳荣；撤销甲良乡、甲站乡、阳凤乡，合并建立甲良镇，辖20个行政村，镇政府驻甲良；撤销播尧乡、觉巩乡、地莪乡，合并建立播尧乡，辖19个行政村，乡政府驻播尧；撤销王蒙乡，将其2个村（高桥村、红光村）并入瑶山瑶族乡，瑶山瑶族乡辖6个行政村，乡政

2016年荔波县城全景

府驻拉片村；划原王蒙乡2个村（板麦村、洞莪村）并入朝阳乡，建立朝阳镇，辖12个行政村，镇政府驻田洞村；水利水族乡（辖7个行政村）、水尧水族乡（辖5个行政村）、永康水族乡（辖10个行政村）、洞塘乡（辖6个行政村）、方村乡（辖11个行政村）、驾欧乡（辖6个行政村）、翁昂乡（辖5个行政村）、捞村乡（辖4个行政村）、瑶麓瑶族乡（辖1个行政村）行政区域和政府驻地不变。建镇并乡撤区后，全县5个镇12个乡均属乡科级建制。

2000年，经省政府批准，撤销佳荣水族乡，建立佳荣镇。

2004年，各乡（镇）开展行政村合并工作，合并后全县有96个行政村、4个居民委员会。

2008年，全县辖6个镇、11个乡（其中5个民族乡）。即玉屏镇、朝阳镇、茂兰镇、立化镇、佳荣镇、甲良镇；洞塘乡、方村乡、播尧乡、驾欧乡、翁昂乡、捞村乡；水利水族乡、水尧水族乡、永康水族乡、瑶山瑶族乡、瑶麓瑶族乡。

第二章 乡镇概况

第一节 玉屏镇

玉屏镇位于县境中部偏北。东与水尧水族乡交界，南与朝阳镇和永康乡相连，西与水利水族乡毗邻，北与三都县周覃镇、九阡镇接壤。总面积160.91平方公里。为县委、县政府驻地，是全县政治、经济、文化中心。镇政府驻县城玉屏。

1978年时为城关镇。1983年2月，城关镇改称玉屏镇，隶属玉屏区。1984年5月，玉屏镇升格为区级镇，辖繁荣、和平、建设、板吉、菜园5个行政村和城北、城南2个居委会。1991年7月“建并撤”时，撤销玉屏区、玉屏镇和时来乡，合并建立玉屏镇。合并后的玉屏镇辖繁荣、和平、菜园、板吉、建设、时来、罗家寨、坡平、板旺、拉岜、福利、拉鱼、石灰坳、尧排、水甫、水春16个行政村和城南、城北2个居委会95个村民小组、32个居民小组。2001年12月，将城南、城北2个居委会划分为城东、城南、城西、城北4个居委会、40个居民小组。2004年12月，合并行政村，将水甫村与尧排村合并为水甫村，石灰坳村、时来村、繁荣村合并为时来村，建设村、和平村、菜园村、板吉村合并为建设村，罗家寨村、板旺村、坡平村合并为板旺村，福利村、拉鱼村合并为福利村，拉岜和水春2个村不变。合并行政村后，玉屏镇辖7个行政村和4个社区居委会。2008年年末，全镇总人口24552人，其中，布依族13798人，占总人口的56.2%；苗族1114人，占总人口的4.54%；水族3490人，占总人口的14.21%；毛南族25人，占总人口的0.1%；瑶族157人，占总人口的0.64%；壮族430人，占总人口的1.75%；彝族22人，占总人口的0.09%；满族33人，占总人口的0.13%；土家族53人，占总人口的0.22%；回族41人，占总人口的0.17%；东乡族5人，占总人口的0.02%；仡佬族17人，占总人口的0.07%；黎族9人，占总人口的0.04%；蒙古族7人，占总人口的0.03%；汉族5146人，占总人口的20.96%；其他民族205人，占总人口的0.83%。

境内属河谷盆地，四面环山，地势平坦，土地肥沃。樟江河从东北向西南环绕城镇、田坝而过，水利条件好。属中亚热带季风气候，年平均气温18.3℃，年平均降水量1320.5毫米，年均日照1272.8小时，无霜期317天。最高海拔933.3米，最低海拔420米，镇政府所在地海拔425米。

镇辖区主要河流有樟江河、水春河。解放前，县城东门外自樟江码头起，经比吉、回龙角、朝阳、寨马码头可达王蒙。共25公里河道，可通航载重1吨左右的船只。各码头每日泊大小木船近10只，日货运量可达10吨左右，主要将沿河两岸乡村所生产的棉、麻、桐梓、菜籽、粮食等运至县城。水春河的三道浪至县城河段水域比较宽阔，木材顺流放排年有2000立方米左右。1966年后，镇辖区内樟江河段先后修筑东风、东升水坝，建造水轮泵站，同时公路运输不断发展，原来的航道水运已成为历史。东风水坝至东升水坝间2公里河段仍可供舢板船航驶。东升水坝至白岩龙王洞205公里段仍能通航。开发水春河漂流后，该河段为县旅游部门机动船接送游客的重要航道。

2008年，全镇有耕地7520.76亩，其中田6660.12亩、土860.64亩，人均耕地0.31亩；有林地面积112983.6亩，草地面积36308.4亩。全镇有非耕地资源9.62万亩，适宜种植水果和水产养殖。野生植物食用类十余科30余种；药用类6个门类100余科；工业用材植物41科。

粮食作物主要有水稻、玉米、黄豆。经济作物有油菜、反季节蔬菜、辣椒、西红柿、麻类、花生等。经农业产业结构调整，农村经济逐步由自给半自给向商品生产转化。2008年，全镇粮食生产4484吨，蔬菜总产11500吨。

至2008年，全镇有私营企业40余家，从业人员1154人，总产值3761万元，上缴税金637万元。

全镇个体私营经济发展到2008年，有私营企业40余家，个体工商户1500余户。

玉屏镇是全县交通枢纽，县城通往各乡（镇）和邻县均开通客运班车，南下广西、广东，北上州府都匀、省城贵阳及重庆、四川皆有货运、客运班车通达。货运车辆有集装箱大型载重卡车及各种不同类型、吨位的货车。客运、货运车辆主要为私营性质。农电网、移动通信信号、广播电视等覆盖率均为100%。

2008年，全镇有小学校（点）11所，在校学生3128人；学前班11个，在班幼儿384人；幼儿园1所，3个班，在园幼儿106人。有专任教师179人。适龄儿童入学率99.80%。镇内有县属中学3所。

有镇卫生院1所，医护人员15人；各村均建有卫生室。县属医疗卫生机构驻镇内。2008年，农村人口参加农村合作医疗率100%。

旅游资源有省级文物保护单位邓恩铭烈士故居、永济泉（东门大井）、水甫石棺墓群、樟江田原风光、水上演艺厅、苗族古建筑风雨楼及国家重点景区水春河峡谷等50个景区、景点、景物。其中，属于世界级的景区、景点4个，属国家级的25个，其余属省、县级景观。

城区建有大会场、体育场、影剧院、医院、商业门市、大型商场等。大街小巷均为水泥路面，有樟江大桥、南门大桥连接城内河两岸。城内有宾馆旅社100多家。城区绿化覆盖率34%以上。创建国家级卫生县城于2004年通过国家评审检查验收，获国家级“卫生县城”称号。镇境属世界非物质文化遗产地范围。

2008年，全镇农业总产值18906万元，工业总产值5352万元，财政总收入1616.4万元。

2008年所辖村（居）、村民小组一览表

表1-1

行政村（居）名称	村民小组总数（个）	村民小组名称
城东居委会	10	—
城西居委会	8	—
城南居委会	12	—
城北居委会	10	—
建设村	21	和平、上菜园、中菜园、下菜园、板吉、板孔、板基、板庙、马道、塘地、播远寨、沙梨园等自然寨
水甫村	10	水甫、水江、水扒、尧排、甲召、水架、洞田、瑶寨等自然寨
水春村	5	水春上寨、水春下寨、更地、更楼等自然寨
时来村	26	旧县、沙地、上白岩、下白岩、官塘、后城、板莪、时来菜园、林场、新寨、鱼塘、罗卜木、石灰坳、河街等自然寨
板旺村	14	上罗家寨、中罗家寨、下罗家寨、板旺、廖家湾、岜腿、回龙角、坡旺等自然寨
拉岜村	8	更乍、播博、拉岜等自然寨

续表1-1

行政村（居）名称	村民小组总数（个）	村民小组名称
福利村	9	内拉鱼、上拉鱼、下拉鱼、上福利、中福利、下福利等自然寨
合计	133	

第二节　茂兰镇

茂兰镇位于县境东部。东与立化镇相连，南与洞塘乡交界，西与水尧水族乡毗邻，北与三都水族自治县九阡镇和县内佳荣镇、瑶麓瑶族乡接壤，东北与广西环江毛南族自治县相邻。总面积为189.4平方公里。镇政府驻茂兰，距县城26公里。

1978年时为茂兰公社。1984年4月，茂兰公社划分为茂兰乡、立化乡和瑶庆水族乡。1991年7月“建并撤”时，撤销茂兰区，将茂兰乡、瑶庆水族乡合并建立茂兰镇，辖场坝、尧朝、瑶埃、长寨、拉伙、洞英、比鸠、罗家、水庆、洞流、拉岩、更坡12个行政村。2004年，合并行政村，原12个村合并为6个村，场坝、尧朝、长寨、拉伙合并为尧朝村，洞英、比鸠合并为比鸠村，洞流、拉岩、更坡合并为洞流村，合并后有尧朝村、瑶埃村、比鸠村、罗家村、水庆村、洞流村6个村，76个村民组。2008年年末，全镇总人口9573人，其中，少数民族人口8555人，占总人口的89.37%。少数民族人口中，布依族5029人、水族3003人、瑶族263人、苗族260人，其他少数民族1018人。

镇境地处贵州高原南部斜坡向广西丘陵盆地过渡地带，属云贵高原余脉。地形呈东北部高、西南部低的向斜形势。属中亚热带季风湿润气候区，气候温和，雨量充沛，年平均气温19.1℃，日均温≥10℃，年平均降水量1500毫米，无霜期290天。最高点罗家村罗家坡海拔1207.8米，最低点茂兰大坝海拔570米，平均海拔750米，镇政府驻地海拔575米。瑶庆、水庆、更坡、洞英、比鸠、拉伙、长寨、尧朝等村寨有裸露型喀斯特地貌零星分布，瑶埃村大部分喀斯特山林地紧靠世界自然遗产地，与茂兰喀斯特森林自然保护区域连接。

境内全镇水资源比较缺乏，历史上被人们称为“干毛难”，仅有茂兰河、水条小河及吉王、更朋、更吉、水庆几条小溪，其地理位置完全处在煤炭开采区内。茂兰河为季节性河流，发源于东北面的罗家村尧柳、保家河、上甲介等溪流，流经茂兰大坝，流向瑶埃坝末端潜入地下。

全镇各类土地面积280万亩，其中裸露型发育喀斯特地貌约占全镇面积的50%。2008年，有耕地面积12000亩，人均耕地1.2亩。有成片荒草坡地和牧草资源近万亩待开发利用。林地总面积219712.35亩，森林面积128042.4亩，活立木积蓄量39.71万立方米。森林覆盖率47.57%。

矿产资源丰富，石灰石遍及各村，煤炭资源以无烟煤分布最广，储量约1.1亿吨，占全县无烟煤总储量的三分之一。水庆村已发现冰洲石，未探明储量。

主要农作物有水稻、玉米、高粱、花生、红薯、棉花、油菜、辣椒以及各种蔬菜等30多个品种。40%的农户有稻田养鱼传统习惯。随着农业生产技术的不断提高和科学种养技术的不断推广，产业结构不断优化，农民传统种植、养殖观念逐渐转变，糖蔗种植、生态鸡、黑山羊养殖等产业逐步代替传统单一的农业耕作，初步形成糖蔗产业为主导，生态鸡、黑山羊、肉牛等养殖业共同发展的新格局。粮食总产量4300吨（其中水稻4240吨），2008年全镇牛存栏2130头，猪存栏2270头，鸡饲养量11200羽（含洞流瑶山鸡繁育基地），鸭存栏2540只。

全镇工业企业有合茂煤矿、兴茂煤矿、富奇煤矿、安匀煤矿、匀茂煤矿、福利煤矿、甲介煤矿等8个，年产量50万吨。煤炭开采是茂兰的经济支柱产业。2008年，全镇有煤炭企业6个，建有2000盏有充电能力的矿灯充电大楼和汽车运输队伍，无镇属企业。

茂兰镇集贸市场物资种类繁多，有工矿机械产品、给排水设备、农用电器、服装、百货、烟酒副食、棉布、小商品、水果、蔬菜、肉类、禽类、蛋类等。

茂兰镇是县内物流的重要集镇之一，是南下广东、广西的主要通道。过境省际公路有县城经茂兰至金城江公路，县城经茂兰至佳荣抵广西驯乐公路，有县城经茂兰至洞塘乡公路。茂兰镇距平寨火车站9公里，距荔波飞机场18公里。每天有县城到茂兰班车和过境客运汽车50余班次。运输业成为茂兰镇农民收入来源之一。2008年，全镇有大小货运车150辆、客运车2辆、农用动力车164辆、私人轿车24辆、摩托车200多辆。农电网、移动通信信号覆盖各村寨，广播电视覆盖率90%。

2008年，全镇有初级中学1所、小学5所（其中花园式小学2所、村级小学3所），有中学在校生940人、小学在校生1148人，在职教师140人。适龄儿童入学率100%。

有镇卫生院1所，医务人员18人；有村级卫生室6个，集体所有制医务人员6人。2008年，农村人口参加农村合作医疗率93.8%。

2008年，全镇工农业总产值11074万元，比1991年增长670.3%。其中，农业总产值3131万元，比1991年增长426.9%；工业总产值7943万元，比1991年增长841.9%。财政总收入128.6万元，比1991年增长111.26%。农民人均纯收入3060元，比1991年增长431.25%。

2008年所辖村、村民小组一览表

表1-2

行政村名称	村民小组总数（个）	村民小组名称
尧朝村	16	场坝组、东风组、浪贬组、比旭组、拉伙四组、拉伙一组、拉伙二组、拉伙三组、长寨一组、长寨二组、长寨三组、几利组、尧所组、浪班组、浪银组、岩家组
洞流村	24	洞流一组、洞流二组、洞流三组、洞流四组、洞流五组、洞流六组、洞流七组、洞流八组、洞流九组、洞流十组、洞流十一组、拉岩一组、拉岩二组、拉岩三组、拉岩四组、拉岩五组、王家寨组、上更叶组、下更叶组、吉讲组、老寨组、平寨组、高岸组、更院组
比鸠村	13	洞英一组、洞英二组、洞英三组、洞英四组、洞英五组、洞英六组、洞英七组、洞英八组、洞英九组、洞英十组、甲惰组、内寨组、下寨组
水庆村	8	水庆一组、水庆二组、水庆三组、水庆四组、水庆五组、水庆六组、水庆七组、水庆八组
罗家组	7	甲介组、保家河组、罗家组、龙洞坪组、下尧柳组、上尧柳组、更排组
瑶埃村	8	长洞组、立卡组、洞开组、丘纳组、丘浪组、瑶寨组、韦寨组、欧家组

第三节　朝阳镇

朝阳镇位于县境中部偏西。东与玉屏镇、永康乡、翁昂乡接壤，南与瑶山瑶族乡相连，西与驾欧乡、播尧乡毗邻，北与水利水族乡交界。总面积166.5平方公里。镇政府驻朝阳村，距县城9公里。

1978年时为朝阳公社。1984年，朝阳公社改为朝阳乡，隶属朝阳区。1991年7月“建镇并乡撤区”时，朝阳乡建为朝阳镇，辖原花高、交朝、拉扶、八烂、田洞、花提、拉香、岜马、洪江、山江及原王蒙的洞莪、板麦等12个村、81个村民小组（含洞纳林场和洪江林场两个组民在内）。2004年，合并行政村，花高、交朝、田洞3个村合并为朝阳村，拉扶、八烂2个村合并为八烂村，拉香、花堤、岜马3个村合并为岜马村，洞莪、板麦2个村合并为板麦村，洪江、山江2个村不变，原村民小组不变。2008年年末，全镇总人口12245人，其中，少数民族人口12046人，占总人口的98.37%。少数民族人口中，布依族9391人、苗族1776人、水族792人，其他少数民族87人。

境内属中亚热带季风湿润气候区，气候温热，四季分明，冬无严寒，夏无酷暑，夏长冬短，雨量充沛，雨热同季，灾害性天气少。年平均气温18.9℃，年平均降水量1300毫米，无霜期315天。日照时数10.5～13.6小时/日，年平均日照1272.8小时，日照百分率为30%左右，属少日照区。最高点在山江村下水银组，海拔1064米，最低点是镇政府所在地，海拔410米。

镇境地势北高南低。地貌主要有山地、丘陵、坝子3个一级地貌类型。其中，山地占总面积70%、丘陵占19%、坝子占11%。2008年，全镇有耕地面积8993亩，其中田7034亩、旱地1959亩。林地面积24510亩，实有林地18194亩。用材林主要有松、杉、柏、樟、泡桐等。

矿产资源主要有烟煤、陶土、石灰岩3种。烟煤主要分布在洪江村的清水塘、拉塘和朝阳村扭头坡一带，储量未查明。陶土储量大，分布广。石灰岩分布广，储量多，且多在公路两侧，开采条件好。

朝阳镇以农业生产为主，有花高、洞阳、塘鸟、花堤、交里、板麦、洪江、水浪等田坝。粮食作物主要有水稻、玉米。朝阳村和八烂村每年种植蔬菜400多亩，主要有豆类、瓜类和叶菜类，是县城蔬菜供应点之一。2008年，全镇农作物播种总面积20353.1亩，总产量4667吨。

全镇有经济林面积3592亩，主要分布在朝阳、八烂、岜马和板麦4个村，主要种植柚子、枇杷、板栗、柿、桃、油茶、油桐等。

大型水利设施主要有鱼胆山引水工程、洪江水库、飞虎山水电站、巴怀水库、鲁翁山塘、洞阳坝提灌站等。岜马、懂架、浪弄、洞边等水源较为缺乏的4个村民组建有规格为30～60立方米水窖30口，蓄水可用于人饮和灌溉，50%以上农户备有小型汽油抽水机用于抽水灌溉，全镇保灌面积75%以上。

养殖业是农户主要经济来源之一。2008年，牛存栏1367头、出栏152头，羊存栏1536只、出栏500只，马存栏280匹，猪存栏2357头、出栏3668头，家禽存栏45132羽、出栏64400羽。扶持养殖户共69户，2008年在洪江村实施养鸡项目。2008年，县扶贫局在朝阳镇洪江村发放鸡苗3万羽，涉及农户317户；在山江村发放鸡苗1万羽，扶持养殖户273户。

2008年，引资100万元，兴建八烂村红柳砖厂和拉良岩石砖厂，两个厂日产红砖6万块。全镇有石场4个，主要分布在扭头坡和板麦洞纳林场组一带，年产值20万元。

食品加工业主要有酿酒和米粉加工，94%以上农户有加工技术，属粗加工，自给自足，部分出售，市场占有量小。

镇内有朝阳农贸市场1个，每5天赶一次场，主要交易物资有粮食、水果、蔬菜等农产品及日杂商品。2008年，镇市场有日杂商品零售店18家、批发店3家、建材商店8家。

镇有省道206公路过境20公里，村、组全部通公路，其中板麦、朝阳、八烂、洪江、岜马5个村道路已硬化。镇内有上交朝渡口和新平寨渡口。2008年，全镇有营运面包车（含家庭用车）25辆、东风牌汽车5辆、农用车15辆、大型拖拉机3台、小型拖拉机30台、摩托车1000余辆、机动三轮车23辆。

镇境内有大七孔电站和飞虎山电站，农电网覆盖各村农户。移动通信信号覆盖全镇各村寨，2008年年末全镇有农村固定电话989部、移动电话1528部，互联网用户45户。广播电视覆盖率80%。

全镇有中学1所，14个班，在校生688人；有中心小学1所、村小5所、教学点1个，共45个班，在校生1169人；有幼儿园1所，3个班，在园幼儿90人。共有教职员工96人。适龄儿童入学率100%，小学在校生辍学率为零，初中阶段入学率达100%，辍学率控制在2.14%以内。“两基”和“普九”目标完成。朝阳小学于1991年获省教育委员会颁发“贵州省提高初等教育质量实施计划（JIP）项目先进学校”称号，于2005年被州教育局评为“黔南州普及中小学实验教学示范学校”。

全镇有镇卫生院1所、村卫生室5个，医务人员总计15人。卫生防疫坚持预防为主，建立镇、村卫生保健网，实现人人享有初级保健目标。2008年，农村人口参加农村合作医疗率92.47%。

2008年，全镇工农业总产值4758万元，比1991年增长2803万元。其中，农业总产值3758万元，比1991年增长2223万元；工业产值1000万元，比1991年增长580万元。财政总收入21.4995万元，比1991年增长21.95%。农民人均纯收入2675元，比1991年增长314%。

2008年所辖村、村民小组一览表

表1-3

行政村名称	村民小组总数（个）	村民小组名称
朝阳村	13	上花高组、下花高组、下交朝一组、下交朝二组、下交朝三组、上田洞组、中田洞组、下田洞组、前播用组、后播用组、上寨平组、中寨平组、下寨平组
八烂村	15	板罗组、拉扶组、内吉毛组、外吉毛组、塘上组、当老组、寨省组、八烂一组、八烂二组、八烂三组、八烂四组、八烂五组、新寨组、更坡组、鲁翁组
岜马村	15	双桥组、觉巩组、花堤组、大寨组、新平寨组、供老组、岜马组、懂架组、挠降组、寨鸠组、拉良组、交里组、上拉香组、中拉香组、下拉香组
板麦村	17	洞边组、弄浪组、上寨马组、下寨马组、上婆组、中婆组、下婆组、外麦组、中麦组、内麦组、上寨莪组、下寨莪组、巴怀组、拉早组、拉庙组、下冷组、洞纳林场组
山江村	10	弄雅组、更佑组、上水银组、下水银组、拉正组、拉义组、坡团组、大寨组、懂更组、拉棒组
洪江村	10	林场组、干龙组、拉偶组、马浪组、拉佑组、向阳寨组、上拉岜组、下拉岜组、浪者组、坡庙组

第四节　佳荣镇

佳荣镇位于县境东北部。东与黔东南州从江县加勉乡交界，南与广西环江县驯乐苗族乡接壤，西与县内茂兰镇和瑶麓瑶族乡相连，北与三都县九阡镇及榕江县水尾乡和从江县光辉乡毗邻，是黔桂两省（区）、3地州（黔南、黔东南、河池）、5县（荔波、三都、榕江、从江、环江）、8乡镇（佳荣、驯乐、九阡、茂兰、瑶麓、加勉、水尾、光辉）的接合部及边贸中心。总面积362.8平方公里，是贵州省土地面积最大的乡（镇）。镇政府驻佳荣，距县城52公里。

1978年时设佳荣公社，属茂兰区。1984年，佳荣公社改为佳荣乡。1991年，佳荣乡与水维水族乡、岜鲜水族乡合并建立佳荣水族乡。2000年3月，建立佳荣镇，辖威岩村、坤地村、拉滩村、高里村、拉毛村、岜鲜村、拉先村、拉祥村、拉易村、水维村、大土村、甲料村12个行政村共129个村民小组。2008年年末，全镇总人口17184人，其中，少数民族人口15466人，占总人口的90%。少数民族人口中，水族8966人、布依族3712人、苗族2505人，其他少数民族283人。

镇境处于月亮山麓西南侧，地形东北部高、西南部低，是云贵高原南部斜坡逐步向广西丘陵盆地过渡地带，属云贵高原余脉。年平均气温15℃，年平均降水量1600毫米，无霜期280天。最高点月亮山次峰海拔1468米，最低处何家寨海拔300米，镇政府所在地海拔671米。

全镇有各类土地总面积54.96万亩，有效农用耕地10557.7亩，其中农田8763.1亩、旱地4794.6亩。林地面积40万亩，森林面积22万亩。其中，速生杉木林7万亩，大板栗7000亩，稀疏林地3万亩，自然林8万亩，灌木林2万亩。活立木积储量137.95万立方米。森林覆盖率62.41%。林产品有木材、香菇、木耳等。境内稀有野生植物有红豆杉、桫椤、榉木、单性木兰、格木、紫檀木、黄洋木等。野生中药类有大黄草、小黄草、大血藤、小血藤、杜仲、官桂皮、穿心莲、十大功劳、桔梗、瓜娄壳、天冬、水草等50多个品种，堪称荔波野生中草药材的宝库。

成片草场主要有拉毛、水碰、俄羊、姑爽、拉祥、平木、拉亮、拉滩等十多处，大多是坡度较缓的荒山草坡，总面积13万亩，总载畜量6500多头（按每20亩载畜1头计算），待开发利用。

矿产资源主要有煤、铁矿、铅铲矿和重晶石、石灰石等。煤矿主要分布在姑偿、拉滩、拉蒋3个井田，总储量6300万吨。

境内溪河纵横，主要有甲料河、水维河、坤地河、拉易河、兰靛山河、拉滩河、姑爽河等。拉滩、拉易、甲料3条河流水能蕴藏量2.72万千瓦，可开发量9170千瓦；拉先河自然落差95米，水能蕴藏量8600千瓦，可开发量6020千瓦；拉吴流经坤地新寨小河、水维小河等都可开发小型水电站。

农作物主要有水稻、玉米、红薯、高粱、油菜、大豆、小米、棉花、辣椒、甘蔗和各种蔬菜等。农业生产通过调整产业结构，改良品种，推广水稻、玉米高产品种和早熟蔬菜、果树、甘蔗等种植，促进农村经济由自给半自给逐步向商品化、产业化方向发展。养殖业以饲养牲畜、家禽为主。2008年，粮食总产量5083吨。全镇大牲畜存栏6470头，出栏1430头；猪存栏7740头、出栏5040头；家禽出栏12450羽。

工业主要有煤炭和铅锌、铁矿开采，镇内有金达、恒姑、威桑、长城4个煤矿，年产煤30多万吨，远销广东、广西。县招商引资引进的铅锌选矿厂2个落户境内。

1995年，佳荣乡被列为贵州省“双百小城镇”试点后，镇党委、政府充分利用区位优势，制定《佳荣镇总体发展规划》，同时实施佳荣新的农贸市场和集镇建设改造，成为全县小城镇建设的示范。佳荣集贸市场处于黔南州、黔东南州、河池地区交界地带，是县内较大的市场之一。1996年建成佳荣乡人饮工程，结束佳荣没有自来水的历史。

全镇村村通公路，佳荣至从江县边界公路全长70公里，县城至佳荣客运班车以及过境班车每天有10余班次。农电网覆盖各村寨，70%的农户用上自来水，移动通信信号、广播电视覆盖全镇，80%以上农户拥有电视机、电饭煲等家用电器，部分农户拥有电冰箱、洗衣机，一些农户建起砖混结构住房。

2008年，全镇有小学15所，在校生1631人，教职员工83人，适龄儿童入学率100%；有初级中学1所，在校生887人，教职员工52人。

有镇卫生院1所、村级卫生室12个。2008年，农村人口参加农村合作医疗率90%。

境内有大土苗族风情、文大天池、坤地布依族风情、红七军会师旧址、七彩河奇石风光、原始提水水车（何家）、桫椤峡谷风光、甲料水族风情、水维民族风情、月亮山探险游等景点10个待开发。

2008年，全镇工农业总产值11877万元，比1991年增长104.92%。其中，农业总产值4479万元，比1991年增长543.06%；工业总产值7398万元，比1991年增长240.8%。财政总收入103.23万元，比1991年增长854.55%。农民人均纯收入2318元，比1991年增长668.01%。

2008年所辖村、村民小组一览表

表1-4

行政村名称	村民小组总数（个）	村民小组名称
威岩村	18	威岩二组、威岩三组、威岩四组、威岩五组、威岩六组、威岩七组、威岩八组、威岩九组、威岩十组、平木一组、平木二组、拉吾厂、拉吾一组、拉吾二组、上寨、中寨、独家、宋家
坤地村	17	坤地一组、坤地二组、坤地三组、坤地四组、坤地五组、坤地六组、坤地七组、坤地八组、洞独组、弄力上组、弄力中组、弄力下组、何家组、坡脚四组、坡脚五组、新寨组、木林组

续表1-4

行政村名称	村民小组总数（个）	村民小组名称
拉滩村	10	恒姑组、上拉奖组、下拉奖组、拉滩组、拉基组、岩洞口组、上俄羊组、下俄羊组、巴灰组、瑶几组
高里村	8	高里一组、高里二组、高里三组、干角组、水碰一组、水碰二组、后山组、移民组
水维村	10	李家组、郭家组、林场组、中寨组、湾寨组、岜毛组、大坪组、老寨组、上卡组、四两寨组
大土村	5	大土组、棚上组、河应组、小傲组、代家组
甲料村	11	谢家组、更折组、甲料一组、甲料二组、甲料三组、甲高组、柳寨组、杨家组、林场组、窝羊组、拉塘组
拉易村	6	拉易一组、拉易二组、拉易三组、拉易四组、拉易五组、拉易六组
拉毛村	14	拉毛一组、拉毛二组、拉毛三组、拉毛四组、水排组、拉亮一组、拉亮二组、拉亮三组、拉亮四组、拉亮五组、拉亮六组、拉埃一组、拉埃二组、拉埃三组
岜鲜村	7	岜鲜一组、岜鲜二组、岜鲜三组、岜鲜四组、地牙一组、地牙二组、地牙三组
拉先村	11	拉先一组、拉先二组、拉先三组、拉先四组、拉先五组、拉先六组、拉先七组、拉学一组、拉学二组、拉学三组、拉学四组
拉祥村	11	拉祥一组、拉祥二组、拉祥三组、拉祥四组、拉祥五组、拉祥六组、拉祥七组、拉祥八组、小寨组、拉学组、新寨组

第五节　立化镇

立化镇位于县境东南部。东与广西驯乐苗族乡交界，南与洞塘乡、广西环江县相连，西与洞塘乡接壤，东北与茂兰镇毗邻。总面积93.1平方公里。镇政府驻立化村，距县城34公里。

1978年，立化属茂兰公社管辖。1984年，立化从茂兰公社划出，建立化乡，隶属茂兰区。1991年7月，立化乡建为立化镇，辖洞湖、应昂、立化、尧明4个村34个村民小组。2004年，合并行政村，应昂村并入立化村。2008年年末，全镇总人口3656人，其中，少数民族人口2852人，占总人口的78%。少数民族人口中，布依族2456人、水族105人、瑶族164人、苗族127人。

境内地势较高，地形起伏不平，地貌类型多样。年平均气温18.5℃，年平均降水量1450毫米，无霜期299天。最高点洞湖海坡海拔830米，最低点尧明村才困组，海拔410米，镇政府所在地海拔600米。

土地主要为石山、半石山坡、丘陵田土、坡地、谷地。2008年，有耕地面积2341亩，其中田2048.52亩、土292.48亩，人均耕地0.64亩。有可开发利用非耕地7万亩。

林地面积10.75万亩。其中，国家公益林23656亩，地方公益林27709亩，商品林56166亩，活立林木积蓄6.5万立方米。森林覆盖率50%。世界著名的喀斯特漏斗森林位于境内。

矿产资源有煤矿、特大型白云石矿、铅锌矿、硫铁矿等。煤矿储量14570万吨，品质优良，占全县无烟煤储量的43.6%，主要分布在立化村和洞湖村。

境内溪河纵横，有大小河流十多条，主要有拿云小溪、更若小溪、拉薅小河、韦老小溪、伍家河等。伍家河水库属小（2）型水库，库容64万立方米，总干渠长11.5公里，灌溉面积800亩。

农作物主要有水稻、玉米、红薯、油菜、大豆、糖蔗和各种蔬菜等。畜牧业生产主要有农户饲养的大牲畜、家禽。

工业企业有更班、平寨、林宏、安平、高荣、下寨和高坡7个煤矿，年生产能力99万吨，无镇属企业。立化镇是县内最大的煤炭中转站及主要集散地，全县85%以上的煤炭在立化集散出境远销广东、广西。

镇境有广西金城江通达立化的铁路专线。立化是荔波县南下的主要门户，也是黔南州南下经济通道的“次南门”。南距广西河池100公里。荔大公路、金平铁路贯穿全镇，交通便利。

农电网、移动通信信号覆盖全镇各村寨，广播电视覆盖率70%的农户用上自来水，95%以上农户拥有电饭煲、电视机等家用电器，部分农户建起混凝土住房。

全镇有小学1所，为农村寄宿制小学。2008年，有在校生538人，有教师32人。适龄儿童入学率99.72%。

有镇卫生院1所，洞湖村、尧明村建有村卫生室。农村人口参加农村合作医疗率90%。

2008年，全镇工农业总产值26551万元，比1991年增长3106.2%。其中，农业总产值1141万元，比1991年增长1077.4%；工业总产值25410万元，比1991年增长3432.1%。财政总收入1402.56万元。农民人均纯收入3219元，比1991年增长915.5%。

2008年所辖村、村民小组一览表

表1-5

行政村名称	村民小组总数（个）	村民小组名称
立化村	19	更班组、岜巩组、岜欧组、余家组、韦老组、塘马组、瑶寨组、伍家组、黎家组、岜昔一组、岜昔二组、平寨组、应昂组、蒙寨组、交士组、十二索上组、十二索下组、海荣组、高望组
尧明村	8	才困组、上拉薅组、下拉薅组、更龙组、玉寨组、塘岜组、卢寨组、韦寨组
洞湖村	7	洞湖一组、洞湖二组、洞湖三组、洞湖四组、洞湖五组、洞湖六组、洞湖七组

第六节　甲良镇

甲良镇位于县境西北部。东与三都县恒丰乡交界，东南、南与方村乡毗邻，西南与播尧乡相连，西与独山县甲里镇、西北与独山县打羊乡、北与独山县基长镇接壤，东北与独山县塘立乡相接。总面积192.2平方公里。镇政府驻甲良村，距县城36公里。

甲良由布依语“更良”译为汉文而得名。1978年时为甲良公社。1984年，甲良公社改为甲良乡。1991年7月“建并撤”时，甲良乡、甲站乡、阳凤乡合并建立甲良镇，辖甲站、板培、甲高、甲新、纳核、中怀、丙外、金华、七星、甲良、洞庭、金对、桥头、梅桃、石板、新场、大利、拉守、甲岸、益觉20个村。2004年，合并行政村，将20个村合并为甲良、甲新、丙外、甲高、甲站、梅桃、新场、益觉、石板9个村165个村民组。2008年年末，总人口25000人，其中，少数民族人口24500人，占总人口的98%。少数民族人口中，布依族19599人、水族4655人、苗族74人、侗族172人。

境内属南亚热带季风湿润性气候，四季分明，春季阴雨多雾，夏季多雨凉爽，秋季少雨气清，冬季阴冷干燥。年平均气温15.8℃，年平均降水量1279.7毫米，无霜期282天。

镇境地处云贵高原向两广丘陵下降的过渡带，地势西、西北高，南低，地形以山地为主。主要山脉有介于甲站河和黄江河间的洞庭—干广—更榜山脉、西部的三孔桥—阳凤—老场—马鞍山—羊山山脉。最高峰坡友峰海拔1095米，最低处更让寨河田坝海拔787.6米。

境内河流属珠江流域，有甲站河、甲午河、黄江河、洞庭河、董奎河、阳凤河、甲岸河，河流总长度92.3公里。河网密度0.48公里/平方公里。最大河流原为甲站河，20世纪80年代被上游忙雍水库截流，水量骤减，常断流。黄江河从西北方向的三孔桥至更让寨脚，流经境内拉干、船口、尧农、更榜，长23公里，主要支流有洞庭河、董奎河等。

2008年，全镇有耕地面积18258亩，其中农田面积13703亩、土地面积4555亩，人均耕地0.73亩。林地面积18.7万亩，森林覆盖率56.8%。

已探明矿产资源有煤炭、铁矿、陶土、石灰石等。煤炭储量3000万吨，已开采10万吨。其他矿产有待开发。

斗牛之乡——荔波甲良

粮食作物以水稻、玉米种植为主。经济作物主要有辣椒、茶叶、葡萄、杨梅、桃子等。阳凤片区土质适宜种植超级稻及优质大米，亩产大米800公斤；梅桃、金对适宜种植本地线辣，亩产1000公斤。甲良、甲站地区适宜种植水稻、玉米、西红柿等农作物，玉米亩产450公斤，西红柿亩产6200公斤。2008年，全镇粮食总产量4015吨，其中水稻2749吨、玉米719吨，人均占有粮食163公斤。茶叶种植面积2500亩，提子种植350亩。

畜牧业以猪、牛、马、羊和家禽为主。2008年，牛存栏4120头、出栏2845头，猪存栏6390头、出栏16230头，家禽存栏46087羽、出栏26108羽。

全镇有煤矿企业3家、采石场3个、木材加工厂1家。

招商引资500万元，在镇政府驻地懿井亭东南面建农商贸易市场1个，总面积48000平方米。

境内有独山—荔波过境公路37公里、甲良—麻尾过境公路16公里、甲良—塘立公路等，甲良客运站已竣工投入使用。2008年，乡村通邮率100%，有固定电话用户0.1万户，电话用户普及率56.2%；移动电话用户1.1万户，互联网宽带接入用户456户。农电网覆盖各村寨。广播电视覆盖率90%。

2008年，境内有幼儿园1所，在园幼儿150人，专职教师10人；有小学14所，在校生1850人，教职工126人，小学适龄儿童入学率100%；有初中1所，在校生1905人，专任教师92人，初中适龄人口入学率99%，小学升初中入学率100%；九年义务教育覆盖率达99.8%。

镇文化站有500平方米的文化综合楼，有1200平方米容纳600人的电影院1座，图书室有藏书1万多册，资产总计65万元。镇文化站多次获得全省、全州“先进文化站”“先进单位”称号。甲良镇于1994年获文化部授予“全国文化先进乡镇”称号，于1996年被省文化厅评为“先进单位”。

有镇卫生院1所，设病床19张，有职工41人；有村卫生室5个，服务9个行政村2.46万人。2008年，农村人口参加农村合作医疗率94%。

镇内民族节日主要有斗牛节、六月六布依族歌节、水族端节。土特产有甲良辣椒、梅桃毛尖、阳凤大米和甲良鸭。风景名胜有三孔桥、洞庭风景名胜区和黄江河景区。待开发旅游资源有洞庭国家级保护树种五针松。

2008年，全镇工农业总产值7899万元，比1991年增长531.3%。其中，农业总产值6849万元，比1991年增长426.6%；工业总产值1050万元，比1991年增长2103.3%。财政总收入508.9万元，比1991年增长259.3%。农民人均纯收入3320元，比1991年增长562.1%。

2008年所辖村、村民小组一览表

表1-6

行政村名称	村民小组总数（个）	村民小组名称
甲良村	25	马道、对门沟、蔡家队、老街、机关、牛行一组、牛行二组、拉干、干广、吊井、上塘米、下塘米、林场、金对二组、金对三组、金对四组、干尧、洞庭一组、洞庭二组、洞庭三组、拉料、上甲言、下甲言、小甲言、板六
梅桃村	16	尧付、梅桃、懂奎、更让、上更榜、下更榜、桥头、尧琼、纳排一组、纳排二组、马安一组、马安二组、岜打、岜领、船口、尧农
丙外村	17	上寨一组、上寨二组、中寨、下寨、杉木林、上岜聋、下岜聋、岜银、水蒙一组、水蒙二组、本同、定坝、交抹、甲阶、干塘、以奎、懂条
甲新村	16	者上、者下、懂夯、更打、纳怀、班拉、上新、下新、吉林、甲午、高坡、大寨、其恶、懂丙、板卜、大甲
甲高村	17	高坡、甲左、甲莽、孔抹、甲抓、上湾河、下湾河、纳核上、纳核下、更流、纳拉、平寨、三甲、懂平、纳业、拉抹、后寨
益觉村	15	更标、地龙、益觉、甲瞒、把然、过也、大水、小水、上么、下么、月亮一组、月亮二组、甲岸一组、甲岸二组、月光
新场村	35	牛寨一组、牛寨二组、牛寨三组、拉守一组、拉守二组、拉守三组、下河、上新、下新、平竹、拉瓢、庭全、上利、下利、拉岜、甲吝、甲岭、月呆、更兰、拉岬、打郎、新场一组、新场二组、水头一组、水头二组、下寨、上老场、下老场、拉拐、上交朝、下交朝、播完、交甲、上把明、下把明
甲站村	12	新寨、懂丙、觉更、觉巩、板培、板勇、务平、洋拉、朋宾、把琴、塘连、水蒙
石板村	13	塘龙、上燕、下燕、更内、甲银、弄丈、地兰、把盘、石板一组、石板二组、石板三组、上塘冗、下塘冗

第七节　洞塘乡

洞塘乡位于县境东南部。东南与广西环江县相接，西与永康乡、翁昂乡相连，北与立化镇、茂兰镇接壤。总面积201平方公里。乡政府驻懂朋村，距县城33公里。

1978年时为洞塘公社。1984年，洞塘公社改为洞塘乡。1991年8月“建并撤”时，洞塘乡行政区划不变，有木朝村、三合村、懂朋村、计才村、板寨村、久安村、尧所村、洞腊村。2004年，原10个村合并为木朝村、懂朋村、尧所村、板寨村、久安村、洞腊村6个村74个村民小组。2008年年末，全乡总人口8631人，其中，少数民族人口5825人，占总人口的67.49%。

乡境地处世界自然遗产地、中国南方茂兰喀斯特自然保护区核心区内，是荔波县世界自然遗产地的重要地区。属中亚热温润气候，年平均气温17.5℃，年平均降水量1350毫米，无霜期330天。最高点海拔1230米，最低点海拔400米，乡政府所在地海拔560米。

2008年，全乡有耕地面积7589.5亩，其中农田面积5610亩、土地面积1979.5亩。岩石及森林面积165000亩，有灌木及草坡105000亩，是国内中亚热带喀斯特地貌上原生性森林植被保存较完好的地方，生长乔木树种达500种，有被称为活化石的银杏、鹅掌楸等多种珍稀树种，还有全国独有的一属一种掌叶木和射毛悬竹、席竹等。

矿产资源主要有煤矿，分布在洞腊村、久安村和尧所村，洞腊村罗家寨（塘房组）煤矿理论贮量180万吨，尚未开采，其它地点由于贮量小、煤层薄、分布不均，不能大规模开采，以保护为主。尧所村洞腮组、巴格组一带有白云石矿近2000万吨，含丰富的金属元素镁、钙等。此外，在喀斯特核心区内还有少量的铁矿。

由于自然地理条件的差异，历史上境内自然划分为“上四保”“下四保”两大片区，“上四保”为木朝（含老场）、新街、和平（今懂朋村）、三合，“下四保”为尧所、板寨（含计才）、久安、洞腊。“上四保”土质多为沙质土，保水性能差，地面水资源缺乏，无河流，天旱成旱洞，下雨成池塘，“洞塘”因此而得名。这一片的村寨农业生产靠天降雨，水利设施落后，玉米生产较稳定。“下四保”土质多为黏壤土，有小河沟贯穿田间，水源较丰富，水稻产量稳定。

全乡以农业生产为主。粮食作物主要有水稻、玉米，经济作物主要有油菜、大蒜、生姜、糖蔗、木薯等，林、果产品主要有酸梅、五倍子、泡竹、楠竹、山木、杜仲、九阡李、栽秧李、板栗等，酸梅果是乡内特产。2000年后，全乡加强农业产业结构调整，在稳定粮食生产的基础上，发展其他经济作物。2004年后，先后推广桑树和甘蔗种植，并通过招商引资引进九曲湾公司进驻洞塘办糖厂，调动农民种蔗积极性。2008年，全乡粮食总产量3300吨、玉米总产量1000吨、油菜籽总产量100吨，甘蔗种植面积1200亩，产量5000吨。

畜牧养殖以猪、牛、家禽为主。1985年开发畜牧饲料，发展养殖业。2008年年末，牛存栏2021头，出栏1250头；猪存栏2242头，出栏2015头；家禽存栏5万羽，出栏3万羽；有饲料经营点3个。

境内有水电站3座，于2001年并入国家电网，农户通电率100%。

荔大公路和红茂铁路过境，全乡通村公路率100%，洞塘车站建成使用。全乡移动通信网络覆盖率95%。广播电视覆盖率100%。

2008年，全乡有九年一贯制学校1所、村级完全小学3所，在校学生1380人，教工78名。适龄儿童入学率98%。

有乡级卫生院1所、村级卫生室6个，有乡卫生医务人员7名、村卫生室人员8名。2008年，农村人口参加农村合作医疗率60%。

境内历史英雄人物有抗日英烈全正熹、抗美援朝英雄金朝贵。红七军板寨会师旧址坐落于板寨村。

境内喀斯特原始森林自然生长2万亩梅花，树龄在200年以上的珍稀古梅数百株，有“十里梅海”“万亩梅林”之称，集中连片的野生梅林被评为“中国野生梅之乡”。梅园花期30多天，每年春节前后，满山遍野绽放的红梅、白梅、绿梅、黄梅，争奇斗艳，成为全县的旅游景点。从2006年起，县内每年举办一次梅花节，吸引大量游客观花赏景。

境内有以洞塘景区为主的茂兰保护区文化体验游路线，有县投资建成的五眼桥、九洞天、野梅箐、三友园、打卦亭、古铁艺作坊、古榨油坊、石上森林、红七军会师旧址纪念展馆、黎明关遗址、茂兰保护区展示中心、七彩报春谷、洞良展演场等景点及旅游设施。

2008年，全乡工农业总产值1203万元，比1991年增长900%。其中，农业总产值901万元，比1991年增长700%；工业总产值302万元，比1991年增长160%。财政总收入45万元，比1991年增长35%。农民人均纯收入1980元，比1991年增长980元。

2008年所辖村、村民小组一览表

表1-7

行政村名称	村民小组总数（个）	村民小组名称
木朝村	12	老场组、瓦厂组、洞良组、木朝组、洞更组、岜町组、俄芽组、拢拥组、田洞组、大山脚组、舒家组、水井湾组
懂朋村	19	洞白组、单林组、新街组、老街组、九龚组、懂朋组、娃寨组、落卡组、懂亮组、洞翁组、立孟组、山口组、么阳组、白岩组、浪岜组、石板组、九街组、甲务组、甲纠组
板寨村	16	洞旧组、里忙组、里根组、交忙组、卡记组、坡格组、五圩组、板王组、瑶寨组、板老组、板江组、甲党组、交乐组、上寨组、中寨组、下寨组

续表1-7

行政村名称	村民小组总数（个）	村民小组名称
尧所村	9	下寨组、堡上组、甲乙组、必几组、加别组、洞腮组、必左组、必达组、巴格组
久安村	9	刘家组、王同组、坡恒组、三组、四组、五组、六组、七组、八组
洞腊村	8	肯甫组、蒙寨组、塘房组、新寨组、塘边组、架立组、洞腊组、塘蒙组

第八节 方村乡

方村乡位于县境北部。东与水利水族乡交界，南与播尧乡相接，西北与甲良镇毗邻。总面积53.81平方公里。乡政府驻双江村街上组，距县城30公里。

1978年时为方村公社。1984年，方村公社改为方村乡，属股级机构，属甲良区管理，辖交进、交挠、丙花、拉街、板平、尧并、把抹、六合、双江、红坭、寨近11个行政村59个村民小组。1991年7月“建并撤”时，方村乡区划不变，升为正科级机构。2004年，将11个行政村合并为拉街村、尧并村、红坭村、丙花村、双江村5个行政村60个村民小组。2008年年末，全乡总人口9608人，其中，少数民族人口9206人，占总人口的97.9%。少数民族人口中，布依族9031人、水族125人、壮族50人。布依族人口占总人口的94%。

境内属中亚热带季风气候区，气候温热，四季分明，冬无严寒，夏无酷暑，夏长冬短，无霜期长，雨量充沛，日照充足，雨热同季，灾害性天气少。年平均气温16℃，极端气温最高时36.5℃，极端最低气温-5℃，霜期每年11月30日有霜，次年2月20日终霜，无霜期282天。年平均降水量1300毫米。地势东北高、西南低，最高点海拔1468米，最低点海拔800米，乡政府驻地海拔820米。

境内河流均属珠江流域，有溪、河5条。三岔河以西称甲良河（黄江），以东称甲站河。溪沟有桥罗、板央、末万、鲁吉等，5条溪沟汇成方村河，方村河是县境第二大河。地下水为岩溶型地下水，主要集中于双江村东部的龙井、新安村的拉门、红坭村的甲逮一带。南面河谷深切，除方村大坝外，丘峦起伏，沟河纵横，植被覆盖广，南部龙井山水秀丽，被誉为“第二小七孔”。

2008年，全乡有耕地面积8124亩，其中田6000亩、土2124亩；有可开发荒山荒坡35400亩；林地主要分布在丙花村、拉街村，森林覆盖率42.6%；草地分布尧并、把抹、双江、红坭4个村。

矿产资源主要有烟煤、铁矿、方解石、石灰石、陶土。煤矿分布在双江、尧农、打蚌、干沟、拉门、拉街村、甲练、岜明；铁矿在双江拉力、打蚌一带；石灰石主要分布在红坭村的浪抹，双江村的打棒、拉门等地；双江大坝的陶土品位为全县第一。

方村乡为农业乡。农作物以种植水稻、玉米、辣椒为主，养殖业以饲养猪、鸡、鸭、鹅为主。2008年，粮食总产量3229吨，种植辣椒2900亩、金秋梨486亩、椪柑580亩。年末，牛存栏3288头、出栏2356头，猪存栏5230头、出栏3124头，家禽存栏2.5万羽、出栏1万羽，肉类总产量182吨。

全乡比较大的自然村寨都有农户自办的小型农家店，经营日常生活用品。

境内小水电并入南方电网，在方村建有变电站，农电网覆盖全乡。有方村板郎、丙花、板廷、交进、拉岜、塔脚等电灌站、机灌站和水轮泵站，以及鲁阳、鲁末小型水库2座，保灌面积1000亩以上。全乡有机耕机械9台、小型拖拉机5台、农用汽车16台、电动机109台、加工机械2500台。

全乡各村、组均通公路，每天有从乡驻地到县城的客运班车2班。乡内无专业邮电网点，村民的邮件均到县城或邻近的甲良镇办理，书报、杂志订阅由邮递员投送。移动通信信号覆盖全部村寨，乡政府驻地机关单位已使用计算机办公，个别农户家庭已开始拥有计算机。广播电视覆盖率100%，拥有电视机的农户达95%。

2008年，全乡有初级中学1所、村级小学5所，有学前班4个班，共有教职工75人。适龄儿童入学率100%。

有乡卫生院1所，有医务人员5人，病床8张。全乡无村级卫生室。2008年，农村人口参加农村合作医疗率93%。

2008年，全乡工农业总产值3944.2万元，比1991年增长531.3%。其中，农业总产值3539万元，比1991年增长426.6%；工业总产值405.2万元，比1991年增长2103.3%。财政总收入221.45万元，比1991年增长259.3%。农民人均收入2496元，比1991年增长562.1%。

2008年所辖村、村民小组一览表

表1-8

行政村名称	村民小组总数（个）	村民小组名称
红坭村	16	董斗组、上塘马组、下塘马组、寨近组、上末万组、下末万组、甲莪组、塘八组、板站组、六合一组、六合二组、丰寨组、红坭组、者火组、板交阳组、鲁末组
双江村	22	上板勇组、塘桥组、板廷组、鲁吉、板平一组、板平二组、板央、上交挠组、下交挠组、小寨组、上拉岜组、下拉岜组、交进一组、交进二组、交进三组、交进四组、街上组、板牙组、板郎组、下板勇组、普脚组、板麦组
丙花村	3	拉甲组、丙花组、者吕组
尧并村	12	拉往组、尧并二组、尧并三组、尧并六组、上尧更组、下尧更组、尧并四组、尧并五组、把抹组、新寨组、更贵组、更信组
拉街村	6	播马组、甲练组、过又组、桥罗组、拉街四组、拉街五组、拉挂组

第九节　播尧乡

播尧乡位于县境西北部，地处两省区（广西、贵州）、3县（南丹、独山、荔波）、9乡镇（方村、水利、朝阳、芒场、麻尾、懂岭、三棒、甲里、甲良）交汇处。东与水利、朝阳接界，南与驾欧乡毗邻，西与独山县董岭乡接壤，北与独山县阳凤和县内甲良镇、方村乡相邻。总面积186平方公里。乡政府驻和平村甲算组浪棵梨，距县城30.5公里，距小七孔景区20公里，离麻尾火车站30公里。

1978年时为播尧公社。1984年，播尧公社改为播尧乡。1991年8月“建并撤”时，撤销播尧、觉巩、地莪3个乡，合并建立播尧乡，辖19个村，即和平、豆村、中心、星尧、架桥、丙楼、尧花、黎明、寨索、星庞、觉巩、拉美、联江、地脉、地莪、太阳、拉强、拉平、新桥，乡政府驻和平村播尧场坝组。1993年，乡政府驻地迁到和平村甲算组浪棵梨重新规划建设。2004年，合并行政村，原19个行政村合并为和平、中心、架桥、尧花、觉巩、黎明、联江、地莪、拉平9个村152个村民小组。2008年年末，全乡总人口19291人，其中少数民族人口19204人，占总人口的99.55%。少数民族人口中，布依族17476人、水族385人、苗族1273人、侗族32人、壮族38人。

境内地势西北部高东南部低，是县境喀斯特地形的重要组成部分。属高地亚热带季风温润气候，冬无严寒，夏无酷暑，年温差小，气候温热，四季分明，春季温暖，夏长冬短，无霜期长，雨量充沛，日照充足，雨热同季，灾害性天气少，无霜期285天。年平均气温16.1℃，年平均最低温度8.8℃，极端最高温度36.3℃。年平均降水量1200毫米。最高点中心村尧蒙组海拔1300米，最低点觉巩村星庞组海拔770米，乡政府所在地海拔860米。

2008年，全乡有耕地面积14487.05亩，其中田11970.45亩、土2516.6亩；有林地面积123153亩，其中经济林84353.8亩、疏林地12283.5亩、灌木林地26149亩、未造林地366.7亩；有草地面积46860亩，载畜量2300余头；有水域面积3546.9亩，其中河流2905.1亩。境内适合种植水稻、玉米、大豆、小麦、高粱、荞子、辣椒、棉花、芝麻、小米、稗子、烤烟等农作物，可开发种植松树、杉树、板栗、麻竹、桃子、李子、香菇、葡萄、五倍子等植物。

矿产资源主要有煤矿，分布在五七、拉万、架桥、麻庄、拉棒、母约、星尧、觉巩等地，储藏量8000万吨。境内硫矿、铁矿未开采。

全乡以农业生产为主，95%以上的耕地种植粮食作物，少部分土地种辣椒、花生、棉花等经济作物。2004年，乡党委、政府对农业产业结构进行调整，是年全乡发展烤烟670亩，总产值53万元。2005年，烤烟种植发展到1050亩，总产值64万元，创税13万元。2008年，水稻种植11560亩，玉米种植4100多亩，粮食产量达6800吨，其他作物如油菜种植9920亩，亩产量达100～150公斤；马铃薯种植800亩，亩产量1500～2000公斤。另外，还种植桑蚕485亩，收蚕茧98吨，产值78万元。全乡有各种机耕农具十余台，稻谷脱壳、磨面、榨油实现机械化。

农户素有饲养生猪、家禽、牛、马、羊及养鱼的传统习惯，养殖业成为农民家庭主要的经济来源之一。2008年年末，牛存栏3985头，马存栏1385匹，猪存栏6580头、出栏4285头，羊存栏535只，家禽存栏25560羽。

境内建有大小水库4座、引水工程2处，灌溉面积2700亩。有机电抽水工程十余处和电灌站2座。内角水库、打拉水库、地莪水库、联江水库，每年投放32万尾鱼苗喂养，年可捕鲜鱼5吨。2005年后，大部分村寨群众开始利用稻田养鱼，全乡每年稻田养鱼面积2000亩以上，收获鲜鱼3～4吨。2008年，稻田养鱼2400亩，推广良种鱼35万尾。开展山塘、池塘、稻田生态养鱼示范，水产总产量46吨。

全乡工业以采煤为主，在五七、拉万、麻庄、架桥、拉棒、母约、打更等地建有煤井，年产量5万吨。2003年后，原煤生产由县统一经营管理。

甲良—麻尾公路贯穿乡境，全乡村、组全部通公路。农电网覆盖各村寨。辖区有过境邮路2条，信件和报纸杂志由甲良邮电支局送达。移动通信网络覆盖全乡。广播电视覆盖率100%。

2008年，全乡有小学13所、中学1所，每所学校建成新教学楼，播尧中学建有学生宿舍、学生食堂、多功能厅。有在校小学生1872人、中学生1004人。适龄儿童入学率99.68%。

有乡卫生院1所，各村有卫生室。2008年，农村人口参加农村合作医疗率91%。

2008年，全乡工农业总产值7056万元，比1991年增长5616.91万元。其中，农业总产值5613万元，比1991年增长4289.08万元；工业总产值1443万元，比1991年增长1327.83万元。财政总收入33.629万元，比1991年增长32.329万元。

2008年所辖村、村民小组一览表

表1-9

行政村名称	村民小组总数（个）	村民小组名称
和平村	17	豆村一组、豆村二组、豆村三组、豆村四组、麻庄组、地腊组、老场一组、老场二组、甲算一组、甲算二组、甲算三组、尧细组、更鸭组、更鹅组、拉仰上组、拉仰下组、麻尧组
架桥村	9	架桥一组、架桥二组、架桥三组、过内组、岜文组、新把查组、老把查组、董毫组、降毫组
中心村	12	新寨上组、新寨下组、中寨组、利齐组、董文组、上尧蒙组、下尧蒙一组、下尧蒙二组、已固上组、已固下组、董拉组、董细组
尧花村	15	浪板组、更港组、董老上组、董老下组、董马组、大寨组、更塘组、丙楼上组、丙楼下组、麻巩组、更伟组、丙王一组、丙王二组、拉鸟组、拉类组

续表1-9

行政村名称	村民小组总数（个）	村民小组名称
黎明村	9	打拉组、甲老上组、甲老下组、寨英组、拉力组、岜好组、浪兰上组、浪兰中组、浪兰下组
觉巩村	28	觉巩组、浪抹组、拉曰组、拉干组、巴竹五组、巴竹六组、下巴竹组、董后组、共塘组、董大组、祥母组、更坡组、拉纳组、董雄组、交弄组、坡易组、上桃组、下桃组、板拜组、巴念组、拉塘组、交庞组、新寨组、甲能组、拉江组、拉美组、新场组、尧蒙组
联江村	13	曼井上组、曼井中组、曼井下组、甲令组、纳朗组、甲村组、巴明上组、巴明下组、地温组、六香组、寨票上组、寨票中组、寨票下组
地莪村地莪村	32	地莪组、场坝组、巴脚组、上弄迈组、下弄迈组、地脉一组、地脉二组、把扎一组、把扎二组、拢望组、田湾组、洞括组、鱼村组、洞丢上组、洞丢中组、洞丢下组、更类组、太阳二组、太阳三组、太阳四组、更方上组、更方中组、更方下组、更正组、更卡组、上甲雷组、下甲雷组、上昔村组、下昔村组、拉棒组、上台村组、下台村组
拉平村	16	拉柳一组、拉柳二组、上董平组、下董平组、卡上组、新寨组、拉寨一组、拉寨二组、拉久组、塘必组、母约组、拉强组、强岜组、上中弄组、下中弄组、小河组

第十节　驾欧乡

驾欧乡位于县境西南部。东与朝阳、瑶山乡毗邻，南与广西南丹县接壤，西与独山县黄后乡交界，北与播尧乡相连。总面积110.7平方公里。乡政府驻绿林村拉圭，距县城45公里。

1978年时为驾欧公社。1984年，驾欧公社改为驾欧乡，隶属朝阳区，乡政府驻拉欧。1991年7月“建并撤”时，驾欧乡行政区划不变，辖绿林、新街、拉欧、拉关、板潭、联山6个行政村61个村民小组47个自然寨。1996年，乡政府迁到绿林村拉圭。2004年，将6个行政村合并为绿林、联山、拉欧、新街4个村行政村（六林村、拉关村合并为绿林村，拉欧村、板潭村合并为拉欧村）。2008年年末，全乡总人口7800人，其中，少数民族人口7263人，占总人口的93.1%。少数民族人口中，布依族6630人、水族102人、瑶族10人、苗族521人。布依族人口占全乡总人口的85%。

境内气候属暖温带大陆性季风气候，冬暖夏凉。年平均气温16.7℃，最高气温40℃，最低气温-4℃。全年无霜期300天，年平均降水量1200毫米，年日照时数1200～1300小时。最高点拉克腊海拔840米，最低点板潭海拔730米，乡政府驻地海拔756米。

2008年，全乡有耕地面积5620亩，其中农田面积4350亩、土地面积1270亩；林地面积76963亩，森林覆盖率19.18%；可利用草地面积63611亩。

矿产资源主要有煤矿，分布在东部的板潭、南部的新街三道湾、西部的拉金、北部的拉崩，煤层厚度为0.4～1米，总储量80万吨。

农业生产以种植农作物为主。粮食作物主要有水稻、玉米、豆类、薯类等。杂交水稻、杂交玉米种子普及率96%以上。经济作物主要有油菜、辣椒等。2008年，全乡粮食总产量2985吨，人均粮食382.7公斤；油菜总产量180吨。

境内清水塘灌区灌溉面积590亩，巴槽引水渠灌溉面积1150亩，有电灌站7座及清水塘人饮工程1个。

从1981年实行林业“三定”至2008年年末，累计造林3.12万亩，林木覆盖率59.56%，活立木蓄积量24.46万立方米。

畜牧业以牛、猪、马、家禽为主。2008年年末，牛存栏2183头、出栏210头，马存栏482匹、出栏45匹，猪存栏5723头、出栏5800头，家禽存栏1.4万羽、出栏2.8万羽。

境内有联江河（驾欧河段）长7.5公里，建有大七孔电站，总装机容量4.8万千瓦/3台，工程总投资2.3亿元，单独运行多年平均发电量3.23万千瓦时，联合运行多年平均发电量4.76万千瓦时。

省道206公路过境21公里，全乡村、组全部通公路。2008年6月开工修建麻尾—驾欧高速公路17公里，境内长5公里。

2008年，全乡有固定电话用户414户，占总户数的19.2%，移动通信信号覆盖全乡。农电网覆盖各村组农户，广播电视覆盖率100%。乡政府驻地有宾馆酒店3家、旅游特色商品店1家、信用社1家、超市2家、集贸市场1个。

全乡有小学4所，2008年在校生745人，有专任教师43人。适龄儿童入学率100%，小学升初中升学率100%。

有医疗卫生机构1个，医务人员6人；联山、拉欧2个村建有卫生室。2008年，农村人口参加农村合作医疗率85%。

境内有小七孔风景区的水上森林、野猪林、天钟洞、卧龙潭、鸳鸯湖、龟背山喀斯特森林等景点。

从2002年起，县委、县政府投资590元，将乡内生活在小七孔景区的拉关村上几定、下几定、拉贯、拉蒙、翁龙5个组的村民87户340人实施异地移民，搬出景区，在乡政府驻地拉圭建移民新村，占地总面积99.97亩，新建民房78栋，总建筑面积14000平方米。

2008年，全乡工农业总产值1233万元。其中，农业总产值877万元，工业总产值356万元。财政总收入31万元，农民人均纯收入1620.5元。

2008年所辖村、村民小组一览表

表1-10

行政村名称	村民小组总数（个）	村民小组名称
联山村	17	么定组、上拉美组、中拉美组、下拉美组、内冲忙上组、内冲忙下组、外冲忙组、拉崩组、岜乃组、上简应组、下简应组、拉保组、更挠三组、更挠四组、更挠五组、更挠六组、更挠七组
拉欧村	17	上岜故组、下岜故组、上水塘组、下水塘组、中寨组、拉寨组、大寨组、交挠组、拉欧一组、拉欧二组、拉欧三组、拉欧四组、拉欧五组、拉金组、黄寨组、甲林场组、乙林场组
绿林村	17	新寨上组、新寨下组、更坡组、平寨上组、平寨下组、大寨一组、大寨二组、大寨三组、拉圭组、更灶组、拉贯组、上几定组、下几定组、翁龙组、拉蒙组、牛角组、拉克腊组
新街村	12	新街一组、新街三组、新街四组、新街五组、新街六组、新街七组、新街八一组、新街八二组、新街九组、塘八组、更标组、翁吉组

第十一节　翁昂乡

翁昂乡位于县境东南部，东南与广西环江县川山镇木伦接壤，西北与朝阳镇交界。总面积157.8平方公里。乡政府驻敦伦，距县城26公里。

1978年时为翁昂公社，隶属朝阳区。1984年，翁昂公社改为翁昂乡。1991年7月“建并撤”时，翁昂乡行政区划不变，辖拉内、巴乐、洞常、尧桥、己陇5个村。2004年，合并行政村，原5个村合并为己陇、拉内2个村41个村民小组。2008年年末，全乡总人口4414人，其中，少数民族人口4267人，占总人口的96.67%。少数民族人口中，布依族4007人、瑶族100人、水族80人、壮族50人、苗族30人。

境内气候凉爽。年平均气温26℃，全年无霜期330天，年平均降水量200毫米，年日照时数1200小时。最高点海拔1000米，最低点海拔450米，乡政府驻地海拔810米。

2008年，全乡有耕地面积6242亩，其中农田面积4763亩、土地面积1479亩；森林面积186045亩，森林覆盖率75%，森林资源居全县各乡（镇）第二位，林区生长药用植物桔梗、乌梅、桂皮、大通草、续断、金银花、黄草、水草、白芨、灵芝、龙胆草、天冬、黄精、葛根、桑根、黄柏、杜仲、厚朴、山药、木瓜、小血藤、车前草、青天葵等；有草场面积4995亩。

境内有大小溪流24条，宜于分段养鱼、筑建水库、建小型电站。

矿产资源主要有硅石和褐铁矿2种。硅石储量2500万吨，分布在吉腊一带，品位为97%～98%，质量达一级和二级品。褐铁矿主要分布拉内、吉腊、吉洞、拉佑等地。

翁昂乡以农业生产为主。由于乡境海拔高，水稻生长周期长，收割晚，日照充足，颗粒饱满，大米晶莹光亮，油质糯性，称为上品，远销邻县各地。林下养鸡被称为“虫草鸡”，堪为席上珍品，批量销售。乡内竹鼠、小本黑猪及野外蜜蜂移家养殖、稻田养鱼等在部分农户中形成养殖规模。中草药材种植规模较大、产量较高的有板蓝根。2008年，全乡水稻种植面积4617亩，总产量1973吨；玉米种植面积1250亩，总产量413吨。年末，牛存栏2606头、出栏451头，马存栏235匹，家禽存栏6639羽、出栏5843羽。

境内传统工艺品有已拢竹编斗笠、晒席、箩筐等竹器，竹编工艺品以花鸟虫鱼、凤凰祥兽、山川河流、风景名胜为图案，编成玲珑精致的装饰品作为旅游产品外销。

县城经永康至捞村公路贯穿乡境，全乡村、组全部通公路。农电网覆盖各村寨农户，移动通信信号覆盖全乡，广播电视覆盖率90%以上。

乡内有六年制小学校3所，2008年，有在校生420人，有教职工25人。适龄儿童入学率80%。

有卫生院1所，医务人员7人，病床7个；有村级卫生室3个，医务人员3人。农村人口参加农村合作医疗90%。

乡内布依族保持传统习俗，布依族群众使用纯布依族语，是研究布依族语言的佳地。翁昂民歌为布依族有代表性的古老曲调，是布依族民歌保存与流传较完整的地方，在每年全县“六月六”布依族歌节上，翁昂乡男女歌手连年夺冠。

民居建筑保持“吊脚楼”风格，是考察布依族民居的佳地。翁昂是布依族舞蹈“矮人舞”“花棍舞”“傩戏舞”的发源流传地。民间布依族古籍《抱落跎》、布依族古文字（天地日月等），是研究布依文字历史的原始材料。

翁昂乡地处喀斯特世界自然遗产地核心地区，四分之三的面积属于茂兰保护区区域。境内有大小溶洞151个，洞内钟乳凝聚、洞水滴嗒，天然雕饰，是尚未开发的旅游资源。

2008年所辖村、村民小组一览表

表1-11

行政村名称	村民小组总数（个）	村民小组名称
拉内村	22	山中组、坡费组、彩拉组、懂莽组、江风组、江蚁组、浪彩组、肯西组、拉类组、洞情组、理想组、巴弓组、巴乐组、贬和组、洞杂组、弄朋组、敦伦组、纳蛮组、板甫组、肯岜组、坡丹组、拉内组
己陇村	19	花达组、肯益组、比把组、洞多组、坡报组、洞常组、洞应组、拉八组、拉塘组、拉洞宁组、吉洞组、拉佑组、尧桥组、干排组、久伟组、己陇组、莫干组、林场组、吉腊组

第十二节　捞村乡

捞村乡位于县境最南端，东南与广西环江县川山镇毗邻，西南与广西南丹县里湖乡交界，北与瑶山乡相连，东北与翁昂乡接壤。总面积96.17平方公里。乡政府驻群力村大寨组，距县城50公里。

1978年时为捞村公社。1984年，捞村公社改为捞村乡，隶属朝阳区。1991年7月“建并撤”时，捞村乡行政区划不变。全乡辖4个行政村37个村民小组。2004年，合并行政村时，捞村乡保留原4个村。2008年年末，辖区总人口3733人，以布依族为主，占总人口数的92%，瑶族占5%，苗族、壮族、水族、汉族等其他民族占3%。

乡境地处云贵高原向广西丘陵过渡的斜坡地带，地貌整体为典型的喀斯特山地，山高坡陡，基岩裸露，峰林峰丛发育，谷地洼地狭小。捞村河将全乡由西北向南深切为二（切割深度达400米以上），并在乡政府所在地形成3平方公里的河谷丘陵及溶蚀盆地。最高点海拔1017米，最低点海拔300米，乡政府所在地海拔330米。

境内气候属中亚热带温暖湿润一年三熟农业气候区，乡中心河谷地带年平均气温20℃，大于0℃积温7000℃，大于10℃积温6300℃，为全县最高值区。最冷月1月平均气温9.6℃，最热月7月平均气温28℃。年平均降水量1240毫米，年平均相对湿度68%。年日照时数1137小时，无霜期达350天。乡境三分之二地区属于典型的喀斯特森林地貌，降水较充沛，空气湿润，气候温和，高山丘陵一年四季林木葱茏。

乡内打狗河和捞村河成“V”字形，均属雨源性河流，水资源总量150亿立方米，其中地表水资源量140亿立方米。全乡蕴藏水能资源6万千瓦，至2008年已开发3.05万千瓦。

2008年，全乡有耕地面积4620亩，其中农田面积2055亩、土地面积2565亩，人均耕地1.24亩，人均基本农田0.57亩。以坡耕地为主，水田主要分布在沿河两岸及巴弓、尧莪、洞勤。林地面积8.9万亩，有林业用地11.5万亩，其中划入茂兰国家级自然保护区0.5万亩，森林覆盖率54%。有林场面积7435亩，活立木储量2.74万立方米。有野生动植物1000种以上。林产品以木材、油桐为主，干笋、五倍子、香菇、木耳等有一定产量。有天然草场5.24万亩。

全乡以农业生产为主。粮食作物主要有水稻、玉米。养殖业以饲养生猪、牛、羊为主。改革开放后，经过农业产业结构调整，开始由传统型农业向现代型农业转变，但生产力水平仍较低。2003年，省委、省政府将捞村乡定为全省100个一类贫困乡进行扶贫开发攻坚，贫困人口逐步越过温饱线。

境内招商引资落户工业企业3家，总投资2.05亿元。引进的捞村红糖加工厂项目投资200万元，至2008年，带动全乡成为种植、加工一体化的甘蔗产业之乡，甘蔗种植规模达4000多亩，占全乡耕地面积的80%。引进的浪祥水电站项目投资2亿元，装机容量2×15000千瓦，年发电量14200千瓦时，年均税收500万元。引进的平岩小型水电站项目投资300万元，装机容量500千瓦。3个引资企业开创了捞村乡工业生产的历史。

乡政府所在地建有农贸市场1个，为黔桂两省区边境贸易的重要市场。

2008年，村村通公路，村民小组通公路率90%，实现道路硬化村民小组20个。农电网覆盖各村寨农户。乡内邮件由朝阳邮政分局每周送达一次。移动通信信号覆盖全乡。95%以上农村家庭拥有电视机，广播电视覆盖率100%。

2008年，有捞村小学1所及巴公、力书教学点2个，全乡教职工18人，教学班12个（其中有1个学前班），在校学生297人（其中学前班53人）。适龄儿童入学率99%，初中毛入学率100%。

全乡人口出生率年均控制在6‰以内，年自然增长率控制在4.5‰以内。

乡有卫生院1所，有村卫生室4个。2008年，农村低保供养人口覆盖全乡4个村1087人。农村人口参加农村合作医疗率92.75%。

境内旅游资源主要有打狗河峡谷风光、平林古桥奇树生态生物景观、平林打拉河自然风光、千年榕树群景观等。

2008年，全乡工农业总产值2657万元，比1991年增长278.65%。其中，农业总产值1707万元，工业总产值950万元，财政总收入32.63万元，农民人均纯收入2604元。

2008年所辖村、村民小组一览表

表1-12

行政村名称	村民小组总数（个）	村民小组名称
群力村	14	浪祥组、盘龙组、洞勤组、尧莪组、山脚组、纳汉组、板江组、大寨组、坡所组、久么组、久利组、更见组、洞更组、更乱组
平岩村	11	平岩组、上平林组、下平林组、林场组、更甲组、更岜组、内弓组、外弓组、平寨组、坡黑组、洞龙组
力书村	5	洞作组、拉仰组、长洞组、央卜组、更布组
巴平村	7	岩脚组、八架组、弄哄组、弄拉组、弄要组、高傲组、哄后组

第十三节　水利水族乡

水利水族乡地处县境西北部。东与玉屏镇相连，南与朝阳镇交界，西与方村乡和播尧乡接壤，北与甲良镇和三都县恒丰乡、周覃镇毗邻。总面积126.28平方公里。乡政府驻水利村，距县城16公里。

1978年时为水利公社，隶属玉屏区。1984年5月3日，成立水利水族乡。1991年“建并撤”时，升格为科级建制，行政区划不变，辖水利、水岩、水丰、水龙、水丙、尧棒、洞托7个村50个村民小组。2004年，合并行政村，水龙村、水丙村2个村并入水利村，原7个村并为5个村49个村民小组。乡内居住水族、布依族、瑶族、苗族等民族。2008年年末，全乡总人口6443人，其中，少数民族人口6096人，占总人口的94.6%；水族人口4707人，占总人口的73.1%。

境内以石山居多，占46%，平地少石山主要以灌木林居多，有少量松林木、杉林木，属喀斯特地貌，地下水资源丰富。年平均气温15.8℃，年平均降水量1300毫米，无霜期305天。最高点海拔1223米，最低点海拔675米，乡政府所在地海拔885米。

2008年，全乡有耕地面积4389亩，其中农田面积3692亩、土地面积697亩。有林地8.8万亩，其他用地1.82万亩。有森林面积4.16万亩，森林覆盖率51%。有三所坟和熊山两个较大林区，优势树种为马尾松、杉和杂木及竹类。活立木积蓄量14万立方米。有天然草场6.86万亩。

境内矿产资源缺乏，已探明地下矿藏有少量煤矿、铁矿、硫矿、铁矿等。其中煤储量318万吨，未开发。

全乡以农业生产为主。粮食作物以水稻、玉米、马铃薯、红薯为主。2008年，粮食总产量2083吨，其中水稻1686吨；油料作物种植面积0.26万亩，产量287吨；蔬菜种植面积0.9万亩，产量717吨，主要品种有西红柿、西瓜、白菜等。实施西红柿嫁接种植和错季节商品蔬菜种植。通过荒坡土地流转，开发种植茶场3000多亩、油茶2000亩、西红柿1000亩。

乡内有规模养殖场6个，年出栏生猪5000余头、家禽100万羽，养殖小区趋于标准化、规模化。2008年年末，大牲畜存栏2850头、出栏463头，猪存栏2970头、出栏1160头，家禽存栏7900羽、出栏5835羽。

境内有岜甲、拉干引水渠2条；有岜甲、董荣、高寨、岜忙等水库4个；有小型蓄水工程6处、小水池6口，蓄水150万立方米；有灌渠8公里，有效灌溉面积1987亩，保灌面积714亩。44个村民小组有人饮工程。

2008年，全乡村村通公路，通村公路里程46公里，通组公路里程85公里，未通公路村民小组1个，大部分自然村寨实现路面硬化。农电网覆盖各村组农户，移动通信信号覆盖全乡，全乡广播电视覆盖率85%。

全乡有小学校5所，2008年，有在校生609人，有教职工49人。适龄儿童入学率99.2%。有乡级成人文化技术学校1所。

乡有卫生院1所，设病床9张，有医护人员7人；有村级卫生室5个。2008年，农村人口参加合作医疗率88.2%。

乡内卯节、额节是水族的重要节日。水利卯节是头卯。

境内山青峰奇，已开发观音峰景区，待开发利用的有方村河拉应峡谷、兰顶山森林、较大的水族村寨等自然风光和人文景观。

2008年，全乡工农业总产值1753万元，比1991年增长588.25%。其中，农业总产值903万元，比1991年增长438.34%；工业总产值850万元，比1991年增长923.91%。财政总收入11.89万元，农民人均纯收入2150元，比1991年增长762.41%。

2008年所辖村、村民小组一览表

表1-13

行政村名称	村民小组总数（个）	村民小组名称
水利村	20	老街组、纳恶组、抵朵组、岩寨组、大寨内组、大寨外组、抵瓦组、孔庭组、高寨组、旧寨组、洞的组、板达组、板头组、拉打组、岜忙上组、岜忙下组、水龙三组、水龙四组、水龙五组、水龙六组
水丰村	10	大寨上组、大寨下组、水碾组、下寨组、板尧组、漂田组、拉吕组、懂吊组、岜领组、懂外组
水岩村	10	大寨上组、大寨下组、拉干上组、拉干下组、抵河组、拉小组、上水降组、下水降组、懂红组、母达组
洞托村	5	上洞托组、下洞托组、湾寨组、尧票组、兰电山组
尧棒村	4	拉偶组、拉纳组、拉更三组、拉更四组

第十四节　水尧水族乡

水尧水族乡位于县境中部偏东北，东与瑶麓乡毗邻，东南、东北与茂兰镇接壤，西南与永康乡相连，西北与玉屏镇交界。总面积90.7平方公里。乡政府驻水尧村板央寨，距县城13公里。

1978年时为水尧公社，隶属城关区。1980年，隶属玉屏区。1984年5月3日，成立水尧水族乡，辖水尧、水功、水捞、水扒、拉交5个村46个村民小组。1991年7月“建并撤”时，水尧水族乡升格为科级建制，行政区划不变。1998年7月，成立水瑶新村。2004年，合并行政村，水尧村和水扒村合并为水尧村，整合后全乡辖水尧、水功、水捞、水瑶新村、拉交5个行政村46个村民小组。乡内居住水族、布依族、汉族、瑶族、苗族等民族。2008年年末，全乡总人口7822人，其中，水族人口占总人口的79.3%，其他民族占20.7%。

水尧乡地貌特征类型根据县境地貌类型，海拔高程、剥蚀和侵蚀程度以及地貌形态，划分为山地、丘陵、坝子3个一级地貌类型，7个二级地貌类型。水尧乡南部属7个二级地貌类型中的第一类，中切低中山：海拔652～1031米，切割深度小于500米，大于200米，坡度25～35度，类型属翁昂中切岩溶低中山。中和北部属7个二级地貌类型中的第二类，浅切低中山：海拔800～1100米，切割深度小于200米，坡度15～25度，类型属水功浅切低中山。地处低山丘陵地貌，地势北高南低。地形受地质构造较明显，向斜成谷，背斜成山，与全县一样形成山地与谷地由西而东相间排列，主要山脉和水系沿地质构造走向发育，组成全县山脉与河流谷地成北偏东向长带状相嵌分部的格局，水尧乡属水尧—翁昂乡低中山格局。年平均气温16.8℃，年平均降水量1400毫米，无霜期275～310天。最高点海拔1031米，最低点海拔652米，乡政府驻地海拔700米。南面的水尧村、拉交村、水瑶新村土壤主要为石灰土，北面的水功村、水捞村土壤主要为黄壤沙石土。

2008年，全乡耕地面积4789亩，其中农田面积4229亩、土地面积560亩，有可开发利用非耕地资源9654亩。林地面积9654亩，优势树种为马尾松、杂木、灌木等，活立木积储量362万立方米。有成片草场3.44万亩，主要分布在北面的水功村。

境内已探明的煤炭储量1971万吨，占全县煤储量的6.28%，为低灰中硫高热无烟煤，煤质好。

全乡农业生产以种植业为主，粮食作物主要有水稻、玉米等。在推广粮食作物良种良法确保粮食产量基础上，调整产业结构，发展糖蔗种植。糖蔗产业逐步形成规模，由零星种植发展到规模连片种植，逐步形成产业效应，成为农户增收产业之一。2008年，全乡粮食总产量2569吨；种植糖蔗1826亩，产量4930吨。县委、县政府引进日榨甘蔗6000吨的九曲湾制糖有限公司落户水尧村。

养殖业主要有生猪养殖和鱼养殖，2008年年末，水尧乡大牲畜存栏2937头，生猪存栏2893头，家禽存栏13564羽。2008年全乡完成稻田养鱼1500亩，全年推广良种鱼苗45万尾，全乡坑塘养鱼35亩。

境内有新寨煤矿、的为煤矿、岜合煤矿、吉党煤矿等煤矿企业4个，是县内主要产煤乡（镇）之一。2006年，引资兴建水尧友谊页岩砖厂并投产，年产红砖1200万块。2008年，在董罕组新建小康页岩砖厂，产红砖1000万块。

荔大公路横贯全境，全乡村、组全部通公路，荔波机场位于境内；农电网覆盖各村寨农户；移动通信信号覆盖85%；广播电视覆盖率92%。

2008年，全乡有中心小学1所、村级完全小学4所、办学点1个，在校学生942人，有教师58人。适龄儿童入学率100%。

乡有卫生院1所，水功、水捞、水扒3个村建有卫生室。每村有防疫保健人员1人，开展卫生防疫、妇幼保健、新法接生等工作。2008年，农村人口参加合作医疗率86%。

2008年，全乡工农业总产值9080万元。其中，农业总产值912万元，比1991年增长51.7%；工业总产值8168万元。财政总收入30.25万元。农民人均纯收入2187元，比1991年增长69.7%。

2008年所辖村、村民小组一览表

表1-14

行政村名称	村民小组总数（个）	村民小组名称
水尧村	20	打里组、坡顶五组、坡顶六组、老场组、董响组、大寨一组、大寨二组、大寨三组、大寨四组、岜莫组、板央二组、板央一组、糖芽组、董伟组、董见组、懂夯组、懂路组、水扒二组、水扒一组、洞力组
水捞村	8	水捞组、懂罕组、巴平组、孔伞组、马安一组、马安二组、岜合一组、岜合二组
水功村	5	杨柳组、上更组、底朵组、下更组、板独组
拉交村	10	拉交一组、拉交二组、拉交三组、拉交四组、拉交五组、拉交六组、拉交七组、拉交八组、拉交九组、拉交十组
水瑶新村	3	水瑶一组、水瑶二组、水瑶三组

第十五节　永康水族乡

永康水族乡位于县境中部。东与洞塘乡、茂兰镇相连，南与洞塘乡、翁昂乡交界，西与朝阳镇、玉屏镇接壤，北与水尧水族乡毗邻。总面积103.5平方公里。乡政府驻太吉村，距县城15公里。

1978年时为永康公社。1984年5月3日，成立永康水族乡，辖尧兰、尧古、西竹、母早、吉洞、董亥、德门、太吉、白岩、甲棒10个行政村42个村民小组，隶属玉屏区。1991年7月“建并撤”时，永康水族乡行政区划不变。2004年，合并行政村，尧兰村与尧古村合并为尧古村，母早村与西竹村合并为西竹村，吉洞村与董亥村合并为董亥村，太吉村、德门村两村不变，甲棒村与白岩村合并为白岩村。2008年年末，全乡总人口6105人。其中，水族人口4411人，占全乡总人口的72.25%；布依族人口1612人，占全乡人口总数的26.40%；其他民族人口82人，占全乡人口数的1.34%。

境内年平均气温16.8℃，年平均降水量1350毫米，无霜期350天。最高点海拔1200米，最低点海拔300米，乡政府所在地海拔730米。

2008年，全乡耕地面积5323亩，其中农田面积4376亩、土地面积947亩；林地面积109060亩，占全乡总面积的70.39%；草地面积27650亩，占全乡总面积的17.84%。境内矿产资源缺乏。

全乡农田主要种植水稻及油菜，旱地主要种植玉米及豆薯类和棉花、辣椒、板蓝根等。2008年，全乡粮食总产量4000吨（其中玉米800吨）。

养殖业以家庭经营方式为主，家家户户饲养水牛、黄牛，主要用以耕田。由于县委、县政府发展养殖业优惠政策的鼓励，各村小型规模养殖户逐渐增多，至2008年，全乡有小型规模养殖户10户，品种涉及牛、猪、羊、鸡、鸭、鱼等。

2005年，县军华畜牧发展有限责任公司投资210万元，在永康建碧峰养殖场，占地3500余亩，进行生态循环立体种养殖，研发养殖无公害、绿色、有机畜牧产品生产及销售。2006年，州政府认定改企业为“州级农业产业化重点龙头企业”。2007年9月，国务院副总理回良玉由贵州省委书记石宗源、省长林树森陪同到该基地视察，给予高度评价。

水利工程主要有排洪渠、引水渠、山塘、水库、提灌站等。排洪工程涉及44个村13个村民组，引水渠道涉及4个村10个村组。用于农田灌溉的水库仅有吉洞村师母水库，水库蓄水量4万～5万立方米，灌溉农田300～400亩。

境内有私营企业投资开办的建筑材料加工场1家，主要加工出售块石、碎石、石粉等建筑材料，产品主要供应县城及永康乡、水尧乡等周边乡（镇）建筑工地。

县城通往翁昂乡和洞塘乡的公路通过乡境，途经甲棒、白岩、太吉、母早、尧古、尧兰等村寨。德门、西竹、吉洞、董亥等村及自然村寨全部通公路。农电网覆盖各村寨农户，移动通信信号、广播电视覆盖各村组，拥有电视机农户占总户数的95%。乡政府驻地机关单位已使用计算机网络办公，农村个别家庭开始拥有计算机。拥有电视机的农户达全乡总户数的95%。

全乡有小学4所，2008年在校生728人（含学前班52人），适龄儿童入学率100%。

有乡卫生院1所，医务人员5人，设病床10张；有村级卫生室4个。2008年，农村人口参加合作医疗率81.2%。

境内已开发的旅游景区及景点有尧古布依民族村寨、国家级茂兰喀斯特自然保护区、永康穿洞抗日遗址等。水族的端节和额节是境内隆重的节日。

2008年所辖村、村民小组一览表

表1-15

行政村名称	村民小组总数（个）	村民小组名称
西竹村	6	西竹一组、西竹二组、西竹三组、母早一组、母早二组、母早三组
尧古村	10	尧古一组、尧古二组、尧古三组、尧古四组、尧古五组、尧古六组、尧兰一组、尧兰二组、尧兰三组、尧兰四组
太吉村	5	太吉一组、太吉二组、太吉三组、太吉四组、太吉五组
董亥村	6	董亥一组、董亥二组、董亥三组、吉洞一组、吉洞二组、吉洞三组
德门村	6	德门一组、德门二组、德门三组、德门四组、德门五组、德门六组
白岩村	9	白岩一组、白岩二组、白岩三组、白岩四组、甲棒一组、甲棒二组、甲棒三组、甲棒四组、甲棒五组

第十六节 瑶山瑶族乡

瑶山瑶族乡位于县境南部。东与翁昂乡毗邻，南与捞村乡接壤，西与驾欧乡、广西南丹县里湖乡交界，北与朝阳镇相连。总面积110平方公里。乡政府驻拉片村，距县城32公里。

1978年时为瑶山公社。1984年5月，恢复建立瑶山瑶族乡，辖拉片村、英盘村、菇类村、懂别村4个村22个村民小组，总面积61.25平方公里。1991年8月9日，撤销瑶山、王蒙两乡，合并建立瑶山瑶族乡，辖原王蒙乡的高桥村、红光村和原瑶山瑶族乡的拉片村、英盘村、菇类村、懂别村共6个村46个村民小组。2004年合并行政村，英盘村并入拉片村，懂别村并入菇类村后，乡下辖4个行政村，即高桥村、红光村、拉片村和菇类村。乡内有瑶族、布依族、水族、苗族、汉族、壮族等民族居住，瑶族集中居住在拉片村、菇类村、英盘村及董别村4个村，布依族、苗族、水族、汉族和壮族主要分布在高桥村和红光村。2008年年末，全乡总人口5688人，其中，瑶族人口2672人，占全乡总人口的46.98%；布依族人口2323人，占总人口的40.84%；水族人口348人，占总人口的6.12%；苗族、汉族、壮族等民族人口345人，占总人口的6.07%。

境内属于典型的喀斯特山区，亚热带湿润气候，热量丰富，雨量充沛。无霜期313天。

土壤以红壤为主，有黄壤石灰土分布，土层深厚，肥力较强。

2008年，全乡有耕地面积3900亩，其中农田面积2400亩、土地面积1500亩。有林业用地面积146493.45亩，其中有林地18175亩，占总区域面积的11.8%；灌木林地面积6154.2亩；未成林造林地6638.4亩。森林覆盖率61.55%。名贵树种有黄杨木、楠木、蓝靛木等。境内退耕还林工程造林面积

3977.82亩，个人自发造林面积1.6万亩，以杉木为主。林产品主要有油桐籽、木耳、杜仲、酸梅、水果、蚕等。

粮食作物主要有水稻、玉米、小麦、豆类、小米、薯类等。旱稻是瑶族长期保留的珍贵品种，已有200年种植历史，种植面积不大，但耐旱力强，米质好，亩产只有200公斤，是瑶族馈赠客人、建房挂房脊、婚嫁、丧葬等活动的礼品。经济作物主要有油菜、辣椒、土烟、花生、麻等，以油菜、辣椒为主。杂交水稻、杂交玉米良种推广面积逐年扩大。其中，杂交水稻良种推广面积占水稻种植总面积的85%以上，油菜种植农户已普遍使用油菜育苗移栽技术。乡内建有提灌站1个，灌溉面积2526亩。2008年，全乡粮食总产量1909.9吨。主要推广杂交水稻种植面积2500亩；种植杂交玉米面积1400亩，其中玉米育苗移栽1200亩；全乡种植油菜1824亩，其中油菜育苗移栽900亩。

养殖业以猪、牛、羊、鸡、鸭、鹅为主。拉朝鸡是县内较为有名的优良鸡种，高桥村、红光村每年有成批鸭、鹅上市。瑶山有珍贵鱼种娃娃鱼。1994年，黑山羊在瑶山23个点28户饲养成功。2008年，瑶山鸡存栏1.83万羽、出栏1.83万羽，全乡水产品产量8吨，良种鱼苗推广358万尾，其中淡水养鱼近2000亩，稻田养鱼面积200亩以上。

全乡村、组全部通公路，农电网覆盖各村组，移动通信信号覆盖全乡，广播电视覆盖率90%以上。乡文化站建有瑶族歌舞表演队，对外宣传瑶山瑶族特有的民族文化。瑶山男陀螺队代表贵州省参加全国第八届少数民族运动会夺得金牌。拉片村四组村民谢友明被选为第29届奥运会圣火在贵州传递的火炬手。瑶山瑶族“猴鼓舞”已列为国家级非物质文化遗产。

2008年，全乡有小学2所、中学1所，在校中小学生660人，教师总计65人。适龄儿童入学率99.63%。瑶族初中学生获“两免一补”（免书费、免杂费，获寄宿生生活补助）。初中戴帽班于1993年9月设立在王蒙小学，直到1995年，由香港影业集团董事长邵逸夫先生捐资80万港币和省、州、县配套资金共同在王蒙市场周边修建了瑶山第一所农村独立民族中学，即瑶山民族中学。1997年3月瑶山民族中学正式投入使用，教学服务于瑶山、驾欧、捞村三个边远贫困乡。在校学生415人，8个教学班，29位教职员工，专任教师29人，大专学历14人。

有乡卫生院1所、村级卫生室5个，卫生院有医务人员8人。计划免疫适龄儿童服苗率100%，新法接生率93%以上。农村人口参加农村合作医疗率90.79%。

境区内有大七孔、小七孔国家级旅游风景名胜区，有拉片、懂蒙、拉柳等民族村寨旅游点。

2008年，全乡工农业总产值3442.5万元，比1991年增长907.56%。其中，农业总产值2128.7万元，比1991年增长613.47%；工业总产值1313.8万元，比1991年增长406.49%。财政总收入46.85万元，比1991年增长544.76%。农民人均纯收入1625.43元。

2008年所辖村、村民小组一览表

表1-16

行政村名称	村民小组总数（个）	村民小组名称
拉片村	12	岜么组、林场组、尧沙组、拉片一组、拉片二组、拉片三组、拉片四组、懂保组、拉朝组、英盘一组、英盘二组、英盘三组
高桥村	16	外孟塘组、拉庆组、拉柳组、白腊坳组、坡旧组、下脚组、上脚组、拉转组、拉过组、巴楼一组、巴楼二组、巴楼三组、上海利组、下海利组、内孟塘组、下洞组
红光村	8	洞更组、洞干组、拉烘组、甲林组、更类组、江懂组、界排组、塘上组
菇类村	10	懂蒙组、懂书组、板告组、朝沙组、更咸组、懂别组、九加组、更龚组、拉更莫组、懂瓜组

第十七节 瑶麓瑶族乡

瑶麓瑶族乡位于县境东部，东南与茂兰镇交界，西与水尧水族乡相邻，北与佳荣镇接壤。总面积25.99平方公里。乡政府驻瑶麓村，距县城30公里。

1978年时为瑶麓公社。1984年，恢复建立瑶麓瑶族乡，属茂兰区。1991年“建并撤”时，瑶麓瑶族乡行政区划不变，辖1个村（瑶麓村）13个村民小组。2008年年末，全乡总人口1553人，青瑶村民占全乡常住人口总数的99.8%。

境内属于亚热带季风性湿润气候，气候温热，四季分明，夏长冬短，无霜期长，雨量充沛，日照充足，雨热同季。年平均气温17.3℃，年平均降水量1320.5毫米，无霜期280～290天。最高点汉按山海拔951米，最低点打里下坝海拔630米，乡政府所在地海拔640米。

2008年，全乡有耕地面积1360亩，其中农田面积870亩、土地面积490亩；林地面积33679亩，森林覆盖率62.25%；草丛植被1200亩。

矿产资源主要有煤、重晶石。煤矿主要分布在机远坝、甲丙坝。重晶石储量未探明。

粮食作物主要有水稻、玉米、大豆、高粱、红薯、荞子、饭豆等。水稻有黏稻和糯稻，糯稻主要有摘糯和打糯2种。乡内逐步推广杂交水稻、杂交玉米种植。经济作物主要有油菜、花生、辣椒、棉花等，除油菜、花生外，其他种植面积较少。2008年，水稻种植面积870亩，平均亩产425公斤；杂交玉米平均亩产325公斤；杂粮种植面积较少，荞子、高粱等已不种植；油菜种植面积583亩，产量43吨。

养殖业主要有猪、羊、牛、鸡、鸭等，是农户的主要经济收入之一。2008年，牛存栏867头、出栏108头，羊存栏313只、出栏86只，猪存栏1237头、出栏780头，家禽存栏21370羽、出栏20130羽。

境内有引水灌溉工程1处，引水渠道全长20.4公里。其中，主干渠8.7公里，支渠2.3公里，配套支沟9.4公里，灌溉白岩脚坝、瑶麓坝、洞力坝、打里坝、洞干坝等共800亩，保灌面积400亩。有提灌站1处，灌溉面积40亩。在洞闷建有人饮提灌站。

1985年年底在甲丙建的岜豆煤厂于2000年停产关闭。鑫塬煤矿进行技术改造后，2008年扩大为年产9万吨。

境内有县城经茂兰至佳荣县道918过境公路7.4公里，有瑶麓—茂兰、瑶麓—佳荣、瑶麓—水庆村3条乡（镇）公路，村民小组全部通公路。农电网覆盖各组、农户，移动通信信号覆盖全乡，广播电视覆盖率90%。

2008年，乡内有中心完全小学1所，在校学生161人，有教师7人。适龄儿童入学率100%。

有村卫生室1个，设病床4张，有医务人员1人。2008年，农村人口参加农村合作医疗率95%。

民族节日主要有大年（春节）、小年、卯节、“熟霞”祭祀节（“熟霞”瑶语）、尝新米节、播种节。

2008年，全乡农业总产值867万元，比1991年增长880.8%；财政总收入22万元；农民人均纯收入2485元，比1991年增长977.7%。

2008年所辖村、村民小组一览表

表1-17

行政村名称	村民小组总数（个）	村民小组名称
瑶麓村	13	上韦组、下韦一组、下韦二组、覃家一组、覃家二组、覃家三组、打里一组、打里二组、欧家组、洞干组、洞闷组、卢家一组、卢家二组

第三章　自然地理

第一节　地形　地质　地貌

一、地形

荔波县地处贵州高原南部斜坡，为贵州高原与桂东丘陵的过渡地带。地势总趋势北高南低。东北隅月亮山次峰海拔1468米，南部打狗河和甲料河出境处海拔300米，县城海拔425米，全县平均海拔758.8米。

县境地形受地质构造控制较明显，向斜成谷，背斜成山，形成山地与谷地由西而东相间排列，主要山脉和水系沿地质构造走向发育，组成全县山脉与河流谷地成北偏东向长带状相嵌分布的格局。

由西而东为：甲良—播尧低中山，方村河谷中丘；水利—驾欧低中山，樟江河谷低丘、低山；水尧—翁昂低中山，三岔河谷低山、低丘。山地中多有小河流沿背斜轴或断层发育。

河流水系发育程度受岩石性质控制较明显。山地多为碳酸盐岩类，喀斯特发育，地表水流小而短，谷深流激，多盲谷和伏流，地下水系较发育。碎屑岩分布的丘陵及低山地，地表水发育较好。

东北隅为樟江，三岔河—茂兰和甲料河分水岭，山高水低，河谷深切，河流沿古陆边缘断层发育。

二、地质

县境内沉积岩层广布，有新生代陆相碎屑岩、中生代海相碎屑岩和化学岩、古生代海相化学岩、碎岩和泻湖相煤系、元古代浅变质海相、碎屑岩和化学岩等，未见火成岩分布。

第四系，主要分布于樟江、方村河、茂兰河等河谷地带及零星散布于山间盆地、岩溶洼地及洞穴之中，结构松散，透水性强。上层为黏土、亚黏土及亚沙土，下层为沙砾、泥砾及沙泥质胶结的卵石层，二元结构明显，厚度小于30米。

第三系，仅见于县城附近。上部为紫红色钙质粉沙岩，下部为紫红色砾岩，厚度0～250米。

三叠系，出露于樟江中下游和方村河两侧地带，结构致密，隔水性好，上统缺失。分中三叠统和下三叠统。中三叠统，灰绿、黄绿色黏土页岩与钙质砂岩互层，上部夹薄层为石灰岩，厚度610米以上。下三叠统，上部永宁组为灰绿色页岩，中厚层砂岩夹薄层瘤状灰岩；其下为灰色薄层致密灰岩，下部飞仙关组为灰绿、紫红色泥质灰岩夹钙质页岩、灰褐色页岩；底部有灰绿色含砾黏土岩，厚度大于405米。

二叠系分布较广，灰岩节理发育，透水性较好，煤系地层有一定隔水能力。分上二叠统和下二叠统。上二叠统，上部大隆组为钢灰色硅质岩夹页岩，中部长兴组为深灰色薄至厚层燧石灰岩夹薄层硅质岩及黏土岩，底部吴家坪组为黑色页岩夹硅质岩和煤，有3个煤组，西部煤炭地质储量为2.2亿吨，局部含黄铁矿和铝土岩，厚度411～1071米。下二叠统，上部茅口组为浅灰、灰色中厚层至块状石灰岩；下部栖霞组为深灰、黑灰色中厚层致密灰岩，含泥质、有机质、燧石结核和条带；底部为黑色钙质页岩和灰白色中厚层石英沙岩夹页岩，局部夹煤。厚214～981米。

石炭系，出露广泛，分布面积大，灰岩是主要溶洞含水层。地下水系发育，煤系有相对隔水作用。分上石炭统、中石炭统和下石炭统。上石炭统，灰白、灰色厚层至块状细结晶灰岩，厚度47～427米。中石炭统，上部为灰白色厚层石灰岩夹少量白云岩和燧石灰岩，下部为白色粗粒白云岩，厚度182～710米。下石炭统，上部大塘阶上司段为灰、黑色中厚层灰岩；中部大塘阶旧司段为石英砂岩夹炭质和砂质页岩，东部有可采煤3层，储量3.14亿吨；下部岩关阶汤巴沟段为深灰、黑灰色泥质灰岩夹泥岩；底部岩关阶革老河段为中厚层石灰岩。厚度227～2003米。

泥盆系，出露于东北部个别地区，结构致密，节理不发育，有一定隔水性。下统缺失。上泥盆统，上部为泥岩、页岩夹硅质岩；下部为泥质灰岩及炭质页岩。厚度182～1082米。中泥盆统，上部为泥岩、页岩夹炭质泥岩，下部为含硅质泥岩夹泥灰岩，底部夹石英砂岩，局部有底角砾岩。厚度182～1089米。

寒武系和震旦系，仅出露于东北隅少数地段。寒武系的上寒武统，为灰色、黄绿色页岩、钙质页岩及混质灰岩等；中寒武统，为深灰、灰黑色中厚层石灰岩和炭质灰岩夹碳质页岩及沙质页岩、白云质灰岩；下寒武统，为黑色炭质页岩，底部为黑色薄层硅质岩夹块状或结核状磷块岩。震旦系的上震旦统，为灰色中厚层白云岩、中部黑色炭质页岩；下震旦统，为浅变质岩类，上为水渍砾岩，中为黑色炭质页岩，下为水渍含砾泥岩，底部为厚层细粒砂岩夹炭质页岩和含砾砂岩。

县境地质构造经历加里东、燕山和喜马拉雅山三大地壳运动历史阶段。各期的构造特征反映了不同地质力学环境，每一期旋回的升降及与之相应的沉积剥蚀是量变的过程，每一期强烈的褶皱断裂是质变的飞跃。所以该区地壳运动的规律是从沉降到上升，从沉积到褶皱剥蚀。

根据形态和构造线方向，分为两大体系：一是形态的褶皱为主，控制性构造线方向北东向的华夏系构造；二是构造形态以断裂为主，控制性构造线方向北西向的古陆边缘折断构造。

华夏系构造定形于燕山运动。褶皱、背斜、向斜相间排列，主要褶皱由西而东为：

阳凤背斜，位于塘弄、月光一带，轴向北东5～10度，县内轴长11.4公里，南北西端伸入独山县境，轴部地层为下石炭统。

已故向斜，位于尧蒙、已故一带，轴向北东25～30度，轴长7.6公里，南北两端消失于甲良断层，轴部地层为中石炭统。

豆村背斜，位于岜领、豆村、尧细一带，轴向北东5～25度，县内轴长19公里，北端在甲良西南消失于断层，南端伸入独山县境，轴部地层为中石炭统。

方村向斜，位于甲站、觉巩、驾欧一带，轴向北东10～25度，县内轴长34.5公里，南端在拉美扬起，北端伸入三都县境，两翼倾角内向外变缓，为一

荔波典型的喀斯特地貌

发育完整的长轴褶皱，轴部地层为中三迭统。

围寨背斜，位于拉达、水降、水丰一带，轴北东10～25度，县内轴长24公里，北端伸入三都县境，南端在洪江倾没，轴部地层为下石炭统。

水浦背斜，位于水江、鱼塘一带，轴向北东20～30度，北端伸入三都县境，南端消失于断层，轴部地层为上泥盆至上石炭统。

围寨背斜和水浦背斜，组成偏东向“Y”字形复背斜。

荔波向斜，位于罗布木、坡平、寨省、拉转一带，轴向北东25～40度，县内轴长36公里，北端伸入三都县境，南端伸入广西境内，西翼倾角北缓南陡，荔波附近东南翼倒转，向斜形态较对称，轴部地层为中三叠至下二叠统，县城附近有第三系。

翁昂背斜，位于水功、德门、平岩一带，轴向北东20～40度，县内轴长25公里，北端在水庆倾没，南端在平林以南消失于断层，轴部地层为下石炭统。

茂兰向斜，位于俄羊、浪贬、木槽、聋关一带，轴向北东20～25度，轴长31.2公里，北端在俄羊扬起，南端在聋关南消失于断层，轴部地层为中石炭统至下二叠统。

断裂分北北东—北东组和北西—北西西组。北北东—北东组断裂为走向平行或斜交褶皱轴的纵断层，倾向以北西西为主，倾50度以上，断层延伸较远，多伸出县境，沿断层一般可见破碎带和断层角砾岩，有硅化及方解石化现象，为该区主要控制性断裂，形成于燕山期；县城东西两侧形成荔波地堑构造的两条正断层，形成于喜马拉雅期，主要断层有甲岸正断层，甲良正断层，尧棒正断层，水利、水架地垒正断层，荔波地堑正断层，洞塘正断层，板寨和洞腊复瓦式正断层。北西—北西西组断裂为垂直或近于垂直褶皱的横断层，以逆断层为主，倾角斜，断层常切割褶皱轴和北北东组断裂，造成褶皱轴和断层线的东西向移动，断裂形成于燕山期后段，主要断层有岜马逆断层、母右坡逆断层和捞村正断层。

古陆边缘折断构造：县东北隅地区，地层古老，地质构造为古陆边缘折断构造。北东和北西两组断层交错发育，呈网格状分布，多为正断层。北西组断层发育程度较强烈，延伸较远，为控制性构造。两组断层形成于加里末期，定形于燕山期，主要断裂有北西组和水维正断层、拉毛正断层、洞伞正断层；东北组的高里正断层、拉先正断层、平木正断层。

三、地貌

县境地貌类型，根据海拔高程、剥蚀和侵蚀程度以及地貌形态，划分为山地、丘陵、坝子3个一级地貌类型、7个二级地貌类型。其中，山地占总面积的71.63%，丘陵占18.2%，坝子占10.17%。7个二级地貌类型划分及分布：

（一）中切低中山

海拔800～1468米，切割深度小于500米、大于200米，坡度25～35度。面积为114.35万亩，占总面积的31.23%，成6片分布于全县各地。

拉易中切低中山　分布于水维东部和北部、岜鲜东部和东北部，为全县屋脊地带，面积为12.79万亩，占总面积的3.49%。

罗家寨中切低中山　分布于茂兰镇东北部、立化镇北部、佳荣镇南部，面积10.15万亩，占总面积的2.77%。

播尧中切岩溶低中山　分布于播尧乡中部、甲良镇西部地带，面积12.37万亩，占总面积的3.38%。

尧棒中切岩溶低中山　分布于水利乡、朝阳镇西部及驾欧乡东西、南大部和甲站、方村、地莪、觉巩等地东部边缘地带，面积27.05万亩，占总面积的7.39%。

翁昂中切岩溶低中山 分布于翁昂乡、永康乡大部及洞塘乡西部、水尧乡南部及瑶山、朝阳两乡（镇）东部、捞村乡北部边缘地带，面积45.93万亩，占总面积的12.54%。喀斯特植被自然保护区在该片区内。

蓝靛山中切低中山 分布于水利乡东部，面积6.07万亩，占总面积的1.66%。

（二）浅切低中山

海拔800～1100米，切割深度小于200米，坡度15—25度，面积10.43万亩，成两片分布。

拉埃浅切低中山 分布于佳荣镇中部、岜鲜南部和水维乡西部边缘，面积5.89万亩，占总面积的1.6%。

水功浅切低中山 分布于水尧乡中部和北部、玉屏镇东北部和瑶庆乡水庆村西部边缘地带，面积4.56万亩，占总面积的1.75%。

（三）中切低山

海拔500～800米，切割深度小于300米、大于200米，坡度15—25度，面积136.93万亩，成3片分布。

中部——南部中切岩深低山 分布于玉屏、朝阳两镇东部和西部边缘及瑶山乡西部、捞村乡东部和西部，面积55.75万亩，占总面积的15.23%。

东北部中切低山 分布于佳荣镇东南部和西北部、水维西南部、岜鲜中部和西部，面积22.40万亩，占总面积的6.12%。

东部一东南部中切岩溶低山 分布于茂兰、洞塘、瑶庆及立化等广大地区，面积58.78万亩，占总面积的16.05%。

（四）深切中丘

海拔700—900米，切割深度小于200米、大于100米，坡度15—25度，面积50.92万亩，成3片分布。

阳凤深切中丘 分布于阳凤和播尧西部，面积6.07万亩，占总面积的1.66%。

方村河深切中丘 分布于方村河两侧广大地区，面积36.24万亩，占总面积的9.89%。

水利深切中丘 分布于水利乡拉达河和朝阳镇洪江河两侧地区，面积8.61万亩，占总面积的2.35%。

（五）深切低丘

海拔300～500米，切割深度小于200米、大于100米，坡度15—25度，面积6.78万亩，成3片分布。

甲料河深切低丘 分布于甲料河两侧地带，面积1.44万亩，占总面积的0.39%。

三岔河深切低丘 分布于三岔河两侧地带，面积4.08万亩，占总面积的1.11%。

捞村河深切低丘 分布于捞村乡中部捞村河与打狗河汇合地带，面积1.26万亩，占总面积的0.34%。

（六）浅切低丘

海拔380—500米，切割深度小于100米，坡度5—15度，面积8.58万亩，成两片分布。

樟江浅切低丘 分布于樟江河两侧地带，面积8.58万亩，占总面积2.34%。

水春河浅切低丘 分布于水春河与樟江河汇合处，面积0.39万亩，占总面积的0.1%。

（七）低盆地坝子

在上述6种地貌类型片块中发育的山间盆地、溶蚀盆地、河谷台地、峰丛洼地、峰林谷地等小地貌统称“坝子”，切割深度一般10—15米，地势平缓，坡度5—15度，海拔310—830米，属低盆地类型，是农业主要耕作区，面积37.22万亩。其中，山间盆地9.26万亩，溶蚀盆地16.46万亩，河谷台地3.30万亩，峰丛洼地2.13万亩，峰林谷地6.07万亩。

第二节 土壤 植被

一、土壤

全县的土壤共划分为7个土类、14个亚类、76个土属、233个土种。

（一）红壤土类

红壤土类面积37.33万亩，占全县土地总面积的10.1%。分为红壤、黄红壤、粗骨红壤3个亚类。

（二）黄壤土类

黄壤土类是县内主要土壤资源之一，面积95.40万亩，占全县土地总面积的26.05%。各乡（镇）均有不同数量分布，以东部的茂兰区和北部的甲良区分布面积最广，垂直分布在海拔750米以上的丘陵山地及低中山，根据成土作用的组合及发育程度，分为黄壤、粗骨黄壤2个亚类。

（三）红色石灰土土类

红色石灰土土类面积0.61万亩，占全县土地总面积的0.17%。零星分布在玉屏、朝阳、王蒙、捞村4个乡（镇）。此土类有机质分解较彻底，土体中有机质含量较其他石灰土低，肥力中下等。

（四）石灰土土类

石灰土土类是县内面积最大、范围最广的土壤类型。总面积202.52万亩，占全县土地总面积的55.3%。全县各乡都有不同数量分布，其中比较集中连片的有翁昂、洞塘、茂兰、永康等乡。根据成土条件，成土母质及局部地形和人为生产的影响，划分为黄色石灰土、石卡拉土2个亚类。

（五）紫色土土类

紫色土土类面积1.33万亩，占全县土地总面积的0.36%。主要分布在樟江河谷第三紫色岩类的风化母质上，分钙质紫色土、中性紫色土和酸性紫色土3个亚类。

（六）潮土土类

潮土土类面积0.29万亩，占土地总面积的0.08%。主要分布在樟江沿河两岸一级阶地或超河漫滩上以及茂兰、瑶麓等乡，因地处沿河两岸，水源条件较好，地下水位高，具有返潮回润的特点，抗旱能力强，肥力中等，质地疏松，多已开垦为农耕地。

（七）水稻土土类

水稻土土类是县内主要的耕作土壤类型。面积21.1万亩，占全县土地总面积的5.76%，占耕地面积71.84%。各乡（镇）都有分布，多在海拔400～800米的低山丘陵坡旁、岩溶洼地、山间谷地、坝子及沿河两岸的地段。根据成因、水型及诊断土层的发生学特征，划分为渗育型、潴育型、潜育型3个亚类。

二、植被

（一）天然植被

在自然植被中，温暖性针叶林植被34.23万亩，暖性针、阔叶混交林植被67.55万亩，落叶阔叶林植被2.26万亩，常绿阔叶混交林植被29.68万亩，竹林植被1.62万亩，灌木林植被14.49万亩，草丛植被2.06万亩，灌丛草植被1.56万亩，林草丛植被16.32万亩，经济林1.05万亩。

成片森林植被以阔叶混交林为多，其次是以松、杉为主的常绿针叶林。阔叶混交林集中分布在甲料河、三岔河、樟江和方村河下游沿岸；针叶林分布于樟江流域和方村河上游地区，岩杉、侧柏等耐寒针叶树木零星分布在县东北部、东部和西北部的温凉山区；泡桐、枫木、樟树、香椿、油桐、罗拐、梓木以及干、水果树的核桃、板栗、桃、李、梨等阔叶树种，主要分布在东北部和东部海拔1000米以下的温凉山区以及全县各地的“四旁”（路旁、水旁、寨旁、宅旁）地带。

草场植被，可供放牧面积19.43万亩，占全县总面积的5.33%。其中，以东部和中部的山区面积较大，占牧地面积的68.1%，西北部（甲良地区）仅占31.9%。草场大部集中在海拔800米以下的低中山和丘陵缓坡地区，占牧地面积的86.7%。成片草场共有397片，其中1万～2万亩5片。草场可利用面积3.62万亩，这类草场地势平缓，土质和水热条件较好，适宜牧草生长，年可采割鲜草2～3次，青绿期10个月以上，年产鲜草10.85万吨，理论载畜量1.21万牛单位。

（二）人工植被

县内地形地貌复杂，山谷纵横，起伏较大，致使耕地分散，多不连片。其分布特点是田多分布在河流两岸和山间、槽谷地带；土多分布在低丘、中丘的缓坡地区。

人工植被中，草本类有一年一熟旱作组合型，一年两熟旱作组合型；一年一熟水田组合型，一年两熟水田组合型；一年两熟蔬菜组合型，一年三熟蔬菜组合型，一年四熟以上蔬菜组合型。面积174.18万亩。此外还有人工种草0.33万亩。木本类有人工造用材林53.54万亩，人工造经济林1.8万亩。

第三节 水 文

一、河流水系

（一）地表水

境内河流均属龙江水系珠江流域。全县较大的河流水系有打狗河水系（包括樟江干流和方村河支流）、三岔河水系和甲料河水系。全县集雨面积大于20平方公里或河道长于10公里的河流共30条。县内河道总长1048公里，其中各河流主河道长483.95公里，河道密度0.47公里/平方公里。县内属上述3条水系的河流流域面积2375.1平方公里。其中，打狗河水系的流域面积1708.4平方公里，占71.93%；三岔河水系流域面积579.18平方公里，占24.39%；甲料河水系的流域面积87.52平方公里，占3.68%。

地表水径流分布基本上和降水分布趋于一致，一般是东北多，西南少，中部较多。东北部甲料河流域径流大于1000毫米，中部地区700毫米，西北部地区小于600毫米。在季风气候条件下，径流的季节变化大。冬季（12—2月）是河流的最枯季节，径流量仅为全年的6%；春季（3—5月）径流逐渐增多，径流量占全年的26.42%，3月尚属旱季，4月下旬才开始进入雨季，所以径流量增加不大；夏季（6—8月）径流量最多，高达全年的51.47%；秋季（9—11月）径流逐渐减退，径流量占全年的16.11%。径流的年际变化也较大，偏丰年径流总量为22.13亿立方米，平水年18.07亿立方米，偏枯年14.43亿立方米，特枯年为10.68亿立方米。

1.打狗河水系　包括打狗河流域、樟江河流域及其支流方村河、拉达河流域，由北至南贯穿县境，在捞村出境，进广西境内汇入龙江河，流域总面积为3745.22平方公里，其中县内为1708.4平方公里。

樟江河流域：樟江河是县境内最大的河流，发源于月亮山南麓，流经3个乡（镇），在王蒙与方村河交汇，主河道长53.1公里，最大流量3704立方米/秒，最小流量2.92立方米/秒，平均流量35.72立方米/秒，年均总水量11.29亿立方米，其中县内径流量6.82亿立方米。

方村河流域：方村河发源于三都县阳安乡，由北至南流经三都县廷牌、和勇进入荔波境内，经甲站、方村、地莪、觉巩、驾欧等地，在驾欧板潭入洞成伏流，从王蒙内孟塘出露汇入打狗河，主河道长138.2公里，最大流量1937立方米/秒，最小流量2.42立方米/秒，平均总流量28.92立方米/秒，年均总水量9.12亿立方米，其中县内径流量3.49亿立方米。

打狗河流域：打狗河为樟江下游，主河道长52.6公里，河段最大流量769方米/秒，最小流量1.96立方米/秒，平均流量12.01立方米/秒，年均总水量4.46亿立方米，其中县内径流量1.7亿立方米。

拉达河流域：拉达河发源于水利乡孔廷北侧，东北流经拉达入三都县，称水令河，转向流至水江，称水甫河，沿县界东南流，注入樟江，主河道长9.9公里，最大流量148立方米/秒，最小流量0.06立方米/秒，年均总水量0.42亿立方米，其中县内径流量0.38亿立方米。

2.三岔河水系　三岔河发源于立化镇洞湖村，自北向南流经洞塘，经蒙寨出境，流入广西环江汇入龙江河，主河道长20公里，最大流量2606立方米/秒，最小流量1.16立方米/秒，平均流量14.43立方米/秒，年均总水量4.7亿立方米。

3.甲料河水系　甲料河发源于佳荣镇大土，流经甲料、洞独、何家寨出境，经广西驯乐、上潮、环江注入龙江河。甲料河水系在境内流域面积92.63平方公里，县内主河道长22公里，最大流量507立方米/秒，最小流量0.22立方米/秒，平均流量3.11立方米/秒，年均总水量1.24亿立方米，其中县内径流量为0.98亿立方米。

（二）地下水

境内地下水分为岩溶型地下水、山区基岩裂隙地下水、松散层孔隙水3种类型，以岩溶水类型为多，主要集中于南部和东南部瑶山乡、永康乡、翁昂乡、洞塘乡、茂兰乡一带和西部的播尧乡、驾欧乡。上述地区均为岩溶比较发育的石灰岩地区，总面积850平方公里。这些地区地表水径流小，大部分降水由地面潜入地下，形成地下水。河流常呈潜流与明流交替的状况，很难截然分开。

二、水质

境内绝大多数水质符合饮用水卫生标准。污染较为严重的是三岔河水系，立化一段氨氮含量为0.06毫克/升，总硬度为31.4毫克/升。伍家河口酸碱度为5.2度。这一段河水氨氮含量大于卫生标准20～30倍，主要是开发煤矿的工业废水和矿碴导致水质污染，但到巴格河段已逐渐净化。水尧河友谊桥一段污染程度与伍家河相似。方村河邑乃河段氨氮含量0.12毫克/升，瑶所河口和樟江龙王洞河段氨氮含量0.04毫克/升，有不同程度污染，但经过数公里流程，都自行净化或淡化。按水质的7个项目标准分析，根据省级、县级水资源规划试行规范，全县水质为一级水和二级水。

三、水能资源

境内河流落差大，水能资源丰富。全县河道累计落差6342米，水能理论蕴藏总量34.9万千瓦，可开发量24.43万千瓦。

已开发利用的水电站14座，装机43台，容量97390千瓦，占可开发量的3.99%。

第四节　气　候

一、气候特点

根据气候带划分，荔波县属于中亚热带季风湿润气候区。由于地理纬度较低，境内山峦起伏，河谷深切，地形地貌复杂，气候类型多样，因而具有亚热带高原山地季风湿润气候特征。总体特征是气候温热，四季分明，冬无严寒，夏无酷暑，夏长冬短，无霜期长，雨量充沛，日照尚足，雨热同季，灾害性天气少；在不同的地形、地势影响下，温度的地区差异显著，日照差别大，雨水时空分布不均，有明显的雨季和旱季。多年气象资料表明，干旱、低温、洪涝及绵雨等主要的农业自然灾害天气时有出现，其范围大小和危害程度各地不同。

二、气温

气温分布的总趋势是南高北低。地势每升高100米，气温大致下降0.55℃。河谷地带与同高度的山地比，东西向槽谷比南北向槽谷、南坡比北坡、封闭型谷盆地比同高坡地气温高。樟江河谷是县内气温的高值区，捞村乡（海拔350米）年平均气温19.2℃，为全县最高。另外，洞塘乡、立化镇的三岔河谷和佳荣镇甲料河谷为县内两个温度次高区。县境西北部甲良镇（除方村河谷外）和水利乡以及县的东北部邕鲜和水维北部海拔均在800米以上，是县内气温低值区，年平均气温16.3℃；最低的水维拉易（海拔930米）年平均气温15.5℃。

县内各地平均气温的年际变化不大。县城年平均气温18.5℃，最高年19.0℃，最低年18.2℃，相差0.8℃。月平均气温年际变化较大，尤以冬季各月明显。县城1月平均气温为8.5℃，最高的2010年为10.4℃，最低的2011年为4.3℃，相差6.1℃；7月平均26.4℃，最高的2011年为27.4℃，最低的2008为25.7℃，相差1.7℃。

常年最热月为7月，最冷月为1月。1月平均气温各地均在5.5℃以上，极端最低气温在-4.3℃以上。县城历年极端最低温度为-4.3℃，出现在1983年12月22日；极端最高气温39.2℃，出现在1984年8月3日。超过35℃的天数，平均每年有8.6天；超过37℃的天数平均每年仅4天，夏季炎热但不酷热。

境内地形地势复杂，气候的垂直变化和地形小气候明显。各地四季的起止时间和长短亦不相同。地势比县城高的地区夏季比县城短，其余各季比县城长；地势比县城低的地区反之。

县城气温日较差年平均为8.5℃，一年中，8—10月的日较差月平均大于9.0℃，夏季（5—8月）日较差均大于8.0℃，平均最低气温均低于23.0℃，这是境内夏季白天炎热而夜间较凉爽的又一气候特点。

县内霜少，无霜期在270天以上。无霜期分布大致是河谷地区大于280天，海拔在800米以上地区280—300天左右。

各地气温极值温度表

表1-18

地 名	极端最高气温（℃）	极端最低气温（℃）	地 名	极端最高气温（℃）	极端最低气温（℃）
气象站	39.2	-4.3	翁昂乡	37.2	-6.3
玉屏镇	39.2	-4.3	甲良镇	36.9	-6.6
永康乡	37.4	-6.1	方村乡	36.9	-6.6
水尧乡	37.7	-5.8	播尧乡	36.8	-6.7
水利乡	36.5	-7.0	茂兰镇	38.3	-5.2
朝阳镇	39.3	-4.2	瑶麓乡	37.8	-5.7
瑶山乡	38.9	-4.6	佳荣镇	37.6	-5.9
捞村乡	39.7	-3.8	立化镇	38.6	-4.9
驾欧乡	37.2	-6.3	洞塘乡	38.0	-5.5

各月平均日较差表

表1-19

月 份	1	2	3	4	5	6	7	8	9	10	11	12	年均
平均日较差（℃）	6.9	7.2	7.7	8.6	8.6	7.9	8.5	9.5	9.9	9.0	9.3	9.0	8.5

各地霜期表

表1-20

地 名	初霜	终霜	霜期	无霜期	地 名	初霜	终霜	霜期	无霜期
	（日/月）	（日/月）	（天）	（天）		（日/月）	（日/月）	（天）	（天）
气象站	16/12	10/2	57	308	翁昂乡	19/12	8/2	52	313
玉屏镇	16/12	10/2	57	308	甲良镇	29/11	27/2	91	274
永康乡	3/12	23/2	83	282	方村乡	29/11	27/2	91	274
水尧乡	3/12	23/2	83	282	播尧乡	29/11	29/11	91	274
水利乡	26/11	1/3	96	269	茂兰镇	9/12	9/12	70	295
朝阳镇	19/12	8/2	52	313	瑶麓乡	3/12	3/12	82	283
瑶山乡	3/12	24/2	84	281	佳荣镇	1/12	1/12	87	278
捞村乡	27/12	29/1	24	331	立化镇	7/12	7/12	74	291
驾欧乡	1/12	25/2	87	278	洞塘乡	9/12	9/12	70	295

三、日照

县境地处低纬度地带，太阳可照时数在10.2—12.9小时/日之间。县城附近平均年日照时数1076.3小时，日照百分率为24.3%，在全国属少日照区，光能资源不是很富裕。

县境地势复杂，日照受地形条件影响较大，各地日照差异也大，特别是南北向的峡谷地带，因山体对阳光遮蔽角度大，日照条件更差。佳荣镇的何家寨位于甲料河谷，是南北向深谷，全年日照数只有667.0小时，年日照百分率仅18%，比同一地区的佳荣镇威岩坝年日照数少22%，天空状况（如云量、阴雨日数）对日照也有明显影响。佳荣片区是县内多雨中心，年降水量比县城偏多26%，雨天明显比县城多，其地形遮蔽与县城相近，但日照时数比县城少15%。

日照时数的地理分布总趋势是西部比东部多，西部年日照时数大于1020小时，东部小于1020小时。季节分布是夏季多，冬季少。5—10月各月平均日照数85小时以上，特别是7月、8月、9月的日照数均在127小时以上，日照百分率为33%—34%，平均每天有日照4.5小时。

县城各月日照时数和日照百分率表

表1-21

月 份	1	2	3	4	5	6	7	8	9	10	11	12	全年
日照时数（小时）	42.5	40.3	53.6	73.5	91.6	86.7	125.0	156.3	139.3	98.3	91.5	77.6	1076.3
日照百分率（%）	12.8	12.7	14.4	19.2	22.1	21.1	29.8	38.8	37.8	27.5	28.0	23.7	24.3

四、风

县境处于东亚季风区内，冬季盛行偏北风，夏季盛行偏南风。由于地形对风向和风速的影响，迎风面和背风面、峡管和峡谷的走向风速差异很大，局部地区还出现山谷风、坡风、尘卷风等。县气象站定时观测的最大风速为西南风18.2米/秒，出现在2004年8月4日。1978—2008年共出现大风1次。县城年平均风速为1.11米/秒。

累年各月平均风速表

表1-22

月 份	1	2	3	4	5	6	7	8	9	10	11	12	年均
风速（米/秒）	1.4	1.5	1.6	1.4	1.1	0.9	0.8	0.8	0.9	1.0	1.0	1.1	1.1

五、降水

县境属亚热带季风气候，降水充沛，年降水量的年际变化不大，但各月降水分配不均，有明显的雨季和旱季，夏半年为雨季，冬半年为旱季。

降水量的分布大致是从东北向西南递减。佳荣片区为全县的多雨中心，年均降水量1526.7毫米，比县城年均雨量1211.9毫米多26%；瑶山片区年均降水量1037.5毫米，比县城少14%。降水量的地理分布差异较大，大部分地区在1196毫米左右，80%以上的保证率降水量大于1012毫米。

降水主要集中在夏季。6—8月各雨量均在176毫米以上，占全年总水量的53%左右；冬季（12—2月）仅占全年总水量的7%左右；秋季（9—11月）占15%左右；春季（3—5月）海洋季风逐渐增强，降水占全年雨量的25%左右，3月降水量只有45.7毫米左右，4月增至94.9毫米以上。常年于4月下旬进入雨季，4—10月降水量占全年降水量的86%。10月以后，海洋季风减弱，逐渐为南下的大陆季风取代，降水量显著减少。

各年进入雨季的时间差异较大。县城雨季平均开始日期为4月23日，平均结束日期为10月22日，雨季平均长183天，多数年份的雨季出现在4月下旬至5月上旬。

各年降水量的变化小，但月降水量的年际变化很大。县城年平均水量为1121.9毫米，最多的为1590.3毫米（1979年），最少为919.0毫米（1981年），最丰年与最少年相差671.3毫米。历年各月相对距平更为突出，如县城常年8月降水量为176.2毫米，而1979年8月多达452.5毫米。

夏季多为大雨、暴雨。据县气象站1978—2008年气象资料统计，平均每年出现大雨以上日数为14.4天。其中，暴雨4.3天，大暴雨0.3天，未出现特大暴雨。30年间，日雨量大于50毫米曾出现过37次，1994年6月27日雨量达172.8毫米，为最大雨量；最长连续降雨日数为20天，出现在1998年6月27日，雨量为169.4毫米；最长连续无雨日数为32天，出现在1995年12月7日—1996年1月7日，其次为31天。

县境冬季降雪较少。1978—2008年，县城平均每年降雪日数2.7天，县城积雪数累计12天，平均每年0.4天。县内地势较高地区降雪和积雪稍多一些，平均每年降雪日数一般不超过5天。冬季降雪多为冰粒，其次为雪花。每次降雪时间较短，雪量也不大。仅1983年1月20日夜间一次降雪和2003年1月5—6日降雪在20厘米以上。

冰雹在荔波出现较少，大部分出现在3—5月间，都为小冰雹，降雹的时间短、范围小。1978—2008年共出现冰雹18次，平均每年0.6次，冰雹直径一般不超过1厘米，局部地区偶尔出现鸡蛋、鸭蛋大的冰雹，但数量少。入侵荔波的冰雹路径主要有三条：一是从独山县基长、狮山进入荔波县阳凤经甲良、甲站入三都县境；二是月亮山南麓，从三都县入境，经拉易、甲料进入广西环江县境；

三是从独山县甲里、墨寨进入荔波县播尧，经觉巩、驾欧、瑶山、朝阳到永康、洞塘入广西环江县境。县内其他地方也偶有降雹，但次数少，多不成灾。

全县各雨量站各月平均降水量

表1-23　单位：毫米

站名	1月	2月	3月	4月	5月	6月	7月	8月	9月	10月	11月	12月	全年降水量
气象站	26.2	34.7	45.7	94.9	161.9	253.2	214.2	176.2	86.7	60.6	36.7	20.9	1211.9
佳荣	29.6	40.5	60.5	131.5	206.3	281.6	293.4	206.3	115.5	76.2	50.1	35.2	1526.7
茂兰	25.9	35.9	56.2	126.6	176.5	276.5	286.5	192.5	116.2	70.5	46.2	26.1	1435.6
瑶山	21.3	25.2	39.2	86.2	147.2	234.1	192.3	156.3	79.1	15.2	23.1	18.3	1037.5
甲良	26.2	36.2	46.4	89.6	143.2	343.4	198.2	156.3	79.3	51.2	32.3	20.3	1222.6

荔波县各地各季节降水量

表1-24　单位：毫米

站名	春季（3—5月）		夏季（6—8月）		秋季（9—11月）		冬季（12—2月）		全年雨量
	雨量	占全年（%）	雨量	占全年（%）	雨量	占全年（%）	雨量	占全年（%）	
县城	302.5	25	643.6	53	184.0	15	81.8	7	1211.9
佳荣	398.3	26	781.3	51	241.8	16	105.3	7	1526.7
茂兰	359.3	25	755.5	53	232.9	16	87.9	6	1435.6
瑶山	272.6	26	582.7	56	117.4	12	64.8	6	1037.5
甲良	279.2	25	377.7	53	162.8	15	82.7	7	1222.6

六、空气湿度、蒸发、云量、地温

据县气象站1978—2008年30年资料，县城年平均相对湿度为79%，各月平均相对湿度在74%～84%之间。夏季相对湿度较大，6—8月超过80%；冬季较小，12—2月在75%左右。历年最小相对湿度为9%，出现在1993年12月26日。各年最小相对湿度大都出现在冬半年。

1978—2008年县气象站对水体蒸发观测显示：县城年平均蒸发量1247.1毫米，冬半年（11—3月）各月超过72毫米，夏半年（4—10月）各月超过127毫米，以8月的155.8毫米最多。

县城年均总云量为8.1成，春夏云量较多，3—8月大于8成，秋冬云量较小，9—2月小于8成。

地面温度年平均为20.5℃，地面最高温度年平均为32.7℃，地面最低温度年平均为14.7℃；地面极端最高温度为67.9℃，出现在1988年7月20日，地面极端最低温度-6.9℃，出现在1999年12月23日。地中5厘米年均温度19.8℃，地中10厘米为19.9℃，地中15厘米为20.2℃，地中20厘米为20.1℃。

第五节　自然资源

一、植物资源

境内植物按其用途分为食用、药用、工业用、保护和改善环境用及特殊种质五大类。在茂兰喀斯特森林保护区有国家一级保护植物10种、二级保护植物169种。

（一）食用植物

有以壳斗科的栗、青杠类，凤尾蕨科的根茎类，蔷薇科的果实类等为主的淀粉植物；有以多种食用真菌为主的蛋白植物；有以茶属、花椒属、胡桃属为主的油脂植物；有蔷薇科、桑科、芸香科、柿树科等10科32种可供食用的维生素植物。还有为人类间接食用的植物性饲料、饵料及蜜源植物。

（二）药用植物

有700余种，包括中草药植物、兽用中草药植物以及土农药植物，其中以中草药植物较为丰富。具有重要价值、已有大量和一定数量收购的达百余种，较珍贵和产量较大的有桔梗、乌梅、桂皮、大通草等；产量较多的有官桂皮、续断、银花叶、小瓜石斛、黄草、水草、白芨、灵芝菌、金樱子、益母草；其他较名贵的有牛膝、龙胆草、天冬、黄精、葛根、桑根、山慈菇、水球子、泡参、山乌龟、灵芝草、鹿含草、麦冬、茯苓、黄柏、杜仲、厚朴、山药、木瓜、女贞子、小血藤、板蓝根、十大功劳、黄栀子、天丁片、车前草、青天葵。

（三）工业用植物

工业用植物中，用材植物以松科、杉科、柏科、樟科为主，共41科126种；纤维植物以荨麻科、桑科、锦葵科、棕榈科为主；鞣科植物以壳斗科、蔷薇科、杨梅科、漆树科等为主；芳香植物以樟树科、芸香科等为主；工业用油植物以松科、樟科、大戟科为主；树脂和树胶植物以松属、野茉莉属、枫香属为主；经济昆虫寄生植物以五倍子蚜虫寄生植物盐肤木、白蜡虫寄生植物白蜡树属为主。

（四）保护和改善环境植物

具有抗污染性能的植物有乌桕、大叶桉、细叶桉、泡桐、苦楝、女贞、柳树、刺槐、梧桐、榆树、榕树等；适于石灰岩山地造林的有30余种，如香椿、枫香、化香、臭椿、红椿、青杠栎、黄枝油杉、侧柏等；观赏植物有桂花、夜荷花、小叶黄杨、玫瑰、山茶、杜鹃、五针松、兰草等60余种。

（五）特殊种质植物

列为国家保护的珍贵树种有二级保护树种香果树、杜仲、伞花木、掌叶木、鹅掌楸、短叶黄衫，三级保护树种八角莲、任木、黄枝油杉、白辛树、广东五针松、半枫荷、南方铁杉等20种。

二、动物资源

县境属于森林覆盖较大的山区，野生动物种类繁多。哺乳纲有黄毛猴、短尾猴、猕猴、蝙蝠、穿山甲、野兔、鼯鼠、松鼠、竹鼠、狐狸、黄鼠狼、野猫、熊、水獭、旱獭、豹、黑熊、獐子、刺猪、野猪、野牛、岩羊、黄麂、刺猬等。爬行纲有蛇目盲蛇科有眼镜王蛇、眼镜蛇、乌梢蛇、银环蛇、金环蛇、翠青蛇、烙铁头蛇、五步蛇、竹叶青、青竹标等；蜥蝎目有龙蜥、壁虎、龟、鳖、狗龙等。鸟纲有斑鸠、野鸡、松鸡、寒鸡、竹鸡、秧鸡、水野鸡、八哥、画眉、鹭鸶、野鸭、猫头鹰、啄木鸟、乌鸦、喜鹊、猴面鹰、鹰、鹧鸪、家燕、布谷鸟、山雀、翠雀、小云雀、麻雀等。水生动物据1984年调查，樟江河（包括捞村河）、方村河两大河流中有30余种，主要经济鱼类有青鱼、草鱼、鲢鱼、鳙鱼、鲫鱼、鳜鱼、馄青、偏青、鱼球、红鲤、竹鲤、蛇鱼等，还有鳝鱼、青虾、泥鳅、蚌、螺以及爬行类的鳖（即甲鱼）、蟹，两栖类的鲵（即娃娃鱼）、蛙等。鲵主要分布在樟江河流域的水维、岜鲜、时来龙王洞，王蒙的大七孔、小七孔等河流中；鳖在全县各河流均有分布，以中部和西部的时来、朝阳、王蒙、捞村、方村、地莪、觉巩、翁昂地区出产较多。

在茂兰喀斯特地区，有国家一级保护动物3种、二级保护动物32种，还有茂兰特有种38种。

三、矿产资源

境内矿产主要有煤、铁、铅锌、碳酸钙、方解石、石灰石、白云岩等，有矿点46个，其中以煤炭分布最广，储量最多。另外还有冰洲石、硅、铜、水晶以及贵重金属异常反应现象。

（一）煤炭

境内大部分地区都有煤系地层和煤层分布，分有烟煤和无烟煤2种。无烟煤集中分布于东部茂兰向斜东西两翼，含煤地层为下石炭统，以祥摆组为主。烟煤多分布于方村向斜东西两翼，荔波向斜两翼亦有矿点分布，含煤地层为二叠系梁山组和吴家坪组。

无烟煤经广西、贵州地质队普查和勘探，总储量3.1亿吨，分布在洞塘乡、立化镇、茂兰镇、水尧乡、瑶麓乡境内。烟煤地质储量2.2亿吨，分布在播尧乡、甲良镇、驾欧乡境内。

（二）铁矿

主要有赤铁矿、菱铁矿和褐铁矿，前两者为沉积型，后者为风化淋滤表生矿产。

1.赤铁矿　贮存于下石炭统祥摆组和下二叠梁山组，有水条、拉槽、水利、水庆4个矿点，属高硅、高铝、贫铁矿石，尚难利用。

2.菱铁矿　矿体贮存于下石炭统摆佐组炭岩中，含铁45%～60%，为高品位矿石，估算储量278万吨。

3.褐铁矿　境内褐铁矿分为赤铁矿风化的褐铁矿、煤系中黄铁矿氧化的褐铁矿和铅锌金属矿氧化的铁帽型褐铁矿，多有分布，主要矿点为水省、拉街、拉力、拉先、坤地等。储量8394.52万吨（未审批）。

（三）铅锌矿

县境东北部为广西白城铅锌含矿带延伸部，有奴亚、干田坝、拉先、坤地等矿点。

（四）硅石矿

翁昂硅石矿，产于下石炭统旧司组。C+D级储量74.68万吨，远景储量2500万吨，质量达一级品和二级品。

（五）石灰石矿

石灰石矿分布面广，下石炭统马坪组、中石岩统黄龙组和上二叠统茅口组灰岩较为丰富，质量上乘，除作水泥石灰石外，尚可作电石和制碱灰岩。

（六）白云岩

产于中石炭统黄龙组，主要分布于凉水井、洞腮、水扒等地，未开发。经地质部门调查，矿床特点是质优、量大，矿石品质高镁低硅磷，少钾钠，具有开采前景。

（七）方解石

主要在岜昔、洞腮等地，尚未开发。

（八）陶土

县境内陶土比较丰富，分布在甲良、方村、玉屏、水利、立化，有一定开采价值。

第六节　自然灾害

境内自然灾害主要有干旱，其次是洪涝、秋绵雨、大风、冰雹、低温，夏季高湿高温及植物病虫害等，个别年份出现地震。

一、旱灾

境内属季风气候，冬半年主要受北方冷气团控制，常年冬、春少雨，严重影响小麦、油菜越冬作物的生长。加之春旱频繁，不能满足水稻播种的需水，影响水稻的适时播种和栽插。冬干春旱严重影响水电站发电，影响工业正常生产，部分地区的人、畜饮水受到影响。夏季雨水虽多，但时空分布不均，常出现不同程度的夏旱，影响水稻、玉米等春播作物的产量。

每年出现中等以上旱情的频率均在50%以上，每年都有不同程度的干旱发生，80%左右的年份冬干春旱。中稻适宜播种期内（4月底以前）有打田水的概率仅40%。夏旱几乎每年都有不同程度发生，每5—6年发生一次重旱，10年左右发生一次特大旱。进入20世纪80年代后，雨量持续偏少，干旱尤为频繁，在水稻生长季节，几乎每年都出现一段严重的干旱时段。

干旱的地理分布与年降水量基本一致，冬干和前春旱南部比北部地区重，后春旱西部地区比东部地区重，夏旱以西南为重。此外，播尧、瑶山、永康、洞塘等乡的部分地区，由于喀斯特溶岩地貌发育，植被又遭到破坏，土层瘠薄，降水很快由地面径流转为地下潜流，地面水缺乏，干旱频繁，灾情更重。

1981年7月1日—8月25日共56天，总雨量仅102.9毫米，只有正常年份同期的四分之一，水稻减产3成以上。

1985年7月8日—8月19日共43天，降水量仅103.6毫米，只有正常年份同期的1/3，水稻减产36%。

1985年12月—1986年2月，总雨量仅57.4毫米，比常年减少2成。1986年3月—5月31日，总雨量215.8毫米，比常年偏少3成。

2002年6月20日—7月15日，全县遭受干旱，农业直接经济损失2312.5万元。

2003年8月1—22日，全县遭受伏旱天气，17个乡（镇）1.62万人受灾，大牲畜1.15万头饮水困难。农作物受灾面积102900亩，成灾面积49500亩，重旱48150亩，干枯5250亩，水田缺水84000亩。

二、风灾、雹灾

境内的风灾、雹灾往往同时出现，但次数少。1978—2008年，县城未出现8级以上大风，年均出现冰雹0.3次。

1979年4月18日夜间降冰雹，甲良区的3个乡、6个村、29个村民组，朝阳区的1个乡1个村的油菜、小麦、包谷等受到不同程度损失；夜间雷电击死玉屏镇板吉村村民1人。

1980年4月12日夜间，全县范围内出现大风、大雹、雷阵雨，阳凤、播尧、觉巩、地莪、甲良、方村、水利、时来、水尧、永康、茂兰、洞塘、朝阳、玉屏14个乡（镇）受大风、冰雹袭击，夏收作物严重受灾，损坏房屋915间，其中全部倒塌53间。这次大风、冰雹、雷阵雨天气从4月12日晚23时30分发生至4月13日凌晨2时结束，从西北方向入侵，先下雨，后刮大风和下冰雹，冰雹直径最大的有鸡蛋大，冰雹、大风持续15分钟左右。

1984年5月2日夜间，境内各地出现大风伴大雨，玉屏镇建设村两株直径1米的大树被吹倒，压垮房屋2间，伤6人；朝阳、甲良、茂兰、洞塘等乡被吹倒民房107间，甲良被大雨冲坏灌渠200余米。大风大雨对已成熟的油菜造成损失。

2002年4月5日，佳荣镇威岩、拉吾、坤地等村相继遭受龙卷风袭击，造成237栋房屋受损，电线杆折断10根、倾斜25根，卫星电视设备损坏4套，木仓被摧毁232栋，经果林受灾200余株，平木砖厂厂房砖柱被吹倒，轻伤1人。

三、洪涝灾

荔波地势高差大，河谷深切，河道虽较宽，但流速快，洪水易涨易落。暴雨主要对洞塘、翁昂、永康等喀斯特发育地区的低洼地造成水淹田土的洪涝灾害。

1983年6月19—22日，全县普降暴雨，暴雨中心在县东北部佳荣、水维片区。佳荣4天总雨量377.1毫米，县城196.9毫米，甲良100.7毫米。这次暴雨冲坏和淹没部分农田，沿河农作物受到损失。

1995年6月25日，全县普受洪涝灾害影响，大部分农作物均被淹或被冲毁，出城公路全部中断，共造成水稻、玉米、房屋、公路、桥梁、水利设施等经济损失800万元。

2000年6月10—20日，全县普降大到暴雨，降水量141.6毫米。其中，樟江上游地区降水量达149.1毫米，樟江河县城段洪水位达422.25米，超警戒水位3.25米，超危机水位1.75米，水流量2820立方米/秒，是县内有水文记录以来的最大洪水，造成的灾害为历史罕见。这次洪水造成全县17个乡（镇）、169个村、1230个村民组、27653户、124438人受灾，成灾人口87350人，绝收户数8536户、人口38412人，被困人口52470人，紧急转移安置人口8960人，无家可归619人，泥石流造成1人死亡、2人重伤、6人轻伤。洪水涌进县城、朝阳镇和王蒙集市，进水深达2米，时来坝、南门坝、朝阳坝、方村坝等被洪水淹没。农作物受灾面积108150亩，耕地毁损面积25500亩；房屋倒塌1535间（其中居民住房1465间），损坏房屋5760间；淹死大牲畜457头；县城及大部分乡（镇）自来水、交通、通信中断；损坏堤防35处共长8.5公里，损坏护岸23处，冲垮山塘20口，冲毁各类渠道114条共125公里，损坏各类水利灌溉设施62处，损坏各类人畜饮水工程28处，15.2万人、4.5万头大牲畜饮水困难；洪水冲走、损坏64所学校的课桌凳1000余套，3000余名学生被迫停课；县城4条出城公路、70%的通乡公路完全中断，矿山公路多处垮塌，樟江河上的5座钢索桥被毁。全县因灾造成的直接经济损失19490.5万元（其中农业经济损失5460万元），间接经济损失26000万元。

2001年6月20日傍晚，受雷雨大风天气影响，全县普降暴雨，造成河水暴涨，部分乡（镇）受灾严重，造成居民房屋倒塌91户共409间，损坏房屋3654间，农作物受灾面积38865亩，成灾面积33840亩，绝收5025亩，农业直接经济损失2529万元。

2002年5月9日，全县普降大到暴雨，造成直接经济损失1420万元。

2003年7月6日，玉屏、茂兰、水尧、播尧等6个乡（镇）遭受大暴雨袭击，直接经济损失320万元。

2004年4月24日，甲良、立化、翁昂、洞塘、水利等乡（镇）遭暴雨灾害，直接经济损失186万元。

四、病虫害

境内气候温热湿润，夏长冬短，各种病虫害容易发生。

（一）水稻病虫

共有18种，危害严重的有稻瘟病、纹枯病、稻飞虱、稻纵卷叶螟，其次是二化螟、三化螟、黑尾叶蝉、白翅叶蝉、赤枯病、胡麻叶斑病、稻曲病、稻蓟马、负泥虫、稻包虫、稻蝗、稻螟蛉、稻象甲、平根叶蝉等。

（二）旱地粮食作物病虫

主要有玉米锈、玉米丝黑穗病、玉米螟、黏虫、甘薯黑斑病、甘薯叶蝉、小麦锈病、小麦白粉病、麦蚜等。

（三）油料作物病虫

主要有油菜白锈病、油菜霜霉病、油菜菌核病、油菜软腐、油菜蚜虫、豌豆潜叶蝇、黄豆条跳甲、花生黑斑病、花生褐斑病等，以油菜菌核病、白锈病、霜霉病、油菜蚜虫发生面较广，危害较重。

（四）其他经济作物病虫

主要有红麻炭疽病、立枯病、根腐病、麻叶甲、地老虎、天牛等。

（五）柑橘类病虫

主要有矢尖介壳虫、疮痂病、柑橘红蜘蛛、吹绵介壳虫、锈壁虱、柑橘大实蝇、柑橘溃疡病等。

五、秋风、秋绵雨、霜、雪、冻

（一）秋风

境内秋风大都出现在秋分到寒露之间，以日平均温度连续3天或3天以上低于20℃的开始日期为秋风出现期，最早出现于9月中旬，多数年份出现在10月上旬（概率为57％）。秋风对中稻基本无影响，对双季晚稻危害较明显。

（二）秋绵雨

9—11月连续雨日7天以上的为一次秋绵雨过程。境内80％的年份出现秋绵雨，平均每年1.4次，以10月出现次数多，严重影响“三秋”（秋管、秋收、秋种）生产。

（三）霜、雪、冻

霜、雪、冻在境内危害不大，只是地势较高地区（如水利至甲良一带）每年冬季出现一段雨雪冰冻天气，造成交通和通信线路中断。

1979年2月6—8日，甲良出现雨雪冰冻，中断交通3天。

1983年1月20日19点24分降雪，至21日8点10分降雪停止，雪量21.9毫米。县城平地平均积雪深度为20厘米，3天才全部融化。甲良和佳荣气象哨实测当晚积雪深度分别为33厘米和25厘米。大雪造成输电、通信线路中断，交通堵塞，许多树木被雪压断，给供电、邮电、交通、建筑等行业及群众生活带来损失和困难，但又给冬季农作物补充足够的水分。

2003年1月5—6日，全县各乡（镇）普降暴雪，积雪深度均在20厘米以上，雪量32.4厘米，北部乡（镇）积雪深度在30厘米以上。降雪造成经济损失550万元。

2008年1月13日，境内遭遇持续长达20多天的低温雨雪冰冻灾害，是县内有气象记录以来最严重一次。冰冻对农作物、农户房屋、交通公路、通信线路、水、电等造成毁损，给群众生活带来严重影响。2月1日降小雪1天。强低温冰冻天气造成全县17个乡（镇）不同程度受灾，受灾户数3.44万户，受灾人口17.2万人；农作物受灾面积1.28万亩，绝收面积0.59万亩，主要在朝阳、玉屏、洞塘、捞村、方村、水利、翁昂、甲良等乡（镇），经济损失650万元；因灾倒塌房屋7间，损坏房屋1118间，经济损失94万元；因灾死亡大牲畜2530头，经济损失208万元；因灾造成多处电线杆倒伏、断杆和变速器倒伏，直接经济损失600万元；因灾造成自来水管多处爆裂，部分地区停水，饮水困难人口9万余人，饮水困难牲畜5500余头；灾害造成水利设施损失500万元，交通、运输业损失156万元，林业经济损失1178万元，通信损失500万元。

六、地震

1998年4月16日11时13分，县境发生里氏4.9级地震，是日17时34分、次日2时5分和2时47分又先后发生3.8级、4.1级和3.1级余震，震中在荔波县捞村乡与广西南丹县木伦乡交界处，距荔波县城50

公里，地震殃及全县并波及周边县。地震造成荔波县部分房屋不同程度开裂、歪斜、移位、倒塌，其中以学校受损严重，教室受损580间；公路、桥梁、输电线路、矿山煤井、通信、水利设施等中断；受伤6人。地震造成直接经济损失6000万元。

第二篇
中国南方喀斯特
荔波世界自然遗产地

中国南方喀斯特世界自然遗产项目是中国政府明确的分批次申报的世界自然遗产项目，由贵州荔波领衔，捆绑云南石林、重庆武隆申报。该项目于2007年6月27日第31届世界遗产大会审议通过被列入《世界遗产名录》，成为中国第六个世界自然遗产地。

中国南方喀斯特的重要组成部分——荔波世界自然遗产地主要由茂兰国家级自然保护区、荔波樟江国家级风景名胜区大七孔、小七孔景区组成，荔波遗产地总面积730.16平方公里，核心区295.18平方公里，缓冲区434.98平方公里，遗产地海拔385～1109米，平均海拔747米，以典型锥状喀斯特、地表与地下喀斯特生态系统的完美组合为特征。在荔波遗产地这片土地上少数民族人口占90%，主要包括布依族、水族、瑶族和苗族等，民族文化底蕴丰富，喀斯特环境与少数民族传统文化之间的和谐关系在荔波遗产地保护管理上得到普遍的国际认同。

荔波世界遗产地出露的碳酸盐岩发育于不同地质年代，经过几百万年的喀斯特作用，塑造了显著的锥状峰丛和峰林喀斯特，是世界上同类喀斯特的模式地，形成了特殊而又美丽的地貌景观。满足世界遗产的第七条和第八条评价标准，即“具有超乎寻常的自然现象或非同寻常的自然美和美学价值”“反映地球演化历史主要阶段的杰出范例，包括生命记录，重要的、正在进行的地貌演化，重要的地貌形态或自然地理特征”。遗产地还例证了大陆型热带—亚热带喀斯特森林生态系统发育与演化过程，有潜力满足第九条标准，即“反映陆地、淡水、海岸、海洋生态系统和动植群落正在进行的重要的生态和生物演化过程的杰出范例”。

第一章 自然环境与生态

第一节 自然环境

一、地质地貌

荔波遗产地位于云贵高原向广西丘陵盆地过渡的斜坡地带，在地质构造上隶属于江南台隆西南部的三都—荔波古陷褶断束，处在轴缘凹陷地带。区内地质构造以褶皱为主，断层次之。由石炭、二叠系碳酸盐岩组成的茂兰向斜，保存原生性较强的喀斯特森林主要分布于此向斜南段的石炭系碳酸盐岩石上。

荔波遗产地处中亚热带南部，喀斯特地貌十分典型，形态多种多样，锥峰洼地，层层叠叠，呈现出罕见的喀斯特峰丛景观。地面枯枝落叶垫积填充，蓄存的地表水与地下暗河、泉水并存，暗河、泉水汇集而成清澈的小池。降水和水源丰富，为森林植被的生长发育提供优越的条件，区内无论山峰、盆地，到处都有森林覆盖。

荔波遗产地区在古生代为海侵区，沉积物以浅海相碳酸盐类为主，于中生代末期褶皱隆起，脱离海侵，上升为陆地。新生代造山运动后，陆地持续上升，形成强烈溶蚀的喀斯特峰林、峰丛和低山山地喀斯特地貌。遗产地内分布地层从老到新有石炭系下统大塘组、摆佐组，中统黄龙群，上统马平群及二迭系下统栖霞组、茅口组。其中，摆佐组为该区分布最广，其上喀斯特森林保存最好的地层。区内分布岩石，主要为灰岩和白云岩，且为纯质碳酸盐岩类，仅个别地点为石英砂岩及夹于其中的少量页岩。以白云岩出露面积最大，为喀斯特森林的主要着生基岩，基岩裸露率在70%—80%之间。

遗产地内喀斯特地貌发育，喀斯特形态多种多样，锥峰尖削而密集，洼地深邃而陡峭，锥峰洼地层层叠叠，呈现出峰峦叠嶂的喀斯特峰丛景观。地貌类型以峰丛漏斗和峰丛洼地为主，仅东部有小面积的峰林盆地分布。地貌形态主要有落水洞、漏斗、洼地、槽谷、盲谷等。

遗产地区境地势西北高、东南低，平均海拔880米以上，最高海拔1078.6米，最低海拔430米。其中，西部山峰一般海拔860—1010米，洼地为670—800米；东部山峰海拔为660—820米，洼地为450—600米，山峰与洼地相对高差为150—300米。遗产地区内高程为700米左右的洼地分布最广，形态宽坦，大部均开垦为良田，为主要的农业生产活动区；峰丛漏斗是决定区内喀斯特地貌特征重要的地貌类型；盲谷在区内均有分布，雨季节时洪水排泄不及常酿成内涝，成为适宜耐湿植物生长的有利地形。

二、气候

荔波遗产地区处于中亚热带季风温润气候区，具有春秋温暖、冬无严寒、夏无酷暑、雨量充沛的中亚热带山地湿润气候特点。年平均气温为15.3℃，气温年均差18.3℃，1月平均气温为5.2℃，7月平均气温为23.5℃，≥10℃活动积温4598.6℃，生长期237天。全年降水量1752.5毫米，集中分布在4—10月，年平均相对湿度83%，年日照时数1272.8小时，日照百分率29%，太阳辐射年总量为63289.80千瓦/平方米。

由于区内特殊的森林地貌环境，其气候具有一定的特殊性。气温：4—9月，峰丛洼地随高度增加而升高，10月至次年3月，一般随高度增加而降低，下半年这种地形逆温是喀斯特森林小地形气温垂直分布独具的特色。相对湿度：峰丛洼地、漏斗之底部终年阴湿，各月相对湿度均在90%以上，而山坡的中上部分，相对湿度较低，晴天极为干燥。降水量一般随海拔升高而增加。光照：漏斗底部光照极差，底部年可照时数只相当于顶部的38.5%，晴天的光照强度，底部仅为顶部的34.4%。

三、土壤

荔波遗产地区成土母岩为碳酸盐岩，故其风化发育形成的土壤均为石灰土。剖面构型主要是AF—D型、A—D型和A—AB—D型，属于初始期、幼年期和发育期的石灰土，其中以初始期石灰土占绝对优势。该种石灰土，是石灰岩风化残留物形成的少数细土被与植物残落物和根系交织在一起腐解后形成的棕黑色AF层，其下即为成土母岩。由于成土母岩是纯度较高的白云岩和石灰岩，能形成土粒的重要成分二氧化硅和三氧化二铁含量极低，而含量最高的钙、镁和碳酸盐类在溶蚀过程中随水流失，因此形成的土壤层，仅有20—40厘米，且土被不连片，多存在于岩石缝隙中。石灰土表层pH7.1—7.4，属弱碱性；中下层pH7.5—8.1，属碱性。土壤有机质表层达20%，下层仍可达2%—8%，全氮量含量表层为1%—3%，亚表层和心土层为0.2%—0.5%。全磷和全钾量含量，表层分别为2.14%和0.41%，其速效磷含量为10—20ppm，速效钾为80—290ppm。

遗产地区内石灰土的基本特点：土壤容量因素差，表现为土层薄，土被不连续；土壤质量好，表现为有机质和氮、磷、钾养分丰富。剖面多呈碱性。

四、水文

茂兰喀斯特地区地表水系不发育，尧兰河、尧所河、板寨河及洞腮河均分属区内与之相应的四条地下河系，是地下河明流的局部段落。河流流量较小，枯流量一般均小于50—100升/秒。板寨河、瑶兰河坡降小于18%，尧所河、洞腮河注入山谷时形成总落差约60—80米的跌水。

区内地下水赋存的二元结构是喀斯特森林水文的独特现象，即枯枝落叶垫积层充填的上层喀斯特裂隙水和下层喀斯特水并存，上层水流量小且动态稳定，下层水流量大，动态变化也相对较大。根据地层岩石的含水性质及含水的丰富程度，区内可分为碳酸盐强含水岩组和碎屑岩、泥灰岩弱含水岩组。喀斯特上层裂隙水又称森林滞留水，是森林植被对喀斯特作用的影响的具体表现形式，主要是由喀斯特森林的持水作用形成。森林滞留水按其滞留的地形部位分为森林滞留泉和森林滞留沼泽湿地两大类型，前者遍及全区，凡喀斯特森林茂密的山麓坡下、漏斗洼地中、山鞍坳口上均有分布，致使区内到处是清泉淙淙、流水潺潺；后者普遍见于地势平缓或低洼的密林中，或积水成塘，或形成连片沼泽湿地，局部地段在喀斯特森林内出现类似于寒温带沼泽森林的景观。

区内独特的水文结构，极大地改善了地下水及地表水的循环条件，明显地显示出喀斯特森林的水文效应：不仅使地下水的补给、径流及排泄条件明显改善，而且使大气降水、地表水和地下水的互相转化产生良性循环，改变了喀斯特区的干旱面貌，地表水、地下水动态较稳定，提高了水土保持的能力，有效防止一般喀斯特区旱涝交加的频繁灾害，为森林生长和人类生存、生活和生产创造了良好环境。

樟江河流域：樟江河是县境内最大的河流，发源于月亮山麓，流经3个乡（镇），在王蒙与方村河交汇，主河道长53.1公里，最大流量3704立方米／秒，最小流量2.92立方米／秒，平均流量35.72立方米／秒，年均总水量11.29亿立方米，其中县内径流量6.82亿立方米。樟江小七孔景区是一处融山、水、林、洞、湖、瀑于一体的天然原始奇景。小七孔流域以峰丛洼地、峰丛漏斗为主要特征，锥峰高度多在100～200米之间，河谷开阔，起伏有致，碧水清流，景色秀丽。樟江大七孔景区是以下湖为主体，有水神河、沾水塘、万蛇塘、二层湖等。

第二节　自然生态

1984年4—6月，省林业厅、贵州农学院、贵阳师范学院等16个单位80余名各类专业人员对茂兰喀斯特森林区进行综合考察，涉及19个学科。茂兰喀斯特森林区面积30万亩，森林覆盖率92%，属中亚热带常绿落叶阔叶混交林。该区地处中亚热带向南亚热带过渡的季风气候区，气候温暖、湿润，雨量充沛，形成荔波喀斯特丰富的生物多样性特征，既有许多国家珍稀濒危物种，又有新发现的众多动植物新种，成为许多模式标本的产地，是一个罕见的、巨大的生物资源基因库。

一、植物

荔波遗产地在中国植被分区处于亚热带常绿阔叶林区、东部（湿润）常绿阔叶林亚区、中亚热带常绿阔叶林带，其自然植被除少数地段为藤刺灌丛和灌草丛外，均为发育在喀斯特地貌上的原生性常绿落叶阔叶混交林，是一种非地带性的植被覆盖。遗产地区植物资源十分丰富，系既有温带性质的科属，又有热带性质的科属，自然植被包括常绿落叶阔叶混交林、针叶阔叶混交林、竹林、灌木林、藤刺灌丛等多种类型。

荔波遗产地区有高等植物225科、687属，共计1532种。其中，苔藓植物45科、94属、144种；蕨类植物37科、84属、212种；裸子植物6科、12属、17种；被子植物137科、497属、1159种。药用植物有345种。这些植物中，有些是珍稀和国家紧缺药材，如钩状石斛、半夏等。遗产地区植物列入《IUCN物种红色名录》《中国物种红色名录》的种类涉及27科、67属、121种。其中，极危7种，濒危26种，易危50种，近危32种，无危6种；受到严重威胁的濒危植物共计83种，占总数的68.60%。这些物种的地方性极为显著，如贵州山核桃、狭叶含笑、荔波瘤果茶、白花兜兰等。列入全球红色名录的共18种，其中，极危1种（即卫矛科的十齿花），易危9种，近危7种，缺乏数据1种。

遗产地区的森林植被中，建群植物多为耐旱喜钙的圆果化香、青冈栎、樟叶槭、黄梨木、云贵鹅耳枥、齿叶黄皮、掌叶木、圆叶乌桕、朴树、菱叶海桐、香叶树等。主要森林群落类型有青冈栎、化香林、化香、黄皮林、栲、杜英林、黄杉、化香林、黔竹林等。因地形相对高差不大，植被无明显的垂直带谱。

（一）国家重点保护野生植物

遗产地现有国家一级保护植物10种，二级保护植物150种。一级：南方红豆杉、红豆杉、单性

中国南方喀斯特荔波世界自然遗产地全貌

木兰、掌叶木、硬叶兜兰、白花兜兰、小叶兜兰、带叶兜兰、麻栗坡兜兰、异形玉叶金花。二级：翠柏、福建柏、广东松、短叶黄杉、短叶穗花杉、中华猕猴桃、盾叶秋海棠、八角莲、杜仲、半枫荷、四药门花、喙核桃、油丹、香梅、闽楠、任木、鹅掌楸、香木莲、槽树、龙棕、香果树、黎橡、伞花木、榉树等24种以及兰科的135种（如春兰、墨兰、建兰、虾脊兰、鹤顶兰等）。

（二）特有植物

遗产地区植物因所处的地理环境和喀斯特地貌特殊性及小生境多样性，生长在特殊的石灰岩和白云岩生境中，形成许多该区的特有种。已发现茂兰特有种41种，主要有荔波大节竹、荔波鹅耳枥、荔波瘤果茶、荔波球兰、荔波唇柱苣苔、石山胡秃子、短叶穗花杉、吊丝竹、贵州悬竹、石山木莲、单性木兰、黔南厚壳桂、石山桂、岩生鼠李、石山漆、丛状桂花、石山吴茱萸、少毛唇柱苣苔、短毛唇柱苣苔、大苞短毛唇柱苣苔、箭杆竹、花黔竹、水单竹、抽筒竹、石生鼠李等。此外，还有兰花植物135种，是中国兰花科植物保存最丰富的地区之一，其中白花兜兰等兜兰属植物列为国家一级保护植物。

二、动物

荔波遗产地区水文地质条件特殊，气候温暖湿润，森林保存较好，为野生动物提供了良好的生存和栖息环境。现统计有脊椎动物近400种，其中鸟类16目47科205种，兽类8目24科61种，鸟类有15目40科137种，爬行类3目10科47种，两栖类2目8科34种，鱼类5目10科43种。另有昆虫1300余种，蜘蛛类有146种，陆生贝类有140余种，多足类十余种。主要动物种类有猕猴、黑熊、穿山甲、林麝、白鹇、蛇雕、蟒等，以猕猴和白鹇为优势种群。动物共有45种列入《中国物种红色名录》，其中极危种3种，濒危种4种，易危种38种。发现的动物新属有鞘翅目的步甲科的荔波行步甲属、卵行步甲属、上野行步甲属；膜翅目的长颈蜂科的杨氏长颈蜂属、叶蜂科的颊片叶蜂属；直翅目的露螽科的拟鼓鸣螽属。

（一）国家重点保护野生动物

有国家一级保护动物4种、二级保护动物31种。一级：豹、蟒、林麝、白颈长尾雉。二级：猕猴、藏酋猴、穿山甲、小灵猫、黑熊、斑灵狸、金猫、苏门羚、鸳鸯、红隼、鸢、风头鹰、赤腹鹰、风头鹃隼、褐冠鹃隼、蛇雕、普通鵟、领角鸮、红角鸮、领鸺鹠、斑头鸺鹠、草鸮、蓝翅八色鸫、白鹇、细痣疣螈、虎纹蛙、大鳞金线鲃、长须金线鲃、多斑金线鲃、狭口金线鲃、粗壮金线鲃。

（二）动物特有种

茂兰已发现动物特有种38种，其中绝大部分为昆虫种类和蜘蛛种类。爬行类：荔波壁虎。鱼类：大鳞金线鲃、长须金线鲃、小口缕鱼、荔波盲条鳅。昆虫类：茂兰新蹟、中华诺蹟、琥珀树、茂兰弯茎叶蝉、双带扁头叶蝉、黑带侧脊叶蝉、叉突片叶蝉、端刺丽叶蝉、锥顶带叶蝉、碎斑鱼蛉、双刺粉蛉、茂兰窗溪蛉、三带窗溪蛉、彩翼罗草蛉、茂兰蕈虻、茂兰眼蕈蚊、钩臂眼蕈蚊、丽奇眼蕈蚊、长角齿眼蕈蚊、叉刺迟眼蕈蚊、茂兰迷蚜蝇、茂兰盲目步行虫、王氏盲目步行虫、荔波盲目步行虫、西川氏荔波步行虫。蜘蛛类：黔希蛛、茂兰玛琳蛛、镰形弱蛛、董背泰莱蛛、徐氏弱蛛、茂兰阿纳蛛。软体类：荔波倍唇螺、小七孔倍唇螺。

第三节　自然遗产特征与价值

一、特征

荔波遗产地喀斯特地貌复杂多样，森林生态空间广阔，生物资源丰富，区系成分过渡性特点明显。各种森林植物、各类动物及部分大型真菌，共有2000余种，其中经过鉴定已经发表和有待发表的植物新种40多种，属于贵州和全国动植物分布新记录的有200种以上。

区内地带性植被是以青冈类、栲类为主的常绿阔叶林，乔木层中主要为胡桃科、樟科、壳斗科、榆科、芸香科、无患子科的青冈栎、乌冈栎、栲、香叶树、川桂、化香树等和以华南五针松为主的针叶林。

岩溶森林的特点：（1）常绿阔叶林中混有一定比例的落叶树种，落叶树种达39%～46%，针叶林分布于峰丛山脊两侧。（2）生境的多样性造成物种组成的复杂性，如旱生植物、喜光植物、耐瘠植物、广幅植物和“喜钙”植物等组合的综合体。（3）森林水平结构复杂，树种适应性强。（4）虽然森林的立地条件低劣而严酷，但森林覆盖率高，说明它们在不断克服不利因素发展起来，同时反映这类森林生态系统极为脆弱和不稳定，一遭触动极易解体。

区内的乔木、灌木及各种粗细藤条交织在一起，树根裸露生长于岩山上，树根与岩石纠结为一体，即便树干倾倒也不分离。这些奇特的自然景象，构成别具一格的“喀斯特漏斗森林景观”。

原生性喀斯特森林，由于地貌类型和地形坡位的组合格局，在无明显垂直带分布的情况下，山顶、山脊两侧分布有华南五针松、短叶黄杉、翠柏、黄枝油杉等为优势的针叶阔叶混交林。局部地形平缓且具有土壤堆积条件的地段，如鞍部、垭口，生长着以丝栗栲、杜英等为主的较小面积的常绿阔叶树为优势的片段。绝大部分地段包括不同坡位、洼地、漏斗底部等发育的是常绿落叶阔叶混交林。

区内植被因长期樵采退化形成的灌木林，受经常性火烧和长期放牧形成的藤刺灌丛和灌草丛，是喀斯特森林顶级群落逆向演替中不同阶段的表现，其分布为以村寨为圆心1～2公里半径的范围内，多在坡下部和洼地中。因受人为干扰的影响，特别是灌草丛，即使停止人为干扰，也很难再重新恢复正向演替。

二、价值

区内集中连片的原生性喀斯特森林，主要分布在茂兰国家级自然保护区和荔波樟江国家重点风景名胜区，是迄今地球上残存分布集中、原生性强、相对稳定的喀斯特森林生态系统，植物区系处于贵州区系向广西区系过渡交错地带，动物区系属东洋界体中区西南山地亚区黔中山地丘陵地。

丰富的自然资源，形成独特的绿色喀斯特自然风光。樟江国家重点风景名胜区以喀斯特原始森林和水文景观为特色，整个景区有景点76处，其中一级景点17处、二级景点24处、三级景点35处，为绿色锥状喀斯特独一无二的特殊景观，是融山、水、洞、林、湖、瀑、石多种景物景观于一体的景区。

贵州茂兰国家级喀斯特森林自然保护区、樟江国家级风景名胜区以保存完好的原生性森林、生态系统、生物物种、水体以及人文景观和民族文化为特征。主要体现为：茂兰喀斯特森林是世界上相同纬度仅存的喀斯特森林类型，在世界植被类型中占有重要地位；茂兰喀斯特森林具有重大的科学研究价值，联合国教科文组织将其世界性意义和科研价值列为世界人与生物圈保护区和世界自然遗产地，是属于全人类共有的自然遗产，值得永久性保护。茂兰喀斯特森林独特的水文地质二元结构，对喀斯特地区生态环境的改善具有极大的促进作用；茂兰喀斯特森林生态系统是亚热带喀斯特地区中生物多样性保持最完整、种类最丰富的地区；茂兰喀斯特森林具有极高的美学价值和感染力。荔波拥有世界上相同纬度保存面积最大的喀斯特森林生态系统，被中外专家誉为“地球腰带上的绿宝石”，具有特殊的意义和价值。

贵州茂兰国家级自然保护区重点保护野生植物名录

表2-1

序号	保护级别	种 名	学 名
1	Ⅰ	单性木兰	Kmeria septentrionalis
2	Ⅰ	异形玉叶金花	Mussaenda anomala
3	Ⅰ	掌叶木	Handeliodendron bodinieri
4	Ⅰ	红豆杉	Taxus chinensis
5	Ⅰ	南方红豆杉	Taxus chinensis var.mairei
6	Ⅰ	白花兜兰	Paphiopedilum emersonii
7	Ⅰ	硬叶兜兰	P.micranthum
8	Ⅰ	小叶兜兰	P.barbigerum
9	Ⅱ	水蕨	Ceratopteris thalictroides
10	Ⅱ	中国蕨	Sinopteris grevilleoides
11	Ⅱ	篦子三尖杉	Cephalotaxus oliveri
12	Ⅱ	翠柏	Calocedrus macrolepis
13	Ⅱ	福建柏	Fokienia hodginsii
14	Ⅱ	广东松	Pinus kwangtungensis
15	Ⅱ	黄杉	Pseudotsuga sinensis
16	Ⅱ	短叶黄杉	Pseudotsuga brevifolia
17	Ⅱ	四药门花	Tetrathyrium subcordatum
18	Ⅱ	香樟	Cinnamomum camphora
19	Ⅱ	闽楠	Phoebe bournei
20	Ⅱ	任豆	Zenia insignis
21	Ⅱ	香木莲	Manglietia aromatica
22	Ⅱ	鹅掌楸	Liriodendron chinense
23	Ⅱ	红椿	Toona ciliata
24	Ⅱ	喜树	Camptotheca acuminata
25	Ⅱ	龙棕	Trachycarous nana
26	Ⅱ	香果树	Emmenopterys henryi
27	Ⅱ	伞花木	Eurycorymbus cavaleriei
28	Ⅱ	榉木	Zelkova serrata
29	Ⅱ	多花脆兰	Acampe rigida
30	Ⅱ	花叶开唇兰	Anoectochilus raxburghii
31	Ⅱ	白芨	Bletilla striata
32	Ⅱ	黄花白芨	B.ochracea

续表2-1

序号	保护级别	种 名	学 名
33	Ⅱ	广东石豆兰	Bulbophyllum kwangtungense
34	Ⅱ	伞花石豆兰	B.shweliense
35	Ⅱ	齿瓣石豆兰	B.Levinei
36	Ⅱ	密花石豆兰	B.odoratissimum
37	Ⅱ	梳帽卷瓣兰	B.andersonii
38	Ⅱ	虾脊兰	Calanthe discolor
39	Ⅱ	银脉虾脊兰	C.argenteostriata
40	Ⅱ	三棱虾脊兰	C.tricarinata
41	Ⅱ	长距虾脊兰	C.sylvatica
42	Ⅱ	剑叶虾脊兰	C.davidii
43	Ⅱ	钩距虾脊兰	C.graciliflora
44	Ⅱ	尖喙隔距兰	Cleisostoma rostratum
45	Ⅱ	短序隔距兰	C.striatum
46	Ⅱ	栗鳞贝母兰	Coelogyne flaccida
47	Ⅱ	流苏贝母兰	C.fimbriata
48	Ⅱ	珊瑚兰	Corallorhiza trifida
49	Ⅱ	杜鹃兰	Cremastra appendiculata
50	Ⅱ	惠兰	Cymbidium faberi
51	Ⅱ	春兰	C.goeringii
52	Ⅱ	线叶春兰	C.goeringii var.serratum
53	Ⅱ	春剑	C.goeringii var.longibracteatum
54	Ⅱ	建兰	C.ensifolium
55	Ⅱ	寒兰	C.kanran
56	Ⅱ	多花兰	C.floribundum
57	Ⅱ	台兰	C.fioribundum var. pumilum
58	Ⅱ	兔耳兰	C.lancifolium
59	Ⅱ	无齿兔耳兰	C.javeanicum
60	Ⅱ	长叶兰	C.erythraecum
61	Ⅱ	套叶兰	C.cyperifolium
62	Ⅱ	矮石斛	Dendrobium bellatulum
63	Ⅱ	美花石斛	D.loddigesii
64	Ⅱ	钩状石斛	D.aduncum

续表2-1

序号	保护级别	种　名	学　名
65	Ⅱ	细茎石斛	D.moniliforme
66	Ⅱ	罗河石斛	D.lohohense
67	Ⅱ	细叶石斛	D.hancockii
68	Ⅱ	束花石斛	D.chrysanthum
69	Ⅱ	黑节草	D.officinale
70	Ⅱ	广东石斛	D.wilsonii
71	Ⅱ	流苏石斛	D.fimbriatum
72	Ⅱ	丛生羊耳蒜	Liparis cespitosa
73	Ⅱ	滇南羊耳蒜	L.siamensis
74	Ⅱ	长苞羊耳蒜	L.inaperta
75	Ⅱ	羊耳蒜	L.japonica
76	Ⅱ	见血青	L.nervosa
77	Ⅱ	二褶羊耳蒜	L.cathcartii
78	Ⅱ	紫花羊耳蒜	L.nigra
79	Ⅱ	扇唇羊耳蒜	L.stricklandiana
80	Ⅱ	对叶兰	Listera puberula
81	Ⅱ	钗子股	Luisia morsei
82	Ⅱ	沼兰	Malaxis monophyllos
83	Ⅱ	毛唇芋兰	Nervilia fordii
84	Ⅱ	粗花茎鸢尾兰	Oberonia integerrima
85	Ⅱ	镰翅羊耳蒜	L.bootanensis
86	Ⅱ	足茎毛兰	Eria coronaria
87	Ⅱ	马齿毛兰	E.szetschuanica
88	Ⅱ	匍茎毛兰	E.clausa
89	Ⅱ	半柱毛兰	E.corneri
90	Ⅱ	大花斑叶兰	Goodyera bifora
91	Ⅱ	大斑叶兰	G.schlechtendaliana
92	Ⅱ	绒叶斑叶兰	G.velutina
93	Ⅱ	角盘兰	Herminium monorchis
94	Ⅱ	龙头兰	Pecteilis susannae
95	Ⅱ	黄花鹤顶兰	Phaius flavus

续表2-1

序号	保护级别	种 名	学 名
96	Ⅱ	鹤顶兰	P.tankervilleae
97	Ⅱ	贵州鹤顶兰	P.guizhouensis
98	Ⅱ	云南石仙桃	Pholidota yunnanensis
99	Ⅱ	石仙桃	P.chinensis
100	Ⅱ	细叶石仙桃	P.cantonensis
101	Ⅱ	套叶馥兰	Phreatia formosana
102	Ⅱ	独蒜兰	Pleione bulbocodioides
103	Ⅱ	船唇兰	Vandopsis undulata
104	Ⅱ	带唇兰	Tainia dunnii
105	Ⅱ	叉喙兰	Uncifera acuminata
106	Ⅱ	琴唇万代兰	Vanda concolor
107	Ⅱ	香果兰	Vanilla siamensis

说明：名录种类不全

表2-2

荔波遗产地动物新种名录

序号	中文名	学 名	备 注
1	荔波壁虎	Gekko liboensis	荔波特有
2	荔波盲条鳅	Nemacheilus liboensis	荔波特有
3	小口缨鱼	Sinocrossocheilus microstomacus	荔波特有
4	荔波倍唇螺	Diplommatina liboensis	荔波特有
5	小七孔倍唇螺	D.xiaoqikongensis	荔波特有
6	珍蟹	Daipotamon minos	荔波特有
7	荔波潮虫	Sryloniscus liboensis	荔波特有
8	茂兰盲目步行虫	Sinaphaenops mirubilissimus	荔波特有
9	王氏盲目步行虫	S.wangorum	荔波特有
10	荔波盲目步行虫	S.gralilior	荔波特有
11	西川氏荔波步行虫	Libotrechus nishikawai	荔波特有
12	库本奥工虫	Oodinotrechus kishimotor	荔波特有
13	琥珀树螱	Glyptotermes succineus	荔波特有
14	直颚杆螱	Srylotermes orthognathus	模式种
15	茂兰新襀	Neoperla maolanensis	荔波特有
16	中华诺襀	Rhopalopsole sinensis	模式种

续表2-2

序号	中文名	学 名	备 注
17	白色脊额叶蝉	Carinata albusa	模式种
18	茂兰弯茎叶蝉	Flexocerus maolamus	荔波特有
19	双带扁头叶蝉	Ophiuchus bizonatus	荔波特有
20	褐点窗翅叶蝉	Mileewa mira	荔波特有
21	月斑边大叶蝉	Kolla lunuluta	模式种
22	黑带侧脊叶蝉	Paratkina nigrifa	荔波特有
23	叉突片叶蝉	Thagria furcata	荔波特有
24	端刺丽叶蝉	Calodia opicalis	荔波特有
25	锥顶带叶蝉	Scaphoideus turbinatus	荔波特有
26	黄斑锥头叶蝉	Onukia flaopunctata	模式种
27	锚纹窗翅叶蝉	Mileewa anchora	模式种
28	船茎窗翅叶蝉	M.ponta	荔波特有
29	乳空窗翅叶蝉	M.papillata	模式种
30	暗褐角胸叶蝉	Tituria fusca	荔波特有
31	基褐异脉飞虱	Specinervures basifusca	模式种
32	邻脉尖唇叶蜂	Malluchiella interstitialis	荔波特有
33	碎斑鱼蛉	Neochauliodes discretus	模式种
34	彩翼罗草蛉	Retipenna callioptera	荔波特有
35	双刺粉蛉	Coniopteryx(Coniopteryx) bispinalis	模式种
36	云贵齿粉蛉	Conwentzia yunguiana	模式种
37	锚突重粉蛉	Semidalis anchoroides	模式种
38	茂兰窗溪蛉	Thyridosmylus maolans	荔波特有
39	三带窗溪蛉	T.trifasciatus	荔波特有
40	茂兰鹬虻	Rhagio maolanus	荔波特有
41	茂兰眼蕈蚊	Sciara maolana	荔波特有
42	钩臂眼蕈蚊	S.hamatilis	模式种
43	丽奇眼蕈蚊	Qisclara bellula	荔波特有
44	长角齿眼蕈蚊	Phorodonta longiantenna	荔波特有
45	叉刺迟眼蕈蚊	Bradysia fureata	荔波特有
46	茂兰迷蚜蝇	Milesia muolana	荔波特有
47	镰形弱蛛	Leptoneta falcate	荔波特有
48	徐氏弱蛛	L.xui	荔波特有

续表2-2

序号	中文名	学 名	备 注
49	黔希蛛	Achaearanea qianensis	荔波特有
50	茂兰阿纳蛛	Anahita maolan	荔波特有
51	董背泰莱蛛	Telema dongbei	荔波特有
52	茂兰玛琳蛛	Mallinella maolanensis	荔波特有
53	细尾拟鼓鸣螽	Subibulbistridulous giacilis sp. nov.	新种
54	双瘤新渍	Neopterla bituberculata	新种
55	曲囊新渍	N.flexiscrotata	新种
56	短宽钩渍	Kaminuria brerinata	新种
57	茂兰钩渍	K.maolanensis	新种
58	小齿钩渍	K.microdonata	新种
59	李氏钩渍	K.lii	新种
60	茂兰印度隼蟌	Idocyha maolanensis	新种
61	茂兰普莱蜓	Planaeschna maolanensis	新种
62	剑突拟隐脉叶蝉	Sophonia spathulata	新种
63	弯突脊额叶蝉	Carinata recurvana	新种
64	一点脊额叶蝉	C.unipuncta	新种
65	宽带拟隐脉叶蝉	Sophonia zonulata	新种
66	锚突重粉蛉	Semidalis anchoroides	模式种
67	茂兰窗溪蛉	Thyridosmylus maolans	荔波特有
68	三带窗溪蛉	T.trifasciatus	荔波特有
69	茂兰鹬虻	Rhagio maolanus	荔波特有
70	荔波沟茎飞虱	Sulculus liboensis	新种
71	李氏额凹萤叶甲	Sermyloides lii	新种
72	黄斑峨眉球跳甲	Omeisphaera flavimaculata	新种
73	王氏盲步甲	Sinaphaenops wangorum	新种
74	纤细盲步甲	S.gracilior	新种
75	奇异盲步甲	S.mirabilissimus	新种
76	荔波步甲	Carabus liboicus	新种
77	卵行步甲	Oodinotrechus kishimotoi	新种
78	荔波行步甲	Libotrechus nishikawai	新种
79	上野行步甲	Uenotrechus liboensis	新种
80	黔南行步甲	Trechiotes qiannanicus	新种

续表2-2

序号	中文名	学 名	备 注
81	大环腹三节叶蜂	Arge megacincta	新种
82	尖鞘黄腹三节叶蜂	A.acuminitheca	新种
83	荔波淡毛三节叶蜂	A.libona	新种
84	红背颊片叶蜂	Genatomostethus sculpturalis	新种
85	马氏平缝叶蜂	Nesoselandria maliae	新种
86	荔波平缝叶蜂	N.libona	新种
87	汪氏平缝叶蜂	N.wangae	新种
88	双窝侧齿叶蜂始	Neostromboceros bifovella	新种
89	圆额侧齿叶蜂	N.circtJlofrons	新种
90	斑股侧齿叶蜂	N.maculifemoratus	新种
91	纹胸侧齿叶蜂	N.rugosulus	新种
92	褐腹腔齿角叶蜂	Denticornia bruneiventris	新种
93	后柄尖臀叶蜂	Nesoselandriola pedicella	新种
94	黑角齿柄叶蜂	Busarbia nigrocapa	新种
95	无柄线框叶蜂	Linorbita sessilia	新种
96	刘氏黏叶蜂	Caliroa liui	新种
97	黑胫黏叶蜂	C.pseudocerasi	新种
98	荔波脉柄叶蜂	Busarbidea libona	新种
99	侧沟弓蕨叶蜂	Heptamelus lateralis	新种
100	黑足拟栉叶蜂	Priophorus niger	新种
101	小齿拟栉叶蜂	P.paranigricans	新种
102	线颊锤脉叶蜂	Pristiphora lineogenata	新种
103	光盾麦叶蜂	Dolerus glabratus	新种
104	红胸原曲叶蜂	Protemphytus rufithoracinus	新种
105	贵州片爪叶蜂	Darjilingia guizhouensis	新种
106	白环狭腹叶蜂	Athlophorus albocincta	新种
107	双色细叶蜂	Pachyprotarsis bicoloricornis	新种
108	荔波细叶蜂	P.Libona	新种
109	混斑宽腹叶蜂	Macrophya commixta	新种
110	小斑宽腹叶蜂	M.micromacula	新种
111	小鞘宽腹叶蜂	M.minutitheca	新种
112	方凹宽腹叶蜂	M.quadriclypeata	新种
113	黄痣宽腹叶蜂	M.stigmaticalis	新种

续表2-2

序号	中文名	学 名	备 注
114	细条斑黄叶蜂	Tenthredo tilineata	新种
115	白转横带叶蜂	T.leucotrochanteratina	新种
116	蓝青基叶蜂	Beleses nigrolividus	新种
117	平额异基叶蜂	B.flatofrontalis	新种
118	双斑开片叶蜂	Onychostethomostus bimaculatus	新种
119	黄背大片叶蜂	Megatamostethus fulvitergus	新种
120	淡柄开片叶蜂	O.pedicellus	新种
121	白足真片叶蜂	Eutomostethus albipes	新种
122	临脉玛叶蜂	Mallalchiella interstitialis	新种
123	烟翅真片叶蜂	E.rani	新种
124	冉氏真片叶蜂	E.rani	新种
125	汪氏真片叶蜂	E.wangae	新种
126	黑片弯眶叶蜂	Phymatoceridea nigrotegularis	新种
127	尖鞘弯眶叶蜂	P.acutitheca	新种
128	宽带异鄂叶蜂	Conaspidia latifasciata	新种
129	荔波沟额叶蜂	Corrugia libona	新种
130	短颊杨氏长颈蜂	Yangixiphia brachygenata	新种
131	端黑齿扁蜂	Onycholyda euapicalis	新种
132	粒杨猎蝽	Yangicoris geniculatus	新种
133	华猛猎蝽	Sphedanolestes sinicus	新种
134	李短猎蝽	Brachytonus lii	新种
135	广带蝎蛉	Brachytonus lii	新种
136	茂兰新蝎蛉	Neopanorpa maolanensis	新种
137	凉席泰菜蛛	Telema liangxi	新种
138	科氏纳尔蛛	Wendilgarda coddingtoni	新种
139	黑斑肥腹蛛	Steatoda nigrimaculata	新种
140	弯钩肥腹蛛	S.uncata	新种
141	瘤翅长角象	Gibber brevirostris	新种
142	咖啡拟毛小蠹	Dryocoetiops coffeae	新种
143	尖尾筘齿小蠹	Coptodryas mus	新种
144	粒胸食菌小蠹	Ambrosiodmus asperatus	新种
145	瓜蔓颅沟销冠小蠹	Cosmoderes monilicollis	新种
146	四棘材小蠹	Xyleborus mucronatus	新种

续表2-2

序号	中文名	学 名	备注
147	冠颈材小蠹	X.cristatus	新种
148	核桃小蠹	X.juglans	新种
149	褐腹三齿叶蜂	Canonia rufiventris	新种
150	平盾弯眶叶蜂	Macrophya planate	新种
151	缅甸弯眶叶蜂	Phymatoceridea birmana	新种

第二章 荔波自然遗产地的申报

第一节 组织机构

一、申报领导小组（办公室）

2000年，荔波县委、县政府正式把申遗工作纳入议事日程，并于同年3月成立了国家级茂兰喀斯特自然保护区和国家级樟江风景名胜区申报世界自然遗产领导小组及办公室，组长莫俊国，副组长玉如良、冯关芳、魏鲁明。领导小组下设办公室，办公室设在茂兰国家级自然保护区管理处，魏鲁明兼办公室主任。

2001年2月，荔波县成立国家级茂兰喀斯特自然保护区和国家级樟江风景名胜区申报世界自然遗产前期工作领导小组及办公室，组长逄焕华，副组长潘朝显、陆兴华、黄玉成、张惠明、冯关芳、玉如良、魏鲁明。领导小组下设办公室，办公室设在荔波樟江风景名胜区管理处，张惠明任办公室主任，冯关芳、魏鲁明任办公室副主任。2002年11月，因人事变动，调整申报国家级茂兰喀斯特自然保护区和国家级樟江风景名胜区为世界自然遗产地领导小组。组长逄焕华，副组长潘朝显、陆兴华、黄玉成、龙河云、李天送、华廷龙、冯关芳、魏鲁明。领导小组下设办公室在荔波樟江风景名胜区管理处，冯关芳兼办公室主任。2004年11月，因人事变动，调整申报世界自然遗产地领导小组。组长逄焕华，副组长潘朝显、陆兴华、田景胜、龙河云、华廷龙、李洪、陈昌远、冯关芳、魏鲁明。2005年6月，再次对申报世界自然遗产地领导小组进行调整。组长逄焕华，副组长潘朝显、陆兴华、田景胜、陈稠彪、李洪、陈昌远、冯关芳、魏鲁明。

2005年10月，调整充实荔波申报世界自然遗产地领导小组。组长潘朝显，副组长陈稠彪、李洪、马应忠、程志安、董豫黔、陈昌远、何建飞、冯关芳、魏鲁明。领导小组下设办公室和宣传资料组、环境整治组、后勤保障组3个工作组。2006年3月29日，县成立申遗环境综合整治工作领导小组，由州人大常委会副主任、县委书记逄焕华，县人大常委会主任陆兴华、县政协主席田景胜任顾问，县长陈稠彪任组长，进一步加大环境综合整治工作力度。

二、荔波世界自然遗产管理局

2006年4月29日，成立荔波县遗产管理办公室，为县人民政府直属正科级事业机构，承担全县国家遗产、世界遗产的申报和管理的行政职能，编制6人。5月10日正式挂牌办公，副县长陈昌远兼任办公室主任。遗产地管理主要由茂兰保护局、樟江风景名胜区管理局、县遗产管理办公室进行具体管理。其中茂兰保护局主要行使对茂兰国家级自然保护区进行科研保护和景区开发职责；樟江风景名胜区管理局主要行使对大七孔、小七孔景区进行保护和旅游开发；遗产管理办公室主要承担全县国家遗产、世界遗产的申报和管理的行政职能，负责配合省申遗专家组对荔波世界自然遗产地的申报进行资料的收集、整理以及专家、各级领导到提名地调研考察的对接等。同时与荔波林业局、荔波县环境保护局、荔波县文化局、荔波县水利局、荔波县公安局、荔波县国土局、荔波县畜牧局等职能部门，遗产地所在乡（镇）政府、村、组均各负其责，协调配合，共同搞好遗产资源管理。

2012年3月，荔波县遗产管理办公室更名为“荔波县世界自然遗产管理局”，同年12月升格为正处级单位，统筹全县世界自然遗产地的保护。

三、茂兰保护区管理局

1986年12月，荔波县人民政府批准建立茂兰自然保护区，并划定了范围。1987年4月，贵州省人民政府将茂兰保护区列为省级保护区。1988年5月，国务院批准茂兰保护区为国家级自然保护区。1996年4月，联合国教科文组织将茂兰纳入“人与生物圈保护区网络”，成为世界生物圈保护区。茂兰自然保护区建立后，经贵州省人民政府批准，1988年9月组建贵州茂兰国家级自然保护区管理处（2000年5月，改称贵州茂兰国家级自然保护区管理局），为正县级省属事业单位，隶属贵州省林业厅，编制45人。下设办公室、人事教育科、财务科、科研科、林政科、社区发展管理科、森林派出所、生态旅游管理中心、永康管理站、三岔河管理站、翁昂管理站、洞塘管理站。

四、荔波樟江风景名胜区管理处

荔波樟江风景名胜区管理处是隶属于荔波县人民政府下的副县级事业机构，加挂荔波县旅游事业管理局牌子，实行一套人马、两块牌子、合署办公，内设监察保护科、规划建设科、计划财务科、旅游策划科、管理科、办公室和景区派出所，设有7个管理站、一个绿化环卫大队，内设机构的级别为科级，编制人数30人。1990年8月，贵州省人民政府批准大七孔、小七孔为省级风景名胜区，1994年1月，国务院将大七孔、小七孔列为国家重点风景名胜区。

第二节　世界自然遗产地申报工作

一、宣传与培训

1994年9月18—24日，中央电视台《神州风采》栏目“中国风景名胜摄制组”到樟江风景区拍摄风光片，此片在中央电视台《神州风采》栏目中播出。同年10月15—17日，中央电视台《走向辉煌》栏目委托贵州电视台和黔南电视台到樟江风景区拍摄风光片。1998年，荔波县参加上海“98中国国际旅游交易会”，共发放景区宣传资料2万份。

1995年起，县委、县政府着手世界自然遗产地项目申报的前期准备工作，主要开展探讨、游说、呼吁、资料收集等工作。为荔波申报世界自然遗产奠定基础，2000年6月，荔波县人民政府出台《关于保护森林资源，建立生态县公园县的通告》。通告明确规定要保护好樟江风景名胜区和喀斯特森林保护区，使荔波县的森林资源得到有效的保护。

2000年9月，组织参加重庆旅游交易会，发放宣传资料1万份，初步打开重庆市场。2001年9月，与《贵州日报》《贵州商报》《贵州都市报》、贵州电视台签订《荔波“绿宝石”计划推展协议》，在报纸、电视上进行宣传。2002年3月，中央电视台2频道《金苹果》栏目摄制组到景区拍摄、制作节目。8月，全国十佳卫视到荔波进行“聚焦绿宝石”采风。

2001年10月，荔波县人民政府正式向黔南州政府提出申报世界自然遗产的请示报告。呈报文件指出：荔波县境内拥有世界级的茂兰喀斯特森林自然保护区和樟江国家重点风景名胜区，构成了以自然景观为主体的喀斯特森林景观和水景特色，是目前世界上仅存下来绝无仅有的喀斯特森林生态系统，将荔波申报为世界自然遗产有着重要的现实意义和深远的历史意义，也将填补黔南州、贵州省尚无世界遗产的空白。同年11月，荔波县人民政府将申报世界自然遗产的申请呈报贵州省申报世界遗产办公室。2002年12月30日，黔南州人民政府向贵州省人民政府呈交了《关于申报荔波喀斯特森林为世界自然遗产的报告》。报告指出：荔波喀斯特森林具有唯一性、独特性、代表性、原生性、多样性、观赏性、传奇性等特点，同时荔波地理环境独特，气候条件优越，自然资源丰富，综合优势突出，申报为世界自然遗产理由充分，具有极大的可能性。

2007年6月，世界遗产评估专家组到荔波参加评估会议

2004年4月10日，在贵阳举办“荔波综合旅游区”大型推介活动；4月25日，中央电视台9频道《旅游指南》栏目摄制组到荔波拍摄旅游专题片；5月下旬，中央电视台10频道《地球上的故事》专题拍摄组到荔波拍摄“中国南方喀斯特”申报世界遗产——贵州锥状喀斯特专题片；11月，参加由国家旅游局、上海市政府和中国民用航空总局共同主办的2004年中国国际旅游交易会。

2005年3月中旬，贵阳、上海、重庆三地15家旅行社及《中国旅游报》《贵州商报》对荔波旅游资源进行考察和宣传报道。4月中旬，参加广西桂林举办的“中国国内旅游交易会”。10月，在中国国家地理杂志社主办并与全国媒体联合评选“中国最美的地方”活动中，荔波获“中国最美的森林奖”。

2006年4月3日，荔波县举行申报世界自然遗产誓师大会及万人游行和签名活动，县委、县人大、县政府、县政协领导以及各乡（镇）、县直各部门、社会团体、非经济人士、学生和群众共2万多人参加大会。之后，对机关、乡（镇）、学校进行世界自然遗产知识培训，共培训2.2万人次，发放宣传资料4.1万份，编印《世界遗产与荔波申遗情况介绍》知识手册，申遗工作家喻户晓。

2006年4月，为集中展示“申报中国南方喀斯特”荔波提名地喀斯特地质地貌与洞穴、生态过程及生物多样性、民族文化内涵，迎接IUCN专家组检查工作。遗产管理办公室在茂兰邑町和大七孔景区新建“世界遗产展示中心”，进行内外部装修、布展，增设投影仪、影像及民族银饰、服饰、工艺品等，供游客观赏，利用电子播音系统适时播放“中国南方喀斯特”世界自然遗产地等相关知识。

2006年6月9日注册“中国南方喀斯特”网站域名，2006年10月25日，荔波正式开通“世界自然遗产——中国南方喀斯特”网站，网址为http://www.southchinakarst.cn。

同年7月2—7日，《人民日报》、新华社、《光明日报》《经济日报》《中国文化报》《中国日报》《北京周报》《今日中国》、美国《彼岸》杂志、解放军总参谋部等10家媒体组成的中央媒体记者团到荔波进行为期6天的采访。

2007年4月10日开工建设“中国南方喀斯特”荔波展示中心，11月5日竣工，并正式对外界展出。中国南方喀斯特荔波展示中心建筑面积2820平方米，设有自然展厅4个、民族展厅4个。展示中心已成为荔波青少年课外活动中心。是年，县环境保护局、县科协共同将荔波世界自然遗产展示中心申报为贵州省环境教育基地和贵州省省级科普教育示范基地。

2007年4月，《北京周报》《今日中国》《人民画报》《人民中国》4家中央对外宣传媒体的外国专家及记者共13人到荔波，考察采访“中国南方喀斯特”世界自然遗产申报工作。是年，通过新华社、《贵州日报》《贵州都市报》、黔南电视台、新浪网、新华网等十余家媒体，开展申遗新闻报道。

2007年6月24日，第31届世界遗产大会在新西兰克赖斯特彻奇开幕。荔波县委书记王振金、荔波樟江风景名胜区管理处处长冯关芳参加会议。6月27日大会通过决议，将中国南方喀斯特列为世界自然遗产名录。消息传来，荔波县城一片欢腾，数万人在“樟江园”广场点燃篝火，燃放烟花、载歌载舞、彻夜联欢。6月28日上午在荔波民族中学大操场举行了盛大的庆祝大会，副省长蒙启良，州委书记吴廷述、州长李月成等省、州领导出席了大会，会后参加领导和人员上街庆祝游行。中央、省、州、县电视台等多家媒体对庆祝全程进行了现场报道。荔波终于冲出贵州，走向世界。

二、调研与考察

2001年6月中旬，申遗领导小组赴四川九寨沟、黄龙考察，提出申报世界自然遗产地的意见和建议。

2003年1月6—21日，为了配合“中国喀斯特”申报世界自然遗产工作，迎接联合国教科文组织专家的考察，贵州省申报世界遗产办公室邀请中国科学院地理科学与资源研究所宋林华研究员以及向昌国、梁福源、王福源、张平究4位博士，贵州师范大学杨明德教授、黎道宏教授，贵州工业大学李景阳教授一行对荔波樟江风景名胜区和茂兰自然保护区，独山黄后地下河，罗甸大、小井风景区和板庚中三叠纪构造带，兴义万峰林——万峰湖、西峰林、马岭河峡谷，贞丰双乳峰等地进行考察。通过考察，专家们一致认为，贵州锥状喀斯特景观及其演化具有很高的遗产价值，而未被人为破坏的主要集中在荔波樟江的地貌景观、水文景观、生物景观以及茂兰喀斯特国家级自然保护区。因此，建议贵州喀斯特申报世界遗产的范围包括荔波樟江国家重点风景名胜区和茂兰国家级自然保护区。

2004年6月25日—7月7日，由贵州省建设厅厅长李光荣带队，组织荔波县及兴义、安顺等地共26人，参加在苏州举行的第28届世界遗产大会。同年8月13日，中国科学院地理科学与资源研究所研究员宋林华和贵州师范大学教授杨明德从贵阳乘车赴荔波考察申遗工作途中遭遇车祸，不幸罹难。

2005年6月9日，建设部城建司副司长王凤武、风景园林处副处长左小平由贵州省建设厅副厅长姬保山陪同，到荔波县考察申报“中国南方喀斯特”世界自然遗产工作。同年11月，国际喀斯特自然遗产管理专家、澳大利亚查尔斯特大学教授史密斯应邀到荔波提名地进行考察。

2006年3月19—24日，贵州、云南、重庆3省、市专家和申报地政府领导组成联合考察组到荔波进行实地考察，对荔波提名地提出了12条具体的环境整治意见。24日，荔波县召开紧急会议，根据联合考察组专家和领导提出的12条环境整治意见，对整治工作进行认真梳理和研究，正式启动了环境整治工作。

2006年5月16—17日，贵州省委副书记王富玉、副省长蒙启良代表省委、省政府，率省直20多个部门到荔波实地考察申遗工作，现场办公，并召开申遗专题会议，落实解决荔波在环境整治工作中面临的资金、项目、技术等困难，并形成省委常委会议纪要，督办落实。

同年6月9—11日，IUCN专家、国际著名喀斯特学家、新西兰奥克兰大学教授威廉姆斯偕夫人应邀考察荔波提名地。7月9—12日，国际著名生物多样性专家马敬能博士和中国科学院解焱研究员应邀到荔波进行实地考察，对荔波提名地的生物多样性和迎接IUCN专家考察的路线作评价和建议。2006年8月5—7日，贵州、云南、重庆3省、市专家联合考察组到荔波进行模拟考察。同年9月

2—8日，国际洞穴协会原主席、澳大利亚悉尼大学教授朱丽娅应邀到荔波提名地进行考察。同年9月2—10日，国际著名喀斯特学家、新西兰奥克兰大学教授威廉姆斯和国际喀斯特自然遗产管理专家、澳大利亚查尔斯特大学教授史密斯应邀到荔波提名地进行考察。同年9月8—10日，国际自然保护联盟（IUCN）专家吉米·桑塞尔博士对荔波提名地进行实地考察评估。为期两天的考察达到了预期的效果，荔波提名地向世界自然遗产迈进了具有重要意义的一大步。

三、会议与审定

2003年3月25日，省建设厅在贵阳组织召开“荔波喀斯特森林”申报世界自然遗产名录预选文本初审会，会议原则通过荔波申遗文本。5月13日，荔波县参加贵州省建设厅在贵阳组织召开的贵州锥状喀斯特申报列入“中国喀斯特”世界自然遗产名录预选文本与影像审查会，会议认为，荔波的文本和影像资料内容丰富，资料翔实，条理清楚，图文并茂，符合要求，同意验收。11月6—11日，省邀请中国科学院地理科学与资源研究所、建设部风景名胜专家顾问、研究员宋林华，国家著名喀斯特专家、南京大学俞锦标教授到荔波考察，正式确认荔波为世界自然遗产申报地。11月30日，省建设厅申遗办在贵阳组织召开荔波喀斯特森林申遗初审会，经专家组评审，认为申报文本及所附资料基本符合世界遗产申报要求，建议列入贵州省世界遗产申报名单。

2005年6月9日，建设部到荔波县考察申报“中国南方喀斯特”世界自然遗产地工作。是月，编制完成《“中国南方喀斯特”世界自然遗产提名地贵州荔波锥状喀斯特保护与管理规划》，为荔波喀斯特森林的保护与管理提供具有操作性的依据。9月10日，建设部明确贵州荔波、云南石林、重庆武隆作为“中国南方喀斯特”世界自然遗产的第一批申报单位，并由贵州省牵头组织申报工作。10月25日，完成“中国南方喀斯特”世界自然遗产申报文本。

2006年1月，经国务院批准，中国向联合国教科文组织提交“中国南方喀斯特”世界自然遗产地申报文本及相关资料，确认申报世界自然遗产地依据。3月1日，“中国南方喀斯特”申遗项目通过联合国教科文组织世界遗产中心的筛选，列入预选评估名录，申报项目进入实质性现场考察阶段。同年6月20日，州委、州政府在荔波召开会议，落实荔波申遗工作急需的环境整治资金2000万元，工作经费100万元。

同年9月8—10日，IUCN专家吉米·桑塞尔博士对荔波提名地进行实地考察评估。中国科学院院士袁道先、中国工程院院士卢耀如、中国科学院植物研究所研究员王献溥以及建设部、外交部、中国联合国教科文组织全国委员会的专家一同考察。10日，在贵阳召开IUCN专家考察“中国南方喀斯特”总结座谈会，会后，桑塞尔博士向世界遗产中心提交考察报告，并通过世界自然保护联盟（IUCN）10人小组的审查，同意将“中国南方喀斯特”项目提交2007年6月世界遗产大会表决。

2007年6月27日下午14时25分，第31届世界遗产大会在新西兰克赖斯特彻奇召开。大会审议通过贵州荔波与云南石林、重庆武隆捆绑申报的“中国南方喀斯特”世界自然遗产项目列入世界自然遗产名录，荔波被正式列为世界自然遗产地。大会对“中国南方喀斯特”的评价为：“‘中国南方喀斯特’在喀斯特特征和地貌景观方面的多样性是无与伦比的，代表了世界上湿润热带到亚热带喀斯特景观最壮观的范例”“荔波的锥状和塔状喀斯特同样被认为是世界上同类喀斯特的参照地”。6月28日上午，荔波县在民族中学举行申报世界自然遗产地成功庆祝大会及万人游行和签名活动，并在大七孔景区举行“世界遗产”标志牌揭牌仪式。

第三章 资源保护

第一节 管理机构

1988年9月，省政府行文建立贵州茂兰国家级自然保护区管理处，为省属事业单位（正处级），由省林业厅和县政府共同领导。中共组织、行政事务由荔波县管理，业务及工资、经费等由省林业厅负责，人事商荔波县决定，事业编制40人。每年所需经费由省财政列入省林业厅事业经费预算。茂兰保护区管理处内设办公室、科研科、计财科、管理总站等科室，下设永康、翁昂、三岔河、小七孔4个管理站。1992年1月，建立茂兰保护区森林公安派出所。1993年6月，将护林员队伍精简成立林区治安队，队员分别驻各管理站，专职巡山护林。1995年12月，茂兰保护区管理处成立资源开发公司。1997年7月，茂兰管理处成立多种经营科。

2000年5月，省政府将茂兰管理处更名为贵州茂兰国家级自然保护区管理局，为贵州省林业厅直属正县级全额拨款事业单位，业务和人事由贵州省林业厅直接管理，定编40人（管理人员9人、专业技术人员26人、工勤人员5人），中共党组织关系由中共荔波县委管理，直至2008年。

2012年3月，荔波县遗产管理办公室更名为“荔波县世界自然遗产管理局”，并升格为正处级单位，为统筹全县世界自然遗产的保护和科学利用打下了基础。

第二节 资源保护规划

中国南方喀斯特——荔波世界自然遗产主要由茂兰自然保护区和樟江风景名胜区的大七孔、小七孔景区组成，总面积为73016公顷，占全县总面积的30%，其中核心区为29518公顷，缓冲区为43498公顷，核心区共涉及5个乡（镇）、10个村、51个组、1166户4513人。（本节有关樟江风景名胜区大七孔、小七孔景区的相关内容在旅游篇记述，此处不重记）

一、规划

为有效地保护好茂兰喀斯特森林，1986年12月，县政府行文将茂兰喀斯特森林列为自然保护区，并确定保护区的范围。茂兰保护区涉及洞塘、永康、翁昂、捞村、立化、驾欧和甲良等7个乡（镇）、14个村、96个自然组，共2600余户1万余人。保护管理工作由县林业局负责，并在保护区范围内聘请50名村、组干部作兼职护林员，负责各村、组范围内的护林工作。1987年4月，省政府将茂兰保护区批准为省级自然保护区。1988年5月，国务院将茂兰保护区批准为国家级自然保护区，并明确该保护区是以保护完整的综合自然生态系统为目的，兼有保护珍稀孑遗动植物资源的科研型自然保护区。1996年4月，茂兰保护区被联合国教科文组织纳入国际生物圈保护区网络（MAB）。是年，该区被中国生态旅游专业委员会列为全国22条生态旅游线之一。

2004年12月，茂兰管理局根据国家林业局《关于规范国家级自然保护区总体规划和建设程序有关问题的通知》，委托省林业调查规划院编制《贵州茂兰国家级自然保护区总体规划（2004—2015年）》。此《规划》根据茂兰保护区的区情，遵循自然规律和经济规律，以保护为根本，以发展为目的；以保护工程为基础，以科学研究为重点；以现代化的管理为保障；加大执法、宣传、科研和投资力度，全面发挥保护区的保护、后勤基地（科研、监测、教育、培训）和发展三大功能，逐步将茂兰保护区建设成为一个特色突出、内涵丰富、布局合理、设施完善、功能齐全、管理规范、效益显著、知名度高的国家级自然保护区，实现喀斯特森林生态环境、生物多样性和社区经济的可持续发展。规划期限为2004—2015年，按照茂兰保护区自然资源的特点和主要保护对象的分布状况及保护目的，以保护喀斯特森林生态系统及其珍稀濒危野生动植物为主，将保护区划分为核心区、缓冲区和实验区。

2006年，根据《贵州茂兰国家级自然保护区总体规划（2004—2015）》《荔波樟江风景名胜区总体规划（2002—2020）》《世界遗产公约行动指南（2/2005，UNESCO）》《国际自然保护联盟喀斯特保护地指南》，县政府制定《荔波世界自然遗产提名地管理规划纲要》并实施。《荔波遗产地保护管理规划纲要》由荔波世界自然遗产管理办公室负责协调，组织茂兰自然管理局和樟江管理处共同实施。是年，国家林业局确定茂兰自然保护区为第一批国家级示范建设保护区。

2008年，组织编制《荔波世界自然遗产地保护专项规划》，报省政府审批。（省政府于2009年3月6日第21次省长办公会审查通过。规划保护期为20年，计划投入保护资金6.3亿元）

二、功能区划分

（一）核心区

核心区位于保护区南部与广西木论国家级自然保护区交界一线，即从更查、更独山经万里卡、四北洞、白鹇山、黎明关至罗家洞、干刷、洞洼一带，包括洞杨山、洞多等。核心区面积83.05平方公里，占保护区总面积的39.0%。

核心区保存着发育完好、极为典型的原生性喀斯特森林，森林覆盖率达93.8%。各种地貌类型与森林组合，如漏斗森林、洼地森林、槽谷森林等各种森林群落类型，在核心区均有分布。在干刷和拉笔腊一带，还有一定面积的灌丛植被。茂兰所有的生物物种，特别是国家重点保护动植物种类和茂兰特有种，在核心区内均有分布和栖息。

核心区内禁止任何单位和个人进入，实行绝对保护。如确因科研需要进入核心区时，要事先向保护区管理局提出申请，并经国家林业局或其指定部门批准后，方可在核心区内从事相关科学研究工作。

（二）缓冲区

缓冲区是核心区与实验区的过渡地带，对核心区起保护和缓冲作用，扩大和延伸被保护物种的生长和活动区域。

缓冲区位于核心区外围，总面积81.3平方公里，其主要特征是自然森林生态系统较完整，生物多样性丰富，分布有部分灌木林、藤刺灌丛、灌草丛等不同演替阶段的次生生态系统。

缓冲区尽量减少人为干扰，可有计划地从事科学研究和教学实习等工作，但需事先向保护区管理局提出申请，经主管部门批准后方可进入。

（三）实验区和旅游区

1.实验区。实验区的主要功能是对核心区起到更大的缓冲作用和与周边地区的联系纽带作用，在国家法律、法规允许的范围内和不破坏自然生态环境的前提下，可以开展科学实验、教学实习、参观考察、生态旅游、野生动植物驯养繁殖及其他有益于资源合理利用与生产示范等活动。实验区分为4块：永康乡的尧古、瑶兰；翁昂乡的巴弓、莫干、洞常；洞塘乡的板寨、计才、尧所；洞塘乡的塘边、洞马、蒙寨。总面积29.35平方公里。实验区是保护区内人口最密集、生产活动最频繁、森林资源破坏最严重的地区。

2.生态旅游区。生态旅游区是实验区进行旅游开发的区域。该区位于保护区的东北部，面积19.15平方公里。其主要功能是用于开展喀斯特森林生态旅游，以良好独特的喀斯特森林景观和生态环境为主体，融合自然景观与人文景观，充分利用森林的多种功能，按照生态旅游的理论和宗旨开展旅游活动，从而使观赏游览与科普教育相结合，提高公众保护生态环境、热爱大自然的意识。同时，通过旅游带动社区经济发展，为保护管理积累资金。旅游区的主要景点有青龙潭、金狮洞、九洞天、旺牌山漏斗森林、黄杨沟、水中林、拉滩瀑布等。区内修建简易步道供游人徒步游览。

第三节　保护项目与立法

一、编制保护项目规划

荔波县坚持对遗产保护地“保护第一，规划引领”的原则，组织编制保护项目规划。2010年，组织编制了《荔波世界自然遗产地保护项目专项规划》，并于2011年1月，由省人民政府黔府函〔2011〕18号正式批复。

根据《保护世界文化和自然遗产公约》的规定，各世界遗产地每六年要向联合国世界遗产委员会提交一次定期报告，接受评估审核。2015年度“中国南方喀斯特”项目地须向住建部提交《中国南方喀斯特保护管理规划》《中国南方喀斯特保护管理监测评估报告》。为完成此项工作，县遗产局向省遗产管理部门对接，经征求“中国南方喀斯特”四省七地意见，该《规划》由住建部世界遗产保护研究中心组织国内外专家编制，编制所需费用由“中国南方喀斯特”四省七个世界自然遗产地政府承担。2015年11月30日，中国南方喀斯特世界自然遗产保护管理协调委员会在北京组织召开了“中国南方喀斯特世界自然遗产保护管理规划”专家评审会，该规划通过了由北京大学、中国科学院植物所、北京师范大学等组成的专家组评审。2009—2015年，荔波县按照《保护世界文化和自然遗产公约》国际准则以及国家生态资源保护法律法规和政策的要求，组织编制了《荔波世界自然遗产地保护管理规划》。荔波列入国家生态功能区，取得了联合国教科文组织的帮助，实施了遗产地人文教育的宣传培训和动物资源本地调查。

二、立法

荔波世界自然遗产地申报成功后，县委、县政府努力推进荔波世界自然遗产保护条例立法工作。加强世界自然遗产地统筹保护与管理，使世界自然遗产保护尽快纳入法治化轨道，在国家和省级层面没有立法的情况下，荔波县参照《保护世界文化与自然遗产公约》，借鉴国内先进世界自然遗产地的立法经验，草拟了《黔南州荔波县世界自然遗产保护条例》。2012年3月9日，县人大常委会召开了“荔波县世界自然遗产地立法保护工作部署会”，启动了荔波县世界自然遗产保护之法工作，并于同年6月29日通过了黔南州人大常委会2012—2016年立法规划。

根据黔南州人大常委会立法工作要求，县政府成立了《黔南州荔波世界自然遗产地保护条例》立法工作领导小组和工作组，下设办公室在县世遗局，负责《条例》文本的起草和修改。在领导小组的领导下，县世遗局多次召集县直机关部门和乡镇政府召开征求意见会，征集修改意见，将《条例》呈县委、县人大、县政府、县政协和黔南州相关部门征集意见，形成了《条例》第六稿，并邀请国内专家进行了立法论证。拟于2018年争取黔南州人大审议通过颁布试行。

为使祖辈世代相传留下的珍贵自然遗产完整地保存和传承给后人，形成人人保护世界遗产的良好社会氛围。全县组织县、乡、村、组四级和老中少三代代表共同签订《荔波世界遗产地生态保护公约》进一步提升广大公众对保护世界自然遗产的责任感和使命感。

第四节　生态环境整治与管理

一、环境整治

从20世纪80年代开始，荔波县根据《中华人民共和国宪法》《中华人民共和国森林法》《中华人民共和国环境保护法》《中华人民共和国水法》《中华人民共和国野生动物保护法》《中华人民共和国自然保护区条例》《中华人民共和国风景名胜区暂行条例》等国家法律法规，依法对茂兰自然保护区和樟江风景名胜区进行保护管理。

1995年，县政府制定《荔波樟江风景名胜区管理办法（试行）》。

2000年，黔南州人大常委会制定《荔波樟江风景名胜区管理条例》，2001年7月经省人大常委会批准实施。

2002年3月，IUCN荷兰委员会资助的“小额湿地赠款”项目中“促进少数民族社区参与喀斯特湿地的资源管理”在茂兰保护区启动，为期3年，项目在尧兰、尧古两个民族村寨实施，为社区新增沼气等替代性能源，改变原有的农业产业结构及生产生活方式。是年，洞塘乡尧所村等民族村寨自发制定《村规民约》，对保护区自然资源和生态环境保护进行详细而明确的规定。

2003年，县财政投入500万元，将居住在小七孔景区的89户农户全部搬迁。从是年起，每年支付补偿70多万元，用于拆除影响小七孔景区景观的原有建筑，对荒山荒地、停车场等建设场地进行绿化、美化。2004年，县政府制定《荔波樟江风景名胜区景区监察实施细则》。是年，在樟江景区实施“四区一控”工程（即小康生活区、两高一优农业旅游示范区、樟江田园风光带建设区、旅游开发区和控制环境污染与损坏），成立兰鼎山等6个县级自然保护区。同时，从资金、物资上加大对保护区、景区农户的投入，引导景区农民参与旅游业服务。

2005年，为推进“中国南方喀斯特”申报世界自然遗产荔波预选地的申报进程，迎接国内外遗产专家的考察，制定《“中国南方喀斯特”申报世界自然遗产荔波提名地综合整治方案》，对荔波提名地环境进行综合整治。

2006年，县政府申报实施荔波遗产地保护性基础设施项目，项目资金2860万元。项目内容主要有基础设施、环境整治、展示及科普设施等方面。基础设施包括管理用房、消防设施、安全护栏、垃圾处理等；环境整治包括大小七孔景区及茂兰保护区的生态监测、道路改造、环境绿化等；展示及科普设施含标志标牌、珍稀植物园、科普展示馆及信息咨询设施等。是年3月19—24日，滇、黔、渝3省专家组成联合考察组到荔波进行实地考察，对荔波提名地提出12条具体的环境整治意见，包括拆除小七孔景区内的4个梯级电站、3家宾馆、1所学校、民房，恢复自然植被，考察沿线1000多亩耕地退耕、关闭所有采石场、沿线村寨整治、消除提名地内人工影响痕迹等。是月24日，县委、县政府召开紧急会议，根据联合考察组提出的12条环境整治意见，对整治工作进行研究，正式启动环境整治工作。4月13日，州政府、省建设厅在荔波联合组织召开申遗工作专题会议，明确整治工作的重点和目标，提出整治的内容和时间要求。县财政投入资金400万元，全面铺开申遗环境整治工作，此外争取到奔驰中国公司援助项目14万美元，投入保护区环境整治。同年5月16—17日，省委、省政府率20多个省直部门到荔波现场办公，解决在环境整治工作中面临的资金、项目、技术等困难，并形成省委常委会议纪要，督办落实。从5月27日开始，对保护区内不符合申遗标准的设施、建筑进行拆除。小七孔电站于6月3日凌晨全线停产，至7月1日拆除完毕。电力、电信、移动、联通等单位按照要求将核心区的电力、通信线路全部实行地埋。专家考察沿线的瑶山、驾欧、翁昂、洞塘4个乡退耕土地面积1389.16亩，兑付退耕补偿费共45.79万元。全县旅游公路沿线可视范围内的35家采石场全部关闭，完成40个石场的植被恢复绿化，植被恢复面积1.1万平方米。保护区内共拆除梯级水电站4座、宾馆饭店3家、学校教学楼1栋、职工住宿楼2栋及部分民房，拆除建筑面积共11516.2平方米，拆除后的植被恢复及绿化于7月10日完成，共移植草皮1.7万平方米、移栽大苗1120株，设置和完善区内指示牌、垃圾箱、厕所等旅游服务设施。此外，省、州环境保护局组织相关部门进行环境监测，对小七孔景区水源周边环境实施监控和调查，制定环境整治方案并实施。制作安装茂兰保护区和樟江风景名胜区界碑、标志牌100余块，建成茂兰自然保护区大门及凉水井瞭望台、生态监测站和上山步道安全防护栏。

2007年开展的环境整治项目主要有小七孔环保车营运改造；小七孔湿地恢复建设；景区—县城11座星级旅游公厕新建和改造；小七孔东门—龟背山道路改造；导游培训和民族旅游工艺品制作技能培训；景区垃圾外运，减少人为对环境的污染等。

20世纪80年代至2008年，对樟江沿岸污染源进行整治达40次，强制拆除砖瓦窑50多个，关闭樟江上游煤井20多口。经采取“两禁止、三关闭、二保护”（即禁止砍伐天然林，禁止放火烧山，关闭乡镇林工商公司，关闭杂木市场，关闭木炭市场，保护天然林，保护水源涵养林）的强制措施，以及禁止捕杀野生动物，保护植被、水体，对樟江沿河进行系统绿化，张贴护林防火宣传标语和宣传画，与农户签订护林防火责任书，每个景区周围村组聘请生态保护联络员等，将各种隐患消灭在萌芽状态。至2008年年末，茂兰自然保护区和樟江风景名胜区均未出现破坏地形、地貌和自然环境的行为。

根据省政府21次专题会议精神，省财政和省住建厅自2009年开始每年从省级部门预算中划拨1000万元作为荔波遗产地保护项目专项资金，极大地推动了荔波县遗产地基础设施建设。

二、分片管理

2007年，将荔波世界自然遗产地列入世界遗产名录，分为茂兰自然保护区世界自然遗产地和大七孔、小七孔景区世界自然遗产地两个部分进行管理保护。

1.茂兰自然保护区世界自然遗产地。该区为社区共管，管理措施主要有：

（1）利用电视、广播、张贴标语、发放宣传手册等措施，开展世界自然遗产地保护和林业法治宣传教育。建立林区治安队和保护联防组织，利用法律和行政手段，严厉打击各种乱砍滥伐、乱捕滥猎、毁林开荒等破坏森林资源的违法活动，保护国家珍贵的自然资源。

（2）成立森林防火指挥部，配备交通工具、电台、防火机具，在各个季节，将防火通知书发到辖区内的群众手中，使森林防火工作家喻户晓。

（3）扶持区内群众的生产生活，把发展经济列为管理工作的一个重要内容，扶持群众兴修水利、架桥修路、人畜饮水、照明用电、植树造林，推广农村实用技术，发展教育卫生事业。

（4）编制茂兰生物多样性清单（植物名录、脊椎动物名录、昆虫名录等），为保护管理和决策提供依据。同时，对茂兰珍稀、濒危、特有物种进行专项研究和维护，根据其生长特征、栖息环境等，采取就地保护、迁移保护等措施。

（5）在不破坏和影响自然保护区资源的前提下，以提高社区经济、文化、卫生等事业的发展，增加社区经济总量水平，缓和社区村民与保护区保护资源之间的矛盾。即以生态保护为优先，因地制宜，合理开发；以市场为导向，以科技为支撑，以效益为目标，调动社区居民的保护积极性；逐步解决农村能源建设问题；迁移安置核心区居民；加强社区村民有关技术知识培训教育，提高居民的综合素质；建立农村农业生态示范村、生态示范户，发展社区庭院经济；开展植树造林，绿化荒山荒坡，促进周边农村农业结构调整。

2.大七孔、小七孔景区世界自然遗产地。对该地保护坚持“严格保护、统一管理、合理开发、永续利用”的方针，根据景区资源的观赏、文化、科学价值和环境现状，采取分级保护为主，分类保护为辅的办法，形成分级中有分类的综合分区。整个景区划分为特级、一级、二级、三级保护区和外围保护地带。

特级保护区：小七孔景区野猪林、六十八级瀑布、龟背山；大七孔景区的地峨森林周边。面积为4.6平方公里，占总面积的3.9%。该保护区严格限制开发行为，不得建设有碍风景的设施，限制游人数量，严禁改变地形地貌。

一级保护区：特级保护区外围及水上森林、鸳鸯湖、地峨宫、天生桥等周围，面积为12.8平方公里，占总面积的10.8%。区内严格保护地貌、植被、水文景观的原始性、严禁乱砍滥伐、开山采石等破坏性活动。

二级保护区：指一级保护区外围的水春河沿岸区域，面积71.8平方公里，占总面积的60.4%。属遗产地缓冲区外围，可建设与风景环境相协调的各项设施，严格控制人口数量。

三级保护区和外围保护地带：指二级保护区以外区域和景区外围1公里范围内，包括樟江主要支流水域，实行协调性保护，面积121.6平方公里，区内不得建设有污染的工矿企业，不得破坏景观。

岩溶地貌保护：喀斯特岩溶地貌是景区资源和环境的基础，属典型的碳酸盐溶地貌，易风化冲刷，禁止开山采石和挖沙取土。

森林植被保护：喀斯特森林植被属石头上的森林，一旦破坏将难以恢复，因此，在加强森林保护的同时还进行有计划的封山育林，培育了数十种乡土树种30万株，植树种竹2万余株，保护景观和生态环境。

河流瀑布保护：以樟江为纽带，围绕其支流的河谷溪流和瀑布跌水的水文景观环境进行保护。拆除砖瓦厂，禁止挖沙取土，并种植麻竹、楠竹保水固土，严禁向河流倾倒垃圾、污水。

第五节　宣传培训教育

一、宣传

1994年9月18—24日，中央电视台《神州风采》栏目“中国风景名胜摄制组”到樟江风景区拍摄风光片，此片在中央电视台《神州风采》栏目中播出。同年10月15—17日，中央电视台《走向辉煌》栏目委托贵州电视台和黔南电视台到樟江风景区拍摄风光片。

1998年，荔波县参加上海“98中国国际旅游交易会”，共发放景区宣传资料2万份。

2000年9月，组织参加重庆旅游交易会，发放宣传资料1万份，初步打开重庆市场。

2001年9月，与贵州日报、贵州商报、贵州都市报、贵州电视台签订《荔波“绿宝石”计划推展协议》，在报纸、电视上进行宣传。2002年3月，中央电视台2频道“金苹果”栏目摄制组到景区拍摄、制作节目。8月，全国十佳卫视到荔波进行“聚焦绿宝石”采风。2004年4月10日，在贵阳举办“荔波综合旅游区”大型推介活动；4月25日，中央电视台9频道“旅游指南”栏目摄制组到荔波拍摄旅游专题片；5月下旬，中央电视台10频道《地球上的故事》专题拍摄组到荔波拍摄“中国南方喀斯特”申报世界遗产——贵州锥状喀斯特专题片；11月，参加由国家旅游局、上海市政府和中国民用航空总局共同主办的2004年中国国际旅游交易会。2005年3月中旬，贵阳、上海、重庆三地15家旅行社及《中国旅游报》《贵州商报》对荔波旅游资源进行考察和宣传报道。4月中旬，参加广西桂林举办的“中国国内旅游交易会”。10月，在中国国家地理杂志社主办并与全国媒体联合评选“中国最美的地方”活动中，荔波获“中国最美的森林奖”。2006年6月9日注册“中国南方喀斯特”网站域名。

荔波自然遗产地申报成功后，2007年4月，中国网、北京周报、今日中国、人民画报、人民中国5家中央对外宣传媒体的外国专家及记者共13人到荔波，考察采访“中国南方喀斯特”世界自然遗产申报工作。新华社、贵州日报、贵州都市报、黔南电视台、新浪网、新华网等十余家媒体，也开展了申遗新闻报道。

2007年7月2—7日，全国政协委员、中国对外文化交流协会副会长、文化部原副部长艾青春率领人民日报、新华社、光明日报、经济日报、中国文化报、中国日报、北京周报、今日中国、美国《彼岸》杂志社、解放军总参谋部等10家媒体组成的中央媒体记者团到荔波进行为期6天的采访。2007年10月25日，荔波正式开通“世界自然遗产——中国南方喀斯特”网站，网址为http://www.southchinakarst.cn。

二、培训

按照与联合国教科文组织北京办事处签订的德国奔驰公司捐赠的14万美元合作协议，县遗产办与县委组织部于2008年12月4—6日在县世界自然遗产展示中心举办首期荔波遗产地管理干部培训班，培训县遗产办干部、茂兰管理局、樟江管理处、乡（镇）及县直机关部门干部60人。按照协议约定，2008年完成“世界自然遗产——荔波喀斯特”的光碟的制作编辑、印刷工作，并对7个乡（镇）的村民、干部进行培训，将光碟书籍发放到每个村寨，发放到全县中小学及县城宾馆。是年，县组织编印《荔波世界自然遗产管理干部手册》《遗产地基础管理知识》，制作《荔波世界自然遗产保护专题片》（DVD、VCD），发放到全县领导干部以及遗产地所在乡（镇）、村、组干部手中，VCD专题片发放到每个村寨并在电视台反复播放。同时，分别组织全县相关部门的领导干部以及乡（镇）、村、组干部培训，提高遗产保护意识。

2009年，在住建部和联合国教科文组织北京办事处帮助下，获得奔驰公司“自然之道——奔驰之道”150万元项目援助，编制了《遗产地保护项目专项规划》、编撰了《世界自然遗产荔波喀斯特管理手册》《世界自然遗产喀斯特基础管理知识》和“荔波遗产地保护与管理宣传光碟”，并对遗产地核心区基层管理人员进行了系统的培训和学习，世界遗产概念和价值保护观念深入遗产地的村村组组。

2011年，县遗产管理局组织开展了全县“世界自然遗产保护”演讲比赛活动；2012年在荔波二小开展了“我爱家乡、我爱荔波、说说家乡美——世界自然遗产地基本知识进校园”活动；2013年1月，在全县导游人员培训上进行了世界自然遗产保护与教育的专题培训。取得了良好的效果。2012年6月，配合联合国教科文组织驻华代表处在荔波举办了“中国世界遗产地保护和管理项目”培训，邀请了联合国教科文组织项目顾问英国的Peter Ogden先生、匈牙利的Gabor Szi lag先生进行主讲。中国南方喀斯特、四川大熊猫栖息地、庐山、三清山、武夷山、三江并流等世界遗产管理机构人员及县遗产管理局全体干部30余人参加了培训。共同探讨了世界遗产地利益相关者参与世界遗产事务的技术性问题；剖析了社区参与世界遗产可持续发展的机遇与挑战，分享了世界遗产地管理的成功案例经验，就世界遗产地保护管理项目实施进行了经验交流。

三、展示教育

2006年4月，为集中展示“申报中国南方喀斯特”荔波提名地喀斯特地质地貌与洞穴、生态过程及生物多样性、民族文化内涵，迎接IUCN专家组检查工作，樟江管理处在原大七孔游客中心基础上进行内外部装修、布展，增设投影仪、影像及民族银饰、服饰、工艺品等，供游客观赏，同时利用电子播音系统适时播放“中国南方喀斯特”世界自然遗产地等相关知识。

2007年4月10日开工建设“中国南方喀斯特”荔波展示中心，11月5日竣工，并正式对外界展出。中国南方喀斯特荔波展示中心建筑面积2820平方米，设有自然展厅4个、民族展厅4个。展示中心已成为荔波青少年课外活动中心。是年，县环境保护局、县科协共同将荔波世界自然遗产展示中心申报为贵州省环境教育基地和贵州省青少年活动教育基地。

为了加强世界自然遗产知识的宣传和教育，形成“呵护遗产、人人有责”的社会环境，“中国南方喀斯特荔波世界自然遗产展示中心”于2009年被评为“全国环境保护教育基地”“全国科普教育基地”“贵州师范大学教学科研基地”。于2013年被评为“贵州省科普教育示范基地”，展示中心年接待游客参观4万～5万人。

县遗产管理局还在县城广场开展了世界遗产摄影图片展活动；组织全县中小学生到展示中心参观，全年365天开放展示中心，供游客参观，有效地提高了公众参与意识，增强民众对世界文化、自然遗产的保护和尊重意识，把世界遗产工作置于全社会的支持、监督和保障之下，形成了“呵护遗产、人人有责”的社会环境；编制完成《中国南方喀斯特——荔波世界自然遗产地宣传册》和宣传海报的制作。积极参与县科技局组织的荔波县2015年“3·18”科技日宣传活动，向群众发放宣传手册2000多份。

县遗产管理局还组织评选活动，2012年，经过基层推荐、乡（镇）和部门把关产生候选人，最终评选出22位来自遗产地群众、干部和各有关部门的管理人员在世界自然遗产保护、管理、研究、宣传等方面做出突出贡献，群众公认的先进人物代表进行了表彰。树立了典型，表彰先进，弘扬先进的奉献精神和优良工作作风，激励全县人民为实现世界自然遗产保护、保存和展示做出新的更大贡献。

第六节　巡查与监督

荔波县自2007年以来开展遗产地巡查，确保世界自然遗产完整性保护，独山县麻尾黄后流域是荔波县世界自然遗产地樟江大七孔、小七孔的上游，麻尾工业园区建设是否会对遗产地核心区和核心区群众生产生活造成影响，2013年9月，县遗产管理局组织县环保局、县水利局相关专家及电视台记者到麻尾镇工业园区进行考察。通过深入麻尾工业园区实地调查，初步掌握了麻尾镇工业园区当前的建设情况和存在的问题。根据调查掌握的情况，世遗局、环保局、水利局三家共同形成了联合调查报告分别报送县领导和上级相关部门，引起省委、省政府和重视，省环保厅再次组织专人到麻尾镇工业园区考察，重申世界遗产保护的重要性，强调了保护与发展的协调。2013年9月，县遗产管理局组织人员到遗产地核心区洞塘乡督查环境保护，依据世界自然遗产保护管理要求，要求景区旅游发展公司及农家饭庄限期整改。

2009—2015年期间，县遗产管理局还参与遗产地采矿选址的督察和审核，配合遗产地核心区翁昂、永康、洞塘、瑶山、驾欧等乡镇政府做好矿产选址工作；参与对荔波山水投资公司5个旅游规划进行了审核和评审；对过境高铁建设、架欧—荔波高速公路、小七孔环景区公路等公共基础设施项目进行积极的配合和支持。对小七孔遗产地下游广西水电站的建设进行环保论证，提出了保护世界遗产的要求，暂停了该项目的开工建设。县遗产管理局还配合做好黔南州政协对小七孔污染的提案督办工作。按照住建部、省住建厅工作要求，完成“中国南方喀斯特”荔波世界自然遗产地定期检测报告的上报工作；配合做好国家财政部科学研究所对荔波世界自然遗产保护与利用的研究课题，并通过了国家财政部的评审。

2010年以来，县遗产管理局深入茂兰遗产地对洞塘—翁昂等遗产地核心区进行巡查，调查了解遗产地核心区变化情况，对遗产地核心区共开展巡查检查60余次，还利用开展巡查检查工作的同时，深入遗产地村寨开展遗产保护和森林防火宣传工作。同时，与多部门合作，与茂兰保护区管理局、黎明关水族乡联合行动，核查核心区内村民退耕地情况，查处破坏生态环境行为，反映了遗产地人员生态保护存在的问题和解决办法。

县遗产管理局在此期间与环保局、旅游局等部门对接收集整理荔波县水、空气等监测数据及遗产地核心区人流量等。为改善遗产地内社区居民生活环境，解决社区居民生产生活造成的环境破坏，积极收集相关项目资料，完成了《中国南方喀斯特荔波世界自然遗产地村寨基础设施提升（整改）项目建议书》和《荔波世界自然遗产地尧所村必左组环境整治项目建议书》的编制，并与县财政局沟通联系，落实项目建设。

第四章 科研考察与合作项目

第一节 国内专家科研考察

1981—1983年，贵州农学院林学系派人到茂兰旺牌山一带进行森林植物采集和森林植被调查。此期间，南京林业大学、贵州科学院、中山大学生物系、中国科学院植物研究所等单位，都先后到茂兰作植物标本采集和调查，并发现一些新种。

1984年4—6月，省林业厅、贵州农学院、贵阳师范学院等16个单位80余名各类专业人员对茂兰喀斯特森林区进行综合考察，涉及19个学科。撰写出专题考察和综合考察报告20篇。这次考察基本查清该区自然环境和生物资源，以及属于国家保护的动物、植物种类，考察成果获林业部科技进步二等奖、国家科技进步三等奖。考察报告汇编成《茂兰喀斯特森林区科学考察集》公开出版。这是最早对茂兰喀斯特森林进行系统研究的成果。在此基础上，县政府建立茂兰喀斯特森林保护区。

在综合考察的基础上，对综合考察时未能涉及的学科和未能深入调查的本底资源继续进行调查，先后对保护区内的兰花资源、国家重点保护野生植物资源、昆虫、蜘蛛、鱼类、贝类、竹类资源、森林资源等本底资源状况和生物多样性进行调查，取得这些资源的分布状况、资源量等有关资料。

在开展本底资源和生物多样性研究的同时，保护区管理局会同贵州农学院、贵州师范大学、国土资源部桂林岩溶研究所等有关科研单位，对喀斯特森林生态系统进行一些专题性研究，在喀斯特森林种群结构、群落类型、生物量构成、植物区系组成、猛禽生态学、岩溶作用与碳循环、森林环境恢复等研究领域取得多项研究成果。公开发表有关喀斯特森林和相关动物、植物研究论文30余篇，并将这些研究成果定期汇编成学术研究专集《喀斯特森林生态研究》公开出版，1993年出版第一集，1997年出版第二集。这些研究成果成为荔波县申报世界遗产的重要资料。

1995年5月，保护区管理局与贵州农学院联合，向林业部呈报“中国生态系统研究监测网络——贵州茂兰国家级自然保护区喀斯特森林生态系统定位研究”的课题申请书。同年11月，在南京召开的林业部森林生态系统定位研究站工作会议上通过的《中国森林、荒漠、湿地生态系统研究——监测网络建议发展规划》中，拟定在贵州茂兰国家级自然保护区建立全国唯一的喀斯特森林生态系统定位研究站。1995年12月—1996年3月，省林业厅组织定位站选址小组，在保护区内进行地点实地考察比较，确定地处核心区的板寨白鹇山为定位站站址，向林业部科技司呈报了选址报告。

1996年1月15日，贵州农学院林学系教授朱守谦主持的国家自然科学基金课题“退化喀斯特森林生态系统自然恢复的生态学过程”在茂兰进行研究。是年2月18日，保护区科研人员和贵州农学院林学系教授毛志中在考察中发现喀斯特森林高位湖泊。6月，四川省林业科学院院长、教授、生态学专家杨玉坡和森林生态研究所所长、教授李承彪到茂兰进行生态系统考察。8月，中国科学院院士、国家地质矿产部岩溶地质研究员、中国地质学会岩溶地质专业委员会主任、教授袁道先与全国政协委员、贵州农学院林学系教授周政贤在茂兰板寨的白鹇山考察。9月，著名植物学家、中国科学院植物研究所研究员、兰花专家、教授陈心启到茂兰进行兰科植物考察。

1996—1997年，省林业厅和林业部相继拨给部分资金，在白鹇山先期建立科学研究观测站，安装自动观测仪器对林区降水和水文进行观测。1998年1月，观测站正式建成并开始观测，科研人员在观测站区进行喀斯特森林凋落物等一些科研项目研究。

1998年5月，GEF中国自然保护区管理项目小型科研鼓励基金课题《民族文化与传统生产方式对茂兰保护区的影响》在茂兰进行研究。

1999年4月，茂兰保护区珍稀野生植物白花兜兰参加昆明世博会展览。

2003年1月6—21日，省申遗办邀请贵州省政府聘请的申遗专家、建设部风景名胜专家顾问、中科院博士生导师、地理科学与资源研究所研究员宋林华，贵州师大地质学院教授黎道洪，省地勘院教授李兴中等一行，对荔波樟江风景名胜区和茂兰自然保护区，独山黄后地下河等地进行考察。通过考察，认为贵州锥状喀斯特景观及其演化具有很高的遗产价值，而未被人为破坏的地貌景观、水文景观、生物景观主要集中在荔波樟江景区和茂兰国家级自然保护区。

是年2月11—20日，贵州师大教授屠玉麟、黎道宏，贵州地质设计院高级工程师李中兴，贵州电视台编导包晓竹、蔡大海、刘烨等到荔波考察收集资料。

2003年8月，中国科学院热带林业研究所首席科学家白嘉雨到茂兰考察。

2004年4月，云南、贵州、广西石灰岩地区兰科植物保护育研讨会在茂兰举行。

2005年12月，茂兰保护区被纳入全国野生动物疫源疫病118个监测站之一。

2006年7月9—12日，国际著名生物多样性专家、博士马敬能（中欧生物多样性项目负责人，中国环境与发展国际合作委员会生物多样性工作组主席）和中国科学院研究员解焱应邀到茂兰实地考察，对茂兰喀斯特森林生物多样性和迎接IUCN专家考察的线路作评价和建议。

2007年1月，国家重点基础研究项目（973）在茂兰启动。

是年5月21日，中国科学院武汉植物园博士康明到茂兰进行伞花木考察。

茂兰管理局针对保护区内众多的生物资源，开展珍稀濒危、特有和经济价值大的动物、植物种类驯化、繁殖和人工饲养、培育，建立动物饲养场和苗圃，进行竹鼠、果子狸、猕猴等野生动物人工饲养，在保护区内的瑶族村寨——洞常建立科技扶贫示范点，指导群众人工饲养野生动物。还进行华南五针松、深山含笑、棕竹、红豆杉、鱼尾葵、梅树、龟背竹、兰花等珍稀和观赏树木、花卉的栽培和育苗试验，均获得成功。对保护区内群众编制凉席的黔竹进行资源调查，开展生物量、产量和利用方式研究。

2010—2012年度，获得联合国教科文组织“奔驰中国世界自然遗产地保护管理项目”6.5万美元援助对荔波世界自然遗产地开展“动物物种多样性本底调查”。并于2012年7月通过了联合国教科文组织驻华代表处顾问、中国科学院院士汪松及国内动物多样性专家组的评审。本次调查共收录动物物种1066种，隶属46目195科。被列入IUCN红色名录的有16种，列入濒危野生动植物国际贸易公约（CITES）的有17种，列入中国物种红色名录的有69种，列入国家重点保护野生动物名录的有49种。此次调查发现新纪录4种，新种16种。项目所建荔波世界自然遗产地动物多样性数据库在贵州省尚属首例。

第二节　国外专家科研考察

1989年8月，联合国教科文组织和国际地质科学联合会决定将茂兰作为IGCP（国际地质对比计划）299项研究的考察对比点，IGCP299项（地质、气候、水文与岩溶形成）有23个国家，中国科学院院士袁道先任该项目的首席科学家和工作组组长。1991年7月，中国、日本、美国、德国、伊朗、泰国、英国、意大利、匈牙利等14个国家的52位专家和学者，到茂兰保护区进行为期3天的IGCP国际喀斯特地貌对比考察。

1992年4月，日本土壤学家Kazudo Yoshion到茂兰考察喀斯特森林土壤。

1994年3月，美国2名洞穴研究专家到茂兰作探险洞穴考察。

1995年3月，地质矿产部桂林岩溶研究所邀请斯洛文尼亚洞穴考察队14人到茂兰的瑶所、三岔河等地进行为期半个月的考察。

1998年3月，法国国家科研中心生态与进化功能研究所博士霍曼勒到茂兰考察。

1999年4月，英国伦敦皇家科学院生物学专家艾伦教授到茂兰进行钙化生物沉积物考察研究。

是年5月，英国亚里桑那大学加速器（AMS）实验室教授Warren Belk到茂兰保护区考察。

2000年5月，美国加州大学副教授、博士瓦尔特到茂兰进行翼手目科类种群数量以及栖息环境研究。

2000年11月，全球岩溶生态系统对比科学目标（IGCP448项目）国际执行计划确定茂兰为对比点。

2002年8月，日本林业技术协会理事长弘中义夫、国际事务部部长加藤秀丽等5人到茂兰进行科学考察。

2005年11月，世界保护联盟保护洞穴和喀斯特地形工作组主席、国际喀斯特自然遗产管理专家、澳大利亚查尔斯特大学教授史密斯应邀到茂兰考察。2006年9月2—10日，史密斯与国际著名喀斯特学家、新西兰奥克兰大学教授威廉姆斯，国际洞穴协会原主席、澳大利亚悉尼大学教授朱丽娅应邀到茂兰考察。

2006年1月，中国荔波原生梅花国际研讨会在茂兰召开，韩国、日本的专家参加研讨会。

2007年8月21日，日本东京农工大学原久雄教授到茂兰开展森林生态系统养分循环研究。同年9月10日，澳大利亚西澳林业发展委员会执行主席、植物学家William Hollingwcrth、中国林业科学院科研所研究员李维长到茂兰考察社会林业发展情况。是年11月，东南亚地区生物圈保护区网络（SeaBRnet）第五次会议暨中国生物圈保护区网络（CBRN）第九次大会在茂兰召开，会议以“生物多样性与促进民族文化多样性的保护与可持续发展”为主题进行讨论，参加会议的有印尼、日本、马来西亚、老挝、韩

2006年9月，世界遗产保护联盟首席专家史密斯（左四）在荔波实地考察

国、泰国、新西兰、越南等国家代表及国内所有生物圈保护区、国家级保护区成员代表。

到2008年，茂兰保护区科研部门与美国、英国、日本、法国、斯洛文尼亚等国家的科研机构建立国际合作伙伴关系，共接待17个国家的专家、学者150人次，研究内容涉及森林生态、洞穴生物、生物岩溶、岩溶环境、洞穴形态与发育、古气候、古环境重建、地貌、水文、地质、土壤、陆生贝类、蜘蛛、昆虫、鸟类、兽类、鱼类、两栖类、爬行类、自然景观、人文景观、民族意识、生态旅游和民族地区经济发展模式等学科。

1989—2008年茂兰保护区科研项目一览表

表2-3

序号	项目名称	取得时间	负责人	项目来源	完成时间	执行情况
1	贵州野生灵长类调查（黔南部分）	1989年	冉景丞	贵州野生猫科动物调查	1993年	已完成
2	黔南野生黑熊、豹猫资源调查	1992年	冉景丞	贵州省林业厅	1994年	已完成
3	国际岩溶作用与碳循环对比研究	1992年	冉景丞	ICCP379项目	1998年	已完成
4	黔南野生兰科植物调查	1994年	魏鲁明	贵州野生兰科植物调查之一	1994年	获贵州省林业厅科技进步一等奖
5	荔波县森林资源二类调查	1994年	魏鲁明	荔波县林业局	1995年	已完成
6	茂兰喀斯特森林群落种群结构的研究	1994年	魏鲁明	贵州省自然科学基金	1996年	已完成
7	荔波洞穴研究	1994年	冉景丞	IGCP448项目	2005年	其中部分内容获黔南州科技进步二等奖
8	退化喀斯特生态系统的恢复过程	1995年	魏鲁明	贵州大学	1996年	已完成
9	茂兰喀斯特林区几种猛禽繁殖生态观察	1995年	冉景丞	中国西南野生动物研究青年基金	1998年	已完成
10	茂兰保护区猛禽年动态变化研究	1995年	冉景丞	中国野生动物保护协会	1998年	已完成
11	茂兰喀斯特林区部分隼形目猛禽繁殖生态研究	1995年	冉景丞	贵州省自然科学基金	1998年	已完成
12	亚热带喀斯特林区岩溶作用与碳循环研究	1995年	冉景丞	国土资源部岩溶动力学开放实验室	2005年	已完成
13	茂兰保护区有效管理调查与研究	1997年	魏鲁明	美国福特基金资助项目	1997年	已完成
14	茂兰喀斯特森林降雨及水文观测	1997年	魏鲁明	茂兰保护区	1997年	已完成
15	国际岩溶生态对比研究	1997年	冉景丞	ICCP448项目	2005年	已完成
16	贵州野生动物资源调查	1998年	冉景丞	国家林业局贵州省林业厅	2001年	已完成
17	贵州野生动物资源普查	1998年	冉景丞	国家林业局	2001年	已完成
18	表层岩溶生态系统水分储集运移和植被响应研究	1998年	冉景丞	国家自然科技基金	2002年	已完成
19	民族文化与传统生存方式对茂兰保护区的影响	1998年	陈正仁	国家林业局GEFSRG-9805项目	2002年	已完成
20	中国西南地区陆生贝类资源调查	1998年	冉景丞	管理局自立项目	2003年	已完成
21	亚热带喀斯特森林区岩溶作用与碳循环研究	1998年	冉景丞	桂林岩溶研究所	2004年	黔南州科技进步二等奖
22	退化喀斯特森林生态系统恢复生态学过程及恢复技术研究	1998年	魏鲁明	国家自然科学基金	2005年	已完成

续表2－3

序号	项目名称	取得时间	负责人	项目来源	完成时间	执行情况
23	荔波县白颈长尾雉资源调查	1999年	熊志斌	荔波县科技局	2000年	已完成
24	茂兰竹类资源调查研究	1999年	余登利	荔波县科技局	2000年	已完成
25	茂兰资源昆虫调查研究	1999年	谭成江	荔波县科技局	2000年	已完成
26	茂兰喀斯特森林猛禽资源调查	1999年	熊志斌	茂兰保护区	2002年	已完成
27	中国西南岩溶生态系统研究	1999年	冉景丞	国土资源部重点科技项目	2004年	已完成
28	茂兰保护区生态旅游规划	2000年	魏鲁明	人与生物圈委员会资助项目	2000年	已完成
29	贵州白颈长尾雉资源分布调查研究	2000年	熊志斌	IUCN物种保护委员会	2001年	已完成
30	西南岩溶石山区岩溶水资源潜力及生态环境地质综合调查评价	2000年	冉景丞	新一轮国土资源大调查	2001年	已完成
31	茂兰昆虫研究	2000年	陈会明	贵州省自然科学基金	2003年	已完成
32	茂兰景观昆虫研究	2000年	冉景丞	贵州省重点基金	2003年	贵州省科技进步三等奖
33	茂兰自然保护区鸟类群落多样性研究	2000年	冉景丞	香港观鸟会	2003年	已完成
34	贵州茂兰喀斯特林区白鹇生境选择研究	2000年	熊志斌	贵州省自然科学基金	2004年	已完成
35	茂兰野生兰科植物的研究	2000年	魏鲁明	华南石灰岩地区野生兰科植物保护项目之一	2004年	已完成
36	少数民族社区参与喀斯特森林湿地资源管理	2001年	冉景丞	IUCN荷兰委员会	2003年	荔波科技三等奖、获福特汽车环保奖
37	濒危植物掌叶木种子生态特征研究	2001年	熊志斌	茂兰保护区管理局	2003年	已完成
38	茂兰喀斯特林区蜘蛛多样性调查	2001年	陈会明	管理局自立项目	2004年	已完成
39	茂兰保护区珠江防护林体系建设工程	2001年	姚正明	贵州省林业厅	2007年	已完成
40	茂兰自然保护区二期基本建设可行性研究	2002年	冉景丞	管理局自立项目	2002年	已完成
41	少数民族社区参与喀斯特森林湿地管理	2002年	冉景丞	IUCN物种保护委员会小额湿地赠款项目	2004年	已完成
42	洞穴生物研究	2002年	冉景丞	单位课题	2006年	已完成
43	兰科石斛属药用植物在石漠化治理中的作用研究	2004年	冉景丞	国土资源部岩溶动和学重点实验室	2007年	已完成
44	石斛人工栽培技术在石漠治理中的作用研究	2005年	冉景丞	国土资源部岩溶动力学重点实验室	2007年	已完成
45	茂兰国家级自然保护区珍稀树种造林示范基地	2006年	姚正明	贵州省林业厅	2010年	已完成
46	野生动物疫源疫病监测	2006年	冉景丞	国家林业局	长期	实施中
47	茂兰喀斯特森林区濒危野生雉类分布与生存环境研究	2007年	熊志斌	黔南州科技局	2009年	已完成
48	茂兰喀斯特石漠化生态环境植物多样性调查研究	2007年	熊志斌	贵州地球化学研究所	2009年	已完成

续表2-3

序号	项目名称	取得时间	负责人	项目来源	完成时间	执行情况
49	茂兰喀斯特林区大型土壤动物对凋落物分解过程的贡献研究	2008年	冉景丞	贵州省科技基金	2010年	已完成
50	喀斯特森林水土保持与生物成土作用研究	2008年	冉景丞	省长基金	2010年	已完成
51	茂兰保护区仿野生人工种植铁皮石斛技术研究	2008年	冉景丞	贵州省林业厅	2010年	已完成
52	荔波县野生梅资源调查研究	2008年	魏鲁明	贵州省科技基金	2010年	已完成

第三节 国际国内合作交流

一、国际交流活动

2009—2015年，荔波县积极构建国际保护网络，将荔波世界自然遗产保护纳入世界的舞台。2009年8月中国南方喀斯特三省市与美国猛犸洞国家公园建立了“友好姊妹公园”。2011年4月，在中国“人与生物圈”国家委员会的倡导下，中国生物圈保护区网络成员代表在贵州荔波世界自然遗产地、茂兰世界生物圈保护区共同发表了中国生物圈保护区“生态旅游”《荔波宣言》。主张环境和生态保护优先；尊重和保护文化多样性；实施生态教育；鼓励社区参与，保护地方民众利益的原则。

2012年6月，由中国联合国教科文组织全国委员会秘书处、中国住房和城乡建设部风景名胜区管理办公室、联合国教科文组织驻华代表处主办，贵州省住房和城乡建设厅、黔南州人民政府协办，荔波县人民政府承办“世界自然遗产保护与可持续发展国际论坛”于5月31日—6月3日在荔波召开。参加论坛的有来自世界自然保护联盟、世界遗产中心和加拿大、德国、英国、匈牙利等13个国家、国内18个省（市）40多位世界遗产地官员，以及从事世界遗产保护与管理的专家、学者代表近200人。会议高度评价了荔波积极探索和实践世界自然遗产保护与合理利用，在遗产地所采取的保护性建设和基础设施建设措施，提升了遗产地的环境质量，促进了社区经济的发展，基本实现了世界遗产的保护与可持续发展的“荔波模式”，并形成了具有广泛代表意义的“荔波共识”，为国际世界遗产保护提供了富有成效的经验借鉴案例。为世界遗产可持续发展、社区居民的作用与潜力的发掘、人与自然和谐等方面的工作理清了思路，提供了决策参考。

2013年7月21日，在荔波举办“发展中国家世界自然遗产保护的挑战与探索”国际论坛。在中国联合国教科文组织全国委员会、中华人民共和国住房和城乡建设部、联教科文组织驻华代表处、世界自然保护联盟（IUCN）北京办事处的大力支持下，论坛由生态文明贵阳国际论坛组委会主办，贵州省黔南州人民政府、贵州省住房和城乡建设厅、贵州师范大学协办，贵州省荔波县人民政府承办。包括中国在内的8个国家和地区从事世界遗产管理和研究的官员、专家代表、县直部门、乡镇、企业200余人参加了此次国际论坛。在这次论坛交流中，就世界自然遗产申报理念、遗产地环境压力与生态建设、遗产保护现状与模式、遗产评估与面临的挑战和对策、遗产保护社区参与和共管、遗产地保护立法与政府财政支持、跨国跨地区合作等进行了探索与交流，并形成了富有积极意义的“荔波共识”在国际层面上引起了强烈的反响，论坛的举办达到了预期目标，获得了圆满成功。

二、国内协作活动

荔波县加强与“中国南方喀斯特”第一批世界遗产地三省市的交流与合作，相互促进、共同发展。2009年6月，县遗产管理局牵头组织云南石林、重庆武隆在荔波县举办了首届“中国南方喀斯特保护管理年会”，并形成了“中国南方喀斯特世界自然遗产保护管理联席会议制度”。为此，云南石林、重庆武隆分别于2011年、2012年举办了“中国南方喀斯特保护管理年会”，实现信息共享和交流合作机制。2013年7月，经报请省住建厅、住建部和联合国教科文组织，在荔波县举办了“中国南方喀斯特”三省市保护管理工作年会。会议对“中国南方喀斯特”保护管理委员会的章程、资金、学术期刊进行了研讨，就常态化工作目标和内容形成了共识。

2014年7月11日，贵州省住房和城乡建设厅牵头组织召开的主题为“中国南方喀斯特系列管理框架研讨会”。会议就成立“中国南方喀斯特”世界自然遗产保护协调委员会和对《“中国南方喀斯特”世界自然遗产保护协调委员会章程》及《“中国南方喀斯特”世界自然遗产保护协调委员会资金管理办法》进行了充分研讨，形成了决议，达成了共识。成立了四省市七地联合的“中国南方喀斯特世界自然遗产保护管理协调委员会”，由所涉及省（自治区、直辖市）住房和城乡建设厅（园林局）轮流主持整体的管理协调工作，轮值期为1年。2015年度由贵州省轮值主持。

2015年12月，应中国南方喀斯特保护管理协调委员会工作要求，将在荔波举办“中国南方喀斯特保护管理年会”，讨论轮值换届，推选下任轮值省份和主席，对2015年保护管理工作进行总结和审议财务支出；讨论遗产地保护监测评估报告、科研项目合作、联合捆绑宣传和培训、网站建设等内容。

附1：

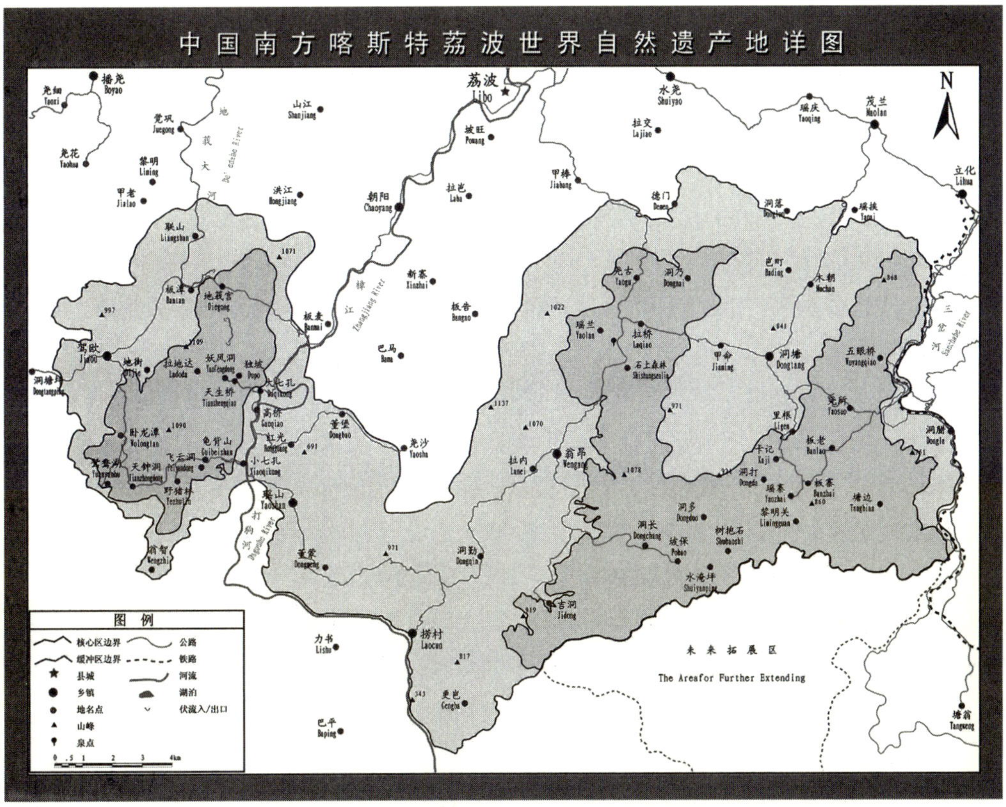

中国南方喀斯特荔波世界自然遗产地详图

附2：

世界遗产委员会决议

决议：31 COM 8B.11

世界遗产委员会

1.已审议文件WHC-07/31.COM/8B和WHC-07/31.COM/INF.8B.2，

2.基于满足世界遗产标准（七）、标准（八），将中国的中国南方喀斯特列入世界遗产名录。

3.通过以下突出普遍价值的阐述：

中国南方在喀斯特特征和地貌景观方面的多样性是无与伦比的。该遗产包括了精心选出的区域，这些区域保护和展示了这些喀斯特特征和地貌景观的最好范例，因而具有突出普遍的价值。中国南方喀斯特是由三个相关联的片区组成的系列遗产，荔波喀斯特和石林喀斯特各由两个部分组成，武隆喀斯特由三个部分组成。

标准（七）：中国南方喀斯特代表了世界上湿润热带到亚热带喀斯特景观最壮观的范例。石林县的石林被认为是最好的自然现象和世界上该类喀斯特的最好的参照。该片区包括了发育在白云质灰岩中的乃古石林和出现在湖泊之中的蓑衣山石林。较其他发育了剑状喀斯特的地区而言，石林包含了更丰富的剑状喀斯特形态，更丰富的形态和色彩多样性，并随不同天气和光的条件而变化。荔波的锥状和塔状喀斯特同样被认为是世界上同类喀斯特的参照地，形成了特殊而又美丽的地貌景观。武隆喀斯特包含了被称为天坑的巨大垮塌洼地和罕见高度的天生桥，天生桥之间延伸着深度很大的无顶洞穴。这些壮观的喀斯特特征有着世界级的品质。

标准（八）：石林和荔波所展示的喀斯特特征和景观都是全球的参照地。在石林县，石林喀斯特发育的主要阶段经历了2.7亿年，跨越了从二叠纪到现今的四个主要地质时期，展示了这种喀斯特阶段演化的特征。荔波出露的碳酸盐岩发育于不同地质年代，经过几百万年的溶蚀，塑造形成了显著的峰丛（锥状喀斯特）和峰林（塔状喀斯特）。荔波喀斯特包含了众多高耸的锥峰和深陷漏斗，以及陷落河流和悠长的河流洞穴。武隆代表了经历了显著抬升的内陆喀斯特高原，其巨大的漏斗和天生桥是中国南方天坑景观的代表。武隆景观包含了世界上最大的江河系统之一、长江及其支流的历史证据。

该遗产得到很好的管理，有明确的管理规划和各利益相关者的有效参与。该遗产具有强大的国际网络支持其持续的研究和管理。三个片区中，武隆由于地处偏远而受到最少的人类（活动）影响，保留了在其他类似地区已被削弱的自然价值。要求在扩展和细化缓冲区方面继续做出努力，保护上游汇水区及下游河段和地下延伸部分，从而维护水质，以达到确保遗产地及其地下作用和生态系统长期保护的水平。在武隆，应考虑对核心区的边界进行扩展，此外，（建立）一个单一的、具景观规模的缓冲区将是一个明显的改进，从而包括芙蓉峡谷以北所有的天坑要素。少数民族的传统保护是（石林和荔波）两个遗产片区的重要特征，要求喀斯特与少数民族（石林的彝族、荔波的水族、瑶族和布依族）文化特征与传统之间的关系在就地管理方面得到持续的认同和尊重。该遗产今后的潜在拓展，要求制定一个有效协同各个遗产片区管理的框架。

4.建议缔约国考虑这是一个较大的世界遗产提名地的第一期提名，并考虑在其随后的提名中考虑是否将整个系列提名合理地缩减为一个（提名地）数量较小的系列提名，并且再用一期申报完成，而不是再用两期申报完成（见IUCN中国南方喀斯特评估报告5.2部分）。标准（九）的潜在申报应该在最终的整个系列提名中考虑。

5.要求缔约国重新考虑武隆片区的边界，从而对IUCN就该（遗产）提名评估（报告）中所提出的有关意见进行处理。

6.敦促缔约国继续做出努力扩展和细化缓冲区以保护提名遗产地的上游汇水区，特别是要确保汇水区必要的长期保护管理得到落实。

7.欢迎认同当地居民有益参与管理提名遗产地的重要性，并要求在进行第二期次提名申报时对当地居民的参与和维护相关的土著社区的传统活动给予特别考虑和注意。

8.同样欢迎缔约国中国有意与缔约国越南讨论该（遗产）提名跨国界情况的意向。

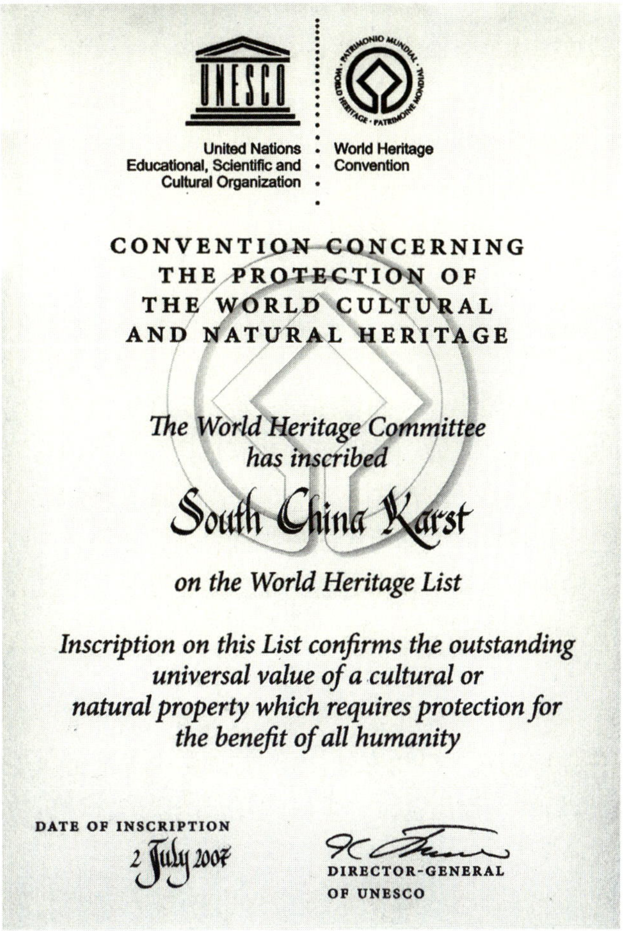

附3：

荔波宣言

在联合国教科文组织（UNESCO）“人与生物圈”计划（MAB）创立四十周年之际，中国人与生物圈国家委员会在贵州荔波世界自然遗产地、茂兰世界生物圈保护区举办“全国生物圈保护区生态旅游”专题研讨会。会议时间，经过全体与会代表酝酿、交流和讨论，一致通过《荔波宣言》。宣言全文如下：

人类正面临一个历史从未有过的挑战：随着全球划时代的到来，消费经济的增长，自然之源的国度消耗，世界范围的生态与环境出现空前危机。为此，人类开始了保护地球家园的行动！中国作为一个负责任的大国，提出了以“生态文明”为主导价值的科学发展，并致力于将这一战略构想落实于各项事业，以主人翁的姿态加入到人类这一伟大行动中。

今天，自然和生态资源的脆弱及不可再生性，与人类的活动对环境和生态资源的巨大耗损的矛盾日益突出。为此，倡导、鼓励和实行生态旅游已成为我们的共识，借此促进人类与自然的和谐相处，实现人类社会可持续发展的美好愿景。

对于生态旅游，我们主张以下原则：环境和生态保护优先；尊重和保护文化多样性；实施生态教育；鼓励社区参与，保护地方民众利益。

我们认可生态旅游的主旨，即生态旅游应该保护好自然资源和生物及文化的多样性，维持资源利用的可持续性，促进保护区自身与社区共同发展，建立人与自然和谐共处的局面，促进生态文明建设。我们相信生态旅游可以在人类与环境之间搭起友好的桥梁，恢复人类与自然间的友好共生关系。我们认为，这些基于创新理念和价值的行为不是人类的义举和善举，而是人类对历史痛定思痛的反省和自觉，是人类自救和救赎!

让我们携起手来，为守护好地球家园贡献每一个人的力量。

附四：

石林决议

2011年11月25日由国家住房与城乡建设部城建司、贵州省住房与城乡建设厅、云南省住房与城乡建设厅、重庆市园林局以及石林、荔波、武隆三地政府部门和遗产地管理部门参加的中国南方喀斯特2011年年会在云南石林举行，经与会者共同讨论商定，形成以下决议：

一、为了加强中国南方喀斯特世界自然遗产的保护和管理，在联合国教科文组织《保护文化与自然遗产公约》的框架下，中国南方喀斯特世界自然遗产建立联合长效工作机制——“中国南方喀斯特世界自然遗产保护管理委员会”（以下简称“管委会”）。

二、管委会设于贵州省住房与城乡建设厅，主任1名由贵州省建设厅主要领导担任，副主任2名由云南省住房与城乡建设厅、重庆市园林局分管领导担任，委员若干名分别由三地政府分管领导和三地管理机构主要领导担任；管委会下设秘书处，秘书长1名由贵州省风景名胜区协会主要领导担任，副秘书长3名分别由云南石林、贵州荔波、重庆武隆三地遗产管理机构主要领导担任。管委会秘书处设专职工作人员负责日常工作。

三、管委会主要工作职责：负责中国南方喀斯特世界自然遗产地保护管理整体协调工作，包括中国南方喀斯特世界自然遗产总体保护规划的制定、对三地遗产保护管理工作的督导、对世界遗产委员会的定期工作报告、构建统一对国内外的宣传平台和开展与国内外其他世界遗产地的培训与交流、学术研讨活动，以及组织专家对三地开展专项工作。

四、组成中国南方喀斯特世界自然遗产管理委员会专家顾问组，聘请国内外专家进行保护管理的专项工作和技术工作。

五、管委会工作经费由云南石林、贵州荔波、重庆武隆共同出资，秘书处建立专项账户进行台账管理，定期进行工作汇报和财务报告。

贵州省住房和城乡建设厅遗产管理办公室
云南省住房和城乡建设厅遗产管理办公室
重庆市园林局
贵州省荔波县世界遗产管理办公室
云南石林风景名胜区管理局
重庆市武隆县世界自然遗产管理委员会
2011年11月25日

第三篇
人口　民族　宗教

荔波县从1978年至2008年进行过三次、四次、五次人口普查，1978年全县总人口118294人。1982年7月全国第三次人口普查，全县总户数24327户，总人口127497人，其中，男性64285人、女性63212人。1990年7月，全县开展第四次全国人口普查，全县总户数29071户，总人口144086人，其中，男性73935人、女性70151人。2000年11月，全县开展第五次全国人口普查，全县总户数43625户，总人口171366人，其中，男性90130人、女性81236人。2008年，全县6镇11乡（5个民族乡）总人口171454人。

荔波县为少数民族聚居区，境内世居民族有布依族、水族、汉族、苗族、瑶族5个民族。1982年第三次人口普查统计，境内常住人口有17个民族和1个未识别民族，全县总人口127497人中，少数民族人口110688人，占总人口的86.82%。人口在100人以上的民族有7个：布依族75039人、水族25812人、汉族16809人、苗族4872人、瑶族3832人、壮族796人、侗族225人。境内世居民族有布依族、水族、汉族、苗族、瑶族5个民族，各民族风情文化丰富多彩。中共十一届三中全会后，县委、县政府加强民族工作，促进各民族大团结、大繁荣。

荔波县有少数群众信仰佛教、天主教、基督教，并有一定的活动。

第一章 人 口

第一节 人口分布

1978年，全县总人口118294人。1980年，全县总人口123510人，全县人口密度为50.5人/平方公里。

1991年，全县5镇12乡总人口为142379人。其中，玉屏镇16281人、永康水族乡5493人、水尧水族乡5795人、水利水族乡5281人、朝阳镇10379人、瑶山瑶族乡5159人、驾欧乡6798人、捞村乡3339人、翁昂乡4073人、茂兰镇8424人、立化镇3197人、瑶麓瑶族乡1432人、佳荣乡13740人、洞塘乡7480人、甲良镇19952人、播尧乡17122人、方村乡8434人。人口密度为58.3人/平方公里。

2008年，全县6镇11乡（5个民族乡）总人口171454人。其中，玉屏镇23152人、永康水族乡6011人、水尧水族乡7427人、水利水族乡6433人、朝阳镇12222人、瑶山瑶族乡5860人、驾欧乡7899人、捞村乡3738人、翁昂乡4482人、茂兰镇9573人、立化镇3753人、瑶麓瑶族乡1537人、佳荣镇16303人、洞塘乡8654人、甲良镇24403人、播尧乡19894人、方村乡10113人。全县人口密度为70.2人/平方公里。其中，密度最高为县城所在地玉屏镇128.6人/平方公里，最低为翁昂乡28.4人/平方公里。

第二节 人口构成

一、性别构成

1978年，全县总人口118294人，其中，男性59000人，占总人口的49.88%，女性59294人，占总人口的50.12%，男女比例为99：100。1991年，全县总人口142379人，其中，男性72689人，占总人口的51.05%，女性69690人，占总人口的48.95%，男女比例为104：100。

从2006年起，县人口计生部门开始统计出生人口性别比。2008年，全县总人口171454人，其中，男性87828人，占总人口的51.23%，女性83626人，占总人口的48.77%，男女比例为105：100。是年，出生婴儿男女性别比为125.03：100。

二、年龄构成

1990年第四次全国人口普查年龄结构分组统计，县内0～19岁67229人，占总人口的46.66%；20～54岁61536人，占总人口的42.71%；55～99岁15320人，占总人口的10.63%；百岁以上老人2人。

2000年第五次人口普查，全县人口年龄结构按5岁进行分组，100岁划分为23个年龄组。其中，第五组20～24岁组占总人口的8.84%，第六组25～29岁年龄组占总人口的10.12%，第七组30～34岁组占总人口的9.91%；第五组至第七组总计49470人，占总人口的28.87%；50岁以上人口29739人，占总人口的17.35%；15岁以下人口48208人，占总人口的28.13%；百岁以上老人8人。

三、城乡构成

1979年，全县非农业人口0.72万人，占总人口的6%，农业人口11.35万人，占94%；城镇人口0.71万人，占5.87%，乡村人口11.37万人，占94.3%。

1991年，非农业人口0.91万人，占总人口的6.39%，农业人口13.37万人，占总人口的93.90%；城镇人口0.78万人，占总人口5.48%，乡村人口13.5万人，占总人口的94.82%。

2008年，非农业人口1.59万人，占总人口的9.27%，农业人口15.55万人，占总人口的90.69%；城镇人口1.51万人，占总人口8.81%，乡村人口15.63万人，占总人口的91.16%。

四、职业构成

1982年，全社会从业人员48200人。单位职工4500人，乡村从业人员43700人；抽样统计集体所有制单位职工共705人，其中从事工业294人，运输业13人，建筑业184人，商业、饮食业132人，居民服务业33人，卫生教育业10人，金融业39人。

1990年，全社会从业人员66400人。其中，乡村从业人员60000人，城镇私企和个体从业人员1100人，单位职工5200人，其他100人。抽样统计全民所有制单位职工共4591人，从事农业、林业、牧业、渔业、水利业246人，工业373人，交通运输邮电业155人，商业、饮食、物资供销业472人，公用事业、居民服务业39人，卫生社会福利业299人，教育、文化艺术和广播电视业1646人，科研、综合技术服务业14人，金融、保险业154人，机关、党政和社会团体1193人。

2008年，全县单位职工7500人，城镇私营企业和个体从业人员3800人，乡村从业人员89600人，其他100人，全社会从业人员总计101000人。其中，第一产业65100人，占64.46%；第二产业4600人，占4.55%；第三产业31300人，占30.99%。

五、文化构成

1982年7月第三次人口普查统计，总人口中，大学毕业生191人、大学肄业或在校12人、高中2742人、初中11098人、小学31041人；12周岁及12周岁以上的文盲、半文盲人口46964人。

1990年第四次人口普查统计，总人口中，大学毕业生107人、大学专科312人、中专1609人、高中2673人、初中16453人、小学57797人；15周岁及15周岁以上的文盲、半文盲人口37299人。

2000年第五次人口普查统计，在6周岁及6周岁以上人口中，小学80202人、初中36986人、高中4775人、中专4779人、大学专科1538人、大学本科287人、研究生2人；文盲和半文盲24274人。

2008年，全县有中等教育在校学生1942人，普通中学在校学生11674人，普通小学在校学生17488人，学龄儿童入学率99.60%。

六、姓氏构成

（一）全县姓氏

据1982年第三次人口普查统计，境内有姓氏200个。2008年年末，全县姓氏共有213个。

213个姓氏为：莫、覃、何、蒙、潘、吴、韦、黎、卢、白、柏、梁、玉、常、张、唐、李、杨、夏、欧、刘、高、罗、王、田、陈、邹、姚、徐、陆、邓、周、滕、钦、龙、全、尹、林、沈、郭、葛、朱、石、肖、谢、黄、郑、雷、廖、彭、芮、孔、蔡、蒋、赵、曾、邬、严、金、赖、程、洪、熊、向、袁、贾、杜、苏、马、龚、侯、路、俞、孙、胡、申、智、舒、游、代、吕、钟、曹、巫、谭、詹、魏、汤、岑、宋、崔、董、范、焦、余、姜、池、温、孟、饶、郝、庄、冉、庞、丁、童、宁、查、安、秦、汪、梅、许、阮、贺、伍、尚、卓、尤、席、涂、邱、皮、兰、聂、于、桑、艾、江、斐、封、乔、陶、傅、粟、花、毛、练、郜、骆、冯、浦、简、颜、康、乐、文、计、钱、易、任、史、瞿、犹、曲、衣、管、班、万、戎、韩、叶、左、咸、古、柯、倪、樊、帅、顾、方、柴、段、符、麦、刁、祝、商、翁、溪、翟、荆、敖、齐、岳、甘、匡、禹、凌、幸、邵、鲁、璩、戴、祁、姬、房、盛、按、费、麻、闵、华、施、逢、瓦、侣、付、传、芦、邸、项、司马。

（二）世居少数民族姓氏

1.布依族姓氏。境内布依族姓氏有罗、卢、杨、覃、蒙、韦、玉、柏、陆、莫、欧、黎、姚、周、白、王、何、李、陈、龙、吴、谭、董、徐、张、梁、邓、宋、向、林、袁、马、饶、全、熊、童36个。人口较多的有莫、覃、何、蒙、韦、罗、姚、欧、黎、吴、柏等姓氏。莫姓主要分布在方村、甲良、阳凤、地莪、驾欧等地；覃姓主要分布在朝阳镇、玉屏镇时来、甲良镇甲站等地；何姓主要分布在捞村、翁昂、瑶山的王蒙、驾欧的拉欧及新街等地；蒙姓主要分布在玉屏镇的板吉村；韦姓主要分布在播尧乡的觉巩及地莪、朝阳镇的洪江及三江等地；罗姓主要分布在永康水族乡的甲棒和播尧乡的老场等地；欧姓主要分布在茂兰镇瑶庆、佳荣镇威岩和立化镇更班附近的村寨；黎姓主要分布在播尧乡的觉巩；姚姓主要分布在洞塘乡久安和板寨；吴姓主要分布在播尧乡的地莪；柏姓主要分布在甲良镇的甲站。其他姓氏主要散居于县城和除瑶麓以外的16个乡（镇）。

2.水族姓氏。境内水族姓氏有潘、蒙、吴、姚、常、韦、欧、何、邓、石、杨、张、谢、王、左、龙、卢、江、全、肖、陆、陈、罗、胡、梁、舒、黄、龚、刘、莫、程、孟、李、朱、田、余、廖37个。境内水族聚族而居，一个村寨或几个村寨甚至一个乡为一个姓氏居住。潘姓主要居住在佳荣镇的拉先、岜鲜、地牙、拉毛、拉亮、拉易、威岩、拉祥、水碰、拉滩、甲料，甲良镇的金华、丙外、七星、甲新，瑶山瑶族乡红光村的甲林寨；蒙姓主要居住在永康水族乡的太吉、德门、溪竹、董亥、白岩、尧古村，甲良镇的板培村、七星村和甲站村的水蒙组以及金华村的上水蒙、更酒组，佳荣镇的拉滩村上拉奖组、下拉奖组，水尧水族乡的懂港、下拉交组，洞塘乡木槽村的陇用、洞白、拉干、必格、九街、卡别组，茂兰镇的水庆、洞流村；吴姓主要居住在水利水族乡，佳荣镇的拉吾和玉屏镇的水浦村，永康水族乡尧古村的拉桥组；姚氏主要居住在水尧水族乡的水尧、水捞、拉交村以及水功村的板独组；常姓居住在水尧水族乡的水功村和茂兰镇的水庆村四组；韦姓散居在朝阳镇的山江村、播尧乡的新桥村拉榜寨、地莪村的地脉组、玉屏镇水浦村的水扒组；欧姓居住在水尧水族乡水捞村的水捞寨、水尧村的董伟组和永康水族乡的白岩村白岩组；何姓散居在茂兰镇洞流村、更坡村组和永康水族乡的尧古村；石姓居住在水尧水族乡拉交村董未组，永康水族乡德门村的吉流寨（第六组）和佳荣镇的甲料村；谢、杨、张三姓散居在甲良镇甲良村的场坝、播尧乡觉巩村寨索组；县城所在地的玉屏镇有韦姓、蒙姓、潘姓、吴姓、姚姓、邓姓等水族家庭迁来居住，中共一大代表邓恩铭家邓氏家族原居住在玉屏镇水浦村板本寨（邓恩铭的故里），后其家庭部分成员迁至县城北街居住（邓恩铭故居）；立化镇的黎家寨以蒙姓为主，也有部分是何、韦、欧和吴；其余姓氏主要分布在县城和县境南部乡（镇）。

3.苗族姓氏。境内苗族姓氏有韦、麻、马、项、田、吴、杨、王、江、陈、龙、肖、唐、全、朱、潘、张、廖、黄、石、林、姜、梁、郭、谭、周、胡、余、罗、彭、李、舒、曹、鲁、刘、任、庄、何、冉、高、金、向、陶、陆、邓、赵、伍、段、冯、贾、白51个。

4.瑶族姓氏。瑶族聚族而居，大分散、小聚居，自成村寨，同一姓氏为寨。白裤瑶姓氏有何、谢、黎、罗、陆、覃、王、兰、韦9个；青瑶姓氏有韦、覃、欧、卢、常、莫6个；长衫瑶姓氏有何、韦、欧3个。

第三节 人口变动

县内常住人口变动因素主要是出生人口、死亡人口的自然变动和外地人口迁入、县内人口迁出产生变化。1999—2008年，从省内、省外迁入荔波居住12841人，从县内迁出省内、省外14945人。也有部分从事经营活动的流动人口在县内临时居住。

1978—2008年全县人口变动情况一览表

表3-1 单位：人

年度	总户数（户）	总人口数	出生人数	出生率（‰）	死亡人数	死亡率（‰）	自然增长率（‰）
1978	24084	118294	—	32.85	—	10.1	22.75
1979	24430	120779	—	—	—	—	—
1980	24647	123510	—	—	—	—	—
1981	24718	126213	—	27.60	—	9.10	18.50
1982	25017	128385	2126	16.56	—	8.62	14.55
1983	25065	130938	3704	28.29	—	12.02	16.26
1984	25645	131163	2311	17.62	1100	8.39	9.28
1985	26020	132832	2295	17.28	—	8.00	10.18
1986	26577	134709	2658	19.73	—	6.70	13.17
1987	27094	136481	2668	19.55	979	7.17	12.37
1988	25022	130428	2711	20.78	931	7.14	13.64
1989	28458	140326	2269	16.17	1218	8.68	7.49
1990	30176	144086	2344	16.56	960	6.66	9.77
1991	31314	142379	2134	14.99	795	5.58	9.37
1992	32623	141488	2115	14.88	809	5.72	9.23
1993	33313	146826	2234	15.49	865	5.89	9.32
1994	34845	148287	2312	15.59	851	5.74	9.85
1995	36158	149757	2408	16.08	893	5.96	10.12
1996	36901	152026	3124	20.54	1212	7.97	12.57
1997	36728	152173	2662	17.49	1008	6.62	10.87
1998	37613	155338	2468	15.89	855	5.50	10.38
1999	38615	158095	2205	13.95	897	5.67	8.27
2000	39023	159538	2268	14.22	990	6.21	8.01
2001	39458	163855	2313	14.12	981	5.99	8.24
2002	40612	164476	2201	13.38	1132	6.88	6.50

续表3－1

年度	总户数（户）	总人口数	出生人数	出生率（‰）	死亡人数	死亡率（‰）	自然增长率（‰）
2003	40936	166143	1880	11.32	1098	6.61	5.94
2004	42621	166581	2838	17.04	1138	6.83	10.22
2005	43338	167579	2022	12.07	1084	6.47	5.61
2006	45024	167351	1896	11.33	1453	8.68	4.91
2007	46022	168121	1847	10.99	1217	7.24	4.98
2008	480243	171454	1824	10.64	998	5.82	4.90

说明：表中空格为数据遗失

第四节　人口普查

1982年7月，全县开展第三次全国人口普查，登记时间为1982年7月1日零时，以1982年6月底的行政区划为统计范围。资料的各项数据包括：有户口的常住人口，持有迁移证和超生子女未落上常住户口的人口，不包括现行军人。登记的项目有姓名、性别、年龄、民族、常住人口的户口登记状况、文化程度、行业、职业、不在业人口状况、婚姻状况、妇女生育总数和存活子女总数，1981年育龄妇女生育状况、住房地址、住户人数、住户1981年出生人数、住户1981年死亡人数，有常住户口已外出一年以上的人数等19项。普查结果：全县总户数24327户，总人口127497人。其中，男64285人，女63212人；大学毕业生191人，大学肄业或在校12人，高中2742人，初中11098人，小学31041人；12周岁以及12周岁以上文盲、半文盲人口46964人；少数民族110731人，少数民族人口占总人口的86.86%。

1990年7月，全县开展第四次全国人口普查，普查登记时间为1990年7月1日零时。普查的主要项目有总人口、家庭户人口、性别构成、民族构成、各种文化程度、人口出生率和死亡率等。普查结果：全县总户数29071户，总人口144086人。其中，男73935人、女70151人；大学本科107人，大学专科312人，中专1599人，高中2693人，初中16434人，小学57712人，文盲、半文盲45834人；少数民族人口127670人，少数民族人口占总人口的88.61%。

2000年11月，全县开展第五次全国人口普查，普查时间为2000年11月1日零时。普查登记的对象是具有中华人民共和国国籍并在中华人民共和国境内常住人口，每个人均在常住地登记。普查的主要项目有总人口、家庭户人口、人口分布、年龄、性别、民族、文化构成等。普查结果：全县总户数43625户，171366人。其中，男性90130人，女性81236人；全县0～14岁人口48646人，占28.39%，15～64岁人口113084人，占65.99%，65岁以上人口9636人，占5.62%；大学（大专）1774人，占1.04%，高中（中专）9213人，占5.38%，初中35504人，占20.72%，小学80101人，占46.74%，文盲、半文盲为19280人，占11.25%；少数民族人口146775人，占总人口数的85.65%。在本地登记人口中，居住在城镇的人口32791人，占总人口的19.14%，居住乡村人口138443人，占总人口的80.79%。

第五节　计划生育

一、计划生育管理

（一）政策法规

1979年，县计划生育委员会制定《计划生育奖励措施》，对完成或超额完成人口出生率、晚婚率、人口自然增长率达到县下达任务数的区、社，以及参加计划生育工作的领导干部、计划生育宣传员、医务人员表现出色的，给予物质或现金奖励。

1980年5月，根据《贵州省计划生育暂行办法》及省、州有关文件精神，制定《荔波县计划生育暂行办法》，从1980年5月1日起执行。

1981年7月，针对农村两包到户后，计划生育奖惩政策兑现不够，农村中非婚生育、计划外生育、超胎生育较多的情况，荔波县出台《关于计划生育的若干规定》，以保证全县人口指标、计生措施、任务的完成。是年12月，县委下发《中共荔波县委　荔波县人民政府关于进一步做好计划生育工作的意见》。

1982年5月，县委下发《关于贯彻执行中发〔1982〕11号、省发〔1982〕12号文件的补充规定》。是年，全县各社队农业生产、计划生育两个合同一起定，把生产、生育指标、任务、措施落实到户，农村干部把农业生产、计划生育指标、任务、措施实行岗位责任制，县包区、区包社、公社包生产大队、大队包生产队，层层落实责任和任务，在干部岗位责任制中对完成生产、生育任务的有奖，完不成任务的减分考核。

1986年，经县政府同意，《荔波县计划生育若干规定》《荔波县对外来从业人员计划生育处理规定》开始试行。

从1988年1月1日起，在全县施行《贵州省计划生育试行条例》。

1992年3月，县政府下发《荔波县人民政府关于计划生育若干问题的补充规定》，对全县各乡（镇）的计划生育管理工作实行乡（镇）干部全员承包责任制，县政府与乡（镇）签订人口与计划生育目标管理责任书。

1997年，县委、县政府下发《关于开展计划生育妇检工作的通告》《关于进一步加强计外费征收、管理、使用意见的通知》等11个文件，县计生局下发有关计划生育工作的18个规范性文件。

2001年，县委、县政府先后下发《关于加强机关单位人口与计划生育工作的有关问题的规定》《关于加强人口与计划生育工作严格控制人口过快增长的决定》《关于严格执行人口与计划生育政策法规的通告》等文件。是年，各行政村（居）都有驻村干部协管计生工作。全县执行县对乡、乡对村签订人口与计划生育目标管理责任书和县与各机关单位签订人口与计划生育管理责任书，执行计划生育“一票否决”制度。

2003—2005年，县委、县政府先后下发《中共荔波县委、荔波县人民政府关于开展创建计划生育优质服务县工作实施意见》等27个文件，开展创建全国计划生育优质服务先进县工作。2005年，经省验收，荔波县获“贵州省计划生育优质服务先进县”称号。2005—2008年，坚持开展创建“国家计划生育优质服务先进单位”活动。

（二）计划生育“三结合”帮扶

从1996年起，贯彻落实省、州关于开展计划生育“三结合”（农村计划生育工作与发展经济相结合、与帮助农民勤劳致富奔小康相结合、与建设文明幸福家庭相结合）的决定。年初，成立由县委书记任组长，县长、县政协主席、县人大副主任、分管副县长任副组长，县34个有关部门负责人为成员的计划生育“三结合”工作领导小组。同时，各乡（镇）对计划生育帮扶户进行调查摸底，应重点帮扶183户，其中独生子女户96户、二女结扎户87户。7月，县委、县政府下发《关于进一步加强计划生育工作的决定》。是年，全县帮扶149户，投入资金总计43.6万元，帮助帮扶户发展林业和养殖业。

1997年，县委、县政府实施计划生育“三结合”的“4321”工程（县四家班子正职领导帮扶4户、副职领导帮扶3户、科局级领导干部帮扶2户、股级至一般干部帮扶1户），四家班子领导挂牌帮扶独生子女户、二孩结扎户共36户，投入资金0.4万元、化肥5吨；县部门领导共帮扶446户，投入资金共17.3万元、化肥15吨，并对446户计划生育帮扶对象建档管理。

1998年，全县“三结合”帮扶对象增加到1140户（其中1998年643户），共投入资金25.5万元、化肥25吨。

1999—2001年，对帮扶对象实行挂牌管理，其间，2000年帮扶户数达1291户，帮扶资金69.88万元。

1999年共完成帮扶1101户，占年任务1039户的105.96%，共投入帮扶资金18万元、化肥25吨，较好地完成了帮扶任务并实行挂牌管理。

2002年，县委、县政府出台《关于认真做好农村独生子女户、二女结扎户养老保险工作的意见》，采取部门集资、社会捐款和政府拨款方式，投入资金共35.44万元，为全县886户农村独生子女户、二女结扎户办理养老保险，每户400元。其中，政府拨款21万元，县民宗局集资1.6万元，其他部门集资捐款12.84万元。

2003年，全县机关单位、干部职工、乡（镇）共帮扶计生户1500户，占州下达年任务1000户的150%，并建立帮扶档案。

2004—2006年，县直部门及乡（镇）投入“三结合”帮扶资金累计436.6万元。2007年，帮扶计划生育户5289户，资金47万元。

2008年，全县按“4321”帮扶工程投入帮扶资金62.14万元，帮扶计划生育户4920户。

是年，开展农村国家级奖扶对象和县级奖扶对象调查、审定、核实上报工作，并兑现农村国家级奖扶对象143户、县级奖扶对象56户，资金共1.94万元，兑现率100%。同时，上报农村独女、双女助学奖励153户，独生子女户父母死亡补助1.7万元。

（三）计划生育“村为主”

1996年，在全县开展创计划生育“合格村”“无多孩生育乡”活动，经州计划生育考核组年终考核，全县创建计划生育“合格村”9个、无多孩生育村37个。

1997年后，县委、县政府将创建计划生育合格村和基本合格村作为计划生育工作重点，计划生育合格村和基本合格村不断增加，至2000年，全县计划生育合格村88个、基本合格村42个，占全县村总数的76%，瑶麓乡成为全县连续三年“无多孩生育乡”。

2001年，县政府将各乡（镇）实行计划生育“村为主”情况列入年度重要考核指标进行考核，全县“村为主”达标村111个，占171个村（居）的65.91%。

2002年，为实现全县80%以上的村基本实现计划生育“村为主”，对“村为主”工作进行逐级考核，层层签订计划生育“村为主”工作目标责任书，同时县计生局加强业务培训。年末，全县创建计划生育“合格村”111个、“基本合格村”31个，省政府对3个村点进行检查验收，均达到基本实现“村为主”工作要求。

2003年，全县开展“村（居）民自治”的村67个，占全县村（居）数的38.51%；实现计划生育“村为主”151个，占全县村（居）数的88.3%；创建计划生育合格村139个，占全县村（居）数的81.29%，创建基本合格村18个，占全县村（居）数的10.53%。

2005年，全县实现计划生育“村（居）为主”村（居）98个；推行“村（居）民自治”的村（居）97个，其中村（居）自治工作达标村25个。

2007年，全县“村（居）民自治”推行面达100%，其中村（居）自治工作达标村40个。

（四）流动人口生育管理

2004年，在县人口和计划生育局下设县流动人口管理中心，编制3人，对流动人口进行规范化管理。

2006年，县政府与县直12个职能部门签订流动人口计生综合治理目标管理责任书，各部门齐抓共管，政策外生育大幅度下降。是年，各乡（镇）在街道、景区、宾馆、学校及流动人口聚信地设置避孕药具发放自取点共235个、自取箱235个，制作自取点提示牌108块、发放点网络图20块，对每个点明确专人负责，保障自取箱内药具不出现空缺。全年流出育龄妇女办证率81.5%，流入育龄妇女验证率98%，信息反馈率100%。

2007年，全县流出人口16311人，其中18周岁以上育龄妇女6958人（已婚育龄妇女4409人），流出人口生育97人；流入人口3918人，其中18周岁以上育龄妇女989人（已婚育龄妇女801人），流入人口生育27人。流动人口出生人数符合政策生育率75.26%。流出育龄妇女办证率96.36%，流入育龄妇女验证率98.94%，信息反馈率100%。

2008年，与周边县（市）开展两地协作管理；在流动人口集中的社区、集贸市场及流动人口聚集地带建立流动人口计划生育协会等，解决流动人口管理和服务难题。是年，全县流出人口16914人，其中18周岁以上育龄妇女7522人（已婚育龄妇女4924人），流出人口生育151人；流入人口3626人，其中18周岁以上育龄妇女836人（已婚育龄妇女771人），流入人口生育30人。流动人口出生人数中，符合政策生育率72.85%。流出育龄妇女办证率98.16%，流入育龄妇女验证率100%，信息反馈率100%。

（五）社会抚养费征收

从1982年12月起，按国家计划生育委员会和财政部下发的《关于加强超生子女费管理的暂行办法》征收超生子女费。

1992年8月，县政府制定下发《荔波县计划生育罚款征收及使用管理办法的通知》，对计划外生育费的清收、使用、管理作出具体明确规定。

1996年，按照省、州有关提取乡计划生育统筹费的文件规定，提取计划生育统筹粮。

1997年，17个乡（镇）社会抚养费实行“乡收县管、财政监督”管理体制，由县计生局设立专户管理，主要用于村计生员的报酬和乡（镇）、村开展计划生育宣传教育工作开支。是年，全县实征社会抚养费44万元，占年任务74万元的60%。

1998—2008年，征收社会抚养费累计480.72万元。

二、计划生育服务

1978—1984年，全县计划生育技术服务由县计生办开展。1984年2月，成立县计划生育指导站，部分乡（镇）配有专职计生员。1985年，全县有已婚育龄妇女18161人，采取节育措施10755人，节育率59.2%。由于计划生育服务工作不断加强，已婚育龄妇女采取节育措施人数逐年增加，至1992年，全县有已婚育龄妇女20375人，采取节育措施18092人，节育率88.8%。

1993年，建方村乡计划生育服务站。1994年，建茂兰镇和瑶山乡计划生育服务站。1996年，建甲良镇计划生育服务站。1997年，建洞塘乡、佳荣镇、驾欧乡计划生育服务站。

1998年，开展计划生育服务站规范化管理达标建设，年底，朝阳、玉屏、茂兰3个镇计划生育服务站经州考核达到规范化管理标准；洞塘、佳荣、驾欧、甲良4乡（镇）建成业务用房并投入使用。是年年底，全县有10个乡（镇）计划生育服务站达到计划生育手术和妇检不出乡（镇）。2000年，9个乡（镇）建成计划生育服务业务用房，并从中专毕业生中择优聘用20名计生业务技术人员充实到乡（镇）计划生育服务站。

2001年，建成村级服务室33个。是年年底，全县17个乡（镇）建成计划生育业务用房共4814.32平方米，投入资金总计224.56万元。

2002年起，开展计划生育优质服务站创建工作。2003年，全县最后一批创建规范化管理达标乡（镇）站的水利、瑶麓通过州级验收合格，县计划生育站创建“计生优质服务一级站”及洞塘乡计生站创建“计生优质服务乡站”经省计生委考核合格。是年，全县完成已婚育龄妇女妇科病普查普治12160人，占已婚育龄妇女数30400人的40%；全县有已婚育龄妇女30400人，采取节育措施27271人，节育率89.71%。

2002—2004年，在计划生育优质服务站创建工作中，全县3年投入经费611.09万元，其中县级441.09万元、乡级170万元。投入站房改扩建经费349.39万元，计划生育服务站业务用房面积由7041平方米增加到11000平方米；投入206.7万元，更新县、乡计生设备434套（件）以及乳腺诊断仪、波姆光治疗仪、多功能手术床、九孔无影灯、酶标仪、B超机等。是年年底，全县有计划生育技术人员84人，开展已婚育龄妇女妇科病普查27649名，普查率为90.8%；对9457名已婚育龄妇女妇科病进行治疗，普治率为70%。

2006年，对县、乡、村三级计划生育、妇幼保健机构进行整合，建乡（镇）计划生育妇幼保健站。

2008年，按照计划生育工作“四优一满意”（环境优美、设施优良、服务优质、管理优秀、群众满意）的要求，投入26万元，完善玉屏、朝阳、驾欧3个乡（镇）站房改造、科室调配及设备配置。至年底，全县计划生育服务机构有技术服务人员111人，其中县级25人、乡（镇）86人；全县有已婚育龄妇女27959人，采取节育措施24658人，节育率88.19%。

三、计划生育宣传

1978年，中共中央批转《关于国务院计划生育领导小组第一次会议的报告》，11月召开全省计划生育工作会议，20—26日，县委、县革委抽调县机关干部30名，到各区、公社，以播放广播、发宣传资料、张贴标语和宣传画等形式开展政策宣传。

1979年6月，省革委颁发《贵州省计划生育暂行办法》，县、区两级计划生育干部于7月开展宣传工作。9月，召开全县计划生育工作动员会，抽调机关单位干部40名，到各区、公社进行计划生育宣传动员，印发宣传资料5000份，书写标语250条，开展宣讲11场次。

1980年5月，县政府出台《荔波县计划生育暂行办法》，全县集中计生宣传人员20人赴各区、公社，利用赶场天向群众发送宣传资料及放电影、广播等30场次。1981年，先后在城关区、朝阳公社、王蒙公社、茂兰区开展4次宣传活动，撰写宣传稿13篇，制作宣传画板20幅，印发宣传资料2000份。

1982—1985年，每年从县机关单位抽调干部，由县委、县人大、县政府、县政协领导带队到区（镇）、乡、村，采取宣讲会、有线广播、放映电影、唱山歌、座谈会、张贴标语等方式，向群众宣传计划生育政策和生育科学知识。

1987年1月20—23日，召开全县计划生育宣传工作会议，并在春节前后开展全县范围内以广播、张贴标语、文艺演出等形式为主的计划生育宣传月活动。《贵州省计划生育试行条例》（以下简称《试行条例》）颁布后，是年11月，举办全县计划生育知识竞赛活动，宣传《试行条例》。

1988—1989年，将《试行条例》及宣传提纲印发至各区（镇）、乡、村、组，并利用宣传车到各区（镇）、乡进行宣传讲解，先后在县城、区公所所在地举办8期宣传栏，邀请州计生指导所放映队到县城及区、乡放映计划生育宣传片，配合开展《试行条例》学习。印发《县人民政府关于计划生育的通告》27857份。

1991年，州优生优育宣传队到茂兰、朝阳、玉屏、瑶山等乡镇开展“三优”（优生、优育、优教）宣传。是年，国家计生委、中宣部国情国策摄制组到荔波摄制专题片。

1992年，重点宣传是计划生育持证生育政策，在乡镇开展禁止早婚、早育，提倡优生优育、节育避孕科学知识宣传教育。

1993年，开展各种宣传教育活动22次，受教育群众9万余人次，占全县总人口的62%。

1994—1996年，开展创建“计划生育合格村”活动。

1998年7月，《贵州省计划生育条例》（以下简称《条例》）颁布实施后，采取多种形式进行《条例》宣传。年内，在县党校举办《条例》学习培训班，培训村支部书记168人；深入甲良、永康、朝阳、玉屏、翁昂、水利6个乡（镇），向干部职工400多人次作宣传讲解；在乡（镇）开展50场次宣传活动，发放《条例》2400本，张贴《条例》3500张。

1999—2000年，开展9次“以宣传教育为主”的计划生育宣传活动，在县城樟江大街设置长期性计划生育宣传灯箱标语牌14块，在荔茂公路沿线用水泥制作长期性宣传标语7块，在小七孔公路集镇地段灯杆上悬挂铁皮制作的长期性宣传标语30块，将《条例》制作成挂历发给全县农户。同时，开展“婚育新风进万家”活动，向已婚育龄妇女发放宣传资料2.8万份。

2002年，开展“村为主”达标宣传活动，从县到乡到村分别召开群众会进行宣传，发放“村主为”宣传资料，举办“村为主”知识竞赛，推动全县计划生育“村为主”达标工作。9月1日施行的《中华人民共和国人口与计划生育法》，并将该法发到群众手中，同时举办演讲比赛。

2003年，重点宣传以《人口与计划生育法》《流动人口计划生育工作管理办法》《社会抚养费征收管理办法》《计划生育技术服务管理条例》，开展“四下乡”（计划生育文化活动下乡、计划生育政策法规解答下乡、计划生育宣传下乡、计划生育技术服务下乡）活动，到甲良、朝阳、佳荣、播尧等乡（镇）文艺演出6场，发放计生宣传资料1.2万份。全年接待育龄群众咨询1.6万人次。

2004—2008年，将宣传教育工作纳入精神文明建设内容，开展“婚育新风进万家”活动，深入农村宣传晚婚晚育、少生优生、“生男生女一样好，女儿也是传后人”的科学文明进步婚育观念，宣传工作投入经费累计25万元。县、乡、村计划生育服务站（室）悬挂温馨画图；在主要公路沿线制作“关爱女孩行动”等大型宣传广告牌；举行“救助贫困母亲”文艺会演；开展送计生文化下乡、山歌唱计生、旅游黄金周送药具上门服务等宣传活动。

四、计划生育协会

1988年5月15日，成立县计划生育协会，并制定协会章程。协会办公室设在县计生委。协会有会员38名，常务理事15名、理事24名。

1990年9月，召开荔波县计划生育协会第一次会议，审定县计划生育协会章程，选举会长、名誉会长、秘书长，通过理事会成员名单。县计划生育协会有会员113名。是年，开始筹建区、乡计划生育协会。

1991年，朝阳、茂兰、玉屏、瑶山、方村、驾欧、水利、翁昂等乡（镇）成立计划生育协会，全县计划生育协会会员增加到467名。

1992年，全县17个乡（镇）全部成立计划生育协会。玉屏镇的16个村、2个居委会和方村乡的11个村成立村级计划生育协会。至年底，全县共有会员1093名。1993年，全县各乡（镇）、居委会均成立村级计划生育协会。1996年，计划生育协会会员发展到1186名。

1999年，全县各乡（镇）计划生育协会及村级计划生育协会全部完成换届调整工作。

2000年，县、乡（镇）计划生育协会配备专职秘书长。同年，县编委同意县计划生育协会编制2名，其中专职秘书长1名（副局级），协会工作人员1名，在计划生育系统编制内调整。2001年6月，县计划生育协会人员列入参照国家公务员管理。

2005年，全县有乡（镇）级协会17个、村级协会98个，会员发展到25340名。全县计划生育合格村协会53个，占协会总村数的54.08%，基本合格村协会25个，占协会总村数的25.51%。

是年，结合全国开展“婚育新风进万家”活动，全县基层计划生育协会成立计划生育文艺宣传队35支，利用各种节日开展文艺宣传活动。

2008年，县计划生育协会免费为农家乐旅游接待的计划生育户开展烹饪技术培训服务150人次；协调农业银行解决计划生育育龄群众乡村旅游小额贷款50户共计256万元；指导开展农家乐的村、组农户成立协会旅游分会，实行统一要求、统一标准接待制度，旅游接待家庭户均增收3500元以上，吸引外出务工人员160名返乡从事农家乐旅游服务。

第二章　民　族

第一节　民族构成

一、民族构成

荔波县为少数民族聚居区，以布依族、水族、瑶族、苗族人口居多。1982年第三次人口普查统计，境内常住人口有17个民族和1个未识别民族，全县总人口127497人中，少数民族人口110688人，占总人口的86.82%。人口在100人以上的民族有7个：布依族75039人、水族25812人、汉族16809人、苗族4872人、瑶族3832人、壮族796人、侗族225人；人口不足100人的民族有11个（含1个未识别民族）：彝族35人、满族26人、毛南族20人、回族11人、蒙古族6人、土家族6人、土族3人、东乡族2人、京族1人、高山族1人、未识别民族1人。

1983年，开展民族识别工作，对县内方村、甲良一带的莫姓家族，茂兰、洞塘、翁昂的“长衫瑶”，瑶山及捞村的“白裤瑶”和瑶麓的“青瑶”等民族成分开展社会调查和考证。1984年，召开“莫姓”和“荔波三支瑶”的民族识别工作会议，明确境内莫家属布依族，“白裤瑶”“青瑶”“长衫瑶”统属瑶族。

1990年，第四次人口普查统计，境内常住人口有22个民族。全县总人口144086人中，少数民族人口127750人，占总人口的88.66%。人口在100人以上的民族有7个：布依族84662人、水族29981人、汉族16336人、苗族6413人、瑶族4791人、壮族1253人、侗族385人；人口不足100人的民族有15个：毛南族70人、土家族36人、满族30人、回族25人、仡佬族19人、彝族41人、土族12人、仫佬族3人、东乡族5人、黎族8人、蒙古族8人、朝鲜族3人、锡伯族3人、白族1人、傈僳族1人。

2000年，第五次人口普查统计，境内常住人口有29个民族。全县总人口171366人中，少数民族人口150591人，占总人口的87.88%。人口在100人以上的民族有9个：布依族93681人、水族35407人、汉族20775人、苗族8540人、瑶族5915人、壮族5720人、侗族485人、毛南族355人、仫佬族148人；人口不足100人的民族有20个。2008年年底，根据县公安局户籍管理年末人口统计，全县常住人口171454人，有22个民族。其中，少数民族人口数157750人，占全县总人口的92.01%。在少数民族人口中，布依族104884人，占总人口的61.17%；水族36639人，占总人口数21.37%；苗族8454人，占总人口的4.93%；瑶族5492人，占总人口的3.20%；壮族1356人，占总人口的0.79%；侗族526人，占总人口的0.31%；毛南族100人，占总人口的0.06%；其他14个少数民族人口共299人，占总人口的0.17%。

第二节 民族分布

布依族、水族、苗族、瑶族4个民族为境内人口较多的世居少数民族。

布依族分布，除瑶麓瑶族乡外，全县16个乡（镇）均有分布。

境内水族主要分布在永康、水尧、水利3个水族乡和佳荣镇。另外还有部分散居在茂兰、立化、朝阳、甲良、玉屏、瑶山、洞塘、播尧、方村等乡（镇）、村寨。

苗族主要聚居在佳荣镇的大土、水维、甲料、坤地、拉祥、拉易、拉吾等区域。散居苗族主要分布在播尧乡的拉美、田湾，朝阳镇的岜马、寨平，洞塘乡的懂朋、塘边、三河，瑶山瑶族乡的坡旧、朝沙、拉庆、下洞、塘上、拉柳、白腊坳、巴楼，驾欧乡的更灶，捞村乡的岩脚，甲良镇的降亳，玉屏镇的新寨、萝卜木。

瑶族分别聚居在瑶山、瑶麓、茂兰、佳荣、洞塘、立化、翁昂、捞村、玉屏、水尧10个乡（镇）、38个自然村寨。在38个自然村寨中，除白腊坳寨为瑶族、布依族、水族、苗族、汉族杂居外，其余37个自然寨全部是瑶族居住。

汉族人口分布广，全县17个乡（镇）中，除瑶麓、捞村两个乡外，其余15个乡（镇）都有汉族居住，其中以城镇和乡村集市所在地居住较为集中，佳荣镇的高里村和洞塘乡的木槽村为汉族聚居地。

壮族主要分布在玉屏镇、洞塘乡、佳荣镇、翁昂乡和立化镇的集市所在地；侗族主要分布在玉屏镇、播尧乡、佳荣镇和方村乡的集市所在地；土家族主要分布在洞塘乡和玉屏镇的集市所在地；毛南族主要分布在洞塘乡和玉屏镇的集市所在地；其他少数民族主要散居于县城所在地玉屏镇。

第三节 世居民族

境内世居民族有布依族、水族、汉族、苗族、瑶族5个民族。

一、布依族

荔波布依族使用本民族语言，布依族青壮年、学生学习汉文，使用汉语与其他民族进行交流。荔波布依语属于汉藏语系壮侗语族壮傣语支，与同语族的壮语、侗语、傣语、水语、黎语等有密切关系，特别是与同语支的壮语北部方言有许多共同点。荔波布依族中有的说“莫话”，莫话介于水语、布依语、汉语之间，是黔南州境内布依族语言的一种，主要分布在荔波县和相邻的独山县，荔波县讲“莫话”群体主要分布在县城西北的方村河流域。北部以方村、甲良两乡镇为主，向西南一直延伸到播尧乡；临近水利乡也有村寨讲莫语，但人口较少。2003年调查，讲“莫话”的人口约18000人，其中讲锦话人口不到3000人。无论莫话还是锦话，当地都认为是讲“麻话”。

布依族文字有方块文字和拼音文字两种。拼音文字是1956年国家文字委员会以拉丁字母为基础创立的布依族拼音文字，曾在全县推广。方块文字是荔波布依族傩书古文字，散存于本民族的经书、傩书手抄本中，已发现的布依古文字有300字。布依族古文字是布依族先生自创，世代传承使用至今，字音只能用布依族语音朗读，字义也只有布依傩书先生能读懂解释其义。布依古文字是在布依地区流传使用上千年、至今仍在民间流传使用的文字。

分布在农村的布依族居住“干栏”式房屋。“干栏”式房屋建筑造型为中间屋脊高两檐矮，房屋开间多为四排三间，不论房屋高低，其高度零头必须带“八”字。“干栏”式房屋为木质结构，主要用材为松木、杉木、白杨木、枫木等。布依族居住屋内一般以正中的一间为堂屋，堂屋正中设神龛，是作供奉祖先之用。神龛前置一方桌，逢年过节作祭祀之用。堂屋的后半间及两头的开间，分别为卧室、厨房等。进入21世纪后，随着社会的进步和发展，部分村寨农户建砖瓦结构或砖混结构房屋。

布依族以大米、玉米为主食，小麦、高粱、薯芋和豆类为辅助，制作成焖饭、二合饭（大米掺玉米）、苞谷粑、米线、饵块粑、豌豆粉、米凉糕等品种。其中，糯米制品如汤圆、花糯米饭和芝麻油团粑最为知名，多用于宴客或馈赠礼品。有的还喜爱捕食松鼠、竹鼠和竹虫，食野生烤鱼。布依族善于制作糟辣、辣面、枫叶黑糯饭、粽子，喜腌制酸肉和泡菜，擅长酿制甜酒、黑糯米酒、刺梨酒、杨梅酒、拐枣酒等。布依族非常注重节日美食，有“四月八”用花糯米饭祭牛王、“六月六”食手抓芭蕉鸡等节日食俗。

布依族人家穿着用布从原料到成衣，一纱一线都是自己动手自给自足。服饰色彩、款式，根据性别、年龄不同，各有特点。青年妇女喜爱穿花色艳丽的土花布，中老年妇女则喜爱深蓝色和青色。礼服以青色为上等。妇女上衣为圆领短衫，下穿蓝青色长裤，其托肩、袖口、裤脚都镶有花边（栏干）。头缠青色头巾、脚穿绣花布底鞋，胸拴银链绣花围腰，颈佩银项圈，手戴银手镯。男装也因年龄不同，穿着也有差异。老年人多穿青蓝色长衫或对襟短衣、长裤，头包青色头帕或戴土布小帽，腰束青布带，脚穿布袜和大口鞋；青壮年多穿对襟短衣；少年儿童喜穿土花服装。

境内布依族妇女擅长纺织，尤以织土花布盛名。按布的底色不同分为白底蓝布、蓝底白布或蓝白混纺作底等类型。布纹有柳条、格格、花椒、梅花、桂花、篱笆、鱼刺、兰尼、反手纱等十几种，花式达150多个。

大多数布依族家庭婚姻保留传统的经择亲、相亲、说亲、订亲到结婚的习俗。部分青年男女由于接受现代思想教育，自由恋爱结婚。

布依族传统舞蹈有矮人舞、刷把舞、龙狮舞、吊丧舞。传统体育项目有踩高跷、赛龙舟、斗牛、滚累、滚铁环、斗独脚鸡、敲鸡崽等，每年“四月八”，甲良、阳凤等地进行斗牛比赛，踩高跷、滚累、滚铁环、斗独脚鸡、敲鸡崽等逐渐消失。

境内布依族传统节日有春节、清明节、“四月八”、端午节、“六月六”“七月半”、中秋节等。其中，以“四月八”、端午节、“六月六”、中秋节最具民族特色。

布依族重情好客，贵宾到来，必有“进门酒”“敬客酒”“交杯酒”“转转酒”“千杯酒”“送客酒”等礼遇，热情接待。

布依族家庭老人病故后，实行木棺土葬，丧葬仪式程序有守气、存遗津、净身、炒包谷、报丧、祭奠、就龙、超度亡灵、出殡、下葬等过程。

荔波布依族有本民族独特的信仰和禁忌。崇拜“天地君亲师”、祖宗、神社等。禁忌较多，如家中老人过世，停丧期间（无论多少天），本家直系亲属和同宗族亲属一律不准吃荤；孝男孝女不准坐凳子，不准睡床，不准穿布、皮鞋，只能穿草鞋或赤脚，直至把亡人入土下葬为止；守灵期间，孝男不准理发，孝女不准洗头，直至七七四十九天烧灵为止。忌鸡早鸣，怕出现火灾。忌猪、牛、马进家。过年、过节或村寨上办喜事、丧事，孕妇不得串门。在外面死亡的人，不准抬进村寨停尸。随着现代科学教育的不断普及，传统的崇拜、禁忌观念在逐步淡化。

二、水族

荔波水族使用本民族语言，青壮年、学生学习汉文，使用汉语与其他民族进行交流。荔波水族语言属汉藏语系壮侗语族侗水语支，与壮侗语族的毛南语、侗语、布依语、仫佬语、壮语有亲缘关系，尤其与毛南语、侗语关系最密切，相通之处达40%。水族学习汉文化，与汉族和其他民族人民长期交往，同时随科学技术不断进步和发展，水语中不断吸收布依语、侗语、壮语、毛南语和汉语以及现代新词术语来丰富本民族语言，加上新事物的层出不穷，水语中也不断出现不少的外来借词。

荔波水族同其他地方水族一样，在水族地区民间使用测吉凶的古老文字，水语称“泐虽”，汉语称为“水文”或“水书”，目前发现有400多个单字，600多个异体字。“水书”不是水族日常通用文字，其文本由“水书”传承者——水书先生口耳相传。这种古文字只作为民间水书先生择日子看风水所用，一般群众难以认识，也不能成为交流思想的工具，但它是研究水族社会历史和哲学思想的可贵资料。国家文字委员会采用拉丁字母拼音，创立水族拼音文字，曾于1984年在各水族乡中心小学中推广，之后主要是民族学类的专家学者在水书研究中使用。

水族村寨大多坐落在平坝边缘或半山槽谷中，少数在山顶建寨。水族村寨四周多留古树竹林，房前屋后喜栽桃、李、梨、橘等果木。园边篱沿爱植棕、漆等经济林木。村寨内外通常有大小鱼塘，寨口依山的大路一侧设立看寨石神，插上木刀木枪，重大节日敬供。水族是农耕民族，村寨大小要根据耕地面积而定。耕地集中、面积大则村寨大；耕地分散、面积小则村寨小。水族村寨的规模大小不等，一般有十几户、几十户，少者只有几户，多者达上百户。村寨成员大多系聚族而居，异姓他族杂居或单家独户的较少。

水族民居以木房为主，有叉叉房、木楼、平房三种。叉叉房是最原始、最简易的民居，是在地上竖两个“人”形叉，叉上用一根横梁连接，两边用小一些的木料斜搭到地面，上面覆盖树皮或茅草，形成一个横放的三角形柱状空间供人居住。平房是在平整好的地基面上直接建立房屋木架，屋顶覆盖茅草或瓦，用树枝或芦苇编成大排围在四周的木柱外边而成，也有用竹席圈围或夯泥土墙的。平房一般为一层加上“人”形屋顶下的阁楼，也有二层加阁楼的。木楼有干栏式木楼和吊脚楼。

水族日常以稻米为主食，种植有小麦、玉米、高粱、小米、荞、红苕、饭豆、洋芋等辅助作物。糯米是水族待客的上品食物。每当节日或亲友走访，主人便蒸糯饭来招待或以糯饭、糯米粑、糯米粽子作为礼物相馈赠。水族在节日喜庆中，最为特殊的饮食为食鱼，在祭祖和祭奠亡灵时要忌荤，但不忌鱼。水族鱼食中要数“鱼包韭菜”的烹饪方法为上。

水族传统服饰的颜色主要为蓝色、青色、绿色、黑色4种，多采用青色、蓝色、黑色自织自染的土布和绿色绸缎制成。基本款式是包头帕、穿右衽大襟衣衫配围腰、长裤、布鞋（女性多为绣花）。按时间、场合分为春夏秋冬盛装、便装。水族土布为水族妇女自种棉花、自制蓝靛，自纺、自织、自染而成。织染的土布花纹主要有斜纹、回纹、鱼骨纹等。传统的印染方式主要有豆浆染、扎线染、蜡染。

水族适龄青年男女确定配偶有三种情形，即男方老人经过几方面衡量觉得某姑娘中意，通过媒妁到女方家提亲；男青年看中某姑娘，便与自家父母商量，由父母出面确定对象直到结婚；男女青年双方通过相恋而确定结婚。迎娶时新郎带一队亲友去女方家迎娶新娘，返回时，女方家派若干至亲青年男女送新娘到新郎家。新婚之夜，新郎新娘不能同房。新娘在新郎家住两天，到第三天新娘回娘家，叫回门。此后新娘在男方家住一些日子便回一次娘家，直至生孩子后才常住男方家。

水族节日按时序排列有清明节、敬霞节、卯节、新米节、端节、艾节、春节等。其中，最具民族特色的是卯节、端节、艾节。

水族注重丧葬礼仪，在丧葬过程中保留着较为完整的原始信仰习俗。水族的丧葬程序十分繁杂，一般包括报丧、入殓、择吉、移柩、安葬、立碑、守服、除服等阶段。

水族的传统舞蹈主要有铜鼓舞、斗角舞、芦笙舞。

水族传统体育项目有赛马、斗牛、板腰、射弓，游艺项目有下拱棋、挑抬棋、舞龙狮等。

水族至今还保留的原始信仰习俗，大体上有崇拜自然、崇拜祖宗和崇拜神灵等。

水族民间古传禁忌较多，如喂养的母猪忌生两个猪仔；喂养的母狗忌生独狗仔；忌猪牛进家，家庭喂养公鸡忌在酉时鸣叫；忌见流星，认为天上流星下坠，地上人畜遭殃；未满月的产妇忌进别人家门；别人家在请水书先生进行某种念咒仪式时，忌不请自登门“冲吉”；出远门或择日办事等，在出走前煮饭夹生不熟，或在吃饭时火坑的火焰发出怪叫声，视为不祥；刚离婚女子忌进娘家村寨；寡妇再婚后，忌进原夫村寨；结婚当天忌打雷或死人等。

三、汉族

汉族从元朝开始入住荔波，明清时期逐渐增多，主要是朝廷派遣官员和军队驻屯，也有部分是商业、小手工业者到荔波定居。抗日战争时期，沦陷区的部分汉族迁入荔波居住。新中国成立后，南下和西进的人民解放军军官转业到荔波工作，各级各类院校的汉族毕生分配到荔波，荔波的汉族人口不断增加。

荔波汉语属北方语区西南官话土语范畴。汉话是县境内各族人民共同使用的交流工具。在语音方面除了县境北部甲良一带受独山汉话声调的影响略有不同外，境内其余地区的汉话与县城汉话的声、韵、调相同，但荔波汉话受广西汉话的声、韵、调影响，与广西汉话相近。

汉族的住房，城镇与农村略有不同。在城镇居住密集，地处街道，房屋建造多属木柱瓦顶结构平房，一般平民的住房比较矮小又窄狭，富有之家雕梁画栋，高大宽敞。自20世纪80年代后，汉族居民新建钢筋水泥结构的多层建筑。在农村的住房与布依族基本相同，一般是木质结构瓦房，较高大宽敞。随着农村经济发展，农村汉族群众兴建砖木结构或钢筋水泥结构新房。但不论城镇或乡村，汉族的住房，家家户户设社龛，列社位，以供奉祖先。

汉族日常饮食较讲究烹调，注重口味，在婚嫁庆典场合，菜肴的花样、烹调、口味更为讲究，县内著名厨师都出自汉族。荔波的臭酸是汉族特有的调味品。荔波特产——风猪，名驰省内外，出自汉族之手。一般人家对腊肉、香肠加工比较普遍，作为年节和待客的佳肴。汉族制作的米花、米片也富有地方特色，经过菜油炸酥，味道香脆，又易于保存。

荔波汉族服饰与周围邻县大抵相同。

境内汉族男女多提倡自由恋爱结婚，婚姻缔结过程，有访亲、订亲、迎亲、会亲等程序，婚礼逐步简化。

汉族的丧葬活动多遵古制，老人过世，孝家子孙、家族及亲友披麻戴孝，遵守成服。停柩三五天，多达六七天，延请道士念经、开路、竖幡、设坛，超度亡魂出殡前还要举行隆重的家祭、宾祭仪式，杀猪宰羊大办宴席，招待亲戚及帮忙人员。随着时代的发展进步，治丧旧俗逐渐改变从简。

汉族的传统节日主要有春节、端午节和“七月半”。其中最隆重的是过大年（春节）。

荔波汉族的工艺美术有银饰、刺绣、镜屏、编织、剪纸、雕刻等。其中，银饰、刺绣、编织享有盛誉。

四、苗族

荔波苗族有三支，语言各异。居住水维地区的红苗和黑苗的语言，不属同一方言，红苗语言属湘西方言，黑苗语言属黔东方言。散居苗族普遍使用汉语，但音调不同于荔波的汉语，他们虽散居各乡，而音调十分一致，与贵阳话相似。荔波苗族语言属汉藏语系苗瑶语族苗语支中部方言中的黔东南部次方言。

荔波苗族使用1956年国家创立的苗族拉丁拼音文字，即黔南地区以都匀坝固为标准音的苗文。自1984年起，苗族拼音文字一直在佳荣镇的水维小学和大土小学推广运用。

境内苗族房屋大多数是吊脚楼。改革开放后，群众生活水平逐年提高，吊脚楼由盖杉木皮改为盖瓦。苗族农户的禾仓均为吊脚禾仓，散居苗族多将禾仓建靠自家房屋。而聚居苗族的禾仓，都建在离寨子100米远的向阳高处。

禾晾也叫“禾穗”，是大土苗族特有的晾晒禾把（谷穗）的木架。大木架由两根粗大的杉木柱和数根穿方构成，形状像汉族地区的牌坊，顶部两侧盖上半米宽的“人”字形杉木皮档雨。通常建在寨旁、溪边。晚秋糯谷、小米、红稗等成熟时，农户将穗条剪摘、捆把，挂在禾晾上风干后入仓。无人看守，也不会失窃。禾晾是大土独有的奇景，进入大土苗寨，其溪水塘边或绿树楼旁，有一排排高达4米的大木架，整齐地围寨而立，构成一个连心架。

苗族主食为稻米，有籼稻和糯稻两类，水维坝区以籼米为主，大土等高寒山区以糯米为主。改革开放后，农户有了打米机，加工大米都用机械加工。杂粮有玉米、粟子、小麦、大麦、节豆、黄豆、薯类、洋芋、高粱、稗子、荞子等，一般不单独食用。

苗族口味嗜酸喜辣，日常生活离不开酸，故有“三天不吃酸，走路打趔趄”之说。由于居住地的地理条件较差，劳动强度大，劳作之余以酒舒筋活血，消除疲劳，家家户户自制酒曲，自酿各种泡酒、甜酒和烧酒。苗家有“无酒不请客，请客必有酒”的规矩，喝酒时多用大碗或竹筒，喝酒对歌，遇上好歌手对唱，从晚上一直对歌、喝酒到天亮。逢年过节，只要走进苗寨，不论走进哪家，均可一醉方归。糯米饭在苗族生活中占有重要地位，逢年过节要吃糯米饭或糯米粑，走亲访友要以糯米饭作礼物；女婿初拜岳父岳母，新媳妇始见公婆，须以糯米饭作为引荐礼物。酸鼠、酸鱼、酸鸟、酸笋、酸韭菜等是大土苗族较出名的风味名菜，也是大土苗族饮食文化的代名词。酸鼠、酸鱼、酸鸟是款待贵宾的席上佳肴。“酸汤鱼”则是水维苗族较出名的风味名菜，是接待宾客的重要菜肴。

佳荣苗族男子上穿对襟短衣，下穿长裤，头包青帕，内有一条白底方格帕为里层，青帕的一端绣轮形花纹，包头时，花纹竖于额前。佳荣苗族妇女的服装均为上衣下裙，有中裙和长裙，女上穿无领对襟衣，下穿长裤，外罩百褶裙。上衣肩部镶圆形托肩，托肩以红色、绿色、蓝色等色压边。长衣过膝，衣摆开口较长，领口、襟边、袖口、衣边均镶4条栏干花边，衣扣两排，每排三对，扣头是圆形铜质（或银质），扣桩长约4厘米。上衣内系围腰，围腰以4片红色、蓝色、绿色镶嵌为菱形，上片绣花。百褶裙分前后两片，上半段为青布，下半段白底蓝色蜡染图案。节日期间，女下装围裙片长至脚踝，外套过膝中裙。中裙后片裙为藏青色或蓝色，前片为百褶裙。特别是跳芦笙舞时，上衣加到六七件，加系前片百褶裙，裙边再加一圈乡花，还缀几十个小银铃，膝部以下系脚笼，脚笼彩带是用苎麻做成6条穗子，染为青色，脚穿黑色布鞋。头发梳成“斗”形。未婚女子参加活动时，均着盛装，戴银帽，佩上银角、银花等头饰，颈项载两三个项圈。手腕载三四副银手镯。全身所戴银饰重达数公斤，最重者可达10公斤。平时装束为胸前系围腰，外罩青布衫，下着长裤和后片百褶裙。年轻女子的服饰加镶嵌绣花边，显得格外艳丽。盛装上的图案采用传统图案，衣袖是重点装饰部位，多使用双头龙、单头双身龙、飞龙、蝴蝶、飞鸟、宗庙等，在领、肩、下摆中多使用变形的龙和变形的蝴蝶，衣襟上为一些虫和几何图案。花带裙和便装上的图案多为生活中所见的一些小动物，如青蛙、鸡、鸭、鱼、小鸟等再配上许多的花草。

散居苗族的服饰，男性头戴黑帕，一圈一圈扎在头上，衣服黑色，竖领，开襟，布纽扣，裤子黑色，大裤腰，大裤裆，大裤脚，用黑布带捆扎。女的头发梳成发髻，盘在脑后，称为“粑粑转”。年轻妇女戴的是黑白双层“锅圈帕”，由一黑一白两张两头带须的帕子，叠成五寸宽，外黑内白包在头上。老年妇女不再追求漂亮，一般只包一张黑帕子。女性的衣服颜色不定，是竖领，满襟，布纽扣。胸前拴围腰，上面绣有梯形彩色图案一块，颜色鲜艳美观。首饰是银项圈、银手镯。小孩的服装最特别的是帽子。帽子是黑色圆形的，项上有突出的拇指大小红色圆球，无遮阳，前沿缀上八个到十二个用银子铸造成的小佛像，叫做“银帽佛”。

佳荣苗族妇女都喜爱戴银饰，尤以黑苗最为重视。银饰主要有银簪、耳环、耳柱、耳坠、手镯、项圈、压领、胸佩和围腰链。头饰品只有蝴蝶形的银簪或叫银针，耳饰品是最常见的首饰，项圈多为三条棱形实心项圈，压领又叫长命锁，由一块心形或蝶形空心的领心和数十个银铃组成，用长约50厘米的粗银丝扭结而成的银链条连接领心，连接处有两块蝶形小银片，整个压领由三只蝴蝶组成，象征着苗族始祖“妹榜妹留”。少则1.5公斤，多则3～5公斤。戴银，一般可分为头饰、项圈、手镯、围腰链以及身上零星饰物，其品种达百余种，工艺颇为复杂。苗族银饰造型以蝶形、鱼形为主，在苗族观念中，蝴蝶是“蝴蝶妈妈”的象征，鱼是企盼民族人丁兴旺的向往。银饰工艺有锻打、压模、錾刻、浮雕、镂刻、扭结、焊接等。苗族的银饰在结构上以对称、均衡、放射为主要结构。

佳荣苗族银饰有男饰和女饰两大类。男饰较简单，有银锁、手箍、手镯、戒指、烟盒、项链、项圈、枪箍等单件饰品；女饰以成套为主，种类较多，有头饰、耳饰、项饰、胸饰、手饰和衣饰等几大类。头饰有银花、银角、银簪、银梳、插针等；耳饰有耳环、耳柱、耳坠等；胸饰有压领、项圈、项链等；手饰有手钏、手镯、手链、戒指等；衣饰有银片、银缀、银泡、银铃、腰链、披肩等。图案多为铜鼓、龙、蝴蝶、鸟、鱼、花等凸纹，顶端明显为变形银羽。三个角尖拴白鸡毛。造型主题充满了宗教观念。其余银饰多为花鸟造型，有双凤朝阳，喜鹊登梅，锦鸡报晓等造型。银饰图案也以花鸟、鱼虫、蝴蝶等为主。在苗族银饰的图案上，多以蝴蝶、牛角、锦鸡、花草为主要内容，蝴蝶是苗族的徽章，银角是苗族图腾的标志，锦鸡是“嘎闹”的族徽，花草是不同支系生活环境的印记。

苗族男女青年婚前有传统的社交活动，如“会姑娘”“跳苗”等都是苗族青年自由恋爱的方式及场所。境内苗族的婚俗，随着时代的发展，观念的改变，已逐步破除姑舅表婚，但同族同姓不准开亲。改革开放后，苗族青年男女到外地工作、打工，也开始与外地青年结合成亲，但当地的民族婚俗仍保持着浓郁的民族情趣。婚姻的缔结形式有自主婚、自由恋爱媒聘婚、媒聘婚三种类型。佳荣苗家的婚姻一般经过谈情、提亲、订亲、接亲、回门五个阶段。

境内苗族节日有跳苗节、谢牛节、龙袍节、种棉节、苗年节、万物收齐节、吃新节、开锄节、开秧门节、解耙节、鸟王节、风浪节、秧苗节等。

苗族有独具特色的完整丧葬习俗，体现浓厚的“灵魂不灭”观念。苗族将丧亡分为正常死亡和非正常死亡两类。寿终、青壮年善死者，称为正常死亡，实行木棺土葬；凶死、产死、夭殇、麻风病死、溺水死、吊颈死等称为非正常死亡，实行火葬或火葬后再土葬。老人正寝寿终称为“白喜”，是家庭的一件大事，必须用厚木棺土葬，并根据死者生前喜爱和家庭经济状况，杀牛、杀马、杀猪或杀羊等祭奠，举行隆重的葬礼，吹芦笙、芒筒、唢呐等送丧，棺材称“寿方”。丧俗有临终、咽气、沐尸、整容、入殓、守灵、停柩、入土、扶山、烧沐巾、满月、挂清等程序。苗族停柩时间为单数天，一般为一天，最多不超过三天。出殓前，请巫师于大门处，一脚踏门外，一脚在门内做法事“分手”，意为解脱死者与活人之联系。整个丧葬程序有落气告亲、停尸装棺、法师念咒、蒸饭作卜、分食祭品、棺木制作、陪葬衣饰、出葬礼仪、安葬仪式、祭祀仪式、扶山仪式等11个环节。

大土苗族崇拜和神，认为人有灵魂，灵魂不死，祖宗虽死犹活，注视活人的一切并干预活人的福祸安危。因此，凡遇有佳肴、逢年过节，出行或重大决策时，都要祭祀祖宗，乞求祖灵保佑，体现大土苗族对祖先虔诚，对老人尊重，以及对自然界的神秘和对神灵的畏惧。崇拜神林、牯牛、蝴蝶、波纹、修狃、岩石、水井、溪桥等。苗族最隆重的祭祖活动为“吃鼓藏”。“吃鼓”有大鼓藏、中鼓藏、小鼓藏之分。满60年甲子而举行的为大鼓藏，满30年举行的为中鼓藏，满12年举行的为小鼓藏。尤以间隔12年一祭最为普遍。苗族“吃鼓”有“醒鼓”“祭鼓”“送鼓”等程序，分三年进行，寅年“醒鼓”，卯年“祭鼓”，辰年“送鼓”。“吃鼓”有“黑鼓”“白鼓”之分，“黑鼓”的牺牲品为水牯牛，“白鼓”的牺牲品为猪。此外，还有祭雷神、祭土地神等祭祀活动。

佳荣境内苗族日常生活禁忌主要有女人不准爬楼，杨姓不吃猪心，新雷不干农活，新女婿不准摸锅灶。

境内苗族传统舞蹈有芦笙舞、古瓢舞、踩鼓舞、板凳舞等。

传统体育项目有射击赛、捉鱼赛、摔跤赛、拔河赛、陀螺赛。

五、瑶族

境内瑶族语言属汉藏语系苗瑶语族苗语支荔波方言组，下分瑶麓土语、瑶山土语和瑶埃土语。瑶麓、瑶山、瑶埃的瑶族长期各居一方，极少往来，各自使用本支土语，故三支瑶族之间语言不通，交谈借助布依语、汉语。三支瑶族从服饰上区分，称为青瑶、白裤瑶、长衫瑶。

（一）白裤瑶

瑶山地区白裤瑶村寨大都坐落在山谷的山腰、山脚或坡坳之中，村寨分布稀散，传统居住房是栽上几根木柱叉叉，围上竹篾，盖上茅草的“叉叉房”。20世纪80年代后，瑶山瑶族建干栏式青瓦木楼。

白裤瑶的禾仓，又称“坛子仓”，是瑶族最具代表性的建筑物。禾仓大多建在寨上中间和坡脚空旷地上，用四只木柱支撑，离地1.6米左右铺上木板，周围用竹篱笆围成圆形，顶上盖茅草避雨。禾仓最奇特的地方是在每根柱子与仓底的结合部，都安装有一只光滑锃亮的椭圆形土陶罐子，用罐子将木柱与禾仓分隔，老鼠无法爬进仓内，具有通风、防潮、防鼠、防虫等功能，仓底空地供人夏季休息和小孩玩耍。在白裤瑶的传统习俗里，一般人不能开仓，如出嫁的女儿、外来的人员都不能开仓进仓，但家族里的任何一个男子、女婿或未出嫁的姑娘都可以开仓进仓。

居住在山里的瑶族有丰富的狩猎经验，将捕捉到的山鼠、山鸟、山鸡、竹鼠、野猪等烘干后贮藏，用于款待客人。瑶族喜食虫蛹，将松树蛹、葛藤蛹、野蜂蛹、蜜蜂蛹等，作为下酒佳品。“瑶山鸡”是荔波瑶族地区的特产，饲养“瑶山鸡”为瑶族主要经济收入。

瑶山白裤瑶摆“长席宴”是沿袭千年的传统，当地人称之为“瑶王宴”。“瑶王宴”是瑶族同胞同甘共苦的一种象征，每逢接媳妇、嫁姑娘、丧葬等红白喜事，全寨男女老少都集中吃“瑶王宴”，周边寨子的人也参加，用木板摆起长长的“餐桌”，几百人一起进餐。参加“长席宴”的人越多，表示主人家的人缘越好。

白裤瑶男子常年穿着一模一样的宽裆紧腿白裤，上穿黑衣，胸前绣有方块白花，女子穿百褶裙，着背牌，服装的基本色调是黑色和白色。男的服装包括上衣、白裤、腰带、绑腿、头帕五大件。妇女穿着上身着黑衣下身穿裙子，包括背牌、头巾、裙子、腰带、绑腿五大件。男性白裤瑶婚前留短发，婚后留长发，把头发卷在白帕之内；上身着黑色矮领无扣土布长袖齐腰短衣，对襟敞胸，衣两侧和背后下端开岔口；下身穿着宽裆紧腿到膝白色短裤，裤脚装饰五条垂直红条；腰间系一条青色土布腰带（或花腰带）。膝下以布带绑腿。白裤瑶女童剃头，寒冬季节，头戴双角黑布帽，帽角在两侧，少女时期留发，婚后用头巾双折包头，包成两角，角在脑部前后，前高后矮，用白色布带系绕头巾。

白裤瑶青年男女自由恋爱结婚。女孩到十六七岁以后，其父母在家中靠门边的地方为其提供一间阁房，窗户朝外，开关自如，夜幕降临或是逢节日时，男子便到女孩子的窗前唱情歌、吹牛角、吹竹箫、吹木叶，意在向女子求爱，如果女孩子中意，便打开窗户让男子进屋。男女恋人通过几个月或一两年时间交往后，双方确立为意中人，男方告知母亲，请媒人到女方家拜访商谈提亲。婚后女子随夫居住。在白裤瑶的婚恋习俗中，常有包办婚姻、逼婚现象，但很少离婚。女孩子要出嫁时，男方按习俗要给女方母舅家一笔“母舅奶钱”，母舅才认可外甥女婿。随着时代的进步，以对情歌求爱的方式和婚前女子躲避男方家人的习俗在逐步改变。

白裤瑶普遍实行棺木土葬。凡十岁以下的小孩夭亡，一律不殓入棺，而且不能跟祖坟埋在一起，全村所有夭亡的小孩都规定在低凹的地方掩埋。十岁以上的人死亡，都视为大人，一切按常规办理。逝者安葬入土后，在寨子摆“长席宴”，几百人一起进餐。三日后，内亲、寨邻又至坟上盖泥土，并聚餐。此后不再奠祭，清明不扫墓。

白裤瑶认为神无处不在，山有山神，水有水神，天有天神，地有地神，家有家神，还有寨神、门神、灶神、圈神、井神、树神、石神、洞神等。白裤瑶有“架花桥”、立“花娘牌”等添粮补寿习俗，用这些习俗祈求老人、小孩健康长寿。为祈求神的保佑，建房下基石时要敬供鲁班，新房入住前要敬供屋神、门神、土地神、（猪牛）圈神，种植下种要敬供雷公。有老人过世，要准备棺材和背牌，举行敲铜鼓和砍牛仪式。

白裤瑶普遍禁食鹅肉、羊肉、狗肉和猴肉。当他们听到第一声春雷以后，七天不出工，第二次减为五日，第三次减为三日，谓之“忌雷”。每个村寨都有一株风水树，谓之“神树”，不准砍伐。家门前挂着象征门神的木刀、狗爪和鸡毛，绝对不允许乱摸乱动。已婚女子不得进外家的粮仓或开外家的酸坛。生育小孩，必须由产妇自己接生，不但外人不能去帮助她，就连他的母亲、姐妹、妯娌也不准前去助产。未满月的孩子，除孩子的母亲外，谁也不准摸、抱孩子。

白裤瑶传统的体育项目有打陀螺、打石陀、射弩、射箭、踩高跷等，其中，瑶山陀螺项目代表贵州省参加全国第五届到第八届少数民族运动会并取得优异成绩。

（二）青瑶

瑶麓青瑶自然村寨用石块垒成又高又厚的围墙相隔，每个寨子都留有一个或两个出入口，出入口都设置一座用杉木柱子、盖青瓦的小寨门（当地称为“丢弯”），门寨外一侧设一个用大块片石搭成的神龛，神龛内放一些奇形怪状的石头，传说这些石头是瑶民先祖请来的“山神”“石神”“土地神”，形成“丢弯果瓦”，供人节日奉贡。

青瑶住房建筑多为干栏式木瓦吊脚楼，住房较为低矮，上半部镶木板，下半部围用石片围隔，楼上住人，楼下为厩，饲养牲畜，具有冬暖夏凉的特点。堂屋正对大门的板壁上装设一香火台“以洼”，在香火台框边插上锦鸡、野鸡等漂亮的珍禽羽毛作为装饰，以显示这家主人是打猎高手及荣誉的象征展示。各户均在自己的住房旁边用粗木竖起一个四五米高，七八米长的晾架，称为“禾廊”，专供晒包谷和糯谷用。青瑶特地为未婚女儿设置一间“厢房”，在房间的板壁上设一个能观察“厢房”的小孔，谓之“谈婚洞”。男女青年夜间通过“谈婚洞”表达爱慕之情。

青瑶男女都有便装和盛装。男性的盛装，上衣外边左胸部处有绣花纹禾包，腰带系花腰带，帕巾包头，外面一块两端一定有刺绣花纹和须线，脚笼绑腿彩带，一般节日喜庆走亲访友才着盛装，平时便装。妇女盛装特别，披带背牌，花边条飘带挂背面两侧，头髻别插银簪3—5根，佩带银项圈5—7根，胸前挂上银鸟3—5个，腰上系3—4条彩带，脚笼彩带绑腿，衣裙花纹图案鲜红耀眼，色彩艳丽。妇女在节日喜庆的日子里，特别是参与迎亲送亲的青年女孩，必须穿戴盛装。改革开放后，男女平时穿着逐步改变为以汉族服装为主，男子已改留短发，妇女平时不佩戴银饰，不别头簪。

青瑶青年男女恋爱自由，婚姻自主。青瑶女孩十八岁后，就让她单独住进专门为她修建的“寮房”，即屋大门侧面的一个房子，开始与青年小伙子谈情说爱。姑娘的床头板壁上凿有一个小孔，这就是“凿壁谈婚洞”，瑶语称之为“K笛”，每当夜深人静，小伙子就到“K笛”与姑娘谈情说爱，通过交谈和长久的接触交往，了解后，方能选定自己的恋爱对象。双方就可相互馈赠银项圈等定情信物，互定终生。青瑶婚礼程序先是订婚。男女订婚后，一般在半年至一年的时间内多为由男方父母择日结婚，时间一般选择在农历十月至次年二月底前。结婚后，先由新郎家办客邀请女方家（外家）哥弟吃“认亲饭”，过后新郎新娘邀请房族哥弟回门拜访岳父母。

青瑶至今仍沿袭洞葬。老人病故，亲戚寨邻向遗体告别后便一律回避，由儿媳妇替死者洗身换衣。尸体在出殡前才入棺。入殓时，由儿媳妇抬死者的头和脚，大儿子扶腰，房族同辈分的男女扶身，“媳妇替老大”，这是规矩，儿媳妇不能推脱。棺材进洞要看时辰，有专人推算。一般是晚上十时以前进洞，少数是白天进洞。亲戚与寨邻都来送葬。送葬者，包括直系儿孙都不戴孝。出发前，鸣铁炮三响，吹“八仙”。祭祀活动在葬洞前的平地上举行。埋葬后，家中不设神龛，不供香火，仅在三早及七早祭一下，而所谓的祭三祭七，到时候亲友也来致哀，以后就不再祭祀，也不扫墓。洞葬的规矩有八岁以下儿童死亡不能洞葬；几个寨子（即几个姓）合用一个洞，洞内按姓氏划定葬区，同姓五代以内堆放在一起，不相混淆，棺材堆放不分辈分、年龄、性别，自下而上按先后顺序叠放；棺材上不署姓名牌位；非正常死亡者棺材，或置放在洞口，或沿岩壁，也有直接火焚的。

青瑶信奉的鬼神较多，主要有山神、寨神、家神、爱情神、生育神、保育神、地基神、大门神、落魂神等。为保佑儿童祛病消邪，家家大门顶上挂有小木刀三把，雉鸡毛数根，干谷穗几点。瑶麓青瑶信奉怪石、巨树，每个村寨都在村口寨门设有土地庙，供奉寨神。所谓庙宇，仅是一座简陋石盒，里面放数块奇形怪状、中间穿孔的石头，坐落在入寨路口处的大榕树下。每年大年三十，全寨合资购买食品家家户户男性老幼聚集，在土地庙前举行迎春祭祀、烧香、烧纸，祈求全寨人丁兴旺、风调雨顺。当寨内发生重大事情时（如出现瘟疫），也要集体在土地庙前祭祀，封寨三天，寨门有专人把守，不准生人闯入。全部封寨活动妇女都不能参加。

青瑶的禁忌主要有结婚时接亲、送亲队伍不得同走一条路；妇女“坐月子”禁食荤，满月才能开荤；坐月妇女不能到别家串门；禁忌雷鸣和急风暴雨；开春后直到收割，听到雷声，要放枪鸣炮，并不出工一天等。

（三）长衫瑶

长衫瑶房屋建筑大都是干栏式青瓦木楼，木楼高，开间宽。楼底为畜厩及堆放农业工具与柴草，楼上住人，并以板壁相隔。

长衫瑶男子蓄发绾锥髻，身着青色长衫，故称“长衫瑶”或“长袍瑶”。长衫瑶服饰领襟相连，领口袖口白色，无扣，腰系青色布带。长衫瑶中男女留长头发，头包青色帕，包头帕长约2米，妇女头帕上还别银簪。头帕两端各绣有一方形图印，图中各绣有两条鱼纹。头帕的中间绣有三个小人头的方形图印。包头时三个小人头图在额前，表示家庭和睦美满；一头鱼纹在脑后，表示夫妻鱼水情深，形影不离，和谐到老；另一头鱼纹插入额前帕内，表示牢牢地把握住爱情过上甜蜜生活。长衫瑶男子头上包帕，帕巾中央绣有正方形印鉴式的图案，头帕一年四季包在头上，常年身穿长袍长裤，一身不变。长衫瑶少年儿童戴三角形帽子，帽子前方绣有三十几个小人头，表示伙伴越多越好。长衫瑶妇女身着右衽无扣短衣，穿背牌，背牌绣有各色的大方形图案。妇女手腕戴着各式银手镯，胸前佩戴五根至九根扁型银项圈，下身围三四条蜡染绣花百褶裙，后套围片，腿套脚笼，系有绣球带拴住。

长衫瑶的婚姻多为自由恋爱缔结。男女青年开始谈恋爱时，以走亲访友的方式到亲戚家的寨上物色对象，与姑娘对歌谈情，如双方有意便互赠信物，传递爱意，并请媒人谈合，同时得到父母及族中家人的同意后，男方选择吉日良辰，带领姑娘回自己的家看父母，并邀约寨上的青年男女和亲朋好友，摆席设宴同贺。次日，男方寨上姊妹随同姑娘前往娘家回门，第二天房族各家都杀鸡、杀鸭邀请姑娘吃“开口饭”，女方寨上摆设酒宴邀请陪同姊妹吃“认亲饭”。婚期的当天，新娘家按习俗在自家大门前摆设“拦门酒”，专门恭候男方所邀来的结亲队伍。接亲人每人必喝一碗酒，吃一块肥肉，才允许男方进入女方家门。次日还要举行新娘“八字酒”。新娘家族按习俗，女方陪送嫁妆的多少来定摆放酒碗的数量，让新郎接亲人员自行饮尽方能接纳嫁妆出门。新娘随新郎一行人到女方家按习俗只顾饮酒而饭吃不饱，男方家还需派专人送饭送荤菜在接亲人员返家途中食用一餐，饭毕启程。临近家门时，新郎和新娘脱鞋赤脚携手同走专门制作的新竹楼梯进入家门，以竹象征新郎和新娘未来的生活节节高升。婚后第三天新郎携新娘备足一定礼物回门返娘家酬谢舅亲，女方家全体房族用佳肴美酒殷勤款待新姑爷，用餐的方式有各家各请，也有几家联合宴请。至此，婚礼程序全部结束。

长衫瑶仿效周边民族由洞葬改为土葬。长衫瑶老人病故后，丧家须在堂屋设灵堂，供奉亡灵神祇。并杀牛祭祀，牛角挂在堂屋左侧房柱上方以示纪念。亲朋寨邻送酒及糯米参加吊唁，并敲铜鼓三天三夜。青年男女在丧家的寨中举行“打竹把”“板腰”等传统性群众活动。丧家对参加吊唁者供食一餐。送葬时，要请道士先生来“开路”。坟茔无固定葬地，由丧家任意选中。

长衫瑶主要信仰神庙，在洞塘瑶寨的田坝中，仍然保留着两坐庙宇，一座叫“老虎庙”，一座叫“田庙”，每年春节后，集体进行隆重的祭祀活动。

长衫瑶坐月妇女严禁到处乱跑，不准串门，不准喂牛、喂猪，不准做农活，有些老年人“忌腿”，不肯轻易出门，特别不愿参加丧葬活动。男子参加祭祀活动，女子不许动手用铁器。在举行丧葬仪式时，本家族的人不准吃肉。打新雷以后不准食鼠。胸前绣有白花的上衣，只有男子才能穿。

县内瑶族都过春节、清明节、端午节、中秋节，还有自己特有的传统节日陀螺节、小年、卯节、播种节、熟霞祭祖和尝新米节、庙节等。

第四节　民族事务

一、民族经费管理使用

从1980年成立县民族事务委员会起，中央、省、州下拨的民族经费，由县民委管理，县民委根据各少数民族生产、生活需要的轻重缓急情况立项目，投入经费，予以扶持。2001年以后，每年开展项目立项、论证工作并向省、州申报项目资金，对上年度项目的扫尾工作进行督促、检查、验收。项目资金管理由以拨代支改为报账制，实行项目建设的共同责任制。

水书研究与挖掘

1980—2008年，中央、省、州、县拨付民族经费总计1636.9万元。民族经费主要投向为：投入农业、林业、牧业生产总计179.1万元，购买各种农业机械505台、化肥119吨，购买水稻、玉米良种及树苗、果苗、种牛、种猪、鱼苗，举办农业技术培训班120期，培养少数民族农业技术人员7000余人；投入群众生产生活总计788.3万元，兴建人饮工程323处，维修电站5处及驾设、维修输电线路93处，补助农村特困户和无房户建房

659栋（建筑面积共52464平方米，户均79.6平方米），打造民族村寨改建民房180户；投入教育总计277.2万元，补助修建教学楼11814平方米，维修校舍6224平方米，添置教学设备体育器材、课桌凳，补助困难少数民族学生25575人次；投入文化体育事业总计158.3万元，主要用于补助民族节日活动（如布依族“四月八”斗牛节、“六月六”歌会和端午节龙舟赛、水族卯节、瑶山瑶族陀螺赛等），开办布依族、水族、苗族的民族语言文字学习班和“双语”教学班，为县民族文工队购置乐器、服装、道具以及文工队员的工资补贴费，补助“水书”和布依“傩书”的搜集、整理，补助各乡（镇）建立电视差转台、文化站和民间文艺队等；投入交通基础设施总计452.3万元，补助新修乡村公路76条375公里，维修乡村公路65条90.4公里，新建大小桥梁43座，维修桥梁23座，资助部分村寨寨内道路硬化等；投入医疗卫生事业总计44.8万元，补助边远乡村卫生院、村卫生室修建医务用房816平方米，添置各种医疗设备779台（件），购买部分常用药品，解决农村群众就医难问题。2007年8月，瑶山瑶族学生谢高丽（女）和瑶麓瑶族学生韦熙考上大学，由于两名学生的家庭因贫困无力供子女上学，县民宗局向州民宗委申请后每人获得助学金3000元。

1980—2008年全县民族经费收支统计表

表3-2　　单位：万元

年度	民族经费来源					民族经费投向					
	总计	中央	省	州	县	农林牧生产	群众生产生活	教育	文化体育	交通	其他
1980	21.0	5.0	10.1	5.1	0.9	3.9	8.3	6.6	0.3	1.1	0.8
1981	58.8	20.0	25.0	13.5	0.3	10.8	23.1	18.6	0.9	3.1	2.3
1982	48.8	17.5	21.0	10.0	0.3	14.3	12.6	5.3	1.1	9.5	6.0
1983	44.9	15.5	19.0	10.0	0.4	11.3	9.3	5.3	1.4	15.2	2.4
1984	54.3	19.0	23.5	11.5	0.3	6.5	16.5	10.4	4.4	3.3	13.0
1985	22.1	7.5	9.8	4.5	0.3	3.8	5.1	8.0	3.0	2.0	0.2
1986	31.3	12.0	13.5	5.5	0.3	2.4	10.5	11.6	1.8	1.1	3.3
1987	34.7	12.0	15.0	7.4	0.3	2.0	11.0	10.8	2.2	4.9	3.8
1988	41.9	14.0	18.0	9.5	0.4	0.6	8.5	15.0	5.2	1.0	8.6
1989	37.1	12.5	16.2	8.0	0.4	3.2	10.6	11.4	1.9	2.9	7.1
1990	41.8	14.1	18.1	9.1	0.5	1.0	15.6	6.3	14.3	2.0	2.6
1991	32.0	11.0	13.5	7.0	0.5	0.7	8.0	7.2	5.2	4.3	6.6
1992	29.3	10.0	12.5	6.4	0.4	0.7	7.6	7.5	1.3	0.2	12.0
1993	37.2	12.5	16.0	8.0	0.7	0.5	5.1	19.0	2.0	1.5	8.9
1994	32.0	7.3	15.5	8.5	0.7	2.0	6.5	2.9	1.6	1.4	2.6
1995	31.2	10.5	13.5	6.5	0.7	0	13.6	4.0	1.9	3.8	7.9
1996	32.0	10.5	13.5	7.2	0.8	0.6	10.1	5.3	0.7	8.7	6.6
1997	28.0	9.5	11.8	5.9	0.8	2.5	7.0	6.0	2.0	7.0	3.5
1998	60.0	20.0	23.0	16.0	1.0	0	36.0	4.5	0	13.5	6.0

续表3-2

年度	民族经费来源					民族经费投向					
	总计	中央	省	州	县	农林牧生产	群众生产生活	教育	文化体育	交通	其他
1999	62.2	20.0	25.0	16.2	1.0	1.3	15.8	5.0	0.4	8.6	6.2
2000	59.6	23.0	23.0	12.6	1.0	1.0	25.6	2.0	5.0	23.5	2.5
2001	90.2	33.0	37.0	19.0	1.2	1.5	41.7	11.0	2.0	30.0	4.0
2002	69.7	23.5	27.0	18.0	1.2	0	17.3	11.0	5.0	35.0	1.4
2003	75.0	25.0	29.0	19.5	1.5	3.2	20.3	7.0	6.0	34.4	4.1
2004	85.5	28.0	40.0	14.0	3.5	4.6	14.0	8.2	23.0	33.0	2.7
2005	56.4	15.0	18.0	18.5	4.9	6.0	11.0	6.0	5.0	26.5	1.9
2006	121.2	45.0	56.0	15.0	5.1	31.0	27.0	27.0	0.0	27.0	8.3
2007	126.7	39.1	47.0	20.6	20.0	29.0	11.0	15.0	14.0	86.0	7.7
2008	172.0	50.0	60.5	41.5	20.0	38.0	24.0	25.0	47.0	38.0	0
合计	1636.9	542.0	671.0	354.5	69.4	179.1	427.6	277.2	158.3	452.3	142.2

二、少数民族干部培养

1978年，县委、县政府对少数民族干部陆续采取短期培训与长期专业培养相结合的方式，有计划地选送部分中等专业学校毕业生或在职干部到县、州党校和各类大专院校学习深造。

从1983年9月起，县委、县政府每年选送部分少数民族学生到黔南州民族干部管理学校学习，培养少数民族干部。

1987年后，县委、县政府鼓励各单位干部职工参加自学成才考试，对自学成才取得毕业证书者，每科给予考试费补助20元。是年，全县有少数民族干部1533人，占全县干部总数的62.41%。

1992年，瑶山瑶族一名女学生谢珍妹初中毕业，她是瑶山唯一完成初中学业的女孩，但其中考总分未达到录取分数线，为培养瑶族女干部，县政府责成县民委向省、州招生办反映瑶山没有瑶族女干部，谢珍妹是新中国成立后瑶山唯一读完初中的女学生的情况，后来谢珍妹被破格录取进入黔南民族干部管理学校学习。

1994年，县委、县政府鼓励全县各族干部参加在职学习，并报销学费。由县人事局和县委党校牵头，在县委党校开设脱产中专班、函授大专班和本科班，全县在职干部职工报名参加学习的人数达60%以上。

2000年秋，县委、县政府作出培养“村级青年干部队伍”的决定，并连续3年委托县职业中学开设“村级科技干部班”，培养村级少数民族后备干部200人。

至2008年，全县行政、事业单位干部共4201人，其中少数民族干部3647人，占干部总数的86.81%。县级领导干部中少数民族干部占68%，科级领导干部中少数民族干部占85.3%；行政单位中少数民族干部占81.43%，事业单位中少数民族干部占88.16%。

三、民族政策法规宣传

中共十一届三中全会后，县委、县政府实施《中华人民共和国民族区域自治法》《国务院实施

〈中华人民共和国民族区域自治法〉若干规定》《贵州省实施〈中华人民共和国民族区域自治法〉若干规定》（以下简称“一法两规定”），重视对“一法两规定”的学习、宣传和贯彻执行。县人大常委会将“一法两规定”等法律、法规印制成《民族工作法律手册》1000册，发送到县机关、乡（镇）、村、组学习。县民族工作职能部门对学习、宣传、贯彻执行“一法两规定”常抓不懈，利用有线广播、有线电视等媒体开办民族法律、法规专栏节目，采用墙报、黑板报、张贴宣传标语等方式开展学习、宣传活动，利用场天到各乡（镇）集市发放法律、法规等资料，开展法律、法规和民族政策咨询服务。

1990年7月31日，县委、县政府行文要求全县干部职工认真学习、贯彻执行“一法两规定”。1995年、1996年、2002年，先后牵头举办全县干部职工民族知识竞赛活动，全县17个乡（镇）和县直各单位干部职工参与竞赛答题，并参加黔南州民族知识竞赛摇奖活动，均获三等奖。

自“一法两规定”颁布实施到2008年，共编印《法律工作手册》和法律、法规单行本1.7万册，县直有关部门和乡（镇）办墙报、黑板报共395期，全县张贴宣传标语2000多条（幅）。

四、民族文化研究

（一）民族古籍整理

1.《水书》古籍整理。2002年3月，荔波县参与申报的《水书》入选国家档案局、中央档案馆首批《中国档案文献遗产名录》，11月，县人大常委会作出《关于开展拯救水书工作情况汇报的审议意见》，要求县政府将《水书》征集抢救工作列入政府议事日程。之后，县政府成立《水书》抢救工作领导小组，开始《水书》抢救工作。

2003年3月，县政协六届一次会议上，68名委员联名提出《关于挖掘古老民族文化，开发利用水书，申报为世界文化遗产的提案》；县第十四届人大一次会议作出《关于抢救整理开发利用古老文化——水书并申报为世界文化遗产的决议》。

2005年12月8日，县政府颁布《荔波县水书抢救保护工作实施办法》，组织收集民间珍藏的《水书》，在县档案馆建立《水书》展示厅。

2006年6月，申报的“水书习俗”项目获国务院批准入选首批《国家级非物质文化遗产》。

2007年5月，成立荔波县民族研究所。民族研究所为县民宗局下属副科级事业单位。同时在县民族研究所加挂荔波县水书研究院牌子。是年10月，县民族研究所组织译注《水书·泐金》卷，由贵州省档案局（馆）与荔波县政府合编，贵州人民出版社正式出版。

2008年3月，《水书·庚甲》《水书·泐金》《水书·金银》入选首批《国家珍贵古籍名录》。2008年年底，完成《水书·金银》卷注译并交由贵州人民出版社出版。至此，全县收入县档案馆收藏的《水书》原件9107册。其中，1000余册经注录后载入《中国少数民族古籍总目提要》网，2000册馆藏《水书》列入国家图书馆数字资源联合建设工程项目。

2.布依文古籍整理。2007年3月，成立县布依文古籍研究馆，下设陈列室、研究资料室、办公室。10月，成立县布依文古籍申报工作组，工作组撰写出布依傩书的申报专卷、情况简介，整理出“布依族古文字表”。

2008年3月，组建荔波县古籍专家委员会，邀请省、州古籍专家参与“布依文古籍”评审鉴定。11月，正式将《献酒备用》《解书神庙》《汉皇书》《关煞向书注解》《接魂大全》等5部布依文古籍申报第二批《国家珍贵古籍名录》。

（二）民族研究

为保护、挖掘、弘扬和传承境内少数民族文化，1989年，成立贵州省水家学会荔波中心组。1994年，成立贵州省苗学会荔波工作委员会。2003年，成立荔波县布依学会。2004年8月，贵州省苗学会荔波工作委员会更名为荔波县苗学会。2005年，成立荔波县水家学会、荔波县瑶学会。

以上学会成立后，分别对本民族的历史、政治、经济、文化、艺术、科学、教育、体育、卫生等方面开展调查研究和学术交流活动，先后编撰出版《荔波布依族》（上、下集）、《荔波水族》《荔波瑶族》《荔波苗族》《荔波布依族古歌集》《荔波少数民族考略》等7本历史文献书籍。

第五节　民族团结

中共十一届三中全会后，县委、县政府加强民族工作，促进各民族大团结、大繁荣。1980年8月成立县民族事务专门工作机构。1981年6月8日，县委行文批转县委组织部《关于干部要求更改族别问题的处理意见》。

1982年6月22日，县政府行文成立县“民族团结月”活动领导小组，贯彻落实州七届人大二次会议关于从1982年起每年8月开展全州“民族团结月”活动的决定，各区、公社也成立“民族团结月”活动领导机构，指定专人具体办公，进一步改善和发展社会主义民族关系，增强各民族人民之间的团结。1983年7月，县中医院莫珍友（布依族）、韦荣芝（女，布依族）获国家民委、人事部、中国科协联合授予“在少数民族地区长期从事科技工作者”称号。

1988年9月21日，县十届人大常委会第八次会议审议了《关于贯彻落实少数民族政策、发展民族地区经济工作情况汇报》。

1989年，玉屏一小苗族女教师吴洪芬获国家民委、人事部、总工会授予“模范优秀教师”称号。

1990年7月31日，县委办、县政府办印发《关于认真开展民族团结月活动的通知》，在全县开展民族团结月活动。

1993年9月、1996年1月，县十二届人大常委会先后2次审议县政府关于开展民族工作的情况报告。1998年9月、1999年5月，县十三届人大常委会分别审议县政府《关于我县民族乡经济发展情况的报告》《关于我县贯彻〈民族乡行政工作条例〉情况的报告》。

1999年7月18日（农历六月初六），县民族事务局与县委宣传部、文化局共同举办全县首次布依族“六月六”传统歌节活动。

2000年，佳荣镇大土村支部书记龙贵雄（苗族）获国务院授予“全国劳动模范”称号。

2003年，省委、省政府召开“贵州省第四次民族团结进步表彰大会”，瑶麓乡政府何继恩获省委、省政府授予“民族团结先进个人”称号。

2005年11月10日，县委组织部、县委统战部、县法制办和县民宗局联合举办全县民族宗教工作培训会，17个乡（镇）分管宗教工作的副书记、政法委书记、社会事务办主任、公安派出所及94个村（居）党支部书记、村委会主任等280多人参加了培训会，树立加强民族团结、维护社会稳定的大局意识。

2007年6月4日，县民宗局组织召开以“如何在新时期抓好民族工作”为主题的专题座谈会，布依族、苗族、水族、瑶族4个民族学会的会员参加座谈。

2008年8月25日，县民宗局牵头，会同县司法局、文体广播电视局、科协、妇联等单位利用场天开展“民族团结月”系列宣传活动，悬挂横幅标语10条，展出图片50幅，发送资料4000份，接受群众咨询150人次。

第三章 宗 教

第一节 宗教活动

一、佛教

1978年，县内信奉佛教仅几人，因相继离世，至1990年仅有信徒1人。玉屏镇周守珍（女）受其父影响信奉佛教，曾到贵阳黔灵山弘福寺学教，获宗教界“皈依证”“菩萨戒牒”“五戒证”三证，入门后法名“通贞”，在自己家中设“静心室”进行佛教活动。1991年，发展老年人5名加入佛教，5名老年人先后取得宗教界“皈依证”。每年农历二月、六月、九月的十九日为佛教节日，即观世音菩萨圣诞日、成道日和出家纪念日，每逢这三个日子，教徒和信教群众聚集举办观音庙会。2003年，经州、县两级民宗部门实地考察，为“静心室”发“宗教活动场所临时登记证”，“静心室”成为境内唯一合法宗教场所，信教人员在合法场所烧香、拜佛、念经，正常开展爱国爱教活动。至2008年，全县有佛教在册人员292人。是年5月，四川汶川地震发生后，信教人士17人向灾区捐款1050元。

二、天主教

20世纪90年代后，一些外出打工的群众在外地加入天主教后带入荔波，也有外来传教人员传入。2008年年初，全县登记天主教在册人员34人，主要分布在县城，甲良镇的纳核村、石板村，方村乡寨近村、红泥村，播尧乡的豆村等。由于人数少、规模小，居住分散，没有固定的活动场所，因此，他们都到独山的三棒等处教堂参加活动。

三、基督教

1995—1996年，甲良镇石板村莫某某等9人，由当时在平塘县教书的美籍华人李某和在独山教书的美籍华人李某出资，介绍他们到广州白云区汉高镇学习基督教90天，学习结束后回乡传教，未能发展。2002年，县内有基督教在册登记人员12人。2003年8月，永康太吉村溪鸟组蒙某某和瑶山懂别村谢某某到贵阳医学院附近教堂学习基督教10多天后，带回《圣经》、十字架、圣像、光碟、教历等进行宣传、发放。2004—2008年，有美国、韩国等外籍基督教教徒以旅游观光为名，到水利乡的水丰、水岩，佳荣镇的拉祥、水维、拉埃、拉学、拉平、岜鲜，甲良镇的甲良、甲新，瑶山乡的菇类等地散发基督教宣传资料。到2008年，全县有基督教在册人员42人。

第二节　宗教管理

2001年，荔波县民族事务局更名为荔波县民族宗教事务局。2002年1月，按县政府办《关于印发荔波县民族宗教事务局职能配置内设机构和人员编制规定的通知》，将宗教管理职能纳入县民族宗教事务局。

是年年底，全县有信教人数100人，其中佛教56人、天主教32人、基督教12人。

2003年8月，成立县宗教工作协调小组，各乡（镇）相应成立宗教工作协调小组，对全县174个村的248名协调员进行登记。是年，有基督教教徒以支教为名，到茂兰小学传教，散发《圣经》、基督教宣传资料等，发现后及时处理。

2004年6月，在县民族宗教事务局设立县宗教事务管理所，为正股级事业单位。7月，县民宗局举办全县各乡（镇）宗教工作协调小组正、副组长和县直机关分管领导培训班，学习宗教理论和宗教政策。同时，开展《宗教管理条例》宣传，发放宣传资料，张贴宣传标语；在城镇开展咨询服务并发放《条例》500多本、宣传资料210份，接受群众咨询87人次，受理群众咨询服务58人次。在宣传中，发现美国、韩国等外籍人员借旅游为名，到水利乡的水丰、水岩，佳荣镇的拉祥、水维、拉埃、拉学、拉毛、岜鲜，甲良镇的甲良、甲新，瑶山乡的菇类等村寨散发宣传资料，县民宗局立即与统战、公安等部门联合进行查处4起。

2005年7月，县宗教事务管理所在水利乡纳莪组收缴《改变历史的耶稣——耶稣爱水族人》155本、宣传宗教水语光碟848张，并对传教者进行教育。

2007年7月，在方村中学收缴有关宣传耶稣书籍和有关资料，并对外国传教人员作口头警告，并责令其限期出境。同年在宗教调查中，发现玉屏镇时来二组农民麦某某在其住处开设宗教聚会点“德福堂”，无宗教界发给的证件，不具备合法条件，不能对外开放和接收社会上的人员到该处从事宗教活动，且在其活动中掺杂有封建迷信内容，不属宗教信徒，其宗教活动为非法，责令其停止活动。

2008年，全县有信教人员368人，其中佛教292人、天主教34人、基督教42人。

第四篇
中国共产党地方组织

1978—2008年，中共荔波县召开了第四次、第五次、第六次、第七次、第八次、第九次、第十次代表大会。历届中共荔波县委领导全县人民贯彻执行中共中央的一系列方针政策，结合荔波县实际，在煤炭工业开发、“三农”（农业、农村、农民）问题，扶贫开发、发展旅游业、精神文明建设、城乡建设、文化教育卫生事业等方面制定和实施了改革开放、经济建设的举措，使荔波经济社会得到前所未有的发展。同时，县纪律检查委员会强化党风党纪教育与廉政建设，县委各部门不断深化机关改革，整顿机关作风，加强党组织建设，对党员开展“三讲教育”“三个代表”重要思想学习等思想建设，各项党务工作得到改善和提高。

第一章　中共荔波县委员会

第一节　工作机构

1978年，县委工作机构有县委办公室、县纪律检查委员会、县委组织部、县委宣传部、县委党校、县信访组等6个。

1980—1985年，先后成立县直属机关党委、县委保密委员会、县委统战部、县委政法委员会、县委农村工作部、县委和政府联合信访科、县史志编纂委员会办公室、老干部科等8个工作部门。

1990年，成立县委机要局、县保密局。

1994年，对县委工作机构进行改革，撤销农村工作部、机要局、保密局的独立建制，工作职能并入县委办，对外挂保密办牌子；撤销联合信访办公室的独立建制，工作职能分别并入县委办、政府办；撤销老干局的独立建制，行政职能并入组织部；撤销对台办的独立建制，工作职能并入统战部，对外挂县委台湾工作办和政府台湾事务办的牌子；宣传部含精神文明指导和对外宣传工作，与人武部共同承担国防教育工作。县委工作机构有1办（县委办）、3部（组织部、宣传部、统战部）、2委（政法委员会、直属机关党委）共6个。

2001年，县级党政机构改革后，县委工作机构为8个：纪律检查委员会（监察局与其合署办公，实行一套工作机构，两个机关名称的体制）；县委办公室（含政策研究工作、机要局〔密码工作领导小组办公室〕、保密委员会办公室〔保密局〕，为副科级机构）；组织部（离退休干部工作局归口组织部管理）；宣传部（精神文明建设指导委员会办公室设在宣传部）；统一战线工作部（含对台工作）；政法委员会（社会治安综合治理委员会办公室与其合署办公，维护社会稳定领导小组办公室设在政法委，为正科级机构）；机构编制委员会办公室；直属机关党委。至2008年，上述工作机构设置不变。

县纪律检查委员会　1978年10月，恢复成立中共荔波县委纪律检查委员会。1981年1月，改称中共荔波县纪律检查委员会，仍属县委工作机构。1984年2月，根据中共中央文件精神，升格为县委领导机构之一。1988年，在各区、镇及县粮食局、县教育局、县供销社设纪检组。1993年，县纪委、县监察局合署办公，人员编制10人。2001年，县纪委（监察局）内设办公室、控告申诉室、纪检监察室、案件审理室、执法监察室、党风廉政建设室（加挂纠风室的牌子），行政编制13人（纪委5人、监察局8人）。2007年12月，控告申诉室更名为县纪委信访室。2008年，县纪委在县直属机关单位派驻纪检组13个，县纪委（监察局）内设机构增设综合室，行政编制增加到14人。

县委办公室　1994年，县委办公室内设秘书信息股、督查调研股、综合股，人员编制18人。

2001年对县委办公室的职能进行调整，内设机构为机要局、保密局（保密委员会办公室）均为副科级机构和督查政研室、秘书股、信息股三个职能室及机关后勤服务中心（事业单位）。行政编制16人，事业编制7人，直至2008年机构不变。

县委组织部荔波县委建立后就设立组织部。1992年2月，县委知识分子联系小组办公室变更为县委知识分子工作领导小组办公室，升格为正科级机构，挂靠组织部。2001年12月，知识分子办公室变更为组织部内设股室，另设办公室、组织股、干部股、干部监督办公室。并建立党员电教中心，为组织部下属股级事业单位；县委离退休干部工作局归口组织部管理。2005年5月，成立荔波县农村党员干部现代远程教育办公室，为组织部管理的副科级事业机构。2007年，增设信息股，为组织部内设正股级机构，人员编制在组织部已有编制中调整。至2008年机构未变。

县委宣传部　1994年4月，县委宣传部内设机构有办公室、宣传通讯科、理论教育科、对外宣传办公室、精神文明办公室、国防教育办公室。宣传部人员编制5人。2005年，在宣传部设县新闻中心。2008年，人员编制6人。

县委统战部　1982年，恢复建立县统一战线工作部。1987年10月，县委成立对台工作领导小组，下设办公室，副科级机构，无正式编制，由统战部兼管。1990年8月，设立县政府台湾事务办公室，隶属县政府领导，挂靠统战部管理。1991年7月1日，人员增加到4人。1994年4月，撤销台办独立建制，工作职能并入统战部，对外加挂县委台湾工作办公室和县政府台湾事务办公室两块牌子，至2008年机构不变。

县委政法委员会　1982年5月，成立县委政法委员会。1991年5月，成立社会治安综合治理办公室，与政法委合署办公，至2008年未变。

县直机关党委　1980年6月成立县直属机关党委，正科级单位，内设机构有办公室，行政编制3人。到2008年实有人员5人。

县离退休干部工作局　1985年3月，成立县委老干部科，设在县委组织部。1987年10月，县委老干部科改为县委老干部局，归县委组织部管理。1990年，县委老干部局改为县离退休干部局，由县委、县政府共同管理。1996年12月，县离退休干部局更名为县离退休干部工作局。1999年10月，县老龄委员会、老年大学与县离退休干部工作局合署办公，实行三块牌子、一套人员。2001年12月—2008年，县离退休干部工作局归县委组织部管理。

县机构编制委员会办公室　2001年11月之前，县机构编制委员会办公室挂靠县人事劳动局。2001年12月，单独设置县机构编制委员会办公室，列入党委机构序列。

县委党校　1999年，县人事劳动局在县党校加挂荔波县干部培训中心牌子。2008年4月、10月，先后加挂清华大学现代教育远程教学贵州荔波站、黔南广播电视大学荔波工作站牌子。是年，县委党校编制13人，实有13人，其中专职教师5人（高级讲师1人）。内设办公室、教务科、总务科、学员科。学校占地面积9240平方米。有计算机网络教育、多媒体背投教育、中央党校远程教育C级站。

县委党史研究室　1984年5月，成立县史志编纂委员会，下设办公室。1985年8月，成立县委党史资料征集委员会办公室，史志机构分设。1990年5月，中共荔波县委党史资料征集委员会办公室改称为中共荔波县委党史研究室。1999年10月，县委党史研究室和县地方志编纂委员会办公室合署办公，两块牌子、一套人员。2003年5月，县委党史研究室和县地方志编纂委员会办公室合并，名称为荔波县史志办公室，为县委、县政府直属正科级事业单位，内设办公室、党史科和方志科，为股级科室。至2008年，机构设置不变。

第二节 党员代表大会

一、第四次党员代表大会

1981年1月18—23日，中共荔波县第四次代表大会在县城召开。大会应到代表281名，代表全县3229名党员，实到代表264名，特邀代表3名、列席人员24名。大会总结第三次县党代会以后，特别是粉碎“江青反革命集团”以后的工作，动员全县党员和各族人民团结一致，努力完成中共十一届三中全会后党中央提出的各项工作任务。会议强调要坚持和改善党的领导，提高党的战斗力，抓好党的组织建设、思想建设、作风建设，充分发挥各级党组织的战斗堡垒作用和共产党员的先锋模范作用；严格执行党的民主集中制，充分发扬民主；加强各级领导班子建设，抓好培养、选拔干部工作。大会审议通过第三届委员会作的《坚持和改善党的领导，提高党的战斗力，为加快我县社会主义现代化建设而奋斗》的工作报告。大会选举产生中共荔波县第四届委员会委员25名（其中，少数民族11名、妇女3名）、候补委员4名；选举产生县纪委委员7名；选举产生出席中共黔南州第四次代表大会代表26名。中共荔波县委四届一次全委会选举产生常务委员11名，王元当选书记，张国治、柏文熙、吴洪铭当选副书记。

二、第五次党员代表大会

1985年3月27日—4月1日，中共荔波县第五次代表大会在县城召开。大会应到代表208名，代表全县党员3381名，实到代表196名，列席人员19名。大会对第四届委员会工作报告和县纪委工作报告进行讨论，肯定第四次代表大会后县委贯彻执行中共十一届三中全会和十三大的路线、方针、政策，按照新时期的要求，全面拨乱反正，清除“左”倾错误影响，坚持马克思主义实事求是的思想路线，坚持四项基本原则，工作重点转移到经济建设上，实施改革、开放、搞活的一系列措施，经济工作有了较大发展，党风和社会风气明显好转，其他各项工作都取得较好成绩。经过审议，大会通过《关于中共荔波县第四届委员会工作报告的决议》《关于中共荔波县纪律检查委员会工作报告的决议》。大会选举产生中共荔波县第五届委员会委员25名、候补委员4名；选举产生县纪委委员7名。中共荔波县五届一次全委会选举产生常务委员8名，李秀振当选书记，蒙院芬、张海、饶昭德当选副书记。

三、第六次党员代表大会

1988年9月9—12日，中共荔波县第六次代表大会在县城召开。大会应到代表202名，代表全县党员3816名，实到代表188名，另有列席代表15名。大会听取和审议第五届委员会作的《深化改革，同心同德，为逐步建立社会主义商品经济新秩序而奋斗》的工作报告及县纪委工作报告。会议认为，自1985年3月第五次代表会以后，县委按照中央“巩固、消化、补充、完善”的方针，结合荔波实际，提出“依靠省州，面向两广，开发山区，兴县富民”的经济发展战略，符合县情，并经各单位努力，物质文明建设和精神文明建设都取得了较好成绩。经过审议，会议通过《关于中共荔波县第五届委员会工作报告的决议》《关于中共荔波县纪律检查委员会工作报告的决议》。大会选举产生中共荔波县第六届委员会委员27名、候补委员2名；选举产生县纪委委员11名。在中共荔波县六届一次全委会上选举产生常务委员8名，李秀振当选书记，蒙院芬、张海、饶昭德、王化莹当选副书记。

四、第七次党员代表大会

1992年1月14—17日，中共荔波县第七次代表大会在县城召开。大会应到代表185名，代表全县3862名党员，实到代表179名，另有特邀代表10名、列席代表33名。大会听取和审议并通过第六届委员会作的《中国共产党荔波县委员会工作报告》、县纪委工作报告。会议决定进一步解放思想，进一步改革开放，进一步发展生产力，进一步加强对农业和农村工作的领导。全力推进发展商品的经济体制改革，全力推进建设民主的政治体制改革；切实加强党的建设，切实加强精神文明建设，以改革总揽全局，加快资源开发步伐，加快支柱产业的发展，加快基础设施的建设，加快工农业生产后劲项目的实施，加快脱贫致富速度，提高全县各族人民物质和文化生活水平，切实打好“八五”计划关键仗。大会选举产生中共荔波县第七届委员会委员33名、候补委员2名；选举产生县纪委委员13名；选举产生出席中共黔南州第六次代表大会代表12名。在中共荔波县七届一次全委会上选举产生常务委员11名，王化莹当选书记，龙文榜、饶昭德、吴秀全、刘朝武当选副书记。

五、第八次党员代表大会

1996年12月17—19日，中共荔波县第八次代表大会在县城召开。出席这次会议的代表220名，代表全县4847名党员，另有特邀代表26名、列席代表67名。大会听取和审议并通过第七届委员会作的《励精图治，开拓进取，为实现跨世纪的宏伟目标努力奋斗》的工作报告、县纪委工作报告。会议决定：以后的工作要以邓小平建设有中国特色社会主义理论和党的各项方针政策为指针，艰苦创业，扎实苦干，团结一致，励精图治，强化以农田水利基本建设为重点的农业基础地位，强化教育基础设施建设，强化以交通为重点的基础设施建设，强化投资环境硬件基础设施建设，推进全县各项工作的发展；在党的组织建设和思想建设方面，要把两个文明建设中关键在于党的建设作为中心工作来抓。大会选举产生中共荔波县第八届委员会委员31名、候补委员4名；选举产生县纪委委员17名。在中共荔波县八届一次全委会上选举产生常务委员9名，张仕福当选书记，玉如敏、黄玉成、王家健当选副书记。

六、第九次党员代表大会

2001年6月26—28日，中共荔波县第九次代表大会在县城召开。大会应到代表220名，代表全县5705名党员，另有特邀代表11名、列席代表83名。大会听取和审议并通过第八届委员会作的《明确新目标，迎接新挑战，拓展新思路，开创新局面，为夺取荔波两个文明建设的更大胜利而努力奋斗》的工作报告、县纪委工作报告。会议决定要高举邓小平理论的伟大旗帜，按照“三个代表”重要思想的要求，认真贯彻落实党的十五大、十六大、省九次党代会精神以及各项方针政策，坚持解放思想，实事求是，坚持以经济建设为中心，坚持发展才是硬道理，坚持“三个有利于”，带领全县各族人民开拓创新，奋发图强，大力加强以农业和交通为重点的基础设施建设，调整产业结构，进一步明确建设经济强县目标，大力发展旅游业和加大扶贫攻坚力度，提高经济运行质量和效益，努力开拓城乡市场，加快小城镇建设和非公有制经济发展步伐，促进荔波经济再上新台阶。大会选举产生中共荔波县第九届委员会委员31名、候补委员4名；选举产生县纪委委员17名。在中共荔波县九届一次全委会上选举产生常务委员10名，逄焕华当选书记，潘朝显、王家健、龙河云当选副书记。

七、第十次党员代表大会

2006年10月23—25日，中共荔波县第十次代表大会在县城召开。大会应到代表245名，代表全县6319名党员，实到代表243名，另有特邀代表27名、列席代表95名。大会听取和审议第九届委员会作的《观念再更新，思路再开拓，目标再明确，步伐再加快，为全县实现“十一五”经济社会发展目标而努力奋斗》的工作报告、县纪委工作报告。会议决定以邓小平理论和“三个代表”重要思想为指导，用科学发展观统领经济社会发展全局，切实加强党的的先进性建设和执政能力建设，团结和带领全县人民始终坚持以经济建设为中心，围绕建设国际化专业旅游城市的目标，进一步选准调优发展思路，坚定不移地实施和推进旅游强县、旅游兴县、旅游富县、旅游活县、旅游热县的发展战略，积极推进城乡统筹发展，建设社会主义新农村，加快城镇化、农业产业化进程，优化经济结构，壮大综合实力，建设更加和谐富裕文明的新荔波。大会选举产生中共荔波县第十届委员会委员37名、候补委员7名；选举产生县纪委委员21名。在中共荔波县十届一次全委会上选举产生常务委员9名，王振金当选书记，陈稠彪、王云生当选副书记。

第三节 重要会议

一、全体委员会议

中共荔波县第四届委员会任期内共召开全委会6次。第三次全委扩大会于1982年12月14—19日召开，会议传达省委工作会议精神，学习中共十二大文件，讨论如何开创荔波社会主义现代化建设新局面，确定20世纪末全县的奋斗目标和经济翻番路子、措施及如何抓好三个根本好转（财政经济党风和社会风气好转）等问题。第四次全委扩大会于1983年11月25—30日召开，主要学习《邓小平文选》《中共中央关于整党的决定》，审查计划生育、秋种等各项工作完成情况。第五次全委扩大会于1984年8月10—14日召开，主要传达省委五届三次全会精神，州委、州政府经济工作会议精神，提出1984年提前实现“六五”计划和1985年实现经济翻番的计划和措施。第六次全委会于1985年3月24日召开，会议汇报荔波县第五次代表大会准备情况，讨论修改县委工作报告。

中共荔波县第五届委员会任期内共召开全委会4次。第二次全委会于1985年6月30日召开，会议通过《关于第二期第二批整党的安排意见》。第三次全委扩大会于1985年9月23—26日召开，主要学习中央关于整党工作的相关文件，县委常委作对照检查。第四次全委扩大会于1987年1月8—9日召开，会议审定召开第六次县党代会的相关事宜，通过了《关于1987年加强社会主义精神文明建设的实施意见》。

中共荔波县第六届委员会任期内共召开全委会5次。第三次全委会于1990年1月16日召开，贯彻落实十三届五中全会精神，部署1990年各项工作任务，作出《关于认真搞好治理整顿和深化改革的决议》。

中共荔波县第七届委员会任期内共召开全委会7次。第三次全委会于1993年7月16—17日召开。会议研究下半年党风建设和经济工作。第五次全委会于1993年11月20—22日召开，传达学习中共中央关于学习《邓小平文选》第三卷的决定和江泽民总书记在学习《邓小平文选》第三卷报告会上的讲话；传达贯彻中国共产党贵州省第七次代表大会精神；传达贯彻全国、全省、全州组织工作座谈会议精神；研究部署下步工作。第七次全委扩大会于1995年12月27—28日召开。会议审议通过《中共荔波县委关于制定荔波县国民经济和社会发展“九五”计划和2010年远景规划的建议》。

中共荔波县第八届委员会任期内共召开全委会7次。第二次全委扩大会暨党员代表会议于1997年6月7日召开，会议听取中共荔波县八届委员会第一次会议以来的工作报告；审议和通过《中共荔波县委关于加强社会主义精神文明建设的决议》；选举产生出席中共黔南州第七次代表大会代表。第三次全委扩大会于1997年11月1—2日召开，主要内容是贯彻学习党的十五大精神，传达省委七届七次全委会和州委七届二次全委会精神，动员全县广大党员、干部和各族群众进一步解放思想，更新观念，把荔波县改革开放和各项建设事业全面推向21世纪。第五次全委扩大暨全县经济工作会于1999年3月5—7日召开，会议贯彻落实中央、省、州经济工作会议精神，总结荔波改革开放二十年的经济工作，研究和部署全县跨世纪的两个文明建设，提出荔波跨世纪的发展战略及发展目标，通过《中共荔波县委、县政府关于进一步加强农业和农村工作的决定》。第六次全委扩大会于2000年2月20日召开，会议贯彻落实州委七届五次全会精神，表决通过《关于召开中国共产党荔波县第九次代表大会的决定》《中共荔波县委关于制定荔波县国民经济和社会发展第十个五年计划的建议》。

中共荔波县第九届委员会任期内共召开全委会8次。第二次全委扩大会暨全县经济工作会于2002年1月16日召开，会议传达全省、全州经济工作会议精神，总结2001年全县经济工作，安排布置2002年经济工作。第三次全委扩大会暨全县经济工作会于2003年2月10日召开，会议传达中央、省、州经济工作会议精神，总结2002年全县经济、计划生育、税费改革工作，安排布置2003年经济工作的目标和任务。第四次全委扩大会于2003年5月29日召开，传达学习《中共贵州省委、省人民政府关于加快旅游业发展的意见》，研究部署旅游发展工作，通过县委、县政府《关于加快旅游业发展的决定》《关于招商引资的若干规定（试行）》《关于引资的奖励办法》《关于鼓励和扶持旅游产品开发经营的若干规定》。第五次全委扩大会于2004年9月1—2日召开。会议传达学习中央、省、州关于西部大开发文件，讨论通过县委、县政府《关于加大力度实施西部大开发战略的若干意见》。会议总结前几个月的工作，明确后几个月的工作重点，确保顺利完成全年各项目标任务。第六次全委扩大会于2004年11月8日召开，会议深入贯彻落实党的十六届四中及省委九届六次、州委八届八次全委扩大会议精神，突出把加强党的建设要求落到实处，推进全县经济社会持续健康发展。第七次全委扩大会于2005年8月19日召开，贯彻落实省委、州委全会精神，进一步落实总书记胡锦涛视察贵州时的重要讲话精神，总结上半年工作并部署下半年工作，研究提出进一步做好新形势下人口和计划生育工作、国土资源工作、环境保护工作、水利建设工作和林业工作的意见。第八次全委扩大暨全县经济工作会于2006年1月9日召开，总结2005年和“十五”期间的各项工作，讨论通过“十一五”规划建议（草案），部署2006年全县经济工作目标任务。

中共荔波县第十届委员会从2006年10月起至2008年年底共召开全委会5次。第三次全委扩大会于2008年1月10—11日召开，贯彻落实党的十七大和省第十次、州第九次、县第十次党代会及中央、省、州经济工作会议精神，总结上年经济工作，分析形势，部署全年各项工作任务。第四次全委扩大会于2008年4月19日召开，会议研究荔波当前和今后一个时期“整脏治乱”城乡清洁工程建设工作，讨论通过《关于进一步加强“整脏治乱”城乡清洁工程建设工作的决定》。第五次全委扩大会于2008年8月14日召开，会议贯彻落实省委十届三次、州委九届五次全会精神，总结上半年工作，研究部署下半年经济社会发展任务，审议通过递补十届县委委员的决定。

二、常委会议

中共荔波县委常务委员会议，一般邀请人大常委会主任和政协主席列席，根据议题需要，邀请政府分管领导或相关部门（单位）、乡（镇）负责人列席。

第五届委员会任期内共召开常委会议48次。1986年8月召开的常委会议学习《中共贵州省委转发省委组织部〈关于加强乡镇干部队伍建设的意见〉的通知》，研究决定加强乡（镇）干部队伍建设的相关问题，议定原则上按每个乡平均8人编制配齐。12月召开的常委会议议定1987年精神文明建设工作要做11件实事，其中有加强农村文化站（室）建设、建设农村广播网、筹建科技阅览室和图书室、修复邓恩铭故居等。1987年5月召开的常委会议学习中央〔1987〕13号、16号文件并提出贯彻落实的意见，议定既要抓好政治上坚持反对资产阶级自由化，又要抓好“双增双节”运动，贯彻的效果要落实在兴县富民上，实现“商品经济上要有一个新的突破，精神文明建设要有一个新的发展，经济工作要上一个新的台阶”。1988年3月召开的常委会审定1987年两个文明建设表彰会先进集体、先进个人名单，决定表彰49个单位62名先进个人。

第六届委员会任期内共召开常委会议27次。部分常委会议情况：1989年6月召开的常委会议定，要继续抓好治理经济环境，整顿经济秩序，深化改革开放工作；坚持“背靠两省州，面向两广，开发山区，兴县富民”开发荔波经济的基本出发点，坚持抓好振兴荔波经济的七个系列生产项目。8月召开的常委会议听取7月、8月开展计划生育第二次突击的工作情况汇报，认为工作取得历史性的突破，决定在年内适当时候召开全县计划生育表彰大会。1990年2月召开的常委会决定从县直机关抽调150名干部，由县四家班子领导带队分业、分口、分头实行承包责任制下到基层工作，主要抓好农业、煤炭生产和和实施“温饱工程”等扶贫项目；决定撤销荔波政府驻深圳联络站。12月召开的常委会议提出按期完成“八五”计划的措施要求：一手抓“白色”，即抓粮食，另一手抓“黑色”，即抓煤炭生产，第三是抓“绿色”，即抓种植业和植树造林。同时抓好第三产业、旅游、服务业的发展。1991年1月召开的常委会决定建立县精神文明建设指导委员会，将樟江大街的建设列为1991年精神文明建设工作的一件大事来抓。3月召开的常委会议决定抽调县、区、乡200名干部组成宣讲队下基层开展为期15天的七中全会精神宣讲。4月召开的常委会议议定于4月5日开展纪念邓恩铭烈士就义六十周年活动。10月召开的常委会议同意修建邮电大楼同步匹配自动电话1000门。

第七届委员会任期内共召开常委会议122次。部分常委会议情况：1992年召开的常委会议，深入学习邓小平南巡讲话和党的十四大精神，进一步理顺发展荔波经济的思路和政策，提出旅游搭台、经济唱戏；抓东西两翼煤田开发，促减重增值转换；后劲增强，电力先上；重视场坝、搞好田坝；以粮为本，靠山治富等经济发展思路。1993年4月召开的常委会决定县汽车站搬迁至酒厂处，争取省交通厅计划投资400余万元新建一个功能齐全的汽车站。9月召开的常委会议提出扶持瑶山脱贫、实现温饱的意见，议定在人才、资金、政策上倾斜。1994年5月召开的常委会议定从5月起至9月全县分四个层次和四个阶段开展解放思想大讨论；研究“两瑶”地区扶贫开发试验区有关问题，议定从1994年开始5年内对“两瑶”的扶贫政策。11月召开的常委会专题讨论加强煤炭产运销管理，提高煤炭综合经济效益的问题，议定在平寨火车站设立煤炭外销装车协调组、在时来村沙地设立煤炭税费征收站、建立井口煤炭价格监督组、建立煤炭企业欠缴税费清收组。12月召开的常委会同意县委、县政府关于贯彻《中共贵州省委、省人民政府“关于加快个体、私营经济发展的意见”》的实施意见，对于兴办“四型”企业的干部职工，允许脱离原工作岗位，带职带薪五年。1995年7月召开的常委会原则同意县教育局提出的多渠道筹集“普及九年义务教育”经费的办法和措施，干部、职工按工资总额1%计征，离退休人员减半征收。12月召开的常委会议同意县扶贫开发办公室、县项目开发办公室、县招商引资办公室“三办”合署办公。1996年5月召开的常委会议定上海知青在荔波工作要求提前办理退休的可按干部管理权限报批后按照有关规定办理退休手续，退休后不再留任原工作岗位。

第八届委员会任期内共召开常委会议96次。部分常委会议情况：1997年3月召开的常委会决定撤销原荔波县“两瑶”地区扶贫开发试验区管理委员会，组建瑶山扶贫攻坚工作队，从县直机关单位抽调24名年富力强、有工作经验的干部进驻瑶山乡21个村民组，任期三年。确定荔波至大沙坡公路工程、独山经甲良至荔波的公路立项动工、完成樟江河谷“小康带”四区一控建设的规划并启动实施、兴建荔波民族中学教学楼等1997年要办理的十件实事。1998年1月召开的常委会研究县农机厂的深化改革等问题，议定聘请贵州省交通厅公路局局长龚明福和中国工商银行贵州省分行信贷处处长齐跃南为荔波县经济顾问。4月召开的常委会议定聘请贵州省政府副省长楼继伟为荔波县特别经济顾问。10月召开的常委会议定，同意把县城至小七孔公路作为旅游公路进行改造，按帕尔玛三级油路规模改造建设，计划投资500万元。11月召开的常委会议定聘请贵州省计划委员会交能处处长陈勇为荔波县经济顾问，省人大常委会副主任步智信为荔波县特别经济顾问。1999年1月召开的常委会议审定1999年工作的总体思路，即“一个中心”“两个加大”“三个重点”“四个确保”“五个到位”“六项改革”“七个突破”“八个常抓不懈”（简称“12345678”思路）；研究城乡绿化和创建国家级卫生县城、旅游县城问题；研究县城文明工程创建方案和制作县城“亮丽工程”户外宣传广告牌的有关事宜；议定编制荔波县跨世纪发展思路小册子和《荔波宣传》画册的相关问题。3月召开的常委会议定独荔公路建设、荔大公路收费、荔波国家电网建设等相关问题。5月召开的常委会议审定县委、县政府《关于广泛深入持久地开展创建文明单位、文明行业和争做文明公民活动的决定》《荔波县开展创建文明单位、文明行业和争做文明公民活动具体实施方案》，议定6月4日召开创建“三文明”活动动员大会。2000年1月召开的常委会议定在县中队—地矿宿舍—板吉加油站—县食品厂一带建设荔波广场。3月召开的常委会研究国家级茂兰喀斯特自然保护区和樟江风景名胜区申报“世界自然遗产”“五创”（创建全国园林城市、中国优秀旅游城市、全国卫生县城、全国文明县城、全国喀斯特森林生态公园县）工作，议定同意成立国家级茂兰喀斯特自然保护区和樟江风景名胜区申报“世界自然遗产”和“五创”工作领导小组。6月召开的常委会议定筹办邓恩铭烈士诞辰一百周年纪念活动有关事项，即成立纪念活动领导小组；召开一次较大型的纪念性座谈会，特邀省州老领导到荔波作革命传统教育和党性教育；修缮邓恩铭烈士事迹陈列室。7月召开的常委会议研究“三讲”教育工作、扶贫开发与小康建设工作，原则同意“三讲”教育实施方案和《荔波县今后三年扶贫开发与小康建设实施意见》，同意县直机关赴瑶山乡党建与扶贫工作队于2000年7月15日收队；议定表彰抗洪抢险救灾先进集体50个，先进个人150名，编辑《伟大的抗洪精神》一书。

第九届委员会任期内共召开常委会议123次。部分常委会议情况：2001年8月召开的常委会议定加大对外宣传工作，宣传荔波以机场开工为切入点为契机，举办一场大规模、高档次、高规格的宣传活动。11月召开的常委会听取县级机构改革编制情况汇报，原则同意关于行政单位内设机构的设置。2月召开的常委会研究布置县直机关作风教育整顿工作，提出2002年“围绕一个目标，突出两个重点，加强三个基础，调整四大结构，培育五大产业，实现非均衡推进经济发展”的工作思路和措施。2002年1月召开的常委会议定关于广西红茂矿务局破产改制重组的4条应对措施和意见。9月召开的常委会议定要在2004年实现国家卫生县城称号，同意召开创建国家卫生县城动员大会，议定对荔波籍瑶族大中专毕业生实行免试分配工作等政策鼓励和导向瑶族同胞子女入学。2003年1月召开的常委会议同意全县于4月1日开始实施医疗保险工作。2月召开的常委会研究板寨红七军会师旧址修葺工程建设问题，议定在人大会前举行开工仪式。5月7日召开的常委会专题研究防治非典工作，决定从县直部门抽调百名干部（每个单位2～3名），由单位领导带队下村入户，深入农村抓好防治非典工作和各项经济建设工作。8月召开的常委会议定召开学习“三个代表”重要思想动员大会的相关事宜。2004年3月召开的常委会议定原则同意社区建设的工作实施方案，议定3月20日在县民中球场召开建设贵州优先发展重点旅游区（荔波）动员大会。6月召开的常委会议定成立县政府机构改革工作领导小组，原则同意政府机构改革方案和实施意见。2005年1月召开的常委会议定要突出“三农”工作，确保农业增效、农民增收；议定开展保持共产党员先进性教育活动的有关事宜。9月召开的常委会同意全面启动全县农村合作医疗卫生制度改革，按国家政策匹配农村合作医疗补助专项资金。10月召开的常委会议定原则同意“走进中国最美丽的地方——荔波”大型采风策划方案和“中国荔波万亩野生梅文化旅游首游式”策划方案。2006年1月召开的常委会议定于是年2月12日正式开工改造樟江大街，5月1日完成县旅游局游客中心至大十字段的改造，10月1日完成全部改造工作。3月召开的常委会讨论关于推进社会主义新农村建设事宜，议定成立社会主义新农村建设协调领导小组，原则同意县委、县政府《关于推进社会主义新农村建设的意见》，当年要抓好10个社会主义新农村建设示范点。9月召开的常委会研究荔波水泥厂有关事宜，议定同意依法对荔波水泥厂进行改制，并议定关于改制成本的测算、债务的清理和分摊、职工生活费、改制主体的确认等问题。

第十届委员会任期内，从2006年11月起至2008年年底，共召开常委会议46次。部分常委会议情况：2007年2月召开的常委会研究议定承办全省第二届旅游产业发展大会的相关事宜。8月召开的常委会研究议定县城客运车辆升级换代相关问题，原则同意政府关于县城客运机三取缔的政策措施和补助标准。2008年1月召开的常委会议定同意给予20万元作为县民族中学2007年度的高考奖励，从2008年起，县委、县政府要出台促进教育发展及高考奖励办法。2月召开常委会议定合并召开申遗成功、第二届旅发会、年度目标管理考核3个总结表彰大会。3月召开的常委会传达全州农村工作会议精神，议定结合会议精神出台农业农村工作实施意见，产业调整以蔗、桑、畜、果、蔬、茶为主，其中以糖蔗为重点。

第四节　重大决策

一、改革开放，经济建设

1990年1月16日中共荔波县六届三次全委会作出《关于认真搞好治理整顿和深化改革的决议》。一是提高认识、坚定信心，认真搞好治理整顿，深化改革；二是明确治理整顿、深化改革的工作目标和任务；三是落实好农业的倾斜政策，集中力量抓好粮食生产；四是搞好工业生产、稳定经济增长；五是在治理整顿中进一步搞好财贸金融工作；六是进一步发展教育、卫生、科技、文化事业；七是加强党的领导，充分发挥各级党组织的核心领导作用、战斗力作用和党员的先锋模范作用。

1992年5月19日，县委、县政府作出《关于加快工业改革步伐切实提高经济效益的决定》。22日，县委、县政府又作出《关于在县城建立商业开发区的决定》，明确在玉屏镇建立的商业开发区定名为荔波商业开发区。开发区范围：樟江西路，即黄泥坡以南至两所坟；樟江南路、樟江北路，即南起荔波民族中学、北抵茂兰喀斯特森林自然保护区管理处。

1992年7月16日，县委、县政府作出《关于建立旅游开发区的决定》。一是旅游开发区定名为樟江风景名胜旅游开发区。其范围包括：小七孔、大七孔、水春河3个风景区及其缓冲地带的生活服务区，玉屏镇服务中心、王蒙服务中心，以及拉片村、水春村、水扒村、罗家寨4个民族旅游村寨。二是凡在旅游开发区的指定范围内投资兴建接待服务设施，其投资方调节税可按5%征收。从营业日起免征十年所得税，免征三年的产品税、增值税。免征五年的房产税、奖金税、个人收入调节税。三是凡在旅游开发区的指定范围内征地进行建设性投资的，只交征地费用，耕地占用税只收三分之一，免征十年土地使用税。四是在旅游开发区内兴办文化娱乐设施可享受两三条的优惠待遇。五是鼓励全民、集体和个人到风景区管理处指定的景区内设立临时摊点经营饮食和照相，出售旅游商品。六是在景区的总体规划指导下，投资开发大七孔、水春河的景点建设或交通建设的单位和个人，投资用于景点建设额在300万元以上的，可按景区总投资的比例分成二十年的门票收入，并免收同期的所得税和个人收入调节税。

1994年12月，根据省委、州委关于加快非耕地资源开发的决策和要求，经反复论证，县委、县政府对加快全县非耕地资源发展提出十条实施意见：一是把非耕地资源开发引入市场竞争机制；二是非耕地资源属国家和集体所有；三是县土地主管部门对非耕地资源有裁定权；四是依法完善非耕地资源开发手续；五是允许非耕地使用权再次有偿转让；六是非耕地资源开发不受地籍、户籍、国籍限制，凡到荔波县投资从事非耕地开发的都予以鼓励支持；七是非耕地开发者对开发的产品享有经营自主权；八是非耕地林木实行计划性间伐或更新采伐；九是建立非耕地资源开发基金；十是建立健全非耕地开发组织机构。

1995年9月，县委出台《关于招商引资的若干规定（试行）》《招商引资奖励办法（试行）》。

1999年3月5日，县委、县政府作出《关于创建科技先进县的决定》，强调牢固树立“科学技术是第一生产力”思想，坚持党委和政府对创先活动的领导，通过深化改革和增加科技投入，加强科技队伍建设，建立科技新体制，提高全民科技文化素质。主要任务和目标是：一是大力推进农业和农村科技进步；二是广泛开展科技兴县、兴厂、兴企活动，创建科技型工业企业；三是组织实施好科技扶贫工作，打好扶贫攻坚战；四是继续抓好各类示范工程，逐渐向高效农业转化；五是大力推动社会发展领域的科技进步。

1999年3月，县委、县政府作出《关于创建生态县、公园县的决定》。一是建立健全机制，切实加强领导；二是加强天然林的保护与管理；三是加大城乡绿化工作力度；四是进一步开展城乡“四化”达标活动。

1999年12月，县委印发《关于荔波县跨世纪发展思路的决定》。决定用《荔波县跨世纪发展思路》替代《荔波县国民经济和社会发展“十五”计划和2015年远景目标纲要》。《跨世纪发展思路》将荔波县县域经济定位为以旅游为龙头及其相关产业发展的经济体系；以煤炭为龙头的及其矿产品开发粗加工的经济体系；以绿色产业为龙头的及其非耕地资源开发和绿色产品深加工的经济体系；以粮食为龙头的及其农林牧副产品深加工的经济体系。快速健康地实施农业产业化，壮大和充实县域经济，增强县域经济实力，同时以强化四大基础，调整四大结构，打好两个攻坚，实施三大战略，抓住一个关键为具体目标和措施，运用超常规思维，采取超常规手段，实现超常规跳跃式发展。《决定》要求荔波县人大常委会要及时组织讨论，并形成相关决议，荔波县人民政府要在县委《决议》和人大《决议》的基础上，制定切实可行的实施方案。

2000年8月，县委根据省委办公厅、省政府办公厅1997年有关划定革命老区的文件精神，决定成立荔波县划定革命老区领导小组及办公室，组织人员按照有关划定革命老区的标准，调查核实、收集整理1930—1938年间中共在荔波的革命活动史料，申报革命老区县。省委办公厅、省政府办公厅于2002年12月批复，同意划定荔波县为革命老区。

2004年9月2日，县委召开九届五次全委（扩大）会议，形成《中共荔波县委关于加大力度实施西部大开发战略的决议》，明确全县加大力度实施西部大开发的总体目标是力争发展速度高于全省、全州平均水平，GDP年均增长11.35%左右。

2006年1月，县委九届八次全委（扩大）会议明确“十一五”时期经济社会发展的奋斗目标是实现国民经济又快又好发展，综合经济实力迈上新台阶，经济自我积累、自我发展能力明显增强；初步建立较有发展后劲的特色优势产业体系，基本完善以交通、水利为重点的城乡基础设施体系和“绿色荔波”生态经济保障体系，为建设生态与经济、经济与社会、城镇与农村协调发展，人与自然和谐，人民生活宽裕，开放文明的新荔波奠定较好基础。

2007年11月25日，为推进农业产业化发展，向全面建设小康社会目标迈进，县委、县政府决定发展高产高糖甘蔗产业，下发《关于发展高产高糖甘蔗产业的意见》，提出引进大型糖蔗加工龙头企业，大力发展糖蔗生产，推动农业产业化进程。增强糖业市场竞争力，逐步建立“企业+基地+农户”的运行模式，把企业与蔗农联结成为风险共担、利益共享的共同体。《意见》还提出“2008年在现有1万亩的基础上扩大种植4万亩，实现年榨原料蔗25万吨；2009年种植面积达到9万亩，年产原料蔗35万吨；2010年全县甘蔗总面积13万亩，实现年产原料蔗65万吨”的发展目标。

2007年11月25日，为加快糖蔗产业的发展步伐，县委召开全县糖蔗产业发展大会，部署全县糖蔗生产工作。

2008年3月3日，县委召开常委扩大会，专题研究糖蔗产业发展工作，之后发出《关于扎实推进2008年度糖蔗种植工作的紧急通知》，以政策措施和行政措施保障全县17个乡（镇）糖蔗种植面积达4万亩，实行干部风险共担、效益共享责任制，进行糖蔗种植风险抵押。

二、“三农”问题（农业、农村、农民）

1979年，县委根据《中共中央关于加快农业发展若干问题的决定》在全县农村实行联产承包责任制。1983年，县委下发《关于开展建设“文明村”“文明单位”的意见》，明确指导思想、建设的形式和内容。

1993年7月，县委和县政府就减轻农民负担采取3条措施：1.农民依法纳税，村提留和乡统筹费用，必须严控在上半年农民人均收入的5%以内。各种摊派、集资、达标活动，行政事业性收费，一律停止执行；2.清理1992年平价分配和奖售的柴油、汽油和化肥等农用物资的兑现情况。没有兑现的，继续列入1993年供应指标；3.成立减轻农民负担领导小组，设立专门的办公室，对全县农民负担问题进行调查研究，并及时汇报和解决。

1994年4月，县委、县政府制定“两瑶”开发试验区扶贫开发措施。扶贫目标：瑶山3年脱贫85%，5年脱贫解决温饱。主要措施：1.加大扶贫领导力量。从县直机关抽调骨干组建试验区管理委员会，工作脱离原单位到“两瑶”地区任职3年，明确3名副县级干部专抓试验区工作，有关部门带项目安排专人到两瑶地区实施。2.制定优惠政策。由管委会拟出两瑶地区对内搞活，对外开放以及调动干部职工、农民群众发展经济脱贫致富积极性的各项优惠政策，报县审定出台。3.资金倾斜安排。县财政每年拨出一定专款作为两瑶地区扶贫开发试验区的启动基金，列入财政预算；上级安排两瑶地区各项扶贫资金由管委会统一安排。4.加强监督。县委、县政府定期听取两瑶地区扶贫开发工作汇报，及时解决扶贫工作中出现的问题。

1997年3月5日，县委决定，撤销县“两瑶”（瑶山、瑶麓）地区扶贫开发试验区管理委员会，组建瑶山扶贫攻坚工作队，从县直机关单位抽调26名干部到瑶山瑶族乡驻组挂村开展扶贫工作。时间为3年，不脱贫不脱钩。同时，县委、县政府出台《关于瑶山扶贫工作的实施意见》。

1997年9月，县委、县政府发出《关于开展结穷亲帮致富的实施意见》，将任务、责任明确到人，落实到户。对未脱贫的计划生育户实行挂牌帮扶，实施“4321”工程，即县四家班子领导正职帮扶4户，副职帮扶3户，科（局）级干部帮扶2户，股级以下干部帮扶1户，并从政策、资金、技术、物资、市场5个方面落实具体帮扶措施。

1999年3月，县委八届五次全委会通过《关于进一步加强农业和农村工作的决定》。第一，全面贯彻落实党在农村的基本政策，进一步深化农村改革。第二，积极调整和优化农村经济结构，发展农业产业化经营，努力提高农村经济效益。第三，大力实施科教兴农战略，努力提高农业科技含量。第四，大力加强农业基础设施建设，切实改善农业生态环境，提高农业综合生产能力。第五，切实加大扶贫攻坚力度，推进农村小康建设。第六，抓好千里农村经济示范带建设。

三、精神文明建设

1987年，县委五届四次全委会议通过《关于一九八七年加强社会主义精神文明建设的实施意见》。1991年，建立县精神文明建设指导委员会，常抓精神文明建设工作。1997年，县委八届二次全委会批准县委《关于进一步加强社会主义精神文明建设的决议》。《决议》对十一届三中全会后全县精神文明建设情况进行总结，对加强思想道德、文化建设、精神文明创建活动等提出以后14年社会主义精神文明建设的指导思想和奋斗目标。

1993年1月，县委对乡镇机关社教工作作出安排。社教工作，主要进行建设有中国特色社会主义理论教育，把思想认识统一到党的十四大精神上来，理清乡镇深化改革和加快建设步伐的思路。要求乡镇领导班子中的主要问题得到解决，党员和干部的思想作风、工作作风有明显改进，明确并坚持以经济建设为中心开展各项工作，以科技为先导的农业社会化服务体系建设有新的进展；乡镇企业有新的发展路子，农村商品经济有新的发展规划和措施。坚持“两手抓，两手硬”，注重精神文明建设，对突出的行业不正之风得到纠正；群众反映强烈而不能够解决的突出问题得到解决；理顺关系，明确职责，各项规章制度建立健全，并得到贯彻执行，有关业务部门延伸到位并较好地发挥作用。

1997年6月，中共荔波县八届二次全委会作出《关于进一步加强社会主义精神文明建设的决议》。

1999年，县委、县政府作出《关于广泛深入持久地开展创建文明单位、文明行业和争做文明公民活动的决定》，活动以创荔波美好形象，面向新世纪为主题，以全面提高公民文明素质和城乡文明程度为目标，通过不懈努力，使全县范围的优美环境、优良秩序、优质服务和优雅言行取得明显成效。

四、干部工作，法制建设

1993年11月，县委决定开展落实离休干部待遇进行检查，主要内容有：一是政治待遇，是否在重大节日（元旦、“七一”、国庆）组织他们开展活动或进行慰问，是否定期组织他们学习，过组织生活，通报工作情况，是否经常走访和看望他们，是否通知他们参加应参加的会议，该听的报告；二是生活待遇，是否按规定体检，患病及时治疗，按规定发给各种补贴，报销医药费以及住房情况。

1997年3月28日，在全省广泛掀起学“大关”精神的热潮中，县委结合县内实际，向全县各行各业发出“远学大关，近学大土”的号召，同时针对极少数部门和乡（镇）的个别干部职工不讲学习，不讲政治，不注意机关形象，作风不踏实、不严谨，脱离基层、脱离群众的不良现象，县委作出整顿机关工作作风的决定，整顿机关工作作风，密切党群和干群关系。

1997年7月，为培养村级后备干部，县委、县政府决定在县民族职业中学举办“科技村干部培训班”，培训班由县民族职业中学主办，县委党校协办。招生名额100名，学制两年。学员经考试、考核成绩全部合格后，由县民族职业中学发给经州教育局验印的职业高中毕业证书，国家承认学历，不包分配，由县委组织部择优安排到各村担任科技村民委员会副主任。

1998年6月，县委作出《关于开展依法治县工作的决定》。一是明确依法治县工作的指导思想和基本任务；二是深入开展法制宣传教育，提高干部群众的法律意识和法制观念；三是进一步落实执法责任制和冤案、错案责任追究制，提高依法行政、公正司法的水平；四是完善制约机制，加大监督力度；五是改善法律服务，建立健全法律服务体系；六是加强组织领导，保证依法治县工作顺利进行。

2005年8月，县委九届七次全委（扩大）会通过《中共荔波县委深入推进惩治和预防腐败体系建设实施办法》，并将惩治和预防腐败体系建设任务分解落实到全县各级各部门各乡（镇），对中央的《实施纲要》作出总体部署。

第五节　重大活动

一、解放思想大讨论

1978年12月，中共十一届三中全会胜利召开后，县委印发《关于组织在职干部学习马克思主义政治经济学的意见》，在全县党员干部中学习马克思《政治经济学批判》序言、恩格斯《反杜林论》和毛泽东《改造我们的学习》《关于正确处理人民内部矛盾的问题》等重要理论文章。在学习理论的同时，进行实践是检验真理的唯一标准的解放思想大讨论。

1994年2月，县委成立解放思想大讨论领导小组，围绕“八七”扶贫攻坚计划应采取的措施；对支柱产业——煤炭开发中的产、供、销存在的问题和应采取的措施；对农业资源（重点是非耕地资源）的开发应采取的措施和优惠政策的实施；发挥边境优势，落实州委、州政府“南下通道经济”战略应采取的新举措；进一步发展非公有制经济，鼓励农民进城经商办企业，搞活县城及集镇经济发展应采取的新举措；围绕旅游开发应开辟的项目和应制定的优惠政策6个专题，组织动员全县机关、企事业单位和各乡（镇）全体干部职工开展解放思想大讨论。

1996年8月，根据中央“西部大开发”战略决策，县委在全县开展“解放思想、抢抓机遇、实施‘西部大开发’专题大讨论”活动。

二、机关作风整顿

1992年3月9日，县委针对一些党员干部和领导干部中存在的官僚主义、形式主义和个人主义，发出《关于整顿机关作风的意见》，从3月16日开始到3月底进行机关干部思想整顿、纪律整顿、作风整顿，整顿主要以自我教育、自我检查、自我纠正、自我完善为主。

三、农村社会主义教育

1992年8月，县委成立县农村社会主义教育（简称“社教”）活动领导小组，从县机关中抽调干部150人组成第一批农村社教工作队，组织集中培训后，分赴80个行政村进行宣讲。农村社教分为思想教育、组织整顿、促进发展、考核验收4个阶段进行，为期4个月。工作队按照县委《关于在全县农村开展社会主义教育活动的通知》要求，向农民宣讲中共十三届七中、八中全会精神以及《中共中央关于进一步加强农业和农村工作的决定》。各村委会成立扶贫帮困组、科技兴农组、治安联防组、民事调解组等，加强社教工作。

12月，抽调县机关干部147人组成第二批农村社教工作队，分赴88个行政村开展为期4个月的农村社教工作。两批社教工作队共297人进村入户宣讲中共十四大精神，覆盖全县168个行政村的每个自然寨，农民群众受教育面达到85%以上。社教活动结束后，经县委、州委验收，全部合格。

四、“三讲”教育

2000年7月，县委根据中央和省委、州委关于深入开展以“讲学习、讲政治、讲正气”为主要内容的“三讲”党性党风教育活动的统一部署，召开“三讲”教育动员大会，在县机关单位开展“三讲”教育活动。分“思想发动、学习提高”“自我剖析、听取意见”“交流思想、开展批评”“认真整改、巩固提高”4个阶段进行。在“自我剖析、听取意见”阶段收到群众意见1439条，为群众办理102件实事，接待群众来信来访103件，全部办结。教育活动达到中央提出的“思想上有明显提高，政治上有明显进步，作风上有明显转变，纪律上有明显增强，干群关系上有明显改善”的要求。

五、“三个代表”重要思想学习教育

2001年2月，县委根据中央和省委、州委的部署，开展学习“中国共产党始终代表着中国先进生产力的发展要求，始终代表着中国先进文化的前进方向，始终代表着中国最广大人民的根本利益”的“三个代表”重要思想教育活动。学习教育活动分为学习培训、对照检查、整改提高3个阶段，全县106个县机关和17个乡（镇）干部职工4064人参加学习教育，并写读书笔记和学习心得，科级干部449人深入168个村，与村支部、村委会签订办实事承诺书，为群众办实事415件，撰写调查报告533份。县、乡、村干部参加学习考试4000多人，考试合格率90%。

六、保持共产党员先进性教育

2005年1月，按照中央和省委、州委关于开展保持共产党员先进性教育活动部署，县委围绕“提高党员素质、加强基层组织、服务人民群众、促进各项工作”的目标，在全县开展保持共产党员先进性教育活动。学习活动分学习动员、分析评议、整改提高3个阶段、两批进行，至11月底结束。68个单位114个基层党组织参加第一批教育活动；应参加教育活动的党员1113名，实际参加教育活动党员1107名，占比99.5%。参加第二批先进性教育活动的有乡（镇）党委和企业、学校、居委会基层党组织，全县参加教育活动的党员覆盖面达99%。在教育活动中，全县投入资金310万元，为群众办好事、办实事1032件。在集中整改阶段工作结束后，县委开展“回头看”“回头查”活动，对问题较多、群众意见较大的单位，进行认真“补课”。

第六节　县委办公室工作

县委办公室围绕县委的重大决策和工作部署，开展协调服务工作，办文、办会、收集和综合处理信息、办理接待，为县委领导及县委常委的决策工作提供服务，保障县委工作正常运行。2001年，机构改革时对县委办职能进行调整，增加对机要密码和保密工作的管理及政策调研、督查职能，增加县重要外事接待的协调工作。

一、文秘工作

县委办文秘工作主要围绕县委的工作承办文稿的起草、传递、送审、印发、归档、电话通知接转、下传等日常工作及县委会议的综合服务等，即办文、办会、办事，搞好服务。

1987—1988年，起草、印发县委文件44个，县委办文件68个，处理中央、省、州各类文件1933件，处理各类请求、报告、批件、信件334件。1992—1993年，起草、记录、印发县委文件、常委会议纪要及常委办公会议纪要89个，县委办文件37个，各类通知、情况汇报、简报27个。1994—1995年，完成文件起草并印发县委文件（通知）80个，常委会议纪要10个，县委办文件（通知）78个，共印发22188份。处理中央、省、州各类文件4510件。1999—2000年，编发县委文件208个，县委办文件217个，处理上下来文来函2044份，主办、协办、服务各种会议170余次，参与接待活动47次。2002—2008年，起草、记录、印发县委文件741个，常委会议纪要及常委办公会议纪要96个，县委办文件1301个，办公室专题会议纪要43个；共印发各类文件256633份；收发中央、省、州来文49659份；接待来信来访300余人次，主办、协办、服务各类会议241次。

二、信息工作

县委办信息工作主要围绕中央、省委、州委、县委的中心工作收集和综合处理信息，负责党务信息的收集、编报和反馈，编有《荔波信息》《荔波情况》，信息由办公室领导和干部收集、撰写。1987—1988年，《荔波信息》出刊26期，刊载信息114条；编辑《荔波情况》20期；上报省、州信息110条，被采用61条。1994年，设秘书信息股。1993—1995年，编发《荔波信息》《荔波情况》30多期，上报省、州信息195条，被采用115条。1999年，《荔波情况》从第九期更名为《荔波工作》。2001年，设信息股。1999—2008年，编发《荔波信息》《信息专报》等各类刊物361期，上报省、州信息2475条，被采用527条。

三、督查、政研工作

1994年，县委办内设督查调研股。1996年，建立县委政策研究室，规格为正科级，挂靠县委办公室。1997年，政研室开展投资环境调查，调查组对矿山开发、个体私营企业等方面进行调查，撰写专题材料11篇提交县委讨论，为制定更加优惠的政策吸引外来投资提供参考。1998年，政研室参加县调查组赴兴义地区开展煤炭市场调研，撰写《兴义地区煤炭市场调查报告》，为县政府调整煤炭规费决策提供依据。1999年，荔波被列为贵州省农村税费改革试点县之一，由政研室负责制定具体实施方案和指导各乡（镇）开展此项工作，通过调研学习湄潭县经验、深入乡（镇）测算农民收入和人均负担等，把好工作的各个环节，全县税费制度改革于是年11月底结束，总结上报相关材料。同时，督查部门牵头或参与财政税收、计划生育、春耕生产、矿山安全、公路交通建设、半年和年终各项指标完成情况等督查活动30余次，上报督查材料43期。2001年，督查政研工作职能并入县委办，为内设股室。2003年，以省委书记钱运录协调帮助荔波解决的几个重大项目为督查重点，多次开展督查，及时反馈进展情况，及时总结汇报。2003—2008年，上报督查材料218期，办理督办、批办件80件，办结46件；电话督查520次；开展专项督查调研30次、专题调研6次、一般调研18次，完成各类调研文章75篇。组织有关部门围绕退耕还林、“三基本”、农业产业结构调整、建设贵州省优先发展重点旅游区和黔南民族生态旅游区、社会主义新农村建设、新型农村合作医疗、种桑养蚕、基层组织建设等工作开展调研。

四、机要工作

1982年，县委办设传真室，负责机要工作。此后，机要工作部门先后设置为县委办机要局、县委机要局。机要工作部门主要负责全县党政军领导机关、要害部门的核心机密信密码传递工作，承担县委、县政府及其各工作部门秘密信息及文电的译传办理，负责县委及办公室文件上传、下传。

五、保密工作

县保密机构成立后，依法履行全县保密行政管理职能。从1990年开始，保密局每年会同相关部门开展2次以上的保密检查。1991—1992年，完成17个单位的定密工作。1992年，制定“二五”保密法制宣传教育规划，将保密宣传与全县普法教育同步进行。同时，放映《中华人民共和国保守国家秘密法》及其配套法规影像25场（次），1400多干部职工受教育。是年，开展确定保密要害部门（部位）工作。1994年，对复印、印刷、废旧收购站进行检查，开展测绘成果保密检查。

1995年、1998年、2004年，先后组织全县干部开展保密法自答题活动、参加全国“奥士达杯”保密知识竞赛、全省举办的保密技术知识竞赛，参加人数累计2388人。

1998年，涉密工作人员实行保密培训考试、持证上岗工作，71个单位425人通过培训考试合格获得上岗证。1998年，开展查缴泄密数据光盘工作，对30个有计算机的单位进行全面检查。1999年，组织有关单位开展为期10天的查缴泄密非法出版物工作，对县城和乡（镇）的书店、书报销售点、个体书摊及图书租赁点进行检查。2003年对涉密网络、计算机及其系统上国际互联网进行保密检查，基本摸清全县各单位计算机配备、使用情况。2005年，对全县17个乡（镇）和县部门的涉密人员122名进行保密法律法规和现代化办公、通信、计算机安全保密技术知识培训。2004—2006年，会同机要局等单位对20多个县直机关密码电报管理情况、对70多单位的计算机及其网络保密管理情况进行专项检查，对全县党政机关进行保密大检查。

1978—2008年历届中共荔波县委领导任职一览表

表4－1

届 次	职 务	姓 名	性别	民族	任职起止时间（年、月）	备 注
第三届	第一书记	张聚国	男	汉族	1978.1—1978.2	
	第二书记	傅金玉	男	汉族	1978.2—1978.10	
	书 记	王 元	男	布依族	1978.10—1981.1	主持县委工作
	副书记	柏文熙	男	布依族	1978.1—1981.1	
		吴洪铭	男	苗族	1978.1—1981.1	
		刘治中	男	汉族	1978.1—1979.6	
		张国治	男	汉族	1980.8—1981.1	
	常 委	杨昌映	男	汉族	1978.1—1981.1	
		韦国丰	男	水族	1978.1—1981.1	
		吴国仁	男	水族	1978.1—1981.1	
		蓝恩保	男	瑶族	1978.1—1981.1	
		袁青田	男	汉族	1978.1—1979.11	
		何建飞	男	布依族	1978.1—1981.1	
		刘治中	男	汉族	1978.1—1979.6	
		逄树萼	男	汉族	1978.1—1981.1	
第四届	书 记	王 元	男	布依族	1981.1—1984.11	
	副书记	张国治	男	汉族	1981.1—1983.12	
		柏文熙	男	布依族	1981.1—1983.12	
		吴洪铭	男	苗族	1981.1—1985.3	
		李秀振	男	汉族	1982.6—1985.3	1984.11—1985.3主持县委工作
		蒙院芬	女	布依族	1983.12—1985.3	
		张 海	男	汉族	1984.9—1985.3	
	常 委	双维汉	男	汉族	1981.1—1983.7	
		李振川	男	汉族	1981.1—1983.6	
		吴国仁	男	水族	1981.1—1983.12	
		杨昌映	男	汉族	1981.1—1985.3	
		潘长辛	男	汉族	1981.1—1984.4	
		李德余	男	汉族	1981.1—1985.3	
		欧崇顺	男	布依族	1982.4—1985.3	
		汪克强	男	汉族	1983.12—1984.11	

续表4－1

届 次	职 务	姓 名	性别	民族	任职起止时间（年、月）	备 注
第四届	常 委	蒙强炳	男	水族	1983.12—1985.3	
		饶昭德	男	汉族	1983.12—1985.3	
		何道生	男	布依族	1983.12—1985.3	
第五届	书 记	李秀振	男	汉族	1985.3—1988.9	
	副书记	蒙院芬	女	布依族	1985.3—1988.9	
		张 海	男	汉族	1985.3—1987.10	
		饶昭德	男	汉族	1985.3—1988.9	
		王化莹	男	汉族	1987.11—1988.9	
	常 委	韦绍忠	男	水族	1985.3—1988.9	
		何道生	男	布依族	1985.3—1986.6	
		蒙强炳	男	水族	1985.3—1988.9	
		龙文榜	男	汉族	1985.3—1988.9	
		蒙熙林	男	水族	1986.11—1988.9	
第六届	书 记	李秀振	男	汉族	1988.9—1990.2	
		王化莹	男	汉族	1990.2—1992.1	
	副书记	韦绍忠	男	水族	1988.9—1991.7	
		王化莹	男	汉族	1988.9—1990.2	
		蒙院芬	女	布依族	1988.9—1988.12	
		饶昭德	男	汉族	1988.9—1992.1	
		吴秀全	男	布依族	1989.4—1992.1	
		龙黄宗	男	汉族	1990.3—1992.1	挂职
	常 委	蒙强炳	男	水族	1988.9—1992.1	
		龙文榜	男	汉族	1988.9—1992.1	
		蒙熙林	男	水族	1988.9—1992.1	
		李国庆	男	汉族	1988.9—1989.1	挂职
		覃相和	男	布依族	1989.4—1992.1	
		高金林	男	苗族	1990.4—1990.11	挂职
		王家健	男	布依族	1991.1—1992.1	
第七届	书 记	王化莹	男	汉族	1992.1—1994.6	
		饶昭德	男	汉族	1994.6—1996.12	
	副书记	龙文榜	男	汉族	1992.1—1993.3	
		饶昭德	男	汉族	1992.1—1994.6	
		吴秀全	男	布依族	1992.1—1993.1	

续表4－1

届 次	职 务	姓 名	性别	民族	任职起止时间（年、月）	备 注
第七届	副书记	刘朝武	男	汉族	1992.1—1996.12	
		龙黄宗	男	汉族	1992.1—1992.10	挂职
		李跃南	男	汉族	1992.4—1994.1	挂职
		玉如敏	男	布依族	1992.11—1996.12	
		黄玉成	男	汉族	1994.10—1996.12	
		张仕福	男	汉族	1995.3—1996.12	
		谷德志	男	汉族	1996.3—1996.12	挂职
		刘国福	男	水族	1996.4—1996.12	挂职
		龙河云	男	苗族	1996.4—1996.12	
	常 委	黄玉成	男	汉族	1992.1—1993.6	
		蒙强炳	男	水族	1992.1—1996.12	
		王家健	男	布依族	1992.1—1996.12	
		蒙熙林	男	水族	1992.1—1996.12	
		田景胜	男	水族	1992.1—1996.12	
		陈曼丽	女	汉族	1992.1—1993.6	
		冉孟华	男	汉族	1993.6—1996.12	
		史晶富	男	汉族	1995.7—1996.12	
第八届	书 记	张仕福	男	汉族	1996.12—2000.10	
		逄焕华	男	汉族	2000.10—2001.6	
	副书记	玉如敏	男	布依族	1996.12—1999.12	
		黄玉成	男	汉族	1996.12—2001.6	
		王家健	男	布依族	1996.12—2001.6	
		谢继成	男	汉族	1997.1—1997.12	挂职
		严 肃	男	汉族	1997.3—1998.2	挂职
		潘建春	男	水族	1997.3—1998.3	挂职
		王心平	男	汉族	1997.3—1998.3	挂职
		田景胜	男	水族	1997.11—2001.6	
		胡智勇	男	布依族	1998.2—1999.2	挂职
		张惠明	男	布依族	1998.3—2001.6	
		赵廷昌	男	汉族	1998.3—1999.3	挂职
		任 平	男	汉族	1998.3—2001.3	挂职
		潘朝显	男	水族	1999.3—2000.3	挂职
		袁先顺	男	汉族	1999.3—2000.3	挂职

续表4-1

届 次	职 务	姓 名	性别	民族	任职起止时间（年、月）	备 注
第八届	副书记	刘君昂	男	汉族	1999.12—2000.12	挂职
		杨吉泉	男	汉族	2000.3—2001.3	挂职
		周忠斌	男	汉族	2000.4—2001.4	挂职
		欧开灿	男	汉族	2001.3—2001.6	挂职
		张军伟	男	汉族	2001.4—2001.6	挂职
	常 委	蒙熙林	男	水族	1996.12—1999.4	
		田景胜	男	水族	1996.12—1997.11	
		史晶富	男	汉族	1996.12—2001.6	
		莫俊国	男	布依族	1996.12—2000.11	
		杨永英	女	布依族	1996.12—2001.6	
		任 平	男	汉族	1998.3—1999.4	挂职
		何惠明	男	汉族	1999.10—2001.6	
		高勇华	女	回族	2001.6—2001.6	
		程国庆	男	汉族	2001.6—2001.6	
		华廷龙	男	水族	2001.6—2001.6	
第九届	书 记	逄焕华	男	汉族	2001.6—2006.2	
		王振金	男	汉族	2006.2—2006.10	
	副书记	潘朝显	男	水族	2001.6—2005.11	
		王家健	男	布依族	2001.6—2003.8	
		龙河云	男	苗族	2001.6—2005.4	
		陈稠彪	男	苗族	2005.4—2006.10	
		谭志鹏	男	汉族	2003.1—2006.8	
		王云生	男	汉族	2006.8—2006.10	
		欧开灿	男	汉族	2001.6—2002.3	挂职
		张军伟	男	汉族	2001.6—2002.3	挂职
		李小建	男	汉族	2002.3—2002.12	挂职
		潘仁英	女	汉族	2002.3—2003.3	挂职
		李天送	男	汉族	2002.4—2003.12	挂职
	常 委	何惠明	男	汉族	2001.6—2003.3	
		高勇华	女	回族	2001.6—2006.9	
		程国庆	男	汉族	2001.6—2003.1	
		华廷龙	男	水族	2001.6—2005.4	
		黄佩忠	男	汉族	2001.6—2006.3	

续表4－1

届 次	职 务	姓 名	性别	民族	任职起止时间（年、月）	备 注
第九届	常 委	李 洪	男	汉族	2001.6—2006.10	
		高晓昀	女	汉族	2006.9—2006.10	
第十届	书 记	王振金	男	汉族	2006.10—	
	副书记	陈稠彪	男	苗族	2006.10—	
		王云生	男	汉族	2006.10—	
	常 委	李 洪	男	汉族	2006.10—	
		马应忠	男	布依族	2006.10—	
		陈雪良	男	汉族	2006.10—	
		陆德高	男	汉族	2006.10—	
		韦鸿敏	男	布依族	2006.10—	
		高晓昀	女	汉族	2006.10—	

说明：1985年3月—1987年12月期间，县委常委增加2人，调离2人

第二章 纪律检查

1978年10月，恢复成立中共荔波县委纪律检查委员会。1981年1月，改称中共荔波县纪律检查委员会，仍属县委工作机构。1984年2月，根据中共中央文件精神，升格为县委领导机构之一。1988年，在各区、镇及县粮食局、县教育局、县供销社设纪检组。1993年，县纪委、县监察局合署办公，人员编制10人。2001年，县纪委（监察局）内设办公室、控告申诉室、纪检监察室、案件审理室、执法监察室、党风廉政建设室（加挂纠风室的牌子），行政编制13人（纪委5人、监察局8人）。1994年12月，控告申诉室更名为县纪委信访室。2008年，县纪委在县直属机关单位派驻纪检组13个，县纪委（监察局）内设机构增设综合室，行政编制增加到14人。

第一节 全体委员会议

1985年4月，第五届县纪委第一次全委会选举产生常务委员5人，其中书记1人、副书记1人。

1988年9月，召开第六届县纪委第一次全委会，选举产生常务委员5人，其中书记1人、副书记1人。

1992年1月，召开第七届县纪委第一次全委会，选举产生常务委员5人，其中书记1人、副书记1人。1995年5月4—5日，召开第七届县纪委第七次全委扩大会议，参加会议的有县纪委委员、乡（镇）纪委书记、县直机关纪检组组长、监察室主任等72人。会议审议通过县纪委常委《加强认识，狠抓落实，努力取得1995年反腐败斗争新成效》的工作报告。

1996年12月，召开第八届县纪委第一次全委会，选举产生常委5人，其中书记1人，副书记2人。1997年4月、7月、11月，第八届县纪委先后召开6次全委扩大会议，参会人员扩大到不是县纪委委员的乡（镇）纪委书记、县直机关纪检组组长、监察室主任。会议主要学习中共中央《关于党政机关厉行节约制止奢侈浪费行为的若干规定》及中纪委召开的3次全国纪检监察机关电视电话会议精神。1998年3月，召开第八届县纪委五次全委扩大会议，传达总书记江泽民在中纪委第二次全委会上的讲话精神和省纪委第九次、州纪委第三次全会精神，总结1997年工作，部署反腐败工作。1999年3月，召开第八届县纪委六次全委扩大会议，学习总书记江泽民在中纪委第三次全体会议上重要讲话和中纪委第三次全会精神，审议通过县纪委常委会所作的《任务明确 狠抓落实 努力搞好新形势下的纪检监察工作》的报告，会议通过县纪委第六次全体会议决议。

2001年6月，召开县纪委九届第一次全委会，选举产生常务委员5人，其中书记1人、副书记2人。第九届县纪委共召开两次全委会。

2006年10月，召开第十届县纪委第一次全委会，选举产生常委7人，其中书记1人、副书记2人。2008年3月28日，召开第十届县纪委第二次全委扩大会议，传达贯彻第十七届中纪委第二次全委会和省、州纪委全委会精神。会议从加强创新体制和机制，加强宣传教育和案件检查等方面对2008年反腐倡廉工作进行全面部署。

第二节 党风党纪教育与廉政建设

一、党风党纪教育

1979—1984年，党风党纪教育主要是学习《关于党内政治生活的若干准则》，利用正面、反面典型材料，加强党员教育，清理和纠正招工、招干、户口农转非、工作调动和分配住房中的不正之风。

1985年，从各单位抽调71人组成3个组，由县委领导带队，开展党内纪检工作大检查。

1986年2月，县纪委根据中央关于整党中“统一思想、整顿作风、加强纪律、纯洁组织”的要求，对党员、干部进行系统、全面的党章、党的基本知识和职业道德教育，培训区、乡主要领导干部50人及县机关、企业事业单位干部400人。

1987年3月，举办县直机关科局长学习班，学习《坚持四项基本原则，反对资产阶级自由化》。6月，举办农村支部书记学习班2期，主要进行党性、党风、党纪教育。7月，下发《关于提倡婚事新办丧事从俭的决定》。年内，2名县级党员领导干部因大操大办儿女婚事被通报。

1991年，组织全县乡（镇）纪委书记参加州纪委组织的乡（镇）纪委书记培训班；组织党员干部观看《普通一官》《焦裕禄》《中流砥柱》《大决战》等影片；组织全县43个单位92名党员参加贵州省纪委教育室和《贵州党风》举办的“党风党纪知识百题竞赛”，获三等奖1名、鼓励奖2名。

1993年，举办科（局）长学习班，主要学习《执政党的纪律问题》等内容。

1995年6月，县纪委召开县直机关党员领导干部大会，传达中纪委和省纪委、州纪委关于专项治理文件精神，通报全县专项治理情况。是年，通过组织收看电影教育片《复活》《领导干部的楷模——孔繁森》，加强党风党纪教育。

1996年，开展党纪政纪普及教育知识竞赛活动，全县千余名党员干部参加；编印《荔波县领导干部廉洁自律学习手册》发给全县科（局）级以上领导干部学习。

1997年，县纪委创办《党风与廉政》刊载中央“八项规定”发给全县基层党组织学习。组织学习中央颁布的《中国共产党领导干部廉洁从政若干准则》，发放530份。

1998年，组织党员、干部1200人参加全国、全省开展的《中华人民共和国行政监察法》知识竞赛活动，获中纪委表彰1人、省纪委表彰2人、州纪委表彰3人，县纪委获组织奖。

1999年，通过在县有线电视台播放《中国共产党纪律处分条例》电视系列片，各单位组织干部职工观看。2000年，发放警示教育资料880套，在县有线电视播放电视教育片《警钟》，组织全县干部职工收看中央电视台《焦点访谈》播出的许运鸿案件及电视片《责任的呼唤》《一代廉吏于成龙》。是年，开展警示教育知识竞赛，参加竞赛共1800人。

2002年，组织全县党员、干部学习《关于加强和改进党的作风建设的决定》，在县有线电视播放改进党的作风建设专题讲座。

2003年，征订《典型案例选编》，发给副科级以上干部学习；在县有线电视台播出先进典型人物电视剧《一心为民好书记——郑培民》《忠诚卫士》《大地有江河》等，同时播放慕绥新、马向东等反面典型案例剖析光碟；开展副科级以上领导干部廉洁从政知识测试，参加测试457人，其中县处级30人。

2004年4月，县机关单位购买《江泽民论党风廉政建设和反腐败斗争》《黔南典型案例警示教育读本》发给干部职工学习；组队参加州纪委、州委组织部、州委宣传部、黔南电视台举办的全州党内法规知识竞赛活动，获全州第三名。

2005年，开展反腐倡廉形势政策宣传，全县制作板报36期。2006年2月，将州纪委编写的《甘洒热血写春秋》发给全县副科级以上干部学习。是年，举办学习贯彻落实《建立健全教育、制度、监督并重的惩治和预防腐败体系实施纲要》宣传专栏3期。

2007年，在全县开展党风廉政宣传信访下乡活动，播放《牛玉儒同志先进事迹报告会》《绝路》等电教片，发放宣传资料1000余份，受教育群众5000人。组织收看中央电视台《焦点访谈》栏目播出的中共中央纪委关于严格禁止利用职务上的便利谋取不正当利益的若干规定专题片，办党风廉政宣传教育专栏6期。

2008年，开展廉政文化创建活动，制作反腐倡廉广告牌6块，组织参加州纪委举办的“做党的忠诚卫士，当群众的贴心人——纪念改革开放暨纪检机关恢复重建30周年”诗歌朗诵和演讲比赛。

二、廉政建设

1979—1981年，县纪委开展“文化大革命”中冤假错案复查平反以及一些历史案件改正工作。同时，对婚丧嫁娶讲排场、比阔气等歪风开展自查自纠。

1984年，县委下发《关于迎接党风大检查实现今年党风明显好转的意见》，县纪委领导在全县三级干部会上作全县党风状况专题发言，着重纠正“招、转、调”和分配住房中的不正之风。1985年起，县纪委开始督促检查基层党组织开好民主生活会，重点对党风情况进行检查。

1989年，县纪委先后召开4次全县廉政建设大会，到会人数总计6000余人。10月，县委六届二次全委扩大会作出《加强自身廉政建设15条规定》，同时，县政府出台《为政清廉13条规定》。之后，各单位制定廉政制度。是年，县委设置廉政建设科。

1990年，先后召开全县廉政建设大会、廉政肃贪大会，重申廉政纪律，公开处理违纪违法人员14人。

1991年12月31日，县委、县政府作出《关于禁止党员、干部、职工赌博的规定》。

1992年3月，县委发出《关于整顿机关作风的意见》，从3月16日开始，至3月底结束。主要在机关中开展思想、作风、纪律整顿，采取以自我教育、自我检查、自我纠正、自我完善为主的方式加强纪律教育。

1993年9月，建立县委反腐倡廉领导小组，同时召开县机关反腐倡廉动员大会，重点在党政机关、司法行政机关、经济管理部门，以中央提出的“五项规定”“十一个不准”的要求进行自查自纠。

1994年4月，县委印发《关于贯彻落实省纪检、监察工作会议精神的意见》，要求切实纠正部门和行业不正之风，一是狠刹乱收费，特别是要切实减轻农民负担；二是要认真落实“收支两条线”的规定，把合理收费和依法罚没的收入列入财政收入，切实解决自收自支、收费提成问题；三是县以上党政机关办的经济实体还未脱钩的，要按中央和省的规定脱钩；四是继续纠正用公款旅游、大吃大喝的不正之风。

1996—1999年，督促全县机关、乡（镇）、企事业单位党组织开好一年一度的领导干部廉洁自律专题民主生活会，开展清房、超标使用小汽车和挂军警车牌号清理。1999年，清理用公款安装的私人电话，收缴封存移动电话136部、传呼机284个，经公开处理，收回资金21万元。当年节约通信费用30万元；查封1个国营单位违规配备更换小轿车1辆，价值30万元。

2000年，县委出台《荔波县党风廉政建设责任制》后，县纪委建立领导班子成员联系督查党风廉政建设责任制及落实纠风责任追究制。是年，全县制定党风廉政建设责任制单位94个，建立领导干部廉政档案396卷。

2001年，落实领导干部不准收受礼金、有价证券的规定，清查领导干部收受礼金情况，领导干部上交收受的礼金共1.3万元。

2002年，对全县32名县级领导干部配偶、子女从业情况进行公示；两名领导干部将接受的礼金上交国库共1.1万元；在国有企业领导干部廉洁自律5项规定执行情况检查中，依纪依法收缴3名领导干部违规兼职兼薪款共6万元；制定《关于改进党政机关事业单位移动电话、传呼机管理的试行办法》，重申《严禁非专职驾驶员驾驶公车的规定》。

2003年6月，县委下发《关于不准用公款大吃大喝的有关规定》。县纪委对超标、超编使用小汽车进行清理，共查93个单位，查出超标小汽车2辆；查处违反规定驾驶公车肇事的乡（镇）领导干部2人；追究矿山安全事故责任人7人。

2004—2005年，县委、县政府出台《关于狠刹国家机关及其工作人员大操大办酒席的规定（试行）》以后，查处违反规定的党员干部4人，大操大办酒席的风气得到遏制。2005年9月，开展国家机关工作人员和国有企业负责人投资入股煤矿清查工作，全县进行自查自纠单位113个，经查，查出国家机关工作人员和国有企业负责人2人投资240万元入股办矿，已撤资退股。是年，对党政机关超标准配备、挪用专项资金购配小汽车以及公车私挂进行清查，查出5个单位公车私挂小汽车9辆。

2006—2007年，执行领导干部个人重大事项报告制度；开展领导干部任前廉政谈话；进行干部诫免谈话6人次；查处违反规定操办酒席干部1人；清理党政机关干部拖欠公款115人总计131万元，全部追回。2007年，科级干部述职述廉47人。

2008年，县委、县政府发出《关于分解落实2008年党风廉政建设和反腐败工作任务的通知》，将党风廉政建设和反腐败工作任务分解落实到牵头单位27个、协办单位32个，县委主要领导分别与17个乡（镇）、58个县直部门主要负责人签订党风廉政建设责任书。

第三节　案件查处与行政监察

一、案件查处

1978—1980年，查处违纪党员34人，其中开除党籍16人，撤销党内职务4人，留党察看4人，党内严重警告10人。其间，1979年对“文化大革命”“清队”“一打三反”等运动中受处理的122名干部进行复查113人，其中维持结论74人、改变原处分39人。

1981年，主要纠正“四清”“反右倾”“反左”“文化大革命”4个时期的冤假错案，按照“全错全纠，部分错部分纠，不错不纠”的原则，平反纠正221人，其中，“文化大革命”时期120人，“四清”时期4人，“反右倾”时期5人，“反左”时期和其他错误92人。是年，查处违纪党员10人，其中，开除党籍3人，留察4人，撤销党内职务1人，严重警告和警告处分各1人。

1982—1984年，查处违纪党员32人，其中，开除党籍17人，留党察看9人，严重警告、警告各3人。

1985年，查处违纪案件8件，其中官僚主义3件，贪污、受贿各1件，计划生育超生1件，乱搞两性关系2件。复查历史案件3件，其中恢复党籍3人、安排工作1人。上缴财政违纪款7.5万元。

1986—1992年，查处违纪党员96人，其中，开除党籍18人，留党察看30人，严重警告23人，警告18人，通报批评1人，免予处分2人，批评教育4人。被查出党员的错误性质贪污、贿赂、包庇、违反财经纪律、腐化堕落、道德败坏、违反计划生育政策等。

1993年起，县纪委、县监察局合署办公后，负责全县党政机关和干部违法案件的查处。

1993—2008年全县违纪违规案件查处情况统计表

表4－2

年度	立案（件）	结案					受党纪处分（人）	受政纪处分（人）
		总计（人、件）		乡科级干部（人）	一般干部（人）	其他干部（人）		
		人	件					
1993	20	20	20	1	7	12	19	1
1994	26	23	26	—	17	6	15	11
1995	12	12	12	—	9	3	6	6
1996	22	21	22	3	11	7	10	12
1997	12	11	12	1	7	3	4	8
1998	19	19	19	—	18	1	5	14
1999	45	33	45	5	30	8	13	32
2000	37	33	37	6	21	6	10	27
2001	20	15	20	6	6	3	10	10
2002	24	20	24	5	14	1	7	17
2003	36	33	36	9	11	13	15	21
2004	31	31	31	25	1	5	12	19
2005	43	43	44	15	20	8	18	26
2006	23	23	23	10	7	6	13	10
2007	17	17	19	4	11	2	6	13
2008	14	14	14	5	8	1	1	13

二、行政监察

1993年7月，成立减轻农民负担领导小组，设立专门办公室，对全县农民负担问题进行调查研究。同时出台减轻农民负担3条措施：1.农民依法纳税，村提留和乡统筹费用，必须严控在上半年农民人均收入的5%以内。各种摊派、集资、达标活动，行政事业性收费，一律停止执行。2.清理1992年平价分配和奖售的柴油、汽油和化肥等农用物资的兑现情况。没有兑现的，继续列入1993年供应指标。3.成立减轻农民负担领导小组，设立专门的办公室，对全县农民负担问题进行调查研究，并及时汇报和解决。

是年11月—1994年2月底，对落实离休干部待遇情况进行检查，在各单位开展自查基础上，离退休干部局重点抽查。

1994年，县纪委（监察局）对成人高考、招干、征兵、税费征收等工作开展监督。

1995年，县纪委（监察局）参与县政府征兵、招工、招干、招生监督。年内，取消公路收费站和检查站13个，清理乱收费10.2万元，减轻农民负担17.3万元。

1996—1997年，对中小学校乱收费，公路“三乱”（乱设站卡、乱罚款、乱收费）、减轻农民负担等问题进行检查。1997年，对建设行业、涉农部门和部分中小学乱收费问题进行执法检查，挽回经济损失5.08万元。1998年，查处违规收费小学1所，将违规收取的费用3.9万元全部清退；村务公开执法立案5件，办结4件，转相关单位处理1件，涉及违规金额29万元；对扶贫资金和农用物资价格质量进行专项检查。

2000年，对中小学校收费、减轻农民负担、医药购销不正之风、重特大责任事故调查、国债资金管理、粮食改革政策措施落实、落实收支两条线规定、有形建筑市场规范运作和建设工程招投标等情况进行执法检查，初查案件9件，转立案2件。

2003年，对经营性土地使用权招标拍卖和挂牌出让进行行政效能监察，对国债资金、“天保工程”、社保资金、扶贫资金、“希望工程”等专项资金使用情况进行执法监察。是年，参加重特大安全责任事故调查84起。

2005年，开展专项资金管理使用情况、《中华人民共和国行政许可法》贯彻执行及严格土地管理情况监督检查。

2006年，开展行政效能监察、治理商业贿赂工作，共查办商业贿赂案件4件，涉案金额35万元。

2007年，开展治理商业贿赂工作，查处医药购销领域商业贿赂案件2起，涉案金额4万元，分别给予当事人党纪政纪处分。

2008年，对安全生产和矿山安全责任事故进行监督检查，查处安全责任事故案件2件6人。

第三章 组织工作

第一节 基层组织建设

一、基层组织

1978年，全县有党员3079人。其中，女性373人；工业22人，农业2292人，机关648人，其他135人；少数民族2512人；大专以上学历41人。

1979年7月，撤销工交办、财贸办、农林办、教卫办4个核心领导小组，分别建立工交、财贸、农林、教卫4个党组，至1980年撤销。1980年9月建立县政府党组。11月，建立县人大常委会党组。1981年3月建立县检察院党组。1984年建立县经委党组，5月建立县政协党组、县教育局党组。1986年7月建立县计委党组。

1984年4月，实行社（镇）机构改革，公社改称乡，同时茂兰公社划分为茂兰、立化、瑶庆3个乡。1984年5月玉屏镇升格为区级镇，镇党委同时升格直属县委领导。

1986年后，按照"坚持标准，保证质量，改善结构，慎重发展"的原则，着重在党组织力量薄弱的地区和单位，特别是在科技、文教、卫生以及生产第一线发展已具备入党条件的工作骨干入党。

1987年12月底，县委下辖4个区、1个镇党委和25个乡（其中6个水族乡、2个瑶族乡）党委。同年底，全县30个区（镇）乡党委领导中，正、副书记59人，大专以上文化程度共有17人。

1988年，对全县2853名农村党员进行培训。

1990年，全县基层党组织吸收39名具有大专以上文化程度知识分子和195名具有中专、高中文化程度知识分子入党。

1991年，全县发展党员87人。其中，生产第一线工人农民61人，机关干部和知识分子26人。

1992年，全县培养入党积极分子370人，发展党员231人，其中农民162人，占70.13%。

1996年，全县基层党组织举办入党积极分子培训班18期，共培养入党积极分子1440人。全年发展党员290人。

1997年，发展党员334人，其中，企业和农村生产第一线196人。

2000年，全县党员5705人，其中工业347人、农业3524人、科技教育文化卫生594人、机关1240人。

2002年，继续抓好农村基层组织建设"三级联创"工作，年底，全县达到"五个好"村党支部18个，基本达到"五个好"村党支部21个。达到"六个好"乡（镇）党委2个，创建基层满意县部门12个。

2004年2月，成立县建筑工程有限责任公司党支部，有党员9人。同月，成立贵州明德实业公司党支部，有党员17人。

2005年，农村基层党组织着力培养政治素质强、个人致富能力强、带领群众共同致富强的“三强”领头人。

从2007年开始，在全县农村党员中实施“党员创业导富工程”，县委出台《荔波县关于实施“党员创业导富工程”发挥农村党员“双带”作用的意见》《关于建立党内激励关怀帮扶生活困难党员和鼓励党员创业导富的意见》，在资金、政策、项目、技术上给予优先扶持，共向省、州争取项目63个，资金520万元，1000多名党员通过导富项目增收致富。是年，全县在册“导富党员”1200余名，进入新一届村级领导班子76名；涌现出玉屏镇板旺村党支部、拉岜村党支部、福利村党支部、朝阳镇八烂村党支部等一批先进典型。

二、组织整顿

1985年7月—1986年年底，全县分三批整党，在整党中发展新党员218名。

1988年，县委要求全县广大干部在工作中树立深化“五个观念”，即任务观念、纪律观念、求实观念、服务观念、政绩观念。对基层党组织进行整顿和对党员进行民主评议，共整顿党支部145个。

1989年4月，县委同意组织部《关于我县推行民主评议党员制度的实施意见》《关于处理不合格党员的暂行规定》，在全县开展民主评议党员活动，按照中央和省委提出的“一定要坚持党章规定的党员条件”“教育、管理、表彰、处置”四个相结合，“把对党员的教育贯穿始终，把思想政治工作贯穿始终”的两个始终和“优秀、合格、基本不合格、不合格”四个档次的精神进行评议。县、区、乡机关和事业单位在第二季度完成评议；厂矿、企业单位和农村在第三季度完成评议。

1992年，对全县168个村党支部进行整顿、调整和补充，新任党支部书记19人。同时，在村党支部开展民主评议党员活动，应参加评议2617人，实际参加评议的党员2598人，占99.27%，评议出不合格党员4名。

1994年，按照省委提出的“配好一个班子，选好一个支部书记，找好一条致富路子，建好一套管理制度”的要求，从县直机关、乡（镇）机关选派227名干部下村蹲点开展帮扶工作。年底，全县村党支部具备“四个一”条件34个，占农村党支部总数的20.24%；村党支部开展“双带”（党员带头致富，带领群众共同致富）活动160个，占农村支部总数的95.24%；1671名党员开展“双带”活动，联系农户2689户。通过帮扶脱贫1561户，占联系户的58.05%。

1995年，对全县后进村进行组织整顿，共整顿党支部36个。整顿后，完善一套经营体制、选准一条致富路子的村有16个，占44.4%；已健全一套好的管理和服务制度的村30个。年底，省、州从留存的党费中拨给4000元，县匹配4000元，用于补助农村60岁以上的贫困党员。

1996年，对农村基层党组织进行重点整顿，建立“后进”“软弱”“瘫痪”“半瘫痪”档案卡及村后备干部档案。

1999年2月5日，县委作出《关于在副科级以上党政领导班子和领导干部中深入开展以“讲学习、讲政治、讲正气、讲团结、讲奉献”为主要内容的党性党风教育的实施意见》。开展“五讲”教育的步骤和方法：开展“五讲”教育要采取自上而下的方法，分级分批进行。在时间安排上，县委常委班子成员的“五讲”教育要从4月开始，县委抓的试点工作于4月下旬开始，5月底在县直机关和各乡镇展开。一个领导班子开展学习教育的时间一般为两个月左右，全部工作要在11月底以前完成。具体步骤分为准备阶段、思想动员学习提高阶段、总结反思，对照检查阶段、认真整改、健全制度阶段、总结检查阶段。

2002年年底，全县达到“五好”村党支部18个，基本达到“五好”村党支部21个。

1978—2008年全县党组织统计一览表

表4-3

年度	党组织（个）			党员（人）		
	基层党委	党总支	支部	总数	其中	
					女	少数民族
1978	24	3	236	3079	373	2512
1979	24	5	247	3117	383	2512
1980	25	3	259	3195	376	2610
1981	24	4	266	3201	379	2618
1982	26	4	265	3229	383	2629
1983	25	4	271	3237	383	2658
1984	26	4	282	3381	415	2727
1985	25	6	284	3602	419	2924
1986	27	5	294	3688	434	3013
1987	26	4	303	3762	442	3089
1988	7	4	303	3844	451	3144
1989	8	3	314	3762	442	3086
1990	8	3	322	3853	466	3159
1991	8	7	319	3862	473	3200
1992	20	7	328	4043	507	3351
1993	21	7	336	4238	537	3546
1994	21	7	333	4373	556	3680
1995	21	14	345	4587	581	3847
1996	21	15	348	4847	652	4093
1997	21	15	361	5155	731	4380
1998	19	15	366	5371	776	4563
1999	19	14	358	5556	828	4751
2000	19	12	364	5705	877	4893
2001	19	9	360	5863	916	5075
2002	19	9	358	5980	964	5169
2003	21	9	350	6107	1031	1094
2004	21	9	342	6232	1061	1184
2005	21	9	355	6319	1093	1287
2006	21	9	352	6391	1086	1346
2007	21	9	352	6565	1158	1486
2008	21	9	352	6690	1206	1579

第二节　干部队伍管理

一、干部管理制度改革

1978—1979年，全县干部由县委组织部管理。1980年后，县政府直属部门干部、国有企业干部、公社一般干部划归县人事局管理，县委组织部代县委管理全县科级领导干部和非领导职务干部，直接管理县委、群众团体、人大常委会、政协、法院、检察院、工商联七大类机关的一般干部。这种管理模式一直延续到2001年。

1999年3月，县委制定《关于进一步加强干部管理工作的意见》，规定对干部的管理权限、录用、聘用、调整、选拔、平时和年终考核审查、干部档案保管、降职、辞职、辞退、违纪处理、离退休有关手续的办理。

2001年，全县党政机构改革后，乡（镇）一般公务员管理从县人事局划入组织部管理。

2005年，贯彻省委组织部《关于对违规配备干部进行纠正的通知》精神，对县政府工作部门主要领导交叉任职，不再新配专职党组书记或副书记；对政府工作部门党、政正职分设造成超额配置的，出台具体调整办法，采取提前退职、交流到缺职单位、保留职级改任副职、男年满55周岁、女年满50周岁改任同级非领导职务等措施，消化多设职位；建立干部监督督查员制度，聘请5名老干部和纪检、审计、信访等部门干部为干部监督员，发挥纪检监察部门和干部监督员对干部任用工作的监督作用。

2006年，县委出台《关于对领导干部实行离任审计加强管理监督的通知》《关于大中专毕业生安置工作有关问题的决定》。2007年，出台《关于研究干部问题的有关规定》《关于干部考察工作的有关规定（试行）》。2008年，县委出台《荔波县委管理干部任前公示办法（试行）》《关于实行党政领导干部试用期跟踪考察的管理意见》，制定《领导干部打招呼制度》《领导干部诫勉制度》《荔波县领导干部个人重大事项报告制度》《关于进一步加强干部人事工作纪律的意见》等有关干部人事制度改革配套文件。是年，实行干部考察员认证制，全县聘任干部考察员38名。

二、干部队伍建设

（一）干部选拔任用

1979年11月27日，县委批转组织部《关于设立镇人民政府、人民公社管理委员会和进一步调整好领导班子的意见》。镇政府和人民公社管理委员会的领导班子实行直接选举。至1980年4月，选举工作结束。

1987年9月3日，县委、县政府决定，从行政部门选调45周岁以下，身体健康，高中、初中文化程度，有一定工作能力的干部充实政法和经济工作部门。

是月，县委批转组织部《关于认真做好乡镇党委换届选举工作的报告》，按照“德才兼备”的原则和干部“四化”的方针，根据“相对稳定、调整充实、适当交流、积极慎重地推进干部制度改革，进一步完善领导班子群体结构”的要求，调整和配备乡（镇）党委领导班子。

1993年4月10日，全县17个乡（镇）领导班子换届选举工作结束，共选出新一届乡（镇）人大主席团常务主席17名、副主席1名，乡（镇）长17名、副乡（镇）长54名。有14个乡（镇）选出女副乡镇长，6个乡（镇）选出科技副乡（镇）长。

1994年9月1日，县委批转组织部《关于做好乡镇党委换届选举工作的报告》，按照干部队伍“四化”方针和“德才兼备”的原则，以及中央“基本稳定，个别调整，提高素质”的要求，从发展市场经济的能力上调整配备乡（镇）党委领导班子。

1999年3月，科级领导干部拟任实行常委票决制度，由举手表决改为无记名投票表决。

1999年、2002年、2007年，荔波县三次面向全县、全州公开选拔教育局副局长、旅游局副局长、团县委副书记等共12个副科级职位领导干部。

2002年，县委出台《关于在全县党政机关中推进中层干部竞争上岗的实施意见》，打破“领导说了算”“论资排辈”等用人模式。

2007年7月20日，县委组织部开展初任科级干部廉洁自律培训，88名初任领导干部参加培训

2002年8月，实行领导干部定期定岗交流制。2006年6月，按照中央的规定，对在同一职位工作超过规定年限的，进行岗位交流。到2008年，全县对科级干部进行平职交流789人次。其中，乡（镇）与乡（镇）间交流197人次，乡（镇）与部门间交流216人次，部门与部门间交流273人次，单位内部轮岗交流103人次。2002—2008年，全县共45个单位开展了竞争上岗，共选拔股级干部325名。

（二）后备干部培养

1984年8月，县委召开三级干部会，首次开展后备干部推荐，以无记名投票的方式，民主推荐产生县第三梯队后备干部人选。被推荐人员的条件为35岁以下大、中专毕业生。经民主推荐和县委常委会讨论考察后，确定县第三梯队后备干部20人。其中，男性18名、女性2名；平均年龄26.25岁；大专文化13人、中专文化4人、高中文化3人；助理工程师1人；少数民族15人。县委决定，第三梯队后备干部作为县委管理干部，其档案归县委组织部管理。对后备干部采取动态管理，按照“优者上、良者育、劣者汰”原则，实行“一年一淘汰，一年一补充”制度。1985年，县委对后备干部队伍进行调整，调出4人，增补4人。是年，县委从第三梯队干部中选拔担任副科级干部3人。

此后，后备干部选拔培养列入县委组织部的一项经常性工作。

1994年8月，县委选拔青年干部11人到广西自治区环江县、宜州市挂职学习，担任乡（镇）党委副书记、乡（镇）长助理等职务，为期3个月。从县直机关选调青年干部18人到县内14个乡（镇）挂职锻炼，为期18个月。

1998年7月，县委从播尧、甲良、茂兰、朝阳4个乡（镇）各选派乡（镇）长1名和村领导到瓮安县进行为期1个月的挂职学习锻炼。

2006年，乡（镇）换届从中层干部和副科级后备干部中选拔6名优秀青年干部充实到乡（镇）领导班子。2006—2008年，提拔的59名干部中有51人是后备干部。

2008年，县委采取“一推双考”办法推荐选拔后备干部，即由各乡（镇）和机关单位推荐，组织部再对推荐的人员进行文化考试和德绩考评。全县推荐上报196人，经过“双考”后列为后备干部141人。县委对后备干部坚持一年至少一次集中培训。

二、干部理论学习教育

1986年3月24日，组织部联合宣传部和党校作出《关于干部理论学习的意见》，从是年到1989

年，每年组织在职干部至少学一门理论，各类干部用4年时间把应学理论课程基本学完。5月2日，县委成立理论教育函授领导小组，主抓各级干部马克思主义哲学、政治经济学、科学社会主义、中国革命史的学习。

1987年5月9日，县委对干部政治理论学习作出安排，强调各级干部要把《坚持四项基本原则反对资产阶级自由化》《建设有中国特色的社会主义》两本书作为主要学习内容，同时深入学习中央文件和党报党刊上有关重要社论和文章，学习结束时进行考试。

1988年4月30日，组织部、宣传部分批组织农村党员干部317人、农村党员266人学习中共十三大文件精神。

是年6月30日—7月15日，县委党校举办“社会主义商品经济理论”学习班2期，培训经理、厂长、股长以上领导干部共182人。

1989年5月，举办社会主义初级阶段理论和党的基本路线学习班2期，共培训各机关单位和学校的股长、经理、科局长干部324人。10—12月，科局级以上干部分期分批到党校脱产学习5天，主要学习中共十三届四中全会精神和江泽民在庆祝中华人民共和国成立40周年大会上的讲话。

1990年7月25日，县委印发《关于当前组织在职干部认真学习马克思主义理论的几点意见》，要求全体干部和职工自学为主，集中学习为辅。各区、乡和县直机关部、办、委、局的党支部建立中心学习组，进行学习辅导。

1991年4月6日，县委号召全县干部职工认真学习焦裕禄的模范事迹，加强自我教育，加强思想改造，努力搞好工作。

1993年7月6日，县委批转组织部、宣传部《关于全县党员、干部深入学习建设有中国特色社会主义理论的安排意见》，在8—9月举办科局领导干部、企事业党组织理论教育骨干和乡（镇）书记培训班4期。是年，举办建设有中国特色社会主义理论培训班2期，每期5天，培训县直机关部、办、委、局、独立厂、场、公司负责人、党组负责人242人；举办新任二级班子培训班1期，培训乡（镇）长24人，县科局干部14人；向上调训干部46人，其中，贵州大学秘书班7人，州乡（镇）人大主席团专干班17人，州领导干部科技讲习班4人，州女乡（镇）长培训班13人，州党校青干班3人，省、州妇干班2人。

1996年6月14日，县委印发《1996—2000年全县干部教育培训规划》。

三、干部监督

1978年，根据中央和省、州有关落实干部政策的文件精神，县委成立落实干部政策工作领导小组，抽调专人对历次政治运动发生的案件进行复查，至1990年年底，复查处理案件共270件。其中，全错全改187件，部分错部分改24件，维持原结论59件。撤销刑事处分或劳动教养的88人，恢复党籍17人，恢复公职144人（其中收回安排工作111人，补办离退休和退职手续15人，恢复工作籍18人），撤销其他处分45人；补发工资19人，清退财物4人，一次性补助102人；对已故的12人，落实政策后发给安葬费、抚恤金和遗属生活困难补助。1992年年底，平反冤假错案20件。

1987年5月12日，县委批转组织部《关于进一步完善和改进干部管理工作的意见》。《意见》对适当下放部分干部管理权限和分级管理作明确规定，强调局级单位任免干部，党组织成员必须有3人以上参加，在研究领导干部的子女、配偶调动和提拔时，领导干部不许插手或干预。

1990年5月，县委进行干部任期工作考核。考核的范围和对象是县人大常委会决定任免的县政府各工作部门的正职领导干部；县政府决定任免的各工作部门的副职和荔中的正副职领导干部；县人大办及人民法院、人民检察院的副职领导干部。

1993年12月9日，组织部发出《关于继续开展民主评议党员的通知》，开展民主评议党员活动，民主评议坚持以正面教育为主，将教育、管理、表彰、监督融为一体。

1995年2月，中共中央颁布《干部任用暂行条例》，按条例规定对全县干部选拔任用和对领导干部进行监督。

1999年2月25日，县委发出《关于加强干部纪律管理的实施意见》，要求：第一，必须严肃党的政治纪律；第二，必须严肃党的组织纪律；第三，必须严肃经济工作纪律；第四，必须严肃党和群众的工作纪律。实施意见提出，从是年起，对各乡（镇）及县直机关各部门的党风廉政责任制实行一票否决权。

2000年4月29日，县委印发组织部《关于批转执行“三个制度”“一个意见”的请示》。“三个制度”即领导干部打招呼制度、领导干部诫勉制度、领导干部报告个人重大事项制度，“一个意见”即《关于进一步加强干部人事工作纪律的意见》。

2001年7月18日，县委办、县政府办发出《关于清理国家机关干部、职工收养子女的通知》，清理时限为1998年1月1日至2001年7月21日，清理对象为全县党政机关、企事业单位干部职工（包括离退休干部职工）。

2003年，对不胜任现职的科级领导干部作降职处理28名，对工作不负责任或违反有关规定拒不执行组织决定的科级干部作撤职处理5名，对有违纪行为的科级干部予以免职处理3名。

2004年，制定《领导干部任期经济责任审计实施意见》，对离任领导干部进行经济责任审计。是年，组织部与纪检监察部门共同调查核实群众举报的干部问题3件（次）。

1978—2008年全县干部统计一览表

表4－4

年度	干部总数（人）	其中			
		女性	少数民族	共产党员	大专以上文化
1978	1816	440	890	604	183
1979	1876	452	971	621	179
1980	1940	453	1012	579	168
1981	2039	520	1132	560	178
1982	2104	524	1181	540	206
1983	2150	528	1170	552	199
1984	2205	554	1248	612	198
1985	2171	507	1094	640	211
1986	2333	622	1443	691	238
1987	2456	657	1583	356	288
1988	2566	693	1648	715	233
1989	2662	777	1798	752	371
1990	2739	840	1890	751	388
1991	2816	826	1971	751	414
1992	2874	861	2091	756	438

续表4－4

年度	干部总数（人）	其中			
		女性	少数民族	共产党员	大专以上文化
1993	2960	895	2164	756	456
1994	3126	964	2357	785	509
1995	3260	1069	2458	780	543
1996	3671	1265	2841	902	638
1997	3798	1356	3039	989	731
1998	3851	1412	3148	1091	884（本科138）
1999	3946	1453	3266	1097	1021（本科152）
2000	4064	1527	3297	1178	1252（本科228）
2001	4181	1577	3452	1225	1531（本科245）
2002	4141	1581	3487	1249	2133（本科383）
2003	4247	1611	3613	1325	2431（本科478）
2004	4258	1614	3608	1315	2780（本科579）
2005	4299	—	3684	—	—
2006	4293	1642	3728	1416	3240（本科769）
2007	4342	1677	3961	1445	3407（本科1020）
2008	4201	1725	3859	1503	3668（本科1089）

第三节　知识分子和人才工作

1978年，全县有科技人员297人。其中，工程技术人员44人，农业技术人员83人，卫生技术人员140人，科研人员1人，教学人员29人；中专152人、大专84人、其他61人。

1984年，成立落实知识分子政策领导小组，开展落实知识分子政策工作，向全县有中专以上毕业文凭的干部职工发放知识分子补贴。从知识分子中提拔到县级、科（局）级领导岗位共33人。

1985年9月，县政府对县内荔波籍任教20年以上、外县籍任教15年以上的教师颁发荣誉证书，对有5人以上从教的家庭和对教育工作有显著贡献的教师分别授予“教育之家”“辛勤园丁”称号。

1986年1月，县委、县政府决定，凡在县内工作具有中专毕业以上文化程度、取得技术员以上职称或经自学考试获得国家承认中专以上毕业证书的干部职工，分别按资历、工作年限、工资级别，发给每人每月7元、5元、3元不等的书刊资料费。

1987年，县委、县政府以解决配偶户口、工作等优惠条件，向县外、州外、省外招聘教师、技术人员和干部到荔波县工作。

是年8月11日，县委、县政府印发《关于鼓励科技人员、干部职工到城乡承办企业从事开发性生产的有关暂行规定》。

1991年6月29日，县委决定对1966年年底以前高中毕业的中小学公办教师和党政机关、企事业单位干部，按中专学历发给知识分子补贴和浮动工资。

1992年2月，知识分子联系小组办公室更名为中共荔波县委知识分子工作领导小组办公室，升格为正科级机构，挂靠县委组织部。是年，将在乡（镇）连续工作满5年、县直单位工作满8年的干部职工的浮动工资转为固定工资，为1985年以后受省级以上表彰的先进个人44名晋升一级工资，安排家属子女工作70户，解决部分知识分子夫妻分居、住房困难等问题，吸收知识分子入党53人，表彰893人（其中省、州表彰46人）。3月9日，县委、县政府在《关于表彰先进科技工作者的决定》中，对王清源等17名先进科技工作者予以表彰，并授予“1991年荔波县先进科技工作者”荣誉称号。

1993年、1995年，招聘教师（英语、语文教师）共40名。此后，以提供每人20～30平方米的周转住房1套及办公电脑1台等优惠条件，陆续从云南师范大学、广西师范大学、大连外国语学院、天津外国语学院、西南大学、浙江师范大学、昆明理工大学、重庆师范大学、河南大学、南京理工大学、四川外国语学院、温州大学等院校招聘一批外省籍毕业生到荔波任教。1995年3月17日，县委、县政府对蒙学诗等27名知识分子、科技人员进行表彰，并授予“荔波县1993年至1994年优秀知识分子、科技人员”称号。

1997年1月7日，在县城召开全县教育表彰会，首次利用教育基金的增值额，对近几年为发展荔波教育事业辛勤耕耘、成效显著的先进集体28个、先进个人81人进行表彰。

1998年6月29日，县委、县政府作出表彰优秀知识分子、科技人员的决定，受表彰的优秀知识分子、科技人员32人。

2000年，在县城沙梨园片区无偿划拨土地27亩建设教师新村，解决150户教师住房困难。

2001年，知识分子办公室改为组织部内设机构。

2002年，全县招聘原煤生产技术干部6人（其中工程师2人、助理工程师4人），选派科技副乡（镇）长16人。

2003年，全县招聘原煤生产技术管理人员2人（助理工程师）。招聘煤炭安全监督管理人员35人，一年后转正31人。

至2008年，全县有专业技术人员2906人（不含省、州垂管部门人员），是1978年的10倍。其中，教学专业技术人员2054人，农业专业技术人员198人，工程专业技术人员196人，医疗卫生专业技术人员394人，其他专业技术人员64人。已评聘专业技术职称人员2708人，其中，高级职称41人、中级职称622人、初级职称2045人。招聘外省籍教师共75人。

第四节　远程教育

2003年8月，县委成立农村党员干部现代远程教育工程领导小组，启动全县农村党员干部现代远程教育工作，制定《关于全县农村党员干部现代远程教育工程实施意见》，明确开展农村党员干部现代远程教育工作的总体目标和主要任务，落实远教工作的实施步骤和经费。各乡（镇）党委相应成立领导小组，实施农村党员干部现代远程教育工程。是年年底，县委将农村党员干部现代远程教育工程列入2004年10件实事之一。2004年11月，全县建成60个村级远程教育站点。

2005年5月，成立县农村党员干部现代远程教育办公室，为县委组织部管理的副科级事业机构，内设综合股、业务股。

是年8月14日，正式启动实施“贵州省农村中小学现代远程教育工程”。覆盖全县117所中小学校和办学点，项目总投资261万元，国家和地方按2∶1比例投入资金，省以下即省、州、县按5∶3∶2进行资金配套。

2006年，对全县远程教育站点进行调整，利用信息管理系统对远程教育工作进行科学管理，采取从远程教育资源网中下载刻录、购买或与涉农部门协调刻录等方式收集教学光盘，建立近3000小时的县级教学资源库。8月14日，全县远程教育站点通过省级评估验收。

2007年，推行“科普+远教”合作模式，组建远程教育种桑养蚕、糖蔗种植和果蔬种植农技服务队，向群众提供技术咨询服务，帮助解决技术难题。同时，实施以“1个村级远程教育示范点创建10户远程教育示范户带动50名党员群众脱贫致富”为目标的远程教育“115”示范工程，把“115”示范工程纳入“党员创业导富工程”建设体系进行运作，县委对示范乡（镇）、示范村和示范户在政策、项目、资金、信息等方面进行扶持，发挥示范带动作用。10月，“种桑养蚕技术”“瑶山作证”课件获全州组织系统技能比武二等奖。22日，县委在瑶山中学召开全县远程教育村校结合工作经验交流现场会，推广“小手牵大手”村校结合工作模式。

2008年4月，清华大学在县委党校建立教育扶贫远程教学站。7月，“科普+远教”咨询服务厅正式启动，同年，全州农村党员干部现代远程教育工作现场会在荔波县召开，荔波县“科普+远教”合作模式作为典型经验在全州推广。利用教育扶贫远程教学站点资源优势，开办中小学校长教育管理培训班。11月，开展远程教育进社区工作，全县4个社区全部安装远程教育设备。

第四章 宣传工作

第一节 干部理论学习

1978年，全县党员、干部重点学习中共十一届三中全会精神。1979年5月，县委印发《关于全县公社以上在职干部理论学习的意见》，重点学习中共中央关于国民经济发展“调整、整顿、改革、提高”八字方针。

1980年4月，县委印发《关于在职干部政治学习安排意见》，上半年重点学习邓小平《目前形势和任务》的重要讲话，下半年重点学习社会主义经济规律理论知识。

1981年1月，宣传部印发《认真组织机关干部学习〈关于建国以来党的若干历史问题的决议〉的意见》，举办县、区机关副科（局）长以上党员干部（含厂矿企业领导干部）培训班；各区以公社为单位，培训农村党员。

1982年3月，县委印发《关于在职干部理论学习的意见》，以《马克思主义哲学》《政治经济学》《科学社会主义》《陈云同志文稿选编》为学习重点，要求打破“两个凡是”，坚持实践是检验真理的唯一标准，树立以经济建设为中心的思想。采取“小集中”读书班为主，理论讨论和自学为辅的方式进行学习。

是年，先后举办全县科（局）长以上领导干部经济理论集中学习班，学习内容为社会主义制度下按劳分配问题、商品和货币价值规律、价格政策等在“四化”中的作用、社会主义农业体制改革和社会主义经济计划管理等知识；举办县、区、公社领导干部学习《邓小平文选》、中共十一届六中全会报告《全面开创社会主义现代化建设的新局面》培训班2期，每期10天，培训167人；举办学习中共十二大精神培训班4期，参加学习552人；举办县、区机关干部职工宣讲报告会，培训3320人；举行学习中共十二大理论考试，参考391人，及格率达95%。

1983年1—8月，全县开展新党章轮训。

1986—1987年，举办以《马克思主义哲学纲要》为主要内容的哲学理论培训班6期，每期10天，培训500余人次。举行哲学考试，参试党员、干部、职工1300余人，合格率95%。

1988年，在全县党政机关和党员、干部中开展学习贯彻中共十三大精神和党的基本路线教育活动。3月，举办县、区、乡干部培训班2期，培训干部317人，主要学习社会主义初级阶段如何发展生产力、如何发展商品生产的理论。4月，举办全县干部群众学习中共十三大文件知识竞赛活动，县、区组织参赛队17个共70名队员参加竞赛。5月，区、社党委举办农村党员干部学习中共十三大文件轮训班，受训2353人，受训率93%。6月，开办全县领导干部学习社会主义商品经济理论培训班，每期培训时间1周，共培训182人（其中副县级以上领导干部11人，科局级干部68人，企业厂长、经理以上干部103人），参试干部171人，及格率100%。是月，组织县机关干部参加全省商品经济理论统一考试，参试干部319人，参试率81.7%，及格率98.4%。

1989年，在县委党校开办4期科（局）长干部学习班和党支部书记学习班，每期脱产学习1周，共培训337人，经考试，全部合格。年底，组织干部职工参加全省干部职工基本路线教育开卷考试，参加考试518人，及格率95.6%。

1990年，开展以中共十三届五中全会《关于加强党同人民群众联系的决定》为主要内容理论学习，重点学习毛泽东《改造我们的学习》《关于领导方法的若干问题》，邓小平《在中国共产党全国代表大会上的讲话》《论坚持四项基本原则，反对资产阶级自由化》等文章，举办县机关股长以上干部（含离退休干部）培训班4期，每期1周，共培训236人。

1991年1月，县委印发《关于学习党的十三届七中全会精神的安排意见》。2月，召开全县思想政治工作理论研讨会，县直机关党支部书记、各系统工会主席、团委书记50人参加会议，收到思想政治工作论文10篇，评出优秀论文3篇予以奖励；成立思想政治工作理论研究会。7月，印发《关于认真学习江泽民总书记在庆祝中国共产党成立70周年大会上的讲话的通知》，以党的建设理论为主要学习内容，组织全县党员干部学习党建理论知识。

1992年，重点学习中共十四大文件精神和邓小平在武昌、深圳、珠海、上海等地视察时的重要谈话（简称“南巡谈话”）。举办中共十四大精神培训班3期，培训党员干部职工400余人；各乡（镇）分别举办中共十四大文件学习培训班，参加培训3662人，其中党员和入党积极分子2253人。是年，组织全县党员干部职工参加全省学习中共党史理论统一考试，参考单位83个，参考人数599人，及格率98.2%，为考试及格的干部职工颁发由州委讲师团验印的合格证。

1993年5月，举办新任二级班子领导干部理论培训班2期，每期1周，共培训168人，培训内容为坚持党的基本路线一百年不动摇、解放和发展生产力、建立和完善市场经济体制、县域经济发展问题等，县委书记、副书记、县长、县纪委书记分别授课。

1994年，干部理论学习以《邓小平文选》第三卷为主要内容，县委中心学习组以自学为主，每月集中学习2次；举办全县二级班子领导干部读书班4期，每期5天，参加读书班学习共110人；各乡（镇）党委按照《关于全县举办农村党员、干部学习〈邓小平文选〉第三卷培训班的安排意见》，利用乡（镇）业余党校举办学习班，17个乡（镇）共培训农村党员、村组干部、入党积极分子2580人，占应参训人数的82.2%；机关、部门、厂矿、居委会等单位组织职工群众学习原文后加以讨论，写心得体会和学习总结。

1995年3月，县委决定在全县开展学习邓小平理论、学习党章的“双学”活动。县委中心学习组以《中共中央关于加强党的建设几个问题的决定》为重点，集中学习48人次；县直机关党员干部集中学习810人次；举办理论教育“双学”轮训班5期，对全县行政村的村支部书记和村主任进行轮训，应培训人数336人，实训人数328人，参训率97.62%。

1996年5月，开展学习《爱国主义学习纲要》及迎接香港回归祖国知识教育。6月，组织干部职工参加全省“以史为鉴，莫忘国耻，热爱祖国，振兴中华”为主题的读书教育活动，全县提交答卷540人，经省、州组委会对试卷评定，获奖8人，受省、州组委会表彰。7月，举办纪念中国共产党成立75周年“双学”知识抢答赛，评出一、二、三等奖6名，优秀奖6名，组织奖2名。《邓小平文选》第三卷学习活动持续到1998年。

2000年，根据中共中央关于开展“三讲”教育活动的要求，采取集中学习、专题讲座、调研报告会、民主生活会、写心得体会等方式，在县直机关、企事业单位、乡（镇）开展“三讲”教育活动。

2001年，开展党员、干部职工学习“三个代表”（中国共产党始终代表中国先进生产力的发展要求，代表中国先进文化的发展方向，代表中国最广大人民的根本利益）重要思想理论学习活动。

2002年11月以后，重点学习中共十六大精神。2003—2004年，与组织部、党校、机关党委联合举办县、乡（镇）副科级以上领导干部培训班共4期，结束后在各级机关、单位、企事业、学校和村党支部的干部群众中开展中共十六大精神的宣讲，要求干部职工写心得体会，举办学习贯彻中共十六大精神经验交流会或宣讲会、报告会，把学习、宣传、贯彻中共十六大精神引向深入。在农村，宣传部发放《农民教育读本》《“三个代表”重要思想惠及百姓千村万户》等宣传书刊1000余册，引导农民劳动致富、科技兴农。

2005年，在全县各级党组织全面开展以学习、宣传、贯彻、践行科学发展观为主的保持共产党员先进性教育活动，重点学习总书记胡锦涛视察贵州的重要讲话。

2006年，在继续开展宣传、学习科学发展观和保持共产党员先进性教育活动的同时，宣传学习《中国共产党权利保障条例》。是年，县委宣传部开展庆祝中共建党85周年和庆祝长征胜利70周年“弘扬长征精神，建设美好荔波”主题宣讲活动。

2007年，县委印发《中共荔波县委关于学习宣传贯彻党的十七大精神的通知》，在全县开展学习中共十七大精神活动。是年，围绕贯彻落实科学发展观，以“继续解放思想，坚持改革开放，促进社会和谐，开创社会主义现代化建设的新局面”为主题，组织开展“理论进基层”活动，组建6个宣讲工作组，到各乡（镇）宣讲20场（次）。举办干部学习培训班15期，参加学习3000人次。

2008年，举办学习中共十七大精神报告会2次，邀请省、州讲师团和专家组到荔波宣讲。开展“十七大精神进企业、进农村、进社区、进学校、进军营”活动，培训理论骨干24人，举办宣传讲座23次、形势报告会2次，听讲人数总计达2万人次。

第二节　政策宣传与对外宣传

一、政策宣传

1978年12月，中共十一届三中全会召开以后，广泛宣传新时期的基本路线、基本方针、总任务及四项基本原则，着重宣传《中共中央关于加快农业发展若干问题的决定》。1979年，重点宣传中共中央关于经济体制改革的决定、邓小平关于社会主义初级阶段理论和党的基本路线。1980年，开展“以经济建设为中心”的宣传活动。

1981年，开展中共十一届六中全会精神宣传活动，重点宣传六中全会《关于建国以来党的若干历史问题的决议》。1982年，重点宣传农村土地承包制“两不变”（生产资料公有制不变和农业生产责任制长期不变）、“三兼顾”（做到国家、集体和个人利益兼顾）的政策。1983年，宣传党中央《关于当前农村经济政策的若干问题》的精神，教育农民群众树立劳动致富的思想。1984—1988年，主要宣传经济体制改革各项政策。

1989年，县委发出通知，要求必须旗帜鲜明地反对动乱，必须与党中央保持高度一致，坚决反对资产阶级自由化。

1990—1992年，全县开展中共十三届五中全会《关于加强党同人民群众联系的决定》宣传活动及农村时势政策宣传。宣传贯彻《中共中央关于进一步加强农业和农村工作的决定》，在县、乡（镇）机关中抽调297人组成农村社教工作队，深入168个行政村进行农村政策、党的基本路线、劳动致富、加强基层组织建设等宣传，农民受教育面达到85%。

1993年，着重宣传邓小平“坚持党的基本路线一百年不动摇”的重要论述。

1994—2001年，开展“八七”扶贫攻坚计划、煤炭产业和非耕地资源开发、黔南州“南下通道经济”战略、发展非公有制经济以及发展旅游产业等方面的政策宣传。

2005年10月28至11月1日，百位名家百家媒体走进荔波，图为大型采风活动恳谈会现场

2002年，宣传“四引”工程（引导农民脱贫致富奔小康，引导农民学习科技知识，引导农民开展文化体育活动，引导农民美化家园），在各乡（镇）建立“四引”工程示范村18个。

2005年，重点宣传中共中央总书记胡锦涛视察贵州时的重要讲话，紧扣全县经济社会发展形势展开讨论。

2007年，根据县委《关于学习宣传贯彻党的十七大精神的通知》，宣传部向全县各级党组织发出《关于学习宣传贯彻党的十七大精神工作安排意见》，县委讲师团分赴17个乡（镇）宣讲共20余场（次）。

2008年，邀请省、州讲师团、专家组到荔波举办“学习十七大精神报告会”，与组织部等部门举办“十七大精神进企业、进农村、进社区、进学校、进军营”宣讲活动，通过宣传讲座、形势报告会等形式，深入宣传中共十七大精神。

二、对外宣传

1978—1986年，对外宣传工作围绕县委、县政府中心工作进行。1987年，围绕关于“依靠省州、面向两广、开发山区、兴县富民”的战略决策，以宣传煤炭支柱产业为中心，向外宣传荔波。

1988—1989年，围绕小七孔风景区开发利用和自然保护区申报工作，通过国家和省内外各种报刊、广播、电视等媒体宣传荔波，扩大荔波的知名度。

1990年，围绕县内矿产资源、红色旅游资源、绿色旅游资源和少数民族文化资源开展对外宣传工作。

1991年，开展县城和乡（镇）整脏治乱以及创建国家卫生县城、国家文明县城活动，通过各种宣传媒体加强对外宣传，吸引国内外宣传媒体记者到荔波进行采风、采访报道。

1996年8月8日，黔南州举行建州40周年庆典，荔波在成就展活动中，重点推介茂兰喀斯特森林国家自然保护区、小七孔、大七孔和水春河景区、樟江田园风光带及荔波布依族、水族、苗族、瑶族等民族的民俗风情，同时展示荔波的工农业建设成就、自然资源、投资优惠政策等方面的情况，发放风景名胜区旅游折页和投资指南8000余份。12月，编辑出版《荔波画册》，发行5000册。

1997年5月，省委、省政府在贵阳举办贵阳机场通航庆典暨贵州省招商引资洽谈会，荔波县在省展览馆举办为期1个月的宣传展览，推介荔波旅游资源和民族土特产、争创国家卫生县城和文明县城等方面的成果。

2001年，对外宣传工作围绕县委、县政府“生态立县、旅游强县”的战略部署，申报世界自然遗产地为外宣工作的重中之重。11月8日，县委、县政府在荔波樟江园广场举办“庆祝荔波机场奠基典礼暨荔波自然风光演唱会”。庆典活动邀请蒋大为、毛阿敏、刘秉义等国家著名歌唱家到荔波演唱，中央、省、州电视台及广播电台进行现场直播。

2005年，成立县新闻中心，隶属宣传部，并将荔波网交由新闻中心管理。

是年，在《多彩贵州》栏目中，开展“荔波旅游形象大使选拔赛”“中国游——贵州‘美丽之星'电视大赛""中国绿宝石之旅少数民族服饰展选拔赛""徒步穿越茂兰喀斯特科考"等活动，由贵州电视剧制作中心拍摄的《邓恩铭》4集电视剧在中央电视台播放。

2006年，与中国国际广播电台合作，邀请美国、法国、韩国、泰国、印度、阿根廷等国家的20多家电视台、电台记者到荔波采访，分别用43种语言向这些国家的人民宣传荔波，提升荔波的国际知名度和美誉度。

2007年6月27日，"中国南方喀斯特"正式列入世界遗产名录，荔波成为贵州省第一个、中国第六个世界自然遗产地。7月，县委、县政府在北京举办"贵州·荔波申报世界自然遗产成功记者见面会"，推进荔波"世界自然遗产地"宣传。同时，在全县范围内广泛开展荔波申遗成功的大型宣传活动。

2008年，分别在上海、广州、深圳、重庆等地举办"喀斯特王国·多彩贵州"旅游推介会，宣传荔波旅游。在《黔南日报》刊载荔波专版，并在全国各大报刊宣传荔波，提高荔波知名度和美誉度。

第三节 新闻报道

1978—1989年，各区所在地建有广播放大站，播放荔波新闻节目。部分稿件被黔南人民广播电台、贵州人民广播电台采用、《黔南日报》《贵州日报》。

1990—1996年，中央、省、州的报刊、电台、电视台等新闻单位采用荔波稿件数量逐年增加。随着电视机的逐步普及，电视新闻逐步取代广播新闻。2002年停办广播新闻节目。

2005年，出台新闻奖励办法，提高通讯员积极性，对外宣传稿件量逐年增加。

2008年5月，荔波电视中心更名为荔波电视台。

1990—2008年全县在州级以上新闻单位用稿情况统计表

表4-5　　单位：篇

年度	州级新闻单位采用	省级新闻单位采用	国家级新闻单位采用	年度	州级新闻单位采用	省级新闻单位采用	国家级新闻单位采用
1990	110	30	1	2000	360	148	51
1991	215	85	2	2001	358	149	57
1992	270	80	2	2002	365	155	62
1993	94	110	5	2003	420	206	65
1994	410	80	18	2004	458	216	68
1995	112	70	18	2005	510	230	80
1996	184	84	22	2006	540	240	85
1997	283	108	30	2007	608	268	105
1998	300	121	40	2008	810	320	160
1999	351	130	42				

第四节　精神文明建设

一、组织精神文明创建活动

1982年，成立荔波县精神文明建设领导小组，下设办公室，隶属县委宣传部，1990年改称精神文明建设委员会。1988—1990年，在全县干部职工、群众和青少年中开展“讲文明、讲礼貌、讲卫生、讲秩序、讲道德”“心灵美、语言美、行为美、环境美”“热爱祖国、热爱社会主义、热爱中国共产党”的“五讲四美三热爱”活动，弘扬中华民族传统美德和民族精神。

1991年11月15日，县委要求县直各机关、企事业单位和乡镇，组织干部职工、中学教师、青年学生，学习《中国人权状况》（白皮书），正确认识中国人权的发展历史和现状，认清西方资产阶级人权观念的虚伪性和欺骗性，从而提高思想认识，坚定社会主义信念。

1992年4月6日，县委、县政府转发荔波县法制宣传教育领导小组提出的《荔波县1992年法制宣传教育工作的安排意见》。1992年，全县法制宣传教育工作的主要任务是：以宪法为核心，以专业为重点，突出抓好学习宪法、企业法、全国人大常委会《关于加强社会治安综合治理的决定》。普法学习以机关干部特别是乡、镇、科局以上领导干部、执法人员、宣传教育工作者和青少年为重点。坚持理论联系实际，学用结合，把普法同党和政府的中心工作相结合，同农村社会主义思想教育相结合，同社会治安综合治理相结合。

1993年12月25日，开展纪念毛泽东诞辰100周年活动。活动期间，县直各单位、各乡（镇）宣传毛泽东生平业绩，播放毛泽东早期革命题材影片，举办歌颂毛泽东的歌咏比赛等。

1994年3月18日，县委、县政府发出《关于表彰见义勇为青年莫秀强、少年蒙黔俊的通报》，授予莫秀强“见义勇为青年”、蒙黔俊“见义勇为少年”称号，并号召全县人民、广大青少年向他们学习。

自1995年起，组织开展文明村寨和“十星级”（爱国星、教育星、科技星、法制星、和睦星、婚育星、新风星、勤俭星、公德星、环卫星）文明户创建活动。同年9月5日，县委、县政府印发省委、省政府《关于开展向优秀教师田沛发同志学习的决定》，在全县范围内开展“远学孔繁森，近学田沛发”的学习活动。

1996年6月，开展精神文明建设工作调研活动，调研总课题为“荔波县精神文明建设工作现状及对策”，内容为思想道德和文化建设等8个分课题。同年，开展精神文明创建活动中，每两年进行一次检查评比，评出县级、州级文明单位、文明乡（镇）、文明示范窗口、精神文明先进工作者、文明公民等，由县委、县政府和州文明办予以命名表彰。至2008年，全县共评选出州级文明单位12个，州级文明乡（镇）7个，州级文明示范窗口3个。

1997年6月26日，县委、县政府作出向大土村学习的决定，号召全县各级各部门学习大土艰苦创业、敢于挑战、因地制宜、抓住机遇、大胆地向荒山荒水进军，打好贫困山区的扶贫攻坚的精神。是年11月30日，县委组织800多名团员青年开展以“服务社会，情系万家”为主题的“青少年讲文明、树新风”活动。

1998年11月，邀请老领导到各乡（镇）中小学进行热爱祖国、热爱家乡宣讲，介绍荔波历史和改革开放的变化，教育学生爱祖国、爱家乡。

1999年6月1日，县委、县政府作出《关于广泛深入持久地开展创建文明单位、文明行业和争做文明公民活动的决定》，要求以提高全县公民文明素质和城乡社会文明程度为目标，以群众拥护不拥护、高兴不高兴、满意不满意为基本标准，通过深入开展群众性“三文明”创建活动，使全县范围的优美环境、优良秩序、优质服务和优雅言行取得明显成效。6月3日，印发《荔波县开展创建文明单位、文明行业和争做文明公民活动具体实施方案》。6月4日上午，县委、县政府在县人民大会场召开动员大会，活动正式在全县展开。

2000年2月20日，县委作出《关于贯彻执行中央、省州委〈关于加强和改进思想政治工作的若干意见〉的意见》，要求进一步提高对加强和改进思想政治工作重要性的认识；思想政治工作要坚持正确的方针原则；全县开展思想政治教育工作要动真来实；积极探索新形势下思想政治工作的新规律和新方法；常抓不懈，稳定推进，把思想政治工作任务落实到基层；切实加强党的领导，建立健全思想政治工作机制。

2001年，开展学习、宣传、贯彻《公民道德实施纲要》，把依法治国和以德治国紧密结合起来，推行道德规范，提高公民道德素质，加速社会主义“四化”建设步伐。

是年，在各中小学普遍开展争做有理想、有道德、有纪律、有文化的“四有”新人活动，举办演讲比赛、歌咏比赛；各学校贯彻实施《中国小公民道德建设计划》，普遍开展“我做合格小公民”倡议活动（做父母的小帮手，做礼貌的小标兵，做小朋友和同学的小伙伴，做保护环境的小卫士，做主宰自己的小主人）；贯彻执行《中华人民共和国未成年人保护条例》。2003年，开展“四引”（引导农民勤劳致富奔小康，引导农民学习科技知识，引导农民开展文体活动，引导农民建设美化家园）工程文明新村创建活动，选定17个乡（镇）的18个村（组）实施“四引”工程。

2002年，县文明办牵头，向广西南丹县、环江县发起倡议，由3个县的宣传部、文明办牵头，在3个县毗邻的南丹县里湖乡、小场乡，环江县木伦乡、驯乐乡、都川乡，荔波县驾欧乡、瑶山乡、洞塘乡、佳荣镇等边界乡（镇）共同开展联创精神文明示范带活动。联创活动以构建边界和谐，繁荣边界贸易，有利于解决山林水事纠纷，开展边界文化体育交流和科技交流活动，帮助农民发展经济，共同脱贫致富为目的。3个县签订协议书，共同开展创建活动。2003年，荔波、环江两县共同确定荔波县佳荣镇、洞塘乡、立化镇，环江县驯乐苗族乡、川山镇为两地跨省联创精神文明工作示范带，每年开展两次以上联谊活动。

2004年，开展争做“三好”（好公民、好建设者、好家庭）道德实践活动。

2005—2006年，开展“八荣八耻”（以热爱祖国为荣，以危害祖国为耻；以服务人民为荣，以背离人民为耻；以崇尚科学为荣，以愚昧无知为耻；以辛勤劳动为荣，以好逸恶劳为耻；以团结互助为荣，以损人利己为耻；以诚实守信为荣，以见利忘义为耻；以遵纪守法为荣，以违法乱纪为耻；以艰苦奋斗为荣，以骄奢淫逸为耻）宣传教育，结合“公民道德宣传月”，开展“八荣八耻”进机关、进厂矿、进农村的文明宣传活动，举办“知荣辱、树新风、促和谐”读书演讲比赛活动。2005年，县委印发《关于创建全省文明县城的决定》，要求各单位坚持把人民群众参与、受益和满意作为创建工作的出发点和落脚点，不断提高公民的文明素质、思想道德素质、科学文化素质，把荔波建成环境优美、秩序安定、生活方便、文化活跃、团结互助、共建共享、居民称心的文明县城。2006年3月，县文明委印发《关于文明社区暂行管理办法》，县委、县政府作出《关于进一步加强“整脏治乱”城乡清洁工程建设工作的决定》，印发《荔波县贯彻〈贵州省城市市容和环境卫生管理条例〉实施办法》，县文明办制定印发《荔波县城镇市民守则》，在全县开展创建活动。同年7月，县委召开创建全国文明县城动员大会，机关单位开展“创文明机关，做人民满意的公务员”活动，窗口行业开展微笑服务、诚信服务，景区开展服务质量达标活动；政法军警、文明办开展“独荔公路平安大道”创建活动；宣传文化系统开展“实效年”主题创建活动，形成全民参与、集中整治的氛围，营造良好的政务环境、法治环境、市场环境、人文环境、生态环境和生活环境。2007年，省委、省政府授予荔波县“贵州省文明县城”称号。2008年，获中央文明委授予“全国文明城市”称号。

2007年，开展“整脏治乱”专项行动和“满意在荔波”主题活动。

自2008年起，用3年时间在全县实施公民道德建设工程——“满意在荔波”。制定实施《荔波县2008年度“整脏治乱”专项行动实施方案》《荔波县“整脏治乱”专项行动目标综合考核暂行办法》《公民道德建设工程——“满意在荔波”主题活动（2008—2010年）纲要》《公民道德建设工程——“满意在荔波及文明县城”创建活动实施方案》，对环境卫生、交通秩序、基础设施建设、窗口行业优质服务、作风建设等进行整治。

二、精神文明阵地建设

1986年，中共甲良区委、区公所组建电影队、广播电视站和文艺宣传队，在全县首开“以文养文”“以电（影）养文”的创业之路。经过几年实践，积累了部分资金，在全镇开展群众性文化体育和文明创建活动，利用秧歌队，老年文艺队、体育竞技队在村寨开展文明宣传。1988年，镇政府拨出资金4.5万元，征地修建文化站，至1991年9月，建成全县第一座独立办公文化站，被评为黔南州“一级文化站”，获“贵州省文化站达标单位”称号，1993年12月又获“贵州省农村精神文明建设先进单位”称号。1994年，该站申报建立精神文明活动中心，得到中央文明办支助资金12.5万元，重新建设电影电视大厅、体育场、图书馆、多功能厅、科普橱窗等，固定资产达70万元。该中心在各个节日期间分别开展布依族小年赛马、篮球比赛、拔河比赛、布依歌对唱、猜谜语、斗鸡比赛、“六月六”斗牛文化节等活动。

1995年，中央文明委实施“百县千乡宣传文化工程”建设，县文明办向州、省文明办申报茂兰镇精神文明活动中心建设项目，经审核批准，省、州、县三级财政配套资金共20.5万元，修建镇政府综合楼1幢，划拨一层楼给文明中心管理使用，1997年建成。

1996年12月，甲良镇获“贵州省首批文化先进镇”称号。

2001—2008年，陆续向州、省、中央文明办申报建设精神文明活动中心并投入使用，其中获中央文明办资金累计112.5万元，省财政配套累计资金57.25万元，州财政配套累计资金20.5万元，县财政配套累计资金89.25万元，乡财政配套累计资金20.5万元，共计投资300万元。全县精神文明阵地有县宣传文化活动中心、甲良镇精神文明活动中心、驾欧乡精神文明活动中心、佳荣乡精神文明活动中心、播尧乡精神文明活动中心、瑶山瑶族乡精神文明活动中心、捞村乡精神文明活动中心。

第五章　政法委及综治工作

第一节　协调监督工作

1982—1990年，县政法委建立重大案件报告制度，要求各政法机关凡重大案件立案、结案均报告政法委，对重大案件进行集体讨论和分析案情，跟踪督查督办案件。监督推行《岗位责任制》《目标管理责任制》《错案追究制》，建立公安、检察、法院、司法在诉讼活动中的协调机制，形成互相配合、互相制约的工作格局。

1991年，县政法委在组织抓“严打”战役的同时，指导协调公安、检察、法院、司法等部门抓好疑难案件查处工作，组织召开政法部门主要领导会议，研究排查刑事案件，列出3起重大拐卖人口案重点侦破。

1991—1997年，协调处理案件22件（次）。

2004年，评查政法机关办理的案件165件，从严监督执法机关执法办案活动，促进公正执法。

2002—2006年，受理涉法案件15件，妥善处理15件。

2008年，协调处理案件6起。在协调处理重点疑难案件和有争议案件中，采取召开政法委员办公会议，集体分析讨论，形成决议后交由政法机关职能部门办理的办法协调办案。

第二节　社会治安综合治理

1978年后，社会治安管理按照“预防为主，治安管理从严”的方针，预防各类治安案件发生。1987年后，贯彻新颁布的《治安管理处罚条例》，加大治安案件处罚力度。

1981年7月—1982年2月，开展严厉打击犯罪分子的斗争，进行3次集中行动，依法从重从快惩办一批杀人、放火、抢劫、强奸和其他严重破坏社会秩序的现行犯罪分子。

1983年8月，按照中共中央、省委从重、从快、从严的方针，打击各种刑事犯罪活动。

1985年1月16日，县委同意社会治安综合治理领导小组《关于开展全县社会治安综合治理工作的意见》，要求各级组织按照中共中央文件精神及中央政法委员会的部署，采取各种措施，进行社会治安综合治理。

1986年3月15日，县委批转县政法委《关于县普法和社会治安综合治理工作会议纪要》，并指出：做好普法工作是治理社会治安，实现党风和社会风气根本好转的重要保证。

1987年6月8日，为维护城乡社会治安，预防和减少犯罪，促进社会主义精神文明建设，县委通报一批参加赌博的党员、干部和职工名单，并按照党纪、政纪和《治安管理处罚条例》进行严肃处理。

1988年4月，成立打击拐卖妇女儿童犯罪活动办公室，办公室设在县政法委。8月31日，县委和县政府批转社会治安综合治理领导小组《关于社会治安综合治理工作的实施安排意见》，在农村实行治安综合治理承包责任制，各乡成立治安管理办公室，区（镇）建立治安巡逻队，乡村普遍推行《乡规民约》或其他形式的群众自治公约。

1991年5月，成立县社会治安综合治理委员会，全县4区1镇25个乡相应成立社会治安综合治理领导小组，开展综合治理工作。是年7月“建并撤”后，全县17个乡（镇）相继成立综治委和综治办，明确专（兼）职工作人员，建治安队9个34人，建护村队6个20人。是年，在全县落实治安承包责任制。

1992年3月31日，县委、县政府印发《荔波县社会治安综合治理5年规划》《荔波县社会治安综合治理达标活动实施方案》《荔波县社会治安综合治理达标活动考核细则》。

至1993年，全县有982个村民组27930户与村、组签订治安承包责任状，分别占全县应签组、户的82.73%、85.75%。是年，全县组建群防群治队伍747个3811人。其中，治安联防队24个174人，护村队123个1367人，护寨队549个2066人，护厂护矿队8个31人，护校队43个173人。此外，有守楼护院人员23人，组建义务消防队274个1036人。是年，对84户特种行业、78家娱乐场所进行清理整顿，签订治安合同书，亮证营业。重新登记暂住人口2871人。

1996年，县政法委与宣传、文化、工商部门先后组织开展禁赌、扫黄、查禁卖淫嫖娼等专项清理整顿活动11次，取缔、查封和拆除带有色情服务的包厢、赌博娱乐场所，捣毁卖淫窝点，清理登记房屋租赁和外流人员。

自1998年起，每年5月定为“综治宣传月”，县政法委在每年“综治宣传月”“6·26”禁毒日、“12·4”法制宣传日开展大型治安宣传活动，发放宣传资料，播放宣传光碟，进校园授课，提高全民治安防范意识和普及法律知识。

2001年2月28日，县委办、县政府办下文成立荔波县“打黑除恶”领导小组。4月18日，县委、县政府召开全县社会治安，整顿和规范市场经济秩序工作会议，贯彻落实全省社会治安，整顿和规范市场经济秩序工作会议精神，部署全县社会治安、整顿和规范市场经济秩序工作。

2002年，在全县推行跨县、跨乡（镇）、跨村三级治安联片联防机制，与三都、独山两县落实村级边界治安防范组织值班制度，县际边界接壤部分乡（镇）之间签订治安联防公约。玉屏镇以“农村连片联防、城镇分区治理”为目标，跨出县域，与三都县周覃、九阡两镇开展治安联防协作；水利、甲良、方村实施跨村、跨乡（镇）治安联防。是年，共建县级治安防范组织3个、乡（镇）治安防范组织16个、村级治安防范网络组织33个。同时，开展机关单位、楼群院落治安防范，制定平安工程总体目标、治安防范措施、门卫守护人员职责、安全文明公约，逐步建立单位、小区、院落治安值班室。在县城辖区划分民警责任区5个，矿区成立厂矿治安联防队7个，加强企业、厂矿单位的治安防范。政法综治机关每年与各乡（镇）签订综治责任状，各乡（镇）按照属地管理原则，与部门、村（居）、组签订责任状，年终兑现奖惩。签订综治责任状制度实施到2006年止。

2003年，全县各乡（镇）、村组建治安联防队45个336人，创建安全小区101个、安全文明单位54个、安全文明村寨189个。

2005年，启动黔、桂两省（区）边界治安联防协作机制，召开黔、桂两省（区）边界治安联防会议6次，黔、桂两省（区）、8县（市）、5乡（镇）边界治安暨文明共建协作会议5次，分别签订边界治安联防协作协议，共同维护边界治安秩序。

2008年8月15日，县委印发《关于加强和改进政法工作的意见》，将社会治安综合治理纳入县委、县政府对乡（镇）、部门的目标管理考核内容，实行一票否决制。

是年，建成乡（镇）综治工作中心17个、村（居）委会综治工作站94个，成立调解室80个。乡

（镇）建立治安联防队115个1200人；乡（镇）、村（居）委会建立治安巡逻队127个2350人；县城组建公安协勤专职队伍30人，常备民兵应急分队30人，专职保安队110人，协管治安员50人，城区治安维稳队220人，校园警务室47个配备专职保安人员65人。全年投入200万元在县城街道、星级宾馆安装视频监控摄像系统。在荔波电视台开办《平安荔波》《法制播报》等法制栏目，建立义务治安信息员队伍100余人。

第三节　维护社会稳定与平安创建

一、维护社会稳定

（一）矛盾纠纷排查与调处

1978年，每个生产大队有治保主任，专职抓治安保卫工作。1986—1990年，全县有治安保卫委员会181个（其中机关15个）1128人，有治安保卫小组915个1324人。

1992年，成立县维护社会稳定工作领导小组，下设维稳办，制定《荔波县矛盾纠纷排查化解工作机制》《荔波县矛盾纠纷排查化解责任查究制度》《荔波县维稳工作督查机制》《荔波县应急处突工作预案》等。

1994年，县内发生较大的群体性事件3起，经深入细致地做群众的思想工作，以及依法进行疏导劝阻，事态得到平息。此后，每年年初、年中、年末，县政法委召集维稳成员单位对各种不稳定因素和突出矛盾纠纷隐患进行排查，针对因企业改制、城镇开发扩建拆迁、征地补偿以及农村山林土地水事纠纷引发的较大矛盾纠纷或群体性事件进行预防。

1996年8月9日，县委办、政府办印发《荔波县社会治安综合治理第二个五年计划（1996—2000年）》和《荔波县社会治安综合治理“平安工程”实施方案》。

1999年5月4日，成立县维护稳定工作领导小组，成员由县直有关单位、人武部及玉屏镇负责人组成，在县委政法委设领导小组办公室。

2000年5月22日，县委转发《荔波县依法治县领导小组2000年工作安排意见》。

2001年2月23日，县委办、县政府办转发《荔波县“扫黄”“打非”领导小组关于2001年“扫黄”“打非”集中行动实施意见》。

2005年，妥善处理群众性事件5起，其中，涉及50人以下的3起，50人以上至200人以下的1起，200人以上的1起。2002—2006年，民间矛盾纠纷在乡（镇）、村两级及时得到调解处理，化解在萌芽状态。五年间调处民间纠纷2359件，调处成功2228件，其中妥善处理影响较大的矛盾纠纷18起。尤其对因征地、山林、水利、租包合同、工程移民、金融、集资以及劳资等纠纷，按照“可散不可聚，可顺不可激、可解不可结”“教育疏导，依法处理，防止激化”的原则，进行教育疏导和依法调解。

2008年8月，县委批准成立荔波县维护社会稳定工作促进会。

至年底，全县政法部门调处群体性事件271起，预防群体性事件苗头384起，调解各类纠纷13575件，依法处置冲击党政机关、堵塞交通、非法集会等违法违规事件121件。

（二）平安创建

1998年起，以创建“平安工程”为重点落实各项安全防范措施，印制规章制度和职责10余项，以玉屏镇综治办和石灰坳村作为基层综治办及村级治安室规范建设试点，以地税局、中国人民银行作为机关创建“安全文明小区”“安全文明单位”试点，随后在全县铺开。至11月底，全县建成治安室127个、安全小区37个、安全文明单位56个，人防、物防、技防措施落到实处，通过省综治检查组考核验收。此后，持续开展“平安工程”创建活动。

2006年，县委出台《荔波县平安建设实施意见》，启动“平安荔波”创建活动，以“平安村寨”“平安乡镇”“平安单位”“平安楼栋”“平安小区”“平安院落”“平安车站”“平安码头”“平安校园”等为目标开展创建工作。

至2008年，在平安创建宣传活动中，发放入户宣传资料25万份，书写永久性标语50幅，与农户签订平安创建各项承诺书13万份。以“八好八少”（治安防控网络好、刑事治安案件少，矛盾排调机制好、群访重访事件少，法制宣传教育好、少年违法犯罪少，齐抓共管落实好、涉黄赌毒现象少，移风易俗氛围好、邪教非法活动少，民主管理体制好、安全责任事故少，环境美化家居好、家庭邻里纠纷少，精神文明行为好、整脏治乱污染少）为主线，围绕“实现一个目标、打牢两个基础、突出三个重点、筑牢六条边界线”（实现平安荔波建设一个目标，夯实平安村寨、平安社区建设两个基础，抓住城区、矿区、景区三个重点治安防控区域，筑牢独山、三都、从江、榕江、南丹、环江6条边界线）为重点，开展平安创建工作。年末，全县命名平安家庭46897户，占全县总户数48689户的96.32%；命名平安村（居）96个，占全县98个村（居）的97.96%；创建平安乡（镇）17个，占100%。全县建安全小区39个、平安单位93家、平安村（居）98个、平安乡（镇）17个、和谐矿区7个、无毒村（居）81个、无邪教村（居）85个。

第六章 统战工作

第一节 落实政策

一、起义、投诚人员政策落实

1979年9月，县委成立落实对国民党起义、投诚人员政策办公室，接待来信来访，调查核实当事人历史情况，对照文件精神，落实政策。到1987年，全县共排查224人，来信要求落实起义投诚政策的22人，认定身份为起义、投诚人员12人。其中，属于国民党军官5人、士兵2人；属于地方武装游击部队4人；司法审判官1人。根据每人家庭经济来源和困难情况，每人每月补助10～100元不等，由州委统战部拨款到县委统战部，专款专用。经对照政策，不属于起义、投诚范围10人，均作出文字结论，函送解释。1993年，县委统战部又为宽释人员和起义、投诚人员4人追加生活费补助。

二、革命武装游击队认定

1979年，对部分来信来访反映荔波游击队的性质认定问题，引起县委重视，上报州委联合调查，州委向省委呈报《关于"荔波人民游击队"结论意见的报告》。省委组织批复同意州委《关于"荔波游击队"结论意见的报告》，并对"荔波游击队"进行定性："'荔波游击队'是在全国解放战争胜利形势的影响下，为反对国民党反动政权和土匪势力而自发成立的进步武装力量，独山、都匀解放后，是我党领导组成的一个革命武装组织。这支武装力量，对于解放荔波、配合我军剿灭土匪，维持社会治安，做出了积极的贡献。"批复文件要求原来对"荔波游击队"及其成员强加的一切诬蔑不实之词和造成的冤假错案，应一律予以平反纠正，恢复名誉。文件对平反后的安置作出规定："'荔波游击队'的成员，在接受党的领导后，服从分配并一直坚持革命斗争的，干部参加工作的时间（工人的工龄）从接受我党领导之日（周覃、九阡、方村从1949年11月20日，佳荣从1950年9月）算起，当时因各种原因未分配工作，以后又重新参加革命工作的，一律从重新参加革命工作之日算起。"

三、非中共知名人士政策落实

杨家骝，荔波县方村人，1904年出生。任国民党上校团长，1938年9月29日，在江西率部与侵华日军交战，血洒疆场，英勇为国捐躯。之后，国民党中央委员会追认杨家骝为抗日阵亡陆军少将。县委统战部与县民政局共同收集相关资料逐级向上申报，1992年10月2日，省政府追认杨家骝为革命烈士。

印尼华侨吴德福，广东揭阳人，1951年3月到荔波参加革命，曾任玉屏镇镇长及六区副区长、区长，于1954年被定为反革命入狱，刑期7年，出狱后1960年病故。1981年州中级法院为其平反。

1996年，县委统战部为吴德福举行迁葬仪式，从福泉迁到荔波安葬，在县城召开会议，平反昭雪，恢复政治名誉。

抗日战争时期，国民党空军飞行员全正熹，驾机与日本机群空中多次作战达3个月，摧毁日军机场、港口等多处阵地，最后血洒长空，壮烈牺牲。2006年，荔波县为纪念全正熹抗日功绩，在他家乡洞塘乡尧所村修葺烈士故居并立石碑，镌刻颂扬烈士的诗文。

第二节　统战宣传

1988年4月，为系统广泛宣传统战理论知识，统战部与广电局利用有线广播在全县开展统战知识讲座，包括理论基础及统战范围、对象、性质、任务、基本方针等。统战部还根据工作安排进行各项统战工作电视宣传和会议宣传培训。同时，注重加强对海外宣传工作，在每年召开的台属、侨属座谈会上和走访慰问台属、侨属活动中，面对面宣传中共中央对台方针、政策。

1992年6月12日，在召开的台属、侨属座谈会上，学习传达县委、县政府出台的《关于加快荔波县经济建设的有关规定》等文件。

1993年，编写对外宣传稿件7篇。其中，送州台办1篇，在县内广播站播出3篇，座谈会宣传讲稿3篇。鼓励台属、侨属加强与海外亲人联系，欢迎他们到荔波县参观考察，为荔波建设服务。

第三节　党外人士与非公经济人士工作

1982年4月之前，统战工作由县委宣传部兼管。

1982年4月，统战部恢复设立后，对被错划为右派和在“文化大革命”（1966—1976年）中被打成“牛鬼蛇神”、受到不公正处理的非党知识分子陆续给予平反。

1982—1987年，并向县委推荐安排落实副科级干部4人、副县级干部4人。其间，1985年为助理工程师以上党外知识分子建档立卡37人。

1988年7月，建立非党知识分子联络员制度。

1989年5月，为98名股级党外干部建档立卡，选出13人报请县委批准作为副科级党外后备干部。之后，每年进行党外后备干部人员调整并建档。

1991年7月，制定《关于培养选拔党外干部工作规划》措施。

1984—2008年，党外干部和非党知识分子中，被选为县人大代表18人、县政协委员210人。1988—2008年，先后向县委推荐批准安排副科级干部40人、正科级干部3人、副县级干部10人。2008年统计，全县有在职副县级党外干部4人，其中，副县长1人，人大副主任1人，政协副主席2人；有正、副科级党外干部33人。

第四节　台湾事务

1988年起，县政府每年拨出专项慰问经费，在中秋节和春节期间召开台属、侨属座谈会和上门走访慰问。传达学习中共对台方针政策，了解台属、侨属的生产生活情况，积极帮助解决他们的困难和问题。

1993年经县人民政府批准，同意在商业大街划地400平方米给回乡台胞尚顺发建房定居。

1996年，对首批赴台探亲的台属进行行程前教育，交代注意事项。办理台胞回乡定居1人。接待回乡探亲台胞90人次，接待台属（胞）来访50人次，处理涉台信件20件（次）。

1997年6月28日，召开县直涉台涉外部门工作会和台属、侨属座谈会，传达学习“和平统一、一国两制”“八项主张”、《中国公民往来台湾地区管理办法》、中共中央总书记胡锦涛在《告台湾同胞书》发表30周年时的讲话，以及对台经贸法规等文件。

2005年3月，组织台属学习《反分裂国家法》，利用赶集在县城设点宣传，印制宣传资料2000份，分发到各乡（镇）进行宣传。

2008年，全县有台属35户145人，有涉台婚姻6对，主要分布在玉屏镇、朝阳镇、洞塘乡、驾欧乡等，无定居台胞。全县有港澳同胞2人、海外侨胞10人。海外同胞在荔波的亲属共182人。

第七章　其他党务

第一节　离休退休干部工作

1978—1984年，离休干部由县委组织部管理。1985年，县委成立离退休干部工作机构，管理和服务新中国成立前参加革命工作的离休干部。

1990年后，县离退休干部局管理和服务对象为新中国成立前参加革命工作的离休干部和副县级以上退休干部（含享受副县级待遇退休干部），其余退休人员由所在单位管理和服务。

一、政治待遇

县委、县政府每年按规定组织离休干部学习中央、省、州有关文件，在一定范围内传阅中央、省、州发至县级的有关文件，县委、县政府主要领导定期向离休干部通报全县工作和经济、社会发展情况及国内外政治形势，使离休干部及时了解党的路线、方针、政策和国家大事。

县党代会、人代会等重大会议，均安排离休干部或离休干部代表参加，请老红军上主席台就座。县委、县政府举行重大活动，都请离休干部代表参加讨论。县委、县政府每年举行一次离休干部迎春座谈会或茶话会，全县所有离休干部、副县级以上退休干部均受邀参加。此外，各单位在各种重大节日召开该单位离退休干部座谈会，向离退休干部通报单位工作情况，听取他们的意见、建议和要求。每年为离退休干部订阅党刊，为他们的政治学习提供资料。

在离退休干部比较多的部门或单位，组建离退休干部党支部。至2008年，全县共建立4个离退休干部党支部。对没有单独建立离退休干部党支部的单位，要求离退休党员干部参加原支部党组织生活，使他们不脱离原支部的管理，并鼓励其在身体条件许可的情况下，参加相关公益活动，尽党员的义务。

每年“七一”、中秋节、国庆节、老年节、春节等重大节日，县领导都走访看望部分离退休干部，各单位召开离退休干部座谈会。县离退休干部工作部门对离退休干部进行经常性走访，及时了解离退休干部的身体、学习和生活状况，反映他们的意见和要求，合理解决他们的实际问题。

二、生活待遇

在历次离退休费调整中，县内各相关单位严格按照中央和省、州文件规定办理离退休干部增加离退休费及调薪工作，按时足额兑现。

1989年，县政府拨款3万元，新建县老年大学教室和办公室共80平方米、室外活动场地374平方米，作为离休干部学习和活动的场所。

20世纪90年代末，受企业改制的影响，部分企业濒临倒闭，出现特困企业，在这些企业出现拖欠离退休干部工资、医药费现象。为解决好拖欠离退休干部“两费”问题，1998年1月4日，县委以《中共荔波县委关于我县企业单位离休干部“两费”开支渠道问题的批复》，同意从1998年起全县各企业单位离退休干部的“两费”统一列入县财政预算，转各企业单位主管部门管理和发放。自此，全县所有离退休干部的工资、医药费报销和所有按文件规定应该发放的经费都得到保障。用县财政作为企业部门离退休干部“两费”经费的保障机制，走在全州乃至全省的前列，得到省、州肯定。

1978—1994年，离退休干部原在单位所住房屋，符合文件规定标准的予以保留，需要建新房的，按省、州文件规定发给建房补助费。1995年住房制度改革后，按改革后的文件规定执行，全县离退休干部住房均有保障。

1998年起，全县各单位包括企业单位的离退休干部遗孀生活补助费统一由县离退休干部工作部门办理发放。2004年，离退休干部遗孀每月生活补助费由原280元增加到400元，离退休干部的医药费实报实销，离退休干部遗孀的医药费按50%给予报销。

2004年，县委、县政府决定将原玉屏二小的教学园区划给县离退休干部工作局作为老年活动中心。

2005年5月，省离退休干部工作局下发《关于解决有特殊困难离休干部及离休干部遗孀有关生活待遇问题的通知》，7月，县委对全县“离休干部无工作遗孀给予医药费困难补助”的问题作出决定，同意按省的新规定发放，如遇白血病、尿毒症、癌症等重病的进行个案处理，以原发放的补助金额为基数补足50%予以报销。县医院设离退休干部专用病房，离退休干部就医优先。到2008年，县内离退休干部的生活待遇全部得到落实。

三、社会活动

1985年，部分离退休干部不怕劳累、不计报酬、发挥余热积极服务社会。是年，全县评出离退休干部先进个人6人，其中出席州离退休干部工作先进代表大会1人。

1986年，离退休干部积极参加整党和“巡视”工作，帮助单位清理档案、账目等。

1987年，部分离退休干部坚持开展调查研究、咨询等活动，积极解决民事纠纷。

1990年，县离退休干部在各行业中发挥作用24人。其中，原单位返聘6人，在各种老年组织中工作4人，从事种植和渔牧养殖业10人，参加服务和管理离退休干部工作2人，参加学会、协会组织并任职2人。有56人参加关心下一代协会工作，配合各有关单位对青少年开展革命传统教育6场，受教育人数3225人。

1991年“七一”，召开离退休干部“老有所为”先进工作者表彰会，表彰离休干部13名、退休干部10名。各乡（镇）单位的关心下一代协会组织离退休干部开展关心教育下一代活动。县机关离退休干部自发组织“夕阳红”协会，开展书法、绘画、工艺、农艺、文艺、体育活动和各种娱乐活动。

1992年，县政府拨专款为老年门球队赴广西参加两省（区）、10县（市）老年门球联赛。老年节期间，组织玉屏镇、甲良镇等5个中老年文艺队、花灯队、民歌队进行两场文艺晚会演出，参加演出的中老年人200多人次，观众达万人。是年，离退休干部根据自己的专长和爱好，受原单位返聘3人，撰写回忆录3人，在居委会工作8人，种植养殖业8人，在老年大学任职2人，参加各种学会、协会143人。

1994年老年节期间，组织离退休干部门球、钓鱼、斗鸟、棋类、书画等8项文体比赛，参加比赛活动的离退休干部100人次。

1995年，在纪念抗日战争胜利50周年之际，组织离退休干部16人组成宣讲队，分4个组，分别到玉屏、甲良、朝阳、茂兰4个片区及县城各中小学校进行爱国主义宣讲活动，听宣讲学生有5000

余人。

1996年，离退休干部10人组成城镇卫生监督队，对县城卫生情况进行监督；在庆祝老年节和《中华人民共和国老年人权益保障法》颁布实施活动中，离退休干部自编自演文艺节目，用布依族歌曲、水族歌曲庆祝老年节，宣传《中华人民共和国老年人权益保障法》。

1997年，成立由离退休干部、老教师、老劳模、在职干部等30人组成的爱国主义教育宣讲团，分4组到全县4个片区各中小学进行“庆回归”、纪念“七七”事变60周年和纪念“八一”建军70周年的爱国主义教育宣讲活动，听取宣讲报告的青少年学生近万人次。

1998年，离退休干部25人组成创省级卫生县城工作督查组，每天轮流执勤，对县城卫生进行督查。年内，组织县情报告团，请离退休干部分别到县民族中学、职业中学，玉屏、甲良、茂兰、朝阳等中小学开展爱祖国、爱家乡县情宣讲活动，听取宣讲师生5000人次。

1999年8月，县委宣传部组织相关部门共同举办“深入揭批法轮大法文艺晚会”，离退休干部100余人自编自演，以花灯、歌剧、小品、快板等节目揭批“法轮功”邪教组织反科学、反社会、反政府的真面目。11月，8名离退休干部组成老干部爱国主义宣讲团，分赴13所中学及5所中心小学开展爱国主义教育活动，受教育师生达万余人。

2004年，在关心下一代工作、老年教育工作中做出突出成绩的两名离退休干部获州委组织部、州老干局授予“先进离退休干部”称号。

2005年，建立由离退休干部组成的县经济开发促进会，到州内外10个县（市）参观考察后，就发展旅游业向县委、县政府建言献策。该会还引进元胡药材到驾欧、水利、永康3个乡种植。

2008年，离退休干部在甲良、播尧、方村、驾欧、朝阳、玉屏6个乡（镇）兴办韩国“朝天王”辣椒种植示范点；在玉屏镇尧排组建立甘蔗种植示范基地，送给该组群众化肥3吨，邀请技术员到该组田间地头给群众讲解甘蔗种植技术，赠给农户《甘蔗种植技术》33册，该组24户种植甘蔗107.8亩。

四、老年大学

1989年3月10日成立荔波县老年大学，学制2年。县老年大学以“老有所学，增长知识，老有所乐，丰富生活，老有所教，陶冶情操，老有所养，促进健康，老有所为，服务社会”为宗旨，根据老年人的特点安排课程，开设政治理论、老年卫生保健两门必修课，同时根据时事需求和老年人的特点、兴趣和爱好，先后开设荔波县情、家用电器、法律、书画、音乐、舞蹈、庭院经济、旅游知识、花卉栽培、盆景栽培、剪纸等课程。教学工作坚持寓教于乐、少而精的原则，多学科、多层次、知识性、趣味性、实用性相结合，并采取多形式、多渠道的教学方式开辟第二课堂，充实教学内容。

在“三八”妇女节、“五一”劳动节、重阳节、中秋节、教师节等节日期间，组织文艺演出，先后与独山、龙里、罗甸、三都、州直机关、省军区老年大学以及广西环江、南丹县老年大学联欢，组队参加省、州、县的各项比赛活动。通过书画展、文艺演出、组织宣传小组等形式，组织学员参与社会活动，学员深入社区、学校开展创建卫生县城、申遗宣传。学员们自编自演舞蹈、小品、山歌等节目宣传荔波，如自编舞蹈《土布利吉》曾在省、州老年大学会演中获银奖和金奖。

至1999年县老年大学成立10周年时，招收学员总计6届、9个班257人（离休干部63人、退休干部职工194人），毕业250人。

2004年8月，成立玉屏镇老年大学。10月，成立茂兰镇老年大学。

2007年5月，县老年大学升格为正科级事业单位，编制增加为4人。

2008年8月，成立玉屏镇板吉老年大学。至年末，有县办老年大学1所，在校学员160人；有乡

（镇）办老年大学3所，村办老年学校1所，每所学校每年有学员60人左右。县、镇、村老年大学（学校）已毕业学员1070人。

1989—2008年县老年大学招收学员情况统计表

表4-6

时 间	班数（个）	学员人数（人）	毕业人数（人）	学员届次	备 注
1989.3—1990.12	1	48	38	一	
1991.3—1992.12	1	51	44	二	
1993.9—1995.7	1	52	44	三	
1995.8—1997.7	1	51	50	四	
1997.9—1999.6	2	88	44	五	
1999.10	3	105	—	六	综合班、书法班、综合班
2001.8—2003.6	3	108	46	七	综合班、书法班、综合班
2003.8—2005.6	3	166	109	八	综合班2个、健身班1个
2005.8—2007.9	3	—	—	九	文艺班、书画班、综合班

五、经济开发研究促进会

2003年10月，县委、县政府发出《关于成立荔波县经济开发研究促进会筹备工作领导小组的通知》，成立县经济开发研究促进会（以下简称县经促会）筹备组，在县老干局设办公室，筹备工作正式启动。12月19日，县经促会召开成立大会并挂牌，州经促会会长罗平义出席会议并作讲话。会议聘请县经促会名誉会长5名，会议民主选举会长1名、常务副会长1名、副会长9名、常务理事19名，选举秘书长1名、副秘书长4名。大会选举县经促会理事38名，其中农业科技组9名、工业经济组9名、财贸金融组7名、民营经济组6名、招商旅游经济组7名。县经促会由县老干局主管。设农村经济组、工业经济组、财贸金融组、民营经济组、招商引资组等办事机构5个。

2004年，县经促会共召开全体会议4次、常务理事会议12次、专题会议3次，开展调研7次。先后向县委、县政府写出《茂兰镇乡镇企业发展基地规划与发展》《煤炭收费明白卡的制定》《板蓝根、早桃、蔬菜发展种植》《兴建糖酒批发市场》《开拓樟江风景名胜区旅游市场》《樟江天然食品厂发展》《招商引资政策实行情况》7个专题调研报告。

2005年，共召开全体会议4次、常务理事会议10次、专题会议4次，开展调研8次。撰写《瓮安县新技术炼焦考察报告》《关于加快兴建拉刚电站的建议》《关于茂兰四个冶炼厂反映问题的报告》《关于县商业局糖酒公司批发市场建设和困难企业职工建房的建议》《赴都匀市就硅矿冶炼生产考察的报告》《赴荔波樟江天然食品有限责任公司调研的报告》《关于我县水书抢救和“申遗”工作的调查报告》《关于阳风司玉明养牛场调研报告》8个专题报告和建议。

2006年，共召开全体会议4次、常务理事会议9次、专题会议5次，开展调研5次。撰写《关于加强县城养犬管理的调研报告》《关于“荔波不夜城”项目尽快落实兴建的建议》《关于对粮食等四个部门（粮食部门、物资总公司、商业总公司、供销社）开展调研的报告》《关于我县种桑养蚕工作亟待解决的几个问题的建议》《关于荔波县民中消防绿化引水工程的调研报告》5个专题调研报告。

2007年，召开全体会议4次、常务理事会议8次、专题会议3次，开展调研8次。县经促会工业经济和民营组7名理事，分2个组对立化、茂兰、佳荣、瑶麓、水尧、洞塘、播尧7个乡（镇）煤炭生产销售环境情况进行调研，并撰写《煤炭生产销售环境情况的调研报告》，提出6点工作建议，得到县委、县政府的重视，并采取措施改善煤炭生产销售环境。

2008年，召开全体会议4次、常务理事会议6次，开展16次调研。撰写《关于荔波县世界自然遗产有关问题的调研报告》《关于对部分乡镇糖蔗种植情况的调研报告》《关于水泥厂、九曲湾糖厂、茂兰冶炼厂的考察调研报告》《关于播尧—驾欧断头公路修复问题的调研报告》4个专题调研报告。

至2008年，县经促会开展调研、考察活动46次，写出调研报告31个。此外，县经促会促成州内县（市）经促会在荔波召开联席会暨旅游专题研讨会；引进贵州恒丰公司捐赠价值2万余元的衣物、鞋子支援贫困瑶山中学学生；联系农工党贵州省委为水利卫生院捐赠价值0.8万元药品；联系省慈善总会支持永康尧古布依学生覃某免医疗费2万元；帮助驾欧新街村开展板蓝根种植促进农民增收；引进浙江客商投资20万元开展中药元胡种植试验；在甲良镇开展韩国“朝天王”辣椒试验种植；帮助茂兰冶炼厂解决生产用电困难问题；为水利乡母达组协调资金、水泥硬化村寨道路878米。

六、维护社会稳定工作研究促进会

2008年6月，成立县维护社会稳定工作研究促进会，县四家班子领导王振金（县委书记）、陆兴华（县人大主任）、陈稠彪（县委副书记、县长）、董豫黔（县政协主席）、王云生（县委副书记、县纪委书记）、陆德高（县委常委、县政法委书记）、高晓昀（县委常委、县委组织部部长）、李德余（县政协原主席）、柏文熙（县委原顾问）、吴洪铭（县人大原主任）等任名誉会长，县政协原主席黄玉成任会长，县委原书记饶昭德任常务副会长，有理事55人、常务理事23人，与县经济促进会合署办公。县维护社会稳定工作研究促进会成立后，开展化解重大矛盾纠纷，撰写维稳工作调研报告等工作，国家信访局在2008年8月的情况交流上撰文向全国介绍荔波的经验。

第二节　县直属机关党组织建设

一、机关党员代表大会

1987年10月15—17日，召开中共荔波县直属机关第一次党员代表大会，选举中共荔波县直属机关第一届委员会委员5名。

1991年10月24—25日，召开中共荔波县直属机关第二次代表大会。应到代表117人，实到代表105人，代表县直机关710名党员。会议听取和审议中共荔波县直属机关第一届委员会工作报告；选举中共荔波县直属机关第二届委员会委员9人；选举县直属机关纪委委员4人；选举出席县第七次党代会代表84人。

1996年10月21日，召开机关党员代表大会。会上，县直机关党委书记作此届机关党委工作情况报告；选举出席县第八次代表大会代表45名。

2001年5月21日，召开县直机关党员代表大会，参加会议代表128人，选举出席县第九次代表大会代表41人。

2002年1月19日，召开机关党员代表大会，选举出席第十六次全国党代会代表候选人5人，省党代会代表候选人10人，州党代会代表9人。

2006年10月18日，召开机关党员代表大会，应到会代表149人，实到会代表145人。会上，县直属机关党委书记向大会作县直属机关党委五年主要工作情况报告；选举出席县第十次代表大会代表43名。

二、基层组织建设

1978年，县直机关有党总支3个、支部52个，有党员102名。

1979—1980年，在党员中开展马列主义、毛泽东思想和“四项基本原则”的学习活动。

1981年，与县委宣传部、组织部联合组织学习党的十一届三中全会精神并进行考试，参加考试的党员人数370人。

1982—1983年，举办党员干部培训班5期，316人参加学习。

1984年，举办县直机关中青年知识分子学习班1期，85人参加学习。党委委员下基层上党课13次，参加听课人数111人。

1987年，举办党务骨干培训班1期，支部书记、副书记37人参加培训。与县委宣传部共同举办科局长培训班，学习《坚持四项基本原则，反对资产阶级自由化》和邓小平《建设有中国特色的社会主义》等，113人参加学习。

1988年，在商业系统党总支开展民主评议党员试点。取得经验后，1989年在县直机关全面开展民主评议党员活动，参加评议党员668人，评为优秀的61人、合格的597人、基本合格的6人、不合格的4人。

1988—1989年，以学习测验、知识竞赛等方式开展中共十三大精神学习活动。

1989—1990年，查处违纪党员4人，其中受党内警告2人、严重警告1人、开除党籍1人。

1991年1月中旬—2月初，在县直机关各总支、支部开展先进支部和优秀党员评选活动，共评出先进支部19个、优秀党员55个，并召开有500名党员参加的表彰大会。是年，新建农委、计委、经委党总支3个，恢复卫生党总支。举办发展党员对象培训班（入党积极分子）2期，65人参加；举办入党积极分子培训班1期，44人参加培训。“七一”期间，举办纪念中国共产党71周年百题知识竞赛，组织在职党员干部开展学习党史、党章、党风、党纪等知识，发出试卷650份，收回试卷411份，对成绩优异的48人颁发奖状和奖品。

1993年，与县委组织部、团县委共同下发《关于认真做好推荐优秀共青团员作为党员发展对象的意见》。举办党务干部培训班，168名党务干部参加培训。举办第七期发展党员对象培训班，50名积极分子参加培训。“七一”前夕，为纪念毛泽东诞辰100周年和中国共产党成立72周年，组织开展重温入党誓词活动，767名党员参加。

1994年，开展民主评议党员活动和“创先争优”活动，于“七一”期间表彰先进党支部12个、优秀党务工作者15名、优秀党员24名。

1995年，在县直机关开展“向领导干部的楷模——孔繁森学习”活动。对党支部书记进行岗位培训2次，参加人数126人次。

1996年5月，对县直机关党支部“三会一课”“四薄一册”进行大检查，合格率为72.3%。是年，开展民主评议活动，参加民主评议的党员905人，评为优秀的78人、合格的825人、不合格的2人。

1997年4月17日—5月9日，各总支、支部开展《中国共产党发展党员工作细则（试行）》贯彻执行情况检查，并将检查情况报告机关党委。年内，按期改选支部13个、新建支部3个、恢复支部1个。

1995—1997年，每年“七一”期间，组织开展“学理论、学党章”知识竞赛。

1998年，组织开展学习党的十五大知识竞赛。

1999年，与县委组织部联合举办有95名党员参加的农村农业经济村干班。

2000年，民主评议党员968人，评为优秀的85人、合格的883人。

2001年，与县委组织部、宣传部联合举办纪念中国共产党成立80周年知识大赛，县直机关有37个党支部组队参加。向县委推荐表彰先进党支部6个、优秀党务工作者6人、优秀党员7人。

2003年，组织开展了民主评议党员活动，推荐优秀党员12人受到县委表彰。

2001—2003年，在县直机关党组织中开展“三个代表”重要思想学习教育和贯彻中共十六大精神活动。

2004—2006年“七一”期间，先后有县农业局支部、国税局支部、县民中支部、地税局支部等先进支部及优秀党员蒙应团、覃秋云、吴冬梅、李映江、夏配明、覃正巧等受州委表彰。

2006年，在县直机关单位党组织中全面开展保持共产党员先进性教育活动。

2007—2008年，以学习贯彻中共十七大精神及新《党章》《中国共产党基层组织工作条例》《中国共产党纪律处分条例》《中国共产党党内监督条例》《中共中央关于加强党的执政能力建设的决定》等为重点，加强党员理想信念、政治纪律、组织纪律教育。

2008年，开展县直机关党的基层组织建设年活动，印发《县直机关基层党建工作标准和县级示范单位创建方案》，重点开展县乡企（煤炭）局、县林业局、县医院3个不同行业党支部的示范支部创建工作。同时，按照“五好党支部”标准，对机关软弱涣散基层党组织进行整顿，创建“四型机关”“三优一满意”部门，在州委党建活动督查组的历次检查中均受到好评，满意率达95%以上。是年，在全州“创先争优”活动中，县国税局党总支、县人口计划生育局党支部获州委党建办命名“五好”党总支、党支部称号。“七一”期间，受县委表彰的县直机关基层党组织8个、优秀党务工作者2人、优秀党员12人，受州委表彰先进支部1个、优秀党员1名、优秀党务工作者1名。年内，民主评议党员1242人，评为优秀71人、合格1170人、不合格1人；对县直机关各支部党建工作开展情况进行目标管理量化考核。

从1991年开始举办入党积极分子培训班后，每年培训入党积极分子不间断，至2008年共举办18期。

1980—2008年县直属机关党组织统计表

表4－7

年度	基层党组织（个）		党员人数（人）			
	总支	支部	总计	正式党员	预备党员	发展党员
1980	3	52	422	398	24	—
1981	4	53	431	415	16	22
1982	4	52	445	431	14	10
1983	4	56	442	428	14	8
1984	4	61	539	462	77	75
1985	6	63	595	526	69	53
1986	5	64	608	578	30	25
1987	4	68	633	605	28	30
1988	4	70	647	621	26	14
1989	3	71	679	669	10	7
1990	3	75	694	679	15	12
1991	7	78	710	686	24	22

续表4－7

年度	基层党组织（个）		党员人数（人）			
	总支	支部	总计	正式党员	预备党员	发展党员
1992	7	81	769	717	52	15
1993	7	84	767	715	52	51
1994	7	81	867	824	43	49
1995	7	86	867	824	43	36
1996	8	88	943	891	52	42
1997	8	92	1018	949	69	35
1998	8	95	1027	958	69	61
1999	9	96	1054	1014	40	47
2000	9	95	1101	1065	36	34
2001	9	95	1126	1084	42	39
2002	9	91	1154	1109	45	34
2003	10	103	1246	1213	33	25
2004	9	102	1256	1225	31	17
2005	9	96	1291	1265	26	23
2006	8	101	1346	1321	25	16
2007	8	99	1353	1338	15	10
2008	7	91	1397	1356	41	27

第三节　党校教育　党史研究

一、党校教育

（一）干部培训

1978年后，县委党校每年举办乡、村级领导干部培训班2期、机关干部培训班1～2期，每期培训人数140～160人，培训时间为一个星期，学习内容根据参训对象确定，机关干部培训以学习马克思主义、毛泽东思想、邓小平理论为主，乡村干部培训以中央、省、州、县的文件精神和中央、省关于发展农业、农村经济政策为主，学习结业时每个参训学员写心得体会。

1981年，全县新任公社干部在县委党校脱产学习1年，年底结业返回原岗位工作。1981—1983年未安排机关干部及乡村干部到县委党校学习。1984—1994年，每年按计划开展干部培训。

1995—1999年，每年举办培训班4期，每期40余人。另有系统、部门委托举办短期专业培训班。从2000年起，县委组织部不再安排干部到县委党校学习，另行安排培训地点，党校教师参与授课，县委党校此后不再承担干部培训任务。

（二）学历教育

从1984年开始，县委党校与贵州省广播电视大学挂钩，联合在县内招生开办中央电大荔波党政专业大专班，每年考试录取学员24人（含三都4人）到县委党校进行为期3年的脱产学习，毕业后回原单位。

1992年，县委党校挂靠州委党校，举办黔南州委党校荔波党政中专班，招新生48人，脱产学习2年，学习期间由老师分别带队到各区、乡开展社会调查，学员于1994年毕业后回原单位。

（三）函授教育

从1994年9月起，县委党校与省、州党校联合招生办学。是年，经过考试录取学员68人为省委党校经济管理专业荔波函授大专班学员，学期3年。

1997年9月，招收行政管理大专班，录取学员20人。

1998—2000年，每年报考党校的考生有300余人，1998年、1999年，每年录取250人，学习法律、经济管理等专业。从1999年9月开始，开办法律函授班本科班，每年招1～2个班。1994—2008年，在党校取得函授毕业文凭的学员近2000人。2008年，省委党校宣布停止招生后，县委党校停办函授教育。

（四）理论宣讲

中共十一届三中全会召开后，县委党校抽调老师配合县委宣传部等单位，组成宣讲组到各单位、公社宣讲十一届三中全会精神。1982年，参加县委组建的社会主义思想教育工作队下乡宣传社会主义思想。1986年，在机关单位宣讲哲学、社会主义经济学。1992年，老师参加社会主义思想教育工作队下乡驻村，开展为期3个月的社会主义思想教育活动。2001年，校领导、教师全部参加县委“三个代表”重要思想教育活动宣讲组、督查组，到各机关、乡（镇）进行为期1年的“三个代表”重要思想宣讲。之后，参加全县“保持共产党员先进性”教育活动宣讲。

二、党史研究

（一）党史资料征集

1985—1990年，重点做好中共一大代表邓恩铭烈士资料的收集。多次赴山东济南、青岛等地展开调查，收集到大量有关邓恩铭革命活动的文物史料，为1990年7月1日邓恩铭烈士故居革命事迹陈列室开馆布展提供了文物史料。1997年、2001年、2002年，先后赴北京、山东、武汉等地开展邓恩铭相关史料补充征集，为2003年扩建的邓恩铭故居提供馆藏文物史料。

2003—2004年，开展对红七军一纵队、二纵队在荔波进行革命活动的历史调查，并收集整理文物史料，为2004年7月建成开馆的红七军板寨会师旧址纪念馆提供了文物、图片、史料。

2005年，根据国防大学苏士甲教授提供有关荔波县南街人蒙九龄参加革命的线索，为核实、征集这一史料，2006—2008年，组织人员先后赴中央党史研究室，湖南、广东、江西等地展开调查，获取有关蒙九龄投身革命的大量史料。确认蒙九龄1922年参加途经荔波的滇军前往广州讨伐革命叛军，后考入黄埔军校第三期。1926年5月，黄埔军校毕业后参加北伐战争、八一南昌起义和湘南起义。此外，还收集了黄埔军校荔波籍学员全正熹、杨家骝、梁孟、姚戡、覃德操、黄觉民等相关记载的资料和信息。

2006年12月5日经县委同意后，县委办印发《荔波县2006—2010年党史工作规划》。县史志办公室围绕工作规划，于2007—2008年，根据老红军、将军肖锋编著的《长征日记》（上海人民出版社出版，2006年4月第1版）中有关“中央红一师一、二、三团于1935年4月15日至19日，先后长征途经黔南的平塘通州城，周覃、九阡和荔波场、朝阳、拉欧”的记载，史志办开展中央红军过荔波课题调研，经过走访调查证实，红一方面军红一师1935年4月18日在荔波场宿营，此间，红军通过宣传，有17名青年参加红军。

（二）党史书籍编研

1987年10月，县委党史资料征集委员会编辑出版17万字的《荔波的解放（内部资料书）》，详细介绍荔波两次解放的经过，摘录曾经参加荔波解放的解放军将士、游击队领导人的回忆录等；1990年6月，收集整理出版8万字的《邓恩铭遗作选》和7万字的《邓恩铭》（贵州人民出版社），《邓恩铭遗作选》收录了邓恩铭烈士的家书、工作函件、文章、漫画等42篇。《邓恩铭》一书介绍了邓恩铭小时候在荔波家乡生活、学习的经历、故事，然后远赴山东求学，走上革命道路的英烈事迹。两书出版后，成为研究邓恩铭烈士的重要文献。1992年2月，编辑出版10万字的《红七军在荔波》（贵州民族出版社），记载红七军一纵队、二纵队游击黔桂边区，在荔波板寨会师、开展革命活动以及攻打榕江的历程、事迹、故事。1994年3月，编辑出版10万字的《荔波英烈》（贵州人民出版社），记载荔波籍在外的革命英烈和到荔波从事革命活动以及为荔波的解放和建设牺牲奉献的革命英烈的事迹。该书成为全县爱国主义和革命传统教育的生动教材。

1996—2008年，县史志办先后编纂出版《中国共产党荔波县历史大事记（1930.4—2001.12）》《荔波革命老区史料汇编》《中国共产党荔波县历史（1921—1978）》（第一卷）、《中国共产党荔波县历次代表大会简介（1954—2006）》等党史资料书籍。其间，创办了《荔波党史通讯》《征集与研究》《党史纵横》等内部刊物。

（三）党史宣传教育

2001年8月，在聚焦绿宝石活动中，将本县红色之旅推上卫视作宣传推介，同时制作《绿色林海中的红色经典》影像光碟进行红色文化宣传。2002年，协助配合省州电视台、山东电视台、青岛党史办联合拍摄《青山赤子》《山海魂》《邓恩铭》《邓恩铭故乡行》等党史专题片。

2004年6月，协助拍摄专题电视片《红色故里——荔波》；9月下旬，《战略要地——黎明关》电视专题片上星播放；10月，协助拍摄《红星闪耀在贵州》等革命历史宣传教育专题片，利用电视、网络、报刊等载体，宣传荔波革命老区的发展变化。

2005—2007年，配合老年大学和关工委，深入县内中小学宣讲党史。全县各类招聘考试，把县情、党史列入考试内容之一。2002年后，在《贵州党史》《史志林》等刊载荔波老区历史事件或人物调研文章30余篇。

第五篇
地方人民代表大会

1980—2007年，荔波县召开了县第八届、第九届、第十届、第十一届、第十二届、第十三届、第十四届、第十五届人民代表大会。每届大会的代表都履行代表各项权利，听取和审议县人大常委会工作报告、县政府工作报告、县法院工作报告、县检察院工作报告以及县国民经济和社会发展计划报告、县财政预算及预算执行情况报告，批准通过有关报告，选举县人大常委会领导和县人民政府领导。在县人民代表大会闭幕期间，县人大常委会开展了代表视察、专题调研、审议决议、工作监督、人事任免、议案处理等工作。同时，全县乡（镇）人大也开展有关工作。

第一章 县人民代表大会

第一节 代表选举

1979年12月—1980年1月，开展县第八届人民代表大会代表选举工作，选出代表255名。其中，工人10名，农民154名，解放军1名，干部69名，知识分子10名，其他劳动者11名；妇女47名；少数民族192名；非中共党员83名；年龄最大76岁，年龄最小22岁。

1984年2—11月，开展县第九届人大代表选举工作，共选出代表155名。其中，农村代表占72.91%，城镇代表占27.09%；工农和其他劳动者代表74名，干部代表52名，知识分子代表27名，军警代表2名；妇女代表30名；少数民族126名（布依族84名，水族30名，瑶族6名，苗族、壮族各2名，侗族、蒙古族各1名）；初中以上文化程度占67.74%；最小年龄19岁。

1987年2—6月，开展县第十届人大代表选举工作。全县登记选民7.21万人，参加投票选举的选民6.29万人，参选率87.24%。依法足额选出人大代表129名。其中，工农和其他劳动者60名，干部58名，知识分子10名，军警1名；非中共党员35名；妇女23名；少数民族占78.29%；大专以上文化程度占16.27%；年龄最大70岁，年龄最小20岁。

1989年12月21日—1990年3月9日，开展县第十一届人大代表选举，1989年12月21日开始到1990年3月9日结束。全县有选民7.61万人，实际参加投票选举的选民6.52万人，参选率85.68%。选出人大代表143名，占应选代表146名的97.95%。其中，工农和其他劳动者63名，干部70名，知识分子9名，武警1名；妇女28名；少数民族111名；非中共党员48名；初中以上文化程度占76.53%；年龄最大67岁，年龄最小22岁。

1992年2月1日—3月25日，开展县第十二届人大代表选举工作，依法足额选出县人大代表148名。其中，工农和其他劳动者77名，干部和知识分子71名；妇女代表28名；少数民族116名（布依族72名、水族28名、苗族8名、瑶族4名、其他少数民族4名）；非中共党员40名；大专以上文化程度31名；年龄最大70岁，年龄最小19岁。

1997年11月—1998年1月，开展县第十三届人大代表选举工作。全县有选民9.46万人，参加选举的选民8.94万人，参选率94.5%。依法足额选出人大代表158名。其中，工人、农民和个体工商户、居民共84名，干部、知识分子73名，武警1名；中共党员106名；妇女39名；少数民族128名（布依族83名、水族25名、苗族11名、瑶族4名、其他少数民族5名）；大专以上文化占28.48%；年龄最大59岁，年龄最小19岁。

2002年11月下旬—2003年1月9日，开展县第十四届人大代表选举工作。全县有选民10.36人，参加选举的选民9.97万人，参选率96.24%。依法足额选出人大代表158名。其中，妇女31名；少数民族133名；非中共党员45名；本科以上文化程度35名；非公有制2名，农民82名；上届连任代表45名；

年龄最大60岁，年龄最小21岁。

2006年10月11日—12月15日，开展县第十五届人大代表选举工作。全县有选民12.54万人，参加选举12.23万人，参选率97.53%。依法足额选出人大代表158名。其中，非中共党员34名；妇女31名；少数民族140名；干部73名，农民46名，工人37名，军警1名，非公有制1名；上届继任46名；大学以上文化程度占33.5%；年龄最大62岁，年龄最小27岁。

第二节　代表大会

一、县第八届人民代表大会

1980年3月18—22日，荔波县第八届人民代表大会第一次会议在县城召开。出席会议代表255名，列席人员208名。会议听取和审议县革命委员会工作报告和县人民法院、县人民检察院工作报告，并分别作出决议；听取议案审查委员会的议案审查报告；对代表提出的5件议案转为代表建议、批评和意见，交由县政府办理。大会依法选举县第八届人大常委会委员9名，柏文熙当选主任，吴国仁、覃家有、王大贤、覃寿奇、白正明当选副主任；吴洪铭当选县长，李德余、周志宏、蒙明儒、汪克强当选副县长，何宪均当选县法院院长，覃兴奎当选县检察院检察长。大会选举出席州第七届人大代表28名。届中任命蒙院芬代理县长，韦绍忠、袁希柳代理副县长。

县第八届第二次、第三次、第四次会议先后于1981年8月、1982年3月、1983年3月在县城召开，听取和审议县人大常委会、县政府、县法院、县检察院以及计划、财政等6个工作报告。第三次会议依照法律程序撤换和补选县人大常委会委员2名；第四次会议听取县人大常委会关于第九届人大代表名额和换届选举工作的说明。

二、县第九届人民代表大会

1984年11月23—28日，县第九届人民代表大会第一次会议在县城召开。到会代表155名，列席人员178名。大会听取和审议了县人大常委会工作报告、县政府工作报告、县法院工作报告、县检察院工作报告以及县国民经济和社会发展计划报告、县财政预算及预算执行情况报告，会议审议通过上述6个报告，批准当年国民经济和社会发展计划和财政预算。大会依法选举县第九届人大常委会委员12名，吴洪铭当选主任，吴国仁、覃寿奇、杨昌映、白正明当选副主任；蒙院芬当选县长，韦绍忠、刘朝武、袁希柳当选副县长；何礼新当选县法院院长，莫俊国当选县检察院检察长。届中补选黄玉成为副县长。

县第九届第二次、第三次、第四次会议先后于1985年3月、1986年3月、1987年4月在县城召开，听取和审议县人大常委会、县政府、县法院、县检察院以及计划、财政等工作报告。第三次会议依法补选县人大常委会委员3名，选举出席州第八届人大代表32名。

三、县第十届人民代表大会

1987年8月25—31日，县第十届人民代表大会第一次会议在县城召开。应到会代表129名，实到会128名，列席人员148名。会议听取和审议县人大常委会工作报告、县政府工作报告、县法院工作报告、县检察院工作报告以及县国民经济和社会发展计划报告、县财政预算及预算执行情况报告，会议审议通过上述6个报告，批准当年国民经济和社会发展计划和财政预算。对代表提出的4件议案转为代表建议、批评和意见，交由县政府办理。大会依法选举县第十届人大常委会委员11名，吴洪铭当选主任，杨昌映、韦恩和、李文桓当选副主任；韦绍忠当选县长，李德余、刘朝武、黄玉成、何毅当选副县长；玉如敏当选县法院院长，莫树成当选县检察院检察长。

县第十届第二次、第三次会议先后于1988年3月、1989年3月在县城召开，听取和审议“一府两院”、人大常委会、计委、财政等工作报告。其中，第二次会议补选县人大常委会委员1名。

四、县第十一届人民代表大会

1990年4月26日—5月2日，县第十一届人民代表大会第一次会议在县城召开。出席会议的代表143名，列席人员138名。会议听取和审议县人大常委会工作报告、县政府工作报告、县法院工作报告、县检察院工作报告以及县国民经济和社会发展计划报告、县财政预算及预算执行情况报告，会议审议通过上述6个报告，批准当年国民经济和社会发展计划和财政预算。大会依法选举产生县第十一届人大常委会委员11名，吴洪铭当选主任，韦恩和、李文桓、张帮礼当选副主任；韦绍忠当选县长，龙文榜、刘朝武、黄玉成、陆兴华选副县长；玉如敏当选县法院院长，莫俊国当选县检察院检察长。第三次大会依法补选龙文榜为县长、覃顺芳为副县长。届中增补蒙强炳为副县长。

县第十一届第二次、第三次会议先后于1991年3月、1992年3月在县城召开，听取和审议“一府两院”、人大常委会、计委、财政工作报告。

五、县第十二届人民代表大会

1993年4月19—24日，县第十二届人民代表大会第一次会议在县城召开。应到代表148名全部到会，列席人员118名。会议听取和审议县人大常委会工作报告、县政府工作报告、县法院工作报告、县检察院工作报告以及县国民经济和社会发展计划报告、县财政预算及预算执行情况报告，会议审议通过上述6个报告，批准当年国民经济和社会发展计划和财政预算。大会依法选举县第十二届人大常委会委员15名，覃顺芳当选主任，杨世钧、何建飞、蒙镇贤、韦国菊当选副主任；玉如敏当选县长，蒙强炳、陈曼丽、陆兴华、莫俊国、谭成华当选副县长；莫刚灿当选法院院长，谭义勇当选检察院检察长。届中增补刘秀云、龙河云、王永波为副县长。

县第十二届第二次、第三次、第四次会议先后于1994年3月、1995年3月、1996年4月在县城召开，照例听取和审议6个工作报告。第四次会议补选莫永开为县人大常委会副主任。

六、县第十三届人民代表大会

1998年3月9—14日，县第十三届人民代表大会第一次会议在县城召开。应出席代表158名、实到会158名，列席人员140名。会议听取和审议县人大常委会工作报告、县政府工作报告、县法院工作报告、县检察院工作报告以及县国民经济和社会发展计划报告、县财政预算及预算执行情况报告，会议审议通过上述6个报告，批准当年国民经济和社会发展计划和财政预算。对代表提出的6件议案转为代表建议、批评和意见，交由县政府办理。大会依法选举产生县第十三届人大常委会委员13名，陆兴华当选主任，何建飞、王朝贵、蒙镇贤、韦国菊、莫永开、姚锦超当选副主任；玉如敏当选县长，莫俊国、龙河云、莫仲禹、王永波、潘永会当选副县长；张海青当选县法院院长，谭义勇当选县检察院检察长。届中增补张惠明、杨承志为副县长。

县第十三届第二次、第三次、第四次、第五次会议先后于1999年3月30日—4月1日、2000年4月、2001年3月、2002年3月在县城召开，照例听取审议6个工作报告。第四次会议依法补选潘朝显为县长、余认生为县法院院长；选举出席州第十一届人民代表大会代表18名。

七、县第十四届人民代表大会

2003年3月8—12日，县第十四届人民代表大会第一次会议在县城召开。应到会代表158名，实到会代表157名，列席人员125名。会议听取和审议县人大常委会工作报告、县政府工作报告、县法院工作报告、县检察院工作报告以及县国民经济和社会发展计划报告、县财政预算及预算执行情况报告，会议通过上述6个报告，批准当年国民经济和社会发展计划和财政预算。会议对代表提出的议案《关于抢救整理开发利用水书议案》，经大会表决通过转交县政府办理。大会依法选举县第十四届人大常委会委员10名，陆兴华当选主任，莫仲禹、程志安、莫永开、姚锦超、王永波、潘永会当选副主任；潘朝显当选县长，龙河云、杨承志、董豫黔、朱丽琼、莫春开当选副县长；余认生当选县法院院长，罗莎当选县检察院检察长。届中增补杨昌齐、陈昌远为副县长。

县第十四届第二次、第三次、第四次会议先后于2004年3月2—5日、2005年3月4—5日、2006年3月2—6日在县城召开。照例听取和审议规定的6个工作报告。第四次会议大会依法补选陈稠彪为县政府县长。

八、县第十五届人民代表大会

2007年1月6—9日，县第十五届人民代表大会第一次会议在县城召开。应到会代表158名，实到会147名，列席人员135名。会议听取和审议县人大常委会工作报告、县政府工作报告、县法院工作报告、县检察院工作报告以及县国民经济和社会发展计划报告、县财政预算及预算执行情况报告，会议通过上述6个报告，批准当年国民经济和社会发展计划和财政预算。会议对代表提出的7件议案转为代表建议、批评和意见，交由县政府办理。大会依法选举县第十五届人大常委会委员14名，陆兴华当选主任，莫仲禹、王永波、潘永会、付洪当选副主任；陈稠彪当选县长，李洪、马应忠、陈昌远、朱丽琼、冯发新当选副县长；李昌书当选县法院院长，朱启松当选县检察院检察长；选举出席州第十二届人民代表大会代表18名。

县第十五届第二次会议于2008年2月在县城召开。会议听取审议规定的6个工作报告；依法补选县第十五届人大常委会委员1名，补选张英为副县长。

第二章 县人大常委会

第一节 工作机构

1980年3月，县人民代表大会设常务委员会，为县人民代表大会的常设机构。1981年8月，在县人大第八届第二次会议上，讨论通过设立县人大常委会办公室。办公室设主任1人，下设人事秘书、代表联络信访和法律监督3个组开展日常工作。

1987年8月，人大常委会内设教科文卫工作委员会、法制工作委员会、财政经济工作委员会、代表民族工作委员会。

1993年，县人大常委会增设信访科（副科级）。1998年，增设农村经济工作委员会，同时增设行政科（正股级）。

2003—2008年，县人大常委会工作机构有办公室、教科文卫工作委员会、财政经济工作委员会、法制工作委员会、代表民族工作委员会、农村经济工作委员会；内设机构有信访科（副科级）、行政科（正股级）。

1980—2008年县人大常委会各届任职情况一览表

表5－1

届 次	职 务	姓 名	性别	民族	任职时间（年、月）	备注
八届人大常委会	主 任	柏文熙	男	布依族	1980.3	
	副主任	吴国仁	男	水族	1980.3	
		覃家有	男	布依族	1980.3	
		王大贤	男	汉族	1980.3	
		覃寿奇	男	布依族	1980.3	
		白正明	男	布依族	1980.3	
九届人大常委会	主 任	吴洪铭	男	苗族	1984.11	
	副主任	吴国仁	男	水族	1984.11	
		覃寿奇	男	布依族	1984.11	
		杨昌映	男	汉族	1984.11	
		白正明	男	布依族	1984.11	

续表5－1

届　次	职　务	姓　名	性别	民族	任职时间（年、月）	备注
十届人大常委会	主　任	吴洪铭	男	苗族	1987.8	
	副主任	杨昌映	男	汉族	1987.8	
		韦恩和	男	水族	1987.8	
		李文桓	男	汉族	1987.8	
十一届人大常委会	主　任	吴洪铭	男	苗族	1990.5	
	副主任	韦恩和	男	水族	1990.5	
		李文桓	男	汉族	1990.5	
		张帮礼	男	汉族	1990.5	
十二届人大常委会	主　任	覃顺芳	男	布依族	1993.4	
	副主任	杨世钧	男	侗族	1993.4	
		何建飞	男	布依族	1993.4	
		蒙镇贤	男	水族	1993.4	
		韦国菊	女	布依族	1993.4	
		莫永开	男	布依族	1996.4	届中补选
十三届人大常委会	主　任	陆兴华	男	布依族	1998.3	
	副主任	何建飞	男	布依族	1998.3	
		王朝贵	男	畲族	1998.3	
		蒙镇贤	男	水族	1998.3	
		韦国菊	女	布依族	1998.3	
		莫永开	男	布依族	1998.3	
		姚锦超	男	布依族	1998.3	
十四届人大常委会	主　任	陆兴华	男	布依族	2003.3	
	副主任	莫仲禹	男	布依族	2003.3	
		程志安	男	汉族	2003.3	
		莫永开	男	布依族	2003.3	
		姚锦超	男	布依族	2003.3	
		王永波	女	苗族	2003.3	
		潘永会	男	水族	2003.3	
十五届人大常委会	主　任	陆兴华	男	布依族	2007.1	
	副主任	莫仲禹	男	布依族	2007.1	
		王永波	女	苗族	2007.1	
		潘永会	男	水族	2007.1	
		付　洪	男	汉族	2007.1	

第二节　常委会议

县第八届人大常委会共召开会议28次。会议听取和审议县政府有关经济、文化、卫生、民政、民族等工作和县法院、县检察院执法情况的报告，对事关民生重大问题的处理作出相应的决议和决定。其间，通过审查修改，于1981年5月13日第九次常委会批准公布实施《荔波县综合农业区划的报告》《关于加强城镇建设管理实施办法》《关于加强城镇清洁卫生管理暂行办法》。

县第九届人大常委会共召开会议24次。会议听取和审议“一府两院”（县政府、县法院、县检察院）工作报告，对事关民生重大问题的处理作出相应的决议和决定。其间，通过审查修改，于1985年7月16日第六次常委会批准公布实施《荔波县城土地确认为国有的暂行规定》《关于乡镇（街道）、企业、城镇服务行业排污费核计征收的办法》。

县第十届人大常委会共召开会议25次。会议听取和审议“一府两院”有关工作报告，对事关民生重大问题的处理作出相应决议和决定。其间，通过审查修改，于1987年9月15日第二次常委会批准公布实施《关于进一步加强预算外资金管理的决议》《关于组织各族人民讨论宪法修改草案的决议》。

县第十一届人大常委会共召开会议23次。会议听取和审议“一府两院”有关工作报告，对事关民生重大问题的处理作出相应的决议和决定。其间，通过审查修改，于1991年3月5日第七次常委会批准公布实施《县政府关于动用1991年县级财政预备费的议案》《关于贯彻实施〈中华人民共和国残疾人保障法〉的决议》《关于红茂矿务局在我县开采的原煤要增加交纳资源补偿费的决议》。

县第十二届人大常委会共召开会议36次。会议听取和审议“一府两院”有关工作报告，对事关民生重大问题的处理作出相应的决议和决定。其间，通过审查修改，于1996年1月8日第15次常委会批准公布实施《关于荔波县城1996—2010年总体规划修编的决议》。

县第十三届人大常委会共召开常委会议35次。会议听取和审议“一府两院”有关工作报告，对事关民生重大问题的处理作出相应的决议和决定。其间，通过审查修改，于1999年3月16日第九次常委会批准公布实施《关于茂兰喀斯特森林自然保护区管理的暂行办法》。

县第十四届人大常委会共召开会议39次。会议听取和审议“一府两院”有关工作报告，对事关民生重大问题的处理作出相应决议和决定。其间，通过审查修改，于2003年7月8日第三次常委会通过《关于组织代表评议县农业局技术服务工作的决定》。

县第十五届人大常委会召开会议16次。会议听取和审议“一府两院”有关工作报告，对事关民生重大问题的处理作出相应决议和决定。其间，通过审查修改，于2007年9月10日第五次常委会通过《关于组织代表评议县卫生局农村合作医疗卫生工作的决定》。

第三节　代表工作

一、代表联络

从县八届人大开始，在县直机关和24个人民公社建立代表小组31个。以地区统一编组，在全县4个区建立4个中心联系组，建公社联系组20个、生产大队代表小组135个。区、社代表联系组每半年开展一次活动，代表小组每季度开展一次活动。1991年建镇并乡撤区后，以乡（镇）编组。2008年，全县有人大代表小组82个。

二、代表视察

（一）省、州人大代表视察

1980年后，省、州人大代表到荔波视察的内容涉及农业生产、林业生产、农民收入、民族政策、计划生育、水旱灾害、法律法规实施、国民经济指标完成情况、国有企业改革改制、交通通信电力建设、普法工作等。视察组现场察看建设中的独（山）荔（波）公路、荔（波）大（沙坡）公路、荔（波）小（七孔）公路、麻（尾）驾（欧）高速公路、大七孔电站、小七孔电站、移民新村、水尧机场等工程。参加视察组的成员为驻县的省或州人大代表，省、州机关的下选代表莅临参与视察。至2008年，县人大常委会接待省、州人大代表视察组共28次。

（二）县人大代表视察

县人大代表每年开展一次以上视察活动，视察内容为落实生产责任制、生产救灾、群众生活、社会治安、教育工作、农村基层政权建设、民族区域自治法贯彻实施、民族乡经济文化建设、喀斯特森林资源开发利用、双扶（扶贫扶优）周转金投放使用、义务教育的贯彻实施，普及法律常识，人民代表大会决议的贯彻执行等专题，组织委员和代表深入县直部门、学校、各乡（镇）、村（居委会）、组进行33次视察，针对视察中发现的问题和人民群众的迫切要求，及时召集政府和职能部门共同研究解决办法。如广西红茂矿务局在茂兰采煤造成污染和占地问题，县人大常委会决定由县人民政府与广西协商，由红茂矿务局拨给“三废”治理经费和占地补偿费。

（三）县人大常委会视察

县人大常委会每年就国民经济和社会发展计划落实、减轻农民负担、反腐倡廉、荔大公路、农村公路建设、茂兰人饮工程、煤炭产供销以及对《贵州省计划生育条例》《全国人大常委会关于加强社会治安综合治理决定》等法律法令贯彻实施情况，组织常委会成员和部分代表进行28次视察。如1995年根据省、州人大的安排，协同省、州人大代表进行视察活动2次，先后对荔波县国民经济、社会发展计划和财政预算执行情况、《中华人民共和国农业法》贯彻实施情况，对方村、永康、水尧、驾欧4乡经济发展情况以及人民群众最关心的问题进行视察。每次视察结束均写出视察报告，并召集政府及职能部门共同研究处理。

三、专题调查

1980年、1981年，县人大常委会由4名副主任以稳定和完善农村生产责任制、农村经济政策贯彻落实情况为题，组织人大代表先后开展两次专题调查。第一次分别赴水利、方村、甲站、茂兰、洞塘、佳荣、水维7个公社的21个大队63个生产队进行调查，第二次先后到洞塘公社的三合、和平，水维公社的甲料、拉易4个边远山区大队进行深入调查。调查结束后写出报告，并召集政府及职能部门参加情况通报会，要求交通、水电部门及时改变边远地区的落后状况，得到交通、水电部门重视并予以解决。

1993—1994年，县人大常委会针对全县有关经济指标落实情况、“双扶”（扶贫、扶优）资金使用、乡镇企业征税及瑶埃村散居瑶族待遇等问题，组织人大代表开展4次专题调查，写出调查报告，建议政府及职能部门及时解决。

2000年，甲良镇群众强烈反映三孔桥水利工程质量存在严重问题，县人大常委会组织人大代表及时会同甲良镇政府和有关单位深入工地进行调查，召开现场会议，作出令其停工整顿，加强工程质量管理，保证质量的决定。经过教育整顿后，该工程竣工验收时被评为优质工程。

2005年，县人大常委会根据群众反映的市场管理混乱，部分商人短斤少两坑害群众的问题，组织人大代表参与督促工商行政部门加强依法行政，开展市场整顿，维护市场秩序。

四、代表评议

1993年起，县人大常委会内年组织县内省、州、县人大代表组成评议小组，分别对县乡企局、农业局、卫生局、人事局、交通局、县法院、县检察院的工作进行评议。评议小组在评议工作中，充分肯定受评议部门成绩的基础上，对工作中存在的问题，提出具体的意见和建议，对受评议单位的工作作出实事求是、客观、公正的评价。

第四节 监 督

一、法律监督

县第八届人大常委会听取和审议县政府关于贯彻实施《中华人民共和国地方各级人民代表大会和地方各级人民政府组织法》《中华人民共和国宪法修改草案》的执法情况汇报并作出相应决议。

县第九届人大常委会听取和审议县政府关于贯彻实施《中华人民共和国婚姻法》《中华人民共和国民族区域自治条例》的执法情况汇报并作出相应决议。

县第十届人大常委会听取和审议县政府关于贯彻实施《黔南布依族苗族自治州自治条例》《中华人民共和国森林法》的执法情况汇报并作出相应决议。

县第十一届人大常委会听取和审议县政府关于贯彻实施《中华人民共和国土地管理法》《婚姻登记办法》的执法情况汇报并作出相应决议。

县第十二届人大常委会听取和审议县政府关于贯彻实施《中华人民共和国义务教育法》《中华人民共和国选举法》的执法情况汇报并作出相应决议。

县第十三届人大常委会听取和审议县政府关于贯彻实施《中华人民共和国统计法》《中华人民共和国治安管理处罚条例》的执法情况汇报并作出相应决议。

县第十四届人大常委会听取和审议县政府关于贯彻实施《中华人民共和国村民委员会组织法（试行）》《中华人民共和国水法》的执法情况汇报并作出相应决议。

县第十五届人大常委会听取和审议县政府关于贯彻实施《中华人民共和国经济合同法》《中华人民共和国食品卫生法》的执法情况汇报并作出相应决议。

1996年4月，全国人大内务司法委员会调研组到荔波县检查贯彻实施《中华人民共和国妇女权益保障法》情况。

1997年6月，全国人大民族委员会执法检查组到荔波检查贯彻实施《中华人民共和国民族区域自治法》中关于教育、卫生、文化等方面规定的执法情况。与此同时，州人大常委会到荔波县进行《民族乡行政工作条例》贯彻实施情况检查，并部署荔波县开展《贵州省职业技术教育暂行条例》《中华人民共和国妇女权益保护法》《中华人民共和国未成年人保护法》《中华人民共和国教育法》《中华人民共和国环境保护法》《中华人民共和国食品保护法》等10部法律执行情况检查。县人大常委会按州人大常委会的要求开展检查后，将检查情况报送州人大常委会。

二、工作监督

1986年5月，县第九届人大常委会召开第九次会议，听取和审议1986年荔波县关于《中华人民共和国森林法》《中华人民共和国土地管理法》贯彻执行情况报告，对县内森林资源减少和资源被破坏提出批评意见。会后，县政府及时召开有关部门会议，增加资金投入，发布保护森林布告，对森林资源实施保护。

1994年8月，县第十二届人大常委会召开第九次会议，听取和审议1992年荔波县关于《依法治县的实施方案的报告》，作出《关于依法治县的决议》。

1997年6月，县第十二届人大常委会召开第28次会议，听取和审议1997年荔波县关于《村民委员会建设的情况的报告》，作出《关于进一步加强村民委员会建设的决定》。

2000年4月，县第十三届人大常委会召开第13次会议，决定对全县执法单位开展落实执法责任制情况大检查。促进“一府两院”依法行政、公正司法。

第五节　人事任免

县人大常委会按照法律规定，对“一府两院”行使人事任免权。

1980年3月—1984年10月，县第八届人大常委会任命县政府组成人员45名；任命县人大常委会工作人员2名、县法院工作人员23名、县检察工作人员12名。免去县政府工作机构工作人员职务13名、县人大机关工作人员职务1名、县检察院工作人员职务1名、县法院工作人员职务1名。县人大常委会接受县长、副县长的辞呈并同意辞去县长职务1名、副县长职务3名，同时任命代理县长1名、副县长2名。

1984年11月—1987年7月，县第九届人大常委会任命县政府组成人员27名、县人大常委会机关工作人员2名、县检察院工作人员6名、县法院工作人员5名。免去县政府工作机构工作人员职务4名、县法院工作人员职务1名。

1987年8月—1990年4月，县第十届人大常委会任命县政府组成人员26名、县检察院工作人员6名、县法院工作人员4名。免去县政府工作机构工作人员职务2名、人大常委会机关工作人员职务1名、县检察院工作人员职务1名。

1990年5月—1993年3月，县第十一届人大常委会任命县政府组成人员30名、县检察院工作人员5名、法院工作人员2名。免去检察院工作人员职务5名。

1993年4月—1998年2月，县第十二届人大常委会任命县政府工作机构工作人员5名，县法院工作人员10名、县检察院工作人员7名。任命县政府副县长2名、代理县长1名。免去代理县长职务2名、县政府组成人员职务2名、人大常委会机关工作人员职务1名、县法院工作人员职务3名、县检察院工作人员职务1名。

1998年3月—2003年2月，县第十三届人大常委会任命县政府副县长5名、县政府组成人员60名、人大常委会机关工作人员3名、人大常委会委员3名、县法院工作人员35名、县检察院工作人员13名。免去县政府副县长职务2名、县政府组成人员职务16名、人大常委会机关工作人员职务3名、县法院工作人员职务15名、县检察院工作人员职务2名。

2003年3月—2006年12月，县第十四届人大常委会任命县政府组成人员30名、人大常委会机关工作人员6名、县检察工作人员6名、陪审员5名。免去县政府组成人员职务2名、人大常委会工作人员职务6名。

2007年1月—2008年12月，县第十五届人大常委会任命县政府组成人员26名、人大常委会机关工作人员2名、县法院工作人员5名。免去人大常委会委员2名、县法院工作人员职务2名。

第六节 议案与建议

在历次县人代会上，代表提出的议案、建议、批评和意见，属于议案的由人民代表大会审议，属于建议、批评和意见的由县人大常委会代表工作委员会分类整理后交县政府及职能部门办理，要求办理单位在接到议案和建议之日起3个月内办理完毕并答复代表，政府及职能部门办理结束后向县人大常委会作专题汇报。

自第八届人民代表大会第一次会议至第十五届人民代表大会第二次会议的28年间，代表提出的议案共10件，提出的建议、批评和意见共3100多件，涉及荔波工业、农业、城市建设、城市管理、教育、文化、卫生等经济和社会生活的各个方面。

上述议案、建议、批评和意见，历年均按《关于办理人民代表议案、建议、批评和意见的程序》及时交政府和职能部门办理。县政府给予高度重视，针对议案提出的问题，多次召开专题会议，及时研究对策，认真负责抓落实，如对县第十四届人民代表大会第一次会议上提出的《关于抢救整理开发利用水书议案》及第四次会议上提出的《关于加强樟江河治理议案》，县政府对这2件议案办理情况分别作出详细答复。水书已被列入首批“中国档案文献遗产名录”和“国家级第一批非物质文化遗产代表作名录”。目前正在启动申报“世界记忆工程遗产名录”和“世界人类口头与非物质文化遗产名录”。关于加强樟江河治理议案的办理情况是召开专题会及时部署。明确分管旅游、城建、农业的副县长牵头组织职能部门负责落实樟江综合治理规划编制等工作；加大宣传力度，提高全民保护樟江意识；制订切实可行的工作计划、确保治理工作取得实效。

县人大常委会将增强代表议案、建议办理实效作为支持和保障代表依法履职的重要环节。在办理中注重办复方式的创新。一是在加强综合分析、实行统一交办的基础上，将代表反映比较集中的突出问题作为重点跟踪督办案，由常委会领导和有关工委负责督办。二是对涉及多个部门的代表建议，由主办单位牵头负责，相关单位参加，共同办理。三是加强与代表沟通，注重办理实效，要求办复前进行面商，办复后要有回访，代表对办理不满意的必须重办，近期不能办理的，必须向代表说明理由。

“一府两院”对历年的建议、批评和意见均及时认真办理，绝大多数已得到解决，对条件尚不具备，暂时不能解决的也作出明确的答复。2005年5月，根据荔波县委常委第93次会议安排，关于县人民医院和县中医院资产重组问题，有关代表到周边县进行调研，并在县医院和中医院召开座谈会，走访村（居）群众，通过调研，听取群众的意见及卫生部门反映的问题和困难。提出建议县委、县政府尽快将乡（镇）卫生院人事、财物转移到县卫生局分管，并妥善解决卫生系统退休职工的福利待遇问题。

第三章　乡（镇）人民代表大会

第一节　代表选举

乡（镇）人大代表的选举与县人大代表选举同步进行，自十三届人大以后，县人大代表改为五年一届，乡（镇）人大仍为三年一届，十四届人大以后，县、乡（镇）人大代表选举同步进行改为五年一届。

代表实行普选，县内年满18周岁的公民，除依法剥夺政治权利者外，均享有选举权和被选举权。每次选举均成立选举委员会，按选举法规定，选举乡（镇）人民代表大会的代表。乡、镇人民代表大会代表的选举，历届均采用直接选举方式，1984年前采用等额选举办法，从1984年的第八届人大开始，改等额选举为差额选举。由本乡（镇）选民直接选出。从1980年第七届人大起县人大代表采用直接选举方式产生，即由选区的选民直接选举县人民代表大会代表。县、乡（镇）人大代表的选举，一律采用无记名投票。

“文化大革命”期间，普选制度遭到破坏。粉碎“江青反革命集团”后，1980年恢复普选制度。全县划分乡（镇）人大代表选区共339个；县人大代表选区66个。代表候选人的产生采取以选区或选民小组为单位，由各级党组织和选民提名推荐，酝酿协商的办法。

从1980年开始，乡（镇）代表组织陆续建立，全县包括县机关和24个社镇，共建立31个代表小组。到县九届人大以后，逐步增加。以地区统一编组建立区中心联系组4个，社镇联系组20个，村组代表小组135个。

1988年以后，为进一步加强县、乡两级人大代表工作的开展，县人大常委会聘任区、镇人大工作联络员，明确各区、乡、村代表小组定期开展代表活动，密切同人民群众的联系，自觉接受人民群众的监督。

1991年撤区并乡建镇后，以乡（镇）统一编组，逐渐建立和完善代表的学习和活动。通过以会代训和经常性的培训，着力提高乡（镇）人大代表的履职能力和整体素质。每年每个季度进行一次代表培训，围绕乡（镇）重点工程和重大事项经常组织代表开展视察和执法检查，极大地调动乡（镇）人大代表的工作积极性，充分发挥乡（镇）人大代表的作用。

2008年，县十五届人大统计包括县机关和17个乡（镇）共分为82个代表小组。

第二节　乡（镇）人大主席团

1991年8月前，全县有4区1镇25个乡设人大联络员1名，各乡设人大常务主席1名，主席多数由乡党委专职副书记兼任。

1991年10月建镇并乡撤区后，全县17个乡（镇）经选举产生人大主席团，属乡（镇）人民代表大会的常设机构，设常务主席1名，较大的乡（镇）由党委书记兼任人大主席团主席，设专职副主席1名，设主席团成员3～5名。乡（镇）人大主席团1年召开1次乡（镇）人大会议，每3个月召开1次主席团会议，听取和审议乡（镇）政府及所属相关部门工作报告，讨论该乡（镇）重大事项。主席团办理或督促办理人大代表建议、批评意见，组织县人大代表和乡（镇）人大代表视察工作。

1995年，根据《中华人民共和国地方各级人民代表大会和地方各级人民政府组织法》的规定，乡（镇）人大常务主席改称乡（镇）人大主席团主席，各乡（镇）均设有专职人大主席团主席1名。根据工作需要，玉屏、永康、茂兰、佳荣、朝阳、播尧、甲良、驾欧等乡（镇）增设常务副主席1名，负责日常事务工作。乡（镇）人大主席团正、副主席均由乡（镇）人民代表大会选举产生。

1996年，乡（镇）人大选举独自进行，县人大常委会加强指导，选出乡（镇）人大代表767名。代表大会选举产生乡（镇）人大主席团主席17名、副主席1名，选举产生乡（镇）长17名、副乡（镇）长55名、科技副乡（镇）长16名。

2008年，乡（镇）人大主席团设专职主席1名，为正科级。乡（镇）人大主席团围绕同级党委、政府的总体工作目标和代表议案、建议，建言献策、议政督政。

第六篇
地方政府

1980年3月—2008年12月，县政府历经8届7次换届，第八届至第十一届政府每届任期3年，第十二届至十五届政府每届任期5年。1978年中共十一届三中全会以后，县人民政府贯彻执行中共中央的农村经济政策，在农村实行家庭联产承包责任制，发展农业生产。

20世纪80年代，县政府按县委提出的“依靠省州，面向两广，开发山区，兴县富民”的经济发展战略，在抓商品粮基地建设的同时，开发以万亩柑橘、万亩乌梅、万亩泡桐、万亩杉木、万亩泡竹为重点的工程，以煤炭开发和开发大七孔、小七孔水电站为重点等一系列发展经济建设项目，县政府坚持稳定家庭联产承包责任制，增加农业投入，推广科技兴农，农业和农村工作全面发展，煤炭工业产、供、销稳步增长。使全县经济不断发展。20世纪90年代，县政府不断深化改革开放，进一步搞好煤炭开发。在农村实施“温饱工程”，解决贫困人口的温饱问题，实施国家“八七”扶贫攻坚计划，建立“两瑶”扶贫开发试验区，到1996年，多数贫困户越过温饱线，成为全省率先解决温饱先进县之一。进入21世纪后，县政府在农业工作方面以增加农民收入为中心，全面推进农业农村经济持续健康发展；在工业生产方面进行煤矿技改、扩界和资源整合；在生态建设方面加强樟江河河道治理，启动石漠化治理工程，创建国家级生态示范区工作通过国家验收。旅游和社会事业方面申报为全省优先重点发展旅游区之一获得成功。教育事业通过“两基”复查和“普实”验收和实施广播电视“村村通”工程，实施新型农村合作医疗。2007年捆绑申报的“中国南方喀斯特”世界自然遗产在第31届世界遗产大会通过，成为中国第六个世界自然遗产地，实现贵州世界遗产零的突破。全县经济建设、文化事业全面发展，启动“国家园林城市”“中国优秀旅游城市”创建工作。2008年，“国家卫生县城”通过复查验收，县城获得“全国文明城市”称号。2008年年末，全县国内生产总值113378万元，比2007年增长23.94%；全社会固定资产投资总额68357万元，比2007年增长11.56%；社会消费品零售总额32317万元，比2007年增长26.24%；财政总收入18216万元，比2007年增长25.33%；农民人均纯收入2618元，比2007年增长21.3%。

第一章　政府工作机构

第一节　县政府领导成员

1978—1980年2月，荔波县政府工作由县革命委员会取代，县革委主任、副主任由中共黔南州委组织部任免。

1980年3月，县委、县革委根据省革委《关于政权派出机构和企事业单位不再设革命委员会的通知》，撤销全县企事业单位的革委会和4个区革委，恢复各科、局和区公所政权机构。在县第八届人民代表大会第一次会议上，根据《中华人民共和国地方各级人民代表大会和地方各级人民政府组织法》的规定，将荔波县革命委员会改为荔波县人民政府，县政府由县长、副县长和所属委、办主任、科（局）长组成。

1980年3月—2008年12月，县政府历经8届7次换届，第八届至第十一届政府每届任期3年，第十二届至十五届政府每届任期5年。

县人民政府原办公大楼，2013年7月1日迁出办公

1978—2008年历届县政府领导任职一览表

表6－1

届 次	职 务	姓 名	性别	民族	任职时间（年、月）	备注
县革委	主 任	张聚国	男	汉族	1978.1—1978.2	
		吴洪铭	男	苗族	1979.6—1980.3	
	副主任	袁青田	男	汉族	1978.1—1979.11	
		傅金玉	男	汉族	1978.1—1980.3	
		柏文熙	男	布依族	1978.1—1980.3	
		覃家有	男	布依族	1978.1—1980.3	
		吴国仁	男	水族	1979.3—1980.3	
		李德余	男	汉族	1979.3—1980.3	
		韦国丰	男	水族	1979.7—1980.3	
		周志宏	男	布依族	1979.7—1980.3	
第八届	县 长	吴洪铭	男	苗族	1980.3—1983.12	
	代县长	蒙院芬	女	布依族	1983.12—1984.11	
	副县长	李德余	男	汉族	1980.3—1983.12	
		周志宏	男	布依族	1980.3—1983.12	
		蒙明儒	男	布依族	1980.3—1983.12	
		汪克强	男	汉族	1980.3—1984.11	
	代理副县长	韦绍忠	男	水族	1983.12—1984.11	
		袁希柳	男	汉族	1983.12—1984.11	
第九届	县 长	蒙院芬	女	布依族	1984.11—1987.8	
	副县长	韦绍忠	男	水族	1984.11—1987.8	
		刘朝武	男	汉族	1984.11—1987.8	
		袁希柳	男	汉族	1984.11—1985.8	
		黄玉成	男	汉族	1986.3—1987.8	
第十届	县 长	韦绍忠	男	水族	1987.8—1990.4	
	副县长	李德余	男	汉族	1987.8—1990.4	
		刘朝武	男	汉族	1987.8—1990.4	
		黄玉成	男	汉族	1987.8—1990.4	
		何 毅	男	布依族	1987.8—1990.4	
第十一届	县 长	韦绍忠	男	水族	1990.4—1991.12	
		龙文榜	男	汉族	1992.3—1993.3	
	代县长	龙文榜	男	汉族	1991.12—1992.3	
		玉如敏	男	布依族	1993.3—1993.4	
	副县长	龙文榜	男	汉族	1990.4—1991.12	

续表6－1

届次	职务	姓名	性别	民族	任职时间（年、月）	备注
第十一届	副县长	刘朝武	男	汉族	1990.4—1993.4	
		黄玉成	男	汉族	1990.4—1993.4	
		陆兴华	男	布依族	1990.4—1993.4	
		覃顺芳	男	布依族	1992.3—1993.4	
		吴兆全	男	汉族	1992.7—1993.4	挂职
		蒙强炳	男	水族	1992.12—1993.4	
第十二届	县长	玉如敏	男	布依族	1993.4—1998.3	
	副县长	蒙强炳	男	水族	1993.4—1997.2	
		陈曼丽	女	汉族	1993.4—1995.2	
		陆兴华	男	布依族	1993.4—1998.3	
		莫俊国	男	布依族	1993.4—1998.3	
		谭成华	男	汉族	1993.4—1998.3	
		吴兆全	男	汉族	1993.4—1997.4	挂职
		谢继成	男	汉族	1995.5—1997.12	挂职
		刘秀云	女	汉族	1995.7—1996.9	
		龙河云	男	苗族	1997.1—1998.3	
		王永波	女	苗族	1997.1—1998.3	
第十三届	县长	玉如敏	男	布依族	1998.3—1999.12	
		潘朝显	男	水族	2001.3—2003.3	
	代县长	潘朝显	男	水族	2000.11—2001.3	
	副县长	莫俊国	男	布依族	1998.3—2003.3	
		龙河云	男	苗族	1998.3—2003.3	
		王永波	女	苗族	1998.3—2003.3	
		莫仲禹	男	布依族	1998.3—2003.3	
		潘永会	男	水族	1998.3—2003.3	
		任平	男	汉族	1998.4—2001.3	挂职
		吴惠明	女	汉族	1998.6—2001.6	挂职
		李太盛	男	汉族	1999.6—2001.6	挂职
		张惠明	男	布依族	2000.11—2001.7	
		杨承志	男	苗族	2002.5—2003.3	
第十四届	县长	潘朝显	男	水族	2003.3—2005.5	
	代县长	陈稠彪	男	苗族	2006.1—2007.1	
	副县长	龙河云	男	苗族	2003.3—2005.5	
		杨承志	男	苗族	2003.3—2006.12	

续表6－1

届 次	职 务	姓 名	性别	民族	任职时间（年、月）	备注
第十四届	副县长	董豫黔	男	汉族	2003.3—2007.1	
		朱丽琼	女	汉族	2003.3—2007.1	
		莫春开	男	布依族	2003.11—2007.1	
		杨昌齐	男	布依族	2003.11—2007.1	
		陈昌远	男	布依族	2003.9—2007.1	
		李 洪	男	汉族	2006.12—2007.1	
		马应忠	男	布依族	2006.12—2007.1	
		冯发新	男	汉族	2006.12—2007.1	
第十五届	县 长	陈稠彪	男	苗族	2007.1—	
	副县长	李 洪	男	汉族	2007.1—	
		马应忠	男	布依族	2007.1—	
		陈昌远	男	布依族	2007.1—2008.1	
		朱丽琼	女	汉族	2007.1—	
		冯发新	男	汉族	2007.1—	
		张 英	男	布依族	2008.7—	
		丁蜀生	男	汉族	2007.10—2008.10	挂职
		金必煌	男	汉族	2007.10—2008.10	挂职
		曾 静	女	汉族	2007.10—2008.10	挂职

第二节 县政府工作机构

1978年5月，县革委所辖工作部门21个，即荔波县革委办公室、荔波县劳动局、民政局、公安局、计划委员会、统计局、财政局、粮食局、工建交办公室、县全民国防教育办公室、教育局、交通局、水利局、农业区划办公室、林业局、社企管局、县供销合作联社、科学技术委员会、农业局、轻工局、知识青年上山下乡办公室。

1983年12月22日，县委、县政府《关于党政机关改革方案的请示报告》呈请州委、州政府审批，县政府工作部门设1办6委22个局（共29个部门），即县政府办公室（含战备工作）、经济委员会（由经济委员会、原财贸办公室、工交办公室、农林水办公室合并组成）、计划委员会（含农业区划工作）、科学技术委员会、计划生育委员会、民族事务委员会、体育运动委员会、统计局、物价局、劳动人事局（由人事、劳动局合并组成，保留编委名称）、民政局、财政局、税务局、工商局、粮食局、商业局、卫生局（含爱国卫生运动委员会）、建设局、教育局（含职工教育工作）、林业局、农牧局（由农业局、畜牧局合并组成）、水电局、公安局、司法局、交通局、广播事业局、农业机械局、轻工业局、社队企业局。

1984年2月，经报请州委、州政府批示后，确定荔波县政府工作部门保留25个，即政府办公室、计划委员会、科学技术委员会、统计局、劳动人事局、物价局、民政局（退伍军人和军队离、退休干部安排工作）、司法局、公安局、林业局、水利电力局、财政局、税务局、粮食局、商业局、工商行政管理局、教育局（含体育运动委员会）、卫生局（含爱国卫生运动委员会）、交通局（原工交局的交通部分）、城乡建设环境保护局、计划生育委员会、民族事务委员会、广播电视局、文化局、审计局。其中，劳动人事局由劳动工资局、人事局组成，保留编制委员会名称；经济委员会由经济委员会、原工交局的工业部分以及手工业联社组成；农牧局由农业局、畜牧局合并组成，教育局由教育局、体育运动委员会合并组成，保留体育运动委员会名称。

此后至1986年，先后成立文化局、审计局、县体育运动委员会、县地方志编纂委员会办公室、县档案局（与原档案馆合并）、土地管理局。1989年1月，成立县旅游局。

1994年，进行县级机构改革，根据州政府审批的荔波县县级机构改革方案，县政府工作机构设26个，即政府办公室、经济贸易局、粮食局、农业局、教育局、统计局、工商行政管理局、审计局、民政局、财政局、公安局、人事劳动局、卫生局、计划生育局、旅游事业局、县志办、档案局、民族宗教局、国土资源管理局、建设局、司法局、交通局、文体广播电视局、乡镇企业局、水利局、林业局。

1994年2月，县委、县政府成立“荔波县扶贫项目开发领导小组”，设立扶贫办挂靠县政府办公室。

1995年5月，成立县项目开发办公室，挂靠在县政府办。是年年底，将县委招商引资办与县政府项目开发办、扶贫办合并为县扶贫开发办，实行一套机构、三块牌子合署办公。10月，成立县煤炭工业局，与乡（镇）企业局实行两块牌子、一套人员合署办公。11月，成立县山林、土地、水事权属争议协调处理办公室，设在县政府办。1996年年底，调处办与县委、县政府联合信访办合并，改称为县联合信访局，对外加挂调处办牌子，为独立建制单位。

1996年10月，国土资源局与地质矿产局正式分设。11月，成立县环境保护局，为独立建制。12月，将农村经济工作委员会从教育局分立，更名为县农业办公室。

1997年3月，将畜牧管理的职能从农业局分离出来，成立县畜牧局；将文体广播电视局分设为文化体育局和广播电视局。10月，县政府在贵阳设立荔波县人民政府驻贵阳办事处（后于2001年7月撤销）。是年，县科学技术委员会改建为县科学技术局。

1999年10月，县志办与县委党史研究室合并，为县史志编纂委员会办公室。

2001年10月，进行政府行政机构改革，设置工作机构28个，即政府办公室（含外事、侨务、人防、信访、法制和经济实体改革调研等工作）、发展计划局（含招商引资和外协工作，挂招商引资局牌子）、经济贸易局（含非国有经济管理工作）、教育局、科学技术局、民族宗教事务局、公安局（含国家安全工作）、监察局（与纪委机关合署办公，不占政府机构限额）、民政局（含老龄工作委员会办公室）、司法局、财政局（含国有资产管理工作）、人事劳动和社会保障局、国土资源管理局、建设局、交通局（含战备支前运输工作）、水利局（含小水电建设和防汛抗旱工作）、农业局（含农机、畜牧和区划工作）、林业局、环境保护局、卫生局（含爱国卫生工作）、计划生育局、审计局、统计局、粮食局、乡镇企业局（加挂煤炭工业管理局牌子）、文体广播电视局、物价局、资本营运公司。

2002年1月，撤销农业区划办，其职能并入县农业局。

县政府办公室 1978年时为荔波县革命委员会办公室。1980年3月改称荔波县政府办公室。1994年4月，将外事办工作职能并入县政府办公室（保留外事办牌子）。1997年10月，设立荔波县政府驻贵阳办事处，于2001年7月撤销。2002年1月—2008年12月，县政府办公室设秘书股、信息督查股、外事办公室、行政管理股和法制办公室。

县劳动人事和社会保障局 1978年10月成立县人事局。1984年2月，人事局与劳动工资局合并为县劳动人事局。1994年1月，劳动人事局更名为人事劳动局，同时，将劳动安全委员会办公室工作职能并入人事劳动局。2000年6月，成立县社会保险事业局，隶属县人事劳动局，为副科级事业单位。2002年1月，县人事劳动局更名为县人事劳动和社会保障局，社会保险事业局更名为县社会保险服务中心，仍为人事劳动和社会保障局下属副科级事业单位，至2008年机构不变。

县民政局 1978年已成立县民政局，隶属县革命委员会生产指挥部，1980年3月后隶属县政府。2002年1月，将县老龄委员会更名为县老龄工作委员会，其办公室设在县民政局。

县民族宗教事务局 1980年11月，成立县民族事务委员会。1994年1月，民族事务委员会改称县民族事务局。2001年3月，民族事务局更名民族宗教事务局，至2008年机构不变。

县公安局 1978年已恢复建立在“文化大革命”中撤销的县公安局。1982年设朝阳区派出所。1984年，设林业公安派出所，属县林业局编制，业务受县公安局和林业局双重领导。1985年，城关区派出所改为玉屏镇派出所，增设玉屏区派出所。1987年，县交通监理职能划入县公安局，设县公安交警队。至1991年，县公安局内设机构有办公室、政保科、经文保科、治安科、刑侦队、预审科、政工科、看守所、行政拘留所、法制科、消防科、交警队，下属机构有玉屏区、朝阳区、甲良区、茂兰区4个区和玉屏镇5个派出所。1992年，撤销4区1镇派出所，组建16个乡（镇）派出所。1994年，建公安巡警队。是年12月，县公安交警队改建为县公安局交警大队，为副科级机构，属县公安局和州交警支队双重领导。1999年，成立禁毒大队、樟江风景区治安派出所。2002年，成立经济犯罪侦察大队、国内安全保卫大队、公共信息网络安全监察科、治安大队（下设基层基础科、户政科）、监管大队（下设看守所、行政拘留所），成立刑侦3个中队（一中队、二中队、三中队）。2008年，撤销经济犯罪侦察大队、监管大队。至年末，县公安局内设机构有指挥中心、国内安全保卫大队、治安管理大队、刑事侦查大队，交通管理大队、禁毒大队、政工监督室、法制室、警务保障室、巡逻特警大队、公共信息网络安全监察大队、看守所、行政拘留所，下设机构有16个乡（镇）派出所和1个景区派出所（瑶麓瑶族乡未设派出所），全县公安系统实有人员156人。

县发展和改革局 1978年，县计划委员会隶属县革委生产指挥部，内设建设组、物价组、物资组。1981年，建设、物价、物资工作与计委分离，另建相应局级机构，计委编制5人，未设内设机构。2001年，县计委改为县计划局，内设办公室、发展投资股、以工代赈办公室，行政编制12人。2003年10月，县计划局改为县发展计划局。2004年，县发展计划局改为发展和改革局，内设机构不变，下设改革研究中心（为参照公务员管理事业单位，编制3人），至2008年机构不变。

县统计局 1978年，统计工作由县革委生产指挥部计划统计劳动办公室负责。1982年11月，成立县统计局。1984年4月，成立县农村抽样调查队。1988年2月，建立区、镇统计站和乡统计组。1991年，成立各乡（镇）统计站。至2008年，县统计局内设办公室、业务股、普查中心，共有人员10人。乡（镇）统计站无正式编制，统计工作由乡（镇）明确专人负责。

县财政局 1978年，县财政局有人员6人，4个区有财政工作人员共8人。1985年，4区1镇建立财政所，乡设财政员。1987年，在县财政局设“三查”办公室、财政信用资金管理所、国库券推销办公室。1990年，在县财政局设中华会计函授站。1991年，全县区、乡“建并撤”后，撤销原区镇财政所，新建乡（镇）财政所17个。1994年，设国有资产管理办公室。1998年8月，成立预算外资金管理局，属县财政局副科级机构。2002年1月，成立县会计核算中心，属县财政局管理的事业单位；成立县农税征收管理局，属县财政局管理的副科级机构。2003年5月，成立县政府采购中心，为县财政局下属正股级事业机构。2006年11月，将县农税征收管理局改为基层财政管理局。至2008年，全县财政系统实有人员132人，其中乡（镇）88人。

县经济贸易局 1978年10月，县工交办改为县经委。1984年2月，县工业交通局的工业部分与轻工业局合并组成县经济委员会。1994年4月，撤销县经济委员会、对外经济协作办公室，合并为县经济贸易局；撤销商业局，改建为商业贸易总公司；撤销物质局，改建为物质贸易总公司；撤销轻工局，改建为城镇集体联社。同时，将以上两司一社的行政职能并入经济贸易局。2002年1月，劳动安全委员会办公室职能从县人事劳动和社会保障局划入县经济贸易局，挂荔波县安全生产委员会办公室牌子。

县全民国防教育办公室 1978年4月，成立县全民国防教育办公室，为县委、县政府联合办事机构。1989年1月，全民国防教育办改设在县委宣传部。2002年1月，县国教办改设在县政府办公室（在县人武部办公），为县委和县政府常设办事机构，规格为正科级。

县信访局 1978年，县委、县革委分别成立县委、县革委信访组。1979年11月，成立信访领导小组，由县委书记任组长。1984年3月，成立县委、县政府联合信访科。1990年5月，信访科改为县委、县政府联合信访办公室。1994年，撤销县委、县政府联合信访办公室独立建制，并入县委办公室。1996年4月，恢复县委、县政府信访办公室。1997年2月，撤销县委、县政府联合信访办公室，成立县委、县政府信访局，与县山林土地水事权属争议协调处理办公室合署办公。2002年，信访局并入县政府办公室，为副科级机构。县山林土地水事权属争议协调处理办公室职能划归国土资源局。2005年10月，恢复县信访局正科级机构规格，行政编制3名。

县教育局 1978年1月，文化、教育机构合并为文化教育局。1984年2月，文化、教育职能分开，设教育局，将县体育运动委员会并入教育局。1985年5月，体育运动委员会分出单设。1992年，在各乡（镇）设教育辅导站。2004年，撤销教育辅导站，由各乡（镇）中心完小管理所该乡（镇）小学教育教学工作。

县文体广播电视局 1978年5月，建立广播事业局，与县广播站实行局站合一。1984年4月，改为县广播电视局。1994年4月，撤销县广播电视局、文化局和体育运动委员会，合并成立县文化体育广播电视局，下辖各乡（镇）广播电视站。1996年1月，建立县有线电视中心，隶属县文体广播电视局。1997年2月，文体广播电视局分设为文化体育局和广播电视局。2002年2月，撤销文化体育局和广播电视局，合并组建县文体广播电视局，至2008年机构不变。

县国土资源局 1986年9月，建立土地管理局。1994年4月，撤销原矿产资源管理办公室和土地管理局的独立建制，合并组建国土资源管理局，对外加挂矿产资源管理局和环境保护局两块牌子。1996年6月，地质矿产管理环境保护职能从国土资源管理局分离出来，成立县地质矿产局，对外仍挂荔波县环境保护局牌子。1996年8月，将县国土资源管理局更名为县国土局。是年11月，将县环境保护职能从县地质矿产局分离出来，单独成立荔波县环境保护局。2002年1月，国土资源管理局与地质矿产管理局再次合并，建立县国土资源局。

县建设局 1982年6月，建立荔波县城乡建设环境保护局。1994年1月，撤销县城乡建设环境保护局，改建为建设局。1999年2月，成立县公共事业管理局，隶属建设局下属副科级事业单位。

县交通局 1978年4月，县革委工业局与县革委交通局合并为县工交局。1984年2月，恢复交通局。1989年11月，成立公路交通运输管理所，为副科级机构。1998年3月，将公路养护工区更名为县乡公路管理所，为副科级单位。上述两个机构均隶属县交通局。2003年4月，县港监所与船检所合并更名为地方海事处。2008年6月，县乡公路管理所更名为县公路管理所。县交通局主管的事业单位有县公路管理所、公路运输管理所、路政中队、代管征费稽查所、地方海事处，主管的国有企业有汽车客运站、县道路收费站。

县水利局 1978年前已成立水利电力局。1991年“建并撤”后，撤销城关、甲良、茂兰、朝阳4个区水利站。1994年4月，县水利电力局更名为县水利局。1996年12月，县水利局更名为县水利电力局。1999年4月，供电系统从水利电力局中分离单设机构。是年11月，县水土保持站更名为县水土保持执法监督站，增设县水政监察大队。2002年1月，县水利电力局正式变更为县水利局。2005年10月，增设县河道管理所、县茂兰水管所、县威刀水库管理所、县洪江水库管理所。2008年年底，县水利局下属事业单位共11个。

县农业局 1978年前已成立县农业局。1984年2月，农业、畜牧机构合并为农牧局。1991年“建并撤”后，撤销区级机构，成立17个乡（镇）农业技术经营管理综合服务站。1994年6月，撤销农牧局，改建为县农业局。2002年1月，撤销县畜牧局、县农业机械管理局、县区划办，其职能并入农业局，同时组建县农业机械技术服务中心。2003年4月，县畜牧局单设。2007年5月，成立县农村能源环保办公室，为县农业局下属正股级事业单位。2005年3月，成立县农业综合执法大队。至2008年年底，县农业局内设机构共14个，下辖17个乡（镇）农业服务中心（含农机站）。

县林业局 县林业局于1978年前已建立。1997年，县林业局下设16个行政事业单位和1个独立核算企业。2008年，县林业局有基层单位27个，其中独立核算企业1个。

县环境保护局 1996年11月，将县地质矿产局的环境保护职能分离，单独成立县环境保护局，至2008年机构不变。

县卫生局 1978年前已建立县卫生局。1994年，撤销县爱国卫生运动委员会办公室，职能并入县卫生局。2006年1月，成立县新型农村合作医疗管理委员会办公室，为县事业单位二级机构。2008年，县卫生局设置不变。

县司法局 1980年11月，成立县司法局。1988年，成立甲良区、地峨乡、翁昂乡法律服务所。2000年，成立朝阳镇、佳荣镇法律事务所，同时成立县法律援助中心，为县司法局内设副科级行政机构。2008年，县司法局内设机构有政工科、县依法治理办公室（法制宣传教育股）、律师公证工作管理股、基层工作管理股、法律援助工作管理股（也称法律援助中心）、办公室（计财装备股），派出机构除瑶麓瑶族乡外的16个乡（镇）司法所。

县监察局 1988年4月成立县监察局。1993年5月至2008年，县监察局与县纪委合署办公。

县科学技术局 1978年2月，县科技局改为县科学技术委员会。1997年8月，县科学技术委员会更名为科学技术局，至2008年机构不变。

县计划生育局 1978年，县计划生育办公室设在县卫生局。1984年5月，计生办改称县计划生育委员会。1994年1月，县计划生育委员会更名为县计划生育局，至2008年机构不变。

县审计局 1984年3月，成立县审计局。2002年5月，县审计局内设机构调整为法制综合股、财政金融投资审计股、行政事业经贸审计股、经济责任审计股，至2008年机构不变。

县乡镇企业局（县煤炭工业局） 1978年8月，建立县社队企业管理局。1984年2月，改名为乡村工业公司，由行政管理单位变为企业单位。1985年10月，政企分设，恢复县乡镇企业局。1990年4月，增设玉屏、茂兰2个区煤炭管理所和水尧、茂兰、洞塘、瑶庆、立化、佳荣6个乡煤炭管理站，属县矿业管理办公室和县乡镇企业局的派出机构。1991年“建并撤”后，建立乡镇企业管理站。1995年4月，成立县煤炭工业局，与县乡镇企业局合并办公，并明确县乡镇企业局、县煤炭工业局的主要职能。2001年11月，征费管理职能下放在各乡（镇）设立的乡镇企业管理站。2003年8月，县煤矿安全生产监督管理局与县乡镇企业局、县煤炭工业局合并，设立煤炭执法监察大队。2004年1月，撤销县煤矿安全生产监督管理局，其职能转入县煤炭工业管理局。2005年4月，撤销县乡镇企业局（煤炭工业管理局）下属的县煤矿安全生产监督管理站（煤炭监察大队），其煤矿安全生产监督管理职能划入县安全生产监督管理局。

县物价局 1978年，县物价工作由县计委负责，设物价组。1981年8月建立县物价局。1984

年，下设物价检查所，为副科级事业单位。1994年1月，县物价局并入县工商行政管理局，对外仍使用县物价局公章，挂县物价局牌子，内设物价股，保留物价检查所。1998年8月，恢复县物价局建制。2004年5月，县政府成立县煤炭价格调节基金管理委员会，办公室设在县物价局。2007年4月，物价检查所更名为价格监督检查局。

县旅游事业管理局 1990年，成立县旅游局。1994年1月，改为县旅游事业局。2002年1月，县旅游事业局更名为县旅游事业管理局。1999年2月，荔波樟江风景名胜区管理处与县旅游局合并，实行两块牌子、一套人员合署办公，荔波樟江风景名胜区管理处定名为中国荔波樟江风景名胜区管理处，属荔波县政府领导下的副县级事业单位。2002年6月，成立荔波县旅游发展委员会。2003年5月，县旅游发展委员会下设办公室，为副县级机构，主管全县旅游发展工作。

县扶贫开发办公室 1986年，成立县扶贫项目开发领导小组，在县政府办公室设扶贫办公室。1992年，建立县贫困地区经济开发领导小组办公室，履行扶贫项目开发职责。1996年3月，将项目开发办公室和招商引资办公室并入扶贫办公室，实行三块牌子、一套人员合署办公。是年4月，县贫困地区经济开发领导小组办公室更名为县扶贫开发领导小组办公室。是年9月，县扶贫开发领导小组办公室更名为县扶贫开发办公室，为正科级机构；2002年，县政府明确县扶贫开发办公室为政府常设议事机构，保留招商引资职能。是年，县政府成立农业综合开发办公室，与扶贫开发办公室合署办公。

中国樟江风景名胜区管理处 1991年7月，成立县喀斯特森林风景名胜区管理处，为副科级机构。1992年6月，更名为荔波樟江风景名胜区管理处。1999年2月，定名为中国荔波樟江风景名胜区管理处，升格为副县级事业单位，与县旅游事业管理局合署办公。

县档案局 1986年2月，成立县档案局，与县档案馆实行局馆合一，至2008年机构不变。

县农业办公室 1990年2月，成立荔波县农村经济委员会。1991年1月，农经委与县委农村工作部合署办公。1994年4月，农工部与农经委合并组建为荔波县农村工作委员会，属政府系列。1996年12月，农村工作委员会更名为荔波县农业办公室。

畜牧水产局 1978年，县畜牧机构隶属县农业局。1980年，设立县畜牧局。1984年年底，县畜牧局与县农业局合并为县农牧局。1991年，建镇并乡撤区后，在新设立的17个乡（镇）设立畜牧兽医站。1997年3月，恢复县畜牧局。2002年，县畜牧局又并入县农业局。2003年6月，畜牧工作从农业局分离，设立畜牧水产局。2008年，县畜牧水产局内设机构有法规股和畜牧执法大队，直管17个乡（镇）畜牧兽医（水产）站。

县遗产办 2006年4月，成立县自然遗产办公室，至2008年机构不变。

县安监局 2004年8月，成立县安全生产监督管理局，将县卫生局的职业卫生监督检查和危险化学品经营资格审查、登记、发证的职能划归县安监局。2005年4月，将县经贸局的安全生产综合监督管理职能划入县安监局，县安委会办公室并入县安监局，加挂县安全生产委员会办公室牌子。同时，县乡镇企业局（县煤炭局）的煤矿安全生产监督管理职能划入县安监局，县公安局的烟花爆竹生产经营单位安全生产监督管理职能划归县安监局。县安监局、县安全生产委员会办公室正式挂牌。至2008年，机构不变。

县招商引资局 1995年7月，成立县招商引资办公室，与县扶贫办、县项目办合署办公。2004年10月，招商引资机构单列，建立县招商引资局，内设办公室、综合股、业务股、外来投资者投诉中心及行政服务中心。2008年，实有工作人员12人。

县供销合作联社 1978年前已建立县供销合作社。1983年，县供销合作社改为县供销合作社联合社，至2008年未变。

第三节　区、乡（镇）机构

一、区及公社管理机构（1978—1990年）

1978年12月，根据省革委《关于政权派出机构和企事业单位不再设革命委员会的通知》精神，撤销城关区、朝阳区、茂兰区、甲良区4个区革命委员会，恢复区公所。各区公所设区长1人、副区长1～2人，其任免由县委负责，实行委派制。区公所设秘书、司法助理员、民政助理员、武装部部长、妇女主任、青年干事各1人。区公所下属机构有财政所、供销社、银行营业所、税务所、工商所、林业站、教育组、卫生院、水管所、公安派出所、粮管所、兽医站、农业技术推广站、文化站和广播站。

1980年4月以后，撤销区、公社革委会。全县24个社、镇先后召开社员代表大会，宣布废止革命委员会，恢复公社、镇管理委员会，选举管理委员会组成人员。

1983年12月，城关区管理委员会改为玉屏区管理委员会，城关镇管理委员会改为玉屏镇管理委员会，城关公社管理委员会改为时来公社管理委员会。1984年4月，茂兰公社划分为茂兰、立化、瑶庆3个公社后，分别成立茂兰、立化、瑶庆3个公社管理委员会。5月，玉屏镇升格为区级镇，镇管理委员会直属县政府领导。

1984年4—6月，全县5个区（镇）、25个乡先后召开人民代表大会，改社、镇管理委员会为乡（镇）人民政府。选举乡（镇）长、副乡（镇）长。其中，经贵州省政府批准，成立瑶庆、水维、岜鲜、永康、水利、水尧6个水族乡政府和瑶山、瑶麓两个瑶族乡政府。乡政府设乡长1人，副乡长1人或2人，秘书、武装部部长各1人。同时，建立基层群众性自治组织村民委员会，设主任、妇女委员、调解委员各1人。村民委员会下辖村民小组。

二、乡镇机构（1990—2008年）

1991年7月，实施建镇并乡撤区后，撤销4个区管委会，时来乡、王蒙乡、朝阳乡、茂兰乡、立化乡、瑶庆乡、水维乡、岜鲜乡、甲站乡、地莪乡、觉巩乡、阳凤乡12个乡分别并入玉屏镇、朝阳镇、瑶山瑶族乡、甲良镇、播尧乡、茂兰镇。至此，荔波县政府延伸机构增加为5镇12乡（其中6个民族乡）共17个乡（镇）政府。

乡（镇）政府领导班子每届任期3年。属于县政府的局级建制。同时，县直部门中的财政、税务、土管、公安、农牧、民政、教育、卫生、广播、文化、计划生育等机构延伸到乡（镇），配备专职人员开展工作。

2000年3月，撤销佳荣水族乡和乡政府，建立佳荣镇及镇政府。

至2008年，县政府辖6镇11乡（其中5个民族乡）共17个乡（镇）人民政府。

第二章 施政纪要

第一节 重要会议

一、全体会议

县政府全体会议由政府组成人员出席，必要时由政府办通知有关乡（镇）和有关非政府组成部门的负责人列席会议。全体会议一般由县长或常务副县长主持召开。一般情况下，政府全体会议每半年举行一次，特殊情况下可以提前或延期召开。全体会议的议题主要是研究和决定县政府工作中的重大决策、重大事项，制定发展目标等。

历年全体会议议定的重大决策、重大事项有：

1981年7月，全体会议要求全县各公社（镇）落实划定林业“三定”（稳定山权林权、划定自留山、确定林业生产责任制）任务。

1982年3月，召开全体会议，传达省政府批准水甫石棺墓群为省级文物保护单位；邓恩铭故居为省级重点文物保护单位。

1983年5月，洞塘公社洞腊大队与广西环江县河顿大队因交界处土地归属纠纷发生争议引起互相斗殴，县政府召开会议决定，由广西环江县、荔波县、五县联防办公室三方派出代表，共同调查协调解决。

1983年7月24—26日，在荔波县召开两省（区）煤田开发会商会。会议商定了煤田开发范围等12个问题。确定红茂矿务局向荔波交资源补偿费和提供荔波紧缺物资等事宜。

1984年2月28日，在全体会议上传达县委、县政府《关于延长责任田土承包期至2000年不变的决定》。

1985年8月，县政府全体会议研究召开第一个教师节庆祝大会，向在荔波县境内外县籍任教15年、荔波籍任教20年以上的先进教师个人颁发荣誉证书，对5人以上从教家庭颁发“教师之家”奖状。

1986年，国务院公布荔波为国家级贫困县后，政府研究确定扶贫方案。

1987年9月，县政府全体会议决定动工兴建瑶麓人畜饮水工程（1990年6月竣工）。

1989年，政府召开会议，建立县直机关支农联系点制度并确定各单位在乡（镇）的支农联系点，开展全县性扶贫工作。

1990年11月，县政府全体会议作出“七年消灭荒山，十年绿化荔波”的决定并要求各区、乡（镇）主要负责人与县政府签订绿化承包责任状。

1991年6月17—20日，全体会议主要分片检查农业生产“双抢”工作完成情况、农业适用技术推广及科技兴农情况、办示范点情况等，总结各区、乡在“双抢”工作和科技兴农、农业适用技术推广经验，并进行评比。

1993年12月12日，召开政府全体会议，传达州委全委扩大会议精神，并就完成和超额完成当年财税征收任务，提高财政收入基数作重要讲话。同时，会议还对“两费”和乡（镇）收取的煤炭生产扶持基金、生产发展基金的上解作详细规定。

1994年4月21—22日，召开全县工业会议。会议主要传达全州工业会议精神，总结上年工业生产情况，分析当前工业生产形势，研究部署1994年的工业生产任务。

1995年5月4日，召开全县煤炭工作会议。通报了1995年第一季度全县煤炭生产任务完成情况，布置第二、第三、第四季度工作。

8月30日，召开全县粮食定购和农业税征收工作会议。会议传达省、州有关文件精神，部署1995年秋粮入库和农业税征收工作，表彰上年度秋粮入库先进单位。

1996年5月15日，召开全县“双抢”工作会，贯彻省委、省政府5月13日召开的“双抢”电话会议精神，通报当前的生产形势，部署“双抢”工作。

12月20日，召开全县冬季农业工作会议。会议对全县上年冬是年春的农田基本建设工作进行回顾，对是年冬下年春的农田基本建设工作进行部署。会上组织讨论《关于大力发展商品牛羊的决定》。

1997年3月7日，召开了荔波县农村工作会议。传达贯彻全州农村工作会议精神，并对全县1997年度的农业和农村工作进行部署。县政府与17个乡（镇）领导签订了《耕地保护责任书》《杂交玉米营养袋（块）育苗定向移栽责任状》《水稻宽窄行规范化栽培责任状》《畜禽防疫双轨目标管理责任状》。

1998年3月，部署瑶山扶贫3年计划实施工作。

2000年1月、6月，全体会议先后研究《关于加快发展全县农业产业化经营的意见》《关于荔波县今后三年扶贫开发与小康建设的实施意见》。

2001年2月13日，召开县四家班子领导和有关部门负责人参加的关于申报“世界遗产地”前期工作会议，同意申报“世界自然遗产地”并成立申报“世界自然遗产地”工作领导小组及其办公室。会议强调要加大宣传力度，做好“申遗”的规划工作。

2002年12月24日，全体会议传达省委办公厅、省政府办公厅《关于划定荔波县为革命老区的通知》。

2003年2月，县政府全体会议研究部署在春节期间县城开展“盛世灯火映樟江”大型灯展活动有关事宜。

12月，全体会议研究根据州政府领导的意见，同意将大七孔电站移交给黔南广能电力有限责任公司。

2004年8月，全体会议研究决定，为全县贫困高中生、初中生和小学生发放助学金。是月30日，县政府举行贫困学生助学奖励基金颁发大会，对1217名学生进行救助，资金总计26万元。

2006年3月，全体会议讨论通过《关于深入开展普法和依法治县工作第五个五年规划的决定》。

7月，政府全体会议召集涉旅部门负责人研究“中国南方喀斯特”申遗事项的有关事宜和外国专家赴荔波进行模拟考察事宜。

2008年3月，经全体会议讨论决定《关于加强农业基础建设促进农业发展、农民增收的意见》。

10月31日—11月7日，县境普降大暴雨，为历史上深秋大暴雨的唯一记录。县政府全体会议研究决定立即开展抗洪抢险救灾的措施。

二、政府常务会议

县政府常务会议由县长、副县长、办公室主任组成。会议由县长或由县长委托常务副县长召集和主持。必要时，由县委、县政府确定与议题有关科局负责人列席会议。一般情况下每两月召开一次，特殊情况可以提前或延期召开。议题一般由县政府办公室主任根据县长或常务副县长的指示确定会议内容，会后，根据会议讨论的决定事项形成会议纪要并印发。

常务会议的主要议题：传达贯彻党中央、国务院、省州党委和政府及县委的重要指示、决定和命令；讨论和通过提请县人民代表大会及其常委会审议的报告和议案，研究执行县人代会及其常委会的决定；讨论和审定向省、州党委和政府的重要请示、报告；讨论各乡（镇）、各工作部门请示县政府决定的重要事项；准备县政府全体会议的议题；分析形势、通报重要情况；讨论决定县政府工作中的其他重要问题。

历年常务会议讨论决定的重要事项有：

1983年10月，召开常务会议传达省政府黔府通217号文件《贵州广西两省（区）关于红茂矿务局在荔波境内开发煤田若干问题的会商纪要的通知》，对实施该纪要的具体问题进一步安排和落实。

1984年2月，召开常务会议传达中央文件《关于延长农民责任田土承包期为20年不变》的精神。

1985年4月，县政府常务会议决定在全县范围内征收农林特产税，并颁布实施办法。

5月2日，县政府召开第31次常务会议，讨论修改评选县劳模暂行条例；讨论修改县政府廉政建设的决定。

1986年10月，常务会议研究部署全县工业普查工作的有关事宜，要求一年内完成工作任务。

1987年6月，召开常务会议，具体落实县委、县政府“依靠省州、面向两广，开发山区，兴县富民”发展全县经济的战略决策。

1988年2月，县政府研究决定，抽调部分科（局）长和农技干部下乡帮助农民大种烤烟。

1989年1月，县委、县政府决定在全县建立县机关支农联系点制度。同时县城开展创建省级卫生县城活动。

6月13日，召开第32次常务会议，学习党中央、国务院《告全体共产党员和全国人民书》《邓小平同志在军以上干部会议上的讲话》精神，研究政府下一步工作打算。

1990年1月，政府部署落实县委决定两年内实现第二个经济翻番，重点抓好“粮、煤、林”的稳定增长。7月，常务会议布置落实省委、省政府《关于开展建镇并乡撤区工作的指示》和县委《关于荔波县开展建镇并乡撤区工作的安排意见》。

1992年7月，传达省政府批准将荔波喀斯特森林风景名胜区更名为荔波樟江风景名胜区，同时，研究建立荔波县旅游开发区的有关事宜。

1993年4月，政府常务会议布置对遭受冰雹大风受灾地区群众的救援工作。

1994年1月，常务会议安排落实国家“八七”扶贫攻坚计划。

1995年12月，召开常务会议，研究成立荔波县教育基金会。

1996年4月7日，召开常务会议，研究全县税费征收管理站、产销管理和实施事宜。会议针对检查站内部存在的一些问题制定了措施，研究县政府办《关于批转平寨煤炭税费征收管理所对税费征收站违纪违章处罚暂行实施细则的通知》，要求各乡（镇）、站所加强职工教育，加强内部管理，堵塞税费流失，为财政增长做贡献。

12月，县政府常务会议研究加强农田基本建设、表彰先进单位和个人等工作（含绿化造林、冬修水利、以工代赈、坡改梯工程、畜禽防疫等）。

是年，深圳市委、市政府对荔波县进行对口帮扶，县政府在常务会议上多次研究深圳对荔波贫困乡（镇）的教育卫生、农业设施开发等扶贫项目的落实措施。

1998年4月16日，荔波发生4.9级地震，县政府召开紧急会议，部署对受灾群众进行抢险救灾工作。

11月2日，经常务会议讨论后，县政府公布《关于实施稳定和完善农村土地承包关系的工作方案》，从1994年起，耕地承包期再延长50年，非耕地资源开发使用期再延长60年。是年，在全县农村颁发了土地经营权证书。

1999年，常务会议多次研究《关于创建生态县、公园县的决定》《关于创建科技先进县的决定》《关于进一步加强农业和农村工作的决定》《关于农村税费制度改革的实施方案》；研究部署冬修水利、坡改梯、绿化造林、农情信息网络实施、病虫害综合防治等农业和农村工作。

2000年7月13日，县政府常务会议研究整治樟江河遭受特大洪灾后的“白色污染”问题。之后组织茂兰保护处、樟江风景处和环保、国土、林业、水电、建设等有关部门以及玉屏镇、朝阳镇、瑶山乡，召开“保护母亲河”行动规划会，确定樟江流域内的环境保护、绿化规划、防污排污、桥梁建设、河道开发等事宜的落实。

11月24日，召开常务会，研究《荔波县旅游发展规划》编制工作。

2001年7月13日，政府常务会议研究关于樟江北路安居工程建设和荔（波）—大（哨坡）公路二期工程的落实事宜。之后，两个工程相继开工建设。

2002年10月，县政府常务会议议定向州政府提出申报世界自然遗产的请示；讨论研究全县林业工作暨强化樟江沿岸林业生态建设的落实措施。

11月，县政府常务会议议定向省政府申遗办公室提出申遗事宜。

2003年4月29日，召开常务会议，落实“非典”防治工作。

6月，常务会议研究决定，由县政府发出《关于加快旅游发展的决定》《关于鼓励和扶持旅游商品开发经营的若干规定》《关于招商引资的奖励办法》。

8月，县政府常务会议研究，同意在县城举办“中国·荔波绿宝石之旅暨贵州少数民族服饰展演”活动以及相关措施。

2004年1月29日，常务会议研究，在全县做好高致病性禽流感防治工作，要求各乡（镇）有关部门组织抓好落实，建立疫情报告制度，在佳荣、立化、洞塘、瑶山、播尧等地设立检查站，杜绝外省（区）禽类进入县境。

2005年1月1日，常务会议传达执行国家免征农业税政策。

5月，常务会议研究“两基”验收申报事宜。

2006年1月9日，常务会议研究在全县农村开展新型合作医疗的相关事宜。会议决定在完善乡镇合医办机构的基础上，要求半月内完成65%的参合率目标。

2007年6月27日，由贵州荔波、云南石林、重庆武隆捆绑申报的“中国南方喀斯特”世界自然遗产项目，在联合国教科文组织第31届世界遗产大会上获全票通过的当日，政府召开紧急常务会议，研究召开庆祝大会事宜。

7月，政府常务会议研究部署第二届贵州旅游产业发展大会的有关事宜，要求各级各部门同心协力为开好这次大会努力工作，涉旅部门进入有效工作程序。

2008年1月中旬，全县遭受强冷冻天气侵袭，县政府于1月20日召开紧急常务会议，部署抗凝救灾工作。

5月19日，四川汶川大地震发生后，县政府召开紧急常务会议，部署动员全县人民向地震灾区捐款捐物工作。

8月4日，召开常务会议，传达省委十届三次会议和州政府二次全体会议精神。会议强调，牢固树立科学发展观，推进“旅游兴县、旅游强县、旅游富县”发展战略，促进经济社会跨越式发展。会议还对职工住房增量补贴、农村低保、危房改造、高考和教育成果奖励、糖蔗种植奖励等议题进行讨论。

三、县长办公会议

县长办公会议由县长、分管工作的副县长和办公室主任组成，必要时政府办分管副主任参会。根据会议内容和议题，由办公室通知相关部门和相关乡（镇）负责人列席。会议由县长或县长委托的副县长主持召开。一般情况下，会议每半月至少举行一次。

县长办公会议主要议题是研究处理县政府日常工作中的重要问题，提出解决办法；通报政府近期工作情况、主要任务和安排近期工作等有关事宜；讨论决定各乡（镇）政府和县属各工作部门有关呈报给县政府的重要请示、报告和请求事项等问题；协调和处理县政府与有关部门的重要工作。

提交县长办公会议讨论的问题，由分管副县长确定。会议讨论决定事项，由政府办公室编写纪要，会议主持人签字。其议定事项的执行，由政府办负责督查督办。

历年县长办公会讨论决定的重要事项：

1984年8月，卫生部赴贵州丝虫病考核调查组，对荔波进行考核，县长办公会议上听取考核调查结论通报，全县经血液调查3620人，未发现微丝蚴阳性。卫生部确认，荔波县达到基本消灭丝虫病目标。

1985年4月25日，召开办公会议传达《荔波县征收农林特产税实施办法》。

1986年11月22日，召开办公会议，研究讨论全县普及初等教育事宜。

1988年4月4日，县长办公会议研究兴修小七孔二级水电站有关事宜，初步规划为1989年7月全面施工，1990年年底基本建成，1991年正式投产，总装机为1000千瓦×2机组。

1989年3月，办公会传达学习中共十三届四中全会公报和中央领导讲话精神；传达县委《关于加强自身廉政建设的决定》《荔波县执行贵州省计划生育施行条例》。

1990年10月，在办公会上通报兴修小七孔—麻尾、佳荣—广西驯乐公路有关事宜。

1991年1月，县长办公会对县政府《关于在全县实施“温饱工程”的通知》进行安排。

1992年3月16日，就建设部专家考察荔波喀斯特森林风景名胜区召开办公会，部署接待、景区规划、考核内容等事项。

1993年8月17日，召开会议，研究程控电话配套资金、交通经费补助、武装民兵训练补助等问题。

1994年6月21日，召开全县工资制度改革工作会议，部署全县机关、事业单位工资制度改革实施工作。

1995年3月1日，荔波与广西红茂矿务局就恢复立化镇十二索矿井的开采事宜，通过县长办公会议进行协商。经过双方协商，达成共识形成纪要。荔波同意和支持红茂矿务局恢复建十二索矿井（后改称高荣矿），原矿区内荔波6个单位已取得采矿权，故重新划定十二索矿井，同时要求做好环境保护工作。明确从1995年1月1日起，原煤补贴费（含资源补偿费）按7元/吨标准执行。

1996年7月，县政府召集职能部门参加县长办公会议，研究部署创建省级卫生县城的方案，制定创建规划、奖惩办法、治理脏乱差措施等。

1997年7月13日，在瑶山召开瑶山扶贫攻坚项目现场办公会议。县四套班子及有关科局领导到会。会议议定，瑶山乡所实施的扶贫项目要结合本乡实际，要覆盖到所有农户，做到村村有林场、户户有果园、家家搞养殖；以物作贷，以物还贷，与农户签订合同；项目覆盖农户每户至少有1000元的扶贫项目资金；成立瑶山扶贫开发公司，负责组织实施。

1998年1月18日，召开县长办公会，讨论研究关于水尧乡大道建设有关问题。决定该工程总投资119万元。大道建设中涉及的征地问题采取公路建设用地处理，工程采取议标形式进行施工，由县交通建设开发公司第二工程处负责承建。

4月11日，在办公会上传达县委、县政府《关于开发荔波县樟江蜜柚的实施意见（1998—2000）》《关于招商引资及争取县外无偿资金的奖励办法》。

1999年3月10日，县长办公会讨论县力达工贸中心建设问题，决定在樟江大街农机厂原址新建工贸中心市场，要求项目建设于翌年4月底前竣工投入使用。

5月17日上午，巴合煤矿3号井瓦检员在清理整改维修巷道时操作失误，引起瓦斯燃烧事故，造成死亡10人、重伤1人、轻伤1人的重特大安全事故。县政府召开紧急办公会议，立即布置抢救及处理缮后工作。

2000年6月19日，召开县长办公会议，议定同意将轻工局房屋划拨给邓恩铭烈士故居，用于烈士故居的改建、扩建；同意把县城有线电视系统和县城官塘坡电视差转台房地产划拨给县有线电视中心，但资产性质不变。

7月27日，召开县长办公会，布置政府机关“讲学习、讲政治、讲正气”为主要内容的“三讲”教育活动。

2001年7月31日，召开办公会议，布置北街安居工程、荔大公路二期工程、县政府大院绿化工程等实施事宜。

2002年4月1日，召开办公会议，听取各位副县长汇报各自分管工作情况。研究决定同意解决玉屏镇居委会成员补贴，同意玉屏镇建设村筹建服务中心大楼，不减免税金；同意公开拍卖县经贸局宿舍区面积约130平方米的空地，拍卖所得拨给经贸局支付办公楼欠款，如有结余作县财政收入；同意制定《荔波县科学技术进步奖励办法》；同意拍卖县百货公司老十字街7个门市，拍卖收入用于支付百货公司所欠银行贷款，但不能减免税费。

7月10日，县政府召开党组成员及县长办公会议，传达州政府全体（扩大）会议精神，讨论通过《荔波县2002—2010年煤炭生产开发规划》《荔波县以工代赈十年规划建设项目》《关于加快老城区改造的决定》。

9月18日，召开办公会议，传达州政府第四次全体会议精神，主要是对前9个月的工作进行总结和对后3个月的工作进行部署。这次办公会还对樟江沿河生态建设、公路沿线沙石场的管理、小七孔景区公路环线等工作进行研究部署。

12月，县长办公会决定，组织人力开展全县大规模打击非法盗采国家煤炭资源集中整治行动，布置炸封非法小煤井343口。

2003年2月，办公会议讨论《政府工作报告（征求意见稿）》。

9月6日，召开办公会议，讨论事项为关于解决时来引水渠整修经费问题；引进资金修建县林业局办公房和新建县幼儿园的问题；关于国土局拍卖农贸市场在建宾馆的问题；关于荔大公路有关问题；关于全县煤炭销售管理工作的有关问题；关于对粮食购销公司资产处置方案。

2004年2月18日，召开办公会，研究关于景区特许经营权转让、文体广电局购置演出音响和灯光设备、盘活粮食局“金谷大厦”资产以及县行政服务中心的开发建设问题。

2005年1月16日，召开办公会，传达州政府《关于行政机关、工作人员行政效能投诉和告诫暂行规定》《关于行政机关、工作人员行政过错责任追究办法》《黔南州行政效能考评暂行规定》

《黔南州政府部门行政首长问责制暂行办法》等；研究调整副县长工作分工；解决独荔公路征用地补偿问题；解决职工医疗保险费筹资渠道问题；解决荔三公路占地补偿问题。

2006年1月18日，召开办公会，专题讨论荔波县“十一五”计划纲要和全县2006年社会发展基本项目计划；研究解决农村独生子女户、双女结扎户、五保户和特困户参加农村医疗改革，同意个人资金部分由政府支付。

2月15日，召开办公会，审定《荔波县国民经济和社会发展第十一个五年计划纲要（草案）》。

11月7日，召开县长办公会议，讨论《政府工作报告》；讨论县水泥厂改制、荔波二中建设、住房公积金贷款清收以及申报世界自然遗产环境整治及基础设施建设项目进行可行性研究。

2007年5月25日，召开办公会，议题有解决小七孔电站拆除后人员安置问题；原县建筑公司和樟江食品公司改制问题；乡（镇）财政收支管理体制问题；讨论通过“中国南方喀斯特”申报世界自然遗产荔波提名地环境综合整治以及2006年技术支撑项目协议书等事宜。

6月24日下午，县长办公会讨论时来坝片区修建性详细规划防洪问题，分别对时来坝片区20年一遇、30年一遇和50年一遇3种情况的防洪标高进行研究核实。

7月2日，召开办公会议，议定关于安全生产问题；关于调整煤炭税费征收标准问题；关于城镇土地使用税问题；关于参股筹建黔南州信用担保机构问题；关于煤矿井下作业人员意外伤亡保险问题；关于安装视频监视系统问题；关于清退农村社会养老保险费问题；关于机关事业单位职工医疗保险筹资比例问题；关于清退机关事业单位养老保险费问题；关于实施农村居民最低生活保障制度问题；关于2007年度审计项目计划问题；关于三都至荔波或独山至荔波高速公路线路走向问题等。

7月21日，召开办公会议，研究新设煤矿等相关问题。会上学习州政府办《关于进一步加强当前安全生产工作的紧急通知》，并对县内8个民用煤矿的建设、当前煤矿安全生产、民爆物品的押运等问题进行分析讨论并形成决议。

2008年1月22日，召开办公会，讨论修改《政府工作报告（初稿）》；研究2008年财政预算安排方案；通报第二届贵州省旅发大会有关事宜；关于集体林权制度改革；关于安置房建设；关于世界自然遗产地退耕还林补偿问题。

10月30日，召开办公会议，贯彻落实省政府省长林树森10月15日在省监察厅《关于呈报〈关于荔波县九曲湾糖厂问题的初查报告〉》上所作的重要批示。议定按照批示要求，对项目善后有关工作进行部署安排，从根本上消除隐患，确保稳定。

四、政府专题会议

政府专题会议是县长、常务副县长或分管副县长对解决某一事项专门召开的会议，一般由县政府办公室根据研究事项的急缓安排会议日期和议程。专题会议由县政府常务会议组成人员或办公室副主任召集和主持。根据会议内容通知政府有关部门和乡（镇）领导参加。专题会议开会时间，可根据工作需要确定。专题会议研究处理县政府日常工作中具体业务问题，即听取有关工作情况汇报或通报有关工作情况；部署近期某项工作；研究处理各乡（镇）或政府工作部门向县政府专题请示的问题；协调有关部门需要解决的问题；研究处理部门工作中具体的业务问题。

专题会议的组织工作由县政府办公室负责。会议纪要由主持人签发。专题会议决定的事项，由县政府办公室督查督办。

重大专题会议有：

1990年3月6日，县政府召开专题会“关于应昂联办煤矿投资事项”专题会议，研究落实开发措施。

12月3日，县政府召开1990年冬1991年春水利建设专题会议，讨论研究水利建设实施项目，确保按质按量完成建设工作任务。

1991年1月3日，召开全县旅游工作会议，就申报国家级风景名胜区景点建设和旅游宣传，以及旅游接待等工作进行研究，对开发景区旅游资源提出构想。

1月8日，召开全县卫生行政工作会议，贯彻落实州政府关于脊髓灰质炎疫苗强化免疫电话会议精神，集中精力搞好全县第一轮脊髓灰质炎疫苗强化免疫工作。

1月17日，县政府和贵阳铁路分局就贵州铁路旅行社在荔波建设旅游宾馆事宜召开专题会议。经过协商，双方就旅游宾馆建设原则、选址、土地征用、管理权限、小七孔铁索桥建设及相关的一些具体问题达成共识，形成纪要。这是首家县外企业到荔波投资参与旅游资源的开发。

4月23—24日，县政府召开煤炭生产经营厂家和检查站会议，主要传达贯彻荔政〔1991〕15号《关于加强对公路运输渠道原煤税费征收管理的通知》。

8月6—7日，召开全县煤炭工作会议。会议贯彻全州工业会议精神，部署落实抓紧抓好原煤生产和销售，清理“三角债”货款等。

1992年2月27日，县政府召开工业经济专题研讨会，对县经委职能及工业经济发展提出新思路。

6月17日，召开全县铁路治安综合治理会议，贯彻《中华人民共和国铁路法》《铁路运输安全保护条例》。会议决定建立荔波县铁路治安综合治理领导小组，要求沿线乡（镇）、村成立相应机构，认真搞好铁路治安工作。会议决定出台《荔波县政府关于整顿铁路治安秩序的通告》。

9月8日，县政府召开关于樟江大街二期工程质量专题会，研究落实路面标高质量等存在问题。

11月6日，县政府召开全县计免工作会议。贯彻落实州政府11月5日召开的关于搞好第二轮脊髓灰质炎强化免疫电话会议精神，部署全县计免工作。

1993年2月21日，荔波县政府、广西环江县政府就两地水泥厂联合经营荔波县水泥厂问题召开会议。双方经过充分协商，达成联合经营的协议，并形成会议纪要。

5月18日，县政府召开全县煤炭安全生产工作会议，布置1993年煤炭安全生产工作。

7月11日，县政府召开全县计免保偿工作会议，总结全县计免保偿工作经验，部署落实计免保偿工作任务，迎接全州计免保偿工作经验交流会在荔波召开。

10月26日，县政府召开全县教育工作会议。要求着力抓好“双教”（普教和农教）工作，迎接省州验收。针对对全县复查发现的10个方面的问题进行安排整改。

11月18日，县政府召开全县第二次消灭脊髓灰质炎强化免疫工作会议，传达全州计划免疫工作会议精神，贯彻落实国务院召开的消灭脊髓灰质炎强化免疫活动月的电话会议精神。

12月25日，召开全县农村社会养老保险工作会，贯彻省政府和全州农村社会养老保险工作会议精神。

1995年3月20日，县政府召开关于确定普洛段营业税纳税地点和大沙坡工程建设专题会议，落实有关实施措施。

5月9日，县政府召开全县文化工作会议，贯彻全州文化工作会议精神，研究部署全县文化部门实施“九五”计划。

1996年5月6日，县政府召开全县国土资源管理工作会议，传达贯彻省州土管、矿管、环保工作会议精神，部署1996年国土资源管理工作任务。

6月7日，县政府召开全县清理检查预算外资金工作动员会议。会议传达全省、全州清理检查预算外资金工作会议精神，部署全县清理检查预算外资金工作事宜。

1997年1月24日，县政府召开荔波县教育工作会议，传达全州教育工作会议精神，总结1996年荔波教育工作，布置1997年工作任务。县政府与各乡（镇）签订1997年工作目标责任状。

5月8日，县政府召开全县文化工作会议。会议主要是贯彻落实省、州文化、宣传、文联工作会议精神，布置1997年文化工作。

5月17日，县政府召开全县煤炭安全生产工作会议。主要是总结1996年的煤炭安全生产工作，研究部署1997年全县煤炭安全生产工作。

1998年10月30日，县政府召开开发建设县城农贸综合市场专题会议。决定由县房地产开发公司筹资兴建，建好后工商部门参与管理。

1999年4月14日、4月27日、5月3日，县政府先后召开关于煤炭产运销问题专题会议，主要内容有建立煤炭促销队伍；加强对站台经营秩序的管理；采取“双让利和两保护”的政策加强原煤的运销；加大对原煤的打假力度，提高荔波煤炭在“两广”的信誉。

2000年6月，荔波遭受50年一遇大洪灾，7月6日，县政府组织召开县直有关部门及乡（镇）、村党政领导关于清理樟江河白色污染、荔小公路绿化用地和樟江沿河吊桥修复等有关问题会议。对洪水损毁的樟江沿河吊桥进行修复，以解决沿河岸群众生产生活的实际困难。同时治理白色污染。

6月21日，都匀供电局、县政府及有关部门负责人召开关于建设荔波茂兰110千伏变电站事宜专题会议，议定拟建110千伏茂兰变电站，选址茂兰镇浪炳原；县政府承诺所选站址用地征拨包干费不超过8000元/亩，荒山、石山免费征拨；县政府负责提供茂兰镇电力负荷发展规划及工业小区规划等资料，并保证变电站生活用水及消防用水；都匀供电局负责上报省电力公司并立即开展变电站及输电线路的勘测设计工作；变电站年内动工建设，争取于2002年8月竣工投入运行。

2001年8月15日，县政府就县会计核算中心成立运作等有关事宜召开专题会议，对增加财政收入、控制财政支出、加强预算外资金管理、制止铺张浪费和治理“三乱”、私设“小金库”等违纪行为提出要求。

10月7日，召开荔波机场开工筹备专题会，研究拆迁事宜和开工庆典活动有关事宜。

2002年6月18日，县政府召开农口系统负责人会议，要求各部门努力寻求农业农村发展的新思路，积极调整农业产业结构，要找准新的切入点，努力培植经济增长的新亮点，促使农民增收、财政增长。

6月25日，县政府召开退耕还林工作专题会，听取县林业局作《荔波县退耕还林工程调查情况》汇报和县粮食局关于《荔波县退耕还林粮食供应实施方案》的汇报。会议议定全县退耕还林粮食兑现粮种为中籼稻谷；退耕还林粮食兑现标准为每亩退耕地每年补助稻谷150公斤；对退耕还林粮食兑现的条件和程序作出了明确规定和要求。

11月13日，县政府召开专题会议，研究茂兰、佳荣两镇人饮及县城防洪堤工程建设问题。会议决定由县自来水公司负责实施茂兰镇人饮工程，年底前开工建设；由县水利局负责实施佳荣镇人饮工程，待县政府与州水利局协商一致后再具体施工；县城防洪堤工程年底前动工，工程设计防洪能力为50年一遇，工程设计要结合创建公园县、生态县的特点，达到合理规划、科学设计、突出特色的要求。

2003年4月4日，县政府召开小七孔景区移民搬迁工作专题会，有关部门和驾欧乡政府参会，就移民搬迁涉及的林木补偿、移民证办理、新居水电安装、新建学校以及坟山征用补偿等问题逐一落实解决。

10月10日，县政府召开打击非法小煤窑专题会议。对全县的非法小煤窑治理工作作出部署并进行清理。

是日，召开卫生工作会议，一是解决县疾控中心业务用房的建设问题；二是决定将县中医院、县保健站合并组建成为一所具有民族特色、功能较为齐全和初具现代化的“荔波县第二人民医院”，院址建在时来坝开发新区。

2004年1月12日，县政府召开专题会，研究清理拖欠工程款和拖欠民工工资问题。会议要求各级各部门要认真抓好清欠工作，着重清理和兑现2003年以前拖欠的工程款以及拖欠的农民工工资，做到尽早尽快兑现，确保社会稳定。

1月29日，县政府召开高致病性禽流感防治工作专题会，传达《省人民政府办公厅转发国务院办公厅〈关于加强高致病性禽流感防治工作的紧急通知〉》精神，分析县境禽流感防治工作所面临的严峻形势，要求全县各乡（镇）结合实际，制定和完善各项防范措施，并组织抓好落实；各有关部门要根据各自职责，制定高致病性禽流感防治应急预案，确保一旦发现疫情，能立即投入力量，迅速控制和扑灭疫情。会议决定在与广西接壤的佳荣、立化、洞塘、瑶山、播尧等乡（镇）设立检查站，实行24小时值班制度，坚决堵住外来疫区的禽类进入县境。

6月16日，县政府召开专题会议，对佳荣镇、茂兰镇人饮工程等问题进行协调。会议还对佳荣镇坤地村与威岩村公益事业建设、农田水利建设等作出决定。

8月11日，县政府召开自来水水源点保护工作专题会，要求对水厂水源点严格进行保护和执法，加强排污监控等事项予以落实。

10月28日，县政府召开消防工作专题会，研究开展全县火灾隐患大整改、大排查、保平安活动，并以县政府文件下发执行。

2005年5月19日，县政府召开旅游工作会议，对导游培训、文化产品开发、冬季旅游推介、民族村寨建设、抗战60周年纪念活动等事项进行研究。

6月13日，县政府召开冬季旅游工作专题会议，围绕冬季旅游“扩景点、强宣传、拓市场”的旅游发展思路，以荔波万亩梅花旅游节活动为载体，以南部旅游（即茂兰自然保护区与红色文化旅游）线路的隆重推出为切入点，以樟江风景名胜区为依托，围绕观梅、赏梅、品梅，全面推动荔波冬季旅游。

10月12日，县政府召开水书抢救工作专题会，对水书抢救原则，申报“世界非物质文化遗产”，研究破译及其保护等事项进行落实。

2006年1月19日，县政府召开新型农村合作医疗工作专题会，研究提高全县新型农村合作医疗参合率措施（2005年年底全县农村参合率仅20.84%），要求在完善乡（镇）合医办组织机构的基础上，要确保在1月25日前完成州下达的65%参合目标。

1月，县政府专题研究举办首届“中国·荔波万亩梅花报春节暨原生态文化旅游月”活动相关事项。

5月31日，县政府召开关于荔波机场土地征用、补偿专题会，研究解决办法等有关措施。

7月9日，县政府召开加强财政税收工作专题会议，会议强调，在进一步加强财源建设的同时，加强对国有资产经营的管理，加强对非税收入的管理，促进财政增收。会议要求严格支出预算管理，控制或压缩一般性开支，以缓解财政收支矛盾。

2007年1月，县政府召开专题会议，研究举办“中国·荔波万亩梅花报春节暨2007年贵州赏花游首游式”活动有关事项。

3月11日，县政府召开关于时来农贸市场建设工作专题会。会议决定划拨土地用于时来农贸市场建设项目。该项目由玉屏镇政府牵头，做好时来农贸市场的建设和市场运作等相关事宜，以确保该农贸市场发挥出应有的经济效益和社会效益。

9月20日，县政府召开第二届贵州省旅发大会资金管理及相关融资工作专题会，研究落实各种措施。

10月22日，县政府召开全县煤炭生产专题会，要求安监局和煤管局实行安全生产“周报制”，所有煤矿企业实行安全生产“日报制”；要求加大打击非法无证小煤窑的力度，着力抓出成效。

2008年1月17日，县政府召开会议，专题研究向建设银行贷款加快景区与城市建设等有关问题。同日，县政府召开专题会议，研究“荔波荡漾”大型山水实景演出后勤保障、基地项目建设用地等相关问题。

1月，县政府召开专题会议，研究部署第三届“中国·荔波万亩梅花报春节暨2008年贵州赏花游”首游式各项事宜。

1月27日，县政府召开专题会议，研究冰冻期间煤电油运保障工作，要求采取有力措施，做好冰冻期间煤、电、交通运输以及油、气等的保障供应。

3月29日，县政府召开专题会议，研究捞村乡群力村更乱组滑坡地质灾害有关问题。会议要求有关部门要立即采取有效措施，保证地质灾害治理工作按时完成，确保当地人民群众生命财产安全。

8月7日下午，县政府召开关于集体林权制度改革工作专题会，听取县林业局（林改办）对林改工作进展情况的汇报，分析林改工作中存在的困难和问题，对下步林改工作进行安排部署。会议要求严格执行林改政策，规范林改操作程序，进一步加强林地矛盾纠纷调处力度，加强对林改工作的督查和指导。

是月21日，县政府召开专题会议，研究部署贯彻落实全省小煤矿瓦斯治理与综合利用现场会议精神，同时研究岜合煤矿及其他民用煤矿地面建设、供电等问题。

第二节　施政重大决策与绩效

1978年中共十一届三中全会以后，县革委执行中共中央的农村经济政策，在农村实行家庭联产承包责任制，发展农业生产。同时，工业以煤炭为拳头产品，加强原煤产、运、销和安全生产管理。1979年，全县国内生产总值2485万元，比上年增长6.97%；全社会固定资产投资总额93万元，比上年下降9.71%；社会消费品零售总额918万元，比上年增长2.68%；财政总收入144万元，比上年增长13.39%；农民人均纯收入152元，比上年增长6.29%。

1980—1984年，县政府按照中共中央“调整、改革、整顿、提高”和以“计划经济为主，市场调节为辅”的方针，稳定农业生产责任制，充分发挥资源优势，发展粮、林、水电、畜牧业、社队企业生产和商品经济。1984年年末，全县国内生产总值3735万元，比1980年增长36.07%；全社会固定资产投资总额210万元，比1980年增长66.67%；社会消费品零售总额1624万元，比1980年增长65.04%；财政总收入211万元，比1980年增长88.39%；农民人均纯收入208元，比1980年增长23.08%。

1985—1987年，县政府按县委提出的“依靠省州，面向两广，开发山区，兴县富民”的经济发展战略，在抓商品粮基地建设的同时，开发以万亩柑橘和万亩乌梅为重点的果品系列，以5万亩泡桐、3万亩杉木、1万亩泡竹为重点的林产品系列，以猪、牛为主的畜产品系列，以煤炭为重点的矿产品系列，以开发大七孔、小七孔水电为重点的能源建设系列，以综合食品加工为重点的农副产品加工系列，以恢复和发展风猪、凉席、民族土花布为重点的名优特产品系列项目；开展全县种植业、土地资源进行调查，查清各地资源、社会经济条件、特点、优势和潜力，为发展农业生产和经济建设提供依据。县政府与广西煤炭厅、区经委、红茂矿务局、柳州铁路分局以及广东省的一些单位建立协作关系，开展横向经济联系。三年中，全县经济得到发展，至1987年年末，全县国内生产总值4730万元，比1985年增长50.16%；全社会固定资产投资总额142万元，比1985年下降5.23%；社会消费品零售总额2364万元，比1985年增长27.92%；财政总收入319万元，比1985年增长76.24%；农民人均纯收入209元，比1985年增长11.77%。

1988—1989年，县政府贯彻执行国家治理经济环境、整顿经济秩序、全面深化改革的方针，保障改革和建设顺利进行。坚持稳定家庭联产承包责任制，增加农业投入，推广科技兴农，农业和农村工作全面发展，煤炭工业产、供、销稳步增长。至1989年年末，全县国内生产总值8904万元，比1988年增长28.12%；全社会固定资产投资总额281万元，比1988年增长50.27%；社会消费品零售总额2915万元，比1988年增长1.64%；财政总收入953万元，比1988年增长89.84%；农民人均纯收入366元，比1988年增长32.13%。

1990—1992年，县政府先后发出《关于保护樟江两岸防护林的通告》（1991年）、《关于进一步搞好煤炭产运销和安全工作的通知》（1991年）、《关于切实搞好国营煤矿筹建工作，加快巴合煤矿建设的决定》（1991年）、《关于开征农村教育费附加的通知》（1991年）、《关于切实抓好教育工作的通知》（1992年）、《关于修筑县城樟江大街道路的决定》（1992年）、《关于在全县国营流通企业进行“四放开”改革的通知》（1992年）等重要文件。农业农村工作方面，实施“温饱工程”，推行“行政部门包任务、技术部门包技术”的岗位目标责任制，解决贫困人口的温饱问题；制定实施《荔波县渔业捕捞许可证管理实施办法》，保护和合理利用渔业资源。工业方面，清理整顿矿山，封停取缔非法采矿小煤窑、危及交通安全小煤窑、危及永久性建筑小煤窑及污染严重小煤窑等。基础设施建设方面，完成县城樟江大街、水春河旅游便道、朝（阳）—王（蒙）公路改建等重大项目建设，按期建成朝（阳）—麻（尾）公路项目首次获省交通厅公路施工先进县；落实大七孔电站一期工程建设投资渠道。旅游业方面，决定建立荔波旅游开发县，获省政府批准。1992年年末，全县国内生产总值14202万元，比1990年增长52.24%；全社会固定资产投资总额344万元，比1990年增长19.11%；社会消费品零售总额4168万元，比1990年增长34.76%；财政总收入1112万元，比1990年增长5.9%；农民人均纯收入390元，比1990年增长32.65%。

1993—1997年，县政府先后出台《荔波县农村社会养老保险基本方案》（1993年）、《关于加强煤炭生产的意见》（1993年）、《关于推行畜禽防疫双轨目标管理责任制的（试行）意见》（1994年）、《荔波樟江风景名胜区管理暂行办法》（1995年）、《荔波县城镇国有土地使用权出让转让暨土地有偿使用暂行规定》（1995年）、《荔波县城镇市容环境卫生城建监察管理办法》（1997年），发出《关于做好国营工商企业第三轮承包工作的通知》（1993年）、《关于加强粮食市场管理的通知》（1994年）、《关于认真完成教育任务迎接高标准扫盲验收的通知》（1995年）、《关于开展农村社会养老保险工作的通知》（1997年），批转《荔波县实施九年义务教育规划》（1995年）、《荔波县农村实施初级卫生保健规划》（1995年）。农业农村方面，1993年秋粮入库再次名列全州第一，实现“七连冠”；实施国家“八七”扶贫攻坚计划，建立“两瑶”扶贫开发试验区，从1994年起连续3年从财政拨出扶贫启动资金20万元投入“两瑶”扶贫；争取到国家扶贫资金2858万元，改善“两瑶”生产生活条件，被省委、省政府评为扶贫开发县；1995年，全县森林覆盖率达31.72%，与省政府签订的十年绿化荔波的目标提前5年实现；1996年，全县新增已解决温饱的贫困人口27210人，贫困人口由上年的63020人下降到38810人，多数贫困户越过温饱线，成为全省率先解决温饱先进县之一，受省委、省政府表彰；利用深圳商贸投资控股公司捐赠资金100万元，兴建水尧瑶族移民新村，实施移民搬迁70户。工业方面，县城自来水改扩建工程总投资200万元，水质达到合格标准，供水能力成倍增长；县水泥厂与广西都川水泥厂实现联营。基本建设方面，建成大七孔水电站及玉屏、茂兰、播尧、驾欧、朝阳、甲良等农贸市场；樟江大街二期、三期工程和樟江南路竣工投入使用；荔波县被评为全州小城镇建设先进县，受州政府表彰；荔大公路和水尧—茂兰13.6公里路基工程改建全部竣工，荔（波）—小（七孔）

公路29公里、阳凤至独山墨寨县际断头公路，经验收评为优良工程。瑶山扶贫公路10.4公里通过验收；建成茂兰人饮工程，驾欧人饮灌溉工程动工建设，小七孔至大七孔电站35千伏输电线路架设完毕。社会事业方面，全县17个乡（镇）“双教”验收合格，州政府发给“双教”合格证，省教委发给“实现基本无盲单位”锦旗；承办全省少年游泳比赛；儿童计划免疫保偿工作成效显著，在荔波召开全省计免保偿现场会；全县已基本消灭小儿脊髓灰质炎，丝虫病防治工作成绩显著，经卫生部专家考核，确认已达到消灭丝虫病的标准，公布为全国基本消灭丝虫病县；全县村卫生室的覆盖面从上年的44.8%上升到88%；经省、州考核评审，被省政府授予“省级卫生县城”称号；开展创建“平安工程”活动，维护社会稳定。1997年，全县国内生产总值30092万元，比1993年增长88.87%；全社会固定资产投资总额5566万元，比1993年增长264.03%；社会消费品零售总额6821万元，比1993年增长49.06%；财政总收入4568万元，比1993年增长159.84%；农民人均纯收入1206元，比1993年增长170.40%。

1998—2002年，县政府先后出台《关于实施稳定和完善农村土地承包关系的工作方案》（1998年）、《关于深化粮油流通体制改革的实施意见》（1998年）、《关于加强基本农田保护区土地管理的规定》（1998年）、《荔波县城市居民最低生活保障制度暂行办法》（1998年）、《荔波县农村最低生活保障线暂行办法》（1998年）、《关于创建文化先进县的实施意见》（1999年）、《荔波县城镇市容环境卫生、城建监察管理办法》（2002年），发出《关于开展土地利用总体规划编制和基本农田保护区划定的通知》（1998年）、《关于保护森林资源制止毁林开垦和乱占林地的通知》（1998年）、《关于取缔非法小煤窑的通告》（2002年）、《关于划定水土流失重点预防保护区、重点治埋区、重点监督区的通知》（2002年）、《关于强化樟江沿河林业生态建设的决定》（2002年）、《荔波县县城建设拆迁补偿安置办法（暂行）的通知》（2002年）、《关于实施〈荔波县旅游发展总体规划〉的通知》（2002年），批转《荔波县文化带建设实施意见》（1998年）。项目建设上，以农业基础建设和以生态建设为重点，1998年以工代赈坡改梯工作被州委、州政府评为全州先进县，植树造林工作获全州优质造林县并获“全国造林百佳县”称号；进行农田水利渠道防渗、山塘整修，建小水窖（池），解决农村饮水困难；实施农网改造并全部完成；实施农村沼气、退耕还林、农村人饮工程建设，治理水土流失，蔬菜、酸梅、麻竹、蜜柚、茶叶等生产项目初步形成产业化经营。对国有企业进行改革改制，已进行产权制度改革的企业6户，占改革改制企业总数的27.3%；已进行租赁、承包、国有民营等改革形式改革的企业16户，占改革改制规划企业户数的72.7%；同时，对煤炭生产企业进行安全集中整治，加大维简费投入，全面强化技术改造，提高生产效益。公路新（改）建99公里，新增公路里程32.88公里；荔波机场作为省、州的重点建设工程，已开工建设。全县已有142个村（居）委会基本实现计划生育“村为主”，通过省政府验收；开展争创“国家级卫生县城”活动。2002年，全县国内生产总值44343万元，比1998年增长29.36%；全社会固定资产投资总额13261万元，比1998年下降18.10%；社会消费品零售总额15029万元，比1998年增长75.47%；财政总收入7008万元，比1998年增长32.53%；农民人均纯收入1255元，比1998年增长0.08%。

2003—2006年，县政府先后出台《荔波县城镇职工基本医疗保险实施办法（试行）》（2003年）、《荔波县政府采购管理办法》（2003年）、《关于对樟江大街进行景观改造的决定》（2006年）、《关于在县直机关开展行政效能建设工作的意见》（2006年），发出《关于加强非公有制经济管理的通知》（2003年）、《关于进一步加强我县征集抢救水书工作的通知》（2004年）、《关于命名我县第一批县级非物质文化遗产代表作名录的通知》（2005年），完成《荔波樟江风景名胜区总体规划》修编。这几年中，县政府在农业工作方面：按照中共中央、国务院和省委、省政府关于“以增加农民收入为中心，全面推进农业农村经济持续健康发展”的总体要求，建“三小”工程、水利工程、沼气池，进行基本农田治理，推广小型农业机械耕作，实施以种植业、养殖业和扶贫攻坚为主要内容的助民增收“五个十”示范工程，带动农业增效、农民增收；制定全县2006—2010年种桑养蚕发展规划，以“公司+农户+基地”模式发展种桑养蚕业。工业生产方面，进行煤矿技改、扩界和资源整合，完成技改矿井22口，大部分煤矿年生产能力从3万吨提高到6万吨以上，提高煤炭产业规模化管理水平；打击煤矿违法生产和非法盗采行为，取缔非法小煤窑。生态建设方面，加强樟江河河道治理，禁止在樟江河两岸毁林开荒等破坏樟江两岸生态的行为；启动石漠化治理工程，继续实施退耕还林、天保工程、珠防工程建设，完成重点造林工程3.5万亩；以创建国家级生态示范区为载体，通过采取旅游扶贫开发、自然保护区建设、景区保护建设、生态移民、封山育林、农村能源改造、立体农业基地建设等有力措施，区域生态环境保护取得显著成效，创建国家级生态示范区工作通过国家验收。旅游和社会事业方面，申报为全省优先重点发展旅游区之一获得成功，名列全省首位；争取国债资金和其他专项资金支持旅游项目建设，建成观音峰景区一期工程、瑶山游客中心及停车场、表演场等设施，完成茂兰游线规划与建设；组织实施世界自然遗产项目申报工作；2006年举办“中国荔波万亩梅花报春节暨原生态文化旅游月”活动，开发荔波冬季旅游；教育事业通过“两基”复查和“普实”验收；实施广播电视“村村通”工程；实施新型农村合作医疗，完成县疾控中心及县传染病区建设项目。此外，2005年参加“中国最美的地方”评选活动，获得“手机网络人气奖”“中国最美的十大森林”两项殊荣。2006年，全县国内生产总值76873万元，比2003年增长45.28%；全社会固定资产投资总额46265万元，比2003年增长137.01%；社会消费品零售总额21817万元，比2003年增长32.19%；财政总收入12948万元，比2003年增长57.77%；农民人均纯收入1751元，比2003年增长28.75%。

2007年，县政府先后发出《关于禁止在退耕还林地、樟江沿河两岸及公路沿线可视范围内开荒复耕的通知》《关于推进全县供销社系统企业改革改制意见》等重要文件。年内，实施板寨、水甫、板旺、木朝、拉片等10个新农村示范点和5个民族文化村寨建设，“两瑶”民族村寨改造成为全县新农村建设和民族团结示范村寨；实施易地扶贫搬迁705户2859人；建成“三小”工程1000口，解决农村人口8000人的饮水困难；实施“万村千乡”市场工程，新发展连锁农家店90家。开展煤矿整顿关闭与整合，全县煤矿优化整合为27对；打击非法盗采、非法运销煤矿行为，维护煤矿生产秩序。捆绑申报的“中国南方喀斯特”世界自然遗产在第31届世界遗产大会通过，成为中国第六个世界自然遗产地，实现贵州世界遗产零的突破。承办第二届贵州旅游产业发展大会暨首届中国南方喀斯特文化旅游节、机场通航庆典和世界人与生物圈网络国际会议、全国山地户外运动锦标赛等系列活动。职工养老、失业、医疗、工伤保险和城市、农村低保等保障性措施落实到位，发放城镇低保金240万元、农村低保金（特困救助）257万元；发放农村医疗救助金32.29万元，农村“五保”供养金29.57万元。全面启动“国家园林城市”“中国优秀旅游城市”创建工作，实施出租汽车从事县城客运经营项目，实现县城客运车辆升级换代。

2008年，在年初遭受特大冰冻灾害后，县政府以保民生为首要任务，奋力抗灾救灾，迅速开展电网、工业、旅游、危房改造等灾后重建工作。争取到中央扩大内需首期投资3651万元，支撑县域经济持续增长。新增和改造茶园2000亩；特色水果产量达1741吨；推广瑶山鸡养殖67万羽，实施养羊饲草面积3500亩。煤炭产业通过强化安全监管、挖掘生产潜力，全年原煤产销量达130万吨，实现税费收入1.35亿元。AAAA级景区创建工作通过国家旅游局专家组现场验收；全县旅游经济直接收入1877万元，旅游业社会综合收入15016万元。荔波机场荔波至深圳航线正式开通运营，城区道路总长已达23.6公里，城镇化率达30.6%；建成通村公路200公里。招商引资在建项目17个，累计到位资金3.16亿元，比上年增长21%。建立城镇居民基本医疗保险制度，基本实现应保尽保；新型农村合作医疗参合率达94.75%；“国家卫生县城”通过复查验收，县城获得“全国文明城市”称号。

2008年年末，全县国内生产总值113378万元，比2007年增长23.94%；全社会固定资产投资总额68357万元，比2007年增长11.56%；社会消费品零售总额32317万元，比2007年增长26.24%；财政总收入18216万元，比2007年增长25.33%；农民人均纯收入2618元，比2007年增长21.3%。

第三节 重要活动

一、申报“中国南方喀斯特”世界自然遗产

1995年，开始启动世界自然遗产申报工作，通过11年的努力，至2005年9月，建设部正式确定云南石林、重庆武隆和贵州荔波联合以“中国南方喀斯特”共同申报世界自然遗产，并作为2006年全国唯一的申报项目。为确保申报工作取得成功，2006年4月3日，召开荔波申报“中国南方喀斯特”世界自然遗产誓师大会，举行游行和万人签名活动。8月6日，建设部及“中国南方喀斯特”申报自然遗产三省（市）模拟考察团的领导、专家到荔波考察指导工作。2007年6月27日，第31届世界遗产评审会上获全票通过，列世界遗产名录，成为贵州第一个、中国第六个世界自然遗产地。

二、首届万亩梅花报春节暨原生态文化旅游月

2006年1—2月，县委、县政府为利用丰富的野生梅林资源开发冬季旅游，举办首届“中国荔波万亩梅花报春节暨原生态文化旅游月”活动。“棋圣”聂卫平参加了这次活动，同时举行了黔桂两省（区）猛牛争霸赛、民族民间特技表演、国际野生梅梅花研讨会、山地自行车大赛等活动。2007年1月、2008年1月，分别举办了第二届、第三届梅花节旅游月活动。

三、第二届贵州省旅游产业发展大会（筹备）

黔南州承办的全省第二届旅游产业发展大会决定在荔波召开后，2007年2月13日，县委常委会研究相关筹备工作。之后成立贵州省第二届旅游产业发展大会荔波执委会，加强与省、州对接，开展筹备工作。为做好全省第二届旅游产业发展大会筹备工作，县委、县政府决定实施的建设项目有县城北山口公路改造；驾朝公路建设；驾朝公路联山、拉欧大桥；小七孔环保车辆营运招商；翁昂至董莽公路改造工程；县城环境整治及旅游公路沿线环境整治；机场公路建设；演艺中心及多功能会议厅建设；露天会场建设；世界自然遗产展示园区一期工程建设；樟江大街立面改造；樟江大桥装饰工程；15座旅游厕所建设；宾馆改造工程；旅游公路及樟江河道绿化美化工程；小七孔水上森林延伸及湿地建设；水春河码头建设、游客中心建设；旅游信息系统建设；新农村乡村旅馆建设；美食街改造及特色旅游商品销售一条街改建；恩铭大道建设等。同时，县委、县政府研究出台旅发大会建设项目招商引资优惠政策确保各项目启动实施。

2007年11月6日，第二届贵州省旅游产业发展大会在荔波如期举行，国家部委及省党政部门领导，国内外旅游机构、旅游企业代表以及致力于喀斯特文化旅游研究与发展的各界人士出席大会。第二届省旅发大会以“整合资源、夯实基础、创新机制、加快发展”为主题。大会期间，举办“首届中国南方喀斯特文化旅游节”开幕式暨文艺演出，以及黔南旅游考察、经贸招商、旅游招商推介及签约、中国南方喀斯特文化旅游座谈会等活动。

第三章 其他政务

第一节 信访工作

一、来信来访

1978年后，在信访部门办理信访工作的同时，县委、县政府领导适时到信访部门值班，接待群众来访，县信访局做好接访记录、服务等。

1979年11月，县委决定每个星期六为县委常委、县革委领导接待日，县领导轮流在县委信访组接待来访群众。

从1981年3月16日起，县委常委、县人大常委副主任、县政府副县长轮流于每星期日下午到信访组接待人民来访，处理人民来信。

1996年1月1日《信访条例》颁布施行后，县信访局将《信访条例》《贵州省信访条例》《贵州省群众逐级上访制度试行办法》《黔南州山林土地水事权属争议协调处理暂行办法》宣传活动，制作宣传栏，利用赶场天在县城和乡（镇）进行宣传，将编写打印《信访政策、法规咨询问答》《山林土地水事权属争议调处政策、法规及程序咨询问答》2000册宣传资料分发给群众。同时，还将国家、省的《信访条例》制成录音带，通过广播进行广泛深入的宣传。

1997年6月5日，县委、县政府印发《荔波县乡镇、县部门目标管理考核办法（试行）的通知》，将信访工作列入目标考核内容之一，对因不及时疏导，引发进京上访的乡（镇），此项工作不得分。7月25日，县委印发《关于建立县四家班子领导接待群众信访制度的决定》，决定每月的5日、20日为县四家班子领导接待群众信访工作日，将县四家班子领导搭配组成6个接待组，每个接待日均由县委、县人大、县政府、县政协的1名领导轮流参加接待工作。8月22日，县委办、县人大办、县政府办联合印发《荔波县信访（调处）工作目标管理考评试行办法》。8月25日，召开全县信访（调处）工作会议，县四家班子领导、县直有关部门和17个乡（镇）领导等110人参加会议，学习国家《信访条例》和《贵州省信访条例》《贵州省群众逐级上访制度试行办法》，并将这3个法规性文件汇编发给与会县直有关部门、乡（镇）、村（居）委会，将《黔南州山林土地水事权属争议协调处理转行办法》印发各乡（镇）。

2000年，县信访局实行年度目标考核制度，于年初制定《荔波县信访局（调处办）年度工作目标考核办法》，年终进行考核。

2001年9月11日，县委、县政府印发《关于调整县四大班子领导和县公安局、法院、国土局领导接待群众信访日成员的通知》，组成接待组6个，每个组由县四家班子领导各1人和公安局、法院、国土局的领导或有关股（室）负责人各1人共7～9人组成。

2003年11月9日，成立群众重复上访问题专项治理领导小组，开展群众重复上访问题专项治理工作，全面排查重复上访情况，进行群众重复上访问题专项治理。

2004年7月27日，县委办公室、县政府办公室联合印发《关于健全和完善各乡镇及县直有关部门信访工作网络的通知》，要求进一步建立、健全和完善全县信访网络。8月12日，县委办公室、县政府办公室联合印发《关于建立荔波县处理信访问题协调联席会议制度的通知》，对联席会议的职责、成员单位（29个）、工作规划、工作要求、办公室职责和工作规则5个方面作出明确规定。10月12日，县委办、县政府办联合印发《关于进一步完善荔波县处理信访突出问题及群体性事件联席会议制度的通知》，就联席会议的主要职责、工作原则进行了补充和完善，并根据当时群众信访中反映比较突出的问题，成立“农村土地征用问题”“城镇房屋拆迁问题”“国有企业改制问题”“涉法涉诉问题”“企业军转干部问题”等6个工作小组，明确牵头部门和各组组长。

2005年1月4日，县委办公室、县政府办公室联合印发《关于对全县处理信访突出问题及群体性事件工作进行督查的通知》，成立4个督查分组，组长均由县委副书记或常委担任，开展信访突出问题及群体性事件工作督查。

2006年6月14日，开展重点地区和敏感部位非正常上访集中整治行动。

2008年9月3日，县委、县政府印发《关于启动信访工作责任追究制的通知》，实行信访工作责任追究制。

是年，按照中央、省、州的要求，开展“县委书记大接访”活动。7—12月，县委书记、县长接访34次，其他县级领导接访152次，县直部门接访381次。信访事项涉及的55个部门和乡（镇）负责人到现场办公，形成“领导包案接访，部门负责办理，相关单位配合”的信访工作格局。全年接待群众来信来访147批（件）552人次。其中，个体信访104批206人次，集体信访43批346人次。涉及的问题有土地征用6件、房屋拆迁18件、企业改制6件、涉法涉诉11件、劳动社保10件、农村农业40件、民政8件、其他48件。县级领导负责处理15件，落实责任单位43件，化解信访问题和矛盾纠纷89件。

二、信访案件办理

1995年11月—2002年2月，县信访局（调处办）受理山林所有权争议案件33宗、土地所有权争议案件24宗，共计57宗。调查处理结束52宗，办结率91.2%。未办结的5宗于2002年3月分别移交有关职能部门办理。在办结案件中，经过调查，促成争议双方或多方达成书面协议处理15宗；县政府行文作出处理决定36宗。调查处理后，不服县政府处理决定向州政府提出行政复议7宗，州政府均维持县政府的处理决定；不服县政府的处理决定或不服州政府复议决定向县法院提出行政诉讼16宗，县法院经过开庭审理作出一审判决均维持县政府的处理决定；不服县法院一审判决向州法院提起行政诉讼14宗，经州法院开庭审理后作出二审（即终审）判决，均维持县法院一审判决。

第二节　档案管理

一、档案整理

全县第三次清理积存档案经过3年工作，到1978年年底，县级党政机关已有27个单位完成清理积存零散文件任务，尚有5个单位未完成，有7个单位未清理；53个企业有6个开始清理；4个区中朝阳区完成任务；24个公社中完成任务的有6个，未完成的有6个，未启动的有12个；154个生产大队中完成任务的有4个，未启动的有150个。1979年，按黔南州档案局“清积扫尾”的要求开展清理工作，至11月中旬，全县有清积任务共221个单位，完成任务的有117个单位，占53%；未完成的单位有33个，未启动的单位有71个（均为大队）。第三次清理积存档案工作到此结束。

1980年8月1日，县委办发出《关于开展档案鉴定工作的通知》，县成立档案鉴定领导小组，要求各单位明确一位领导抓此项工作。1981年7月，对具有永久保存价值用复写纸书写的档案文件采用复抄的办法进行补救，对划分不当的保管期限重新划定。共抄写县委办、文教局、县人委办1950年后共1189卷中的复写文件，并划出永久667卷、长期403卷、短期119卷。

1986年8月至10月，开展第四次清理积存档案工作，主要清理历年积存文书档案和会计档案。同时，贯彻执行《机关档案工作条例》，组织档案进馆，建立平时立卷归档制度，做好平时立卷归档，不再出现新的积存。经过220人3个月的突击，共整理档案7553卷。县机关局级以上应清档案单位61个，已清理结束并移交的单位29个，已清理结束但未移交的单位20个，正在清理的单位12个；三级机构应清理档案单位33个，已清理结束并移交的单位14个，已清理结束但未移交的单位8个，正在清理的单位11个；4区1镇中有2区1镇已移交；25个乡中已清理并移交的单位14个，已清理结束但未移交的单位2个。全县应清理会计档案单位101个，已清理结束82个单位，共清理会计档案44552卷（册）。年底共接收64个单位移交进馆档案5225卷（含4个撤销机构档案），其中永久2812卷、长期2309卷、短期104卷、卡片2229张、资料75册，馆藏档案达到12041卷、资料70种2703册。

1994年，对1991年“建并撤”时突击进馆的档案按规范要求重新整理，由3380卷整理为1129卷。

1995—1998年，县档案局主要针对档案达标工作要求组织人员对部分县直机关单位进行档案整理归类指导。

1999年4月，县委办转发县档案局、农业局《关于做好第二轮土地承包经营档案工作的通知》后，至12月底，全县第二轮土地承包经营档案325卷全部接收进县档案馆，并于2000年4月被黔南州档案局、黔南州农业局评为“第二轮土地承包经营档案工作一等奖”。

2001—2002年，全县退耕还林还草工程结束，其档案立卷归随之完成，共形成永久档案117卷、长期档案7卷。2002年，对退耕还林工作档案进行整理验收。

2002年5月28日，县政府办公室下发《关于加强林业重点工程档案管理工作的通知》，制定了《林业重点工程档案的归档范围及保管期限》《林业重点工程档案验收标准》，要求各乡（镇）党委、政府及县直有关部门将1998年12月在荔波县启动实施的天然林资源保护、世界银行贷款贫困地区林业发展、珠江防护林建设和退耕还林还草四大工程建设与档案管理工作同部署、同检查、同验收。

是年，在全县农村税费改革中，县农村税费改革办公室、县档案局联合下发《关于加强我县农村税费改革档案管理工作的通知》，并制定农村税费改革档案验收标准。至2003年5月，全县农村税费改革档案的立卷归档工作完成，归档立卷共305卷（永久、长期），9—10月通过考评验收。档案立卷一式两份，其中一份移交县档案馆，另一份分别交各乡（镇）档案室。

2003年6月，黔南州荔波机场建设开发有限责任公司与荔波县档案局联合印发《荔波机场建设工程项目档案管理工作会议纪要》，县档案局协助机场整理档案，经3个月整理，完成470卷一式两份档案归档。

2007年，全县开始集体林权制度改革，对其档案整理归档工作进行同步安排。集体林权制度改革文书档案采用《归档文件整理规则》新方法进行整理，到2008年，集体林权制度改革仍在进行中。

2008年12月30日，县档案局印发《荔波县档案馆档案收集实施细则》《荔波县档案馆接收档案标准》。

二、档案管理

1989年4月3日，在州委办、州政府办转发州档案局的《关于在全州开展机关档案室上等级活动的意见》中，荔波县列为第二批从1990年开始定级升级的单位。根据州档案局《机关档案室等级标准考评细则》，县档案局有重点地开展档案达标监督指导工作。至1992年年底考评，县税务局、县区划办、县石油公司达到省标县直一级标准，县保险公司达到省标县直二级标准，这4个单位成为全县第一批档案管理规范化、标准化单位。1993年，县档案局发出《关于对县机关、企事业档案管理已达标升级单位进行复查的通知》，对达标单位进行复查，巩固达标成果。1991—1995年，全县有16个单位升级，其中达一级8个、二级4个、三级4个。

1996年，县财政投资40万元、建筑面积1122平方米（其中库房面积779平方米）的新档案馆验收并投入使用。

1999年，县档案馆达标工作列入州、县两级档案部门当年目标管理考核主要内容。县财政拨款7万元增添档案馆设备，编案卷目录181本、全引目录51本、专题目录11本、资料分类目录3本，汇集全宗卷98盒，鉴定开放全宗档案24个，设置档案利用接待室、阅览室、展览室、业务室，完善各种规章制度，统计档案利用效果。年底考评，县档案馆行政管理、建筑与设备、基础业务建设、档案信息资源开发利用指标达到《贵州省地县综合档案馆目标管理考评标准》二级。

2000年，县委办、县政府办下发《关于依法治档、全面开展档案达标升级工作的实施意见》，加强档案管理工作。是年12月，县委组织部与县档案局联合下发《关于认真做好乡（镇）、村级档案管理达标工作的通知》，开展乡（镇）、村档案达标管理工作。2001年，县委办、县政府办下发《关于对未达标单位档案工作进行考核验收的通知》后，县政府与未达标乡（镇）和科局级单位签订《档案达标责任书》，县财政拨出31.25万元达标工作专项经费，乡（镇）财政共投入10.2万元基础设施经费。至2001年年底，全县17个乡（镇）和5个县直单位通过省标一级验收，5个县直单位通过省标二级验收。2002年7月17日，荔波县人大常委会召开第35次会议，首次听取审议并通过县档案局所作的《关于荔波县档案达标升级工作的情况报告》。是年11月，全县174个村（居）委会建立“有档案、有柜子、有制度、有人管”的“四有”村级档案室。2002年3月，县内机关、团体、企事业单位19个获州政府档案达标升级工作“先进单位”称号。

从2002年5月起，全县执行《归档文件整理规则》，试行计算机管理档案。8月，县国税局、县地税局和县科协率先安装计算机档案管理软件。随后，县物价局、县财政局、县烟草局、县供电局、县医院、县纪委、县国土局、县建设局8个单位进入执行新规则、运用计算机管理档案行列。

是年，县会计核算中心成立后，县档案局与县财政局又联合下发《关于加强会计档案管理和移交工作的通知》，并制定会计档案管理规章制度，加强会计档案管理。

2003年6—11月，县档案局先后印发《荔波县国家重点建设项目档案管理登记办法》《荔波县国家建设项目（工程）档案验收办法》《荔波县重点工程档案管理暂行办法》并予以实施。

是年，全县新增升级单位20个，其中升一级的7个单位全部应用计算机管理档案。至此，12年累计全县升级单位90个，占应升级单位112个的80.36%。

自2006年后，中央和省下拨国家重点档案抢救和保护项目经费共74万元，县级配套经费85.5万元，修建特藏库房及修复室，建立辅助档案保存的数字视频防盗监控系统、自动报警气体灭火系统、远程恒温恒湿监控系统，档案基础设施得到改善。

2006—2008年，中央、省下拨国家重点档案抢救和保护项目经费共74万元，县级配套经费85.5万元，修建特藏库房及修复室，建立辅助档案保存的数字视频防盗监控系统、自动报警气体灭火系统、远程恒温恒湿监控系统，档案基础设施得到改善。

三、档案收藏

2008年，县档案馆馆藏有文书、历史、会计、人事、声像、古籍、电子数据、实物8种资料，总藏量49491卷（件、册、盒），档案全宗164个。其中，文书档案29204卷（件、盒），历史档案115卷（盒），人事档案1710卷（盒），会计档案2100卷（盒），实物档案26件，声像档案1312张（件），古籍9924册，图书资料5100册。馆藏水书古籍9217册，馆藏布依傩书古籍282册。

馆藏档案中，时间最早的一件历史档案为清咸丰年间（1851—1861年）蒙老夏与吴秀富买卖山地的契约，因其量少，皆归入民国档案为主体的历史档案全宗保管，另有大清律例刑案汇纂集成；民国档案最早的一件为1914年贵州省国税厅筹备处的纳税凭单；馆藏历史人物档案有中共一大代表邓恩铭、革命烈士蒙九龄的资料，有贵州历史名人周西成、刘其贤、韩文焕、王家烈的相片及同学、同人集体照片；馆藏革命历史档案分中国共产党创立、土地革命战争时期、抗日战争时期、解放战争时期4个阶段收藏；馆藏汉文古籍共425册；馆藏有牛角水书、马尾绣、证书等实物档案。

四、档案利用

1980—1998年，县档案馆提供利用档案资料总计5600卷册、2050人次，复印资料1.57万页。

1999年11月，开展第一批档案鉴定开放工作，共鉴定24个全宗3419卷档案，鉴定后决定开放3071卷，暂不开放348卷，实际开放卷数占鉴定卷数的89.82%。

2005年，建立现行文件阅览中心，为搞好利用服务，县档案馆公开向社会承诺，除正常工作日按上班时间查档外，实行双休日、节假日不休假制度；查档来人来电来函均可；查档一律免费。2006—2008年，共接待查档3521人次，调阅档案6049卷（册），为全县干部职工工资改革、农村山林土地纠纷调解、城镇建房拆迁、编史修志等提供依据资料。

五、古籍抢救

（一）水书抢救

水书长期散存于民间。1993年10月，贵州省水家学会荔波中心组成立水书抢救小组。2002年3月，国家档案局、中央档案馆将水书古籍列入首批《中国档案文献遗产名录》。7月21日，在水尧水族乡召开荔波县拯救水书座谈会，开始全面抢救征集水书工作。11月16日，召开全县水书先生暨征集抢救水书会议，参会的43名水书先生无偿捐赠祖传水书原件77本，县档案馆对征集的水书进行登记、注录、消毒、修补、裱糊、编号、上柜保护，并扫描录入电子文档保存。2003年3月12日，县第十四届人民代表大会第一次会议作出《关于抢救整理开发利用古老文化——水书并申报为世界文化遗产的决议》；3月15日，在政协荔波县委员会六届一次会议召开期间，68名委员提出关于挖掘古老民族文化，开发利用水书，申报为世界文化遗产的提案；5月，县档案局、县民宗局、县文体广播电视局、县水家学会作出《关于表彰欧海金等水书先生对征集抢救水书做出贡献的决定》；10月，县委、县政府成立荔波县水书征集抢救工作领导小组。2004—2005年，县政府将水书抢救工作列入政府要办的“十件实事”，发出征集抢救通知，制定抢救工作实施方案和办法。2005年10月，与中山大学合作，挂牌成立中山大学荔波水书研究基地。是年12月，成立荔波县水书申遗领导小组。2006年6月，国务院批准水书习俗列入《第一批国家级非物质文化遗产名录》。2007年1月，县政府与黔南民族师院、黔南州水书抢救办公室在都匀召开中国水书文化首届国际学术研讨会。2008年4月，县档案馆珍藏的《庚甲》

《泐金·纪日》《金银》3部水书列入全国首批《国家珍贵古籍名录》，县档案馆被评为首批51家“全国古籍重点保护单位”之一，为全省获此殊荣的两家单位之一，是全国唯一获此荣誉的县级档案馆。

至2008年12月，征集到水书原件9137册，居全省之首。

（二）布依族古文字档案（布依文古籍）抢救

布依族古文字档案（布依文古籍）包括布经书和傩书，散存于布依族民间，由布依文先生传承。2006年，翁昂乡率先开展布依傩书抢救工作，恢复翁昂乡傩戏表演队，表演傩书剧目，引起国内外专家学者和新闻媒体的关注，得到县委、县政府的重视。2008年12月3日，县档案局与县布依学会联合召开布依傩书申报第三批《国家珍贵古籍名录》工作会议，议定从原馆藏傩书中精选出6册年代最为久远的傩书进行译注，聘请省内历史学、语言学、文字学、版本学、档案学、民族学、宗教学等专家进行鉴定，规范傩书及其传承人员的名称，傩书正式定名为《荔波布依傩书》，其传承人员称为傩书先生。全县征集抢救傩书工作正式启动。至2008年年底，征集进馆的布依族古文字档案（布依文古籍）636册，其中傩书282册、经书354册。

六、执法检查

1988年5月，县政府办公室批转县档案局、司法局《关于对〈中华人民共和国档案法〉贯彻执行情况进行检查的通知》，对县机关77个单位进行检查。经检查，全县30个区（镇）、乡完成任务29个，正在清理1个；有清积任务的局级单位61个，完成1985年以前清积任务的51个；有清积任务的三级机构33个清理结束，其中移交县档案馆单位18个。会计档案清理中，全县81个会计核算单位，只1个未清理，其余全部清理结束。

2002年11月，对全县档案未达标的42个单位进行档案达标执法检查。2003年，档案达标单位20个，累计达标单位90个，占应达标单位112个的80.36%。

其他年份每年组织一次机关、企事业单位和重大项目建设单位档案常规业务执法大检查。

七、宣传教育

2003年8月后，县档案馆建档案展览室，利用珍藏档案进行宣传教育。先后举办荔波文物图片展、水书习俗文化展、水族文化习俗展等。

2005年春节期间，在县城广场举办“荔波县档案局文物图片展”，在“五一”黄金周，举办水书布展览。此外，会同县教育局将文物图片等宣传资料在“荔波县少年活动中心”展出。

2006年10月，制作水书相关文字、图片，在中共荔波县第十次代表大会期间展出。

2006—2008年，利用每年“梅花节”活动，在永康乡瑶古村进行水族文化展览宣传。

每年“6·9”档案宣传日、“12·5”法制宣传日，开展档案法律法规宣传。

2003—2008年，中小学生、干部职工、社会各界人士、中外游客或专家学者参观展览达6万人次。

八、信息化建设

2006年，档案信息化工作起步，采取“定人、定机、定量”措施，进行档案数据条目录入。到2008年7月，完成馆藏档案24325卷、37.22万条文件级数据条目录入工作，成为全州县级档案馆全面完成馆藏档案条目录入工作的档案馆之一。并在全州县级档案馆中率先建成贵州省档案信息三级网站。

第三节　地方志编纂

1984年10月，县委办批转县史志办关于《荔波县志》编纂方案后，第一轮社会主义新方志《荔波县志》编修工作全面启动。1986年11月，县政府批转县地方志编纂委员会《关于“七五”计划期间完成荔波县修志任务的报告》。是年，县志编纂委员会发布《荔波县县志资料征集的通知》，向社会广泛征集荔波县的历史资料。至1993年，完成《荔波县志》初稿总纂，1994—1996年，按照地方志书三级审稿制度，《荔波县志》经县志编委会初审、州史志办复审、省志办终审后，于1996年11月定稿付印，1998年5月正式出版发行，历时14年，全书127.5万字。参与编写该志人员有100多人，查阅档案7300多卷，制作资料卡1.32万份。

1998年5月，县委、县政府决定编修《荔波县情》，上限1991年，下限1997年12月。资料由各部门、乡（镇）提供，县志办整理编纂，1999年12月完成初稿，2000年4月送州史志办审查，是年10月内部印刷出版发行，全书136万字。为《荔波县情》提供资料的单位101个，参与编写人员有104人。

2008年3月，县人武部编纂的《荔波县军事志》定稿付印，内部出版。8月，县国税局、地税局、财政局共同编纂的《荔波县税务志》定稿付印，内部出版。是年，启动播尧乡、茂兰镇、佳荣镇、玉屏镇等乡（镇）志编纂工作。

第四节　招商引资

一、招商引资政策

1995年，招商引资工作起步，按照“一事一议”原则，进行招商引资项目洽谈。

1997年9月，县委、县政府颁布实施《关于招商引资奖励暂行办法》。

2001年9月，县委、县政府制定印发《荔波县投资兴业优惠政策》，终止执行原《关于招商引资奖励暂行办法》。同时，颁布实施《荔波县引资奖励办法》。

2003年5月，县委、县政府颁布试行《关于招商引资的若干规定》《关于引资的奖励办法》，同时终止执行原《荔波县投资兴业优惠政策》《荔波县引资奖励办法》。

是年下半年，建立“一站式”服务中心，启动“一站式”服务工作，县监察局、工商局、质监局、国税局、地税局、国土局、建设局、煤炭局、环保局、供电局、消防大队等单位向县委、县政府作出服务工作书面承诺，公开办事程序及工作职责，各安排1名“一站式”服务大厅工作人员，为外来投资者提供方便、快捷、高效的服务。2005年，县政府办公室发出《关于切实做好外来投资“一站式”服务中心工作的通知》，加强服务工作。

二、招商引资项目

1995—2008年，全县招商引资引进项目累计226个，引进到位资金140275.29万元。重大项目有金锣湾商业步行街购物广场、樟江部落（翡翠商旅文化城）、今典华庭（怡景苑）、三力大酒店、城市出租车、小七孔景区环保观光车、水尧制糖厂、捞村浪祥水电站等。

1995—2008年招商引资实绩统计表

表6－2

年度	项目数（个）	到位资金（万元）	年度	项目数（个）	到位资金（万元）
1995	5	1500.00	2002	22	5237.00
1996	7	2105.00	2003	21	7304.00
1997	7	2673.00	2004	16	11000.00
1998	12	3018.00	2005	16	17298.00
1999	13	2816.71	2006	28	21189.00
2000	13	3905.78	2007	24	22933.00
2001	25	4106.80	2008	17	35189.00

重大项目简介：

金锣湾商业步行街购物广场 金锣湾步行街购物广场位于县城樟江大桥头原老电影院片区，占地面积8400平方米。该项目包括大型超市、休闲、步行街等，步行街长200米、宽42米，两旁有商铺110间，项目总投资2000万元，由黔南天力房地产开发公司投资建设，2002年2月动工修建，2005年1月竣工投入使用，是荔波县第一个招商引资旧城改造项目。

三力酒店 位于县城樟江大桥桥头北侧，占地4000平方米，主体建筑1.3万平方米，建筑总高54.2米，楼高14层，为三星级酒店，总投资4000万元，由重庆客商周平投资建设。2002年9月动工修建，2006年1月竣工投入使用。该项目是县内第一个三星级酒店。

城市出租车 2003年，贵州安盛经济发展有限公司投资350万元，在荔波县注册荔波安盛出租车有限公司，项目实施后投资方购进轿车50辆，投放县城出租车市场，原人力三轮车和机动三轮车在县城停运。

浪祥水电站 浪祥水电站位于捞村乡群力村浪祥组，由贵州荔都水电发展有限责任公司投资建设，2003年9月动工修建，2006年4月发电。装机2×1.5万千瓦，年发电量12000万千瓦时，所发电量全部输入国家电网。电站总投资1.8亿元，每年上缴国家税收200万元以上。

樟江部落（翡翠商旅文化城） 位于县城樟江园广场（现邓恩铭广场）旁，是集“吃、住、娱、购、游”为一体的多功能民族文化旅游城。占地面积3000平方米，建设项目主要有四星级涉外酒店、商住楼、民族风情街、民族歌舞广场、少数民族文化展示馆等，总投资2亿元，由荔波县鑫懋源房地产开发公司（外地客商在荔波注册成立的公司）投资建设，2005年9月开工建设，是荔波县招商引资重点项目，至2008年仍在建设中。

今典华庭（怡景苑） 位于县城樟江园广场南则，县水利局宿舍前，项目占地1904平方米，为商住项目，建筑楼层14层。由黔南康诚房地产开发有限公司投资建设。2005年12月开工建设，项目总投资2000万元。

小七孔景区环保观光车 2007年4月，北京美嘉环球旅行社有限公司投资4200万元，在小七孔景区实施环保观光车项目建设。其中，车辆投资1800万元，经营配套服务设施2400万元。2007年8月投入运营。

水尧制糖厂 水尧制糖厂项目位于水尧乡水尧村塘芽组，占地230亩，设计规模日处理甘蔗6000吨，总投资3.6亿元。2008年5月，项目由广西富方投资公司投资建设，并在荔波注册荔波县九曲湾制糖厂有限公司。

第七篇
地方政协

政协荔波县委员会1984—2008年，召开了一届至七届全体会议。每次会议都听取和审议常委会工作报告、审议提案审查委员会关于提案办理情况报告、通过大会各项决议。县政协发挥政治协商、民主监督、参政议政的职能作用，不断搞好调查研究，坚持“长期共存，互相监督”“肝胆相照，荣辱与共”的方针，广交朋友，联络感情。每届政协都开展委员提案、委员视察调研、文史资料编辑、联谊活动、智力支边工作，在新形势下，研究新问题，开拓新领域，创出新局面。

第一章 政协荔波县委员会

第一节 委员构成

历届县政协委员的安排，坚持统筹兼顾、合理安排的原则，注意扩大团结面和广泛的代表性，体现“大团结、大统一”的精神，重点安排教育、科技、医药卫生界及知识分子的名额。

1984—2008年历届县政协委员界别情况一览表

表7－1

界别构成	委员人数（人）						
	一届	二届	三届	四届	五届	六届	七届
中共	5	6	7	7	7	8	8
无党派	1	2	1	2	2	2	2
共青团	3	2	4	3	3	3	3
总工会	2	2	3	3	3	3	3
妇联	2	2	3	3	4	4	4
工商联	2	4	1	3	2	5	10
供销合作社	1	3	—	—	—	—	—
文艺	1	4	3	1	1	—	—
科技	12	14	17	17	20	18	17
农林	5	8	8	9	10	10	9
教育	15	15	17	18	19	19	18
体育	1	1	1	1	1	—	—
医药卫生	10	13	12	13	15	12	12
少数民族	13	12	15	18	20	23	25
侨联小组	2	—	—	—	—	—	—
特邀人士	12	27	25	25	29	29	31
工商经济	—	—	8	—	—	—	—
新闻	—	2	—	—	—	—	—

续表7-1

界别构成	委员人数（人）						
	一届	二届	三届	四届	五届	六届	七届
科协	—	—	—	3	3	3	2
经济	—	—	—	9	10	10	8
新闻文化体育	—	—	—	—	—	2	3
合　计	16个界别共87人	16个界别共117人	15个界别共125人	16个界别共135人	16个界别共149人	15个界别共151人	15个界别共155人

第二节　全体委员会议

一、第一届全体会议

1984年11月21—27日，政协第一届荔波县委员会第一次会议在县城召开，出席会议委员87名。会议听取和审议县委统战部关于召开政协荔波县委员会第一届第一次会议筹备工作报告。全体委员列席县第九届人大第一次会议，讨论协商县政府和县法院、县检察院工作报告。大会确定第一届委员会工作任务是组织委员和各界人士学习政治理论、时事政治和科学技术；充分发挥社会主义民主，发挥人民政协政治协商和民主监督的职能作用；协同有关部门进一步落实统战政策；围绕社会主义物质文明和精神文明建设开展工作，组织活动；做好祖国统一、文史资料的征集和编写以及做好智力支边工作。会议通过政协第一届荔波县委员会第一次会议决议《关于提案审查情况报告的决议》。会议选举产生政协荔波县第一届委员会主席1名、副主席4名、常务委员21名，蒙明儒当选主席，李德余、艾福田、常青、何正刚当选副主席。会议期间收到委员提案68件。

第一届第二次、第三次、第四次会议分别于1985年3月22—25日、1986年3月6—12日、1987年4月8—11日在县城召开。每次会议均听取和审议常委会工作报告及提案工作报告，通过大会决议，列席县人民代表大会。其间，第三次会议协商增补委员2人，增选常委2人。

二、第二届全体会议

1987年8月25—31日，政协第二届荔波县委员会第一次会议在县城召开，出席会议委员117名。会议听取和审议政协第二届委员会筹备工作报告；听取和审议第一届常委会工作报告；审议提案审查委员会关于提案办理情况报告；通过大会决议。全体委员列席县第十届人大第一次会议。会议明确第二届委员会的六项工作，进一步加强对人民政协的性质、地位、作用的学习和宣传，充分发挥政治协商、民主监督的职能作用；进一步调动委员和各界人士的积极性，发挥人民政协的智力库优势；进一步推动委员和各界人士学习，在区、乡建立委员联络组，县城建立中心学习组，组织委员学习；进一步搞好调查研究，加强对工作组的领导；继续宣传中共统一战线政策，坚持“长期共存，互相监督”“肝胆相照，荣辱与共”的方针，广交朋友，联络感情，为实现祖国统一贡献力量；在新形势下，研究新问题，开拓新领域，创出新局面。会议选举产生政协荔波县第二届委员会主席1名、副主席4名、秘书长1名、常务委员23名，蒙明儒当选主席，艾福田、常青、何正刚、李继芳当选副主席。会议期间收到委员提案131件。

第二届第二次、第三次会议先后于1988年3月16—19日、1989年2月28日在县城召开，听取和审议常委会工作报告及提案工作报告，通过大会决议，列席县人民代表大会。

三、第三届全体会议

1990年4月26日—5月2日，政协第三届荔波县委员会第一次会议在县城召开，议委员125名，列席人员25名。会议听取和审议政协第二届常委会工作报告、提案审查委员会关于第二届第三次会议以后提案办理情况报告和提案审查委员会关于提案审查情况的报告。全体委员列席县第十一届人大第一次会议。会议通过大会决议，决议强调，20世纪90年代是推进祖国和平统一、振兴中华民族的重要历史时期，人民政协对于维护政治、经济和社会的进一步稳定发展负有重大责任，必须以高度的政治责任感和使命感，积极参政议政，为全县的稳定发展发挥更大作用。会议选举产生政协荔波县第三届委员会主席1名、副主席4名、秘书长1名、常务委员20名，李德余当选主席，艾福田、何正刚、李继芳、蒙育崇当选副主席。会议收到经济建设、文化教育、宣传、医药卫生、党政管理、水利电力、劳动人事、法制建设、城建、交通、农林牧生产、职工福利、计划生育等方面的委员提案152件。

第三届第二次、第三次会议分别于1991年3月26—31日、1992年3月24—30日在县城召开，听取和审议政协常务委员会工作报告及提案工作报告，通过大会决议，列席县人民代表大会。

四、第四届全体会议

1993年4月19—24日，政协第四届荔波县委员会第一次会议在县城召开，出席会议委员135名，列席人员25名。会议听取并审议政协荔波县第三届委员会常务委员会工作报告；听取和审议第三届第三次会议以后提案工作情况报告；通过会议决议。全体委员列席县第十二届人大第一次会议。会议选举产生政协荔波县第四届委员会主席1名、副主席6名、秘书长1名、常务委员20名，黄玉成当选主席，艾福田、欧崇顺、李继芳、杨智英、杨志枰、王朝贵当选副主席。

第四届第二次、第三次、第四次、第五次会议分别于1994年3月13—17日、1995年3月22—25日、1996年4月22—26日、1997年3月10—14日在县城召开，听取和审议常委会工作报告及提案工作报告，通过大会决议，列席县人民代表大会。

五、第五届全体会议

1998年3月7—13日，政协第五届荔波县委员会第一次会议在县城召开，出席会议委员135名。中共荔波县委书记张仕福到会作重要讲话。会议听取并审议政协第四届常委会工作报告；通过第五届委员会第一次会议提案审查情况的报告；通过第五届委员会第一次会议决议。全体委员列席县人大第十三届第一次会议。会议选举产生政协荔波县第五届委员会主席1名、副主席6名、秘书长1名、常务委员20名，黄玉成当选主席，程志安、冉孟华、杨志枰、卢付银、邓群芳、李荣庆当选副主席。

第五届第二次、第三次、第四次、第五次会议分别于1999年3月29日—4月5日、2000年4月7—10日、2001年3月21—25日、2002年3月17—19日在县城召开，听取和审议政协常务委员会工作报告及提案工作报告，通过大会决议，列席县人民代表大会。其间，第五次会议增选田景胜为副主席。

六、第六届全体会议

2003年3月7—11日，政协第六届荔波县委员会第一次会议在县城召开，出席会议委员149人，特邀县领导和老领导29名，列席人员40名。会议听取和审议政协第五届常委会工作报告；审议通过政协荔波县第六届委员会第一次会议决议和提案委员会关于第六届第一次会议提案审查情况的报告。全体委员列席县第十四届人民代表大会第一次会议。会议选举产生政协荔波县第六届委员会主席1名、副主席6名、秘书长1名、常务委员21名，田景胜当选主席，何建飞、卢付银、邓群芳、李荣庆、付洪、冯发新当选副主席。

第六届第二次、第三次、第四次会议分别于2004年3月9—11日、2005年3月3—5日、2006年3月21—25日在县城召开，听取和审议常委会工作报告及提案工作报告，通过大会决议，列席县人民代表大会。

七、第七届全体会议

2007年1月5—8日，政协第七届荔波县委员会第一次会议在县城召开，出席会议委员155人，特邀县领导和老领导29名，列席人员40名。中共荔波县委书记王振金到会并作重要讲话。会议听取和审议政协第六届常委会工作报告；审议通过第七届委员会第一次会议决议和提案委员会关于第七届委员会第一次会议提案审查情况的报告；通过大会决议。全体委员列席县第十五届人大第一次会议。会议选举产生政协荔波县第七届委员会主席1名、副主席4名、秘书长1名、常务委员23名，董豫黔当选主席，程志安、莫永开、李荣庆、莫春继当选副主席。

第七届第二次会议于2008年2月17—19日在县城召开，会议听取和审议第七届常委会工作报告及提案审查委员会关于第七届第一次会议以后提案办理情况报告和提案审查委员会关于提案审查情况的报告，通过大会决议，列席县人民代表大会。

1984—2008年县政协历届领导任职情况一览表

表7-2

届次	职务	姓名	性别	民族	任职时间（年、月）	备注
第一届	主席	蒙明儒	男	布依族	1984.11—1987.8	中共党员
	副主席	李德余	男	汉族	1984.11—1987.8	中共党员
		艾福田	男	汉族	1984.11—1987.8	中共党员
		常青	男	水族	1984.11—1987.8	无党派
		何正刚	男	布依族	1984.11—1987.8	无党派
第二届	主席	蒙明儒	男	布依族	1987.8—1990.4	中共党员
	副主席	艾福田	男	汉族	1987.8—1990.4	中共党员
		李继芳	女	汉族	1987.8—1990.4	无党派
		常青	男	水族	1987.8—1990.4	无党派
		何正刚	男	布依族	1987.8—1990.4	无党派
第三届	主席	李德余	男	汉族	1990.4—1993.4	中共党员
	副主席	艾福田	男	汉族	1990.4—1993.4	中共党员
		何正刚	男	布依族	1990.4—1993.4	无党派
		李继芳	女	汉族	1990.4—1993.4	无党派
		蒙育崇	男	水族	1990.4—1993.4	无党派
		欧崇顺	男	布依族	1991.3—1993.4	中共党员
第四届	主席	黄玉成	男	汉族	1993.4—1998.3	中共党员
	副主席	艾福田	男	汉族	1993.4—1998.3	中共党员
		欧崇顺	男	布依族	1993.4—1998.3	中共党员

续表7－2

届 次	职 务	姓名	性别	民族	任职时间（年、月）	备 注
第四届	副主席	李继芳	女	汉族	1993.4—1998.3	无党派
		杨智英	男	侗族	1993.4—1998.3	无党派
		杨志枰	男	苗族	1993.4—1998.3	无党派
		王朝贵	男	汉族	1993.4—1998.3	中共党员
		程志安	男	汉族	1996.4—1998.3	增补
第五届	主 席	黄玉成	男	汉族	1998.3—2003.3	中共党员
	副主席	程志安	男	汉族	1998.3—2003.3	中共党员
		冉孟华	男	汉族	1998.3—2003.3	中共党员
		杨志枰	男	苗族	1998.3—2003.3	无党派
		卢付银	男	瑶族	1998.3—2003.3	中共党员
		邓群芳	女	汉族	1998.3—2003.3	无党派
		李荣庆	女	布依族	1998.3—2003.3	无党派
		田景胜	男	水族	2002.3—2003.3	中共党员
第六届	主 席	田景胜	男	水族	2003.3—2007.1	中共党员
	副主席	何建飞	男	布依族	2003.3—2007.1	中共党员
		卢付银	男	瑶族	2003.3—2007.1	中共党员
		邓群芳	女	汉族	2003.3—2007.1	无党派
		李荣庆	女	布依族	2003.3—2007.1	无党派
		付 洪	男	汉族	2003.3—2007.1	无党派
		冯发新	男	汉族	2003.3—2007.1	无党派
第七届	主 席	董豫黔	男	汉族	2007.1—	中共党员
	副主席	程志安	男	汉族	2007.1—	中共党员
		莫永开	男	布依族	2007.1—	无党派
		李荣庆	女	布依族	2007.1—	无党派
		莫春继	男	布依族	2007.1—	中共党员

第三节 常委会议

第一届常委会共召开常委会议17次，分别学习《坚持四项基本原则，反对资产阶级自由化》《建设有中国特色的社会主义》和中共中央《关于经济体制改革的决定》《关于进一步搞好农村经济的十项政策》《中共中央关于社会主义精神文明建设指导方针的决议》，通过县政协《关于学习和贯彻中共十二大文件的决议》等。

第二届常委会共召开常委会议15次，讨论《关于坚持和完善中国共产党领导的多党合作和政治协商制度的意见》，审议通过《关于贯彻中共十三届四中全会精神的决议》，传达中共中央、国务院和北京戒严部队的一系列重要决策、通告等。

第三届常委会共召开常委会议15次，学习、宣传和落实中共十四大报告精神，对有关全局的大事提出意见和建议，协商讨论加快全县改革开放和加速经济发展步伐等重大问题。

第四届常委会共召开常委会议22次，先后学习《人民日报》社论《高举邓小平理论伟大旗帜阔步前进》、中共十五大精神传达提纲；听取县政府工作通报和县工商局关于县城农贸市场建设情况的通报，与会委员就全县农贸市场建设现状作认真分析，给工商局提出吸纳社会闲散资金加强县城农贸市场开发的建议；讨论协商《中共荔波县委关于制定荔波县国民经济和社会发展“九五”计划和2010年远景目标的建议》《荔波县人民政府关于荔波县国民经济和社会发展“九五”计划和2010年远景目标纲要报告（征求意见稿）》，与会委员提出修改意见和建议43条。

第五届常委会共召开常委会议26次，分别听取县政府工作情况通报、听取并讨论县政府工作报告征求意见稿；协商讨论县政府“十五”规划纲要报告征求意见稿；听取并讨论县政府关于全县财税工作情况的通报；听取县教育局与团县委关于“希望工程”及项目进展情况和县公安局禁毒工作情况的通报；听取并讨论县计生局关于贯彻《贵州省计划生育条例》和独生子女优惠政策执行情况通报；听取县教育局关于“两基”工作情况、县林业局关于珠江防护林工程情况和县计生局关于人口与计划生育情况的汇报；听取并讨论茂兰自然保护区管理处关于发展全县生态旅游规划的意见等。

第六届常委会共召开常委会14次，分别学习《中国人民政治协商会议章程》、中共中央总书记胡锦涛关于“领导干部‘做官先做人，万事民为先’”的重要批示和《中共中央关于印发〈“三个代表”重要思想纲要〉的通知》《中共中央关于在全党兴起学习贯彻“三个代表”重要思想新高潮的通知》《十六届三中全会公报》《中共中央关于完善社会主义市场经济体制若干问题的决定》《中共中央、国务院关于促进农民增加收入若干政策的意见》《中共中央关于进一步学习和贯彻实施〈中华人民共和国宪法〉的通知》《中共中央办公厅关于学习贯彻〈中国人民政治协商会议章程〉的通知》《宪法》及宪法修正案、《政协章程》及政协章程修正案，中共十六届四中全会公报、《中共中央关于在全党开展以实践“三个代表”重要思想为主要内容的保持共产党员先进性教育活动的意见》《胡锦涛在贵州考察工作结束时的讲话》《中共中央关于进一步加强中国共产党领导的多党合作和政治协商制度建设的意见》《反分裂国家法》《中共中央关于加强人民政协工作的意见》、胡锦涛“七一”重要讲话精神、全国政协《关于学习贯彻〈中共中央关于加强人民政协工作的意见〉的决定》《全国政协副主席、中央统战部部长刘延东在黔南调研时的讲话》和中共贵州省委《关于加强人民政协工作的实施意见》等；分别传达省政协第九届第二至四次会议精神、中共贵州省委第九届第七次全委会议、省政协人口环资委工作会议和州政协第九届常委会议精神等；听取县政府通报经济社会发展运行情况，听取并审议县政府《关于荔波县国民经济和社会发展第十一个五年规划纲要的报告（草案）》，审议县政府工作报告；听取县政府相关部门关于县城建设、畜牧业发展、荔波机场建设、“申遗”工作、调整农业产业结构、水书征集抢救、社会主义新农村建设；专题研究县人民医院、县中医院整合问题，协商水书申报第一批国家级非物质文化遗产代表作名录工作。

第七届常委会共召开常委会议22次，分别学习政协第十届全国委员会第五次会议决议、胡锦涛在中纪委第七次全体会议上的讲话、《中共中央关于加强人民政协工作的意见》《中国人民政治协商会议章程》，学习十七大会议精神、省长林树森在荔波调研时的重要讲话、省建设厅关于荔波樟江风景名胜区建设规划等有关文件；分别传达省两会、州政协十届一次全会和省政协提案工作等会议精神；听取县政府工作报告（草案）、2008年“十件实事”“十项重点工作”、荔波县国民经济和社会发展计划执行情况及国民经济计划（草案）报告、荔波县财政报告情况和财政预算（草案）

等报告；听取县政府旅发大会工作进展情况通报，听取县政府相关部门关于煤矿整合情况、农村合作医疗、糖蔗种植及蔗糖加工生产等情况通报。会议讨论确定年度调研课题、旅游商品开发经营问题、糖蔗种植管理问题、非公经济经营管理和发展的问题（含和谐煤矿建设问题）；分别就樟江河谷农业旅游观光、旅游文化包装、“两基”迎国检、巩固教育成果、乡村旅游的现状及发展、应对危机抓发展、沉着应对挑战求跨越、发挥群团工作在构建和谐社会中的作用、巩固优化煤炭支柱产业在荔波经济发展中的作用等问题提出意见和建议。

第四节　工作机构

1983年4月，中共荔波县委作出建立荔波县政协的决定。是年8月，省委批准成立荔波县政协。1984年1月，县委确定组成荔波县政协第一届筹备小组。10月15日，成立政协荔波县第一届委员会筹备委员会，召开了第一次会议，正式成立县政协。1990年5月以前，设办公室、提案审查委员会、文史资料委员会。1998年3月，县政府智力支边办公室设在县政协。荔波县政协第一届、第二届、第三届所有工作均由办公室统一安排落实，第四届（1993年4月—1998年3月）开始增设提案委、文史委、支边办（县政府挂靠机构），至2008年年底，政协内设机构不变。

第二章　主要工作

第一节　委员提案

1984年11月—1987年4月，政协第一届荔波县委员会召开全委会3次，收到委员提案共304件，共办理完毕207件，办复率97.18%。

1987年8月—1989年2月，政协第二届荔波县委员会召开全委会3次，收到委员提案共237件。

1990年4月—1992年3月，政协第三届荔波县委员会召开全委会3次，收到委员提案共387件，办复率100%。

从1995年起，提案委对提案工作建立“提案委员意见回执卡”制度，要求承办单位在给提案人回复提案办理意见的同时，随件寄去“提案委员意见回执卡”，恳请提案人收阅办复意见后，须填写“回执卡”，签上自己满意或不满意的意见，返送县政协提案委，对不满意的，提案委督促承办单位妥善办理，力争提案人满意，促进提案办理质量提高。

1993年4月—1997年3月，政协第四届荔波县委员会召开全委会5次，收到委员提案共494件，办复率100%。其中，政治生活、经济建设119件，财贸26件，教育、科技、文化、卫生、环保140件，城建、交通32件，农业、林业、牧业、水电77件，法制建设47件，旅游开发31件，其他22件。提案委提案进行整理归类，拟定承办单位，县政府办公室、县政协办公室联合召开提案办理工作会，将提案送达相关单位办理，办复率100%。在第四届第五次会议上，有18名委员联名提出《建议在樟江大街十字路口处设立交通安全指示灯》提案，得到县委、县政府高度重视，拨出9.5万元安装交通安全自动控制指示灯。

从第四届第一次会议起，每年进行好提案、提案办理先进单位和提案积极奖评选表彰。

1999年，根据《中国人民政治协商会议章程》有关规定，结合荔波县提案办理工作情况，县政协积极配合县政府研究制定《关于办理县政协委员提案的暂行规定》，并以县政府文件下发政府各工作部门贯彻执行。

1998年3月—2002年3月，政协第五届荔波县委员会召开全委会5次，收到委员提案共742件，办复率100%。其中，政治生活、经济建设392件，教育、科技、文化、卫生、体育231件，人事、劳动、政法及其他119件。县第五届政协委员陈建军撰写《关于对教学质量有特殊贡献的中小学教师实行“重奖”的建议》的提案，在交提案的当天得到其他9名委员签名支持，交办后得到县委、县政府的高度重视和承办单位的认真办理，是年，县政府拨款5万元、县教育局出资3万元作教育发展基金和高考奖励基金，对教学质量有特殊贡献的中小学教师实行重奖激励。该提案当年被评为好提案。此后，县委、县政府每年都拨出资金对教学质量有特殊贡献的教师进行奖励。

在第五届第三次会议上，有11名县政协委员联名提出《关于尽快将荔波旅游发展纳入国民经济发展计划和财政预算的建议》提案，得到县委、县政府采纳，在制定的《跨世纪发展思路》中将旅游业作为后续支柱产业进行培育。

县政协从第五届起，对在届内连续被授予“提案办理先进单位”的承办单位进行表彰，第五届表彰奖励连续5年被评为先进的提案承办单位有县政府办、农业局、教育局、交通局。

2003年3月—2006年3月，政协第六届荔波县委员会召开全委会4次，收到委员提案共431件，办复率100%。其中，经济建设280件，教育、科技、文化、卫生、体育99件，政法、人事劳动、统战及其他52件。在2003年的提案工作中，制定《关于办理政协提案实施意见》，并以县委办文件下发到各部门贯彻执行。同时，推行主席、副主席领衔督察重点提案工作制度，并制定《荔波县政协关于主席、副主席领衔督察重点提案实施办法》，加强提案办理工作制度化、规范化。县政协六届常委陈建军在六届一次会议上政协委员提出《关于在我县建立政府采购审计制度的建议》的提案，得到县委、县政府的重视，为防止政府采购工作暗箱操作，在办理政府采购中都邀请县纪委、审计人员参加招标采购。此提案被评为好提案。

在第六届第二次会议上的委员提案《关于解决甲良中学师生饮水问题的建议》被县水利局采纳后，积极筹措资金80多万元落实该建议，解决甲良中学师生及甲良镇政府所在地饮水问题。

第六届中受表彰奖励的提案承办单位共36个。

2007年，县政协根据《中共中央关于加强人民政协工作的意见》，修订《荔波县办理政协委员提案暂行规定》，以县委文件下发实施，为提案工作规范开展提供机制保障。

2007年1月—2008年2月，政协第七届荔波县委员会召开全委会2次，收到委员提案共248件，办复率100%。其中，经济建设167件，教育、科技、文化、卫生、体育53件，政法、统战及其他28件。提案被采纳或部分采纳208件。在第七届第一次会议上，县政协委员提出《关于禁止佳荣铅锌选矿厂污水处理流入樟江的建议》的提案，县环保局商请州环境监测站、县防疫站等部门技术人员多次深入佳荣镇境内的2个铅锌选矿厂，对污水进行采样分析鉴定，提出整改方案和时限，定期到厂进行跟踪督查，促使企业加强对生产废渣和尾矿库污水渗漏的治理，取得成效。

2008年2月县政协七届二次会议期间，审查立案提案132件。其中，经济建设98件，教育、科技、文化、卫生、体育25件，政法、统战及其他9件。交付34个承办单位办理，办复率100%。提案被采纳或部分采纳114件，占立案数的86.4%。

在七届二次会议上，县政协委员提出《关于建立健全干部职工体检制度的建议》的提案，得到县委主要领导的批示并提交县委常委会议研究，同意建立干部职工每两年体检一次的制度。

1993—2008年，县政协评选表彰好提案共164件、提案办理先进单位共133个（次）、获提案积极奖共48人次。

第二节　视察调研

一、视察

1987年，县政协组织科技工作组政协委员对县内家庭果园及瑶山林场的杉木生产进行视察。

1992年10月，组织州、县政协委员13人对荔波民族中学和县水电局进行为期一周的视察，形成《荔波民族中学视察报告》《荔波县水电局兴办经济实体视察报告》，提出的建议得到被视察单位采纳。

1996年11月，组织县政协委员20人对治理小吃街脏、乱、差情况及米行从新农贸市场搬迁回老农贸市场（东门）形成粮食市场的情况进行视察。

2005年，组织县政协委员28人对阳凤裕民生态养殖场、观音山养殖示范区、石灰坳瑶山鸡养殖场等规模养殖基地进行视察。

2007年，组织县政协委员先后对糖蔗种植情况和蔗糖加工基地、县城家禽屠宰脱毛摊点卫生状况、佳荣镇铅锌选矿厂排污情况、县城临街商铺打麻将现象等进行视察，提出整改意见和建议，引起县委、县政府的重视。

2008年，结合开展“整脏治乱”工作，组织部分政协委员先后对玉屏、朝阳、瑶山、驾欧等乡（镇）及小七孔景区的“整脏治乱”工作进行视察，对视察单位存在的问题提出整改意见和建议，引起各乡（镇）及景区管理部门的重视并进行改进。

1984—2008年共组织政协委员视察88次，撰写视察报告52篇。

二、调研

第一届县政协委员开展调研活动11次，撰写调研报告11篇。

第二届县政协委员开展调研活动10次，撰写调研报告10篇。

第三届县政协委员开展调研活动5次，撰写调研报告5篇。

第四届县政协委员开展调研活动12次，撰写调研报告12篇。其中，1995年5月，针对当年的提案中关于县农机厂的生存发展问题，组织县农机局、财政局、人劳局、工商联、政府办等单位的州、县政协委员和单位负责人，到县农机厂开展调查研究，写出《关于对县农机厂目前状况的调查和建议》的调研报告和《关于重视和帮助农机厂抓好管理和生产的建议案》，报县委、县政府后得到重视和采纳，县委、县政府重新组建农机厂新的领导班子，并派有县政协领导组成的工作组进驻农机厂进行厂风整顿，使该厂生产与经营管理步入正轨。

第五届县政协委员开展调研活动10次，撰写调研报告10篇。其中，1998年，围绕县委、县政府“创建公园县、生态示范县，培育旅游业成为支柱产业”的中心工作，组织科技界政协委员成立调研组，开展樟江上游流域涵养林保护情况调研活动，实地考察佳荣拉学河、水维河和水春河沿岸林区，查明樟江河水资源的变化状况和山林采伐、木材营销情况，写出《关于樟江上游流域涵养林保护情况》的调研报告，并形成建议案，得到县委、县政府的重视和采纳，关闭了乡（镇）木材市场，同时，向州、省呈报要求建立月亮山自然保护区的建议。2001年，为解决农村群众必要的生活烧柴问题，寻求植造薪柴林的可行性，组织部分政协委员和县农办、扶贫办、林业局等单位负责人赴广西凤山、天峨等地考察学习任豆树推广种植情况，写出考察调研报告，提交《关于推广种植任豆树的建议案》，县委、县政府采纳并责成县林业局研究执行。

第六届县政协委员开展调研活动8次，撰写调研报告8篇。其中，2005年，根据县委的安排，针对县人民医院和县中医院是否重组整合问题，组织部分政协委员及政协机关副科级以上干部成立3个调研组开展专题调研，采取分发问卷表、召开座谈会、社会走访、专访有关科室等形式深入调查，并召开第六届第九次政协常委会进行专题协商，认真讨论，征求各方面意见，在充分分析利弊的基础上形成调研报告，提出不重组整合的建议，得到县委的采纳。

第七届县政协委员开展调研活动9次，撰写调研报告9篇。2007年7—8月，针对群众反映强烈的市场猪肉价格上涨过快问题，组织部分政协委员和县畜牧局、物价局、商业总公司等相关部门负责人到9个乡（镇）和生猪规模养殖场、专业户中调研，写出《荔波县生猪生产情况调研报告》，阐明猪肉价格上涨的原因，提出对策及建议5条，得到县委、县政府的重视和采纳。2008年5月，组织部分政协委员到永康、洞塘、茂兰、水利、播尧、瑶山、捞村、朝阳等乡（镇），采取一看二访三听的调查方式，详细了解全县糖蔗种植田间管理情况和存在的问题，写出《荔波县糖蔗种植管理情况调研报告》，针对存在的问题提出建议6条，得到县委、县政府的重视和采纳。是年9月，组织部分政协常委赴湖南绍山市、江西九江市、浙江省等地考察具有地方特色的旅游商品开发情况，对他们旅游商品生产管理模式和经营方式作细致的调查研究，写出《地方特色的旅游商品开发调研报告》，指出荔波县特色旅游商品市场存在的5个问题，并提出对策和建议，得到县委、县政府的重视和采纳。

第三节　文史资料编辑

1985年12月，为纪念抗日战争胜利40周年，编辑出版《荔波文史资料第一辑（抗日专辑）》，全书3.8万字，正文收录文章26篇。

1987—1990年4月，编印《文史资料》共11期共11万字；征集稿件80篇共25万字，表彰征集撰稿人员10名；与省、州及独山、丹寨、环江展开协作，交换资料，共同整理编辑出版文史资料书《黔南事变》；征集月亮山游击队和红七军进驻翁昂开展革命活动史料以及何老幺收留红七军伤员治伤养病的珍贵史料，与从江县交换有关佳荣乡月亮山游击队革命活动和莫御的资料；收集荔波县建置沿革，红七军在荔波、月亮山农民起义，邓恩铭烈士轶事及遗诗等。

1990年5月—1993年4月，编辑出版第二辑《荔波文史资料》、第三辑文史资料《荔波诗词集》，《荔波诗词集》收录了明代至当代600余年间荔波58名诗词作者的作品443首；翻印荔波名人覃金锡（即覃二如）的遗著《赘赘篇》。

2000年7月，编辑出版《贵州旅游文史系列丛书·荔波卷》，主要内容为大七孔景区、小七孔景区、水春河景区、茂兰景区、红色文化、民族文化旅游资源介绍。

2002年，出版第四辑文史资料《教育专辑》，收录文章52篇共11万字，内容包括荔波教育史考，清末至民国的私塾和公学教育，新中国成立后全县普教、扫盲、幼教、职教和师范教育等。

2005年，收集整理汇编第一届至第五届县政协全委会资料《政协文集》，内容包括中共荔波县委领导讲话、政协中共党组请示、中共荔波县委批复、筹备工作报告、开幕词、常委工作报告、提案工作报告、提案审查报告、会议决议、闭幕词等文献，共20万字。

2006—2008年，征集整理县内各民族文化史料，参与承编中国少数民族文史资料书系之一《水族百年实录》。

第四节　联谊活动

1991年，与荔波县相邻的黔、桂两省（区）部分县政协为促进毗邻地区联谊协作，建立黔、桂两省（区）8县（市）政协联谊协作会议制度，参加联谊的8个县（市）为金城江、天峨、南丹、环江、独山、三都、平塘、罗甸。1991年8月20日和1992年10月14日，先后两次由荔波县政协牵头组织召开预备会议，协商讨论，明确联谊协作会议的宗旨，制定章程。1992年12月10—12日，在荔波县举行黔、桂两省区8县（市）政协联谊协作会第一次年会，贵州省政协发来贺电，两地州（广西河池地区、黔南州）政协主席在会上作讲话，中共荔波县委书记、县长在会上作讲话，各县（市）政协主席、秘书长交流政协工作、智力支边工作经验，介绍各县（市）基本情况及经济开发情况。会上，通过协商洽谈，达成意向性协作项目协议34项，金额共22万元；交换协作项目7项，价值250万元。会议充分肯定在少数民族地区和贫困山区开展横向联系，加强区域合作，逐步形成有特色的区域经济，是发展社会主义市场经济的必然趋势，政协之间的联系协作是经济发展的客观要求。此后，增加广西罗城、凤山、宜山（宜州）县和都匀市为联谊协作会成员，定名为“黔桂两省区十二县市政协联谊协作会”。

2005年11月16—18日，黔、桂12县（市）政协第十四次联谊协作会议在荔波县城召开。会议的主要议题是全面贯彻落实党的十六大、十六届四中全会、五中全会、全国政协十届三次会议精神，研讨政协怎样为构建社会主义和谐社会多做贡献，交流为构建社会主义和谐社会取得的成绩和经验。通过理论研究和工作探讨，不断推进新时期政协工作，促进县（市、区）小康社会建设进程。参加会议的有金城江、宜州、凤山、天峨、南丹、环江、罗城、都匀、独山、三都、平塘、罗甸等各县（市、区）政协主席、副主席、秘书长（或办公室主任）。

第五节　智力支边

1984年11月，成立县智力支边联系小组办公室，围绕县委、县政府的中心工作，开展智力支边活动。

一、教育支边

1986年4月，邀请贵州省艺术学校教师、民革党员郑皓如到荔波，帮助县文化局文工队训练队员和编排节目，为期1个月。

1987年1月，邀请民革贵州省委副主委杨瑞芝等6名教师到荔波进行支边讲学。

1991年，与教育局配合，采取请进来、派出去、走下去的方式，请省、州教师到荔波讲学，组织县内教师赴贵阳、平塘考察学习共3批92人次，组织县内有教学经验的教师17名到乡（镇）学校开展支边教学活动，为教育办实事。

1998—2004年，从香港恩慈基金会慈善企业家黄佩球引资总计17.25万元，资助佳荣镇大土村小学建教学楼，改善办学条件，帮助该校贫困学生70名。

1998年，从香港田家炳基金会引进价值1.6万元图书，捐赠给甲良中学、甲良小学及玉屏中学、茂兰小学。

1999—2002年，从美籍华人树华基金会引进资金2万元，资助县民族中学贫困女学生40名。

1999—2003年，从州寒窗基金会引资0.78元，资助考入高校的贫困学生8名。

1999—2008年，从美籍华人燃灯基金会引资57.96万元，先后资助佳荣镇的拉先小学、拉学小学、拉毛小学、拉易小学、高里小学、水碰小学、拉亮小学、拉吾小学，翁昂乡的洞常小学，永康乡的尧古小学、甲棒小学，方村乡的红坭小学，洞塘乡的木朝小学，甲良镇的金华小学、甲岸小学共15所小学建教学楼和帮助贫困学生；资助县民族中学和县职业中学共243人。同期，从农工党贵州省委、农工党湖北省委、农工党广东省委引进资金共7.46万元，先后资助瑶山民族中学少数民族学生393人，奖励该校优秀教师6人。

2000—2007年，从江苏省爱德基金会引进资金共55.17万元，用于新建玉屏镇水扒小学、水利乡水龙小学、茂兰镇吉王小学、洞塘乡肯甫小学以及三合小学、瑶山乡董蒙小学、播尧乡拉美小学、佳荣镇甲料小学、朝阳镇岜马小学、捞村乡力书小学、永康乡董亥小学、永康乡德门小学等12所小学教学楼，资助爱德项目学校贫困学生共1341人。

2002年，从民主建国会贵州省委会引进价值1.5万元图书744册，捐给县内第一批爱德项目学校6所。

2003—2004年，温州市公路管理处爱心人士盛国俊捐赠1.8万元，资助茂兰中学贫困学生40人。

2004年，邀请九三学社黔南州委副主委、黔南师院数学系副教授李强到荔波开展“解读新课程标准”专题讲学，参加听讲学的教师共336人。

2005年，香港爱心人士梁惠琼向永康乡德门村徐于亮小学捐赠毛衣133件，邬采霜捐赠围巾133条（折合人民币0.47万元）。

是年，美国科技教育协会吴章镕在驾欧乡建立爱华公共图书馆，捐赠的书刊价值5700美元，分5年捐付。至2008年，已捐赠书籍2263册（折合人民币1.4万元）。

2007年，九三学社黔南州委向永康乡捐赠价值0.6万元的书籍、棉被。

2007—2008年，香港爱心人士梁惠琼夫妇向永康乡德门村德门小学捐赠价值6.8万元的学习用具、体育器材、生活用品等。

2008年，从香港“两地一心”慈善机构引资25万元，补助新建佳荣镇拉祥小学、播尧乡觉巩小学教学楼。从香港慈恩基金会引进资金15.15万元，用于新建方村乡方村小学教学楼13.35万元，并奖励播尧乡觉巩小学、瑶山乡瑶山小学、永康乡尧古小学优秀学生共90人。从深圳慈善会引资3.57万元，资助播尧乡播尧中学、迎春小学、中寨小学贫困学生150人。从美国教育生活基金会引资2.28万元，资助县民族中学高中部瑶族学生13人。

二、卫生支边

1985年12月，邀请芜湖地区医院五官科主任医师杨景云到荔波支边，指导县医院五官科医生提高喉梗阻的早期诊断与治疗抢救技术，接诊五官科患者，并举办学术讲座2次。

1985—1993年，争取省人民医院到县人民医院定点支边，省人民医院每年派医务专家到荔波开展医疗智力支边活动共35人次，共计服务204天，对县医务人员培训340人次，为离退休干部、县级干部、高级教师、农艺师、工程师体检共计271人次，开展专家门诊，为患者就诊3200多人次。

1997年，从省人民医院引进资金0.65万元，用于改善瑶山卫生院设施。

2000年，从中国初保基金会引进价值5万元的医药器材资助县医院。

2002年11月8日，邀请贵阳医学院、中医学院的医学专家3人到荔波开展医学讲学培训，培训医务人员共89人。是年，从农工党贵州省委引进价值3万元的医药用品捐赠给县医院和瑶山乡卫生院。

2003年8月5日，邀请贵州省人民医院、贵阳医学院附属医院、贵阳中医二附院的3名医学专家到荔波县进行3个专题医学培训，共培训40人。

2004年4月15日，邀请世界知名学者、全国著名皮肤病防治专家、全国政协原委员、贵阳医学院教授韦国仁到荔波开展医疗义诊，义诊人数108人。是年，从省卫生厅引资8万元，补助新建翁昂乡卫生院业务用房。从农工党贵州省委引进价值1万元的医疗药品和器械捐赠给翁昂乡卫生院。

2005年11月8日，邀请贵阳医学院、省妇保所的3名专家到荔波县进行3个专题医学讲学培训，培训医务人员131人。

是年，农工党贵州省委为翁昂乡卫生院捐赠价值0.6万元的药品，同时为该乡20户贫困户捐赠大米500公斤、弹花被20床、棉衣20件，折合人民币0.35万元。2007年，又为水利乡卫生院捐赠价值0.8万元的药品。

2007年3月6日，邀请省州医学会妇产科、省人民医院妇产科、遵义医学院妇产科的4名专家到荔波进行4个专题医学讲学培训，培训医务人员共计88人。

2008年，从香港慈恩基金会引进资金3.11万元，新建永康乡尧古村卫生院。

三、农业技术支边

1986年1—5月，县支边办邀请省特等劳模、省农科院副院长李桂莲先后5次到荔波传授早菜栽培技术，并重点培养种早菜的示范户6户。

1991年7月，组织农民技术员17人赴三都县、贵阳市花溪区和白云区、罗甸县参观学习；是年9月，邀请农业专家到荔波讲学，试种紧凑型山东掖单苞谷良种。是年10月，组织县相关部门、乡（镇）、村“两委”（党支部委员会、村委员会）及养蚕示范户共42人，赴广西环江县考察种桑养蚕产业。

1992年8月，组织县、乡供销社主任、洞塘乡领导和种植五倍子示范户共18人，赴遵义、道真县考察五倍子人工培植技术。回县后，邀请遵义地区科委高级农艺师杨树槐到荔波进行技术培训，参加学习的有洞塘乡农民95人。11月，组织朝阳镇拉扶村农民8人，赴广西河池市、宜山县考察广西沙田柚生产，并争取列入省科协扶贫项目，获得无息贷款2万元，在拉扶村发展沙田柚200亩。

1993年，先后举办实验和推广强力增长素、油菜育苗、蔬菜、沙田柚、烤烟、五倍子生产技术培训班5期，由县政协委员中的农业技术干部传授技术，参加培训的农民233人次。

1994—1996年，举办乡土人才培训班31期，培训人员4281人次；举办其他培训班18期，培训人员440人次。邀请专家、教授及专业技术人员讲学达108人，其中，省38人、州13人、县57人。

1997年、1999年，从农工党贵州省委引进资金0.65万元，在瑶山乡开展科技养殖培训，在朝阳镇交朝村实施沼气池示范建设。

1997年，从黔南州水电局、卫生局、民委引进资金6万元，修建茂兰水庆人饮工程；从黔南州水泥厂、都匀水泥厂、福泉、都匀化肥厂引进价值1.3万元的水泥、化肥，支持瑶山乡路面硬化和农业生产。

2002年9月，邀请县科协领导到瑶山乡高桥村、玉屏镇拉岜村、拉鱼村实地开展柚树栽培管理技术培训，培训农民共210人。是年，从三都县引进皇竹草在玉屏镇尧排村示范种植，种植面积2亩，其中1.8亩作留种用，0.2亩作饲料用草。

2002—2008年，先后从江苏省爱德基金会引资36万元，在朝阳镇拉扶村、花高村建沼气池100口，在玉屏镇水甫村、水春村建沼气池300口，在玉屏镇水甫村实施“爱德”经果林建设项目面积200亩。同时，请县农业局技术员对实施“爱德”经果林项目的农户开展现场管理技术培训及农业适用技术现场培训18次，培训人数共684人次。

2004年5月12日，组织农业技干11人参观贵阳花溪区蔬菜、白云区花卉、乌当区果树生产基地。

2005年6月24—25日，邀请省畜牧兽医学校畜牧专家5人到荔波县开展2天的畜牧讲学培训，共讲6个专题，培训120余人。

2008年，从香港黄族宗亲会引进资金3.57万元，资助播尧乡地莪村冰灾重灾户176户。

四、经贸支边

1990—1991年，县支边办协助县经委、县乡企局举办矿长、安全员、瓦检员技术培训班，邀请贵阳煤炭学校、红茂矿务局专家到荔波讲学。

1991年5月，组织商业等10个单位24人参加湘、黔、桂3省（区）融安产品展销会，推销产品，洽谈业务，沟通情况，交流经验。6月，举办企业管理培训班1期，邀请省民主建国会领导授课，参加学习的有供销社、商业局、经济委员会系统厂长、经理共34人。

1993年9月，为帮助洞塘乡开发酸梅资源，对酸梅进行精加工，筹办以酸梅为主的果脯系列食品加工，赴平塘考察，牵头写出建厂可行性报告，报州扶贫办立项。为发展乡镇企业，组织县有关部门和玉屏镇领导赴独山、贵定、贵阳考察冷冻牛肉、酱菜加工、奶牛发展项目。

1997年，引进都匀商人剂驿泉投资110万元，在茂兰开发亨发煤矿。此后没有再引进经贸支边项目。

第八篇
社会团体

中共十一届三中全会以后，荔波县各人民团体逐步恢复和建立，在中共荔波县委的领导下，人民团体发挥群众性、广泛性的作用，投入到改革开放、经济建设、文化建设、生态建设之中。1978—2008年，工会组织开展职工教育、劳动竞赛、民主管理、权益维护。共青团开展少先队、希望工程、创建青年文明号、志愿者行动、春晖行动等活动。妇女联合会维护妇女儿童的合法权益，开展“双学双比”“五好文明家庭”和“巾帼建功”的创建活动。工商业联合会维护会员权益，开展联谊、光彩事业活动，推动非公有制经济的发展。科学技术协会开展科普教育，建立科普网站，培训农村技术人才。文学艺术界联合会繁荣社会主义文化，创作出一批艺术成果，为人民群众服务。残疾人联合会权益保障，在康复、就业、特殊教育、助残等方面做了大量工作。

第一章 工 会

第一节 组织建设

1978年，县设有总工会，在机关单位、企业设基层工会。

1985年，全县有基层工会100个，会员3247人，占职工总数的81.76%。

1990年，企业改制重组和农民进城务工人员不断增加，基层工会组织不断发展。1991年，全县建基层工会119个，会员4598人，占职工总数4831人的95.18%。

2000年，县总工会下设县工人俱乐部、县职工服务中心。

至2008年，全县有基层工会288个，会员17627人，其中农民工会员11443人。

第二节 代表大会

第四次工会代表大会 1984年6月18—20日，荔波县第四次工会代表大会在县城召开。应到会代表127人，实到代表127人。其中，妇女37人，占代表总数的29.13%；少数民族35人，占代表总数的27.56%；共产党员52人，占代表总数的40.94%。大会听取和审议县总工会第三届委员会工作报告，并作出决议；选举产生县总工会第四届委员会委员21名、县总工会经费审查委员会委员5名；选举出席州工会第四次代表大会代表16名。全委会选举产生常务委员7名，主席1名、副主席1名。

第五次工会代表大会 1989年4月1—3日，荔波县第五次工会代表大会在县城召开。应到代表131人，实到123人；列席代表37人，实到23人；特邀代表21人。大会听取和审议第四届委员会工作报告和经费审查工作报告；选举产生县总工会第五届委员会委员13名、经费审查委员会委员5名。全委会选举产生常务委员5名，主席1名、副主席1名。

第六次工会代表大会 1995年9月19日，荔波县第六次工会代表大会在县城召开。应到会正式代表88人，实到会正式代表76人，列席、特邀代表10人。大会听取和审议第五届委员会工作报告和财务工作报告；选举产生第六届工会委员会委员15名、经费审查委员会委员5名。全委会选举产生常务委员7名，主席1名、副主席1名。

第七次工会代表大会 2001年11月1日，荔波县第七次工会代表大会在县城召开。应到会正式代表107人，实到会正式代表101人，列席、特邀代表28人。大会听取和审议第六届委员会工作报告和经费审查工作报告；选举产生县总工会第七届委员会委员21名、经费审查委员会委员5名。第七届第一次全委会选举产生常务委员7名，主席1名、副主席2名。

第八次工会代表大会 2007年9月6日，荔波县第八次工会代表大会在县城召开。应到会正式代

表107人，实到会正式代表103名，特邀、列席代表64名。大会听取和审议第七届委员会工作报告和经费审查工作报告；选举产生县总工会第八届委员会委员21名、经费审查委员会委员4名。第八届第一次全委会选举产生常务委员7名，主席1名、副主席2名。

第三节　工会活动

一、职工教育

1978年，县总工会主要以培训方式，开展职工思想教育和劳动技能学习。1980年4月，县总工会与县科协联合举办科技英语学习班，参加学习的职工100余人。1981年9月，县总工会聘请教师3人，开办职工初中文化补习班，主要补习语文、数学和英语，参加学习的职工30人，学习时间一年。除职工培训外，对部分农民工开展技能培训。1981—1988年，全县培训职工、农民工累计1470人次。1989年11月，县总工会组织培训基层工会主席、财务委员和经审委员共110人。1990年10月，县总工会举办女职工委员培训班，培训骨干59人。1993年，举办工会干部和职工培训班2期242人。1995年，先后开办《中华人民共和国工会法》《中华人民共和国劳动法》（以下简称“两法”）学习班2期98人。1996年，举办邓小平建设有中国特色社会主义理论和工会业务知识培训班9期，培训全县专职、兼职工会干部545人次。组织工会主席、厂长、经理以及职工学习“两法”165次，参加学习人数4000多人次。1997年，举办集体合同知识培训班2期，参加学习的有企业法人、工会主席等112人。1998年，全县各系统工会、基层工会举办中共十五大报告、邓小平理论培训班28期2150人。县总工会举办中共十五大精神知识竞赛，参赛人员5958人次，参赛面达职工总数的72%，职工受教育面98.7%。1999年5月、11月，县总工会举办基层工会干部理论和业务培训班2期92人次。2001年，组织全县企业职工学习贯彻中共十五大及十五届四中、五中、六中全会精神，学习总书记江泽民在建党80周年大会的讲话和“三个代表”重要思想。2004年，全县工会参加省总工会举办的《贵州省工会条例》知识竞赛，参赛职工占全县职工总数的60%。2007年，全县工会组织开展各种学习教育活动，参加学习的职工总计3150人。县总工会举办基层工会干部培训班2期60人。2008年，各级工会利用农民工夜校、职工夜校开展以稳定就业、促进就业为主要内容的技能培训活动，受训职工、农民工845人。

1989—2008年，全县累计培训职工、农民工25631人次。

二、劳动竞赛

1978年，全县城乡各条战线开展“农业学大寨”“工业学大庆”的社会主义劳动竞赛活动，以“大寨”“大庆”为榜样，机关职工做好本职工作，企业、社队搞好生产。年末，评选出先进单位5个、先进厂矿班组55个、先进生产者和先进工作者136名，在县城召开千人大会，给予表彰奖励。

1980—1986年，荔波银饰社开展民族银饰产品革新竞赛活动，生产出“荔兴”牌水族龙头手镯。该产品于1985年10月被轻工部、国家民委评为全国少数民族用品优质产品。1986年10月，“荔兴”牌布依族四季手镯在全省旅游品、工艺品、民族用品评比展销会上被评为优秀民族用品，获省轻纺工业厅、省旅游局和省民委“兴黔杯奖”。

1988年4月，县总工会与团县委、经委、科协联合发出《关于组织青年职工开展荔波县第一届“振兴杯”五小成果竞赛活动的通知》，要求团组织和各基层工会组织青年职工参加“振兴杯”的小建设、小发明、小设计、小革新、小改造的“五小”成果竞赛活动。

是年11月，公安局工会、县总工会职工马复明分别被评为全省工会财务先进单位、优秀财务工作者，受省总工会表彰。

1998年，小七孔镇电站职工蒙洪炳荣获贵州省“五一劳动奖章”。

2000年，荔波县总工会获全州工会财务工作竞赛评比二等奖，受州总工会表彰。

2001—2008年，全县被评为全省、全国先进工作者，受省部级表彰的职工28人。

三、民主管理

1996年，成立县企业解困工作领导小组，在全县企业开展全员劳动合同制工作。是年，全县95%企业实行全员劳动合同制。

1997年起，县总工会按照《中华人民共和国劳动法》的规定，与县经贸局、县工商联等相关单位合作，共同推动企业员工工资集体协商、集体合同工作制度，在全县国有企业、集体企业中开展工资集体协商和集体合同签订工作，随后逐年普及到非公企业中。

1999年，全县开始实施厂务公开制度。之后，县委、县政府在不同时期制定不同的工作重点，并根据需要及时调整厂务公开民主管理工作领导小组，逐步加大厂务公开、民主管理工作力度，厂务公开、民主管理工作从国家企业、事业逐步发展到集体单位、私营企业。

至2008年年底，全县实施厂务公开的国有企业及规模较大的私营企业共98家。全县签订工资集体协商和集体合同企业126家，占全县企业总数的80%，覆盖职工3831人。

四、职工帮扶

1978—1993年，全县工会组织对困难职工的帮助，主要是解决他们就业、生活、医疗、子女入学等方面的实际困难。

1994年，慰问特困职工27户，发慰问金共1110元；帮助困难职工67人，帮扶资金2.1万元。

1997年，走访困难企业6家，慰问困难职工家庭80户，帮助农机厂、土产公司、服务公司、林工商公司垫付离退休老干部的“两费”6166元。

1998年，县总工会与经贸局、人事劳动局联合成立荔波县特困企业职工互助基金会，制定管理办法，建立困难企业、困难职工档案，元旦、春节期间走访慰问困难职工。慰问企业特困职工94户，慰问金额1.01万元。1999年元旦、春节期间，慰问企业特困职工家庭78户，资金8440元。

2000年，两节期间荔波县总工会筹集了慰问金1.2万元，慰问了企业困难职工家庭80户。

2001年，在县委、州总工会的重视及县总工会的自身努力下，走访、慰问了企业困难职工98户，发放慰问金18800元。

至2008年的30年间，县总工会在元旦、春节、“六一”儿童节慰问及“金秋助学”等活动中，帮扶困难职工、农民工子女2845人次，帮扶资金67.93万元。

五、文体活动

1978—1983年，每年春节、“五一”、国庆等节日都举办拔河、扭秧歌、猜谜语等文体活动。1984年5月，举办纪念“五四”运动65周年“振兴中华读书演讲会”，参加活动400余人。经评选，报州职工读书委员会审定，读书活动先进单位14个，先进辅导员11人，先进个人40人，出席州召开的读书代表大会并受表彰。1986年5月，在县城开展“五一”国际劳动节100周年纪念活动，举办篮球、象棋、围棋、乒乓球、游泳等项目比赛。1988年3月，举办“迪斯科健美操”骨干培训班，参加培训的老、中、青职工110人。5月1日，县首届迪斯科健美操表演赛在县城灯光球场举行，参加表演和比赛的代表队15个共417人。1989年9月，举办荔波县庆祝中华人民共和国成立40周年歌咏比赛，参赛代表队24个共1000人。10月，为庆祝中华人民共和国成立40周年，与县体委等单位联合举办荔波县首届“振兴杯”篮球赛以及职工门球、象棋、围棋、乒乓球比赛，参赛人员200余人。1990年“五一”劳动节期间，举办全县第二届职工健身迪斯科比赛和职工书法、美术、摄影比赛，同时举办职工花卉、盆景、根雕、泥塑艺术作品展览。1993年，元旦、春节、“五一”“十一”等节日期间，开展象棋、围棋比赛和支持北京申办2000年奥运会环城赛跑等活动。与团县委、宣传部、文化局、妇联、体委等部门共同举办“纪念毛主席诞辰100周年”大型歌咏比赛。1998年春节期间，县总工会组织春节游艺、猜谜、舞龙狮活动，“五一”期间举办大型歌咏比赛，夏季举办卡拉OK歌手消夏晚会。金融、保险、税务、教育、卫生等单位组织系统内各种文体活动，投入资金总计8.65万元。1999年7月，开展“爱祖国，爱家乡，迎接新世纪”知识竞赛；国庆前夕，县总工会组织80余人参加钓鱼比赛活动。在全县迎国庆50周年大型文艺调演比赛活动中，30多个参赛队全部是各乡（镇）及县直属机关文化站和基层工会选送，参赛人员200人。是年，全县开展“四有”（有理想、有文化、有道德、有纪律）、“三爱”（爱祖国、爱党、爱社会主义）、“三德”（社会公德、职业道德、家庭美德）为主要内容的创建文明行业、文明窗口、文明家庭的精神文明活动。2001年“五一”劳动节期间，县总工会举办“移动杯”职工篮球运动会，基层工会组织参赛代表队27个。2002年“三八”妇女节期间，县总工会、县妇联组织基层工会女职工组队22个参加拔河比赛；“五一”期间，举办全县职工歌咏比赛，基层工会组队参赛代表队共20个。2008年，开展春节“农民工杯”男子篮球赛和迎奥运“五一”拔河赛。

六、职工权益维护

职工权益保护主要通过县人力资源和社会保障局、经贸局、工商联、安监局等相关单位，共同推动工资集体协商、集体合同制度工作，让职工的合法利益得到保障。县总工会作为县调解委员会成员单位，参加县内发生的劳动争议仲裁案件调解。

1996年，成立县企业解困工作领导小组，县委副书记、县政协主席黄玉成任组长，县总工会、人事劳动局等13家单位负责人为成员，开展全县全员劳动合作制工作。是年，全县95%以上企业与职工签订劳动合同。

1997年，开展“企业平等协商和签订集体合同制度年”活动，至年底，全县应签订集体合同的企业单位29家，已签订27家，签订率93.1%。

至2008年，签订工资集体协商和集体合同126家，覆盖职工2631人。县总工会参与劳动争议案件调解114件，调解结案67件。

七、经费收缴与审查

工会经费来源于各单位按照规定比例提取的工会会费。工会经费主要用于职工开展文体活动、困难补助等。会费使用由经费审查委员会监督审查。1978—2008年，县总工会经费审查委员会召开工会经费审查会议60余次，对县级工会和基层工会开展经费审查60余次，审查基层工会经费368家。

第二章 共产主义青年团

第一节 组织建设

1978年，中国共产主义青年团荔波县委员会有书记、副书记、工作人员各1人。

从1979年起，团县委按照团中央提出的“积极地、有计划地发展新团员”的方针，要求基层团组织发展与管理并重，认真处理好团员数量与质量的关系，先进性与群众性的关系，制定发展团员计划，抓好团员发展工作。

1984年，县编委分配团县委编制3人，其中书记、副书记、工作人员各1名。

1987年后，贯彻“积极有计划地发展新团员，向一切先进青年敞开大门”的方针，按照“坚持标准，保证质量，积极培养，协调发展”的工作要求，除各中学按计划发展团员外，利用培训班、基干民兵训练、预备役集训等机会，发展农村团员。1987—1992年，发展新团员共1230人。

1994年，县级机构改革中，县编委明确团县委不设内设机构，人员编制3人。

2007年后，严格按照“成熟一个发展一个”的原则发展团员。

1978—2008年全县共青团组织基本情况一览表

表8-1

年度	团员总数（人）	基层团委（个）	团总支（个）	团支部（个）	团干部（人）	
					专职	兼职
1978	1975	25	8	173	7	15
1979	3175	24	2	206	12	15
1980	2198	25	7	204	7	15
1981	3126	25	2	198	8	15
1982	3104	24	2	223	33	15
1983	2486	26	6	214	7	15
1984	2788	29	5	214	41	15
1985	3937	30	4	204	10	3
1986	3002	31	6	235	16	16
1987	3263	31	6	237	16	12
1988	2735	31	7	219	7	48

续表8－1

年度	团员总数（人）	基层团委（个）	团总支（个）	团支部（个）	团干部（人）	
					专职	兼职
1989	2618	30	7	254	15	21
1990	3010	30	7	253	9	18
1991	2895	30	7	253	9	19
1992	3189	30	7	256	9	20
1993	3256	30	8	248	9	21
1994	3764	30	8	264	9	26
1995	4123	30	9	256	9	27
1996	4562	30	10	260	12	30
1997	4826	30	10	264	15	28
1998	5342	30	12	264	17	29
1999	6390	30	12	265	18	27
2000	6196	30	12	266	19	29
2001	5890	32	12	267	19	32
2002	5962	31	12	275	21	36
2003	6542	31	12	280	26	36
2004	7263	31	16	298	28	36
2005	7950	31	17	312	28	45
2006	8654	32	17	322	28	49
2007	9456	33	17	345	28	49
2008	10236	33	17	365	28	49

第二节　代表大会

共青团荔波县第八次代表大会　1987年7月13—15日，共青团荔波县第八次代表大会在县城召开。到会代表125人。大会审议通过代表资格审查委员会关于代表资格审查的报告；审议并通过共青团荔波县第七届委员会工作报告。大会选举产生共青团荔波县第八届委员会委员16人；选举出席州第五次团代会代表15人。在共青团荔波县第八届第一次全委会上选举生产常务委员5人，选举产生书记1人、副书记1人。

共青团荔波县第九次代表大会　1992年5月7—8日，共青团荔波县第九次代表大会在县城召开。应到会代表100人，实到代表96人。大会审议和通过共青团荔波县第八届委员会工作报告。选举产生共青团荔波县第九届委员会委员17人；选举出席州第六次团代会代表14人。在共青团荔波县第九届第一次全委会上选举产生常务委员7人，选举产生书记1人、副书记1人。选举出席州第六次团代会代表14人。

共青团荔波县第十次代表大会　1999年7月8—9日，共青团荔波县第十次代表大会在县城召开，应到代表98人，实到代表91人。大会审议和通过共青团荔波县第九届委员会工作报告；选举产生共青团荔波县第十届委员会委员17人。在共青团荔波县第十届第一次全委会上选举产生常务委员9人，选举产生书记1人、副书记1人。

共青团荔波县第十一次代表大会 2006年4月，共青团荔波县第十一次代表大会在县城召开。应到会代表100人，实到代表86人。听取审议和通过共青团荔波县第十届委员工作报告。选举产生共青团荔波县第十一届委员会委员17人。在共青团荔波县第十一届第一次全委会上选举产生常务委员9人，选举产生书记1人、副书记1人。

第三节 组织活动

一、少年先锋队活动

1979年恢复少先队组织后，在各小学校发展少先队员。到1984年，全县建立少先队的学校共130所，有少先队员14245人，有校内辅导员219人。各校组织少先队开展“学雷锋”“为人民服务，做好事，送温暖”“五讲四美”等活动。

1985年，在少先队组织中开展每人一分钱献给中国少年英雄纪念碑和“寻找美、创造美”活动。1988年，按照省的要求开展少先队“达标创优红旗大队”活动。1989年，开展“争创优秀中队，争当优秀少先队员”活动。

1990年，举办少先队辅导员培训班，为担任辅导员的教师发聘书。是年，全县有少先队员14245人，少先队大队26个。

1992年，在团中央、全国妇联等单位举办的全国青少年“社会主义好”读书教育活动中，玉屏一小获“组织奖”，学生尹琪获三等奖，教师韦勇能获优秀辅导员奖。团县委被贵州省未成年人保护委员会评为全省未成年人保护工作先进集体。

1993年12月15日，荔波民族中学初二（四）班学生蒙黔俊勇救落水女孩，团县委授予蒙黔俊“勇敢少年”称号。

1998年4月，组织开展“捐一元压岁钱，为贫困地区小朋友做好事献爱心”活动。6月，开展“同在蓝天下，手拉手情系灾区小伙伴”活动。

2000年10月，玉屏二小少先队员王世祺代表全县少先队员出席贵州省第三次少代会。

2001年4月，玉屏二小少先队开展“手拉手”地球村环保宣教活动；“六一”期间，玉屏二小王世祺作为水族代表参加全国少工委组织的“各民族少年手拉手，新世纪相聚在北京”活动。

2002年10月，县少工委被全国未成年人保护委员会评为“第四届全国未成年保护工作先进集体”。

2004年，组织荔波一小的四年级、五年级学生参加全国“希望杯”综合知识竞赛，获三等奖9人。6月，该校获“希望之星”称号的学生何周玲被选为是年雅典—北京奥运火炬接力手，为年龄最小的火炬接力手。

2005年4月，组织学生2人赴西安参加“全国中小学信息技术创新与实践”比赛，均获二等奖，荔波一小被评为“全国中小学信息技术创新与实践”先进单位。8月，组织学生代表全省希望小学参加全国28个省、市首届歌咏大赛，分别获最佳组织奖、才艺二等奖、古诗文朗诵三等奖和团体总分第四名。

2007年5月，组织荔波一小学生李天浩代表贵州小学生赴澳门参加“五四”青年慈善文艺演出。

2008年年底，全县有少先队大队26个，少先队员总计15739人。

二、希望工程

1989年，争取“希望工程”在荔波实施，并做好前期准备工作。

1993年，全县有失学儿童40名获省青少年发展基金会资助。12月23日，团县委、县委宣传部、直属机关党委、总工会、妇联、财政局、民委、教育局、文化局、工商局等单位联合举办全国第一个“希望工程”社会监督日活动，在县电影院举行“宣传希望工程，为失学孩子献爱心”为主题的文艺晚会，为失学儿童筹集到善款2万元。

1994年3月28日，发出“向瑶山、瑶麓送温暖献爱心”倡议，县直机关单位开展向“两瑶”献爱心活动，参加单位80个，收到捐款6.35万元，衣物、炊具等3257件。是年，全县17个乡（镇）失学少年儿童190名获省青少年发展基金会书费补助，每学期总计6270元。

1996年9月，水利小学校长莫才明、朝阳镇花提小学教师覃家平获全国第四届“希望工程”园丁奖。

1997年7月，上海申美饮料食品有限公司向玉屏一小捐款25万元，对该校进行扩建并将玉屏一小名称改为“邓恩铭可口可乐希望小学”。

1999年1月，团县委获1998年贵州希望工程志愿者劝募行动“希望工程”攻坚奖，受团省委、省青少年发展基金会表彰，玉屏镇教育辅导站覃炳能获个人贡献奖。

2002年，英国皇家医学院教授王执礼由省委办公厅牵线搭桥，捐赠5万元，资助玉屏镇贫困儿童100名。

2004年，在全县发放助学金1.96万元，涉及学校45所，受助学生392人。8月下旬，团省国资委工委向甲良镇贫困学生捐助7.56万元，并举行“助学长征”文艺演出。团县委被评为2004年“全省‘希望工程’工作先进单位”。

2007年，荔波二中获广州合景泰富地产控股有限公司资助110万元。

2008年，协调落实荔波二中希望中学第一期“希望工程款”35万元，并正式开工建设。深圳通大公司资助县内贫困学生5名。是年，为水利小学争取到贵州青年旅行社捐助“希望工程款”2万元。

三、青年文明号创建活动

1995年，首先在县内国税系统开展争创“青年文明号”活动。到12月12日，按照争创“青年文明号”的要求，通过考核，团县委、县国税局命名县国税征收一分局、茂兰国税所为县级“青年文明号”。

1996年6月，县金融系统开展创建“青年文明号”活动，成立创建领导小组，在县人行设办公室。各金融机构参加创建活动的部门13个，7月中旬挂牌服务。1997年1月中旬，金融系统授牌表彰县级“青年文明号”6个，农业银行甲良营业所获“黔南州青年文明号”称号。

1998年5月4日，县国税局立化征收管理分局、县地税局稽查分局、县工矿贸易公司被命名表彰为“1997年度州级青年文明号”。1999年5月4日，县公安刑侦大队、县国税局朝阳国税所、工行县支行营业部、农行县支行营业部被命名为“1998年度州级青年文明号”。2001年，县地税局玉屏征收分局获“2000年度州级青年文明号”称号。2002年，荔波供电局机关、县移动通信公司、县国税局立化征收管理分局、县地税局稽查局、县地税局玉屏分局、县地税局立化分局、县供销社工矿公司获“2001年度州级青年文明号”称号。

2003年4月25日，荔波供电局机关、县电信局营销班、县移动通信公司、县国税局立化征收管理分局、县地税局玉屏征收分局、县地税局立化分局、县地税局稽查局、县供销社工矿公司重新命名为“2002年度州级青年文明号”。

2004年，贵州明德实业有限责任公司获“县级青年文明号”称号。

2007年，县地税局玉屏分局、县地税局办公室、县地税局立化分局、县地税局稽查局、县地税局甲良税务所被评为“2006年度黔南州青年文明号”。

2007年，县地税局玉屏分局、县地税局办公室、县地税局立化分局、县地税局稽查局、县地税局甲良税务所被评为“2006年度黔南州青年文明号”命名表彰。

2008年停止评选“青年文明号”工作。

四、志愿者行动

从1990年起，团县委组织开展青年志愿者活动。

1996年3月5日，县人民医院、玉屏镇卫生院青年志愿者上街设摊开展义诊；玉屏一小、玉屏中学167名师生上街开展“创卫”活动。3月8日，荔波民族中学全体师生开展学雷锋做好事活动，到军烈属、残疾离休干部、无子女退休教职工遗孀家中，帮助他们做家务。

1997年3月7日，团县委组织县直机关团员青年、县武警中队官兵、学校学生等开展以“弘扬时代新风，争为文明公民”为主题的青少年志愿者学雷锋活动，进行县城卫生大规模突击清扫，受市民欢迎。

1998年3月6日，团县委组织县直机关团员青年、荔波民族中学、县职业中学、玉屏中学学生开展“学雷锋青年志愿者创卫活动”。

1998年8月—2000年7月，实施为期3年的青年志愿者扶贫接力计划。为完成扶贫接力计划安排的任务，先后有24名志愿者在荔波县支医、支教、支农。2000年1月，在瑶山支教的志愿者腾明龙获“全国首届十大杰出青年志愿者”称号。7月8日，腾明龙等7名扶贫支教志愿者获省文明办、省人事厅、省教委、团省委授予“贵州省1999—2000年青年志愿者扶贫接力计划优秀青年志愿者”称号，团县委获“贵州省1999—2000年青年志愿者扶贫接力计划先进集体”称号。

2001年7月，县委副书记田景胜获“扶贫接力计划杰出贡献奖”，团县委获“2000—2001年青年志愿者扶贫接力计划组织奖”。

2002年8月，成立县青年助残志愿者行动指导组，在全县范围内招募志愿者，全县志愿者注册412人。

2004年3月5日，团县委牵头，县残联、玉屏镇团委、玉屏镇社会事务办配合，组织团员青年代表、县武警中队战士和少先队员、县医院义诊志愿者共90人召开“向雷锋学习大会”。会后，参加大会人员分为3个服务分队，开展“学雷锋树新风”活动，到城北、菜园、罗家寨等地帮助残疾困难户、孤寡老人。

2007年6月5—12日，组织在县内服务的“三支一扶”（支医、支教、支农、扶贫）志愿者10名到小七孔开展志愿服务活动。在召开省第二届旅游产业发展大会期间，荔波民族中学、县职业中学的学生志愿者600人以及县直机关、乡（镇）青年志愿者500人参与大会服务工作。

2008年3月5日，团县委开展志愿者助残活动，团员青年与残疾人结对帮扶。10月，开展“牵手残疾人、走进残奥会”活动，30名志愿者到孤寡老人和残疾人家中做家务。

从1990—2008年，全县开展志愿者活动并向社会提供各种服务累计5万人次。

五、春晖行动

2005年，团县委响应团省委关于开展“春晖行动”的号召，下发《春晖行动方案（试行）》，号召全县团组织弘扬中华民族扶贫济困、反哺故土的优良传统，发挥“亲情、友情、乡情”情感纽带作用。通过宣传动员、联系沟通，各乡（镇）争取到外乡友人的捐款共80万元，用于学校、卫生、水利、公路、人畜饮水工程建设和种植养殖、加工技术培训等。团县委聘请贵阳市新太乙房地产开发公司董事长罗金鑫为甲良镇甲站村新太乙希望小学名誉校长，聘浙江温州文具有限公司董事长君义为玉屏镇君义希望小学名誉校长，聘省民族研究所研究员黄海为瑶麓乡瑶麓小学名誉校长，聘贵阳市社区生活报社社长彭为民为瑶麓乡瑶麓小学信息顾问。此外，经团县委推荐，县樟江旅行社有限责任公司总经理蒙强武被评为“黔南州外出打工返乡创业带民致富杰出青年”，荔波县人、浙江德赛帝伦鞋业有限公司销售部经理助理吴家顺被评为“黔南州在外乡友情倾家乡参与扶贫助民增收杰出青年”，浙江温岭人、荔波富万家超市总经理李朝英被评为“黔南州外籍乡友黔南创业助推发展杰出青年”。

2007年2月，开展“春晖行动——贵州‘信合’温暖万名贫困母亲”活动暨“我与家乡共话发展座谈会”系列活动，县内60岁以上的贫困母亲110人得到帮助，发放慰问金共1.1万元。之后，团县委结合旅游产业发展需要，聘请应届高中毕业生中考取省内外本科院校的荔波籍大学生185人作为“春晖行动”旅游宣传使者。

2008年9月2日，团县委召开“2008年春晖旅游宣传使者礼聘大会”，礼聘2008年考取省外本科院校的荔波籍大学生20人为“春晖旅游宣传使者”，让他们到校后通过班会、社会活动日、印发宣传资料等多种途径，介绍家乡的优美山水和城镇风光以及城市建设新面貌，借以提升荔波的知名度。

第三章 妇女联合会

第一节 组织建设

1978年，县妇联设主任1人，副主任1人，实有干部4人，无内设机构。是年，对公社、大队、生产队的妇女组织进行整顿，在县级行政事业单位和城关区、城关镇机关建立妇女工作委员会26个、妇女代表小组5个。

1980年，对城关镇、驾欧乡、翁昂乡、永康乡、朝阳镇、岜鲜村、城关公社的36个大队妇女代表会进行整建后，全县有妇代会组织154个、主任153人、副主任141人、委员629人。

1982年11月底，对全县161个大队妇代会整顿基本结束，召开妇代会的生产队1038个，选举产生公社妇女联合会班子成员。

1985年，全县25个乡（镇）于4月以前召开乡（镇）妇代会，选举产生新的领导班子。之后，对全县的村、街道妇代会组织进行调整和充实。

1990年，在县级行政事业单位和玉屏区、玉屏镇机关建立妇女工作委员会26个、妇代小组5个。是年，全县有基层妇女代表组织170个。全县区、乡配备专职妇女干部共22人，永康、水尧、瑶麓、瑶山4个乡未配专职妇女干部。

1991年，全县“建并撤”后，全县17个乡（镇）于1992年9月27日—10月11日先后召开妇代会，选举产生乡（镇）妇女主任17人、副主任10人。全县共175个基层妇代会组织，已整建160个。

1992年，全县17个乡（镇）配齐村妇代会组织168个、居委会5个，配妇女主任173人、副主任175人、委员173人，1245个妇女代表小组均配小组长。有168个乡（镇）建妇女活动室。

1993年9月起，按《中华全国妇女联合会章程》的规定，将妇联主任、副主任称谓改为主席、副主席。

1994年，县政府成立县妇女儿童工作委员会，委员会办公室设在县妇联。

1995年，根据省、州关于加强农村基层妇代会组织建设的意见，对村妇代会进行整顿，每个村配齐妇代会主任1人、副主任1人、委员1人。

1996年，全县168个村分别配备村妇女代会主任168人、副主任170人、委员168人。

1998年，除瑶麓乡妇女干部为兼职外，其余16个乡（镇）均配齐专职妇女主任、副主任各1人。

2001年，全县17个乡（镇）有专职妇女干部17人，各村（居）委会全部建立妇代会组织，共有妇代会主任174人，妇女主任均为村领导班子成员。

2004年，全县行政村合并为98个村（居）民委员会后，对村级妇女组织进行组建。

至2008年，县妇联编制3人，实有人员4人，无内设机构。全县17个乡（镇）有专职妇女干部17人，94个村、4个社区居委会全部建立妇代会组织。

第二节　代表大会

荔波县第五次妇女代表大会　1985年5月6—9日，荔波县第五次妇女代表大会在县城召开。应到会代表141人，实到代表131人。大会听取和审议县妇联第四届执行委员会向大会作的工作报告；选举产生荔波县妇女联合会第五届执行委员会委员23人；选举出席省第五次妇女代表大会代表4人。在县妇联第五届第一次执委会上选举产生常务委员9人，选举产生主任1人、副主任1人。

荔波县第六次妇女代表大会　1992年4月27—28日，荔波县第六次妇女代表大会在县城召开。应到会代表151人，实到代表146人。大会听取和审议第五届执行委员会向大会作题为《积极开拓勇于进取——为经济振兴富民兴县建功立业》的工作报告；选举产生荔波县妇女联合会第六届执行委员会委员21人。在县妇联第六届第一次执委会上选举产生常务委员9人，选举产生主任1人、副主任2人。

荔波县第七次妇女代表大会　1997年12月24—25日，荔波县第七次妇女代表大会在县城召开。应到会代表90人，实到代表86人。大会听取和审议荔波县妇女联合会第六届执行委员会向大会作题为《以经济建设为中心，围绕党的中心工作，为兴县富民发展妇女儿童事业而努力工作》的工作报告；选举产生荔波县妇女联合会第七届执行委员会委员17人。在县妇联第七届第一次执委会上选举产生常务委员9人，选举产生主席1人、副主席1人。

荔波县第八次妇女代表大会　2004年3月，荔波县第八次妇女代表大会在县城召开。应到会代表110人，实到代表102人。大会听取和审议荔波县妇女联合会第七届执行委员会向大会作题为《与时俱进　开拓创新为兴县富民和妇女儿童事业的发展而奋斗》的工作报告；大会选举产生荔波县妇女联合会第七届执行委员会委员17人。在县妇联第八届第一次执委会上选举产生常务委员9人，选举产生主席1人、副主席1人。

第三节　主要活动

一、“双学双比”活动

1987年，县妇联本着“实际、实用、实效”的原则，与县科协因地制宜地举办多种形式的实用技术培训46期，参加培训妇女572人次。

1988年，根据州妇联《关于召开1988年度执委扩大会及开展“双百”活动表彰会的通知》，开展“双百”活动，即创一百个先进乡（办事处）妇联和创一百个先进妇代会。至12月中旬，召开全县“双百”总结评比表彰会。

1989年，根据省妇联《关于在全省农村各族妇女群众中开展“双学双比”竞赛活动的通知》精神，成立县“双学双比”（学文化、学技术、比成绩、比贡献）活动协调领导小组，办公室设在县妇联。是年，共培训县、乡、村妇女干部和骨干人员367名，建油菜移栽联系点27个、联系户360户。

1990年3月，全县4区1镇建立“双学双比”协调组织5个，区、乡、村妇联组织建联系点28个，有重点联系户167户、科技示范户16户；办扫盲班（点）175个，学员共3622人，验收脱盲2700人。县妇联与其他部门联合举办实用技术培训班73期，播放科技录像36场，发放农业实用科技资料4320份。同时，通过办好样板田、试验田，全县妇联组织完成半旱式栽培2311亩，其中县妇联在拉渔村完成半旱式栽培172.5亩、秋种油菜160亩。

1991年2月，有8个乡（镇）建立“双学双比”协调领导小组。1992年，召开全县“双学双比”表彰会，表彰“双学双比”先进协调小组3个、先进乡（镇）11个、女能手11人。是年，全县受州表彰的女能手5人。

1992年，举办各种农业实用技术培训班87期，培训项目有水稻半旱式栽培、杂稻制种、早熟蔬菜、种桑养蚕、烤烟种植。全县各级妇联组织妇女配合造林8370亩，全县种植沙田柚760亩，挖窝32600个。表彰“双学双比”先进协调小组3个、先进乡（镇）11个、女能手11人。是年，全县受州表彰的女能手5人。

是年10月，省妇联与县妇联在玉屏镇石灰坳村簸鸟坡联合创办贵州省妇联果树基地，面积200亩，土地承包期为1992年10月—2022年11月。省妇联投入启动资金1万元，县妇联贷款2万元进行建设。

1993年，有2630名妇女参加夜校学习，各级妇联组织举办各种实用技术培训班11期，参加培训的有3970人，协调成员单位办各种实用技术培训班63期，4100人参加。掌握1～2项实用技术的妇女2.1万人，掌握3项以上实用技术的妇女9980人。

1994年，全县举办农业技术培训班158期，培训妇女人数10382人，其中，妇联自办16期，培训人数664人，成员单位举办142期，培训妇女骨干人数9718人，共投入培训经费2.5万元。

1995年，全县办扫盲班296个，有学员3774人。其中，妇女3288人；少数民族3168人。经验收，妇女脱盲3288人。全县参加造林的妇女3850人次；县妇联投入经费0.68万元，举办农业技术培训班16期，培训664人。全县有以妇女为主体的科技示范户664户。在县妇联的19个联系点中，走上脱贫致富路的有40户。全年参加“双学双比”活动的妇女2.56万人。

1996年，县妇联于5月20日、6月20日在玉屏镇举办《妇女纲要》培训会，培训妇女骨干232人。全年举办各种农牧业技术培训班158期，培训妇女6500人次，举办农业骨干培训班85期，培训农民技术骨干589人次，其中妇女参与培训306人次，投入培训经费3.8万元。全县6个乡（镇），26个村组，1446户投入坡改梯工程，妇女投入劳动力1864人次，全县参加扫盲4421人，其中妇女3479人，教员161人，共验收脱盲3566人，其中妇女2456人。

1997年，积极配合教育部门抓好扫盲工作，参加扫盲班学员3500人，其中妇女3150人，脱盲人数3500人。全年举办各类农业实用技术普及培训764期，培训农民64500人次，培训“绿证”学员394人。全年投入培训经费17万元。

1998年，全县参加扫盲妇女3690人，脱盲3690人，占扫盲总人数的90%，投入扫盲资金2.5万元。举办农民技术培训班6期，培训妇女328人，投入资金6.2万元。取得绿色证书的妇女16人。在甲良镇组织80名妇女参加“千万农家女百项新技术”知识竞赛活动。

1999年6月，县政府拨款4000元开展“双学双比”活动。是年，对农村妇女进行实用技术培训共320期3万人次，发放资料1.45万份。投入扫盲资金2.45万元，在全县建立扫盲联系点17个，办扫盲班180个，参加学习的妇女3000余人，其中少数民族妇女占98%。在教学中采用“双语”（汉语、少数民族语）教学，脱盲妇女2524人。

2000年，县妇联建立扫盲联系点17个，办扫盲班115个，全县参加扫盲的妇女2570人，脱盲80%。是年，举办“千万农家女百项新技术”培训班138期，培训3.21万人次，发放资料1.8万份。年内，参加绿色证书培训的妇女90人。

是年7月，省妇联对联办的果树基地作出处理意见，将投资共5.4万元（其中省妇联投入2.8万元、县妇联投入2.6万元）的贵州省果树基地从2000年起由县妇联全权管理，盈亏自负，并命名为贵州省“三八绿色示范基地”。

2001年，全县建扫盲联系点17个，办扫盲班110个班，参加学习的妇女1120人，脱盲1005人。是年7月9—23日，县妇联牵头组织科委、司法局、民政局、农业局等单位，到立化镇、佳荣镇、洞塘乡、茂兰镇、水尧乡、永康乡、翁昂乡、玉屏镇等8个乡（镇）举办妇女农技法律培训班8期，培训妇女510人，发放资料3100份。

2002年，县、乡妇联配合农技部门共举办实用技术培训班674期，培训妇女12126人，发放资料36467份；举办绿色培训班12期，参加培训妇女357人，经考试全部取得绿色证书。全年县妇联举办妇女培训班3期，培训妇女145人，发放资料1500份；配合教育部门举办扫盲班227期，参加扫盲妇女1299人，脱盲916人，各级妇联组织妇女参与植树造林1100亩。

2003年3月，全县举办实用技术培训450期，培训妇女2.25万人次，发放资料2.98万份。举办绿色证书培训班9期，获得绿色证书妇女190人。“三八绿色示范基地”种植大板栗400株、铜谷李200株、九阡李200株。

2004年11月25—26日，“双学双比”成员单位培训捞村、瑶山两个乡的农村妇女100人，在玉屏镇板旺村创建贵州省“美德在农家示范村”。

2005年4月1日，县妇联对农村妇女36人进行科技、保健、知识培训。8月2日，县妇联、农业局与广西环江毛南族自治县农业局联合举办种桑养蚕骨干培训班1期，参加培训70人，妇女占60%。

2008年，县妇联推荐农村妇女骨干10人参加州委组织部、州妇联、州扶贫办举办的全州农村妇女科技知识培训班学习。是年，全县17个乡（镇）培训农村女能手350人次，在玉屏镇板旺村建立农村“巾帼示范村”1个，推选出新型农村妇女骨干17名，带动当地妇女脱贫致富。

二、妇女儿童合法权益维护

1978年，县妇联组织全县妇女学习新《中华人民共和国宪法》，使广大妇女懂得婚姻、家庭、母亲和儿童受国家的保护。

1979年春节前后，县妇联配合有关部门有婚姻家庭问题调查，以省发宣传提纲为主，结合县情，开展正确婚姻家庭观念宣传。

1980—1983年，县、区、公社三级妇联组织接待来信来访累计1062件，全部办结。

1984年，成立县维护妇女儿童合法权益法制宣传月活动领导小组，加强妇女维权工作，并采取以会代训、举办法律培训班等形式，增强妇女的法制观念，维护自身合法权益。

1986年7月5日—8月5日，县妇联与县司法局联合举办全县首届妇女法律知识竞赛活动，参加竞赛活动妇女干部、职工共389人。

1989年，县、区两级妇联举办法律培训班6期，参加培训学员307人。

1990年，县妇联采取层层举办骨干培训班方式，以县、区、乡为单位，集中妇女干部学习73期。是年，针对县内一些单位没有按国务院规定给予女工享受90天产假的问题，县妇联多次向政府和有关单位反映，并向县人大提交专题提案后，县政府下发文件，明确女工产假的享受权利。

1991年，县妇联通过培训、座谈及自编山歌、诗歌等多种形式，向妇女传播有关维权法律知识。同时，配合有关部门举办法律培训班16期，参加学习妇女17332人。

1993年，县妇联与有关单位开展《中华人民共和国妇女权益保障法》《中华人民共和国未成年人保护法》《中华人民共和国婚姻法》《中华人民共和国继承法》等法律宣传，配合县检察院、法院、司法局等单位调查处理各种纠纷80多件、未成年人案件4件，重婚案2件。

1994—1995年，县妇联协助公安机关解救被拐卖妇女、儿童17人。

1996年，在各乡（镇）开展妇女法规培训，受训妇女500余人，发放宣传资料5000余份。

2000年11月3日，县妇联举办妇女干部维权培训班，全县女副乡（镇）长、妇联主席和县妇联执委共40人参加培训。

2002年10月15日，县政府下发《荔波县2001—2010年妇女发展规划》《荔波县2001—2010年儿童发展规划》。县妇联和有关部门于5月16日、5月25日、12月4日、12月5日开展“两纲两法”宣传活动，群众咨询7000人次，发放资料1.66万份。

2003年1月5日，县妇联与县司法局联合成立荔波县法律援助妇联工作站，工作站设在县妇联。3月5日、5月20日、6月26日、7月6日、9月5日，县妇儿工委成员单位开展5次大型妇女、儿童法律法规知识宣传咨询和送法律、送科技、送医药“三下乡”活动，群众咨询5500人次，发放“两纲两法”宣传资料1.21万份。是年6月，县妇联获全国妇联“母亲安康计划”项目即“母亲健康快车”1辆，价值12.8万元。2004年，县、乡妇联在“三八”妇女节维权周，开展维权宣传咨询服务20次。其中，县妇联于3月5日、5月31日开展法律宣传咨询活动，发放“两纲两法”宣传资料2.8万份。2005年3月10日，妇儿工委成员单位在县城榕树花园开展法律宣传咨询活动。2007年5月20日，在县城榕树花园开展法制宣传活动，宣传“两纲两法”，发放《妇女权益保障法》500余份，制作禁毒宣传展板20余块，接受妇女咨询30人次。

2005年，全年各级妇联共接待来信来访225件，其中乡镇妇联接待210件、县妇联接待45件，处理率在95%以上，较好地维护了妇女儿童的合法权益。县法院拓展维权力度，选派特邀5名人民陪审员到省参加培训，县人大常委会为人民陪审员颁发了证书；县公安局坚持从重从快的方针，严厉打击各种侵害妇女儿童合法权益的犯罪行为；县司法局无偿为上访妇女提供法律援助12次，切实维护了妇女儿童的合法权益。

2006年，县乡妇联以“三八”维权周、三下乡活动为契机开展维权宣传咨询服务20余次，同时，认真接待来信来访工作，及时处理信访案件，做到事事有交代、件件有落实。

2008年3月7日，25个妇儿工委成员单位在樟江园广场开展“三八”维权周宣传咨询活动，发放宣传资料2.5万份，展示图片50张，群众咨询1500人次。5月20日、5月30日、8月25日，分别举办了3次法律法规宣传活动。8月，组织县、乡300多名妇女参与省妇联、省综治办、省司法厅举办的“满意在贵州，千万妇女学法”知识竞赛活动。

1978—2008年全县妇联接待来信来访情况统计表

表8－2　　单位：件

年度	来信来访总数	办结	其中	
			妇联系统办理	转有关部门办理
1978	168	168	152	16
1979	158	158	136	22
1980	210	210	192	18
1981	286	286	263	23
1982	201	201	189	12
1983	365	365	300	65
1984	275	275	208	67
1985	165	165	153	12
1986	246	246	218	28
1987	625	625	532	93

续表8－2

年度	来信来访总数	办结	其　中	
			妇联系统办理	转有关部门办理
1988	685	685	562	123
1989	256	256	113	143
1990	624	624	606	18
1991	738	738	653	85
1992	538	538	493	45
1993	397	397	314	83
1994	909	909	900	9
1995	142	142	126	16
1996	63	63	60	3
1997	167	167	156	11
1998	364	364	346	18
1999	325	325	312	13
2000	138	138	122	16
2001	150	150	127	23
2002	167	167	151	16
2003	225	225	198	27
2004	228	228	202	26
2005	235	235	223	12
2006	225	225	217	8
2007	215	215	205	10
2008	167	167	162	5

三、“五好文明家庭”“巾帼建功”创建活动

1979年，在全县开展“五好文明家庭”创建活动。活动中，评选出“三八红旗手”175名、“三八红旗集体”21个，在“三八”妇女节期间进行表彰。玉屏镇板吉村覃爱银被评为全国“三八红旗手”，受全国妇联表彰。

1980—1990年，坚持开展“五好文明家庭”活动，评选表彰“三八红旗手”和“三八红旗集体”“五好文明家庭”。1990年，在创建“五好文明家庭”活动中，评选出“三八红旗手”73名、“三八红旗集体”5个、好婆媳5对、好夫妻4对、好妯娌2对，优秀妇女干部8名。

1993年，在开展“五好文明家庭”创建活动同时开展“巾帼建功”活动。1994年，在创建“巾帼建功”暨“五好文明家庭”活动中，县妇联表彰8个先进集体，5个农村先进“女能人”，6名先进妇女干部，15名先进女能手，5个“美好家庭”，5个模范丈夫。

1995年，在世界妇女大会召开期间，开展“九五世界妇女知识竞赛”活动，印发试卷2000份，共收回试卷1300份，评选出一等奖1名，二等奖2名，三等奖5名。

1997年，县内推荐到州妇联表彰的“五好文明家庭”5户、“三八红旗手”6人、先进集体2个、先进工作者3人。

1998—2003年，每年表彰“巾帼建功”“五好文明家庭”活动中涌现出的“三八红旗手”“五好文明家庭”、先进妇女工作者等。其间，2000年受省表彰的“三八红旗集体”1个、“三八红旗手”1名、“生态环境保护建设女标兵”1名，先进乡镇妇联1个、先进村妇代会10个。

2004年，宣传女能手和“生态建设女标兵”的先进事迹，越来越多的农村妇女走出家门，加入到竞赛活动中。朝阳镇板麦村妇女何应群被评为“全省科技致富带头人”。

2005年，倡导健康、文明、科学的生活方式，引导广大家庭成员特别是妇女树立终身学习的理念、妥善处理好学习、工作和家庭的关系，不断用新知识、新技能充实自己。梁运菊被评为“贵州省林业生态建设女标兵”，谭小辉被评为贵州省城镇妇女“巾帼建功”创业带头人。县妇联在“三八”妇女节期间表彰“三八红旗集体”9个、“三八红旗手”28名、“五好文明家庭”9户、“巾帼文明示范岗”5个、“巾帼建功标兵”5名。

2008年，县妇联主席周宏被省文明办、省妇联表彰为“整脏治乱”先进个人；瑶山乡拉片村何金英获省表彰为“整脏治乱”专项行动优秀家庭；县职业中学老师何明交获省表彰为第六届贵州省“五好文明家庭”；立化镇尧明村玉度宜获“少生快富”先进个人；立化镇妇联主席韦永兰获省妇联表彰为“争先创优”先进个人。

四、少儿工作

1979—1982年，儿童工作以“三优”（优生、优育、优教）为主要内容，以家教为重点，开办家长学校，提高家庭教育水平，大力宣传“三优”工作。1982年“六一”儿童节期间，联合县妇幼保健站免费为800名少儿进行健康体检。

1984年，全县有家长学校6所，共37个班，开办家长培训66期，家长受训4500人，发放资料4500份。

1985年“六一”儿童节前，配合妇幼保健站，给全县875名儿童进行体格检查。

1986年1月，成立县儿童少年健康工作协调委员会。全年为900多名儿童进行健康检查。

1987年，县妇联被省妇联评为“儿童少年工作二等奖”。

1988年8月，根据中央、国务院办公厅文件精神，对4个区5个农村中心幼儿园、22个学前幼儿班的固定资产进行清理造册登记，并移交县教育局。

1989年8月23—25日，县妇联和县教育局联合举办荔波县首届家教培训班，参加培训教育共43人。截至12月，全县已办家长学校3所，家长学员316人。

1990年，全县家长学校3所，参加学习的家长319人，学年授课17次，听课家长5243人次，印发教课资料3676份，家长专栏8期，心得体会404篇，表彰好家长45人，办家教骨干培训班1期，参加人员96人。“六一”前夕，各中小学开展学雷锋、学赖宁演讲会、报告会共5次，参加演讲学生98人次，听讲人数1674人次，办“六一”专刊21期。

1993年，县妇联牵头，教育局、计生局、保健站、防疫站、残联等6家相关单位联合举办乡（镇）妇联主任、副主任，乡（镇）卫生院，乡（镇）教育辅导站负责人共77人参加的“90年代中国儿童发展规划纲要”宣传骨干培训班。

1994年，成立县妇女儿童工作委员会，县政府副县长任主任。是年，全县有家长学校10个班，家教辅导站17个，家教研究会1个。在玉屏中学开办了1个“春蕾女童班”，有学生40人，学制三年（1994—1996年）。

1996年“六一”儿童节期间，慰问残疾儿童和贫困儿童10名，慰问石灰坳小学40名学生。

1997年“六一”儿童节期间，县妇联组织城乡学校、幼儿园召开庆祝大会和进行游行活动。在庆祝大会上，表彰先进教育工作者20人、品学兼优学生18人、好孩子30人、关心和支持儿童工作的领导9人。

1999年6月1日，县妇联在县人民大会场举行首届“农行杯”少儿卡拉OK赛，全县17个乡（镇）小学参加比赛小歌手48名。全年办家长学习班28期，出专栏32期，发放学习资料10050份。

2000年6月1日下午，县妇联在玉屏二小举行少儿故事大王选拔赛，评选出3名选手参加黔南州少儿故事大王比赛。

2002年5月16日，县妇联牵头组织县妇儿工委成员单位县计生局、科协、教育局、团县委、公安局、妇幼保健站、卫生局等单位领导一行27人深入甲良镇利用场天开展《两个规划纲要》以及妇幼保健知识宣传咨询活动。咨询群众达5000人次，发放资料15500份。5月25日，县妇联积极配合普法领导小组在樟江大街开展法律咨询宣传活动，发放资料600份，咨询群众500多人。5月27—30日，县妇儿工委分别到玉屏镇石灰坳小学、立化小学、尧明小学、水尧水扒小学、玉屏二小和县幼儿园进行慰问。7月8日，县妇联组织11名品学兼优的青少年参加州妇联举办的“新世纪，新北京，新科技”夏令营活动。妇儿工委表彰100名品学兼优的学生和30名好孩子。

2003—2006年，与县委宣传部等相关部门组织小公民道德建活动，开展“我做合格小公民”征文评选、“小公民敬老爱老助老”主题道德实践等活动。

2008年，县妇联、县教育局、县民政局、县卫生局、县统计局、县人口计生局、县关工委等8家单位联合印发《荔波县家庭教育工作“十一五”规划》。开展以《荔波县儿童发展规划纲要（2001—2010年）》《小公民道德建设计划》《未成年人保护法》《义务教育法》《儿童权利公约》等法规宣传咨询活动。

第四章　工商业联合会

第一节　组织建设

1988年2月，县工商联筹备小组重新登记老会员47人，同时在国有、集体、乡镇企业、私营企业、个体工商户中吸纳新会员21人，会员发展到68人。

是年9月，正式恢复县工商业联合会，设立执行委员会和常委会，执委会配专职主任委员、副主任委员各1名，内设总务、组织、宣传3个股，各股正、副股长由常务委员兼任，股员3—7人。

1989年1月，县工商联成立经济服务部，实行董事会领导下的经理负责制，独立核算，自负盈亏。

1990年5月，组建百货和服务业同业小组，对小组活动、组长职责任务作出明确规定，加强同业间的自我协调、自我服务、自我管理、自我约束、自我教育。

1991年7月，《中共中央批转中央统战部〈关于工商联若干问题的请示〉的通知》，县工商联将工作重点由国家和集体企业逐步转移到以非公有制经济为主要对象、做好非公经济代表人士工作上，对非公经济人士开展团结、教育、引导、服务工作，并从全县实际出发，发展新会员。

1997年4月9日，成立县商会，与县工商联实行两块牌子、一个机构合署办公。

1998年1月，成立茂兰工商联（商会）分会。

2001年12月，工商联（商会）行政编制2人，设会长1人（不占工商联编制）、副会长2人，秘书长由1名副会长兼任，县商会下设实业服务部，事业编制2人。

2002年5月，成立立化工商联（商会）分会。12月，成立玉屏工商联（商会）分会。2004年9月25日，成立甲良工商联（商会）分会。各分会通过召开会员大会选举产生执委成员，选举产生会长、副会长、秘书长。之后每5年进行一次换届选举。

到2008年，全县工商联（商会）有会员292人，其中企业会员35人、个人会员257人。县工商联（商会）机构设置不变。

第二节　代表大会

县工商联第三次会员代表大会　1988年9月28日，县工商联第三次会员代表大会在县城召开。应到会代表47人，实到代表47人。大会听取和讨论通过《关于恢复荔波县工商业联合会的筹备工作报告》；学习和讨论《中国工商业联合会章程》；选举产生县工商联第三届执行委员会委员22人。县工商联第三届第一次执委会选举产生常委15人，选举产生主任委员1名、副主任委员2名、秘书长1名。

县工商联第四次会员代表大会 1992年5月12日，县工商联第四次会员代表大会在县城召开。应到会代表65人，实到代表61人。大会听取和审议县工商联第三届执委会工作报告，选举产生县工商联第四届执行委员会委员21人。县工商联第四届第一次执委会选举产生常委11人，选举产生会长1名、副会长5名、秘书长1名。

县工商联第五次会员代表大会 1997年4月8日，县工商联第五次会员代表大会在县城召开。应到会代表66人，实到代表58人。大会听取和审议县工商联第四届执委会工作报告；选举产生县工商联第五届执行委员会委员31人。县工商联第五届第一次执委会选举产生常委19人，选举产生会长1名、副会长6名、秘书长1名。

县工商联（商会）第六次会员代表大会 2001年10月27日，县工商联（商会）第六次会员代表大会在县城召开。应到会代表83人，实到代表81人。大会听取和审议县工商联第五届执委会工作报告；选举产生县工商联第六届执行委员会委员31人。县工商联第六届第一次执委会选举产生常委13人，选举产生会长1名、副会长8名，秘书长由1名副会长兼任。

县工商联（商会）第七次会员代表大会 2006年8月10日，县工商联（商会）第七次会员代表大会在县城召开。应到会代表120人，实到代表92人。大会听取和审议县工商联第六届执委会工作报告；选举产生县工商联第七届执行委员会委员39人。县工商联第七届第一次执委会选举产生常委19人，选举产生会长1名、副会长11名，秘书长由1名副会长兼任。

第三节 主要工作

一、会员权益维护

1989年10月，浙江个体服装经营户组成服装展销团到荔波县城进行展销，受到荔波本地服装经营户阻挠，经调解展销活动得以正常开展。

2007年5月，浙江籍某服装经营户与金锣湾门面业主发生门面租赁纠纷，依据《中华人民共和国合同法》予以调解，双方达成谅解继续履行合同。

是年9月，县城旅馆业主集中反映核定营业额偏高问题，通过协调，采取听证方式合理确定各旅馆的营业额。

2008年9月，县职业高级中学扩建，需要征用玉屏镇竹子加工厂，因搬迁费没有得到落实，经协调县政府解决搬迁费5.5万元。

二、联谊活动

1990年，荔波、都匀、独山、平塘、三都工商联发起黔南南部5县（市）工商联联谊会，以“加深了解、增进友谊、互通信息、促进发展”为宗旨，年会采取轮流制。是年，首次联谊会年会在荔波县召开。此后，广西南丹县、河池市、宜州市先后加盟联谊会。

1996年，在荔波召开第七次年会，有黔南州罗甸县和广西环江县加入。

之后，黔南州龙里县、长顺县、福泉市和广西环江县、天峨县、东兰县、都安县、凤山县、巴马瑶族自治县加入联谊会。至2008年，联谊会由黔南州5县（市）联谊会发展成为黔、桂两省（区）18县（市）联谊会。

三、非公有制经济发展

1978年，全县个体工商户17户。至1988年年底，全县个体工商户发展到1129户，从业人员1568人，注册资金263万元。经营网点分布全县各乡（镇），经营范围以副食品、日杂用品、餐饮及农副产品收购、加工、个体运输业、个体旅店业等为主。

1989年，县内非公经济得到全面发展。1997年9月，县委、县政府制定实施《荔波县招商引资优惠政策》。至1998年，全县有私营企业29户，注册资金7629.6万元；个体工商户2012户，从业人员3780人，注册资金2022.2万元。

2004年12月，成立县商会支点担保公司，为非公经济融资提供担保服务。

至2008年，全县有私营企业146户，注册资金32755万元；有个体工商户2692户，从业人员4550人，注册资金8211万元。

四、光彩事业

1997年8月，中央、省、州有关领导到荔波县指导开展扶贫帮困光彩事业工作。是年9月，成立县光彩事业推动委员会。

2000年3月，县建设工程公司总经理汪国民捐资10万元，新建玉屏镇石灰坳小学教学楼。

2001年11月，荔波阳凤裕民生态养殖场总经理司玉明为荔波飞机场奠基庆典活动捐资10万元；2005年7月捐资15万元新建永康乡甲棒村小学教学楼。

2003年3月，贵州明德实业有限责任公司董事长赵军华捐资10万元，修建水利乡水龙村办公楼、党员活动室、五保户住房；2005年7月又捐资50万元，新建县幼儿园。

2006年10月，县建设工程公司中共党支部书记金敬春捐资17万元，新建荔波民族中学学生公寓。

2007年3月，荔波县茂兰镇安匀煤矿总经理曾海捐资25万元，修建茂兰镇水庆村通村公路；2008年9月，又捐资18万元进行茂兰镇水庆村道路硬化。

2007年7月，荔波县资源开发总公司董事长全修林、个体工商户韦勇各自捐资20万元，修建县城恩铭广场大屏电视。

2008年1月，荔波县观音峰示范养殖场董事长张黔国捐资44万元，为玉屏镇平抑生猪市场物价。

是年10月，荔波县下寨煤矿矿长朱玉朋捐资25万元，投入立化镇新农村建设。

至2008年年末，荔波县有100多名非公经济人士参与光彩事业活动，在捐资建校、参与新农村建设、社会公益事业、扶贫济困、资助贫困学生等方面，实施项目累计58个，捐资累计1600万元。

1991—2008年全县非公经济光彩事业统计表

表8－3

年度	支教助学		扶贫济困		新农村建设（万元）	自然灾害捐赠（万元）
	资助人数（人）	资助资金（万元）	扶贫人数（人）	扶贫资金（万元）		
1991	1	0.01	—	—	—	—
1992	—	—	—	—	—	—
1993	—	—	20	0.20	—	—
1994	3	0.15	108	1.25	—	—

续表8-3

年度	支教助学		扶贫济困		新农村建设（万元）	自然灾害捐赠（万元）
	资助人数（人）	资助资金（万元）	扶贫人数（人）	扶贫资金（万元）		
1995	—	—	68	0.74	—	—
1996	—	—	17	0.17	—	0.50
1997	1	0.05	50	0.50	1.30	—
1998	12	0.24	210	4.20	2.20	—
1999	—	—	73	0.73	3.80	1.20
2000	83	2.49	268	5.36	3.70	0.86
2001	68	0.32	570	11.40	10.50	3.70
2002	112	3.83	467	14.01	30.80	82.50
2003	92	2.37	300	11.70	20.80	—
2004	136	2.08	450	17.36	13.70	31.50
2005	160	15.30	810	33.60	27.50	70.60
2006	103	17.83	780	32.12	46.50	85.80
2007	63	15.96	1025	42.38	80.60	—
2008	47	13.18	890	57.80	150.70	90.70

第五章　科学技术协会

第一节　科协组织

1980年6月，成立荔波县科学技术协会。首届县科协设学会工作组、科普工作组、青少年科普工作组。1981年后，县科协不设内设机构，人员为事业编制3人。

1982年11月，成立玉屏镇科协。1983年1月，成立朝阳乡科协。1984年6月，时来、水利、永康3个乡成立乡科协。8月，玉屏区、水尧乡成立科协。1990年8月，朝阳乡拉扶村成立西瓜技术研究会，方村乡成立科学养猪研究会。

2001年，县科协人员编制4人，列入参照国家公务员管理。

从2002年起，全县每个村（居）委会均建立科普小组1个，分别配备科技副主任1名。到2008年，全县建立农村专业协会54个。

第二节　代表大会

县科协第一次代表大会　1980年6月24—26日，县科协第一次代表大会在县城召开。应到会代表76人，实到代表76人。其中，林业代表7人、水电代表5人、农机代表5人、农业代表9人、畜牧代表6人、气象代表2人、卫生代表17人、教育代表9人、工交代表5人、社队科研组代表5人、其他代表6人。会议传达贯彻全国科协第二次代表大会精神，围绕全县工业、农业、医药、教育事业，开展献计献策提建议活动，代表提出书面建议共63条。大会讨论通过《荔波县科学技术协会章程》；选举产生县科协第一届委员会委员20人。县科协第一届第一次全委会选举产生常务委员9人，主席1人、副主席3人、秘书长1人。

县科协第二届代表大会　1985年1月24—26日，县科协第二次代表大会在县城召开。应到会代表85人，实到代表85人。大会听取和审议县科协第一届委员会工作报告，讨论修改并通过《荔波县第二届科协章程》《县农村基层科普协会组织通则》。会议期间，有21名代表为全县经济发展提出书面建议57条。大会选举产生县科协第二届委员会委员24人。县科协第二届第一次全委会选举产生常委12人，主席1人、副主席3人。

县科协第三届代表大会　2004年5月9—10日，县科协第三次代表大会在县城召开。应到会代表96人，实到代表96人。选举产生县科协第三届委员会委员31人。县科协第三届第一次全委会选举产生常务委员11人，主席1人、副主席2人。

第三节 学会 协会

一、学会

农学会 1980年3月29日成立县农学会，有会员52人。其中，农业20人，植保1人，土化1人，气象6人，畜牧6人，兽医11人，其他7人。理事会由11人组成。农学会下设农业、气象、畜牧3个科学小组。至2008年年底，学会有会员30人。

林学会 1980年2月6日成立县林学会，有会员26人，设常务理事5人。至2004年5月12日，县林学会召开3次代表大会，会员发展到158人。2008年，县林学会有会员135人。

水电学会 1980年4月成立县水电学会，有会员26人。

医学会 1980年5月成立县医学会，有会员56人，分为医疗、防疫、护理3个科学小组。县医学会第一次会议选举理事会成员11人。1983年4月3日召开第二届会议，选举理事会成员15人，会员发展到97人。

财会学会 1982年9月16日成立县财会学会，有会员33人。2008年年底，学会有成员7人。

二、协会

珠算协会 1983年7月27日成立，有会员36人。到2008年12月，协会有成员7人。

青少年科技辅导员协会 1981年5月3日成立县青少年科技辅导员协会，有会员24人。理事会由7人组成，分宣传组、创作组、实验制作组、内外联络组4个活动组。至2008年12月，有会员51人。

科普、美术、摄影协会 1982年1月成立县科普美术摄影协会，有会员31人，理事会由9人组成。1985年12月召开年会，分为美术协会、书法协会、摄影协会3个协会，美术协会有会员17人，书法协会有会员18人，摄影协会有会员14人。

中学、小学语文教学研究会 1988年1月3日成立县中学、小学语文教学研究会，有会员53人。理事会由13人组成。

农村卫生协会 1988年11月10日成立县农村卫生协会，理事会由26人组成，有常务理事11人。

青少年集邮协会 1989年8月28日成立县青少年集邮协会，有会员41人。设名誉理事长1人、理事长1人，副理事长2人，秘书长1人、理事3人。

烹饪协会 2003年8月13日成立县烹饪协会，有会员38人。至2008年12月，有单位会员10个、个人会员46人。设常务理事13人、理事13人，专职工作人员3人。

兰花协会 2006年4月30日成立县兰花协会，有会员51人。到2008年12月有会员51人。

民间科普文艺协会 2003年3月成立县民间科普文艺协会，有会员31人。至2008年12月有会员30人。

瑶山鸡养殖协会 2006年12月15日成立县瑶山鸡养殖协会，有会员54人。至2008年12月有会员54人，常务理事5人，专职工作人员1人。

第四节 科普工作

一、农村技术人才培训

（一）乡土人才培训

1978—1990年，与相关部门采取联合开办农村夜校、组织科技干部下乡、以会代训、举办科技讲座等形式，培训农村乡土人才。共举办培训班1132期，培训乡土人才5.11万人次。评定首批农民技术员并授予证书50人。1990年后，主要培训科学带头人，重点对科技“二传手”进行培训，加快实用技术推广。

2006年，经过培训，选出掌握果树修剪技术较强的农民技术骨干17名组成果树服务修剪队。

（二）农业技术函授

1986年9月，成立农村致富技术函授大学辅导站，学制一年，在全县招生，培训科学致富人才，重点培训农村知识青年、复员退伍军人。第一届招生36名，其中，种植系17名、养殖系16名、加工系2名、乡镇企业管理系1名。1987年11月招收第二届学员68人。1989年结业29人，其中，养殖系15人、种植系14人。1990年6月招第三届学员28人，另外代辅导分校直接在甲良区招生27名，共计55人。学员中，考取县农业局干部2人，提拔为科技副乡长1人。

1997年起，由县委组织部、县科协牵头，在县职业高中和县委党校举办村级后备干部科技培训班，招生对象为25周岁以下的初中、高中毕业生及退伍军人、农村能工巧匠、科技示范户、村组干部。课程设置36门，除传授职业技术学校必修的基础理论课程外，还根据全县实际选修县编乡土教材。经过两年学习期满成绩合格者发给黔南州教育局验印的职业高中毕业证书，县内承认中专学历。

1999年，成立县农村基层干部农技函授学校，农技函授总站及办公室设在县农业局，各乡（镇）建立函授教学点，每年由财政拨专款5万元，对40岁以下具有初中以上文化程度且有一定自学能力的村组干部及后备干部进行农技函授培训，学制2年，开设农业、牧业、林业、乡企、土管、行政6类课程。教材选用部分中专教材和县内编写的乡土教材，如《果树和蔬菜》《土壤与肥料》《种植新技术》《庭院综合生产技术》《果品加工》《玉米栽培》《牛品种改良》《三元杂交猪技术》等。学员课程考试合格，发给毕业证书，县内承认中专文凭。

至2004年，村级后备干部科技培训班招收学员300人，获得毕业证书264人；县农村基层干部农技函授学校招收学员累计508人。

至2008年，全县有农村实用人才2027人。

二、科普活动

1980—1981年，在城关区、朝阳区、茂兰区、甲良区所在地各设宣传专栏1个，开展工业、农业、医药等方面的科学知识普及宣传，创办《荔波科普》2期，合办《科普园地》14期。

1983年6月，在荔波举办西南三省（区）多种经营科普美术展览，参观人数700余人。

1984年，县科协在甲良、朝阳、王蒙、县城举办“破除迷信”图片展览，观众达5000人。

1980—1986年，县科协放科技电影601场，观看群众34500人次；合办科技广播讲座，播出科技广播搞1086篇。

1990年，县科协先后建立方村乡丙花村和朝阳乡拉扶村两个科普村。

1991年，县科协与县妇联组织县妇幼保健站科技人员编写《妇女儿童保健卫生知识问答》50题，印发全县29个单位参与“恩威杯”全国首届妇女保健卫生知识大赛选拔赛活动。1992—1995年，结合基层组织建设“四个一”（一个好的领导班子、一条好的致富路、一套好的管理制度、一支好的干部队伍）工程，到玉屏、甲良、方村、翁昂、捞村等乡（镇）的37个村放映水稻半旱式栽培、养鸡、水稻病虫害防治等科教片37场。其间，县科协于1994年与教育、卫生、防疫、妇幼保健及各乡（镇）科协负责人组成科普宣传队，到7个乡（镇）集贸市场进行科普宣传，每次展出挂图106张，发放资料共4200份。

1996年，县科协与广播部门开办科技广播节目44期，播出科技稿件120篇。

1998年，重点开展“3·18”科技日活动，县级各学会在县城大街进行多学科大型科普宣传，并到各乡（镇）开展咨询，发放各种科普资料共3.4万份。

2000年，结合揭批“法轮功”邪教组织，开展“崇尚科学文明，反对迷信愚昧”大型图片展活动，到学校展出12场（次），观展群众7.5万人次，全县有2000多名中学生写观后感。

2001年，通过自办瑶山早桃示范园，对周围群众进行技术传授，带动周围群众建设标准果园3000亩。

2003年春节，邀请省科协科普大篷车宣传队到荔波县开展科普活动。利用县内举办“盛世灯火映樟江”大型灯展活动宣传荔波科普网站，发送科技资料30种1000册。在防治非典型性肺炎（以下简称“非典”）期间，县科协发送防治“非典”宣传挂图500份到172村（居）和5个检查站，刻录20张防治“非典”光碟发到各乡（镇）进行防治宣传。

2004年，开展大型的“3·18”科普咨询和全国科普日纪念活动，发放各种科技资料共35种6.3万份。

2005—2006年，重点开展种桑养蚕、特色果品种植推广宣传。

2006年3月28日，邀请贵州大学农学院果树和植保专家到荔波作专题讲座，推广特色果品种植新技术，落实“科普惠农兴村计划”。在全县蜜柚种植评比中，拉岜村科普示范户刘秀良获第一名。

2007年，在文化、科技、卫生“三下乡”和科技、文体、法律、卫生“四进社区”活动中，发放各种科普资料及图书1万份。开展“健康进社区”“人口早期教育”“食用三聚氰胺奶粉婴幼儿泌尿系统结石筛查”等系列科普宣传。

2008年3月18日，开展全国科普日系列活动，以“节约能源资源，保护生态环境，保障安全健康”为主题，发放科技资料6800份，发送科普挂图和《科学素质纲要》挂图1000份。

三、科普网站

2001年，在中国科协的资助下，建立荔波科普网（www.lbxq.cn）。随后在玉屏镇、茂兰镇、朝阳镇、甲良镇、佳荣镇等相继开通荔波科普信息站。荔波科普网成为贵州省第一家示范网站。

2008年，利用现代科学信息资源，与县委组织部联合开办“科普+远教”咨询服务厅，发放各种资料及远程教育光盘，为群众开展科普咨询服务。

第六章 文学艺术界联合会

第一节 组织建设

1999年6月，成立荔波县文学艺术界联合会，为正科级单位，设办公室，挂靠县文体局，主席由县文体局局长兼任，设1名专职副主席兼秘书长，无工作人员。县文联成立后，组织成立作家协会、书法家协会、美术家协会、音乐家协会、舞蹈家协会、摄影家协会、诗词楹联协会、民间文艺家协会8个文艺家协会。各协会设主席1名。

2005年1月，县文联单独办公，单列编制，内设办公室，配主席1名、副主席1名兼秘书长。是年年底，派驻会副主席1名，共3人办公。自2005年后，成立花木盆景奇石协会。集邮协会划归文联统一管理。

2008年，县文联设有办公室，有编制3人，有主席、副主席、秘书长各1人，无工作人员。全县有文艺家协会9个。

第二节 代表大会

县文联第一次代表大会 1999年6月18日，县文学艺术界联合会第一次代表大会在县城召开。应到会正式代表25人，实到代表23人。大会听取和审议县文联工作报告；制定文联章程；选举产生县文联第一届委员会委员6名，其中主席1名、副主席1名。

县文联第二次代表大会 2005年1月24日，县文联第二次代表大会在县城召开。应到正式代表88人，实到代表58人。大会听取和审议县文联第一届委员会工作报告；讨论修改文联章程；选举产生县文联第二届委员会委员11名，其中主席1名、副主席3名、秘书长1名。

第三节 文艺活动

一、主要活动

2005年，县文联与县文体广播电视局联合举办“迎春书画、摄影、奇石、花卉、盆景展”活动。5月，由浙江台州人李昌志创办成立了本县唯一一家从事文房四宝、字画装裱、书法培训的古榕斋。店面因县城古榕树得名，牌名由著名书法篆刻家刘江题写。先后有刘正成、曹宝麟、包俊宜、陈加林等书画名家莅临古榕斋。至2008年，有百余中小学生和书法爱好者参加培训，先后有十余人次在国家级、省级赛事中获奖。古榕斋的创办，为青少年学生学习书法提供了平台，同时也活跃了书法爱好者，为促进本县青少年书法起到了积极的推动作用，得到了社会的肯定和赞誉。

2006年6月，县文联组织开展向黔南州建州50周年献礼——荔波山水画集体创作活动。

2007年，在县筹备全省第二届旅游发展大会期间，县文联举办“徐庭炜书画作品展暨徐庭炜作品集捐赠仪式”，黔南州美协会员、县美协原主席徐庭炜向贵州省第二届旅游发展大会捐赠《中国南方喀斯特——荔波山水画册》1000册，县委、县政府向徐庭炜颁发荣誉证书。同时，徐庭炜在县宣传文化中心举办个人书画展。

是年，县文联、教育局、县文广局、荔波古榕斋书法培训中心在县城樟江园广场联合举办首届“古榕斋杯”百名少年现场书法大赛，全县有80名中小学生参加比赛，由县书法家组成评委，对参赛作品评出一等奖3幅、二等奖6幅、三等奖9幅。

二、艺术创作成果

（一）文学类

卢剑平（笔名路泞），2002年4月自选文集《一路不安》编入当代作家丛书。由中国文联出版社出版。2002年参加黔南州中短篇小说大赛，其短篇小说《回家》获二等奖。作家罗世槐的短篇小说《第一桶金》同时参赛，获优秀奖。精短篇小说《金苹果》入选黔南文艺丛书（2002—2003）卷。

（二）美术类

2006年，曹本健获“贵州省优秀美术家”“贵州省有突出贡献美术家”称号，其创作的油画作品《斗鸟乐》《乡场上的午餐》分别获第三届（2006年）、第五届（2008年）全国西部大地情美术作品展优秀奖。

（三）歌曲类

1990年，罗世槐创作的歌曲《村野少女》获贵州省《广播新歌》一等奖。

2005年，姚铜创作的歌曲《咿呀奈》在北京市获全国首届“真维斯杯”文艺展演二等奖。

2005—2006年，魏芳先后获第一届、第二届“多彩贵州”歌唱大赛黔南赛区第一名、第二名，进入黔南州代表队参加全省总决赛。

2007年8月，由何有秋作曲的《人民法院之歌》获全国法院歌曲征集大赛三等奖。

（四）书法类

2008年，申学军书法作品入展中国书坛新人作品展。

（五）摄影类

县摄影家协会共同组稿出版《喀斯特神话》《山水天堂》《瑶山春晖》《中国最美的地方——荔波》等摄影画册。2007年中国摄影出版社出版徐大岭的《映像喀斯特荔波》画册。

熊亚平的2005年摄影作品《法—网》获得贵州省“走进法制”摄影比赛一等奖；2007年摄影作品《沉痛的思考》获得贵州省首届公安警察文化艺术摄影比赛二等奖，摄影作品《梦幻鸳鸯湖》获得首届全国“梅花杯”荔波风光摄影比赛二等奖。

（六）诗词类

蒙照辉作品获黔南州诗词楹联学会举办“歌颂党、赞中华、扬国学”中华诗词大赛二等奖。

（七）舞蹈类

杨长沙编导的《欢乐苗家》获全省文艺调演最佳编导奖，《芒筒芦笙祭祀乐舞》获全国第十六届群星奖三等奖；吴玫、蒙利娟编导的《欢歌喊太阳》获黔南州文艺调演二等奖；吴玫编导的《打猎舞》获贵州省少数民族运动会竞技舞蹈比赛金奖，获全国少数民族运动会竞技舞蹈比赛二等奖，奖黔南州文艺调演二等奖；田儒倩编导的《狩猎》获多彩贵州黔南赛区“民族民间舞蹈”三等奖。

第七章 残疾人联合会

第一节 组织建设

1991年前，全县残疾人工作由县民政局负责。1991年3月21日，成立荔波县残疾人联合会，为正科级单位，实行理事长负责制，有工作人员3名，其中理事长1名，残疾人工作正式与县民政局分离。

此后，逐步在乡（镇）建立残联组织，在村建立残疾人协会，乡（镇）残联和村残协全部配备专职委员。

2007年12月，通过省、州残联的检查验收，荔波县成为中残联基层残疾人组织规范化建设第一批验收合格县。全县17个乡（镇）成立有残联，全县98个行政村（居）成立残疾人协会；乡（镇）残联和村（社区）残协共配备115名残疾人专职委员。乡（镇）、村（居）两级残疾人专职委员务工补贴纳入县级财政预算。

2008年年末，县残联机关有工作人员7名，其中理事长1名、副理事长1名、理事4名。

第二节 代表大会

县残联第一次代表大会 1991年3月21—22日，县残联第一次代表大会在县城召开。大会有代表60人。其中，各区（镇）代表35人，县直机关、企事业单位及人民团体代表25人；残疾人代表31人，占代表总数的51.67%。会议听取县残联筹备领导小组所作的筹备工作报告；选举产生县残联第一届主席团主席1名、副主席4名；推举理事长1名。

县残联第二次代表大会 1995年9月21日，县残联第二次代表大会在县城召开。大会有代表50人。其中，各乡（镇）代表38人，县直机关、企事业单位的代表12人；残疾人代表26人，占代表总数的52%。大会听取和审议县残疾人联合会第一届主席团及其执行理事会作的工作报告；选举产生县残联第二届主席团主席1名、副主席2名；推举理事长1名、理事2名。

县残联第三次代表大会 2001年11月12日，县残联第三次代表大会在县城召开。大会有代表69人。其中，残疾人代表39人，占代表总数的56.52%；各乡（镇）、县直机关、企事业单位代表30人。大会听取和审议大会听取和审议县残联第二届主席团及其执行理事会作的工作报告；选举产生县残联第三届主席团委员23名，选举主席团主席1名、副主席2名；推举理事长1名、副理事长1名、理事4名。

县残联第四次代表大会 2007年6月13日，县残联第四次代表大会在县城召开。大会有代表106人。其中，各乡（镇）代表83人，县直机关、企事业单位代表23名；残疾人代表54人，占代表总数的50.94%。大会听取和审议县残疾人联合会第三届主席团及其执行理事会作的《更新观念　开拓进取　为我县残疾人事业的持续快速健康发展而努力奋斗》工作报告；选举产生县残联第四届主席团委员33名，选举主席团主席1名、副主席2名；推举理事长1名、副理事长1名、理事4名。

第三节　权益保障

一、康复

1991年8—11月，县残联开始对部分乡（镇）的“三康”对象（白内障患者、小儿麻痹后遗症患者、0～7岁聋哑儿）进行抽样调查，为全面普查打基础。

1992年年初，对全县康复对象进行全面普查，经过3个月普查，掌握全县白内障患者、小儿麻痹后遗症患者及0～7岁聋哑儿的基本数据。其中，白内障患者2938名、小儿麻痹后遗症患者678名、0～7岁聋哑儿67名。

是年5月3—6日，省“三康”办公室派遣白内障医疗队到荔波支边，在县医院为20名白内障患者进行手术，术后全部康复。

1998年5—7月，县残联调查，全县有贫困残疾人2005户2195人。其中，残疾扶贫户1400户1400人（指有一定劳动能力和有经营意识户），应救济户605户795人（指无劳动能力和无经营意识户），贫困残疾人占全县残疾人总数的33%。

从1998年起，国家、省、州残联组织在荔波县实施“视觉第一中国行动”“长江新里程计划”“彭年光明行动”“国家彩票公益金康复项目”等残疾人康复项目，全县有1500名残疾人受益。2001年，县残联被省政府残工委评为“视觉第一中国行动”先进单位。

2006年，荔波作为全省第二次残疾人抽样调查的22个抽样县之一，以玉屏镇的城南居委会、城西居委会，朝阳镇的板麦村委会、山江村委会，瑶山乡的高桥村委会、红光村委会，方村乡的红泥村委会、丙花村委会等共8个村（居）委会为抽样调查样本点。抽样调查结果，是年4月1日零时，全县有各类残疾人10597人，占总人口的6.52%。其中，视力残疾1436人，占13.55%；听力残疾3075人，占29.02%；言语残疾207人，占1.95%；肢体残疾2956人，占27.9%；智力残疾593人，占5.6%；精神残疾682人，占6.44%；多重残疾1648人，占15.55%。

至2008年12月，全县完成白内障手术613例，白内障患者520人重见光明；完成小儿麻痹后遗症患者矫治手术46例，其中38名小儿麻痹后遗症患者丢下拐杖；完成聋儿听力语言训练15例，其中11名残疾聋儿走进义务教育课堂；完成聋儿听力语言训练32例、智残儿童启智训练25例、脑瘫儿童训练10例、肢体矫治手术26例、肢体康复训练52例、低视力配镜25例、装配矫形器26例、假肢安装34例，残疾人辅助用具供应860件。在“视觉第一中国行动”“长江新里程计划”“国家彩票公益金康复项目”中，全县有1500名残疾人受益。

二、就业

1991年，开始安置残疾人就业。是年，全县安置残疾人就业3人。1992年，全县安置残疾人就业5人，其中合同制工人1人。同时对部分残疾人进行培训，通过培训后能自食其力的残疾人55人。

1993年，宣传国家对残疾人的各项优惠政策，鼓励残疾人从事个体业、自谋职业。全年安置残疾人5人。对农村残疾人，以短期培训的方式，帮助他们发展农副业，在技术、资金方面优先照顾。全县残疾人通过培训后就地稳定就业123人，通过培训和帮助实现脱贫致富15人。1994年，残疾人通过培训扶持脱贫致富78人。在事业、企业单位安置残疾人就业3人。1995年，安置城镇有一定劳动能力的残疾人7人；组织134名有一定劳动能力的农村残疾人参加培训。

1996—1997年，按照集中与分散就业相结合的原则和多层次、多渠道、多形式的安置办法，安置部分有劳动能力的残疾人就业。同时，县残联会同人事劳动、民政等部门对全县企事业单位残疾人劳动就业状况进行调查摸底，加大对企业的监控，向各企业提出“无论企业有何种困难，残疾人不能脱岗”的要求，得到工商、税务、民政等部门支持，全县两年分散安置残疾人13名。

1998年，县残联开展残疾人求职登记、能力评估、技术培训和职业介绍等工作。依据《中华人民共和国残疾人保障法》《贵州省实施〈中华人民共和国残疾人保障法〉办法》《残疾人就业条例》的有关规定，向用人单位和私营企业推荐残疾人就业。通过技能培训、推荐就业，至2001年年底，为残疾人进行求职登记104人，帮助扶持残疾人个体从业32人。

1998—2001年，县残联举办各类残疾人职业技术培训班7期419人次；推介11名残疾人到事业单位和私营企业就业。

2002—2005年，县残联每年举办农业技术、职业技能等培训班，农村、城镇残疾人参加培训后掌握了一定技能，被推荐到企业就业17人，自主就业8人；农村残疾人利用学到的农业技术从事种植业生产实现脱贫50人。

2006年，在残疾人抽样调查中培训各类残疾人66人。其中，培训后回乡从事种养业15人，并为他们争取贷款13万元，减免税费3万元。

2007—2008年，举办实用技术培训班1期，培训农村残疾人41人；举办残疾人职业技能培训班1期，培训有一定劳动能力又有经营意识的残疾人35人。推荐8名残疾人到企业就业。

三、特殊教育

1998年，县残联贯彻执行《特殊教育条例》，争取“扶残助学”“盲童入学”“彩票公益金助学”“希望工程”捐助等项目资金，以及协调减免杂费等方式，帮助轻度残疾儿童少年就近随班就读，帮助“三类”（视力、听力、智力）残疾儿童少年到贵阳、贵定和独山等地特殊教育学校就读。

至2008年年底，全县466名各类残疾失学儿童得到救助，扶助资金共4.9万元。其中，学校减免学杂费60人，州残联救助11人，县残联救助40人，“希望工程”救助27人。全县残疾儿童少年入学率从2001年的56.6%上升到2008年的71%，并通过省、州“两基”验收。

四、权益维护

县残联配合司法等相关部门制定《荔波县残疾人法律援助工作办法》，建立残疾人维权法律援助机构，聘请常年法律顾问，开展“扶残维权行动”。为残疾人提供法律服务7680人次，免费为残疾人办理案件28件；创建残疾人维权示范岗，县立化镇司法所、播尧乡司法所被省司法厅、省残联命名为“全省残疾人维权示范岗”。

县残联成立残疾人信访机构，对残疾人来信来访反映的困难和问题，协调有关方面帮助解决，正确处理好维稳与维权的关系，全县没有出现残疾人群体上访和进京上访现象。

第四节　助残活动与文体活动

一、助残活动

1991年起，每年5月的第三个星期日为“全国助残日”，县残联根据当年“全国助残日”活动的主题，开展形式多样的“全国助残日”活动。

1998年，县残联争取到扶持残疾人养猪、养羊项目贷款56万元，采取直接帮扶、户贷帮扶、干部帮扶、乡贷帮扶，以及基地辐射等帮扶方式，在玉屏镇、佳荣镇、朝阳镇、茂兰镇、翁昂乡等5个乡（镇）扶持残疾人贫困户280户，涉及残疾人430人。是年12月，根据《国家“八七”扶贫攻坚计划》，县残联、县扶贫办起草《荔波县残疾人扶贫攻坚计划》，将残疾人的扶贫攻坚计划纳入全县扶贫攻坚工作的总体规划中，按照“统一安排、统一部署、统一扶持、整体提高”的扶贫攻坚目标组织实施。

1999—2000年，县残联争取到扶贫贷款62万元，以小额到户的方式发放给贫困残疾人家庭252户，解决温饱411人。

2001年，县残联、民政局解决残疾人特困户生活费476人，资金2.85万元。全县落实干部与残疾人结对帮扶110人。

1991—2008年，在“全国助残日”活动中，为残疾人办实事、办好事共517件，帮助残疾人解决生产生活中的实际困难1.54万人次，解决资金41.6万元，发给救济粮81吨。其中，贫困残疾人得到现金和实物帮扶525人，帮扶资金和物资折款4.82万元；为残疾人发放法律宣传资料7550本（册）；免费为残疾人办理各类涉诉案件26件，其中乡镇办理16件、公证处办理2件、中心法律服务所办理3件、法律援助中心办理5件。

至2008年年底，城镇残疾人纳入最低生活保障88人，农村贫困残疾人纳入最低生活保障986人。

二、文体活动

1991年10月，县残联组织残疾人参加黔南州首届伤残人田径运动会，开创荔波伤残人参加体育竞赛的先例。运动会上，荔波选手何庆尤（肢残）获得男子上肢组A6级3000米赛跑第一名，高泉波（聋人）、尚利生（语言障碍）分别获男子聋哑组100米赛跑、400米赛跑第四名，韦利萍（语言障碍）获女子聋哑组100米赛跑第五名。

1992年7月，组织残疾人棋类爱好者参加黔南州残疾人棋类比赛，李玉萍（肢残）获女子肢残组弹子棋第一名，何庆尤（肢残）获男子肢残组象棋第一名，唐真强（肢残）获男子肢残组象棋第二名，韦利萍（语言障碍）获女子聋哑组弹子棋第二名，荔波代表队获团体总分第三名。

1999年10月21—26日，选派伤残运动员蒙学俊、胡应奎参加黔南州残疾人代表队，出席在贵阳举行的第二届全省残疾人运动会，蒙学俊获得男子聋哑组100米仰泳、100米蝶泳、100米自由泳第一名，胡应奎获得男子聋哑组800米赛跑、1500米赛跑第三名并获道德风尚奖。获奖运动员受到省、州、县的表彰和奖励。

2002年、2006年，残疾人运动员覃建红（智残）两次代表贵州省参加全国第三届、第四届特殊奥林匹克运动会，获得金牌2枚、银牌3枚、铜牌1枚。

2005年，聋哑运动员吴胜茂参加第三届全省残运会，获男子羽毛球比赛第三名。2006年5月，吴胜茂参加在昆明举行的第六届全国残运会，获男子羽毛球比赛第六名。2008年11月，吴胜茂参加在浙江嘉兴举行的第二十一届聋奥会选拔赛暨2008年全国聋人锦标赛运动会，获男子羽毛球双打第二名。

第九篇

人力资源　社会保障　民政

1978年改革开放以来，全县机关、事业单位进行了人事制度改革，实行了干部聘用制度，1990年以后，一直实行招考录用干部制度，面向社会招考选拔录用行政、事业单位工作人员。1993年8月，国务院颁布实施《国家公务员管理条例》以后，开始推行国家公务员制度同时按国家规定对专业技术人员进行管理。1994年，根据中央有关机构改革精神，按照政企分开和精简、统一、高效的原则，进行县级机构改革。1996年进行乡（镇）机构改革。1983年，成立县劳动就业培训中心，进行就业培训，提高劳动者素质。2003年，成立县就业工作领导小组，制定就业再就业工作实施方案。20世纪80年代初，境内开始劳务输出。2004年，荔波县被州政府授予“劳务输出先进县”称号。1978年以后，干部职工工资福利不断提高。社会各项保险制度逐步建立，社会各项管理制度和社会救助与福利制度逐步完善。

第一章 人力资源与劳动就业

第一节 人事制度改革

1986年，进行人事制度改革，实行干部聘用制度，主要是机关、事业单位面向社会招聘人员，应聘者经考试，由用人单位或劳动人事部门考核审查同意后办理聘用手续。被招聘者与用人单位签订合同，合同期满可以续聘、解聘或辞聘，属于农业人口的被聘用人员，不转粮户关系，仍保留责任地。是年，县农业局招聘农经员6人。

1987年4月起，实行国家工作人员非领导职务晋升制度，对全县国家机关、事业单位干部身份人员明确非领导职务，是年评定晋升不同级别的非领导职务共488人。

1988年，面向社会公开招考干部，为公安、法院、财政等部门招聘22人，为教育、卫生部门录用30人。1989年，为公安、法院、财政、税务等部门和区、乡录用干部共76人。

1990年以后，一直实行招考录用干部制度，面向社会招考选拔录用行政、事业单位工作人员。

按照县委、县政府《关于大中专毕业生安置工作有关问题的决定》，从2000年1月起，所有大专毕业生、中专毕业生安置一律实行“凡进必考”办法，择优录用，增加工勤人员也实行考试聘用制度。本科毕业生仍由县大中专毕业生分配领导小组统一安排。

2002年起，县内公务员、党的机关工作者和参照公务员管理的事业单位录用人员，实行全省统一招考录用制度。是年，由省统一招考，县内录用33人。2003年，录用大学毕业选调生4人。2004—2008年，招考录用人数总计73人，其中选调生14人。

第二节 公务员管理

1978年11月，中共中央发出《关于实行干部考核制度的通知》后，对干部进行了一次考核鉴定。1980—1992年，对干部考核采取领导评议和群众评议相结合的方法进行。

1990年起，在全县党政群机关单位全面推行年度考核制度，对工作人员的德、能、勤、绩进行考核，分为优秀、称职、不称职3个等次。是年，全县参加考核的工作人员3414人（含事业单位），评为优秀415人、称职2732人、不称职223人、未定等次44人。年度考核结果作为提拔、晋升技术职务、奖惩、培训、辞退、增资的依据。

1993年8月，国务院颁布实施《国家公务员管理条例》以后，1994年，县土地管理局被列为全省6个公务员试点单位之一，开始推行国家公务员制度。

1996年5月，对全县拟过渡为公务员的人员进行集中培训，并组织参加全省统一考试。参训人员915人，合格909人。

1997年以后，对一般干部的考核采取平时考核和年终考核相结合、定量考核与定性考核相结合的办法。平时要求个人如实填写《平时考核纪实手册》，季度末由单位主管领导审核一次，年终作为考核依据。对担任副科级以上领导职务的干部，主要采取届中和任期考核相结合的办法，考核由任免机关组织进行。1998年4月，全县机关及乡（镇）第一批过渡为国家公务员796人。

自1999年起，年度考核增加“基本称职（基本合格）”等次，凡是考核被定为基本称职（基本合格）的人员，安排离岗到州参加学习培训，经过半年考察后再重新确定等次。

2005年，按照《中华人民共和国公务员法》管理全县公务员队伍。2007年，按照《行政机关公务员处分条例》对违纪违规公务员进行处分。县内国家工作人员年度考核制度一直延续至2008年。

第三节　专业技术人员管理

1978年7月，全县从事科技工作的专业技术人员共297人，对专业技术人员没有进行统一管理。

1980年，对科技干部进行技术职称考核评定。至1982年年底，经考核合格、套改、评定和晋升技术职称162人。其中，工程师8人、助理工程师38人、技术员59人、主治医师4人、主管医师2人、技术员一级51人。

1983年6月，对全县科技人员的分布情况进行全面普查，全县有科技人员417人。其中，直接从事技术工作403人；在公社工作182人。

1988年10月，对事业单位专业技术职称进行改革，实行专业技术人员聘用制，对取得专业技术任职资格的人员发资格证和职称聘任证书，职称与工资挂钩。职称改革后，每年正常进行事业单位职称评聘，符合条件者，经申报、评审，晋升专业技术职务。

1989年12月—1990年1月，对全县专业技术人员进行普查，获初级以上职称总计2141人（包括1983年以前评得职称及国家机关中已评定职称未聘用的45人），其中高级20人、中级288人、初级1833人。

1990年开始，对专业技术人员实行年度考核制度，考核分为称职、基本称职、不称职3个等次。是年，考核受聘的专业技术人员1398人，其中不称职5人。

1995年，开展机关、事业单位技术工人等级考评工作。

2002年4月，对建筑行业技术工种进行职业技能鉴定，共鉴定60人。

至2008年年末，全县获专业技术任职资格人员2954人，其中高级78人、中级987人、初级1889人。

第四节　编制管理

一、机构改革

（一）县级机构改革

1994年，根据中央有关机构改革精神，按照政企分开和精简、统一、高效的原则，进行县级机构改革。

在党委工作部门改革中，撤销农村工作部、机要局、保密局、信访局独立建制，工作职能并入县委办；撤销老干局独立建制，行政职能并入组织部；撤销对台办独立建制，工作职能并入统战部。党委部门改革后由11个调整为6个，调整后的机构有县委办公室、组织部、宣传部、统战部、政法委员会、县委党校。

在政府工作部门改革中，撤销外事办独立建制，工作职能并入政府办；撤销旅游局行政系列建制，改为县政府直属事业单位；撤销计划委员会、经济委员会、经济协作办独立建制，合并组建计划和经济贸易局；撤销商业局、物资局、轻工局行政序列建制，改为公司，其行政职能并入计划和经济贸易局；撤销农牧局、农村经济委员会独立建制，合并组建为农业局；撤销教育局、科学技术局、合并组建教育科技局；撤销工商行政管理局、物价局、标准计量局独立建制，合并组建工商行政管理局；撤销计划生育委员会，改建为计划生育局；撤销土地管理局、矿产资源管理办公室独立建制，合并组建国土资源管理局；撤销体育运动委员会、广播电视局、文化局独立建制，合并组建文体广播电视局。改革后政府工作机构由44个调整为24个，调整后的机构有县政府办、计划和经济贸易局、粮食局、农业局、教育科技局、统计局、工商行政管理局、审计局、民政局、财政税务局、公安局、人事劳动局、卫生局、计划生育局、民族事务局、国土资源管理局、建设局、司法局、交通局、文体广播电视局、乡镇企业局、监察局、水利局、林业局。

人大机关、政协机关、纪检监察部门、检察机关、审判机关、武装部、直属机关党委按有关规定设置，任命群众团体机构按《宪法》和有关规定设置。全县县级行政编制按350名（不含公安、检察、法院、司法、人武部的编制）核定。

2001年，按照州的统一部署，进行党政机构改革。改革以精简、统一、效能和一件事情由一个机构管理为主的原则，对党委和政府工作部门进行调整。即：将机构编制委员会办公室单独设置，列入县委工作部门；机要局、保密委员会办公室设在县委办，为副科级机构；信访办设在政府办，为副科级机构；撤销计划和经济贸易局独立建设，分别组建发展计划局和经济贸易局，招商引资职能划入发展计划局，挂招商引资局牌子，将安全生产管理职能由人事劳动划入经济贸易局；撤销国土局和地质矿产局，合并组建国土资源局；建立统一的人事劳动和社会保障行政机构。

政府机构由原来的31个精减为25个。县级机关行政人员编制按24%的比例精简，由356名减为271名。同时精简领导职数，县委设书记1名、副书记3—4名，县政府设县长1名、副县长4—5名；非领导职数按领导职数的50%设置；县委、县政府工作部门一般设正职1名、副职1—2名，少数工作量大的副职不超过3名，非领导职数按领导职数的50%配置。调整后，全县有党政工作部门总计35个、政府事业单位3个。其中，县级党的工作机构有纪律检查委员会（与监察局合署办公）、县委办公室、组织部、宣传部、统一战线工作部（含对台工作）、政法委员会、机构编制委员会办公室、直属机关党委8个；政府工作部门有政府办公室、发展计划局、经济贸易局、教育局、科学技术局、民族宗教事务局、公安局、监察局（与县纪委合署办公，不占机构限额）、民政局、财政局、司法局、人事劳动和社会保障局、国土资源管理局、建设局、交通局、水利局、农业局、林业局、环境保护局、计划生育局、卫生局、审计局、统计局、粮食局、乡镇企业局、文体广播电视局、物价局（与物价检查所合署办公，不占机构限额）27个；政府议事协调机构有农业办公室、扶贫开发办公室（农业综合开发办公室）2个；政府事业单位有旅游事业局、档案局与档案馆实行局馆合一体制（一个机构两块牌子）、供销合作社联合社3个。

人大机关、政协机关、检察机关、审判机关、群团机关按《宪法》和有关规定设置。

2004年，进行政府行政管理体制改革，对政府部分工作机构和职能进行整合，即：将人事劳动和社会保障局承担的企业工资总额、经营者年薪和其他主要负责人工资标准审核工作划入经济贸易局；将承担的安全生产管理职能并入县安全生产监督管理局；将县发展计划局改组为县发展和改革局；将县政府办承担的经济体制改革和盐业管理职能划入发展和改革局；在县安全生产委员会办公室的基础上组建县安全生产监督管理局，为县政府委托行使安全生产监督管理职能的直属事业单位；将县计划生育局更改为人口和计划生育局；县政府法制办公室设在县政府办，为正科级机构。

经过调整，县政府设政府办公室、发展和改革局、经济贸易局、教育局、科学技术局、民族宗教事务局、公安局、监察局（与县纪委合署办公，不占机构限额）、民政局、财政局、司法局、人事劳动和社会保障局、国土资源管理局、建设局、交通局、水利局、农业局、林业局、环境保护局、人口和计划生育局、卫生局、审计局、统计局、粮食局、乡镇企业局、文体广播电视局、物价局（与物价检查所合署办公，不占机构限额）等工作部门27个，设农业办公室、扶贫开发办公室（农业综合开发办公室）政府议事协调机构2个，设旅游事业局、档案局（与档案馆局馆合一，一个机构两块牌子）、供销合作社联合社、安全生产监督管理局政府事业单位4个。

（二）乡（镇）机构改革

1996年，对全县乡（镇）类别进行调整，玉屏镇、朝阳镇、甲良镇、茂兰镇、立化镇、水尧水族乡、佳荣乡、播尧乡、洞塘乡9个乡（镇）为二类，瑶山瑶族乡、水利水族乡、瑶麓瑶族乡、永康水族乡、翁昂乡、方村乡、捞村乡、驾欧乡8个乡为三类。

1997年，进行乡（镇）机构改革，二类乡（镇）机构设置4～5个，党委工作机构设党政办公室、政法委员会（与治安综合治理办公室合署办公）、人民武装部（不占机构限额），政府机构设民政办公室、计划生育办公室、科教文卫办公室。三类乡（镇）机构设置3～4个，党委工作机构设党政办公室、政法委员会（与治安综合治理办公室合署办公）、人民武装部（不占机构限额），政府机构设民政办公室、计划生育办公室。全县乡（镇）党群机关总编制核定461名。

2001年，实施乡（镇）机构改革，划分县乡事权，理顺条块、行政层级关系。即设在乡（镇）的农技、农经、水产、畜牧农机、乡镇企业管理、文化、广播电视、计划生育服务、水利、林业等事业机构和人员交由乡（镇）管理，业务由县主管部门领导；设在乡（镇）的公安、司法、土地、卫生、教育等机构和人员由乡（镇）与县主管部门双重领导，以县主管部门为主。乡（镇）机构行政编制按总数16%的比例精简，事业单位按财政供养人员20%压缩。行政机构改革后，各乡（镇）党委机构不变，政府机构设社会事务办、计划生育办、经济发展办、城镇管理办（在建制镇设置）4个。事业机构改革后，设置以乡（镇）管理为主，业务受主管部门指导的事业机构有农业服务中心、文化服务中心、水利站、林业站、乡镇企业管理站5个；设置实行双重领导，以主管部门管理为主的事业机构有国土资源所、教育辅导站、卫生院3个；设置实行考核、工资、福利以乡（镇）管理为主，人员编制以业务主管部门管理为主的事业机构有计划生育服务站、财政所2个。派出机构有公安派出所、人民法庭、司法所3个。

二、人员编制管理

1987—2000年，县编委办设在县劳动人事局。2001年机构改革，县编委办单独设置，列为县委工作部门。

县属行政、事业单位经县委、县政府批准的各部门“三定”方案，凡涉及机构名称的变更、增设、职能调整、隶属关系的改变、领导职数和人员编制的增减，都必须按照审批程序，书面报编委办审核，提出方案经编委会或县委研究审批。在控制机构编制方面，除上级党委、政府和机构编制部门有明确要求外，对各部门要求的机构编制事项都进行严格控制，原则上不增加机构和编制，职能调整和任务增加的部门，由部门内部调剂解决；对财政补贴的事业单位，原则上不增加机构和编制，对因工作确需增加的，也要按照“撤一建一”和总量控制，“只减不增”的原则从严控制。

在空编补员方面，各乡（镇）、各部门每年3月底前按“空编补员计划审批表”的要求，向编委办报送本年度的用编计划，县编委办审核后提交县编委会审批，下发年度用编计划。用人单位报人事调配工作领导小组研究人员招考录用或调动。

在人员工资审核方面，各乡（镇）、各部门每季度前按照《工资基金审核制度》的要求，将本单位“工资基金审批表”先报编委办审核人员在编情况后到人社、财政部门核发工资。在“机构编制管理证”审验方面，各（部门）单位在每年3月份之前要到县编委办进行“机构编制管理证”年审，以保证机构和人员编制相统一。

三、事业单位登记管理

2001年2月，根据国务院《事业单位登记管理暂行条例》及实施细则的规定，设立县事业单位登记管理局，挂靠县编委，实行两块牌子、一套人员管理体制。是年12月，县事业单位登记管理局作为常设办事机构单列，为编委办的副科级机构。2002年5月，正式启动全县事业单位登记法人登记管理工作，全年登记单位180个，登记率85%，登记发证168个。到2008年，事业单位登记管理工作步入规范化。

第五节 就业与劳务输出

一、劳动就业与培训

1983年，成立县劳动就业培训中心，进行就业培训。全年举办培训班8期，培训768人。

1984年，成立县劳动服务公司，主要进行职业介绍、就业培训。是年，企业单位招工实行合同制。合同制工人在合同期内，工资升级、奖励、津贴、补贴等，均与固定职工同等享受。1987年，对城镇待业青年及新工人进行就业前和上岗前培训，共培训181人。

1990年，县人事劳动服务公司更名为荔波县劳动人事局劳动就业办公室。1984—1990年，小七孔电站劳动服务公司、玉屏印刷厂劳动服务公司、商业劳动服务公司、待青社、军地劳动服务公司5家劳动服务部门安置待业青年367人。1991—1998年，安置待业青年就业3164人。

1998年，建立县再就业服务中心，开展全县国有企业下岗职工摸底调查，全县有国有企业下岗职工149人，全部纳入再就业服务中心管理。

1999年，安置待业人员就业535人，促进下岗职工再就业76人。

2000年，对县内劳务市场进行统一管理，制定劳务市场管理办法。同时，对县城的板车和搬运工进行登记和集中管理，统一待工、合理安排。是年，统筹就业培训542人。举办第一期从事美发美容人员在岗培训班，培训27人，学员经过考试全部获初级美发美容职业资格证书。

2001年，成立县劳动职业介绍所，隶属县人事劳动局管理。

2000—2002年，全县新增就业1628人，下岗职工再就业272人。

2002年，开展全县建筑行业首期技术工种职业技能鉴定，分别鉴定建筑行业的砌筑工、钢筋工、混凝土工、架子工、电焊工等工种技能等级，参加鉴定人员68人。全年统筹就业培训549人。

2003年，成立县就业工作领导小组，制定就业再就业工作实施方案。自是年起，为国有企业下岗职工再就业人员办理“再就业优惠证”。2005年，“再就业优惠证”办理对象由国有企业下岗职工扩大到集体企业下岗职工及享受城市居民最低生活保障且失业一年以上的城镇其他登记失业人员。

2006年，根据省劳动和社会保障厅《关于实施“五年百万农村劳动力技能就业培训工程”的通知》，县职业高级中学列为贵州省农村劳动力技能就业培训定点机构。

2007年，县劳动就业办公室更名为县就业局。年内开展“零就业家庭”就业援助工作，“零就业家庭”出现一户、帮扶一户，达到动态为零。至2008年，“零就业家庭”42户就业58人。

2008年，就业和再就业培训234人，其中持证下岗人员150人、农民工技能培训84人。

2003—2008年，办理“再就业优惠证”404本。全县新增就业2789人，促进持证下岗职工再就业780人，其中促进“4050”（40～50岁）人员就业51人。

二、劳务输出

20世纪80年代初，境内开始劳务输出。1983年，到广东东莞、深圳务工256人。1988年，开始有组织地进行劳务输出，是年输送到广东企业务工83人。到20世纪90年代，劳务输出人数逐年增多，1995年为427人，1998年为722人。

2003年，17个乡（镇）成立劳务输出服务站，县设驻广东省罗定市劳务输出管理站，开展劳务输出跟踪管理服务工作。

2004年，县委、县政府召开首次劳务输出工作表彰大会，表彰劳务输出先进集体5个、先进个人15人，广东省罗定市政府领导和十余家用工企业代表到会祝贺。是年，荔波县被州政府授予“劳务输出先进县”称号。

1995—2008年全县劳务输出统计表

表9－1 单位：人

年度	输出人数总计	其中有组织输出	年度	输出人数总计	其中有组织输出
1995	427	—	2002	3462	672
1996	480	—	2003	2365	843
1997	680	—	2004	2562	956
1998	722	—	2005	6902	1115
1999	3262	627	2006	4612	1192
2000	3427	632	2007	5091	1196
2001	3426	646	2008	4216	671

第六节 工资 福利

一、工资制度改革

1978年，县内国家机关、事业单位、工商企业均统一实行等级工资制。

1985年，按国务院《关于国家机关、事业单位工作人员工资制度改革方案》，对全县国家机关、人民团体、企业事业单位工资进行改革，国家机关、事业单位执行以职务工资为主的结构工资制度，基本工资由基础工资、职务工资、工龄工资组成（教师和护理人员分别增加教龄和护龄津贴）。工改后，普通中小学校（幼儿园）从1985年1月起，国家机关和事业单位从1985年7月1日起执行新工资，全县62个国家机关、人民团体、事业单位，2364人参加改革，人均月工资70.24元，比改革前人均增加21.56元，增长44%。企业的工资改革按照省政府的规定执行，即提高工资原类别，调整偏低工资标准，改革企业内部的工资分配，理顺工资关系。

1994年8月，按照国务院制定的《国家机关、事业单位工资制度改革方案》，进行工资制度改革。国家机关工作人员（工勤人员除外）实行职级工资制，基本工资由职务工资、级别工资、基础工资、工龄工资4个部分组成；事业单位专业技术人员实行专业技术职务工资制，工资由专业技术职务工资和生活津贴2项组成，其中中小学教师（幼儿园）、护士另增加职务工资的10%，列入工资基数。事业单位工资来源实行财政全额拨款、财政差额拨款、自收自支三种办法。机关工勤人员和事业单位人员的工资构成中固定部分和生活津贴部分，全额拨款单位分别占70%、30%比例，差额拨款单位分别占60%、40%，自收自支单位分别占55%、45%。全县参加工改3812人。其中，财政全额拨款单位3398人（机关1140人、事业1849人、离退休409人）；差额拨款事业单位在职287人（含离退休20人）；自收自支单位127人（含离退休29人）。在职人员人均月增资72.5元，离退休人员人均月增资104.5元。

2006年，根据国务院《关于改革公务员工资制度的通知》和人事部、财政部《关于印发事业单位工作人员收入分配制度改革方案的通知》及省政府《关于印发机关事业单位收入分配工资制度改革实施意见的通知》，对工资收入分配制度进行改革。按照国家公务员制度管理和参照公务员管理的事业单位工作人员（除工勤人员），仍实行职级工资制，基本工资由职务工资和级别工资2项构成；技术工人实行岗位技术等级工资制，由岗位工资和技术等级工资2项构成；普通工人实行岗位工资制，只有岗位工资一项。事业单位专业技术人员、管理人员、工勤人员实行岗位绩效工资制，基本工资为岗位工资和薪级工资、绩效工资、津贴补贴4项。

全县参加工资改革在职人员4487人，人均月增资262.1元。其中，机关单位1359人，人均月增资307.33元；事业单位3128人，人均月增资242.44元。全县离退休人员1199人，人均月增离退休费271.54元。同时，对艰苦边远地区津贴进行调整，荔波县属于二类地区，最低增加40元，最高增加50元，人均增加27.70元。工资改革后，工作人员的职务（岗位、技术等级）工资相对固定，随着职务（岗位、技术等级）的变动而升降。事业单位人员年度考核晋升薪级工资，每年一次；机关人员两年考核、五年考核，分别晋升档次（岗位）、级别工资。新工资制度从2006年7月1日起执行。

二、工资调整

1978年，按2%的升级指标，对全民所有制单位中生产、工作成绩优异、贡献较大和提职后工资偏低的人员考核升级。当年，全县职工总数2734人，升级55人。

1980年年初，根据国务院《关于职工工资升级的几项规定》，按“劳动强度、技术高低、贡献大小”三个条件进行考核，择优升级，领导干部、一般干部、工人的升级指标分别计算，互不占用。城镇集体所有制事业单位的职工，参照全民所有制单位调资政策自行安排。调资一般升一级，个别表现突出并有重大贡献的升两级。全县升级人数1195人，占职工总数的41.8%。

1982年，按教育部《关于调整中小学教职工工资的办法》和卫生部《关于医疗单位部门职工调整工资方案》及体委有关规定，对全县中小学、卫生、体育部门人员工资进行调整，1978年年底以前参加工作的教职工升一级，少数教学成绩显著、贡献较大、教龄较长，与同类人员相比工资偏低的优秀骨干教师升两级；卫生部门中已取得技术职称的中级技术人员工资低于卫校12级的升两级。调资于1982年9月结束，从1981年10月起执行。

1982年9月，按照国务院的规定，调整1978年年底前参加工作的全县国家机关、事业单位正式职工工资。全县国家机关、事业单位有固定职工1803人，列入调资范围的有1497人，批准升级1436人。

1983年，根据国务院批转劳动人事部《关于1983年企业调整工资和改革工资制度的报告》，按照“职工工资要体现同企业经济效益挂钩，同职工个人劳动成果挂钩”的原则，对全县企业职工工资进行调整。企业职工调资每升一级，国家拨增资指标3.5元摊为成本，不足部分由企业自有奖金（即奖励基金）支付，一年后仍按“两个挂钩”考核，企业经济效益不断提高，升级职工仍符合条件升级者，升级增加的工资可全部摊入成本，对经常性亏损企业缓调。

1985年11月，根据省委组织部《关于解决部分离休干部工资级别偏低问题的通知》，对全县

1945年9月30日前参加革命工作的机关、企事业单位离休干部，现行工资不到行政19级和1949年9月30日前参加革命工作，现行工资级别不到行政20级的（国营企业非国家机关行政干部的工资，按本人标准工资相对应的行政工资级别），可分别按行政19级、20级工资额计发离休工资。全县离休干部55人，符合条件6人，人均月增资17.67元。

1987年，对1985年列入国家机关和事业单位工资制度改革的国家机关、事业单位及经批准已经实行机关、事业单位工资制度的企业工作人员工资进行调整。全县机关、事业单位工资升级589人，人均月增资4.50元。企业单位调资以企业经济效益、工人自身劳动成果为考核依据，增资总额控制在企业总人数人均1.8元以内。全县企业职工工资升级271人，人均月增资4.87元，升级人数占职工总数的37.7%。

1988年5月，根据国务院、省政府及省工改办关于提高中小学教师工资标准的通知精神，全县中小学教师工资待遇提高10%。全县教师1141人，人均月增资7.06元。新工资从1987年10月起执行。

是年11月，按省、州统一部署和要求，调整全县国家机关、事业单位部分工作人员工资，至1989年1月底审批结束，1988年年底全县国家机关、事业单位有职工2566人，机关工作人员升级724人，事业单位人员升级1842人。

1989年，全县从事护理工作的护士工资也提高10%，全县有57名护士增加工资，人均月增资15.96元。

1990年5月，按《贵州省关于1989年解决国家机关、事业单位工资问题的实施方案》，调整全县国家机关、事业单位工作人员工资。列入调资范围的正式职工，均在原职务工资基础上增加一级工资。同时，提高研究生、大中专毕业生的初期工资和见习期工资待遇，改革大中专毕业生定级工资办法，提高离休、退休人员待遇。全县机关、事业单位参加调资在册职工2950人，普调一级2732人，调升二级2253人；提高初期、见习期人员工资待遇206人。增资额从1989年10月1日起执行。

1991年11月起，对全县1989年10月1日以后参加工作的大中专生（含“五大”毕业生）和高中生、普通工人、技术工人等，按省人事厅《关于调整新参加工作人员工资待遇问题的通知》的规定，调整工资待遇。

1993年5月，对企业工资进行调整，以1990年年末在册正式职工人数为准，下达升级指标，晋升一级工资。全县进行调资的企业46个，参加调资职工925人（国营634人、供销217人、集体74人），150名新参加工作职工的初期工资也进行了调整。

是年，根据省委组织部、老干局、人事厅、财政厅《关于给我省国家机关、事业单位离退休人员增发离退休费等问题的通知》，对原已按国务院和省政府规定增发10%离休费的人员，依据本人离退休时的职务（含享受待遇）或工作年限，改按同职务同工作年限在职人员奖励工资标准增发离退休费，自1992年3月1日起执行。

1994年，提高企业等级工资及考核升级工资。全县参加调资国有企业31个共789人，供销企业7个共270人，集体企业4个共87人；考核升级企业42个职工总计2884人，不升级企业职工262人，新职工提高工资标准63人。

1997年，根据人事部和省人事厅文件精神，调整机关、事业单位工资标准和离退休人员离退休生活费。全县1997年6月30日在册职工参加调资4061人，人均月增资20.89元；离退休人员、退职人员共641人，人均月增资39.15元。同时，提高新参加工作人员的试用期工资标准和转正定级工资标准。

是年，对企业离退休人员养老金、离休金作出调整，并相应增加生活补贴。当年，考核升级企业6个，职工205人，人均月增资40.10元。

1999年7月，调整全县机关、事业单位工作人员工资标准，参加调资4026人，人均增资119元；718名增加离退休退职人员的生活费，人均月增加111.5元，最低80元，最高140元。22名企业离休人员按机关行政人员待遇增加离休费，人均增加173元。同时，调整新参加工作人员试用期工资和转正定级工资标准。

2001年1月，调整机关事业单位工资标准，机关单位工作人员调整基础工资和级别工资，事业单位人员（含机关工作人员）调整职务（岗位、技术等级）工资。全县有在职人员4167人，人均月增资101.5元；839名离退休人员增加离退休生活费，人均月增加100.5元。是年10月，再次调整机关、事业单位工作人员工资标准和离退休人员生活费。在职人员调整职务（岗位、技术等级）工资，共审批4117人，人均月增资78.5元；离退休人员888人，人均增加离退休费81元。两次调资中，对新参加工作人员的试用期工资和转正定级工资也进行调整。

2003年7月，调整机关事业单位职务（岗位、技术等级）工资，最低增加35元，最高增加80元，从2003年7月起执行。

2008年12月，对党的机关、人大机关、行政机关、政协机关、审判机关、检察机关及工商联机关，以及经批准参照《中华人民共和国公务员法》管理单位的工作人员，实施统一津贴补贴项目、标准、资金来源和发放办法。规范后津贴补贴标准为生活性补贴不分职级，统一标准为人均500元/月；工作性津贴按职级由低至高逐步拉开差距，办事员300元/月、科员510元/月、副科级610元/月、正科级690元/月、副县级860元/月、正县级1030元/月。生活性补贴和工作性津贴所占比例分别为60%、40%。离休人员补贴按同职级在职人员标准全额计发，退休和退职人员补贴分别按同职级在职人员标准的70%和50%计发。全县符合规范补贴范围的公务员单位59个、参照公务员管理事业单位6个，在职人员1359人，人均月增资300元；离退休人员470人，人均月增加164元。新增加的津贴补贴从2008年1月1日起执行。

1978—2008年全县职工工资情况统计表

表9－2

年度	职工工资总额（万元）				职工平均工资（元）			
	合计	国有经济单位	集体经济单位	其他	职工平均工资	国有经济单位	集体经济单位	其他
1978	205	169	36	—	520	528	514	—
1979	217	183	34	—	520	523	486	—
1980	271	239	32	—	653	664	457	—
1981	286	247	39	—	645	650	557	—
1982	306	270	36	—	683	692	600	—
1983	314	278	36	—	710	678	720	—
1984	380	312	68	—	820	821	756	—
1985	415	362	53	—	892	928	663	—
1986	498	441	57	—	1072	1074	814	—
1987	546	471	75	—	1127	1148	938	—
1988	636	558	78	—	1311	1329	1114	—
1989	669	601	68	—	1344	1355	971	—
1990	799	715	84	—	1548	1554	1400	—

续表9-2

年度	职工工资总额（万元）				职工平均工资（元）			
	合计	国有经济单位	集体经济单位	其他	职工平均工资	国有经济单位	集体经济单位	其他
1991	901	786	115	—	1628	1638	1278	—
1992	1252	1085	167	—	2080	2087	1856	—
1993	1457	1252	205	—	2200	2159	2278	—
1994	2154	1993	161	—	3154	3215	2013	—
1995	4122	3298	824	—	5050	5074	3912	—
1996	2811	2564	247	—	4000	4006	3529	—
1997	3501	3202	299	—	4760	4779	4257	—
1998	3329	3011	318	—	4700	4705	4543	—
1999	3875	3627	248	—	5536	5630	4779	—
2000	4241	3962	241	38	9500	9526	6900	4247
2001	5625	5305	285	35	9067	9371	6118	4640
2002	6279	5949	304	26	9838	10232	5090	4942
2003	6545	5874	645	26	9909	10050	8876	7138
2004	7193	6738	426	29	11639	12200	6818	8139
2005	8774	8139	604	31	14726	15213	10564	8611
2006	9621	8902	685	34	15969	16500	11504	9333
2007	11393	10982	360	51	19495	20170	19122	7210
2008	14868	11682	2625	561	19962	19881	22883	13200

三、职工福利

（一）职工洗理补贴

1985年，根据省财政局、人事局的文件，为全县职工（含离退休）发放洗理费每人每月4元，1991年8月提高为8元，1994年5月调整为10元。2008年1月，在机关单位实施统一的公务员规范津贴补贴后，取消洗理费项目。

（二）遗属生活困难补助

1978年，按照省财政厅、民政厅、人事局于1963年联合下发的《关于国家机关、事业单位工作人员牺牲、病故后遗留家属生活照顾的处理意见》，对县内国家机关、事业单位工作人员牺牲、病故后遗留家属，执行生活困难补助政策。补助标准为居住在地、市的遗属每人每月补助12～15元，居住在县以下的遗属每人每月补助8～12元；对参加工作不满5年的，只作一次性抚恤；遗属生活有困难的，由民政部门给予救济。

此后，1980年3月、1986年3月、1988年9月、1991年7月、1994年8月、1996年10月、1999年7月、2001年1月、2003年7月、2007年6月，先后按照省人事厅、省财政厅、省政府办公厅、省委组织部等单位的文件精神，10次提高困难补助标准。2008年，全县享受困难补助354人，人均月享受困难补助费311.76元。

第七节 劳动监察与仲裁

一、劳动监察

1995年5月，县劳动人事局成立劳动监察室，有专职和兼职劳动监察员4人。是年，通过开展《中华人民共和国劳动法》宣传活动，督促用人单位补签劳动合同763份，接待投诉53件。开展《中华人民共和国劳动法》执行情况大检查2次，规范劳动用工，检查国有企业25个，发放劳动法宣传资料100余份。

1996年，开展劳动合同签订情况检查2次，检查国有企业、集体企业38个，督促用人单位订立和补签劳动合同1026份，开展劳动法规知识宣传咨询活动2次，发送政策宣传资料120份。

1997年，按照《贵州省劳动监察规定》《贵州省劳动用工年检规定》，对全县47个用人单位进行检查，用人单位参加用工年检33户，规范劳动用工，涉及劳动者1290人。

1998年，督促用人单位参加用工年检32户。其中，国有企业25户，涉及劳动者813人；集体企业7户，涉及劳动者357人。查处外地私营业主到境内非法招工案件1件，涉及劳动者14人。

1999年，巡视监察全县用人单位51户，企业用工年检32户，开展劳动合同签订情况检查2次，督促用人单位订立和补签劳动合同102份。

2000年，向用人单位宣传并重点检查《贵州省劳动保障监察条例》执行情况，监察用工单位63户，监督检查国有企业7户。检查劳动用工合同30户，涉及劳动者530人。

2001年，监察用人单位66户，重点监察养老保险金和失业保险金缴纳情况，涉及劳动者1370人。审核用人单位规章制度累计200余条，对其中与劳动保障法律、法规相抵触的条款7条进行修改或撤销。参加年检的用人单位37户，涉及劳动者1249人。

2002年，开展劳动用工专项检查4次，重点进行农民工工资追讨和妇女、未成年童工禁忌岗位专项督察。全年开展劳动保障法律、法规宣传2次，发放宣传资料2000多份。查处在县城违规招工案件1件，涉及被误导报名人员13人。

2003年9月，撤销劳动监察室，建立劳动保障监察大队。是年，督促用工单位年检39户，涉及劳动者1109人；到用人单位开展监察196户（次），涉及劳动者1606人。处理劳动监察案件11件，督促用人单位补签劳动合同719份，追缴社会保险费5.34万元。针对劳动合同签订、禁止使用童工情况、农民工工资支付等情况进行专项检查5次，为农民工173人追讨被拖欠工资13.36万元。

2004年，开展各类专项大检查5次，进行日常巡视监察210户（次），涉及劳动者2500人。受理并处理劳动监察案件18件，为劳动者追回被拖欠工资和医疗费18.73万元。用人单位用工年检41户，其中，国有企业27户729人，集体企业8户347人，民营企业6户151人。

2005年，开展“禁止使用童工”“农民工劳动保障权益保护”等专项监察5次，涉及用人单位25个，发现问题并及时整改3个。进行日常巡视监察110户，涉及劳动者1500人。受理并处理劳动监察案件7件，为劳动者追回被拖欠工资和医疗费15.3万元。

2006年，开展农民工劳动保障权益保护及农民工工资支付情况等专项监察3次，涉及用人单位12个；对用人单位实施劳动保障监察180户（次），涉及劳动者3870人次；监察立案处理16件；为劳动者追回被拖欠工资和医疗费等26万元；督促用人单位与劳动者补签劳动合同420份，追缴社会保险费4.5万元。

2007年，组织开展“农民工工资支付情况专项检查”“清理整顿人力资源市场秩序专项行动”等专项执法行动3次。对用人单位实施劳动保障监察250户（次），涉及劳动者4125人次；监察立案处理22件；为劳动者追回被拖欠工资和医疗费等38万元；督促用人单位与劳动者补签劳动合同495份，追缴社会保险费7.6万元。

2008年，开展用人单位遵守劳动用工和社会保险法律法规情况专项检查2次，对用人单位实施劳动保障监察340户（次），涉及劳动者5012人次；监察立案处理25件；为劳动者追回被拖欠工资和医疗费等57万元；督促用人单位与劳动者补签劳动合同580份，追缴社会保险费8.3万元。

二、劳动争议仲裁

1986年，企业招收工人实行劳动合同制，被录用的劳动者要与用人单位签订劳动合同，由劳动争议仲裁机构进行劳动合同鉴证。1987年，在县劳动人事局设劳动争议仲裁办公室，主要进行劳动合同鉴证。根据黔南州劳人局《关于当前开展劳动合同签订、换证、鉴证工作几个问题的通知》规定，用工单位与劳动者订立劳动合同后必须按照有关劳动合同鉴证程序和管理范围划分规定，到当地仲裁机构办理劳动合同鉴证手续，未经鉴证合同视为无效。1990—1999年，根据国家《劳动争议处理办法（试行）》成立了县劳动争议仲裁委员会，由劳动行政主管部门、总工会、用人单位代表（经贸局）三方共同组成，下设仲委办公室在人事劳动局，承担处理劳动者和用人单位的劳动争议工作。劳动仲裁机构每年受理劳动争议案件1～2件。

2000年以后，劳动纠纷事件逐渐增多，争议案件逐年上升。是年受理劳动纠纷案件2件，2002年上升为5件。

2003年，根据国家《劳动争议处理条例》成立了县新的劳动争议仲裁委员会，并明确三方机构由人力资源和社会保障部门、县总工会、企业家联合会（工信局）共同组成，仲委会下设办公室在人社局法规科（股），负责处理劳动者和用人单位的劳动争议。收到申请申诉案件13件，受理8件，其中进行裁决2件、调解6件、不予受理5件。为劳动者落实工伤死亡补助金、抚恤金、一次性伤残补助金、伤残就业补助金、工伤津贴等计19.47万元。

2004—2008年，受理劳动争议仲裁案件76件，依法为劳动者落实工资、工伤（亡）补助金、医疗费、护理费、赡养费、一次性伤残就业补助金等各项待遇总计339.36万元。

第二章 社会保障

第一节 最低生活保障

全县城乡居民的最低生活保障由县民政部门办理。

一、城市低保

1998年10月，县内建立城市低保障制度，标准低、范围小，重点在建立制度。是年，只有玉屏镇居民10户29人纳入。之后，纳入低保范围逐年扩大，享受低保人员逐年增加。

2004年8月，制定《荔波县城市居民最低生活保障制度实施细则》，规定凡在全县城市常住非农业户口共同生活的家庭成员，月人均收入低于保障标准的居民，均可申请享受城市居民最低生活保障待遇。保障范围涵盖在职职工、下岗职工、退休人员、失业人员、无业人员等县内户口全体社会成员。申领审批程序按个人提出申请，社区居委会调查、审核、张榜公布后，上报审批和低保金发放等3个环节办理，做到公开透明、公平公正。

2008年，城市低保制度覆盖全县17个乡（镇），保障标准由每人每月75元提高到每人每月160元。

二、农村低保

2000年，开始在农村实行低保制度，之后逐步扩大低保覆盖面。

2007年，按照国务院《关于在全国建立农村最低生活保障制度的通知》，建立全县农村低保制度。农村居民低保对象是家庭人均年纯收入低于当地农村居民最低生活保障标准的农村居民；因病、因残、年老体弱、缺乏劳动力或劳动能力低下、生存条件恶劣等原因造成家庭生活常年困难的农村居民。是年，纳入低保的农村居民占全县农业人口的7.83%，发放标准每人每年700元。2008年，扩大农村低保面，全县农村低保人口占全县农业人口的15.6%，按每人每年785元发放。

2000—2008年全县城乡最低生活保障情况一览表

表9－3

年度	城市最低生活保障			农村最低生活保障		
	户数（户）	人数（人）	金额总计（万元）	户数（户）	人数（人）	金额总计（万元）
2000	96	295	10.4	305	1259	4.1
2001	260	611	22.0	309	1263	5.3

续表9－3

年度	城市最低生活保障			农村最低生活保障		
	户数（户）	人数（人）	金额总计（万元）	户数（户）	人数（人）	金额总计（万元）
2002	346	789	31.0	1230	4920	13.8
2003	396	931	45.0	236	1064	66.5
2004	628	1078	123.7	534	696	13.6
2005	604	994	108.5	3589	5742	140.3
2006	712	1165	168.1	2286	6356	117.2
2007	769	1261	225.6	4151	10954	197.1
2008	881	1435	286.8	8052	24000	920.0

第二节　社会保险

一、养老保险

（一）企业职工养老保险

1991年，成立县企业职工离退休金统筹委员会，制定《荔波县企业职工离退休金统筹实施方案》。1994年，在原制定统筹方案的基础上，县政府制定《荔波县国营企业固定职工离退休金统筹暂行办法》，规定职工离退休基金实行统一筹集、统一核算、统一调剂、统一使用。统筹的离退休金由劳动人事局养老保险管理股统一管理，专户储存、专款专用，按企业当月报送的离退休人员工资发放名册核定数额下拨给企业。

1998年1月1日起，按照省政府《关于建立统一的企业职工养老保险制度的通知》，建立与全省统一的企业职工基本养老保险制度，个人缴费比例统一按职工本人缴费工资的4%执行，职工个人账户按本人缴费工资的11%建立，基本养老金计发办法、调整办法执行全省统一标准。2000年，县内企业的缴费比例按黔南州规定35%的比例执行。

2000年1月1日起，根据省政府《关于调整全省企业及其职工基本养老保险费比例的通知》，参加统筹的企业，缴费比例高于企业工资总额22%的统一调整为22%，低于20%的调整为20%；从2001年1月1日起，个人缴费比例调整为6%。此后，按照省的文件规定调整企业和个人缴费比例。

2002年，按省劳动保障厅下发的《城镇个体工商户及其从业人员和自由职业人员参加基本养老保险有关问题的通知》，县内个体工商户及其从业人员和自由职业人员当年办理基本养老保险14人。

2003年1月1日起，按照省的文件规定，县内参加基本养老保险统筹的企业缴费比例高于21%的统一调整为21%，低于20%的统一调整为20%。2004年1月1日起，全省基本养老保险单位缴费比例统一为20%，个人缴费为8%。

2005年12月，按国务院《关于完善企业职工基本养老保险制度的决定》，荔波县按省出台的相关配套文件执行，扩大社会保险的覆盖范围，提高统筹层次，统一城镇个体工商户和灵活就业人员参保缴费政策。2007年开始实行州级统筹后，2008年上半年全县实现州级统筹。

2008年，全县个体工商户、自由职业人员参加基本养老保险发展到675人。

1992—2008年全县养老保险费率及单位、个人缴费比例统计表

表9-4

年度	养老保险费率（%）	单位划入（%）	个人缴费（%）	年记账利率（%）
1992	统筹金	—	3	7.56
1993	统筹金	—	3	10.98
1994	统筹金	—	3	10.98
1995	统筹金	—	3	10.98
1996	统筹金	—	3	10.98
1997	统筹金	8	3	7.47
1998	统筹金	7	4	5.67
1999	24.5+5	6	5	3.78
2000	35+5	6	5	3.78
2001	22+6	5	6	2.25
2002	22+6	5	6	2.25
2003	21+7	4	7	1.98
2004	20+8	3	8	2.25
2005	20+8	3	8	2.25
2006	20+8	3	8	2.25
2007	20+8	—	8	4.14
2008	20+8	—	8	4.14

说明：上表“养老保险费率”栏1999—2008年的数据采用“+”号，表示单位与个人的缴费比例相加

1991—2008年全县养老保险参保与基金收支统计表

表9-5

年度	统筹单位数（个）	参保人数（人）	基金收入（万元）	养老保险支付	
				人数（人）	金额（万元）
1991	35	756	29.32	299	27.51
1992	37	1454	47.75	326	45.88
1993	35	1508	55.40	353	45.11
1994	41	1550	68.15	385	57.74
1995	35	1587	138.21	431	116.39
1996	38	1664	139.40	438	123.67
1997	38	1611	147.54	438	130.45
1998	35	1519	160.76	438	130.45
1999	33	1394	119.77	402	117.53
2000	33	1357	137.82	422	178.27

续表9－5

年度	统筹单位数（个）	参保人数（人）	基金收入（万元）	养老保险支付	
				人数（人）	金额（万元）
2001	33	1333	124.65	435	177.00
2002	33	1353	135.00	434	206.00
2003	40	1468	212.00	451	212.00
2004	41	1622	252.81	477	223.70
2005	48	1861	324.38	456	295.71
2006	52	2000	358.11	478	364.95
2007	56	2186	464.13	481	417.46
2008	70	2476	871.04	531	549.52

（二）机关事业单位养老保险

从1999年1月起，按《黔南州机关事业单位社会养老保险制度改革办法（试行）》，正式启动机关事业单位养老保险制度改革，养老保险费筹集以职工工资总额为缴费基数，职工个人和单位分别按2%、3%比例缴纳。个人部分从工资中扣缴；单位缴纳部分，自收自支事业单位和省、州直管部门由单位直接缴纳，财政全额拨款单位由县财政预算缴拨。由于财政未能足额预算缴纳保险费，没有相关配套政策，该项制度未能全面推行。至2007年6月底，全县登记参保单位97个，参保职工4490人，基金累计结余900.18万元。2007年6月，根据州委的决定，对全县机关单位缴纳的养老保险费进行清退。

（三）农村养老保险

1997年9月，成立县农村社会养老保险管理所，属县民政局管理。经半年宣传发动后，全县参加农村社会养老保险有7个乡（镇）222人，收取养老金5.29万元。1998年2月，根据中共中央关于整顿金融机构秩序的决定，停止办理农村养老保险业务。2007年8月，经县政府批准，农村养老保险按照投保基数和历年利息一并退还投保人。

二、失业保险

1993年3月，贯彻落实国务院《国有企业职工待业保险规定》，按照省、州的规定，开展待业保险金统筹管理，缴费标准按企业全部职工及机关事业单位劳动合同制工人工资总额的1%收缴。待业保险金支出主要用于待业职工的救济，后待业保险范围扩大到被开除、除名的职工。

1999年1月国务院《失业保险条例》和2000年6月省政府《贵州省失业保险办法》颁布实施后，待业保险更名为失业保险。此后，失业保险覆盖城镇各类企业、事业单位，基金筹集标准为单位按照本单位工资总额的2%，职工个人按照本人工资总额的1%缴纳，单位招用的农民合同制工人，本人不缴纳失业保险费。职工所在单位和本人按规定履行缴费义务满1年的，非因本人意愿中断就业的，按规定享受失业保险待遇。失业保险待遇的享受期限，缴费年限满1年不满2年，领取期限为3个月；满2年不满3年的，领取期限6个月；满3年不满4年的，领取期限9个月；满4年不满5年的，领取期限12个月；满5年不满6年的，领取期限14个月；满6年，领取期限15个月；以后每增加1年，领取期限增加1个月，最长不超过24个月，领取标准为当地最低工资的70%。

1999—2008年全县失业保险参保及基金收支情况一览表

表9-6

年度	参保单位（个）		基金收入（万元）		基金支出	
	企业	事业	企业	事业	金额总计（万元）	享受人数（人）
1999	730	2746	5.56	1.23	0	0
2000	935	2646	12.00	27.00	0	0
2001	852	3068	18.40	34.60	0	0
2002	867	3098	9.31	26.88	1.50	21
2003	887	3168	13.04	37.43	2.50	22
2004	939	3168	16.30	33.77	2.58	27
2005	1055	3168	16.56	49.26	3.25	33
2006	1075	3168	20.82	65.15	2.60	11
2007	1075	3164	28.64	68.34	11.24	74
2008	1097	3164	49.60	86.90	32.51	73

三、医疗保险

2003年4月起，实施全县机关、事业单位基本医疗保险制度。2005年下半年，全县启动实施企业职工基本医疗保险制度。2003年，制定《荔波县城镇职工基本医疗保险实施办法》，规定用人单位按照全部职工工资总额的7.5%，在职职工按本人工资基数的2%缴纳医疗保险费；基本医疗保险实行社会统筹与个人账户相结合，基金属于县级统筹管理。由于县级财政困难，未能按照规定比例预算单位应缴纳的保险费，采取包干预算方式缴拨。

2008年10月，按州政府颁布实施的《黔南州城镇居民基本医疗保险实施办法》，启动实施城镇居民基本医疗保险，实行全州统筹。

2003—2008年全县医疗保险参保缴费及待遇支付情况一览表

表9-7

年度	参保单位（个）	参保人数（人）	基金征缴（万元）			收入总计（万元）	支出总计（万元）
			个人	财政	企业		
2003	134	5545	900.37	60.00	—	150.37	120.60
2004	134	5460	120.90	150.00	—	270.90	215.10
2005	155	6420	114.80	200.00	21.50	336.30	268.19
2006	176	6653	92.00	200.00	54.00	346.00	355.70
2007	184	6883	98.65	388.00	77.55	564.20	291.00
2008	197	7095	130.88	250.00	90.10	470.98	373.14

四、工伤保险

2005年7月1日起，全县实施工伤保险制度。按照《贵州省实施〈工伤保险条例〉办法》《黔南州工伤保险暂行办法》，实行全州统筹。工伤保险根据不同行业实行差别费率，一类企业0.6%，二类企业1.2%，三类企业2%。对煤矿、冶金、建筑等特殊行业实行特别费率，煤矿生产企业，按产量每吨征收4元，冶金企业按照黔南州上年在岗职工平均工资的3%征收，建筑行业以该项工程总造价的15%作为人工工资，按1.3%费率征收。职工发生工伤首先由人力资源和社会保障工作部门进行工伤认定，认定为工伤的享受应得待遇。是年，全县参保单位32个，参保人数617人，基金收入4.34万元。至2007年，参保单位增加到86个，参保人数1950人，基金收入15.18万元，基金支出15.18万元，享受待遇2人。2008年，参保单位85个，参保人数2400人，基金收入27.68万元，基金支出8.92万元，享受待遇8人。

五、生育保险

2007年7月起实施《黔南州生育保险暂行办法》，实行全州统筹。全县生育保险参保对象为国家机关、事业及企业单位，参保缴费率0.6%。是年，全县参保单位6个，职工425人，基金收入0.51万元。2008年，参保单位8个，参保人数635人，基金收入2.89万元，享受待遇15人，支付金额3.12万元。

第三章 民 政

第一节 村民自治

1984年，公社管委会改为乡政府后，各村建立村民委员会，村民委员会设主任、妇女委员、调解委员各1人。村委会下设村民小组。

1991年，乡（镇）“建并撤”后，全县设村民委员会174个。是年，各村（居）委会分别按照《中华人民共和国村民委员会组织法》《中华人民共和国城市居民委员会组织法》，先后召开村民大会，依法选举产生第一届村（居）民委员会。村（居）委会每届任期3年。选举产生的各村委会制定村民委员会自治章程、村民委员会村规民约、村务公开制度、村级财务管理制度、民主评议村干部制度、两委联席会议制度等各种制度。

2004年，合并行政村，全县设村委会94个、居委会4个，村（居）下设村民小组1210个。

至2008年，各村（居）委会进行7次换届选举。

1991—2007年各村（居）委会换届选举情况一览表

表9－8

届 次	换届时间（年、月）	选举村（居）委会主任（人）	选举村（居）委会副主任（人）	委员（人）
第一届	1991.11	174	174	522
第二届	1993.11	174	174	522
第三届	1995.11	174	174	522
第四届	1998.11	174	174	522
第五届	2001.11	174	174	522
第六届	2004.11	98	98	294
第七届	2007.11	98	98	294

1991—2008年全县村委会村民自治工作情况统计表

表9－9

年度	村（居）委会（个）	设村务公开栏（块）	村务公开期数（期）	召开村民代表会（次）	民主理财小组（个）	村务公开监督小组（个）	民主评议村干部（次）	培训村干部（人次）
1991	174	174	692	640	174	174	265	456

续表9-9

年度	村（居）委会（个）	设村务公开栏（块）	村务公开期数（期）	召开村民代表会（次）	民主理财小组（个）	村务公开监督小组（个）	民主评议村干部（次）	培训村干部（人次）
1992	174	174	865	680	174	174	248	389
1993	174	174	720	610	174	174	276	432
1994	174	174	680	720	174	174	253	396
1995	174	174	860	760	174	174	218	468
1996	174	174	890	690	174	174	298	496
1997	174	174	865	682	174	174	198	463
1998	174	174	780	650	174	174	268	446
1999	174	174	862	673	174	174	245	457
2000	174	174	886	669	174	174	234	432
2001	174	174	880	676	174	174	234	468
2002	98	192	919	678	92	83	254	470
2003	98	192	952	647	84	78	146	447
2004	98	192	967	268	90	86	136	257
2005	98	192	874	253	86	76	141	248
2006	98	192	982	278	92	88	138	256
2007	98	192	239	134	80	70	128	243
2008	98	132	841	211	96	96	121	241

第二节　优抚　安置

一、优抚

1978年，县民政部门按照国家优抚政策落实各项优抚待遇。1979年3—8月，开展全县优抚普查，全县有革命烈士家属24户共123人，6名病故军人有家属35人，3名失踪军人有家属12人，424名现役军人（干部35名），残疾军人41名，复员军人606名，退伍军人1169名。

1982年8月，城关镇、阳凤公社、翁昂公社被评为“优抚工作先进单位”，受州政府、都匀军分区通报表彰。

1983年3月，县政府召开全县拥军优属、优抚工作表彰会，表彰拥军优属先进单位14个，优抚工作先进单位13个，优抚对象先进个人86人。

1986年11月，县政府下发《关于进一步做好烈军属优抚工作的通知》规定，从1987年起，对家居农村的义务兵家属的优待，每户不得少于150元；对城镇义务兵家属的优待，优待经费由镇政府向辖区内的单位和居民户提取；对荣立战功的退伍兵，除按国家有关规定优先安置外，还对其进行一次性奖励，荣获战斗英雄称号的奖励5000元，荣立一等功的奖励2000元，荣立二等功的奖励1000元，荣立三等功的奖励200元，经费由县财政开支。对烈军属推行包户服务制度。

1987年起，在征兵期间定兵的同时定优待，发入伍通知书的同时发军属优待证，送新兵的同时给部队送优待通知书；对革命烈士家属、革命残疾军人、带病回乡的复员退伍军人和参训预备役人员的优待标准及时兑现，建立以青年民兵为骨干的群众性拥军优属组织，推行包户服务制度，帮助没有劳力或劳力不足的烈军属解决生产、生活中的实际困难。是年，拥军优属先进单位，时来、翁昂、阳凤3个乡被评为全县拥军优属先进单位，受县政府表彰。

20世纪90年代后，根据《军人抚恤优待条例》《贵州省军人抚恤优待实施办法》《农民承担费用和劳务管理条例》以及民政部门的有关文件规定，落实县内优抚对象的待遇。

1993年8月，县委、县政府在《关于加强人民武装工作的决定》中，对优抚优待、优待金筹集及标准等作出明确规定。同时规定，凡县籍现役军人，在服役期间获军区以上授予荣誉称号者奖励5000元，荣立一等功奖励3000元，二等功奖励2000元，三等功奖励500元。

1995年6月，茂兰镇政府被评为全州拥军优属先进单位，受州委、州政府、都匀军分区表彰。

1997年起，按照省政府办公厅、州政府办公室关于提高义务兵家属优待金和老复员退伍军人定期补助文件精神，提高优待金标准，按上年度当地农民人均纯收入的70%发放。次年，兑现全县145户义务兵家属优待金每户707元，总计10.25万元；兑现380名老复员退伍军人的定期补助每人450元，总计17.1万元。之后每年的优待金发放标准按当地群众生活水平的提高而逐步提高。

1998年7月，荔波县被评为全州拥军优属先进县，受州委、州政府、都匀军分区表彰。

1999年5月，县政府下发《关于批转县民政局〈关于提高全县义务兵家属优待和老复员退伍军人定期补助的意见〉的通知》，对全县义务兵家属的优待按上年农民实际人均纯收入100%的标准给予兑现；对在乡老复员军人的生活实行定期补助，1999年定补标准按省规定的人年均480元兑现，定补金列入县财政预算，并随着当地群众生活水平的提高而逐步提高。

2003年1月27日，县政府被评为全省拥军优属先进单位，受省委、省政府、省军区表彰。2005年7月29日，州委、州政府、都匀军分区《关于表彰双拥模范城（县）、拥军优属、拥政爱民先进单位和个人的决定》（黔南党发〔2005〕21号），授予荔波县“双拥模范县”称号。

2007年2月10日，省委、省政府、省军区在《关于命名表彰省双拥模范城（县）和双拥先进单位的决定》中授予荔波县“双拥模范县”称号。

县民政局从2006年起每年为全县重点优抚对象缴纳农村合作医疗费，至2008年，3年缴费累计21950元。

1987—2008年全县军属优待金发放情况统计表

表9－10

年度	军属优待金发放			复原退伍军人定期补助		
	义务兵家属优待户数（户）	户均优待金（元）	发放总金额（万元）	享受人数（人）	人均定补（元）	补助总金额（万元）
1987	358	150	5.37	451	180	8.11
1988	172	150	2.58	439	180	7.90
1989	181	150	2.71	411	180	7.39
1990	169	150	2.53	396	180	7.12
1991	214	150	3.21	380	180	6.84
1992	192	200	3.84	380	180	6.84
1993	192	200	3.84	380	180	6.84

续表9－10

年度	军属优待金发放			复原退伍军人定期补助		
	义务兵家属优待户数（户）	户均优待金（元）	发放总金额（万元）	享受人数（人）	人均定补（元）	补助总金额（万元）
1994	177	300	5.31	380	180	6.84
1995	177	300	5.31	380	180	6.84
1996	215	300	6.45	380	300	11.40
1997	145	707	10.25	380	450	17.10
1998	131	800	10.48	293	450	13.12
1999	128	800	10.24	278	640	17.79
2000	171	1152	19.70	267	720	19.22
2001	103	1196	12.32	260	720	18.72
2002	91	1220	11.10	247	900	22.23
2003	91	1255	11.42	231	1152	26.61
2004	87	1360	11.83	209	1152	24.08
2005	92	1490	13.71	190	1652	31.39
2006	106	1700	18.02	176	1900	33.44
2007	105	1808	18.98	159	2248	35.74
2008	97	2160	20.95	146	3209	46.85

二、安置

1978—1979年，接收安置军队转业干部团职2人、营职7人、连排职15人。1982年，接收安置114名复退军人，因战致残3人。

农村退伍军人按照“从哪里来，回哪里去”的原则进行安置，以回农村为主；城镇退伍军人安置，由其父母所在系统接收分配工作；父母无公职的城镇退伍军人由县政府统筹安排；从工作单位入伍的退伍军人，按复工复职安置。

1993年，县委、县政府在《关于加强人民武装工作的决定》中规定，城镇退役军人安置通过考试择优选用。

1994—2000年，复退军人安排工作87人。其中，城镇居民户口32人，农村户口二等功获得者2人，三等功获得者46人，转业志愿兵7人。此期间，荔波县于1997年被州退伍军人和军队离休退休安置领导小组评为“接收安置退伍军人先进单位”。1999年安置县人武部转业干部5人。自2000年起，退伍的农村义务兵，一律不再安置，1999年以前立三等功的退伍兵，可以参加竞争考试安置。

2001—2008年，复退军人正式安排工作53人，均为城镇居民户口，其中伤残军人2人。

至2008年，全县按1993年县委、县政府关于现役军人的奖励规定，荣立三等功以上荣誉获得一次性奖励人员总计109人。

1978—2008年退伍军人安置情况一览表

表9－11

年度	接收安置（人）			立功受奖			安置工作（人）
	总人数	城镇户口	农村户口	立功等级	人数（人）	奖励（万元）	
1978	61	12	49	三等功	3	0.06	15
1979	33	9	24	—	—	—	9
1980	144	15	129	—	—	—	19
1981	142	17	125	三等功	4	0.08	19
1982	114	23	91	—	—	—	25
1983	33	6	27	—	—	—	5
1984	93	19	74	三等功	1	0.02	13
1985	55	9	46	—	—	—	9
1986	58	11	47	三等功	1	0.02	9
1987	76	6	70	三等功	2	0.10	7
1988	40	6	34	—	—	—	5
1989	65	5	60	—	—	—	4
1990	41	11	30	三等功	1	—	10
1991	34	9	25	三等功	9	—	9
1992	38	2	36	三等功	5	—	2
1993	44	5	39	三等功	9	0.45	5
1994	37	3	34	三等功	12	0.60	8
1995	26	4	22	三等功	4	0.20	8
1996	42	7	35	二等功	2	0.80	18
				三等功	8		
1997	46	7	39	二等功	1	1	22
				三等功	16		
1998	38	6	32	三等功	10	0.50	14
1999	35	1	34	三等功	9	0.45	10
2000	16	4	12	三等功	5	0.25	8
2001	59	12	47	三等功	4	0.20	11
2002	57	8	49	三等功	6	0.48	9
2003	42	7	35	三等功	2	0.10	7
2004	54	5	49	三等功	3	0.15	6
2005	48	6	42	三等功	6	0.30	6
2006	24	3	21	三等功	1	0.05	3
2007	45	6	39	三等功	2	0.10	6
2008	60	5	55	三等功	9	0.45	1

第三节　救灾救济

一、灾害救济

境内自然灾害主要有干旱、洪涝、低温绵雨、大风、冰雹以及植物病虫害等，每年都有不同程度的自然灾害发生。

县内发生各种灾害后，县委、县政府及时组织相关单位到灾区抗灾救灾，对灾区灾民的救济按“依靠群众，依靠集体力量，生产自救为主，辅之以国家必要救济”的方针，扶持灾民和贫困户生产自救，发展生产。

为在发生自然灾害后快速向灾区提供人力、物力、财力援助，2004年3月，制定《荔波县自然灾害救助应急预案》；11—12月，先后制定《荔波县重大突发性自然灾害社会捐助应急预案》《荔波县灾民生活评估办法（试行）》《荔波县救灾救济款物使用管理办法》《荔波县灾民民房恢复重建工作方案》《荔波县抗灾救灾工作联席会议制度》，以及建立应急避灾场所等自然灾害救济体系。

2008年1—2月初，县境遭遇持续长达20多天的特大冰冻灾害，农作物、农户房屋、交通公路、通信线路、水、电等严重受损，17个乡（镇）、98个村（居）委会、1241个村（居）民小组不同程度受灾，受灾34396户171980人。灾害发生后，县委、县政府及时安排救济粮91.51吨，拨购粮款27.67万元，解决1525户6101人次粮食困难；安排救济棉被1409床、棉衣709件，救灾捐赠衣物8860件（套），解决926户2418人衣被困难；走访慰问困难群众885户，发放慰问金总计17.7万元；安排购买肉食慰问困难群众资金11.4万元；安排倒塌民房恢复重建及民房维修资金31.8万元，解决灾民及困难群众35户138人住房困难。同时，及时发放农村“五保户”供养经费、城乡低保资金以及重点优抚对象经费等。

1991—2008年全县救灾救济情况统计表

表9－11

年度	受灾人口（万人）	直接经济损失（万元）	发放救济粮（吨）	救济棉衣棉被（件）	恢复被毁坏房屋		救灾资金投入（万元）	救灾物资折款（万元）
					户	间		
1991	8.20	1426.61	320.00	—	—	—	34.80	—
1992	8.40	1524.30	409.00	—	—	—	36.50	—
1993	3.84	1160.00	337.00	—	537	3227	39.80	—
1994	8.30	1467.70	190.00	330	121	726	38.00	—
1995	7.50	546.00	250.00	119	88	530	47.50	0.55
1996	7.26	1383.90	664.50	298	68	410	93.00	1.10
1997	7.79	4842.00	470.00	370	85	509	135.80	2.60
1998	9.85	6782.00	476.00	390	1651	9907	138.00	2.72
1999	7.33	3713.80	169.00	450	33	198	112.00	2.98
2000	9.76	2918.60	280.00	400	1318	7913	180.00	3.20
2001	13.71	5203.00	480.00	420	8	48	186.00	3.30

续表9－11

年度	受灾人口（万人）	直接经济损失（万元）	发放救济粮（吨）	救济棉衣棉被（件）	恢复被毁坏房屋		救灾资金投入（万元）	救灾物资折款（万元）
					户	间		
2002	12.98	5386.00	549.00	420	76	455	179.70	4.60
2003	2.21	5948.00	550.00	560	46	242	111.50	5.80
2004	1.28	5073.00	350.00	720	250	480	107.20	1.65
2005	12.43	3139.00	300.00	750	167	501	176.00	6.80
2006	10.17	9759.00	450.00	1486	64	384	168.00	14.26
2007	4.01	1342.00	324.00	705	153	318	299.40	87.40
2008	1.68	2668.00	469.00	3520	1145	3383	539.00	23.70

二、社会捐赠

2008年1月，县内遭受50年间最大范围的持续冰冻灾害后，县民政局收到社会各界捐款56.5万元，支出55.6万元，其中由县政府统一安排救灾50万元；发放爱心卡100户2万元，雪凝灾害期间几次慰问抢险救灾部队购粮、油、雨衣、手套、生猪、水果、现金等3.6万元。

2008年5月12日，四川汶川发生8.0级特大地震后，县委办、县政府办于5月15日联合发出《关于开展向四川省地震灾区捐款活动的紧急通知》，县委、县政府向全县人民发出《向四川地震灾区捐款倡议书》。到9月10日，全县党政机关、人民团体、社会各界向灾区捐赠款总计113.75万元。其中，县财政预算安排10万元，单位捐款16.31万元，个人捐款87.44万元。捐赠衣物总计1273件，捐赠物资折款2.55万元。全县中共党员缴纳特殊党费18.07万元，捐赠款分4次汇到灾区，捐赠衣物于6月底全部送到州民政局，由州民政局统一送往灾区。

第四节 救助 社会福利

一、“五保户”供养

1978年，对全县“五保户”（保吃、保穿、保住、保医、保葬）实行供养制度。1979年后，县内“五保户”供养救助方式有5种：明确专人照料；由亲属供养；集体提供粮食；划留双份责任地，由他人代耕，包交一定数量粮食；由村组安排巡回流动供养（即吃流动饭）。

1990年，全县有“五保户”376户395人，除依靠集体“五保”外，还进行临时补助，如遇灾情病害或逢年过节，给予临时救济。

1994年1月起，按国务院颁布的《农村五保供养工作条例》的规定，对年满60周岁的无生活来源、无劳动能力、无法定赡养的老年人，实行“五保”供养。为加强农村“五保”供养管理，每年对符合农村“五保”供养条件的人员进行登记造册，入户抽查，及时注销不符合条件或死亡对象，把符合“五保”供养条件的对象纳入供养范围，并建立农村“五保”工作台账，实行动态管理。

自2006年后，按新的《农村五保供养工作条例》，对农村“五保”供养对象实行动态管理，符合条件应保尽保。2007年年底，全面开展农村“五保”排查，符合条件全部纳入供养。

2000—2008年全县农村“五保户”供养情况统计表

表9－12

年度	户数（户）	人数（人）	金额（万元）
2000	162	372	29.80
2001	165	380	30.50
2002	203	455	30.50
2003	156	355	27.30
2004	157	358	28.40
2005	339	359	22.43
2006	337	361	22.56
2007	338	360	29.24
2008	620	680	55.08

二、社会救助

1978年，县民政部门设收容所，收容社会上的游民、难民、沿街乞讨、无家可归的流浪儿童等。对收容的荔波籍人员，采取救济安置，为他们提供一定的生产、生活条件；对外籍人员，收容初审后，遣送到独山或都匀收容站安置。到20世纪90年代，一直沿用收容遣送办法，对收容人员临时安排食宿，然后遣送到其所在地区，交当地政府有关部门管理。1981—2002年，全县收容遣送外籍人员103人次，外地遣送到荔波安置16人。

2003年，将收容所改为县流浪乞讨人员救助站。2003—2008年，全县救助流浪乞讨人员总计57人次。

三、困难群众临时救助

2004年9月，县政府颁布实施《荔波县农村特困家庭对象医疗救助制度实施细则》。2006年11月22日，县政府办发出《关于印发荔波县农村特困家庭医疗救助制度实施方案的通知》。2008年6月25日，县政府办发出《关于印发荔波县城市困难居民医疗救助实施方案（试行）的通知》《荔波县医疗救助实施方案》。

2006—2008年，县民政局为全县农村困难群众24536人缴纳合作医疗保险资金24.54万元；为全县城市困难群众1307人缴纳医疗保险资金2.09万元。对全县五保户，20世纪60年代精简退职老职工、城乡低保户和低收入困难家庭患病人员179人实施医疗救助，救助资金总计39.33万元。

2000—2008年全县城乡临时救助情况统计表

表9－13

年度	城乡困难群众临时救助			社会捐赠
	户数（户）	人数（人）	金额（万元）	金额（万元）
2000	34	103	5.1	24.0
2001	92	292	11.7	—
2002	97	298	14.6	2.8

续表9－13

年度	城乡困难群众临时救助			社会捐赠
	户数（户）	人数（人）	金额（万元）	金额（万元）
2003	193	579	29.0	2.3
2004	173	522	26.0	0.5
2005	157	469	23.5	2.0
2006	238	714	28.6	2.3
2007	525	1575	63.0	8.9
2008	470	1410	56.4	170.2

四、社会福利

（一）福利院

1978年，县内设甲良梅桃孤儿院。1979年4月，将梅桃孤儿院交州管理，更名为黔南州梅桃孤儿老残教养院。

1991年，州拨款2万元，县匹配1.8万元，分别拨给茂兰、洞塘、瑶山、瑶麓、立化等乡（镇）建敬老院。

1996年后，甲良、播尧、朝阳、驾欧、玉屏等乡（镇）先后建立敬老院。

2005年，全县有敬老院10所。2005—2008年，茂兰、瑶山、玉屏、立化等乡（镇）先后撤销。至2008年年底，全县有敬老院6所。其中，甲良敬老院占地80平方米，建筑面积120平方米，床位6张；播尧敬老院占地面积100平方米，建筑面积200平方米，床位6张；朝阳敬老院占地面积120平方米，建筑面积240平方米，床位7张；驾欧敬老院占地面积240平方米，建筑面积360平方米，床位14张；瑶麓敬老院占地面积130平方米，建筑面积260平方米，床位5张；洞塘敬老院占地面积80平方米，建筑面积160平方米，床位7张。各敬老院服务人员由乡（镇）自行安排，年末在院人数33人。

（二）福利彩票发行

从1989年起，发行即开型彩票。

1995年，在县民政局设荔波县福利彩票办理点，业务由州福彩中心统一管理。福利彩票类型有3D、七乐彩、福彩22选5等。

2003年起，县内民政部门开始发行电脑福利彩票，以县民政局为主要发行渠道，建立福利彩票发行网点3个，在各乡（镇）民政股设代办点。

至2008年，全县有福利彩票发行网点16个，彩票网点管理人员16人。

第五节 婚姻及收养登记

1978年，由县各（乡）镇民政部门进行婚姻登记。1981年，国家《婚姻登记办法》颁布实施后，依法办理婚姻登记。

1987年11—12月，开展全县1981—1987年执行《婚姻登记办法》情况检查，1981—1987年年底，结婚4282对，当时申请办理结婚登记652对，占结婚总数的15.2%。检查后补办登记手续583对。

1992年4月，《中华人民共和国收养法》颁布实施后，县民政部门承担收养登记工作。至1994

年，民政部门登记捡拾弃婴12人。

1999年，成立荔波县民政局婚姻登记处，依法办理婚姻登记业务。2002年，在各乡（镇）设立婚姻登记办理点18个（含县民政局婚姻登记处）。2003年，县民政局设婚姻登记处，玉屏、水利、永康、水尧、茂兰、瑶麓、立化、朝阳等乡（镇）辖区内的婚姻登记划由县民政局婚姻登记处办理，将原婚姻登记代办点18个调整合并为10个。各乡（镇）婚姻登记点设在社会事务办公室。

2008年，全县设婚姻登记点13个（县城1个、乡镇12个），各乡（镇）社会事务办公室依法办理婚姻登记业务。

2004—2008年，民政部门登记捡拾弃婴61人，其中，送州福利院50人，留给无子女人抚养11人。

1991—2008年全县结婚登记、收养登记情况统计表

表9－14

年度	婚姻登记（对）		收养登记（人）	年度	婚姻登记（对）		收养登记（人）
	结婚	离婚			结婚	离婚	
1991	1083	2	2	2000	1206	17	18
1992	1097	4	3	2001	1561	22	15
1993	1135	3	2	2002	1594	25	14
1994	1164	5	5	2003	1628	50	11
1995	1186	3	3	2004	1547	65	9
1996	1193	7	7	2005	1552	69	6
1997	1212	4	9	2006	1466	69	9
1998	1256	8	14	2007	1535	69	7
1999	1266	10	12	2008	1586	101	5

第六节　民间组织管理

一、社会团体登记管理

1978年后，县民政部门承担经授权的社会团体登记管理工作，依据国务院《社会团体登记管理条例》，对登记的社团组织按年度开展年检。至2008年，全县登记管理的社会团体14个，注册登记的各社团组织每年年检均为合格。

1978—2008年荔波县社会团体登记管理统计表

表9－15

序号	民间组织名称	业务主管单位	登记时间	登记证号
1	荔波县林学会	县林业局	1980.4.1	社证字第1012-004号
2	荔波县计划生育协会	县计生局	1992.1.1	社证字第1012-001号
3	荔波县消费者协会	县工商局	1992.3.1	社证字第1012-002号
4	荔波县个体协会	县工商局	1992.4.1	社证字第1012-003号

续表9-15

序号	民间组织名称	业务主管单位	登记时间	登记证号
5	荔波县农学会	县农业局	1992.3.1	社证字第1012-005号
6	荔波县集邮协会	县邮政局	1992.10.1	社证字第1012-006号
7	荔波县烹饪饭店协会	县商业局	2003.7.1	社证字第1012-007号
8	荔波县迪斯科协会	县文体广播电视局	2003.9.1	社证字第1012-009号
9	荔波县离退休教职工协会	县教育局	2004.8.9	黔荔社证字第1012-010号
10	荔波县太极拳协会	县文体广播电视局	2004.9.13	社证字第1012-011号
11	荔波县工矿贸易有限责任公司爱心协会	县供销社	2005.6.30	黔社证字第1012-014号
12	荔波县民间民族科普文艺协会	县科协	2007.6.18	黔荔社证字第1012-030号
13	荔波县金秋协会	县文体广播电视局	2008.8.8	黔荔社证字第1012-034号
14	荔波县废旧金属回收行业协会	县经济贸易局	2008.8.21	黔荔社证字第1012-033号

二、民办非企业单位

2003年3月，登记成立玉屏镇城西文艺队，业务由县文体广播电视局主管，业务范围为组织群众性业余文艺活动，进行经验交流及有关讲座学习研究，参加多种形式文艺比赛。

是年9月，登记成立县中老年花灯队，业务由县文体广播电视局主管单位，业务范围为花灯舞剧表演等。

第七节　老龄工作

1987年，成立县老龄委员会。1994年，县老龄委员会更名县老龄工作委员会，开展老年人权益保障工作和组织有利于老年人身心健康的各种活动。

2000年，全县有社区服务中心1个，参加活动的老年人2680人；有涉及老年人法律援助机构1个，开展敬老与法治宣传活动1次。

2001年，按照民政部《实施“社区老年福利服务星光计划”方案》，启动“星光计划”（在3年内使用各级彩票中心发行福利彩票筹集的福利基金的80%和各级政府投资及社会各界资助，在社区居委会和农村乡镇新建或改扩建一批城市社区老年福利服务设施、活动场所和农村乡镇敬老院，以供老年人娱乐、健身和学习）。县委、县政府成立“星光计划”实施工作领导机构，制定《荔波县实施“社区老年福利服务星光计划”方案》和三年发展规划实施计划。通过实施“星光计划”，在4个居委会建立“星光老年之家”，“星光老年之家”成为老年人“老有所养、老有所医、老有所教、老有所学、老有所为、老有所乐”的载体。

2004年，全县有社区服务中心1个，参加活动的老年人2865人；有老年大学1所，在校学员170人；有老年学校2所，在校学员102人。

2008年，全县有老年人口18308人（男8314人、女9994人），老年人占总人口的10.7%。有老年活动中心（室）5个；开展敬老与法治宣传活动3次；有老年大学1所，学员200人；有老年学校4所，在校学员280人；有涉老法律援助机构1个。

2004—2008年，慰问老年人1582人次，金额累计31.5万元。

2000—2008年全县老年人社会保障及救助情况一览表

表9－16

年度	高龄补贴		最低生活保障（人）		特困医疗救助（人）	办理老年优待证（本）
	人数（人）	金额（元）	城镇	农村		
2000	0	0	29	527	—	—
2001	0	0	520	540	—	—
2002	4	2000	317	1750	—	—
2003	5	3900	350	456	—	—
2004	3	3600	456	375	—	—
2005	4	4800	101	4517	16	27
2006	3	3600	155	4517	13	149
2007	1	1200	899	2299	17	218
2008	27	9720	301	6872	21	89

第八节　勘　界

一、县际边界线

荔波县与独山县　荔波县与独山县边界线总长70.93公里。272227262732号界桩为荔波县、独山县、三都水族自治县三县边界线的交点，为单立三面型石质界桩。位于独山县本寨水族乡高核村八组、三都县恒丰乡板孔村打兰村民组、荔波县甲良镇中怀村大甲村民组，距香科（村寨名）东北约650米，边界线的两侧分别为荔波县的甲良镇、原播尧乡、原驾欧乡3个乡（镇）、14个行政村；独山县的本寨乡、基场镇、尧棒乡、甲里镇、董岭乡、打羊乡6个乡（镇）、14个行政村。

荔波县与三都县　荔波县与三都水族自治县行政区域界线长84.56公里，双方边界接边的有8个乡（镇）、21个村委会。8个乡（镇）是荔波县的甲良镇、原水利乡、原玉屏镇、原茂兰镇、原佳荣镇、三都县的恒丰乡、周覃镇、九阡镇。21个村委会是荔波县的中环村、甲高村、板培村、水丙村、洞托村、水浦村、水春村、水庆村、高里村、地牙村、拉学村、拉先村、拉易村，三都县的板孔村、锦奎村、塘党村、洞览村、水条村、水昔村、石板村、甲才村。边界线由西向东走向自荔波、独山、三都3县交会点起到荔波、榕江、三都3县交会点止。共埋设双面型界桩1块。

二、州际边界线

荔波县与榕江县　荔波、榕江两县行政区域界线由东起榕江、从江、荔波3县为边界线交会点，西止榕江、三都、荔波3县边界线交会点，榕江、荔波两县接边线全长8.246公里，呈东西走向。双方边界接壤的有3个乡（镇），即榕江乡的计划乡、水尾乡，荔波县的佳荣镇，两县接边的村委会有计划乡的摆拉村，水尾乡的拉述村，佳荣镇的拉易村。接边双方乡（镇）3个、村委会3个。

荔波县与从江县　荔波从江线北起荔波、榕江、从江3县边界线，南止荔波、从江、环江（广西）3县边界线交会点，呈西北—东南走向，全长18公里。两县接壤的边线涉及2个乡（镇），即荔波县的佳荣镇、从江县的光辉乡。涉及的村有佳荣镇的拉易村、大土村和甲料村，光辉乡的长牛村、党郎村、加牙村共6个行政村。

三、省际边界线

荔波县与环江县 荔波县与环江县两县划定线段走向：自洞汴幅图向东北方向至雷家坡幅图为两县行政区域边界线，界线总长约为119公里。4552007号界桩为单立双面型石质界桩，位于广西壮族自治区环江毛南族自治县川山镇何顿村与贵州省荔波县洞塘乡洞腊村交界处，4552008号界桩为单立双面型石质界桩，位于广西壮族自治区环江毛南族自治县驯乐苗族乡福寿村与贵州省荔波县佳荣镇原新寨村交界处。

荔波县与南丹县 两县接边界线总长63.3公里。4552006号界桩为单立双面型石质界桩，位于广西壮族自治区南丹县里湖乡甲木村更大屯与贵州省荔波县瑶山乡红光村交界处，拉尾组东南250米处的山顶上。

第十篇
政法　军事

1978年改革开放以来，荔波县为荔波经济加快发展、跨越发展保驾护航。荔波县公安部门从1983年起，贯彻执行《中共中央关于严厉打击刑事犯罪活动的决定》，在全县开展严厉打击犯罪分子的“严打”斗争。1991年，开展“反盗窃、破大案、打团伙、抓流窜”破案会战等斗争，保持对严重刑事犯罪的高压态势，打击了犯罪、保护人民、维护社会安定和谐、捍卫国家法律尊严。

县检察机关落实“强化法律监督，维护公平正义”的检察工作主题，按照“加大工作力度，提高执法水平和办案质量”的总体要求，全面履行宪法和法律赋予的监督职能。推进反腐败斗争，履行法律监督职能，为维护司法公正展开工作。改革开放以来，荔波检察机关按照上级院提出的工作思路和奋斗目标，因院制宜，坚持“以人为本，从严治检，执法为本，依法建院”。

县法院在中共十一届三中全会以后坚持“解放思想，实事求是”清理纠正了历史冤假错案，到1987年12月，全部复查结束，让蒙冤受屈者及其受株连的亲友得以昭雪沉冤。县法院不断加强以法官为主体的队伍建设，维护社会正常的生产、生活秩序。贯彻“公正司法，一心为民”的方针，保护民生、维护民权、促进民和、确保民安，为荔波经济社会的发展和稳定做出了积极的贡献。

1982年恢复司法行政工作设立荔波县司法局，2002年，成立16个乡（镇）司法所，基层法律服务逐步深化，人民调解工作全面开展。

律师事业稳步开展，公证工作不断拓展。法律援助工作为困难群众排忧解难。普法依法治理工作取得成果。

1978年，县人民武装部（以下简称人武部）为军队建制，归都匀军分区领导。1986年7月，县人武部移交地方，改为地方建制，名称为“贵州省荔波县人民武装部”。1996年4月，县人武部收归军队，受都匀军分区和荔波县党政双重领导。中国人民武装警察部队荔波县中队、县公安消防中队、民兵预备役开展了军事工作、国防教育、拥政爱民、抢险救灾、支援荔波县经济建设。

第一章 公 安

第一节 案件侦破

一、刑事案件侦破

1978年，全县开展刑事案件侦破统一行动3次，打击各类刑事犯罪分子。

自1983年起，贯彻执行《中共中央关于严厉打击刑事犯罪活动的决定》，开展全县首次严厉打击犯罪分子的“严打”斗争。按照“从重从快、一网打尽”的方针，开展“严打”整治专项行动，逮捕犯罪嫌疑人162人。

1988—1990年，全县发生各类刑事案件813件，破获433起，逮捕犯罪嫌疑人496人，摧毁作案团伙44个，缴获赃款、赃物折款共22.26万元。

1991年，开展“反盗窃、破大案、打团伙、抓流窜”破案会战，破获刑事案件62起，追回损失4.4万元，抓获犯罪嫌疑人80人，摧毁作案团伙8个21人。全年各类刑事案件立案328起，破案163起，破案率为49.7%。抓获犯罪嫌疑人227人，摧毁作案犯罪团伙24个99人。

1992年，开展“打流窜、追逃犯”“打团伙、破大案”“反盗窃”“打拐”等专项斗争，全年破获刑事案件225起，破案率66.96%，抓获犯罪嫌疑人229人，摧毁作案团伙12个47人。

1993—1995年，持续开展“严打”斗争，案件侦破以“严打”的各类案件为重点，先后开展“夏季治安重点整顿”“百日破案会战”“反盗窃、破大案、挖团伙、追逃犯”“打拐”“围歼车匪路霸”等专项行动。3年破案454起，打掉作案团伙89个。其间，在1994年开展的“严打”斗争和专项治理中，重大案件发案68起，破案53起；特大案件发案8起，破案8起。

1996年，按照中共中央开展夏季“严打”斗争的部署，在全县范围内开展夏季“严打”斗争，历时5个多月，破获各类刑事案件104起，抓获犯罪嫌疑人114人。全年破案132起，抓获犯罪嫌疑人212人，打掉作案犯罪团伙27个110人。

1997年，开展春季、夏秋季、冬季3个阶段“严打”斗争，严厉打击抢劫、强奸、杀人等重大恶性案件，缴获一批赃款赃物、危禁物品、枪支弹药和管制刀具。全年破获刑事案件102起，破案率80.3%，抓获犯罪嫌疑人157人，摧毁作案犯罪团伙17个73人。

1998年，开展“破案会战”“打击走私盗抢机动车辆”等专项行动，缴获东风汽车1辆、摩托车8辆、自行车28辆、手榴弹1枚、子弹10发、管制刀具25把、枪支8支，追回被盗耕畜16头（匹），为群众挽回经济损失21.36万元。1999年，刑事案件立案43起，破案82起（其中39起为上年未破案件），抓获犯罪嫌疑人17人。

2000—2001年，刑事案件立案372起，破案193起，抓获杀人犯罪嫌疑人25人、抢劫抢夺犯罪嫌疑人31人、强奸犯罪嫌疑人19人、拐卖妇女儿童犯罪嫌疑人26人，打掉盗窃团伙8个37人、恶势力团伙3个18人，端掉赌博窝点17处316人。

2002年，在打击抢劫、抢夺、盗窃（入室盗窃、机动车辆盗窃）等专项行动中，摧毁犯罪团伙36个117人，缴获摩托车8辆、彩电5台、影碟机3台、手机8部、耕牛15头，各类赃款、赃物价值总计27万元。

2003—2006年，全县各类刑事案件立案901起，破案518起。其中，县公安局于2006年破获佳荣镇“十年尸骨积案”、县城南门枪击杀人案、捞村乡杀妻藏尸案、县城北街杀人抛尸案等命案，实现命案必破目标。

2007年，刑事案件侦破以“打盗抢、抓逃犯”为重点，全年各类刑事案件立案216起，破案150起，抓获犯罪嫌疑人120人。

2008年，全县刑事案件立案423起，破案126起。其中，打掉韦某某恶势力团伙1个，抓获涉恶人员5人；侦破茂兰安匀煤矿保险柜被盗案及茂兰场坝价值近50万元的重型货车被盗案；打掉盗窃摩托车团伙3个、盗窃耕牛团伙2个，追回被盗摩托车23辆、汽车7辆、耕牛9头；抓获网上在逃人员21人（其中外省在逃人员5人）。

二、经济案件侦破

1978年，县公安机关查处挪用单位资金案件1起，涉案金额300元。1979年，查处侵占公款案件1起，涉案金额300元。1980—1984年，查处诈骗案件6起，涉案金额1490元。

1985—1989年，侦破挪用单位资金、金融诈骗涉税等经济案件7起。1990—1997年，侦破虚开增值税发票、金融诈骗、侵占公款等各类经济案件21起。1998—1999年，查获制假煤炭窝点2个，涉及掺假煤炭60吨，查处诈骗案件4起。

2000—2001年，开展“打击货物运输和制售发票”“整顿煤炭经营秩序”“整治烟叶市场”等专项行动。经济犯罪案件立案3起，涉案总价值10万元，追回赃款4.3万元，收缴劣质烟叶6吨、假冒“黄果树”牌香烟150条，摧毁制假窝点2个。

2002年县公安局成立经济犯罪侦查大队，持续开展“打击货物运输和制售发票”“整顿煤炭经营秩序”“整治烟叶市场”等专项行动，侦破省、州督办的特大合同诈骗案、特大虚开抵扣税款发票案、特大票据诈骗案。其中，破获案值1000万元的出口骗税案件1起，抓获犯罪嫌疑人2人；查获制假煤炭窝点1起，涉及掺假煤炭30余吨；市场整治收缴各类盗版书刊192本、光碟50张、劣质烟叶30公斤、假冒劣质商品27种。

2003—2004年，侦破虚开增值税专用发票、挪用单位资金、侵占公款、金融诈骗等各类经济案件11起。其中，2004年的票据诈骗、虚开增值税专用发票、伪造企事业单位印章案件，涉案金额6000万元，造成直接经济损失30万元。

2005—2008年，受理各类经济犯罪案件15起，涉案金额总计1525万元。

第二节　治安管理

一、危险物品管理

从20世纪80年代起，县公安局治安大队根据《关于中、小型化工企业安全生产管理规定》《化学危险物品储存管理暂行办法》《化学危险物品凭证经营、采购暂行办法》《铁路危险物品运输规则》《化学危险物品防火管理规则》《关于违反爆炸、易燃物品管理规则处罚暂行办法》等管理规定，结合全县实际情况，通过组织培训爆破人员，提高爆破技术水平，防止事故发生；坚持爆炸物品管理审核制度，每次核发爆炸物品，先结清上次购进数和消耗数，再办理下次批购手续；加强烟花爆竹经营点和公共场所燃放爆竹管理等措施，对县内危险物品进行严格管理。

1987年2月17日，国务院颁布新的《化学危险物品安全管理条例》后，县公安局培训爆破人员122人，并对原有701人进行年审。通过年审，合格的爆破人员464名。

1991年，爆破员年审369名，审办爆炸物品供应准购证114个，换发烟花爆竹营业许可证117个。1992年，年审爆破员266名，选点建库1处3个，办理爆炸物品准购证411个，办理烟花爆竹许可证135个。1993年，查处违反爆炸物品管理案件6起，收缴流失炸药1113公斤、雷管2600发、导火线100米。1994年，年审爆破员288名，办理爆炸物品准购证179个，查处违反爆炸物品管理案件7起。1995年，开展爆炸物品管理检查活动6次，检查12个乡23个单位。1996年，先后3次对全县7个爆炸物品管理站进行安全检查，共检查炸药库28个。1998年，办理爆破物品准购证213个，审批炸药201吨、雷管1.83万枚、引线1.7万米，收缴非法出售爆竹3510响。1999年，收缴非法枪支64支、管制刀具227把，摧毁制枪窝点2个，销毁土炸药55公斤，查获非法销售炸药780公斤。

2000年，捣毁非法制造爆炸物窝点4个，查处非法销售炸药案件2起，收缴非法炸药303公斤、导火索900米、自制炸药原料硝铵480公斤、爆竹30万响、非法民用枪支947支、管制刀具690把，摧毁非法制枪窝点5个。2001年，收缴非法买卖及储存炸药1490公斤、雷管3878枚、导火索350米，收缴非法民用枪支496支、管制刀具354把，捣毁制枪窝点1个。

2002年，收缴炸药530.54公斤、雷管3140枚、导火索263.63米、民用枪支102支、日式手雷1枚、军用手榴弹2枚、管制刀具242把。处理涉嫌非法持有枪支案5人，判刑4人。2003年，收缴非法枪支58支、枪支零部件11件、黑火药7公斤、铁砂3公斤、火底120枚，没收私造炸药2吨、非法储存炸药284公斤，扣押涉案硝酸铵21吨、雷管700枚、导火索400米，扣押违规储存烟花爆竹81件243万响。下发停业整顿通知书6份，责令停业整改4家。在危险化学物品专项整治中，缴获毒鼠强872克，严控鼠药1.5公斤。2004年，开展危险品专项整治8次，扣押非法储存炸药591公斤、雷管605发、导爆管180枚，扣押违规爆竹200万响。下发停业整顿通知书8份，责令停业整改1家。

2005年，开展民爆物品、危险化学物品专项整治18次，没收、扣押非法储存炸药258公斤、雷管2457枚，提出整改意见120条，下发停产整顿通知书11份。2006年，没收、暂扣非法储存炸药540公斤、雷管100枚，收缴各类违法枪支53支。2007年，收缴非法持有土火枪65支、炸药66公斤、雷管517枚、管制刀具30把。2008年，开展民爆、危险化学物品专项整治26次，检查涉爆单位30家，没有发生重大涉枪涉爆案件。

二、特种行业管理

1978—1987年，依据《城市旅栈业暂行管理规则》，对全县从事特种行业的单位和个人，由辖区派出所民警管理。

1987年11月10日，新的《旅馆业治安管理办法》发布履行后，1988年，对全县从事特种行业的单位和个人进行登记、审核发证后，逐步规范特种物业的经营活动，全年登记全县有从事特种行业的单位52个、个人189人。至1989年，全县特种行业经营户发展到81家。其中，旅馆57家、废金属收购点16家、刻字1家、修理业7家。

1992年，检查旅馆89家（次），取缔旅馆2家，处罚旅馆16家。

1994年，对54家旅馆、12家废金属收购点、1家刻字、7家修理业全部进行规范备案。此后，公安机关每年与有关单位联合开展特种行业和公共娱乐场所清理整顿，对非法经营者依法予以取缔。

至1997年，全县有特种行业经营户110家。其中，旅馆87家床位1810个，废旧金属收购点6家，打字、复印15家，刻字2家。另有公共娱乐场所59家。是年，特种行业及娱乐场所全部实行亮证经营，县公安局与各业主签订《治安合同责任书》。1999年，全县有特种行业105家。其中，旅馆89家，废金属收购点8家，刻字1家，修理业7家。

2001—2006年，每年开展全县特种行业检查，对有违法行为的经营户进行处罚或予以取缔。其间，2001年检查105次，取缔旅馆6家；2003—2005年检查349次，处罚旅馆45家，抓获犯罪嫌疑人34人。

2007年，检查特种行业105次，取缔旅馆6家，处罚旅店19家。

2008年，在全县各大宾馆推广安装旅店业信息管理系统，对临时暂住人员实行动态管理。至年末，全县有特种行业经营户122家。其中，旅店业89家床位3879张，废旧金属收购点9个，打字复印店15家，刻字店1家，娱乐场所8家。县公安局利用旅店业信息管理系统抓获网上在逃人员2名。

三、禁黄禁赌

1978年后，按照公安部的规定，将禁止黄色淫秽物品、禁止卖淫嫖娼、禁止赌博列为社会治安的重要内容进行查处。

1978年后，将禁止黄色淫秽物品、禁止卖淫嫖娼、禁止赌博列为社会治安的重要内容进行查处。

1983年，贯彻执行“治安管理从严”的方针，严厉查处涉黄、赌博案件，全年有赌博人员420名到公安机关自首，缴获赌资1万元。

1986—1990年，查处赌博案件46起，抓获赌博人员220人，收缴赌资1.04万元，罚款1740元。

1991—1997年，查处赌博案件91起，抓获赌博人员228人，没收赌资1.47万元。

1998年，全县开展“打黄扫非”集中统一行动25次，抓获卖淫嫖娼16人，涉赌人员200余人。

1999年，开展集中统一行动27次，依法取缔赌博场所5家，缴获各类淫秽图书杂志165本、影碟146张，查处违法人员220人。

2000年，根据公安部下发的《关于开展加强娱乐服务场所管理、严厉打击卖淫嫖娼赌博吸毒贩毒等社会丑恶现象专项行动的意见》，县公安局制定《荔波县开展加强娱乐服务场所管理、严厉打击卖淫嫖娼赌博吸毒贩毒等社会丑恶现象专项行动方案》，每年开展“打黄扫非”专项整治行动。是年，开展“打黄扫非”专项整治行动5次，查处卖淫嫖娼、赌博案件58起，抓获违法人员182人。2001年，开展查禁黄、赌、毒集中统一行动8次，取缔赌博场所5家，缴获各类淫秽影碟20张，停业整顿网吧2家，查处卖淫嫖娼、赌博案件37起，抓获各类违法人员180人。2003年，取缔赌博场所20余家。2004年，检查公共复杂场所40家、印刷企业2个、书报刊点9个，查缴各类非法出版物200册。2005年，检查公共复杂场所38家、印刷企业2个、书报刊点10个，查缴各类非法出版物190册。2006年，查缴各类非法出版物210册，取缔麻将室3家，捣毁“摇筒”赌博窝点5家，查处卖淫嫖娼案件2起。2007年，检查旅店、发廊、娱乐场所等公共复杂场所76家，查处涉黄案件5起，行政拘留8人。

2008年，检查复杂场所58家、印刷企业5个、书报刊点6个，查缴各类非法出版物530册，取缔麻将室15家，捣毁“摇筒”赌博窝点11家，查处卖淫嫖娼案件3起。

1989—2008年全县治安案件查处统计表

表10－1

年度	受理案件（件）	查处案件（件）	查处违法人员（人）	调解（人）
1989—1990	1395	793	961	268
1991	353	267	407	102
1992	608	462	551	123

续表10－1

年度	受理案件（件）	查处案件（件）	查处违法人员（人）	调解（人）
1993	361	269	528	83
1994	201	162	210	64
1995	264	230	409	—
1996	216	195	291	—
1997	320	299	442	70
1998	315	282	394	250
1999	307	279	340	—
2000	640	556	818	280
2001	613	543	758	—
2002	451	416	521	—
2003	635	608	677	—
2004	441	427	515	—
2005	411	395	457	—
2006	317	279	349	—
2007	102	96	—	—
2008	396	266	—	—

第三节 户政与出入境管理

一、户政管理

（一）户口管理

1978—1981年，县内农业户口归大队、公社管理。1986年后，全县户口统一归口县公安局户政科管理，群众办理户口迁移和户口登记项目变更、更正审批等，由县公安局户政科管理。

1998—2008年全县户政管理人口情况一览表

表10－2

年度	常驻户口（户）	农业转非农业户口（人）	办理居民身份证（人）	办理临时居民身份证（人）	办理小城镇户口（人）	暂住人口（人）	列管重点人口（人）	总人口（万人）
1998	37636	12176	1948	850	92	1612	148	15.37
1999	38634	13526	2376	890	198	1786	152	15.63
2000	39019	12818	3557	960	171	1921	198	15.84
2001	39524	13484	4607	1560	153	2021	213	15.91
2002	40634	14236	7049	2320	265	2100	213	19.98

续表10－2

年度	常驻户口（户）	农业转非农业户口（人）	办理居民身份证（人）	办理临时居民身份证（人）	办理小城镇户口（人）	暂住人口（人）	列管重点人口（人）	总人口（万人）
2003	40929	14467	8460	700	210	3902	229	16.07
2004	42550	14929	8906	2779	201	1891	195	16.40
2005	43253	13884	6395	2000	470	2462	179	16.63
2006	45036	15118	17263	1680	272	3425	170	16.85
2007	45971	15491	2620	1720	54	3725	175	17.01
2008	47969	15964	26800	1346	124	1750	169	17.14

说明：1997年前数据遗失

（二）身份证办理

1987年，根据《居民身份证条例》《中华人民共和国居民身份证实施细则》的规定，县政府成立县颁发居民身份证领导小组及办公室，从县直各部门、区、乡（镇）抽调干部47名，在玉屏镇试点后，全面开展颁发居民身份证工作，在县城国营照相馆定点照相，由各派出所办理，县公安局户政科统一审批送省制作。至1990年年底，全县申请办证7.29万人，占应办证人数的86.6%，经省制证后发证6.37万人，占申请领证人数的87.4%。此后，身份证办理进入常态。

2003年6月，《中华人民共和国居民身份证法》颁布实施后，在办理年满16周岁公民居民身份证的同时，依法办理未满16周岁公民申领的居民身份证。

2008年，全县开始换发第二代居民身份证。

二、出入境管理

从1991年起，根据《中华人民共和国护照法》、国务院《外国人入境出境管理实施细则》《中华人民共和国公民入境出境管理实施细则》《中国公民因私事往来香港地区或澳门地区的暂行管理办法》《中国公民往来台湾地区管理办法》等系列法规、规章，县公安局开始办理出入境证件。1998年7月，成立出入境管理科，并受州公安局出入境管理部门领导。出入境管理科依法管理外国人入出境、过境、居留等事务，根据权限受理外国人的办理签证、居留证申请，受理县内公民使用的因私护照、赴港澳地区通行证件以及大陆居民赴台通行证件，查处外国人、县内公民违反出入境管理法律法规的案件和事件。

1998—2008年出入境人数及涉外案件查处情况统计表

表10－3

年度	办理边境通行证（份）	境外人员临时住宿登记（人次）	受理公民因私出国、出境（人）	查处涉外案件（起）
1998	142	81	1	—
1999	280	77	27	—
2000	285	75	31	1
2001	349	128	24	—
2002	186	281	90	2

续表10－3

年度	办理边境通行证（份）	境外人员临时住宿登记（人次）	受理公民因私出国、出境（人）	查处涉外案件（起）
2003	113	308	23	—
2004	148	274	98	1
2005	48	45	183	2
2006	取消	223	315	—
2007	—	249	75	—
2008	—	732	143	—

说明：1997年前数据遗失

第四节　交通管理

1978—1983年，县内的路政、监理工作由交通局负责，业务属于独山监理所指导。1984年成立荔波县交通监理站，隶属县交通局领导，业务由州监理所负责管理。

1987年，全县城乡道路交通管理划归公安机关统一管理，撤销县交通监理站，建立县公安交通警察队。管理的内容有交通安全宣传教育、交通指挥、交通秩序维护、交通事故处理和车辆检查、驾驶员考核与发牌、发证、路障管理及交通标志、标线等安全设施的设置与管理等。是年，组织设置路标、路牌、标语牌等标志，提醒驾驶人员警惕违章、违纪发生。1989年，开办驾驶员学习班8期，参加学习180人次。

1991年，举办交通安全学习班8期，参加学习143人；培训轻型摩托车、机动三轮车驾驶员45人。

1992年后，每年开展交通安全宣传活动，发放交通安全法规资料，加强交通安全教育；查处、整顿交通违章，重点取缔无牌证车辆。1994年，组织驾驶员学习3次，培训摩托车、小车驾驶员200人。

1995年，成立县公安局交通管理大队。1996年4月，增设茂兰、玉屏、甲良交通警察中队，为正股级单位。

是年5月，县交警大队制定《关于制止公路乱罚款的若干规定》，要求交通民警严格执法、文明执勤。全年开展交通安全教育活动2次。

2001—2003年，开展《交通安全条例》学习活动，每年有800～1000名驾驶员参加学习。

2005年5月，《道路交通安全法》正式颁布实施，开展大型宣传活动16次，发放宣传资料1万份，受教育人数4.1万人次。

从2006年起，按照公安部的部署，开展为期3年的“三基”（抓基层、打基础、苦练基本功）工作。县公安局交警大队以创建学习型队伍为载体，完善基础设施，采取队伍管理规范化、基层管理正规化、交通管理社会化、执勤执法信息化、勤务模式科学化等措施，进行交警“三基”工程建设。至2008年，“三基”工作通过省级验收。

2007—2008年，开展客运车、摩托车专项整治行动，对违法车辆，按照法律法规规定，采取扣车、扣证等手段，做到不消除违法行为绝不放行，严惩驾驶人违法行。

2008年1月，在县内遭受严重冰冻自然灾害中，为防止群众在冰冻期间发生交通事故，县公安局组织交警、治安及基层派出所民警3000余人次，出动车辆500辆（次），上路铲冰除雪，不分昼夜疏导、分流车辆3000辆（次），救助受困车辆60辆，护送转运滞留旅客2000余人，确保冰冻灾害期间的交通安全。4月，根据省编委办公室、省公安厅《关于调整县级公安机关交通管理机构名称的通知》，县公安局交通管理大队名称改为公安局交通警察大队。

1978—2008年全县交通事故统计表

表10－4

年度	交通事故总数（起）	受伤（人）	死亡（人）	直接经济损失（万元）
1978—1986	22	7	1	1.60
1987	5	1	0	0.05
1988	7	2	0	0.08
1989	8	1	0	0.10
1990	12	8	1	0.90
1991	11	7	2	1.70
1992	14	3	3	3.06
1993	13	12	2	2.90
1994	19	21	6	8.49
1995	12	4	3	2.70
1996	15	10	8	4.30
1997	14	9	6	3.80
1998	13	4	6	2.60
1999	4	2	1	1.20
2000	9	6	3	1.60
2001	15	11	8	4.50
2002	36	64	11	14.20
2003	79	154	10	16.80
2004	31	47	6	5.70
2005	26	30	9	18.00
2006	12	7	4	4.50
2007	60	22	13	5.20
2008	71	19	9	6.50

第五节 消防安全管理

一、消防监管

1978年，县公安局设有消防股，开展全县消防管理工作。1979年，全县有义务消防队181个8824人。对15个公社（镇）、21个大队、20个自然寨、9个场坝、4个水利工程、3个煤窑、3个水电站和供电所、10个供销社（店）、2个炸药库、7个厂矿企业、11个粮管所（站）、2个林业飞播区进行大检查，发现安全隐患100多处，整改80处。修订了村寨防火公约。1984年，县公安局消防股改为消防科。1987年，县城配有消防车1辆、水带800米、消防栓18个、灭火机具113个、消防桶10个、水泵2台、水池18个（蓄水量180立方米）。1990年，对50户以上的自然村寨进行防火检查验收，对发现的火险隐患提出整改措施。

1991年起，按照“预防为主、防消结合”的方针和“谁主管、谁负责”的原则，层层建立安全防火组织，以防火为中心开展宣传教育和防火安全检查，组建义务消防队，队以下设指导组、破拆组、供水组、疏散组、警卫组等；各单位、村寨订立防火公约并购置相应防火设备，建立健全岗位防火责任制；主要街道、厂矿及自然村寨成立义务消防队，防火设备主要有水池、水缸、沙包、灭火机、水龙头等。是年，县公安局制定《荔波县公安局1991年防火宣传提纲》，组织消防干警到乡（镇）宣传防火安全知识，受教育6万人次，对39个单位的仓库及55个车间，农村较大村寨30个及城镇居民住宅400户进行防火安全检查，发现不安全因素23处，并责令整改。

1992年，消防部门25个对机关单位、4个乡（镇）政府所在地、4个煤矿、5个汽油库加油站、6座炸药库、4个百货物资仓库、4个供销社、4个粮管所仓库、2个100户以上村寨进行以防火为中心的安全检查，对查出的隐患进行整改。

1993年，开展防火宣传8次，出动防火宣传车30台（次），出动警力75人次，发放宣传资料6500份，张贴标语1500幅，并以播放录像、广播等形式进行声像宣传。

1994—1995年，开展防火安全大检查9次，检查重点单位、公共娱乐场所等439个（次）、村寨52个（次），发现火险隐患152处，整改137处，发出《火险隐患整改通知书》36份，停业整改2处，发放防火宣传资料800份，张贴标语150幅。

1996年，贯彻落实《消防改革与发展纲要》和省政府《关于切实做好全省消防改革与发展工作的通知》精神，制定《荔波县“九五”城镇消防规范方案》，绘制荔波县“九五”城镇消防规范示意图。

1997年8月1日，成立县消防大队。11月，开展全国“119”消防宣传周活动，消防干警出动车辆5辆（次），到5个乡（镇）宣传防火安全知识，发放消防安全宣传资料3000份，受教育人数4万人次，在5个乡（镇）中学进行消防安全教育，播放录像、广播进行声像宣传，张贴标语300幅。年内，对119个防火单位（场所）进行安全防火检查，填写防火检查登记表50份，发出整改通知书34份。

1998年起，按照“预防为主、防消结合”的方针，开展消防安全宣传、教育培训及安全检查，帮助群众提高防火意识，消除火灾隐患，减少火灾事故发生。是年，公安部下发《关于统一公安边防、消防、警卫对外称谓的通知》以后，县公安消防大队对内称中国人民武装警察部队荔波县消防大队，对外称黔南布依族苗族自治州荔波县公安消防大队。县消防大队建立值勤备战制度，实行24小时值班。县政府逐步投入经费，为县消防大队配置消防设施。2008年7月，建成消防站，挂牌成立黔南州荔波县公安消防中队。

二、重特大火灾事故

1982年12月20日，岜鲜大寨失火成灾，受灾52户284人，被烧毁房屋160间，粮食20吨，损失折款4.32万元。

1985年7月10日，岜鲜大寨再次失火，造成27户135人受灾，烧毁房屋79间、粮食37.5吨。

1991年12月28日凌晨3时，佳荣乡大土村发生火灾，造成3户17人受灾，烧死2人，烧毁房屋3栋12间，直接经济损失0.5吨。

1992年9月4日，方村乡交尧村村民莫某用火不慎发生火灾，致使19户114人受灾，经济损失21万元。

1992年11月2日，甲良镇金华村发生重大火灾，烧毁房屋27栋101间、粮食59.5吨，受灾38户153人，直接经济损失10万元。

1992年11月26日，水利乡水封村懂外组村民杨某晚饭后用火疏忽大意，导致房屋起火，烧毁房屋8栋21间，死亡1人，经济损失2万元。

1993年1月9日，甲良镇纳核村发生重大火灾，烧毁房屋125间、粮食66.2吨以及其他物资，致使38户190人无家可归，经济损失25万元。

1998年1月19日14时30分左右，佳荣乡新寨村何家寨组发生火灾，受灾44户203人，烧毁住房105间，烧死生猪100头、耕牛3头、家禽35只，烧毁抽水电动机30台以及大量生产生活用品，直接经济损失32.26万元。

1999年12月22日，甲良镇石板村地兰组发生火灾，受灾14户71人，烧毁建筑面积2700平方米，烧毁粮食57.1吨、玉米11吨，烧死生猪31头，烧毁柴油机3台、粉碎机3台、打米机3台及大量生产生活物资，直接经济损失18.23万元。

2001年9月16日凌晨3时，茂兰镇卫生院第二门诊发生火灾，过火面积120平方米，死亡1人，直接经济损失1.87万元。

2001年12月31日凌晨2时30分，甲良镇甲高村甲抓组发生火灾，受灾16户67人，烧毁建筑物11栋40间共1558平方米，烧毁稻谷31吨、玉米11吨，烧死生猪28头，直接经济损失25.40万元。

2005年11月23日15时30分，甲良镇丙外村以奎组发生火灾，烧毁房屋10栋47间，过火面积1426平方米，烧毁稻谷17.5吨、玉米3150公斤，烧死生猪42头，直接经济损失8.68万元。

2006年1月26日10时20分，播尧乡地莪村更方组发生火灾，烧毁房屋7栋、稻谷22.9吨，火灾过火面积2400平方米，直接经济损失10.19万元。

2007年3月28日17时10分，甲良镇丙外村干塘组潘某某家发生火灾，烧毁房屋16栋，火灾过火面积1600平方米，受灾20户98人，直接经济损12.64万元。

同年12月10日21时10分，甲良镇甲站村板培组蒙某某家发生火灾，过火面积2.15万平方米，烧毁稻谷27.2吨、玉米7.8吨、猪9头、电视机8台、打谷机8台等，直接经济损失12.78万元。

2008年4月29日13时23分，佳荣镇拉易村下寨一、二组发生火灾，过火面积6.5万平方米，烧毁房屋65栋，受灾78户293人，直接经济损失83.47万元。起火原因为潘某某家用电器线路老化短路引燃家中可燃物导致火灾。

1991—2008年全县火灾事故统计表

表10-5

年度	火灾总数（起）	受伤（人）	死亡（人）	直接经济损失（万元）
1991	3	0	1	0.63
1992	5	0	3	12.35
1993	1	0	0	7.65
1994	4	2	0	2.46
1995	5	0	0	43.52
1996	4	0	2	0.51
1997	6	0	1	1.93
1998	6	0	0	69.70
1999	7	0	0	28.40
2000	3	0	0	21.00
2001	14	0	1	82.00
2002	9	0	0	12.00
2003	7	3	0	7.20
2004	5	0	0	16.00
2005	7	0	1	19.00
2006	8	0	0	22.90
2007	5	0	0	14.00
2008	5	0	0	90.90

说明：1978—1990年资料遗失

第六节 缉 毒

1978年后，县公安机关坚持“四禁并举，堵源截流，打防结合，打零包、带大案”的原则，开展“春夏扫毒风暴”“打零包、端窝点”“路上堵、公开查”“打击跨区域贩毒”等系列专项行动，对非法种植毒品原植物进行踏查铲除，对吸毒人员进行管控。

1979年2月—1990年6月，全县共出动警力644人次，基层干部、群众1020人次，在驾欧、捞村、翁昂等乡（镇）开展毒品铲除及宣传教育工作，共铲除罂粟9844株，治安处罚11人。

1991年，开展“禁贩、禁吸、禁种”专项工作，全年铲除罂粟5026株，排查吸毒、涉毒人员14人，破获毒品案件6起，治安处罚9人。

1992年4—5月，在捞村、驾欧、洞塘等乡深山中发现罂粟种植，铲除罂粟共6725株，治安处罚5人。

1993年5月3日，在荔波召开荔波、独山、平塘3县边界禁毒联合专题会议，确定通过情报交流、联合打击、主动出击、交叉打击等形式，强化3县边界禁毒协作工作机制，打击边界涉毒违法犯罪。10月23日，在立化镇平寨矿抓获毒贩4名，缴获烟毒5.5千克。

1994年5月，在捞村、翁昂边界铲除罂粟4亩12210株。

1995—1998年，全县开展禁贩、禁吸、禁种毒品工作，制定和完善工作方案，对吸毒人员按照国务院颁布的《强制戒毒办法》进行强制戒毒。10月，在玉屏镇公路检查站截获海洛因500克，抓获犯罪嫌疑人3名。1997年上半年，铲除罂粟291株，缴获海洛因1.5克。年底，发现吸毒人员52人。1998年，县公安机关开展禁毒行动2次，发放宣传资料500余份，张贴宣传标语30多条，缴获海洛因2克，统计在册吸毒人员25人，对吸毒人员均落实帮教措施。

1999年9月，成立县禁毒会。同时，成立县公安局禁毒工作大队，与刑事侦查大队合署办公，实行两块牌子、一套人员管理体制。县禁毒委会按照“三禁（禁吸、禁种、禁贩）并举，堵源截流，严格执法，标本兼治”的方针，制定禁毒工作方案。公安局禁毒工作大队连续开展围剿毒品犯罪“大行动”，在全县开展禁毒专项斗争，动员全社会参与，破获黎某某、杨某某为首的重大贩毒团伙，缴获海洛因28.6克。全年抓获贩毒人员7人，查处吸毒人员46人，缴获海洛因30克，逮捕5人，报送劳教12人。

2000—2007年，每年“6·26”国际禁毒日前后，通过报刊、广播、电视等新闻媒体及其他形式，集中开展禁毒宣传活动，特别是对在校学生进行毒品预防教育，发放《禁毒教育读本》《毒品预防教育》等书刊，增强全社会的禁毒意识。重点开展对吸毒人员的调查摸底工作，摸清吸毒人员底数，将戒毒出所的吸毒人员纳入派出所的日常性工作进行管理，开展帮教。同时，建立禁毒工作责任制，逐级签订禁毒工作责任书，实行禁毒工作目标管理，开展创建“无毒社区”活动。其间，破获各类毒品案件265起，缴获毒品海洛因等各类毒品233.31克，铲除非法种植罂粟27000余株，打击处理293人。

2008年，开展围剿毒品犯罪专项行动，破获毒品案件17起，缴获毒品152.91克。同时，采取多种形式的戒毒措施，打击吸食、注射毒品的违法行为，全年办理吸食毒品案件30起，劳动教养5人、强制戒毒3人、强制隔离戒毒12人、限期戒毒2人、社区戒毒7人、治安处罚4人。对经强制戒毒后的出所人员，由家庭、单位、常住地公安派出所及基层群众组织共同负责对其后续帮助教育，防止其复吸。对新发现的复吸者，由司法部门对其实行劳动教养，继续帮助其戒毒。

第七节　监所管理

一、监所建设

县看守所自1957年建立起，设计押量50人，设有监室11间，一直使用至2003年，位于县城城西。

2003年8月，投资1426.95万元，新建县看守所监房，新址位于玉屏镇时来沙地，占地面积25亩，监区占地面积3680平方米，活动场所1200平方米，监室960平方米，设计押量200人，监室12间，属中型所，监区等级评定为三级看守所，设卫生所、检察院驻监察室各1个。2005年9月建成投入使用。

二、生活卫生管理

对在押人员的生活管理，坚持严格执行“将上级拨付的给养费用于在押人员吃好、吃熟、吃卫生、吃足定量”的规定。从1991年11月1日起，由每人每月24元标准逐步提高，到2003年每人每月83元。

对在押人员的卫生管理，实行凡进必检制度，即对新入所在押人员进行入所5项疾病检查；驻所卫生医务工作者每天开展巡诊，发现病情及时进行诊治，每月开展一次监室卫生防疫消毒；监督在押人员按规定做好洗、晒衣物棉被及理发、洗澡等日常个人卫生，养成良好卫生习惯；督促在押人员每天坚持锻炼身体，增强体质。

三、在押人员管理

坚持“教育、感化、挽救”的方针，对新入监所人员一律依法办理收押、出所手续，按照规定进行健康检查和人身、物品安全检查。对收押新入所人员，书面或口头告知其享有的合法权益和应当遵守的监规纪律，以及被殴打、欺侮的报告方法，并在24小时内对其进行谈话教育。对新入所人员实行一个星期内进行重点观察，发现问题及时处理。张贴在押人员权利和义务制度，落实在押人员一日生活制度。对未成年在押人员，开展适合其身心特点的教育活动。在依法羁押、收押、提审、会见、出所就医、交付执行执法过程中，履行法定手续，严格按照程序办事，未发生在押人员非正常死亡、脱逃事故。

第八节　110报警服务与信息网络安全监察

一、110报警服务

2003年7月，县公安局投资30万元，建立110指挥中心，常年全天接受市民报警和救急求助，并向社会做出“有警必接、有危必帮、有险必救、严格执法、热情服务”的服务承诺。110指挥中心实行县公安局领导每周轮流带班、局机关各部门负责人每天轮流担任值班长，24小时接警制度。110接处警按一级处警、就近处警、分类处警相结合的处警原则，为群众提供安全服务。之后，县公安局巡警队成立，与城区派出所联合行动，全天候开展城市街巡逻，同时接受110指挥，及时接警处警，县城区实现“巡、防、控”一体化。

2008年12月，县政府投资100万元，在县城主城区建成城市综合管理视频监控系统，监控室设在110指挥中心，建立起110、119、120“三台合一”指挥系统，统一指挥，信息共享、资源共用。

2003—2008年，共接处警2.1万起，通过破案，为群众挽回经济损失300余万元。

二、信息网络安全监察

2002年5月，县公安局成立公共信息网络安全监察科，为股级机构。

2002—2003年，建成县公安局公安专网、公安信息网站；开展“金盾”工程建设，建成县公安局到各派出所公安网络。

2004年，开展重点单位网络安全检查38家（次），网吧安全检查45家（次），处罚网吧5家（次）；处置网上有害信息1000余条；开展全局信息化应用培训5次。是年起，开展网吧信息安全年审工作，年审网吧5家。

2005年，350兆无线通信转信台建成投入使用，实现全县公安机关扁平化、实时化指挥。开展网上舆情处置156次，删除本地有害信息1263条。

2006年，进行350兆对讲机集群选址建设和信息应用建设培训。网吧安全检查45次，处罚网吧5家，网吧信息安全年审5家，处置网上有害信息1000余条。

2007年，检查重点使用计算机单位54家，网站备案13个，网上舆情处置56次，删除有害信息1658条，落地查人6人，网吧安全检查64次，处罚网吧5家。

2008年9月，公共信息网络安全监察科升格为公共信息网络安全监察大队，为副科级机构。是年，检查重点使用计算机单位34家，网站备案6个，网上舆情处置165次，删除有害信息2650条，落地查人3人，网吧安全检查84次，处罚网吧5家。

第二章 检 察

第一节 机构与队伍建设

1978年8月，恢复重建县人民检察院，内设刑事检察科、经济检察科和办公室。1980年8月，县检察院建立检察委员会。1984年8月，县检察院设刑事检察科、经济检察科、法纪检察科和办公室。1985年，设控告申诉和监所检察科。1988年11月，在县检察院设立国家工作人员职务犯罪举报中心，与控告申诉科合署办公。1989年4月，实行侦查、批捕、起诉分离，刑事检察科分为批捕科、起诉科。1990年3月，经济检察科改称贪污贿赂检察科。至此，内设机构有6科1室。1991年，增设民事行政检察科。1997年，成立反贪污贿赂局，在政工科内设法警队。

2002年2月，在机构改革中，将审查批捕科改为侦查监督科，审查起诉科改为公诉科，法纪检察科改为渎职侵权检察科。内设办公室、政工科（含法警队）、侦查监督科、公诉科、反贪污贿赂局（副科级，内设侦查科、职务犯罪预防科、技术科）、渎职侵权检察科、监所检察科、民事行政检察科、控告申诉检察科（举报中心、刑事赔偿工作办公室）。人员编制政法编制32人，2005年增加2人。2005年12月，渎职侵权检察科改为反渎职侵权局。

2008年，县检察院内设机构不变，实有干部职工36人。其中，具有检察官职称21人；法律专业人数占干警队伍的92.7%。

1978—2008年县检察院历任检察长名录

表10－6

姓 名	性别	民族	职务	任职时间	备 注
董聚川	男	汉族	代理检察长	1978.8—1980.3	
覃兴奎	男	布依族	检察长	1980.3—1984.11	县八届人大一次会议选举
莫俊国	男	布依族	检察长	1984.11—1987.8 1990.4—1993.3	县九届人大一次会议选举；县十一届人大一次会议选举
莫树成	男	布依族	检察长	1987.8—1990.4	县十届人大一次会议选举
谭义勇	男	布依族	检察长	1993.3—1998.3 1998.3—2003.1	县十二届人大一次会议选举县十三届人大一次会议选举
罗 莎	女	汉族	检察长	2003.1—2003.3 2003.3—2004.3	2003年1月县十三届人大常委会任命代理检察长；县十四届人大一次会议选举为检察长
韦明尧	男	布依族	检察长	2004.3—2006.10	2004年3月县十四届人大常委会任命为代理检察长，同年4月县十四届人大二次会议补选为检察长
朱启松	男	布依族	检察长	2006.10—2007.3 2007.3—	2006年10月县十四届人大常委会任命为代理检察长；2007年3月县十五届人大一次会议选举为检察长

2004年8月，按照《黔南州人民检察院关于开展人民监督员试点工作实施方案》，县检察院作为全州第一批开展人民监督员制度试点工作单位，成立人民监督员制度试点工作领导小组，开展人民监督员制度试点工作，经州检察院批准，确认史晶富、杨志枰、何建飞、覃宏茂、蒙向川5人为县检察院第一任人民监督员。9月21日，在县第十四届人大常委会第十二次会议上作《荔波县人民检察院关于开展人民监督员制度试点工作专题报告》。

2005年，在开展人民监督员制度试行工作期间，经人民监督员监督评议，依法做出撤销案件决定4件。

2006年，以职务犯罪案件外部监督为重点，通过人民监督员监督，依法做出不起诉决定1件。

2008年，人民监督员对职务犯罪案件5件拟作不起诉、撤案处理和犯罪嫌疑人不服逮捕决定的“三类案件”进行审查监督，均同意县检察机关的意见。

第二节　刑事案件检察

一、案件审查批捕

1978年，全县刑事案件审查批捕工作，由县检察院刑事检察科负责办理，1979年，未受理公安机关提请逮捕案件。

1983年，按照“严打”斗争的要求，对严重危害社会的刑事犯罪分子依法从重从快打击，审查公安机关提请逮捕的犯罪嫌疑人。

1986年，刑事案件审查以重点打击走私套汇、投机倒把、制贩假药假酒、有毒食品和盗砍滥伐林木、买卖土地等犯罪嫌疑人。

1987年，围绕“压大案、反盗窃、打流氓、抓逃犯”和查禁社会丑恶现象等专项斗争开展批捕工作，全年受理公安机关报捕76人，经审查，批准逮捕71人，不批准逮捕5人。

1990年7月，到乡（镇）、村及监管场所宣讲《关于敦促犯罪分子在限期内投案自首的通告》精神，全县有8名犯罪嫌疑人投案自首，收到检举犯罪线索10件。

1997年起，对公安机关管辖案件实行立案监督。是年，对应该立案侦查而不立案侦查的4件案件，要求公安机关说明不立案的理由，经审查认为不立案侦查的理由不能成立2件。

1999年，为使案件不在批捕环节产生梗阻，对重大复杂案件提前介入6件，向公安机关发出《说明不立案理由通知书》3件，公安机关撤回2人。

自2000年后，按照“公正执法、加强监督、依法办案、从严治检、服务大局”20字工作方针开展批捕工作。

2005年，开展“青少年维权岗”活动，通过举办专题讲座等形式，做好对青少年的法治宣教、回访帮扶工作，探索预防未成年人犯罪的方法。全年受理未成年犯罪案7件9人，不批准逮捕2件3人，发出纠正违法通知书2份，追加逮捕1件1人。

2006年，侦查监督部门对诉讼违法行为提出监督纠正意见和检察建议9件（次），对侦查机关应当立案而未立案的案件依法受理和开展监督立案5件，对应当逮捕而未提请逮捕的建议追加逮捕5人，对重大案件提前介入引导侦查9件（次），要求侦查机关提供法庭审判证据意见书14件（次），报请州检察院批准延长羁押期限手续4件。

2007年，在严厉打击刑事犯罪的同时，贯彻宽严相济的刑事司法政策，受理公安机关提请复议不批准逮捕案件2件2人，经审查，依法维持原不逮捕决定2件2人。

2008年，县检察院以“打黑除恶”为重点，成立“打黑除恶”领导小组，制定实施方案，建立涉黑涉恶案件快速办理机制，制定并试行《轻罪案件刑事和解实施意见》，规范轻微刑事案件操作规程。受理立案监督5件，向侦查机关提出要求提供法庭审判证据意见书12件（次），报请州检察院延长羁押期限手续1件。

2001—2008年，立案监督51件，发出纠正违法通知28次，追诉漏犯漏罪21人。

1980—2008年刑事案件审查情况一览表

表10-7

年度	受理提请逮捕犯罪嫌疑人（人）	批准逮捕犯罪嫌疑人（人）	不批准逮捕（人）	公安机关撤回（人）
1980—1982	231	206	23	2
1983	186	166	20	—
1984	121	112	9	—
1985	67	60	7	—
1986	73	68	5	—
1987	76	71	5	—
1988	98	88	10	—
1989	79	75	4	—
1990	246	225	21	—
1991	101	97	4	—
1992	121	104	17	—
1993—1996	366	336	30	—
1997	79	68	11	—
1998	92	83	9	—
1999	76	66	8	2
2000	89	81	7	1
2001	172	142	30	—
2002	113	93	20	—
2003	118	100	12	6
2004	159	136	22	1
2005	137	110	27	—
2006	151	118	31	2
2007	100	85	4	11
2008	130	97	33	—

二、公诉

1978年，县检察机关未受理移送审查起诉案件。从1979年起，受理移送审查起诉案件。

1981—1987年间，先后对审判机关定性不准、判决不当的案件4件提出抗诉，州中级人民法院做出改判。其中，由原定终止犯罪免于刑事处罚改判有期徒刑1年的1件，由原定判处有徒刑3年处罚改判有期徒刑4年的1件，由原定有期徒刑3年改判有期徒刑1年的1件，由原定终止犯罪免于刑事处罚改判有期徒刑1年的1件。

1989年起，审查起诉工作分为批捕、起诉两个部门办理，原自侦案件侦查、批捕、起诉由自侦部门全部办理改为侦查、批捕、起诉3个部门分别办理。

1996年，在受理移送审查起诉案件中，退回补充侦查2件3人。

1997年起，按修改后的《中华人民共和国刑事诉讼法》审查起诉案件，对拟作不起诉的案件，报州检察院批准后不起诉。

1998年，受理审查起诉案件退回补充侦查5件8人。

2007年，受理审查起诉案件退回补充侦查4件4人，积存6件6人，审结率达76.92%。

2001—2008年，县检察机关出庭支持刑事案件公诉466次。

1979—2008年检察机关受理审查起诉案件情况一览表

表10－8

年度	受理审查起诉（人）	决定起诉（人）	免予起诉（人）	不起诉（人）	移送州检察院（人）	其他处理（人）
1979	56	45	—	—	—	—
1980	77	57	6	4	—	10
1981	67	51	5	7	4	—
1982	89	77	5	5	2	—
1983	194	158	19	9	8	—
1984	156	132	12	6	6	—
1985	123	97	19	7	—	—
1986	52	42	3	2	5	—
1987	103	88	9	—	6	—
1988	94	81	4	3	—	退回侦查6人
1989	95	76	9	—	—	不起诉、退回侦查10人
1990	114	96	12	—	6	—
1991	100	90	10	—	—	—
1992	—	—	—	—	—	—
1993	128	112	12	4	—	—
1994	97	97	—	—	—	—
1995	83	76	5	2	—	—
1996	99	89	4	3	—	退回侦查3人
1997	69	64	—	5	—	—
1998	74	61	—	5	—	退回侦查8人
1999	67	61	—	6	—	—
2000	87	68	—	7	4	退回侦查8人

续表10－8

年度	受理审查起诉（人）	决定起诉（人）	免予起诉（人）	不起诉（人）	移送州检察院（人）	其他处理（人）
2001	149	122	—	10	6	移送单位撤回2人、退回侦查9人
2002	88	77	—	11	—	—
2003	109	88	—	8	5	退回侦查8人
2004	149	132	—	—	—	17
2005	107	99	—	—	8	—
2006	133	106	—	—	—	27
2007	34	23	—	1	—	退回侦查4人、积存6人
2008	157	119	—	3	3	退回侦查32人、撤回起诉3人

第三节　民事行政案件检察

从1991年9月起，按照省检察院提出的“边建边干、以干促建、逐步发展”的方针，县检察院设民事行政检察科，依法对法院的民事经济审判活动和行政诉讼活动进行法律监督，对生效的民事行政判决、裁定，认为确有错误的，依法向法院提出抗诉；对正确的民事行政裁判，运用法律做好申诉人的服判息诉工作，避免产生重复申诉。2002—2008年，采用检察建议启动申诉案件再审程序。

1991—2008年民事行政案件申诉情况一览表

表10－9

年度	受理申诉案件（件）	立案（件）	抗诉（件）	息诉（件）
1991	4	—	—	—
1992	9	3	—	—
1993	8	4	—	—
1994	14	6	1	—
1995	17	8	3	—
1996	24	9	6	—
1997	21	6	3	—
1998	27	11	5	—
1999	21	5	1	20
2000	24	5	—	—
2001	24	3	1	—
2002	13	6	3	—
2003	24	6	2	—

续表10－9

年度	受理申诉案件（件）	立案（件）	抗诉（件）	息诉（件）
2004	10	4	2	6
2005	11	4	1	—
2006	6	2	—	—
2007	5	2	—	—
2008	16	8	—	8

第四节 反贪污贿赂与渎职侵权检察

一、反贪污贿赂检察

1979年开始立案侦查各种经济犯罪案件，通过办案，为国家、集体挽回经济损失。

1993年，按照中共中央反腐败斗争的统一部署，查办贪污贿赂等经济犯罪。全年立案侦查的10件案件中，贪污贿赂案3件，挪用公款案件5件，偷税抗税案件2件。

1994—1996年，重点查办党政机关、司法机关、行政执法机关和经济管理部门发生的贪污贿赂等经济犯罪案件，特别是领导干部犯罪案件。

2003年，县委成立预防职务犯罪工作领导小组，发出预防职务犯罪工作实施意见，加强反腐败斗争力度。

2007年，在查办职务犯罪工作中，开展集中查办破坏社会主义市场经济秩序渎职犯罪专项活动和治理商业贿赂专项活动。

1979—2008年反贪污贿赂案件查办情况一览表

表10－10

年度	立案侦查经济案件		为国家、集体挽回经济损失（万元）
	件数（件）	人数（人）	
1979	2	2	1
1980	7	8	7
1981—1983	13	14	13
1984	16	19	3
1985	7	8	5
1986	18	26	23
1987	11	11	19
1988	—	—	—
1989	11	13	12
1990	15	22	40
1991	7	7	8

续表10－10

年度	立案侦查经济案件		为国家、集体挽回经济损失（万元）
	件数（件）	人数（人）	
1992	9	9	9
1993	10	11	12
1994	13	13	13
1995	7	7	6
1996	8	8	18
1997—1998	13	14	20
1999—2000	13	13	26
2001	5	5	23
2002	8	8	23
2003	4	5	10
2004	6	6	29
2005	11	11	80
2006	6	6	20
2007	3	3	30
2008	3	6	50

二、反渎职侵权检察

1978—1980年，主要开展反渎职侵权法纪宣传工作。从1981年起，检察机关开始开展反渎职侵权案件检察。

1987年，针对小煤窑、小矿山无安全措施，经常发生伤亡事故的情况，县检察院法纪科会同有关部门先后派出3个工作组12人次，分别到立化、水尧、茂兰等地矿点调查了解，进行安全检查和依法办矿宣传，协助企业整顿和完善各种规章制度，促进有关部门抓好安全生产，避免渎职案件发生。

1991年，立案查处渎职侵权案件线索11件，立案查处9件12人。其中，玩忽职守案4件5人，非法拘禁案2件3人，重大责任事故案2件4人。移送起诉7件8人，不起诉4人。

1998年后，重点查办国家机关工作人员滥用职权、玩忽职守、徇私舞弊、刑讯逼供、非法拘禁等犯罪案件。

2006年，在查办案件的同时，对有关部门行政执法工作进行跟踪调查，对发现的问题发出检察建议2份。

1981—2008年反渎职侵权案件查办情况一览表

表10－11

年度	受理案件线索（件）	立案侦查		向法院起诉		免予起诉		其他处理	
		件	人	件	人	件	人	件	人
1981	3	2	4	1	1	1	2	—	1
1982	4	3	4	2	3	1	1	—	—
1983	5	3	6	—	—	—	—	—	—
1984	6	4	5	2	3	—	—	—	1
1985	12	7	12	4	7	2	3	1	2
1986	11	8	12	5	7	2	3	1	2
1987	13	11	14	8	9	1	1	—	—
1988	15	9	13	6	6	—	—	—	—
1989	8	6	8	—	—	—	—	—	—
1990	8	6	9	5	6	—	1	—	—
1991	11	9	12	7	8	—	4	—	—
1992	4	3	5	2	3	—	2	—	—
1993	6	3	3	2	2	—	1	—	—
1994	5	4	6	3	4	—	2	—	—
1995	9	6	9	4	7	—	—	1	1
1996	6	5	7	3	4	—	2	1	1
1997	6	4	6	3	4	—	—	1	1
1998	3	2	2	1	1	—	1	—	—
1999	3	1	1	—	—	—	—	—	—
2000	—	2	2	1	1	—	—	—	—
2001	2	1	2	—	—	—	—	—	—
2002	9	7	7	—	—	—	—	—	—
2003	5	1	1	1	1	—	—	—	—
2004	2	1	3	—	—	—	—	—	—
2005	—	1	2	—	—	—	—	—	—
2006	2	1	—	—	—	—	—	—	—
2007	2	1	1	1	1	—	—	—	—
2008	2	1	1	1	1	—	—	—	—

第五节　监所与控告申诉检察

一、监所检察

1985年3月，县检察院设置监所检察工作部门，开展监所检察工作。当年，配合公安机关开展看守所检查3次，到看守所上法制课2次。

1986—1992年，监所部门进行安全检查30次，为被监管人员上法制课28次，提出检察建议17次。

1993年，清理出超期羁押犯罪嫌疑人4名，经检察监督，予以纠正。1994年，对收押、释放犯罪嫌疑人进行监督，在监督中发现，公安看守所收押患有严重疾病犯罪嫌疑人2人、应送劳改而不送劳改人犯3人，发出《纠正违法通知书》1次，提出口头建议7次。

1995年11月，成立驻荔波县看守所检察室，对看守所的执法活动进行监督。在看守所安全防范检察中，发现安全隐患4处，经提出检察建议后消除隐患4处。1996年，在法定羁押期限监督中，对公安环节上超期羁押的5人、检察环节上超期羁押的2人、法院环节上超期羁押的3人，发《违法通知书》4次，提出口头建议12次。1997年，派驻看守所检察室与看守所开展共建文明监管场所活动，建立健全责任制，制定犯罪嫌疑人行为规范，加强犯罪嫌疑人法制教育。1998年，纠正应释放而未立即释放的2人，口头建议5次。

1999—2001年，与公安看守所、武警等单位召开安全防范联席会议3次，协助监管部门查监12次，纠正各种安全隐患6处；宣传“检务公开”5次；清理、纠正超期羁押，向办案机关发出纠正违法通知书、检察建议书28次、口头建议7次。

2002年，为在押人员上法治课6次，受教育300人次，做个别转化教育6次。

2003年，清理、纠正超期羁押，向办案部门发出纠正超期羁押的检察建议书2份、纠正违法通知书3份、案件催办通知书3份，发出安全防范建议书1份，协助监管部门清监、查监13次，消除安全隐患2次。是年，驻看守所检察室获最高人民检察院授予“二级规范化检察室”称号。

2005年后，将刑罚执行监督和执法活动监督作为检察工作的重点，防止超期羁押案件发生。2007年，清理出监外执行罪犯6人，及时向监管机关提出纠正和改进检察建议。

2008年，开展减刑、假释、保外就医专项检查活动，审查保外就医材料2份。对在押人员开展定期法治宣传2次，与在押人员开展教育谈话40人次。

二、控告申诉检察

1978—1984年，控告申诉检察工作无专门机构负责。从1985年起，县检察院内设控告申诉检察工作部门，开展控告申诉检察。

1986年，根据中共中央关于复查历史老案的文件精神，复查“文化大革命”以前经检察院决定免诉、不诉、不批准逮捕和不服法院判决的案件6件6人，经复查后，改变原决定2件2人。

1990年1月，重婚案件由法纪检察部门划归控告申诉检察部门办理。

1990—1992年，举报贪污、贿赂、挪用公款、假冒商标、境外存款隐瞒不报、巨额财产来源不明等7种案件线索交贪污贿赂检察部门受理。

1993—1995年，采取出动宣传车、展示案例、张贴标语、上街设点咨询、发送宣传资料等形式，宣传贯彻最高人民检察院《关于加强举报工作的决定》《奖励举报有功人员暂行办法》。1995年1月1日，《中华人民共和国国家赔偿法》正式实施后，检察院刑事赔偿案件由控告申诉部门负责办理。

1997年6月，最高人民检察院授予控告申诉监察科集体一等功1次。是年，开展“文明接待室”创建活动，控告申诉监察科举报中心接待室获最高人民检察院授予“文明接待室”称号。

1999—2001年，开展法治宣传12次，发放举报、检务公开宣传资料1000份，在咨询点接待咨询180人。2000年，控告申诉接待室再次获最高检院授予“文明接待室”称号。2001年，受理控告申诉来信来访72件，受理举报线索18件（贪污贿赂案件线索13件，侵权渎职案件线索1件，其他案件线索4件）。

2002—2004年，受理控告申诉来信来访207件、举报线索61件、刑事申诉案件线索1件。2003年控告申诉接待室第三次获最高人民检察院授予“文明接待室”称号。

2005年，控告申诉工作推行首办责任制。全年受理控告申诉来信来访41件、举报线索18件、刑事申诉案件1件。

2006年后，开展“清理赔兑未落实案件”专项行动。是年，受理控告申诉来信来访29件、举报线索12件、刑事申诉案件1件。

2007年，在持续开展的“文明接待室”创建中，控告申诉接待室第四次获最高人民检察院授予“文明接待室”称号，成为全州唯一连续获得此殊荣的检察院。全年受理控告申诉来信来访15件、举报线索7件。

2008年，开展“大接访”活动，集中排查化解重信重访，全年未发生涉检案件非法上访和进京上访。受理来信来访39件，其中，检察长接待12件30人、接转批复办结5件。办结州检察院交办的案件6件，办理县人大交办信访2件。受理举报线索2件、刑事申诉案件2件，全部审查处理。

第三章 法 院

第一节 机 构

1978年，县人民法院（以下简称法院）内设机构有办公室、民事审判庭、刑事审判庭，共有工作人员15人。下辖机构有甲良人民法庭，有工作人员1人。

1979年，恢复县法院审判委员会。

1980—1981年，先后建立朝阳、茂兰和玉屏3个人民法庭，3个法庭工作人员共10人。

1982年7月，增设经济审判庭。1987年4月，设行政审判庭、执行庭。1989年，设立立案庭。1991年8月，设告诉申诉庭和政工科。1994年11月成立法警队。1997年，设立政策研究室，告诉申诉庭改为审判监督庭。2000年12月，成立执行工作局，法警队改为法警大队。2002年2月，设立书记官室。2008年5月，设监察室。

2008年年底，县法院内设机构有办公室、民事审判庭、刑事审判庭、行政审判庭、立案庭、审判监督庭、执行工作局、政工科、政策研究室、司法警察大队、书记官室、监察室，人员编制59人，实有人员53人。下辖机构有甲良、玉屏、茂兰、朝阳4个人民法庭，有工作人员共12人。

1978—2008年县法院历任院长名录

表10－12

姓 名	性别	民族	职 务	任职时间	备 注
何宪均	男	布依族	院 长	1978—1980.2	任命
				1980.3—1984.2	县八届人大一次会选举
何礼新	男	布依族	代理院长	1984.2	任命
			院 长	1984.11—1987.8	县九届人大一次会议选举
玉如敏	男	布依族	院 长	1987.8—1990.4	县十届人大一次会议选举
				1990.4—1993.3	县十一届人大一次会议选举
莫刚灿	男	布依族	代理院长	1993.3.19	县十一届人大常委会20次会议任命
			院 长	1993.4—2001.3	县十二届人大一次会议选举
张海青	男	汉族	代理院长	2001.3.16	县十三届人大常委会23次会议任命
			院 长	2001.3—2003.1	县十三届人大四次会议补选

续表10－12

姓　名	性别	民族	职　务	任职时间	备　注
余认生	男	汉族	代理院长	2003.1.22	县十三届人大常委会39次会议任命
			院　长	2003.3—2006.10	县十三届人大一次会议选举
李昌书	男	汉族	代理院长	2006.10.17	县十四届人大常委会30次会议任命
			院　长	2007.1—2008.12	县十五届人大一次会议选举

第二节　刑事案件审判

1978—1980年，刑事审判工作以打击现行刑事犯罪活动，维护社会治安秩序为头等重要任务，优先审理刑事案件。1981年，案件审判实行“依法从重从快”的方针，严惩杀人、抢劫、强奸、放火、爆炸以及其他严重破坏社会秩序的刑事犯罪分子。

1983年，执行全国人大常委会《关于严惩严重危害社会治安的犯罪分子的决定》，依法从重从快审理现行刑事案件，在审理杀人、抢劫、强奸等重大危害社会案件中，判处死刑13人、死缓4人、无期徒刑1人，判处10年以上有期徒刑8人、5年以上10年以下有期徒刑9人。1984年，坚持依法从重从快，稳、准、狠地打击刑事犯罪活动。

1990年，按照中央政法委和省、州有关“严打”指示精神以及最高人民法院《关于竭尽全力维护社会稳定的通知》，审理刑事案件。

1991年，盗窃、抢劫犯罪突出，青少年犯罪严重，并出现贩卖毒品和种植毒品原植物案件。针对青少年违法犯罪突出的问题，县法院根据最高人民法院、全国总工会、妇联、共青团中央、国家教委的联合通知，在刑事审判庭内设立少年法庭，专门审理未成年人犯罪案件。

1992年，坚持“严打”方针和宽严相济的政策，切实开展刑事审判工作。是年，判处5年以上有期徒刑20人，判处5年以下有期徒刑93人，缓刑18人，免予刑事处分3人，宣告无罪2人；退回补充侦查6件9人，建议检察院撤回起诉4件6人。

1993年，开展反盗窃、打击拐卖妇女儿童等为重点的专项斗争。

1994年，受理审结各类刑事案件中，盗窃35件48人，抢劫6件11人，抢夺1件3人，故意伤害8件9人，拐卖人口6件10人，强奸妇女6件6人，奸淫幼女3件3人，贪污4件4人，其他7件13人。判处5年以上有期徒刑的35人，判处5年以下有期徒刑的45人，拘役1人，缓刑9人，免予刑事处分的1人，退回补充侦查6人，撤诉3人，终止1人。

1995—1997年，受理案件退中，退回检察院补充侦察7人，建议撤诉9人，自诉人自动撤诉4人，驳回自诉人起诉3人，检察院撤诉3人。

1999年，受理案件中，适用普通程序审理的34件，简易程序审理的24件；在已结案件中，盗窃16件26人，抢劫11件19人，故意伤害10件13人，重婚3件6人，贪污3件3人，贩卖假币3件3人，交通肇事2件2人，贩卖毒品1件3人，强奸1件1人，其他6件12人；宣告无罪1人，驳回起诉2人，检察机关撤回起诉2人，自诉人自动撤诉2人，按撤诉处理1人。

2000年，审理未成年人犯罪2件2人。

2001年，检察机关撤诉的8人，自诉人撤诉3人，驳回自诉案件6人，中止3人。

2002年，审结盗窃24件32人，抢劫6件14人，故意伤害8件8人，强奸4件4人，交通肇事4件4人，挪用公款3件3人，非法拘禁1件3人，寻衅滋事2件3人，非法持有枪支3件3人，放火1件1人，贪污

1件1人，滥伐林木1件1人，贩毒1件1人，虐待1件1人，聚众哄抢1件1人，故意毁坏公共财物1件1人。在案件审理过程中，适用普通程序审结的案件19件29人，适用简易程序审结的案件42件51人。

2004—2005年，案件审理坚持“严打”方针，快审快结，及时予以严惩，依法严厉打击危害社会秩序和公民生命财产的犯罪活动。特别是审理3次组织几十人挖断矿山专用公路，造成煤矿严重损失的欧某聚众扰乱社会秩序犯罪案；审理潘某盗窃团伙盗窃耕牛10头犯罪案、吴某盗窃团伙盗窃耕牛8头犯罪案等，确保社会稳定。

2008年，审结危害公共安全罪15件15人，破坏社会主义市场经济秩序罪1件1人，侵犯公民人身权利、民主权利罪9件9人，侵犯财产罪34件68人，妨害社会管理秩序罪案15件16人，受理贪污受贿等职务犯罪案件1件3人，渎职罪2件3人。

1978—2008年全县刑事案件审判情况一览表

表10－13

年度	受理案件		审结	
	件数（件）	人数（人）	件数（件）	人数（人）
1978—1979	53	—	—	—
1980	42	—	39	43
1981	44	—	33	33
1982	49	—	36	42
1983	72	108	47	71
1984	99	—	95	—
1985	56	69	57	73
1986	93	—	91	126
1987	74	109	74	109
1988	72	127	72	127
1989	75	146	75	146
1990	135	289	135	289
1991	107	188	107	188
1992	—	—	95	157
1993	—	—	75	120
1994	76	107	76	107
1995	—	—	62	94
1996	—	—	87	156
1997	—	—	40	51
1998	—	—	50	71
1999	58	88	56	85
2000	67	86	67	86
2001	100	164	100	164

续表10－13

年度	受理案件		审结	
	件数（件）	人数（人）	件数（件）	人数（人）
2002	62	81	62	81
2003	—	—	66	85
2004	82	115	82	115
2005	89	111	89	111
2006	71	115	71	115
2007	52	72	52	72
2008	77	115	77	115

第三节 民商案件审判

1978—1980年，以保障全民所有制、集体所有制和个人的合法权益为民事审判工作的重点，依据民事政策、法律、法令的规定，坚持群众路线，依靠群众，调查研究，调解为主，及时审结各类民事案件。

1981—1990年，受理离婚案609件，判决离婚426件，调判不离婚183件。

1991年，所受理的案件中，婚姻家庭纠纷123件，债务纠纷34件，赔偿纠纷11件，房屋纠纷13件，继承纠纷1件，其他纠纷25件。

1994年，玉屏法庭受理县内首宗因彩色电视在保修期内出现故障的产品质量纠纷案件，在诉至法院前，当事人多次找商场负责人、消费者协会均未能解决，玉屏法庭通过向商家宣传《消费者权益保障法》《产品质量法》后，商家同意按原告的要求负责包修出现质量问题的电视机，原告表示同意，双方达成和解。

1995年，审结在全县反响较大的播尧场坝与甲算组土地侵权案、朝阳田洞的抢收稻谷案、甲良梅桃因婚姻引起的群众性抄家哄抢财物案、煤厂劳动报酬纠纷案等。

1996年年初，县法院出台《关于加强民事审判工作的有关意见》，推行一步到庭、一步到位制度，强调当事人举证，各基层法庭开展巡回审判。

1998—2000年，审理案件中，房地产、票据遗失、医疗事故纠纷、因封建迷信引发的侵权纠纷、产品质量纠纷等新类型案件出现。

2002年，受理各类民事案件，涉及企业改制、购销、借贷、农业和农村经济发展、金融等方面。

2008年，民商审判工作按照“能调则调，当判则判，调判结合，案结事了”的办案原则，注重调解，依法调解，有效化解矛盾纠纷，及时审理抚养、扶养关系纠纷、买卖合同纠纷、借款合同纠纷、劳动争议纠纷等案件，在坚持平等保护原则前提下，妥善处理调解和判决的关系。

1978—2008年民商案件审判情况一览表

表10－14

年度	受理案件（件）	审结案件（件）					
		总计	其 中				
			调解	判决	撤诉	其他	
1978—1979	—	120	—	—	—	—	
1980	144	132	—	—	—	—	
1981—1990	—	1140	909	—	—	—	
1991	207	207	130	54	—	23（含撤诉、移送有关部门）	
1992	202	197	122	52	10	13（移送有关部门）	
1993	207	202	—	—	—	—	
1994	261	253	—	—	—	—	
1995	272	264	—	—	—	—	
1996	333	392	188	108	92	4（驳回起诉）	
1997	521	510	—	—	—	—	
1998	750	—	—	—	—	—	
1999	599	572	—	—	—	—	
2000	538	536	—	—	—	—	
2001	344	329	—	—	—	—	
2002	270	262	—	—	—	—	
2003	—	260	—	—	—	—	
2004	1286	1267	—	—	—	—	
2005	396	387	—	—	—	—	
2006	260	247	—	—	—	—	
2007	372	358	—	—	—	—	
2008	634	625	351	—	109	—	

第四节 经济案件审判

1978年至1982年上半年，县法院没有专门审理经济纠纷案件审判机构，各种经济纠纷一般作为民事案件，由民事审判庭审理，国营企业与集体企业之间的经济纠纷或公私纠纷，由行政主管部门调解或仲裁。

1982年7月，设置经济审判庭，初期主要开展经济审判任务、受案范围等宣传工作，各种经济纠纷仍作为民事案件由民事审判庭审理。

1983年开始，经济审判庭按照省高院规定的案件管辖范围收受审理案件。在经济纠纷审理中发现的违法犯罪，及时移送有关部门查处。1983—1990年，审结各类经济案件300件，如期履行和执行203件。1990年，法院派专人分赴广东等地执行9件，为县乡镇企业局供销公司追回售煤款近7万元。

1991—1993年，受理案件83件，标的159.49万元，审结67件。其中，协助县民政部门收回逾期“双扶”贷款13.5万元。

1994年，县法院设立经济调解中心，对部分案件采用调解方式审结。全年受理案件18件，标的57万元，全部审结。

1995年，受理案件52件，标的221.2万元，全部审结。其中，通过普通程序审结13件，通过经济纠纷调解中心调解审结39件；为企业收回各种欠款20万元。

1996年，受理县煤炭局委托清收企业拖欠“两费”后，深入县内矿山、企业，收回欠费共70万元，为企业收回外欠款20万元。为有关厂矿、企业提出司法建议20多条，提供法律服务50余次。全年受理案件70件，标的152万元，全部审结。其中，通过督促程序审结49件，简易程序审结5件，普通程序审结16件。

1997年，受理审结各类经济纠纷案件中，有信贷、融资租赁、购销、其他债务纠纷案件和养路费案件。为有关企业、厂矿提供法律服务30余次，提出司法建议7条；为有关部门开展追欠专项服务，追回各种欠费141万元、拖欠税款3万元。

1998年，多形式、多渠道为企业和个体工商户等提供法律服务，为金融部门及养征部门开展专项收贷和清缴欠费活动，共提出司法建议20多条。1998—1999年，受理审结案件239件，标的500万元。

2000—2001年，受理案件121件，审结116件。受理县财政局和县预算外资金管理局起诉的财政信贷资金和间歇资金案件共16件，涉案170万元。

2002年，撤销经济审判庭，经济纠纷案件划归民事审判庭办理，未审结的案件5件移交民事审判庭审理。

第五节　行政案件审判

1987年4月，县法院设立行政审判庭后，在县属各单位进行宣传，并邀请县直机关领导和有关干部座谈，主动与有关部门理顺行政执法和行政诉讼的关系。是年，受理玉屏镇居民覃某不服土地管理局行政处理决定案，审理后维持土地管理局处理决定。覃某不服，提起上诉，二审撤销原判，重新处理，维护了居民的土地使用权。

1990年10月1日《行政诉讼法》实施后，县法院组织县直机关单位负责人学习。

1994年起，对行政非诉案件，依法行使审查权。是年，审理行政机关非诉申请执行案件9件，裁定准予执行4件，已超过申请执行的期限依法不予执行5件。

1995—2000年，受理行政机关非诉执行案件64件，全部执行完毕。

2002年，受理行政案件2件，即执行县政府申请执行板吉村一农户拒不履行果树补偿决定和交出土地案；播尧乡政府申请执行一农户拒不履行与乡政府签订的拆迁安置协议的房屋案。

2006年，在普法宣传活动中，利用赶集日宣传，发放《行政诉讼须知》等宣传资料500份，普及行政诉讼知识。

1987—2008年行政案件审判统计表

表10－15

年度	受理案件（件）	审结案件（件）				
		总计	维持原判	撤销行政行为	原告撤诉	驳回起诉
1987—1990	11	11	—	—	—	—
1991	7	7	2	1	1	3
1992	9	9	3	3	1	2
1993	13	13	4	1	6	2
1994	11	11	—	—	5	—
1995	11	11	1	2	3	1
1996	14	14	—	—	4	—
1997	8	8	—	—	—	—
1998	10	10	2	1	5	1
1999	14	14	—	—	—	—
2000	7	7	—	—	—	—
2001	8	8	—	—	—	—
2002	2	2	—	—	—	—
2003	7	7	2	2	3	—
2004	4	4	—	—	—	—
2005	3	3	3	—	—	—
2006	3	3	—	—	—	—
2007	2	2	—	—	—	—
2008	3	3	—	—	—	—

第六节　告诉申诉与审判监督

一、告诉申诉

1978—1990年，县法院未设置申诉信访和审判监督机构，告诉申诉来信来访工作由相关部门逐一审查，根据不同情况进行处理。

1991年8月，开展告诉申诉审判工作。是年，受理申诉信访案件286件，其中，转有关审判庭审理123件，转有关部门处理34件，直接解答咨询83件，简易调解46件。此外，根据公安机关的提请意见，经审查后对服刑罪犯裁定准予假释2人。

1992年，告诉申诉庭与执行庭合署办公，在开展执行工作的同时开展告诉申诉工作。全年受理申诉信访案件111件。其中，转有关审判庭审理16件，转有关部门处理95件。对服刑罪犯裁定准予假释2人。

1993年，受理刑事申诉案件6件、民事申诉案件6件、经济申诉案件1件，均裁决予以维持。受理假释案件7件，准许假释7人。接待群众来信来访300人次，处理来信200件。

1994—1996年，收申诉案件30件，通过审理维持26件，撤销1件。接待来信来访1353人次。受理假释案件8件，予以假释8人。提出再审2件，移送州中级人民法院1件。收减刑案件1件，准予减刑。

1997年，撤销告诉申诉审判庭，告诉申诉案件由审判监督庭办理。

二、审批监督

1997年，建立审判监督庭，至1999年收到并审结申诉案件27件，受理审结假释案件3件。接待群众来信来访1750人次。

2000年，信访工作坚持首问责任制和院长、庭长接待日制度，逢休息日与赶场天有干警值班，方便群众。2000—2008年，受理并审结申诉案件95件。2001—2004年，接待群众来信来访1337人次。其间，2003年为经济确有困难的案件当事人减交、免交、缓交诉讼费用1万余元，让经济确有困难的当事人打得起官司，并通过诉讼维护其正当权益。

2007—2008年，进行案件质量监督检查，监督审查案件1071件，编发案件质量监督检查通报24期。

第七节　案件执行

1978—1990年，县法院的执行工作采取审执合一的执行体制，对有执行事项的案件，由审理案件的业务庭同时负责执行。

1992年，经州中院批准，成立县法院驻县土管局、县矿管办、县税务局、县运管所、县稽征站执行室。11月，开展“执行月大会战”活动2次。

1993年，帮助县水电局执行红茂矿拖欠水资源费3万元，此后矿务局每月按时交纳水资源费；在尧排执行胡某故意伤害赔偿案，胡氏兄弟抗拒执行，被依法采取强制措施，既教育群众，又维护法律尊严。1995年，执行黄某房屋拆迁案，执行佳荣场坝违章建筑及甲良非法侵犯他人财产等比较有影响的案件。

1998年，撤销县法院驻县土管局、县矿管办、县税务局、县运管所、县稽征站等单位执行室。

1999年，对列为重点强制执行的128件案件，在开展大规模的执行活动中执结110件，执结率80%。

2001年，开展为期40天的执行工作大会战活动，成立领导小组，制定《荔波县人民法院关于开展执行大会战的工作安排意见》，根据案件基本情况，责任落实到人，敦促义务人履行义务。这次活动执结案件22件，其中强制执行14件、主动履行义务8件。2002年，对涉及扶养费、赡养费等案件，优先予以执行，保证申请人基本生活不受影响。对金融、借贷等案件及时予以执行。针对一些执行有一定难度的案件，采取集中统一执行等措施，提高执行效率。

2003年，试行执行听证、债权凭证登记制度，采取委托拍卖、依法搜查等措施，确保生效法律文书得到执行。如拍卖荔波县群雄有限公司骨科医院固定资产，用以偿付该公司拖欠11个案件申请人的借款220万元；依法强制拆除拒不执行土地管理部门处理决定的甲良镇梅桃村莫某非法占地建的房屋。

2006年，清理并执结旧存案件70件，执行标的118万元。

2008年，开展“规范执行行为，促进执行公正”活动，建立规范执行行为的长效机制，将“规范执行行为，促进执行公正”专项整改融入清理执行积案活动中，严防发生新的执行积案。推行“阳光执行”，及时执结案件，对有财产的但拒不执行的当事人坚决采取强制措施，提高案件执结率，保护当事人合法权益。同时，重点抓超期一年以上、部门保护主义干扰、特困群体为申请执行人、建设领域拖欠农民工工资和中止执行应当依法恢复执行等五类重点案件清理以及州人大、州法院、县委、县人大督办的案件，进行集中执行。是年，按照《全国法院执行案件信息管理系统运行管理办法（试行）》规定，建立执行案件信息系统。

1991—2008年案件执行情况表

表10－16

年度	受理执行案件（件）	执行结案（件）	执行标的（万元）	执行率（%）
1991	253	145	—	57.31
1992	223	167	24.60	74.89
1993	—	—	—	93.00
1994	—	—	23.00	80.00
1995	—	—	32.00	82.00
1996	289	266	10.00	92.04
1997	—	388	100.00	—
1998	530	492	340.00	92.83
1999	482	395	245.00	81.95
2000	105	79	298.00	75.23
2001	165	150	85.00	90.91
2002	86	82	60.00	95.35
2003	95	87	500.00	91.58
2004	156	144	385.00	92.31
2005	139	136	250.00	97.84
2006	114	110	567.00	96.49
2007	92	89	158.82	96.74
2008	127	123	742.74	96.85

第四章 司法行政

第一节 普法宣传教育

1980年11月，成立县司法局，在全县开展法律普及（以下简称普法）工作。1982—1985年，县司法局在全县开展《宪法》修改草案和《民事诉讼法》《经济合同法》《森林法》及以保护妇女儿童合法权益为重点的法律法规宣传，印发资料2798份，培训区、乡、村法制宣传骨干608人，利用宣传车、广播、电影、幻灯等形式进行宣传，受教育48万人次。同时，到机关、企事业单位、学校、乡村上法制课40场（次），办法制宣传栏27期，举办法制演讲会、座谈会等16场（次），张贴标语344条。

1986—1990年，第一个五年普法工作启动（简称"一五"普法），成立县普法领导小组，制定《荔波县普及法律常识五年规划》，分县区机关干部、企事业单位职工、乡（镇）干部职工、村干部及全体居民4个层次开展普法工作，采取广播、讲座、发放资料、集体讨论等方式进行法律知识宣传。"一五"普法期间，全县举办法制讲座26场（次），出动巡回宣传车275辆（次），解答法律咨询360人次，刊出宣传专栏66期，发放宣传资料2.35万份。

1991—1995年，实施"二五"普法，各乡（镇）和县直机关各单位成立相应的普法工作领导小组，开展普法工作。全县"二五"普法以宣传《宪法》为核心，以新《刑法》《刑事诉讼法》《婚姻法》《继承法》《妇女权益保护法》《未成年人保护法》为重点，由"一五"以普及法律常识向以提高公民的法律意识转变。同时在全县开展反"法轮功"邪教组织普法宣传。"二五"普法期间，全县出动巡回宣传车290辆（次），解答法律咨询410人（次），刊出宣传专栏115期，举办法制讲座33场（次），培训普法骨干5218名；发放各类法律法规读本1.45万本，翻印法律法规单行本8500本，自编普法辅导资料5100份，开展普法知识竞赛4次，组织全县干部、职工普法考试5次。

1996—2000年，全县实施"三五"普法，以推进依法治县为主要任务，普法和依法治理相结合，县普法依法治理领导小组利用冬季农闲时期举办乡（镇）领导干部普法培训班4期436人，召开普法工作大会3次。"三五"普法期间，各乡（镇）成立法制宣传志愿者队伍，深入到各村寨进行法制巡回宣传，解答法律咨询460人次，受教育人数达5.7万人次，出动巡回宣传车315辆（次），刊出宣传专栏130期。在每年的"综治宣传月"活动中，各乡（镇）、各部门组织上街宣传等大型法制宣传活动，发各类普法宣传资料累计15.9万份，办宣传专栏960期。

2001—2005年，实施"四五"普法。2001年9月，县委作出《关于开展依法治县的决定》，县人大作出《关于开展依法治县的决议》。全县"四五"普法的目标是"实现提高全民法律意识向提高全民法律素质的转变，实现由注重依靠行政手段管理向注重运用法律手段管理的转变"。在实施"四五"普法中，重点推进各级政府部门政务公开工作，加强基层"民主法制示范村"建设以及对中小学生进行法治教育。2004年3月，县普法依法治理办公室和教育局联合下发《关于加强全县中小学生法制教育工作的实施意见》，并为全县55所中小学聘请法治副校长。2005年，县普法依法治理与民政局联合下发《关于开展依法治村的实施意见》，全县建立民主法制示范村17个，结合全县“四在农家”（富在农家、学在农家、乐在农家、美在农家）乡村精神文明创建活动开展民主法治示范村建设。同时，组建司法律师公证、法律援助、玉屏镇、朝阳镇、茂兰镇、甲良镇、立化镇7个法治宣传志愿团，到乡（镇）、村（居）组开展法治宣传教育活动。“四五”普法期间，每年举行全县行政事业单位人员参加的大型法律知识考试，对副县级以上领导干部举行单独的法律知识考试，试卷交州普治办评改，并建立健全全县干部职工学法用法档案。2001年起，在每年全国“12・4”法制宣传日举办全县法治宣传活动。为全县副科级以上领导干部征订发放《WTO知识读本》《社会主义法制建设基本常识》《依法治国论》等读本8400本，为全县机关、企事业单位干部职工征订发放《干部法律知识读本》5600本，组织法治副校长到中小学校讲授法治教育课235场（次），举办法治讲座56场（次），出动巡回宣传车380辆（次），解答法律咨询660人次，出宣传专栏985期，发放宣传资料25.55万份。

2006年，开始实施“五五”普法，全县开展法律进机关、进乡村、进社区、进学校、进企业、进单位、进景区的“法律七进”活动。是年，县司法局、县普法依法治理建普法网，普法依法治理工作向信息化、规范化迈进。

2008年，在全县开展“学法律、讲权利、讲义务、讲责任”为主题的“一学三讲”法治宣传教育活动。

第二节　人民调解

1978—1980年，民事纠纷由县法院调解。1980年11月，恢复民事纠纷调解组织，至1981年年底，全县24个公社恢复调解委员会，116个生产大队设调解小组，753个生产队设调解员。1982年，公社改设调解领导小组，大队改设调解委员会，生产队设调解员。1984年，4区1镇配司法助理员各1名，县司法局每年集中培训调解人员。1982—1987年，培训调解人员共1332人次，1988年培训2040人次。1990年，全县乡（镇）调解领导小组26个，建立基层人民调解委员会170个（村级168个、街道2个），村民组选调解员1238人。

1996年，针对一些基层调解组织软弱涣散，对纠纷调控不力等状况，县政府发出《关于对我县人民调解组织进行规范化组织建设的通知》，茂兰、甲良、立化、玉屏、播尧、方村、驾欧、洞塘等有司法助理员的乡（镇）对基层人民调解组织进行清理整顿。

2003年3月，县委办公室、县政府办公室发出《关于贯彻〈最高人民法院、司法部关于进一步加强新时期人民调解工作的意见〉的意见的通知》，加大对人民调解工作的规范性管理。4月，县司法局根据《人民调解工作条例》的规定，对全县原有的191个人民调解组织、1678名人民调解员进行调整和充实。调整后的人民调解组织为192个，人民调解员993名，均建档立卡。

2005年，县司法局联合县法院以乡（镇）为单位，对993名新任基层人民调解员和乡（镇）干部进行分批分期培训，共发放各类培训资料8万份、各类业务书籍3000多册。是年，全县民间纠纷主要是山林、土地、婚姻家庭、经济等类型，其中山林纠纷占30%，土地纠纷占30%，婚姻家庭纠纷占13%，经济纠纷占12%，损害污染赔偿纠纷占5%，其他类型纠纷占10%。

2008年10月，县司法局制作各类调解文书印发到各基层调委会。12月，下发《人民调解员调解纠纷补贴标准和管理办法（试行）》，从2009年1月1日起执行。

2002—2008年，县司法局定期或不定期组织开展矛盾纠纷排查调处，及时掌握社会纠纷苗头和动向，把矛盾纠纷化解在基层、化解在萌芽状态，做到“小事不出村（居）、大事不出乡镇、矛盾不上交”。全县调解组织共排查各类民间纠纷4883件，调解成功4697件，调解成功率96%。

第三节 公证事务

1980年，重建荔波县公证处，为财政全额拨款的公益性机构。

1981年9月，公证处办理水尧砖厂申请的《基建工程合同》公证，这是全县第一件公证案件。10月，办理遗嘱证明书公证1件。全年办理公证案件2件。

1982年，办理公证6件，其中《房屋买卖合同》公证2件。1983年，办公证案177件，涉及基建工程合同、承包大桥新建合同、房产分割协议、支援果蔬生产合同、建筑工程合同、鸡舍合同、身份签字合同、借款合同、贷款合同、借用生产周转金合同、扶持重点户合同、建筑电影公司宿舍合同等。

1984—1985年，办理公证案件1165件。公证案件涉及鱼塘、水库、饭店、推土、原煤推销、电站、商店、门市、厂房租用、电站外线管理、临时工、建设电视输电合同、建管工程安装、借款、有偿无息借款合同等，其中有偿无息借款合同及借款类合同500余件。

1986—1989年，公证案件1062件。涉及承包荒山造林合同、百货公司招工合同、买卖房屋契约、招聘合同、租赁合同、调解协议、协议书、收养、终止承包合同、委托培训合同、还款协议、汽车租赁、财产分割、场地租赁、教师进修合同、担保合同、借款合同等。

1990—1991年，办理公证318件，主要是定向招生、聘用人员、承包、贷款等合同。

1992—1999年，公证案件3811件，主要涉及融资、租赁、转让、买卖、遗嘱、继承、赠予、收养子女等合同。其中，当事人申请撤销遗嘱书公证1件。

2000年，公证案件339件，其中，融资租赁18件，县中心贸易市场拍卖5件，养猪贷款8件，商品房预售协议14件，个人住房贷款81件，生姜生产购销合同32件，土地及房屋转让7件，其他公证174件。2001—2002年，公证案件601件。

自2003年起，公证处主要与银行合作，开展银行贷款合同公证及荔波县工矿公司办理汽车购销合同公证。全年公证1735件，其中，信用社贷款协议1204件，建设银行贷款6件，工商银行贷款39件，汽车融资贷款公证221，补偿协议公证14件，其他251件。2004—2006年，公证案件17376件。

2008年，根据省、州文件精神，县公证处改为事业单位。全年办理公证736件。其中，民事168件，主要涉及委托、继承、房屋买卖、证据保全、赠予、现场监督、声明书、遗嘱、亲属关系证明等；经济568件，主要涉及汽车贷款、公积金贷款、借款、荒山承包合同等。

1980—2008年，公证处先后配备注册执业公证员5名，公证助理员12名。

第四节 律师事务

1982年，根据《中华人民共和国律师暂行条例》，设立县法律顾问处，由县司法局工作人员负责相关业务工作。

1987年，建玉屏镇、地莪乡法律服务站。1990年，建玉屏镇、甲良区、瑶庆乡、阳凤乡、觉巩乡、翁昂乡法律服务所6个。各服务所开展民间纠纷调解、民事诉讼代理和非诉讼代理、代写法律文书、解答群众法律咨询等工作。

1989年，县法律顾问处更名为县律师事务所。至1990年，该所担任刑事案件辩护266件，代理民事案件166件，代写法律文书155件，非诉讼代理和参加调解案件5件，解答法律咨询1589人次，受聘担任4家单位常年法律顾问。

1993年、1994年，县律师事务所参加全国律师资格考试取得执业律师资格2名。

1995年，县律师事务所更名为昌言律师事务所，有注册执业律师2名、律师助理3名。2002年，昌言律师事务所通过国家司法考试获得执业律师资格1名。是年，该所有执业律师3名。

1995年起，昌言律师事务所先后接受县政府、交通局、运管所、玉屏镇政府、农村信用合作联社、人民医院、巴合煤矿、明德实业公司等53个行政机关、企事业单位、社会团体的聘请，指派律师担任常年法律顾问，为顾问单位的重大决策提供法律意见、法律论证、法律依据，代顾问单位起草、审查、修改有关法律事务文书，完善顾问单位的各项规章制度，代理顾问单位参加民事、经济、行政诉讼及仲裁、行政复议活动，代表顾问单位对外谈判等，依法维护顾问单位的合法权益。特别是担任县政府的法律顾问，县政府重大法律事务文书都经顾问律师起草、审查、修改。同时，该所组成法律顾问组，代理县政府参加诉讼、仲裁、行政复议、对外谈判、处理群体性纠纷等。

1995—2008年，昌言律师事务所办理刑事辩护案件258件、民事经济诉讼案件392件、非诉案件（含调解案件）297件，解答法律咨询2.3万人次，代写法律文书336份，为当事人挽回经济损失9000万元。

第五章 军 事

第一节 军事机构

一、人民武装部

（一）县人民武装部

1978年，县人民武装部（以下简称人武部）为军队建制，归都匀军分区领导。1979年11月，恢复县委书记兼任县人武部政委制度。1981年4月，县人武部组训科改为军事科，1983年2月又恢复为组训科。1986年7月，根据中共中央、国务院、中央军委《关于县（市）人民武装部改归地方建制有关问题的通知》精神，县人武部移交地方，改为地方建制，名称为“贵州省荔波县人民武装部”，为副县级机构，保留党的委员会，党委书记由县委书记兼任，下设军事、政工2个科和1个办公室。县人武部受县委、县政府和都匀军分区双重领导，领导班子由中共黔南州委和州政府任命。

1996年4月，根据中共中央规定，县人武部收归军队，为团级建制，职能、任务不变，仍是县委的军事工作部门和县政府的兵役机关，受都匀军分区和荔波县党政双重领导。

1979—2008年中共荔波县人武部委员会历任领导任职一览表

表10－17

职 务	姓 名	任职时间	备 注
第一书记	王 元	1979.11—1984.12	县委书记兼
	李秀振	1985.3—1990.2	县委书记兼
	王化莹	1990.2—1994.6	县委书记兼
	饶昭德	1994.6—1996.12	县委书记兼
	张仕福	1996.12—2000.10	县委书记兼
	逄焕华	2000.10—2005.12	县委书记兼
	王振金	2005.12—2008.12	县委书记兼
书 记	袁青田	1977.12—1979.12	政治委员
	李振川	1980.1—1983.6	政治委员
	何道生	1983.6—1985.10	部 长
	蒙熙林	1996.4—1999.1	政治委员
	何惠明	1999.1—2003.3	政治委员

续表10－17

职　务	姓　名	任职时间	备　注
书　记	余品烈	2003.3—2005.4	政治委员
	王安能	2005.4—2006.4	政治委员
	罗国庆	2006.4—2008.12	政治委员
副书记	袁青田	1976.10—1977.12	政治委员
	张明伦	1976.10—1978.5	部　长
	逄树萼	1977.12—1981.5	部　长
	李景松	1981.5—1982.4	部　长
	刘志远	1983.6—1985.10	政治委员
	蒙熙林	1985.10—1996.4	政治委员
	罗玉美	1996.4—1998.10	部　长
	钱明焱	1998.10—2003.3	部　长
	陈雪良	2003.3—2008.12	部　长

1978—2008年荔波县人武部历任领导任职一览表

表10－18

职　务	姓　名	任职时间	备　注
部　长	张明伦	1978.1—1978.5	1971年12月起任职
	逄树萼	1978.10—1981.3	
	李景松	1981.5—1982.4	
	何道生	1983.6—1985.10	
	王朝贵	1986.6—1996.4	
	罗玉美	1996.4—1998.10	
	钱明焱	1998.10—2003.3	
	陈雪良	2003.3—2008.12	
政治委员	袁青田	1978.1—1979.11	
	李振川	1979.11—1983.6	
	刘志远	1984.10—1985.10	
	蒙熙林	1986.6—1999.1	
	何惠明	1999.1—2003.3	
	余品烈	2003.3—2005.4	
	王安能	2005.4—2006.4	
	罗国庆	2006.4—2008.12	

续表10－18

职 务	姓 名	任职时间	备 注
副部长	欧富安	1978.1—1978.4	
	蒙育新	1979.6—1981.7	
	李景松	1980.11—1981.5	
	陈富铭	1980.11—1983.5	
	何道生	1982.2—1983.6	
	莫如高	1983.5—1985.10	
	蒙熙林	1985.8—1986.6	
	王贵明	1998.6—1999.8	
	陈雪良	2000.2—2003.3	
	傅贤能	2003.4—2004.10	
	叶良华	2004.10—2008.4	
	田兴富	2008.4—2008.12	
副政治委员	朱长荣	1978.1—1979.4 1980.11—1983.5	
	张秀启	1978.1—1981.6	
	刘志远	1983.5—1984.10	
	王朝贵	1985.11—1986.6	

（二）基层人民武装部

1978年至1984年3月，全县的区、镇、公社均设人武部。1984年4月，公社改为乡（镇），人武部设置不变。

1991年，全县乡（镇）“建并撤”完成，建立乡（镇）人武部17个，配备专职武装干部28名。

2007年，按照《贵州省县（市、区）人武部全面建设要则》规定，全县划分3个层次开展基层人武部正规化建设。各乡（镇）按规定落实单独的办公室，各种职责、图表上墙，档案资料整理规范，分3年全面实现自动化办公。

到2008年年底，全县有6个镇11个乡人民武装部，有专职武装干部17名。

二、人民武装委员会

（一）县人民武装委员会

1979年，恢复建立荔波县人民武装委员会（以下简称武委会）。县武装委员会由党委、政府、军事机关及县组织、宣传、人事、计经、财政、民政、教育、人防、共青团、工会、妇联、体育等部门负责人组成，县武委会主任由县委书记兼任。至2008年，县武委会设置不变，武委会主任则随县委书记变动及时调整。

（二）乡（镇）人民武装委员会

2005年，在各乡（镇）设立人民武装委员会，乡（镇）党委书记任乡（镇）武委会主任，乡（镇）长任乡（镇）人武部第一部长兼乡（镇）武委会副主任。至2008年，乡镇级武委会设置不变。

三、中国人民武装警察部队荔波县中队

1978年，中国人民解放军荔波县中队受都匀军分区和荔波县武装部双重领导。1982年12月整编为中国人民武装警察部队荔波县中队（以下简称武警中队），移交荔波县公安局代管并举行移交仪式，实行横纵双向领导。1983年1月，更名为“中国人民武装警察部队荔波县中队”，隶属武警黔南支队领导，但仍由荔波县公安局代管。

四、县公安消防中队

1997年8月1日，成立县公安消防大队。1998年，公安部下发《关于统一公安边防、消防、警卫对外称谓的通知》，县公安消防大队对内称中国人民武装警察部队荔波县消防大队，对外称黔南布依族苗族自治州荔波县公安消防大队。

2002年10月，县政府投资35万元建设的县公安消防大队办公楼竣工。

2003年11月，县政府发动社会各界集资27万元，购买载重6吨水罐消防车1辆，结束县消防大队没有执勤车辆的历史。

2004年，县政府划拨建设用地9亩，拨款45万元，修建县消防中队营房。之后，通过政府拨款和单位自筹，陆续投入资金进行场地硬化、围墙等附属设施建设，投入建设资金累计150万元，至2008年7月全面竣工。

2007年，县政府投入69.5万元，购置8吨消防水罐车1台、载重2吨水1吨泡沫的泡沫消防车1台。

2008年年初，县政府通过公安部消防局匹配经费8.8万元，购置价值16.6万元的多倍细水雾消防车1台，消防车数量达4台。

是年7月，县政府投入40万元，建成消防站，挂牌成立黔南州荔波县公安消防中队。与此同时，省消防总队投入60万元，为荔波县消防中队配置个人防护装备。

第二节　民兵预备役

1978年12月，对民兵组织进行整顿和调整。1981年，民兵组织调整分两批进行，主要任务是缩小组建民兵范围，压缩参加民兵的年龄，简化民兵组织层次，严格民兵的政治条件和体格条件，扩大基干民兵分布，把民兵工作制度同预备役制度、民兵工作和战时兵员动员准备工作结合起来。

1983年4月，在荔波县组建中国人民解放军昆明军区预备役第四师第十二团第三营和后勤处，以及昆明军区后勤部预备汽车三团三连。1984年，缩编为中国人民解放军都匀预备役师步兵三团三营，对原建在城关区的城关、水利两个公社的步兵七连调整到甲良区的播尧、觉巩、阳凤和地曦4个乡组建。

1984年6月，根据州委、州政府、都匀军分区《关于中国人民解放军都匀陆军预备役师布局调整的通知》，荔波县原组建步兵第三团（原步兵第十二团）第三营任务不变，撤销原编团后勤处和昆明军区后勤部预备汽车三团三连建制。7月，根据昆明军区、省军区命令对预备役部队进行调整，荔波县设都匀陆军预备役师步兵第三团三营。七连由朝阳、王蒙组建，八连由茂兰、瑶庆组建，九连由甲良、甲站乡组建，机枪连由方村乡组建，炮兵连由水尧、永康乡组建。

1988年，按照“控制发展，自然减退”的原则和“三个便于”（便于活动、便于集中、便于执行应急任务）进行合理编组，把握民兵预备役、服兵役各类人员的年龄条件，做好出入转队和登记工作。通过调查摸底、组织审查、反复核对，完成预备役师三营5个连队、24个基干民兵连、2个独立排、164个普通民兵连的组织调整工作，登记核实退伍军人108名。

1990年，根据《贵州省民兵预备役应急分队建设暂行条例》的规定，组建县民兵应急分队。在县城附近组建第一排、第二排，在肯甫组建民兵独立排兼县应急分队第三排。全县4区1镇25个乡组建应急分队。

1991年，按照省军区、都匀军分区、都匀陆军预备役师《关于在建镇并乡工作中加强民兵预备役部队建设》的指示精神，“建并撤”后，乡（镇）民兵预备役部队编制变为都匀陆军预备役师步兵第三团三营营部仍由玉屏镇和县卫生系统组建；步兵第七连由播尧乡组建，撤销该连原在阳凤乡二排的建制；步兵第八连由朝阳镇和驾欧乡（三排）组建，撤销该连在王蒙三排的建制；步兵第九连由茂兰镇和佳荣乡（三排）组建，撤销该连原在瑶麓乡的编制；机枪连由甲良镇和方村乡（三排）组建；炮连保留永康乡、水尧乡各1个排的建制，撤销该连原在永康乡的2排建制，由水利乡组建。

1994年8月，县步兵第3团3营8连（朝阳镇、驾欧乡）和2个炮兵班（水尧乡、永康乡）共131人参加成都军区组织的西南战区预备役部队师团级干部“团进攻野战阵地（实兵）战术作业军事演习”，八连立三等功1次，全连立三等功6人、获团嘉奖31人。

1996年8月，根据《中华人民共和国预备役军官法》规定，为预备役军官66人分别被授予校官和尉官军衔，并佩戴兵种符号。

2006年，成立空军雷达阵地勤务保障分队。年底，全县有民兵7963人，其中普通民兵7483人、基干民兵480人。

2008年4月，人武部组织全县17个乡（镇）51名民兵，进行为期2天的越野、射击、投弹比武竞赛，并从中选拨出3名民兵参加都匀军分区“军事三项”比武，获得总分第三名，蒙会景获个人全能第一名。7月，县人武部组织荔波“7·18”维稳处突演习，参演人员包括民兵应急分队、民兵卫勤保障分队、民兵通信分队、企业民兵等124名，动用军地车辆80余辆（次）。年末，全县有普通民兵7857人、基干民兵600人。

第三节 征 兵

1978—1987年，县人武部严格按照征兵条件征集兵员，1987年，荔波县被省政府、省军区评为连续14年无责任退兵先进单位，国防部授予“征兵工作先进单位”奖旗。

1990年，荔波县取得连续17年无责任退兵，分别被国防部、省政府、省军区评为“征兵工作先进单位”。11月，国防部、成都军区、省军区和都匀军分区四级征兵办公室负责人到荔波县检查工作。

1994年，各乡（镇）相继成立征兵工作领导小组和工作机构，工作机构分别由公安派出所、卫生院、村委会等负责人组成。配合乡（镇）人武部做好预征对象初检初审等工作。

从1996年起，按《征兵宣传提纲》规定，对17周岁的青年不再征集。

1997年，在征兵命令下达之后，乡（镇）主管领导与县兵役机构签订责任书，征兵工作进一步制度化和责任化。11月18日，省委常委、省军区政委、少将喻忠桂到荔波检查征兵工作。

2006年11月，召开全县冬季征兵工作会议，传达都匀军分区对玉屏镇在2005度被评为“州征兵工作先进单位”的通报，并表彰15个2005年度县级征兵工作先进单位。

2007年8月，利用学生军训时机，在县民族中学进行征兵工作宣传和咨询活动。征兵期间，一些往届高中毕业补习生积极要求报名参军。

2008年，结合荔波县人口少，青年外出务工多，应征青年体检合格率低，兵员征集难度大的特点，县人武部早动员、早宣传，从8月中旬开始，对县内没有考上大学的高中毕业生及各类院校毕业生进行调查摸底，确定为预征对象，发出《关于进一步抓好征兵工作有关问题的通知》，报名应征青年迅速增加。经体检，合格114人，合格率57%。合格人员中，大专4人、中专10人、高中46人（含职高12人）、初中54人；少数民族98人，占总数的85.97%。经复查后，完成征兵任务。

第四节　国防教育

1978年，县委、县政府、县人武部将全民国防教育纳入社会主义精神文明建设内容，在民兵中开展以爱国主义为中心内容的形势战备教育，开展国防教育进入工矿、机关、企事业单位及学校、农村活动。

1990年，成立县国防教育工作领导小组，由1名县委副书记任组长。

从1994年开始，每年侧重对中小学校学生进行国防历史、国防理论、国防法规、国际形势、国防知识教育。同时，进行队列训练、轻武器常识讲解，教育学生从小了解国防，热爱祖国。

1997年，成立县国防教育委员会，仍由县委副书记任主任，在县委宣传部设办公室。

2002年4月，开展《中华人民共和国国防法》颁布一周年纪念活动，组建宣传队，利用场天到乡（镇）进行宣讲，发放宣传资料2万份。此后，每年4月28日“国防教育日”开展国防教育宣传活动。

2003年后，县国防教育委员会由县委书记任主任，办公室设在县政府办公室，设专职办公室主任，具体实施全县国防教育工作。

2004年6月，组织召开国防形势报告会，全县副科级以上领导干部400余人参加。是年，荔波县被省国教委评为“2000—2004年度全民国防教育先进单位”。

2006年，为纪念红军长征胜利70周年，全县各中小学举行以“弘扬长征精神，建设美好荔波”为主题的爱国主义和国防教育演讲比赛。

2007年，将国防教育工作列入各乡（镇）、各部门年终目标考核内容，国防教育同其他工作同部署、同落实、同检查。各乡（镇）、县直机关单位成立国防教育工作领导小组，以主要领导为组长，明确1名副职抓国防教育工作。

2007年、2008年，县委、县政府、县人大常委会、县政协领导于“八一”建军节前到驻地部队开展“军事日”活动。同时，各乡（镇）、县直各单位也分期分批组织“军事日”活动，让干部职工亲身体验军事生活中接受国防教育。司法部门将《中华人民共和国国防法》《中华人民共和国国防教育法》《全民国防教育大纲》列为“五五”普法学习内容。

在历年民兵整组点验期间，利用新闻媒体对各乡（镇）民兵点验活动进行宣传报道，向受点验的民兵预备人员讲授国防知识。

每年利用县内高中新生和职业中学新生入学军事训练进行国防教育。至2008年，全县参加军训并受国防教育的学生达1万人。

第五节 拥政爱民

一、扶贫援建

1995年1—9月，筹集资金7500元，帮助永康乡尧古村完成新修公路建设，解决全村群众运输难问题。

1996年4月，为永康乡德门村筹集资金，联系贷款，引进黑山羊55只由农户放养并取得效益。

1997年4月，与团县委在甲良镇金对村举办高产优质辣椒培训班，近100人参加培训。5月，资助1000元，帮助解决翁昂乡拉内村修建人畜饮水工程资金缺口问题。6月，永康乡尧古村稻田发生虫灾，资助500元购买农药及时发给群众杀虫。

1998年，投入3400元，资助永康乡尧古村维修和架设输电线路、购买油菜种、兴建人畜饮水工程等项目。

1999年1—4月，组织民兵投入坡改梯工程，完成450亩。6月，组织瑶麓乡民兵捐献秧苗给甲良片区群众。

2002年，县公安消防大队资助玉屏镇拉岜村修建4个防火池，并配备水带、水枪、消防水桶等消防设施。

2001—2003年，资助价值2800元水泥，帮助永康乡白岩村进行村组水泥路面硬化；资助水泥10吨、资金4300元，用于永康乡尧古村人畜饮水工程建设；资助水泥10吨、资金1万元，用于洞塘乡板寨村村级建设。

2005—2007年，资助水泥4吨、资金近100万元，帮助洞塘乡板寨村修建引水工程、进村公路、鱼塘、猪圈等，并资助5000元引导1户退伍军人发展餐饮业；资助40吨水泥为玉屏镇和水尧乡部分村组修建水渠；在茂兰、立化、甲良等乡（镇）成立护林、护寨、护矿民兵分队，为群众巡逻保平安；组织民兵为19户优抚对象修建房屋57间1140平方米。

2008年，资助水泥30吨，帮助水尧乡群众建设水渠；派干部职工分3批到瑶麓乡蹲点25天，帮助种植甘蔗发展蔗糖业。

2004—2008年，资助资金7.2万元、实物折款305万元，帮助农户解决化肥、种子等物资需求。

二、抢险救灾

1996—1998年，驻荔波部队参加抢险救灾24次，出动兵力2820人次，出动车辆210辆（次）。救助和转移群众26人。向灾区捐款2900元、捐物300多件。

1999年5月，县人武部组织高炮分队民兵投入人工降雨，进行抗旱。驻军参加抢险救灾29起（其中山火21起、民房火灾8起），出动兵力800余人次，车辆60辆（次），救助和转移群众28人。全年向灾区捐款2000多元、衣物150多件。

2000年6月10日、6月21日，荔波境内连降大到暴雨，驻县部队官兵及时响应县委、县政府的号召，迅速投入抗洪抢险救灾。同年，驻军及民兵参加扑灭火灾5起（其中山火3起、民房2起），出动兵力300余人次、车辆10余台（次）。向灾区捐款4000元、衣物200余件（套）。

2001年，部队在抢险救灾中出动兵力840人次、车辆46辆（次），扑灭火灾19起（其中民房13起、山火6起），救助和转移群众57人，向灾区捐款4040元。

2002—2007年，驻荔波部队在抢险救灾中出动兵力3900人次、车辆323辆（次），扑灭火灾70起（其中民房35起、山火35起），救助和转移群众167人。6年间向灾区捐款26700元、衣物等1940

件（套）。

2008年1—2月，县人武部组织民兵参加抗冻救灾和灾后重建工作，撒防滑沙80吨，铺稻草10吨，疏通大小车辆150辆，运送、架设电杆300根，护送支援都匀燃煤100百吨，外调油料50吨，走访受灾群众16户。在此期间，成都军区第十三集团军第三十七师红军团第六连44名官兵、步兵装甲团123名官兵奉命到荔波援助抗冻抢险救灾工作（电线路抢修），完成抢险救灾任务。在省委、省政府召开的全省抗冻救灾表彰大会上，水利乡武装部部长吴树凡获省委、省政府授予一等功。

是年，驻荔波部队在抢险救灾中出动兵力6000人次、车辆70辆（次），扑灭火灾7起（其中山火3起、民房4起），救助和转移群众73人。全年向灾区捐款4.8万元、衣物300多件（套）。

第十一篇
农业　林业

1978年中共十一届三中全会以后，荔波县进行了农村经济体制改革，首先实施了家庭联产承包责任制的土地使用制度改革。从1991年开始，全县实施以工代赈农田基本建设工程项目，改善贫困山区农民群众的生产条件，发展农村经济，推进农业综合开发。2003年，开始组织申报农业产业龙头企业，2006年，制定并实施《荔波县农业产业县级龙头企业认定和运行监测管理办法（试行）》。至2008年，全县发展农业产业化经营龙头企业共15家。县农业部门组织开展农业科技活动，对各乡（镇）、村、组，开展科技宣传、咨询和培训，培训了一批农业技术干部、农民技术员、科技示范户。1980年11月，成立荔波县农业区划委员会，组织全县农业资源调查，开展农业区划工作。2000年6月成立县农村能源开发办公室后，县内农村沼气开发建设工作。荔波县的林业在1978年至2008年间，开展各种形式的植树造林，同时进行了退耕还林、石漠化治理等工程，不断加强对山林的保护和林政的管理，发展了林业保护了生态。荔波县种植业、养殖业、水利建设、农业机械全面发展，农业生产逐年增加。

第一章 农村经济体制改革

第一节 土地使用制度改革

一、家庭联产承包责任制

1978年，县内土地为生产队所有，生产队的社员集体出工，按工计分，以工分计酬。1979年，根据《中共中央关于加快农业发展若干问题的决定》《农村人民公社工作条例（试行草案）》，全县开始推行定产到组、联产计酬生产责任制。是年，全县有生产队1197个，实行以队派工生产队40个、包产到组生产队23个、包产到劳力的生产队11个、大包干到组的生产队7个、包产到户的生产队739个、包干到户的生产队377个。

1980年，生产队调整为1185个，实行以队派工的生产队1个，包产到组的生产队3个，包产到户的生产队48个，产量到田、责任到户、按产计酬的生产队2个，包干到户生产队1131个。

1984年2月，根据中共中央关于延长责任田承包期的文件精神，县委作出延长责任田承包期的决定，在稳定第一轮承包的基础上，按“增人不增地、减人不减地”的政策和“三不准”（不准将原来的承包地打乱按现有人口重新发包，不准随意打破村组〔原生产队〕土地所有关系的界限在全村范围内重新平均承包，不准任何干部在延长土地承包期工作中以权谋私、假公济私）规定，由村集体组织与农户签订包干到户承包合同，承包期延长至1997年。

二、第二轮土地承包

1997年，中共中央下发《关于进一步稳定和完善土地承包关系的通知》，荔波县委、县政府于1998年9月在玉屏镇开展第二轮土地承包试点，取得经验，11月下发《中共荔波县委、县人民政府关于稳定和完善农村土地承包关系的实施意见》，全县第二轮农村土地延期承包工作全面启动。至1999年4月30日，第二轮土地承包工作全面结束，全县颁发“土地经营权证书”32079份，填证率100%，签订率100%，入户率96%。全县承包面积11.61万亩，其中田9.70万亩、土1.91万亩。第二轮土地承包期延长至2026年。

在第二轮土地延期承包中，清理“四户一人”（死亡户、外迁户、荒芜户、农转非户、农转非人）耕地面积总计1776.05亩，涉及人数1984人。其中，死亡户57.4亩，涉及50人；外迁户111.6亩，涉及129人；农转非户198.71亩，涉及241人；农转非个人1408.34亩，涉及1564人。由村集体和农户签订招标合同面积1678.91亩，实行指定承包面积97.14亩，合同签订率100%。

第二节　农民专业合作社

2007年，《中华人民共和国农民专业合作社法》颁布实施后，荔波县加强农民专业合作社的政策与法律法规宣传，农业部门以培训、走村入户、悬挂宣传标语、发放宣传单等形式开展宣传，提高全县群众对农民专业合作社的认识和知晓率。10月，成立玉屏镇果蔬专业合作社，为县内第一个农民专业合作社。为推动农民专业合作发展，农业、工商部门从全县产业发展情况出发，到乡（镇）、村、组引导种植大户、能人、村干部等领办农民专业合作社。同时，农业部门结合农民专业合作社的产业特点，制定发展规划，开展服务工作。至2008年，全县注册的农民专业合作社有玉屏镇果蔬专业合作社、荔波县益丰源血橙专业合作社、拉岜蜜柚专业合作社、荔波县瑶山鸡养殖专业合作社、茂兰镇强民农机农民专业合作社、朝阳镇兴农果蔬专业合作社。

省级农业高效示范园——甲良方村

第二章 农业综合开发

第一节 农田基本建设

从1991年开始，全县实施以工代赈农田基本建设工程项目，改善贫困山区农民群众的生产条件，发展农村经济。项目在当年中期安排实施，第二年中期完成，并由州组织验收。

1991—1998年，全县坡改梯工程治理面积总计445595亩，其中，优质工程20091亩，合格工程425504亩。坡改梯工程新增耕地面积15342.47亩，围绕坡改梯工程植树造林4334亩。此期间，1994—1998年进行中低产田改造及恢复水毁面积4921亩。

1999—2000年，坡改梯面积5673亩，恢复水毁及中低产田土改造工程6400亩，营造高标准经果林10385亩。工程新增耕地面积114.6亩。

2001年，以工代赈坡改梯工程治理面积5728亩。其中，优质工程3372亩，合格工程776亩。完成配套水池277个。

2002年，以工代赈工程造田298亩，造经果林3840亩，改造中低产田土1100亩。

2003年，以工代赈基本农田建设治理面积5790亩，工程综合优良率为90.22%。工程新增有效农田243.5亩。

2004年，全县基本农田建设任务4800亩，配套小水池469个。工程于2004年8月至2005年4月实施，实际治理面积5525亩。

2005年，全县基本农田建设任务4000亩，配套小水池共575个。工程安排9个乡镇共19个工程点，涉及14个村，32个组，929户3482人（其中一类乡1个、一类村9个）。工程从2005年9月开始实施到2006年5月下旬结束。经验收，综合优质率为67.62%，综合良好率为20.35%。

2006年，全县基本农田建设任务1930亩，财政扶贫资金项目兴建小水池147个，兴建小山塘1座。有工程点10个，工程涉及乡（镇）8个、村10个，村民小组20个，农户1031户4135人。工程从2006年10月开始动工到2007年5月下旬竣工，实际治理面积2005亩。

2007年，全县基本农田建设任务1650亩，财政扶贫资金项目兴建小水池250个、山塘引水渠1条总长1580米，工程涉及10个乡（镇）、20个村，39个村民小组，1716户7536人，工程点26个。工程从2007年10月开始动工到2008年5月下旬竣工，实际治理面积1693亩。

2008年，全县以工代赈坡改梯工程营造茶园任务688亩，项目涉及乡（镇）1个，村1个，农户69户276人。工程从2008年8月开始动工，总投资61.06万元。其中，以工代赈资金20万元，省财政配套35万元，州级财政配套0.6万元，县级财政配套1.2万元，群众投工投劳抵资4.26万元。项目工期10个月。

第二节 农业产业化经营

2003年，根据《黔南州农业产业化州级龙头企业认定和运行监督管理办法（试行）》及州农业产业化办公室《关于在全州开展州农业产业龙头企业申报工作的紧急通知》，开始组织申报农业产业龙头企业。是年，荔波樟江天然食品有限公司通过监测，评为合格州级重点龙头企业。

2006年，制定并实施《荔波县农业产业县级龙头企业认定和运行监测管理办法（试行）》。在各乡（镇）推荐的基础上，通过评审组实地考察评议，认定全县第一批农业产业化经营县级重点龙头企业8家。

至2008年，全县发展农业产业化经营龙头企业共15家，其中州级龙头企业5家，即荔波县军华畜牧发展有限责任公司、荔波晨维生态资源开发有限责任公司、荔波县观音山种养殖示范区、贵州亚博生态开发有限责任公司、荔波县樟江天然食品有限责任公司。

第三节 农业技术培训

1978—1990年，县农业部门组织农业技术人员到各区、乡（镇）开展农业技术培训，先后举办“杂交优势制种”“良种推广”“双季稻栽培”“化学除草”“防治病虫害”“水稻宽窄行栽培”“麻类高产栽培”“果苗嫁接及移栽”“蔬菜栽培”“西瓜和芭蕉引种栽培”等各种农业技术培训班100期，参加学习人员达14488人次。

1991年后，县农业部门采取以会代训、专题培训、门诊服务、场天咨询、广播宣传、创办科技宣传栏、现场指导操作等方式，向农民传授农业实用技术。

1991年，县农业局开办农业广播电视学校，至1997年，共开办13个班、7个专业，招收学员176人，毕业115人，103人获得中专文凭，12人获得大专文凭。1991—1997年，县内举办各类农业技术培训550期，培训人数6.6万人次，发放各类技术资料11.7万份。其中，乡（镇）干部培训12期，培训360人次；农村骨干培训24期，培训人数1200人次；农民培训43期，培训7869人次；妇女培训7期，培训600人次；现场培训110期，培训7700人次。培训内容有杂交稻高产栽培、温室两段育秧、水稻半旱式栽培、再生稻培植、水稻宽窄行栽培、水稻病虫害防治、玉米育苗定向移栽、旱地分带轮作、油菜育苗移栽、水稻制种技术、绿肥种植、蔬菜栽培、果树栽培等。咨询服务2.7万人次，发放资料5万份。7年累计投入培训经费50万元，其中，县级投入2.2万元，乡（镇）级投入4.8万元。1991年至1997年创办《荔波农业》期刊，7年共出刊105期，印发5250份。

2000年，利用农业广播电视学校培训农业科技后备人才，开办中专班10个、大专班2个、农技函授班17个，招收学员共640名。全年县、乡（镇）共开展各种农业技术培训班1017期，培训人数4万人次，印发技术资料4万份。

2002年，举办技术培训班66期，培训村干部、农民技术员以及一般农民群众2.5万人次，开展技术咨询68场（次），咨询人数28536人次，印发各种技术资料3万份。

2003年，农业部门结合“3・18”科技活动日和“三下乡”活动，组织干部分赴各集市、各乡（镇）、村、组，开展科技宣传、咨询和培训，举办各种农业技术培训418期，培训人数3.2万人次。其中，行政干部210人次，农业技术干部321人次，农民技术员151人次，科技示范户456户。发放各种技术资料5万份。

2004—2005年，开展各种技术培训592期，培训4.44万人次，发放各种技术资料7.4万份。发放的资料主要有《油菜育苗技术》《稻瘟病综合防治技术要点》《绿肥栽培技术要点》《稻茬油菜免耕栽培技术要点》《蔬菜栽培技术要点》《脱毒马铃薯高产栽培技术要点》。

2007—2008年，开展以玉米育苗移栽、种桑养蚕、水稻育秧、良种、化肥知识、旱菜种植等为重点的各种农业技术培训256期，培训农民3.89万人次，发放各种技术资料和明白纸5.95万份。

第四节 农业区划

一、综合农业区划

1980年11月，成立荔波县农业区划委员会，组织全县农业资源调查，开展农业区划工作。至1985年8月，全县参加农业资源调查的干部、农经技术人员和专业技术人员221名。基本查清全县地质、土质、气候、生物、水源、矿产等自然条件、自然资源和社会经济条件，撰写专业区划报告11个、专题材料33个。编写《荔波县综合农业区划报告》，整编表格1套、1/20万图册1本。《荔波县综合农业区划》对荔波县的自然资源、农业生产现状和存在问题以及社会经济条件进行了综合评价，提出全县资源优势和开发利用这些资源的制约因素以及应采取的经济技术对策；按照因地制宜、全面规划、扬长避短、发挥优势的原则，提出全县农村经济的发展方向和战略目标，描绘全县农村经济的近期、中期和远期发展蓝图。

《荔波县综合农业区划》按地域分异规划和基本分异指标，将全县划分为5个农业区。

（一）中部低山低丘河谷稻、油、麻、畜、果、油桐、防护林区

该区位于县境中部，为东北—西南走向的樟江河岸地带。其范围包括玉屏、时来、朝阳、王蒙、瑶山、捞村6个乡（镇）共38个村255个村民小组，农业户5074户26569人，占全县农业人口的21.6%。有耕地面积（习惯亩，以下同）2.71万亩，占全县耕地面积的20.87%。其中，田1.94万亩、土0.77万亩。人均占有耕地1.02亩。耕地多分布在比较开阔的谷地上，有500亩以上坝子12个、连片3000亩以上坝子2个。该区是全县粮食主要产区之一，粮食作物有水稻、玉米、黄豆，经济作物有油菜、苎麻、红麻、辣椒、甘蔗、西瓜等。该区耕作技术、推广良种、施用化肥、栽培管理水平较高。

（二）西北部中丘河谷低中山岩溶粮、油、辣、麻、烟、牧、林区

该区位于县境西北部，与独山县和广西南丹县接壤，包括水利、方村、甲良、甲站、阳凤、播尧、地莪、觉巩、驾欧9个乡，共63个村417个村民小组，农业户9787户52278人，占全县农业人口的42.54%。有耕地面积5.44万亩，占全县耕地面积的41.96%。其中，田4.08万亩、土1.37万亩。人均占有耕地1.04亩。耕地多分布于河谷、丘陵和山谷之间，除方村田坝达千亩以上外，其余均为300亩以内的小坝。该区是全县粮食主要产区之一。

（三）东南部低中山低山强岩溶粮、林、畜、药材、席竹区

该区位于县境东南部，与广西环江县毗邻，包括永康、洞塘、翁昂3个乡共24个村156个村民小组，农业户2899户15204人，占全县农业人口的12.37%。耕地面积1.9万亩，占全县耕地面积的14.68%。其中，田1.49万亩、土0.42万亩。人均占有耕地1.25亩。

（四）东部低山河谷岩溶粮、油、煤、牧（牛）发展区

该区位于县境东部，与广西环江县相依，包括茂兰、立化、瑶麓、瑶庆、水尧5个乡共22个村137个村民小组，农业户2988户16605人，占全县农业人口的12.66%。耕地面积17912亩，占全县耕地面积的13.81%。其中，田14819亩、土3093亩。人均占有耕地1.08亩。该区耕地多分布于坡傍和山谷盆地之间。

（五）东北部中切低山低中山粮、林、牧、土特产区

该区地处县境东北部，与从江县、榕江县、三都县、广西环江县毗邻，包括佳荣、水维、岜鲜3个乡共17个村122个村民小组，农业户2258户12245人，占全县农业人口的10.85%。耕地面积11254亩，占全县耕地面积的6.68%。其中，田9225亩、土2029亩。人均占有耕地0.92亩。区内以粮食作物为主，经济作物较少。

二、农业区域开发总体规划

1992年9月，根据全国农业区划委员会的部署，县农业区划部门开始进行全县农业区域开发总体规划编制。总体规划以《荔波县综合农业区划》《第二次土壤普查》等资料为依据，在《荔波县农业后备资源调查评价报告》的基础上，于1994年12月编制完成《荔波县农业区域开发总体规划（1996—2005年）》。《荔波县农业区域开发总体规划》将全县划分为3个农业综合开发区。

（一）东部中低山岩溶粮油林牧土特产开发区

包括茂兰、立化、永康、水尧、洞塘、翁昂、瑶麓、佳荣8个乡（镇）、67个行政村、450个村民小组，有农户9395户48025人，其中农村劳动力24771人。土地面积1831128亩，其中耕地面积61248亩，占全县耕地总面积的33.5%。规划区地貌类型：北部为中山、深切低山，中部为中低山、河谷岩溶、峰丛洼地，南部为强岩溶中低山地貌。海拔大多在500～800米之间，其东北部海拔1000米以上，月亮山次峰海拔1468米，为全县地势最高点。年平均降水量1200～1600毫米，年均气温16～18℃，≥10℃的积温3500～5300℃，无霜期270～300天，农作物可以一年两熟至三熟。区内有中低产田土40620亩，有宜农荒地73220亩，宜林荒山65773亩，低产林地17033亩，未利用草地430470亩，可利用荒水面135亩。

该区土地资源丰富，人口密度低，人均占有量大，林牧及后备耕地资源丰富，是全县农业后备资源最丰裕、开发潜力最大的地区。该区在规划期内农业开发的主要任务是中低产田土改良30675亩；建设杂交玉米育种基地300亩；建设商品粮基地4个乡；建设速生用材林基地77250亩；建设酸梅生产基地20000亩；新增灌溉面积1200亩；解决700人和700头牲畜饮水困难；建设生猪基地，新增猪肉产量1400吨；建设牛羊基地；新增牛羊肉产量230吨；建设工矿区蔬菜基地1770亩。开发顺序安排为先茂兰、立化，次水尧、瑶麓，其次洞塘、永康、翁昂，再次佳荣。

（二）中部低山丘河谷粮油牧渔林果开发区

包括玉屏镇、朝阳镇、瑶山乡和捞村乡等4个乡（镇）、38个行政村、258个村民小组，有农户3817户28876人，其中农村劳动力14981人。土地总面积827035亩，占全县总面积的22.59%，其中耕地38081亩，占全县耕地面积的20.83%。该区地貌类型：中间地带为河谷丘陵，两翼为低山地，樟江河纵贯全区，地势北高南低，海拔大多在400～800米之间，最高处瑶山东缘大河岭海拔1125米，打狗河出境河面高程300米为全县最低点。年均降水量1200～1300毫米，年平均气温17～19℃，无霜期300～330天，农作物可以一年两熟至三熟。区内有中低产田土26297亩，有宜园荒山38295亩，宜林荒山22683亩，低产田92亩，低产林1585亩，未利用草地225450亩，可利用荒水面653亩。

该区土地资源较丰富，地势较为平坦，交通便利，气候温和，农业基础设施较好，发展粮食、蔬菜、水果及林业、牧业、渔业条件优越，农业开发的基础好、潜力大，是全县农业区域开发的重点区。该区在规划期内农业开发的主要任务是中低产田土改良28840亩；建立杂稻制种基地1200亩；在两个镇建设商品粮基地两个；建设优质柚和早桃基地15000亩；建设速生优质用材林基地24000亩；建设经济林基地22500亩；建设樟江防护林10500亩；解决700人和500头牲畜的饮水困难；建设生猪基地，新增猪肉产量814吨；建设牛羊基地，新增牛羊肉产量93吨；建设水产养殖基地，新增水产品产量400吨；建设城郊蔬菜基地11500亩。开发顺序安排为先玉屏、朝阳2个镇，次瑶山、捞村2个乡。

（三）西部中丘河谷低中山岩溶粮油牧林茶烟辣开发区

包括甲良镇、方村乡、播尧乡、水利乡和驾欧乡5个乡（镇）、63个行政村、483个村民小组，有农户12221户56079人，其中农村劳动力27438人。土地总面积100337亩，占全县总面积的27.4%。耕地面积83515亩，占全县耕地面积的45.67%。规划区地貌类型为河谷丘陵和低中山，岩溶出露比较集中。该区海拔大多在800～1000米之间，是全县平均海拔最高的地区，驾欧东部大路坪垭口海拔1152.7米，为该区地势最高点，方村河潜入处海拔730米，为最低点。年平均降水量1160～1300毫米，年均气温15.8～16.7℃，≥10℃积温4682～4799℃，无霜期270～280天，农作物可以一年两熟。

该区有中低产田土57638亩，占耕地面积的68.99%。有宜农荒地6110亩，宜林荒山43456亩，未利用草地116430亩，可利用荒水面322亩。该区土地资源丰富，地势开阔，因地势高而气温相对较低，但土地适种性广，有利于发展多种经营，全区越冬作物种植面积大，复种指数较高，是全县重要的粮食和经济作物产区，是县农业区域开发的次重点区。该区在规划期内农业开发的主要任务是中低产田土改良46830亩；在3个乡（镇）分别建立商品粮基地3个；建设油菜、绿肥良种繁育基地600亩；建设优质茶叶基地5000亩；建设速生优质用材林基地48750亩；建设经济林基地33750亩；新增灌溉面积4495亩；解决4400人和4200头牲畜的饮水困难；建设生猪基地，新增猪肉产量1322吨；建设牛羊基地，新增牛羊肉产量90吨。

三、区划成果利用

第一次区划完成后，县政府根据《综合农业区划》成果资料，确定经济开发方向和重点，编制绿色工程、坡改梯、中低产田土改造、造林基地、封山育林、商品牛羊基地、水利水电工程、商品粮及水果生产基地等系列规划。在实施各项规划过程中，省、州先后分配民族地区补助费472.93万元，不发达地区经费840万元，开发资金和支农周转金477.8万元，专项贴息贷款381.5万元，少边穷贷款282万元，世界银行贷款188万元，粮棉布“以工代赈”189万元，拨改贷资金250万元，“双扶”（扶贫、扶优）资金100万元。至1990年，部分农产品生产基地逐步形成，油菜、辣椒、红麻、西瓜、柑橘等具有一定批量生产能力，蔬菜、肉类、水果等基本满足市场需求。

1996年后，县委、县政府按照全县农业区域开发总体规划，调整产业结构，发展商品蔬菜生产、优质水果、优质辣椒、糖蔗种植等产业。到2008年，全县商品蔬菜生产基地发展到4.18万亩；优质水果基地发展到6万亩，其中投产面积4万亩；桑园面积达到1.246万亩；优质辣椒生产基地面积9852亩；糖蔗种植面积达3.6万亩；优质油菜推广面积达到5万亩。

第五节　农村沼气开发

2000年6月成立县农村能源开发办公室后，县内农村沼气开发建设工作起步。2001年，全县选派农民15人参加州农业局举办的全州第三期沼气技术培训班学习，获得施工合格证。同时，县农业局派技术员参加农业部在贵阳举办的沼气技术培训班学习沼气技术。是年，全县建成沼气池337口，投入点火使用303口，投入以工代赈资金20.55万元，群众自筹资金29.95万元。

2002年，全县用财政扶贫沼气项目资金建成沼气池781口，用以工代赈沼气项目资金建沼气池

418口。全县开展沼气综合利用农户508户。其中，沼液浸种560公斤，沼液喂猪860头，沼液种植蔬菜460亩，沼液喷施果树108亩，沼肥养鱼23亩。2003年，全县农村建成沼气池1073口，其中点火使用668口。

2004年，将翁昂乡拉内村、甲良镇洞庭村建成沼气生态示范村。拉内村建沼气池121户，进行“三改”（即改圈、改厕、改厨）配套建设120户，“三改”率达到99.2%。洞庭村建成沼气池104户，进行“三改”配套建设101户，占建池户的97.1%。是年，“三沼”（水稻沼液、玉米沼液、蔬菜沼液）综合利用推广面积10766亩。其中，水稻沼液浸种5155公斤，涉及建池户1836户，推广种植面积5155亩；玉米沼液浸种2026公斤，涉及建池户824户，推广种植面积1013亩；蔬菜沼液种植面积2180亩，涉及建池户1123户；果树沼肥综合利用2300亩，涉及农户910户；沼液喂猪28头，涉及农户21户；沼肥养鱼118亩，涉及农户47户。全县2010户建成沼气池。其中，建成池641户，“三改”配套1369户。

2005年，全县实施国债沼气项目建设任务1540户，分别在8个乡（镇）的16个村实施，实际完成1243户；实施省沼气五期项目任务1090户，分别在5个乡（镇）的7个村实施，实际完成612户；实施国家农业发展沼气项目任务180户，主要在玉屏镇的时来、菜园、水春3个村实施，实际完成180户，完成“三改”配套建设180户。

2006年，全县建成沼气池1886口，“三改”配套完成1083户。在建成的1886口沼气池中，属于2005年国债沼气项目任务1550户，在甲良、播尧2个乡（镇）的9个村实施，实际建成沼气池1500口，“三改”配套913户；属于省沼六期项目任务150户，在佳荣镇全部建成，“三改”配套64户；属于沼气“双改”扶贫项目任务100户，在洞塘乡木朝村实施，全部建成，完成“三改”配套建设100户。亚行技援配套沼气项目任务200口，在朝阳镇八烂村、驾欧乡新街村和永康乡尧古村以及洞塘乡木朝村实施，实际建成136口，完成“三改”配套建设100户。

是年，在朝阳、驾欧、甲良、播尧设“三沼”综合利用服务点5个实施“三沼”综合利用项目，推广水稻沼液浸种2653公斤，面积2653亩；玉米沼液浸种1572公斤，面积1048亩；沼肥种菜2241亩；沼液种果1320亩；沼液种马铃薯100亩；沼肥喂鱼面积203亩，沼液喂猪307头。

2007年，全县建沼气池2213口，改厕795户，改圈540户，改厨881户。沼肥使用面积8370亩，其中，水稻沼液浸种3100公斤，推广面积3100亩；玉米沼液浸种2250公斤，推广面积1510亩；沼肥种菜2110亩；沼液种果1500亩；沼肥种洋芋150亩；沼肥喂鱼面积418亩；沼液喂猪361头。

2008年，新建乡、村级农村沼气后续服务网点29个，购置沼气后续服务抽液抽渣车3辆、抽渣泵29台、红分线分析仪29台和一批零配件发至各网点。是年，全县建成沼气池1497口，改厕364户，改圈183户，改厨441户。水稻沼液浸种3100公斤，推广面积3100亩；玉米沼液浸种2000公斤，推广面积1353亩；沼肥种菜2560亩，沼肥种果2193亩，沼肥种马铃薯260亩；沼肥喂鱼面积495亩，沼肥喂猪420头。

第三章 种植业

第一节 粮食作物

境内种植的粮食作物主要有水稻、玉米、小麦、荞子、豆类、红薯、马铃薯等。水稻、玉米为大季作物，小麦等为小季作物。

一、品种

（一）水稻

水稻为境内主栽秋收粮食作物，一般为一年一熟或两熟。栽培品种较多，分为籼稻、粳稻、糯稻3种类型，杂交水稻为推广良种。1978—1990年，推广的杂交水稻主要有引进的浙丽1号、地优桂23号、高粱糯、76选、汕优63、D优63、明灰63等品种。随着杂稻种植面积逐年扩大，除粳稻、糯稻以外，杂稻品种取代籼稻品种，到1990年，杂稻种植面积占全县水稻栽插面积的74.7%。

1991年，以“汕优63”为主要品种，是年推广杂稻种94.5吨，1992—1997年，先后引进汕优28、冈优12、汕优多分、特优63、冈优22、K优5号、威优467、协优63等进行示范栽培，经反复试种对比，至1997年，全县共推广杂交水稻良种9种，以汕优63、冈优22、冈优12、Ⅱ优63为当家品种。其中，汕优63适应性强，产量高，质量好。

1998年，全县推广杂交水稻种125吨，品种有冈优22、汕优63、Ⅱ优838、Ⅱ优501、K优5号、金优63、协优63、D优63、威优467等。

2000年，全县推广杂交水稻种130吨，品种主要有冈优22、冈优725、冈优12、汕优63、协优63、K优5号、Ⅱ优501共7种，其中冈优系列占总品种的70%。

2005年，推广的杂稻品种主要有金优63、D优527、协优63、冈优527、冈优725、中九优85、宜香99E-4、富优1号、陆两优106等。

2006—2008年，全县推广杂交水稻种累计334.1吨，连续推广2～3年的品种主要有冈优527、中优85、冈优725、宜香99E-4、D优527、B优827、准两优527、金优725、金优527、协优57、Q优6号等。此外，2006年还推广冈优22、金优117、金优6号、中优7号、冈优608、宜香3003、金优431等品种，2007年新推广协优527、内香优9号、中优177号等品种，2008年新推广T优300、金香优830、川江优527等品种。

（二）玉米

玉米在境内俗称苞谷，为境内主栽秋季作物，在粮食生产中次于水稻。玉米种植为一年一熟，因茬口安排不同分为“早苞谷”“晚苞谷”。杂交玉米为推广良种。

1979年，在甲良和播尧进行杂交玉米制种。1983年，推广杂交玉米种子957公斤。1987年，推广杂交玉米9405.5公斤，主要有中单2号3046公斤、丹玉13号4041.5公斤、南顶1号1568公斤、兴玉1号750公斤，种植面积19994亩，占玉米播种面积的17.31%。

1991年，推广杂交玉米中单2号14960公斤。是年，在茂兰镇洞流村进行杂交玉米制种211亩，制种失败。1992年，引进推广京杂6号种子8271.5公斤、农大60种子900公斤、掖单13种子510公斤。首次引进紧凑型玉米掖单13号，试种成功。1993年，推广掖单13号4550公斤、掖单1号480公斤、农大60号7500公斤。

1995年，引进良种90-1、试201、郑单12、试117、农大60等平展型品种与8001×340、1243、9318、掖单13（CK）等紧凑型玉米进行品比试验，结果为农大60和8001×340效益好，有推广价值。

1997年，推广杂交玉米种30吨，品种以中单2号、掖单13、贵毕303、京杂6号为主，除有部分糯玉米、本地玉米、马牙苞谷外，大部分常规品种被杂交品种代替。

1999年，推广的杂交玉米品种有掖单13号、贵毕303、贵毕302、兴黄单、中单2号、中单9409等。

2000年，县农技站在茂兰镇洞流村进行杂交玉米新组合品比试验，参试品种有贵毕302、贵毕303、农大3138、农大108、剑试1号、海禾1号、中单2号、川单15、黔2609、黔9501与掖单13对照。试验结论：在所有供试品种中，产量都比对照品种掖单13号高，且增产幅度较大，特别是剑试1号，产量高达每亩553公斤，抗性较好，可向高产肥水区进一步推广示范，充分掌握其适应性及稳定性再作推广；品种中单2号建议逐年减少推广；农大108、农大3138可作示范推广，但有早衰现象；农大108后期叶片发红，种植上要注意中后期增施钾肥。

2001年，全县杂交玉米推广面积30507.2亩，占玉米种植面积的93.2%，经测产验收，平均亩产259.32公斤。

2005年，推广的杂交玉米主要品种组合有正大619、临奥1号、登海3号、遵玉3号、正红6号、东单60、农大108、农大3138、西山21等。

2008年，推广的杂交玉米品种组合有正红6号、正大619、遵玉3号等67个品种，推广面积10155.59亩。

（三）小麦

小麦在境内西北部甲良片区种植较多，其他地方种植较少，品种更换少。1980年以后，引进的阿夫、绵阳11号逐步取代其他品种。1991年，杂交小麦种子推广1050公斤。1992年，推广4050公斤，品种为川麦10号。1993年，推广670公斤。1994年、1995年未引进新品种。1996年，引进2400公斤。此后，因未选好品种，小麦产量低，土壤肥料消耗量大，种植小麦的农户少，小麦品种推广更新较慢，到2008年，县内很少引进小麦新品种。

（四）马铃薯

马铃薯在境内俗称洋芋。1978—1998年，县内长期种植本地常规老品种，产量低，种植面积较小，主要作为蔬菜食用。1999年，调整农业产业结构，引进坝薯9号、坝薯10号、中甸红、会-2号等脱毒马铃薯良种50吨，进行试种，种植面积400亩。其中，甲良镇150亩，佳荣镇100亩，驾欧乡150亩。经测产验收，平均亩产1176.32公斤，比本地品种平均亩产增产407.9公斤。由于种植脱毒马铃薯效益明显，2000年，从贵州省农科院引进中甸红40吨、会-2号20吨，在玉屏、朝阳、水利、瑶山等地推广。2002年，引进脱毒马铃薯品种，推广种植面积5498亩。2007年，引进费乌瑞它进行试种，效果较好。2008年，脱毒马铃薯费乌瑞它种植面积达到8306亩，占全县马铃薯种植面积的91.3%。

（五）其他粮食作物

大豆、红薯、大麦、小米、荞子等粮食作物在县内均有种植，除大豆种植面积较大外，其他几种作物种植面积较小，以本地品种为主，群众自由串换。

二、种植

粮食作物是县内的主要农作物，按收获季节分为秋粮和夏粮，夏粮有小麦、大麦、马铃薯等，秋粮有水稻、玉米、大豆、红薯、小米等。

1978年，在全县推广湿润育秧2300亩，用种量115吨；推广湿润秧田加盖薄膜108.8亩，用种量3550公斤；温室育秧用种3834公斤。3种育秧栽插2万亩，占水稻田面积的20%。是年，全县粮食作物种植面积16.73万亩，总产29896.2吨，平均亩产178.7公斤。其中，夏粮播种面积2.61万亩，产量847.7吨；秋粮播种面积14.12万亩，产量29048.5吨。1980年后，推广杂交水稻和杂交玉米良种，推广湿润育秧、湿润秧田加盖薄膜、温室育秧等育秧技术，改进栽培方式，粮食产量逐年增长。1988年，推广水稻半旱式栽培81亩。1989年，推广两段育秧技术。1990年，建两段育秧温室855个，用种3420公斤，移栽面积4542亩。是年，全县粮食总产量39824吨，亩产277.4公斤。

2000年，全县粮食作物实收面积15.87万亩，总产量50144吨。其中，夏粮实收面积1.17万亩，总产1042吨；秋粮实收面积14.7万亩，总产49148吨。2006年，全县粮食作物播种面积171500亩，总产量57700吨。其中，夏粮产量3100吨，平均亩产336.44公斤，比1978年和1990年分别增产157.74公斤和59.04公斤。

2008年，全县粮食作物播种面积16.45万亩，粮食总产量59927.2吨。其中，夏粮总产量2546.3吨，秋粮总产量57380.9吨。

1978—2008年主要粮食作物播种面积及产量统计表

表11－1 单位：亩、吨

年度	水稻		玉米		大豆		小麦		红薯		马铃薯	
	面积	产量	面积	产量	面积	产量	面积	产量	面积	产量	面积	产量
1978	141199	25455	20602	2430	8157	500	24844	890	1654	135	116	10
1979	101424	29965	19994	2110	6319	265	21765	605	1167	105	66	10
1980	98015	29959	21120	2612	7214	433	4079	141	1752	153	122	8
1981	96490	18645	16575	1794	7548	369	3897	182	1750	179	216	33
1982	99937	29783	17143	1999	7272	378	4725	232	1689	181	186	22
1983	99958	31850	17706	2102	7859	414	4344	214	1130	110	208	12
1984	99676	33413	17928	2233	9531	548	3839	185	1728	116	263	17
1985	99266	21335	17380	1992	9257	499	3850	182	1749	151	388	23
1986	94414	30088	20115	2899	9743	636	4742	283	3514	280	623	70
1987	98524	33217	22359	3101	8524	477	4117	264	3882	327	691	82
1988	98907	29950	20330	2884	8262	392	4305	262	3302	5668	567	61
1989	98512	30884	20400	3029	10227	502	6032	287	4118	409	338	60
1990	99189	35250	21277	3156	8905	367	7362	381	4301	442	954	120
1991	99272	35466	23078	3359	8728	284	6200	414	4460	362	1390	288
1992	99033	30470	22226	3037	8377	196	6161	502	3631	282	1788	277
1993	98295	37031	23850	4012	8970	417	6405	372	5025	462	780	136

续表11－1

年度	水稻		玉米		大豆		小麦		红薯		马铃薯	
	面积	产量	面积	产量	面积	产量	面积	产量	面积	产量	面积	产量
1994	—	36115	—	5050	—	662	—	638	—	—	—	—
1995	98340	37128	24195	5057	10080	779	8940	1033	—	—	—	—
1996	—	38414	—	5592	—	926	—	730	—	—	—	—
1997	—	40487	—	5628	—	669	—	769	—	—	—	—
1998	—	41299	—	6975	—	731	—	814	—	—	—	—
1999	9463	31092	3190	7261	1013	935	500	292	2492	186	400	28
2000	6608	39258	2013	8557	941	944	540	692	715	1103	398	501
2001	97046	40632	30507	8670	13948	844	7322	677	10611	1378	5840	537
2002	95804	29256	26300	8670	12405	789	7694	728	6825	1036	5498	543
2003	94991	37637	23850	7355	10595	695	7274	759	9460	1256	7499	930
2004	94054	39802	28943	9401	9055	603	6462	703	6215	1022	9075	1135
2005	91095	40623	31040	10156	10817	842	6126	653	6278	749	11289	1769
2006	94451	41101	34320	11019	10605	858	5449	587	7242	1454	11025	1932
2007	89160	41345	32777	11337	9962	1021	3286	800	4385	1511	12337	1471
2008	95214	43696	30359	10822	9247	855	4567	811	6191	1660	8306	1429

第二节 经济作物

县内经济作物主要有油菜、蔬菜、水果、桑树、甘蔗等。

一、油菜

油菜是县内主要油料作物，以稻田种植为主。1978—1981年，县内种植的油菜品种（含本地）十余种。1982年，引进西南302、72-2、72-4、贵油3号。1983年，引进黔油9号、怀油819品种。在全县播种油菜总面积中，黔油23、胜利油菜、安徽大花占95％以上。1988年，在时来村进行万油17号、秦油2号、西南302、中油821共4个品种对比试验，面积3亩。试验结果为万油17号亩产214公斤，中油821亩产191公斤，秦油2号亩产162公斤，西南302产量最低。1990年，中油821播种面积9915亩，其他品种有云油7号、云油8号、定油1号、西南302。

1990年，农业部门引进油菜育苗移栽技术试种获得成功。县委、县政府对该项技术引起重视，1991年，将油菜育苗移栽作为全县冬季农业重点项目安排落实，与各乡（镇）签订责任状，办示范点，油菜育苗移栽推广面积2万亩，占油菜种植面积的37.5％，油菜单产显著提高。此后，油菜育苗移栽面积和油菜单产逐年增加。1991年，以中油821、万油17为主要品种，配有定油1号、云油7号、黔油9号等品种。1992年，从黔南州种子公司引进蜀杂1号种子150公斤进行推广。1994年，引进油研5号、油研7号840公斤进行推广，效益较好，后继续推广。1997年，油菜栽种以油研5号、油研7号为主，配有群众自留的万油17号等。油菜育苗移栽推广面积4.5万亩，占油菜种植面积的

85.4%。油菜籽年总产量由1991年的2690吨增到1997年的3683吨，年均递增5.27%。2000年，全县油菜实收面积5.41万亩，总产量4067吨。2001年，推广的油菜品种主要有油研5号、油研7号、杂选1号。2005年，全县油菜收获面积5.5万亩，总产量5433吨。2007年，推广的品种有油研7号、油研9号、油研10号、油研11号、黔油14号、黔油16号、黔油20号，以油研7号、油研10号为主。2008年，主要推广黔油14号、油研11号、贵杂4号、中油6303等品种，油菜总产量3838吨，比上年减1606.8吨，减29.5%。

二、蔬菜

县内种植的蔬菜品种主要有白菜、牛皮菜、莲花白、青菜、花菜、莴笋、芹菜、萝卜、胡萝卜、韭菜、番茄、辣椒、西葫芦、南瓜、茄子、豇豆、四季豆、大蒜、洋葱、黄瓜、生姜、芋头、八月豆、篱笆豆、菠菜、豌豆、胡豆、冬瓜、丝瓜、苦瓜、佛手瓜、山药、水芋等，白菜品种以山东系列为主，萝卜以短叶13、南畔洲等为主，辣椒以甲良皱皮线椒、湘研系列为主。

（一）辣椒

县内各地均有辣椒种植，以甲良、播尧、地莪、方村等地为多，且质量上乘。

1978—1990年，县内种植的辣椒品种有4种，以素有“椒中之王”美称的甲良皱皮辣椒为多，其次是小青辣和菜辣。其间，1980年，播种面积3171亩，总产量179.2吨。1985年，播种面积4423亩，总产量300.3吨。1990年，全县种植3797亩，总产192.2吨。

1991年以后，随着蔬菜产业的发展，辣椒品种逐渐丰富，以湘研系列1-9号、洛椒系列等为主，早熟、中熟、晚熟品种相互搭配，辣椒品种增加到18个，菜辣椒成为县城近郊的主栽品种，种植面积120亩。

1993年，全县辣椒种植6410亩，仅甲良、播尧、方村3个乡（镇）就有4200多亩，占种植总面积的65.5%。在玉屏镇，城郊群众选用早熟抗病高产良种，采用地膜覆盖栽培技术种植辣椒，面积不断扩大，1997年种植面积330亩，产品供应水尧、立化、茂兰、佳荣等矿区，销往独山、都匀等地。

2000年，县内种植的菜辣椒以湘研系列为主，主要有湘研1号、湘研9号。

2003年，方村、甲良、播尧种植小皱皮辣椒面积5000亩，产鲜椒300吨，实现产值54万元。菜用辣椒种植面积304亩，主要分布在玉屏、茂兰、朝阳、瑶山、水尧、水利、永康等乡（镇）。

2005年，全县实施优质辣椒种植6300亩，其中蔬菜用辣椒种植面积849亩。品种以洛椒系列为主，主要有洛椒4号、洛椒8号。

2008年，围绕州委、州政府提出的“甲良线椒要融入以独山为主的全州10万亩优质线椒生产圈”的整体思路，县内以播尧、方村、甲良为主，推广优质辣椒种植面积7120亩，比2007年增加2827亩，增长4.2%。其中，甲良3035亩，方村2135亩，播尧1950亩。品种以辣丰3号、辣丰5号两个线椒型品种为主。

（二）荔波水蕨菜

荔波水蕨菜，系蹄盖蕨科菜蕨属多年生草本植物，其植株高达0.5米左右，根状茎粗壮，直立或斜生，木质呈深紫色，枝叶簇生其上，叶柄刚硬，叶片形态随植株成长而改变，幼龄期为一回羽状复叶，成熟期变为二回羽状复叶，小羽片长约5～15厘米，孢子囊群线形、褐色，沿叶缘斜生。

荔波野生水蕨菜自然分布于荔波樟江河谷和喀斯特山区的低海拔的山谷溪边、河岸冲积沙地及石灰岩洞口隐蔽潮湿的地方。荔波水蕨菜是由野生水蕨菜经人工驯化栽培所得，1993年县农业局在玉屏镇菜园村进行了水蕨菜的人工驯化栽培试验，经过多年的摸索和总结，逐渐掌握了野生水蕨菜人工栽培、种苗繁育、田间管理、采收包装、大棚种植等技术，2004年开始由玉屏镇果蔬专业合作社进行小规模生产示范，之后种植规模逐渐扩大，2008年荔波水蕨菜种植面积1000亩，年产量100万公斤以上，产品主要销往贵阳、重庆、湖南等地市场。

荔波水蕨菜于每年的3—10月采收上市，上市周期长，可重复采摘。其薛苔或嫩叶均可食用，可炒食、凉拌、做汤，烹制方便，加工后颜色仍保翠绿，味道独特、鲜美、清香可口，深受大众喜爱。荔波水蕨菜还具有清热解毒、健胃之功效，维生素C含量较为丰富，品质上乘，是可食蕨类中独具特色的蔬菜品种，属一级蔬菜的范畴。

（三）其他蔬菜

1978年，在县城南门菜园建蔬菜专业队1个，解决县城居民蔬菜供应问题。其他边远地区利用园地种蔬菜，以自食为主，少量出售。1985年，开始引进高产良种和先进种植管理技术，培育早熟蔬菜。县委、县政府提出"稳粮增菜"的经济发展战略，即在樟江沿河一带，在保证粮食总产稳定增长的前提下，面向北边县（市）市场，发展早熟蔬菜种植。1988年，邀请贵州农科院蔬菜专家李桂莲到荔波传授早熟蔬菜栽培技术，早熟蔬菜产业得到发展，到1995年，形成以玉屏镇为中心，向朝阳方向发展的早熟蔬菜生产基地及形成蔬菜产、运、销产业化雏形。1997年，早熟蔬菜种植面积2117亩，蔬菜栽培采用地膜覆盖栽培、地膜加小拱棚栽培、大棚栽培、破季节蔬菜栽培等新技术，蔬菜淡旺逐步得到调节，品种多样化。1998年，全县早熟蔬菜栽培面积2816亩。其中，地膜覆盖栽培2578亩，中、大棚栽培10.5亩，双膜小拱棚227.5亩；优质蔬菜种植面积1899亩，总产量3949吨，平均亩产2080公斤，亩产值1840元。

2000年，早熟蔬菜栽培面积增加到3580亩，平均亩产增加到2250公斤，总产量达到8055吨，远销广东省、广西壮族自治区，贵阳市以及凯里、怀化、独山、三都、福泉、贵定、都匀等周边县（市），荔波成为全省第二大早熟蔬菜生产基地，蔬菜种植成为全县中部和北部乡（镇）农村的优势产业。

2005年，全县早熟蔬菜种植种类主要有茄果类、瓜类、豆类和菜用糯玉米等。其中，种植面积超过1000亩的有番茄、四季豆、豇豆和瓜类。年末，全县商品蔬菜生产面积达32400亩，总产量56070吨。

2008年，全县蔬菜种植面积发展到51400亩。其中，商品蔬菜41800亩，占全县蔬菜种植面积的81.32%。在商品蔬菜生产中，冬春菜种植面积22700亩，夏秋菜种植面积19100亩，总产量58600吨。种植种类主要有番茄、大蒜、辣椒、茄子、四季豆、豇豆、西葫芦、南瓜、黄瓜等。

此外，县内群众喜食野生水蕨菜。水蕨菜自然生长在樟江河谷和喀斯特山区低海拔山谷溪边、河岸冲积沙地及石灰岩洞口阴暗潮湿等地。随着荔波旅游业的发展，稀少的野生水蕨菜满足不了市场需求。1993年后，县农业局在玉屏镇菜园村进行水蕨菜人工栽培试验，逐渐掌握野生水蕨菜人工栽培、种苗繁殖、田间管理技术。2004年，由玉屏镇果蔬专业合作社进行水蕨菜小规模生产示范，之后种植规模逐渐扩大。

三、水果

荔波县种植水果历史悠久，品种主要有荔波蜜柚、荔波血桃、荔波枇杷、荔波酸梅、梨、李、葡萄、芭蕉、西瓜、香瓜、柿子及柑橘类的橙、椪柑等，其中以本地优良品种荔波蜜柚、荔波血桃、荔波枇杷、荔波酸梅最为著名。荔波蜜柚、荔波血桃、荔波枇杷、李、橙、椪柑主要分布在玉屏、朝阳等樟江沿河一带及水利；荔波酸梅主要分布在洞塘、翁昂、永康；梨、柿、板栗分布在樟江沿河的其他地区。

1978年起，荔波当地农民简单地从本地品种的荔波蜜柚、荔波血桃、荔波枇杷等品种获取实生苗进行种植，荔波水果种植面积缓慢增加，当时没有面积统计。到1988年，成立荔波县果树蔬菜管理站（荔波县果蔬公司）后，其技术人员开始从本地优良品种的荔波蜜柚、荔波血桃、荔波枇杷筛选出优良单株，建立果苗基地，培育优良本地品种水果苗，实施规模种植。同时引进一些柑橘、橙、梨等其他新品种进行试种成功后，并引进水果苗嫁接技术，建立果苗基地，培育苗木。并且采取改造低产果园和发展万亩果园基地等措施，使果园面积和水果产量逐年上升。改造荔波蜜柚低产果园120亩，水果总产量2650吨。1989年，全县果园面积8039亩，荔波蜜柚6496亩，荔波血桃380亩，荔波枇杷165亩，其他柑橘类513亩，梨185亩，李220亩，葡萄30亩，芭蕉50亩。1990年，采取以苗作贷和无偿发放果树苗40万株给农户栽植等措施发展水果生产，到年底，全县果园面积累计1.4万亩，水果产量2830吨。1991年，种植荔波蜜柚、橘、橙6725亩，荔波血桃2400亩。次年，水尧乡一果农引进苹果种植成功。1993年，县农业局果蔬公司从广西引进沙田柚到荔波试种成功，到1996年开始挂果。1996年，县委、县政府决定开发县内非耕地资源，发展绿色产业，并投入资金以苗作贷发展果树生产，在全县建设万亩沙田柚基地，鼓励群众、干部及各单位种植果树。以荔波蜜柚作为授粉树种植，同时从外地引进先进的栽培管理技术，挂果后，在同样栽培管理条件下荔波蜜柚的表现比沙田柚好，1997年果园开始采取高接换种，1998—2000年，全县近2万亩沙田柚高接换种为荔波蜜柚。

（一）荔波蜜柚

荔波蜜柚是贵州省的名特优水果品种。属芸香科、柑橘亚族、柑橘属。树势：树冠圆头形，树势强，枝条开张下垂。树叶：枝叶茂密，叶片大，长卵圆形，叶经揉后无刺激性味道。花：花多为总状花序或穗状花序，花序带叶或不带叶，以无叶花序居多，亦有少数着生于结果母枝叶腋或顶端的单花，每花序的花量一般1—20朵。果：果形倒卵圆形，果肩圆尖，果面淡黄色，纵径横径比为15.5：16；果大，单果重1500—2500克；皮较薄，平均厚0.7—0.9厘米；囊瓣大，果肉饱满、柔嫩多汁、化渣、酸甜适度、香气浓郁，每100毫升果汁含糖8—11克，酸0.73—1.0克，维生素C48.93—51.98毫克，可溶性固形物10.7—13.6克，可食部分68%左右。

荔波蜜柚一年可抽梢3—4次，春梢为结果母枝，荔波蜜柚花芽分化期在9—12月，盛花期为4月上旬至中旬，幼果膨大期为5—6月，果实彭大期为7—8月，果实充实期为9月，果实开始成熟期为9月底至10月上旬；品质最佳期为10月中旬至11月中旬。

荔波蜜柚富含维生素C以及镁、钙、铜、铁、铝、钛、锰、钒、磷、氯等十多种矿物质营养元素，有“性平，味甘微酸，具有消食和胃，理气化痰，生津止渴”的性能，对气滞腹胀、痰多色白、咳嗽喉痒、消化不良、便秘、醒酒解毒等都有显著疗效。荔波蜜柚肉含有类似胰岛素成分，有降血糖功效，极有益于糖尿病、心血管病患者。荔波蜜柚有白肉、红肉、黄肉等种类，红肉汁胞呈色色素为番茄红素和β胡萝卜素。

荔波蜜柚外形浑圆，象征团圆之意，所以也是中秋节的应景水果。更重要的是柚子的“柚”和庇佑的“佑”同音，柚子即佑子，被人们认为有吉祥的含义，过年的时候吃柚子象征着金玉满堂，柚和“有”谐音，是大柚大有的意思，有着除去霉运带来来年好运势的寓意。

荔波蜜柚品质优良，分别荣获1997年全国早熟柚类评比优质奖、1998年全国第五次柚类评比金杯奖；1999年参加全国柑橘品种结构调整战略研讨会暨柑橘特优新品种展示会上被评为柑橘品种结构调整推荐品种。荔波蜜柚主要分布于低海拔高热地区的玉屏、朝阳、瑶山、捞村等地，2008年年底，荔波蜜柚种植面积达14570亩，产量8520吨。

荔波蜜柚有潜在的广阔市场。荔波蜜柚甜酸适口、化渣、味芳香品质优，深受消费者青睐。荔波蜜柚9月底开始成熟，挂在树上可到次年1月，采收后经简易包装可储存4—5个月。荔波蜜柚耐运输、销售周期长、风险性小，近年来有贵阳市都匀、凯里、遵义等省内县（市）和重庆、柳州等省外直辖市、地级市客商到荔波县抢购荔波蜜柚，果品市场供不应求，外部市场极其广阔。荔波蜜柚不仅是美食果品，而且是令人仰慕的天然保健食品，素有“天然水果罐头”之美称。

（二）荔波血桃

荔波血桃是贵州省的名特优水果品种。属蔷薇科、桃属植物，落叶乔木。树势：树冠宽广而平展；树皮暗红褐色，老时粗糙呈鳞片状。枝叶：小枝细长，无毛，有光泽，绿色，向阳处转变成红色，具大量小皮孔；冬芽圆锥形，顶端钝，外被短柔毛，常2～3个簇生，中间为叶芽，两侧为花芽；叶片长圆披针形、椭圆披针形或倒卵状披针形，先端渐尖，基部宽楔形，上面无毛，下面在脉腋间具少数短柔毛或无毛，叶边具细锯齿或粗锯齿，齿端具腺体或无腺体；叶柄粗壮，常具一枚至数枚腺体，有时无腺体。花：花红色鲜艳，花单生，先于叶开放，直径2.5～3.5厘米；花梗极短或几无梗；萼筒钟形，被短柔毛，稀几无毛，绿色而具红色斑点；萼片卵形至长圆形，顶端圆钝，外被短柔毛；花瓣长圆状椭圆形至宽倒卵形，粉红色，罕为白色；雄蕊约20～30枚，花药绯红色；花柱几与雄蕊等长或稍短；子房被短柔毛。果：果实形状和大小均有变异，卵形、宽椭圆形或扁圆形，长几与宽相等，其果实大、近圆形、色泽鲜艳、离核、口感爽脆、清香味甜、果肉鲜红、故命名为“荔波血桃”。

荔波血桃盛花期为3月上旬至中旬，幼果膨大期为4月下旬至5月上旬，果实彭大期为5月中旬至5月下旬，果实成熟期为5月底至6月上旬。

荔波血桃味甘酸，性温，有生津润肠、活血消积、丰肌美肤作用，果肉中富含蛋白质、脂肪、糖、钙、磷、铁和维生素B、维生素C及大量的水分，对慢性支气管炎、支气管扩张症、肺纤维化、肺不张、矽肺、肺结核等出现的干咳、咯血、慢性发热、盗汗等症，可起到养阴生津、补气润肺的保健作用。

荔波血桃主要分布于玉屏、朝阳、瑶山、水尧等乡（镇）。1991年全县种植面积2000余亩，1995年全县种植面积3000余亩，到2008年年底，全县种植面积已达6210亩，年产量为620吨左右。

荔波血桃品质优、成熟早，5月中下旬开始上市，上市期正值市场新鲜水果短缺，外地客商纷纷慕名前来购买，产品主要销往贵阳市及都匀、凯里等省内县（市）和广西壮族自治区的南宁市、柳州市等省外市场，市场供不应求。

（三）荔波枇杷

荔波枇杷是贵州省的名特优水果品种。蔷薇科、枇杷属植物。树势：常绿小乔木，高可达10米。枝叶：小枝粗壮，黄褐色，密生锈色或灰棕色绒毛；叶片革质，披针形、倒披针形、倒卵形或椭圆长圆形，长12—30厘米，宽3—9厘米，先端急尖或渐尖，基部楔形或渐狭成叶柄，上部边缘有疏锯齿，基部全缘，上面光亮，多皱，下面密生灰棕色绒毛，侧脉11—21对；叶柄短或几无柄，长6—10毫米，有灰棕色绒毛；托叶钻形，长1—1.5厘米，先端急尖，有毛。果：果实球形或长圆形，直径2—5厘米，黄色或橘黄色，外有锈色柔毛，不久脱落；种子1—5粒，球形或扁球形，直径1—1.5厘米，褐色，光亮，种皮纸质。

荔波枇杷花期从9月底至12月下旬，花期较长；幼果膨大期为1月下旬至2月上旬，果实彭大期为2月中旬至4月下旬，果实成熟期为3月底至5月中旬。

荔波枇杷品质优，营养丰富，其主要成分有糖类（葡萄糖、果糖和蔗糖）、蛋白质、脂肪、纤维素、果胶、胡萝卜素、鞣质、苹果酸、柠檬酸、钾、磷、铁、钙以及维生素A、B、C等。胡萝卜素含量十分丰富，并含有人体所必需的8种氨基酸。荔波枇杷果实有润肺、止咳、止渴、和胃的功效。荔波枇杷除了鲜吃外，枇杷肉还可以制成糖水罐头，或酿酒。荔波枇杷不论是叶、果和核都含有扁桃苷。荔波枇杷叶亦是中药的一种，以大块枇杷叶晒干入药，有清肺胃热，降气化痰的功用，常与其他药材制成“枇杷膏”。荔波枇杷中含有丰富的维生素B，对保护视力、保持皮肤健康润泽，促进儿童的身体发育都有着十分重要的作用。

荔波枇杷主要分布于玉屏、朝阳、瑶山、立化等乡（镇）。1989年全县种植面积165亩，1995年全县种植面积约560亩，到2008年年底，全县种植面积已达1360亩，年产量为82吨左右。

荔波枇杷品质优，成熟早，4月上旬开始成熟，5月上中旬为成熟盛期，上市期正值市场新鲜水果短缺，外地客商纷纷慕名前来购买，产品主要销往贵阳市及都匀、凯里等省内省外县（市）和广西壮族自治区的南宁市、柳州市等省外市场，市场供不应求。

四、桑

瑶山瑶族群众有种桑养蚕的传统，但都是自产自销，规模小，没有推向商品市场。

2004年，县内部分农户自发小面积引种、试种、试养桑蚕获成功，开始发展桑蚕产业，品种有沙伦109、桂桑优12、桂桑优62。2006年10月，县委、县政府为推动该产业发展，成立县桑蚕产业发展办公室，设在县农业局，明确专人负责，给予经费支持。2007年，桑园面积发展到17000亩，种桑养蚕户6348户，蚕种发放量25883张，鲜茧产量1044吨。2008年，部分农户转产改种县内新产业品种甘蔗，桑园面积下降到12640亩，有种桑养蚕户4380户，蚕种发放量21583张，鲜茧产量886吨。

五、麻

县内麻类有青麻、红麻2种。1978年，以种植青麻为主。

1979年，从广西引进红麻种，在玉屏、时来、朝阳试种成功，当年收精麻381.8吨。为解决种子问题，从广西聘请麻农作留种技术指导。1982年，进行青麻种子直播118亩，获得成功，亩产精麻29.2公斤；红麻留种254.8亩，收种子3350公斤。1983年，引进红麻种黔红1号、青皮13号。是年，留种581.9亩，收种子18.6吨，平均单产35.7公斤。1978—1986年，红麻种植年均2779.9亩，年均产量343.3吨。

1987—1990年，红麻产品市场购销不稳定，农户种植面积波动大，1987年种植面积下降到545亩，总产103吨，1989年恢复种植面积3453亩，总产295.3吨，1990年种植面积又下降到500亩，总产29吨。青麻也因市场价格低，1990年的种植面积仅232亩，总产11.2吨。此后，青麻、红麻因市场销售不畅，县内较少种植。

六、甘蔗

甘蔗曾在城关、时来、朝阳、王蒙、捞村、翁昂、洞塘等地农户中自主零星栽种，零星出售，无面积产量统计。

2005年，温热条件好的洞塘、立化、捞村3个乡（镇）的群众自发种植糖蔗，面积仅几十亩，到2007年发展为近万亩。3个乡（镇）种植的糖蔗品种主要以台糖16为主。2007年，捞村乡测产最高亩产9吨，平均亩产5.8吨。2008年，全县糖蔗种植面积25851亩，加上2007年的宿根蔗1万亩，糖蔗种植面积35851亩，种植涉及17个乡（镇）、91个行政村、525个村民小组、农户11002户，有连片种植50亩以上的种植点126个，面积13027.95亩，占种植总面积的34.9%。

七、其他经济作物

（一）花生

花生在县内每年都有零星种植，以瑶麓花生最有名，香脆可口，但产量低，种植面积小。

（二）烟叶

县内种植的烟叶分土烟和烤烟两种，以烤烟为主。1986年，在甲良、播尧组织指导农户种植烤烟83亩，1988年发展到1641亩。由于烘烤技术差、烤烟质量低、价格低，1990年种植面积下降到264亩。1991年后，烘烤技术得到提高，烤烟价格提升，种植面积逐年增加。1996年，从瓮安聘请烟农到播尧乡指导当地烟农和到当地承包土地种植烤烟，烤烟面积扩大，1997年种植面积4000亩。因烘烤技术存在的问题没有得到彻底解决，烤烟种植面积又逐年下降。至2008年，全县烤烟种植面积仅245亩。

（三）西瓜

1987年，在城郊时来坝种植西瓜27亩。之后，西瓜种植由时来坝发展到南门坝、坡平、罗家寨。1997年，种植面积1350亩。后因西瓜与早熟蔬菜争地，西瓜种植向拉鱼、福利、朝阳的吉毛方向转移。2004年，全县西瓜种植面积315亩，总产量614吨。2006年，普通西瓜种植面积470亩，袖珍西瓜种植面积3亩，总产量924.2吨。2008年，普通西瓜种植面积520亩，袖珍西瓜种植面积10亩，总产量1060吨。

第三节　耕作制度

一、水田耕作

1978—1983年，县内为提高耕地利用率和单位面积产量，水稻田推行稻—麦、稻—油、稻—菜两熟制。1983年，推广稻田多熟制，由县农技站和城关（玉屏区）农技站配合，在时来乡进行稻田多熟制试验，选用菜（蔬菜）—瓜（西瓜）—稻组合结构，试验面积10.6亩，经过现场验收，第一熟收白菜17500公斤，第二熟收西瓜19000公斤，第三熟收水稻5565公斤。试验成功后，1984年推广面积120亩，到1990年，稻田多熟制推广面积11500亩。其间，1989年有11个村42个村民小组进行四熟制耕作，采取菜—菜—瓜—稻四熟制，即秋季种白菜，冬季种莲花白，春季种西瓜，夏季种水稻。

海拔较高的地区仍采用稻—麦或稻—油两熟制，仍有翻犁炕冬，水稻一熟制情况存在。

至2005年，全县推广稻田多熟制12000亩，主要分布在玉屏、朝阳、瑶山、茂兰、甲良、水尧、永康等乡（镇），采用瓜—稻—菜、菜—稻—菜、苞—稻—菜多熟耕作。

二、旱地耕作

一般推行一年两熟，即玉米—油菜、玉米—荞子、玉米—大麦（或小麦），同时套种豆类、红薯、南瓜等。甲良地区多为一年三熟（玉米—荞子—油菜）。1991年，推广旱地分带轮作2530亩。之后，旱地分带轮作逐渐减少。

三、复种指数

1980年后，农村开展集约经营，提高单位面积产量。1985年，复种指数为148.7%，1990年提高到150%，2006年上升到152%。之后，复种指数逐渐降低。

四、中低产田土改良

1981—1986年，全县有中低产田82800亩，占稻田总面积的82.87%，其中冷田、烂田、锈田13400亩，占稻田13.5%；有中低产旱地28100亩，占旱地面积93.56%。1981—1990年，采取开沟排水，降低地下水位，提高水温和土温，选用高产糯稻品种，合理密植，增加群体结构等措施，对中低产田土进行改造43128亩。其中，1990年的中低产田改造，主要是种植绿肥10300亩，增施有机肥

7500亩，秸秆还田7000亩，改造冷田、烂田、锈田50亩。

1991年，绿肥种植推广18800亩，其中专用绿肥800亩、兼用绿肥18000亩。1998年，秸秆还田17200亩，绿肥翻压还田800亩，坡改梯工程9998亩，恢复水田2094亩。1999年，全县秸秆还田61750亩，绿肥翻压还田450亩，坡改梯工程10700亩，土变田2100亩。2001年，秸秆还田72900亩，绿肥翻压3500亩，以工代赈坡改梯工程4630亩，土变田7330亩，耕作措施改良1680亩。2002年，秸秆还田87000亩，绿肥翻压还田3800亩，工程措施改良9200亩，耕作措施改良1700亩，实施沃土工程15300亩。2005年，绿肥翻压还田30100亩，秸秆还田95400亩。2008年，秸秆还田53000亩。

第四节　植物保护与检疫

一、植物保护

县内植物保护主要是病虫害防治、草害防治、鼠害防治。

（一）农作物病虫害防治

对水稻、蔬菜、果树等作物采取防治措施较多，油菜次之，其他作物因发生面积较小或危害较轻，很少防治或不防治。农作物病虫害防治，按照“预防为主、综合防治、防治结合”的植保方针，采取物理防治、耕作防治、化学防治方式进行防治。物理防治即人工捕捉、放鸭灭虫；耕作防治即选用抗病虫品种，间作轮作；化学防治即采用杀虫剂、杀菌剂。杀虫剂有甲胺磷、敌敌畏、氧化乐果、灭扫利、噻嗪啶、杀虫王、灭虫王、扑虱灵等，杀菌剂有稻瘟净、三环唑、叶枯宁、甲基托布津、代森锌、代森锰锌、硫酸铜等。在病虫害发生时期，县植保站及时发出病虫害预测预报，各乡（镇）农业科技人员根据病虫害发生情况，组织群众进行防治，并开展病虫防治技术培训和病虫防治咨询服务，做好相应农药供应，到田间地头作病虫害防治技术指导。

1978—1987年，全县每年平均发生病虫害面积62600亩，平均每年防治48900亩，占年发生数的78.12%。病虫害最严重的1985年达86600亩，最低1979年42100亩。

1988年，水稻病虫发生面积5万亩，虫害主要有稻飞虱、三化螟、稻纵卷叶螟、稻蓟马、负泥虫、稻苞虫，病害主要有稻瘟病、稻曲病、纹枯病，防治面积91400亩（次）。测报主要利用黑光灯、白炽灯、诱蛾器等工具对迁飞性害虫和境内越冬虫进行诱测，对稻飞虱和黏虫进行系统监测。全年发出病虫情报10期，虫情交流11期。

1989年，全县病虫害发生面积79000亩，占栽插面积10万亩的7.9%，防治面积7万亩，占发生面积的88.6%，挽回粮食损失1050吨。全年发水稻病虫情报8期，其他作物病虫简报3期。

1990年，县内稻飞虱、稻纵卷叶螟大面积发生，省、州先后调进农药23吨，防治面积63500亩，挽回粮食损失3275吨。

1992年，开展油菜菌核病监测、稻飞虱虫源性质观察、稻飞虱天敌调查，进行油菜、小麦主要病虫发生情况监测。1993年，全县稻田综合防治面积2200亩，挽回粮食损失1000吨。1994年，进行油菜病虫综合防治，以时来大坝为主，建立综合样板田500亩，带动全县油菜综合防治11250亩。

1995年，开展稻飞虱监测与综合治理面积57000亩，办样板点7个面积共1000亩，通过防治挽回粮食损失2380.3吨。以穗颈瘟为主的稻瘟病综合防治面积58000亩，办示范点7个，挽回粮食1374.4吨。玉米病虫综合防治实施面积1万亩。

1996年，对稻飞虱和水稻、玉米主要病虫害的监测治理，根据监测，白背飞虱主害代为3代，发生程度为大发生，面积57000亩；褐飞虱为5代，发生程度中等偏重，发生面积3万亩，防治面积86000亩，挽回损失1148吨。在水稻、玉米病虫害发生期发出病虫情报14期，张贴宣传防治告示12次，办黑板报12期，举办防治技术培训班17期。油菜蚜虫综合防治面积24300亩，挽回经济损失70万元。

1997年，选择有代表性的甲良、方村、朝阳、茂兰等乡（镇）作为辅助测报点。全年发出病虫情报19期共1140份，预报准确率达90%以上；开展技术培训342期，培训人数1.71万人次，发放各种技术资料7000余份，利用场天开展咨询服务，咨询人数4万人次。年内，水稻病虫害发生157000亩（次），防治面积168000亩（次）。

1998年，将稻飞虱列为系统测报对象，稻纵卷叶螟、三化螟、稻瘟病、玉米螟、油菜蚜虫、小麦锈病等病虫作为一般测报对象。全年开展技术培训368期，培训人数2.95万人次，印发各种技术资料2000份，场天咨询312期，广播宣传5次。水稻病虫害发生155500亩（次），防治面积147000亩（次），挽回损失1703.5吨。

1999年，发出病虫简报20期，开展技术培训15期，培训人数750人次，印发资料1000份，开展咨询服务470场（次），咨询人数4700人次。

2000年，县农业局与各乡（镇）签订责任状，成立稻瘟病综合防治领导小组和技术实施小组，并拨出专项资金，新建甲良、玉屏、朝阳、茂兰辅助测报站4个和村级农情信息网点169个。各乡（镇）示范点面积共8500亩。同时，成立植保服务队，对方村坝、花堤坝、茂兰坝、南门坝等地进行联防联治。在分蘖期、破口期、齐穗期无偿发放施稻灵4600瓶、三环唑1.6万包。县、乡两级拨出专项资金41.7万元，购进三环唑17吨，背负式喷雾器3000台，实施稻瘟病综合防治面积88200亩。

2001年，玉屏、甲良、朝阳、茂兰辅助测报站反馈病虫信息40次，村级农情信息员反馈病虫信息301次，县植保站发出《病虫情报》26期共1560份，县内病虫测报准确率达80%以上。2002年，全县稻瘟病综合防治4万亩，通过防治换回粮食损失2484吨。

2003年，水稻病虫害发生面积174000亩，防治面积179500亩，防治率达103.16%，挽回损失2622.5吨；玉米病虫害发生面积66000亩，防治面积30400亩，防治率46.1%，挽回损失108.5吨；油菜病虫害发生面积50200亩，防治面积23600亩，防治率47%，挽回损失85.5吨。

2005年、2007年，稻瘟病综合防治面积分别为58000亩、42000亩。

2008年，受连续降雨天气影响，稻纵卷叶螟、稻飞虱和黏虫大量迁入荔波，对水稻、甘蔗、玉米生产构成严重威胁，县农业部门启动《荔波县水稻、玉米重大病虫害防治预案》，成立农作物病虫害防治服务队4个，到各乡（镇）开展病虫害防治。是年，全县水稻稻瘟病综合防治面积45000亩。

（二）草害防治

县内危害农作物严重的杂草有10科21种，危害较为严重的有5种。从1982年开始推广化学除草技术，稻田除草主要选用黔南州植保站监制的除草剂，旱地除草选用品种有乙酰胺、农达、克无踪等。

由于化学除草技术具有省工、省力、节约成本、见效快等特点，受群众欢迎，化学除草成为全县重点农业推广项目得到推广，推广面积逐年扩大。1988年，全县稻田化学除草35000亩，1989年上升到40100亩，防除效果达85%。1990年，推广稻田化学除草面积达46000亩。

1992年，开始推广旱地化学除草300亩。1993—1995年，稻田、旱地化学除草推广面积不断扩大，稻田化学除草面积由1993年的55000亩提高到1995年的8万亩，旱地化学除草面积由1993年的1568亩提高到1995年1850亩。1997—1999年，全县实施稻田化学除草面积分别为73000亩、61500

亩、65000亩，旱地化学除草分别为11300亩、11500亩、15000亩。

2001—2008年，全县稻田化学除草面积保持在75000～78000亩之间，油菜、玉米旱地化学除草面积推广由2001年的22500亩上升到2008年的3万亩。

（三）鼠害防治

1978年后，鼠害防治工作逐渐得到重视。1988年，全县有6个乡开展灭鼠工作，参加灭鼠的农户2800户，印发灭鼠技术资料1600份，农田灭鼠投鼠药28.5公斤，灭鼠2.54万只。

1991年，全县农田灭鼠面积1万亩。1995年，农田鼠害防治16000亩，挽回稻谷损失638吨。1997年，实施农田灭鼠的农户12000户，农田灭鼠面积12000亩。

1998年，农田灭鼠13000亩，灭鼠效果达83.7％。1999—2001年，分春、秋两季灭鼠，灭鼠面积累计48000亩。2002年，农田灭鼠2万亩，挽回粮食损失480吨，防治效果80.84％。

2004年，全县农田鼠害中等偏轻发生，个别地区偏重发生，发生面积共40500亩，化学防治面积2万亩，其中春季灭鼠12000亩，秋季灭鼠8000亩，挽回损失428吨。

2005—2007年，全县每年农田鼠害中等发生，发生面积最小为2006年7万亩，面积最大为2007年107000亩。防治面积最大为2007年56000亩，防治效果为81.8%～85%。

2008年，全县鼠害发生面积123000亩，分春秋两季组织农户3.1万户进行鼠害综合防治，防治面积总计7万亩。农田防治效果为86.8%，住宅户防治效果78.4%，挽回粮食损失1600.3吨。

二、植物检疫

1978—1984年，县内无植保检疫机构，检疫工作由黔南州植检机构负责。1985年，县农业部门开始配备植检员。1986年，对柑橘溃疡病进行普查，检查苗木果树6.16万株，发现病株3.54万株。1987年，检查柑橘苗木30亩86.69万株，烧毁病株7.52万株。之后，继续对曾发生过柑橘溃疡病的果园进行跟踪复查。

1990年，全县发生大面积柑橘溃疡病，焚烧病柑橘苗7.5万株。1993年，因全县发生大面积水稻白叶枯病等疫病害，植保检疫工作逐渐引起重视，配植物检疫员3名，开展全县各类农作物病虫害的检疫工作。

2000年，对樟江蜜柚、椪柑、脐橙的种苗繁殖基地4个和杂交稻制种基地1个进行注册登记，蔬菜检疫200亩，对20个不同作物的美洲斑潜叶蝇进行普查2100亩，杂交稻种调运检疫42.9吨，复检“两杂”良种56.94吨，市场检疫25批次。

2001年，注册登记种苗基地4个，面积1306亩；申报办理“种苗繁育植物检疫登记证”2份，开具产地检疫证3份；实施蔬菜、水果调运检疫共12批次50吨；对全县水果、花卉、蔬菜种子批发销售经营户进行登记注册14户；市场检疫35场（次），检查水果、菜种等100吨；开展植物检疫有关法规宣传咨询31场（次），咨询人数8020人次，印发资料5690份。

2002年，注册登记种苗繁育4户，开具产地检疫证2份，调运检疫307批次150吨，开具调运检疫证书3份，市场检疫36批次155吨。

2003年，办理产地检疫注册登记证4份、产地检疫合格证9份，市场检疫55批次，调运检疫68批次，开调运检疫证书12份。

2004年，注册登记种苗繁育户10户，面积共298.5亩，主要有杂稻制种和柑橘、李子、桃子、梨子、花卉、观赏苗木繁育等。全年开展临田调查53批次，面积36000亩，办理产地检疫合格证7份。市场检疫水果、蔬菜等62批次共558吨、果苗11万株。调运检疫78批次。

2006年，办理产地检疫注册登记证3份、产地检疫合格证8份。市场检疫61批次，检查水果蔬菜916吨、果苗15.5万株。省内调运检疫“两杂”种子7批次共258.7吨，省间调运检疫2批次，品种主要有玉米种子15吨、花卉0.14万株。年内查处“两杂”种子违章案件3件，数量11.79吨，补检5次，罚款共计2550元。

2007年，开展植物产地检疫24批（次），共2.52万株，开具产地检疫合格证2份；开展调运检疫110批次329.8吨，开具省内调运检疫证书2份。查处违章调运“两杂”种子案件2件共13630公斤，补检2次。

2008年，全县检疫备案种子274.9吨；办理种苗繁育基地登记4个，面积55亩；开具省内调运检疫证书2份。

第四章 养殖业

第一节 畜禽饲养

县内畜禽饲养以牛、马、猪、羊、鸡、鸭、鹅为主，有本地品种与引进品种之分，农户饲养的畜禽以本地品种为主。

一、畜类

（一）牛

1.水牛　境内水牛系亚洲沼泽型地方品种，属役用型，少数有缺陷或老、残水牛才被淘汰育肥作肉用。水牛全身毛色多为深灰色或浅灰色，皮肤呈青灰色。在捞村、翁昂等地尚有少量白毛水牛分布，皮肤呈粉红色并有黑色素斑块。水牛分布在低热河谷及丘陵有坝子田较多的地带，是县内农业的主要生产资料，一般一头成年水牛日耕稻板田2亩。从1978年后，全县年末存栏数均在2万头以上，占大牲畜存栏数的60%，存栏最多为2005年3.8万头。成年水牛一般体重370公斤以上。2008年年末，全县水牛存栏21714头。

2.黄牛　境内黄牛系地方品种，属西南黄牛类，也是农业生产的主要生产资料，主要分布在低中山、低山丘陵山坡梯田旱地较多的农村。黄牛特点是适应性强，耐粗放，成熟早，体躯矮小，体质结实，行走灵活，宜山地耕作，日耕板田1亩左右。成年公牛一般体重270公斤，成年母牛一般体重216公斤，除役用外，也有少量作肉用。引进牛品种有黑白花奶牛、西门塔尔、利木赞、安格斯和夏洛莱。这些品种的成年公牛体重800～1200公斤，母牛体重650～800公斤。引进品种黄牛生长速度较快，日均增重1公斤以上，与本地黄牛杂交效果较好，杂交一代牛的初生重为33公斤（本地牛仅为23公斤）。2008年年末，全县黄牛存栏26735头。

（二）马

境内马系地方培育品种，属西南马，历来是农村交通运输的主要动力或辅助动力。其特点是体质结实，性情温顺，适应性强，抗病力强，耐粗放，驮载量大（驮载可达自身体重的50%以上），持久力强（可连续使用半个月左右），善走山区小道。马是县内农村耕地和运输的主要动力之一，也是农民群众的主要财产。一般不作肉用，老、残等被淘汰的才作为肉用。1979年，全县马年末存栏593匹，2008年年末，存栏数增加到10393匹，占大牲畜存栏数16.72%。

（三）猪

境内猪品种有11种。其中，本地培育品种有荔波黑猪、瑶山猪；引进品种有内江猪、太湖猪、陆川猪、长白猪、约克夏和巴克夏等。荔波黑猪属肉脂兼用型，具有耐粗饲、育肥快、产仔率高、适应山区自然环境的特点，为群众喜爱饲养的主要品种。瑶山猪是瑶山地区群众习惯饲养的地方品种，为肉脂兼用型，适应性强，耐粗饲，繁殖力强。引进品种主要是利用其产仔率高、瘦肉率高的优势，与地方品种进行杂交。

1979年后，在全面推行农业大包干责任制中，生猪以承包形式进行饲养，饲养收入归己。1988年，肥猪由按比例平价收购改为议价收购或养猪户自行屠宰销售，激发农户养猪积极性，生猪饲养和存栏量逐年提高。

1998年，在全县推广"四良四改三提高"（四良即良种、良法、良舍、良料；四改即改熟喂为生喂、改单一饲料为配合饲料、改吊架子育肥为一条龙育肥、改喂稀料为干湿料；三提高即提高养殖效益、提高饲料转化率、提高商品率）、"仔猪补饲""生猪快速育肥"等技术，猪肥育出栏周期缩短，养殖效益提高，年末生猪存栏达到7.85万头，肥猪出栏7.95万头。全县养猪100头以上32户，50头以上127户，20头以上1000余户。

2002年以后，县内青壮年多外出打工，农户养猪量下降。到2008年，全县有年饲养万头以上养猪场2个，年饲养量千头以上养猪场5个。年末，全县生猪存栏71862万头，出栏7.31万头。本地猪和瑶山猪大部分被出栏率高、生长快、饲料成本高、效益好的内二元杂交母猪和内三元杂交猪所取代，乡村只有少量农户饲养本地猪、瑶山猪。

（四）羊

境内饲养的羊有本地羊、黑山羊、南江黄羊、大耳羊、波尔羊等7个品种，地方羊品种以白山羊为主，经过不断引种与淘汰，已转变为以黑山羊为主。1978—1987年，山羊的存栏数保持在150只左右，出栏50只左右。1988年，县农牧局从威宁引进黑山羊104只放到驼背树新建的种羊场饲养。1989年末，山羊存栏数150只，出栏102只。1994年，从威宁、沿河等地引进黑山羊1500只，年末山羊存栏数增加到3618只。

1995年，县农牧局成立荔波县畜牧技术开发有限责任公司，以"公司+农户"模式发展山羊养殖，有养殖户72户，年末存栏数7430只。由于"公司+农户"模式的推动，全县农户贷款总计600多万元饲养山羊，到2000年年末，全县有羊养殖户220户，山羊存栏49294只，出栏15081只。2003年，引进波尔羊1对和江黄羊27只到县内饲养。2007年，省扶持荔波150万元，加上农户自筹资金和相关单位融资，总投资280万元，发展山羊生态产业化养殖。是年，引进大耳种公羊131只。2007年，省扶持荔波150万元，农户自筹资金及相关单位融资，总投资336万元，发展山羊生态产业化养殖，在翁昂乡拉内村和已陇村扶持养殖户150户，修建羊舍面积6226平方米，建设人工草地3500亩，技术培训3000多人次。是年，引进大耳种公羊131只，黑山羊能繁母羊3000只。年末，山羊存栏6759只。2008年1月，因冰冻灾害造成2000多只羊死亡，年末山羊存栏下降到4789只。

二、禽类

（一）品种

境内饲养的家禽主要有鸡、鸭、鹅。

1.鸡　境内饲养的鸡有15个品种，本地品种主要有本地鸡、瑶山鸡、乌骨鸡，引进品种主要有来航鸡、罗斯鸡、三黄鸡、柳州麻鸡、闽中麻鸡。本地鸡肉蛋兼用，适应性强，耐粗放，抗病力强，反应灵敏，善飞翔，就巢性强，体形矮小，单冠，皮肤白色，成年公鸡体重1.5～2公斤，成年母鸡1.2～1.7公斤，年产蛋80～120枚。

瑶山鸡耐粗放，适应性强，就巢性强，体型高大，成年公鸡一般体重3.5公斤，成年母鸡体重一般2.5公斤，年产蛋量平均在100枚左右。

乌骨鸡个体较小，全身皮肤及骨肉为乌黑色或紫色，肉质鲜嫩，有较好的滋补价值，年产蛋80枚左右。

三黄鸡即黄羽、黄喙、黄脚鸡，不特指某一个品种，是黄羽优质肉鸡的统称，包括贵州金黄鸡、贵农黄鸡。三黄鸡肉质嫩滑，皮脆骨软，脂肪丰满和味道鲜美，且生长速度、饲料转化率、产肉和产蛋量均较高。成年公鸡体重3.2公斤，成年母鸡体重2.3公斤。母鸡年产蛋190～210枚。

2.鸭　境内饲养的鸭有本地鸭、番鸭等8个品种，以本地鸭为主。引进鸭有双鬼头鸭、谷鸭等品种。本地鸭属麻鸭类，肉蛋兼用，体格较小，体质结实紧凑。成年公鸭体重1.5～2公斤，成年母鸭体重1.2～1.7公斤。年产蛋量150～200枚，蛋重51克左右。

3.鹅　县内饲养的鹅有5个品种，以本地灰鹅为主。引进品种有狮头鹅、四川白鹅和朗德鹅等。本地灰鹅体型长、个体大、头部肉瘤发达。成年公鹅体重5～7公斤，成年母鹅体重4～6公斤，年产蛋60～70枚。本地灰鹅就巢性及护仔性强，耐粗放，生长快。

（二）饲养

鸡、鸭、鹅饲养为县内农村副业，群众习惯于自孵繁殖，圈养和放养结合。中共十一届三中全会以后，县委、县政府鼓励家庭发展禽业，提供贷款扶持。县养殖业主管部门从外地引进良种鸡、鸭推广。1984年，粮食部门开始生产供应饲料，县畜牧站进行技术培训，推广科学养殖技术，并发展养禽业专业户和重点户。年末，禽类饲养量12.52万只，产蛋76.6吨，1988年上升到27.83万只，比1978年增长2.01倍。

1989年，外来工业优质饲料在荔波上市，三黄鸡、肉鸭等肉禽养殖量增加，年末存栏33.5万羽、出栏41.3万羽。1990—2003年，推广快大型（饲养40天出栏，体重2.5公斤以上）肉禽养殖技术，饲养量每年保持10%以上增长速度。

2004年，县委、县政府实施“畜牧兴县”战略，将发展瑶山鸡作为全县经济发展战略，并列为2004年县委、县政府工作“十件实事”之一，提出“大力发展畜牧产业，切实发展好‘瑶山鸡’品牌，力争实现到2010年存栏100万羽的养殖目标，努力把荔波打造成全省生态畜牧业重点县”的要求。是年6月，贵阳绿源禽业公司投资20万元，新建荔波瑶山鸡繁育中心，进行瑶山鸡本品种选育，年提供瑶山鸡苗20万羽。是年起，县委县政府每年投入财政扶持资金，在朝阳、瑶山、玉屏和捞村4个乡（镇）发展瑶山鸡养殖，培育专业户和重点户，年出栏55万羽。

荔波瑶山鸡

2006年，瑶山鸡通过省级评审，获得产品产地论证。到2008年，全县有瑶山鸡规模养殖场23个，其中，年出栏3万羽养殖场5个，年出栏1000羽瑶养殖场15个。瑶山鸡常年存栏28.5万羽。县财政累计投入扶持资金36.1万元。

2007年，通过招商，引进河南客商高合印到翁昂乡拉内村投资兴建荔波县绿原生态虫草鸡养殖场。该企业总投资643.9万元，建标准化鸡圈8栋，建筑面积1920平方米。主要产品是初产蛋和虫草鸡，年生产初产蛋50万枚，上市虫草鸡10万羽；建立了销售网络，以“天然牧咯”为品牌，在县城设产品直销店和虫草鸡食府，并把产品打入广州、上海等市场。

2003—2008年，县委、县政府投入财政扶持资金累计85万元，先后在捞村、甲良和播尧等乡（镇）扶持农户发展肉鹅、蛋鸭养殖。5年中，在甲良镇甲新、甲站等4个村扶持100户发展蛋鸭养殖，养殖蛋鸭1万多羽，打造出“甲站鸭蛋”品牌，年销售鸭蛋100多万枚；捞村、播尧发展肉鹅养殖2万羽，扶持养殖户200户，由于打不开市场，未形成产业，只有少数养殖户滚动发展。

三、兔、鸽、蜜蜂养殖

（一）兔

境内饲养的兔品种有安哥拉长毛兔、新西兰兔、加利福尼亚兔、比利时兔、兰特力斯兔和獭兔6种。1982年，从浙江引进兰特力斯兔33只，分给朝阳、玉屏的部分农户喂养，发展到3000只。1984年后，因兔子销售价格不稳，饲养量逐年下降，至2001年，仅个别农户少量饲养。

2002年，翁昂乡巴乐村农户10户从福泉市引进加利福尼亚兔200只，因未掌握喂养技术，没有发展。

2006年，驾欧乡引进加利福尼亚兔、比利时兔300只，由绿林村30户农户喂养，发展到2000只，因销路不广而停止饲养。

2008年，城镇和旅游区周边有住户养兔，饲养量1.3万只。

（二）鸽

境内饲养的鸽品种有公斤鸽、石岐鸽、姚安肉鸽和王鸽4种。鸽子饲养主要在城镇附近，饲养量较少，年饲养量2000只左右，大多是自己食用或观赏，作商品销售的较少。

（三）蜜蜂

境内饲养的蜜蜂品种有中蜂和意蜂。境内蜜源植物品种繁多，四季分布均匀，面积大，适宜养蜂业发展。1978—1987年，民间养蜂均为中蜂。中蜂适宜山区定点饲养，飞行灵活，晴天、雨天都能外出采蜜，抗敌害、抗螨能力强，产卵弱。1987年，全县养蜂2234群，产蜜6000公斤、王浆1公斤。

1988年，引进意蜂14群，分别在朝阳和玉屏各村寨饲养。

1990年以后，有外县、外省个体养蜂户运进意蜂常年在荔波县内放养，并在荔波传播养蜂技术。县内养蜂规模保持在2000群左右，以饲养意蜂为主。2008年，全县产蜂蜜9000公斤。

1978—2008年畜禽养殖统计表

表11－2

年度	猪（万头）		牛（头）		马（匹）		羊（只）		禽类（万羽）	
	存栏	出栏	存栏	出栏	存栏	出栏	存栏	出栏	存栏	出栏
1978	3.66	2.05	33796	5069	476	24	—	—	92335	—
1979	3.05	1.71	35300	5295	593	30	—	—	—	—

续表11－2

年度	猪（万头）		牛（头）		马（匹）		羊（只）		禽类（万羽）	
	存栏	出栏	存栏	出栏	存栏	出栏	存栏	出栏	存栏	出栏
1980	2.79	1.56	36435	5465	1252	63	—	—	—	—
1981	2.91	1.63	36650	5498	1487	74		—	—	—
1982	3.32	1.86	35111	5267	1675	84	—	—	—	—
1983	3.58	2.00	38469	5770	1908	95	—	—	—	—
1984	3.78	2.12	40535	6080	2063	103	—	—	—	—
1985	4.29	2.40	41391	6209	2233	112	—	—	—	—
1986	4.95	2.47	43537	6531	2295	115	61	—	—	—
1987	5.07	2.10	45598	6840	2549	127	68	—	—	—
1988	5.09	1.99	45158	6774	2635	132	258	—	—	—
1989	5.20	2.10	47800	7170	2953	148	800	108	—	—
1990	5.46	2.61	44850	6728	3273	164	199	—	—	—
1991	5.68	3.18	49291	7394	3872	194	72	—	—	—
1992	5.81	3.25	48766	7315	3969	198	266	—	—	—
1993	6.34	3.55	54875	8231	5417	271	773	—	—	—
1994	6.53	5.62	56000	8550	5595	280	4500	—	—	—
1995	7.53	6.50	59450	8918	5880	294	6275	—	—	—
1996	7.47	6.69	63595	10458	5920	1360	12044	1362	—	—
1997	7.25	7.80	60400	11602	6337	1563	16847	7260	26.60	38.10
1998	8.21	7.95	67340	11300	6055	1655	37200	8475	24.10	36.85
1999	7.25	7.49	61040	11300	7380	1085	33138	7600	35.76	41.20
2000	8.19	7.64	63770	11462	6752	1189	49294	15081	26.30	39.11
2001	8.27	7.35	66937	10475	7023	1910	41890	15081	19.67	20.63
2002	8.36	7.37	67256	10584	7271	2023	14158	7166	20.10	20.67
2003	8.47	8.06	66751	13543	6886	2394	14158	6605	27.02	26.54
2004	9.02	8.24	64227	11560	7181	2929	9285	6182	30.68	29.76
2005	8.30	9.08	68910	11874	10663	1946	14355	10870	45.64	57.13
2006	7.08	7.91	45496	8668	14697	772	4044	4309	25.98	39.88
2007	7.02	7.30	46861	9027	15138	804	6759	4387	26.66	40.93
2008	7.52	7.49	51855	10106	8983	522	10187	5602	33.58	45.55

第二节　水产养殖

一、品种

境内河流中有淡水经济鱼类30多种，主要品种有青鱼、草鱼、鲢鱼、鳙鱼、鲤鱼、鲫鱼、鳊鱼、鳜鱼、中华倒刺鱼（中华倒刺鲃）、鳝鱼、乌鱼（乌鳢）、鲶鱼、黄颡鱼、大刺鳅、斑鳠、大鳍鳠等。水库中有甲鱼，湖、塘、河沟中有青虾，另外还有蟹、螺等甲壳类水产动物。

二、水产养殖

境内河流属龙江水系珠江流域，有河流30条。境内总水面积36155亩，可供养殖、捕捞的水面28100亩。其中，樟江河和方村河面积16554亩，占总水面积45.79%，是县内鱼类自然繁殖和捕捞场所；适宜养鱼稻田39149亩；可供养鱼的山塘、水库面积1782.2亩，占总水面积4.93%。

捕捞渔具主要为网类，有三层挂网、丝网、鲹网、桃丝等。小型围网类有抄网、绞网。底泄网类有拖网、兜网、大拉网、小拉网。张网类有欢、大罾。小型拖网有毛鱼凤网、银鱼凤网。钩类有延绳钩、滚钩、柴钩、线钩。箭泊类有竹箭、塑料箭。

1978—1980年，山塘、小水库养鱼全部由生产队集体放养和管理。实行家庭联产承包责任制后，对鱼塘也进行承包，全县农村山塘、水库承包水面3500亩，占山塘、水库水面的80%。其中，集体承包15处，面积500亩；联产承包10处，面积1000亩；家庭养鱼1000户，面积2000亩。池塘养鱼所需鱼苗量少，由农民自己繁育，年繁殖各种鱼苗120万尾，鲢鱼、鳙鱼、草鱼、青鱼4个品种及部分其他品种鱼类依靠天然鱼苗养殖。

1985年，建水产苗种场，有鱼苗池7口，面积5.6亩，繁殖鱼苗200万尾，培育鱼种20万尾，销售到各乡（镇）。此后，水产苗种场成为县内及邻县的鱼苗主要供应点，每年培育和销售鱼苗100万尾。2005年，水产养殖场被征用后，为解决水产养殖鱼种问题，县水产技术人员自筹资金，租用南门农户池塘6.1亩，临时解决部分农户的鱼种需求问题。

1990—1995年，推广人工配合饲料养鱼，同时推广高密度混养、套养等水产养殖技术，提高养殖产量和经济效益。其间，城郊时来、罗卜木、南门、板吉、坡平、罗家寨等250余亩水田改造为池塘开展水产养殖。1996—2000年，从江苏、湖南、广西等地引进水产良种（无锡建鲤、丰鲤、湘云鲤、湘云鲫等）、名特优新品种（罗非鱼、黄颡鱼、大口鲶、革胡子鲶、斑点叉尾鮰、鳜鱼、武昌、淡水白鲳等）示范推广获得成功，养殖产量稳定，养殖效益突出。2001年，开始批量引进各类水产良种推广，至2005年，累计推广水产良种1000万尾。新技术投入和良种覆盖率的提高，池塘亩产量提升至400公斤以上。

2005年，全县山塘、池塘养殖面积4250亩，水产品产量1080吨。此后，随着城镇化建设步伐加快，城郊池塘先后被征用而停止养鱼。2008年，全县农户利用稻田养鱼2500亩。

三、渔政管理

1978—1985年期间，县内未设渔政管理机构，但渔业捕捞水平及技术、设备落后，渔业资源没有受到严重破坏。

1986年，国家颁布《中华人民共和国渔业法》，贵州省颁布《渔业生产管理条例》之后，县政府在县农牧局设立渔政管理站，配备专职人员，管理全县渔业。同时，根据规定，县政府将樟江河狮子口到东升水坝之间河段划定禁渔区，规定每年4月1日至5月31日为禁渔期，即在禁渔区和禁渔期内，禁止一切捕捞活动，禁止电鱼、炸鱼、毒鱼等破坏渔业资源捕捞行为。渔业管理部门开展渔业法律法规宣传，对河道进行夜间和白天巡查，开展水上巡逻，查处违法捕捞人员。

从1998年起，采取河段承包管理和“群管群治”管理模式，将河段渔业资源管理纳入“村规民约”，村民参与管理。

2000年后，每年向省、州争取增殖放流项目，向河流投放鱼苗。至2008年，每年至少开展增殖活动一次，平均每年向河流投放鱼苗20万尾。

2006—2008年，按照新的《渔业法》《贵州省渔业条例》的规定，县内禁渔期改为每年2月1日至5月31日。

第三节 畜禽疫病防治

一、防治

县内畜禽疫病有90种。其中，传染病有炭疽、气肿疽、结核、口蹄疫、狂犬病等26种；寄生虫病有锥虫病、焦虫病、肝片吸虫病23种；普通病36种；中毒病有有机磷中毒、霉中毒等8种。牛病主要有牛出败、放线菌病、气肿疽；猪病主要有猪瘟、猪丹毒、猪肺疫、蓝耳病、圆环病毒病；羊病主要有山羊痘、羊快疫、羊传染性胸膜肺炎；禽病主要有鸡新城疫、禽霍乱、鸡白痢、禽流感、小鹅瘟、鸭瘟等。

畜禽疫病防治以“预防为主”的方针，采取注射疫苗和环境消毒相结合的措施，对口蹄疫、羊痘、禽流感、狂犬病等易造成重大危害的疫病实行免费强制免疫，猪瘟、鸡瘟、牛出败和羊快疫等疫病由养殖场和养殖户自愿免疫。每年春秋两季，防疫人员逐村逐户进行畜禽防疫注射。畜禽传染病发生后，按照国家法律法规，采取封锁、隔离、捕杀、消毒、药物防治、无害化处理等措施进行处理，及时扑灭各种动物疫病。畜禽普通疾病发生后，采用手术或药物等措施进行治疗，诊疗以兽医人员为主。治疗除使用西药外，还利用中草药进行救治。境内实用的兽用中草药有6个门类100余科700余种，常用的有桔梗、桂皮、大通草、续断、银花叶、小瓜石斛、黄草、水草、白芨、灵芝菌、金樱子、益母草、牛膝、龙胆草、天冬、黄精、葛根、桑根、山慈姑、水球子、泡参、山乌龟、灵香草、鹿含草、麦冬、茯苓、黄檗、杜仲、厚朴、山药、木瓜、女贞子、黄栀子、车前草、青天葵等。

1978年，全县开展畜禽疫情普查，普查结果：牛发病率为3.35%，发病死亡率为48.62%，气肿疽、牛结核、牛出败3种病的死亡数分别占是年牛死亡数的30.98%、7.04%和4.23%；猪发病率为14.44%，发病死亡率68.64%，猪瘟、猪丹毒、猪肺疫3种病的死亡数占是年猪死亡数的45.37%、22.12%和28.51%；家禽发病4.15万只，死亡3.77万只，发病死亡率90.84%，其中鸡瘟、禽霍乱、雏鸡白痢3种病的死亡数分别占是年家禽死亡数的43.6%、49.3%和2.29%。

1987年，推行“春防为主，三检跟上，长年补针，因病设防”措施。是年，茂兰区牛、猪春防注射密度95.76%。1990年，采取普通春防、秋季补针、市场补针、紧急补针相结合的措施，提高全县防疫注射覆盖率，村、组覆盖率分别为97%、86.8%。全年猪防疫注射5.69万头（次），免疫率77.2%；大牲畜防疫注射3.57万头（次），免疫率79.7%。

1990年，全县有经营兽药店铺6家。从是年起，西药兽药市场开放，养殖户可以在市场上购买药品进行防治。

1992年，实行畜禽防疫双轨制，既行政轨和业务轨。行政轨是县乡村层层签订防疫责任书，将动物防疫工作纳入政府系列年终考核重要指标。实施常年防疫，确保完成畜禽免疫密度；业务轨是业务部门负责防疫质量，包括疫苗质量、防疫效果等。是年，大牲畜防疫注射数2.87万头（次），猪防疫注射4.57万头（次），免疫密度分别达到95.9%和84.3%。

1993—1997年，随着畜禽防疫双轨制的逐渐成熟，防疫面、防疫密度均达到100%，没有发生重大动物疫情。

1998年，因全国范围内暴发牛口蹄疫情，荔波县也未能幸免。全县有345户牲畜发生“五号病”，发病牛635头，病猪107头。疫情发生后，县委、县政府先后下发通告、通知等文件17个，拨出扑杀经费6.2万元，采取“早、快、严、小”措施强制扑灭疫情，至12月3日，扑灭病牛359头、扑杀病猪57头。同时，对全县各疫区（点）严密切监控，进行牲畜“五号病”疫苗接种。是年，动用680人防疫队伍，在全县17个乡（镇）、169个村、1189个组开展畜禽防疫注射工作。全县免疫猪丹毒90134头，免疫注射炭疽苗19831头（匹）；免疫注射牛出败36240头，占饲养量82%；免疫气肿疽疫苗7497头，共免疫注射17500只（次），其中，羊四联苗11500只、口疮苗6000只，免疫注射占存栏数48%；全县禽存栏24.1万羽，共免疫各类疫苗88815只，其中，鸡瘟Ⅰ系苗免疫19445只、鸡瘟Ⅱ系免疫59290只、鸭瘟免疫10080只；狂犬免疫500只。

1999年，全县免疫注射猪瘟疫苗111074头，占存栏数72538头的153%，注射猪肺疫苗104365头次，注射猪“五号病”疫苗60189头，占存栏83%；注射猪丹毒104365头。全年免疫注射大家畜炭疽苗19433头（匹），注射牛出败苗32180头，注射气肿疽苗5321头，免疫注射占大家畜存栏的93.3%；注射牛“五号病”疫苗54936头，占牛存栏的90%；注射反应67头，反应死亡16头。免疫注射羊四联苗5391只，占羊存栏的16.3%。家禽免疫注射鸡瘟Ⅰ系苗81676羽，免疫注射Ⅱ系苗82673羽。

2000年，注射猪瘟疫苗90912头份，注射猪三联苗90912头份，“五号病”免疫45378头，占饲养量的42.6%；注射牛出败36359头份，炭疽芽孢苗23435头份，气肿疽菌苗5321头份，“五号病”免疫55150头，占饲养量的89%；免疫鸡瘟Ⅰ系疫苗85820羽、鸡Ⅱ系疫苗177200羽；犬免疫550只。

2000年，全县有兽医门诊18个，诊疗病猪6991头（次）、病牛1949头（次）、病马244匹（次）。

从2001年12月起，除“三不打”（病的不打、瘦的不打、弱的不打）外，畜禽防疫密度要求达100%。到2003年，全县防疫覆盖村组达100%；大牲畜免疫数12.11万头（匹），占饲养量的78%，猪免疫12.33万头，占饲养量的88%。

2004年，畜禽免疫实行牲畜户口簿管理制，按照县不漏乡、乡不漏村、村不漏组、组不漏户、户不漏畜、畜不漏针的“六不漏”目标，对免疫的畜禽佩戴免疫标识。是年，大牲畜常规防疫4.27万头，密度为103.3%，生猪常规免疫15.13万头，密度108.7%；强制免疫牛10.9万头，密度134.7%，猪13.79万头，密度99.19%。全年建牲畜户口簿6.4万户，佩戴免疫标识13.7万枚，消毒圈舍1.06万个，消毒场地3.5万平方米。

2005年，全县17个乡（镇）、98个村、1189个组实施畜禽防疫接种，防疫面100%。免疫猪W为14893头，免疫密度为100%；免疫猪瘟疫苗165122头，免疫密度为100%。免疫猪肺疫16201头，免疫猪丹毒11277头，免疫猪副伤寒10315头。免疫牛W应免数为111688头（次），免疫密度为100%；免疫牛出败33879头，免疫炭疽51024头。免疫羊W应免数为16890只，免疫W疫苗16890只，免疫密度为100%；免疫羊痘8450只。家禽接种鸡新城疫Ⅰ系苗17.6万羽，接种Ⅱ系苗17.3万羽；接种禽流感疫苗29.5万羽。城镇犬饲养量1812只，免疫1067只，免疫率58.9%。全年畜禽驱虫总数为90226头（只），其中，牛驱虫33256头、猪48541头、羊8429头。新增佩戴免疫耳标14.5万枚，新增发放新免疫牲畜户口簿3.4万张，消毒圈舍10620个，消毒场地5.5万平方米。

2006年，猪免疫W苗144332头，密度100%；免疫猪瘟疫苗145232头，密度100%；免疫猪肺疫7210头，免疫猪丹毒5726头，免疫仔猪副伤寒4226头。牛免疫W苗118602头（次），密度100%；免疫牛出败14676头，免疫炭疽36146头，免疫马炭疽4972匹，炭疽疫点及周围村组免疫率为100%。羊免疫W疫苗14989只，密度100%；免疫羊痘7450只。鸡接种新城疫I系苗32.78万羽（次），接种II系苗32.48万羽，密度100%。接种禽流感免疫56.34万羽，密度100%；鸭Q病免疫85967羽，密度100%。犬免疫667只，免疫率65.3%。新增佩戴免疫耳标12.5万枚，猪、牛、羊耳标佩戴率达100%；发放新免疫牲畜户口簿3.1万张，免疫档案建率100%。10%牲畜死亡定点调查17个乡（镇）、17个村、1000户，大牲畜死亡率为0.94%，猪死亡率为4.82%，禽死亡率为11.23%，均控制在国标内。畜禽驱虫总数为159824头（羽、只），其中牛48536头，猪101945头，羊9343只。

2006年，县畜牧局设立05快捷服务中心，24小时开通电话，全方位为全县养殖户提供上门快捷服务。当年为群众提供上门服务586人次。

2007年，免疫猪W苗、猪瘟133709头（次），密度100%；免疫猪肺疫7210头，猪丹毒4771头，免疫仔猪副伤寒3604头，免疫高致病性蓝耳病60190头。W病免疫反应1210头，死亡141头。牛免疫W苗102022头（次），密度100%；免疫牛出败20086头，免疫炭疽36172头，免疫马炭疽4972匹，炭疽疫点及周围村组免疫率为100%。羊免疫W疫苗14757只，密度100%。鸡接种新城疫I系苗18.31万羽（次），接种II系苗22.96万羽，密度100%。接种禽流感免疫41.29万羽，密度100%；鸭Q病免疫73564羽，密度100%。犬免疫2492只，免疫率70%。新增佩戴免疫耳标17.5万枚，猪、牛、羊耳标佩戴率达100%；发放新免疫牲畜户口簿5.5万张，免疫档案建率100%。10%牲畜死亡定点调查17个乡（镇）、17个村、1000户，大牲畜死亡率为0.94%，猪死亡率为4.82%，禽死亡率为11.23%。2007年，建立村级兽医室58个，改善了村级动物疫情诊疗设备。

2008年，生猪口蹄疫免疫1.3万头，免疫密度为应免疫数的100%；免疫猪瘟疫苗13.86万头，免疫密度100%；免疫高致性蓝耳病疫苗13.18万头，免疫密度达100%；免疫猪肺疫0.86万头，免疫猪丹毒0.96万头，免疫仔猪副伤寒0.69万头。牛口蹄疫免疫10.4万头（次），免疫密度为应免数的100%；免疫牛出败1.57万头，免疫牛炭疽5.1万头。免疫马炭疽0.13万匹。羊口蹄疫免疫1.31万只，免疫密度为应免疫数的100%；羊痘疫苗免疫1.1万只，免疫密度为100%。接种鸡新城疫I系苗、Ⅱ系苗76.8万羽，免疫率为100%；接种鸡禽流感疫苗62.42万羽，免疫率为100%。鸭高致病性禽流感免疫11.95万羽，免疫率为100%。犬免疫0.28万只，免疫率77.3%。消毒圈舍10万个，场地9万多平方米。免疫耳标佩戴19.53万枚，猪耳标佩戴率达100%，牛耳标佩戴率达100%，羊耳标佩戴率达100%。免疫档案建立100%。

经过多年畜禽疫病防治，到2008年，县内肝片吸虫病等畜禽传染病得到控制，只有牛出败、猪瘟、鸡瘟有零星发病，没有造成重大损失。大牲畜死亡率已控制在1%以内，猪死亡率控制在5%以内，禽死亡率控制在12%以内，达到国家标准。

二、检疫

从1985年开始，县内对畜禽进行常年性市场畜禽检疫和肉品检疫，重点开展畜禽动物产地检疫、屠宰检疫、运输检疫及市场监督，对动物饲养场（户）、动物产品屠宰加工场所定期进行消毒和畜禽定期驱虫，发现疫情迅速逐级上报，并采取封锁、隔离、捕杀、消毒、药物防治无害化处理等综合措施，及时扑灭各种动物疫病。同时，开展疫病调查和定点监测。是年，在4个区、10个村、500户开展疫病调查，调查牲畜数是全县存栏数的10%，通过调查推算，大牲畜死亡率为1.5%，猪死亡率为6.4%，禽死亡率为16.5%，死亡率偏高。在玉屏区水甫村和朝阳区的洞我村开展定点监测，每村50户，调查猪563头，牛218头。此后，疫病调查和定点监测成为常规工作，每年调查数是全县存栏数的10%，选定2个村为定点监测。1985—1986年，由区畜牧兽医工作人员和乡兽医负责检疫工作。由于检疫工作属新的工作内容，涉及检疫费用问题，只在朝阳区和县城集镇2个地方开展，1985年检疫3150头，1986年检疫5300头。

1987年，设立兽医卫生监督检验所，专门负责检疫，动物检疫成为常规性工作。是年，县农牧局组织各乡（镇）工作人员、乡兽医及兽防站工作人员30多人到州畜牧局进行检疫操作及理论知识轮训，考试、考核合格后，领取检疫员证，持证上岗。年内仅在5个市场开展检疫，检疫猪肉尸6442头，检出病害猪肉尸226头，检疫马肉尸2190头，检出病害肉尸22头，全部作高温无害化处理。

1988—1989年，在全县21个动物及动物产品交易市场安排专人检疫值班，对上市的牲畜和动物产品进行检疫，对没有免疫的健康牲畜进行补免，对检疫合格的加盖检疫合格印章，对染疫动物及动物产品进行焚烧处理。

1990年，全县有畜禽市场15个，进行重点检疫的市场8个，检疫猪1.25万头，验出猪瘟45头、猪肺疫44头、猪丹毒30头、仔猪副伤寒18头、其他65头，补免1.01万头，占检疫总数的80.98%。是年，签发兽医卫生合格证30个、兽药经营许可证6个。

1994年，检疫生猪21969头，补免猪瘟21866头，检出病猪103头；检疫大牲畜1495头，补免炭疽等疫苗834头。全年猪肉尸检疫25268头，牛马肉尸检疫1771头。全年检出病害肉尸164头，均作高温和无害化处理。

1995年，全县活畜市场13个，开展检疫12个，检疫生猪32628头，补免猪瘟29442头，检出病猪390头；检疫大牲畜1557头，补免炭疽等疫苗532头。在全县21个市场和肉摊点肉品检验工作，全年猪肉尸检疫20787头，牛马肉尸检疫1556头。全年检出病害肉尸232头，均作高温和无害化处理。

1996年，全县市场活检生猪22363头补免猪瘟疫苗15389头；大牲畜检疫1217头，补免炭疽疫苗999头；全年上市猪肉尸23063头，检疫22015头；上市牛马肉尸968头，检疫966头。全年检出病害肉尸124头，均作高温和无害化处理。

1997年，全县动物及其产品交易市场增加到21个，重点对兼有活畜市场的13个集市开展检疫，其他市场的检疫工作安排专人负责。全年检疫生猪2.81万头，检疫率99%，检出病猪24头，补免2.79万头；大牲畜检疫0.42万头，检出病马2匹，补免0.11万头；检疫屠宰猪2.49万头、屠宰牛（马）892头（匹），检疫率98.4%，检出病害肉55头（匹）。

1998年，全县有活畜市场13个，开展检疫13个，年内上市仔猪39444头，检疫39444头，补针注射23071头，共检出病猪85头，其中猪瘟29头、猪丹毒34头、猪肺疫22头，对检出的病猪均按国标及有关规定进行处理。上市大牲畜4291头，检疫4291头，补针注射炭疽疫苗1397头。运输检疫1211头（只），其中牛54头、猪134头、山羊1023只。全县有动物产品市场16个，零星销售摊点5个，全部开展动物新产品检疫（验）。全年上市猪肉尸25360头，检疫（验）25342头，检出病害猪肉尸78头，其中高温无害化处理77头、销毁1头；上市马肉尸2466头，检疫（验）2466头，检出病害肉尸1头，高温无害化处理1头；上市羊肉尸61只，检疫（验）61只，检出病害肉尸5只，高温处理5只。

1999年，全年检疫生猪56660头，检出病猪103头，其中猪瘟48头、猪肺疫26头、猪丹毒24头、口蹄疫5头，补注射猪三联苗35238头。检疫大牲畜9093头，检出病畜28头（匹）；检疫羊43只，家禽383只。全年运输检疫大牲畜1432头，中家畜6820头（只），消毒运输车56辆。屠宰检疫，全年共检疫鲜销猪肉31012头，检出猪瘟肉26头，猪丹毒肉13头，猪肺疫肉13头，寄生虫猪肉47头，“五号病”猪肉3头。检疫鲜销牛、马肉3223头（匹），检出“五号病”牛肉尸3头。检出病肉尸按有关规定作销毁和高温处理。

2000年，全年检疫生猪55118头，检出病猪101头，其中猪瘟53头，猪肺疫24头，猪丹毒24头；检疫大牲畜5519头，检出病畜23头（匹），补注射猪三联苗12917头，补注射炭疽芽孢苗3164头（匹）。全县23个场点全部开展检疫工作，检疫人员25人，全年累计检疫鲜猪肉37404头，检出猪瘟肉61头，猪丹毒肉13头，肺疫猪肉7头。寄生虫猪肉11头，“W”病猪5头，牛3头，全部进行无害化处理。

2001年，产地检疫生猪48470头，检疫大牲畜6580头，共检出病畜77头，补注疫苗32928头。屠宰检疫鲜肉尸36799头，检出病害肉尸93头，其中高温无害化处理43头、销毁50头。运输检疫大牲畜785头，检疫中家畜7760头（只），运输车辆消毒156辆。

2002—2004年，每年开展动物及动物产品常规检查、处理。

2005年，县畜牧局设立畜牧执法大队，对全县兽医卫生、药政、渔政和饲料进行执法检查。

2006年，执法大队举办培训班8期，培训639人；利用乡镇赶集日开设畜牧法律法规宣传平台，发放宣传资料20060份，接受咨询10330人次；通过广播宣传、接待咨询、违法图片展示、电视曝光等形式宣传畜牧执法；全年办理“兽药经营许可证”8个；查处违法案件44起，结案42起；在重要集镇建屠宰场8个，每天安排检疫值班人员1人；规范产地检疫报检点26个，每个点每天安排值班人员1人；进行产地检疫站110356头，其中，检生猪97806头，检出病猪28头（猪瘟9头、丹毒8头、肺疫11头），检疫牛8088头，检出病牛2头，检疫羊4462头，未检出病羊；屠宰检疫48691头，检疫鲜猪肉43626头，检出不合格病猪肉24头，检疫鲜牛肉5057头，检出不合格牛肉1头，检疫鲜羊肉8头。全县有7个乡（镇）开展出县境检疫工作，执行凭产地检疫合格证明和免疫标识换证制度，全年出县境检疫12767头（羽），大、中家畜3927头，家禽8840羽，消毒运输车辆195车（次）。

2006年，县畜牧局设立05快捷服务中心，24小时开通电话，为全县养殖户提供上门快捷服务。

2007年，组织畜牧技术干部、村级兽医员、检疫人员培训2期，培训270人次；开展牲畜贩运户、禽苗经营户、规模养殖场管理人员培训会各1期，培训人员129人；张贴标语110多张，悬挂横幅3次，发放宣传资料8500余份。全年产地检疫68086头（只、匹），其中，猪59673头、牛6937头、马165匹、羊1311只；屠宰检疫40084头，其中，检疫猪33531头、牛6327头，马76匹、羊150只，完成任务数的89%，检出病肉尸37头，依法进行无害化处理；出县境检疫1861头，其中猪1460头、牛186头、羊212头、马3匹。是年，建立村级兽医室58个。

2008年，检查兽药市场52场（次）、兽药经营户111户（次），兽药市场质量抽检2次，抽检兽药经营户6户，抽取兽药样品8个，合格2个；对生物制品品种实行建立生物药品保管卡和签领签收发放制度。重点监控州级养殖龙头企业3家、县级养殖场2个和种禽场1个。检查饲料市场51场（次），检查饲料经营户158户，没收过期饲料130公斤，饲料质量抽检3次，抽检饲料经营户10户，抽取饲料样品10个，合格8个，对其中2户粗蛋白未达标准的经营户进行处罚；饲养环节饲料抽检3次，抽检4个养殖场自配饲料样品12个，合格率达100%。完成产地检疫71285头，其中检疫生猪64263头、牛6353头、羊188只、马375匹，检出病猪106头，作限制隔离处理；屠宰检疫39293头，其中，检疫猪34239头、牛4666头、羊188只、马200匹，检出染疫动物产品107头，屠宰检疫率100%。出县境检疫636头。

2008年，全县办理兽药经营许可证43个，签发饲料经营合格证75个。

第四节　饲草　饲料

一、饲草

境内牧草以天然生长为主，也有人工种植，草场牧草种类较多。天然牧草有30余科82种，以禾本科为主的占65%左右，另外还有豆科、菊科、蔷薇科和莎科等。

自然生长的禾本科饲用牧草有细毛鸭嘴草、白茅、野古草、黄背茅、黄茅、白健杆、刚莠竹、芒草、金发草、斑茅、长芒鹅观草、鼠尾粟、金茅、马陆草、假俭草、牛筋草、雀稗、细柄草、桔草、剪股颖等；豆科饲用牧草有葛藤、崖豆藤、野豌豆、山蚂蟥、假木豆、圆叶决明、马鞍羊蹄甲等。

人工种植的牧草，豆科有白三叶、红三叶、苜蓿、草木樨、百脉根（绿肥）、苕子，禾本科牧草有多花黑麦草、高羊茅、鸭茅、冬牧七〇黑麦、多年生黑麦草、桂牧一号、皇竹草、象草、墨西哥玉米等，还种植有菊苣、苦荬菜、鲁梅克斯等菊科和藜科牧草。

从1983年起，县内不断进行优质牧草引种种植。

1984年，开展全县草地资源调查，全县牧草资源面积为1309057亩，占全县土地面积的35.75%。其中，300亩以上面积的连片草场有467片834451亩；300亩以下的零星草场474606亩。在成片草场中，有草丛草场（即草坡草场）543312亩，灌丛草场237933亩，疏林草场53206亩。全县各类草场年鲜草产量913320吨。

1983—1988年，先后在永康、佳荣、玉屏、茂兰、水尧、朝阳等地种植红三叶、白三叶、黑麦草、百脉根、墨西哥玉米、串叶松香草、大翼豆、宽叶雀稗、矮柱花草、象草等牧草5226亩。

1998年，再次开展草地资源调查，全县牧地总面积为899075.9亩，其中，实际利用牧地面积581633.5亩，未利用的宜牧草山317442.4亩。全县各类草场年鲜草产量713320吨。

1999年，引进多花黑麦草、皇竹草、苜蓿、菊苣、鲁梅克斯、羔羊茅、鸭茅等十多个品种进行牧草品比试验。

2000年，全面推广优质牧草种植。2003年，根据州委、州政府提出“农户要增收，畜牧扛大头”的发展战略，县和乡（镇）投入资金用于草地畜牧业发展，拨款补贴种草农户。2003—2006年，县政府划拨种草经费总计33万元，在全县推广种草养畜，种植优质牧草4.1万亩，配套养猪4万头、养牛6.5万头。至2008年，全县年末保留人工草地面积1.5万亩以上，人工草地年鲜草产量75000吨。

二、饲料

县内地产的精饲料有玉米、稻谷、小麦、大麦、黄豆等；块根块茎饲料有红薯、马铃薯、木薯、萝卜等；粮食副产品饲料有糠、麸、糟、渣、菜籽饼等；粗饲科有稻草、玉米秆、豆秆、花生秆、油菜秆、蔗稍等。

1983年2月，省粮食局拨给大型型饲料机组1套，10月开始加工，年底生产饲料75吨。

1984年，进行饲料调查，全县年产精饲料10万吨、粗饲料13万吨。

1985年，成立饲料公司，年加工饲料1070吨。1987年7月以后，实行经营承包责任制。1988—1990年，分别加工饲料1362吨、1510.6吨和2420吨。

1991年外来优质工业饲料进入荔波市场，有猪、禽、鱼等浓缩料和配合料，当年利用1520吨。随着畜禽饲养量的不断增多，优质饲料利用也随之增长，

1996年，农牧局下辖的畜牧技术开发有限公司开办饲料厂，年产优质饲料365吨。

1998—2001年，饲料经营企业发展到105户，年利用优质饲料最多时达到0.94万吨。2001年，畜牧技术开发有限公司饲料厂停产。

2002—2008年，实施退耕还林，农户生猪饲养量下降，优质饲料利用下降，有饲料经营户75户，优质饲料利用量年均0.8万吨。

第五章 林 业

第一节 森林资源

一、森林植被资源

（一）森林植被类型分布

境内森林植被分布和森林群落组成，受地形、气候和水热条件影响，形成不同的森林类型。由于地形差异显著，南北部植被差异大。东北部为在砂页岩发育的土壤上形成的以无患子科、樟科、山茶科为代表的地带性常绿阔叶林区；西北部为以原尾松为主的人工林区，南部为以桑科、壳斗科、金缕梅科为代表的石灰岩植被类型区。县境森林植被类型分为6种。

1.南亚热带沟谷季雨林　分布于佳荣镇南部的甲料河及捞村乡的打狗河河谷地带，属南亚热带，热量充足，雨量充沛，具有特殊的河谷地貌，是典型的沟谷季雨林。组成沟谷季雨林的树种丰富，常见树种有榕树、木棉、血桐、毛麻楝、米稿、沉水樟、香椿、红木荷、大叶朴、乔木杜鹃、山荔枝、桫椤、黑桫椤等。

2.亚热带常绿阔叶林　各乡（镇）均有分布，由于雨量充沛，水热条件好，以湿性常绿阔针林具代表性。喀斯特地貌上的常绿落叶阔叶混交林是在这一地带性气候背景下形成的稳定的森林群落，此区亚热带常绿阔叶林具有较复杂的种类组成和层次结构，为多树种复层异龄林。主要树种有青冈、小叶栲、刺栲、栲树、厚皮栲、甜槠栲、钩栲、细叶青冈、黄樟、猴樟、木荷、楠木、桂皮、马蹄荷等，以壳斗科、山茶科、樟科为多，间有落叶树种枫香、鹅耳枥、白栎、麻栎、光皮桦、响叶杨等。低山丘陵有马尾松分布，沟谷山地和土层肥厚的局部地带有杉木生长。常绿阔叶被破坏地带，常为次生的落叶阔叶林所演替，演替的优势树种为枫香。

3.亚热带常绿落叶混交林　分布于甲良、方村、播尧、驾欧和佳荣等海拔较高地带，建群树种主要有枫香、响叶杨、麻栎、山青冈、鹅耳枥、千金榆、长柄山毛榉、化香、桦木、槭树等，常绿树种有栲属、青冈属、石栎属、栗属、木莲属、木荷属等，低山、低中山有马尾松、杉木，土壤肥沃湿润的山脚山谷有樟木、米稿。下层林木有杜鹃、柃木檵木、盐肤木、木姜子等。

4.针叶林　各乡（镇）均有分布，主要以马尾松、杉木、湿地松为主，兼有少量柏木、华山松、五针松和云南松。马尾松和杉木是境内面积最大的两个主要建群树种。马尾松中龄林以上的林种主要由飞机播种、撒播、点播等形成，中幼林由容器苗造林形成。人工植苗造林主要分布在佳荣、玉屏、朝阳、播尧、甲良、方村、驾欧、立化、水尧、茂兰等乡（镇）。杉木主要分布在佳荣镇的水维、大土、甲料、拉易、拉祥等地，方村、水利、播尧、朝阳、瑶山、茂兰等乡（镇）也有连片分布；湿地松主要分布在佳荣镇、朝阳镇；华山松零星分布在佳荣的大土和拉易；五针松主要分布在甲良的洞庭村和水利乡的岜岭村；云南松主要团状分布在方村河、樟江河、甲料河等河谷低山区。

5.针阔叶混交林　各乡（镇）均有分布，以天然起源为主。针叶树种主要有马尾松、杉木、华山松、五针松和少量柏木、三尖杉、惠花杉、黄坡油杉、罗汉松、红豆杉等。阔叶树种以枫香、青冈、响叶杨、桦木、木荷、栲类为主。多数是多树种复层异龄针阔混交林，常绿树种还有石栎属、栲属、樟属、润楠属、木莲类、杨梅等，落叶润叶树种还有麻栎、山青冈、化香、鹅耳枥、泡桐等。常见的针阔叶混交林有马尾松与青冈，以及马尾松、杉木与栲属、栎属的混交林，主要分布在1200米以下的低中山、低山及丘陵地带。

6.灌木林与灌丛　各乡（镇）均有分布，以培育灌木为目的，为专用防护林。灌木树种有白栎、杜鹃、茅粟、盐肤木、檵木、化香、小米柴、山果蔷薇、马桑、胡枝子等。灌木林和灌丛均有保持水土、涵养水源的作用，有的还具有较高的经济和观赏价值。

除上述6种森林植被类型外，县内还有大量的经果林。油桐林主要分布在佳荣的水维、甲料以及朝阳镇的樟江河两岸；油茶林主要分布在樟江河沿岸和方村、甲良一带，常生长于马尾松林下；茶林主要分布甲良的梅桃、益觉及瑶山的高桥村和播尧的架桥村；杜仲林主要分布在玉屏镇的水扒、瑶山乡的高桥、翁昂乡的尧桥、佳荣镇的拉易、甲料等地；黄柏林主要分布在佳荣镇的大土、甲料、水维和玉屏镇的时来、水甫等地；漆树林主要分布在佳荣镇的水维；盐肤木林在各乡（镇）都有分布，多为天然次生，呈小片或沿山脚呈等高线的带状分布；酸梅林主要分布在洞塘、玉屏、翁昂、永康、瑶麓、佳荣和朝阳等乡（镇）；水果林主要分布在玉屏、朝阳、瑶山等3个乡（镇）的河谷地带，品种主要有柑橘、脐橙、樟江蜜柚、荔波柚、沙田柚、椪柑、九阡李、荔波血桃、黄花李等；干果林主要分布在朝阳的八烂村、花提村及佳荣镇的大土村、水维村和甲料村等地。

（二）森林植被区系

根据县境植被特征、植被群落的地理分布及植被与环境的关系，荔波森林植被类型可划分为山地森林植被区系和喀斯特森林植被区系。

1.山地森林植被区系　1989年，对樟江上游水源涵养林的植被调查，境内山地常态地貌森林植被区共有种子植物104科、286属、558种。其中，裸子植物5科、7属、8种；被子植物99科、279属、550种；木本植物81科、203属、433种，占该区种子植物总科数的77.88%、总属数的70.98%、总种数的77.6%。

2.喀斯特森林植被区系　根据1981—1984年的历次调查、采集，采集标本共3000多号，加上南京林业大学宋祥厚及中山大学许兆然的部分统计，境内喀斯特森林有维管束植物148科、408属、801种、37变种，约占贵州维管束植物的六分之一。喀斯特植物区系中，含6种以上的种子植物有44科、242属、575种。具体为蔷薇科、樟科、茜草科、禾本科、唇形科、蝶形花科、兰科、鼠李科、芸香科、忍冬科、卫毛科、马鞭草科、山茶科、紫金牛科、荨麻科、葡萄科、木兰科、桑科、清风藤科、夹竹桃科等。其中，1属含种数较多，主要有槭属9种、鼠李属14种、荚蒾属9种、卫毛属10种及柿属、山矾属、胡颓子属、冬青属等。

二、森林面积及蓄积量

1984—1985年，开展全县森林资源二类调查，全县有林地面积91.05万亩，有林地林木蓄积393.83万立方米；疏林地面积9.63万亩，林木蓄积14.62万立方米；灌木林面积55.82万亩；散生木及“四旁”（村旁、路旁、水旁、宅旁）树蓄积5.22万立方米。全县活立木总蓄积413.67万立方米。全县森林总覆盖率40.19%。在有林地中，用材林面积40.31万亩，林木蓄积181.34万立方米；防护林面积38.26万亩，林木蓄积188.96万立方米；薪炭林面积9.58万亩，林木蓄积27.42万立方米。

1994—1995年，开展第二次森林资源调查，全县有林地面积161.1万亩，有林地覆盖率31.72%，有林地林木蓄积507.84立方米；疏林地面积1.24万亩，林木蓄积为0.19万立方米；灌木林地面积60.45万亩；散生木及“四旁”树活立木蓄积0.41万立方米。全县总森林覆盖率48.23%，活立木总蓄积513.83万立方米。

2004—2005年，开展第三次森林资源调查，全县有林地面积190.50万亩，活立木蓄积595.45万立方米；疏林地面积0.5万亩，活立木蓄积0.29万立方米；灌木林面积14.49万亩；散生木及四旁树蓄积1.21万立方米。全县森林总覆盖率56.1%，活立木总蓄积量596.96万立方米。

第二节　植树造林

一、社会造林

全县社会造林发展到1979年，造林累计72.7万亩（其中飞播56.24万亩、人工植苗造林16.46万亩），年平均造林8.07万亩。1981年，随着林业“三定”（稳定山权林权、划定自留山、确定林业生产责任制）工作开展，农户造林积极性提高，1981—1990年的10年间，全县累计造林21.03万亩，年均21033.3亩。1990年年底，县委、县政府提出“十年基本绿化荔波”的造林目标。1993年，县委、县政府实施“221155”绿化建设工程，即“营造酸梅2万亩、大板栗2万亩、杜仲1万亩、柚子1万亩、早桃5000亩、麻竹5000亩基地”。之后，县财政每年划拨150万元绿色发展资金用于植树造林，调整林种和树种结构。1991—1999年，全县社会造林累计20.72万亩。其间，植树最多的是1995年，造林3.99万亩；植树最少的是1991年，仅造林1.03万亩，合格面积684亩，占当年任务3万亩的2.28%，被黔南州政府通报批评。1999年春旱严重，经果林完成整地0.35万亩，仅植苗0.12万亩。2000年以后，造林重点转向世界银行贷款造林、退耕还林和珠江防护林体系工程建设，社会造林不再列入考核指标。2000—2008年的9年间，社会造林累计完成6.85万亩，年均0.76万亩。

二、基地植树造林

1984年，全县速生丰产用材林基地建设纳入国家林业建设发展计划，投资方式由拨款补助改为由林业部门向国家农业银行贷款。凡营造速生丰产用材林面积50亩以上，且相对集中连片，农户或承包造林者与林业部门签订贷款造林合同，办理公证手续，落实担保抵押，规划设计批准后，每造林15亩，由林业部门贷款600元，贷款期限为10年。实行分期发贷，有偿服务，冬春造林，秋后验收制度，凡成活率达85%以上的，付给贷款总金额50%，即造林每15亩贷款300元，第二年至第五年，每年贷给60

荔波万亩人工种植杉木林——佳荣大土林场

元，第六年给60元作为幼林抚育直至主伐前的管护费用。林业部门在贷款总额中提取5%的管理费（省、州各1%，县3%），贷款利息由林业部门负责支付。10年期满后，由承包造林者或造林单位在林木有收益时，按每15亩15立方米规格材（国家标准）偿还贷款和垫付利息的单位，即为还本付息，抚育间伐材的规格材可抵交材指标，其余木材归承包造林的单位或个人。是年，县林业局向省造林公司贷款34万元，植苗造林分两个年度实施。1985—1986年，两年营造速生杉、马用材林12片，造林面积累计0.85万亩。其中，原玉屏区副区长吴文礼造林0.56万亩。吴文礼为响应“十年基本绿化荔波”的号召，辞职到水利承包荒山造林，完成造林后，修筑宽18米、长13.3公里的护林防火隔离带。1986年，荔波县获省政府授予“森林面积、蓄积、覆盖率三同步增长县”称号。

1987年年初，县委提出发展5万亩速生丰产用材林基地的项目设想后，于4月委托黔南农校对甲良、方村、播尧的宜林荒山进行踏查，初步规划出2万亩速生丰产泡桐林基地。1988年，县委托贵州省林业勘查设计院对全县5万亩速生丰产用材林基地进行规划，即在甲良、方村、播尧等地实施泡桐速生丰产林2万亩，在水维、佳荣等地实施杉木速生丰产林3万亩。1989年秋，林业部立项批准“荔波县5万亩速生丰产用材林基地建设项目”，下达拨改贷资金250万元，当年划拨到位91万元。

1990—1993年，在水维建成速生丰产杉木林基地3.53万亩，并经林业部中南林勘设计院抽查，成活率达86%以上，保存率达95%，各项生长指标超过部颁标准，被评为良好工程。1998年12月，“荔波县水维3.5万亩速生丰产杉木基地建设”项目获黔南州政府科学技术进步二等奖。

2005年，佳荣镇政府自筹资金，在拉先与拉易结合部营造杉木速生丰产杉木林1.25万亩，经县林业部门核查，成活率达85%以上，保存率94%，林木总本长势良好。

三、贷款植树造林

（一）贴息贷款造林

1990年4月17日，州农业银行、州林业局联合下发《关于林业贴息贷款实施意见》，按实施意见的规定，县内水扒果林场于1991年获项目1个，贷款70万元，造林0.15万亩，其中以酸梅为主的经济林0.1万亩，马尾松播种造林0.05万亩。

（二）世界银行贷款造林

1997年4月，荔波县被林业部世界银行中心和省林业厅世界银行办公室确定为贵州省和中国林业评估试点县。县林业部门按世行中心提出的《贫困地区林业发展项目乡、村社区林业评估（CFA）工作手册》开展试点工作，提交荔波县乡、村的全部成果材料。是年10月，世界银行专家及国务院和林业部相关人员对荔波县的试点工作进行国际项目评估，给予充分肯定，评估成功，为“中国贫困地区林业发展项目”正式立项及转贷实施奠定基础。1999年3月5日，省林业厅批准荔波县世行贷款“贫困地区林业发展项目”县级总体设计。同日，省世界银行办公室批准荔波县“FDPA”人工造林7.21万亩，其中经济林1.15万亩、用材林6.06万亩。经济林中，沙田柚0.63万亩、板栗0.47万亩、九阡李0.05万亩。用材林中，马毛松5.88万亩、杉木0.18万亩。项目贷款期限17年，宽限期7年，建设期6年（含抚育期限）。是年5月，县政府与州政府和州财政局签订转贷协议，转贷资金153万美元。县政府于是年7月分别与朝阳镇、玉屏镇、佳荣镇、播尧乡、甲良镇5个项目乡（镇）签订转贷协议。项目实施后，根据项目区群众提出的减少经济林面积，扩大用材林面积的要求，经省世界银行办公室核准，在项目中期调整项目规模及林种、树种结构。在1999—2001年的3年中，在5个项目乡（镇）完成世界银行贷款造林规模9.16万亩，其中用材林8.12万亩，经济林1.04万亩。用材林中，马尾松容器苗造林7.47万亩，湿地松容器苗造林0.65万亩。经济林中，大板栗嫁接苗造林0.6万亩，优质柚嫁接苗造林0.44万亩，造林规模列全省首位，经省林业厅、国家林业局多次核查，面积核实率100%，良种使用率100%，I级苗使用率100%，造林成活率（保存率）98.9%，环保措施合格率100%，林分平均生长量达标率100%，生长量株数达标率100%，造林密度合格率97.3%，平均整地合格率98.1%，栽植技术合格率98.3%，综合评质为优。造林规模与造林质量仍名列全省第一。2000年6月22日，《黔南日报》以《荔波县引进世行贷款造林成效显著——实施面积均超省、州、县下达的任务指标》为题，对荔波世行造林工作的成效进行专题报道。2001年2月22日，《经济信息时报》以《从倒数第一到正数第一——记荔波县世行贷款造林项目的巨变》为题，对荔波世行贷款林的规模与科技含量进行报道。2004年7月20日，《贵州广播电视报》以《绿海腾龙》为题，撰文对荔波世界银行贷款造林进行报道。同年7月，黔南电视台以《世界银行贷款造林》为题，对县林业世界银行贷款办公室进行专访。

2005年，根据国家林业局世行管理中心《关于做好贫困地区林业发展项目幼林质量摸底调查的通知》，县林业局于是年7月20日—10月13日对县内的世界银行贷款造林地块进行全查，省、州核查后认定：荔波县“FDPA”造林总面积9.16万亩。其中，一类林8.74万亩，占造林面积的95.41%，较全省平均一类林占48.6%的比例高出46.8个百分点；二类林0.42万亩，占造林总面积的4.6%，较全省二类林占34.08%的比例低29.48个百分点；三类林为零，全省三类林平均占项目林的18.7%。荔波世行造林的一类林名列全省第一位，被写进《贵州省贫困地区林业发展项目（FDPA）竣工报告》。

四、退耕还林

2001年，开始进行退耕还林。是年9月28日，贵州省计委、省财政厅、省林业厅、省粮食局下达荔波县退耕还林工程预安计划2万亩。至2002年2月，全县退耕还林0.76万亩，退耕配套荒山造林3.55万亩。2003年，退耕还林1.5万亩，退耕荒造3万亩，退耕人工促进封山育林3万亩。2004年，退耕还林0.6万亩，退林荒造2万亩，人工促进封山育林2万亩。2005年，退耕还林1万亩。2006年以后，主要进行退耕还林工程补植补造和退耕还林巩固后续产业打造，全年完成退耕还林补植造林0.45万亩。2007年，退耕还林0.8万亩。2008年，退耕还林灾后补植补造0.95万亩。

五、珠江防护林体系工程

县境地处珠江流域都江干流上游，属珠江流域防护林工程县。2002年，县内启动珠江防护林体系工程建设，全年珠防工程造林1.51万亩，封山育林1.63万亩。之后，每年营造珠江防护林和封山育林，至2008年，全县7年营造珠江防护林体系工程累计11.38万亩。其中，人工造林4.81万亩，人工促进封山育林6.57万亩。

六、石漠化治理工程

2004年，县林业、国土部门开展全县煤矿区环境治理绿化详查设计。2005年，全县完成喀斯特薪炭林人工点播造林0.5万亩，人工促进封山育林0.5万亩。2007年，人工促进封山育林0.4万亩。2008年，石漠化治理面积1.5万亩。其中，人工植苗造林0.67万亩，人工促进封山育林0.83万亩。全县4年完成石漠化治理工程绿化2.34万亩。其中，人工造林1.17万亩，人工促进封山育林1.17万亩。

七、义务植树与“四旁”绿化

每年“植树节”期间，县内组织机关干部职工和群众开展义务植树活动，对“四旁”进行绿化。

20世纪80年代，“四旁”绿化以种松栽果为主。1993年，组织城镇居民在县城至小七孔公路两侧种植黑荆树800株。1994年春，县政府拨出专项绿化资金，绿化樟江风景名胜区，在水春河风景区和县城至龙王洞河段左岸栽刺竹、苦楝、枫香等800株，在大七孔风景区栽吊竹、白杨、桃子300株，在小七孔风景区拉关至翁龙段栽白杨、苦楝1400株，在县城新街人行道两旁植南洋杉、一品红、假槟榔、鱼尾葵等热带花木200株，形成亚热带风情的绿化格局。2000年以后，对小城镇和省道、县道绿化以及樟江河两岸的河道边进行绿化植物种植。2005年，在樟江两岸植香樟大苗5000株、麻竹45000株、白夹竹25000株。

1978—2008年，义务植树与“四旁”植树累计594.27万株。其中，植树最多的年度为2003年，植树45.53万株；植树最少的年度为1999年，植树0.45万株。

八、飞机播种造林

1982年，在水功播区用飞机播种，总面积26.39万亩，有效面积19.43万亩。1993年春，水庆播区飞机播种总面积10.3万亩，有效面积7.33万亩。播区成效调查均由黔南林业勘设计队进行专业调查，除1993年水庆播区未作成效调查外，对其余播区的成效调查结果为水利播区成效率不足5%，效果评定为失败；茂兰播区成效面积为3.87万亩，每15亩林木株数为2115株，效果评定为差；播尧播区成效面积1.43万亩，成效率为11.75%，林木密度为每15亩2115株，效果评定为差；兰鼎山播区成效面积7.21亩，成效率36.72%，但林木密度仅为每15亩1335株，效果评定为差。2008年，县林业局对水庆播区进行县级调查，成效面积仅0.33万亩，成效率为4.43%，低于成效率最低5%标准，评定为失败，州未核查。

九、封山育林

1978—1984年，县林业部门每年进行封山育林。1985年统计，全县封山育林面积总计664500亩，郁闭成林286995亩，占封山育林面积的43.19%。1987—1994年，全县封山育林面积总计207285亩。

1995年5月，国家林业局批准荔波“九万大山”封山育林项目12片，面积86805亩，投资20.23万元。项目按“以封为主，封育结合”“谁封育、谁受益、谁管护”的原则，做到宜乔则乔，宜灌则灌，培育多树种、多功能、多层次、多效益的森林植被类型。1996年，荔波县获全国绿化委员会授予“全国绿化造林百佳县”称号，获贵州省“全省率先绿化达标先进县”称号。1995—1997年，全县封山育林面积总计133605亩。

2002年，驾欧乡在喀斯特石漠化地带实施封山育林3000亩，恢复和保护小七孔周边植被。

2002—2008年，封山育林面积总计159403亩，有护林员14人，设立封山育林宣传牌5块。

十、育苗

20世纪80年代初，县苗圃开展泡桐埋根育苗和播种育苗。1984年，苗圃有职工17人，推行“定人员、定任务、定投工、定措施、定奖惩”生产责任制，是年培育各种苗木16万株。

1990年，县政府将县苗圃土地30亩划归茂兰喀斯特森林自然保护区管理处作基建用地。

2001年，县政府将县苗圃土地40亩划为城镇建设用地，苗圃人员分散到县林业局和各乡（镇）林业站工作，保留国营苗圃建制及人员编制。是年，省林业厅批准荔波县在水利乡拉干坡设珠防苗圃场1个，面积112.5亩，投资100万元。其中，中央投资80万元，地方配套20万元（中央资金已到位，县林业局自筹资金10万元）。场圃于2004年竣工，是年培育各种阔叶林绿化苗42亩，出苗86万株；种植金秋梨20亩。2005年，育苗45亩，培育阔叶珍贵树种树苗61.7万株。2006年，营林站职工培育桑苗和马尾松容器苗。2008年，种苗由林业专业户承包开发。

第三节 山林保护

一、森林防火

1978年11月，开展护林防火大检查，甲良区甲站公社和朝阳区王蒙公社被评为未发生森林火灾先进社。是年，全县发生森林火灾7起，受害森林面积0.47万亩。

1979年春，发生山林火灾22起，毁林面积3.7万亩。全年查处山林火灾事件7起，罚款6起，追究刑事责任1起1人。

1980年，县林业、公安、检察、法院等部门联合派出宣传车到9个公社、17个点向群众宣传《中华人民共和国森林法》以及国务院和省政府关于坚决制止乱砍滥伐森林的紧急通知，受教育群众达2万人次。

1983年12月21日，县人大常委会作出《关于护林防火的决定》。1984年年初，林业部门又派出防火宣传车到区、社，以放电影、展出破坏森林典型案例等形式，向群众宣传护林防火知识，受教育群众13万人次。1985年，县林业派出所按《中华人民共和国森林法》查处纵火烧毁森林资源案件，森林火灾比1984年下降41%，火灾受害面积控制在有林面积的3‰以内。

1990年，县林业局到各区、乡场坝进行护林防火宣传，印发《森林防火通知书》3万份，张贴《关于严格野外用火管理，防止山林火灾的通知》300份，挂防火标语牌600条（块），要求群众严格遵守《森林防火条例》，做到“五不用火”（不割好防火线不用火，防火人员不到达现场不用火，不准备好打火工具不用火，天干风大不用火，放火后无人看守不用火）。

1993年，出动防火宣传车183辆（次），出动人员381人次，开展下乡宣传78次，召开林区村、组群众防火会18次，举办森林防火培训班15期，树立和刷新护林防火宣传标语牌218块，悬挂护林防火标语145幅，印发森林防火宣传日历3万张、防火宣传资料3.8万份。这一护林防火宣传管控模式一直沿用至2003年。

2004年，因林业工作重造轻管，森林火灾上升，全县发生森林山火44起。其中，森林火灾16起，烧毁有林地林木2.55万亩；森林火警28起，烧毁未成林造林地面积内幼木10.62万亩。造成过火面积13.2万亩，成灾面积和损失规模均列全省之首，县政府按省、州林业主管部门关于查处责任人的要求查处相关责任人。

2005年，省、州林业部门将荔波县的森林防火工作列为重点督查对象，县委、县政府加强森林防火工作组织领导，与各乡（镇）签订《森林防火责任状》，县林业局恢复和改进原森林防火宣传管理模式，森林火灾得到控制。

1978—2008年度全县森林山火统计表

表11-3

年度	发生次数（起）			火场过火面积（亩）	受害有林面积（亩）	森林受害率（‰）
	合计	火警	火灾			
1978	7	0	7	—	4725.00	5.66
1979	22	0	22	4197.20	36964.50	44.32
1980	37	0	37	4100.00	25395.00	30.45
1981	22	0	22	—	1470.00	1.76

续表11－3

年度	发生次数（起）			火场过火面积（亩）	受害有林面积（亩）	森林受害率（‰）
	合计	火警	火灾			
1982	7	0	7	426.23	2720.40	3.26
1983	55	0	55	3349.67	21375.00	25.63
1984	48	—	—	—	15679.50	18.80
1985	20	0	20	—	3765.00	4.13
1986	30	—	—	—	10069.95	11.06
1987	25	17	8	9833.00	45276.00	49.72
1988	6	—	—	1200.00	10470.00	11.50
1989	18	13	5	319.13	846.00	0.92
1990	9	2	7	117.63	687.00	0.75
1991	7	3	4	2202.00	1470.00	0.10
1992	42	21	21	17178.00	37800.00	2.77
1993	7	1	6	26.60	351.00	0.33
1994	4	0	4	91.33	91.95	0.10
1995	4	0	4	42.00	285.00	0.03
1996	13	1	12	546.67	2685.00	2.31
1997	7	3	4	328.00	162.00	0.14
1998	8	1	7	62.27	120.00	0.10
1999	15	5	10	299.33	754.05	0.65
2000	11	7	4	61.37	527.55	0.45
2001	8	4	4	150.20	31.80	0.02
2002	17	5	12	230.20	438.00	0.20
2003	53	47	6	843.30	1674.45	0.80
2004	44	28	16	8798.25	25515.00	0.76
2005	30	14	16	523.79	1505.70	0.19
2006	27	23	4	318.66	994.95	0.52
2007	39	29	10	520.56	1236.00	0.65
2008	53	45	8	882.60	669.75	0.35

二、有害生物防治

境内林木在生长过程中，根、干、枝、芽和花、果、叶常受病原菌和害虫侵袭，并在适宜的环境条件下迅速扩展蔓延。森林病虫害被称为“不冒烟的森林火灾”。

县境内森林害虫种类主要有天牛科、夜蛾科、白蚁科、蝗科、蟋蟀科、蝼蛄科、棉蚜科、蚧科、叶旱科；森林病害主要有杉木苗猝倒病、油桐黑斑病、柑橘痂病、溃疡病和寄生樟科等。

1978年，全县建有森林病虫害固定监测标准地3个，临时监测样地15个，应施监测面积146.86万亩，实施监测面积1.87万亩，监测率为1.27%。森林病虫发生面积1.59万亩，发生率1.08%；防治面积0.04万亩，防治率37.96%；应施产地检疫面积70亩，实施产地检疫面积41亩，检疫率58.57%。

在1979年3月31日—6月25日黔南州首次森林昆虫普查采集昆虫标本3046号中，荔波的昆虫标本有800号。在1980年4月28日—9月28日黔南州森林病害调查采集的林木病害标本1665号中，荔波发现的森林病害有38种（病毒病30种、线虫病8种）。

1984年4月10日—6月15日，贵州农学院、贵阳医学院生物教研室和贵州寄生虫病研究所等部门对茂兰喀斯特森林的昆虫和蚊相进行调查，发现茂兰喀斯特森林中有已知昆虫17目、89科、289种。在289种昆虫中，植食性昆虫占79.1%。在植食性昆虫中，食叶害虫占65.9%，枝梢害虫占10.3%，蛀干及干材害虫占17.9%，地下害虫占5.9%。天敌昆虫有11目、25科、60种，占昆虫种数的20.9%。蚊类有9属48种，其中，按蚊属10种、伊蚊属12种、序蚊属17种，其余蚊属9种。

1986年，开展柑橘溃疡病普查，先后检查22个乡（镇）、63个村、128个自然寨的柑橘苗木6.16万株，发现病株3.55万株。是年年底，县林业局设专职森林病虫专职检疫员1人，兼职检疫员2人。1987年，检查柑橘苗木面积30亩，苗木86.69万株，烧毁病株9.25万株。并对原发和过柑橘溃疡病的果园进行跟踪复查，发现并烧毁病株8.3万株。经连续防治，柑橘林木和苗木长势良好。

1989年4月下旬，贵阳医学院生物学教研室对月亮山的蚊相进行调查，共采集幼虫1380条、成蚊144只，为8属446种。其中，按蚊属7种、伊蚊属11种、库蚊属18种，其余蚊属5个共9种。1990年，发生森林病虫面积115.05亩，由于防治及时，病害未形成灾害。

1991年，在县林业局设县森林病虫防治检疫站，有专职检疫员5人。森林病虫害防治检疫机构组建后，制定全县森林病虫防治管理体系，完善林业有害生物防治工作月历、森林植物检疫管理制度、林业有害预测预报信息反馈制度等，加强有害生物防治工作。是年，全县建立有害生物固定监测标准样地16个，年应施监测面积204.59万亩，实施监测面积192.16万亩，监测率93.92%；防治面积1.23万亩，防治率95.35%；实施产地检疫面积287亩，检疫率100%。1994年，荔波县实现林业有害生物防治“一降三提高”（成灾率下降，防治率提高、监测率提高、检疫率提高）的总体目标，年底，县森林病虫病防治检疫站获贵州省目标达标先进单位二等奖。1996年，该站成为贵州省首批县级森林病虫防治体系规范化管理达标单位。

1997年4月—1998年2月，县林业有害生物防治部门开展贵州省6种森林植物检疫对象专题调查，在境内发现锈色粒肩天牛的零星危害，在朝阳镇发现100亩柑橘林感染柑橘溃疡病，及时进行治理，并为东北林业大学出版的《森林植物检疫对象图册》提供锈色粒肩天牛的彩色照片。

2000年12月，省林业厅批准荔波建立松材线虫病检疫监测点，开展松材线虫病检疫监测。同时，经省林业厅考核，授予县森林病虫害防治检疫站“贵州省森病虫害防治先进单位”称号。

2002年3月，对外来苗木跟踪监测发现水春林场从开阳县调进的李子树苗带有病害，并报请州现场检疫核实，此李树苗所带病害为国家林业局明确的森林植物检疫对象“冠瘿病”，其苗木2200株中，假植苗感疫率69.2%，已上山定植苗感率85.7%。为遏制和避免该病在县境内传播，水春林场将苗木全部拔除焚毁，并对树坑及附近的土坑进行消毒处理，避免检疫对象传播。这次植物情况检疫引起国家林业局重视，于2003年投入荔波林业有害生物防治资金15万元。

1978—2008年全县森林病虫害防治情况统计表

表11－4

年度	森林总面积（万亩）	病虫害发生		病虫害防治		主要发生区域（乡镇）
		面积（万亩）	发生率（%）	面积（万亩）	防治率（%）	
1978	83.40	1.02	0.01	0.04	3.82	—
1979	83.40	0.95	0.01	0.02	1.85	—
1980	83.40	0.58	0.01	0.04	6.27	—
1981	83.40	0.48	0.01	0.04	7.85	—
1982	83.40	0.77	0.01	0.07	9.53	—
1983	83.40	0.05	0	0.01	8.77	—
1984	83.40	1.92	0.02	0.09	4.91	—
1985	91.05	0.50	0.01	0.08	16.42	—
1986	91.05	0.44	0.01	0.04	8.43	—
1987	91.05	0.92	0.01	0.38	41.36	—
1988	91.05	0.16	0	0.06	35.11	—
1989	91.05	0.28	0	0.06	21.35	—
1990	91.05	0.22	0	0.06	26.61	—
1991	91.05	0.18	0	0.10	56.14	—
1992	91.05	0.73	0.01	0.11	15.26	甲良、水利、玉屏
1993	91.05	0.28	0.97	0	61.82	甲良、佳荣、水利、玉屏
1994	91.05	0.21	0.72	0	65.74	水利、甲良
1995	116.10	0	0	0	0	—
1996	116.10	0.11	0.47	0.09	68.30	玉屏、水利
1997	116.10	0.06	0.20	0.04	73.30	水利、播尧、玉屏
1998	116.10	0.06	0.19	0.05	81.80	玉屏、水利、甲良
1999	116.10	0.13	0.44	0.13	99.00	玉屏、朝阳
2000	116.10	0.11	0.29	0.08	71.37	玉屏、朝阳、佳荣
2001	116.10	0.18	0.58	0.16	91.60	玉屏、瑶山、佳荣、甲良
2002	116.10	0.07	0.34	0.06	84.50	甲良、玉屏
2003	116.10	0.08	0.06	0.07	76.85	玉屏、永康
2004	116.10	0.06	0.18	0.05	78.70	玉屏
2005	190.10	0.33	0.23	0.30	90.36	水利、玉屏
2006	190.10	0.38	0.26	0.32	84.20	佳荣、水利、玉屏
2007	190.10	1.51	6.20	1.03	68.40	佳荣、玉屏
2008	190.10	1.29	5.30	0.97	75.00	佳荣、玉屏

第四节　林产品开发利用

一、木材加工

1978年，县林业局购置38英寸带锯1台，成立带锯生产车间（后称木材加工车间），有职工10人，开展木材来料加工业务。1985年以后，随着南方省区统配材计划取消，国营木材加工随行就市。1988年后，逐步有个体户、私营企业经营木材加工。

1994年，全县木材经营加工单位进行清理整顿。整顿后，全县有木材加工企业11户，其中国营1户、民营1户、私营9户。

1995年1月，全县实行木材经营加工许可证制度，所有从事木材经营加工的单位和个人，必须向县级以上（含县级）林业行政主管部门提出申请，经批准发给"木材经营加工许可证"，再到工商行政管理机关办理营业执照后方能从事木材经营加工业务。实行木材经营加工许可证的木材范围，包括木材、竹材及木竹成品、半成品、旧房料、商品柴炭。

2008年年底，全县有木材加工企业57户，其中国有1户、集体6户、民营5户、私营45户，规模较大的有鑫源综合木材加工厂、梅桃旋切木材加工厂、兴林指接板木材加工厂、甲良木材加工厂、甲良刨花木片加工厂、荔波国有木材加工厂等6家，其余均以来料解锯和家具生产为主。

二、木材供销

1978—1984年，木材实行统购统销。1985年，取消木材统购，随行就市自由交易，除运销县外、省外的木材仍由县林业部门审批外，在县内销售的木材由群众自由议价。1985—1990年，县内林业企业收购木材累计1.29万立方米，销售累计1.26万立方米。1991后，木材购销控制在商品年限额指标以内，1991—1995年，收购调运木材45382立方米，年均9076.4立方米。其间，1994年，县内设木材交易集市1个，对木材交易进行集中管理。1996—2000年，收购调运木材23325立方米，年均4665立方米。2001—2005年，收购调运木材31995立方米，年均6399立方米。2006—2008年，收购调运木材18765立方米，年均6255立方米。

第五节　林政管理

一、林木采伐管理

1978年，林木归集体所有。1980年，荔波县列为全省林业"三定"（稳定山林权、划定自留山、确定林业生产责任制）试点县，开展林业"三定"工作，将林木划给农户经营管理。按"以营林为基础，造管并举，造多于伐，采育结合，综合利用"的方针，各社队的荒山实行"谁种谁管谁受益"政策，明确承包责任制50年不变。1981年6月，荔波县被林业部表彰为林业"三定"先进县。到1983年，全县完成山林"三定"工作，县政府签发自留山证、林权证和山林管理证，做到"山有主，主有权，权有责，责有利"，权、责、利结合。

1984年，根据"用材林消耗量低于生长量"的原则，对木材采伐实行"一本账"计划和凭证采伐制度。年度木材采伐计划包括社会流通材（国家统配材、地方自主材）、集体自用材和群众自用材，国有、集体和个人采伐木材，均纳入计划，不准突破。采伐计划由县计划委员会下达，逐级落实到区、乡、村、组，发给"木材采伐许可证"，按计划采伐，无证采伐或者超计划采伐，以破坏森林论处。“木材采伐许可证”由省林业主管部门统一印制，县林业主管部门根据“一本账”计划核发，以乡、村或村民小组为单位进行申请。严禁盗伐滥伐。是年，将“木材采伐许可证”的核发权下放到区公所、乡政府以至村委会，出现乱发证情况，个别区、乡发生倒卖采伐证事件，得到及时制止。从是年起，实施《贵州省关于进一步放宽政策，搞活林业经济若干问题的规定》（简称“贵州林业18条”），贵州林业18条允许农户承包开发荒山和对中幼林进行折价转让。根据这一政策，荔波县制定引资造林，建设商品材基地，折价转让杉木中幼林等措施。

1985年，根据国务院《关于木材经营改革问题的通知》，取消木材统购，开放木材市场，允许林农和集体的木材自由上市交易，实行议购议销，但销往县外、省外仍由林业部门统一审批，使用统一印制的木材运输证。是年，县林业部门按照林业部颁发的《制订年森林采伐限额暂行规定》，编制《荔波县森林采伐限额》（即1986—1990年“七五”限额），确定以村为单位的采伐限额，实行木材凭采伐许可证进行采伐、收购和上市制度。同时，规划建设全县林业基地3个，即东北部杉木林基地3万亩、西北部泡桐基地5万亩和南部泡竹林基地1万亩。1986年，对木材经营单位和个人进行清理整顿，将采伐证核发权收归县林业主管部门。

1987年1月，为便于采伐证的审批和发放管理，商品材采伐证直接由县林业主管部门填发，自用材采伐证由县林业主管部门委托区林业站代发。是年5月，对木材流通渠道进行整顿，重申“木材由林业部门统一管理和进山收购，未经林业部门批准，任何单位和个人不准进山收购木材；林农自产的零星木材在指定的市场凭证销售；私人一律不得贩运和倒卖木材”。

1988年5月9日，国务院批准茂兰喀斯特森林区列为国家级自然保护区后，茂兰喀斯特林区的保护管理工作从县林业局划归茂兰保护区管理处管理。

1990年年初，编制《荔波县“八五”期间森林采伐限额规划》，全县1991—1995年森林采伐限额10.7万立方米。

1991年，实行森林资源采伐限额全额管理，商品材、农民自用材、培植业用材、其他用材和烧柴（含商品薪柴和生活烧柴）统一列入限额范围，规定除生活烧柴外，其余均实行凭证采伐。对商品材采伐许可证发放建立台账，进行总量控制和管理。

1994年，《贵州省森林采伐限额管理办法》施行，县内将超过5立方米以上的农民自用材审批权收归县林业主管部门。

1995年，按黔南州颁布实施的《黔南州中幼林拍卖管理暂行办法》，县林业部门开展中幼林经济价值的评估测算工作，中幼林进入流转交易。

1997年，县委、县政府在全省率先出台“两禁止、三关闭、一保护”（禁止砍伐天然林、禁止放火烧，关闭乡镇林工商公司、关闭杂木市场、关闭木炭市场，保护天然林）林业管理政策。

1998年，国家颁布停止砍伐天然林的规定以及省林业厅发布《关于严禁采伐天然林的紧急通知》后，县政府发出《关于关闭乡镇林工商公司的通知》，决定从1999年1月1日起关闭乡（镇）办的林工商公司，除县林工商公司外，任何组织和个人不得经营木材。原乡（镇）林工商公司的木材执照由林政管理部门注销，其库存木材变价由县林工商公司销售。

1999年4月，县政府发出《关于保护森林资源，建立生态县、公园县的通告》，宣布禁止采伐天然林，特别是喀斯特地貌上的林木，严禁杂木上市，各乡（镇）林业站一律不得经营木材。是年，各乡（镇）分别成立天然林保护工作领导小组，加强天然林保护监督。

2004年，县政府依据2003年中共中央、国务院《关于加快林业发展的决定》及中共贵州省委、省政府《关于加快林业发展的意见》，取消原木、原竹和林业生产用苗的农林特产税和行业收费。

二、行政执法检查

1978年，县内设有茂兰、播尧、甲良、更甫木材检查站。1979年，根据《中华人民共和国森林法（试行）》，实行木材运输凭证管理，加强木材出境监督，依法查处违法运输木材行为。1984年，建林业公安派出所，查处各类林业违法案件。1985年，全县统一使用省林业厅印制的木材运输证。1987年，查处无证运输木材20起，收缴无证运输和无证采伐木材68.36立方米，林政处罚金额7130.30元。

1989年3月21日，根据州政府制定的《木材经营管理暂行办法》，进行全县木材市场清理和整顿，取缔非法经营。

1993年8月，省政府批准荔波县设置茂兰出省木材检查站，配备专职木材检查员4人，兼职检查员2人。原检查站设施路障撤销，实行区域流动检查监督，上岗人员必须持有统一证牌并佩戴专门标志。是年，原条、原木、枕木、坑木、电杆、脚手杆、车立柱、椽材、板方材等各种木材、楠竹和大宗木制品（含半成品），旧房料、树蔸、胶合板、纤维板、刨花板、大宗竹制品（含半成品）和商品柴炭、松香、栓皮、杨梅皮、杜仲皮、厚朴皮、黄檗皮、桂皮、桐籽、木姜子、五倍子、生漆、木耳、香菇、茯苓、竹笋等应交林业税金的产品全部列入运输管理对象。

1994年1月，县林业公安派出所侦破珍贵木材偷运案件1起，截获榉木8.26立方米，价值10万元。

1996年6月，对木材运输证实行“会计出纳式”管理制度，即管证和填证职责分离，管证人员负责证件领交、结算、发放和保管，填证人员负责具体填证工作，并实行木材运输证限额、限品种管理，启用新版“省内木材（林产品）运输证”。

1996—2005年，县林业主管部门除查处一般林业案件外，先后在全县范围内开展“跨世纪绿色保卫行动”“猎鹰行动”“春雷行动”“绿创行动”“破案攻坚战”“天保行动”“天保二号行动”“候鸟行动”“候鸟二号行动”“森林火灾案件破案会战”“林业严打专项行动”等，查处各种破坏森林和野生动植物资源的违法行为。

1997年1月，根据林业部《林业行政执法管理办法》，规范县内林业行政执法，在木材运输等林业行政执法活动中，必须出示“林业行政执法证”。

1998年7月—2001年4月，国家林业局授权荔波县林业公安派出所查处《中华人民共和国森林法》规定的行政处罚案件，处罚时以县林业局的名誉作出行政处罚决定，林业公安派出所参与木材流通运输监督管理。行政执法人员必须持有国家林业局统一核发的“林业行政执法证”。

2001年，经省公安厅、林业厅批准，县林业派出所升格更名为县森林警察大队。2001年5月—2008年12月，国家林业局授权县森林警察大队查处《中华人民共和国森林法》规定的行政处罚案件，处罚时以荔波县公安局森林警察大队或荔波县森林公安分局的名誉作出行政处罚决定。在行政执法中，必须出示“林业行政执法证”。

2008年，县林业综执法大队开展“非法占用林地清理”“绿盾三号”执法活动，受理各类林业案件共368件，查处339件，查处率92.12%。其中，林业行政案件111件，刑事案件8件，处理违法人员210人，收缴无证木材320.69立方米。

1979—2008年全县林业案件查处统计表

表11－5

年度	受理案件总数（件）	侦破处理总数（件）	刑事案件（件）		治安案件（件）		行政案件（件）		受处理人次
			立案	破案	立案	处理	立案	处理	
1978	20	20	—	—	20	20	—	—	20
1979	7	7	1	1	6	6	—	—	7
1985	13	12	2	1	3	3	8	8	12
1986	24	12	3	2	10	9	11	11	12
1987	20	20	3	3	11	11	6	6	20
1988	39	33	9	9	2	2	28	22	33
1989	52	46	16	16	18	18	18	12	46
1990	23	23	9	6	12	12	2	2	23
1991	41	41	26	26	11	11	4	4	41
1992	86	82	9	9	14	14	63	59	82
1993	56	55	2	2	8	7	46	46	55
1994	56	54	2	2	2	1	52	51	54
1995	159	151	5	5	—	—	154	152	157
1996	137	135	6	6	2	2	131	129	137
1997	106	103	—	—	—	—	106	103	103
1998	101	99	3	3	1	1	98	96	100
1999	126	122	5	5	—	—	121	117	122
2000	117	104	6	6	—	—	111	108	114
2001	145	142	2	1	—	—	143	141	142
2002	113	105	3	2	—	—	110	103	105
2003	214	184	7	4	—	—	207	180	184
2004	135	103	2	2	—	—	133	101	103
2005	512	494	4	4	—	—	509	490	494
2006	232	218	2	2	—	—	230	216	218
2007	499	478	3	3	—	—	496	475	478
2008	368	339	8	8	—	—	160	111	210

三、林权制度改革

根据省政府2006年11月《关于深化集体林权制度改革工作的意见》，关于从2006年12月起，利用3年时间，通过改革基本建立起“产权归属明晰，经营主体到位，责权划分明确，利益保障严格，流转程序规范，监督服务有效”的集体林权改革制度，实现“山有其主，主有其权，权有其责，责有其利”的目标和2007年年底省政府《关于推进集体林权制度改革的意见》，2008年1月25日，县政府召开林权制度改革摸底调查会议，对摸底调查进行部署。历时2个月，完成摸底调查工作，全县有林业用地面积2904750亩，国有林地面积303150亩，集体林面积2573400亩。在集体林地面积中，集体管理面积2265750亩，责任山和自留山为193950亩，流转山面积为113700亩。根据林改方案，除茂兰国家级自然保护区30万亩和樟江风景名胜区118650亩（经黔南州林改办同意未列入改革），以及已确权的39000亩退耕还林地和因历史原因无法妥善处置的146850亩林权纠纷地外，应列入这次林权制度改革的林地面积为2269050亩。完成摸底调查后，县政府制定出《荔波县林权制度改革方案》，4月，县委、县政府成立荔波县林权制度改革领导小组，县政府召开各乡（镇）长、分管副乡（镇）长、林业站站长参加的林改动员暨林改业务培训会议，学习中央、省文件精神和相关林改知识，对全县林改工作进行全面部署。各乡（镇）相应成立林改工作领导小组，开展乡、村林改宣传和培训。10月13日，县委、县政府在翁昂乡召开全县林权制度改革现场工作会，推进林改工作进程。

这次林权制度改革的内容有“明晰产权，放活经营，规范收费，规范流转”四个方面，采取6种方式进行改革，即稳定自留山政策，已划定的自留山由农户长期无偿使用，不强行收回；完善责任山政策；产权到户，家庭经营或联户经营；分股不分山，分利不分林；其他承包经营；稳妥处理已经流转的集体山林和个人承包管理的山林。以上6种形式，不论采取哪一种，均召开村民会议或村民代表大会，在征得三分之二以上人数同意后，依法完善或补签家庭承包或流转经营合同，换（发）全国统一式样的林权证。至12月底，全县17个乡（镇）有93个村、1148个村民小组4万多户农村人口完成林权制度改革，确权19036宗，面积达2245500亩，其中公益林确权面积1411500亩，商品林确权面积834000亩。以经营模式划分，自留山经营确权229宗，面积11015亩，占完成总面积的0.49%；责任山经营完成11511宗，面积446328.45亩，占完成总面积的19.87%；集体统一经营均利到户的7031宗，面积172288.65亩，占完成面积的7.67%；流转经营265宗，面积115226.7亩，占完成总面积的5.13%。

2009年12月，全县完成林改勘界确权山林2311500亩，勾绘宗地19036宗，占应参加林改山林面积的100%，占林改总面积的94.08%，发证率97%。全县完成林权制度改革18673宗，面积总计2200500亩，林木、林地发放林权产权证9885本，占勘界林改面积的98.02%。2010年，建立权改文书档案736盒（县级1盒、乡村735盒）、照片档案18卷（县级16卷、乡镇2卷）。是年10月，经州政府对全县林改档案进行检查，档案管理合格率98%，通过州级验收。

第六节　林业规费征收

一、育林基金征收与解交

（一）征收

1978年，县林业局根据省财政厅、林业厅的规定，将集体林区征收甲种育林基金和乙种育林基金提取标准由按1964年1月制定的标准每立方米木材（或每百根楠竹）征收7元（甲种育林基金4元、乙种育林基金3元），改为按1972年修订的标准执行，即国营收购或国营采伐单位缴纳5元，在付给社队的林价（山价）款中代扣2元。代扣的集体林育林基金由县林业局本着“优先用于原缴纳育林基金的社、队”的原则安排使用，此标准执行到1981年。

1982年，根据中共中央、国务院《关于保护森林发展林业若干问题的决定》的规定，适当提高集体林区和国有林育林基金的征收标准，扩大育林基金征收范围，集体林区提取标准由1978年前（1964年1月制定的标准）每立方米木材（或每百根楠竹）7元提高到12元。其中，森工企业、林工商公司收购或组织采伐集体林缴纳甲种育林基金8元，从付给生产队的林价中代扣乙种育林基金4元。国有林育林基金提取标准为凡森工企业、国有林场生产的木材提高到15元，这一标准执行到1985年。

从1985年起，不分甲种和乙种基金，统称育林基金。

1986—1987年，育林基金由按每立方米木材固定金额缴纳，改为由经营单位按集体林农出售木材、竹材价售价的15%提取。国有林育林基金的计征标准，按原规定每立方米木材15元提取不变。

1988年，根据国务院的相关文件规定，育林基金改为对木材经营单位按其收购后的第一次销售价的12%计征，国有林照此标准执行。

2001年，将更新改造资金（维简费）并入育林基金，合并后的育林基金按其木材收购后的第一次销售价的20%计征。至2008年，执行标准不变。

（二）解交

1978—1984年，提取育林基金累计440890元。其中，甲种育林基金275560元，乙种育林基金165330元。甲种育林基金的解交比例为省林业厅15%，州林业局15%，县林业局留用70%。乙种育林基金按规定不上缴，由县林业局专户储存，优先用于交售木材的社队或林农更新造林，3年不造林的由县林业局调剂使用。

1985—1988年，提取育林基金累计258535元，育林基金解交比例为：省林业厅30%，州林业局20%，县林业局留用50%。

1978—1994年间，解交省林业厅的育林基金，省林业厅返还给荔波县99.8%，用于荒山造林绿化。

1989—1999年，提取育林基金累计2398339元。根据省政府办公厅《贵州省育林基金管理暂行办法》，育林基金的解交比例调整为省林业厅15%，州林业局15%，县林业局留用70%。

2000年后，育林基金列入地方财政预算。2000—2008年，提取育林基金累计2791266元，全部列入林业事业经费其他支出科目。

二、维简费（更新改造资金）收取与解交

（一）收取

1978年，更新改造资金按生产木材或收购木材产量，每立方米木材提取5元（1972年制定的标准），执行到1981年。1982年，按生产或收购木材产量，每立方米木材提取10元，此标准执行到1985年。1986—1987年，按集体林农出售木材、竹材售价的10%提取。1988年以后，按收购后的第一次销售价的8%提取。从1993年起，木材更新改造资金称为维简费。2001年，荔波县作为全州试点县，将维简费并入育林基金，合并征收。1978—2000年，全县提取木材维简费（更新改造资金）累计1726904元。

（二）解交

1978—1988年，全县提取木材更新改造资金累计161003元。其中，解交省林业厅70%，解交州林业局20%，县级留用10%。

1989—1999年，提取维简费（更新改造资金）累计1050673元。县林业局根据贵州省政府办公厅出台的《贵州省木材更新改造管理暂行办法》，分别上缴省15%、州15%，县留用70%。

2000年后，维简费征收列入地方财政预算。是年，收取维简费125321元，全部列入县级林业事业经费其他支出科目。

2001年，维简费并入育林基金征收后，不再单独解交。

（三）使用

1978—1999年，县林业局留用支配的更改资金中，除10万元按程序审批用于弘林宾馆的建设外，其余主要投向为林区公路、水运码头、木材加工车间的建设与维护及其木材运输器具的采购。

三、林政管理费收取

从1984年4月起，对森林采伐与木材（含竹材）流通实行发证管理，在办理木材运输证时，按木材1.5元/立方米收取林政管理费。1988年4月1日起，按国家经济委员会、林业部、财政部、国家物价局、国家工商行政管理局《关于整顿和调整南方负担问题的通知》，将林政管理费由1.5元/立方米调高到3元/立方米。增加部分主要用于森林防火，林政管理费收取制度执行到2000年年底。

四、森林植被恢复费

从2002年起，按照2000年省政府公布的《贵州省征占用林地补偿费用管理办法》的规定，收取森林植被恢复费。2002—2008年，全县收取森林植被恢复费累计1863830元。收取的森林植被恢复费主要用于县内异地造林开支。

1978—2008年全县林业规费征收统计表

表11－6 单位：元

年度	总计	育林基金提取	更改资金（维简费）提取	林政管理费	植被恢复费
1978	120543	61817	58726	—	—
1979	93666	48034	45632	—	—
1980	93912	48160	45752	—	—
1981	67936	34839	33097	—	—
1982	166430	90780	75650	—	—
1983	130416	71136	59280	—	—
1984	168660	86124	71770	10766	—
1985	128099	65412	54510	8177	—
1986	125706	74581	41852	9273	—
1987	96664	54291	34210	8163	—
1988	116624	64251	39431	12942	—
1989	144058	84279	49249	10530	—
1990	150052	89827	54321	5904	—
1991	130913	79549	43501	7863	—
1992	146212	83409	55306	7497	—
1993	452272	293558	141257	17457	—
1994	627822	437773	174260	15789	—
1995	534940	382451	132164	20325	—
1996	457273	324849	115207	17217	—

续表11－6

年度	总计	育林基金提取	更改资金（维简费）提取	林政管理费	植被恢复费
1997	403372	261155	124019	18198	—
1998	316302	225204	70533	20565	—
1999	243974	136285	90856	16833	—
2000	359083	217571	125321	16191	—
2001	214284	214284	—	—	—
2002	535157	256157	—	—	279000
2003	339757	339757	—	—	—
2004	518300	518300	—	—	—
2005	374526	374526	—	—	—
2006	640000	290800	—	—	349200
2007	1430647	291957	—	—	1138690
2008	384854	287914	—	—	96940

第六章 水 利

第一节 水利工程

一、蓄水工程

（一）水库

1978年前，全县修建水库12个，1978—1990年建成的水库8个。这些水库中，因渗漏等问题难于除险加固，不能发挥效益的水库6个（洞考水库、内角水库、甲老水库、夜寨水库、向阳水库、岜芒水库）。

洪江水库 位于县城南部洪江河上游，距县城17公里，1978年前建成，是荔波县建成的第一座以灌溉为主，以防洪、发电为辅的综合利用工程，附属电站利用水头160米。洪江河源于朝阳水银村南侧，流向南，经拉佑、拉岜、围寨等村入洞为潜流，在飞虎山山洞出露，明流400米后再潜入地下，在朝阳拉良汇入樟江。坝址以上流域面积4.2平方公里，水库利用水量207万立方米。20年一遇洪水流量21立方米/秒，200年一遇洪峰流量83.7立方米/秒。水库校核水位17.5米，设计洪水位16米，防洪水位16.5米，正常水位15米，有效库容200万立方米，死库容7万立方米，可利用水面250亩。水库附属工程飞虎山电站，引用流量0.4立方米/秒，利用水头160米。装机CD26-W-45/1×48型水轮机和SE-W59/34-6型各2套共250千瓦。2000年，因水库存在渗漏问题，由黔南州水利水电勘测设计院对其进行除险加固设计。是年，经省水利厅会同省计委组织专家进行审查后，批复并报珠江水利委员会复核通过。2003年，对水库进行除险加固，总投资393.3万元，主要建设项目有坝基及左右岸帷幕灌浆工程、坝体防治及整治工程、新建取水隧洞及放水设施、进库公路改造、自动化监

荔波台江水坝

测系统工程。

威刀水库 位于水尧乡境内，1978年前建成，修建输水干渠4.16公里，砌石构建防渗，支渠5.33公里，全部为土渠。另有铸铁倒虹管条总长2700米。大坝建筑在距水尧乡东面7公里的无名小溪上，小溪属樟江支流，坝址以上流域面积2.2平方公里。水库下游有水尧乡水尧村、打里村稻田1000亩。工程设计灌溉面积1100亩，由于配套不完善，有效灌溉面积为950亩。水库兴建时，由于石土接壤部位未设反滤层，土坝部分土质防渗性能差，与放水涵管接合部位不良，蓄水后涵洞砌体内与坝后有带土浑水流出，迎水坝面多处沉陷，尤以涵洞轴线上最为严重，虽经补救，效果甚微，故一直不准蓄水。2004年，投入中央专项资金390万元，对水库进行除险加固，对大坝上下游坝坡进行放缓处理，上游大坝基础浇筑防渗齿墙、铺设防渗土工膜和帷幕灌浆；扩宽改造正槽式溢洪道，全长103米，溢洪堰进口段宽12米，陡坡段宽6米，架设交通桥1座；新建放水隧洞1条长100米；对原放水管涵进行封堵，建立水库自动监测系统。

鲁捞水库 位于甲良镇，1978年前建成。水库筑坝于阳凤河上游，坝址以上流域面积31平方公里。多年平均降水量1300毫米，年总产水量200万立方米。设计总库容40万立方米，是县内最早建成的小（2）型水库。大坝为土坝，高7.5米，坝长70米，顶宽4米，背水坡比1∶2.5，迎水坡比1∶1.5。大坝左岸设宽浅式溢洪道，宽9米，深2.6米。砌石方涵，宽0.32米，深0.4米。砌石卧管，随左岸坡布置，坡比1∶3。放水孔用人工凿成直径0.2米的圆孔，以木塞关水、放水，共5级。总库容16.5万立方米，有效库容15.5万立方米，死库容1万立方米。有干渠1条长4.4公里，渠道首部有500米为砌石抹面防渗，其余为土渠。土支渠长2.2公里，总设计灌溉面积480亩。

内角水库 位于播尧乡境内，1978年前建成。工程拦蓄方村河支流溪水，坝址以上流域面积1.13平方公里。1979年，临水面抹面体断裂，县水电局拨专款对坝前与整个坝面重新抹面，1980年春全部完工。大坝因施工质量差，整个坝体含有大量的风化页岩，坝体沉陷不均，历年均有异变，抹面防渗体拉裂，渗漏较大，难以处理，属重点病险库之一。

甲介水库 位于茂兰镇比鸠，1978年前建成。该水库为调节茂兰引水工程水量与滞洪，防止茂兰河沿河两岸稻田4100亩受到汛期严重冲刷而建。大坝建筑在茂兰河明流尾端，坝址以上流域面积38平方公里，年均降水量1500毫米，总产水量570万立方米，最枯流量为0.1立方米/秒，20年一遇洪水量221.2立方米/秒，200年一遇洪峰流量293.7立方米/秒。总库容68.16万立方米，防洪兴利库容68.16万立方米。大坝右端底部设放水孔，孔径0.5米，配5吨螺杆启闭机。设计过水量0.5立方米/秒。坝顶溢流，宽42米，深1米，正常泄水量71.3立方米/秒。水库大坝筑于二迭系灰岩基础之上，地质稳定安全。因灰岩岩层节理发育，渗漏现象明显存在，右岸漏水严重，加之启闭机被洪水带来的杂物打弯无法启闭，故调节水量效益差。但滞洪、防止茂兰河两岸水土流失效果好。2008年，获中央特大防汛应急度汛补助费30万元，用于大坝防渗加固应急处理。

水庆水库 位于茂兰镇水庆村，于1979年3月建成，历时3年。水库拦蓄小溪流水，坝址以上流域面积为3.2平方公里，基流量0.008立方米/秒，最大洪峰流量27.3立方米／秒。砌石拱坝，高12.5米，坝顶长71米，总库容20万立方米，兴利库容19.5万立方米，淹没稻田3亩。用直径300毫米闸阀在坝后放水。坝中部溢流，溢流段长40米，深1.2米，干渠长4.5公里（土渠）。灌溉面积700亩。

水维水库 位于佳荣镇水维境内拉学河上游，于1980年建成，历时4年。坝址以上集水面积3平方公里，年均降水量1659毫米，平均年产水量225万立方米，最大洪峰流量82.5立方米/秒。全部由原水维乡村民投劳兴建。砌石拱坝，高12米、长29米、厚2米，总库容23万立方米，可利用库容22.5万立方米。修建干渠1条长0.9公里。控制灌溉面积500亩。有附属电站1座，装机12千瓦，供水维照明及小型副业加工用电。

巴怀水库 位于朝阳镇巴怀，1978年前建成。水库拦蓄樟江河支流无名小溪之水，集雨面积0.8

平方公里，最大洪峰流量6.3立方米/秒，洪水总量16万立方米。水库总库容22万立方米。其中兴利库容17.8万立方米，死库容4.2万立方米。控制灌溉面积310亩。2007年，总投资85万元对该库除险加固，主要进行大坝整治、溢洪道改造、放水设施改造和管理房建设。

董更水库 位于瑶山瑶族乡红光村董更组，又称红光水库，1978年前建成。由红光村民投劳，国家投资1.59万元，群众集资0.3万元建成。工程有砌石拱坝1座，高13.5米、顶宽2.4米、长60米，总库容14.6万立方米。设计灌溉面积400亩，由于渠道配套不完善，有效灌溉面积仅150亩，保证灌溉面积仅100亩。1998年，对该库进行除险加固。

水江水库 位于玉屏镇水甫村，1978年6月动工，1979年2月建成。大坝建筑在樟江无名小溪之上，流域面积0.7平方公里。水库淹没面积18.8亩，总库容10.6万立方米，兴利库容9.1万立方米，死库容1.5万立方米。渠道0.65公里，有效灌溉面积100亩。

立新水库 位于播尧乡地莪场坝旁，1978年前建成。水源为泉水，常年不枯，为地莪场坝村民饮用。基流未查实，坝前地表流域面积1平方公里，推算最大洪峰流量6.8立方米/秒。水库淹没面积12亩，总库容10万立方米，兴利库容9.5万立方米，死库容0.5万立方米。有土质干渠4公里。有效灌溉面积200亩，保证灌溉面积150亩。

卧龙坝水库 位于驾欧乡拉关村翁龙组（小七孔景区内），于1985年11月由黔南州水电勘测设计院设计，县水电局组织施工，1987年11月竣工。水库拦截打狗河支流小七孔河。坝址上游流域集水面积260平方公里，多年平均来水量1.7亿立方米。最大流量472.4立方米/秒，最小流量0.4立方米/秒。总库容20万立方米，兴利库容20万立方米。有干渠1条长3000米，隧洞1座300米，用于小七孔一级电站发电。2006年申报世界自然遗产地将小七孔电站拆除后，卧龙坝水库列入小七孔景区卧龙潭景点进行管理。

朋宾水库 位于甲良镇甲站村，于1978年前动工修建。该工程属珠江流域方村河支流地下水。集水面积2平方公里，年均降水量1100毫米，多年平均来水量130万立方米，最大流量33.8立方米/秒，最小流量0.01立方米/秒。坝体为土石混合坝，高19米，灌溉渠道开挖时因资金不足而停工。1989年9月，由县水电局设计和施工，在修建朋宾人畜饮水及灌溉工程时，继续完成原开挖干渠591米，新开挖2条渠道总长826米，建渡槽1座长15米，安装倒虹管3条总长702米。总库容35.5万立方米，兴利库容27立方米，设计灌溉面积712亩，实际灌溉面积580亩。

把查水库 位于播尧乡地莪村上台组，工程历时9年，于1985年11月竣工。水源属珠江流域方村河支流架桥河。挡水建筑物为砌石连拱坝，坝高24米，坝顶长120米、宽2米，总库容275万平方米。以发电为主，装机3台570千瓦。库水进入台村引灌渠，有效灌溉面积500亩。该电站建成后交由甲良区管理，1991年撤销区后由播尧乡、方村乡、甲良镇共同管理。1998年后由都匀供电局代管使用。

（二）山塘

2008年年末，全县有山塘74口，总蓄水量83.89万立方米，灌溉面积1192亩。

波甲山塘 位于水利乡水利村。坝址以上集雨面积为0.42平方公里，主河道长1.14公里，该坝址建于20世纪40年代，由群众自发修建，因施工技术差，没有清除坝基处山洪冲积形成的砂石，山塘不能正常使用。2007年，投资16.85万元对波甲山塘进行改建、扩建，设计有效库容6.2万立方米，兴利库容6万立方米，灌溉面积210亩。以农业灌溉为主，具有一定调节能力。

拉杆山塘 位于水利乡水利村。坝址以上集雨面积为0.22平方公里，主河道长1.08公里。山塘为群众自发修建，因施工技术差，溢洪道断面较小，不能满足行洪要求，山塘不能正常运行。2007年，总投资14.26万元对拉杆山塘进行改建、扩建，设计有效库容1.8万立方米，兴利库容1.6万立方米，灌溉面积100亩。以农业灌溉为主，具有一定调节能力。

二、引水工程

2008年年末，全县有引水工程13处，总投资534.04万元，渠道总长65.782公里，管道总长15.43公里，灌溉面积6566亩。

瑶庆引水工程　位于茂兰镇，建于1979年12月，1980年12月竣工。工程水源属珠江流域瑶庆河支流上更叶地下水。最枯流量0.01立方米/秒。有效灌溉面积1500亩，挡水建筑物为浆砌石重力坝，坝高2米。有干渠1条长600米，支渠7条总长11500米，隧道1座长110米，渡槽3座共187米。2008年1月，因冰冻灾害受损，重建恢复渠道投资10万元。

坤地引水工程　位于佳荣镇，又称拉圭引水工程，1978年前建成。工程水源属珠江流域甲料河支流拉吾厂河和尧洛河，两条河最枯流量0.01立方米/秒，有效灌溉面积600亩。工程使用木渡槽和土渠输水，老化快，输水损失较大，效益逐年降低。为保证灌溉，1991年12月—1993年2月，县水利局进行维修配套，建成挡水建筑物浆砌重力坝2座，坝高1.5米，干渠4条总长11962米，支渠2条总长978米，隧道99米，倒虹管2根总长165米，渡槽5座总长124米，灌溉面积增加到1500亩。

瑶麓引水工程　位于瑶麓瑶族乡，建于1986年。工程水源属珠江流域茂兰河支流水条河，最枯流量0.01立方米/秒，有效灌溉面积1000亩。工程所有渠道处在熔岩线上，运行后渠道漏水严重。1995年进行渠道维修和干渠延伸配套建设。

六林引水工程　位于驾欧乡，1978年前建成。工程水源属珠江流域方村河支流驾欧段。曾和红星水轮泵站灌渠以及巴槽引水工程连通运行。1983—1985年，进行渠道防渗处理。有干渠1条长6500米，有效灌溉面积600亩。

小七孔引水工程　位于县城南部小七孔景区内，1978年前建成。工程水源属珠江流域打狗河支流小七孔河，最枯流量0.4立方米/秒。有效灌溉面积650亩。挡水建筑物为浆砌石重力坝，拦水坝高5米，干渠1条长6200米，专渠1条长2000米。

台村引水工程　位于播尧乡台村，1978年前建成。工程水源属珠江流域方村河支流架桥河，集雨面积29平方公里。挡水建筑物为浆砌石连拱坝，坝高24米，库容375万立方米。工程有干渠1条长6040米，支渠5条总长15820米，倒虹管1根长300米，渡槽8座共223米。

水甫引水工程　位于玉屏镇水甫村，1978年前动工兴建，因资金不足停工，后于1983年续建，1984年竣工。工程水源属珠江流域樟江河支流水甫山沟，最小流量0.01立方米/秒。建于1984年，有效灌溉面积600亩。挡水建筑物为浆砌石重力坝，坝高2.2米，库容0.5万立方米。有干渠1条长3750米，专渠3条总长3300米，倒虹管1根长37米，渡槽2座总长51米。

鱼胆山引水工程　位于朝阳镇，1978年前建成。工程水源属珠江流域樟江支流地下水，集雨面积1.7平方公里，年均来水量1105万立方米，最小流量0.01立方米/秒。有效灌溉面积800亩。挡水建筑物为土石坝，坝顶高14.5米、宽7米、长43米，干渠1条长2000米，支渠3条总长7000米。

打拉引水工程　位于播尧乡黎明村，1978年前建成。工程水源属珠江流域方村河支流尧花河。集雨面积175平方公里，年均来水量1.05亿立方米，最小流量0.4立方米/秒。1982年1月进行维修配套，1983年11月竣工。有效灌溉面积1200亩。挡水建筑物为浆砌石重力坝，有干渠1条长11400米，支渠1条长1800米，倒虹管4根总长608米，渡槽1座长45米。2007年12月，进行防渗改造2公里，干渠补漏4公里，总投资35万元。

茂兰引水工程　位于茂兰镇，1978年前建成，是县内唯一的国有灌区。工程水源属珠江流域柳江支流的茂兰河。集雨面积38平方公里，年均来水量2660万立方米，最小流量0.08立方米/秒。有效灌溉面积2850亩。1982年，由县水电局进行配套维修，挡水建筑物为浆砌石重力坝，坝高2.5米，总干渠1条长4439米，左干渠1条长8624米，右干渠1条长3817米，支渠5条总长2023米，渡槽3座总长

104米。

清水塘引水工程位于驾欧乡拉欧村清水塘，2009年3月年建成。2008年12月，进行渠道加固防渗处理和干渠延伸建设，修建板潭干渠1条长1800米，为C15砼渠道；修建拉欧干渠1条长1400米。工程总投资33.99万元。其中，2008年财政预算内以工代赈资金15万元，群众自筹及投劳折资18.99万元。

丁家沟引水工程 位于佳荣镇大土村，工程为续建项目，于2008年10月组织施工，对原有的4公里土渠进行节水改造，解决佳荣镇大土村195亩农田灌溉用水困难问题。采用引水低坝处理技术，铺设DN160毫米P伏C-柴管道3.29公里，渠道防渗加固0.72公里，工程总投资38.23万元。其中，2008年度中央以工代赈资金30万元（含劳务报酬6万元），群众投工投劳8.23万元。

三孔桥引水工程 位于甲良镇石板村，1978年前建成。工程水源属珠江流域方村河支流的黄江河。集雨面积225平方公里，年均来水量1.5亿立方米，最小流量0.45立方米/秒。挡水建筑物为石灰砂浆砌料石坝1座，坝高6米。有干渠1条长9500米，支渠2条总长2800米。倒虹管1根348米，渡槽2座总长104米。沿线拉干及甲良场坝分别建有附属电站，工程形成固定资产11.2万元。1999年，进行两次渠道防渗处理，工程总投资148.75万元，增设倒虹管1根长330米，完成总干渠防渗7.44公里，支渠建设2.9公里，灌溉农田2073亩及水浇地，恢复改善人畜饮水3994人、804头。

捞村洞考引水工程 位于捞村乡，工程于2000年9月开工，2001年6月竣工。工程原为洞考水库配套工程，2000年水库报废后，从洞勤西面山中长流的岩溶地下水引水，最枯流量0.05立方米/秒，正常流量1立方米/秒。灌溉农田1111亩。修建洞勤干渠1986米，拦河坝1座长13.5米，溢洪口1个，消力池2个，沉沙池1个，公路桥2座，维修原洞考引水渠3736米，盘龙干渠防渗2200米，洞勤、纳汗、大寨支渠防渗7850米。工程总投资31万元。2006年，投资10万元进行工程整改和维修，完成维修水源拦水坝1座，干渠维修6100米，修建渡槽1座。

地我引水工程 位于播尧乡地莪村，水源为地下水。工程于2004年8月动工修建，是年11月竣工。上坝干渠1360米，支渠280米，下坝干渠1860米，有效灌溉而积417亩。工程总投资15.4万元。

水维引水工程 位于佳荣镇水维村。工程水源为山溪水。工程建于2004年8月，是年11月竣工。干渠长400米，朱家引水渠400米，夯提引水渠长400米，姑柳引水渠长1000米，有效灌溉面积600亩。工程总投资15万元。

板寨引水工程 位于洞塘乡板寨村，1978年前建成。工程水源为地下岩溶水，最枯流量0.03立方米/秒，河两岸各修引水渠1条，均为土渠。2002年1—8月，进行“三面光”建设，完成拦河坝维修加固11米，左干渠长4600米，涵洞6米，公路涵洞32米，五圩、板王、板寨支渠防渗1480米，倒虹管安装392米，灌溉板寨村农田655亩、水浇地15亩。工程总投资23.3万元。其中，以工代赈资金20万元，县级财政资金3万元，群众自筹资金0.3万元。

拉扶引水工程 位于朝阳镇拉扶村，工程建于20世纪80年代。因渠道及渠系建筑物年久失修，过水能力下降，严重影响灌溉列入2001年度以工代赈水利改造工程，由县水利局设计并实施，2003年1月动工，是年4月竣工。设计灌溉面积650亩，有效灌溉面积650亩。改造维修拉扶主干渠740米（过水流量0.08立方米/秒），新建板乐支干渠780米（过水流量0.025立方米/秒），新建当老支干渠400米（过水流量0.025立方米／秒），改造樟江河段倒虹管长165米，电力提灌站设备更新，安装IS100-80-160提水机组1台（套），装机15千瓦，出水流量每小时120吨，提水扬程28米，提水机房维修，新建工程管理房35平方米，形成固定资产20.4万元。

甲料村引水工程 位于佳荣镇甲料村。2000年，该工程列为以工代赈项目，由县水利局设计并组织实施，设计浇灌面积650亩。2004年4月动工修建，2004年7月完工。建挡水坝5座，坝高均为2米，坝长均为8米，建甲料引水渠道4.98公里、谢家引水渠道4.9公里、窝阳引水渠道4.65公里。工程总投资31.9万元。其中，2000年度以工代赈资金20万元，1999—2000年春水利建设经费6万元，县及受益群众自筹资金总计5.9万元。

老街引水渠道工程 位于甲良镇。工程水源属珠江流域方村河支流黄江，坝址以上集水面积225平方公里，多年平均来水量1.5亿立方米，最大洪水量282立方米/秒，最小流量0.45立方米/秒。该工程是甲良镇三孔桥引水灌溉工程总体工程的一部分，三孔桥引水灌溉工程渠道于2000年已修建到甲良镇，后因资金困难，其余渠道未修建。2005年2月动工修建老街引水工程，是年7月完工。设计灌溉面积680亩，有效灌溉面积680亩。老街支渠长1.7公里（引水流量0.023立方米/秒），甲良干渠长0.88公里（引水流量0.23立方米/秒）。工程总投资28万元。其中，2004年度以工代赈资金20万元，县自筹资金8万元。

拉祥引水灌溉工程 位于佳荣镇，工程于2000年1月动工修建，6月竣工。修建拦河坝2座，干渠3.5公里，支渠2.06公里，钢筋砼渡槽90米，倒虹管680米。灌溉农田800亩、土变田50亩、水浇地200亩。工程总投资37.99万元。

尧花烟水配套工程 位于播尧乡。工程水源为尧花河水。2008年3月动工建设，7月竣工。新建懂老干渠0.7公里，维修原懂老渠道1.5公里，新建巴杆干渠2.2公里，新建容积18立方米集水池6口，泵站维修1座。工程总投资60万元，灌溉烟地800亩。

花高引水渠 位于朝阳镇花高村。2008年1月动工修建，3月竣工。总投资10万元，修建容积5.25立方米的沉砂池1口，安装倒虹管382米，渠道长500米。灌溉稻田360亩。

朝阳节水灌溉工程 位于朝阳镇境内，涉及朝阳镇八烂、田洞、寨平3个行政村。工程于2008年4月动工修建，12月竣工。建成渠道清淤维修382米，修建容积500立方米的调节水池1口，新建塑料大棚11栋，安装输水管道及钢管8719米，安装微灌、喷灌管道系统所需各种配件等。工程总投资115.8万元。工程节水灌溉面积510亩。其中，喷灌示范区200亩，人工管灌示范区300亩，大棚灌溉示范区10亩。

立化平寨引水工程 位于立化村。水源为山泉水。工程于2007年2月动工修建，5月竣工。工程总投资16万元，安装倒虹管412米，渠道长1890米。灌溉农田370亩。

三、提灌工程

全县有小（2）型以上提水工程47处。其中，电灌25处、机灌3处。

播尧拉江灌溉工程 位于播尧乡拉美村，工程于2002年11月动工修建，2004年竣工。工程水源为地下溶洞水，采用动力提水方式解决。工程修建拉江蓄水池40立方米、拉美蓄水池30立方米，机房1栋12平方米，提水管钢管162米，输电线路300米，30千伏安变压器1台，安装潜水泵2台，装机容量分别为18.5千瓦和11千瓦。渠道长2450米。有效灌溉面积160亩，解决418人、360头牲畜饮水困难。

拉岩提灌站 位于茂兰镇拉岩村。工程水源为地下溶洞水，于2002年3月动工，同年6月完工，规模为小（2）型。建提水站1座19平方米，安装200QJ50-53/3、175QJ50-60/5型潜水泵2台，装机容量分别为18.5千瓦和11千瓦，架设10千伏输电线路1.1公里，安装Sq-30KNA变压器1台，安装提水管2条（直径100毫米焊接管100米、直径125毫米焊接管380米），闸阀3个，回阀1个，建10立方米高位水池1口，8立方米缓冲池4口，安装倒虹管2根共803米（其中直径105毫米预制管603米，直径100毫米PE管200米），渡槽2座，渠道2条共1319米，受益面积515.76亩，工程总投资22.27万元。

干尧提灌站 位于甲良镇干尧组。工程水源为地下水。2007年2月开工，同年4月完工。安装提水机泵1套及提水管道48米，修建机房6平方米。修建渡槽（25厘米×25厘米）377米，架设电缆150米，工程总投资9.2万元，解决200亩稻田灌溉用水。

拉扶水轮泵站 为1978年已建工程，位于朝阳镇拉扶村和交朝村之间的樟江河上游。砌石拦河坝1座，坝高5米，坝长160米，总装机5台（左岸3台、右岸2台），过水流量14立方米/秒，提水扬程18米，输水管道880米，建干渠1条长800米，支渠2条总长2600米，有效灌溉面积1000亩。

波平水轮泵站 1978年前建成，位于玉屏镇樟江河上，坝高1.5米，砌石坝一座长175米，过水流量0.9立方米/秒，提水扬程13米，安装406水轮泵2台，输水管道长40米，灌溉渠道1条500米，有效灌溉面积200亩。

板麦水轮泵站 1978年前建成，位于朝阳镇樟江河下游板麦拦河坝，坝高2米，坝长50米，过水流量1立方米/秒。安装60-6水轮泵4台（河流左右岸各2台），输水管道80米，渠道2条共750米，有效灌溉面积380亩。

寨票水轮泵站 1978年前建成，位于播尧乡方村河寨票拦河坝，坝高4米，坝长70米，安装30-18水轮泵2台，60-17水轮泵2台，60-6水轮泵2台，过水流量左岸0.7立方米/秒、右岸0.5立方米/秒，提水扬程90米，输水管道470米，干渠1条1500米，支渠2条共2400米，有效灌溉面积270亩。

迎春水轮泵站 1978年前建成，位于播尧乡方村河下游觉巩段拦河坝，砌石坝高4米，长100米，过水流量3.5立方米/秒，提水扬程40米，输水管道620米，安装60-17水轮泵2台、60-6水轮泵2台、40-17水轮泵3台，干渠2条总长1200米，支渠3条总长3000米，有效灌溉面积200亩。该工程主要给打拉引水工程补充水，另外发电40千瓦。

者吕水轮泵站 1978年2月竣工投入使用。位于方村乡黄江河拦河坝，坝高3.5米，坝长52米，过水流量2立方米/秒，提水扬程36米，左岸安装30-18水轮泵2台、右岸安装40-17水轮泵2台，输水管道长310米，干渠1条800米，支渠2条共900米，有效灌溉面积400亩。

里根电灌站 1978年3月竣工投入使用。位于洞塘乡里根组地下水源，安装17千瓦电动机1台，配8813水泵，扬程22米，出水量0.22立方米/秒，输水管长30米，渠道1条长1300米，10千伏输电线路1条4公里，30千伏安变压器1台，灌溉面积80亩。1978年3月竣工投入使用。

王家寨电灌站 位于茂兰镇。该工程于1978年11月动工修建，1979年2月完工。安装JQ3-180-4/18.5千瓦电动机1台，6K-12水泵1台，提水扬程17米，输水管长22米，渠道1条长2000米，有效灌溉面积150亩。另外，工程专用线路1条7公里，安装30千伏安容量变压器1台。

中心电灌站 位于播尧乡，于1978年2月竣工投入使用。工程水源为地下水，安装JQS10-40深井泵40千瓦2台，提水扬程57米，渠道4条总长500米。建专用线路1条长8公里，安装50千伏安变压器1台。工程有效灌溉面积500亩。

方村电灌群 位于方村乡。水源为方村河水，分为大桥、交进、板郎3个站，为方村电灌群。1993年10月动工修建，1994年完工。有效灌溉面积970亩，安装18.5千瓦电动机3台、200QJ-50-52/4等型号水泵3台、30千伏安变压器3台，渠道3条总长400米，输水管长1790米。提水扬程分别为38米、84米、42米。工程总投资20.5万元。其中，国家补助17.5万元，自筹3万元，群众投劳7000多个工日。

岜打电灌站 位于甲良镇梅桃村岜打组。水源为地下水。1978年11月动工，1979年4月完工。安装17.5千瓦电动机1台、6112水泵1台、30千伏安变压器1台，出水管道长24米，扬程18米，渠道2条总长2.4公里，有效灌溉面积320亩。

母约电灌站 位于播尧乡。该工程水源提方村河水。1989年11月动工，1990年4月完工。安装14.5千瓦电动机1台，68-12水泵条1台，扬程39米，输水管长78米，渠道1条1500米。有效灌溉面积100亩。2009年1月，投资10万元对机房和提水管进行改造、维修，更换水泵，作渠道防渗处理500米。

比鸠电灌站 位于茂兰镇。该工程提茂兰河水。1981年10月动工，1982年12月完工。两级提水，第一级扬程30米，第二级扬程42米，输水管道400米，安装30千瓦电动机2台、3K-9水泵2台，架设10千伏输电线路4.5公里，安装100千伏安变压器1台，建渠道1条长1000米。总投资2.4万元。有效灌溉面积180亩。

洞英电灌站 位于茂兰镇。该工程提茂兰河水。1978年10月动工，1980年12月完工。提水扬程40米，安装37.5千瓦电动机2台、6814水泵2台，输水管道长40米，灌溉渠道4条长1公里。有效灌溉面积120亩。

邑国电灌站 位于茂兰镇。该工程水源为溪水，1979年10月动工，1980年12月完工。提水扬程19米，安装17千瓦电动机1台，输水管长80米，渠道2条总长1000米，有效灌溉面积100亩。

炳王电灌站 1978年前建成，位于播尧乡。该工程水源为尧花河上游，提水扬程37.2米，安装31.5千瓦电动机1台，输水管道长60米，渠道1条长1200米，有效灌溉面积250亩。

白岩电灌站 1978年前建成，位于玉屏镇。该工程水源为樟江河水，提水扬程28米，安装30千瓦电动机1台、50千伏安变压器1台，输水管道长28米，渠道2条共2.5公里，有效灌溉面积240亩。

拉美电灌站 位于驾欧乡。该工程于1983年10月由县水电局设计施工，1984年6月完工抽水。扬程38米，安装18.5千瓦电动机1台，30千伏安变压器1台，输电专用线1条长1.5公里，输水管道长80米，渠道1条长1.07公里，有效灌溉面积150亩。

福利电灌站 1978年前建成，位于玉屏镇。该工程水源提樟江河水。原为机灌站，后改为电灌站，扬程25米，安装18.5千瓦电动机1台，输水管道长115米，渠道1条长2000米，有效灌溉面积150亩。

新平寨电灌站 位于朝阳镇。该工程水源提樟江河水。1978年4月动工，1979年1月完工。安装7.5千瓦电动机1台，3B-33水泵1台，提水扬程25米，输水管道长30米，安装20千伏安变压器1台，渠道长1.3公里，有效灌溉面积150亩。

浪祥水轮泵站 1978年前建成，位于捞村乡浪祥组。该工程堆石坝拦截打狗河河水。坝高2米，坝长250米，过水流量0.47立方米/秒，提水扬程60米，左岸安装40-17水轮泵2台，输水管道长72米，渠道1条长8000米，有效灌溉面积250亩。2006年，建浪祥电站后，水轮泵站改为电灌站。

木槽村孟家电灌站 位于洞塘乡木槽村。工程水源为地下溶洞水。工程于2003年1月动工，同年5月完工。安装潜水泵200QJ80-55/5、200QJ50-65/5各1台，装机容量分别为18.5千瓦和15千瓦。安装50千伏安变压器1台，建电力提水机房15平方米，新建舒家坪干渠1条长1160米（其中渡槽468米），建弯头干渠1条长1600米，建圆形高位水池1座，安装直径100毫米出水钢管2条共222米。工程总投资22.6万元。工程新增灌面332亩。

董老提灌工程 1978年前建成，位于播尧乡。工程水源为尧花河水，原修建的提灌站渠道未经防渗，漏水严重，提水机械年久老化。为恢复和增加灌面，2002年9月动工修整，2003年2月完工。新建泵房23平方米，安装提水机泵2台套，装机2×18.5千瓦，新增直径100毫米提水钢管180米，渠道防渗4.98公里，架设10千伏线路0.5公里，安装50千伏安变压器1台。有效灌溉面积650亩。工程总投资32.87万元。

黎明村寨英提灌工程 位于播尧乡黎明村。工程于2001年3月动工，同年5月完工。水源为地表水。建机房15平方米，建容积150立方米蓄水池1个，渠道长1.7公里（东干渠0.88公里、西干渠0.82公里），安装倒虹管270米、直径150毫米提水钢管200米，安装水泵1台，架设10千伏输电线路700米，安装30千伏安变压器1台。工程总投资15.9万元。有效灌溉面积300亩。

水捞村电灌站 位于水尧水族乡水捞村。工程于2004年9月开工，2005年3月完工。水源为地下水。建机房33平方米，建电灌站2处，装机2台（套），容量分别为7.5千瓦和11千瓦，渠道3条总长

2.32公里，倒虹管2座总长362米，安装提水管总长150米，架设输电线路950米，安装30千伏安变压器1台。工程总投资21.95万元。有效灌溉面积500亩。

久安电灌站 位于洞塘乡久安村。工程于2005年4月开工建设，同年7月完工。水源为地下水。建泵房28平方米，安装离心泵1台（套），装机功率22千瓦，安装直径150毫米提水镀锌钢管长224米，安装30千伏安变压器1台，架设10千伏输电线路1500米，架设380伏低压线路30米，渠道长1.56公里。工程总投资21.7万元。有效灌溉面积380亩。

浪邑提灌站 位于茂兰镇场坝村。工程于2005年4月开工，同年7月完工。水源为珠江流域柳江支流茂兰河，集雨面积30平方公里。建机房28平方米，安装水泵机组1台（套），装机功率22千瓦。安装直径125毫米提水钢管长260米，安装30千伏安变压器1台，架设10千伏线路500米，建渠道3条共1.7公里，茂兰提灌主干渠维修700米，新建直径150毫米钢管倒虹管1条长700米。工程总投资35.2万元（2004年度以工代赈资金30万元、自筹5.2万元）。新增灌溉面积200亩。

第二节 防汛抗旱

一、防洪工程

全县建有防洪工程4个。

茂兰防洪堤工程 属荔波县2006—2008年度扶贫办农发土地治理水利工程措施项目。工程位于茂兰大坝（比鸠至瑶埃）。项目区辖比鸠、尧朝、尧埃3个村57个村民小组2138户8401人，耕地面积8768亩（稻田4768亩、土4000亩）。工程由黔南州水利机械化施工队承建，于2006年10月开工建设，2009年4月全部完工，建成防洪河堤5.52公里。总投资434.21万元，其中，财政资金388.55万元，县级配套资金5.21万元，群众投工投劳1.98万个工日折资54万元。工程建成后，消除了茂兰大坝（项目区）4600亩农田洪涝灾害，新增除涝面积3400亩，改善除涝面积800亩。

县城防洪堤工程 位于县城樟江大桥上游左右岸及下游左岸。1998年，县政府委托贵州省水利水电勘测设计院规划设计，2001年完成设计。设计保护城区面积9.1平方公里，保护人口3万人，按防洪标准30年一遇设计施工，为三等工程。分2003年、2007年两期建设，工程建成左岸碾压大堤和衡重式浆砌石堤1854.82米（樟江大桥以下至官塘河岸左岸堤长1184.89米，樟江大桥上游河道左岸堤长669.93米），建成樟江大桥上游右岸防洪堤103.87米。工程总投资810万元。

茂兰河道疏浚工程 河道疏浚工程位于茂兰大坝长寨、立卡、瑶埃、韦寨河段，为2008年度农发土地治理水利措施骨干工程之一。工程由四川三和恒生建筑工程有限公司承建，2008年10月开工建设，2009年4月全部完工，总投资64万元，完成疏浚河道6处，土石方开挖清运6.15万立方米。通过项目工程实施，原河道弯曲、狭窄、淤堵部分得到清除，使行洪不再受阻，解决了茂兰下坝区1000亩以上农田的排涝问题，新增除涝面积1000亩。

消水洞疏浚工程 位于茂兰镇茂兰下坝瑶埃村河段末端，为2008年度农发土地治理水利措施骨干工程之一。项目区辖瑶埃、尧朝2个村、11个村民小组2210人，耕地面积3451亩。工程由四川三和恒生建筑工程有限公司承建，2008年10月开工建设，2009年4月全部完工，完成疏浚消水洞0.84公里，土石方开挖清运2.44万立方米，总投资193万元，为计划的96%。工程根除了茂兰河长期的排洪障碍，解决茂兰大坝水患问题，新增除涝面积2000亩。

二、抗旱应急水源工程

2004—2008年，建抗旱应急水源工程4个。

播尧乡太阳村应急水源工程 2004年9月20日开工，2005年1月10日竣工。总投资36.86万元，其中抗旱经费25万元，其余为地方自筹。建有机房及高位蓄水池、输水管道等，解决太阳村268户1520人、510头大牲畜饮水困难及消防用水。

甲良镇甲站应急水源工程 于2006年建成，总投资33.41万元，其中抗旱经费20万元，其余为地方自筹。建有高位清水池、调节蓄水池、输配水管网，解决993人、645头牲畜的饮用水量。

播尧乡巴竹抗旱应急水源工程 于2007年建成，投入抗旱经费15万元。建有水源处理1处，30立方米高位清水池1口，安装输配水管道总长8.8公里及水表、闸阀、龙头等100套。供水范围为觉巩村巴竹五组、六组，解决100户473人、300头大牲畜的饮水困难。

播尧乡地莪村弄迈组应急水源工程 于2008年建成，总投资32.18万元，其中抗旱经费20万元，其余为地方自筹。建有水源处理1处、机房及50立方米高位蓄水池1口，安装管道2.35公里。工程解决530人、192头大牲畜饮水问题。

第三节 水土保持

一、综合治理工程

樟江河拉鱼段小流域水土保持综合治理工程 2001年1月，开始实施樟江河拉鱼段小流域水土保持综合治理工程，是年6月竣工。该工程距离县城3公里，涉及行政村2个共1347人，治理水土流失面积8平方公里。实施的水土保持项目有经果林1800亩，水保林2800亩，封禁治理6908亩，保耕措施392亩，坡改梯100亩，拦山沟2000米，蓄水池450立方米/20口，机耕道4公里，沼气池50口。项目总投资72万元，其中，国家补助48万元，受益群众自筹24万元。是年6月，通过州级验收，并与受益部门签订项目移交协议，交玉屏镇管理。该工程实施后，樟江河拉鱼段小流域植被覆盖率提高0.8个百分点，每年减少水土流失量2.27万吨，项目区生态环境得到改善，对当地群众发展种植经果林起到示范带动作用。

朝阳小流域水土保持综合治理工程 2008年12月底，在朝阳镇八烂村更坡组和水利乡水利村高寨组动工修建朝阳小流域水土保持综合治理工程，2009年10月竣工。实施的水土保持项目有经果林195亩，水保林4394.25亩，封禁治理7490.85亩，保土耕作418.35亩，蓄水池6口，沉沙池6口，截排水沟3公里，机耕道2276米（其中泥结石路面757米，砼现浇1519米），防护步道3008米，示范碑1块。项目总投资100万元，其中，国家补助90万元，地方自筹10万元。项目建成后，减轻各类自然灾害和洪涝灾害对下游的危害，提高当地土地利用率，对周边群众起到示范带动作用。

二、生态开发示范项目

2003年12月，在朝阳镇境内的2个行政村开工建设樟江河水土保持生态开发示范区，2004年6月完工，治理水土流失面积14.3平方公里，涉及人口1896人。实施的水土保持项目有经果林762.6亩，水保林5580亩，封禁治理13736.55亩，沼气池36口，保土耕作1275亩，坡改梯95.85亩，蓄水池35口，沉沙池35口，截排水沟3公里，机耕道5公里，防护步道1.5公里，河堤护坎0.315公里，示范碑2块，封禁牌10块。项目总投资143万元，其中，中央预算内专项资金100万元，地方匹配43万元。项目于2004年12月通过州级验收，2005年11月通过省级验收。项目实施后，示范区内森林覆盖率提高31个百分点，年增加涵养水量37.89万立方米，减少水土流失量3.1万吨。

第四节 水利管理

一、水利工程管理

1978年，在县水电局下设水利队、机电队、水利管理组和行政组，对水利工程实施管理。1980年，根据《贵州省水利工程管理办法》，划出水库大坝周围50米、渠道上下两侧10米、水库正常蓄水位以上108米，作为水利工程管理范围和保护地段。

1981年，实行水利工程管理责任制，县水电局、农机局抽出干部63人组成工作队，到农村开展水电管理责任制工作。按照“谁建谁有、谁用谁管”的原则，将水利工程管理责任落实到社、队，全县落实水利工程管理责任制324处，落实管理人员744人，有效灌溉面积48501亩。其中，农村电站32处，落实责任制31处，总装机1634千瓦，落实管理人员79人。在已落实水利管理责任制的324处水利工程中，除茂兰引水工程属全民所有制外，其余323处均属集体所有制。茂兰引水工程属国营灌区归县管理，建立茂兰灌区管理所，有正式职工5人，亦工亦农人员3人，群众管水员46人。

是年12月，县水电局组织人员深入各工程地点，调查落实责任制及合同兑现情况，召开合同兑现经验交流会。

1984年，县水电局下设水电管理股，区建水利管理站，水电工程建成后，建立工程管理委员会或管理所（站），负责工程管理具体工作。小工程设有专管人员。

1984年11月，在全县引水工程落实责任制和“三查三定”（查安全定指标，查效益定措施，查综合经营定发展计划）基础上，对小（2）型以下工程88处（报废18处、实有70处）逐个进行检查核定。经检查核定，13处小（2）型以上水库中险库有内角、水庆2座，病库有洪江、董更、巴怀、洞考、威刀、水维、甲界、鲁劳8座。对病险水库分别作除险、加固和输水渠道防渗处理。对小（2）型以上提水工程47处落实责任制后均有人管理，机械故障得到及时维修，运行正常。全县水轮泵站19处57台中，因多数在流沙层筑拦河坝，坝址易位或垮塌。板浪水轮泵站因垮坝报废；者吕、迎春水轮泵站曾出现垮坝，经维修后，成为打拉饮水工程配套部分，发挥效益。是年，全县先后更换40型、60型水轮泵整机42台。

至2008年年底，全县有主要水利灌溉工程530处。其中，小（1）型水库2座，小（2）型水库16座，山塘351口，引水渠71条，固定提水站90处，总蓄水、引水、提水能力1085万立方米，有效灌溉面积4.2万亩，乡镇供水站7个，农村饮水工程166处，解决饮水困难8.6万人。建成防洪堤两处0.9公里，治理水土流失面积24.5平方公里。水利部门水电站8座23台，总装机8.5万千瓦。全县各种水利工程形成固定资产7亿元。

二、农村饮水安全管理

2005年，根据《全国农村饮水安全工程“十一五”规划》，成立以县政府分管副县长为组长，县发改局、财政局、审计局、水利局、各乡（镇）及有关县直部门为成员的农村饮水安全工程规划领导，组织编制《荔波县“十一五”农村饮水安全工程规划》，召开全县“十一五”农村饮水安全规划技术培训会，水利部门派业务技术骨干到各乡（镇）、村、组进行农村饮水调查摸底。之后，在全县实施“十一五”农村饮水安全工程。2005—2007年，实施农村饮水安全项目21个，覆盖17个乡（镇）的50个村民小组，解决17005人、13361头牲畜的饮水安全问题。项目经县级验收后移交受益村组使用和管护。

2008年，根据农村饮水安全的4条规定（水质达到国家饮用水卫生标准；水量保证，每人每天供水量不低于40～60升；用水方便，取水往返不超过10分钟；供水保障，供水率达80%以上），县政府批复同意县水利局成立荔波县乡镇供水服务公司，作为全县农村饮水安全工程管理机构，负责全县农村饮水安全工程开发利用，管理和维护服务。公司依法自主经营，自负盈亏，并依法享有民事权利，承担民事责任。该公司制定《集中式供水或乡（镇）政府饮水安全工程管理办法》，明确农村饮水安全工程效益1000人所在地供水，工程建设后交由荔波县乡（镇）供水服务有限公司负责管理；对农村饮水安全工程效益500人以上1000以下的集中式供水工程，工程建设后由乡（镇）供水管理站合理收取水费，维护工程正常运行；对农村饮水安全工程效益在500人以上1000以下的分散式供水工程，如选用多个水源或采用水窖形式解决农村饮水安全效益的工程，工程建成后由工程所在村组的村民委员会或村民小组管理，也可由受益农户成立用水户协会进行管理，管水组织适当收取水费，确保工程长期发挥效益；对农村饮水安全工程效益在500人以下的饮水安全工程，工程建设后由村民小组或受益农户成立用水户协会进行管理，并适当收取水费，确保工程长期发挥效益。公司根据各个供水工程具体情况，核算供水价格，报县物价部门批准后实行计量收费。

三、水费征收

1978年11月，县水电局、县计委联合印发《电费和水费征收规定》，变压器在320千伏安以下用户，实行单一电价；水轮泵站，每亩计收水费0.60～0.80元，引水自流灌溉工程每亩计收水费0.80元。1982年，推行水利工程承包责任制以后，部分工程根据需要和负担能力，水费征收标准略高于县的规定，有的还加收水费粮。1989年，全县70处小（2）型以上工程计收水费总额8.3万元。

2001年，实行农灌水费改革，进行水价成本核算，全县农村供水成本价为每亩52元，分三步执行：第一步为每亩15元，第二步为每亩38元，第三步为每亩52元。在执行过程中，根据县级经济状况及群众的实际承受能力，降低标准执行，自流按每亩15元，提灌每亩7元（电费另计）计算，由乡（镇）水利站和财政所共同征收，乡管村用。征收的水费，5%作为乡（镇）干部工作经费，5%作为乡（镇）财政部门代收手续费，3%作为县级水行政主管部门管理费上解省、州，70%返还各水利工程，用于发放工程管理人员工资和工程简单维修，余下部分交财政专户储存，专款专用。2005年取消农业税后，停征农田灌溉水费。

第七章 农业机械

第一节 农机经营

1978年，成立荔波县农业机械供应公司，属国营企业，经销平塘产100型碾米机，湖南产30型粉碎机、电动机、柴油机等农业加工机械。1978年、1979年、1980年，分别销售农业机械78台（套）、80台（套）、84台（套）。1981年以后，销售农业机械种类逐年增多，销售量连年上升，是年销量114台（套），1984年销量上升到208台（套），1987年上升到303台（套），1990年上升到404台（套），1993年上升到511台（套），1996年上升到624台（套），1998年上升到700台（套），2001年上升到817台（套），2003年销售量达898台（套）。1978—2003年，县农机公司销售农业机械累计11437台（套）。2004年，县农机公司不再经销农业机械，农机销售全面市场化，个体经销、集体经营农机产品已达5～6家。

从2005年起，执行国家农机购机补贴优惠政策。2005—2008年，全县农户购买农机累计40394台（套）。其中，加工机械24687台、运输机械2505台、拖拉机2723台、排灌机械5215台、耕整机2937台、其他农机2327台（套）。

第二节 农机作业服务

1978年，县内开始引进推广农业机械，以粮食加工机械为主。是年，县农机部门检修农业机械30台（次），参加检修人员15人次。1979年，检修农业机械35台（次），参加检修人员17人次。

1980年，引进排灌机械40台，出勤率121台（次），机灌面积803亩。之后每年排灌机出勤率、机灌面积连年上升，到1990年排灌机械出勤率792台（次），机灌面积3959亩。

1991—1997年，县农机部门组织技术人员到乡、村、组，协助农户检修农业机械，7年检修农业机械3465台（次）。

1998年，根据全县农业机械分布情况，在发展城郊及坝区农业机械的同时，向深山高坡边远地区推广机械，为农户提供农机具租赁、修理、零配件供应和农机手操作培训等服务，动员有机户为无机户服务，并组织农机耕作服务队，配合有机户开展机械耕作。年内，安排拖拉机4台，在时来坝、南门坝、朝阳片区开展机耕和机收作业。春耕、三秋期间，全县拖拉机、耕作机械、提灌机械、收割机械、运输机械、农产品加工机等农业机械出勤共1685台（次），完成机耕面积15210亩、机电灌溉面积12909亩。农机部门培训农机人员696人，组织机械收割250亩。农机技术人员全年检修耕作机械及排灌机械709台（套）。

1999年，农机技术人员下乡4040人次，检修农机具860台（次），农机出勤21957台（次）。其中，排灌机械1404台，农产品加工机械2724台，大、中、小型拖拉机及农用车750台（套）。完成机耕面积15495亩。邀请广西河池农机推广站出动柳林牌收割机1台，与县内收割机2台进行三秋收割服务，机械收割面积410亩。

2000年，组织大型拖拉机3台、微型拖拉机2台及技术员6人，到驾欧、茂兰、瑶庆等乡（镇）灾区无偿为农户机耕1500亩，解决灾区农户秋种难问题。全年农机出勤21250台（次），完成机耕20160亩，机电灌溉面积31955亩，机械收割面积450亩，检修农机具315台（次）。

2001年，组建茂兰镇拉伙村村级农机合作服务队，配有耕整机28台，县农机部门向服务队赠电焊机1台、小立式钻床1台、切割机1台、砂轮机1台、修理工具1套。是年，全县组织农机检修队4个，赴茂兰、玉屏、朝阳、甲良四大片区，协助乡（镇）、村农机技术员检修农机具1785台（次），帮助比鸠村检修二级电灌站1座。全年农机出勤率20896台（次），机耕19565亩，机灌36253亩，机械收割水稻535亩。

2002年，按省、州农机部门的部署，县农机部门与县工商部门联合开展农机市场整顿与打假活动，派出技术员和执法人员56人次，重点抽查经营门市23个，查出无产品商标、合格证、推广许可证的潜水泵、柴油机、碾米机等机具78台及农机安全性能差的劣质配件200件，并作封存处理。全年全县检修农机具2008台（次）。农机出勤37873台（次），机耕22425亩，排灌28125亩。

2003年，建立茂兰场坝村、更坡村、长寨村村级农机服务队3个，省、州为这3个服务队分别配备钻床、电焊机、切割机各1台及修理工具等设备。年内，组织惠水县收割机2台、广西河池地区收割机5台及县内收割机3台，在时来、南门、茂兰、朝阳坝区进行跨区机收作业服务，全县机械收割面积5800亩。是年，全县机耕25830亩，机灌27240亩，检修农机具4957台（次）。

2005年，成立农机服务队2个。组织县内、县外收割机13台跨区作业，机械收割面积8100亩。

2006年，组建机械收割服务队8个，投入收割机20台，完成水稻机械化收割面积12800亩。成立农机服务队3个。全县农业机械出勤18726台（次），机耕57825亩，机灌36090亩，检修各类农机具8347台（次）。

2007年，引进省外联合收割机19台、省内7台，组织县内收割机3台，进行收割服务，收割面积15660亩。组织县内收割机1台外出跨区收割，收割面积820亩，这是县收割机第一次外出跨区进行收割服务。成立农机服务队3个。

2008年，成立甲良镇新场村农机服务队、立化镇尧明村农机服务队和茂兰镇强民农机农民专业合作社，至此，全县农机服务组织发展到16个。农机部门组织省外收割机22台、省内（惠水、都匀、平塘、独山）收割机6台、县内收割机3台，到部分乡（镇）进行机械收割，收割面积22380亩。全年农机出勤达24325台（次），机械耕作81311亩，机械灌溉43602亩，各类农机具检修8673台（次）。

第三节　农机技术推广

1978年，根据全县田间作业机械发展缓慢的现状，农业机械技术推广工作以田间作业机械为主，采取农户集资购买、国家补贴方式，促进农业机械化发展。是年，引进平塘100型碾米机20台、湖南产30型粉碎机30台、单缸采油机10台。1979—1997年，每年引进先进农机到县内推广，主要有背负式收割机1台（1979年）、大中小型拖拉机20台（1980年）、脚踏打稻机300台（1981年）、家用小型碾米机和粉碎机100台（1982年）、单轮耕整机100台（1983年）、果树打坑机10台（1984年）、排灌机械200台（1985年）、变形拖拉机50台（1986年）、微耕机20台（1987年）、动力脱粒机300台（1988年）、榨油机4台（1989年）、手动植保机械50台（1990年）、磨浆机60台（1991年）、机动打稻机400台（1992年）、水稻抛秧机1台（1993年）、动力潜水泵100台（1994年）、机动植保机械50台（1995年）、运输型拖拉机50台（1996年）、微型拖拉机15台（1997年）等。

1998年后，按照引进示范、宣传培训、群众自愿购机的原则，进行农业机械技术推广。是年，推广耕整机15台、微拖2台、化肥深施器27台（套）。县农机部门购置背户式联合收割机1台，开展机收作业服务示范，成为黔南州引进的第一台联合收割机。1999年，推广水稻直播机1台。

2000年，在南门大坝、拉鱼坝召开机收、机耕演示会2场，推广耕整机、微拖、机动脱粒机。

2001年，重点引进推广新机具、新技术、新产品，主要有家庭小型精加工碾米机251台、人力脱粒机450台、小型联合收割机1台。

2002年，农机技术人员在玉屏、朝阳、播尧、甲良、茂兰等乡（镇）召开机耕现场演示会8次，在玉屏、茂兰、朝阳等镇进行机械收割现场演示4次。

2004年，开展科技兴粮、农机科技下乡活动，分别在茂兰、朝阳、瑶山片区开办农机培训班3期，培训农机操作人员2000人次，印发农机常识和技术宣传资料3200份，接受咨询860人次。

2005年，农业机械推广执行国家农机购机补贴政策。是年，省下达荔波县省级农机具购置补贴资金10万元，按30%的比例补贴购置农机具，并争取农发项目配套资金5.78万元，集中资金补贴茂兰镇农户购买川龙拖拉机2台、中型拖拉机3台、旋耕机3台。全年补贴资金11.25万元，农民投入资金21.3万元，购置耕作机械50台（套）。通过办理助农增收示范点，培训农机操作手和种粮户400人，向农户推广5种型号的农机具100台（套）。

2006年，省下荔波县农机购机补贴和累加资金补贴总计25万元，补贴对象为粮食主产区的农机户、种粮大户、计生户和农机服务队。是年，省级资金补贴25.01万元，争取到农业发展资金补贴4.07万元，州级补贴0.2万元，农户自筹投入52.26万元，农户享受补贴达37.3%（含农发资金），购机共64台（套）。其中，收割机1台，大、中型拖拉机5台，小型拖拉机20台，微耕机22台，单轮耕整机8台，锄草机1台，旋耕机等其他配套机械7台（套）。

2007年9月，省农机部门在朝阳洞阳坝召开贵州省跨区机械收割现场会，组织收割机5台和大、中拖拉机2台，进行机收、机耕演示。

是年，全县获中央补贴项目资金50万元、省级补贴5万元、省级累加8万元、州级补贴1.5万元，对粮食生产坝区的农机户、种粮大户和农机服务队进行补贴，累加补贴率38%。全年兑现购机资金补贴51.3万元，其中，中央补贴36.51万元、省级补贴5.01万元、省级累加补贴8.28万元、州级1.5万元，补贴农户购机161台（套）。

2008年，省、州安排荔波县中央购机补贴资金53.5万元、省级14.5万元、州级1万元，总计69万元。其中，农机推广经费10万元列入县财政预算，专项用于购机补贴和农机推广工作。年内，从中央灾后农业恢复重建补贴资金中安排30万元用于累加补贴农户购置农业机械，并利用农发项目农机购置资金进行捆绑使用，提高农户购买农机具的补贴额。全年实施中央购机补贴资金53.5万元、省级补贴资金14.25万元、州级资金1万元、县级财政补贴2.86万元、农发补贴2.2万元、中央灾后建设补贴资金蔗机补贴17.8万元，补贴农业机械293台，购机补贴率38%—50%（按机具类型差额补），带动群众自筹投入购机资金107.47万元。

第四节　农机监理

1978年，开始实行拖拉机、农用车和驾驶员年检年审制度，规定每年4—7月进行年审检验。

1984年，县内始开展农机监理工作，按照“安全第一，预防为主”方针，开展各种形式的农机安全宣传活动，抓好路检路查和年度检审验工作。是年，监理人员上路查车65天，参加人员130人（次），纠正违章72起。此后每年坚持上路查车，纠正违章和无证驾驶行为。1985—1997年，农机监理人员上路查车1229天，纠正违章3303起。

1998年，结合全国“安全生产周”“安全月”活动，开展路检路查，纠正无证驾驶、无牌行车行为，进行安全宣传教育。监理人员全年上路查车126天，纠正违章470人次。

1999年，在全县“安全生产周”和整顿城镇交通秩序等活动中，上路查车118天（次），纠正违章840台（次），查处无证驾驶63人。乡村道路发生农机事故5起，其中，公安交警处理1起，农机安全监理站处理4起。

2000年，结合交通安全专项治理、安全月、安全周等活动，开展农机路检路查203天，纠正违章拖拉机、农用车875台（次），查出无证驾驶人员85人、无牌照行车111辆。是年，培训驾驶员92人，核发牌证140车（副）。年内发生农机事故4起，均由农机安全监理站处理。

2001年，开展“打回潮、查隐患、反违章、压事故”专项治理活动，查处各类农机违章300起。其中，拖拉机、农用车违章载人30起，无牌行车94台，无证驾驶50次，其他违章126起。年内，补检拖拉机、农用车126台，更换各型驾驶证83个，核发号牌120副，换发行驶证410本。全年发生农机事故2起，死亡1人、重伤2人、轻伤2人，直接经济损失1.15万元，均由农机安全监理站处理。

2002年，在“黑车非驾清理”“安全月”活动中，农机安全人员查出全县无证驾驶65人，无牌照行车77台。经教育，参加驾驶员培训班学习培训63人，车辆检验上户111台。全年办理机车入户197辆，培训并发驾驶证76本，换证、遗失补证、增驾共110本。发生无证驾驶偷开他人农用车造成翻车死亡1人农机事故1起，由县农机安全监理站处理。

2003年，开展“农机安全生产大检查、大整改”“安全月”等活动，上路查车216天，纠正和处理违章载人138起、无证驾驶90起、无牌行车130起、未检机车上路180起、未审驾车116起、其他违章326起。

2004年，在贯彻实施《中华人民共和国道路交通安全法》和“安全月”活动中，农机执法人员上路查车和开展安全宣传活动210天，参加人数860人次，群众咨询3500余人次，发放资料8500多份，悬挂横标8幅，张贴小标语50多条，展出事故警世宣传栏5个。纠正处理各类农机违章440起。

2005年，农机执法人员到乡（镇）开展宣传教育活动126人次，接受咨询的群众2300多人次，发放交通安全资料8000多份，悬挂交通安全横标6幅，张贴小标语30条。是年，开展J类驾驶证、农用车清理和移交工作，将J类驾驶证人员276人、农用车299台移交交警部门管理。

2006年，开展拖拉机专项整治活动中，农机执法人员对“黑车非驾”“无牌无证”人员进行清理，注册、挂牌、发证共188台。全年新注册拖拉机22台、拖拉机驾驶员34人。

2007年，在“五一”“十一”等节日安全大检查和“安全月”活动中，农机执法人员发放资料2500份，张贴安全标语60份，悬挂安全展板5场（次），上路检查拖拉机130台，查处无牌无证40台、违章载人4起、无证驾驶50人。

2008年，县安监局、公安交警、交通、运管、农机监理等部门，到全县各乡（镇）开展安全宣传教育及农机安全大检查。在宣传活动中，发放宣传资料5000份和农机事故警示资料3000份，受教育群众1万人。在安全大检查中，查处拖拉机350台。其中，无证驾驶25人，无牌行驶30台，持公安执照拖拉机195人，带病车辆上路行驶5台，违章载人2台。全年检验拖拉机365台，占应检数667台的54%；审验拖拉机驾驶员188人，占应审数302人的62.3%。是年，制定《荔波县重特大事故救援预案》《荔波县联合收割机跨区作业安全管理规定》。

1978—2008年全县农机年检情况统计表

表11－7

年度	检验拖拉机、农用车		审验驾驶员	
	总数（台）	占应检验数（%）	总数（人）	占应审验数（%）
1978	138	49.3	150	72.0
1979	142	49.6	155	72.5
1980	146	49.9	159	72.8
1981	147	50.0	161	73.0
1982	149	50.3	163	73.0
1983	150	50.5	168	73.2
1984	155	50.8	170	73.5
1985	159	51.2	174	73.8
1986	163	51.4	178	74.0
1987	168	51.8	180	74.4
1988	170	52.0	184	74.7
1989	175	52.4	188	74.9
1990	180	52.8	192	75.4
1991	190	53.2	198	75.8
1992	200	54.4	200	76.0
1993	210	55.5	210	77.0
1994	220	56.4	190	78.0
1995	240	57.3	222	78.4
1996	280	58.8	254	79.0
1997	320	59.0	288	80.0
1998	365	60.8	327	84.9
1999	414	66.0	371	90.9
2000	410	65.0	315	87.0
2001	465	90.0	285	73.0
2002	544	78.0	512	95.0
2003	657	90.0	438	82.6

续表11－7

年度	检验拖拉机、农用车		审验驾驶员	
	总数（台）	占应检验数（%）	总数（人）	占应审验数（%）
2004	455	83.2	436	83.8
2005	112	66.0	85	50.0
2006	146	42.2	95	61.3
2007	518	96.4	100	61.7
2008	365	54.0	188	62.3

第十二篇
“两瑶”扶贫与扶贫攻坚

由于历史和地理条件等原因，瑶山、瑶麓两个瑶族乡经济一直发展缓慢，瑶族人民生活十分贫困。1980年，新华社记者杨锡玲到荔波县瑶山乡采访，所见所闻，在新华社内参登载了反映瑶山人民仍然过着穷困落后生活的报道，引起时任中共中央总书记胡耀邦的高度重视。胡耀邦批示：“少数特别落后地区要派大员去用心研究，切实帮助那里的人民在两三年内翻过身来。”时任中共贵州省书记池必卿于1981年3月3日提出：“耀邦同志的意见，我们要认真执行。”同时提出了省里要派大员深入“两瑶”，用心研究，切实帮助贫困地区解决有关问题。

荔波县委、县政府为了帮助荔波“两瑶”人民早日脱贫，对瑶山地区采取了一些特殊政策，同时，荔波县委、县政府对“两瑶”扶贫攻坚展开了两大战役。从实施“八七”扶贫攻坚至2008年年末，共实施扶贫开发项目819个，投入扶贫资金2.29亿元。农民人均收入不断提高，基本实现村村通电、通公路、通电话，贫困地区群众已经从根本上改善生产生活条件，实现了减贫摘帽。

第一章 “两瑶”扶贫

第一节 特贫乡瑶山、瑶麓

瑶山乡、瑶麓乡是瑶族人民聚居区。在解放前瑶族人民基本没有固定的田土，只是进行赶山吃饭，山上砍火捞，种小米、荞子、红稗等杂粮为生，兼营狩猎。种在坡上的庄稼不施肥，不杀虫，广种薄收，一地种上2～3年，剥尽地力后又重新搬居新地，重新开荒种植，又实行刀耕火种，赶山吃饭。居住的房子也是适应其游农生活，砍林作叉叉房，用茅草盖，用草围，更无什么厕所，极易搬居，一丢就是到新开荒地重新搭起，纯属游农民族。解放后，经过土地改革分得捞村、王蒙等地地主的田土，才开始有固定田土，部分农民住上固定的土木结构瓦房，在20世纪60年代部分瑶族农民结束了“村无常址，户无定居”的流动性生活。

有史以来，“九山半水半分田”的恶劣生存环境使其成为“两瑶”贫穷落后的代名词。瑶山乡、瑶麓乡耕地少，开荒多，农地距村寨远，花劳力多，文化科技落后。瑶麓乡所在地海拔高度660米，年平均气温16.9℃，年降水量1400毫米左右，又地处喀斯特山区，水源不足，干旱严重，人畜饮水困难，地瘠人贫，是个穷山区。由于历史和地理条件等原因，20世纪80年代初，瑶山、瑶麓两乡经济发展缓慢，瑶族人民生活仍很贫困。

1980年5月，新华社记者杨锡玲与贵州省民委副主任韩发敏到荔波县瑶山公社采访，所见所闻，反映了瑶山人民仍然过着穷困落后的生活，迫切需要党和政府采取措施，尽早改变面貌。住房及生活方面，杨锡玲反映瑶山许多赤脚光身挺着大肚子的孩子，妇女光着脚丫，衣服褴褛，几乎不能遮羞。据当地负责人介绍瑶山是荔波最穷的公社，已经连续三年人均收入在40元以下，分配粮食约150公斤，由于粮食不足，不少人长期吃着芭蕉芋。农民的住房破破烂烂，全公社304户，只有14户是瓦房，其余都是茅草房。杨锡玲记者在瑶山寨串门，所到之处，家家的房子都是又脏、又稀、又漏风，室内几乎没有什么家具，少数人家有床，多数人家没有床，只睡在草窝和木板上，少数人家有棉絮，也是又黑又破，襟襟吊吊。政府几乎每年都要发一些棉被救济他们，但他们一领到棉被，就把被里被面做裙子用，光棉絮睡不了两三年就又黑又烂了。由于衣着单薄，房子又不能御风寒，一年有八九个月要烤火取暖。白天他们在火塘边做饭、吃饭，晚上，几块板子放在火塘旁边一家人围火取暖“睡觉”。

农业生产方面。农业生产很落后，除粮食外，几乎没有什么多种经营。耕作方法还是刀耕火种，靠山吃饭，粮食产量很低，1979年一个劳动日只有两角一分钱，1980年一些生产队开始实行包干到户，生活稍好一些。仍还有个别生产队没有定居下来，称他们为“过山瑶”，今年在这座山，明年又搬到那座山去，有时连公社干部也不知道他们搬到哪里去了，他们的行李很简单，一个铁三脚架，一两个顶罐，几个粗陶碗，加上粮食等东西也不过几百斤。

教育文化卫生方面。瑶山的教育卫生文化事业很落后，87%的人是文盲，95%的妇女不会讲汉话，全公社都没有一个大学生或中专生。瑶山公社小学设备很简陋，既没有儿童读物，也没有文体活动，孩子们唯一的娱乐就是养鸟。1979年这个学校有280个学生，1980年却只有74个学生了，学生经常不上课。这所小学有8名教师，都是“文化大革命”中初级师范学校的毕业生，实际只有高小文化水平，算术老师只会一百位数以内的加减法，一百位以上就不会了。杨锡玲到过的拉更莫生产队，全队有9户人家60人，只有4个人识字，10个适龄儿童没有一个入学。瑶山公社只有一个医生，因为农村付不起医药费，医院关门医生回家种田去了。全公社没有一个新法接生员，妇女生孩子仍是旧法接生，妇女和婴儿的生命得不到保障，死亡率达千分之十三；妇女不穿内裤，经期不用卫生纸，得妇科病的人很多。杨锡玲在瑶族村寨串了二三十户人家，只有公社妇女主任家有面盆、毛巾。文化生活更是缺乏，在这里看不到电影、戏剧，听不到音乐。解放三十年，县里的电影队没有到过这个公社，据说只有毗邻广西的一个区电影队到这里放过一次电影。

新华社记者杨锡玲写的《贵州瑶山见闻》于1981年2月22日新华社内参第492期全文刊载，引起时任中共中央总书记胡耀邦的高度重视，胡耀邦批示：“少数特别落后地区要派大员去用心研究，切实帮助那里的人民在两三年内翻过身来。”

时任中共贵州省书记池必卿于1981年3月3日提出：“耀邦同志的意见，我们要认真执行。”同时提出了省里要派大员用心研究，切实帮助贫困地区解决有关问题。

第二节　“两瑶”扶贫举措

为了帮助荔波“两瑶”人民早日脱贫，各级党委和政府领导十分重视，1981年3月，贵州省委书记池必卿、副省长王朝文到瑶山调查，深入瑶乡村寨，访贫问苦，一个星期就将70平方公里的瑶山跑了近80%。之后，时任贵州省政协副主席、省委统战部部长王思明，副省长张玉芹、龚贤永，时任贵州省委书记胡锦涛，副书记王思齐等省领导先后到瑶山视察。1993年1月，中共贵州省委召集有关部门到瑶山现场办公，确定每年由省下拨瑶山小学学生“三包两免”（包吃、包住、包穿、免教育费、免学杂费）资金15万元，列入省财政预算。同时要求有关部门尽快修通瑶山公路。1994年6月9日，中共中央政治局常委、全国人大常委会委员长乔石亲临瑶山视察指导工作。黔南州委先后选派近10名干部到瑶山挂职帮扶，社会各界纷纷伸出援助之手。

1997年4月，县委、县政府为确保扶贫目标的实现，制定了7条保障措施。1.从1994年开始的5年内，凡“两瑶”属县级管理的税费，按收支两条线的原则如数返回乡政府，作为乡政府扶贫开发基金。2.按程序办理有关手续，5年内减免“两瑶”各瑶族村的农业税。3.县政府每年拨出20万元专款作为“两瑶”脱贫起步和发展经济项目配套资金，并列入县财政预算，连续5年。4.每年无偿提供营造用材林的树苗，并采取以苗作贷方式供应经济林的树苗，其他农用物资确保供应。5.建立和完善医疗卫生网络，在3年内解决一些村的医疗器材和药品，逐步改善缺医少药状况。6.采取多种形式分期分批为“两瑶”农户培养农业技术员，培训村组干部，组织劳务输出。7.增设民族教育课，筹建瑶山民族职业中学，培养瑶山本民族的乡土人才。

荔波县委、县政府对“两瑶”扶贫攻坚展开了两大战役。第一战役是1994—1996年，建立“两瑶”扶贫开发试验区管委会，选调3名副县级干部和8名县直部门骨干驻乡3年，与乡党委、政府共同抓扶贫中心任务，抓扶贫政策落实，抓扶贫项目实施，采取政策先导，科技先行，经费保障的超常规手段，主要加强以公路交通、通电照明、科技教育、人口与计划生育领域建设，全局启动种养业，为实现总目标夯实基础。3年间共集纳资金705.489万元，实施35个扶贫项目，1994年建成和发挥效益的项目32个，瑶胞人均占有粮食和人均纯收入分别由1993年年底的160公斤和170元增加到1996年年底的229公斤和469元，贫困面貌发生了一定变化。但由于瑶山贫困程度深，第一战役还没有根本解决脱贫问题。为此，县委、县政府于1997年4月又成立了“瑶山扶贫工作队”，展开了攻坚战。从县直机关选派年富力强会种植技术、懂养殖管理、能操作加工的26名中专以上文化程度、副股级以上干部分驻24个瑶族村民组，带资金（每户1000元扶贫启动资金），带任务（每年每组3～5户脱贫），带技术（教会每个瑶胞至少掌握1～2门适用技术），带指标（每年每户增粮增钱定指标），定组、定户、定时间稳定脱贫。工作队员驻组期间工资向上浮动一级，完成任务好的转为固定工资，并提拔重用；完不成任务的扣回原浮动工资，继续驻组直至瑶胞脱贫。决战总体目标是从根本上解决瑶胞绝对贫困问题，达到人均吃粮330公斤，人均纯收入800元。瑶族贫困人口70%稳定解决温饱，30%逐步迈进小康行列。1997年开了个好头，瑶胞人均占有粮食提高到319公斤，人均纯收增加到624元。并已发展种植项目5类，养殖项目5类，宜种则种，宜养则养，宜加则加，短平快项目与中长期项目相济，家家有优势，户户有项目，挖地造田，半山腰搭鸡棚，寨前建卫生圈，家家投入，老人小孩参与，将新“两瑶”带进21世纪。

第三节 “两瑶”扶贫资金投入与项目

瑶山瑶族乡、瑶麓瑶族乡因受地理条件限制，经济发展缓慢，生活贫困。两个乡被省定为“两山”（麻山、瑶山）特贫乡。

1985—1993年，国家投入资金累计500万元，用于瑶山乡修建公路、人饮工程和教育设施等建设。

1994年，团省委、省民委、省扶贫办等十多个单位联合发出倡议书，倡议全省人民向“两山”献爱心。之后瑶山、瑶麓两乡得到省、州、县32个部门和干部、职工的无偿捐助和专项扶贫资金扶持。1995—1996年，黔南州水电局投资45.23万元，乡自筹5万元，共计50.23万元，投入维修瑶麓总干渠和新修配套支沟，使瑶麓农田较集中而又较大的8个坝子均得到了灌溉，有条件的部分苞谷地进行了土变田。这一扶贫项目既解决了农业生产用水，也解决了全乡人民群众的生活用水，使瑶麓瑶族乡生产和生活基本实现了水利化。同时以工代赈资金20万元，对边远村寨的洞闷组照明用电线路和人畜饮水工程，使全乡13个村民小组全部有了照明用电。贵州神奇制药公司董事长张芝庭先生扶持瑶麓发展养殖业，共投入扶持资金28万元。其中，1994年扶持资金10万元发展饲养黑山羊，1996年又扶持资金18万元发展养猪，给瑶麓乡脱贫创建路子。1995—1996年，贵州省教委、省林业厅、黔南州教委、州卫生局、州民委等部门均扶持瑶麓乡上万元资金，改善学校、卫生院人畜饮水、发展种植业等项目。

在“八七”扶贫攻坚期间，投入两个瑶族乡扶贫资金共860万元，实施项目105个，主要有“三小”（小山塘、小水窖、小水池）工程、民房改建工程、移民工程、土变田工程、人饮工程、教育工程以及种养项目等。

2001—2008年，瑶山瑶族乡实施扶贫项目42个，投入资金1850万元，建设项目主要有整村推进项目、民族村寨建设、人饮工程、公路建设、农网改造、茅草房改造、移民工程、农民技能培训等。通过项目实施，全乡新建改建公路85公里，农村电网改造21公里，新建和改造人畜饮水工程管网20公里，建人饮水池54个，修灌溉小水窖（池）230个、引水渠28公里，解决1870人、1450头大牲畜饮水困难；完成坡改梯724亩，土变田464亩，人均耕地由原0.3亩增加到0.71亩；实施异地移民127户488人，就地改造建房358户，草房户由1993年551户减少到5户；完善拉片、懂蒙、拉柳3个民族村寨基础设施建设，培育22户农家饮食接待点，2005年5月开始接待各地游客，户均年收入2万元；组织群众技能培训40期1万人次；劳务输出全乡累计外出打工人数1330人，劳务经济成为瑶族群众收入的主要构成；全乡4个村基本实现计划生育“村为主”；小学、初中学生入学率分别达到99.5%、92%，瑶族初中在校生由1993年的13人增加到2008年的100人。2005年、2006年、2007年均有瑶族学生考取大学，结束瑶山瑶族无人考取大学的历史。

瑶麓瑶族乡在“八七”扶贫攻坚中得到扶贫项目18个，总投资484万元。其中，无偿资金384万元，贷款100万元。项目覆盖全乡381户1564人。解决饮水困难701人，开展农民技术培训并转移劳动力459人次，解决贫困人口温饱问题253人。到2008年，人均占有粮食406公斤，比1993年增加189公斤；人均收入1683元，比1993年增加1358元。全乡贫困人口由1993年1412人下降到293人，全乡整体越过温饱线。计划生育工作连年被州、县表彰为无多孩乡。全乡于1996年通过基本实现九年义务教育县级验收；组组修通公路，户户通电，有电视机的农户占75%。

第二章 扶贫攻坚

第一节 “八七”扶贫攻坚

1994年2月，国家开始实施“八七”扶贫攻坚计划（即“在20世纪末最后的7年内，基本解决了全国8000万农村贫困人口的温饱问题”），当年，全县扶贫工作以落实“八七”扶贫攻坚计划为重点，至8月底，完成全县贫困户调查摸底工作，制定《荔波县“八七”扶贫攻坚计划》，明确1994—2000年的工作目标。全县“八七”扶贫攻坚将“两瑶”（瑶山、瑶麓）作为扶贫工作的重中之重，组建专门工作机构，投入人力、物力、财力，动员社会各界力量开展“两瑶”扶贫工作。

一、培养科技干部，增加科技含量，提高劳动者素质

1994年开始的“八七”扶贫攻坚中，县委首先抓住培养跨世纪科技后备干部，提高劳动者素质，增加科技含量，增粮增收这个百年大计。从着力培养村级班子入手，先是对全县168个村新当选的336名村支书、村委会主任进行为期一周的上岗轮训，1997年接着从全县17个乡（镇）报考的220名回乡高中、初中知识青年、复员退伍军人、能工巧匠中，通过笔试、面试和复试筛选100人到县委党校脱产学习农业、农村经济管理、土地、会计、税收等基础知识，森林、畜禽、饲料、房地产经营和实践知识，以及土壤、肥料、人口与计划生育等方面的专业课程；拟用3年时间连续举办2～3届这样的培训班，为每个村级班子配备1～2名专职科技后备干部，并作为21世纪初科技副乡（镇）长的后备人选。与此同时，另一方面同步加大劳动力素质培养力度，每年投入20余万元，采用以会代训，现场培训，专业指导等手段普及和推广农业适用技术，用2～3年时间达到每村有10个科技示范户，每组有5个科技示范点，每个劳动力掌握1～2门农业科学技术。继续巩固扶贫攻坚举措“四不变”成果，即定点帮扶不变，明确28名副县级以上干部和县直73个部门定点包村帮扶，不脱贫、不脱钩；扶贫资金投入逐年加大不变，以10%的比例逐年递增；重点突破战略方针不变；计划生育工作与扶贫开发

瑶山重点扶贫项目——水窖项目

相结合不变，继续实施“4321”工程，即正县级干部帮扶4户，副县级干部帮扶3户，科局级干部帮扶2户，股级以下干部帮扶1户。同步加大农业基础设施建设，因地制宜，在2000年前建成2000个小水窖，1000个小水池，200个小山塘，100个机提灌站，使旱涝保收面积提高到85%以上，夺取粮油丰产丰收，保证吃饭问题。

荔波县继1996年在全省率先越过温饱线之后，1997年又解决了1万贫困人口的脱贫，农民人均纯收入1220元，较上年净增210元。县委、县政府正视全县还有2.5万人口贫困程度深、自然条件差、劳动力素质低这一事实，继续带领全县实施扶贫攻坚。采取点上扶贫，以瑶山为重点，实施重点突破；面上扶贫，以抓好村级科技后备干部培训，提高劳动者素质，增加科技含量，增强农业基础设施建设，增粮增收；以调整产业结构，培育新的支柱产业和新的经济增长点，合理布局工业建设区，建立小康带创收为己任，先让部分人富裕起来，带领全县人民奔小康。

二、改善生活生产条件，培育新的经济增长点

1997年，全县积极培育新的支柱产业和新的经济增长点。县委、县政府在“稳定以农业为基础，以煤炭为龙头”的基础上，着力培育旅游支柱产业。自1989年开发建设景区以来，共集纳投入景区建设资金1644万元，改善交通环境，提高旅游接待条件，已建成具备一定档次和品位的吃、住、娱、游、购、行一体的旅游服务网络。8年间共接待游客76万人次，实现旅游经济效益13261.14万元，完成营业税928.33万元，利润4572.06万元，解决长期性就业人员430人，季节性就业人员150余人，通过旅游业脱贫3800户12370人。

至2000年“八七”扶贫攻坚结束，中央、省、州、县及深圳市累计投入扶贫资金19449.48万元。其中，扶贫专项资金13125万元，以工代赈资金2685.13万元，财政扶贫资金679.35万元，其他扶贫资金（含社会各界、深圳捐资）2960万元。全县实施扶贫项目309个。其中，种植业项目61个，投入资金1220万元；养殖业项目55个，投入资金2366万元；基础设施项目86个，投入资金2618万元；教育卫生项目43个，投入资金2262万元；其他项目64个，投入资金983万元。年底，全县贫困人口由1993年的10.6万人降至2.88万人（含返贫人口），7年累计解决77200贫困人口的温饱问题，贫困率由1993年年底的76.8%下降到19.2%，农民人均纯收入由1993年的345.7元增加到1196元，农民人均占有粮食由1993年的250公斤增加到340公斤，基本解决温饱问题。7年累计完成坡改梯3.7万亩，新建基本农田0.42万亩，农民人均基本农田由1993年的0.27亩提高到0.35亩；农户户均饲养商品畜由1993年的1.9个黄牛单位提高到2.1个；新修公路438公里，全县17个乡（镇）全部通公路，169个村中通公路132个；人畜饮水困难由1993年的6万人/4.75万头匹降至4.7万人/2.08万头匹，累计解决1.3万人/2.67万头匹牲畜的饮水困难；治理水土流失3.65万亩，水土流失面积由1993年的56.25万亩降到48.9万亩；全县通程控电话的乡（镇）17个、村43个，通电的村153个，新建广播电视地面卫星接收站的村153个；全县190所中小学校（包括办学点）改造校舍104所8.3万平方米；乡乡有卫生所，新建村级卫生室121个；修建小水池、小水窖1.3万口，建沼气池2000多口。农业总产值14819万元，比1993年增长2.35倍。粮食总产量5.15万吨，比1993年增长3.24倍。

三、定点帮扶，挂职扶贫

从2001年起，全县扶贫工作实行领导干部和机关单位与贫困村挂钩定点帮扶制度，副县级以上领导干部定点联系乡（镇）和一类村贫困村，县直各部门包村扶贫。是年，中共贵州省委作出《关于加大新阶段扶贫开发工作力度的决定》并在全省开展“百乡千村”扶贫工程（全省100个一类重点贫困乡、1000个一类贫困村），荔波县的捞村乡列为省定一类贫困乡。

荔波县2002年被列入国家扶贫开发工作重点县，2011年被纳入滇桂黔石漠化片区集中连片特殊

困难地区县。全县户籍人口18万人，其中农业人口15.87万人，占88.17%，按照农民年人均纯收入2300元的新贫困标准统计，农村贫困人口5.12万人，占农业人口的32.26%，到2013年年底，农民年人均纯收入5934元。

从2004年起，县委、县政府对捞村乡进行重点倾斜扶持，实施整乡推进工程。同时，县内的一类贫困村列为每年扶贫开发的整村推进村。2005年起，县委每年选派县机关干部到贫困乡村挂职扶贫。年末，捞村乡整乡推进实施扶贫项目88个，投入专项资金701.6万元。其中，水利建设项目12个，共121.88万元；交通建设项目14个，共102.5万元；种植业项目18个，共127万元；养殖业项目23个，共124万元；农田基本建设项目9个，共67.5万元；其他项目12个，共158.72万元。农民人均纯收入从2002年的680元增加到2005年的1380元，人均占有粮食从310公斤增长到410公斤，贫困人口解决温饱问题1855人；村通公路率100%，村通广播电视率100%，农户通电率99.9%。人畜饮水困难基本得到解决；农户居住条件得到改善，茅草房和危房已全部消除；基本普及初等义务教育，基本扫除青壮年文盲；乡有文化活动中心、广播电视站和远程教育接收站，村村有远程教育接收点；乡村综合卫生服务机构齐全；人口自然增长率5.47‰，低于全县平均水平。捞村乡基本实现通水、通电、通路、通广播电视、通电话“五大目标”。

在整村推进扶贫开发中，全县扶持农户发展经果林种植3万亩，种植茶叶1.1万亩，建沼气池5200口，农田基本建设3.4万亩，改造中低产田1.2万亩；举办各类培训班1058期，推广农业新技术165项，掌握1门以上农村实用技术2万人，实现劳动力转移就业0.8万人。获贴息资金243万元，整合信贷资金4860万元。在整合信贷资金中，种植业贷款2200万元，养殖业贷款2500万元，其他行业贷款160万元。项目覆盖农户3130户，累计解决4.12万人饮水困难，解决贫困人口温饱问题3.8万人，帮助8.4万低收入人口实现增收。

四、资金扶贫，目标考核

2005年以来，全县共扶持贫困农户1.5万户65000人，投入扶贫资金14718.07万元。其中，中央财政扶贫资金6648.17万元，地方财政配套1926.6万元，以工代赈资金3832.3万元，东西扶贫协作资金803万元，定点帮扶资金1508万元。发放小额贴息贷款8071.4万元，贴息资金540万元。其中，种植业贷款4741万元，养殖业贷款3330.4万元，其他行业贷款540万元。举办各类培训班1675期，培训164083人次，8000多人实现了劳动力转移就业，覆盖农户16500户66000人。实施了103个贫困村的整村推进。

到2013年年底，全县农业完成增加值50329万元，占全县地方生产总值的15.37%；粮食总产量达到4.56万吨，比2005年减少1.01万吨；生猪出栏8.69万头、大牲畜出栏1.19万头，肉类总产量0.92万吨；商品蔬菜产业基地完成种植4.2万亩，桑树园4485亩，糖蔗种植面积3.36万亩，辣椒生产基地1.5万亩，优质水果产业基地4.3万亩，茶园基地达2.69万亩。培植出了军华畜牧发展有限责任公司，观音山种养殖示范区等一批扶贫龙头企业。同时，乡村旅游业进一步增强。至2013年年底，全县旅游共接待人数49.12万人，是2005年22.03万人的2.2倍，年均增长22.2%；实现旅游综合收入6.03亿元，是2005年0.84亿元的7.14倍，年均增长63.68%；旅游直接收入1990万元，是2005年557.8万元的3.57倍，年均增长37.43%。乡村旅游从业人员达3.5万人。6个乡（镇）实现减贫摘帽，减少贫困人口5万人，农民年任均纯收入从2005年的1654元提升到2013年年末的5934元。

县委、县政府还实施扶贫考核机制，相应出台了《荔波县“减贫摘帽”实施意见》《同步小康工作实施意见》，建立了激励机制和问责机制，将扶贫开发工作纳入县政府各部门及各乡镇年度目标绩效考核范围。荔波县坚持按照《贵州省财政扶贫资金项目管理暂行办法》《贵州省财政扶贫资金专户管理暂行办法》《贵州省财政扶贫资金报账制管理实施细则》和《贵州省扶贫资金管理办法》的要求管理使用财政扶贫资金。使扶贫资金最大限度地使用在贫困农户身上。2013年国家审计署对荔波县2010—2012年度扶贫资金进行审计，审计署认为荔波县扶贫经审计数据反映，贫困人口逐年减少，农村贫困人口从7.37万人减少到6.46万人，贫困发生率从46.43%降到40.72%；贫困农民人均收入增长较快，贫困农民年人均纯收入从3528元增加到5124元，年增长22.62元；贫困地区生产生活条件逐步改善，新修及改扩建公路396.41公里，新增自来水供应能力0.59万吨，解决0.33万人交通出行，7.46万人安全饮水问题。

2006—2013年，荔波县争取的小额到户贷款贴息资金526万元，项目贷款贴息资金196.88万元。小额到户贷款贴息项目共带动金融贷款7680万元，覆盖全县17个乡（镇）、96个行政村，扶持4078户，其中贫困农户3567户。项目贷款贴息共带动4家扶贫龙头企业，共带动金融贷款6563万元，项目在提升龙头企业融资能力的同时，对发展区域农业产业化起到促进作用。通过开展扶贫到户小额贴息贷款，促进了农村特色产业发展，壮大了农民群众的经营实力，进一步拓展了贫困农户增收渠道。

五、创建示范村

2008年11月，省民委把瑶山乡拉片村列为全省12个民族团结进步示范村之一进行创建。2009年3月，乡党委、政府以《瑶山乡总体规划》和《拉片村村庄整治规划》为基础，结合瑶山区位优势、民族文化资源优势，编制完成《2008—2010年拉片民族团结进步示范村项目规划方案》，方案以民族文化展示为主，通过景点打造、环境整治、群众素质培训等方面的建设，带动第三产业的发展，使群众通过劳动力的转移、旅游的开发走上增收的道路。2011年，瑶山拉片民族村寨荣获“贵州最具魅力民族村寨专家特别推荐奖”，并成功申报为国家AAA级景区，2012年5月1日正式列为多家旅行社必游景区，成为荔波县第一个国家AAA级的民族文化景区，懂蒙民族村寨被列为省级民族保护村寨，荣获“省级历史文化名村”称号。

2006年，全县启动扶贫工作“富帮穷”“亮点带动”战略，对农村勤劳能干、有奉献精神的生产能人、经营大户和回乡青年免费提供农村实用技术培训，并给予扶贫贷款扶持，带动其他贫困户共同致富。同时，鼓励非公有制经济人士利用其资金、技术和信息方面的优势参与扶贫开发建设。2001—2008年，全县扶贫工作投入和整合包括农业综合开发资金、以工代赈资金、信贷资金、少数民族资金及深圳对口帮扶资金等在内的各种支农经费13500万元。其中，扶贫专项资金4223万元，以工代赈资金2968万元，信贷扶贫资金4860万元，其他扶贫资金（含社会各界、深圳捐资）1449万元。实施扶贫项目共510个，解决饮水困难3.13万人，建“三小”（小山塘、小水库、小水窖）工程3016口，坡改梯4万亩，异地移民969户4074人，建生态养殖示范基地8个，培植养殖示范户200多户，改造和修建村组公路及生产便道280公里，新建和改造校舍5.57万平方米，补助贫困学生6800名。从实施“八七”扶贫攻坚至2008年年末，共实施扶贫开发项目819个，投入扶贫资金2.29亿元。

第二节　对口帮扶与定点帮扶

一、对口帮扶

1996年，中共深圳市委、市政府按照中共广东省委、省政府的部署安排，对荔波县进行对口帮扶。深圳市对口扶持荔波的主要单位和部门有深圳市商贸投资控股公司、深圳市盐田港集团、深圳市光明新区及深圳市对口扶持办公室。至2008年，深圳市委、市政府以及社会各界无偿援助荔波县资金总计3060万元（不含捐赠物资）。

深圳市对口扶持办公室帮扶　1996年、1999年，深圳市对口扶持办公室支持荔波县共105万元，建设茂兰人畜饮水、播尧寨票漫水桥、捞村卫生院、佳荣大土输电线路以及小七孔水厂等工程项目9个。2000年，投入资金30万元在瑶山瑶族乡政府驻地拉片建设移民新村，兴建民房30栋2550平方米（每栋85平方米），实施移民搬迁，将该乡长期居住在深山区的30户112人搬迁到移民新村。2003—2006年，帮扶552万元，援建项目22个。主要项目有拉片村人畜饮水和沼气工程；翁昂乡移民工程道路硬化；已陇、拉内通村公路和水利工程；佳荣镇水维村农田灌溉及人畜饮水和通村公路工程；洞塘乡木朝村通村公路建设、民房改建、“一池三改”（沼气池、改厕、改圈、改厨）沼气项目、道路硬化；板寨村饮水工程和道路硬化；甲良—中怀公路建设；永康乡白岩村移民工程；播尧地莪人饮工程、村寨道路硬化等。22个项目共修建村级公路34.37公里、沼气池154口，改造民房61户，解决2682人、2371头牲畜饮水困难和320亩农田灌溉用水问题。2007—2008年，扶持项目10个，资金295万元。实施项目有玉屏镇拉鱼新农村示范点建设，改造民房73栋共24185平方米；白岩村移民搬迁工程建设，搬迁和改造民房37户，修排洪沟500米，道路硬化1600平方米；播尧乡地莪村7个自然村寨道路建设共14129平方米，人畜饮水工程2处；翁昂乡拉内村贬和公路建设4.8公里。改善农户住房状况110户，解决农户饮水困难750户5400余人，改善群众生产生活环境1340户7000余人。1996—2008年，该办帮扶荔波资金累计982万元。

深圳商贸投资控股公司对口帮扶　1997年，捐资315万元兴建深圳商贸荔波民族中学教学大楼，建筑面积5200平方米，有教室43个、办公室12个。1997—2000年，捐资60万元建设播尧中学多功能厅；捐资210万元兴建深圳商贸茂兰希望小学、深圳商贸朝阳希望小学、深圳商贸花堤希望小学、深圳商贸金对希望小学、深圳商贸罗家寨希望小学、深圳商贸佳荣希望小学，每所学校30万元；捐资12.5万元建深圳商贸方村拉街希望小学。1999年，捐资95万元建设深圳商贸甲良中学学生宿舍楼，建筑面积2120平方米，解决该校住校学生800人的住宿问题；捐资100万元在水尧乡建设移民新村，建民房70栋，将瑶山瑶族乡地处边远深山区、石山区的4个贫困村、3个村民组、70户340名瑶族群众搬迁到移民新村，购买黑白电视机70台（每户1台）、床架210张和棉被210套（每户各2张床架和3套棉被），户户水电安装到家，村寨道路全部实行硬化，建有小学校、村卫生室和远程教育接收站等；开展“深黔携手，扶贫济困”深圳—荔波“1+1”结对助学活动，捐资32万元资助贫困学生3200名。2000年6月21日，荔波遭受特大洪涝灾害，荔波—小七孔樟江河上的钢索吊桥4座被冲断毁坏，深圳商贸控股公司捐赠130万元，维修被冲毁的钢索桥，同时向灾区群众捐赠衣物、生活用品等救灾物资。1999年，捐助60万元改扩建甲良茶叶加工项目，2000年，捐助50万元建设黑山羊养殖示范基地。2002年，总投资480万元建深圳商贸荔波县人民医院住院部大楼，建筑面积4212.3平方米，其中主体工程建设投资239万元，医疗设施、办公设备、医院供氧系统、传呼装置等设施投资241万元。同时，另捐助5万元为县医院购置医疗仪器。新住院部大楼建成后，增加床位50个，提高了住院病人的接纳能力，全院病案甲级率由原85%上升到95%。

1997—2002年，该公司向荔波教育事业捐赠款累计1435万元，援建中学4所、小学151所，新增建筑面积2.6万平方米，学生和教师的教学环境得到改善。

深圳市盐田港集团对口帮扶　2006—2008年，深圳盐田港集团捐资450万元兴建荔波二中盐田港教学楼，有教室50个，建筑面积6808平方米，改善该校2500多名学生和138名教师的教学环境。盐田港集团职工捐赠8万元，设立荔波盐田港中学贫困学生助学基金，用于奖励品学兼优的贫困学生。

深圳市光明新区对口帮扶　2007年，深圳光明新区捐赠100万元建设翁昂乡市场光明新街项目，硬化市场和街道共5260平方米，修建排水沟435米，改变市场街道“脏、乱、差”状况，方便群众生产生活。2008年，荔波遭受雨雪冰冻灾害，光明新区发动干部群众及社会各界为荔波县募捐

10万元用于灾后重建。其中，用于兴建方村乡交进提灌站5万元，解决农田灌溉用水问题2000亩，项目受益570户2100人；美盈森环保科技股份有限公司向永康乡白岩村移民新村捐赠5万元实施道路硬化2580平方米，改善37户158人的居住环境。

其他单位帮扶　2001年，深圳巨帮公司竹园宾馆捐赠彩色电视机30台，分别赠送甲良、朝阳、茂兰和拉街的4所小学。是年，深圳市布吉中学向荔波中学捐资8万元配置多媒体教室设备，捐赠的图书资料价值2万元，资助贫困学生115名共3万元。

二、定点帮扶

1996—1999年，州水利局投入资金累计145万元兴建驾欧乡巴槽人畜饮水工程，解决该乡六林和新街两个村人畜饮水困难问题。

1998年，省教委向荔波县翁昂乡已垅村困难党员46户和教师发放慰问金1万元，向已陇村党支部捐活动经费5000元。

2002—2006年，定点帮扶荔波县的国家林业局捐赠20万元建设驾欧乡六林小学；资助贫困学生50人共28154元，向六林小学赠送书籍价值7500元及计算机等价值3.8万元；支持荔波杨梅基地建设项目资金95.2万元；建立林业站办公用房5个共25万元，补助护林防火经费15万元；补助县林业工作业务经费10万元。

是年，省教育厅捐资15万元帮助茂兰中学建设种养殖实训基地；捐资15万元为翁昂小学购置课桌、床架和图书；捐资20万元为捞村小学购置计算机、文具、办公桌等。

附录：

扶贫决战在瑶山

仲夏，走进荔波县瑶山瑶族乡，被一种精神感动着。一支中专以上文化、科员以上职务的国家干部队伍活跃在田间地头，他们在24个瑶族村民组盖起了茅草棚，与2770多瑶胞同吃、同住、同生产、同劳动。肩负着瑶山扶贫的攻坚决战的使命，既是指挥员，又是坚战斗者。

历来缺水没电的董别村更龚组有24户人家，户户住草房，有16户只能吃苞谷稀饭。县乡镇企业局驻组队员何祥文带去局里捐献的6000元钱新建水池，把局里给自己盖瓦房的2000元挤出1000元买自来水管，自己住茅屋，让118名瑶胞喝上清洁卫生的自来水。

距离乡政府20多里的拉朝组10多户人家，户户种杂交玉米，搞温室育秧，宽窄行栽种，工作队员把农业科技送到边远农家。

这支队伍刚驻组就进入了角色。为从根本上解决瑶胞绝对贫困问题，县委、县政府从县直机关选调会种植技术、懂养殖管理、能操作加工的26名年轻干部，组成“瑶山扶贫攻坚工作队”，担负起扶贫攻坚大决战的使命。正、副队长总领全盘，24名队员分驻24个瑶族村民组。带资金、带任务、带指标驻组3年，定组、定户、定目标，不脱贫、不脱钩。

4月2日，工作队到位上岗，一些布依族、水族小伙子被难住了，语言互不相通。朝沙组队员杨宇声接连跑了5家问不着组长是谁。队员们利用星期天，找回家的学生当翻译、做向导，挨家挨户调查，与组长交换意见。白天指导瑶胞生产，晚上挑灯夜战分户建卡，拟写《瑶山乡瑶族村现状分析及项目实施报告》。

为加快脱贫步伐，县供销社赊销12.3万元的尿素、氨氮让瑶胞给苞谷追肥。县工商局、教育局等20多个单位纷纷捐钱献物，维修水窖33个、水池11个，新建水窖7个、公厕1座，维修公路3公里，建加工点2个。

5月中旬，瑶山乡党委、乡政府，工作队共同组织村支部书记、村委会主任、部分村民组长、工作队员到罗甸大关参观学习，大家被大关12年坚持劈石造田的艰苦奋斗精神打动了，振奋地说：“大关能做的，我们瑶山也能做到”。

工作队员有信心，村组干部有带头奔富欲望，然而最急需的是资金，乡政府扶贫工作队队部办公室“瑶山乡瑶族村民组情况暨发展计划一览表”和“瑶山乡瑶族村民组基础设施项目统计表”清楚显示出扶贫项目和脱贫步骤，而资金到位情况一栏仍然空白。工作队员耐不住了。7月13日，县里“四大班子”一把手以及十多个相关部门负责同志亲临瑶山召开扶贫攻坚项目现场办公会，成立了瑶山扶贫开发公司，兑现每户瑶胞1000元启动资金，落实种植项目5项：杉木林1300亩，桃李120亩，杜仲200亩，酸梅150亩，香菇6000瓶；养殖项目5项：黑山羊1260只，牛265头，猪210头，鸡10700只，鸭2500只；加工项目5个：打米机5台，柴油机5台。投入贴息扶贫贷款100万元，以物作贷，宜种则种，宜养则养，宜加则加，短平快项目和中长期项目相济，坡改梯1200亩，造田370亩。家家有项目，户户有任务。乡党委、政府负总责，扶贫攻坚工作队领办实施，科技副县长谭成华、政协副主席杨志平负责技术培训、项目指导，瑶胞受益。

开山造田，选坡栽树半山腰搭鸡圈……在这109平方公里的大地上，开始了前所未有的扶贫攻坚决战。

（原载《贵州日报》1997年7月31日）

第十三篇
工业　乡镇企业

中共十一届三中全会以后，荔波县的工业发展主要是以煤炭开发为主导，起步于20世纪70年代中后期，为加快荔波县经济建设的步伐，大力开发煤炭资源。煤炭开发对全县财政收入的贡献率逐年增加，1992年，全县运销原煤67.5万吨，产值3780万元，当年财政收入为1112万元，煤炭运销税费占财政收入50%以上，成为荔波县重要的支柱产业。到2007年，煤炭产运销实现的税费占全县财政收入80%以上，成为全县经济发展的第一支柱产业。2008年，煤炭产业通过强化安全监管、挖掘生产潜力，实现产量、效益双提升，全年原煤产销量达130万吨，实现税费收入1.35亿元。同时，20世纪80年代初开始水电开发建设，电力工业也有了长足的发展。其他工业随着国家工业体制的改革、乡镇企业的发展，逐步改制朝着有利于生产，有利于经营管理，有利于市场竞争的方向发展。

第一章 煤炭工业

第一节 煤炭资源与开发决策

荔波县煤炭资源丰富，全县17个乡（镇）中有13个乡（镇）蕴藏着煤炭资源。无烟煤分布于荔波县东部的茂兰煤田，面积450余平方公里。茂兰煤田划分为罗家寨、打油寨、十二索、平寨、更班、甲介、拉奖、拉滩、荒草坪、水庆、水功、姑爽、巴合、应昂、上寨15个井田。

20世纪70年代初，经广西壮族自治区第一、第六、第九地质队联合勘探，于1974年9月提交《贵州省荔波茂兰煤田普查勘探报告书》，广西桂地审〔1974〕12号文批准，茂兰煤田探明工业储量为3.14亿吨。茂兰煤田的无烟煤属低灰、低中硫、高发热量的优质煤。此外，荔波县中西部的荔波向斜和方村向斜有烟煤分布，经贵州省地勘单位的地表普查，估算地质远景储量约2.2亿吨。

荔波县煤炭资源的开发有着得天独厚的优势：一是地理区位优势，荔波县与广西壮族自治区的环江县、南丹县接壤，而广西壮族自治区和广东省都是贫煤地区，销售市场广阔。二是交通便利，1976年修通了广西金城江至荔波县立化镇的铁路专用线直达矿区，在县境内设有肯甫、平寨和更班3个车站。另有三条柏油公路通达广西。三是煤层埋藏浅，为缓倾单斜煤层，易于开采。

荔波县的煤炭开发起步于20世纪70年代中后期，特别中共十一届三中全会以后，加快了经济建设步伐，大力开发荔波县的煤炭资源。

县委、县政府提出“依靠省州、面向两广、开发山区、兴荔富民”的经济发展战略，荔波县煤炭开发进入较快的发展阶段。县委、人大、政府、政协领导班子认识一致。县委一把手、二把手亲自抓，分管县长具体抓，人大、政协献计出力，产煤乡镇党政领导亲自组织，亲自到产销第一线，形成了一套班子、一个整体的功能，从实践中培养锻炼出一批创办乡镇企业的骨干队伍。

20世纪90年代荔波更班矿区

县综合、主管部门发挥职

能作用。县经委把开发煤炭资源作为重点项目抓，乡镇企业局、矿管办、安委会按职能分工具体抓。县经委坚持一月召开一次协调会，及时解决原煤生产、运输、销售、安全中存在的问题。每月一次向铁路申报运输车皮计划，及时协调原煤进站台、组织车皮等工作。乡镇企业局、矿管办、安委会每年都分期分批举办矿长、质检员、安全员、机电员培训班，以提高他们业务技术素质，增强安全意识，保证安全生产，科学采矿。煤炭开发对全县财政收入的贡献率逐年增加，到2007年，煤炭产运销实现的税费占全县财政收入80%以上，成为全县经济发展的第一支柱产业。2008年，煤炭产业通过强化安全监管、挖掘生产潜力，实现产量、效益双提升，全年原煤产销量达130万吨，实现税费收入1.35亿元。

第二节　县内企业开采煤矿

荔波煤炭资源的开采主要经历零星开采、全面开采矿山整治，关井压产煤矿整合，全面提升办矿水平的几个阶段。民国时期（1912—1949），荔波就开始有人开采煤炭，直至20世纪70年代初期，都处于零星开采阶段，主要用于当地烧石灰、烧砖瓦。解放后，先后开办过罗布木煤厂、五七煤厂、拉开煤厂等，由于对煤炭资源不清，缺乏开采技术，加之管理不善，连年亏损，都被迫停产。20世纪70年代中后期，广西地质队对荔波煤炭资源勘探结束，专用铁路修通荔波，广西红茂矿务局开始对荔波的煤炭资源进行开发。1978年改革开放后，荔波煤炭资源开采全面展开。到20世纪90年代中期，全县形成了国家、集体、个体等多元化投资办煤矿的格局。加上当地群众和外来民工的乱采滥挖，当时在开采高峰年份，全县各类小煤矿井口数量多达1000个。1995年，全县煤炭产销量首次突破100万吨。煤炭开采带动了荔波经济的发展，出现了一些“万元户”和小康村。荔波财政收入也逐步形成以煤炭税费为主的格局。

一、县内企业开采

1978年，茂兰、洞塘、水尧、佳荣等公社先后兴办小煤窑。1980年，茂兰区、城关区和甲良区的8个公社、39个大队近100个生产队2000多人，在春播和秋种结束半年多时间内，进入甲介、水捞、甲良等十多个采煤区乱挖滥采，挖独眼井（洞）600个，采用明火照明、明火放炮，进行私人开采。

1982年，茂兰区成立社队企业办事处，配备人员34名，有载重汽车8辆、小汽车2辆，负责各乡原煤产、运、销工作，并直接经营水庆、幸福桥、恒姑、交土4个煤厂，年产原煤2.5万吨。之后各乡先后成立社队企业办公室，负责该乡原煤产、运、销。1984年以后，茂兰、立化、洞塘、佳荣、瑶庆5个乡的煤井逐年增多，从业人员多的乡达500人。社队企业办事处改为乡镇企业办事处。为适应原煤生产发展，产煤乡成立销售公司，配置专人负责原煤运销业务。1985年，茂兰区原煤产量16万吨，占全县原煤总产量的73%。

1987年，荔波县以扶贫贷款265万元扶持乡（镇）新建年产原煤各2万吨的骨干煤井11个：水庆煤井、下甲介煤井、岜项煤井、水条煤井、军民煤井、水功煤井、应昂煤井、姑爽煤井、威桑煤井、上莪羊煤井、下莪羊煤井。1990年先后投产。1990年原煤产销51.38万吨，产值1531.14万元，比1985年的21.6万吨增加产销量29.78万吨。

1988年，全县有采煤企业128家、煤井400个，设计生产规模年产2万吨煤井18个。由于煤矿开发缺乏规划，煤层埋藏较浅薄、易开采，1991年，全县有煤矿110对，总产量51.98万吨。到1997年，境内有小煤井1000余个，总产量112.54万吨。

二、联合办矿

荔波县根据黔南州提出经济联合“积极主动，优惠待人，让利在先，微利也干”的原则，1987年，水尧乡与四十一集团军联合开发水捞军民联办煤矿，双方共同投资，建成年产2万吨矿井。1989年，立化镇、县财政局与柳州铁路局联合开发应昂煤矿，计划年产3万吨，双方各投资120万元。由于联合把双方利益捆一起，按照“平等互利，祸福与共，利益均沾，共同发展”的原则，双方发挥各自优势，引进了资金、人才、技术，增强了煤炭开发的后劲，增加原煤生产新的生长点。

三、铁路协作

搞好与铁路协作关系，荔波县乡镇矿是“以运定产、以运定销”，运出多，销售就多，运多就能多出效益。必须依靠铁路，力争多得车皮装煤外运、外销。县委、县政府一把手、二把手经常赴广西走访铁路局、铁路运输段（站），争取铁路的支援，从1983年以来日均由2个、6个车皮到20世纪90年代初期增加近30个车皮，1992年通过运出的原煤达42.17万吨，占销售原煤的64%。

四、国营岜合煤矿

由于小煤窑开采浪费煤炭资源，生产很不安全，县政府决定兴建地方国营岜合煤矿，1985年9月，贵州省计委批准《岜合煤矿计划任务书》。分期进行，先建设年产9万吨的岜合煤井，总投资761万元。1990年开始建矿，打巷井深528米，打煤层，厚度1米以上，投入正规开采，定名为荔波县岜合煤矿。为荔波经济建设的起飞打下了基础。

第三节　广西红茂矿务局开采煤矿

1978年，广西红茂矿务局已在荔波境内建有平寨、更班、打油寨3个国有煤矿。1983年7月24—26日，贵州省人民政府和广西壮族自治区人民政府就红茂矿务局在荔波县境内开发煤田的若干问题进行了会商。参加会商人员在察看了更班、平寨、巴格、打油寨等矿点之后，听取了红茂矿务局和荔波县人民政府的汇报，对双方所提问题，本着有利于民族团结，有利于地区经济发展和互助互利的原则，双方经过协商，本着尊重历史、照顾现状的原则，同意由广西红茂矿务局继续开发茂兰向斜的更班，并达成一系列互利互惠的协议。

1984年4月18日在四省区五方经济协调会议第一次会议期间，贵州省代表和广西壮族自治区代表就茂兰矿区扩建及进一步开发问题进行协调。同年9月1—3日，黔南自治州和广西煤炭厅在都匀市进行了第一次会议，10月25—27日在南宁市进行第二次会谈，达成以下协议：1.关于茂兰西部煤田的开发范围问题；2.关于照顾民族自治地方的经济利益问题；3.关于铁路运输问题；4.关于茂兰西部矿井供电问题；5.关于矿区公路建设问题；6.关于开发井田征用土地问题；7.关于帮助荔波县培训技术人员问题；8.关于供水问题；9.矿区服务网点为当地群众服务；10.小煤窑超合同售给红茂矿务局的煤的加价。

1989年3月，平寨、更班、打油寨3个煤矿进行采矿权申请登记，均获采矿许可证，持证开采荔波煤矿。到1990年，茂兰矿区共开工矿井5对，已建成投产3对，有两对矿井因压缩基建等原因中途停（缓）建。

平寨矿，矿井位于茂兰煤田东翼的南部。金城江至荔波公路经过矿区。洛茂煤矿铁路专用线经井田东侧，井口离洛茂铁路终点站平寨车站1公里。1971年12月矿井动工建设，1977年9月建成投产。

1972年7月，矿井初步设计生产能力为30万吨/年，服务年限35年。1985年2月15日，核减矿井生产能力为15万吨/年。1990年，矿井保有地质储量1577.7万吨，可采储量1183.3万吨，按矿井核定生产能力15万吨/年计算，尚可服务56年。

更班矿，矿井位于茂兰煤田东翼的中部。金城江至荔波公路经过矿区。从平寨火车站有专用线直延到矿井井口工业广场的地面煤仓。1971年8月矿井动工兴建，由矿务局矿建工程处施工，1977年12月移交投产。1972年2月，矿井生产能力初步设计为90万吨/年，服务年限44年。1973年12月，矿井生产能力修改为60万吨/年。1979年，矿井生产能力核减为30万吨/年。1989年年底，矿井保有地质储量4192.1万吨，可采储量2515.26万吨，按矿井核定生产能力30万吨/年计算，尚可服务84年。

打油寨矿，矿井位于茂兰煤田东翼南端，离金城江至荔波公路5.5公里。矿井在洛茂煤矿铁路专用线肯甫车站设装车站，井口至肯甫车站8公里。矿井于1976年12月筹建，称红茂矿务局第三矿建处。1977年6月580平硐开工。1980年1月国家压缩基本建设，矿井下马停建。同年4月，矿井由矿务局接管后开始以小煤窑生产煤炭。1981年9月，压缩井型改建，矿井建设重新上马。之后，矿井一边生产，一边基建，1986年12月竣工投产。1976年11月，矿井生产能力初步设计为20万吨/年，服务年限16.7年。1980年5月，矿井生产能力修改为6万吨/年，服务年限36.1年。1989年，矿井生产原煤6.6万吨，首次达到生产能力。1990年年底，矿井保有地质储量149.7万吨，可采储量112.3万吨，按矿井生产能力6万吨/年计算，尚可服务13年。

2000年，高荣煤矿（基建矿井）位于十二索井田，建于1977年，为打油寨矿的接替矿井，设计服务年限34年。2000年年产原煤6万吨的打油寨煤矿因资源枯竭闭坑。2002年7月，由红茂矿务局投资兴建的平寨、更班、打油寨、高荣4个煤矿因经营困难而政策性破产。

2002年7月，贵州省青少年发展基金会下属企业贵州青利工贸有限公司出资720万元，收购重组红茂矿务局的平寨、更班煤矿、高荣煤矿，更名为贵州青利公司荔波分公司平寨煤矿、更班煤矿，并将高荣煤矿出卖给私人，重新注入资金，对矿井各系统进行整改，经省、州验收合格后恢复生产。

附：

贵州省黔南自治州、广西区煤炭工业厅
关于开发荔波县茂兰西部煤田的会谈纪要

根据1983年7月27日《贵州、广西两省区关于红茂矿务局在荔波县境内开发煤田若干问题的会商纪要》关于：“茂兰向斜其他十二个井田，广西如需开发，由两省区另行商议”的精神，黔南自治州和广西煤炭厅曾于1984年9月1—3日在都匀市进行了第一次会议；这次又于10月25—27日在南宁市进行第二次会谈，参加南宁会谈的有贵州省黔南自治州州长罗平义、州计委主任罗富敏、州外协办副主任马保华、州经委工程师黄达光、州政府秘书杨仁章、荔波县委书记王元、县政协副主席李德余、县经委主任蒙映禹，有广西煤炭工业厅厅长陆育德、副厅长孙振东、厅总工程师王同良、办公室主任高光才、基建处副处长黄德雄、生产处副处长张力、计财处副处长白铭义、厅高级工程师鲁令杰、红茂矿务局党委书记陈福兴、局总工程师郑兆安等18位同志。双方代表就开发

荔波县茂兰西部煤田问题交换了意见。双方本着加强团结协作，进一步开发和利用煤炭资源，搞活和促进地区的经济发展原则，在团结、融洽、友好的气氛中进行了充分的协商。现将会谈纪要如下：

一、关于茂兰西部煤田的开发范围问题

广西煤炭工业厅要求新增开发水功等6个井田，黔南自治州同意将水功、拉奖、拉滩3个井田先划给广西开发，广西提出增开上寨井田，黔南州表示可以考虑，其余井田广西仍需开发，以后再议。

广西在进行矿井设计时，要分别征求县、区、乡的意见，在兼顾群众利益的原则下，现已开办的小煤窑，仍继续开采外，还应划出一些浅矿段供荔波县小煤窑开采，但应不危及大井安全生产，不损坏大井地面工业建筑。

二、关于照顾民族自治地方的经济利益问题

红茂矿务局在茂兰西部矿井生产的煤炭，每运出一吨，按坑口价格的13%付给荔波县资源开发补偿费，今后国家开征资源税红茂局应照章纳税，如全部上交国库，广西仍按13%付资源开发补偿费；如资源税县有分成，则按冲减分成后的差额付给资源开发补偿费。

在付给13%的补偿费后，如广西在茂兰西部矿井能实现盈利，县则不再参与利润分成，矿区工商税，按规定继续向荔波缴纳。

三、关于铁路运输问题

按原商定荔波县茂兰地区生产的小窑煤的50%由红茂矿务局收购，其余需用火车外运的，仍由荔波县按原途径提报车皮计划，广西煤炭厅提请自治区经委、计委、柳州铁路局等有关部门尽量给予解决。

四、关于茂兰西部矿井供电问题

从红茂矿务局平寨矿到水功矿的高压输电线路由红茂矿务局负责架设，在供电设计中要考虑到荔波县巴合矿的初期用电负荷和当地农民用电负荷。

岜合矿的分路供电设施由荔波县解决。

待荔波县大七孔水电站建成后，水功等矿井可利用水电资源，但不并入广西电网。双方使用电力资源的费用按电表计量核收。

五、关于矿区公路建设问题

为开发岜合、水功井田按四级公路标准，所修的公路经方案比较后，如需新建新路段（瑶庆至岜合联办煤厂）由荔波县和广西煤炭厅各负责一半投资，如需改造水尧至水功老线，这段公路的改造费用由广西负责，公路建成后交荔波县有关部门管理，广西方面按规定付给养路费。修筑公路所征用的土地，由荔波县按国家规定办理有关手续。

六、关于开发井田征用土地问题

广西煤炭厅开发各井田所需用的土地，应本着“少占少用，先征后用”的原则，按国务院关于《国家建设征用土地条例》及贵州省有关规定办理征地手续。

七、关于帮助荔波县培训技术人员问题

广西煤炭厅和红茂矿务局可为荔波县按计划代培一定数量的煤矿中等技术干部和主要技术工种的工人，对岜合井田的开发可提供技术咨询。

茂兰西部矿井的安全救护工作，由红茂矿务局照顾。

八、关于供水问题

广西煤炭厅开发茂兰西部水功等井田的供水问题，由荔波县协同广西煤矿设计院和红茂矿务局在现场商定解决，荔波县提供方便。

九、广西矿井设计中的矿区卫生所、商店，可为当地群众服务，荔波县、区等到矿区开设服务网点，广西煤炭厅表示欢迎，矿井生产用合同工，广西方面要适当照顾到当地农民。

十、荔波县提出的小煤窑超合同售给红茂矿务局的煤，每吨加价五元的要求，广西煤炭厅同意从今年十一月一日开始执行。

与会同志认为：这次会谈是成功的，今年随着茂兰西部煤田的开发，将会促进荔波县的经济建设，并推动红茂矿务局的生产发展，同时也加强了双方协作关系，其意义是重大的，双方愿意在今后的友好交往中，为取得新的成绩，为加深友谊和合作做出更大的努力。

贵州黔南自治州代表　罗平义　王　元

广西煤炭厅代表　孙振东

1984年10月27日

第四节　煤矿管理

一、安全生产管理

（一）管理机构

1978—1984年，煤炭矿山的安全工作由县社队企业局负责。1985年起，煤炭矿山的安全工作由县乡镇企业局负责。1995年后，安全管理工作划归县煤炭工业局（与县乡镇企业局实行两块牌子、一套人员合署办公）。

2003年4月，为加强对煤矿安全生产的监督管理，专门成立了荔波县煤矿安全生产监督管理局，编制60人，并公开向省内外招聘了40名煤炭专业技术人员。同月，为使荔波拟提交省、州进行复产验收的53对煤矿能顺利通过验收，特将新招聘技术人员实行驻矿管理，每矿安排有一名驻矿人员，为煤矿整改提供技术帮助和指导。

2003年8月，县煤矿安全生产监督管理局与县乡（镇）企业局、县煤炭工业局合并为县煤炭工业管理局，设立煤炭执法监察大队，负责对全县煤炭生产经营秩序的整顿与规范进行执法监察监管。在主要产煤乡（镇）设5个乡（镇）煤炭安全管理站，原驻矿技术人员全部划入5个乡（镇）煤炭安全管理站。

2004年9月，原乡（镇）煤炭安全管理站14人调整到国土资源所工作，5个乡（镇）站实行垂直管理，人员编制不变，人员配置为茂兰站5人，立化站4人，佳荣站3人，水尧站3人，播尧站2人。县煤炭工业局设立煤矿安全监督管理站，人员配置13人，主要工作负责煤矿安全“包保”监管，内设监管一站、监管二站，每站有煤监人员6人。2005年4月，成立荔波县安全生产监督管理局，全县煤炭矿山安全工作由县安监局负责，5个乡（镇）煤炭安全管理站工作职能调整到县安监局，撤销煤矿安全监督管理站，不设站的乡（镇）辖区内的煤矿由县安监局直接监管。2008年5月县煤炭工业局更名为县煤炭工业管理局，职能不变。

（二）矿山安全监管

1978—1984年，县内开采的煤炭资源埋藏浅，易开采，对开采技术和开采设备要求不高，发生安全事故率低。

随着煤矿挖掘向深层延伸，安全问题逐渐突出。1985年后，按照“安全第一，预防为主”的原则，进行安全管理。全县划分为8个采煤片区，每片区由所在乡、村和煤炭管理所（站）及主要厂矿负责人组成生产安全领导小组，各厂矿配备安全员、瓦斯检查员、放炮员。

1988年，县矿管部门投资28万元购买矿灯、干式变压器、轻轨等设备，供给区、乡小煤窑。1989年，增添风筒2000多米、瓦检器20台，改善生产安全条件。同时，对茂兰片区227个煤矿（井）进行检查，对事故隐患大的74个煤矿责令关闭。1990年，除区、乡每月开展一次自查外，全县进行4次大检查，对存在安全隐患的煤矿进行整改。

1983—1990年，全县发生伤亡事故101起，死亡140人。对矿山事故处理按照“三不放过”（事故原因分析不清不放过，事故责任者和群众没有受到教育不放过，没有采取切实可行的防范措施不放过）原则，及时查处。2002年2月，县煤炭工业局从广西红茂矿务局等单位选6名工程师调到该局专门从事煤矿安全生产技术工作，充实了县煤炭工业技术人才。

2003年4月，县煤矿安全生产监督管理局公开向省内外招聘煤炭专业技术人员40名，实行技术人员驻矿管理安全生产制度，每矿安排驻矿人员1名，为煤矿整改提供技术帮助和指导。县煤矿安全监督管理大队分两组，对全县煤矿安全生产工作进行包片、包矿、包安全的安全检查。同时，制定煤矿“包保”制度，煤监人员按包片、包矿制度管理矿山安全。

2003—2004年，由中介机构为县内38对煤矿安装瓦斯监测监控设备。此后，煤矿生产事故逐年下降，从2003年的事故27起、死亡66人、重伤10人、轻伤13人下降到2008年的事故7起、死亡7人。

二、从业人员培训

1995年后，县煤炭工业管理局以安全科和生产科为主，对煤矿矿长、瓦斯检验员、安全员及煤矿民工岗前培训，采取集中学习和现场培训的方式进行。

1998—2001年，执行国家“关井压产”“停产整顿”“复产验收”等规定，县安全生产管理部门根据国家对煤矿设备、设施及图纸、资料、培训等的要求，实施分级培训，矿长由二级以上培训机构培训发证，特殊工种（瓦检员、安全员、电工、绞车工）为三级以上培训机构培训发证，井下从业人员由四级以上培训机构培训发证。2001年起，全县煤矿实行持证上岗制度，煤矿从业人员必须进行岗前培训，考核发证，持证上岗。

2007年11月—2008年，在县煤炭工业管理局增设荔波县四级煤矿安全技术培训中心。该中心经过师资培训，完善教学设施后，提请州煤炭工业管理局审查和现场验收，符合煤矿从业人员办学条件，同意成立荔波县四级煤矿安全技术培训中心。

2003—2008年全县各类煤矿人员培训统计表

表13－1 单位：人

年度	矿长		安全矿长		特种作业人员（含安全员、瓦检员、电工、绞车工、水泵工）		民工岗前培训
	培训	复训	培训	复训	培训	复训	
2003	53	—	—	—	140	127	1000
2004	17	25	—	—	289	155	750
2005	20	—	51	—	301	49	820
2006	17	8	47	—	52	8	902
2007	3	20	—	—	123	—	—
2008	9	—	—	—	114	—	580
合计	119	53	98	—	1019	339	4052

第五节 煤矿企业整顿

1998年，国家煤炭产业政策作了重大调整，全国开展煤炭行业秩序治理整顿，煤炭行业实施关井压产后，全县小煤矿数量才逐年减少，办矿规模和水平逐步提高。

1998年后，按照国务院《关于关闭非法和布局不合理煤矿工作的通知》《关于关闭非法和布局不合理煤矿有关问题的通知》和省、州煤炭行业关井压产工作会议要求，县委、县政府成立关井压产工作领导小组，制定实施方案，开展全县煤矿关井压产工作，关闭布局不合理和非法小煤矿60处119口，压产45.28万吨。其中，在国有井田范围内关闭13口，压产13万吨。

全县缺乏矿产资源开发总体规划和煤炭开采开发规划，导致煤炭资源无序开采开发，造成了地表及浅部资源的极大破坏和浪费，矿区环境污染严重。2000年以后，通过对煤炭行业的安全专项整治，取缔和关闭布局不合理和不具备安全生产条件的小煤矿，到2002年，全县保留矿井约70个。

2002年，根据国务院和省、州政府的要求，在全县范围内开展煤矿清理整顿，经过县煤炭行业主管部门和煤矿业主的整改，是年，提交省、州级验收的煤矿中，有16对通过州级验收。2003年，全县提交验收煤矿53对，经省级验收，合格煤矿25对，不合格煤矿13对，列入限期整改煤矿15对。2004年，县煤矿管理部门再次将2003年度验收未合格的煤矿和列入限期整改的煤矿提交省、州主管部门验收，验收合格煤矿23对。至此，全县验收合格煤矿48对。2004年全县煤炭产销量178.15万吨，创荔波县煤炭开采以来的最好成绩，煤炭对全县的财政收入占75%以上，煤炭产业的支柱地位更加凸现。

2005年11月，茂兰镇安匀煤矿、甲介桥头煤矿、荒草坪煤矿、福利煤矿、水庆煤矿，立化镇高荣煤矿，水尧乡的为煤矿、吉党煤矿，播尧乡麻庄煤矿，瑶麓乡甲丙骨干煤矿，方村乡尧农煤矿的《技改方案》《安全设施设计》《安全预评价》通过州、省评审，获得技改项目资格，开始技改建设。2005年年底，贵州省煤矿整合工作会议在荔波县召开，全县煤矿整合工作正式启动。

2006年，县政府请贵州省煤矿设计研究院编制《荔波县整合矿、生产结构调整及合理矿权设置方案》，同年年底，省人民政府黔府函〔2006〕203号予以批复。全县有22对煤矿整合为10对，14对煤矿作技改扩能、扩界，保留煤矿2对，在建煤矿1对，历史遗留问题煤矿1对，有资源而无煤矿的乡（镇）新设矿井9对。

获新建煤矿9个：洞塘乡新立煤矿、甲良镇新设煤矿一井、甲良镇新设煤矿二井、驾欧乡新设煤矿一井、驾欧乡新设煤矿二井、方村乡新设煤矿、水利乡新设煤矿一井、水利乡新设煤矿二井、瑶山乡新设煤矿。

2007年1月，根据国务院办公厅《关于进一步做好煤矿整顿关闭工作的意见》和国家安监总局等11个单位《关于加强煤矿安全生产工作规范煤炭资源整合的若干意见》及省政府《关于进一步促进煤炭工业健康发展的意见》，全县进行煤矿整顿关闭与整合，按煤矿资源整合工作要求，委托有资质单位编制《荔波县煤矿整合和调整资源布局方案》报省、州审批。同时，成立荔波县煤矿整顿关闭与整合工作领导小组，制定《荔波县煤矿整合实施方案》，发出《关于加快推进全县煤矿整合工作的补充通知》，县煤炭工业管理局成立3个推进煤矿整合工作小组，逐矿、逐人进行交流协调。根据省政府的批复，将22对煤矿整合为10对，整合矿井业主和被整合矿井业主双方进行经济补偿协商，由整合矿井业主对被整合矿井业主进行经济补偿。至5月，全县22对整合的煤矿全部签订整合协议。至6月底，全县煤矿整合办证结束，整合后的煤矿全部在省工商管理部门进行企业名称核准登记和办理矿权变更登记。

经过资源整合后，矿井设计年生产能力为15万吨的有5对，矿井设计年生产能力为9万吨的有5对。煤矿进行扩界扩能14对，其中，扩界扩能后，年生产能力由3万吨提高为9万吨的煤矿有13对，年生产能力由6万吨提高为9万吨的煤矿有1对。

至2008年年底，全县煤矿数为32对，设计年生产能力357万吨。

所有整合和扩能扩界煤矿的相关审批手续全部办结。

附：

重点煤矿企业简介

岜合煤矿 岜合煤矿位于岜合井田。设计占用储量408万吨，划定采区面积4.5平方公里，设计生产能力为15万吨/年，其中岜合矿井年产9万吨，前期年产3万吨，服务年限30年。1990年3月，荔波县与柳州铁路局经济开发总公司签订联合开发协议，年底协议终止，由荔波县自办。1991年4月，进行采矿权登记，获采矿许可证。1998年7月23日，荔波县政府办公室下发《关于同意国有岜合煤矿改制方案的批复》同意该矿进行股份制改革，由国有企业转变为国有控股煤矿企业，煤矿职工持有县政府配给的工龄股和矿龄股部分股份。2003年，在全县煤矿清理整顿中，岜合煤矿经州级验收合格。

更班煤矿 位于更班井田。建于1971年8月，总投资3558万元。探明储量4196.5万吨，设计利用储量3675.6万吨，矿区面积16.94平方公里，核定生产能力30万吨/年，服务年限70年。投产后年产原煤20万吨。1989年3月进行采矿权申请登记，获采矿许可证。

平寨煤矿 位于平寨井田。建于1971年，总投资857万元。探明储量2044.87万吨，设计利用储量1876.34万吨，矿区面积8.57平方公里，核定生产能力15万吨/年，服务年限80年。投产后年产原煤10万吨。1989年3月进行采矿权申请登记，获采矿许可证。

水庆煤井 矿井位于水庆井田。设计占用储量59万吨，可采储量40.39万吨，生产规模2万吨/年，服务年限13.5年。1988年9月县矿管办审核，进行采矿权申请登记，获采矿许可证。

下甲介煤井 矿井位于更班井田。设计占用储量195.7万吨，可采储量137万吨，生产规模2万吨/年，服务年限46年。1989年11月县矿管办审核，进行采矿权申请登记，获采矿许可证。后因地质灾害毁坏主巷，工程停建。1992年，改巷续建，正式投产。

岜项煤井 矿井位于更班井田。设计占用储量52.8万吨，可采储量42.23万吨，生产规模2万吨/年，服务年限15年。1989年进行采矿权申请登记，获采矿许可证。

水条煤井 矿井位于上寨井田，设计占用储量44万吨，生产规模2万吨/年，服务年限10年。1988年9月进行采矿权申请登记，获采矿许可证。

军民煤井 矿井位于岜合井田。设计占用储量71万吨，可采储量29.99万吨，生产规模2万吨/年，服务年限16年。1991年4月进行采矿权申请登记，获采矿许可证。

水功煤井 矿井位于水功井田。设计占用储量39.5万吨，生产规模2万吨/年，服务年限9年。1989年2月进行采矿权申请登记，获采矿许可证，正式投产。

应昂煤井 矿井位于应昂井田。设计占用储量74.1万吨，可采储量50.38万吨，生产规模2万吨/年，服务年限17年。1988年10月，经县矿管办审核，进行采矿权申请登记，获采矿许可证。之后主体工程停建。1992年续建。

姑爽煤井 矿井位于姑爽井田。设计占用储量55.3万吨，生产规模2万吨/年，服务年限12.5年。1988年6月，经县矿管办审核，进行采矿权申请登记，获采矿许可证。主巷掘进80米未出煤，主体工程停建，保留煤矿机构开办小煤窑。

威桑煤井 矿井位于拉奖井田。设计占用储量67.5万吨，可采储量15.87万吨，生产规模2万吨/年，服务年限15年。1989年11月，经县矿管办审核，进行采矿权申请登记，获采矿许可证。主巷掘进40米未出煤，主体工程停建，保留煤矿机构开办小煤窑。

上我羊煤井 矿井位于拉滩井田。设计占用储量351万吨，生产规模2万吨/年，服务年限80年。1988年8月，经县矿管办审核，进行采矿权申请登记，获采矿许可证。主巷掘进20米未出煤，主体工程停建，保留煤矿机构开办小煤窑。

第二章 电力工业

第一节 水电开发

小七孔梯级水电站 分4级建站，总装机7台5260千瓦，总投资1015.04万元。4个梯级电站因申报世界自然遗产于2006年3月拆除。

一级电站：于1985年8月上报《荔波县小七孔一级水电站设计任务书》，12月建立小七孔一级电站工程指挥部，1986年1月5日正式开工，1987年10月竣工，12月14日正式向县城送电成功。电站大坝高7.5米，渠道长4060米，引用流量2.2立方米/秒，总装机630千瓦×2.35千伏线路3.4公里，总投资211.25万元。

二级电站：1989年年初动工修建，1990年年底建成投产。工程引水流量2.36立方米/秒，渠道长3000米，工程总投资339.79万元。（补充装机容量）

三级电站：1991年12月动工修建，1994年竣工。总装机1000千瓦，总投资304万元。

四级电站：坝高2米（坝顶高程438.55米）、长22米，引水渠长760米、宽2.3米、深2米，设计过水量3.6立方米/秒，工作水头38米，装机容量500千瓦×2，年发电量600万千瓦时，输电线路长28公里，附设2个变电站、8个电灌站，总投资120万元。

交朝水电站 位于朝阳乡交朝村，利用鱼胆山引水工程渠道流水量0.15立方米/秒，跌水取得18米水头，安装12千瓦发电机1台。

巴克水电站 位于洞塘乡巴克寨，距县城40公里。1983年3月广西河池地区水电局勘测设计。1984年7月动工建设，1985年9月竣工试车运行。总容量640千瓦和HZ240-WJ-60型水轮机2台，配电板4块。装1台S1-60型800千伏安变压器为主变，将400伏电压升至10千伏，通过1条1.2公里10千伏高压输电线路，送入三岔河电网，两站并网运行。总投资117.12万元。

大七孔水电站

飞虎山水电站 位于朝阳乡寨平村飞虎山。1979年6月县水电局勘测设计，总投资（包括农田灌溉部分）50万元。1982年7月竣工投产，年发电1.4万千瓦时。

平岩水电站 位于捞村乡平岩村。1982年，由县水电局勘测设计，是年动工兴建，1983年5月建成投产。年均发电量40万千瓦时。架设6～10千伏高压输电线路8公里，400伏低压输电线路10公里。总投资12.7万元。2006年，扩容改造装机为1260千瓦，后因管理原因退出电网运行。

尧花水电站 位于播尧乡尧花村。县水电局勘测设计，1978年1月建成投产，总投资38.5万元。安装H1300－WJ－42型水轮机1台，TDW200－8型发电机功率200千瓦配套，装机为200千瓦/台。架设6～10千伏高压输电线路35公里，400伏低压输电线路50公里。年均发电量12万千瓦时。后因水源枯竭退出运行。

拉旧水电站 位于永康乡的拉旧。1978年由县水电局勘测设计，1979年动工兴建，1981年4月建成投产，总投资30.5万元。装机容量为150千瓦×2。架设6～10千伏高压线路8公里，400伏低压线路7.7公里。年发电量6.8万千瓦时。

把查电站 位于播挠乡把查寨。工程建设因经费不足，历时10年，至1985年11月工程竣工，总投资148.6万元。装机570千瓦，年发电量40万千瓦时，向甲良区7个乡、18个村供电。2001年11月由供电局投资改低压屏柜、发电机组、升压站设备及坝体等设施，于2002年3月并入国家电网。

第二节 供 电

1978—1998年，全县各乡（镇）由小七孔一级至四级水电站供电。1999年9月建成110千伏线路，从麻尾110千伏变电站降压运行输送国网电到荔波。自此，全县17个乡（镇）中，除立化镇、佳荣镇部分村组由广西电网供电，甲良部分村组由独山供电局供电外，其余均由荔波供电局供电。

2000年12月29日，荔波供电局分别与邻县三都、从江和广西南丹、环江达成供电营业区边界划分协议，双方确认按县级行政区域边界线为供电营业区边界线，有关相互跨区供电事宜另订委托供电协议予以明确，双方供电营业区平面图上同一边界分别盖章以示确认，并作为协议有效证件。

2002年，荔波供电局对县内供电管理区域重新划分：用电营业科负责供电区域为东到水江东界，南到电视塔为界，西到水电局果园为界，北到鱼塘为界；甲良供电所负责甲良镇、方村乡、播尧乡、水利乡行政区域，供电区域为东到三都恒丰，南到水利下水龙，西到独山县董岭，北到洞亭；瑶山供电所负责朝阳镇、瑶山乡、驾欧乡、捞村乡行政区域，供电区域为东到玉屏镇内拉鱼，南到捞村乡巴平村高傲组，西到独山县洞塘坪煤厂，北到朝阳镇山江村拉偶组；水尧供电所负责水尧乡、康永乡、翁昂乡行政区域，供电区域为东到水扒，南到翁昂吉洞，西到打里组，北到水功煤厂、岜合煤厂；佳荣供电所负责佳荣乡行政区域，供电区域为东到大土村，南到坤地村何家寨组，西到高里村，北到拉先村拉易组；茂兰供电所负责茂兰镇、洞塘乡、立化镇、瑶麓乡行政区域，供电区域为东到更排，南到洞塘拉纠，西至瑶庆，北到水条煤厂。

2004年11月18日，荔波供电局与广西环江县电业总公司协调，达成购电协议，由荔波供电局在荔波县的何家寨10千伏支线27号杆处安装高压计量装置1套，作荔波供电局向环江县电业总公司售电计量。

2005年8月8日，县移动公司委托荔波县电力实业公司对第二批村通基站电力线路及配电变压器、高压计量箱进行安装施工。第二批村通基站为阳凤、觉巩、巴格、梅桃、洞庭、坤地、尧棒、甲新、架桥、甲介、瑶庆、曼井、洪江、必忙共计14个。2006年，根据申报世界自然遗产地工作的要求，对大七孔、小七孔及茂兰自然保护区内的电力线路进行改造。2008年，实施无电地区通电工程，向255户无电户供电。

第三节 电网建设

一、供电线路建设

1978年，县内供电线路有小七孔经朝阳至荔波35千伏输电线路7.1公里，产权属县供电所。

1986年，建荔波变电站至水尧35千伏输电线路11公里。线路经黔南州水电局批准建设，向岜合等重点煤矿供电，投资26.5万元，1987年5月11日交付使用，产权属县供电所。

是年，县内输电线路有高压线总长336公里。其中，35千伏线路27.1公里，6.3～10千伏线路308.9公里；低压（380～400伏）线路540公里；升压变压器35千伏1处1台，1000千伏安；配电变压器为3～10千伏安共88台，总计8635千伏安。至1990年，全县供电输电线路共1017.2公里。其中，高压线路35千伏48.8公里，6～10千伏412.7公里；低压线路（380～400伏）555.7公里；变电站2座3500千伏，配电变压器111台，总计9585千伏安。

1992年，建成水尧至茂兰输电线路10.7公里，投资26.34万元，产权属县供电所。同年，完成茂兰及水尧35千伏降压站安装。

1993年，对播尧乡豆村中心电灌站线路进行改造，架设朝阳—岜马、瑶山乡—乡林场、王蒙—浪弄、纸厂—回龙角提水站、荔波—永康长弯6条10千伏26公里输电线路。同时，州水电局进行荔波中心变电间隔出线、水尧降压站、茂兰35千伏变电工程安装。

1994年，建成驯乐—坤地10千伏9.6公里（其中新增5.6公里、改造4公里）和董棚—立孟10千伏3公里、低压3公里及县中心变电站—水泥厂10千伏0.6公里输电线路施工。

1995年，建成介牌—拉朝、联山—黎明、甲介—拉奖、佳荣—拉吾、拉亮—拉祥等10千伏输电线路21.1公里输电线路。

1996年，建成水利乡孔庭—尧棒7.2公里、地莪—洞丢5.5公里、洞塘乡立孟—必克3.4公里、瑶庆—洞闷5公里等10千伏输电线路。

1997年，建成小七孔—大七孔8公里35千伏输电线路，瑶山—捞村、朝阳—山江、董更—董保—瑶沙3条10千伏输电线路。

1999年9月15日，省电力工业局批复都匀供电局，同意110千伏麻尾—荔波输电线路先降压为35千伏运行，将荔波县电网并入110千伏麻尾变电站运行。荔波小七孔电站上网执行省电力工业局小水电上网补充管理规定。是年11月30日，荔波110千伏变电站竣工正式通电运行。

2000年，架设荔波机场10千伏输电线路1.5公里。完成独荔公路10千伏输电线路改线。建成35千伏佳荣变电站，结束佳荣镇部分村、组长期靠广西供电的历史。

2004年7月，由都匀供电局投资建设35千伏王蒙变电站，新架设35千伏输电线路5条，总长27.29公里。2005年9月29日正式投运，负荷转移成功后，交荔波供电局管理运行并维护。

2005年9月，实施县城电网建设与改造工程。县城电网改造工程总投资163.22万元，农网完善化工程投资840万元，樟江大街电缆工程投资1500万元。至2006年11月27日，县城电网改造工程完成10千伏输电线路11.6公里，400伏输电线路10.81公里，220伏输电线路4.7公里，安装配变10台、真空断路器8台。

2006年，根据申报世界自然遗产地工作的要求，对大七孔、小七孔及茂兰自然保护区内的电力线路进行改造。即西门出口处至原小七孔一级水电站处10千伏架空线路改造入地，电缆长约9公里；水尧—翁昂公路穿过保护区内10千伏架空线路改造入地，电缆长3.5公里。

2007年7月，实施荔波樟江大道电缆入地211工程，建设10千伏架空线路0.49公里，10千伏电缆4.86公里，配电变压器3150千伏安，配电设备（含分支箱、环网柜等）10个。是年10月中旬工程竣工。

2008年，按都匀供电局下达的计划，实施立化35千伏输变电扩建工程，总投资1049万元，其中35千伏系统工程310万元，变电部分投资739万元；实施2008年度无电地区通电工程，建10千伏线路3.5公里，400伏、200伏线路3.67公里，配变安装5台，总投资100.7万元，向无电户255户供电。

二、农村电网改造

1999年12月，全县正式启动实施农村电网改造工程，分两期进行。2001—2002年，进行第一期工程建设，新建10千伏线路486.35公里，改造10千伏线路276.84公里、400伏线路189.75公里、220千伏线路214.76公里，安装及改造配电变压器525台，安装真空断路器17台。工程总投资3085.76万元。全县13500户农户进行电网改造，占应改造户数的43%。农户安装一户一表13500户。2002年6月11日，全县第一期改造工程通过省、州审核验收合格。

2002年4月24日，第二期农网改造工程开工，至2003年3月，全县二期改造工程结束，改造10千伏线路270.23公里、400伏线路92.487公里、220伏线路76.57公里，安装配电变压器231台，安装真空断路器13台。农户安装一户一表36000户，占全县总户数的97%。工程总投资1588.76万元。2004年4月，第二期改造工程通过省、州验收。至此，全县乡（镇）、村、户通电率均达100%。新建的110千伏三都至荔波供电线路、110千伏荔波至茂兰供电线路和110千伏茂兰变电站投入运营。经农网改造和新建工程实施，全县形成以110千伏和35千伏线路为主网架结构的供电网。

至2004年12月底，第一期、第二期农村电网建设与改造工程全部结束，投资5700万元。全部工程扩建和新建变电站4座，建设和改造10千伏线路1068公里、400伏线路283公里、220伏线路286公里，更换耗能变压器210台，配电台区改造762台。农网建设改造工程完成后，全县乡（镇）通电率100%，村通电率100%，户通电率99.5%。

第三章 工业体制改革与其他工业

第一节 管理体制改革

1978年改革开放以后，县委的工作重心转移到经济建设上来，工业才获得较快发展。除发展煤炭和电力工业外，还先后办起了机压铁锅厂（年产铁锅1.3万口），县纺织器材厂（年产值17.35万元），县综合厂（1978年加工棉絮9123床，生产算盘5.19万架），酒厂（年产酒100吨），鼎罐厂，梅桃土陶厂，城关、甲良、朝阳缝衣社（年产值74.55万元），糕点厂（年产值36.4万元），农机厂（年产各种型号水轮泵及配件6000余台件），砖瓦厂，县水泥厂（旧厂年产500号水泥7000吨，1998年无偿转让给广西环江县经营。2005年承包方代表携款潜逃，企业倒闭。后县里招商引资，于2006年易址重建新厂），甲良磷化厂，铅锌冶炼厂，荔明冶炼厂，樟江天然食品厂等企业。2009年完成规模工业产值88037万元。

1978—1981年县内工业企业由县工交局管理。1984年2月，全县工业划归县经济委员会管理。1994年，工业由县经济贸易局管理。1980—1985年，工业企业逐步实行利润包干、厂长负责制。1986年后，全县工业企业实行承包经营责任制。1990年，县属集体企业县工艺美术社、县铁木加工厂因不适应市场需求，产品销售不畅，按《中华人民共和国企业破产法》的规定，依法实施破产。1996年，县农机厂由岜合煤矿托管。

第二节 国有企业改制

1998年，县委、县政府根据国家工业企业改革改制的有关规定，对县内国营工业企业进行改制。改制以“三个有利于”（有利于生产、有利于经营管理、有利于市场竞争）为准则，对改革改制企业进行调查分析，在征求职工意见后，采取资产经营权转让、股份制等方式进行改制。是年，国有工业企业应改革改制户7户、实际改制户7户，改制面100%。即国有岜合煤矿进行股份制改制，职工参股经营；将县水泥厂转让给县属企业广西都川水泥厂经营；对县农机厂采取买断全部资产办法进行改制，与县邮政部门达成买断协议，以280万元价格一次性买断该厂全部资产；对县粮油工贸公司实行风险抵押承包经营；对县酒厂依法实施倒闭；自来水公司和小七孔电站两个企业按照国有小型企业“三改一加强”（改组、改革、改造、加强管理）的改革方针和两个企业的实际，采取加强企业管理，实行岗位目标与工效挂钩的办法进行改革。

2001年，对经营困难、亏损严重的县乡镇企业供销公司进行破产清算、土地、房产等资产评估，将资产分离重组，对职工进行改制安置。2007年，对县樟江食品厂进行改制，资产通过公开拍卖转让，所得转让款483.1万元用于职工一次性安置。

至2008年，全县国有工业企业改制9户（县农机厂、县水泥厂、县岜合煤矿、县酒厂、粮油工贸公司、乡镇企业供销公司、自来水公司、小七孔电站、县樟江食品厂）。

第三节　其他工业

一、建材工业

1978年，县内有建材企业仅荔波水泥厂1家，设备生产能力为年产水泥7000吨。至1985年，该厂职工人数从1975年建厂时的8人增加到85人。1979—1986年，年均产量2492吨。1987年，企业实行经营承包经营责任制，1988年生产水泥4100吨，产值23.70万元，1995年生产水泥1165吨，1997年生产水泥达16403.5吨。

1998年6月，经荔波县政府和广西环江县政府协商，双方本着自愿的原则，达成无偿转让协议，将全部资产产权无偿转让给广西环江县经营，转让前退休的9名职工工资仍由该厂发放，其他退休人员纳入社会保障管理。2002年，该厂进行技术改造，改造后年生产能力为4万吨，企业注册资金348万元，全厂在职职工147人（其中荔波员工87人）。技改后，因经营不善，管理混乱，加上新增债务，企业出现拖欠养老金和退休职工工资情况，2003年4月，广西环江县方未征求荔波方意见，将该厂全部机械设备及在职人员转让给贵阳鹤翔贸易有限公司承包经营（承包期2003年4月至2005年4月，年承包费50万元）。该公司承包后，承包方委派的法人代表于2005年3月下旬携款外逃，造成企业瘫痪，全厂停产。

为妥善处理职工问题，荔波县政府根据县内旅游业发展规划，决定对荔波县水泥厂进行搬迁新建，对该厂土地及资产进行清理，采取对外拍转让和置换办法，将所得款项一次性安置职工和退休人员。2006年年初，经招商引资，荔波水泥厂搬迁新建工程正式启动，企业改制同步进行。2008年12月28日，该厂正式投产。是年，原水泥厂改制和职工安置全部完成。

二、加工业

（一）机械加工

1978年后，县农业机械加工厂是县内唯一的国有机械加工企业。其间，该厂工艺设备陈旧落后，难以适应市场经济发展需求，处于亏损状态。1996年，县委、县政府决定由岜合煤矿托管经营。由岜合煤矿管理后，组建矿山机械修造厂，但仍因设备陈旧，产品科技含量低，不适应市场需要，加上管理不善，托管近两年，企业再度进入困境，面临破产。1998年，县政府成立农机厂改制工作领导小组，进驻该厂，对资产进行全面清查，并听取企业负责人及职工的意见，提出破产解体分割拍卖方案，拍卖所得，首先妥善安置离退休职工及在职职工，其次补缴国家税费及偿还债务，不足部分按依次足额解决的办法进行。经与邮政部门协商，达成以280万元（除机械设备外）一次性买断全部资产。此后，县内没有规模化生产的机械加工业。

（二）银饰品加工

银饰品是县内少数民族妇女传统的装饰品，部分乡村有银匠小量加工。1982年，成立荔波县民族银饰社，1986年更名为荔波县民族银饰厂，以原老艺人为基础，招收新工人，当年共有职工8人，生产银饰品1400多件。

银饰厂加工所需白银，由省、州有关部门拨给指标，由银行供应。加工成品统一交县民族贸易公司经销。另外承接民间来料加工。产品主要有耳环、项圈、项链、戒指、小孩帽幅花泡、水族桂花围腰链、木银梳、别簪钻花、布依族双链钻花、帐钩单链钻花、全堂帽幅（缀十八罗汉）、瑶族银鸟、苗族头饰花、项链花以及造新屋的粱泡花等38个品种，商标为“荔兴”牌。

1985年，荔波产银饰品水族龙头手镯获省优质奖、轻工业部优质奖。

1986年1月，组织县内名、优、特产品赴广州穗深商场参加全国部分省、市迎春商品展销会。同年，银饰品瑶族银鸟被评为省民族用品优质产品，获省轻纺工业厅、省旅游局和省民族事务委员会“兴黔杯奖”；银饰品布依族四季手镯在全省旅游品、工艺品、民族用品评比展销会上被评为民族优秀产品，1987年又获省优质奖。

1987年，荔波县工艺品布依族双面麒麟、少数民族白银甲子属相、白银小孩吊铃手镯选入全国工艺美术展览，在北京民族文化宫展销时，被抢购一空。

1994年，县经济贸易局与县轻工局合并，县银饰厂属县经济贸易局下属的国有企业。主要产品有水族龙头手镯、水族富贵手镯、布依族四季手镯、银手链、银戒指、银碗筷、酒杯、酒壶等100余种。其中，龙头手镯、四季手镯、民族银鸟获部优、省优产品称号。1990年，该厂获“贵州省少数民族用品生产先进企业”称号。1994年获省有关部门“产品质量信得过”证书。2006年在“开磷杯”多彩贵州旅游商品“两赛一会”评比中获“能工巧匠”称号。

（三）竹篾编织

竹篾编织是县内传统加工业。1978年国庆节，凉席厂送两床编织花纹隐现天安门图案和“荔波”二字的凉席到北京参加展览，参观者给予了较高的评价。1979年10月，荔波送凉席到北京少数民族产品展销会展销，展销品销售一空。之后，东南亚部分国家和地区向荔波订货。1980年后，因凉席原料泡竹林逐年退化，竹篾收购量不能满足生产需要，凉席产量逐年下降，1981年仅生产217床。在县城郊板庙村附近新建的凉席厂，终因原料缺乏，于1981年12月由县财政拨款7000元，对在厂职工按工龄长短给予一次性补助费。后至2008年，凉席生产由集体转为个体，产品自产自销。乡村有部分农户编织竹篾制品竹篮、簸箕等，利用赶场天销售。

（四）工艺美术品加工

1982年4月，将原工艺美术组更名为荔波县工艺美术社，属集体企业，有工人8人。生产镜片、镜屏、印字等。产品除部分自销外，由县农资公司包销。该社利用县内资源，开发工艺产品，年产值2万多元，年利润2000元。

1985年后，增加新品种，并兼营化工原材料，营业额上升到7万元。1987年后，受物价上涨、原材料供应紧缺、产品销售不畅等因素影响，生产处于停滞状态。1989年，调整产品结构，在原生产镜画、堆画、牌匾的基础上，增加竹编、藤编、松球、羽绒、绣品等，为旅游业提供旅游工艺品，年产值3万元。1990年，生产镜画4755面，编织工艺品1.2万件，产值4.12万元。

1991年以后，经营管理不善，产品销售不畅，企业处于停滞状态。1997年，该厂宣布破产。

（五）铁、木器具加工

1978年，境内铁器、木器加工企业有县鼎罐厂、甲良铁制农具厂、铁木加工厂。1983年建县纺织器材厂。1987年9月，县手工业联社与广西桂平县联营开办机压铁锅厂（厂址玉屏镇）。是年，时来乡兴建拼花地板厂。

上述企业在改革开放中，因产品不适应市场经济发展需求，长期处于亏损状态。县鼎罐厂于1982年撤销；甲良铁制农具厂于1986年停产；铁木加工厂于1991年停产；县纺织器材厂于1990年停产；机压铁锅厂于1990年2月停产；时来拼花地板厂于1991年停产。

县内民间仍有部分个体户加工铁器、木器，利用赶场天销售。

三、酿酒

1978年，县内有地方国有企业县酒厂生产散装白酒。1981年以后，县酒厂购进饮料设备，开始生产各种果汁饮料。同时将散装白酒改为瓶装白酒，注册商标为“古榕老窖”“龙王醇”。1981—1987年，生产白酒988.5吨，年均141.2吨。1988年春，由驻广西解放军第四十一集团军地炮旅承包经营，承包期3年。到1990年，该厂固定资产原值26.6万元，全厂职工33人。1991年，承包期满，县政府结合城镇建设的需要，撤销县酒厂建制，按企业破产程序申报破产，原企业职工进行分流安置。县内民间仍有个体户生产销售白酒。

四、印刷

1978年，县内有荔波中学印刷厂和县综合厂印刷车间开展印刷业务。

荔波中学印刷厂1978—1979年年均产值0.27万元。1980年进行技术改造，增添设备，实行定额管理、超产奖励办法，1981年产值上升到2万元。1990年，该厂有职工6人，产值2万元，固定资产原值2.5万元。1991年以后，该厂实行承包制承包给个人，承包方每年上交承包费方式经营。县综合厂印刷车间有印刷工人11人，承接县内大部分印刷业务，1988年产值4.99万元，1989年产值10.9万元，1990年产值8.74万元。1991年以后因经营管理不善而停业，职工自谋职业。1999年8月，企业职工大会决定，对该厂资产进行拍卖，一次性安置职工，解除职工身份。2000年年初该厂解体。

1978—2008年全县工业总产值统计表

表13－2

年度	企业数（个）			总产值（万元）		
	总计	其中		合计	其中	
		国有	非国有		国有	非国有
1978	6	4	2	140	81	59
1979	7	5	2	160	91	69
1980	7	5	2	180	110	70
1981	7	5	2	200	110	90
1982	7	5	2	210	120	90
1983	7	5	2	220	130	90
1984	7	5	2	250	140	110
1985	8	5	3	270	150	120
1986	12	5	7	290	160	130
1987	13	6	7	450	190	260
1988	13	6	7	750	464	286
1989	12	6	6	1512	706	806
1990	12	5	7	1854	827	1027
1991	14	6	8	2572	836	1736
1992	12	5	7	2622	1022	1600

续表13－2

年度	企业数（个）			总产值（万元）		
	总计	其中		合计	其中	
		国有	非国有		国有	非国有
1993	9	5	4	2730	1145	1585
1994	7	5	2	2900	1800	1100
1995	15	6	9	2930	1900	1030
1996	7	5	2	3260	2080	1180
1997	7	5	2	3423	2100	1323
1998	6	4	2	2412	1795	617
1999	6	4	2	3475	1121	2354
2000	6	4	2	3453	2428	1025
2001	5	4	1	3278	3278	0
2002	5	4	1	3656	3656	0
2003	18	6	12	15531	3972	11559
2004	20	6	14	23983	8972	15011
2005	27	6	21	26597	10087	16510
2006	27	6	21	35814	10555	25259
2007	29	5	24	47331	9368	37963
2008	25	3	22	71008	5690	65318

1978—2008年全县工业主要产品产量统计表

表13－3

年度	原煤（万吨）	发电量（万千瓦时）	水泥（吨）	砖块（万块）	铁制农具（万件）	原木（立方米）	酒（吨）	食用植物油（吨）
1978	7.57	236.40	—	165.10	2.29	13450.00	99.54	11.00
1979	6.20	160.30	1267.00	232.80	1.70	6862.00	153.80	22.20
1980	7.97	162.00	1171.00	197.90	0.65	6880.00	157.40	37.00
1981	10.60	278.20	1600.00	146.70	2.36	4486.00	70.40	112.20
1982	8.78	285.00	1347.00	186.00	1.78	7322.00	188.00	320.00
1983	9.72	352.58	2112.00	201.55	1.16	5928.00	198.20	292.20
1984	18.07	400.00	3312.00	150.00	1.05	7177.00	114.60	395.00
1985	20.00	380.00	3756.00	62.00	1.60	6566.00	205.80	124.60
1986	22.59	500.80	3342.00	49.00	0.75	24728.00	131.50	145.73
1987	33.02	529.89	2782.65	734.49	6.11	12488.00	80.00	221.23

续表13－3

年度	原煤（万吨）	发电量（万千瓦时）	水泥（吨）	砖块（万块）	铁制农具（万件）	原木（立方米）	酒（吨）	食用植物油（吨）
1988	42.12	629.00	4100.00	493.60	3.50	15861.00	181.00	200.00
1989	50.86	638.40	3700.00	603.90	—	18230.00	216.80	100.00
1990	51.40	857.00	1400.00	621.00	—	15020.00	61.00	200.00
1991	51.98	943.05	3300.00	682.90	—	44178.00	—	400.00
1992	66.15	1016.50	2100.00	665.26	—	45137.00	—	200.00
1993	77.71	1167.00	100.00	1386.67	—	4400.00	—	300.00
1994	91.02	1775.00	10000.00	—	—	—	—	—
1995	109.15	2032.00	11600.00	—	—	—	—	—
1996	123.00	2160.00	13000.00	—	—	—	—	—
1997	110.80	2500.00	15300.00	—	—	—	—	—
1998	105.80	2109.00	14600.00	—	—	—	—	—
1999	76.00	2172.00	13200.00	6731.60	—	4748.00	—	—
2000	62.98	2358.00	20800.00	9952.90	—	5818.00	—	—
2001	69.25	3573.00	21600.00	14830.00	—	9023.00	—	—
2002	76.56	5118.00	19700.00	—	—	—	—	—
2003	144.25	5238.00	15100.00	12892.50	—	—	—	—
2004	178.15	19876.00	20000.00	16900.00	—	—	—	—
2005	117.39	16407.00	4000.00	19202.00	—	—	—	—
2006	111.29	31076.00	—	15425.00	—	—	—	—
2007	117.60	41426.00	—	22815.00	—	—	—	—
2008	130.72	37755.00	—	17945.00	—	—	—	—

第四章 乡镇企业

第一节 企业门类

1978年后，全县社队企业逐渐发展，有乡（镇）办、村办、组办、联户办、户办企业；企业有农业、工业、建筑、建材、交通运输、商业饮食服务、其他行业7类。

1988年，全县乡（镇）有企业1245个。其中，工业企业896个、建筑业2个、交通运输业39个、商业饮食业277个、其他企业31个；乡（镇）办企业46个、村办企业18个、联产办企业7个、个体办1174个。

1990年，全县乡（镇）有企业2002个。其中，工业企业1642个、建筑业1个、交通运输业116个、商饮服务业243个；乡（镇）办企业35个、村办企业16个、联户办企业2个、个体办1949个。

2000年，全县乡（镇）有企业2721个。其中，工业企业1433个、建筑业52个、交通运输业534个、商饮服务业702个；集体企业54个、私营企业10个、个体办2657个。

2008年，全县乡（镇）有企业2181个。其中，农业企业6个、工业企业83个（煤矿企业31个）、建筑企业6个、交通运输企业744个、商业饮食服务企业1342个；集体企业4个、私营企业90个、个体办2077个。

第二节 企业经营管理

一、生产经营

1978—1980年，社队企业中，零星的、流动性大的经营项目，如农村“五匠”（铁匠、木匠、竹匠、石匠、泥水匠），实行定额经营管理，由社队确定收入和提交生产队金额，如期完成交生产队金额的，由生产队评工记分，参加统一分配；超额完成的，给予适当奖励；完不成定额的，适当扣减工分。集体煤矿产、供、销由社队统一管理，实行收益分成，一部分交生产队用于农田基本建设和社队福利事业，一部分由企业用于扩大再生产、支付职工工资和职工福利。1980年以后，农村“五匠”先后转为个体经营，不再向社队提交定额款，收益全部归个人。一些仍由社队经营的项目，逐步推行经营承包责任制，由乡、村与承包人签订承包经营合同，承包内容包括产品、产量、产值、收入、利润、财产保护、安全措施、利润提成、职工工资、福利等指标。

乡（镇）煤矿企业实行厂长负责制，管理人员实行计时工资和超产奖励办法。生产以井口定人员，实行计件工资制，新建煤井按掘进米工资承包，采煤实行吨煤工资承包或按煤井口承包上交等办法。区、乡煤矿管理部门按合同进行监督检查，为企业搞好协调服务。

1983年，按贵州、广西两省（区）《关于红茂矿务局在荔波县境内开发煤田若干问题的会谈纪要》精神，红茂矿包运包销荔波生产原煤的50%，每年年初双方签订购销合同。

1985年后，乡镇企业局对直属单位和企业实行承包目标责任制，每年年初签订承包合同任务书，承包合同包括全年产量、销售、产值、税前利、两费收入、企业管理、改善生产条件、安全生产、开拓新项目等内容。1989年签订“一、二、三”的承包目标责任制，即直属企业（供销公司、水捞联办煤厂及其派驻广西金城江中转站），要完成税前利润100万元，两费收入200万元，企业上缴财政300万元的目标。年终直属企业实现税前利润80万元，其他两项指标均超额完成承包任务。

各乡（镇）产的原煤，由区、乡供销公司或企业自行销售，或通过乡镇企业供销公司外销。

1978—2008年全县乡镇企业主要经济指标完成情况统计表

表13－4　单位：万元

年度	乡镇企业总产值（不变价）	乡镇企业营业收入	乡镇企业增加值	工业增加值	乡镇企业实缴税金	从业人员（万人）
1978	138	125	—	30	4	0.10
1979	188	167	—	34	5	0.13
1980	425	301	—	36	4	0.18
1981	556	408	—	38	10	0.15
1982	555	440	—	40	13	0.19
1983	516	463	—	46	16	0.15
1984	978	634	—	50	20	0.20
1985	785	710	—	56	19	0.25
1986	917	748	—	65	23	0.29
1987	1260	917	—	98	45	0.34
1988	1579	1874	—	109	62	0.64
1989	2031	3318	—	116	90	0.48
1990	3216	3311	—	133	125	0.30
1991	3550	3629	—	134	180	0.64
1992	4807	4979	—	135	416	0.61
1993	9161	9099	—	154	715	0.71
1994	15391	15370	—	177	1454	0.63
1995	22575	19009	—	186	1655	0.74
1996	27650	27728	—	195	2018	0.64
1997	39382	37432	—	205	2548	0.85
1998	47728	48579	7557	608	—	1.11
1999	25121	25552	15904	168	1772	0.40
2000	23059	21958	18393	96	1386	0.40

续表13－4

年度	乡镇企业总产值（不变价）	乡镇企业营业收入	乡镇企业增加值	工业增加值	乡镇企业实缴税金	从业人员（万人）
2001	21774	21017	20352	109	1723	0.35
2002	62205	62454	22812	105	2799	0.82
2003	60215	61890	26521	2861	2548	0.86
2004	63939	71916	32011	8550	4189	0.90
2005	79599	91197	34798	3426	4755	0.95
2006	91610	99033	35213	14591	5128	1.03
2007	103717	107007	28899	25824	5784	1.09
2008	125919	131214	33819	29426	7208	1.17

二、行业管理

1978年，煤炭等矿产业归县工业局（工交局）管理，手工业归手工业管理局管理，零星的铁、木、竹加工等分别由公社、大队、生产队管理。

1980年，社队办煤炭企业划归县社队企业局管理，社队企业局派煤管员驻城关区、茂兰区，对社队煤炭产、供、销进行统一管理。新办煤厂由社队企业局审查批准。同年，成立社队企业供销矿产公司，隶属县社队企业局，为全县社队企业矿产品的产、供、销服务。1981年，茂兰区成立区煤炭管理办事处后，茂兰片区社队采煤业由茂兰办事处管理，水尧、甲良片区由社队企业矿产公司管理。1984年，社队企业局更名为乡村工业公司，1986年10月更名为乡镇企业管理局。后增设玉屏、茂兰两区煤炭管理所，水尧、茂兰、洞塘、瑶庆、立化、佳荣6个乡（镇）煤炭管理站。至2008年辖区内乡（镇）企业的产、运、销，厂矿安全生产，账务和管理费、国家税金等，由2所6站进行检查、督促、管理。

第十四篇
旅游业

荔波位于贵州南部，属中亚热带季风湿润气候区，总面积2381平方公里，辖8乡（镇）1办。人口18万人，其中少数民族占总人口的92%以上，主要有布依族、水族、苗族、瑶族等少数民族，民族风情古朴浓郁。荔波是中共一大代表邓恩铭的故乡。境内同时拥有国家级樟江风景名胜区和茂兰国家级自然保护区，民族文化神奇迷离，红色文化传奇惊人，旅游资源十分丰富。

自1984年建立茂兰自然保护区，1990年建立樟江风景名胜区以来，荔波旅游经过20多年的持续打造和开发，形成了大七孔景区、小七孔景区、茂兰景区、水春河景区生态游，以邓恩铭故居及板寨红七军会师旧址为代表的红色旅游，瑶山古寨、尧古布依寨民族风情游，以及茂兰梅园赏花游，还推出《水韵樟江》民族文化实景演艺、竹筏漫游樟江等旅游产品，荔波县的旅游业逐步从单一的生态观光旅游向多元化旅游过渡。荔波县先后获全省首批优先发展重点旅游区、革命老区、国家卫生县城、全国科普示范县、国家级生态示范区、中国最美的地方、全国十大最具潜力景区、中国最佳山水旅游文化名县、中国最佳民族生态旅游名县、国际王牌旅游目的地、世界人与生物圈保护区等美誉称号。2007年，荔波正式列入世界自然遗产名录，成为中国第六个、贵州第一个世界自然遗产地。2003年5月29日，中共荔波县九届四次全委（扩大）会通过《中共荔波县委、荔波县人民政府关于加快旅游业发展的决定》，2015年7月30日，中共荔波县第十一届委员会第五次全体会议通过《中共荔波县委关于实施全域旅游发展战略的决定》，两个决定加速发展了荔波旅游业，使产业优势突显，旅游业已成为荔波县重要的经济支柱产业。

第一章 自然旅游资源

荔波县自然旅游资源主要以“中国南方喀斯特”荔波自然遗产地为主体，遗产地主要包括由茂兰国家自然保护区、荔波樟江国家级风景名胜区大七孔、小七孔景区组成，荔波遗产地总面积730.16平方公里，核心区295.18平方公里，缓冲区434.98平方公里，遗产地海拔385—1109米，平均747米，以典型锥状喀斯特、地表与地下喀斯特生态系统的完美组合为特征。2007年6月27日，第31届世界遗产大会审议通过，荔波被列入世界遗产名录，成为中国第六个世界自然遗产地。

第一节 荔波樟江国家级风景名胜区

荔波樟江国家级风景名胜区地理坐标为北纬25° 12′—25° 34′，东经107° 39′—107° 93′，总面积118.8平方公里。樟江景区以典型、丰富、集中的喀斯特地貌和水文为基础，以大片中亚热带喀斯特原始森林为特色，具有美学价值和科研价值，为世界少见。景区内具有代表性的自然景点58处。1990年8月，省政府公布荔波樟江风景名胜区为全省第二批省级风景名胜区。1994年1月，经国务院审查批准，樟江风景名胜区公布为全国第三批国家重点风景名胜区。2009年荔波樟江景区（大七孔、小七孔景区）正式获国家AAAA级旅游景区称号。2015年7月，樟江景区正式获得国家AAAAA级旅游景区称号。

景区内由于山峦起伏，河谷深，地形地势复杂，气候略有差异。年均气温18.3℃，年降水量1320.5毫米。全年无霜期308天，平均相对湿度80%。最热月为7月，月平均气温26.4℃；最冷月为1月，月平均气温8.4℃。冬无严寒，夏无酷暑。

风景名胜区在地质构造上，属于江南台降西南部的三都—荔波古陷褶断束，处在轴缘凹陷地带。由石灰岩二迭系碳酸盐岩组成的茂兰向斜，南北贯穿全区，控制着这里地层岩石的分布及其产状。保存的原生性喀斯特森林，主要分布于向斜南段的石灰系碳酸盐岩上。

风景名胜区位于云贵高原向广西丘陵盆地过渡斜坡地带，景区内喀斯特地貌十分发育，喀斯特形态多种多样，锥峰尖削而密集，洼地深邃而陡峭，锥峰洼地层层叠叠，呈现出峰峦叠嶂的喀斯特峰丛景观。景区地势西北部高于东南部，景区内最高海拔1078.60米，最低海拔400米，平均海拔800米。景区河流属龙江水系，归珠江流域。

一、景区景点分布

荔波樟江风景名胜区的景观类型以自然景观为主（包括地貌景观、水文景观、植被景观等），人文景观为辅（包括田园景观、民居民俗等），均具有鲜明特色。景区内的山、水、树、石无不生奇。又因地貌、水文和植被的不同组合，形成各有特色的景区。

樟江风景名胜区总体分为奇秀的小七孔景区、神奇的大七孔景区、奇险的水春河景区和一条恬静的樟江风光带。三大景区和一条风光带，总体上是景外有景、景中有洞，洞中有洞、洞中有景，林中有水、水中有林，山、水、洞、林、湖、石、瀑融为一体。

自然景点中，特级景点有野猪林、地峨森林、六十八级瀑布、龟背山，一级景点有水上森林、鸳鸯湖、地峨宫、天生桥（天门）、水春峡，二级景点有卧龙潭、小七孔桥、风神洞、恐怖峡、白岩、姊妹峰、樟江夜月、试胆浪、锦绣田园，三级景点有地峨洞、飞云洞、天钟洞、拉牛天坑、笑天河（二层河）、大七孔桥、龙戏九珠、涵碧潭、拉雅瀑布、苦竹滩、水甫石棺、朝阳晨曦、永济泉、马尿滩，四级景点有地峨河、夕照归途、天然图画、铜鼓桥、长滩、坡峻枫林、万鸟洞、清溪、古榕树、水神峡、龙泉洞。

（一）小七孔景区

小七孔景区位于县城的西面，距县城25公里，是一处融山、水、林、洞、湖、瀑于一体的天然原始奇景，享有超级盆景的美誉。该景区以峰丛洼地、峰丛漏斗为主要特征，锥峰高度多在100—200米之间，河谷开阔，起伏有致，碧水清流，景色秀丽。

小七孔景区自然景点有铜鼓桥、小七孔古桥、涵碧潭、响水河谷、龟背山原始森林、水上森林、翠谷、野猪林、飞云山瀑布、拉雅瀑布、鸳鸯湖、天钟洞、蝙蝠洞、卧龙河、卧龙潭15个。

铜鼓桥　该桥位于小七孔景区东大门处，横跨樟江河，始建于1993年，重建于2001年（2000年荔波境内遭遇特大洪水将原铜鼓桥冲毁）。铜鼓桥长126米，净跨60米，宽2.4米，高25米，桥身两端采用瑶山瑶族铜鼓造型，故称此桥为“铜鼓桥”。

小七孔古桥　位于景区之首，景区之名由桥而得。这是一座小巧玲珑的七孔古石桥，桥长25米，桥面宽4米，拱高4米，建于清道光十五年（1835），昔为沟通荔波至广西的重要桥梁。桥由麻石条砌成，桥身爬满藤蔓和蕨类；古色古香的桥下是绿得令人心醉的涵碧潭。两岸古木参天，巨大的虬枝沿着桥伸臂，宛如巨伞撑在桥上。在桥的东岸立有一块“万古兴桥碑”，有一副对联为“群山岩浪千千岁，响水河桥万万年”。

涵碧潭　位于响水河与樟江河交汇处。两河交汇前，一坝堵水汇成涵碧潭，又名七孔塘，是喀斯特潭景观。小七孔桥横跨潭腰如玉带缠身，潭头尾浪花飞溅，潭边古木森森，从两边向中间伸展迎合，水潭中的小岛上，吊竹丛生，苇草如篷，绿树成荫。清澈如镜的潭水把群山、古树、桥景、绿荫映入水中，倒影粼粼，波光烁烁，山光潭景，分外迷人，桥上人影倒立，桥下鱼儿悠游，似人鱼合欢水底，趣味无穷。潭脚坝下的滚水帘瀑与平静如璧的江水交相辉映，又呈天然美景。樟江水清，响水更洁，大雨过后樟江水浊，响水依然清澈如常，汇合处依旧泾渭分明。响水为何清如许，因自喀斯特森林来。这也是喀斯特森林的特殊水文效应的奇观。月色当空，静影沉璧，渔歌晚唱，这是涵碧潭的又一绝景。

响水河谷　小七孔风景名胜片区内的喀斯特暗河明流，河床为层层岩石叠积，全长1.6公里，落差110米，仅跌水瀑布达68级之多，通常又叫作“六十八级瀑布”。河谷水声隆隆，波浪滔滔，数里之外可闻水声，故有响水河之名。河谷两岸群峰耸峙，谷底河水奔流，四周古树参天，浓荫蔽日，绿色罩地。在这高山深谷间，流水飞溅，涌泉飞腾，与伏流明河汇到一起，构成层层叠叠的大小瀑布、险滩、深潭。多级的瀑布群形成几段奇特的动态水景：下段河床低缓，层层跌水低瀑布，又绕平塘浅滩翻滚，如一壶壶琼浆倒入玉盘金杯，响水声如琴如瑟，好似节日盛典，奏乐燃鞭，铮铮悦耳。中段河水从乱石堆、钙化堆上跨越飞下，有如撒珠落玉，暴雨倾盆，又如铁马金戈，千军鏖战，波声震谷，响水河壮丽景观就在于此。上段河水从峡谷口往下层层泻落，形成二三十米的叠叠瀑布，仰观如银河落天际，侧赏如白练腾空，雨雾迷漫山谷，在阳光照射下呈现艳丽彩虹，蔚为奇观。水声如雷，振动群山回音盘绕，如雷电轰鸣，断人话音，手语传情。上段河水的暗河伏流在密林中穿行，时隐时现，哗哗作响，不知是险滩激流还是瀑布飞奔。也说不清是森林中的流水，还是流水上的森林。天然如此奇观，岂能不使人醉迷入神。

龟背山原始森林 响水河伏流出口洞就在龟背山脚下，上下龟背山，要涉一处跳蹬跨响水河，涉水跋山，或是跋山涉水，都令人久久难忘。龟背山原始森林是典型的喀斯特森林奇观的缩影。森林茂密，古树参天的林里珍稀树种遍布，奇花异草，如龟背竹、虾背兰、棕竹、大血藤、白纹藤，交叉盘结丛生，还有苔藓争艳，一片碧绿。高大数人围的古乔木，竟是在严酷的悬崖峭壁和裸露的石灰岩上，或在崩塌的巨大孤石上生长出来。还有各类树木藤萝叮咬青山繁茂生长，有的盘根错节，把发达的根系直插裂隙孔窍及微妙的石缝之中；有的大树根紧抓住一块孤立巨石挺拔生长，把巨石拱离地面几十厘米高；有的无缝可钻，把粗大的树根伸到几米远的岩坎下入石缝吸取营养，人们对此无法辨认它是杆还是根；有的顽强抗争，挤破山岩，达到石破天惊的地步；还有那枯树上寄生的蒲兰，光岩石上组成罗网的薜荔，攀附上升几米高的麒麟尾，无不显示出喀斯特森林植物顽强的生命力。在这里是不能从外貌来判定树木花草的老幼尊卑的。胸径仅几厘米小树木，已是五六十年的高龄，胸径三四十厘米的大树木，已阅历了几个世纪的沧桑。这满山的芸芸众生，乍看去貌不惊人，但它们当中，有古遗的珍稀树种，有全国或全省的部分新种，有名贵的中草药材，珍奇的野生观赏植物，是一个独特植物宝库，有珍贵的科研价值。喀斯特单一地质条件下的复杂生态环境，严酷生态环境中的顽强生存竞争，把多与少、优与劣，奇妙地统一起来。这个孕育奇秀的喀斯特生态系统又像一本丰富而深刻的教科书、活标本、活材料。无怪乎人们赞誉它为“绿色的宝地”，要积极地保护它、利用它，评它为世界上绝无仅有的奇特景观。

水上森林 亦名瑶池，长约600米，分上下两段。河谷里丛生着茂密的乔木和灌木，形成一道翡翠屏障。这些树木当地群众称之为“合欢树”，学名叫“溪畔冬青”。清澈的河水从河床的杂木林中穿涌而下。年复一年、日复一日地冲刷，河床已没有了一粒泥沙，连磐石也被激流磨光了棱角而变得“圆滑”起来，但树木却像多情的汉子，死死扎根在河床妻子的怀抱里，纹丝不动。美丽的爱情之树四季常青。这种“水在石上淌，树在水中长”的奇景，人见人叹。

水上森林中，石上盘根错节，枝间古藤缠绕。游人手攀拽藤、足踏盘根，沿河穿行，踩瀑践浪，有惊无险而趣味无穷。

生长在石头上的森林，已经令人惊叹不已，走过这片石上流水、水上有树的水上森林，我们该怎样去赞叹这大自然稀有的极致。这里的千百株树木，全部植根于水中顽石，又通过顽石深深扎根于河床中，水中有石，石上有树，树植水中。奔腾而来的水具有排山倒海的力量，它可以吞没和毁灭一切，但都无法动摇这里的每一棵树。这里水疾如风，浪急如火，人在水中站立不稳，树在水中纹丝不动。每一棵生命之树，也正是在这岩石与流水中，显示出生生不息、绵绵不绝的精神风采。

翠谷 在响水河最上游的上几定村、下几定村，是一个封闭的峰丛洼地。群山苍翠欲滴，田野郁郁葱葱，翠谷因此得名。这里密集的峰丛耸入云天，山峰上原生性森林密布，山腰云雾缭绕，清新悦目。青峰下小桥、流水、人家，布依族人民保留着古朴淳厚的风俗。木板房、吊脚楼、土花布、银首饰、女织男耕、翻撬锄地，还有从高山上引水建起的小水电站。昼夜机声隆隆、明珠点点，给寂静的山村增添了繁华。森林、山村、电站互相协调，使游客倍感舒适。

野猪林 又称野竹槽漏斗森林。是下几定东南群山中的大片喀斯特漏斗森林，从漏斗底部到天边山沿，有重重叠叠的丛林密布。漏斗底部有几百亩翠竹杂生在林木丛中。整个漏斗像一个绿色大旋涡，飘旋在林海之上。在漏斗森林西南的暗河出口，遇洪水暴发时，喷出的水柱可飞过十几米高的树梢，水消不及，很快把漏斗变成几十米深的山塘，还有部分水从东北面的山洞泻流入响水河，而形成数十米高的山洪瀑布，水势凶猛，水雾漫山，水声雷动，异常壮观。

这片漏斗森林中，常有各种野兽出没，在漏斗底部的暗河、水塘里，还有娃娃鱼（大鲵，国家二类保护动物）和黄角鱼，山外村民常到这里来打猎、捕鱼，只因有一次碰到一条人体粗的大蟒后，大家才不敢轻易进山。但是每遇旱灾之年，村寨里的人总要邀集一些强壮勇敢的人冒险到这里投石求雨，说只要把大石块投入喷水的暗河口，顷刻间便会乌云四起，风雨大作。

拉雅瀑布 为小七孔四级电站的水渠溢水形成，水量较大，落差30米，坠入响水河，瀑布靠近路边，人车必须从瀑布旁边经过。由于视点低而近，给游人形成仰视观景，加大了高耸感，瀑布下落时又分三叠，水束腾空，细雾迷蒙，声如雷鸣，与响水河谷互为陪衬相得益彰。在瀑布前留影游客达十之八九。瀑宽10米，落差30米，逼近仰视，但见瀑首悬蓝天，旁缀白云，几疑天河自空而降。水量较大的时候，瀑势如山倒，吼声状雷，颇为壮观。瀑布腾空喷泻，横向坠落，同响水河纵向错落的68级跌水瀑布构成一幅绝妙的立体交叉瀑布群景观。瀑在路侧，人在瀑下，倍觉酣畅和亲切。瀑布溅喷的水雾飘飘洒洒，纷纷扬扬，给游客以扑面凉爽和美的享受，可一洗征尘的暑热和劳乏，顿觉轻松和振奋。

鸳鸯湖 在卧龙村西南面，有两个水面相通的喀斯特盲谷湖，象镶嵌在喀斯特森林中的一双巨大光亮的碧玉。其中一个布依语称叫“王盘”，一个叫“王玛”，现称鸳鸯湖。也许确曾有鸳鸯栖息过，但是这个新的命名主要点在其两湖并连相依。鸳鸯湖水面宽约20公顷，水深处达30米，水色碧绿，明洁如镜。湖周围土岸、石岸相间，岸高处达七八米，低处仅一两米。也有几处坡岸长满灌木水草，一直浸入湖中。泛舟湖上，只见岸边古树参天，老干虬枝与攀附其上的藤萝、苔藓，一起低垂湖面。阳光透过林荫，树影波光交织，满湖滴翠、铺金，山风拂来，林啸声、水流声、鸟鸣声交错齐响，悦耳旷心，令人陶醉。最迷人的是湖西南区，几个岛屿之间，巷岔交织，水面纵横，迂回开合，宽窄交错；狭窄处如水上林荫巷道，宽阔处如水上森林天窗，交错处如盘里迷宫，野趣无穷，舟上回味久长，被人称为喀斯特森林的绝景。这宁静清幽的山湖景色，隔五六年也会遇上一次周期性的洪水滔天，被惊涛骇浪打破。这是因为湖下边的暗河入口受堵，泄水能力所限，山洪一时消不了，而淹没整个山谷变成一片汪洋，可惜这种壮丽的景观也是难以看到一次，故被评为国家级景物景观。游人中有“不到鸳鸯湖等于不到小七孔”之说。

天钟洞、蝙蝠洞 天钟洞位于海拔859米的半山上。洞内有3层，总长约2000米。洞厅高大，前后相通，廊道迂回，空气新鲜流畅，钙化堆积物虽未十分发育，但形态生动，景色迷人。由石花、石树、石盘、石幔、石笋、石柱、石葡萄等组成的一幅幅溶洞景观，有的如宫殿楼阁，有的如虫鱼禽兽，有的如田园沃野、林、树、塔、屋，有的如深山飞瀑，有的如莽莽雪原，还有些小景物，如明镜高悬、天狗望月等更是栩栩如生。东部大厅中央一樽形如天钟的巨大钙化堆积物巍然屹立，犹似镇山护洞之宝，无需撞击，已给人声震寰宇的幻觉，成为天钟洞的象征。这一溶洞的出现，应归于大自然造化之功。在很久很久以前，这里还是一片汪洋大海，波及全球的燕山造山运动，使地壳大幅度抬升，导致这里的地层断裂变形，原生的地下暗河通道，已上升到海拔859米的山腰。又由于这个不均匀的造山运动，曾有过多次间歇，便形成了这多层次溶洞和这里多台阶漏斗和洼地的奇特景观。

洞内宽敞、平缓，老幼皆可行动自如，洞外石阶梯320级，游人可由此登山进入洞中，后洞直通鸳鸯湖畔，对游览起着调剂作用，是山、水、洞、林、湖融合一体成为这一绝景的组成部分。

蝙蝠洞与天钟洞相距100米。洞顶有硕大的钟乳倒悬，像只凌空飞翔的蝙蝠，故名。洞厅巨大钟乳石如柱、如塔、如花木禽兽，千姿百态，栩栩如生。洞中有暗河、阴湖、幽壑深邃，神秘莫测。洞深数公里，从贵州地进，可从广西界出。中间有钟乳巨石似雄鸡翘首，人称“鸡鸣黔桂”。

卧龙河 又名清溪，鸳鸯湖与卧龙潭之间一段暗河明流。因常发洪水显威，故名卧龙河。其左岸一群高峰耸矗，右岸一坝良田沃土，夹岸的古树浓荫蔽日，几乎将这段明流又重变为绿荫“暗河”。远处望去只能看见那条弯弯曲曲的林带，无法看见河流的真面目，只有沿溪划船，穿过那一道道绿荫深邃，一处处的澄塘、苇荡、陡岸、深潭、湍流、险滩和密林峡谷，一直穷尽水源，才能领其全貌意境。在澄塘、苇荡、溪水碧绿平静的地方，水鸟三五群集，点水雀吱吱叫唤，一派轻松欢乐，一切似乎都静悄悄，只有落叶花瓣的漂流，始觉溪的流动。在溪边陡岸，怪石排列，如象、如牛、如兽、如禽、如鬼怪妖魔各霸一程，使人毛骨悚然，思绪万千。深潭、水坝，鸟兽难越，人迹罕至。枯藤老树在水上交错纵横拦阻，行船到此，也只得攀藤牵枝抚树前行。在湍流险滩边，残存许多古代水车的遗迹，不得不令人回忆到古农田水利的雅风。滩为其残存水坝乱石堆造成，浪花飞溅，流水激船，不折篙摧桨，休想前行一尺。逆流而上，依旧密林峡谷岩阻林封藤拦，山重水复，只觉处处艰难，道道迷津，不知何处是尽头。船行河上，心情舒畅，景美物奇，诗情画意尽人品赏。“林尽水源”时，“天台别有路，桃洞尚存源”的诗意涌上心头。卧龙河畔布依村风情和卧龙河的卧龙桥，陪衬着溪流佳景更显得多彩迷人。

卧龙潭 原名翁龙潭，喀斯特暗河——卧龙河的出露口。从地表看它只是卧龙河的源头，近年又从这里筑坝引水发电后入响水河，成两河的总水源。暗河从崖底下涌出，潭面上不见踪影，只有坝上泄流的渠水形成雪崩似的滚水瀑布，才感到卧龙河在潭底翻动，潭边怪石奇树林立，古木森森，潭外水声轰鸣，雾雨蒙蒙，四周高山紧锁，水潭犹如地底深渊，即便不相信龙的存在，也感到有龙的象征和龙潭虎穴般的意境。每遇山洪暴发，涛涌浪奔，真有蛟龙显威之势，顷刻之间，十里田园被淹，千亩山林受没，一片汪洋大海，浩瀚惊人。

（二）大七孔景区

大七孔景区距县城22公里，距小七孔景区3公里。景观峻险神奇，气势雄峻磅礴，极富惊险性、神秘性、奇特性。大七孔景区景点有大七孔桥、山神峡、天生桥、水神河、地峨峡、地峨宫、清水塘、万蛇塘、二层湖、笑天河、龙头山、喀斯特森林、地峨宫大洞口等。

大七孔桥 又名双溪桥。在王蒙乡孟塘村附近的打命河（又名孟塘河）上，有大型石桥1座，7孔，高7米，宽4.5米，长35米，横跨东西。修建于清道光二十七年（1847年），落成于道光三十年（1850）为阖邑绅民捐建，称“万善桥”，后因桥被洪水冲毁一孔，交通中断。清光绪三年（1877），重修复改名双溪桥，是中华人民共和国成立前荔波县境内第一大石拱桥，通往广西南丹县的重要桥梁。现今通向小七孔公路经过桥上，是旅游区的重要桥梁和景物之一，桥畔有“双溪桥序”石碑。又因大桥有七孔俗名大七孔桥。

山神峡 打命河两岸悬崖峭壁，形成天然峡谷，逆打命河前行1公里，左岸有座宽、高100多米峭崖直冲云霄，堆堆钟乳放异，丛丛翠林闪彩，像斑斓的彩画贴在绝壁之上，它的中央有由下斜着向上排列成“一”字形的3个洞穴，深邃黝黑。其中最大的一个岩洞口，也是最高的一个洞口，从岩石缝中长出一排青翠欲滴的绿树。这里河谷深邃、岚气缭绕、危岩层叠、峭壁矗立、视线窄狭，仰望天空一线，前后远望穷目。人们在这里如大声说话，两岸绝壁上就有沙石乒乓落下，飞沙走石，不身临其境，是不能信服的。

天生桥 方村河伏流出露不远，有一横跨河两岸的天然巨岩，是喀斯特地貌奇观之一，俗称天生桥，又谓仙人桥。高60米，厚10米，桥孔宽20多米，河水流过桥后，还形成2米多高的宽大瀑布。仰观桥孔下，只见巨型钟乳悬挂，桥脚、桥侧的裂隙石缝长出绿色草丛灌木，藤萝花卉缠裹桥身，真是满目琳琅、五颜六色的自然大彩桥。桥下瀑前水激浪涌，小船不能靠近，必须停船，把船扛在肩上攀登危岩，越过瀑布，又才放船逆流行舟在暗河峡谷之中。此景惊险，别具一番风险乐趣。有诗赞道：“蛟龙腾云下人间，心随白浪舞翩翩。五岳苏杭不堪恋，天生桥下做神仙。”

水神河 为喀斯特地下河的一处大天窗。从河面上仰望天空，天似圆盘一个，真是“井下观天，天小也”。而两岸峡谷笔直耸立，阴森森令人不寒而栗。传说很久以前有个布依族青年渔郎，在一个细雨绵绵、雾霭蒙蒙的初夏，来到这段河里捕鱼，遇见一个漆黑溜光的水怪物，在河中蠕动前行，吓得他忙拜跪求神保佑，怪物方缓缓游去，过后也无影无踪。从此谁去捕鱼都必须烧香敬神始捕到鱼，否则必空手而归。水神的传说不胫而走，水神河因而得名。

地峨峡 这是方村河进入暗河道前的一段明流，是一处宽不过50米，高100多米的深幽河谷。两岸悬崖峭壁上生长各种奇树异草，涨水期河流汹涌澎湃，枯水时节，潺潺细流。人沿峡谷行，惊险又安全，因为峭壁上可进入暗河的小径旁有密密的小树挡着，行人不怕会掉下河去，步入此景情趣无穷。

地峨宫 驾欧乡板潭村干引（布依语干即洞）内的地下龙宫和地下大湖。宫中神秘莫测，上有天窗，仰望如太阳当午。侧有裂隙通外，观之如一弯残月，数颗晨星。湖中有沙滩，沙滩上有根大树干直立，如定海神针。湖边暗河出水处形成高20米的大瀑布。

顶天杉：在地峨宫喀斯特地表高山顶上，生长着一棵珍稀的三尖杉大树，苍劲古雅，巍然挺立，直插云霄，顶天立地，特意独立，杰出挺拔。远望有擎天气派，于喀斯特森林中如鹤立鸡群，气势非凡。树高20米，冠幅20米，胸围3.5米，胸径1.2米，树皮粗厚成鳞，宛如巨虬，枝杆婆娑，如大盖伞，树脂芬芳，清心爽气。最奇妙处，为独其能生长在生境极其严酷的喀斯特山的顶峰而如此粗壮。

清水塘 驾欧乡板潭村对面河有20亩水面的山塘，俗称清水塘。塘坎用块石砌成，约高3米。塘中央有地下深洞，直径2米多，清泉从洞中向上喷涌，终年不涸，清澈不浑，涨涸变化不大，最大为1.5立方米/秒，最小是0.5立方米/秒。村民在塘中增设凉亭一处，架桥直通亭阁，游人可从桥上至凉亭览胜。塘水现利用来碾米、灌田、发电。古时村民是从今喷水洞口往下20米深处，用2米多长的竹竿吊桶汲取阴河水饮用。清光绪年间（1875—1908），有人发现阴河外流之洞口不大，就用几口铁锅重叠堵住出水洞，水即受阻向上升起从人进出之洞口喷出，村民甚喜，随即筑坝拦水，饮用其水，还用以碾米、灌田。现在塘中央喷水洞口仍隐约可见石梯阶往喷水洞口下去的遗迹。清水塘为喀斯特地貌形成的奇特上升大泉（龙洞水）。其水源在朝阳镇的山江村，水入洞后，复经砂石滤清，再由清水塘喷出，因此，四季水清不浑，就是大雨水涨时节，各江河塘库水均浑浊，唯此处之水清澈如故，清水塘因而得名。因道路崎岖，交通不便，游人不多。

万蛇塘 驾欧乡新街村拉布龙寨边有口水塘，俗称万蛇塘，塘水终年不涸，每遇夏旱时，出现成千上万的水蛇汇聚于此塘中。当人们近塘边，人影在水中倒映，水蛇即钻进塘边石隙或塘内巨石下藏身，不时伸出头来探察外边的动静，稍注意数数，就见每块石头下伸出数十条蛇头。但村人依然到水塘里汲水饮用，人不伤蛇，蛇也不伤人。这奇特景观形成的原因是，拉布龙寨位于六林、新街季节河的下游，这条河内夏日水蛇甚多，水蛇不能离水，所以旱年河水枯竭时，散居数十里河中的水蛇汇聚于此塘中，真是名不虚传的万蛇塘。此景只能在夏旱之年出现，别时则无，实属难遇的奇景。

二层湖 在笑天河上游，比笑天河高30多米，又比其上游的方村河低100多米。是方村河伏流后又出现的一个明湖。有1平方公里面积，是喀斯特峰谷中的一个湖泊。湖四周覆盖着密密的原始森林，湖水清澈透底，湖边有许多树生在湖水中，又是一水中森林奇景。

笑天河 是方村河伏流后又出现的一段明流。落差48米，河中银浪滔滔，涛声隆隆，震撼山谷，有如笑天，故名。水出自王蒙乡聋顶村高山岩溶地带的乱堆石中，奔流500多米后再伏流至天生桥露出。这段河床陡、流急，从高处鸟瞰，是极富有原始野趣的山村水态。

龙头山 是俯瞰地峨宫片区景物的观赏点。从这里极目远眺，只见连绵起伏的山峦排山倒海般涌向天际，它们矫健的躯体上都披挂着喀斯特原始森林，使眼前望不到尽头的空间里舒展着的是浩瀚无垠的绿色海洋。在这里极目舒天，尽情尽兴地饱览层峦叠翠、烟云缭绕、气韵生动的壮观景致。

喀斯特森林 景区是一片喀斯特森林，植被完好。森林滞留泉水叮咚。森林中的岩洞尤其显得活跃。洞顶滴水如连珠，洞里有如千百只水晶玉盘，水流涓涓，凉意沁心。常有猕猴等野生动物到此饮水。游人到此，一饮此水，有如琼浆玉液，精神为之大振。

地峨宫大洞口 这是方村河（淇江）流经地峨峡进入地峨宫暗河的落水洞口，外面看去是一个高100多米的大洞口，从洞侧小路进入洞内可以看到洞内景物，有水洞、有旱洞，进洞口处如大蘑菇似的堆积物一层叠，河水一入洞穴就有一个落水洞，大部分河水翻腾而去，少部分水流又从洞底进入，形成层层暗河，天然的千姿百态景物，令人惊叹不绝。

（三）水春河景区

水春河景区距县城13公里。景区以奇险奇峻为特色，长13公里，奇峰绝壁夹急流，构成“十三道浪七重滩”的奇险景观，是风景区最长、最大的峡谷。已开发的漂流项目被称为“黔桂第一漂”。

景区两岸绝壁夹峙，怪石突兀。岩壁上天然形成的奔马和绿毛龟，像凝固的浮雕。乘一叶轻舟泛流而下，但觉云在水底飘，船在山上行，人在画中游。水春河景区自然景点有水春河峡谷、玉泉滩、龙王洞、万鸟洞、江上夕阳、螺蛳山、玉屏山等23个。

玉泉滩 在水春河中段，滩边巨石裂隙涌泉似玉带，故名。泉水清凉甘洌，饮之回味无穷。滩水湍急，落差甚大，激流冲浪荡舟更富于刺激性。舟过长滩进入白岩下，水平如镜，水深碧绿，河中有巨石桌一处，石上有九凹俗称九大碗，相传为龙王宴席处，自然风景和美丽的传说交融，别有一番情趣。

龙王洞 白岩脚下有洞称龙王洞，洞前樟江水深，人不能涉，非舟船不能入，两边悬崖非猿类不能行，自古为人迹罕至之境。每逢乱世，城乡居民常避乱于此。清咸同乱世和民国33年（1944）12月3日日本侵略者进犯，县城和时来村民，多在龙王洞一带躲避。前人有诗道：“凿空盘古来开天，龙洞临江台住仙。一叶扁舟辞热客，十分清气落冷肩。人惊赤帝行秋令，我与青山认旧缘。弹指避秦人散尽，茫茫谁与话桑田。”

万鸟洞 水春布依族寨上游7公里处的河段两岸，绝壁峭岩夹峙，绿树葱茏：在名为虎刀壁的陡岩上，有个巨大的岩洞，洞里穴居成千上万只山燕子。每当阳光初照、旭日东升时，山燕子成群结队飞出洞来觅食，往来不绝于洞中，像蜜蜂般有蔽日遮天之势，响声震谷，鸣声悦耳，蔚为壮观。

江上夕阳 一天奔波旅游，舟过长滩后，向县城回归的情景。时已残阳西下，晚霞当空，陶醉在诗情画意中归去。荔波八景仍在游趣之中：樟江夜月、月点波心、波涵月影、水天月色互相掩映。联云：“扫尽云烟来玩月，踏平坎坷不生波。”对世事憎贬之意，旧日有之。今已是解放，人民政府在樟江上架起虹桥，修建堤坝，景色倍添，目不暇接。东郭晓烟，西峰霁雪，南堰奔涛，北郊落照，沙市围渔，梨井春光，洞天消暑，都一一展现在眼前，使人眼花缭乱。在暮色苍茫的山光水色之中，迷蒙舒畅地醉倒在山环水绕的大自然宏宇之中，神也朦胧，情也朦胧。

螺蛳山 位于县城西1公里，形似田螺。山上稀疏林木中有一排排古墓。其中有明土司蒙教露之坟。山势宏伟壮观。山左侧流水清清，常年不涸。山右侧为烂田湾，土肥地沃，山前为黄泥坡，平地起伏，波浪翻滚，实称得上山川秀丽，林茂粮丰的好地方。

玉屏山 玉屏山拔地而起200米，屹立于荔波县城北，右侧营盘坡，左侧将军山，后靠石龙岩，前环诸黄土小坡，形状端庄，松杉成林，异草丛生，山色秀丽。山临县城，为县城之天然屏障，故称玉屏，玉屏镇因此得名。清乾隆初年（约1738），山被雨水冲刷崩裂两处。至道光二十五年（1845），全县捐资培补，以土填平。每年农历五月初五（端阳佳节）承沿布依族习俗，倾城男女青少年，身着白色衬衫，手提粽子，三五成群攀登玉屏山，或游戏，或竞赛，骑骑马，远远望去遍山皆人。从玉屏山巅俯瞰县城如玉盘盛景，樟江如玉带环腰，大桥如飞龙跨渡，幕幕景色，使人目不暇接。

（四）樟江田园风光带

樟江田园风光带以樟江河流域两岸的田园、名胜古迹、人文景观为主要特征，风光带全长30公里。风光带两岸由近及远，农田村落、低丘远山交相辉映，风光秀丽，有主要自然景点3个。

第二节　国家级茂兰喀斯特森林自然保护区

国家级茂兰喀斯特森林自然保护区、国家级樟江风景名胜区以保存完好的原生性森林、生态系统、生物物种、水体以及人文景观和民族文化为特征。主要体现为茂兰喀斯特森林是世界上唯一仅存的喀斯特森林类型，在世界植被类型中占有重要地位；茂兰喀斯特森林具有重大的科学研究价值，联合国教科文组织已将其世界性意义和科研价值列为世界生物圈保护区；茂兰喀斯特森林独特的水文地质二元结构，对喀斯特地区生态环境的改善具有极大的促进作用；茂兰喀斯特森林生态系统是亚热带喀斯特地区中生物多样性保持最完整、种类最丰富的地区；茂兰喀斯特森林具有极高的美学价值和感染力。荔波拥有世界上相同纬度仅存的喀斯特森林生态系统，被中外专家誉为“地球腰带上的绿宝石”。

茂兰自然保护区涉及洞塘、永康、翁昂、捞村、立化、驾欧和甲良7个乡（镇）、14个村、96个自然组。1987年4月，省政府将茂兰保护区批准为省级自然保护区。1988年5月，国务院将茂兰保护区批准为国家级自然保护区，并明确该保护区是以保护完整的综合自然生态系统为目的，兼有保护珍稀孑遗动植物资源的科研型自然保护区。1996年4月，茂兰保护区被联合国教科文组织纳入国际生物圈保护区网络（MAB）。是年，该区被中国生态旅游专业委员会列为全国22条生态旅游线之一。

茂兰自然保护区内的生态旅游区是实验区进行旅游开发的区域。该区位于保护区的东北部，面积19.15平方公里。其主要功能是用于开展喀斯特森林生态旅游，以良好独特的喀斯特森林景观和生态环境为主体，融合自然景观与人文景观，充分利用森林的多种功能，按照生态旅游的理论和宗旨开展旅游活动，从而使观赏游览与科普教育相结合，提高公众保护生态环境、热爱大自然的意识。旅游区的主要景点有青龙潭、金狮洞、九洞天、旺牌山漏斗森林、黄杨沟、水中林、拉滩瀑布等。区内修建简易步道供游人徒步游览。

说明：有关茂兰自然保护区资源本志第二篇详记

第二章 人文旅游资源

全县有人文景点18个。其中，位于小七孔景区6个、大七孔景区5个、水春河景区6个、樟江风光带1个。一级景点有邓恩铭烈士故居，二级景点有瑶山民族村，三级景点有水春布依族村寨、水扒水族村寨，四级景点有龙定布依族村。

第一节 红色旅游资源

荔波县是中共一大代表邓恩铭的故乡，又是革命老区，红色旅游景点有邓恩铭故居、板寨红七军会师旧址、黎明关抗战遗址、永康穿洞等，是开展革命传统教育和爱国主义教育之地。2004年12月，根据国家《2004—2010年全国红色旅游发展规划纲要》，县委编制《荔波红色旅游发展规划》，同时请专家对邓恩铭烈士故居、板寨红七军会师旧址、黎明关抗战遗址、永康穿洞等线路进行评审，报省批准，列为贵州省七条红色旅游精品线路之一。

一、邓恩铭烈士故居

邓恩铭，男，水族，1901年1月生于荔波县玉屏镇水浦村，是中国共产党第一次全国代表大会代表，中国共产党的创始人之一，1931年4月在山东济南牺牲。邓恩铭烈士故居位于县城玉屏镇向阳北路，房屋建于清光绪年间。1905年，邓恩铭家从水浦村迁居此处。故居坐西南向东北，平面呈长方形，由正房、豆腐房、天井、陈列室、游客服务中心和后院空地组成，总占地面积1200平方米。

1982年2月，省政府将邓恩铭烈士故居正式公布为第一批省级重点文物保护单位。1990年年初，县政府筹资对故居进行维修，并进行故居内物件复原陈列，在故居后院新建180平方米的陈列室，用汉白玉雕塑邓恩铭烈士半身像，设邓恩铭生平事迹展览，1990年7月1日正式对外开放。1995年，省政府公布邓恩铭烈士故居为贵州省爱国主义教育基地。

2005年，为弘扬邓恩铭烈士“不懈追求真理、矢志献身革命”的崇高革命精神，县委、县政府筹资560万元，启动邓恩铭烈士故居保护建设一期工程，将陈列室扩建为230平方米，重新设置长73米的邓恩铭烈士生平革命事迹展览，对复原陈列和辅助展览作调整充实，用较大篇幅介绍少年邓恩铭的事迹。2006年10月，修葺布展后的邓恩铭烈士故居重新对外开放，并成为贵州省全民国防教育基地。

二、板寨红七军会师旧址

中国工农红军第七军第一、第二纵队板寨会师旧址位于荔波县洞塘乡板寨村，距离县城40公里，是县内红色旅游景区的重要组成部分。板寨会师旧址馆舍由旧址房屋、板寨会师陈列馆及馆前广场三部分组成，占地面积3600平方米。

板寨会师旧址坐北面南，为青瓦顶、穿斗式砖木结构，是典型的庭院式民居，由朝门、两厢（一楼一底）、正房（一楼一底）、天井组成，建筑面积540平方米，占地面积405.8平方米。

1981年，荔波县政府将板寨会师旧址公布为文物保护单位。

2003年年初，县委、县政府筹措资金300万元，对板寨会师旧址进行修缮，同时在旧址内进行复原陈列，布置展厅540平方米、展线长120米，展出红七军将士的大刀、床、桌、椅、凳、马灯等文物展品46件（套）。2004年7月正式对外开放。2006年，省政府公布板寨会师旧址为省级文物保护单位。2007年，列为荔波县青少年学生校外活动中心德育基地。2008年，省内外党、政、军机关、企事业单位干部职工、部队官兵、大中小学生等社会各界人士到板寨红七军会师旧址接受革命传统教育达2万人次。

三、黎明关抗战遗址

黎明关位于荔波县洞塘乡板寨村。建于清道光二十五年（1845），是清代至民国时期荔波至广西古驿道上的关隘之一。黎明关前方为百米深谷，两侧为陡山悬崖，只有一条山间小路通行，地势险要，易守难攻。黎明关历来为兵家必争之地。1930年，红七军第二纵队越过黎明关挺进荔波县境，成为第一支入黔的中国工农红军队伍。1944年11月25日，爱国军民在黎明关阻击侵黔日军，打响贵州抗日第一枪，成为抗战遗址。1950年春，中国人民解放军一三八团在此堵击残匪。

2004年，县委、县政府筹资对黎明关及步道进行维修，新建纪念牌坊、观景台、碑记、休息长廊、停车场等十多处辅助设施，开发为红色旅游景点。2005年，黎明关正式对外开放。2006年6月，省政府公布黎明关为省级文物保护单位。

四、永康穿洞抗日遗址

永康穿洞抗日遗址位于县内永康乡白岩村穿洞寨。永康穿洞是清代至20世纪70年代广西经永康进入荔波县城的必经之路。因石板路从隧洞中穿过故称穿洞。1944年11月，日本侵略者进犯荔波县境，是月27日攻陷黔桂边境重要关隘黎明关后，企图直冲荔波县城，迅速进取独山。但从黎明关到荔波县城不到40公里的山路上，受到重重阻击。日本侵略者第三十四联队于是年12月2日进抵永康，并开始进攻固守穿洞的守军部队，以密集炮火向穿洞阵地中的守军射击，守军坚守穿洞，激战两天，日本侵略者毫无进展，并死伤严重。结果日本侵略者的另一支军队向左迂回吉洞、董亥、巴灰（今朝阳）冲进荔波。穿洞守军被迫后撤。日本侵略者一部通过穿洞占领荔波。为纪念此次战斗，中共荔波县委、县人民政府于2006年筹资在穿洞抗日遗址立碑以示后人，并开辟为红色旅游景点，游客逐年增多。

第二节　少数民族文化风情

荔波是少数民族聚居县，世居少数民族有布依族、水族、苗族、瑶族，每个民族都拥有各具特色的民族传统文化，有源远流长的民族风情，有独特的民居建筑，有丰富多彩的民族节日，形成迷人的景观。

一、民族节庆活动

县内每年布依族的“四月八”斗牛活动，“六月六”山歌对唱，水族“卯节”卯坡对歌，

"端节"庆贺丰收，瑶山瑶族猴鼓舞、铜鼓舞表演，苗族的传统舞蹈芦笙舞、板凳舞等，吸引四方游客。

二、民族村寨

大土苗族村寨 佳荣镇大土村是县内典型的苗族村寨，位于海拔1000米以上的月亮山东南麓的半山腰上，距镇政府所在地15公里。大土村辖5个村民小组、210户800多人，苗族人口占总人口的95%。大土苗族村寨仍保持着传统民居建筑，保留有传统风俗习惯，每到浸种撒秧、新米成熟、春节、祭祖时，家家户户要身穿盛装，吹笙跳舞，进行庆祝。大土村组建有一支15人的芦笙乐队和一支100余人的苗族舞蹈队，他们的演出为义演，参加过荔波县申遗活动、梅花节、低碳活动、省第二届旅游发展大会"荔波荡漾"文艺演出等多项大型活动，为荔波人民和外来游客献上精彩的演出，展现大土苗寨的风土人情。

江风布依族村寨 江风布依族村寨位于翁昂乡境内，地处世界自然遗产地茂兰自然保护区腹地，距县城28公里，距翁昂乡政府所在地2.5公里，在荔波旅游景区环线内。寨前近处田园铺展，远处山川环绕。村寨的四周，古树参天，村庄、田园和山水交相辉映，溶洞神秘莫测，有着得天独厚的山水田园风光。村寨较为完整地保留着古色古香的布依族民居、古塔、古桥、古法造纸坊、天然神峰等古迹，特别是民居建筑，以杆栏式木质结构楼房为主，瓦盖两层重檐，二层曲栏回廊。建筑分散布局，小巷连接家家户户，户与户道路纵横交错，宛如网状，如同迷宫。每逢春节和农历三月三、四月八、六月六、九月九等传统节日，或遇上婚丧嫁娶重大活动，村民自发组织在一起，表演布依傩戏、矮人舞和唱布依古歌、花灯戏等，自娱自乐。江风布依族村寨自然、独特、纯朴的民风民俗受游客青睐。

水利水族大寨 水利水族大寨位于荔波观音峰景区内，距县城20公里，交通方便。这里背依青山，前傍田园大坝，风光秀丽。村寨完全保持着水族的传统民居建筑，房屋多是木质结构、瓦顶。平房、楼房和吊脚楼均采用穿斗架，每架五柱、七柱不等。寨内水族穿无领长衫、青布长裤、彩色围腰以及银项圈、银耳环、银头饰等，有端节、卯节及石棺墓、抢亲、神山祭祖等习俗。水族古老文字"水书"在寨内有传承。卯节是寨上隆重的节日。

瑶山民族村 瑶山民族村位于瑶山瑶族乡拉片村。这里风景优美，环境优雅，距小七孔景区3公里，距县城30公里。瑶族风情古朴浓郁，他们由于长期生活在边远山区大山深处，交通落后，偏僻、闭塞，与外界交往少，保存着一些古老习俗。瑶族独特的服饰，传统的蜡染刺绣，狂劲的歌舞，奇妙的婚俗，神秘的丧葬以及恢宏的瑶王宴等令人惊叹。瑶山因此成为荔波民族风情旅游胜地，受游客青睐。2001年，国家补助653.92万元、县投入54.88万元，建设瑶山新村、瑶族文化展示厅、瑶族风情演艺场、瑶王府、标志性雕塑、村景步道、石水景观、景区绿化、旅游标牌等，旅游基础设施不断完善，瑶山民族村建设初具规模。瑶山民族旅游填补了樟江景区人文景观的空白。

瑶麓青瑶寨 青瑶是瑶族的分支，聚居在瑶麓瑶族乡，位于县城东部，地处喀斯特地区，距县城34公里。瑶麓瑶族乡青瑶寨有省级文物保护单位"省立水庆小学""瑶族婚碑"；有省级非物质文化遗产"瑶族打猎舞"和独具特色的凿壁谈婚等民俗文化。2007年，瑶麓瑶族乡被文化部授予"打猎舞之乡"称号。青瑶寨住房为平地吊脚楼、两层"禾廊"、上楼石阶，衣着保持绣人物、楼廊和两节裤、脚笼彩带等服饰传统，佩戴简洁粗放的银项圈、银鸟、头簪等首饰，谈婚论嫁沿袭"谈婚洞"习惯，丧葬仍完整保存独具特色的古代自然洞穴式悬棺。此外，还建有县级"单性木兰"保护区。瑶麓青瑶寨具有新奇、神秘、不可复制、唯一、独特的文化特点和环境优势，瑶麓青瑶寨地处世界遗产地内，成为旅游地。

第三章　景区建设

第一节　景区开发

1985年，县政府实施小七孔梯级电站开发项目时，担任小七孔电站开发指挥部负责人的县水电局工程师艾福田踏勘发现电站周围10公里范围内的喀斯特森林覆盖区，存在原始的自然景观，融山、水、洞、林、湖、瀑、石等自然风景为一体，具有旅游开发价值。于是，艾福田向县委、县政府作开辟旅游景点供游人参观的专题汇报。经县委、县政府研究同意，在建设小七孔梯级电站的同时，在不破坏资源和保护自然景观的前提下，由电站指挥部修筑简易步道，增设必要照明灯光，开发拉雅瀑布、水上森林、龟背山、天钟洞、鸳鸯湖等几个景点，供游人参观。

1988年12月，县政府向州政府呈报兴办旅游开发项目报告。1989年1月，州委、州政府在小七孔景区召开全州旅游工作会议，会上，十余家企业出资共40万元，扶持景区基础设施建设。是月11日，县委、县政府决定，成立喀斯特森林旅游资源开发领导小组，同时向州政府申报建立荔波喀斯特森林风景名胜区。1990年2月，经州政府向省政府申报，省政府批准已开发的小七孔至鸳鸯湖景区定名为荔波喀斯特森林风景名胜区。8月，省政府公布荔波喀斯特森林风景名胜区为贵州省第二批省级风景名胜区。12月，县政府向州、州向省逐级呈报请示，要求将该景区列为国家级风景名胜区。1991年2月，省政府向国务院正式申报将荔波喀斯特森林风景名胜区列为国家重点风景名胜区。

1992年3月，受国务院委托，建设部委派北京林业大学教授孙筱祥组成专家考察组，对该景区申报为国家级景区进行实地考察。专家组考察后认为：小七孔、大七孔、水春河景区和樟江田园风光带，是一个质量非常高的风景名胜区，也是人类宝贵的共同财富，完全具备申报国家级风景名胜区的条件。上述4个景区喀斯特地貌上的水景特色明显，专家组建议以水取名。经县政府研究，更名为荔波樟江风景名胜区。4月，经县向州、州向省呈报更名请示，省政府于6月批准同意将原荔波喀斯特森林风景名胜区更名为荔波樟江风景名胜区。9月，省政府批准，划定小七孔、大七孔、水春河3个景区及其缓冲地带的生活服务区、玉屏镇服务中心、王蒙服务中心，以及拉片、水春、水扒、罗家寨等4个民族村寨为荔波樟江风景名胜区旅游经济开发区。

1993年3月，县、州、省政府逐级向建设部申报将樟江风景名胜区列为国家级重点风景区。是月下旬，国务院组织国家级风景名胜区调研工作组，委托建设部总规划师储传亨任组长，率领12名专家、学者对樟江风景名胜区进行实地考察调研。是年5月，樟江风景名胜区列入建设部向国务院报送审定的第三批国家级重点风景名胜区调研情况的报告。1994年1月10日，国务院发布第三批国家重点风景名胜区名单，荔波樟江风景名胜区列为国家级重点风景名胜区，景区正式名称为中国·荔波樟江重点风景名胜区。3月12日，省政府在贵阳举行新闻发布会，宣布贵州省的荔波樟江、赤水和马岭河峡谷列为国家级重点风景名胜区。

1996年9月3日，荔波樟江风景名胜区水春河漂流“首漂式”在荔波县城举行，中央有关部委、省、州、县有关部门及上海市、广西壮族自治区的相关领导和嘉宾近300人参加“首漂式”。

1998年，开发天钟洞景点，填补小七孔翠谷以西至鸳鸯湖旅游空白带。1999年3月，推出卧龙河、鸳鸯湖生态旅游长廊漂流项目。2004年2月，荔波综合旅游区被省政府确定为全省首批优先发展重点旅游区。

2006年，将被誉为“中国野梅之乡”的洞塘开发为梅园景区。至2015年，每年举办“中国·荔波万亩梅花报春节”活动，填补荔波冬季旅游市场空白，率先在全省打破旅游的季节限制。

经省物价局批准，2009年4月18日，荔波樟江景区大七孔、小七孔景区门票开始调整，小七孔景区门票调整为旺季110元/人，淡季90元/人，大七孔景区调整为旺季55元/人，淡季45元/人。

2011年，为改变荔波旅游南热北冷格局，延长游客在荔波旅游时间，经过市场调研、周密策划和多次试漂，在确保安全的前提下，推出水春河自助漂流产品。该项目的推出，使水春河景区游客量倍增，漂流人数突破历史纪录，日接待量最高可达3000人以上（超过往年的100%以上）。2011年9月推出了竹筏游樟江项目，其亲水性、娱乐性都非常强，让游客在领略樟江沿岸秀美风光的同时，还能感受到浓郁的少数民族风情。

2012年4月，《水韵樟江》大型实景演出正式与游客见面。2013年，原荔波旅游资源开发公司组建为贵州荔波旅游发展（集团）有限公司，注册资本金达11010万元，集团公司共有5家子公司，即：荔波县天水旅游有限公司、荔波县丽水旅游有限公司、荔波县水春河漂流旅游有限公司、荔波县峰水旅游有限公司、贵州小七孔文化演艺公司。

2013年5月，樟江经典文化游项目正式启动。2015年，樟江景区门票收入首次突破1亿元，达11300万元。11月23日，贵州省省长陈敏尔在《打造贵州旅游景区升级版于荔波旅游景区专题调研报告》作出了“荔波景区是打造贵州旅游升级版的重要品牌，要全力支持其做美、做优、做强、做亮”的重要批示。2014年5月大七孔、小七孔景区主要景点及游客集散地实现Wi-Fi覆盖。2015年5月，小七孔推出“古来里”卧龙民族文化园互动项目。

第二节　基础设施建设

1992年，获专项资金160万元，县自筹部分资金，开始进行景区基础设施建设。1994年，景区列入国家重点风景名胜区后，投资不断增加，基础设施建设得到加强和完善。2002年后，按照景区的总体规划进行建设。

2006年，全省第一届旅游产业发展大会上确定2007年第二届旅游产业发展大会在荔波举办后，县委、县政府开展景区、城区各项功能建设，至2007年11月全省第二届旅发大会召开前，投入297.62万元建成县城和景区旅游公厕15座；投入287.12万元建成小七孔景区水上森林湿地；投入190.66万元改造小七孔东门至龟背山景点道路路面；投入127.77万元创建AAAA级景区；改造星级宾馆标间500个。

2008年，在贵州省旅游基础设施建设项目获得的新增中央预算内投资7000万元中，荔波获2860万元（中央预算内投资2000万元、地方配套860万元），全部用于基础设施建设。是年年末，景区共建成主要景点步道40多公里、旅游公路58公里、码头20座、桥梁5座、休息亭廊4座、水冲式厕所18座120个蹲位、停车场13个、水位调节坝1座、综合管理大楼1幢、管理站13个。

2009年，为加强景区旅游基础设施建设，完善景区旅游服务硬件设施，根据景区情况，实施建设了大七孔、小七孔景区游览步道、亭廊、厕所等，总投资185万元。

2010年，根据省建设厅的《关于下达2010年荔波世界自然遗产地基础设施建设补助资金的通知》，下达荔波世界自然遗产地基础设施建设补助资金1000万元，其中，大七孔、小七孔景区规划编制及基础设施建设项目补助资金280万元，组织实施景区规划编制及基础设施建设项目有：1.鸳鸯湖景点建设项目：新建、改建游览步道（新建仿木石步道2000米、改造石步道1000米）、新建服务管理用房200平方米、新建观景台3处、新建观景桥2座（吊桥、平桥各建一座）、标志标牌、新建廊1座250平方米、新建亭2处、改造公厕1座及环境整治及绿化；2.水上森林景点建设项目：新建、改建游览步道800米，计划总投资为20万元；3.大七孔景区恐怖峡景点建设项目：新建吊桥廊亭约120平方米、新建公厕1座；4.樟江风光带景区详细规划编制，以上建设项目已完成。

2011年，根据省建设厅《关于下达2011年荔波世界自然遗产地基础设施建设补助资金的通知》文件精神，下达的荔波世界自然遗产地基础设施建设补助资金1000万元，其中，景区规划编制及基础设施建设项目补助资金270万元，组织实施景区规划编制及基础设施建设项目有新建、改建游览步道3公里、安全护栏3公里、小七孔景区廊1座、亭3处、水春河景区码头2处、公厕2座，大七孔吊桥加固及维护，大七孔、小七孔景区供电线路改造，大七孔、小七孔景区详细规划编制，以上建设项目已完成。

同年，根据国家发改委和省发改委《关于2011年国家重大遗产地保护投资计划安排有关事项的通知》，安排的荔波世界自然遗产地保护性基础设施建设项目，项目总投资2000万元（中央预算内投资1500万元、地方自筹500万元）实施建设项目有：1.保护管理设施：改建看护用房2处450平方米（含卫生室60平方米）、新增消防器材2套、新建森林消防水窖60个、新建安全护栏2公里、新建避雷安全设施6套、新增监控点15处、新建垃圾处理设施40处、新建景区厕所2座、改造3座。2.环境整治：绿化美化18亩、道路改造2.5公里、桥面改造20米、新建巡防步道8公里、河道整治4.5公里、沙坡加固900平方米。3.科普教育设施：新建1个1300平方米科普教育信息中心。截至2015年以上项目完成95%。

2012年，荔波县投入2500万元资金用于樟江景区创建AAAAA级旅游景区相关环境整治及改造建设项目主要有：景区各景点标志标牌的制作安装及完善，改造大七孔、小七孔景区停车场（点）8处共5750平方米、小七孔龟背山停车场扩建1400平方米，大七孔、小七孔及水春河景区游客服务中心室内外改造，新建小七孔景区廊亭4座、仿石凳100处，水上森林岔口瑶池景观改造，步道改造500米、绿化维护2500平方米、景区厕所改造5座，垃圾收集清理设施、设备、景区商铺建设80间，小七孔东、西大门停车场的生态化工程，分别对景区旅游步道、护栏、景点摄影台进行外装饰改造，对景区部分景点大门形象建设，新建部分旅游基础设施和景观建设等基础设施建设。

2013年，为全面建设荔波精品旅游景区，打造荔波旅游升级版，樟江旅游景区实施建设了景区旅游基础设施扩容升级建设，项目总投资为8500万元，建设项目主要有：新建景区大门、小七孔景区水体景观项目（包括5池、2湖、1瀑布群）、步道、护栏、休息亭廊、星级厕所、生态停车场、标志标牌、智慧景区系统（含东西大门和大七孔LED电子屏）、门禁系统升级、大小七孔连线观光公路（新建桥2座，四级标准观光道路1条）等。至2013年实施建设以来，已完成小七孔景区水体景观打造，建设湿地550亩，大七孔、小七孔景区3个大门建设，景区游览步道3.3公里、休息亭廊10座，新改建景区星级旅游公厕7座，建设景区内生态停车场21800平方米，完成了水春河景区码头扩容工程及部分夜游灯光景观工程，景区标志标牌按AAAAA级旅游景区标准设置标志标牌460块，完成王蒙至东门停车场1.82公里公路拓展工程，拉雅瀑布至二级站人车分离栈道工程约1.5公里，大七孔、小七孔连线观光公路1.2公里建设，完成小七孔龟背山景点步道改造，小七孔天钟洞景点木栈道建设等。智慧景区建设：在大七孔、小七孔景区游客服务中心安装LED大屏显示屏3个，在各景点游客集中的地方安装信息发布屏19个，广播语音发布系统16处，电子信息触摸屏7个等设施，在小七孔景区西门游客服务中心建设了智能停车场系统，景区门禁系统已升级完成，并投入运行。

2014年，大七孔、小七孔游客集散中心及水春河游客集散中心项目总投资11300万元，2014年完成投资6550万元。大七孔、小七孔景区游客集散中心建设规模及内容包括：景区形象大门、大七孔、小七孔景区入口专用公路、旅游服务中心、管理房、休息亭廊、景区五星级旅游厕所、景区公安分局办公楼、商铺、生态停车场、绿化、美化、景区标志、标牌及电子显示屏设备安装及配套设施等。

水春河景区游客集散中心项目位于县城时来，项目建设用地面积为2422.72平方米，总建筑面积14054万平方米，内设有监控信息收集、发布、指挥中心，旅游咨询服务及旅游交易中心，酒店、餐饮服务（标准客房132间、拥有可一次性容纳400人餐厅），商场购物等旅游综合服务管理房等。

荔波旅游信息服务中心项目包括荔波大剧院、天泰国际大酒店暨信息文化中心，总投资18000万元（大剧院9500万元、天泰国际大酒店暨信息文化中心8500万元）。

景区扩容升级项目已完成小七孔景区东、西大门、小七孔景区水体景观打造（湿地）、步道、护栏、休息亭廊、星级厕所、生态停车场建设，景区更换标志标牌、大小七孔连线观光公路建设正在实施建设。2014年度共完成投资11680万元。

2015年，新建旅游基础设施建设项目。大七孔、小七孔游客集散中心及水春河游客集散中心项目总投资11300万元，2015年计划投资7500万元，其中，大七孔、小七孔景区游客集散中心4000万元、水春河景区游客集散中心（暨荔波文化旅游信息服务中心）3500万元，2015年项目完成投资7354万元，其中，小七孔景区游客集散中心1695万元、水春河景区游客集散中心（暨荔波文化旅游信息服务中心）5659万元。

荔波旅游信息服务中心项目包括荔波大剧院、天泰国际大酒店暨信息文化中心，总投资18000万元（大剧院9500万元、天泰国际大酒店暨信息文化中心8500万元），2015年荔波大剧院完成投资2828万元。大剧院院场部分于2015年5月28日投入使用。天泰国际大酒店暨信息文化中心正在进行室内给排水及消防管网安装。

2015年，景区扩容升级项目已完成大小七孔连线观光公路，小七孔龟背山景点步道改造，大七孔景区环线木栈道建设步道、护栏、休息亭廊、星级厕所等建设。2015年度共完成投资10182万元。

1992—2015年荔波樟江风景名胜区基础设施建设情况一览表

表14－1

年度	项目总数（项）	主要建设项目	投入资金（万元）			备注
			总计	专项资金	自筹资金	
1992	10	小七孔至鸳鸯湖至西门旅游公路、鸳鸯湖下湖长廊、小七孔一级站餐厅、小七孔景点游览步道、鸳鸯湖下湖码头、水春河一道浪码头、景区零星建设及维修工程等	290.47	170.00	120.47	
1993	5	水春河码头、水春河漫水桥、水春河步道等	31.86	—	31.86	
1994	5	小七孔拉雅瀑布路段路面加高、大七孔步道建设、大七孔吊桥建设等	20.00	—	20.00	
1995	8	小七孔西门管理站、水春河河道疏浚、小七孔零星建设等	38.72	—	38.72	
1996	9	小七孔东门管理房、小七孔西门售票房、卧龙潭景点观景台、景点公厕等	30.33	—	30.33	

续表14－1

年度	项目总数（项）	主要建设项目	投入资金（万元）			备注
			总计	专项资金	自筹资金	
1997	24	小七孔和水春河景区部分景点的管理房、码头、旅游步道、公厕、停车场、输电线路、通信设施等	211.69	126.01	85.68	含征地费
1998	17	东门至龟背山段道路硬化、鸳鸯湖至天钟洞公路建设、天钟洞景点洞内外设施（灯光、步道、护栏）、管理房、公厕、停车场等	246.60	118.80	127.80	含征地费
1999	15	鸳鸯湖上湖、卧龙潭等景点的滑道、码头、管理房、公厕、输电线路改造、杨家桥休息长廊及码头等	67.72	33.00	34.72	
2000	16	东大门改造、龟背山至西大门公路改造、鸳鸯湖至天钟洞公路改造、尧排至水春公路改造、停车场、旅游车道及供水设施、小七孔古桥至响水河至龟背山步道、飞云洞至野猪林至翠谷步道、龟背山至水上森林至翠谷步道改造、鸳鸯湖至天钟洞步道改造、步道护栏新建等	1328.53	710.00	618.53	含征地费
2001	10	铜鼓桥管理房及附属工程、小七孔东门至龟背山路面加宽、鸳鸯湖至天钟洞路面加宽、翠谷至野猪林公路及附属设施等	246.30	136.13	110.17	
2002	14	大七孔栈道、大七孔护栏、大七孔步道、大七孔垃圾处理场、小七孔管理房、水春河管理房、水春河步道及护栏、水春河调节坝、景区苗圃基地、公厕等	1261.36	1091.24	170.12	
2003	20	大七孔游客中心、东门游客中心、西门游客中心、小七孔景区绿化、西门停车场等	269.50	—	269.50	
2004	16	西门停车场扩建、水春河土石方工程（左岸、右岸）、大七孔河道土石方工程、水春河河道挡土墙（右岸）等	315.78	—	315.78	
2005	18	水龙观音峰景区旅游开发建设（管理大厅、观音亭、停车场、公厕、游览步道、输电线路及其他设施）、驾欧至朝阳旅游公路等	1965.20	1000.00	965.20	
2006	27	大七孔入口公路改造、停车场、供水管道铺设、标志标牌、输电线路工程、环保公厕、大七孔停车场及排泄沟环境整治等	418.07	—	418.07	不含旅发会项目资金
2007	13	小七孔景区水上森林湿地、县城和景区旅游公厕、改造小七孔东门至龟背山景点道路路面、AAAA级景区创建等	485.00	—	485.00	不含旅发会项目资金
2008	18	消防设施、防火瞭望台、安全护栏、环卫设施、环境整治、道路改造、巡护步道、监控系统、湿地建设等	1250.00	—	1250.00	不含旅发会项目资金
2009	8	景区游览步道、亭廊、厕所	185.00	—	185.00	
2010	14	鸳鸯湖景点（仿木步道、石步道、管理用房、观景台、观景桥、标志标牌及环境整治绿化）；水上森林步道、大七孔恐怖峡厕所、吊桥长廊等	280.00	280.00	—	
2011	28	看护和管理用房、消防设施、安防设施、监控设施、垃圾处理设施、景区厕所、景区步道、护栏、亭廊、码头、绿化、道路改造、巡防步道、自然灾害防范工程等	2270.00	1770.00	500.00	
2012	48	景区停车场（点）、标志标牌制作、游客公共休息设施和景观设施、厕所更新改造、旅游购物场所整治等	2500.00	80.00	2420.00	
2013	115	东大门、西大门工程，景区木结构景观、厕所、停车场、步道、栈道、道路、桥及智慧区建设等。大七孔、小七孔及水春河景区旅客集散中心、大剧院、景观小品建设等	9050.00	1000.00	8050.00	银行贷款

续表14－1

年度	项目总数（项）	主要建设项目	投入资金（万元）			备注
			总计	专项资金	自筹资金	
2014	75	大七孔、小七孔及水春河景区旅客集散中心、大剧院、景观、厕所、停车场、步道、栈道、智慧景区建设等	11680.00	1250.00	10430.00	银行贷款
2015	15	景区旅游厕所改造及新建、步道、栈道及智慧景区建设等	10182.00	900.00	9282.00	银行贷款
合　计			44212.75	8495.18	35717.57	

2011年2月，中共中央政治局常委、国务院副总理李克强到荔波考察，对荔波旅游产业发展寄予厚望。同年，中共贵州省委书记栗战书、省长赵克志在贵州省旅游产业发展大会上强调荔波旅游产业的建设。2012年，《国务院关于进一步促进贵州经济社会又好又快发展的若干意见》（国发2号文件）对贵州旅游发展提出明确意见，并明确文化旅游发展创新区为贵州省五大战略定位之一，荔波旅游发展迎来了前所未有的发展机遇。国家提出建设黄果树、荔波、梵净山、雷公山等精品景区，《贵州省生态文化旅游总体规划》中将荔波纳入“十大门户”和“六大旅游走廊”之一。荔波机场列为“一干十六支”的航空网络；规划荔波为全省10个三级集散中心之一，组成贵州旅游集散体系；列为十大旅游产业集聚区，建设荔波旅游产业集聚区。2013年，在全省5个100工程中，荔波被列入了100个旅游景区中的21个重点示范建设景区。荔波县委、县政府明确了“以党的十八大精神”为指引，以打造世界知名、国内一流的旅游目的地和休闲度假胜地为目标”的旅游发展战略，围绕旅游抓配套设施建设，围绕旅游抓经济结构调整，围绕旅游抓城镇规划建设，围绕旅游抓招商引资工作，围绕旅游抓城乡统筹发展，围绕旅游抓民族文化开发，围绕旅游抓自然生态保护，着力建设美丽生态荔波，按照“景城互动、城景一体”的发展思路，将荔波建成景色优美的山水景观城，独具魅力的文化体验城，幽雅恬静的人居环境城。

第三节　发展乡村旅游

一、朝阳镇寨莪花海

寨莪花海是朝阳镇精品美丽乡村建设项目，规划面积870亩，花海面积达220亩，在原有100亩花海的基础上，结合民居特色、周边田园风光种植玫瑰、马鞭草、鼠尾草、格桑花、油葵等花卉。花海每年从5月开花一直持续到10月。盛开的紫色花卉是马鞭草和鼠尾草，而玫瑰花的花期则分为两季，第一季的花期为4月至5月，第二季的花期为9月至10月。点播在两边山坡的格桑花花期为6月至10月，格桑花的花朵轻盈如蝴蝶，油葵每天都用笑脸追逐着太阳，就如调皮的孩子一般，而鼠尾草和马鞭草的花朵犹如紫色的精灵降落人间，玫瑰花的热情奔放随时感染着过往的游客。花海栈道全长1100米，栈道尽头的摄影台可以让游客休息和观赏美丽的景色。

寨莪自然寨居住着83户336人，均为布依族，房屋依山而建，错落有致，有精品旅游客栈，一次可承接30人团队的用餐和住宿。为了开发漳江沿河风光带，打造了木屋及帐篷营地功能区，该功能区共建有8栋木屋和100顶帐篷，所有建筑全部临河而建，游客在此即可一览沿河风光，又可亲身下水嬉戏，是夏天避暑游玩的好去处。木屋区距离花海和寨莪布依族自然寨不到一公里，三个功能区互相映衬，有机结合，旅游接待服务中心、旅游公厕、停车场的修建让整个景点的旅游接待能力得到进一步提升。

寨栽民族村寨，除了具有原始、古朴、幽静、野趣之外，更有一种灵动和秀丽的美。在自然中巧妙地融休闲、度假、娱乐于一体，成为人们远离车马喧嚣、回归自然，享受宁静、放松身心的乡村旅游好去处。

二、瑶山拉片民族村寨

瑶山拉片民族村寨全寨122户631人，是一个纯瑶族聚居的少数民族村寨。2014年，国家民委授予其“中国少数民族特色村寨”。地处黔桂边缘，是贵州高原向广西丘陵过渡地带，属南方喀斯特地区岩溶地貌，紧靠荔波县大七孔、小七孔景区，特殊的地貌与周围美丽迷人的田园景观融为一体，气候宜人，环境幽静，置身其间，心旷神怡，是度假避暑的好去处。村内至今仍然完整保存“白裤瑶”丰富多彩的民风民俗，拥有自己独具一格的建筑文化（禾仓、吊脚楼）、服饰文化（蜡染、刺绣已列为国家级非物质文化遗产）、铜鼓文化（猴鼓舞已列为省非物质文化保护）、陀螺文化、瑶族风情演出等，是乡村民族旅游、体验少数民族风情的理想之地。2012年，瑶族古寨旅游人次达3万人，总收入500多万元，已成为国家AAA级景点。在贵州日报报业集团、省民委、省住建厅、省文化厅、省旅游局等共同承办，展现贵州独特的民族民间传统文化和丰富的乡村旅游资源的活动中，瑶山乡拉片村凭借幽美迷人的环境及独特的民族文化成功入围“贵州最具魅力民族村寨”。

三、驾欧乡联山村（联山湾）

联山湾位于荔波县驾欧乡，是依山傍水式的布依族群居区，以闻名天下的小七孔景区和大七孔景区为依托，以山秀水美的乡村田园风光和布依族农耕文化为特色，以山水景观为灵魂，联山湾风光秀丽，水洁风清，水面平静，视野宽阔，两岸青山翠绿，村庄错落有致，仿佛是一首田园山水

乡村旅游景区——联山湾

诗，被许多游客称为“世外桃源”。由于自然风光优美、民族风情浓郁，通过专家、游客、网友的综合评定，联山湾先后获得了“中华民族文化名牌景区”和“中国最佳文体休闲旅游品牌景区”的荣誉称号。2010年5月22日，在贵州日报报业集团首届新闻作品奖表彰大会上，由莫雄亮、韦开典两位作者以联山湾为素材写的《荔波农民自创民谣唱火家乡旅游》的文章，荣获二等奖。浓郁的布依民族风情和山水农耕文化色彩的乡村民谣——《联山湾》使其成为热门的乡村旅游点。

四、水葩古寨

水葩古寨是荔波农业休闲观光旅游的新亮点，有水葩古寨旅居庄园投入150万元进行建设。水葩古寨旅居庄园拥有展示厅1栋，游客接待中心1栋，KTV房1栋，客栈4栋，住宿木屋9栋共111个床位，餐饮木屋2栋可同时容纳200人就餐。旅居庄园后续还将投入资金进一步增加庄园服务等设施，使这座庄园打造成生态环境优美，旅游和休闲功能完善的精品美丽乡村旅游目的地。

五、江风布依村

江风布依村位于荔波县东南部翁昂乡境内，地处世界自然遗产地茂兰世界级自然保护区腹地，距荔波县城28公里，距茂兰保护区重点科考景区——凉水井“石上森林”5公里，属于荔波旅游景区环线，交通十分便利。江风村寨四面环山，到处田园铺展，古树参天，溪水常流；村庄、田园和山水交相辉映；溶洞神秘莫测，有着得天独厚的山水田园风光。村寨较为完整地保留着古香古色的布依居民、古塔、古桥、古法造纸坊、天然神峰等古迹。这里建筑的规划布局也很有考察，房屋做工精细，建设样式优美，很有布依民居特色。每栋建筑正面基本上都朝一个方向，外表相似，分散布局，小巷连接家家户户，户与户道路纵横交错，宛如网状，如同迷宫。这里的布依风情更为浓厚。每逢春节、农历三月三、四月八、六月六、九月九等传统佳节或遇上婚丧嫁娶重大活动，村民都会自发组织在一起，表演布依傩戏、矮人舞和唱布依古歌、花灯戏等欢度节日。布依古歌悠扬委婉，声调中带着浓浓的乡音，浓厚的和声宛如天籁，让人回味无穷。

第四章 旅游综合管理

第一节 景区保护

从1986年起，在景区开发建设的同时，按照“严格保护、统一管理、合理开发、永续利用”的原则，对景区各种资源实施保护和利用。

1992年7月，风景管理处与县公安局联合发出《关于加强荔波樟江风景名胜区管理的通告》，禁止乱砍滥伐、毁林开荒、伐薪烧炭、放火烧山、捕捉野生动物，禁止开山采石、开挖土方和破坏景区环境、景物、景观。1995年3月实施《荔波樟江风景名胜区管理暂行办法》。

2001年7月，实施《黔南布依族苗族自治州荔波樟江风景名胜区管理条例》。2004年，县政府颁布实施《荔波樟江风景名胜区监察实施细则》。

1995—2004年，10年间查处破坏景区资源事件20余起，捣毁在景区内烧炭的炭窑30多个。2002—2003年，荔波县政府对小七孔景区实施了景区移民工程，共计移民89户。

2007年，根据景区资源的观赏、文化、科学价值和环境现状，结合世界自然遗产地保护，以及景区中水体、土壤、空气、植被等生存环境状况，对景区进行分级分类保护。分级保护即将景区划分为岩溶地貌、森林植被、河流瀑布、名胜古迹、民族民俗五大类，以分级保护为主，分类保护为辅，分级中有分类，保护景区的自然景观特色和科学文化价值。2008年，实施小七孔景区环保车使用项目，限制汽车进入小七孔景区，北京美嘉环球旅行社有限责任公司经过竞标获得环保车项目特许经营权。同年。制定《荔波樟江风景名胜区古树名木保护暂行办法（试行）》，对景区古树名木实施挂牌、建档管理，记录生态环境和生长情况。持续对景区生态停车场进行绿化，景区内种植本土树木，增加景区森林覆盖率。每年邀请州、县环保部门对景区水质进行监测。

2014年11月3日，荔波樟江景区举行创建无垃圾景区启动仪式，创建良好的景区风貌

1978年以来一直加强景区森林防火工作，组建景区义务消防队伍，每年在小七孔景区开展消防演练；制定景区森林防火预案，建立景区森林防火巡查机制，与周边村组实施景区森林防火联防联控。2009年，在小七孔景区卧龙潭、天钟洞后洞和大七孔景区板潭、坡旧分别修建了4座火情瞭望台，对大七孔、小七孔景区森林防火实施动态监控，同年购置了40万元大七孔、小七孔景区遗产地消防设施设备。2011年开始开展无烟景区建设工作。2015年年初，环大七孔、小七孔景区公路竣工通车，小七孔景区实现封闭管理。2015年10月获得首批37个“中国森林氧吧”称号。

从20世纪80年代开始严格保护景区水体、土壤、植被、大气，查处破坏和影响景区环境、景物、景观的违法行为，景区水体、土壤、植被、大气得到提高，自然山体完整，森林覆盖率达到75%以上。

第二节　旅游服务

一、旅游交通

县城距贵新高速公路、黔桂铁路36公里，通往县外公路全部为柏油路或水泥路，游客可从贵州的独山、麻尾、三都、凯里，广西的南丹、环江进入荔波景区。

1999年5月，经县旅游部门与铁路部门联系，利用金茂铁路资源，开通“樟江号”柳州—泗亭旅游列车。是年10月，开通金城江—荔波旅游列车，在平寨下车。2002年7月，开通广东湛江—荔波旅游列车，在泗亭下车。2005年6月，开通南宁—荔波旅游列车，在泗亭下车。2008年8月1日，荔波机场正式通航，增加旅游航空线路。

樟江景区南靠黔桂铁路线，北邻国道210，东靠荔波机场，贵新高速公路已接通小七孔景区，县城通往各景区的交通主干道全面贯通，使荔波基本形成了以航空、铁路、公路为主的便捷顺畅的立体旅游交通网络。截至2015年，景区共新建停车场17座，贯穿整个景区的主要道路总长15.15公里，新建成游览步道约23公里，使景区内旅游基础设施得到了全面改善，内部交通十分方便。招商成立了专业的景区交通企业——荔波美嘉环球旅游开发公司，购置100多部中高档旅游观光中转车，负责承载游客在景区游览。

为加强景区资源保护与管理，樟江景区2013年以来贷款0.5亿元用于景区扩容升级，实施了大七孔、小七孔景区集散中心项目，该项目总投资1.5亿元，建设内容包括旅游服务接待中心、管理房、生态停车场（可同时容纳2000辆小车、300辆大巴），该项目是集票务、咨询、停车、购物、餐饮于一体的多功能项目，2015年“五一”投入使用。投资3.2亿元的环景区公路已建成通车，彻底改变省道206贯穿小七孔景区的现状，为大七孔、小七孔景区的封闭式管理奠定了良好的基础。

同时进一步完善了主要的交通设施，包括：1.荔波航线开发，引进云南英安航空“荔波号”飞机入驻荔波机场，在原有航班的基础上，于2014年4月加密开通了荔波至贵阳、荔波至重庆、荔波至广州、荔波至深圳的航班。2015年开通了荔波至成都、海口、上海、昆明、南宁等航线。组建了荔波县航空旅游咨询服务有限公司，运营英安航空公司“荔波号”航班。2.增设荔波县城及麻尾至大七孔、小七孔景区旅游专线车，使旅游专线车由原来的每天2个班次增加至现在的每天10个班次以上，为游客构建更为舒适、便捷的交通环境。3.按照AAAAA级景区标准将大七孔景区停车场全部改造为生态停车场，并合理设置景区大车、小车停车区域，规范停车场标志标牌。

二、宾馆饭店

县内旅游业兴起后，随着游客的不断增多，县城的宾馆、饭店也逐渐增加。2000年6月，经黔南州星级宾馆初评领导小组评定，荔波县阳光大酒店为黔南州第二批旅游涉外定点单位，这是荔波县第一家旅游涉外定点接待单位。

2002年，荔波旅游宾馆饭店业进入快速发展时期。11月，荔波华城阳光酒店被贵州省旅游局评定为三星级旅游饭店，成为全县第一家星级宾馆。2003年10月，县旅游局组织荔波星级旅游宾馆中层以上管理人员十余人参加贵州饭店有限公司、贵州新迪酒店管理公司举办的第三期酒店管理人员业务培训班，参加学习人员取得国家旅游局颁发的“全国旅游行业管理人员岗位培训证书”。是年，组织县内宾馆申报星级宾馆，申报成功16家，其中三星级1个、二星级9个、一星级6个。2004年2月，州旅游局、县旅游局联合开展全州星级饭店复核工作，加强星级饭店管理。此后，每年对县内星级饭店进行复核检查。2007年，荔波三力酒店被评定为四星级酒店，为县内第一家四星级酒店。2008年，县城拥有宾馆酒店112家（其中四星级1家、三星级7家、二星级20家、其他84家），床位数达11600张。同时二级乡村旅社20家，住宿床位60多张，可容纳近百人就餐，主要分布在荔波至小七孔景区沿途、洞塘板寨等地。县城主次街道还分布有大小餐馆近100家，有小吃街1条，各种特色饭菜、特色小吃供顾客选择、享用。截至2015年，全县有宾馆酒店近200家，12000个床位，其中，星级酒店34家、在建五星级酒店4家、四星级酒店5家。建成一批富有乡村特色的“农家乐”，据有关资料统计共有365家。

三、旅行社及导游

2003年，取缔非法旅行社1家，查获虚假旅游广告1起。2004年12月，荔波县樟江旅行社有限公司经省旅游局批准挂牌成立，为县内第一家旅行社，主要经营国内旅游业务。2007年9月，荔波深黔山水旅行社有限责任公司经贵州省旅游局审核批准挂牌成立，颁发“国内旅行社业务经营许可证”，主要经营国内旅游业务。

2000年6月，县旅游局组织县内导游人员参加省旅游局举办的导游培训班，7人参加全国导游人员资格考试。2003年4月，全省旅游景区（点）导游员资格考试黔南考区设在荔波。考试前，县旅游部门聘请省内高校旅游专业教师对县内考生79人进行理论知识、现场导游、礼貌礼仪等培训。在全州参加考试的91人中，荔波通过资格考试76人。2004年3月，县旅游局在全县导游队伍中开展“树新风、树形象”主题教育活动，通过培训、检查等方式，加强导游队伍管理。

2005年5月，在州旅游局面向全省公开招聘的60名专职导游统一培训中，荔波县通过培训考试获得州旅游局颁发的景点导游证10人。2006年2月，县旅游局向社会公开选拔10人参加省旅游局委托省旅游学校举办的学制一年导游讲解员强化培训班，全部通过考试获得省旅游局颁发的全省旅游行业培训合格证。2007年7月，从县机关、乡（镇）、学校抽调近两年刚毕业的大学生50人进行为期3个月的导游集中培训，承担省旅发大会期间导游任务，获得县旅游局颁发的景点导游证，成为兼职导游人员。至2008年，全县获得国家级导游资格证人员15人。截至2015年，全县有旅行社13家（其中分社8家），旅游定点接待单位9家。

四、旅游商品

2003年，县委、县政府制定《关于鼓励和扶持旅游商品开发经营的若干规定》，鼓励和扶持社会各界投资开发旅游商品。到2008年，县内开发的旅游商品主要有风猪、青梅酒、瑶山鸡、酸肉、米片、牛皮糖、瑶山血粑鸭、水族银饰、水族马尾绣、布依土花布、民族服饰、凉席、竹编、芒编、藤编等。县城及景区有旅游购物商店30余家，其中大型购物超市有富万家超市、大鹏购物中心、永汇超市、世纪华联超市，购物商场主要集中在县城主街道，部分景区内设有购物商店。截至2015年，全县旅游商品店10家、摊点近100个、生产企业5家。

第三节 旅游安全与卫生管理

一、安全管理

1992—2015年，先后在景区内设景区监察大队、监察保护科、景区派出所、景区执法大队、景区社会治安综合治理办公室、景区治安联防队、民兵连等安全管理机构。成立景区治安大队。景区治安以巡逻防范为主，同时组织群众参与景区治安管理，增强景区监控能力，及时排出影响游客安全的隐患。景区安全管理严格按照建设部颁发的《风景名胜区安全管理规定》执行。樟江景区管理处与县政府签订《水上安全管理责任书》，先后制定《樟江景区安全检查制度》《消防安全教育培训制度》《樟江景区安全事故的报告和调查处理制度》《防火巡查制度》《防火检查制度》《灭火和应急疏散预案演练制度》《消防安全巡查制度》《消防器材管理制度》等，在危险段增设安全警示牌，增设专职安全员。定期、不定期组织人员对景区的安全设施进行检查，发现隐患，及时排出。

景区设置专职安全员、巡逻员、水上救护员70余人进行日常设备检查、巡逻及定点蹲守等。在旅游旺季时增加安全人员30人，总计人数达100人。同时制定和完善15项景区旅游安全预案，4项特殊情况安全处置预案，签订《荔波樟江景区旅游安全管理工作责任书》。署汶么管理站根据其安全责任区域，每天进行巡查。定期组织工作人员进行安全专业知识业务培训，对应急预案进行演练，确保樟江景区应急反应迅速。

在景区的危险地带设置了安全防护栏、防滑网、警告标志、水上拉网等安全防护设施。配置消防灭火设备，安装了监控系统，景区摄像头达100个，全面监控景区旅游安全情况。在景点、栈道、桥梁、步道及其他易发危险地段设有中英文对照、规范、醒目的安全警告标志，游览须知标牌及安全警示符号。在小七孔、大七孔景区内各设有医务室一个，配备专门医务人员和常用药品，为游客提供基本医疗服务。并成立荔波樟江景区水上救援中心，有专业救生员9人，配备内部救援电话，与荔波县医院签订了专门的运送协议，确保实施快速有效的救援。

二、卫生管理

1992年，成立景区绿化环卫大队，负责景区的环境卫生工作，并组建由当地村民群众组成的景区卫生保洁队伍，制定保洁制度，划定保洁范围，由保洁员专门负责景区环境卫生工作。对景区内的单位、住户划定卫生责任区，实施“门前三包”，进行定期、不定期检查，发现问题，及时通知整改。在全省“黄果树杯”城市环境综合治理竞赛活动中，樟江景区管理处获1998—1999年度成绩显著奖、2002—2003年度第三名。

多年来，景区不断完善各项环卫管理制度，定期对保洁人员进行业务培训，实施景区环卫巡查考核奖惩制度，实现景区垃圾日产日清。2013年11月樟江景区实施全国首个无垃圾景区创建工作，为游客免费提供环保垃圾袋。到2015年年底，景区有专职保洁员91人（游旺季时会临聘部分保洁人员），配置垃圾转运站5座，垃圾清运车4辆（其中1辆为小型三轮摩托清运车），洒水车1辆，各式垃圾箱（桶）300个，旅游厕所26个（其中星级厕所22个）。

第四节 景区达标管理及创建AAAAA级景区

一、达标管理

2003年10月，根据省文明办、建设厅、旅游局联合下发的《关于评选第二批文明风景区的通知》，荔波风管处、县旅游局成立创建贵州省第二批文明风景名胜区领导小组，开展文明风景区的创建工作。2004年3月，州文明办、州建设局、州旅游局受省文明办委托，组成检查组，对荔波樟江风景区创建文明风景名胜区的各项工作进行检查验收。2004年11月，经省文明办组织评选后，荔波樟江风景名胜区被评为全省第二批省级文明景区。

2007年3月，成立荔波县AAAA级旅游景区申报领导小组，在县旅游局设办公室，开展AAAA级旅游景区申报工作。按照AAAA级旅游景区《服务质量与环境质量评分细则》标准要求，樟江景区分别从旅游交通、游览、旅游安全、卫生、邮电服务、旅游购物、综合管理、资源及环境保护8个方面对景区进行整改、完善。2008年11月26日，荔波樟江景区通过国家旅游局旅游景区质量等级评定组评审验收，专家组认为，荔波樟江风景名胜区完全达到国家AAAA级景区标准。2009年1月，获国家AAAA级旅游景区。

从2003年至2015年荔波樟江风景区达标管理荣获：2013年12月，荔波樟江景区获得《国家生态旅游示范区》称号。2014年1月，荔波县荣登2013年“美丽中国”十佳旅游县（区）。2014年9月，荔波樟江景区入选广东国民休闲旅游示范单位。2014年12月，荔波樟江景区被评为贵州十佳旅游景区。2014年年底，樟江景区被评为贵州旅游最具公众影响力“十大品牌”。2015年7月，荔波樟江景区成功申报为国家AAAAA级旅游景区。

二、创建国家AAAAA级旅游景区

创建荔波樟江景区为国家AAAAA级旅游景区工作从2009年启动，时任省委书记栗战书、赵克志分别在贵州省第六届、第七届、第八届旅游产业发展大会上强调荔波要积极创造条件实现AAAAA创建目标，贵州省、黔南州旅游局每年安排经费给予景区建设补贴，并将荔波樟江景区创建国家AAAAA级旅游景区作为近几年的一项工作重点纳入议事日程。2012年8月，黔南州人民政府在州十三届人民代表大会第一次会议的政府工作报告中指出：“要把荔波世界自然遗产地、平塘……打造成AAAAA级景区”。县委、县政府成立了“荔波县创建国家AAAAA级旅游景区工作领导小组”，由县委书记、县人大主任、县政协主席任顾问，县长任组长，县四家班子相关领导任副组长。领导小组负责整个创建工作的组织协调，多次召开专题会议研究解决创建工作中存在的困难和问题。为营造全民参与创建的氛围，县委、县政府召开全县创建动员大会，组建创建工作机构，营造创建氛围，制定工作方

2012年8月2日，荔波AAAAA级旅游景区创建启动

案，落实工作责任，加强督促检查。2009年10月与云南广目经济信息咨询有限公司签订《技术服务协议》。聘请该公司指导荔波樟江景区申报国家AAAAA级旅游景仅编制相关文本资料。2013年3月，荔波县政府与德安杰环球顾问集团密切合作，对申报文本进行4次修改，同时该集团还聘请国家旅游局、中国地理研究院的相关专家和学者到荔波进行创建相关知识培训，均取得了良好的效果，在2013年10月15日国家旅游局组织的景观质量评审会上，专家组组长刘峰认为："荔波是我现在到的1000多个县市景区中最美的，它的水是可以亲近的，山是非常有特色、有灵魂的，它的美令上帝吃醋，完全符合国家AAAAA级旅游景区的景观质量标准"。专家组对申报文本也给予高度赞扬，专家组认为："申报文本的精美堪称是全国所有申报文本中的典型范本。"

为确保创建成功，县委、县政府对照《服务质量与环境质量评分细则》，从旅游交通、游览、旅游安全、卫生、邮电服务、旅游购物、综合管理、资源及环境保护8个方面进行整治，从2009年至2015年，通过国家投资、银行贷款等方式投入景区软硬件设施建设资金近2亿元，不断完善景区的软硬件设施建设。2009年以来，主要完成外部交通环境改善、环景区公路建设、智慧景区项目、景区扩容升级、规范标示标牌、旅游宣传促销、景区接待设施、景区规范管理、资源环境保护等方面的项目建设。2013年10月15日，荔波樟江景区创建国家AAAAA级旅游景区通过国家旅游局组织的景观质量评审后，县委、县政府着手筹备迎接国家旅游局组织的专家暗访工作，要求景区工作人员做到每天都是暗访日，做好景区的管理和服务。还多次评聘有关旅游专家对景区进行模拟暗访和明察，发现的问题进行整改。旅游部门高质量制作专题片为创建添色。在2013年10月15日国家旅游局组织的景观质量评审会上，专家组认为："荔波旅游资源富集，汇报材料专题片制作水平起点高，质量好，多角度介绍了旅游资源"。

县委、县政府超前谋划，营造创建氛围。通过召开动员大会，悬挂横幅，发放传单，安装大型户外广告牌，在电视、报刊、网络等媒体专题报道等形式，营造浓厚的创建工作氛围，使全县上下深刻认识到AAAAA级旅游景区创建工作事关荔波旅游形象和旅游品牌的提升、事关荔波旅游经济的优化升级、事关荔波能否成功跻身全国一流旅游景区行列，意义重大，影响深远。使群众积极参与创建工作。为了AAAAA创建工作，县政府在县级各有关部门抽调精兵强将，会同景区的专业工作人员一起集中办公，结合景区实际，制定《荔波县创建国家AAAAA级旅游景区工作实施方案》，统一部署，强化指导和督查，落实工作责任。

2014年11月10日，国家旅游局专家组对樟江景区进行了暗访，2014年12月24日，荔波樟江景区收到全国旅游景区质量等级评定委员会发来的《关于对贵州省荔波樟江景区暗访情况》的通报后，县委、县政府首先成立了以分管副县长为组长，相关部门领导为成员的整改领导小组；其次，召开专题会议，研究部署整改问题；制定整改方案，落实整改责任，明确整改时限。2015年1月25日，完成全部整改任务。

2015年7月5日，全国旅游资源规划开发质量评定委员会再次组织专家对荔波樟江景区的服务质量与环境质量进行了实地检查，经过专家评定，荔波樟江景区的服务质量与环境质量得分955分，达到国家AAAAA级旅游景区标准。2015年7月13日，国家旅游局公布了国家AAAAA级旅游景区名单，荔波樟江景区榜上有名，成为贵州第四个，黔南首个国家AAAAA级旅游景区。

第五章 旅游宣传与经济效益

第一节 宣传活动

1986年，《人民日报》、中央电视台、中央人民广播电台、上海《文汇报》（海外版）到荔波采风，报道小七孔景区资源。小七孔景区被联合国教科文组织誉为“地球腰带上的绿宝石”“石头上的森林”，开始吸引国内游客。同时，旅游管理部门组织县内摄影爱好者到景区拍摄各景点照片，在贵阳、都匀等地展出，吸引游客。此后，新华社贵州分社记者周浩荣的摄影报道，州人大常委会原副主任王巩汉的《荔波风光天下奇》、州文联作家杨路塔的《小七孔传说》等专著，对宣传荔波小七孔旅游产生广泛影响。

1998年，樟江景区管理处投入资金15万元，与省建设厅、省建设报社在《贵州建设报》刊登“荔波樟江风景名胜区”专版，在《贵州风景名胜》画册上专版刊登樟江景区的图片和文字介绍。是年10月，参加上海1998年中国国际旅游交易会，这是荔波县首次参加大型国际旅游交易会。

1999年，编辑出版画册《地球腰带上的绿宝石——荔波》；在县城及贵阳等地设置大型旅游宣传灯箱广告牌；参加在昆明举办的1999年国内旅游交易会；制作完成《荔波风光天下奇》宣传光盘。

2000年8月，参加重庆旅游交易会，与重庆部分旅行社达成合作协议。10月，参加上海国际旅游交易会。11月，参加昆明国际旅游交易会；在《贵州日报》《贵州都市报》《贵州商报》、贵州电视台等新闻媒体进行报道宣传；11月，中央电视台《正大综艺》《绿色时空》栏目和贵州电视台《今晚快看》《开心旅程》栏目、武汉电视台《天涯伴君行》栏目及成都电视台拍摄荔波风光专题片；与中央电视台、贵州电视台国际部等新闻单位协作拍摄景区宣传片。

2002年，组织参加武汉、重庆、西安、南京、上海等地5次大型国际、国内旅游交易会，发放各种宣传资料2万份；中国台湾自由自存杂志社、贵州都市报社、贵州新报社记者到荔波景区开展采风活动并进行报道；贵州电视台摄制《一生必游之地——荔波》；全国10家卫视在荔波开展“聚焦绿宝石”大型采风活动；贵州电视台《新旅游》栏目摄制组拍摄荔波旅游资源和少数民族风情。

2004年4月，黔南州组织都匀、独山、平塘、三都、荔波5县（市）在贵阳、桂林、河池举办大型旅游推介活动。6月，参加杭州旅游交易会。9月，参加第四届重庆旅游交易会。11月，参加上海国际旅游交易会；中央电视台《旅游指南》栏目、西部频道、贵州电视台、厦门电视台、黔南电视台、国家地理杂志社、两岸四地摄影家、《世界博览》等媒体记者到荔波采风。

2005年，邀请北京、香港、深圳、重庆、广州、南宁、贵阳等地200家旅行社、媒体到荔波采风；参加黔南州在贵阳、桂林举办的旅游推介会。3月，参加黔南州政府在北京举办的黔南旅游推介会。4月，参加桂林国内旅游交易会。6月，参加州政府在深圳举办的黔南旅游推介会。10月，参加龙里药博会及省旅游局在北京举办的红色旅游宣传周活动。11月，参加昆明国际旅游交易会。12月，县委、县政府在贵阳举行“荔波梅花节”新闻发布会；县委、县政府举办“百位名家、百家媒体走进中国最美的地方——荔波”大型采风活动。

2006年，在贵州电视台、中央电视台《请您欣赏》栏目、武汉电视台、南宁电视台等电视媒体展开宣传；在《贵州日报》《贵州都市报》《南宁晚报》《贵州旅游时尚》等报纸杂志上进行旅游宣传。

2007年，组织宣传人员到南宁、柳州、广州、深圳、贵阳等地宣传第二届梅花节活动，参加苏州国际旅游交易会，广州旅游交易会，在贵阳—新寨、贵阳—黄果树、贵阳—毕节、南宁—水任等高速公路上设立旅游广告牌。

2008年，在贵阳、重庆、成都、南宁、广州、深圳、珠海等地举办第三届梅花节推介活动，参加郑州国内旅游交易会，参加黔南州在南宁、河池举办的黔南旅游推介会，在《当代贵州》刊载8期荔波专题宣传页。

2009年至2015年，建立有荔波樟江景区网站（www.lbzjjq.com）和荔波旅游官方网站（www.liboly.com），荔波旅游官方微信、微博宣传平台。开展媒体营销。利用电视、报纸、杂志等媒体大力宣传景区资源和旅游。邀请著名歌手韩磊到荔波景区拍摄大型MTV宣传片《萨尔银多的梦》，先后制作了电视宣传片《荔波风光天下奇》《荔波有多美》《喀斯特神话》《梦幻荔波》等近10部，其中《美丽的荔波》等宣传片在贵州电视台多次播放，《多彩贵州——樟江景区》在凤凰卫视进行了专题介绍。中央电视台《民歌中国》《乡村大世界》《走遍中国》和《请您欣赏》等栏目也对景区进行了介绍。2015年又制作了《山水天堂荔波》中英文版、《荔波冬韵》旅游视频宣传片上传到优酷、土豆等媒体进行宣传，制作《心灵的港湾荔波》视频并在中国香港、澳门、台湾地区及亚洲进行投放，与土豆网合作，拍摄《荔波旅游囧记》上、中、下三集，每集浏览量突破100万次，拍摄《小苹果》等视频，与乐途网合作，加入乐途旅游目的地。在《中国旅游报》《贵州都市报》等省内外各大报纸及成都、重庆、南宁等地主要报刊发布荔波旅游宣传信息。在中国旅游新闻网、中国广播网、贵州旅游时讯、金黔在线等数十家网站播发荔波旅游新闻和相关宣传信息；与上海景域集团开展荔波旅游网络营销及线下推广合作；与北京德安杰合作开展荔波旅游新媒体营销等活动。

荔波旅游宣传营销在2009年至2015年间，组建旅游联盟，与省内黄果树、龙宫、西江苗寨、南江大峡谷、织金洞、梵净山等主要景区组建了贵州精品旅游景区联盟，联合营销。

开展主题营销，利用贵广高铁即将开通的契机，走进珠江三角开展“跟着高铁去旅游”主题营销活动。还精心策划“爱在荔波”浪漫主题系列活动，与贵阳广播电视台联合举办2014年“‘10·27’爱在旅途，情定荔波”大型户外相亲活动。荔波广告宣传除常规性的宣传广告外，在香港地铁灯箱、高速公路、贵阳龙洞堡机场新航站楼、空调列车、荔波机场、县城及景区出入口等重要载体投放平面和视频宣传广告，制作荔波旅游专线车车身旅游宣传广告，景区休息亭廊图片广告，自办了《荔波旅游报》，印制了画册、折页、套封、明信片、手提袋等多种宣传资料。

第二节　节会活动

一、梅花报春节

2006年1月12日，举办首届“中国·荔波万亩梅花报春节暨原生态文化旅游月”活动，活动时间一个月。省、州、县部分领导出席开幕式，近百家新闻媒体现场采访报道开幕式盛况，上万名游客参加节庆活动。活动当天下午，九段围棋手、享有“棋圣”称号的聂卫平应邀到万亩梅花园，与黔南州选拔的12名选手进行围棋对弈，并作围棋演示，解答围棋爱好者提出的各种问题。活动期间，推出黔桂两省（区）陀螺邀请赛、黔桂两省（区）猛牛争霸赛、书画、奇石、根雕、盆景、摄影展等系列活动，大七孔景区、小七孔景区的门票实行5折优惠，吸引数万名游客到荔波观光。

2007年2月2日，举办第二届“中国·荔波万亩梅花报春节暨2007年贵州赏花游首游式”活动，活动时间一个月。活动期间，除观赏清逸脱俗、幽香扑面的梅花外，还举办情醉梅乡民族歌舞演唱会、“梅林清音”、百名“花仙子”古筝演奏等15个异彩纷呈的主题活动；九段围棋手聂卫平，著名讲棋师王元、毛佳君到荔波参加活动，与围棋爱好者对弈；对散客和旅行社团实行景区门票优惠政策，吸引游客观花赏景。

2007年11月，第二届贵州旅游产业发展大会文艺演出

2008年1月22日，举办第三届“中国·荔波万亩梅花报春节暨2008年贵州赏花游”活动，活动持续一个月。1月22日活动开幕式当天，凡组团到樟江景区旅游免收门票，漂游服务费优惠50%；5车以上自驾车队，张贴活动主题车身贴的，免收所有景区门票。1月23日—2月21日，樟江景区门票4折优惠，小七孔天钟洞门票、鸳鸯湖船票、大七孔游船票优惠50%，水春河漂游服务费6折，万亩梅园景区门票5折。

二、第二届省旅游产业发展大会及交易会

2007年11月6日，在大七孔景区召开由黔南州承办的全省第二届旅游产业发展大会。大会期间，举办首届中国南方喀斯特文化旅游节、中国南方喀斯特世界自然遗产展示中心开馆仪式、中国南方喀斯特文化旅游座谈会、招商引资签约仪式、荔波机场通航仪式等活动。当晚，举办大型文艺晚会，演出山水情景剧《荔波荡漾》，贵州卫视直播晚会实况。

另外，樟江景区还采取“走出去，请进来”的方式对景区进行推荐，多次参加了贵州省旅游商品交易会、中国国际旅游交易会、2014年广州国际旅游展览会、第十七届海峡两岸旅游行业联谊会、2014年第十一届东亚（辽宁）国际旅游交易会、2014年杭州国际旅游交易会、2014年第三届上海国际自驾游博览会、第三届中国（北京）国家服务贸易交易会、四川成都音乐节、2014年重庆狂欢节、2014年北京旅游博览会等大型旅游推介活动。邀请省内外旅行社、知名人士到荔波采风，并与旅游企业合作，大力开展宣传。

2009—2015年，荔波县旅游又新推出《水韵樟江》民族文化实景演艺、竹筏漫游樟江、樟江经典文化游等旅游产品，旅游业逐步从单一的生态观光旅游向多元化旅游过渡。荔波县先后获全省首批优先发展重点旅游区、革命老区、国家卫生县城、全国科普示范县、国家级生态示范区、中国最美的地方、全国十大最具潜力景区、中国最佳山水旅游文化名县、中国最佳民族生态旅游名县、国

际王牌旅游目的地、世界人与生物圈保护区等美誉称号。2013年1月5日，第三届中国旅游产业发展年会在北京隆重召开，全国旅游行业盘点2013年度行业收获，展望2014年度产业走势，发布“2013年中国旅游风云榜”。荔波上榜，成为2013年“美丽中国”十佳旅游县（区）。

第三节 旅游经济效益

县内旅游业兴起后，县委、县政府实施“旅游强县、旅游兴县、旅游富县、旅游活县、旅游热县”的发展战略，将旅游业作为龙头产业进行投资开发，经不断打造和向外推介，1996年，荔波被中国生态旅游专业委员会列为全国22条生态旅游线之一，游客不断增多，旅游收入不断增长。2003年6月，县委、县政府出台《关于加快旅游发展的决定》。2004年2月，省政府将荔波综合旅游区确定为贵州省首批优先发展重点旅游区。全县旅游业经过20多年开发建设，从无到有、从小到大，旅游综合收入连年上升。“一业兴、百业举”的社会和经济效益十分突出。景区自开放以来，取得了良好的社会效益，带动了地方社会就业，截至2015年，景区工作人员有90%以上为本地人。景区旅游发展对地方经济带动作用显著，拉动了本地“食、住、行、游、购、娱”六大产业。

荔波旅游发展加速，产业优势突显，已发展成为荔波重要的经济支柱产业。全县旅游接待人次从2008年的187.2万人次增加到2012年的405万人次，年均增长率为21.2%。旅游综合收入从2008年的13.4亿元增加到2012年的34.41亿元，年均增长率为26.6%。樟江景区旅游接待人次从2008年的78.9万人次增加到2012年的161万人次，年均增长率为19.5%。樟江景区门票收入从2008年的1301万元增加到2012年的5800万元，年均增长率为45%。

2014年，荔波樟江景区旅游接待人数达555.36万人次，景区直接收入1.42亿元，全县旅游综合收入达54.9亿元，实现了历史性突破。

1990—2015年全县旅游收入统计表

表14－2

年度	旅游人数（万人次）	综合收入（万元）	年度	旅游人数（万人次）	综合收入（万元）
1990	—	10.00	2003	22.00	5020.00
1991	—	15.00	2004	28.00	6400.00
1992	3.00	64.32	2005	55.00	8400.00
1993	3.20	180.00	2006	98.00	17000.00
1994	5.70	440.00	2007	116.52	8.89（亿元）
1995	5.30	681.60	2008	187.20	13.40（亿元）
1996	4.60	1144.00	2009	221.30	16.30（亿元）
1997	4.10	1720.00	2010	263.10	20.67（亿元）
1998	4.60	1981.60	2011	322.40	25.88（亿元）
1999	9.00	2077.60	2012	405.80	34.41（亿元）
2000	10.00	2340.80	2013	521.90	44.73（亿元）
2001	16.00	3828.00	2014	636.80	54.90（亿元）
2002	22.00	5268.00	2015	1000.20	86.75（亿元）

第十五篇
商贸　供销合作社

荔波县商业贸易部门、供销合作社1978年以来适时进行了一系列改革，国营企业和供销合作商业推行6种类型的承包经营方式，改变了过去统得过死的现象，使封闭经济变为开放经济。1992年3月，为加快商业体制改革步伐，县商业局成立“四放开”领导小组，在全县商业系统逐步推行“四放开”做法。1993年，进一步深化商业体制改革，转换企业经营机制，全面推行国有民营承包。至年底，百货、民贸、食品、糖酒、饮食5个公司35个柜组推行“国有民营”，占整个国营商业门户柜组的96%。2004年12月，县成立企业改革领导小组，商业下属各公司清产核资和资产评估并制定实施方案。在国有商业不断改革机制的同时全县商业个体户蓬勃发展，几乎所有的当街房间，都被开发成了门市。2006年起，县商业系统实施“万村千乡市场”工程。到2008年，全县个体工商户达近3000户，从业人员4000多人。2008年，金锣湾被评为“全国百城万店无假货”示范街，大鹏购物中心为“百城万店无假货”示范店。

2004年9月，县政府成立荔波县供销社系统改革领导小组，2005年3月，由县长担任组长，加强改革改制工作领导。供销社按“界定权责、量化资产、全员安置、置换身份、优化整合、转换机制、谨慎稳妥、稳定发展”的总体思路，进行改革改制。到2008年年底，全县参加改革改制的供销社所属企业7个公司，人数142人。

第一章 商 业

第一节 商业体制改革

一、行政管理机构改革

1978—1994年，县商业局管理全县商业企业，商业局的内设机构有办公室、业务股、保卫股、财经股，行政编制11人。1995年机构改革，县商业局改为县商业总公司，原商业局的行政职能划归县经济贸易委员会。1996年，商业行政管理职能划属县商业总公司，县商业总公司政企合一。

2002年7月，县商业总公司改为县商业贸易总公司，其行政职能（包括屠宰办事业编制5人）划归县经济贸易局，县商业贸易总公司保留总经理、财务、统计各1人，下有百货公司、民族贸易公司、食品公司、饮食服务公司、糖酒公司5个公司。2006年8月，总公司人员增至4人，至2008年机构人员不变。

二、企业管理体制改革

1978—1983年，商业企业实行计划管理体制。1983年，属于县商业局管理的药材公司划属县经济委员会管理。

随着经济体制改革的推行，食品公司于1983年实行承包经营，以站、场、柜、组、点为单位，职工工资与销售额挂钩。

1984年，糖烟酒公司将卷烟销售业务划归烟草公司，改为糖酒公司，并从1984年起实行承包经营，以门市、组为单位，按营业额提成，工资浮动。

1985年以后，百货公司实行承包经营责任制，以柜、组为单位，按营业额百元含量比例分配工资。

1989年起，按照政企分开、所有权与经营权适当分离的原则，落实企业经营自主权和经营责任制，企业自主经营、自负盈亏。国营商业推行6种类型的承包经营方式，即按完成销售任务保基本工资，超产奖励，完不成任务按完成比例递减工资；工资和奖金与购销业务挂钩，试行浮动工资，上不封顶，下不保底；按工资和奖金占购销任务总额的比例，以实际完成任务计发工资和奖金（每百元销售含工资量）；按基本工资三七开或四六开，以少部分工资与购销任务挂钩，超产多发，完不成任务扣发；以柜、组为单位，利润包干；对边远的小门店、饮食服务业，实行租赁经营承包，定期上交承包租赁费。推行不同形式的承包经营后，商品品种增多，店容店貌得到改善，提高了服务质量。但利润大包干类型曾出现包盈不包亏问题。到1991年，除县饮食服务公司以外，商业各工业品销售公司都实行统一进货，设有批发部，对内调拨，对外批发。零售门市、柜、组实行百元含量工资制或按档案工资发放。

1992年3月，根据省、州、县政府的要求，成立“四放开”（经营放开、价格放开、用工放开、分配放开）工作领导小组，推进商业体制改革进程。10月，县商业局组织各公司经理到都匀参加学习“四放开”经验，之后，在商业系统逐步推行“四放开”。

1993年3月起，县商业系统转换企业经营机制，全面推行国有民营承包制。6月，县民贸公司通过对门市、柜、组测算，拟订承包方案，职工代表大会讨论通过后，首先实行国有民营个人承包经营，成为商业系统的示范单位。9月，百货、民贸、食品、糖酒、饮食服务5个公司35个柜、组先后实行国有民营，占整个国有商业门市、柜、组的96%。职工自筹资金，自由组合，自主经营，自负盈亏，统一纳税，包干上缴，逐年递增，定人、定商品、定铺底资金、定标底，公开竞争承包，合同“一定五年”不变，打破企业对门市、柜、组管得过死现象。国有民营承包后，消化库存商品价值60万元。1994年，增加国有民营柜、组5个。

1995年11月，在商业系统推行全员劳动合同制，各公司法人与公司职工分别签订劳动合同。

1997年，商业系统除盐业批发和食品公司猪肉、牛肉加工外，其余各公司的批发和零售门市部全部实行国有民营承包制度。9月，县商业系统各公司法人代表与公司工会主席签订集体劳动合同。年底，商业局组织各公司经理学习都匀市糖酒公司股份制改革经验后，起草全县商业企业股份制改革试点方案和县百货公司、民贸公司股份制试点测算办法。由于条件不成熟，企业上报的测算方案未得到县政府批复，股份制改革停止。

2000年，县盐业公司资产、人员整体划归贵州盐业（集团）公司。

2003年，县政府调整充实县国有企业改革改制工作领导小组，启动新一轮国有企业改制工作，百货、民贸、食品、糖酒、饮食服务5个公司列入改制范围。各公司制定改制方案和职工安置方案，因改制条件不成熟，未获国有企业改革改制工作领导小组批准。直至2008年，商业所属5个企业仍为国有企业。

第二节　商业企业经营

一、商品销售

1978—1990年间，各商业企业在实行承包经营前，按计划开展商品购销活动，企业实行承包经营责任制后，自主经营。由于市场逐步放开，商品批发业务量减少，经营重心转为商品零售。

1991年1—2月，县民贸公司举办总额20万元的有奖销售活动，百货公司采取优惠让利5%销售活动。4—10月，百货公司与朝阳供销社、茂兰供销社联合举办总额60万元的有奖销售活动。各商品购销企业开展送货下乡活动，推销库存积压商品，全年送货下乡达105人次。是年，商业系统商品销售总额704.57万元。各公司对门市、柜、组开展“创文明商店，优质服务”竞赛和“物价、计量信得过单位”评比活动。经过物价、计量部门年终检查评比，百货公司新大楼及第二门市部、糖酒公司十字街门市、饮食服务公司综合门市被评为“物价法规信得过单位”。

1993年6月，县商业局根据各公司经营特点和管理状况，修订商业经营管理制度，各公司制定相应实施细则，规范经营管理和经营行为。

1994年，针对百货公司和民贸公司的库存积压、欠款多的情况，县商业局重点协助百货和民贸公司处理库存积压商品，利用赶场天摆摊设点推销压库商品还贷。

1997年，商品批发和零售门市部以增收节支减亏增盈为中心，以减人增效为原则，压缩行政人员。糖酒公司除保留1名经理负责全面工作外，其他人员一律参与承包，会计、统计以返聘的形式聘用。

2002年，商业系统退取增值税款3.94万元。其中，百货公司1.8万元，民贸公司1万元，糖酒公司0.75万元，食品公司0.19万元，饮食服务公司0.2万元。

2008年9月，县商业贸易总公司牵头组织全县旅游商品企业参加商务部在广西南宁举办的东盟博览会，县内生产的旅游产品土花布、凉席、青梅酒、梅桃毛尖、荔波米扁、布艺娃娃等20余种系列产品参加展览。在开展全国“百城万店无假货”活动中，县城金镠湾商业街被评为全国“百城万店无假货”示范街，大鹏购物中心被评为全国“百城万店无假货”示范店。

二、酒类专卖管理

1989年9月，成立荔波县酒类专卖局，与县商业局合并办公，两块牌子，设办公室，行使酒类专卖批发、出售、发证、管理职能。

1991年8月，在全县范围内清理取缔私人小酒厂、小作坊6户，补交专卖利润486元，并补缴偷税漏税款和市场管理费。9—12月，发放酒类专卖许可证236份、批发许可证2份。1995年，市场放开，停止酒类专卖。

荔波最早的三星级酒店——三力酒店，2006年3月28日开业

2006年1月，商务部《酒类流通管理办法》实施后，7月，县政府发布《关于酒类流通管理备案登记的通告》，规定荔波县境内从事酒类生产、批发、零售的企业经营户，从2006年7月1日起实行酒类流通管理备案登记制度和溯源制度（随附单）；酒类流通备案登记范围为从事白酒、啤酒、葡萄酒、黄酒、果露酒、进口酒等其他酒的生产、批发、零售、餐饮、酒吧等娱乐场所的经营企业、个体工商户；取得酒类营业执照60天内主动向县酒类流通管理办公室办理备案登记（30天内完成办理变更），否则将按《酒类流通管理办法》第二十七条规定处以2000元罚款，并向社会公告；从事酒类经营的生产、批发、零售企业、经营户从2006年7月1日起向供货方索取有效产品质量合格证和随附单等有关资料；原有库存处理3个月过渡期，对未销售完的库存及时向酒类流通管理办公室提出延期申请，否则按《酒类流通管理办法》第十八条处以5000元以下罚款，并向社会公告。县商业总公司按《酒类流通管理办法》开展酒类流通备案登记工作，到玉屏、茂兰、甲良、朝阳、佳荣等镇检查酒类销售门点、宾馆、酒吧等30多家。全年全县备案登记9户，发放随附单7份。2008年，全县备案登记酒类经营户12户。

三、生猪定点屠宰管理

在1998年1月国务院颁发《生猪屠宰管理条例》后至1999年，县商业管理机构派4名干部参加省商务厅举办的生猪定点屠宰行政执法培训班学习，并取得贵州省行政执法证。

2001年，组织屠宰商户学习《生猪屠宰管理条例》《贵州省生猪屠宰管理办法》，印制宣传资料，利用赶场天设摊宣传定点屠宰的法律法规，讲解非法屠宰的危害性。是年，执法人员对全县生猪屠宰行业市场进行检查，依法取缔私屠滥宰窝点7个，对符合生猪定点屠宰的王蒙、驾欧、朝阳、甲良、佳荣、玉屏屠宰场颁发生猪屠宰许可证。

2002年6月，生猪定点屠宰工作划归县经贸局管理。2005年6月，全县生猪屠宰业务由县商业贸易总公司管理，由于涉及行政执法权，县屠宰办仍保留在县经贸局。是年，全县社会总屠宰量23005头。其中，定点屠宰22105头，机械化屠宰15755头（国有食品店屠宰）。屠宰加工费22万元。定点屠宰检出病猪3头。

2006年，开展屠宰市场巡查和市场执法200人次，取缔私屠滥宰窝点3个，销毁病死猪肉100公斤。2007年，对全县3个重点屠宰区域进行清查整治，印发宣传资料2000份，发放整改通知书4份，取缔私屠滥宰窝点5个，缴获私宰肉400公斤，县城定点屠宰率达100%、乡（镇）定点屠宰率95%。全年全县社会总屠宰量27390头。其中，定点屠宰24735头，机械化屠宰17500头（国有食品店屠宰）。屠宰加工费35万元。

2008年1月起，按中央财政对东、中、西部地区实行屠宰环节病害猪无害化处理差别补贴政策，根据省财政厅印发的《屠宰环节病害猪无害化处理财政补贴资金管理暂行办法》的规定，病害猪损失补贴对象为提供病害猪的货主和自宰经营的企业，财政补贴标准为每头500元；无害化处理费用补贴的对象为进行无害化处理的生猪定点屠宰企业，财政补贴标准为每头80元，按省、地、县财政4：3：3的比例进行补贴。因州、县级财政未匹配补贴资金，县内实际补贴资金为病害猪损失每头补贴380元，无害化处理费每头补贴60.8元。是年，全县社会总屠宰量31125头。其中，定点屠宰29391头，机械化屠宰18873头。屠宰检出病猪469头。屠宰加工费47万元。病害猪无害化处理补贴生猪469头，补贴金额27.2万元。

四、“万村千乡市场”工程

2006年起，县商业系统实施“万村千乡市场”工程。6月，成立荔波县大鹏生活资料配送中心和荔波县农资日杂公司农资配送中心，在茂兰镇正式挂牌开业第一家大鹏购物中心农家店，全年挂牌营业14个。2007年，全县建“万村千乡市场”工程农家店90个，占计划70个的129%。其中，生活资料农家店63个，生产资料农资店27个。2008年未建“万村千乡市场”工程农家店。

五、“东桑西移”工程

2006年，商务部为调整茧丝绸行业和区域结构，启动实施“东桑西移”工程。是年，全县种桑苗12000亩，收鲜茧490吨。2007年，种桑养蚕涉及全县17个乡（镇）、81个村，桑园面积共16977亩，种桑养蚕户6500户，比上年增加4724户。全县发放蚕种25883张，比上年上升229.05%，生产鲜茧1044吨，比上年上升230.97%，收购蚕茧1035吨，比上年上升215.35%。农户种桑养蚕收入总计1759.5万元，户均收入2707元。

2008年，部分农户转产改种县内新产业品种甘蔗，桑园面积下降到12640亩，有种桑养蚕户4380户，蚕种发放量21583张，鲜茧产量886吨。

第三节　国营服务业

1978—1982年，县饮食服务公司有饮食门市3个，副食综合门市2个，冷饮门市、国营旅社、照相馆、理发社、刻字店、糕点车间、豆腐车间、洗澡堂各1个。县饮食服务公司销售总额21.04万元，费用总额6.05万元，费用水平28.74%，上缴税金1.03万元，利润0.95万元。

1984年起，服务行业市场放开，除国营旅社由县饮食服务公司经营外，县饮食服务公司实行承包经营责任制，将营业网点承包给职工经营。

1993年10月后，县饮食服务公司全部实行国有民营。1997年，县饮食服务公司将国营饭店仓库、办公室等改造修建成荔波县商业综合市场，新建2层楼房1栋，设有门面32间及国有旅社客房21间（中档床位30个），国有旅社由公司自营，门面、场地出租，部分职工参与承包经营。实行国有民营改革后，该公司每年增加收入近40万元。至1999年，县饮食服务公司扭转了长期亏损的局面。

2000—2005年，县饮食服务公司根据县内旅游业发展趋势，逐年改造，提升国有旅社旅游接待能力。至2008年，县饮食服务公司保持原经营发展状态。

第二章　粮油经营

第一节　粮食流通体制改革

1978—1982年，荔波县执行国家粮油统购统销政策，县内粮食政策性企业与经营性企业并存。1983年以后，国家允许农民将完成征购任务后的余粮进入市场交易，粮食市场实行多渠道经营，除县粮食部门开展议价业务发挥主渠道作用外，允许供销社、其他合作商业和农民个人经营粮食。县粮食企业参与市场竞争，议价业务由县内发展到县外、省外。

1993年7月，为适应粮食购销体制改革，县政府批准成立荔波县粮油贸易总公司，与县粮食局两块牌子、一套人员运行。1994年，县级机构改革，保留县粮食局与粮油贸易总公司，仍实行两块牌子、一套人员体制，人员编制6人。

1998年，进行以“三项政策、一项改革”（按保护价敞开收购农民余粮、粮食收储企业实行顺价销售、粮食收购资金封闭运行和加快国有粮食企业自身改革）为重点的粮食流通体制改革，严格执行国家粮食收购政策。县内符合《粮食收购条例》规定的国家收储企业，可从事粮食收购活动。未经批准，任何单位和个人不得直接向农民和其他粮食生产者收购粮食。

是年，根据国务院《关于深化粮食流通体制改革的决定》，按照深化粮食流通体制改革的要求，县粮食局与县粮油贸易总公司分设，政企分开，粮食局人、财、物等方面与粮食企业彻底脱钩，企业成为独立自主、自主经营、自负盈亏的经济实体。

1999年3月，经县政府批准，县粮食局对原粮食企业进行调整，撤销县粮油贸易总公司和县粮食局内部结算中心、县粮食局直属库、各片区粮管所及其粮油贸易公司，通过人员和资产重组，成立县粮食购销公司、荔波县粮油饲料工贸公司。县粮食购销公司按照国家粮食购销政策，对全县政策性粮食业务实行统一收购、统一销售、统一核算、统一库存制度，内设经营科、计财科、储运科、办公室，下设玉屏、朝阳、甲良、茂兰4个经营部。经营部实行报账制，各经营部下设粮站（点）沿用原名称。新建的县粮油饲料工贸公司作为经营性企业，按市场需求，从事粮食政策性业务以外的生产经营活动。通过改制，粮食系统会计核算单位由原6个变为3个（县粮食局、县粮食购销公司、县粮油饲料工贸公司）。县粮食局的核算由原行政单位企业核算逐步向预算管理转变，但依然承担行业核算的监督、汇总上报管理工作，并负责清缴下拨企业的各项政策性补贴款。县粮食购销公司由原粮食局内部结算中心及4个粮管所合并而成。在人员安置上，实行定岗、定员制度，除经营量较大的粮站保留2人以外，其余粮站只留1人，对收购数量较小的粮站（点），粮食入库结束后采取集并方式，粮点不再保留人员；对部分身体差、业务素质低、达不到退休年龄的职工，采取内部退养办法进行安置。县粮油饲料工贸公司采取门面承包、经营承包、自愿停薪留职等形式安置人员。

2002年后，县粮油饲料工贸公司由于经营不善、资金缺乏、负债严重，没有开展经营活动。2003年，县粮食购销公司撤销玉屏经营部。

根据2002年省政府《关于深化粮食流通体制改革的意见》，从2003年起，原则上全面实行粮食购销市场化，取消定购，全面放开粮食收购，结束由粮食部门统一收购、统一价格、统一销售的历史。同时，按照省、州粮食改革工作部署，进行国有粮食购销企业改革，在保持稳定的前提下实施改组、减员分流，坚持公平、公开、公正的原则，职工重新竞聘上岗。县粮食购销公司经改革，原在册职工68人中，签订解除劳动关系协议55人，企业内部退养13人；对解除劳动关系人员重新聘用36人，自谋职业19人。

2008年6月，县政府启动县粮油饲料工贸公司企业全面改革改制工作，制定企业改革改制及职工安置方案，经过职工大会讨论，改革改制方案于是年12月上旬经县政府批准实施。按照改革方案，该公司职工43人中，办理正式退休6人，内部退养10人，签订解除劳动关系协议27人。职工安置资金总计538.8万元（一次性支付改制成本331.2万元，后续相关费用207.6万元），至12月底，县政府向职工兑现一次性补偿费共199万元，兑现退休、内部退养人员有关费用，县粮油饲料工贸公司改革改制工作结束。

至2008年年底，县粮食购销公司下设经营部3个、粮食收购站（点）16个，在岗人员75人。

第二节 粮油收购

一、粮食收购

1978年，粮食征购继续实行“一定五年”不变政策，全县全年征购任务4000吨。1979年，对边远贫困社（队）的粮食征购任务进行调整，免征瑶山、瑶麓2个贫困公社和138个贫困社队的征购任务，减少460个生产队征购基数。调整后，全县征购任务为3003.6吨。

1980—1982年，全县贯彻执行粮食收购起征点规定，对未达起征点的农户免征粮食，3年间起征点减免原粮3555吨。1983年，国家允许农民将完成征购任务后的余粮进入市场交易。

1985—1987年，按中央和省政府关于调整农村粮油政策的规定，取消粮食统购，改为合同订购，定购品种为稻谷、小麦、玉米，其他品种实行议价收购。其间，完成定购粮8205吨，年均完成定购2735吨，占年均产量32205吨的8.5%。农村年均留粮29470吨，占年均产量的91.5%。1988年，停止执行起征点规定，继续实行“依率计征”政策。1990年，应征贸易粮1393.9吨，减免151.5吨，实际入库贸易粮1242.4吨。为保证粮食收购任务的完成，县政府每年拨款抢修险桥险路，组织机关干部深入基层协助区乡组织粮食入库，并通告“在征收任务尚未完成期间不准粮食进入市场自由交易”。1990年，完成定购粮1643吨，占州下达贸易粮包干任务1500吨的109.5%，定购入库及结账进度名列全州第一。

1991年1月，国务院发出《关于调整粮食购销政策有关问题的通知》，县内从当年秋粮收购开始，将粮食合同定购改为定购，作为农民应尽义务，必须保证完成任务。1991—1993年，全县粮食定购任务按1990年包干指标执行。为确保定购任务完成，县政府每年颁布关于加强粮食市场管理的布告，规定：“粮食收购期间其他单位和个人都不准到市场设摊收购和到农村直接收购粮食。未完成定购粮任务的农户不得在市场内外出售粮食，违者由政法机关传讯”。粮食部门的定购粮入库工作从1987年到1993年连续7年获全州第一名，受州政府嘉奖。

1991—1996年，国家对议价粮收购不作统一定价，由基层企业结合当地市场粮价以及交通运输情况，以“购得进、销得出”为原则，自行确定具体收购价格。

1996年起，按国务院和省政府的有关文件规定，每年随定购粮任务下达给农户“三粮”（水费粮、计划生育粮、教育费附加）任务，粮食部门按任务数组织收购入库。

1997年7月，中共中央、国务院作出按保护价敞开收购农民余粮的决定后，至2002年，县国有粮食企业按保护价敞开收购农民余粮，不拒收、不限收、不停收、不“打白条”，在粮食收购站（点）公布定购价和保护价。

2003年，取消粮食定购，全县国有粮食购销企业粮食收购量保持粮食市场放开前的水平，实现粮食购销从“计划主渠道”向“市场主渠道”转变。

2004年5月，根据国家宏观调控政策，放开全县粮食购销市场。是年，按国务院颁布的《粮食流通管理条例》的规定，鼓励多种所有制市场主体从事粮食经营活动。县内从事粮食经营活动的经营者，在粮食行政管理部门办理粮食收购资格许可证及在县工商行政管理部门办理登记后，可从事粮食收购活动。

2005—2008年，随着粮食购销市场化，县国有粮食购销企业面向市场，改变传统收购方式，采取走村串寨预约收购、集贸市场设点收购、委托代购等方式，常年收购粮食。

二、油菜籽收购

1978年，全县油菜籽收购，不论交售数量多少，按固定比例40%作统购价，60%按超购价计付。随着农村经济政策放宽，国家提高油菜籽收购价格，全县油菜籽连年大幅增产。1982年，全县收购油菜籽折油（按国家规定的30%定折率折算）816吨。

1984年，按国家规定，完成油菜籽收购任务后，不再实行加价，允许多渠道经营。全县按省统一规定的浮动价格，随行就市，议购议销。县粮食部门按国家指令性计划组织油菜籽收购，在油菜籽收购任务未完成前，除粮食部门外，任何单位和个人不得以任何形式收购油菜籽。

1991年起，油菜籽收购按指导性计划执行。为提高农民种植油菜籽的积极性，县政府将油菜籽收购价格在国家定价每50公斤70.40元基础上提高3.6元，并实行返饼返油和化肥奖售政策。是年，州下达荔波县油菜籽收购计划1600吨，实际完成2641吨。

1992年，全省油菜籽收购不分计划内、计划外，实行“综合定价，敞开收购”办法，每50公斤中等油菜籽综合价为60元，各地可根据市场价格的变化情况作适当调整，但上浮不得超过10%，下调不得超过5%。荔波县当年油菜籽收购价格按省定综合价执行，不上浮、不下调，全年收购油菜籽3271吨，创历年最高量。

1994年，执行全省统一油菜籽收购价格。是年，全县油菜籽收购实际完成237吨，仅占州下达计划的15.8%。

1995—1997年，油菜籽收购价格，根据当年市场价格确定。

1998—1999年，油菜籽收购价按省规定的每50公斤110元执行，明码标价，挂牌收购。

2000年，根据省政府《关于做好夏季粮油收购工作的通知》，放开全县油菜籽市场，允许经批准的其他部门、企业入市收购经营。县粮食企业根据市场供需变化，自行定价收购。

2001年，根据省政府《关于做好2001年夏季粮油收购工作的通知》，油菜籽收购取消指导性计划，根据生产和市场供求情况组织收购。2001—2008年，全县油菜籽市场全面放开，县国有粮食企业随行就市收购油菜籽。

1986—2008年全县粮油总产量及粮食部门收购情况一览表

表15－1 单位：吨

年度	粮食总产量	粮食收购		油菜籽总产量	油菜籽收购实绩
		粮食收购实绩	其中：定购		
1986	34528	3508	2053	1677	1476
1987	37758	2228	1571	1967	1328
1988	34136	2825	1500	1638	1009
1989	35243	3365	1500	756	498
1990	39824	3528	1500	1593	1452
1991	39200	2604	1565	4260	2641
1992	35000	4748	1522	3033	3271
1993	42500	3661	1674	1140	412
1994	44400	2949	1473	1286	237
1995	47100	3261	1500	2233	918
1996	47100	3299	1500	2949	641
1997	49400	2891	1500	3660	1038
1998	51900	3723	1630	3979	330
1999	41327	3575	914	2126	427
2000	51500	3834	2465	5259	194
2001	53095	2704	—	3628	392
2002	41401	2324	—	3418	1150
2003	49297	3332	—	4556	1200
2004	53763	3358	—	5290	1554
2005	55800	3649	—	5433	1795
2006	57728	4867	—	5711	1318
2007	58328	5886	—	5444	1172
2008	59927	4766	—	3898	3651

说明：1.粮食收购实绩为贸易粮；

2.1978—1985年数据遗失。

第三节 粮油供应与仓储、加工

一、粮食供应

（一）城镇粮食供应

1978年，县内城镇居民口粮实行定量供应。定量供应执行国家规定的按人分等定量供应办法，按照居民的居住地区、劳动差别、年龄大小，分别核定每人的等级和每月供应的标准，凭证、凭票购买粮食。1993年7月1日后，粮食价格和粮食经营企业全面开放，城镇居民粮食定量供应标准和工种定量标准执行到1993年年底。但进入第四季度后，外县和邻省的一些粮商到荔波抢购粮食，导致县内市场粮价上涨，大米涨到每公斤3.20～3.30元，并且上市量锐减，群众生活和社会安定受到影响。为平抑市场粮价，保障群众粮食供给，县政府发出《关于认真做好当前粮食供应工作的通知》，从1994年12月1日起到1995年8月底止，城镇非农业人口由粮食部门凭原发购粮证定量供应大米、菜油（菜油只供应到1995年4月底），当月有效，过期不补，不能提前购买。同时制定粮油供应价格。粮源从县级储备粮中解决。1995年8月，县政府批复县粮食局《关于对城镇非农业人口粮油供应问题的请示》，同意从1995年9月起实行全年供应，供应数量、价格、办法按1994年的文件规定执行。此后，随着县内粮食市场逐步稳定，城镇居民粮油由市场供给随行就市。

（二）农村粮食供应

从1978年后，国家对粮食征购任务进行调减，县内农民负担减少。1979年，按照国家出售议价粮供应一般缺粮户的规定，对因灾减产、口粮低的重灾社队给予“补缺定销”，已收新粮的地方停止供应。1980年，继续执行农村统销政策，凡口粮人均在起征点以上（包括实际分配粮食已达到起征点）的生产队，国家不再返销粮食，由于某种原因造成的个别缺粮户，由社（队）自行调剂解决；极个别必须由国家返销的，一律按调整后的统销价作价返销。是年，向全县农村议销粮食130吨。

1983年，对农村缺粮户实行议销，对因灾缺粮的农户实行借销，个别受灾严重的由民政部门救济解决。民政部门给予的生活救济粮作返销处理。

1986年，对缺粮、缺钱的“双缺户”以外的缺粮户供应中价粮，由乡政府出证明，粮食部门凭证供应，供应不超过1个月；对经济收入较好的缺粮户供应议价粮。农村粮食供应的对象主要是“双缺户”“五保户”、烈属和军属。此外，还注意对边远乡村和弱智农户以及种植经济作物但产品滞销造成困难的农户予以口粮安排。

1993年7月1日以后，按照国家粮食流通体制改革方案，农村救济粮和缺粮户返销粮，价格随行就市，粮食部门保证供应，销售对象主要是“双缺户”及受重灾缺粮的农户。

1998—2006年，省、州每年下拨救灾救济粮款，解决受灾群众的生产和生活问题。全县救灾粮源，由县粮食部门从市场收购的大米中解决，民政部门按市场价加合理费用，从粮食部门购买粮食发给群众。2007—2008年，县内民政救济粮实行政府招标采购，粮食企业参与竞标。

（三）军粮供应

1978—1982年，县粮食部门按照中央军委后勤部、粮食部《军事系统各类人员粮食定量标准暂行规定》的有关规定，向县武警中队、县公安局消防科、县武装部供应粮食，部队凭全国通用粮票和贵州省地方粮票购粮。1983年1月，改为凭“军用粮油豆供应证”供应。1995年，改为使用军用粮票，粮食部门凭票供应大米、面粉，菜油、大豆按议价价格供应。

1998—2008年，按照国务院、中央军委《关于深化军粮供应体制改革的通知》，军粮供应执行“先前方、后后方，先军队、后地方”的供应原则，军供大米、面粉由省政府安排，县国有粮食企业是军粮供应的主渠道。

二、菜籽油供应

1978—1981年，实行菜籽油定量供应。同时，按国家规定，每逢“五一”、国庆、春节、元旦四大节日，在定量外增加食油供应0.4—0.25公斤。1982年以后，按省的规定，取消节日补助，改为按月暂时补助供应食油0.25公斤。此后，每人每月实际供应0.5公斤。

1991年8月1日起，按省的统一规定，对城镇非农业人口的定量食油供应实行“保留定量，定点供应，统一价格，多买不限，当月定量，当月有效”的办法。是年，菜油销售110.6吨，其中平价销售83.3吨。1992年，菜油销售153.4吨，其中平价销售145吨。

1993年，根据省政府办公厅转发省粮食局《关于认真做好粮价放开后粮油购、销、调、存工作意见的通知》，食油购销价格和经营全面放开，从4月1日起，取消定量供应政策。食油购销价格放开和经营放开后，菜油销售部分城乡，敞开供应，价格随行就市。

三、粮食议价销售

1979年，国家允许粮食议购议销。1983年，县粮食部门全面开展粮食议购议销业务，议价粮食主要由企业自主销售。

1994年，县政府办公室发出《关于进一步加强粮食市场管理的紧急通知》规定：除允许部分在县内市场流通调剂余缺外，凡调出县境的粮食必须经县政府批准，方可调出。否则，一律查扣没收。

1995年，县政府同意粮食企业根据市场行情，对议价粮采取边购边销的办法，组织销售，时间不限，数量不限。

1996—1997年，粮食市场销售不畅，县粮食企业库存积压。根据州政府有关文件精神，县粮食局制定粮食促销奖励办法，各基层粮食企业按照县粮食局的统一部署，组织促销人员外出推销议价粮，将库存议价粮全部销售。

从1998年粮食流通体制改革起至2008年，全县粮食销售全部随行就市。

四、陈化粮处理

随着农村经济体制改革不断深入，县内粮食连年丰收，粮食市场放开，粮食部门按保护价收购的粮食不能顺价销售，粮食部门粮食积压，粮食品质陈化，仓容紧张。1999年，根据国家关于陈化粮处理的有关规定，县国有粮食企业经县政府批准，对库存陈化粮进行销售处理，共销售处理企业周转粮（稻谷）2061吨；经州政府批准处理企业周转粮（稻谷）3200吨。陈化粮处理均由粮食购销公司提出申请，通过县粮食局、县技术监督局共同实地抽样封签送省粮油产品质量监督检验中心进行检验，取得陈化粮鉴定报告后，由粮食、财政、农发行、技监、物价等部门共同研究，提出销售处理意见，书面报告县政府和州政府批准，在粮食、财政、物价部门监督下，粮食企业组织销售。

2001年7月，县粮食购销公司部分政策性陈化粮品质下降，经县政府同意，县粮食购销公司以等量对冲办法销售陈化粮稻谷503吨，所销售的503吨陈化粮稻谷，用2001年收购的保护价新粮抵库。销售陈化粮产生的收购价差价，用县级粮食风险基金弥补。

五、粮油仓储

（一）仓库建设

1978年，县内粮食仓储容量770吨。之后逐步新建部分仓库，增加仓容，到1990年，全县有粮仓44栋，库容量13475吨。

1991年，全县有储粮站（点）23个，粮油仓库建筑面积9417平方米，库容量13685吨。其中，质量完好面积3694平方米，库容量6050吨；需大修面积2102平方米，库容量3303吨；待报废面积3621平方米，库容量4332吨。粮油仓库占地总面积83543平方米。1992年，新建县粮食局直属仓库840平方米和甲良粮管所甲新粮点仓库105平方米，改造觉巩粮点仓库160平方米。1993年，改造茂兰粮管所立化粮点仓库142平方米。经过逐年仓储建设，到1996年年末，全县国家粮油仓库建筑面积共10257平方米，总容量16153吨。

1998年12月，县粮食部门向农业发展银行贷款20万元，新建播尧粮站仓库317平方米，容量762吨；新建拉圭粮点仓库184平方米，容量300吨。2000年4月，新建阳凤粮站晒坝面积806平方米。8月，省财政拨款20万元，新建甲良粮站仓库305平方米，容量500吨。12月，向农发行贷款25万元，新建佳荣粮站仓库432平方米，容量600吨。2001年1月，向农发行贷款40万元，新建朝阳粮站仓库571平方米，容量1000吨。2003年，处置立式油罐14个、卧式油罐9个、沉淀罐5个，总容量212.5吨。

至2008年年底，全县有粮油仓容14686吨。

（二）粮油保管

1978年以后，全县粮油保管工作贯彻“以防为主，防治并举”“以防为主，综合防治”的方针，严格执行国家《粮食保管暂行办法》，推行“四包”（包人员、包粮食、包器材、包费用）定额管理制度，每年开展春、夏、冬3次粮油保管大普查，开展“四无”（无虫害、无霉变、无鼠雀、无事故）粮仓活动，确保国家储粮安全，降低保管费用。

从1985年起，县粮食管理部门有计划地在全县各粮管所推广应用“双低”（低氧、低药量）储粮防治技术。1987年，按照《国家粮油仓库管理办法》《粮油储备技术规范》，进行仓库管理，仓库管理逐步制度化、规范化，减少粮油损耗，争创“四无”粮仓。1988年，经省、州粮食局验收，获“四无粮仓县”称号。1991年，“四无”粮仓仓储工作获全州评比第一名，受州粮食局嘉奖。

1992年，按照国家粮食储备局《国家储备粮油管理暂行办法》的规定，实行“三专”（专人管理、专仓储藏、专账记载）、“四落实”（数量落实、质量落实、品种落实、地点落实），对国家储备粮油与商品粮油进行分开储存和分类管理。县粮食局和储备单位建立“国家储备粮油专卡”详细记载，并进行责任跟踪督查。同时，推广单管风机储粮技术，电子仪表测温普及率达100%。1992—1993年，每年进行3次普查，“四无”粮仓和“四无”粮油比例均在90%以上，科学保粮50%以上。

1994年2月，根据国家粮食储备局《关于加强国家粮油仓储管理工作的通知》，在“四无”基础上增加“账实相符”内容，即按“一符四无”粮仓要求对国家储备粮油进行普查。

1996—1997年，各粮管所、库规范粮油保管制度，建立“三板”（保管员职责板、粮情检查记录板、数量质量分仓卡片板）、“两本”（粮情检查记录本、分仓实物账本）、挂牌（外墙标志牌）、建卡（库存粮油保管出入库专卡）制度，“一符四无”粮仓和“一符四无”粮油比例两年均达90%以上。

1998年以后，全县科学储粮工作主要采取“双低”储粮、机械通风、单管风机对高温粮处理等方式，巩固“一符四无”粮仓。1999年，经全省粮油保管交叉复查，达到“一符四无”县标准。

2001年4月，根据省政府办公厅《关于开展全省粮食清仓查库工作的通知》及全省清查粮油库存会议的安排，开展清仓查库工作。通过清查，荔波县粮油数量、质量、品种与会计、统计、保管“三统一”。荔波县的粮食保管工作经验在2001年全省粮食工作会议上作经验交流。

2005年，省、州再次进行粮食保管交叉检查，荔波县保持“一符四无”县标准。此后停止进行粮食交叉检查。

六、粮油加工

1978年，县粮油加工厂大米加工车间经过上年投资7300元进行技术更新改造后，大米加工实现机械化。各区粮管所购置有小型榨油机，油料加工实现半机械化，每年加工油料600—700吨。

1980年，投资1.5万元，增设面条机1台，加工面条供应城镇居民。

1983年，各粮站使用95型榨油机，油脂加工实现机械化，全县所收油料仅够加工半年。

1990年，增设FM-300型500包/日产（3班）复式磨联合生产机组，解决县内小麦加工、面粉供应问题。

1993年，粮油市场放开后，油脂上调任务少，县内供应实行“以产定销”办法，除县粮油加工厂外，各区粮管所根据季节加工生产。此后，随着各粮管所加工设备老化和粮油库存不足，各粮管所不再开展粮油加工业务。

2006年10月，县粮食局争取到省财政厅、省粮食局资金30万元，在县城建设日产大米30吨应急生产线1条，2007年4月正式投产使用，结束荔波县粮食购销收原粮卖原粮的历史。2008年8月，省财政厅、省粮食局又划拨30万元，对应急生产线进行技术改造，加工精米。

七、粮油调运

1978—1990年，县内除1980年、1983年、1984年分别调出粮食1300吨、285吨、90吨外，其余年份平均每年由国家调入粮食1350吨，弥补库存，保证城乡粮食供应。

1980—1989年，年平均收购油菜籽（菜籽折油）265吨，菜油调拨除1979年调入15吨和1985年无外调以外，其余年份平均每年为国家调出179.5吨。

1991年，州粮食局下达荔波县接收省外小麦1200吨、玉米300吨，接收水患地区稻谷100吨（实际接收110吨）；从荔波调往都匀大米300吨，实际调出283吨，调出油菜籽计划170吨，实际调出730吨。

1992年，县外调入粮食3712吨，县内调出粮食776吨、油菜籽604.8吨。

从1978年至1993年7月，县内粮油调运一直实行指令性计划，即州粮食局下达调拨计划后，县粮食局根据全县的仓容、品种、供应数量情况，将计划落实到各粮管所及粮站（点）。从1993年7月起，国家取消指令性计划，县粮食系统内粮油调剂按合同购销量进行调拨。

2000年3月，按照省政府对黔南州新建粮库装新粮的任务安排，州粮食局安排荔波县调往都匀国家储备库稻谷3800吨，这是县内历年调运规模最大的一次，县粮食局成立调粮领导小组，制定“四定”（定时间、定数量、定质量、定职责）责任制，层层落实任务，基层粮站干部职工做好服务工作，运粮车随到随装。是年，全县销售调粮4522吨，在全州率先提前完成任务。

至2008年，县粮食局历年调出粮油，坚持执行好粮、好油外调的原则，做到合理运输、安全运输，调运人员对调出的粮油质量、数量负责，在调运过程中，没有出现运输事故和粮油污染事故。

八、饲料加工

1982年之前，县内无饲料加工企业，对计划外的饲料供应，仅限于粮油副产品的糠、麸之类。1982年10月，县政府拨款3.5万元，由县粮食局筹建饲料公司，1983年竣工后，省粮食局于是年7月为饲料公司配置价值4.19万元的大型饲料机1台，10月开机生产混合饲料供应市场。

1985年3月，县饲料公司正式成立。随着饲养业快速发展，饲料供应供不应求。是年，县饲料公司投入资金4.56万元进行扩建，1986年竣工投入使用。同时，县饲料公司为保护生猪饲养户的积极性，采取让利办法，以5%的利润率定价销售。

1988年7月，县饲料公司实行经营承包责任制。1993年，县饲料公司与县粮油加工厂、粮油贸易公司、粮食招待所合并成为县粮油饲料工贸公司，继续进行饲料加工，供应市场。

第三章 盐品专营 卷烟专卖

第一节 盐品专营

一、盐品供应

1978年，县盐业公司专营批发，供应全县各零售单位和基层供销社。食盐供应实行全县统一价格，农牧业集体用盐实行优惠价。1980年，农村耕牛承包到户后，农牧业用盐停止执行价格优惠政策。1986年，食盐价格实行城乡差价。1990年，县盐业公司有盐仓面积524.4平方米，各区供销社均建有盐仓，全县食盐库存量可保证供应3个月。

1991年，盐业公司除经营食盐批发业务外，设有零售网点销售食盐。

1996年，按照国务院要求，对食盐进行加碘小袋包装，全年包装加碘盐915吨。1997年，食用盐全部进行加碘包装，全年包装加工碘盐810吨。

1998年，延伸食盐批发网点，扩大批发量，增加销售量。2000年，食盐入库量900吨，对每次入库食盐进行碘测试，做到测试有记录，把好仓库环境卫生关、盐品合格入库库存调运关，对不合格碘盐不发放市场销售。县内食盐经过县防疫站不定期测试，碘盐合格率达到98%以上。

2001年3月，按照州物价局、州盐务分局联合发出的《关于加强食盐价格管理的通知》，进行小包袋装加碘食盐复合膜更换。

2003年，荔波盐业公司原有办公用房、仓库被县政府征用后，县政府协调租用的县糖酒公司100平方米仓库库存量小，公司与甲良供销社（年存盐量250吨）、茂兰供销社（年存盐量100吨）、佳荣个体户（年存盐量60吨）、立化镇个体户（年存盐量40吨）、朝阳镇个体户（年存盐量80吨）等签订食盐购、销、存协议，保证食盐销售工作正常运转。

2004年，推行食盐营销网络配送制，以“便于管理，方便群众，布局合理，辐射到位”为原则，合理规划布局盐品经营店。由于部分食盐零售户对盐品营销网络配送方式不理解，随意改变食盐零售价格，造成辖区内营销网络配送工作和盐业市场价格不稳定。6月，开展食盐零售价格检查，对乱涨价的食盐零售户进行说服教育。是年，购进多品种盐14.4吨投放市场，售出11.5吨。

2005年，盐业公司拓展多品种盐业务，开辟工业用盐和畜牧用盐市场，对农村养殖散户和规模养殖场进行专项调查后，建立用户档案，开展畜牧用盐的购进、销售、服务和联系工作。全年销售多品种盐11吨、工业用盐38吨。

2006年6月，新品种纸塑精盐上市销售，取消乡（镇）复合膜食盐包装点，由县盐业公司直接配送盐品到各乡（镇）的委托批发点。年末，全县有盐品经营户229户。

2008年，以销售纸塑袋装盐为主，复合膜袋装盐销量减少。2006—2008年，全县累计销售多品种盐20.5吨、工业用盐162.15吨、畜牧用盐46.95吨。

1978—2008年全县食盐财务指标完成情况一览表

表15－2

年度	销售量（吨）	销售总额（万元）	费用总额（万元）	税金（万元）	利润（万元）
1978	581.70	15.57	2.30	0.12	2.51
1979	653.50	16.37	2.07	1.11	1.82
1980	669.00	16.61	2.59	0.87	1.47
1981	709.00	18.71	2.75	0.89	1.80
1982	838.00	21.84	2.80	2.00	2.24
1983	695.35	18.39	2.80	1.00	1.92
1984	724.85	19.11	2.92	1.08	2.05
1985	843.40	22.81	3.16	1.88	2.49
1986	878.20	23.96	3.09	1.43	2.80
1987	758.40	20.06	3.34	1.54	3.42
1988	740.80	28.10	2.80	3.33	8.80
1989	104.67	43.20	5.40	3.36	4.70
1990	669.90	38.40	4.50	2.38	3.70
1991	—	42.60	4.20	4.37	4.24
1992	—	42.74	4.40	3.44	4.02
1993	—	47.57	7.20	2.97	−0.43
1994	—	52.69	4.08	4.47	2.72
1995	—	70.18	6.23	3.51	2.00
1996	—	88.56	7.10	4.13	1.29
1997	—	87.50	6.84	3.48	1.40
1998	—	90.50	6.69	5.22	0.80
1999	—	86.76	7.74	5.42	6.29
2000	964.20	90.06	18.46	5.86	0.79
2001	953.30	104.63	23.82	63.77	0.65
2002	881.30	107.74	30.79	0.87	0.20
2003	837.90	103.86	29.32	9.69	0.78
2004	679.20	102.37	36.21	5.79	0.62
2005	754.50	127.20	27.30	8.22	1.72
2006	540.00	77.94	3.22	5.33	−1.60
2007	800.00	110.60	41.20	1.58	4.80
2008	750.00	152.20	61.06	18.04	31.59

二、盐政管理

1978年，县盐业公司由县商业局管理。

1995年，盐业公司与商业局、百货、民贸公司合建综合楼，盐业公司拥有门面2间及职工住房产权2套。

1995年，建贵州省盐务管理局荔波县盐务管理支局，与县盐业公司合署办公，两块牌子、一套人员，盐务管理支局行使县政府的盐政管理职权，统一管理县境内食盐调拨和运销。

2000年10月，县盐业公司资产、人员划归贵州盐业（集团），建立贵州盐业（集团）荔波有限责任公司，仍然负责荔波县辖区内食盐供应和管理工作。是年，贵州盐业（集团）荔波有限责任公司有盐仓565.6平方米，库存量可保证全县供应3个月。

2001年3月，根据国家经贸委《关于开展打击非法经营食盐专项行动的紧急通知》和省经贸委制定的打假行动方案，县政府组织物价、质监、公安、交通、商业、工商、防疫、盐务等部门召开专题会议，部署打击非法经营食盐专项行动，成立由县政府办公室主任为组长的联合行动协调小组，对全县范围尤其是毗邻地的盐业市场、零售网点进行清查，重点清查立化镇、佳荣镇、驾欧乡等地区盐业市场，对临时性（季节性）加工酸梅、李子、笋子、养羊、腌牛皮等个体户进行登记，取缔不按指定地点购进食盐的个体户，规范全县盐业市场。5月，县政府组织卫生、工商、物价、商业、盐务等单位开展第八届“防治碘缺乏病日”活动，在县城设摊开展宣传咨询服务，设置宣传栏8个、图片展板5块，发放各种宣传资料2000份，张贴、悬挂标语80条。在宣传活动中，结合现场进行食盐测碘实验，让群众认识碘盐、非碘盐、食用复合膜包装碘盐的区别。

2002年5月，第九届“防治碘缺乏病日”活动以“科学补碘、健康成长”为主题，在“5·15”宣传日前后，通过电视宣传盐业政策、法规，到乡（镇）开展“执法月”宣传，发放各种宣传资料2000份。是年，贵州盐业（集团）荔波公司被县政府评为“诚信纳税户先进单位”。

2003年9月，县政府根据省、州关于对盐业经营进行联合检查的通知，成立联合检查组，对全县食盐经营店进行检查。检查中，从甲良供销社、茂兰供销社的包装批发点2个及门市、市场摊点50个抽取食盐50公斤进行检查，被抽检的食盐数量足、卫生好，各盐业零售门市严格执行省定批发零售价格，未发现违法违规现象。是月，县城试行食盐配送制度。

2005年春，因荔波县销售的食盐是一级精制盐，广西河池地区食盐是二级盐，两地食盐价格悬殊，荔波盐业公司向州盐业公司反映这一情况后，州盐业公司于2005年6月组织独山、荔波、平塘、罗甸等县盐业公司经理前往广西河池地区协调，召集边界接壤市场协调会、边界接壤市场管理座谈会、相关市场委托批发户恳谈会，规范边界间市场行为。

2007年，开展第十四届“防治碘缺乏病日”活动，以“坚持食用碘盐，预防出生缺陷”为主题，在县城开展“5·15”宣传日活动，在各乡（镇）以学校为重点，采取一个学生带动一个家庭的方式，进行防治碘缺乏病宣传，设立碘盐示范小学3个（佳荣镇坤地小学、洞塘乡板寨小学、瑶山小学）。是年，荔波盐务支局在盐政执法中，按《食盐专营办法》规范全县盐业市场秩序，依法吊销甲良片区不按指定区域购进食盐的个体户2户的食盐零售许可证。

2008年4月，荔波盐业公司组织人员到各乡（镇）食盐市场，特别是与广西接壤地区的市场进行全面检查，全县食盐市场与广西接壤地区食盐市场稳定，食盐价格基本衔接。是年，加大县城各大宾馆、食品生产加工企业、农副产品批发市场、集贸市场以及商场、超市等用盐户用盐情况检查力度，加强交通枢纽地区盐业市场检查，向食盐经营户发放《食盐专营办法》及宣传资料500份。

第二节 卷烟专卖

一、机构

1984年，成立县烟草专卖局、烟草公司，实行一个机构、两块牌子体制，内设行政办公室、财务股、专卖股、销售股，有员工11人，专卖执法人员5人，隶属黔南州烟草专卖局（公司）。1991年，员工增至16人，其中聘用长期合同工8人。1999年，成立甲良稽查中队、茂兰稽查中队、玉屏稽查中队，专卖执法人员增加至22人。2004年11月，根据国家、省的相关文件规定，取消县烟草公司法人资格，经营业务划归黔南州烟草公司管理，县公司的资产、负债、所有权益并入黔南州公司统一核算。同时，进行片区整合，设立稽查大队、内管办、专卖股，三块牌子、一套人员合署办公，并将三个稽查中队整合为一个稽查中队，专卖执法人员减少至12人。2008年年末，县烟草专卖局（公司）有在册正式员工28人，聘用在岗员工19人。专卖股定编10人。

二、专卖管理

（一）证件管理

1984年，根据《烟草专卖条例》，对国有集体、个体卷烟经营户实行专卖许可制度，全县办理准购证223个，其中国有集体2个、个体221个。在准购证年检换发中，对不符合经营规定的不予发证。

1991年，实施《中华人民共和国烟草专卖法》，对原经营许可证进行换发，共换发集体许可证6个、个体专卖许可证674个。1998年，经省级审核，换发国有集体许可证4个、个体专卖许可证1243个。2003年，进行5年一次的许可证到期换发，共换发国营集体许可证6个，个体许可证减少至721个。

2006年后，将专卖执法转变为服务型管理方式，对一年内违规2次以上的违规经营户。同时，对专卖执法人员亦相应办理执法证件，进行专卖技能鉴定。至2008年，全县专卖执法人员持有执法证件具有执法资格人员7人，占执法人员数100%；通过技能鉴定6人，其中获高级专卖管理员1人、中级专卖管理员3人、初级专卖管理员2人。

（二）市场监管

1984年后，县烟草专卖局在市场监管中，针对“假、私、非”卷烟销售违法行为隐蔽、分散、执法难度大的特点，与工商、公安、质监等部门配合，对卷烟市场和经营者实行动态管理，成立零售户自律小组，由稽查员分片管理，对所管辖区进行日常检查和突击检查，以及开展专项检查，打击违法行为。2006年，检查零售户11542户（次），查处烟草违法案件29起。其中，一般程序案件8起、简易程序案件21起；查获初烤烟叶5580公斤、烟丝455公斤、卷烟183.2条，收缴罚没金额4.75万元。2007年10月，与县公安部门联合查处违法运输假冒卷烟案件1起，查获假冒卷烟360件，案值105万元，成为县烟草专卖局成立后查获数量最多、案值最大的假冒卷烟案件。2008年，查获卷烟案件1起，抓获犯罪嫌疑人2人。是年，县烟草专卖局稽查大队被评为全州打假先进集体，1人评为全省打假先进个人。1984—2008年，查处涉烟案件70余起。

三、卷烟销售

1985年起，卷烟销售一直由县烟草公司统一门店销售，设立公司下属卷烟批发站。1985—1991年，年平均销售卷烟4966箱，年均销售总值510万元。1992—1998年，年平均销售卷烟6500箱，年均销售总值762万元。

2002年，对卷烟销售组织体系进行改革规范，在重点乡（镇）重新设立基层站点，并在城区实行“全面访销、全面配送、访送分离、专销结合”的城网运行模式，在重点乡（镇）实行“重点访销、多级配送、访送一体、专销结合”的农网运行模式，推行零售户户籍化管理，对零售户实施全面调查摸底、建卡立档，将零售户按经营情况划分为A、B、C三类，实行分片分类管理和动态管理，做到一户一证、一户一档、一户一号、一户一牌、一户一卡。是年年底，卷烟零售户由2001年的480多户增至650多户，平均访销送货率95%，市场占有率100%。全年销售量5331箱，销售总值3097万元。

2004年，县烟草专卖局制定《荔波县卷烟零售点合理布局方案》，全县办理许可证限额为700户，占比控制在5.2‰。同时，对零售户采取“严进宽出”措施，控制全县零售户数量，撤销基层站点，由县公司集中电话访销，实行访送分离制度。1999—2005年，年平均销售卷烟5603箱，年均销售总值3960万元。

2006年4月，成立以州公司为主体的区域卷烟营销部，由州公司集中访销。2006—2008年，年平均销售卷烟4495箱，年均销售总值4224万元。

第四章 供销合作社

第一节 供销合作体制改革

一、改革改制

1983年3月，县供销社在茂兰区供销社进行供销社体制改革试点后，在全县4个区供销社全面铺开，6月，区供销社体制改革结束。8月，对县供销社进行体制改革，成立县联合社，县联合社人员、工资、经费全部与财政脱钩，所提经费列入经营成本。

1987年，在全系统推行经营承包责任制。经营承包形式主要有定任务保工资、超额提成，纯利包干，百元销售含工资率计酬等。各区基层社、各公司与县联社签订承包经营责任状，基层社百货门市实行核定基数、上缴利润、自负盈亏的经营承包责任制。全县13个地理位置偏僻、交通不便、长期亏损的分店和门市试行租赁制。

1991年，全系统推行目标管理百元计酬经营承包形式，压缩利润大包干、租赁范围，改变承包中失控、以包代管现象。1992年8月，全县供销社系统贯彻落实经营、价格、用工、分配“四放开”政策，工业品门市全部由职工承包经营。

1997年9月，县供销社联合社人员、工资纳入财政预算。

1999年8月，县供销社食品厂改为县天然食品有限公司，划归县经济贸易局管理。

2004年9月，县政府成立荔波县供销社系统改革领导小组，由县政府分管领导任组长，领导小组办公室设在县联社。2005年3月，县政府调整充实领导小组，县长担任组长，加强改革改制工作领导。10月，茂兰供销社按“界定权责、量化资产、全员安置、置换身份、优化整合、转换机制、谨慎稳妥、稳定发展”的总体思路，首先进行改革改制，成立由行政、党支部、职工代表、分社经理组成的领导小组，改革方案经过全体职工讨论、审议通过，报县改革领导小组批准

荔波县供销社大楼

实施。2007年6月，朝阳供销社进行改革改制。

到2008年年底，全县参加改革改制的供销社所属企业7个（土产公司、农资日杂公司、工矿贸易公司、朝阳供销社、甲良供销社、茂兰供销社、玉屏供销社），人数142人。改革改制实行全员解除劳动合同关系，职工按每年工龄1300元标准，领取一次性安置补助费。全系统一次性买断工龄解除劳动合同关系共90人。已经完成改革改制企业（朝阳供销社、甲良供销社、茂兰供销社）筹备组建股份制企业。

二、社员代表大会

1983年8月23—24日，荔波县供销社第四届社员代表大会在县城召开，参加大会代表203人。会议听取和审议第三届理事会工作报告，审议通过县供销合作社联合社章程；选举荔波县供销合作社联合社第四届理事会、监事会。会议选举产生理事会主任和副主任各1名，监事会主任和副主任各1名。

1986年9月16—18日，荔波县供销社第五届社员代表大会在县城召开，参加会议代表131人。会议听取和审议第四届理事会工作报告，讨论修改县供销合作社联合社章程；选举产生第五届理事会主任和副主任各1名，监理会主任和副主任各1名，理事6名，监事5名，专职监察员1名。

此后，供销社改制经营，停止召开社员代表大会。

第二节　经营网点

1978—1982年，县供销合作社有下属企业土产公司、农资公司、城关供销社、朝阳供销社、甲良供销社、茂兰供销社6个。城关供销社有城关、永康、水尧、水利分销店4个，有代销店13个；朝阳供销社有朝阳、王蒙、瑶山、捞村、拉圭、翁昂分销店6个，有代销店15个；甲良供销社有甲良、方村、甲站、地莪、觉巩、播尧、阳凤分销店7个，有代销店14个；茂兰供销社有茂兰、洞塘、瑶庆、瑶鹿、佳荣、水维、岜鲜、立化、肯甫分销店9个，有代销店9个。

1983年，县供销合作社改为县供销合作社联合社。茂兰供销社增设甲介分销店。1984年5月，成立县供销社贸易公司，有职工27人。1985年，城关供销社更名为玉屏供销社，在三都县周覃区设立分销店，建翻砂厂；甲良供销社建翻砂厂、碎石加工厂。

1986年，撤销茂兰供销社甲介分销店。1987年，撤销县供销社贸易公司。1988年10月，成立县供销社食品厂，职工8人。

1991年，全县取消代销店。是年，土产公司下设蚕业公司，人员从土产公司职工中调配。

1994年，全县供销社有行政机构1个，供销社企业8个，基层分销店25个，干部职工共265人。

1997年，开办村级综合服务部11个。

2000年，县供销合作社有企业及社涉企业7个共197人。其中，批发零售贸易企业1个191人，餐饮企业3个3人，服务企业3个3人。全部职工人数207人。

2002年，甲良供销社撤销觉巩分销店。2003年，茂兰供销社启动商业步行街网点建设，撤销水维分销店。2004年，甲良供销社撤销阳凤分销店，茂兰供销社撤销岜鲜分销店。2005年，甲良供销社撤销地莪分销店。

2008年，县供销社联合社有企业7个，有批发零售贸易企业产业活动单位65个。全系统有职工110人，其中，县财政支付工资人员12人。

第三节 购销业务

1978年后，供销社改进经营方式，抓骨干品种购销。在购销旺季，延长营业时间，增设货摊，赶转转场，召开各种类型物资交流会，多渠道进货，扩大购销额，至1980年，向市场提供工业品、副食杂品1850种，议购商品占全年收购总值的58.5%，比1979年上升21%。

1985年，全系统经营利润18.34万元，流动资金比年初增加1.76万元，全县商品流转计划主要指标超额完成。

1990年，由于贷款紧缩，贷款利率上浮，各种收费标准提高，企业资金周转不灵，主要经济指标完成情况下滑，供销社系统亏损15.8万元。此后连年亏损，1993年亏损达58.1万元。

1995年，农民在农业生产上投资增加，化肥需求量增大，化肥价格涨幅高，平均上涨38%，化肥销售出现淡季旺销，季节性投资趋减。全年销售化肥9900吨，较上年同期多供应3180吨，比上年增长47.3%。全系统商品销售收入上升，亏损单位减少，基层社无亏损单位。除土产公司、食品厂无启动资金开展业务外，其余6个核算单位均超额完成年计划。全县利润亏损12.2万元，比上年少亏损11.8万元。1996年，全系统创利润总额1.3万元，实现扭亏为盈。1997年，上缴税金37.8万元，利润总额9.6万元。

2000年，商品流转购销业务下降，8个独立核算单位，亏损企业2个。化肥市场经营渠道增加后，农资市场占有率降低，农业类商品如粮食、辣椒等价格持续下降；生活消费品市场竞争加剧，全系统仅工矿贸易公司超额完成计划，其余企业、基层社经济效益全部下滑。全县化肥销售量5956吨，比上年减少1173吨，下降17.6%。化肥销售量为1993年到2000年8年中最低点。

2002年，全县8个独立核算单位中，亏损单位2个。土产公司全年未开展业务，无销售收入，处于瘫痪状态，靠门面出租收入发工资。

2005年，全县供销社系统商品销售利润总额69.8万元，比上年减少33.9万元，下降32.82%。在7个独立核算单位中，盈利单位2个、持平单位4个、亏损单位1个。上缴各种税费总额169.3万元。全县化肥销售量11704吨，比上年增加1131吨，上升幅度10.7%。

2008年，全县商品销售净利润额23万元，比上年增加5.3万元，上升29.94%。7个独立核算单位中，盈利单位4个、亏损单位3个。上缴各种税费总额96.8万元。全县化肥销售量10770吨，比上年增加1324吨，上升14%。

1978—2008年全县供销社系统购销情况一览表

表15-3 单位：万元

年度	国内纯购进总值		国内纯销售总值		
	总计	其中农副产品采购	总计	生活消费品销售总额	生产资料销售总额
1978	137.6	115.1	430.9	326.8	104.1
1979	167.9	135.4	455.7	338.9	116.8
1980	181.9	148.2	513.1	391.8	121.3
1981	511.4	366.4	591.9	421.5	170.4
1982	244.7	116.6	622.7	489.9	132.8
1983	255.2	133.7	563.1	420.8	142.3

续表15－3

年度	国内纯购进总值		国内纯销售总值		
	总计	其中农副产品采购	总计	生活消费品销售总额	生产资料销售总额
1984	242.1	129.8	581.6	454.5	127.1
1985	398.3	182.9	727.8	539.9	187.9
1986	290.2	132.5	631.3	466.0	165.3
1987	292.0	102.7	671.9	467.9	204.0
1988	567.7	258.6	774.7	520.9	253.8
1989	461.9	132.2	760.2	529.7	230.5
1990	492.5	190.0	804.2	523.2	281.0
1991	371.0	107.3	820.0	456.2	363.8
1992	485.3	156.5	837.7	419.8	417.9
1993	358.0	48.3	811.7	529.7	282.0
1994	409.2	216.3	324.8	120.4	204.4
1995	398.3	182.9	727.8	539.9	187.9
1996	290.2	132.5	631.3	466.0	165.3
1997	3108.2	48.5	1615.4	555.4	1060.0
1998	3230.6	40.7	1418.4	372.4	1046.0
1999	3351.1	17.5	4251.7	3314.5	937.2
2000	3062.2	12.3	1083.1	308.5	774.6
2001	2575.5	43.2	2752.5	326.9	2425.6
2002	2584.5	14.9	1363.0	303.0	1060.0
2003	2795.9	0	2866.7	238.4	2628.3
2004	4215.7	0	4542.0	162.2	4379.8
2005	4903.9	0	4766.4	141.3	4625.1
2006	3265.7	0	3684.0	133.0	3551.0
2007	4741.7	0	5315.3	138.6	5176.7
2008	4648.9	—	4938.0	142.0	4796.0

第五章 石油 物资

第一节 石油经营

一、管理体制

1979年，成立荔波县石油煤炭公司，隶属县商业局，1981年停止煤炭经营。1985年，县石油煤炭公司划归贵州省石油总公司，名称改为贵州省黔南石油分公司荔波支公司，自主经营，独立核算，自负盈亏。

1998年6月，荔波支公司随省石油总公司整体划入中国石化集团公司，属中石化黔南石油分公司的派出管理部门，称荔波片区，不再是独立核算单位。经营管理实行经理负责制，年度工作按集团、省、州公司统一下达的各项任务考核指标组织实施。资金费用管理实行收支两条线；商品物流控制实行进、销、存“五统一”（油品统一采购、车辆统一管理、人员统一调配、运力统一安排、费用统一结算）；财务稽核按国家会计法及系统内部会计制度办理；账账、账实相互核对程序为每月盘点结算制；商品定价严格执行省、州物价局制定的价格，同时，根据市场供需情况在物价部门统一指导下适时调整。

2000年，按照中石化集团公司的要求，对企业人员、资产进行整体重组改制，精简内部机构，撤销办公室、财务室，设经理1名，委派会计1名，职工买断工龄或者改变用工身份，引进劳务工，同工同酬。财务实行费用报账制，对加油站实行量、利、费考核，在人、财、物上无支配权，人员全部实行一年一聘制。

二、业务经营

1979—1991年，石油经营主要是供应全县工农业生产、交通运输、民用照明用油，批零兼营，油品销售以计划分配为主，市场调节为辅，车辆、机具用油凭证定量供应，不足部分计划外议价补充。设县城外老油库、狮子口油库2座，甲良、朝阳和茂兰供销社分别有简易油库供应农村用油。油价实行国家定价。

1992年起，取消凭证定量供应。1993年，在立化镇、城西建加油站各1座。随着国家对石油市场放开，县内出现社会加油站、加油点十余个，如友谊桥、凉水井、更甫、板麦等。是年，荔波支公司与县农场在时来建造加油站1座，合资经营，利润分成。

1992—1995年，油品除少量农业抗旱救灾专用油按平价供应外，其他油品按市场价供应执行省物价局统一制定的价格。1996年起，油品一律按市场价销售。

1998年，新建茂兰、甲良加油站。2000年，荔波—金城江公路改道，车流量减少，销售量萎缩，关闭立化镇加油站。与县农场合资建造的时来加油站，因双方发生责任权利纠纷，2001年9月通过法院裁定，双方终止合营。

2001年，配合市政建设，对樟江中路城西加油站就地改造。是年，在时来寨脚建加油站。茂兰、甲良加油站实行内部员工个人承包经营，到2003年收回，自营自管，实行吨油包干制。

2004年，城西加油站改造成荔波首座IC卡加油站，实现卡机联动，停止手工调价。2006年，城西加油站安装HAN阻燃隔爆系统。2008年，投资80万元对城西加油站进行加油站标准形象改造。

三、安全管理

县内石油经营企业始终坚持安全生产各项规章制度，将安全生产贯穿整个经营过程，加大加油站安全设施资金投入，对新上岗员工进行岗前培训，对在岗员工进行复训，推行班前会制度，每天、每星期、每月对员工进行安全教育。对安全隐患进行排查，不留死角，消灭隐患。制定和完善应急预案，每年开展消防演练，提高员工处置突发事件能力，全县石油经营未出现安全事故。

1979—1997年全县石油销售情况一览表

表15-4　　单位：吨

年度	汽油	柴油	煤油	润滑油
1979	234.00	259.30	116.40	—
1982	349.70	230.10	191.00	—
1983	327.30	255.40	204.30	—
1984	485.90	257.50	190.10	—
1985	653.50	375.30	231.00	—
1986	690.00	378.90	277.60	—
1987	773.30	450.90	239.80	—
1988	841.00	699.00	249.00	—
1989	859.00	819.00	257.00	—
1990	760.00	797.00	382.00	—
1991	1149.00	694.00	354.00	38.00
1992	972.00	611.00	356.00	47.00
1993	644.00	1200.00	195.00	51.00
1994	848.00	1052.00	70.00	52.00
1995	1020.00	2409.00	78.00	46.00
1996	588.00	1885.00	146.00	23.00
1997	505.00	1150.00	155.00	10.00

说明：1998年后不是独立核算单位，无统计数据。

1979—1997年全县石油销售指标完成情况一览表

表15-5　　单位：万元

年度	销售总额	费用总额	费用水平（%）	税金	利润
1979	32.95	3.83	11.62	—	0.66
1980	50.18	6.17	12.30	0.08	1.79
1981	54.27	6.60	12.16	0.19	1.37
1982	54.04	6.37	11.79	0.16	1.21
1983	60.61	7.23	11.93	0.13	2.15
1984	75.96	8.58	11.30	0.52	2.42
1985	103.29	10.82	10.48	1.79	3.03
1986	113.82	11.98	10.53	2.68	5.26
1987	136.71	13.03	9.53	3.29	7.10
1988	205.00	23.00	11.22	9.60	7.60
1989	274.00	27.40	10.00	16.00	9.00
1990	250.00	23.00	9.20	12.00	8.60
1991	324.00	35.00	10.80	8.24	11.06
1992	397.00	44.00	11.08	11.00	9.53
1993	602.00	46.00	7.64	11.14	11.25
1994	557.00	81.00	14.54	14.00	7.20
1995	906.00	119.00	13.13	16.10	4.50
1996	637.00	79.00	12.40	12.00	3.00
1997	466.00	72.00	15.45	12.00	3.30

说明：1998年后不是独立核算单位，无统计数据。

第二节　物资经营

一、物资体制改革

1978年，县物资局政企合一，按计划管理全县物资供应。1984年，国家实行生产资料价格双轨制以后，撤销县物资局，建县物资供应公司。1989年12月，恢复建立县物资管理局，属政府职能部门，行政编制5人，下设机电建材科、金属化轻科、生产资料科、财务科。机电建材科、金属化轻科、生产资料科实行分科承包，超额分成，亏损自补。

1990年5月，县政府决定不再设物资管理局，建立县物资贸易总公司，以物资贸易总公司为管理机构，但不挂牌，对外仍保留原物资管理局的管理职能，物资贸易总公司对外以物资管理局行文。下辖县物资供应公司、县生产资料服务公司。物资供应实行计划内指标和计划外指标双轨制。物资供应公司负责物资统配计划供应，生产资料服务公司负责计划外物资供应。物资供应公司、生产资料服务公司实行自主经营、独立核算、自负盈亏制度，向总公司上交管理费，承担原县物资管理局5个行政人员的工资、福利、医疗等费用。

1996年，将县物资贸易总公司下属的县生产资料服务公司和物资供应公司进行撤并，注册为荔波县物资贸易公司，下设物资贸易科、生产资料科，开展销售经营业务，至2008年不变。

二、业务经营

1978—1983年，县物资经营部门主要组织调拨国家计划分配的生产建设物资，按物价部门的规定收取运杂费、管理费，不盈不亏，略有结余。

随着国家经济改革深入，生产资料市场逐步放开，物资企业参与市场竞争。1987年，在茂兰增设物资销售点。1989年以后，国家逐步取消物资计划供应，县内物资企业供应范围缩小。1994年，物资企业开始出现亏损。

1998年，县物资贸易公司放弃常规经营的建材、金属、化轻、机电、汽车等业务，以国家专控的民用爆炸物资经营为主。民爆物品由州物资总公司提供。1999年5月，县物资贸易公司向县政府提出民爆物品单列直供申请，经县政府同意，并向省民爆器材行业管理部门申报，7月，获民爆物品单列直供资格。是年，向银行贷款80万元，对民爆器材仓库基础设施进行改造，修筑库区安全围墙355米，建造30立方米高位消防水池，并改造库区道路。

2001年，设茂兰民爆物品销售管理站，负责佳荣、洞塘、立化3个乡（镇）民爆物品销售管理。2002年，企业扭亏为盈，还清银行贷款80万元。

2006年9月，国家颁布新的《民用爆炸物品安全管理条例》，县物资贸易公司作为全县唯一经营销售民爆物品的企业，按照新《民用爆炸物品安全管理条例》及民爆器材行业管理部门的规定和要求，重新制定民爆器材购进、运输、储存、销售各项安全管理制度，建立健全各岗位工作职责及库区安全防范制度，请北京国泰民康安全技术中心对民爆器材仓库进行安全评价，按照评价要求对民爆器材仓库的道路、炸药库、雷管库、消防水池和安全围墙、大门等进行改造扩建，在库区安装电子网络全程安全监控系统，投入技改资金共300万元，于2007年按照新标准通过省国防科工办验收，获民用爆破器材销售经营凭证。同时，加强员工法治教育和安全培训，持证上岗，依法经营。

1978—2008年全县主要物资销售情况一览表

表15－6

年度	销售总额（万元）	利润（万元）	钢材（吨）	水泥（吨）	炸药（吨）	汽车（辆）	轮胎（套）
1978	127.00	2.62	308.67	1988.00	100.67	—	89
1979	109.00	4.20	365.00	1730.00	210.00	—	237
1980	199.90	2.70	265.00	2434.00	48.00	—	—
1981	73.00	0.95	296.00	1800.00	44.00	3	30
1982	85.00	2.90	325.00	1285.00	51.00	11	99
1983	98.60	2.05	217.00	2381.00	—	13	94
1984	117.84	2.37	345.00	2256.00	—	10	—
1985	164.00	3.19	552.00	1658.00	76.00	10	103
1986	213.00	4.50	550.00	2140.00	—	15	—
1987	215.00	3.53	594.00	1874.00	120.00	15	—
1988	198.00	4.90	433.00	1653.00	185.00	34	223

续表15－6

年度	销售总额（万元）	利润（万元）	钢材（吨）	水泥（吨）	炸药（吨）	汽车（辆）	轮胎（套）
1989	347.00	10.80	666.00	2390.00	242.00	17	307
1990	268.00	21.26	567.00	2485.00	220.00	—	278
1991	300.00	10.00	700.00	2000.00	300.00	15	100
1992	340.00	11.00	800.00	1000.00	310.00	15	40
1993	350.00	12.00	1000.00	300.00	305.00	10	30
1994	400.00	−5.00	100.00	—	320.00	12	20
1995	320.00	−6.00	—	—	330.00	10	—
1996	300.00	−4.00	—	—	340.00	10	—
1997	540.00	7.70	—	—	400.00	30	—
1998	448.00	1.60	—	—	400.00	10	—
1999	264.00	4.10	—	—	445.00	10	—
2000	404.00	18.70	—	—	450.00	5	—
2001	404.00	5.50	—	—	440.00	—	—
2002	336.00	−3.80	—	—	450.00	—	—
2003	556.00	23.30	—	—	600.00	—	—
2004	754.00	41.00	—	—	700.00	—	—
2005	579.00	35.70	—	—	618.00	—	—
2006	678.00	37.00	—	—	649.00	—	—
2007	625.00	21.00	—	—	526.00	—	—
2008	960.00	71.00	—	—	677.00	—	—

第十六篇
经济综合管理

1978年，全县实行计划经济管理体制，1985年以后，改革计划管理体制，对国民经济管理逐步扩大指导性计划和加大市场调节作用，将农业生产计划改为指导性计划，工业生产计划只对几种产品实行指令性计划。全县国民经济逐步由计划管理向宏观调控转变，通过宏观经济指标和宏观经济政策，指导经济社会发展。

1978年以来，县工商、物价、食品药品监督、国土资源、统计、审计等经济管理部门，不断进行机构改革和管理职能的转变，发挥经济管理部门的作用，使全县改革开放，经济建设不断地发展。

第一章 计划管理

第一节 计划管理体制改革

1978年，全县实行计划经济管理体制。工农业产品的调拨供应、生产生活资料、劳动力分配等实行统一计划、统一分配，紧俏商品实行凭证供应、持票购买。1980年以后，按照国家“调整、改革、整顿、提高”的方针和市场经济相结合的原则，制订国民经济发展计划，主要农产品实行指导性计划，生产、流通领域实行指令性计划。一类物资实行统购、统配；二类物资实行派购，优先订购、收购和分配供应；三类物资由市场自由调节。

1985年以后，计划部门贯彻国务院批转国家计委《关于改进计划体制的若干暂行规定》，改革计划管理体制，对国民经济管理逐步扩大指导性计划和加大市场调节作用，将农业生产计划改为指导性计划，工业生产计划只对几种产品实行指令性计划。全县国民经济逐步由计划管理向宏观调控转变，通过宏观经济指标和宏观经济政策，指导经济社会发展。

1987年后，国民经济计划按开放搞活的政策进行宏观调控，将农业生产放在第一位，发展粮食生产、多种经营，增强农业后劲；工业生产抓企业挖潜改造，提高生产水平，发展乡镇工业，重点抓原煤生产；流通领域推行各种形式的承包经营责任制。

1999年，按照县政府提出的“依靠省州，面向两广，开发山区，兴县富民的经济战略”，以“发挥优势，提高效益，抓好基础，增强后劲”为目标，制订国民经济和社会发展计划，扩大指导性计划，缩小指令性计划。

2008年，经济发展只安排指导性计划，生产经营全部由市场调节。

第二节 计划编制与执行

一、计划编制

县计划部门在国家每个五年计划时期和全县经济社会发展的不同阶段，按照县委、县政府关于全县经济社会发展的战略部署，制订全县经济社会发展计划，主要有长期计划、中期计划、年度计划。计划部门每年年初编制的全县经济社会发展年度计划，经各个行业对计划的各个方面、各项指标进行讨论，达到科学、合理、切合实际和具操作性后，报请县人大常委会审核、修改，经县人代会讨论通过后下达执行。

1981年、1986年，先后制订“六五”时期、“七五”时期全县国民经济和社会发展计划。1991年5月制定《荔波县国民经济和社会发展十年规划和第八个五年计划》。1994年8月制定《荔波县

“九五”和2010年市场建设发展规划》。1996年5月制定《荔波县国民经济和社会发展“九五”计划和2010年远景目标纲要》。1997年6月制定《荔波县国民经济和社会发展项目库》。2001年3月制定《荔波县国民经济和社会发展第十个五年计划纲要》，2006年9月制定《荔波县国民经济和社会发展第十一个五年计划》。

二、计划执行

中共十一届三中全会后，全县贯彻落实中共十一届三中全会精神，按照“调整、改革、巩固、提高”的方针，逐步实行对外开放、对内搞活的经济政策，工农业生产得到迅速发展，至1984年，实现州委提出的提前一年实现“六五”计划的目标。

1985年“六五”期末，由于全县遭受严重旱、虫灾害，粮食比上年减产38.97%，经济作物、养殖业均比上年增长；主要工业产品煤、电、水泥、饮料酒分别比上年增长3.21%、2.7%、13.4%、79.58%。“六五”期末，农业、轻工业、重工业比重有所变化，农业产值占工农业总产值的比例由1980年的81%降为79%，轻工业由7.29%上升到8.42%，重工业由11.62%上升到19.4%。

1986—1990年“七五”期间，以“发挥优势、提高效益、打好基础、增强后劲”为目标，锐意改革，在改革中发展。“七五”期末，各项经济指标均比“六五”期末有较大提升。

1991—1995年“八五”期间，全县按照中共中央“抓住机遇、深化改革、扩大开放、促进发展、保持稳定”的基本方针，不断完善各项改革制度，加强和改善宏观调控。1995年，主要经济社会发展指标均超额完成“八五”预定计划。

1996—2000年“九五”期间，县委、县政府抓住中央实施西部大开发、扩大内需、增加投资、拉动经济增长的机遇，以提高经济效益为中心，把加强管理、调整结构、加快进步放在突出位置，在质量、效益、品种上下功夫。集中力量加强重点项目的建设，大力发展南下通道经济，搞好县域经济的合理布局，扶持边远贫困地区的经济发展。加强经济建设，到2000年“九五”期末，全县国内生产总值24166万元，占计划的100.69%，比上年增长13.46%。

2001—2005年“十五”时期，县委、县政府把加快发展作为富民兴县的第一要务，坚持抢抓争上，务实真干，着力抓住西部大开发、新阶段扶贫开发、中央加大少数民族地区扶持力度三大机遇，加快富民兴县步伐。2005年“十五”期末，全县国民生产总值完成81520万元，占计划数81500万元的100.02%，比上年增长14%。

2006—2008年，全县以科学发展观统领经济社会发展全局，以人为本，创新发展思路，加强基础设施建设、生态建设和环境保护，着力推进经济结构调整，壮大特色优势产业，转变经济增长方式，努力扩大经济总量。同时，以打造国际化专业旅游城市为目标，围绕旅游发展新型工业经济、城镇经济、农业产业化经济，开展社会主义新农村建设，构建富裕荔波、秀美荔波、和谐荔波。2008年年末，全县国民生产总值完成11.34亿元，占州计划数10.5亿元的108%，比上年增长13.24%，完成年度计划11亿元的103.09%。

1978—2008年主要经济指标完成情况一览表

表16－1

年度	国内生产总值（万元）				全社会固定资产投资总额（万元）	社会消费品零售总额（万元）	农民人均纯收入（元）
	合计	第一产业	第二产业	第三产业			
1978	2323	1646	391	286	103	894	143
1979	2485	1760	419	306	93	918	152

续表16－1

年度	国内生产总值（万元）				全社会固定资产投资总额（万元）	社会消费品零售总额（万元）	农民人均纯收入（元）
	合计	第一产业	第二产业	第三产业			
1980	2745	1702	494	549	126	984	169
1981	2947	1838	534	575	157	1158	174
1982	3202	1985	576	641	151	1315	213
1983	3475	2155	625	695	150	1498	214
1984	3735	2315	672	748	210	1624	208
1985	3150	2178	468	504	150	1848	187
1986	3692	2258	810	624	143	2233	195
1987	4730	2956	854	920	142	2364	209
1988	6950	3716	2041	1193	187	2868	277
1989	8904	5044	2523	1337	281	2915	366
1990	9329	5237	2672	1420	157	3093	294
1991	10194	5777	2710	1707	184	3563	377
1992	14202	7426	3454	3322	344	4168	390
1993	15933	7802	4092	4039	1529	4576	446
1994	18540	8122	4982	5436	4228	5780	697
1995	24029	9782	6656	7591	5407	6939	861
1996	27506	10516	7385	9605	4605	6715	1119
1997	30092	10882	7680	11530	5566	6821	1206
1998	34279	12340	8369	13570	16191	8565	1254
1999	35626	10946	9668	15012	6698	10356	1156
2000	38710	14824	10271	13615	8861	12400	1196
2001	41489	16145	10285	15059	12898	13602	1220
2002	44343	15745	12434	16164	13261	15029	1255
2003	52913	15676	16117	21120	19520	16504	1360
2004	59338	19020	18653	21665	31916	20073	1495
2005	67645	20222	22489	24934	35442	22172	1654
2006	76873	21742	25212	29919	46265	21817	1751
2007	91475	23573	31690	36212	61276	25600	2159
2008	113378	31230	39265	42883	68357	32317	2618

第三节 建设项目

一、基础设施建设项目

中共十一届三中全会后到2008年30年间，特别是“九五”“十五”期间，全县执行中央“扩大内需，实施积极的财政政策拉动经济增长”的方针，以西部大开发为契机，加快了交通、能源、水利、旅游和城镇建设为重点的基础设施建设。1978年全县只有8条通乡公路，2008年全县通乡公路达到67条789公里，实现乡乡通公路。总投资1亿多元完成独荔公路改造，总投资6790万元完成荔大公路改建，总投资3.96亿元新建荔波机场，总投资6742.13万元（其中国债资金1000万元）新建小七孔景区游客中心、步道、栈道、停车场等203个项目。总投资1600万元（其中国债资金1500万元）修建茂兰保护区旅游公路，总投资280万元改建县城4条出城公路，总投资750万元完成县城街道硬化工程，硬化率达到100%。2007年，承办全省第二届旅游发展大会，总投资2.26亿元对县城设施进行全面整改，新建邓恩铭广场、乡镇小区和教师新村，新建县人民医院、县中医院和县计生站，扩建县民族中学，新建玉屏二中，总投资3406万元新建和改建38所城乡中小学校。通过土地置换和招商引资的形式新建了200多万平方米的住宅楼和商品楼，县城面积从1978年的0.6平方公里扩大到6平方公里。

二、“以工代赈”项目

“以工代赈”是指政府投资建设公共基础设施工程，受赈者参加工作建设获得劳务报酬，以此取代直接赈济的一项扶持政策。因荔波是一个边远贫困县，加之计划部门在跑项目、争资金上做出了辛勤努力，荔波县从国家1991年实施“以工代赈”项目以来，争取到项目资金5005.75万元，对推动荔波经济加快发展发挥了巨大的作用。

1991年开始实施“以工代赈”项目到2008年，全县“以工代赈”项目总投资达6581.39万元。其中，“以工代赈”资金5005.75万元，地方自筹1576万元。建成项目130个，主要包括交通道路工程、通信线路改造工程、农田水利工程、坡改梯工程、易地移民工程等。通过实施“以工代赈”项目共新建和改造县乡公路和通村公路562.8公里。其中，小七孔—麻尾、甲良—麻尾、玉屏—播尧、荔波—南丹、荔波—大沙坡、甲良—阳凤、翁昂—捞村、阳凤—墨寨、佳荣—从江为四级公路，共206.8公里；荔波—麻尾、荔波—南丹为三级油路，共66.8公里；实施易地移民工程包括驾欧拉圭移民新村、水利拉打移民新村、洞塘瑶寨移民新村、永康甲棒移民新村、甲良干塘移民新村、方村更信移民新村等建设项目，共移民192户800人；坡改梯及基本农田建设96841亩及防洪、排洪人饮提灌、病库治理等项目。

三、绿色产业

1992年，县政府下发大力发展绿色工程的1号文件，出台一系列优惠政策。如招商引资奖励政策，机关干部领办开发性实体的鼓励政策，利益分配和征地、贷款方面的优惠政策等。1993年后，安排财政资金185万元，热作资金100万元，“以工代赈”资金350万元用于发展绿色产业。

1996年，省委、省政府作出《关于大力发展绿色产业的决定》后，荔波县成立绿色产业办公室，计划部门在下达年度计划时，下达绿色产业建设年度计划，把绿色产业建设作为主要考核指标之一，有关职能部门和各乡（镇）要成立相应的组织和领导机构，加强绿色产业的建设和领导，并在县绿色产业总体规划指导下，编制乡（镇）绿色产业建设规划。

为加快荔波绿色产业的发展，县委、县政府提出“山顶植树子，山腰栽果子，山下办厂子，河边种竹子，田坝种稻子，山内建四园三场，山外找销售市场”的设想和“山上抓基地，山脚抓加工，山外抓市场”的发展思路以及“221115”绿色工程（即建设2万亩酸梅基地，2万亩板栗基地，1万亩沙田柚基地，1万亩杜仲基地，1万亩茶叶基地，5000亩早桃基地）的实施方案。

“九五”期间计划新建5.2万亩商品羊基地，2万头商品牛基地，1万亩沙田柚基地，1000亩猕猴桃基地，2万亩板栗基地，2万亩酸梅基地，5万亩坑木林基地，1000亩黄草基地，18万只乌骨鸡生产基地，3600亩辣椒生产基地，3000亩笋竹基地，5000亩菌业生产基地并新建辣椒酱食品加工厂和酸梅系列产品加工厂共76个项目。

四、计划项目监督

计划项目列入监督的范围有农业生产主要是各种农作物的种植面积和产量，以水稻、玉米、油菜等种植面积为考核重点；工业以总产值、产品产量为检查考核指标。1980年后，增加利润考核指标，即商业供销主要对纯购进、纯销售、农业生产资料供应、农产品收购、社会商品零售额以及主要商品收购量、供应量进行检查考核；物资部门主要对调拨、供应和物资库存量进行检查考核。属工业品生产资料如钢材、水泥、木材、石油、烧碱等，分别由物资、石油、农机、林业等部门负责；属于日用品工业品、生活资料、农产品收购和农业生产资料供应，由商业、供销、粮食、医药、外贸等部门负责。1986年，贯彻中共中央关于进一步活跃农村经济十项规定后，对粮食、油料、肥猪等农产品取消统购政策，改为合同订购和市场收购。药材除麝香、黄檗、杜仲、厚朴4个品种仍由国家统一经营外，其余均允许多渠道经营，县计划部门管理监督的品种只限于国家计划价部分。同时，根据国务院公布的《专项控制商品目录》，机关、事业单位购买属控制审批的商品由计划部门审批。

1984年以后，生产建设项目单位工程投资50万元以下，非生产性建设20万元以下由县计划部门审批，报上级计划部门备案。1986年3月贯彻国务院《关于控制固定资产投资规模的若干规定》以后，县计划部门对基建项目审批权为5万元以下。对投资超过县审批权限的生产性和非生产性项目须报送《项目建议书》和《可行性研究报告》，经县政府同意后立项上报。对一般性基本建设要申请立项、申报建设用地计划，并有设计部门的设计图纸，用于基建的资金，先存入建设银行，经财政、审计、建设银行等部门签署意见后，由县计划部门下达基建计划或报上级计划部门审批，列入专项资金开支。建设用地在3亩以下的，由用地单位申请，县政府审批后，由计划部门下达用地指标；超过3亩以上的报州级以上计划部门审批。农村和城镇居民建房用地，由土地管理部门在当年计划部门下达的个人建房用地计划指标内，根据各户具体情况掌握审批。所有基本建设须经县计划部门批准并发放开工许可证方能破土动工。

列入年度计划的“以工代赈”项目，都必须按规定进行审查、评估、论证，没有立项的项目列入项目库，下年继续申报。项目实施按照“四制”（项目法人责任制、招标投标制、工程监理制、合同管理制）和《以工代赈资金管理使用办法》的要求执行。

第二章　工商行政管理

第一节　管理体制

1978年，县工商行政管理局内设业务股、企业管理股、办公室。1982年，内设机构设行政（秘书）股、市场管理股、合同管理股、工商企业管理股。1983年10月，增设立化工商所。1988年设经济监督检查所。

1991年，个体劳动者协会、消费者协会挂靠县工商行政管理局。全县工商系统有干部职工54人。

1994年1月，县级机构改革，县工商行政管理局、技术监督局、物价局合并建立县工商行政管理局，内设办公室、计量市场股、企业登记股、物价股、财务室、经济检查所、计量测试所、物价检查所，人员定编行政18人、事业12人，下设玉屏、朝阳、甲良、茂兰、立化5个工商行政管理所。县个体劳动者协会、私营企业协会、消费者协会3个社团组织仍挂靠县工商局。1998年5月，成立县“3・15”快速反应执法队和信访接待室。

1998年11月，国家工商行政管理局在《工商行政管理体制改革方案》中明确规定，省以下工商行政管理机关实行垂直管理。之后，省委、省政府印发《关于贵州省工商行政管理体制改革的实施意见》，1999年6月，县委办、县政府办转发县工商技监体制改革领导小组《关于工商技监行政管理体制改革的实施方案》，确定工商、物价、技术监督三局分离，工商、物价、技监合理分配财产和人员。县工商局实行省、州垂直管理。

同时，对已建成使用并由工商部门管理的各类市场实行管办脱钩，全县市场在清产核资后，分别交县政府国有资产营运中心或县工商局下属市场服务中心经营。市场服务中心为事业性质、企业管理单位，自收自支，自负盈亏。

1999年12月7日，成立县市场服务中心。

2001年9月，在全省工商行政管理机构改革中，按照州工商局印发的《荔波县工商行政管理局、所职能配置内设机构和人员编制方案及实施意见》，县工商局内设办公室、政策法规股、注册登记股、执法监督股（“12315”投诉中心、经济检查中队），下设玉屏工商所（编制14名）、茂兰工商所（编制10名）、甲良工商所（编制10名），直属事业机构有机关服务中心（为局属股级事业单位，事业编制5名），建立县工商局“12315”投诉中心。全县工商系统行政编制45名（局机关行政编制11名、工商所编制34名），离退休干部工作人员单列编制1名，后勤事业编制5名（不含消费者协会事业编制）。县工商系统有36人取得国家机关公务员资格。至2008年，行政管理体制不变。

第二节 市场管理

一、集贸市场管理

（一）集贸市场建设

1978年后，对“文化大革命”期间和之前被个人或单位占用的市场场地进行清理收回。1980年，县工商局按“因地制宜、形式多样、立足长远、方便群众、逐步配套、因陋就简、讲求效益、分期实施、狠抓当年”的原则，制定市场发展规划，提出建设方案。是年，甲良建成集市场棚53间、面积969平方米，平整水泥地面2385平方米。之后，立化、洞塘、佳荣、翁昂、播尧、地莪、方村、甲站等集市相继整地建棚，到1990年，全县修建集贸市场18个，市场面积达到34059平方米。

1991年，县工商部门投资4.4万元，改造扩建茂兰市场、立化市场、平寨市场、朝阳市场、玉屏市场、佳荣市场。1992年，投资2.4万元改扩建翁昂市场、水尧岜合市场、播尧老市场、方村老市场、拉圭老市场。

1993年，经县政府批准，以县工商局贷款承建承还方式建设荔波综合市场，1994年12月30日建成投入使用，总投资194万元，市场总面积5874平方米，设个体固定门面90间、固定摊位49个、活动摊位172个，主要经营农副产品、食品、工业品等。是年，投资39.17万元改扩建阳凤市场、王蒙市场、捞村市场、玉屏小吃街。

1994年，改扩建玉屏综合市场、地莪市场，其中工商部门投资玉屏综合市场254万元。1995年，投资172.89万元改扩建甲良牛马市场、播尧市场、茂兰市场、洞塘市场。1996年，投资100.03万元改扩建茂兰市场、佳荣市场、甲良市场、播尧市场、朝阳市场、玉屏市场、洞塘市场。

1998年10月，县政府办公室批复同意洞塘乡在肯甫设立边贸市场，实行“统一规划、统一征地、统一管理”办法，按规定办理土地征用手续，市场建设所需费用自筹解决。

1999年，全县有城乡综合集贸市场18个，即立化镇更班集贸市场、立化集贸市场、播尧乡农贸市场、甲良镇阳凤市场、播尧乡地莪市场、茂兰农贸市场、佳荣农贸市场、洞塘农贸市场、朝阳市场、王蒙市场、拉圭市场、捞村市场、翁昂市场、方村乡农贸市场、甲良市场、繁荣市场、西门鸡鸭仔猪市场、县综合农贸市场。这些市场中，西门鸡鸭仔猪市场、县综合农贸市场为工商部门独建，其他市场为工商部门与乡（镇）合建。

2001年9月，县城力达市场建成并正式投入使用，总面积22506平方米，市场内有固定门面200间、固定摊位127个、活动摊位118个，主要经营建材、家电、家具、副食品、工业品。

至2008年，全县有城乡集贸市场19个。

（二）集贸市场管理

1978—1980年，对集贸市场开展经常性监督检查，主要查处不准上市交易的物资、产品。1981年，对城关、甲良、播尧、朝阳、茂兰5个集贸市场进行整顿，治理脏、乱、差，统一规划，定点挂牌，按行归市，改善市场秩序。

1985—1986年，开展创建文明市场活动，各市场备公平秤，为消费者复秤，赶场天有专人检查，发现问题及时处理。

1987年后，工商部门采取定点、定摊、定人员的办法管理市场，商户亮照经营，商品明码标价，管理人员严格查处违法违章行为，取缔无证商贩。在市场内设信息专栏，公布黔南州主要集市主要商品价格行情。

1996年11月，成立朝阳市场服务所，在朝阳和拉圭市场增设服务摊板120个，实行收费管理。

1997年，朝阳、王蒙、拉圭、捞村、翁昂5个市场对肉行摊位实行服务收费管理。

1999年10月，按公平、公正、公开的原则，对玉屏综合农贸市场肉行摊位使用权公开招标竞租，竞标中标金额25.27万元，使用期限1年。2000年10月，再次对玉屏综合农贸市场肉行64个摊位使用权进行公开招标竞租，中标金额22.84万元。

2001年12月，根据省政府办公厅关于工商行政管理机关与所办市场脱钩的文件精神，县工商局将自办的县综合农贸市场移交县国有资本营运公司管理，佳荣农贸市场移交荔波新欣市场开发服务部管理。

2003年5月，将县城农贸市场内无固定门面的百货、成衣、五金、铁具等摊位迁至力达市场内设摊经营，重新划行归市。

2004年1月起，按市场管办脱钩的规定，茂兰镇政府收回茂兰农贸市场经营管理权，同时承担该市场维修、环卫及扩（改）建责任，茂兰工商所购置的所有摊位全部移交茂兰镇政府，镇政府补偿工商所2万元。

2005年3月，县政府将县综合农贸市场肉行国有土地使用权和地上建筑物（肉行场棚）经营权进行公开拍卖，玉屏镇建设村以291万元取得该肉行的经营使用权，期限50年。

二、市场监督检查

1978—1990年，市场监督以打击投机倒把、走私活动，清理整顿无照经营，查处假冒伪劣商品为重点，查处违法违规行为。其间，查处投机倒把案件75件，违章案件439件；无照经营172户，短斤少两20起；销毁变质饮料、罐头等。

1993年后，重点对“三无”（无商标、无厂址、无合格证）产品、猪牛肉、饮料等商品进行检查，对查出的假冒伪劣商品、超期变质商品、注水肉等进行公开销毁处理。

1998年，对茂兰、甲良、朝阳、王蒙、玉屏、立化等主要集贸市场和街头路边食品摊点营业证照、销售假冒走私商品、制售“三无”产品和销售超期变质产品等行为进行检查整顿，对非法出版物及美容、美发、娱乐、保健服务业的违法经营进行查处。全年开展市场检查97次，检查国营、集体、个体工商户共1937户（次），查处无照经营64户；查处市场违规案件172件，罚没款0.76万元；查处违法违章案件206件，罚款共计2.5万元。查处的商品主要有注水牛肉、注水猪肉、各类超期变质商品、假冒商品等。没收不合格衡器类113台（件），对无照经营有奖猜谜活动进行查处。

1999年1月，开展主要集贸市场巡回大检查，检查经营户226户，对违反明码标价规定的商户6户、短斤少两液化气经营户2户予以处罚。国庆节前夕，检查各类门市、摊点1372户，查处无照经营11户和不按行归市、违章设摊14户，没收并销毁超期变质食品。

2000年，先后开展“红盾打假护农”“揭谎月”“百城万店无假货”专项治理活动；对经营夏季饮食、熟食行业进行整顿，经营者与工商所签订卫生责任书。

2001年，在“十一”国庆节假日期间，检查各行业经营户528户，收缴各种超期、变质食品、啤酒、饮料等商品，取缔无经营资格商户6户，对违法经营户罚款800元，受理旅游投诉2起。全年查处制售假冒伪劣食品、销售过期变质食品案件132件，捣毁制假窝点2个。

2001年12月—2002年1月，开展安全过冬、过元旦、过春节打假专项行动3次，检查市场6个、经营户1451户。检查中，收缴不合格计量器具、盗版光碟、劣质商品、注水肉等；查处无照经营28户、超范围经营4户；查获假冒进网许可证1起，罚款2万元，退赔消费者款项共4.29万元。

2002年5—6月，县政府组织县直相关部门对全县各集贸市场的经营主体、经营秩序进行专项整治2次，重点检查集贸市场、建材市场、加油站、旅游市场，捣毁制售“三无”矿灯窝点4个，没收劣质商品和不合格器具，查封过期农药、“三无”商品，没收各类非法音像制品、盗版书刊；对5个不具备经营条件的加油站发出通知限期整改，取缔3户不达标加油站。

2003年8月，开展的食品、药品两个“放心工程”市场监督检查，查处无照经营案件1件，没收过期变质食品、假冒中药材、假茅台酒等。

2004年，重点对奶粉市场、儿童食品市场、夏秋时令食品市场进行检查，收缴“飞鹿”牌奶粉400克包装27包、“花溪”牌奶粉500克包装5包及各类过期变质食品2300公斤。元旦、春节、“五一”、国庆等节日期间，集中检查各旅游景点4次，旅店、宾馆78家，餐馆24家，旅游产品商店7家。同时，建立景区维权投诉站，设立消费者投诉导向牌，并在小七孔设旅游消费维权投诉站，及时处理游客投诉。

2006年春节期间，开展以食品、餐饮、住宿、家禽、烟花爆竹等行业为重点的专项整治，检查市场16个，检查副食品经营户370户、超市2个、餐饮经营户123户、禽类及其制品经营户56户、水产品经营户21户、酒类经营户8户、肉类经营户65户。

2007年11月，县工商局为玉屏片区、茂兰片区、甲良片区聘请群众食品安全监督管理员7人。

2008年，工商部门在元旦、春节期间检查市场14个及食品、饮食经营户626户；在国庆节期间检查食品经营户1018户（次）。同时，重点检查含三聚氰胺问题奶制品，没收问题奶粉，对未经检验的液态奶作下架处理。

三、专业市场管理

（一）粮食市场监管

1994年粮食市场放开，县内粮食市场逐渐繁荣。1998年11月，县政府批准县工商局、粮食局共同成立粮食市场稽查队，下设玉屏、朝阳、甲良、茂兰、立化5个片区稽查分队，按照《粮食收购条例》，查处粮食购销违规行为。

1998年12月—1999年1月，对甲良、播尧、阳凤等市场进行巡查，查处非法收购粮食案件25件，依法没收粮食7.48吨。1999年，查处倒卖粮食案件25件，没收粮食12.89吨。

2000年，实行粮食经营台账制度，要求所有收购、经营、加工粮食的企业及个体工商户建立粮食经营台账。全年发放粮食经营、加工、用粮台账160份，办理“粮食收购资格证”10个，查处粮食经营违法违章案件16件。

2004年4月，建立粮食市场统计报告制度，明确粮食包括大米、面粉、玉米、大豆，市场包括超市和连锁店，各工商所每月1日前将粮食统计月报表报县工商局。

2006—2008年，每年对全县粮食市场进行专项检查，主要检查综合市场、粮食经营企业（门市）、个体工商户及其经营的大米、面粉、玉米等，查处粮食购销和粮食食品经营加工的违法违规行为。

（二）屠宰市场监管

1998年前，县内畜禽屠宰长期为屠户或群众自宰自销，无定点屠宰场地，没有进行统一管理。

1999年3月，县工商局市场巡查组对肉食市场进行突击检查，查处牛肉注水户2户，对注水牛肉作没收销毁处理，并在电视台曝光。6月，占地3016平方米的玉屏镇新建屠宰场投入使用，设宰牛场、宰猪场、宰鸡台、疫检所，同时进行畜禽屠宰管理检查和上市肉品检疫，县城生猪定点屠宰率达100%。此后，玉屏、甲良、朝阳、茂兰、立化5个镇实行畜禽定点屠宰，定点屠宰率100%。11月，个人经营的屠宰场关闭。

2001年8月，根据国家工商总局《关于立即开展肉食品市场专项整治紧急通知》，县工商、卫生、检疫、公安等部门联合开展全县食品市场、屠宰场清理整顿，逐一检查各市场，对有注水肉、病害肉行为的定点屠宰场取消其定点资格，予以关闭，查处有关责任人。

2005年6月起，按照“定点屠宰、集中检疫、统一纳税、分散经营”的原则，对县城生猪（畜禽）定点屠宰场实行集中检疫、统一收费管理。

2008年3月，县物价局、财政局、商业贸易总公司、畜牧局、工商局、环保局联合发出《关于规范生猪饲养屠宰销售环节收费的通知》，取消生猪屠宰、猪肉销售市场管理费。

（三）汽车配件市场监管

随着改革开放的深入，县内汽车不断增加，汽车配件经营户逐渐增多，工商部门不定期开展汽车配件市场监督检查。

2001年，县工商局与有关单位对县内报废汽车拆解拼装情况进行专项检查，检查汽车修理及配件经营23户、摩托车修理及配件经营15户、废旧物资回收6户，对查出的“三无”产品作暂扣处理。

2004年4—5月，工商、质监、物价、公安、经贸、税务等部门组成专项整治小组，对全县汽车市场开展专项整治，检查汽车配件市场门市41个、汽车维修点22个，没收未经强制性认证汽车轮胎、摩托车轮胎及“三无”汽车配件价值3万元，查处假冒摩托车配件案件3件。

2006年3—4月，开展全县车用电瓶液市场专项整治，检查汽车、摩托车修理厂及零配件经营门市31户，重点检查擅自勾兑、质量不达标、标志内容不规范等问题，查出并没收超期、“三无”电解液5瓶。

（四）其他要素市场监管

1999年5月，县工商局、消费者协会、妇联组成检查组，在县城开展妇女用品、美容美发服务质量及标示、广告、宣传等专项检查。通过检查，没收冒牌化妆品10盒。

2001年1月，对县城钢材门市部和建筑队自备钢材进行突击检查，查处没收劣质钢材经营户3户，没收劣质钢材2171.5公斤，罚款0.45万元。

2003年7月，对全县制、售、使用纤维制品的经营者和集团使用絮用纤维制品的单位进行专项整治，主要检查以絮用纤维作填充物的棉絮、被子、褥子、毯（毡）子、枕头、棉衣、床垫、沙发、靠（座）垫等产品。共检查絮用纤维制品经营户192户，使用纤维制品的医院18家、学校6所、幼儿园4所、宾馆（旅店、招待所）207家，未发现有假冒伪劣絮用纤维制品及“黑心棉”现象，检查中取缔无照经营户3户。

四、市场专项治理

（一）农资市场专项治理

农资市场放开后，县工商部门每年进行对农资市场进行检查，查处违法违规农资经营行为。1991—1997年，查处非法经营种子案件2起，单位和个人非法倒卖化肥252.99吨，其中假冒伪劣化肥17.5吨。

1999年，开展农资市场专项治理，查处倒卖化肥违法案件7件，取缔无照经营13户，查扣尿素5.44吨、复合肥33吨、碳铵4.9吨、磷肥2.198吨。

2000—2001年，每年3月开展“红盾护农”执法行动，对营农业生产资料的单位及个体工商户进行全面检查，与经营农业生产资料经的单位及个人签订《经销农业生产资料责任书》，防止假冒伪劣商品进入市场。两年查处无照倒卖化肥案件3起，收缴尿素249包、复合肥85包、碳铵20包，对假冒伪劣农药予以没收。

2002年上半年，对县内农资公司、供销社、农牧三站（农业技术推广站、农村合作经济经营管理站、畜牧兽医站）的农资经营点33个及个体经营户14户进行专项治理，查扣无检验报告单的三元素复合肥70包、喀斯特复合肥62包、铁农牌三元复合肥720包，共19.3吨；立案查处4户，查处无照经营3户。

2004年，开展“红盾护农”行动，集中检查4次，检查经营农资企业和个体工商户58户，同时要求农资经营户建立购销台账，将农资商品纳入重点商品质量监管关口前移范围。

2006年7—8月，县工商、畜牧、药监部门联合开展全县农资市场专项检查，没收并销毁假冒伪劣、违法经营农资商品2786公斤。全年检查化肥经营户48户、农药经营户28户，立案查处各类农资案件5起。

2008年5月，按照省农业厅、省工商局《关于建立农业生产资料商品经营台账的通知》，县工商局、农业局共同行文，规定从2008年5月20日起，凡在荔波县境内经营种子（含蚕种、甘蔗种）、种苗（含桑苗）、农药、肥料、农膜、农业机械、植保器械以及《贵州省农产品质量安全条例》规定的其他农业投入品的单位、个人，均应依法建立农资商品经营台账。至年底，全县有化肥经营户34户、种子经营户96户、农药经营户40户建立健全农资进货台账。全年农资市场专项整治行动查扣和收缴涉假种子65公斤、化肥1.6吨。

（二）动物市场专项治理

1999年，县工商局查出从广西贩运到荔波县内的带病仔猪36头，与兽医检疫、公安部门联合在立化镇当场焚烧销毁，并通过电视新闻曝光。

2003年7月，开展全县经营野生动物场所和屠宰场专项检查，检查经营户、宾馆、饭店、冷冻库等717户，取缔无照经营2户，未发现有国家禁止销售的野生动物及熟食品和从事收购贩运、加工野生动物及其制品行为。

2004年2月，针对县外高致病性禽流感疫情蔓延流行的情况，县工商局发布通告：全县农村集市、菜市场等一律停止现场屠宰加工活禽；临时关闭王蒙、捞村、驾欧、立化、平寨、播尧、更班、佳荣等边界集市活禽交易；严格执行索证索票制度，在市场上经营的禽类制品必须持产品检验检疫合格证和进货发票；严禁疫区禽类及其产品进入县境，对进货渠道不明或无产品检验检疫证的禽类制品，责令其立即停止销售，要求各经营户做好库存、销售记录，对没有检疫证明运入县内的各类禽产品，一律堵回原地不准进入县境内，经检查为带病禽类产品的，就地没收、扑杀、掩埋；对违法经营活禽及其产品、哄抬物价、扰乱市场经营秩序的，严厉查处。

2006年，开展野生动物保护“绿盾行动”，县工商局、林业局、茂兰保护局林业派出所等单位检查县城的宾馆、饭店57家，没收活体国家重点二级保护野生动物果子狸2只、死体果子狸6公斤及竹鼠8只、野山羊肉4公斤、野猫1只，放生国家重点二级保护野生动物白鹇4只、野生鸟7只，将死体进行焚烧处理。是年，县工商局制定《荔波县高致病性禽流感防控工作方案》《荔波县工商行政管理系统市场防控高致病性禽流感应急预案》。

2007—2008年，加强全县出入境禽畜检查，堵截病禽、病畜流入市场。

（三）原煤市场检查

1993年，查处掺假原煤4344吨，罚款8.78万元。

2000年7月，平寨煤管所和县工商局针对县内原煤掺假情况，共同组成原煤打假工作组，对各煤厂、站台和运输线上的原煤质量进行突击检查，发现有不同程度掺假现象。检查中，通过宣传教育，增强矿主和煤炭经营户的法律意识。

2001年，根据国务院关于对煤炭生产企业进行全面综合治理的要求，与煤炭主管部门对全县煤炭生产企业进行全面检查。共检查30户，责令停业整顿24户，查处无照经营5户，罚款1.9万元，没收假煤30吨。

2003—2004年，县工商局在各矿区公路沿线市场巡查164次，捣毁立化镇更班凉水井、更班二凤井、水尧乡友谊桥等3处长期性掺假窝点，现场查处在原煤中掺入煤矸石、黑泥沙等违法行为19次（车），销毁掺杂使假原煤2600吨。通过原煤掺假治理整顿，2005年后，县内原煤掺假现象得到遏制。

（四）鼠药市场专项治理

2001年12月—2002年1月，县工商局对剧毒性鼠药市场进行专项治理，检查市场5个、经营摊点302个、副食及饮食店47个，访查居民用户108户，没收鼠药1245瓶，查处无照经营4户。

2003年9—10月，根据省工商局《关于深入开展毒鼠强市场专项整治的通知》，在全县范围内展开专项检查，检查零星销售鼠药经营户10户，收缴禁止销售的鼠药1148包、饵料150包，没有发现生产毒鼠强和危险化学品的窝点。

2004—2008年，结合县内鼠药市场销售情况，不定期开展毒鼠强专项治理，查禁剧毒性鼠药。

（五）商品展销监管

1999年6月，县政府办公室对外来商品展销有关问题发出通知，规定从1999年7月1日起，常规商品展销（指成衣、百货等）必须经县政府批准，未经批准举办的商品展销活动，视为非法经营活动，由工商、税务等部门按法规予以处罚；对高新商品展销，展销商应出示能够说明该商品的各种证件及手续，由县商会、工商、质监等部门审验审核，报县政府批准后方可举行展销活动。

是年9月中旬，重庆某公司在荔波县进行商品展销活动，经工商局、质监局查实，所展销的商品均无进货证明，大部分属于商家处理品，部分商品属于“三无”产品、假冒产品，根据国家工商局颁布的《商品展销会管理办法》《中华人民共和国产品质量法》的规定，县工商局、质监局责令其立即停止展销，对查获的假冒伪劣商品按有关法律法规处理。

（六）校园周边经营秩序监管

2000年3月，根据全省整顿校园及周边环境经营秩序电视电话会议精神，县工商局印发《关于整顿校园及周边环境经营秩序的通知》，规定：不准核发在学校门前设置台球、电子游戏机和其他有可能危害治安、影响教学和师生身心健康的经营项目的营业执照；不准核发在学校周边地区流动的个体营业执照，不得批准新的摊商到学校周围经营；学校周边200米内，严禁开办集贸市场，不得开设酒吧间、歌舞厅、录像室、台球室、电子游戏室等经营项目；加强对学校周边商业摊点的监督管理。5月初，对13所学校的校内外经营情况进行清理整顿，检查校办食堂5个，校内个体经营户15户，校外200米内个体经营户32户。经检查，校内及校外200米内均无卡拉OK厅、游戏机室等娱乐场所。检查发现校办食堂均无证照，个体经营户无营业执照3户。对未办照的经营户经进行批评教育并补办营业执照。

2006年，执法人员对23所学校及周边经营秩序进行专项检查，检查各类饮食摊点126户（次），签订食品经营责任书63户；没收超期变质小食品、“三无”食品等，取缔无照食品加工户1户、其他无照经营户4户、各类无照商业流动摊点8户；对卫生较差的食品经营户2户发出警示，对无证、无照经营户6户发出限期办理证、照通知；立案查处无照食品经营案件1起；查处无证经营网吧3户。

五、非法传销查处

2002年，根据国家、省、州工商局关于迅速开展广泛宣传、深入揭批、严厉打击传销和变相传销行为的有关通知，县工商局利用黑板报等形式揭露传销和变相传销的欺骗性和危害性，提高群众自我保护意识。2—10月，出动执法人员651人次，对全县范围内的外来经营者、各出租屋、招待所及城乡接合部等场所进行检查，未发现有传销和变相传销行为。

2006年11月，县工商局、公安局印发《荔波县工商、公安机关联合打击传销专项行动工作实施方案》，成立联合打击传销专项工作领导小组，2006年11月—2007年8月，对社区、城乡接合部出租屋、乡（镇）等进行重点检查整治。

2008年3月，县政府成立打击传销专项行动工作领导小组，在县工商局设办公室。是年，开展无传销社区（村）创建工作，以玉屏镇建设村和城东社区为创建示范单位，在该社区（村）成立有居（村）委会、工商所、派出所参加的社区打击传销领导小组，制定各项管理制度和监督制度，签订《创建无传销社区（村）责任书》。同时，组织开展咨询活动，在社区（村）设立宣传栏、警示牌，悬挂宣传标语，向群众发公开信，提高群众识别和自觉抵制非法传销的能力。

第三节　企业登记管理

一、企业注册登记

1978年，全县企业未进行注册登记。1979年，在开展农村、城镇街道工业企业、社队企业、城乡工商业、工业部门产品质量、使用商标等全面清理中，对国营企业208户、集体企业13户和个体工商业20户进行登记，核发执照。1981年，对工业企业和商业网点重新复查登记，换发营业执照。

1988—1990年，根据国务院《关于清理整顿各类公司的决定》，对1986年后党政机关经商办企业成立的各类公司进行清理，符合公司登记条件的给予办理换照手续，不符合公司条件的予以撤销。

1998年8月，县工商局对注册登记的企业进行清查，查出“三无”（无资金、无经营场所、无人员）企业6户，依法注销。11月，根据中共中央、国务院、中央军委关于军队不再从事经商活动的通知，注销县内军办企业。

是年，在全县注册登记的企业中，国有企业102户（法人企业100户）、集体企业340户（法人企业154户）、有限责任公司12户、联营企业6户、私营企业29户。在年内新登记注册的企业28户中，有限责任公司4户、私营企业4户、集体企业20户。

1999年，企业注册登记实行登记程序公开、收费项目公开、“受理、审核、发照”公开的“三公开”审批程序。9月，根据《中华人民共和国公司法》《企业法人登记管理条例》依法注销企业19户。

2000年，根据国务院《关于关闭非法和布局不合理煤矿有关问题的通知》和省、州煤炭关井压产工作会议精神，注销县内煤炭企业22户。10月，注销其他企业17户。

2002年，企业变更29户，企业注销114户（国有、集体74户，私营企业40户）。2003年1月，注销企业93户，新注册企业26户（内资企业18户、私营企业8户），注册资金3296万元。2003年1月，对93户企业予以注销。

2004年，新增的18户内资企业中，法人2户、分支机构16户。全年注销企业21户。

2005年，企业注册登记实行“一审一核制”，工商所直接办理个体注册登记工作。年内，通过“一审一核制”办理企业注册登记112户。

二、企业年检

1979年，对208个国营企业，13个集体企业和20户个体工商业进行登记，核发执照，并建立经济户口。1981年，对工业企业和商业网点重新复查登记，换发营业执照。

1993年，根据省工商局《关于贯彻〈商品交易市场登记管理暂行办法〉的实施意见》的通知，加强市场监督管理。通过1994—1997年的登记年检，普遍对市场主办单位及负责人进行有关法规的宣传学习，督促其建立健全各项规章制度。每年的年检登记从4月中旬开始，于4月30日前完成。

1998年，注册登记的企业共489户，注册资金7629.6万元，比上年分别增长12%和24%。其中，国有企业102户（法人企业100户）、集体企业340户（法人企业154户）、有限责任公司12户、联营企业6户、私营企业29户。新登记注册企业28户，其中，有限责任公司4户、私营企业4户、集体企业20户；办理法人代表变更登记11户。全年应检各类企业432户，实际参加年检430户，年检率达99.5%。无正当理由不参加年检2户，占0.5%。私营企业应检28户，实检28户，年检率100%。对不按时参加年检的企业除批评教育外，处罚款总计4000元。对超出规定，长期不开展经营活动的2户企业作注销处理。

1999年10月30日，全县注册登记企业396户，注册资金13921万元。其中，国有企业125户（法人企业43户）、集体企业211户（法人企业85户）、有限责任公司20户、私营企业40户。年度新登记注册企业42户，其中，有限责任公司15户、私营企业21户、集体企业8户。在企业注册登记中，实行登记程序公开、收费项目公开、“受理、审核、发照”三分开的审批程序。在具体操作上，按照“受理、资质审查、实地调查和核准”的程序规定，做到一人把关，各负其责，按章办事，确保登记工作的严肃性，避免登记工作中以情代法的舞弊现象发生，对符合登记条件的，及时受理，在两个工作日内将执照发到企业手中。

2000年，共年检企业402户，占应检数410户的98%，基本完成了年检任务。截至11月30日，全县共有企业480户，其中，法人企业170户、私营企业62户、非法人企业243户。

为确保企业按期参加年度检验，强化工商监管职能，利用县有线电视媒体进行宣传，并由各个工商所把通知发放到企业手中，督促各企业按时提供有关材料参加年度检验。截至2001年年检期限，全县登记注册企业445户，实际年检407户，年检率达91.5%。

2002年，全县通过年检国有、集体企业349户（其中法人116户、非法人233户）、私营企业43户，个体验照贴花1580户。截至10月30日，全县国有、集体企业350户，注册资金13146万元；私营企业43户，注册资金4104万元。年度内变更企业29户，注销企业114户（其中，国有、集体企业74户、私营企业40户）。注销企业户数较多的原因是原登记的企业有相当部分是名存实亡的企业，历年未进行清理。

2003年，年检内资企业应检284户，扣除21户煤炭生产企业因国家整顿小煤窑，企业正在整改，不能参加年检外，实际已检252户，有11户企业无正当理由不参加年检。私营企业应检企业68户，已检50户，扣除12户煤炭生产企业因国家整顿小煤窑政策正在整改，不能参加年检外，应检而无正当理由未参加年检6户。此次年检，彻底清理一批“三无”企业，按有关规定分别予以注销和吊销，共注销、吊销企业104户。

2005年，私营企业应年检83户，参检78户，年检率94%，办理变更登记18户；内资企业应检195户，参检183户，年检率94%，办理变更登记10户。依法查处未按时参加年检企业34户，罚款1.51万元。

三、企业分类管理

2003年，对企业资信级别进行分类，将年内经营情况良好、无违法违章行为的企业定为A类企业，有违法违章或者不良信贷行为的企业定为B类企业，有严重违法违章或资不抵债的企业定为C级企业。经分类，全县有A类企业1601户、B类企业336户、C类企业56户。

从2005年起，按分类标准将企业分为A、B、C、D四类，即守信企业、警示企业、失信企业、严重失信企业4个类型。年内，在册企业350户中，有A类企业325户、B类企业25户。

2006年11月，登记注册企业321户，其中A类企业317户、B类企业4户。2007年，新登记注册企业49户，均为A类企业。2008年年末，全县在册企业341户，其中A类企业340户、B类企业1户。

四、企业信用申报审核

1990年，申报参加县级“重合同、守信用”企业14户，通过评选，县农资公司、外贸公司获1989年度“重合同、守信用”企业。

1991年，申报参加县级“重合同、守信用”工商企业28户，经县政府审核认定，县农贸公司、县建筑公司、县建筑公司、县生产资料公司、木藤工艺品厂5个单位被评为“重合同、守信用”企业。

1994年，对全县企业发出参加“重合同、守信用”活动通知，有37个企业参加了评比活动，8个企业荣获1994年度“重合同、守信用”称号。

1996年，全县几十家企业参与“重合同、守信用”评比活动，通过评比，县农资日杂公司、工矿贸易公司、医药公司、县建筑公司、玉屏镇建筑公司、甲良中学建材厂、甲良粮油贸易公司、电力实业公司获1996年度县级“重合同、守信用”单位。其中，县农资日杂公司连续7次评为县级“重合同、守信用”单位，因业绩突出，推荐参加省级“重合同、守信用”企业评比，1997年5月，县农资日杂公司获荔波县首家省级“重合同、守信用”单位。

1997年，全县开展“重合同、守信用”企业活动。是年，获“重合同、守信用”企业有荔波县农资公司、荔波县工矿贸易公司、荔波县建筑工程公司、荔波县玉屏镇建筑公司、荔波县医药公司、荔波县甲良粮油贸易公司、荔波县甲良中学建材厂、荔波县种子公司、荔波县贵康木地板厂、荔波县瑶山建筑队。

1998年11月5日，根据《中华人民共和国公司法》《企业法人登记管理条例》和中共中央、国务院、中央军委关于军队不再从事经商活动的通知精神，对本县军办企业“荔波县民兵基地招待所”予以注销。涉及该企业的有关证照一律作废。11月25日，县工商局研究决定取消隶属荔波县武装部的“荔波县佳荣长城煤矿”经营资格，停止一切经营活动。将证、照、印件移交工商局。

1999年9月，根据《中华人民共和国公司法》《企业法人登记管理条例》《企业登记管理条例施行细则》，对19户企业予以注销。

2000年5月，根据国务院国发〔1998〕43号文件《关于关闭非法和布局不合理煤矿有关问题的通知》和省、州煤炭关井压产工作会议精神，对22个企业予以注销。此外，依据《中华人民共和国公司法》《企业法人登记管理条例》《企业法人年度检验办法》，10月，对17家企业依法予以注销。

2003年1月12日，对93户企业予以注销。

2004年12月20日、28日，分别发布企业注销公告，共注销企业21户。

2005年，开展“重合同、守信用”单位复核、申报、公示、发证工作，重新复核省级“重合同、守信用”企业2户（荔波县建设工程有限责任公司、贵州明德事业有限责任公司），新申报省级“重合同、守信用”企业1户、州级3户。

2006年，个体工商户注销1162户，企业注销64户。

2007年，考核认定省级诚信个体工商户，本县有刘汉搁、朱元志、龙光珍、李朝英；省级诚信私营企业，荔波县有荔波县建设工程有限责任公司、贵州明德事业有限责任公司。

2008年，复核省级“守合同、重信用”企业4户，州级“守合同、重信用”企业7户，新申报州级“守合同、重信用”企业4户。

第四节　商标管理

1979年11月，恢复商标统一注册工作，县内企业申请注册的商标，由县工商局初审、省工商局复审后，报国家工商总局注册。

1998年，发现县内新办的1户个体饮料厂从广西市场购买广西荔浦饮料厂商标标志使用，经管理人员宣传讲解《中华人民共和国商标法》后，主动将违法商标当场烧毁，事后自行设计制作该厂商标报县工商局备案。

2002年，查处假冒“五粮液”“剑南春”商标案件1起。

2003年，县工商局建立注册商标管理档案，对商标进行规范商标管理。是年，对全县专卖店、总经销商36户进行商标专项检查，查处销售假冒茅台酒商标案件1起。

2004年10月，县工商局受理深圳铜锣湾百货公司投诉黔南州天力房地产开发有限责任公司在荔波县开发的铜锣湾商业购物广场与其公司注册的“铜锣湾广场”商标侵权投诉，根据《中华人民共和国商标法》《商标法实施细则》的有关规定，责令黔南州天力房地产开发有限责任公司在荔波县开发的商业购物广场停止使用“铜锣湾商业购物广场”名称，并在一个月内更改名称。

2006—2007年，查处各类商标违法案件5起。

至2008年8月，国家工商总局商标局已注册和受理荔波县申请的商标如“小七孔”“大七孔”“吉妮丽吉”“瑶麓花生”“金主”“荔波荔”等共25个。其间，有3户业主申请注册商标，分别是“阳凤大米”“甲良辣椒”“荔波土花布”。本年度申请注册农产品商标2件，其他商标1件，另有两件农产品商标正在申请注册中。没收印有奥林匹克标志服装64件，没收未经登记印有奥运标志广告1800份。

第五节　广告管理

1978年后，随着市场逐步放开，县内出现一些零星户外字牌广告，工商部门对户外广告进行定期或不定期检查。1982年国务院发布《广告管理暂行条例》后，县内开始对广告进行规范管理。1990年，县工商局、宣传部、文化局、广播电视局对全县的户外广告进行清理，对2户手续不齐的广告业主作停业整顿处理。

1995年，《中华人民共和国广告法》正式施行，通过宣传，从事广告制作的业主和进行户外广告宣传的企业、个体工商户陆续到县工商部门办理相关手续并接受监督管理。

1998年，县工商部门对户外广告实行审核制度，在全县主要集镇设置广告专栏8个，定点张贴经审核的户外广告，对未经审查的路边文字广告予以清除。全年查处各类未经审核的户外广告535份。1999年，县政府组织工商、城管、爱卫会等部门对不符合要求的广告栏和乱张贴的户外广告进行全面清理，保持市容整洁。是年检查户外广告18户，立案查处虚假广告2起，并在县电视台曝光。

2000年4月，县工商局、县消费者协会在全县开展以打击虚假广告、虚假宣传、虚假告示为重点的“揭谎”专项治理活动查获虚假户外广告351条、虚假媒体广告2条、虚假店堂广告6条，当场没收销毁；对名称不符的户外广告3户限期整改。是年，按《店堂广告管理办法》的规定，到县工商局办理广告发布审批手续96户。全年没收非法广告4000余张，查处违法广告案件18起。

2001年，全县有户外广告媒体1户、户外广告经营户7户。2002年，进行广告经营资格年检和从业人员培训，登记个体店堂广告42户、户外广告18户、媒体广告1户，取缔不规范广告8户，没收非法印刷品4200份，查处各类广告违法行为3起。

2003年，取缔不规范广告8户，没收非法印刷品广告4000份，查处各类广告违法行为8起。

2004年“3·15”消费者权益保护日，县工商部门上街开展《中华人民共和国广告法》宣传活动，印发《中华人民共和国广告法》宣传资料4500份。5月18日、10月25日，两次组织县樟江天然食品厂、水泥厂等8家企业及有关单位进行《中华人民共和国广告法》培训。全年登记户外广告34条、印刷品广告3户，查处擅自发布户外广告案件10件。

2005年，开展“打虚假、树诚信”广告专项整治行动。1—3月，专项整治药品、医疗、食品广告；4—6月，专项整治农资、农业机械、兽药、饲料、“致富信息”广告；7—9月，专项整治房地产（含物业管理）、印刷品（固定和非固定）、不良内容广告；9—10月，专项整治电视、网站、声讯服务台广告。全年查处广告违法行为8起。

2006年，全年受理户外广告登记77件，开展广告监测4次，监测广告156条（次），查处擅自发布户外广告案件3起。

2007年，通过监测登记户外广告64起，查处违规户外广告7起。

2008年，开展广告市场检查5次，检查个体经营户138户，检查旅游、食品、农资广告145条，叫停烟草广告发布行为1起，立案查处广告案件16起。全年登记户外广告79件。

第六节　经济合同管理

1982年，县工商局内设专门机构开展经济合同管理和鉴证工作。1985年，成立经济合同仲裁委员会后，合同纠纷由仲裁委员会仲裁。

1987—1989年，全县签订经济合同16482份。1987—1990年，鉴证合同192份，检查合同执行情况701份，调解仲裁经济合同纠纷63件，处理不符合规定和无效合同19份。

1993年，调解仲裁企业合同案件5起，为企业挽回经济损失11.5万元。1994年，检查合同188份。1996年，鉴证合同22份。

1997年起，开展企业经济合同检查，促进企业依法旅行合同。是年，检查企业合同19户63份。1998年，检查企业购销合同31份，全部履行率80%，部分履行率20%。

1999年10月，开展合同欺诈专项整治工作，检查国有、集体、私营企业10户，没有发现合同争议、合同欺诈、合同违法等问题。是年，监督合同当事人履行合同28份，金额2831万元，办理企业动产合同抵押登记7户。

2000年，鉴证合同37份，监督合同当事人履行合同413份，金额3968万元。

2001年6月，县工商局立案查处荔波县南方药用动物蚂蚁养殖场户主与合伙人在县境内与养殖户签订3年期养殖合同，骗签合同19份，金额4.03万元。

2002年，受理抵押、质押登记3件，金额2346万元。

2003年，受理抵押质押登记1件、续展抵押登记1件，抵押、质押共计294.37万元。

2002—2008年，开展合同争议、合同欺诈、合同违法专项整治工作。

第七节　非公有制经济管理

1978年，全县贯彻“调整、改革、整顿、提高”的方针，支持发展个体经济发展，允许个人经营小型手工业、商业、饮食服务、客货运输业及修理业，放宽日用工业小商品上市出售政策。

1981年，根据国务院《关于城镇非农业个体经济若干政策性规定》的精神，对个体工商业采取积极扶持措施，个体工商户发展到112户。

1988年，根据省工商局《关于进一步扶持发展个体经济的若干意见》，重点扶持边远贫困山区个体工商业和转产自营户。这部分个体工商户经过批准，免交办理登记费和一年的工商管理费。1990年，在验照中发现无证经营73户，责成按规定办理执照并补交管理费。

1998年，全县登记注册个体工商户2012户，从业人员3780人，注册资金2022.2万元。

1998年，开始办理个体运输营业执照，全年办理282户，收规费1.5万元。是年，查处无照经营103户，其中，补办营业执照84户，补收拖欠个体工商户管理费2.14万元。依法对违法、违章个体工商户52户进行处罚。年末，全县私营企业中，制造业148户，从业人员290人，注册资金78万元；交通运输业183户，从业人员243人，注册资金1042.6万元；批发零售贸易、餐饮业1317户，从业人员2493人，注册资金632.7万元；社会服务业356户，从业人员736人，注册资金261.3万元；其他行业8户，从业人员21人，注册资金7.6万元；农业、林业、牧业、渔业302户。

1999年，按州工商局《关于开展个体工商户亮照经营检查专项治理的通知》要求，检查主要集镇和景区个体工商户568户的亮照经营情况，发现无照经营15户，未亮照经营23户，未验照贴花5户，超经营范围5户。全年查处无照经营88户。

2000年9月，通过4年一次个体工商户营业执照换照，全县有注册个体工商户1717户；验照贴花1650户，占应验照贴花数的96%；建立个体档案1775卷。年末，全县个体工商户发展到1733户，比上年同期增长2.8%，全年新开业415户，注销42户。

2001年，查处各类违法违章经营户40户，罚款0.6万元，补交管理费0.78万元。

2002年年底，全县在册工商户中，因歇业自动流失等原因注销509户。个体户流失量大的主要原因为广西红茂矿务局设立在立化镇的3个煤矿破产，矿区工人撤离，从事个体经营的家属随之撤回广西，未到工商部门办理注销手续；全县治理整顿小煤窑，部分矿区个体户因小煤窑关闭而歇业；2003年，新增个体工商户378户。

2004年7月，县工商局实施省工商局推行的企业登记“一审一核制”，以委托书形式，授权茂兰、玉屏、甲良工商所直接办理个体工商户注册登记，授权注册登记审查员、核准员。到年末，工商所办理个体工商户注册登记365户（其中新开业个体工商户306户、变更38户、换照21户），全县新增个体工商户728户，注销275户。

2005年，个体工商户歇业注销91户，自动流失注销120户。通过验照贴花，查处无照经营14户。是年，全县工商系统实行“阳光收费”制度，县工商局制定《个体工商户管理费阳光定费实施办法（试行）》，至9月，全县纳入“阳光收费”的个体工商户1446户，占总数的72%。实行“阳光收费”后，全县工商部门共清理应缴未缴个体工商户管理费7.8万元。全年支持、引导农民从事个体经营417户，免收工商登记费0.8万元、个体管理费5万元、市场管理费3万元。全年新增个体工商户359户。

2006年，按《个体工商户委托登记管理办法》《个体工商户分类监管指导意见》，个体工商户登记监管工作纳入企业信用监管范围。全县个体工商户2386户中，A级户2357户、B级户29户，无C

级户、D级户。全年新增个体工商户476户。

2007年，全县个体工商户新开业登记注册545户，均为A级户。

2008年9月1日起，全国统一停止征收个体工商户管理费，县工商局开展排查核对工作，将预收的个体工商户管理费全部逐笔全额清退。是年，全县个体工商户中，A级户2892户、B级户14户，无C级户、D级户。全年新增个体工商户706户。

1979—2008年全县非公有制经济发展统计一览表

表16－2

年度	个体工商户			私营企业		
	户数（户）	从业人员（人）	注册资金（万元）	户数（户）	从业人员（人）	注册资金（万元）
1979	17	17	0.47	—	—	—
1980	—	—	—	—	—	—
1981	112	—	—	—	—	—
1982	141	149	—	—	—	—
1983	571	626	22.23	—	—	—
1984	725	779	19.55	—	—	—
1985	838	1011	—	—	—	—
1986	1149	1377	129.89	—	—	—
1987	1287	1578	142.00	—	—	—
1988	1405	—	—	—	—	—
1989	1374	1885	—	—	—	—
1990	1562	2027	344.00	—	—	—
1991	—	—	—	—	—	—
1992	—	—	—	—	—	—
1993	1630	2165	445.60	28	596	172.00
1994	1803	2474	1598.90	23	410	142.00
1995	1909	2669	1927.60	23	410	142.00
1996	1575	2044	1565.00	31	483	190.00
1997	1846	3550	1709.30	29	465	207.00
1998	2012	3780	2022.20	34	272	1143.40
1999	1685	3186	1796.00	40	—	—
2000	1733	—	—	—	—	—
2001	1956	2490	782.00	—	—	—
2002	1879	2317	715.00	83	926	5225.00
2003	1865	2333	2101.00	89	—	10618.00
2004	2384	2822	5299.00	86	2112	12181.00

续表16－2

年度	个体工商户			私营企业		
	户数（户）	从业人员（人）	注册资金（万元）	户数（户）	从业人员（人）	注册资金（万元）
2005	2588	3037	6442.92	—	—	—
2006	2386	4100	5700.00	—	—	—
2007	2456	2736	7956.00	132	—	16116.00
2008	2906	3121	8697.91	122	—	25045.85

第三章 物价管理

第一节 价格改革

1978—1979年，县内物价实行国家统一定价。1980年2月，对县内三类农副产品和完成派购任务的二类农副产品实行议购议销。是年8月，在坚持粮油统购统销、统一调拨的前提下，进行粮油议购议销。

1982年后，工业品价格实行工商企业协商定价，不受进销差率、地区差率、批零差率等作价方案的限制。同一商品允许在同一市场、不同商店之间价格不同。

1985年，改粮食统购为合同订购，实行定购比例价，对合同定购以外的粮食及其他农产品价格全部放开，由市场调节。同时，取消生猪派购，实行有指导的议购议销。放开缝纫机、国产手表、照相机、自行车、电风扇等工业消费品价格。

1986年，放开全部小商品价格。对一类、二类日用工业品和部分生产资料，允许生产、经营单位实行有限度的上下浮动价格，以现行牌价为中准价，允许上浮不超过10%，下浮不超过20%或不限。计划外购进的工业品，实行批发价，售完价格撤销，下批同类商品，可按原价销售，也可以另行定价。

是年6月，县内农产品价格管理实行国家定价、国家指导价和市场调节价3种形式。全县农产品属国家定价的有合同定购的粮食、油菜籽，属国家指导价的有猪肉、麝香、杜仲等，木材实行议购议销。

1989年，适当提高粮油合同订购、统购中的部分品种价格，调整食盐零售价格并实行城乡差价，调整公路客运票价，调低农用薄膜销售价格等。至1990年，县内物价形成政府定价、政府指导价、市场调节的格局。

1991年，化肥实行综合价，改变历年化肥销售平价、议价分开的“双轨制”，实现化肥平价议价并轨。

到1992年，全县商品90%的零售价格，85%的农产品收购价格，80%的生产资料出厂价格制定权向生产者和经营者放开。1993年后，价格管理重点转向加强宏观调控，促进市场价格朝规范有序方向运行。

从1998年5月1日起实施《中华人民共和国价格法》《收费许可证管理办法》。

2003年，大多数商品价格已经放开，并执行省政府印发的《贵州省定价目录》。至2008年，除水、电、食盐、石油、成品油等商品实行政府指导价和政府定价外，其他商品和服务价格均实行市场调节。

第二节 价格监督检查

1984年起，开始常年性价格监督检查工作。1985年10月，根据省物价局《关于开展物价大检查的紧急通知》，开展全县物价大检查，主要检查企业、事业单位，包括各种行政性、经营性收费单位。

1986年，全县有价单位统一使用州物价局制作的商品价格标签，商品销售明码标价。

1990年3月，根据国家物价局颁布的《关于商品和收费实行明码标价制度的规定》，首先在邮政、医疗、公安、交通等部门实行收费项目、收费标准公开制度，之后在全部收费单位实施。

2001年6月，县物价局根据群众举报，依法检查广西地铁公司金城江管理段（立化平寨）收费情况，查出违法收取“铁路货物运输延伸服务费”594万元。此案经贵州、广西两省（区）物价局及荔波县政府共同协调，以罚款30万元结案。

2002年9—11月，根据省物价局转发《国家计委关于开展农村电价和农网改造收费专项检查的通知》，县物价局对县供电局的电价及全县农网改造收费情况进行专项检查，查出违法超标准收取电费236.01万元，后经清退和县政府协调处理，以罚款15万元结案。

2003—2008年，每年开展市场物价和水价、客运票价、景区门票、涉农收费等价格专项检查，查处价格违法案件共29起，挽回经济损失1500万元。

第三节 收费管理

一、行政事业性收费管理

根据中共中央办公厅、国务院办公厅1993年10月颁布的《关于治理乱收费的规定》，从1994年起，在全县实行行政事业性收费年度审验制度，按《贵州省行政事业性收费管理条例》《贵州省行政事业性收费管理条例实施细则》，对各项收费进行管理。

2001年，县物价部门与县财政局按照《贵州省“收费许可证”管理办法》《贵州省经营性服务性价格暂行管理办法》，开展行政事业性收费整顿，向合格收费单位发“收费许可证”。

从2002年起开展年审工作，完成上年度“收费许可证”年审636本（行政事业性198本、经营性438本），新办证214本（行政事业性18本、经营性196本）。2003年，完成“收费许可证”年审734本（行政事业性221本、经营性513本），新办证71本（行政事业性6本、经营性65本）。2004年，完成“收费许可证”年审750本（行政事业性221本、经营性529本）。2005—2008年，每年4月底前完成上年度“收费许可证”年审工作，年审率达100%。

2008年9月，县物价部门召开大七孔、小七孔和水春河景区门票价格听证会，确定景区门票价格。

二、涉农收费管理

2002年，县物价局在全县推行涉农收费公示制，要求全县收费单位对收费项目、标准、依据、监督电话进行公示，并在乡、村、组设立公示牌、公示栏，规范涉农收费行为，提高涉农收费透明度，加强涉农收费管理和监督。2005年，按省物价局、省财政厅公布的收费项目，全县取消收费项目26个，降低收费项目1个，涉及部门10个。

第四章 质量技术监督

第一节 管理体制

1978—1981年，计量工作由县科学技术委员会代管。1982年后，由县物价局管理。标准化和产品质量工作由县经济委员会管理。

1985年4月，成立县标准计量管理所，为县经委下属机构。1986年9月，县标准计量管理所升格为县标准计量管理局，下设县计量检定所。

1992年，成立县技术监督局，将县经委质量管理职能划入县技术监督局。

1994年2月，县技术监督局、工商行政管理局、物价局合并建立县工商行政管理局，对外仍保留县技术监督局的牌子和印章，内设计量市场股，保留计量检定所。

1999年8月，技术监督工作从工商局分离，单设县技术监督局，归省技术监督局垂直管理。

2001年，县技术监督局更名为县质量技术监督局，内设业务股、计量测试所、办公室、代码办公室。至2008年，县质量技术监督局的管理体制、职能、内设机构不变，实有人员9人。

第二节 计量管理

一、计量器具管理

1978—1981年，计量管理工作主要是对市场使用的衡器进行不定期检查。1982—1986年，荔波县的计量检定工作由独山县计量局代管。1987年，县内计量检定由州标准计量局计量检定科兼管。1988年，县标准计量局开展部分计量检定工作。6月，在《中华人民共和国计量法》颁布两周年全州实施情况交叉检查中，对县经委、水泥厂、百货公司等部门的计量单位和计量器具进行检查，在用器具合格率为87%。

1989年，对县水泥厂进行计量器具定升级整顿，年底，该厂计量定级通过验收合格。1990年11月，广西红茂矿务局平寨矿因破坏计量器具准确度，此案经两个月调查取证后，按照《计量违法处罚细则》的规定，没收该矿违法所得7万元，对当事人处以罚款500元。

1991—1993年，在全县宣传《中华人民共和国计量法》，对全县地中衡和各部门、个体工商户的衡器检定154台（件、次）。1992年，查处计量违法案件13起，为消费者挽回经济损失16万元。

1997年10月，查处破坏计量器具准确度案件1起。

1998—2002年，主要对大衡器进行检定。

2003年，开展全县计量器具调查，全县有地中衡11台、500型衡器163台、案秤（包括弹簧秤）

91台、杆秤1万支、CT机1台、B超机2台、心电图机4台、脑电图机2台、天平5台、压力表6块。对调查中发现的违法行为依法处理。

2008年，全县有地中衡17台、500型台秤145台、案秤112台、CT机2台、B超机5台、心电图机5台、脑电图机3台、天平7台、压力表132只、流量表4561只、电流表5200只、燃油加油机35台。

二、衡器改制

1987年起，对全县衡器示值进行改制。至1990年，粮食、供销、商业部门改制衡器123台（件），个体户衡器改制4000台（件）。1991年10月改制结束。

第三节　标准化管理

1978—1988年，县内国营工业企业有水泥厂、农机厂、酒厂。水泥厂产品执行国家标准，农机厂执行行业标准，酒厂没有统一的国家标准和行业标准。1989年3月，制定县酒厂“古榕老窖”“夜榕大曲”“樟江大曲”白酒生产技术标准。同时，为县轻工局制定“银饰工艺品”产品质量技术标准。

1989年4月，因酒厂承包给四十一集团军地炮旅，原制定的标准不适用其生产技术要求，1989—1990年重新制定“荔波大曲”“贵州粮液”“龙王醇”“古榕”“白酒”5个产品生产技术标准。

1990—1991年，制定县供销社食品厂“辣酱”系列产品生产技术标准。这些产品标准随着企业产品停产而消失。

1991年，按照《贵州省工业企业标准化水平评定办法（试行）》，县水泥厂通过州技术监督局标准化考核验收。

1998年，省经委下发《贵州省县以下工业企业消灭无标生产工作的意见》后，全县开展消灭无标准生产工作。2001年10月，经州技术监督局实地考核，荔波县成为消灭无标准生产合格县。

至2008年12月，全县标准备案51个。其中，国家标准26个、行业标准12个、地方标准13个。

第四节　质量管理

1978—1990年，县内工业产品质量管理对象有县水泥厂、酒厂、农机厂，市场产品质量管理对象有农业生产资料及生活用品。其间，县质量管理部门对县水泥厂、酒厂、农机厂的产品质量进行抽样检查30次，进行市场商品质量检查3次，对查出的劣质商品电冰箱、电风扇、洗衣机等及变质商品进行收缴。

1993年3月，在县城进行《中华人民共和国产品质量法》宣传，发放《中华人民共和国产品质量法》单行本1000册。1994年3月，在县城、朝阳、立化、甲良等地组织企业、个体工商户进行《中华人民共和国产品质量法》知识培训，培训企业人员17人、个体工商户163人。

1996年3—9月，先后在朝阳、县城、茂兰、立化等地组织企业负责人和个体工商户参加《中华人民共和国产品质量法》及相关法律法规培训3次，培训企业人员45人、个体工商户376人。

1995—2000年，查处农业生产资料四大类产品139次。其中，抽样送检19批（次），不合格2批（次）。2000年7月，县水泥厂因水泥质量问题，在玉屏中学建设过程中发生不凝固事故，责令其停产整顿并赔偿用户水泥15吨。

2002年，广西雅脉水泥厂在荔波县销售不合格水泥，县质量技术监督局对该厂处罚款2000元，并责令其赔偿用户水泥30吨。2003年，没收销毁伪劣电线17卷，罚款800元；查处长虹电视机爆炸案2件，厂方赔偿用户1万元。2005年，取缔非法生产地条钢作坊1户，没收地条钢16吨，罚款4万元。

2008年，县内纳入质量管理的企业有县水泥厂、樟江天然食品厂、矿泉水厂、胶合板厂及食品小作坊10户、白酒小作坊13户、米粉加工作坊20户、建材生产厂10户。其中，责令停产整顿4户，取缔1户，整改32户。对广西雅山建材有限责任公司的水泥质量问题，责令其赔偿佳荣镇用户11户共20万元。

2000—2008年，全县查处各类产品质量案件13起。在“3·15”消费者权益日上，先后将收缴的假冒伪劣产品当众集中销毁5次。

第五节　特种设备安全管理

1989年前，县内特种设备主要有锅炉、压力容器，由县劳动部门管理，对各单位的锅炉、消毒锅、充气泵、氧气瓶等进行检查登记，建立安全管理制度。1989年，县酒厂压力容器人为原因造成爆炸事故，死亡1人。

1990年后，随着全县经济不断发展，特种设备种类、数量逐渐增加。

2002年6月，将特种设备安全管理职能和管理人员从县劳动部门划到县质监部门。2003年4月，在全县宣传《特种设备安全监察条例》，发放《特种设备安全监察条例》单行本2500册、《气瓶产品安全质量监督检查规则》单行本500册。

2004年，检验液化气瓶6741只，没收检验不合格的液化气瓶146只和超期使用存在安全隐患液化气瓶271只。是年，取缔未取得液化气安全资格的销售商1户，处罚未经检验合格气瓶继续充装液化气的销售商2户。

2004年起，每年6月特种设备安全宣传月期间，县质监局组织进企业、进社区、进学校宣传活动，与消防单位联合在企业、社区、学校开展安全演练。

2004—2008年，开展电梯安全演练5次，参加演练人员500余人次；进行锅炉安全演练4次，使用单位及消防、安监等部门37家参加演练，参加演练人员400余人次。

2008年年底，全县特种设备有锅炉30台、压力表261块、电梯16台、压力容器4件、旅游观光车56辆、行车6台、液化气瓶4153个，纳入日常监督管理的特种设备共计4291台（件）。

第六节　组织机构代码管理

1993年，根据国务院批转国家技术监督局等部门《关于建立企事业单位和社会团体统一标识制度报告的通知》精神，按全省的统一部署，在县技监局设代码办公室。自1994年1月1日起，全县执行统一代码标识制度，每年为县内行政、事业、企业、社会团体等机构办理统一代码。

2005年，代码办理与全国联网，实现网上赋码。2006—2008年，代码办公室连续3年受省代码办表彰，代码工作人员杨若记三等功。

至2008年年底，全县共办理组织机构代码651户。其中，行政21户、事业134户、企业478户、社团15户、村级机构3户。

第五章　食品药品监督管理

第一节　管理体制

1978年，食品管理职能属县工商局，药品药政管理职能属县卫生局。

1986年，成立县食品质量检查领导小组，同时建立区、乡食品卫生监督监测网点，配备区、乡食品卫生检查员。是年9月，成立县药品检验所，属县卫生局正股级事业单位。在各乡（镇）配备药品检验员，在县医院、中医院设立药事管理委员会，县防疫站、保健站、皮防站及17个乡（镇）卫生院设立药事药政监督小组。1990年，全县有食品卫生监督员5人、药品监督人员4人、食品卫生检查员17人。

2001年12月，成立黔南州药品监督管理局荔波分局，内设办公室、综合业务股、纪检监察室。2002年6月，荔波分局更名为荔波县药品监督管理局。2004年3月，县药品监督管理局更名为荔波县食品药品监督管理局，加挂荔波县食品药品稽查局牌子，内设办公室、食品安全股、药品监督股。职能主要是食品综合协调及药品的监督管理，编制9人，其中公务员编制8人、工勤编制1人。至2008年，仍属省以下垂直管理机构。

第二节　食品安全监督

1979年8月，国务院颁布《食品卫生管理条例》后，县食品卫生管理部门在食品卫生管理上，制定全县食品卫生监督管理制度和监督员岗位责任制，实行目标管理；在食品监督上，对食品行业从业人员每年进行一次健康检查，审发复验健康证和卫生许可证，定期或不定期检查食品生产经营厂、场、摊点，定期检测冷饮、糕点、酒、酱油、餐具、肉制品。至1990年，全县现场监督1557人次，警告并限期改进66户（次），责令追回不合格食品15户（次），责令停业整顿15户（次），罚款9户。追究刑事责任、民事责任案件各1件。

1991年，开展食品监督检查，停业整顿6户，限期改进4户，销毁过期变质食品57公斤。1992年，巡回监督985户（次），限期改进59户，责令追回产品34户，处罚38户，销毁过期变质食品1323公斤。1993年，对全县食品生产经营单位211户检查821户（次），巡回监督364户（次），警告6户。

1995年，县内发生村民因食用病死牲畜肉、死因不明牲畜肉引起中毒事件3起，中毒82人，经抢救无效死亡2人。

1996年起，食品监督工作延伸到甲良、朝阳、立化、佳荣等乡（镇）。1997年，巡回监督共

2938户（次），处罚136户（次），销毁过期变质食品31户（次）共270公斤。

1998年9月，开展全县饮食行业卫生专项监督检查，对各乡（镇）街头路边副食摊点进行清理整顿，销毁过期食品11个品种。同时发放宣传资料1000份，张贴标语178张。年内，督促副食、饮食从业人员进行健康检查，受检人员528人，受检率92.23%。在全年检查的食品经营442户中，核发营业执照342户，对没有营业执照的补办登记手续，对不具备条件的予以取缔。

2001年12月—2008年间，食品生产环节的发证许可及监督归质监局，食品流通环节的发证许可和监督归工商局，餐饮服务环节的发证许可和监督归卫生局，农产品种植归农业局，食品综合协调归食品药品监督管理局。

2004年6月26日中午，县幼儿园发生幼儿群体食品中毒事件，34名幼儿出现中毒症状，其中中毒症状严重的10名幼儿住院治疗。经调查，事故原因是幼儿食用了该幼儿园6月25日从县城台北面包房定购的面包500盒。县工商部门依法查封涉嫌引起食物中毒的经营场所台北面包房。为防止此类事件再次发生，食品管理部门立即对全县食品市场和食品加工作坊进行排查，严查加工、经营假冒伪劣食品违法行为，没收过期变质食品；对小吃、食品等商品经营进行重点检查，凡是证照不全的予以取缔。同时决定每月不定期开展食品市场检查，将不合格食品依法清出市场。

是年，县工商局制定《食品市场巡查制》《食品安全信息公示制》《食品准入制》《食品企业信用分类监管制》《不合格食品退市制》。同时制定并实施《食品安全专项整治实施方案》《荔波县工商局应对市场突发情况紧急工作预案》。

年内，开展儿童食品、夏令食品和中秋节、国庆节食品市场专项检查整治，检查食品经营户1460户（摊、次）、月饼加工作坊9户，索取食品经营相关票证220份，摸清食品经营户底数1216户，立案查处无照经营饮食业行为5户，责令熟食店（摊）进行卫生整改3户，不符合卫生标准的月饼下柜82公斤，没收过期变质食品及省、州文件要求查处的“飞鹿”牌、“牧原”牌、“花溪”牌奶粉，责令无照经营小商户停止营业2户，责令违法违章经营户立即改正3户，发出预先警示通知书26份。

2005年，食品安全监督部门与食品经营户签订食品安全责任书614份。开展酒类、奶粉、奶制品、包装食品等专项执法检查，检查酒类经营户212户，立案查处11户，没收假冒泸州老窖（特曲）酒248瓶；查处涉及食品案件18件，罚款0.52万元；依法收缴过期变质食品1600公斤。

2006年，通过个体工商户验照贴花、企业年检和市场巡查等方式，对食品经营户进行注册登记、证照、经营状况等检查，主要检查食品经营企业和个体工商户是否有出租、出借、转让营业执照等违法违规行为。经检查食品经营超市、集市、食品生产企业、个体工商户、饮食企业等，查处食品违法案件12起，取缔无照经营9户，销毁假冒伪劣食品价值1.3万元，签订食品经营责任书505份。

2007年，推行商品准入制度，按国务院《关于加强食品等产品安全监督管理的特别规定》，县食品安全监督部门与食品经营户签订食品安全责任书362户，签订率100%；规范流通领域商品经营者进货检查验收、验证验票、购销台账、协议准入、商品质量承诺、不合格商品退市以及市场开办者质量管理责任等自律制度，县城超市建立进货索票索证制度达100%，乡（镇）、社区食杂店建立进货台账制度达100%。

是年，按照省、州加强农村食品市场监管工作部署和要求，开展农村食品市场整顿年活动，重点整治城乡接合部、县城、乡镇、农村集贸市场和旅游景点、车站，以及辐射农村的食品批发市场、推销会，农村的食品经营超市、批发市场、食品商店、食品加工作坊、农村集贸市场和临时性食品摊点，重点整治品种有粮、油、肉、蔬菜、酱油、食醋、禽蛋及其制品、水产品、奶制品、豆制品、酒、饮料、糕点、儿童食品、保健品及糖果制品、茶叶（包括边销茶）、酱腌菜、蜜饯、可可制品、焙炒咖啡、淀粉及淀粉制品等食品。

2008年春节前后，开展为期一个月的春节“民生红盾”行动，重点检测米、面、油、肉、蛋、水产品、奶制品、豆制品、调味品、米粉、腌制品、干货制类产品、水果、蔬菜、进口食品等高风险食品，对涉嫌不合格的食品进行抽样送检，对质量不合格的食品依法查处。元旦、春节、“五一”、清明、端午、中秋、“十一”等节日期间，检查食品经营户1830户（次），强制不合格食品、无标志食品下柜。

年内，食品安全管理部门与食品经营户续签《食品安全责任书》427份；组织食品经营户参与申报食品安全示范店12户；从部分集贸市场、超市、服务场所销售的干腌制品、膨化食品、乳饮料制品、豆制品、肉类制品、果蔬汁6类食品抽取样品85组进行现场检测，干腌制品检测合格率为93%，膨化食品合格率为96%，乳饮料制品合格率为97%，果蔬汁合格率为93%，豆制品合格率为95%，肉类制品合格率为92%。

自县外市场发现含三聚氰胺问题奶制品后，食品安全监督部门组织执法人员开展含三聚氰胺问题奶制品清理，检查经营户813户（次），收缴不合格奶粉12.2公斤，下柜未经检验液态奶1192公斤、婴幼儿奶粉和普通奶粉1742公斤。

第三节　药品监督管理

一、监督检查

（一）药品市场监督检查

1978年后，甲良、朝阳、茂兰3个卫生院加工中药制剂21个品种，县医院加工部分中草药针剂自用及供各区卫生院使用。

从1985年《中华人民共和国药品管理法》颁布实施到1990年，全县进行药品检查388次，查出伪劣药品1310种，其中，劣质药品746种、假药564种。

1991—2001年，县药品检验所定期对全县药品经营使用单位的药品和市场药品进行监督检查，立案查处假劣药品、医疗器械案件73起，取缔假证、无证行医售药138人次。

2002年，对全县药品经营、使用单位114户进行监督检查，监督覆盖面、建档率100%。检查发现使用过期失效药品20户共73批（次）；从无“药品经营企业许可证”单位和个人手中购进药品2户，挂靠经营1户，购进药品未建有药品购进记录50户，建有不完整的药品购进记录23户，经销进口药品未按规定索取《进口药品口岸检验报告书》等资质存档备查7户。对查出的违法行为，依法给予警告、限期改正、没收药品、罚款等行政处罚。

在2003年药品经营、使用单位检查中，发现从无“药品经营企业许可证”的个体药店购进中药饮片的中医个体诊所1户，使用过期失效药品14户共114批（次），立案查处5户。

2004年，市场监督检查308户（次），监督覆盖率达97.3%。全年查处案件19起，发现违法张贴药品广告2户，移送县工商部门处理。

2005年，对全县药品经营、使用单位171户监督检查340户（次），监督覆盖率100%。检查发现药品使用单位14户使用劣药（使用过期失效药品11户、使用不合格药品3户）共60批（次）。全年查处药品案件30起，医疗器械立案查处1起。

2006年，对全县药品经营、使用单位161户进行全覆盖监督检查，发现药品使用单位从无药品（生物制品）经营资格的企业购进药品、生物制品4户，发现药品经营使用单位使用过期失效药品5户共35批（次），立案查处案件28起。

2007年，在全县药品经营、使用单位153户全覆盖检查中，发现药品经营企业经营超效期药品1户3批（次），药品经营企业超许可范围经营生物制品2户，药品经营企业从无药品经营资格的个人手中购进药品2户，医疗机构使用假劣药品（抽验不合格）13户。全年立案查处21起，没收假劣药品21批（次）。

2008年，全县有药品经营、使用单位160户，全年检查160户319次。查处案件4起，没收假劣药品7批（次）。

（二）专项检查

2001年起，药品监督管理部门每年按照省、州的部署，开展药品、药械、违法药品广告等专项检查。至2008年，开展专项检查项目共23项。同时，对国家、省、州文件明确要求查处的假药进行专项检查。

2001—2008年药品专项检查情况一览表

表16－3

项　目	检查时间	检查情况
氧气使用专项检查	2001年	检查医疗单位19户，未发现使用工业氧气
医疗器械专项检查	2002年	发现未建立一次性使用医疗器械销毁制度3户，未发现使用过期一次性医疗器械和重复使用情况
	2003年	医疗器械使用单位均建立一次性医疗器械销毁制度，未发现有重复使用和使用不合格产品及过期一次性医疗器械情况；发现从无“医疗器械经营许可证”单位购进一次性使用医疗器械的个体诊所2户并进行立案查处
	2004年	发现少数医疗单位在购进医疗器械时未按规定索取产品注册证，未发现假劣一次性医疗器械
	2005年	发现医疗机构2户从非法渠道购进一次性使用无菌器械
	2006年	发现药品零售企业2户经营假冒避孕套，立案查处
	2007年	规范各类药品、医疗器械展示活动，取缔无证经营保健品和化妆品违规企业2户
	2008年	未发现有重复使用和不合格的医疗器械
大输液专项检查	2002年	大输液购进渠道正规，未发现药品经营和使用单位非法擅自配制行为
	2003年	县内无大容量注射剂生产企业，没有医疗机构取得制剂许可，未发现不规范、外观质量沉淀、变质等现象；经营企业按规定建有仓储、销售和药品质量管理制度
	2004年	经营企业建有仓储、销售记录和药品质量管理制度，未发现有沉淀、变质等现象
一次性使用小儿输液品专项检查	2002年	未发现药品经营和使用单位销售、使用违法产品
中药材、中药饮片专项检查	2002年	抽验县中医院的五加皮等5个品种中药饮片，有3个不合格，作没收销毁处理并予以警告
	2004年	城乡集贸市场销售的药材均为地产中草药材，无中药饮片、毒性中药材和濒危动植物中药材销售；中药饮片检查未发现掺杂掺假、以次充好、过期变质等质量问题
	2005年	未发现质量问题
	2006年	未发现掺杂掺假、以次充好、霉变、异味和过期等质量问题
	2007年	抽验16批（次），经州药品检验所检验，不合格8批（次），进行立案查处
	2008年	州稽查局抽验县医院、县中医院的中药材、中药饮片，对检验出的不合格中药饮片，由县食品药品监督管理局立案处罚

续表16－3

项 目	检查时间	检查情况
中成药添加化学药品专项检查	2002年、2004年、2008年	中成药非法添加化学药品专项检查3次，未发现中成药添加化学药品的药物
橡胶避孕套专项检查	2003年	未发现不合格避孕套
特殊药品专项检查	2003年	使用麻醉药品、精神药品的医疗机构均严格按照特殊药品管理规定对麻醉药品和精神药品实行“五专”（专人保管、专柜加锁、专用账册、专用登记、专用处方）管理，未发现流弊社会现象
	2004年	药品批发企业、药品零售企业和个体诊所未经营使用特殊药品，未发现超剂量使用和流弊社会现象，对个别未建立健全特殊药品管理制度的医疗机构责令立即改正
	2005年	未发现特殊药品流弊社会现象
	2006—2007年	被检单位购进渠道合法，做到“五专”管理，未发现超剂量使用和流弊社会现象
	2008年	被检单位采购渠道从具有特殊药品经营资格的企业购进，在使用过程中严格按照特殊药品的管理规定进行管理、使用，未发现特殊药品流弊社会现象
结核血清诊断试剂专项检查	2003年	未发现应查处的结核血清诊断试剂
精神药品专项检查	2003年	使用二类精神药品单位凭医生处方发药，并有专柜保管；对个体诊所未建有二类精神药品购销记录及收支账目，提出限期整改意见。未发现有超限量使用及流弊社会现象
“非典”相关产品专项检查	2003年	查出药品、药械过期失效药品41批（次）；医疗单位医疗器械、设备完好，使用功能正常
疫苗专项检查（生物制品流通专项检查）	2004年	未发现违规经营、使用疫苗和超效期疫苗
	2006年	冷链设备运转正常，疫苗储存条件符合规定，未发现使用超过效期及质量异常的疫苗
	2007年	发现县疾控中心未索取加盖供货方印章的生物制品批签发合格证或者检验报告书，未建立供货方运输设备、时间和温度记录，未定期对疫苗进行检查记录，未建立完整的购进、分发记录，责令限期改正
兴奋剂经营专项治理监督检查	2008年	县内无药品生产和批发企业，有药品中转库1家、药品零售企业25家。未发现中转库违规经营蛋白同化制剂、肽类激素等药品，未发现零售药店经营蛋白同化制剂、肽类激素等药品，对个别药店含兴奋剂物质未标注有“运动员慎用”字样的药品责令下柜停止销售
药品分类管理专项监督检查	2008年	发现个别药店存在个别非药品与药品混置，个别处方药与非处方药未严格分柜摆放，个别处方药未凭医师处方销售，少部分药品按用途分类放置、陈列类别标签放置不够准确等问题，给予警告、责令限期整改
违法药品广告专项监督检查	2004年	发现违法张贴药品广告2户，移送县工商部门处理
	2008年	发现药品零售企业1户发放违法药品广告，移送工商部门处理
其 他	2002年	未发现应查处的“地乌胶囊”和假药“安友”牌清肝明目丸等违法药品
	2003年	未发现省、州文件要求查处的药品
	2004年	假劣藏药检查未发现假劣藏药
	2005年	未发现经营、使用省、州文件要求查处的假劣药品；未发现非法回收药品的单位和个人
	2006年	发现省、州文件要求查处的双黄连口服液33支、盐酸萘福泮注射液88支，进行集中销毁
	2007年	未发现省、州文件要求查处的“假人血白蛋白”“假狂犬疫苗”“氧氟沙星栓”“马来酸曲美布汀片”等药品。县内无药品生产企业，药品包装、标签和说明书日常检查，未发现标明功能主治或适应证超出规定范围等问题

续表16-3

项　目	检查时间	检查情况
其　他	2008年	“瘫清胶囊”“人免疫球蛋白”等假劣药品专项检查，未发现文件要求查处的假劣药品
	2008年	对非法回收药品、非法邮购药品进行专项检查，未发现有非法回收、非法邮购药品违法行为

二、农村药品监督网络和供应网络建设

2004年起，在全县农村开展药品“两网”（监督网络、供应网络）建设，17个乡（镇）聘请药品协管员18名，94个村聘请药品信息员94名，覆盖率达100%。各行政村有药品供应点66个，覆盖率70.21%；药品配送到乡（镇）实现全覆盖；药品配送到村49个（应配送75个），覆盖率65.33%。2005—2006年，全县行政村有药品供应点78个，覆盖率82.97%；药品配送到村58个（应配送70个），覆盖率82.86%。2007—2008年，乡（镇）药品监督网覆盖率100%；行政村有药品供应点81个，覆盖率86.17%；药品配送到乡覆盖率100%；配送到村70个（应配送81个），覆盖率86.42%。

三、GSP认证管理

2003年7月起，在县内药品经营企业开展《药品经营质量管理规范》（GSP）认证工作。7月，组织各药品经营企业实施GSP认证动员培训。2004年，现场指导药品零售企业进行GSP认证申请8家，经省GSP审评认证中心审查，均于9月通过GSP认证。2005年，县城药品零售企业14家全部通过GSP认证。2006年，药品零售企业通过GSP认证16家（县城1家、乡镇15家）。2007—2008年，对已通过GSP认证的药品零售企业实施跟踪检查，均符合《药品零售企业GSP认证检查评定标准》。

四、药品不良反应（ADR）监测

2006年，根据《药品不良反应监测管理办法》的规定，县药监部门与卫生部门联合发出《关于加强全县药品不良反应监测工作的通知》，加强上市药品监测，确保公众用药安全。全年收集上报药品不良反应报告52例。2007年，收集上报药品不良反应共70例。2008年，收集上报药品不良反应45例，医疗器械不良事件5例。

第六章　国土资源管理

第一节　管理体制

1980年，县矿业管理所并入县社队企业局。1982年4月前，土地征用、划拨由县民政局办理。1982年5月，土地征用、划拨改由城建局管理，1984年9月划归县农牧局管理，农牧局设土地管理股。1986年9月，成立县土地管理局，人员编制增至4人。1988年6月，县土地管理局下设建设用地地籍管理站、法规监督站、勘察规划队。是年，法规监督站改为法规监察站，勘察规划队改为勘测规划队。

1988年11月，县政府委派各乡（镇）党委或政府一名领导兼任乡（镇）土地管理员。

1989年2月，在4区1镇建立土地管理所，受县土地管理局及当地党政双重领导，4区1镇编制17人。是年7月，建立土地监察队，为事业单位，编制3人。

1990年4月，县矿产资源管理办公室与县乡镇企业局合建玉屏区、茂兰区2个煤炭管理所和水尧、茂兰、洞塘、瑶庆、立化、佳荣6个煤炭管理站，聘用管理人员18名。

1994年6月，县土地管理局与县矿管办、环境保护局合并，更名为县国土资源管理局。

1996年6月，县国土资源管理局更名为县国土局，将矿管、环保职能划出，另设县地质矿产局。国土局内设办公室、测绘管理股、法规监察股，下设建设用地地籍管理站、土地监察大队、土地勘测规划所、土地开发中心、富园开发公司。各乡（镇）设国土所。

1997年，乡（镇）国土所改为县国土局派出机构。全县国土系统人员编制64人，其中行政编制12人、事业编制52人（县国土局13人、乡镇国土所39人）。

2007年5月，按照县政府《关于印发荔波县国土资源局职能配置、内设机构和人员编制规定的通知》，设县国土资源局（加挂荔波县测绘管理办公室牌子），内设办公室、人事教育股、执法监察股、规划股、地籍与测绘管理股、用地管理股、矿权管理股、资源环境股；下属事业机构县国土资源执法监察大队（升格为副科级事业单位），建立县国土资源技术信息中心（股级事业单位），保留土地矿产勘查所、国土资源开发中心2个股级事业单位；乡（镇）国土资源所事业编制由39人调整为51人。撤销县国土资源规划设计室、建设用地地籍管理站、地质环境监测站。至2008年年末，全县国土资源系统机构不变，实有人员76人。

第二节 土地资源管理

一、土地调查

（一）土地资源详查

1988年7—8月，根据国务院、省、州政府部署，县政府抽调农业区划土壤普查的业务骨干及区、乡土地管理员和部分村、组干部65人，以觉巩乡为重点，调查小片区宜农荒地、闲散土地和废弃地资源。12月，成立县土地资源详查技术中心组，从1989年2月开始土地资源详查工作，到1995年8月全面结束。详查汇总全县各地类面积为耕地310989.5亩（净面积259767.3亩），园地1812.6亩，林地2028038.9亩（有林地1335494.2亩），牧草地609232亩，工矿居民点30274.4亩，交通用地5288.9亩，水域26814.3亩，未利用地619266.5亩。以上8类土地共计3631717.1亩，与州统一接边控制面积相符，比全县总辖区面积3661500亩（即2441平方公里）少29782.9亩，其原因是省内按州统一接边量算统计，东北部与从江、榕江接壤部分在地类调绘时未达到境界线。

（二）土地变更调查

1996年，按省、州统一部署，开展土地变更调查，使用1/2.5万的乡（镇）土地利用现状图，实地进行逐个图斑对照、勾绘、登记、统计、平衡。调查结果：与土地资源详查结果比，耕地减少310.6亩，有林地减少16.6亩，牧草地减少51.0亩，未利用土地减少16.6亩；园地增加61.6亩，城镇用地增加173.3亩，交通用地增加234.1亩，水域增加1.6亩，其他各地类平衡。

2005年，根据省、州安排，进行全县土地利用变更调查。年初全县各地类面积为农用地3041950.8亩、建设用地42769.5亩、未利用地479824.8亩，年末各地类面积为农用地3042598.7亩、建设用地43046.4亩、未利用地478900亩。其中，农用地年内减少2258.2亩，年内增加2906.1亩，净增值为647.9亩；建设用地年内减少0.5亩，年内增加277.4亩，净增值276.9亩；未利用地年内减少930.3亩，年内增加5.5亩，净增值−924.8亩。

2007年，全县土地利用变更调查结果为农用地3042265.6亩，比上年减少180亩；建设用地43709.9亩，比上年增加510.1亩；未利用地478569.6亩；其他土地222.2亩，比上年减少2.4亩。

（三）耕地资源调查

2000年9—12月，按照国土资源部和省、州国土局制定的土地资源调查评价项目实施方案和技术规定，以土地利用总体规划、土地开发复垦规划、废弃地调查报告等为基础资料，确定调查重点区域，开展耕地资源调查。调查项目主要有耕地后备资源、坡耕地。调查工作以土地利用现状图为工作底图，经实地校核、外业调绘，写出《荔波县耕地后备资源调查评估报告》《荔波县耕地调查评价报告》。耕地后备资源调查情况为全县耕地后备资源12867.8亩。其中，甲介河流滩地可新增和恢复耕地900.1亩，佳荣镇水碰村天然草地可开发4000亩，水利乡天然草地可开发2410亩，永康乡开发320亩，水尧乡可开发3500亩，播尧乡可开发830亩，甲良镇可开发500亩，玉屏镇水春可开发407.7亩。坡耕地调查情况为全县有坡耕地76766.96亩。其中，15～25度坡耕地60921.56亩（坡地37645.79亩、梯田23275.77亩），大于25度坡耕地15845.4亩（坡地13070.25亩、梯田2775.15亩）。坡耕地在全县各乡（镇）均有分布，甲良、播尧、佳荣、方村、朝阳5个乡（镇）坡耕地占全县坡耕地的71.37%。根据坡地生态保护情况、工程设施完善度、有无侵蚀和其深岩所占比重等进行评价，评出宜耕坡地3413.56亩，占同类面积的56.04%，不宜耕地3507.03亩；大于25度宜耕梯田1979.45亩，不宜耕梯田795.70亩。1995—2000年，全县退耕还林1324.9亩。

二、土地权属管理

（一）土地所有权

实行联产承包责任制以后，将集体土地承包给农民耕种，农民有使用权，所有权属集体。

1988年，在甲良、朝阳、茂兰3个区和立化乡开展机关单位、城镇居民和农宅地籍调查。经逐个宗地审查，报县政府批准登记发证，机关单位、城镇居民住宅地发“国有土地使用证”，农宅用地发“集体土地建设用地使用证”。

1989年9—12月，开展全县土地权属划界工作，完成乡、村划界1304.75公里，签订边界协议书360份，调处边界纠纷181起。权属划界经省、州技术中心组检查验收，合格率为92.5%。

（二）土地使用权

1.土地使用权登记

1988年，在县城开展地籍登记、发证工作，全县申请登记国有土地767宗，发证748宗。

1989—1994年，国有土地使用权登记102宗，集体土地使用权登记87宗，面积总计12073.51平方米。

1995年，全县开展土地使用制度改革，县政府颁发《荔波县城镇国有土地使用权出让、转让暨土地有偿使用暂行规定》，除不以出让方式获国有土地使用权的用地项目外（如教学用地、交通用地、医疗卫生用地等），凡在县内申请使用国有土地的单位、集体、个人，一律按照国务院55号令和省政府6号令以及县政府的规定，以出让方式获得国有土地使用权，由县政府管控土地出让一级市场，管好转让、出租、抵押土地的二级市场，防止土地资产流失。

1991—1997年，土地变更登记187宗地，面积59926平方米。1998—2001年，国有土地使用权登记630宗，集体土地使用权登记3909宗，土地使用权抵押登记340宗，面积85476.89平方米。

2001年，土地预登记94宗，面积18354.10平方米。为国有企业改制进行土地资产评估确认共9宗，评估面积28104.24平方米，评估金额1186.90万元。

2002年，土地登记219宗，面积101274.75平方米，发证169宗，面积96274.25平方米。其中，土地变更登记13宗，面积9593.52平方米；土地预登记52宗，面积8095.54平方米；土地使用权抵押登记236宗，面积7560平方米。2003年，集体土地流转4宗，面积56000平方米。

2005年，实行土地使用权登记公开查询制度，全年查询3起。

2008年，国有土地初始登记97宗、变更登记57宗。全年土地使用权查询4宗。

2.土地使用权出让

2001年，协议出让国有土地使用权9宗，面积1390.4平方米，收取出让金3.13万元，全部上缴财政。

2003年起，县内通过招标、拍卖、挂牌形式出让国有土地使用权。是年，拍卖国有土地使用权1宗，面积460.02平方米，地价款40万元。2004年，全县出让国有土地使用权7宗。2005年，国有土地使用权拍卖1宗，面积698平方米；挂牌出让17宗，面积6520平方米。2006—2008年，通过招标、拍卖、挂牌出让国土有地使用权25宗，面积总计463795平方米；协议出让国土有地使用权9宗，面积总计8072平方米。

三、土地开发利用

（一）土地开发与复垦

1991年，开展全县土地复垦资源调查。调查结果：因开矿使耕地下沉或开裂、石尘、水毁而停耕的土地和烧制砖瓦破坏的耕地共435.98亩，其中稻田46.27亩；开发土地2181亩，其中耕地120

亩、非耕地2061亩，非耕地开发利用主要是经济果树林。

1991—1997年，开发土地46612亩，其中耕地1853亩、非耕地44759亩。

1998—2001年，耕地开发1497.80亩，坡改梯工程开发25546.05亩（含改造中低产田和恢复水毁面积），非耕地开发35800亩。玉屏镇洞托瑶族新村、水尧乡移民新村老牛场等6个土地开发项目，新增耕地824.19亩，投资总计102.32万元，受益人口7098人。

2002年，土地开发复垦1200亩。

2001年6月，实施水尧乡梅林耕地开发项目建设，项目由省财政投入专项资金，工程竣工验收合格后按每亩1500元结算。这是县内首次争取到国家无偿投资的最大耕地开发项目。项目规划开发耕地927.75亩，修排灌渠3.53公里，建容积30立方米的蓄水池35个，整理乡村道路和修建机耕道5.99公里，绿化陡坡地184.7亩（兼顾美化环境和水土保持），开发园地面积59.4亩。至2003年4月项目竣工，经省国土资源厅和省农业厅验收合格，并验定增加耕地面积828.34亩，项目受益193户945人。

2003年，对水利、茂兰、立化、洞塘、捞村、翁昂等地后备资源的地理位置、地形、地貌、坡度、水文、土壤、植被等进行论证，确定适宜开发位置。是年，茂兰镇水庆耕地开发项目通过可行性论证，获省国土资源厅批准立项开发并动工建设，2004年第一季度竣工。

2004年，全县耕地开发项目9个，开发面积1650亩。2005年，实施耕地开发项目13个，面积总计2840亩。

2006年，全县开发土地并通过验收，新增耕地933.17亩。2008年，土地开发项目申报项目3个，开发面积总计2025亩。

（二）土地利用总体规划

1996年年底，成立县土地利用总体规划工作领导小组，下设办公室和技术组，经过课题研究、规划文本编制等阶段，至1998年年底，完成县级土地利用总体规划编制，1999年1月通过省专家组评审验收，经省政府批准实施。

2000年年初，启动乡（镇）土地利用总体规划编制及基本农田保护区划定工作。8月，各乡（镇）土地利用总体规划编制及基本农田保护区划定全面完成，通过省专家组验收合格，呈报省、州政府批准实施。

2004年，对《荔波县土地利用总体规划（2006—2020年）》进行修编，基期年（2005年年末）的土地利用现状为全县土地总面积3555248.3亩。其中，农用地3033302亩，占土地总面积的85.3%；建设用地43046.25亩，占土地总面积的1.21%；其他土地478900.05亩，占土地总面积的13.47%。规划的远期目标2020年耕地保有量287730亩，基本农田保护面积252615亩，新增建设用地规模17260.05亩，建设用地总规模61277.7亩，城乡建设用地规模40460.85亩，城镇化率50%，人均城镇工矿用地98平方米。

同时，对乡（镇）土地利用总体规划也进行修编，修编后的《玉屏镇土地利用总体规划》经省政府批复实施，其余16个乡（镇）土地利用总体规划经州政府批复实施。

（三）农用地分等定级工作

2004—2007年，按照国土资源部的统一部署，开展全县农用地分等定级工作。全县农用地分等以部颁《农用地分等规程》为依据，通过调查，计算出农用土地生产潜力，评价农用土地质量。全县农用地总面积331886.55亩，划分自然等别8个（四等至十一等）。其中，四等农用地18759.75亩，占5.65%；五等农用地14717.85亩，占4.43%；六等农用地409.95亩，占0.12%；七等农用地16616.25亩，占5.01%；八等农用地26552.4亩，占8%；九等农用地100657.2亩，占30.33%；十等农用地112764.45亩，占33.98%；十一等农用地41408.7亩，占12.48%。按土地自然生产高低划分：下等地（四等、五等）33477.6亩，占10.09%；中等地（六等至十等）257000.25亩，占77.44%；上等地（十一等）41408.7亩，占12.48%。

四、建设用地管理

国家机关、企业事业单位建设用地，按照有关法规审批划拨。农村住宅用地，1983年以前由大队、生产队审批。1984年以后，根据国务院颁布的《村镇建设用地管理条例》规定，改由土地管理部门审批，农户在获得土地管理部门发给的“宅基地使用证”后，才能用地建房。

1987年起，全县各项建设用地，由计划部门和土地管理部门审查，县土地管理部门将州下达的非农业建设用地指标分解到各乡（镇）。乡（镇）政府有权批准农民宅基地占用非耕地用地申请，凡属占用耕地的，必须送县土地管理部门报请县政府审批。个人建房用地，不允许占用良田好土，个别地方因地理条件特殊确需占用少量良田好土的，按照“占一造二”的原则先造后用。到1990年，因建房占用良田好土而造田补偿共11亩。

1990年，县政府颁发《荔波县居民建房用地管理暂行规定》《关于村镇个人建房用地限额的补充规定》《关于县城土地确认为国有的暂行规定》。1991—1997年，以划拨方式审批国家建设用地项目187个，占用耕地320.65亩；个人建房用地总计1263宗，占用耕地3.32亩。

2000年后，建设用地管理实行有偿有限期使用制度。是年3月，根据《闲置土地处理办法》，收回县内长期不开发的闲置国有土地204.93平方米，进行公开拍卖。

1998—2001年，全县国家建设用地项目24个，用地面积399.3亩，其中占用耕地398.7亩。主要项目有独荔公路、新风广场（现邓恩铭广场）、教师新村等。个人建房用地149宗，用地面积52.95亩，其中占用耕地38.1亩。

2002年，审查报批和办理茂兰、翁昂、甲良、播尧等乡（镇）集镇建设用地100亩；荔波机场、茂兰110千伏变电站、江滨大道、广场东路、二环西路、三力宾馆等征地共86.2亩。2003年，拍卖国有土地使用权1宗，面积460.02平方米。2004年，对外公告招标、拍卖、挂牌出让国有土地使用权7宗。

2005年，审查上报各类项目建设用地9宗。申报建设用地总面积607.95亩，其中耕地353.4亩。全年申报建设占用耕地总面积353.4亩，委托州土地开发中心完成补充耕地353.4亩，做到占补平衡，先补后占。

2006年，以划拨方式供地3宗，总面积175.78亩；实地审查建设项目用地17宗；农村个人建房117宗。

2007年，全县第一批次城镇规划建设用地报批，获省政府批准，总面积312.82亩。农村个人建房用地审查报批222户，总面积35.23亩，其中占用耕地10.94亩。征收土地总面积1260.96亩（稻田989.12亩、旱地271.84亩），共支付征地补偿费3603.59万元。全年核发建设用地批准书25本。

2008年，报批县农副产品加工项目、污水处理工程等项目用地及农村建设用地215宗；划拨供地24宗，面积总计23.05亩。

五、耕地保护

1999年，根据国土资源部、农业部《关于认真贯彻执行〈基本农田保护条例〉进一步做好基本农田保护工作的通知》，以及2000年省国土厅《关于进一步抓紧做好基本农田保护调整划定工作的通知》，2001年4—5月，开展全县基本农田保护调整划定工作。全县耕地总面积310636.05亩，第一次划定保护面积264840亩，保护率85.26%。州下达基本农田保护面积273105亩，保护率87.92%。经调整补充，划入基本农田的果园2518.05亩、茶园1107亩，大于25度宜耕坡地2216.1亩；零星地类中的田1108.2亩、土1320.45亩，补充面积总计8269.8亩，基本农田保护面积达272854.8亩，保护率87.84%，其中稻田171966.6亩、旱地97668.15亩、园地3220.05亩。

2005年，在茂兰镇建立高标准基本农田保护区，面积2861.14亩。

2006年，县、乡、村层层签订基本农田保护责任书，确保基本农田面积不减少、质量不降低。是年，建成朝阳镇高标准基本农田示范区1个，面积1118.7亩。

2008年，开展全县基本农田保护情况检查。同时，向群众宣传基本农田保护政策和法规。年末，全县有基本农田保护面积263249.85亩。

六、土地监察与行政执法

1984年7—9月，根据《国家建设征用土地条例》的规定，县政府与广西红茂矿务局联合组成调查组，对红茂矿务局在荔波县立化乡的更班、平寨、打油寨3个煤井占用土地进行清查，3个矿占地总计1863.64亩，经批准的仅46.16亩。经两省（区）及县、矿领导协商，决定由红茂矿务局补办申请用地手续，并按规定给土地所属乡、村予以补偿。1986年11月，贵州省政府批准上述3个矿征用土地1817.48亩。

1986年9月，成立非农用地清查领导小组，下设办公室，对1982年2月《村镇建房用地管理条例》、5月《国家建设征地条例》颁布实施后的非农业建设用地进行清理，查出各种违法占地面积2423.8亩（耕地201亩）。其中，属先用后报、用而不报、少征多用的2360亩，属买卖土地、越权批地、非法转让土地面积63.8亩。清查后，补办用地手续1864宗共2046亩，收取土地使用费及补偿费5.8万元；拆除违章、违法建厂建窑115宗，恢复耕地113.47亩；给予党纪、政纪处分7人。清查前的1982—1986年，未经批准或骗取批准、乱占滥用土地建房2163起，占用耕地201亩，平均每年占地40亩。1987年清查工作经州政府验收合格。

1988年11月，成立荔波县处理违法占地领导小组，县政府分管领导任组长，4区1镇兼职土地管理员及工商、检察、司法、公安、房管、土地等部门领导为成员，加强土地监察工作。

1991—1992年，开展干部职工“三违”（违法、违纪、违章）建私房清理工作，查出违法占地建房28户，作拆除处理30.2平方米，其余处以罚款并补办用地手续。清查工作经州清房领导小组验收合格。

1994年，对樟江沿河两岸违法占地取土加工砖瓦行为进行清查，取缔违法取土制砖68户，炸毁砖瓦窑21座，责令自行拆窑2座，拆毁砖瓦棚15间，限期自封砖瓦窑20个，自拆砖瓦棚30间。

1997年5—12月，开展全县非农建设用地清查，查出各类非农建设用地1165宗，面积848.10亩（耕地345.75亩）。其中，依法批准用地1024宗828.4亩，未经批准非法占用70宗（面积12.9亩），非法转让土地使用权的71宗（面积6.8亩）。对违法用地141宗依法进行处理。

是年，根据省国土厅《关于在全省范围内开展农村宅基地专项治理的通知》，进行农村宅基地专项治理，全县查处违法用地26户，面积总计2.61亩。

1991—1997年，共发生土地违法案件169宗，违法用地207宗，其中立案查处169宗。

2001年，县国土局建立土地动态巡回检查制度，及时发现、制止土地违法行为，将土地违法案件消灭在萌芽状态。2002年，巡查发现并及时制止土地违法行为20宗，立案查处5宗，查出违法用地245.1平方米。全年调处土地纠纷10宗，调解成功率88.9%。

2003年，开展巡查活动17次，发现和制止土地违法行为18宗，立案查处5宗，查出违法用地面积2.79亩。全年调处各类土地纠纷7件，达成调解协议5件。2004年，通过巡查，制止土地违法行为39宗，立案查处6宗，查出违法用地面积81.56亩（其中非法占用基本农田4宗，面积53.41亩）；调处各类土地纠纷6宗。

2005年，土地执法巡查115次，查处违法占地案件3宗，调处各类土地纠纷5宗。

2006年，动态巡查实行月报制度，对全县用地情况实施全面监控，尤其对群众反映强烈、社会影响较大、违法性质严重的案件，依法严肃处理。是年，申请县法院依法强制拆除驾欧乡1户未经批准私自占用基本农田建筑的房屋25平方米；依法没收地上建筑物3宗，占地面积共504.16平方米。

2007年，查处违法占地案件3宗，调处各类土地纠纷1宗。

2008年，查处土地违法案件1宗，面积167.25亩；制止违法建房案件15宗，面积2.43亩。

七、土地证书年检

根据国土资源部《关于开展1999年土地证书年检工作的通知》和省、州国土部门有关土地证书年检工作文件精神，1999年10月，县人民政府发布《关于开展1999年土地证书年检工作的通告》，至次年5月，用地单位和个人申报年检981宗，占应检宗数的94.4%，通过年检711宗，占应检宗数的68.43%。此后，这项工作停止。

八、城镇基准地价评估

1999年1—6月，按《城镇土地估价规程》要求，在玉屏镇开展基准地价评估工作并通过省、州专家评审验收。

2003年10月—2004年10月，县国土资源局委托州土地经济事务所进行玉屏镇基准地价更新和16个乡（镇）基准地价评估。评估出的基准地价经召开听证会后，报州国土资源局验收。

2004年县城（玉屏镇）各类用地基准地价表

表16－4　（6月30日评估）　单位：元/平方米

均值地域	用地类别			
	商业用地	住宅用地	工业用地	综合用地
Ⅰ	900	600	500	700
Ⅱ	700	500	300	500
Ⅲ	500	300	200	300

2004年16乡（镇）各类用地基准地价表

表16－5　（6月30日评估）　单位：元/平方米

乡（镇）类别	用地类别			
	商业用地	住宅用地	工业用地	综合用地
一类	360	170	145	210
二类	250	150	110	180
三类	200	125	90	130

九、“三无”乡（镇）创建

1992年，在捞村乡开展“三无”（无违法批地、无违法管地、无违法用地）工作试点。之后在各乡（镇）开展“三无”工作，并作为县政府对乡（镇）土地管理工作的年终目标考核内容。1993—1999年，每年将“三无”乡（镇）活动评比纳入土地执法监察年终考核。

2000年3月，县政府制定土地管理“三无”乡（镇）创建活动方案，在立化、洞塘、方村、朝阳、甲良、播尧6个乡（镇）开展“三无”乡（镇）创建活动，年底通过州国土局验收合格。

2003—2004年，巩固全县“三无”乡（镇）创建成果，各乡（镇）国土资源所和县国土资源局建立国土资源一级、二级巡查网络，对辖区内用地行为进行检查。

第三节 矿产资源管理

一、采矿权管理

（一）采矿权登记

1987年，县内开始实行采矿权登记管理制度。是年，县矿管办复核批准全县乡（镇）煤井11个，为水泥厂、其他小煤窑和广西红茂矿务局设在荔波的更班、平寨、打油寨3个煤矿申请登记采矿权，获采矿许可证。

1996年，按县委、县政府的要求规划全县年产2万吨以上小型煤矿33个，年内申请采矿权登记24个（建成投产12个、在建4个、筹建8个）。

至1997年，全县煤炭采矿权申请登记372个，换证注销106个，有效采矿许可证268个。其中，国有煤矿2个，乡（镇）煤矿266个。

2005年，挂牌出让采矿权7个（煤矸石砖厂1个、采石场6个）。

2007年，整合煤矿企业10个，整合后向省国土资源厅报送扩能技改扩界煤矿采矿权变更登记企业3个。年内，挂牌出让采石场10个、煤矸石砖厂5个，挂牌出让石灰岩矿山采矿权7宗。2005—2007年，全县挂牌出让采矿权40宗。

（二）采矿权年检

1991年起，实行采矿权年检制度，每年上半年对上年度矿山企业进行年检，采矿企业每年必须到县矿管部门申请年检，经年检合格方可继续生产。

2002年4月，应参加年检矿山企业61个（包括铅锌、建材），实际参加年检59个，审查合格53个，年检矿山现场检查率95%，通过下井检查发现越界开采6家，责令限期改正。

2003年2月，年检煤矿企业64个、非煤企业7个，年检合格70个（煤矿66个、非煤矿4个）。年检中，矿山现场检查率90%，对不合格的矿山不予年检并限期整改。年检发现资源枯竭、安全隐患大的煤矿企业3个，不予通过年检。县内铅锌矿企业6个、煤矿探矿权企业1个（青利公司）、黄金矿探矿权企业1个（省黄金公司），由州国土资源局年检。

2005年，境内煤矿企业43个、铅锌矿4个，由州国土资源局进行矿山企业采矿权人年检，矿山现场检查率达90%，年检不合格的企业通过整改后评定为合格。

2006年，年检采矿企业46个，年检率100%。查处非法转让采矿权企业6个。

2007年，境内煤矿企业38个、铅锌矿企业3个、石场11个、砖厂6个，由州国土资源局进行年检，年检率98.3%，抽检率65.2%，矿山开采率、回采率等各项指标基本达标。

2008年，全县年检采矿企业76个。其中，省级发证34个、县级发证42个，年检实地抽查企业35个（省级矿山企业15个、县级矿山企业20个），抽查率为46%。查处违法行为3起，其中非法转让1起。

二、矿业秩序整顿

1990年，《贵州省乡（镇）集体矿山企业和个体采矿违法处罚办法》颁布实施，县矿管部门依法对乡（镇）集体矿山企业和个体采矿业主进行管理。

1991年，茂兰镇洞英村部分村民以土地祖籍权属关系为由，强行在立化镇岜项矿区违法建小煤井20口，凿通岜项矿山大巷，哄抢资源，岜项矿被迫停产。12月11日，县政府到矿区召开现场会，宣传矿产资源法律法规和县政府关于保护岜项矿的公告。之后，由公安、矿管、乡企、安委会、立化镇等有关单位检查落实公告实施情况，对未执行政府公告的煤井强制封停。1992年年初，各小煤井又擅自恢复，4月，立化镇政府按县政府的规定进行强制清理。9月，岜项矿山非法小煤井清理结束，炸封非法煤井20个，封闭贯通岜项矿大巷煤井2个，取缔影响岜项矿建设煤井6个，注销采矿许可证6个，没收非法采出原煤2079吨。

1994年，县政府对重点矿区小煤窑进行治理整顿，重点整顿立化、打油寨、水尧3个片区，立化片区查出无证煤井72个。对无证煤井炸封56个、整改16个。

至1997年，县政府治理整顿矿山，封、停、整改煤井累计550口（次），行政处罚200起。

2001年，县政府办发出《关于加强矿产资源管理秩序治理整顿工作的通知》，开展矿产资源管理秩序治理整顿工作。2002年，县委政府组成5个煤炭矿山清理整顿工作组，安排专项经费20万元，于是年8月、11月、12月对全县非法煤井进行3次大规模清理整顿，炸封煤井200口（次）。

是年，建立矿山动态巡查制度和举报有奖制度，对矿山进行经常性检查，重点矿区每周检查2次，非重点矿区每周检查1次。巡查工作实行包片责任制，对检查发现的安全隐患、环境污染、盗伐坑木等行为及时查处。同时，针对境内部分矿山企业矿业权转让、出租、承包不符合规定的情况，对主要矿区进行矿业权集中清理，发现广西红茂矿务局高荣矿违规建设，根据《贵州省矿产资源条例》的规定，省国土资源厅依法注销高荣矿采矿许可证。经严格规范探矿权市场，进入荔波县从事探矿活动的单位持证率达到100%，探矿单位每年按期到省国土资源厅年检。

2003年，开展矿山巡查128次，炸封非法小煤窑245口。2004年，矿山巡查140次，炸封非法小煤窑274口，炸毁违法矿山机械113套，查处非法运输原煤车28辆，遣散民工500人（次），下达停止违法行为通知书300份，下达矿山巡查建议书8份，设立宣传标牌33块、无证煤窑炸封牌100块。

2005年，查处矿山企业越界开采等违法行为，下井测量10次，对越界开采企业下发责令整改通知书。全年炸封小煤窑69口，收缴炸药、电雷管、导火索及毁损钢丝绳、电线、设备等，下达责令停止违法行为通知书28份，送达巡查建议书11份，查处营运煤炭车辆53辆（次），查获无证煤炭产品250吨，教育遣散民工217人。

2006年，制定《荔波县整顿和规范矿产资源开发秩序工作实施方案》，成立县整顿和规范矿产资源开发秩序工作领导小组，下设办公室。划拨专项工作经费25万元，开展整顿和规范矿业开发秩序专项整治工作。县政府与产煤乡（镇）签订炸封取缔非法采煤窝点责任书，县国土资源局与乡（镇）国土资源所签订工作目标责任书，建立“包保”责任制，明确周报制度和量化考核机制。至2007年，县政府两年拨专项工作经费70万元，组织人员3500人次，炸封小煤窑90口（次），现场收缴及捣毁机械设备25套，下达责令停止违法行为通知书60份，送达各乡（镇）政府巡查建议书30份，教育遣散民工120人，行政拘留10人，没收违法所得5万元，罚款3万元，制作“炸封牌”标志100块，予以警示教育。在治理整顿中发现越界开采行为的矿山企业25个，均立案处罚，越界处全部封闭；在排查中发现有非法转让行为的矿山企业18个，全部进行清理。

2007年8月，对水庆煤矿、立化镇恒利煤矿、立化镇双龙煤矿、立化镇三岔河煤矿、茂兰镇德比煤矿5个污染环境严重、安全生产条件较差的煤矿实施关闭。是年，对全县矿山企业总量进行调控管理，煤炭矿山企业由39个压减为28个。

2008年，县委、县政府发出《关于构建和谐矿区的实施意见》，加强矿业秩序管理。同时，督促矿山编制《矿山环境保护与综合治理方案》。全年取缔非法采矿点4个，查处采石场越界开采违法案件1起。

三、矿产资源补偿费征收

1989年起，根据省政府办公厅的文件规定，向乡（镇）集体矿山企业和个体采矿业主征收矿产开发管理费。

1994年4月1日起，向采矿权人征收矿产资源补偿费。1991—1997年，矿产资源补偿费征收累计213.74万元，上缴省、州12.83万元，缴县财政43.13万元。1997年6月，由省、州协调，广西红茂矿务局在荔波开采的3个煤矿的矿产资源补偿费由荔波县地矿局征收。

2008年，执行《贵州省矿山环境恢复保证金暂行规定》，矿山企业按标准缴存保证金。

第四节　地质环境保护

一、地质灾害隐患排查

荔波县地形山高坡陡，河谷深切，岩溶发育，地质环境脆弱，易发生地质灾害。

1999年起，县内每年采取属地排查和部门归口的方式进行汛前、汛中、汛后地质灾害排查，即乡（镇）地质灾害由所在乡（镇）组织排查，部门地质灾害由部门组织排查，排查工作以学校、乡（镇）、村寨等人口密集区、重要工程设施和项目所在地为重点，排查后，县国土资源局对新发现点组织核实确认，提出防治措施。各乡（镇）均存在不同程度的地质灾害隐患，主要为崩塌，其次为滑坡，大气降水和不合理的人为工程活动是诱发自然地质灾害的主要因素。崩塌主要分布在3个水族乡，其他乡（镇）有零星分布；滑坡主要分布在播尧乡、朝阳镇；地面塌陷多为采空塌陷，主要分布在立化镇、茂兰镇和水尧乡；泥石流不发育；地裂缝常与其他地质灾害相伴生。

二、地质灾害防治

境内地质灾害较为易发，县国土资源部门坚持“预防为主，避让与治理相结合”的防治方针，落实防治措施。

2002年，成立荔波地质环境监测站，负责全县地质环境保护、治理和地质灾害防治。是年，省地质环境监测总站向省国土资源厅提交《贵州省荔波县地质灾害调查与区划报告》，确认地质灾害隐患233处，将全县划定为6个地质灾害高易发区、4个中易发区、2个低易发区和2个不易发区。进行汛前地质灾害排查后编制《2002年荔波县地质灾害防灾预案》，提出各隐患点预防措施，未因地质灾害造成人员伤亡和重要财产损失。年内，为景区和地质灾害点居民实施移民搬迁选址8个，其中，立化镇高望组4户、下拉薅组16户、水尧乡水捞组30户实施搬迁。

2003年，全县发现地质灾害隐患270处，其中重要隐患点25处。县国土资源局编制《2003年荔波县地质灾害防灾预案》报县政府批转相关部门组织实施，向隐患点群众发放“地质灾害灾情险情防范明白表”，对蓝淀山不稳定斜坡、拉奖危岩体2个重要隐患点进行应急调查，向县政府提交调查报告；省国土资源厅委派专家到拉交、董亥、肯甫3个重要隐患点进行应急调查；在水捞危岩体书写禁止在危岩体危险区范围内活动的永久性标语；对回龙阁滑坡群危险区范围内仍在耕种的农户，致函玉屏镇政府责令立即停止耕种；对西竹、穿洞危岩体危险区范围进行划定，确定应搬迁农户。同时，通过县有线电视台进行地质灾害科普宣传，提高群众防灾避灾治灾的意识；建立健全地质环境监测档案，建立全县地质灾害档案和环境地质灾害台账。

2004年起，县政府与县直有关部门及乡（镇）于年初签订地质灾害责任书，各乡（镇）政府成立地质灾害防治防灾领导小组，将地质灾害防治作为党政的重要工作。此外，有3个村成立地质灾害防治机构。是年，对重要地质灾害隐患点巡查64点（次），建立巡查台账和记录，针对巡查情况，列出重要隐患点报县政府，向受地质灾害隐患险情威胁的住户发地质灾害明白表428份，编制16个重要地质灾害隐患点防灾预案。同时，对重要地质灾害隐患点划出危险区域并要求危险区域内的农户尽快搬离危险区，禁止从事砍伐、放牧、采石等诱发危险事故的活动。全年发生地质灾害5起，造成房屋损毁22栋，无人员伤亡。

2005年，建立县、乡、村（组）、户四级群防网络，有7个村成立地质预警防治机构。全县建立地质灾害监测点61个，实行动态监测，发放地质灾害防灾明白卡713份。全年发现地质灾害隐患点240处，实施地质灾害受胁户搬迁避让6处共105户。9月，省国土资源厅地质环境监测总站对荔波县急需搬迁的重要地质灾害隐患点进行调查复核，有重要地质灾害11处，急需搬迁595户2700人，并向省政府报告。是年，回龙阁滑坡群治理可行性研究报告通过省、州立项治理。年内，地质灾害造成房屋、公路、渠道、小水电站、水坝等毁损，直接经济损失100万元。

2006年，执行汛期值班、地质灾害速报和月报制度。是年发生地质灾害6起，房屋受损4栋，无人员伤亡。全年组织地质灾害点巡查120次。实施4个乡（镇）的7个地质灾害隐患点受威胁户搬迁75户307人。

2007年，在永康乡开展地质灾害应急预案演练。2008年7—8月，与104地质队、贵州大学资源与环境学院青年志愿者组成宣讲组，开展农村地质灾害防治知识培训，参训7681人。是年，在灾害点设立警示标志，向灾害点周边居民、单位发放防灾工作明白卡2000份；对瑶山小学、水尧中学、朝阳镇洪江村拉岜组3处重大地质灾害隐患进行调查，提出防治措施。全年发生地质灾害10起，造成直接经济损失207.33万元，无人员伤亡；开展“地质灾害防治百日督查专项行动”、“5·12”汶川大地震后灾害点巡查110次；搬迁受地质灾害威胁户90户。

附：

回龙阁滑坡群治理

2000年4月，发现玉屏镇回龙阁水利局果园区水池开裂。6月，省国土资源厅委派省地质环境监测总站对该区进行调查，发现该区为滑坡区。7月，县政府请求对该滑坡进行勘察治理，获省国土资源厅项目安排。2001年12月—2002年3月，省地矿局第二工程勘察院对该滑坡区进行勘察，回龙阁水利局果园区为滑坡群。2005年，省政府拨治理经费100万元。9月，县国土资源局委托省建筑工程勘察院对回龙阁滑坡群进行治理工程设计。2006年3月动工治理，是年9月竣工。2007年1月，该滑坡群治理工程经州国土资源局、州财政局组织专家验收组验收，评定为合格工程。

第五节　测绘管理

一、地图市场检查

1998年7月，县政府主持召开县直机关有关单位负责人座谈，会议确定：凡外地到荔波县推销各种地图，必须持有测绘主管部门审查批准的经销证明方可销售，否则一律以非法买卖予以没收。

2002年年初，对全县市场公开销售的各种地图11幅进行登记。6月，整顿和规范全县地图市场秩序，对县城和立化、茂兰、佳荣等集镇地图零售点进行专项检查5次，清理不符合规定的测绘图件，没收盗版中国交通地图册3本、世界地图挂图10张、中国地图挂图13张，并对当事人进行批评教育。

2003年，对县城及各乡（镇）地图市场进行专项治理整顿3次，没收盗版世界地图挂图20张、中国地图挂图17张。

2004年，开展地图市场秩序综合治理，检查各地图销售点和小卖部、小地摊的地图，对发现的盗版和“问题”地图强制没收。

2006年，开展测绘产品市场（世界地图、中国地图挂图）专项检查。2007—2008年，开展地图市场秩序治理整顿。

二、测量标志检查

1999年，对县境内测量标志进行实地勘察，全县有国家二等三角点13个、二等水准点23个。其中，完好三角点6个，完好率46.15%；完好水准点11个，完好率47.83%。对完好的测量标志办理委托保管手续，10月，省国土资源厅委托州验收组验收通过。

2000年，县国土局与省测绘一院开展县城4个GPS网点设点工作，在原测量标志基础上延伸网点2个，工程通过省国土资源厅验收。

2004年，开展县城建设工程损毁测量标志检查，共检查三角点13个、水准点23个、GPS点4个，发现水准点被公路建设损毁1个，报州国土局重新测定并埋设。是年，开展区域内独立坐标系统使用情况检查，经检查全县拥有测量队伍的4个单位的坐标系，没有发现使用独立坐标现象，所有测量均引用国家坐标施测。

2005年，全县设立GPS网点4个，完成省国土资源厅下达荔波县GPS（E）级控制网选点、埋设任务。

2008年，开展6个乡（镇）7个GPS（C级）网点复核工作。

三、测绘资料保密检查

2000年，县国土局与保密局联合向各测绘单位、用图单位发出《关于开展测绘资料保密检查的通知》。经检查，测绘资料归档整齐，专柜存放，专人管理，借阅手续齐全，无擅自转让、转借、复制和向第三方借资料的现象。

2002年，开展测绘成果保密检查。2004年，对全县拥有测绘成果的单位进行测绘成果保密专项检查，无失密、泄密情况。

第七章　安全生产监督管理

第一节　安全生产教育

一、安全宣传

1988—1999年，为防止事故发生，县安委会通过出动宣传车、书写标语、电视讲话、专门会议、录像、广播、宣传画、专栏、咨询、发放资料等形式进行安全宣传，宣传内容主要是安全生产法律法规、政策制度及专业生产规程，通报全国、全省、全县发生的重大安全事故，作警示教育。

2000—2001年，每年开展一次“安全生产宣传周”“百日安全生产无事故”活动。2002年后，“安全生产宣传周”改为“安全生产宣传月”，每年按照全国安全月活动安排，开展安全宣传和“关注安全、关爱生命”主题活动，每次都由县安委办牵头组织县交通、乡企（煤炭）局、农机局、林业局、电力局、交警大队、消防中队、人保公司、财保公司等部门分赴各乡（镇）进行安全生产宣传、咨询。至2004年，县安委会出动宣传车382辆（次），利用广播电视宣传630场（次），张贴标语4560幅，发放宣传资料16.71万份，编发简报260期，受教育群众9万人次。

2005—2008年，县安委会牵头组织成员单位出动宣传车开展宣传60场（次），发放安全生产宣传资料12万份，张贴安全标语600幅（条），电视播出宣传讲座6次，展出挂图、展板2000块，报刊宣传9次，出墙报19期。

二、安全培训

1983—1987年，县安全管理部门举办煤矿培训班，先后培训矿长69人、瓦斯检验员80人、爆破员157人。1988年后，县安委会成员单位按照各自职能组织培训，县安委办主要负责特种作业技术培训。1988—2004年，共培训电工200人、焊工160人、架子工300人。

2005年10月，在县安监局增设县安全技术培训中心。是年11月，增设县煤矿安全培训中心。两个培训中心两块牌子、一套人员。2006年4月，培训中心经省煤矿安全监察管理局批准，获煤矿安全三级资质。

2006年3月，县内朝阳烟花爆竹厂取得安全生产许可证。2008年，增加烟花爆竹批发经营企业1家。以上2家企业按照要求派出人员参加省安全培训中心举办的安全管理人员、守库员、仓库报关员培训班培训，通过考核取得合格证书。

2006—2008年，全县举办特种作业人员培训37期，培训2005人；开展煤矿从业人员培训107期，培训6346人；烟花爆竹零售经营从业人员培训265人。

第二节　安全生产管理

1978—1986年，安全工作管理制度由生产企业自行制定实施。县安委会成立后，安全生产管理实行行政主要领导负责制，县政府每年召开专题会议，并行文部署安全生产工作。

1987年起，县安委会坚持“安全第一、预防为主”的方针，到企业、矿山、工地、营业场所实施检查，定期或不定期对小煤窑安全设施和各企业压力容器使用操作规程进行检查。检查内容主要有安全生产工作组织领导、安全生产规章制度建设和执行、安全生产责任制落实、安全设施配置、安全经费投入、安全隐患整改、安全教育培训以及安全事故处置等情况。在煤矿企业安全检查中，对煤矿独眼井进行查封，对违章作业矿井限期改正，对没有“一长三员”（矿长、瓦斯检验员、爆破员、安全检查员）的煤矿限期配齐。县政府每年开展1～2次全县安全生产大检查，在每年的安全生产宣传月、“百日安全无事故”、春运及元旦、春节、“五一”“十一”等节日期间，集中开展煤矿、交通运输、旅游、建设等为重点的安全大检查，平时开展专项检查。

2004年8月，县政府下文组建县安全生产监督管理局后，贯彻安全生产工作的方针政策及法律法规，编制全县安全生产工作规划，拟订全县安全生产工作的政策和规章，指导、协调、监督有关部门和乡（镇）的安全生产监督管理工作。

2005年起，县政府常务会议或县长办公会议定期专题研究全县安全生产工作，定期或不定期召开煤炭安全生产工作专题会议，召集相关部门负责人汇报和研究安全生产工作。2006年，按《黔南州安全生产“一票否决”实施办法》，全县安全生产工作实行“一票否决制”。2007年7月，县政府决定，对县内各煤矿提取安全生产事故责任保证金和收取各煤矿违反安全生产责任制违约金。即生产规模为年产9万吨以下（含年产9万吨）的，煤矿提取事故责任保证金30万元；生产规模为年产9万吨以上至15万吨（含年产15万吨）的，煤矿提取事故责任保证金50万元；年内发生煤矿安全事故死亡人数在3人（不含3人）以下的，每死亡1人收取违约责任金5万元；死亡人数在3人以上10人（不含10人）以下的，每死亡1人收取违约责任金10万元；发生死亡人数在10人以上的重特大煤矿生产安全事故的，按相关政策及法律规定处理，并收取全部违约责任金。

2004—2008年，全县组织安全检查886次，查处各类生产违章1731余起，下整改通知书1440份。5年间，发生各类安全事故190起，死亡141人，伤160人。

第八章　统　计

第一节　统计管理

1978—1987年，统计部门认真执行统计制度，按时填报各种统计报表。

1988年，对20个县属行政单位、8个全民所有制独立核算工业企业、2个集体所有制独立核算工业企业的统计报表进行检查清理，同时检查40个单位的统计报表数字质量，对不认真执行统计报表制度的单位和个人进行处理。是年11月，县十届人大常委会第九次会议审议县政府关于贯彻实施《中华人民共和国统计法》的情况汇报，作出《关于贯彻实施〈中华人民共和国统计法〉的决议》。

1989年4月，开展全县统计法规执行情况大检查，对违法统计情节严重的铁木加工厂依法给予罚款，对其他一般违法行为进行批评教育并限期改正。

1993年6月，县统计局根据《中华人民共和国统计法》《实施细则》的有关规定，对屡次迟报劳动工资定期报表的单位处以罚款，对直接责任人给予通报批评。

1995年10月，开展“统计法规执行情况检查月”活动，在各统计调查单位自查的基础上，县统计局对县内固定资产投资、乡（镇）工业总产值、社会商品零售总额三方面的统计数据质量和统计违法活动进行重点检查，检查单位11个，没有发现虚报、瞒报等统计违法行为。

2000年8—10月，开展统计法律法规知识竞赛活动，全县有300余名干部职工参加竞赛。

2001年7—8月，在全县范围内开展各机关、企事业单位统计执法大检查。针对检查中发现的问题，及时提出整改意见和建议，特别是对瑶麓乡多次迟报统计报表的情况提出了批评意见。

第二节　调查　普查

一、统计调查

（一）人口变动抽样调查

1991年，开展人口变动情况抽样调查，抽中4个小区，4个调查小区共计361户，调查结果：1991年1月1日零时人口数为1826人，1991年12月31日24时人口数为1796人；当年出生婴儿18人，出生率9.94‰；死亡人口17人，死亡率9.39‰；迁入9人，迁出40人。

1994年10月，人口变动抽样调查抽中调查点2个镇、2个乡，7个小区、17个村民组，人口总计483户2305人。调查结果：1994年10月1日零时人口总计2305人，其中男1142人、女1163人；出生人口54人，出生率23.43‰；死亡人口18人，死亡率7.81‰；自增率15.62‰。

1995年10月，开展1%人口抽样调查，抽中调查点3个乡、2个镇，18个小区，调查结果：1995年10月1日零时总户数961户，其中家庭户958户、集体户3户；总人口4270人，其中男2204人、女2066人；性别比为（女为100）100：107；出生101人，出生率23.65‰；死亡40人，死亡率9.36‰；自增率14.39‰。

2005年11月1日零时，在15个乡（镇）36个村（居）委会36个小区开展1%人口抽样调查。调查分住户调查、个人调查。住户调查内容主要包括居住、环境、设施等基本情况，个人调查内容主要包括年龄、性别、受教育程度、就业、迁移流动、生育、社会保障等指标。调查结果：登记总户数914户、总人数3661人。其中，常住人口3661人、出生人口16人、死亡人口10人、外出半年以上人口271人。

（二）粮油生产抽样调查

1993年5月，对夏季粮油主产区的甲良、播尧、茂兰、朝阳、玉屏等5个乡（镇）进行夏季粮油生产随机抽样调查，走访农户27户151人，调查小麦种植面积10.6亩，亩产66.5公斤；油菜种植面积62.9亩，亩产24.6公斤，户均收获油菜籽57.41公斤，人均占有油菜籽10.33公斤。

二、普查

（一）农业普查

1996年，全县抽调1600人开展第一次农业普查，普查时点为1996年12月31日零时。普查结果：农业从业人员70400人，大牲畜存栏72000头，年末猪存栏81500头，羊存栏16847只。

2006年，开展第二次农业普查，普查时点为2006年12月31日24时，时期资料为2006年度。普查对象为县境内的农村住户、城镇农业生产经营户、农业生产经营单位、村民委员会和乡镇人民政府。普查主要内容包括农业生产条件、农业生产经营活动、农业土地利用、农村劳动力及就业、农村基础设施、农村社会服务、农村居民生活，以及乡（镇）、村民委员会和社区环境等方面的情况。普查结果：住户农业从业人员77233人，单位农业从业人员449人；年末猪存栏70758头、牛45496头、羊4044只；农村常住劳动力资源90991人，其中，整劳动力73411人、半劳动力17580人。

（二）工业普查

1986年10月—1987年10月，开展第二次工业普查。普查对象为县内全民所有制工业和集体所有制工业。普查项目为企业规模、开工日期、职工人数、生产能力、固定资产原值和净值、设备使用、原材料燃料消耗、产、供、销、经济效益情况以及职工文化结构、年龄结构、劳动工资等。普查结果：企业单位数28个，1985年工业总产值957.8万元（1980年不变价），工业净产值473.4万元（现价），1985年全民所有制和集体所有制工业企业职工年末人数2679人，月平均2104人；产品销售收入709万元，产品销售税金35.8万元，工资总额266.6万元，利润总额98.5万元，企业留利43.5万元；年末工业企业职工人数2679人，其中，工程技术人员6人、管理人员204人、服务人员19人。

1995年，开展第三次工业普查，普查对象为县内全部工业企业和附营工业单位。普查项目为工业企业基本情况，财务状况，劳动情况，工业产品生产、销售、库存总值，主要工业产品产、销、存，附营工业单位生产情况，工业企业原材料、能源消费与库存，能源加工转换，工业企业科技活动情况，主要工业技术经济指标，主要工业产品生产能力，主要工业生产设备及新旧程度（已安装设备），主要工业生产设备技术状况（已安装设备），主要工业产品质量，主要工业产品销售收支情况，工业企业部分合资基本经营情况。经清查，初步掌握有乡及乡以上工业企业63个，村以下企业663个。

此后，国家将工业普查内容融入经济普查工作，不再单独进行工业普查。

（三）经济普查

2004年下半年至2005年，开展全县第一次经济普查，普查对象为个体经营户和经营单位。个体经营户普查结果：全县个体经营户涉及13个行业（未涉及房地产），主要集中在零售业、交通运输电信业、餐饮业等行业。工业占4.97%，建筑业占0.92%，交通运输电信业占27.04%，批发业占0.39%，零售业占47.75%，住宿业占1.94%，餐饮业占7.62%，租赁和商务服务业占0.5%，教育业占0.11%，卫生和福利业占0.75%，居民服务业占3.96%，文化、体育和娱乐业占1.2%，其他服务业占2.85%。单位普查结果：清查单位总数814个（含38个本部），其中，法人单位490个，产业活动单位324个。法人在外的产业活动单位35个，无在外产业活动单位。

2008年，进行第二次经济普查，普查的标准时点为2008年12月31日，时期资料为2008年度，普查对象为县内从事第二产业和第三产业的全部法人单位、产业活动单位、个体经营户。普查结果：乡镇企业2181个，工业企业25个，普通中学学校11所，普通小学81所，卫生机构24个，固定电话用户19054户。

（四）第三产业普查

1993年下半年开展首次第三产业普查，普查年度为1991年、1992年。普查结果：1991年全县党、政、企事业机关单位有825个，1992年有850个；1991年城乡个体户有1875户，1992年有1427户。1991年个体户总数中城市654户、农村1221户，1992年城市565户、农村862户。个体户按行业分类：1991年，交通运输业206户、商业1065户、饮食业450户、服务业94户、修理业60户；1992年，交通运输业240户、商业758户、饮食业283户、服务业104户、修理业104户。

（五）基本单位普查

1996年4—10月，开展第一次全国基本单位普查，普查工作通过检查验收，各项数据质量符合上级要求，完成荔波县第一次基本单位普查登记工作，被评为全国第一次基本单位普查的先进集体，获国家先进个人1名、省级先进个人1名。

2001年，开展第二次全国基本单位普查，普查的标准时点为2001年9月30日。普查内容包括各类单位的基本标志、主要属性、基本状态及主要总量指标，个体经营户的基本经营活动情况。

第九章　审计监督

第一节　政府审计

1984年3月县审计局成立，至2008年，县审计局共依法独立实施完成审计监督项目358项。其中，县级财政预算执行审计13项，乡镇财政预决算审计18项，金融保险审计21项，专项资金审计43项，行政事业企业审计47项，企业审计49项，基建投资审计58项，外资运用审计32项，经济责任审计48项，各种资金审计调查29项。查处各类违规违纪资金27422.04万元，其中，违规资金9872.38万元，管理不规范资金14561.3万元，损失浪费资金205.89万元，其他问题资金2782.47万元。作出审计决定处理处罚涉及金额15527万元，其中应上缴财政2811.25万元。审计发现的主要问题有资金管理不规范、挪用、偷漏税款、截留应缴财政资金、虚列支出、乱挤乱摊成本费用、隐瞒利润等。针对审计中发现的问题，向被审计单位提出整改意见和建议，并作出处理决定。向纪检监察部门移送处理案件1件1人，向司法机关移送处理案件6件7人。

一、财政金融审计

1988年，对朝阳区财政所1987年度的财政决算审计，是全县财政金融审计的开始，审计查出违规资金9.75万元，损失浪费金额0.75万元，管理不规范资金7.68万元。

1990年，对茂兰区财政所1989年度财政决算进行审计，查出违规违纪资金21.61万元，审计机关依法作出罚款1.18万元、责令清缴、调整相关账务等处理决定。

是年，对县农业银行1989年度财务收支情况进行审计，查出乱挤乱摊成本费用5.69万元，乱列营业外支出0.24万元，违反控购制度购买专控商品1.81万元等问题。

1997年，开展1996年度县级财政预算执行和其他财政收支审计，审计发现少列预算收入37.52万元，应缴未缴财政收入2.13万元，挪用专项资金12.15万元，违反规定发放补助费1.4万元。此后，县级财政预算执行情况审计成为每年法定必审项目。

1984—2008年，全县实施财政金融审计52项，其中，县级财政预算执行情况和其他财政收支审计13项，乡（镇）财政预决算审计18项，金融审计21项。查出问题资金18378.26万元，其中，违规资金5956.27万元，管理不规范资金11014.88万元，损失浪费124.57万元，其他问题资金1282.54万元。审计作出处理处罚决定涉及金额11595.93万元，其中，应当上缴财政1236.88万元，其他资金作归还原渠道、调账等处理。

二、行政事业企业审计

1984年，审计县乡镇企业局1978—1984年账务情况，发现漏缴1982年、1983年企业管理所得税

0.68万元，应缴未缴财政回收款0.51万元，挪用支农款1.13万元，用企业经费支付行政管理费0.01万元，转移支农资金0.57万元，福利费超支0.04万元，烤火费超支0.03万元，无证作账0.85万元等问题。

1985年，对乡村工业供销公司1982—1984年煤炭经营的财务情况进行审计，查出滥发奖金、乱摊成本费、违反专控商品制度、欠缴能源交通基金、漏缴税金等违规违纪资金16.56万元，以及内部控制制度不健全、财务人员不执行现金管理制度、账务管理混乱等问题。

1985年，对县水泥厂1984年度财务收支情况进行审计，发现会计制度不健全，账务较混乱，查出违规资金1.12万元。

1990年，对县农机厂进行1988—1989年承包经营责任审计，查出杨某以权谋私问题，审计机关依法移送检察机关查处。同年，查出原朝阳乡乡长覃某某、甲良水管站站长陈某某贪污水利经费问题，审计机关依法移送司法机关、监察机关查处。

1998年，对小七孔电站1997年度资产、负责及损益进行审计，查出违规违纪资金1.64万元。

2001年，对贵州盐业（集团）荔波有限责任公司2000年度财务收支进行审计，查出私设“小金库”、隐瞒收入、虚列支出、挤占费用、未提足折旧、财务处理不合规、购进包装物未入账等问题资金总计26.86万元。

2004年，对县扶贫办2001—2003年财政扶贫资金管理使用情况进行审计，查出挤占财政扶贫资金弥补行政经费11.25万元，擅自调整、变更扶贫项目计划129.28万元。审计机关依法作出追回被挤占资金，补齐相关调整变更手续的审计决定。

2005年，对县工商局2004年度财务收支进行审计，查出拖欠应缴未缴预算收入、隐瞒行政性收费收入、预算外资金收支未纳入单位财务账内统一核算等问题资金总计17.89万元。

2007年，对县林业局2006年度财务收支情况进行审计，查出罚没收入、补助支出未纳入单位账内统一核算等问题资金总计38.2万元。

1984—2008年，实施行政事业、企业审计项目总计139项，其中，行政事业审计47项，企业审计49项，专项资金审计43项。查出问题资金4288.48万元，其中，违规资金2549.08万元，管理不规范资金1628.22万元，损失浪费金额47.93万元，其他问题资金63.25万元。审计决定作出处理处罚涉及金额2761.04万元。向司法机关移送案件4件，涉案人员5人；向纪检监察机关移送案件1件，涉案人员1人。

三、经济责任审计

1998年，将领导干部履行职责情况纳入审计监督范围，开展行政、事业、企业领导经济责任审计工作。

1998—2008年，县审计局累计实施经济责任审计项目48项49人，审计查出违规资金765.35万元，管理不规范资金452.12万元，其他问题资金597.51万元，损失浪费资金15.2万元。审计作出处理处罚金额累计23.19万元，向纪检监察机关移送案件2件，相关人员受党纪、政纪处分2人。

四、固定资产投资审计

1985年，对县林业局科技干部宿舍基建资金来源进行审计，查出基建超计划投资2.4万元，漏缴建筑税0.69万元。

1986年，实施基建审计项目3项。在县卫生防疫站1984—1986年基建资金来源审计中，发现漏缴建筑税、挤占防治项目经费等问题。

1987年，对县水电局1986年投放瑶山人畜饮水工程效益进行审计，发现可收回设备资金4.3万元未及时收回。

1989年，对水尧乡谊岜公路工程进行审计，查出多付工程款和漏缴税费5.55万元。

1993年，对县农经委职工住宅楼工程竣工决算进行审计，发现工程竣工决算手续欠完善，超建设规模25.04平方米，超投资计划5.71万元。

1994年，实施樟江大街公厕、小吃街工程、交通局办公及住宅楼、福利村、水春村人畜饮水工程等投资项目审计5项。

2005年，开展工程项目竣工决（结）算审计5项，依法审减工程价款32.01万元。

1985—2008年，投资项目审计累计48项，送审工程价款总额4129.56万元，审计认定工程价款金额3908.63万元，累计审减工程价款220.93万元。

五、外资运用项目审计

1995年起，县内开展外资运用审计工作。是年，对世界银行贷款农村卫生人力开发项目（2539-CHA）1994年卫Ⅳ项目进行审计。

1997年，对世界银行贷款农村卫生人力开发项目（2539-CHA）1996年卫Ⅳ项目执行情况进行审计，查出管理不规范资金0.92万元，其他问题资金14.55万元。审计要求项目主管单位对存在的问题进行整改。

1998年，对当年县教育贷款办公室世界银行贷款贫困省教育发展项目实施情况进行审计，发现其他项目挤占世界银行项目资金24.96万元。审计依法建议尽快追回被挤占资金。

2000年，对世界银行贷款造林项目办公室1999年度世界银行贷款贫困地区林业发展项目（4325-CHA）实施情况进行审计，发现虚增项目工程支出及世界银行贷款资金0.19万元。审计依法作出整改决定。

2007年，对县内世界银行贷款IX项目妇幼子项目2006年度财务收支和项目执行情况进行审计，发现省、州、县级配套资金不到位29.7万元、报账原始凭证内容不完整涉及金额6.99万元等问题。

1995—2008年，对世界银行、外国银行援助、贷款的发展项目实施情况审计32项，查出问题资金1517.02万元，其中，违规资金148.93万元，管理不规范资金1272.51万元，存在其他问题资金95.58万元。审计依法作出处理处罚决定涉及资金57.91万元，其中，应上缴财政0.65万元，应归还原渠道资金41.64万元，应调账处理0.92万元，其他方式方法处理14.7万元。

1984—2008年审计项目统计表

表16-6　　单位：万元

年度	审计项目总计（项）	审计总金额	查出违规违纪金额	审计处理应上缴财政	核减基建工程款
1984	6	—	18.60	—	—
1985	13	—	55.96	26.74	—
1986	14	—	84.03	33.15	—
1987	12	821.28	28.48	6.98	—
1988	49	1317.62	236.72	38.20	—
1989	20	2148.99	118.60	22.24	—
1990	15	4283.16	98.24	35.90	—
1991	73	4399.90	155.77	30.97	—

续表16-6

年度	审计项目总计（项）	审计总金额	查出违规违纪金额	审计处理应上缴财政	核减基建工程款
1992	19	3633.41	54.79	4.07	—
1993	10	1278.83	21.63	23.67	2.13
1994	12	2167.27	53.27	52.40	—
1995	13	—	57.74	13.98	—
1996	33	—	82.60	7.59	—
1997	30	—	101.00	23.00	—
1998	32	—	342.00	7.00	126.00
1999	30	—	534.00	138.00	26.00
2000	40	—	1289.00	52.00	141.20
2001	56	—	1026.00	129.00	379.00
2002	65	—	929.00	59.00	6.00
2003	41	—	651.00	384.00	45.00
2004	31	—	280.50	—	20.50
2005	32	—	531.00	138.00	213.00
2006	34	—	746.00	185.00	952.00
2007	70	—	990.00	45.00	657.00
2008	33	—	545.00	55.00	183.00

第二节　内部审计和社会审计

一、内部审计

1984年前，县内部分国有企业开展内部审计工作，主要是对企业内部财务收支状况进行审查和监督。1984年，县审计局成立后，每年对各单位内审工作进行检查和指导，定期组织内审人员参加省、州内审协会举办的各种培训，提高内审人员的审计能力，规范内部审计程序，内审工作领域不断扩大。

1995年7月，审计署颁布《内部审计工作规定》后，县内审工作由企业扩大到部分行政事业单位和学校，审计内容由单一的财务收支审计扩大到单位内部管理和经营情况审计，审计业务进一步规范。内审工作因受机构编制限制，大部分单位没有设立专门内审机构，只明确专（兼）职内审人员，仅县信用联社、县教育局等部分单位设立专门内审机构，配备专职内审人员，内审工作正常开展。到2008年年底，全县开展内部审计工作的单位发展到20家，审计人员通过内审资格考试并获“内审工作从业证书”16人。

二、社会审计

1989年1月，成立荔波县审计事务所，隶属县审计局，属独立核算、自负盈亏事业单位，开展社会审计工作。所长从县审计局抽调人员担任，其他人员为聘用。

1998年5月，县审计局根据国家有关文件规定，行文撤销荔波县审计事务所，成立兴荔会计师事务所。

1999年8月，兴荔会计师事务所不具备从事社会审计资格，县审计局行文撤销兴荔会计师事务所，不再组建新的社会审计机构。此后，县内的社会审计项目请县外社会审计机构实施。

第十七篇
财政　税务　金融

中共十一届三中全会以后，县级财政体制不断进行改革，贯彻“发展经济，保障供给”的财政总方针，结合当年财政管理体制，县委、县政府加强财源建设，在加强稳固煤炭工业、抓好农业综合开发利用的同时，将旅游业作为财政收入支柱产业之一进行扶持，带动第三产业发展。至1990年年末，全县财政收入突破千万元；至2004年，全县财政总收入突破亿元；2008年全县财政总收入达到18216万元。财政支出坚持“一要吃饭、二要建设”“量入为出，确保重点”的原则，将支出控制在财力允许的范围内。县财政还实施了预算外资金管理、政府采购管理、会计集中核算、国有资产管理，进行了农村税收改革和煤炭税费征收等工作。

1983年，中央对税务系统实行垂直管理，是年，按中央税制改革的规定，进行税制改革，实施国营企业第一步利改税，对国营企业征收国营企业所得税。1984年10月，全面实行国营企业第二步利改税。1994年9月28日，按照中央实行分税制的要求，县税务局分设为荔波县国家税务局、荔波县地方税务局。按国家、贵州省税收规定开展国税征收管理和地税的征收管理。

1978年以来，县金融系统推进改革，开展各项金融服务，发展信贷业务、存款业务、保险业务，加大对农村贷款的投入，增设网点。1978年至2008年，全县金融系统不断加强自身建设及监管，业务不断发展。

第一章 财 政

第一节 财政体制改革

1978—1979年，县财政实行“定收定支，一年一定，收支挂钩，增收分成，下年使用”的管理体制。

自1980年起，根据省政府的决定，将原管理体制改为“划分收支，分级包干，超支不补，结余留用，一定五年”。县对各单位和区实行财政包干。

1984年，县级财政执行州对县“定额补助，增收归已，超支不补，一定五年”的财政体制。

按照国务院1985年3月21日发出的《关于实行“划分税费，核定收支、分级包干的”财政管理体制的通知》，县财政实行“划分税种，核定收支，分级包干”的管理体制。荔波县按照财政收支范围，确定定额上解、定额补助数。

1987年1月，县政府将财政权力下放到区，建立区级财政，并对区、镇实行“定收定支，收入全解，超收分成，支出下拨，节支留用，超支不补，一年一定”的管理体制。收入部分为工商税、农林特产税和其他收入。

1988年，对区级财政实行“定收定支，超支不补，超收五五分成，一年一定”的财政体制。

1991年，根据省、州关于“一级政府，一级财政”的指示精神，开展建镇并乡撤区财务清理和建账工作。1992年，财政预算首先对各乡（镇）人员进行核定，确定人头经费，实行“分级包干，定收定支，超收分成，差额补助”的管理体制。

1996年年初，按照省委、省政府的要求，根据全县实际和电力、旅游、煤炭等行业发展前景，县政府同省政府签订扶持县级财政上台阶合同。之后，县委、县政府制定新的财政管理办法，即从1996年起，将原来执行的“定收定支，超收分成，超支不补，分级包干，增长分成”改为“划分税种，核定收支，分级包干，增长分成”的管理体制，以适应财税改革要求，实现财政收入上台阶增长目标。

1999年，实行“定收定支，总额结算，超收分成，短收不补，一定一年”的管理体制。

2001—2003年，将乡（镇）划分为4种类型：一类为玉屏镇、立化镇、茂兰镇，二类为甲良镇、播尧乡、水尧乡、佳荣镇，三类为洞塘乡、瑶麓乡、瑶山乡、朝阳镇，四类为永康乡、水利乡、翁昂乡、捞村乡、方村乡、驾欧乡。各乡（镇）按类别核定收支基数，确定收支递增比例，超收全留，超支不补，一定三年。即以2001年下达的收支预算数为基数，各乡（镇）收入预算按一、二、三、四类分别以10%、9%、8%、7%的比例递增（不含农业税和农业税附加加征），超任务部分全额返还，支出按10%逐年递增。同时，对完成年度预算考核目标的按一、二、三、四类乡（镇）分别给予一次性奖励，对未完成年度考核目标的给予同等额度处罚。

2004年2月，按“核定收支基数，确定递增比例，超收全留，超支不补”的原则，对乡（镇）财政管理作出规定：收入基数，以各乡（镇）2001—2003年财政收入实际完成数的平均数为基础，结合税源结构因素，确定2004年乡（镇）财政收入任务数，以后每年度按上年任务数递增13%作为当年任务数；支出基数，编制内在职人员工资、编制内在职人员每人每年300元基本办公费、遗属补助费、每个乡（镇）1名驾驶员和1名炊事员工资作为2004年各乡（镇）支出基数，以后每年增加10%办公费。

2007年12月，县政府按照财政部2006年发出的《关于进一步推进乡财县管工作的通知》和省财政厅2007年发出的《关于进一步推进我省乡财县管工作的通知》，发出《荔波县人民政府关于推进乡财县管改革的实施意见》，决定从2007年下半年起，对玉屏镇、水利乡、水尧乡、永康乡进行“乡财县管”改革。改革以乡（镇）为独立核算主体，实行“预算共编、账户统设、集中收付、采购统办、票据统管”的管理方式，由县级财政主管部门直接管理并监督乡（镇）财政收支，同时调整乡（镇）财政所管理体制和职能。至2008年6月，全县推进“乡财县管”改革工作全部结束，从2008年7月开始，全县17个乡（镇）全面推行“乡财县管”体制。

第二节　财政预算

1978年后，贯彻“发展经济，保障供给”的财政总方针，县财政局在每年按“量入为出”的原则，结合当年财政管理体制，测算各项收入和支出指标，编制当年收支预算方案报县政府，县政府将县级财政预算方案提交县人民代表大会审议批准执行。

1985年，全县4区1镇财政员负责编制各区镇级、乡级财政预算、决算报表。

1995年1月1日《中华人民共和国预算法》实施后，依法进行财政预算。

2002年3月，根据中央财政预算改革精神，县政府发出《关于2002年在公安局等5个单位试行编制部门预算的通知》，明确2002年先在公安局、建设局、乡企局、国土资源局、水利局5个部门进行部门预算编制试点工作。改革试点的5个单位按照规定和要求，开展清理预算外资金收入、清理国有资产、清理各项支出的“三清理”和确定单位预算外资金收入、确定单位的国有资产家底以及国有资产收益、确定正确合理支出范围的“三确定”工作，测算出当年收支预算。

2006年，在总结2002—2006年对5个单位实行部门预算试点工作经验的基础上，于2006年12月制定《荔波县部门预算改革试点实施方案》。从2007年开始实施至2008年，预算单位由5个增加到19个。

各乡（镇）财政所根据县政府各年度的财政预算管理体制的具体规定，在年初编制乡（镇）财政收支预算方案，报县财政局审核同意后，提交该乡（镇）人代会审议通过后实施。

第三节　财政收支

一、财政收入

1978年后，县委、县政府加强财源建设，在加强稳固煤炭工业，扶持骨干煤矿建设的同时，抓好农业综合开发利用，集中财政、信贷、扶贫等项资金，加快全县粮、林、烟、油、桐、茶、木耳、酸梅等商品基地建设，开辟新财源。同时，将旅游业作为财政收入支柱产业之一进行扶持，带动运输、饮食、服务等第三产业发展，实现税收增长。至1990年“七五”计划期末，全县财政收入突破千万元，至2004年，全县财政总收入突破亿元。

至2008年，县财政获上级补助资金累计33560万元。其中，增值税和消费收返还1234万元，所得税基数返还841万元，体制补助240万元，一般性转移支付补助3325万元，民族地区转移支付补助1733万元，调整工资转移支付补助4900万元，义务教育补助603万元，农村税费改革补助1341万元，缓解县乡困难转移支付3530万元，农村义务教育国债补助1229万元，专项补助14584万元。

1978—2008年全县财政总收入统计表

表17－1 单位：万元

年度	总收入	与上年比（%）	其中	
			工商税收入	农业税收入
1978	127	24.51	89	38
1979	144	13.38	91	53
1980	112	−22.22	90	22
1981	138	23.21	124	14
1982	150	8.70	119	31
1983	214	42.67	150	64
1984	211	−1.40	166	45
1985	181	−14.22	161	20
1986	262	44.75	189	73
1987	319	21.76	226	93
1988	502	57.37	357	145
1989	953	89.84	645	308
1990	1050	10.18	666	384
1991	1101	4.86	709	392
1992	1112	1.00	804	308
1993	1758	58.09	1335	423
1994	2483	41.24	1873	610
1995	3167	27.55	2292	875
1996	3822	20.68	2891	931
1997	4568	19.52	3461	1107
1998	5288	15.76	3958	1330
1999	5299	0.20	3684	1615
2000	5689	7.34	4049	1640
2001	5686	−0.05	4376	1310
2002	7008	23.25	5455	1553
2003	8200	17.09	6722	1478

续表17－1

年度	总收入	与上年比（%）	其中	
			工商税收入	农业税收入
2004	10351	26.14	8726	1625
2005	11897	14.94	10529	1368
2006	12948	8.83	11178	1770
2007	14535	12.26	12206	2329
2008	18216	25.33	15531	2685

说明：1994—2008年的工商税收入系国税、地税之和。

二、财政支出

1978年以后，财政支出坚持“一要吃饭、二要建设”“量入为出，确保重点”的原则，将支出控制在财力允许的范围内，严格按照县人代会审议通过的支出预算安排拨款。各年支出安排着重于保障及时足额地拨付财政供养人员的工资和国家机构正常运转的必须经费，公检法司、教育、医疗卫生、科技、农口、民政救济、社会保障、基础设施建设等重点支出并逐年增长。

1998年10月，实施综合财政计划以后，对预算内、预算外资金统筹管理，各单位在预算支出方面未出现较大突破现象。同时，通过加强车辆费、电话费、会议费和接待费管理监督，严格控购商品报批手续，控制支出过快增长。

2003年，根据省政府办公厅《转发省财政厅〈关于加强财政性资金管理意见〉的通知》，县财政局制定《荔波县财政资金拨付管理暂行办法》，规定预算资金拨付必须遵循按预算安排、按用款计划、按项目进度和按规定程序办理的“四按”原则。

1978—2008年全县财政实际支出统计表

表17－2 单位：万元

年度	可用财力	支出合计	其中			
			人员经费		公用经费	项目经费
			经费小计	供养人员（人）		
1978	430.40	389.40	124.61	—	35.04	229.75
1979	505.92	449.26	148.65	2158	39.34	261.27
1980	512.09	512.09	158.87	—	42.81	310.41
1981	618.93	565.65	194.03	—	48.51	323.11
1982	766.74	608.82	245.22	—	105.10	258.50
1983	866.86	689.34	300.25	—	100.09	289.00
1984	924.54	791.09	328.08	2716	228.00	235.01
1985	1021.54	882.06	324.40	2887	196.21	361.45
1986	945.92	854.48	422.15	2662	188.72	243.61
1987	1006.28	954.34	426.13	2834	206.68	321.53

续表17－2

年度	可用财力	支出合计	其中				
			人员经费		公用经费	项目经费
			经费小计	供养人员（人）		
1988	1224.45	904.91	491.53	—	193.19	220.19
1989	1846.38	1257.06	562.26	—	328.69	366.11
1990	1895.08	1543.31	672.17	3709	444.47	426.67
1991	2310.10	1578.10	773.40	4206	422.80	381.90
1992	2606.40	2151.60	1053.00	3987	393.50	705.10
1993	2862.10	2462.60	1245.50	4043	528.30	688.80
1994	2925.00	3368.90	1870.30	—	557.40	941.20
1995	3389.10	3807.70	2113.30	—	886.20	808.20
1996	3647.20	3881.50	2156.40	4645	976.80	748.30
1997	4043.90	4880.60	2368.70	5205	1399.90	1112.00
1998	5035.00	5863.00	2914.00	5343	1819.00	1130.00
1999	5920.00	7184.00	3856.00	5268	1809.00	1519.00
2000	6493.00	7827.00	3666.00	5455	1550.00	2611.00
2001	9673.00	11749.00	5566.00	5327	1880.00	4303.00
2002	10416.00	11132.00	7441.00	5458	991.00	2,700.00
2003	11961.00	13858.00	7110.00	5520	2482.00	4266.00
2004	15476.00	16966.00	8483.00	6388	3339.00	5144.00
2005	19922.00	20086.00	10950.00	7055	3516.00	5620.00
2006	22373.00	22738.00	13534.00	7095	3759.00	5445.00
2007	30447.00	27517.00	14783.00	7166	8505.00	4229.00
2008	44864.00	40361.00	17487.00	7183	10439.00	12435.00

说明：1.“供养人员”中部分年度没有人数，是因当年的财政总决算报表无供养人员统计。2.部分年度的“实际支出合计”数大于当年的“可用财力”数，是因为有上年结余数在内。

第四节　财政资金管理

一、预算外资金管理

1985年，县财政局根据国务院《关于加强预算外资金管理的决定》，是年，对县属行政事业单位预算外资金收支情况进行统一管理。至1989年，全县完成预算外资金专户储存工作，对预算外资金使用进行合理划拨和严格控制。

1994年，乡（镇）预算外资金纳入财政管理，对各征收站及未办手续、未经批准而私自利用预算外资金购买的汽车、摩托以及现代化办公用品进行清理，列入固定资产管理。

至1997年，全县有预算外资金汇总单位67户。其中，财政部门1户，行政事业单位49户，17个乡（镇）各1户。

从1999年1月1日起，施行县政府颁布的《荔波县预算外资金管理暂行办法》及其实施细则。

是年，县预算外资金管理局与纪检、监察、银行、审计等部门，对全县行政事业单位开设的银行账户进行清查。全县81个行政事业单位（含17个乡镇），在各银行开设账户共190个。其中，允许保留账户140个，撤销账户50个，除部分单位因专项资金特殊需要，允许开设两个账户外，其余单位只能开设一个基本账户，并必须设立财政专户，用于缴存各单位的预算外资金。

是年，根据“预算外资金所有权归国家，调控权归政府，管理权归财政”的规定，按“政府有收入，部门有利益”的原则，对有较大预算外资金收入的单位测定返还比例，建立县政府调控基金。

2000年，执行“收支两条线”管理规定，县直机关单位预算外资金纳入财政专户管理。至2001年，纳入财政专户管理的单位有37个。是年，从预算外资金中提取政府调控基金51万元。

2007年，将景区门票收入纳入县预算外资金管理局统一管理。

1999—2008年的10年间，提取县政府调控基金累计497.75万元。

1997—2008年全县预算外资金收支统计表

表17－3 单位：万元

年度	收入合计	支出合计	年度	收入合计	支出合计
1997	973.60	854.50	2003	966.74	1324.00
1998	908.00	918.00	2004	1551.62	1310.44
1999	1187.00	1245.00	2005	3944.77	3534.62
2000	1665.70	1404.10	2006	6271.32	5061.55
2001	1601.30	1255.60	2007	7653.82	4919.79
2002	1378.90	1493.50	2008	9925.60	8152.37

二、政府采购管理

2002年1月，县政府根据财政部《政府采购管理暂行办法》，颁发《荔波县人民政府采购管理办法（草案）》。

2003年5月，由县政府采购中心负责实施行政事业单位的政府采购业务，参与财政性资金的各项工程招标工作。6月，县政府颁发《荔波县政府采购管理办法》，自2003年7月1日起施行。7月，县政府办公室印发《荔波县2003年政府采购目录及限额标准》。

从2004年起，采购中心每年年初编制全年《政府采购目录及限额标准（草案）》呈报县政府审查，县政府审批后执行。逐步建立健全政府采购工作程序、工作纪律、评标纪律、公开招标采购程序、询价采购程序、邀请招标采购程序、竞争性谈判采购程序等制度，按“公开、公平、公正”原则进行采购，接受县监察、审计部门监督。

2002—2008年全县政府采购情况统计表

表17－4

年度	采购次数（次）	采购车辆（部）	采购一般设备（件）	采购超设备（件）	采购资金预算（万元）	实际采购资金合计（万元）	较预算资金节约（万元）	节约率（%）
2002	15	12	15	—	143.68	127.34	16.34	12.83
2003	20	11	206	8	354.73	303.07	51.66	17.05
2004	26	15	567	1	577.16	499.26	77.90	15.60
2005	53	20	811	3	1319.96	1165.53	154.43	13.25
2006	45	18	1020	2	736.26	655.16	81.10	12.38
2007	44	21	1132	3	794.71	714.50	80.21	11.23
2008	54	20	1341	6	1008.10	895.52	112.58	12.57

三、会计集中核算

2000年7月，荔波县开始实行会计集中核算制度，会计核算中心将首批会计人员30名委派到29个单位工作。2002年，纳入会计核算中心核算的单位有17个乡（镇）和68个县直部门，建立核算账户232个。对业务量大、项目工程多的县公安局、水利局、教育局、卫生局4个单位委派会计进行管理。2004年1月，将县公安局等4个单位的账务纳入核算中心核算。2001—2008年，会计核算中心拒付各种不合法、不规范的票据金额累计383.71万元。

四、乡（镇）财政零户统管

2003年前，乡（镇）预算内资金财务由乡（镇）财政所统一管理，会计基础工作规范。但乡（镇）各单位的预算外资金管理混乱，有的单位收费不缴入财政专户，直接坐收坐支；有的单位没有会计人员，或会计、出纳由一人担任，违反《中华人民共和国会计法》的规定；各单位没有账簿，财政所对各单位收支难以监督。2003年12月，县政府颁发《荔波县乡镇零户统管暂行办法》，自2004年1月1日起，各乡（镇）行政事业单位所有财务收支活动集中到乡（镇）财政所统一办理，由乡（镇）财政所统一开设银行账户进行集中核算。2008年7月，各乡（镇）财政“零户统管”纳入“乡财县管”一并实施。

第五节　国有资产管理与资本营运

一、国有资产管理

全县行政事业单位资产、国有企业资产、国有资本金的管理由县国有资产管理办公室负责。

1990年年底至1991年11月，清理登记全县127个单位的固定资产总额7199.47万元。其中，行政事业单位5501.46万元，企业单位1698.01万元。

1994年，在县级机构改革中，对全县行政事业单位和38个企业的财产进行清理登记，清理核实的国有资产总额为3500万元。清理中，对合并单位的资产、资金、会计档案等进行清理登记，并划转到新的单位统一管理，防止国有资产低价折股、低价出售、公转私有等现象发生。

从1997年开始，每年开展对行政事业单位、国企年度检查，掌握全县国有资产的存量、结构、分布、经营状况和增减变动情况。是年，行政事业单位年检110户，国有资产总额7076万元；企业年检登记29户，国有资产总额3694万元。

1997—1998年，开展全县行政事业单位的非经营性资产转经营性资产清理工作，并征收国有资产占用费。1998年，征收国有资产占用费5万元。

2000年，县政府颁布《荔波县行政事业单位国有资产处置管理实施办法》。自该办法实施起，先后对部分单位的车辆等资产进行处置拍卖，并收取处置费。

从2001年开始，每年在审核国有企业年度决算报表的基础上界定产权，对固定资产的增减变动情况进行逐项核查，在产权明晰的基础上方能办理有关手续，颁发产权证书，核定产权登记年检表，办理产权年检登记，按规定收取年检费。

至2003年，全县征收国有资产占用费单位30个共28.43万元。

2007年3—5月，开展行政事业单位资产清查，全县行政事业单位共134户全部纳入清查范围。

2008年，参与樟江天然食品厂等国有企业改革改制资产清查、核实，防止国有企业资产流失。同时，清理17个乡（镇）的固定资产总计2028.04万元。

二、资本营运

2001年12月25日，成立荔波县国有资本营运有限责任公司，实行总经理负责制，县政府为出资人，任免董事长和监事会主席，董事长由县政府县长担任，副董事长由常务副县长担任，董事由县财政局、发改局、国土局、建设局主要负责人担任，县纪委有关负责人兼任监事会主席，县人大常委会有关负责人和县审计局主要负责人任监事。

2007年2月成立的国有独资企业县农业开发实业有限责任公司为县资本营运公司的下属企业，独立核算、自负盈亏。

（一）国有资产接管

2002年10月，根据县城建设指挥部会议纪要，与县通力民族荔工联营公司签订协议，收回其土地资产，由县国有资本营运有限责任公司承担其债权债务。

2003年，代县政府接管的土地资产有：大会场，政府投入土地2074平方米，2003年估价116万元；文化馆（灯光球场），政府投入土地995平方米，2003年估价83万元。

2004年8月，收购县樟江天然食品有限责任公司原厂区（板庙对面）的国有土地并纳入县城建设土地储备，该宗土地评估价208万元。是年，收购铁锅厂46.3万元。

2005年，会同县国土资源局挂牌拍卖北街种子公司旁国有土地使用权6宗，面积976平方米，出让成交价52.27万元；拍卖时来新城区国有土地使用权9宗，面积1740平方米，出让价95.13万元。

2006年1月，代县政府接管小七孔民族度假村，接收土地25亩及瓦结构房屋10幢。是年3月，用民族路江樟园广场旁6.13亩土地（评估价为329.4万元），等价置换县国家税务局大楼房产和土地，土地纳入县级土地储备。

2008年12月，县国有粮油饲料公司完成改制后，县政府付改制经费53.8万元，县国有资本营运有限责任公司代县政府接收该公司位于向阳中路房产土地，债权债务由县国有资本营运有限责任公司承担。

（二）拆迁安置补偿

2003年，县城不夜城建设项目（后改建为江滨公园），拆迁91户，拆除建筑面积12437平方米，合同补偿金额总计452.85万元，安置被拆迁户建房用地15702平方米。是年，搬迁县看守所、武警中队，拆除建筑面积5463.87平方米，支付搬迁费210万元。

2003—2004年，开发铜锣湾（后改名为金锣湾）商业步行街，拆迁38户，拆除房屋面积7478平方米，合同拆迁补偿金额总计343.38万元，安置被拆迁户建房用地3478平方米。

2004年4月，根据县城建设指挥部的要求，对不夜城、江滨路、铜锣湾建设项目被拆迁户建房基础工程和土石方工程费用进行补偿，支付补偿金总计68.65万元。

2006—2007年，江滨路建设项目共拆迁56户，拆除建筑面积7488平方米，合同补偿金额315.37万元，划地安置26户，安置用地4928平方米，房改房安置10户。

2007年，恩铭大道建设项目拆迁16户，拆除建筑面积3728平方米，合同安置补偿金额249.64万元，划地安置9户，安置建房用地3498平方米。

2007—2008年，民族风情街改造项目拆迁56户，补偿金额145.46万元，划地安置116户，房改房安置18户。按照房屋拆迁政策，支付被拆迁户逾期临时住房过渡补助费70.18万元。

2008年，因物价上涨，将临时住房过渡补助费每平方米2元调整为每平方米5元，增补钢材差价每平方米10元，补偿拆迁户总计46.11万元。

（三）投资建设

2003年5月，与朝阳镇政府签订开发协议书，投资建设朝阳大街和镇开发区，是年7月底前完成征地补偿工作，按每亩1.3万元标准征地16.88亩，支付21.94万元，缴纳各种税费29.96万元，项目于2004年通过审计验收。

2003—2004年，投入196.08万元修建县气象局至广场东路道路。

2005年，县政府决定，县城建设指挥部的业务交由资本营运公司承担，财产、人员、业务同时移交。是年，向建设银行贷款1100万元，用于县土地储备、瑶山民族风情村寨建设、洞塘乡木朝景区建设等项目。

2006年，投入资金1519万元修建时来安置区道路及二环西路路网，硬化路面41898平方米，铺设人行道8334平方米。其中，向国家开发银行贷款500万元用于县城二环西路建设项目，征收土地90.31亩。

2007年2月，向农业发展银行三都县支行贷款3000万元用于世界自然遗产展示园建设。是年7月，向国家开发银行贷款7000万元用于荔波县申报世界自然遗产提名地环境整治及基础设施建设，项目包括小七孔电站拆除及绿化、樟江大街改造、县水泥厂拆除等25个子项目。其中，恩铭大道、江滨路道路工程征购土地407亩，支付征地款1568.56万元（拆迁补偿金265.56万元）；世界遗产地展示园建设项目征地438.42亩，付征地款1229.79万元；县中医院新址、都市山庄、官塘大道等建设项目征地365.3亩，支付征地款1133.56万元。

2008年12月，向农业发展银行三都县支行贷款3230万元，用于板莪寨至南门大桥（江滨路）道路建设。

（四）农贸市场管理

2002年12月，按照国务院《关于工商行政管理部门限期与所办市场彻底脱钩有关意见的通知》，县城综合农贸市场和佳荣农贸市场产权收归县政府，县政府委托县国有资本营运有限责任公司管理，债权、债务及管理这两个市场的新欣市场开发服务部整体移交县资本营运公司。

2003年5月，县政府委托县工商局对力达商场和县城综合农贸市场进行管理，县工商局向县资本营运公司缴纳相应委托管理承包费。6月，县资本营运公司将佳荣农贸市场经营权转让给佳荣镇政府，转让价54.5万元，债权仍由资本营运公司承担，佳荣镇政府分期将转让款交资本营运公司偿还银行贷款。

2005年5月，县政府决定终止县资本营运公司委托县工商局代管县城综合农贸市场和力达商场协议，县政府收回经营管理权，交县资本营运公司管理。2007年5月，县资本营运公司投资68万元对市场进行场棚、摊位改造，2008年1月投入使用。

（五）煤矿企业人身意外保险业务

2005年6月，县政府根据《中华人民共和国煤炭法》第四十四条“煤矿企业必须为煤矿井下作业职工办理意外伤害保险，支付保险费”的规定，以及《国务院办公厅关于进一步加强煤矿安全生产工作的紧急通知》等有关文件要求，下发《荔波县人民政府关于在全县煤矿企业实行井下作业人员意外伤害保险的通知》，指定由县国有资本营运有限责任公司兼业代收保险费，与荔波人寿保险公司共同负责为各煤矿企业办理人身意外伤害保险业务和理赔事项。规定：因煤矿安全生产责任事故死亡的赔付20万元以下，意外伤害医疗费最高不超过10万元；各煤矿企业支付保险费的标准按实际销售原煤每吨10元缴纳；对全年没有发生任何伤残事故或没有发生死亡事故的煤矿企业，县政府分别按企业全年缴纳的保险费总额的15%或10%给予奖励。

2005年7月，县资本营运公司与县人寿保险公司签订保险代理合同，为全县煤矿企业办理煤矿井下人员意外伤害保险业务。是年，全县煤炭企业43家全部参加保险。7月1日—12月31日，共发生意外伤害事故117宗，其中死亡8人，伤、残109人，县人寿保险公司赔付医疗费及伤残金等总计198.4万元。

2006—2008年，煤炭合法投资企业投保率100%，发生安全事故共死亡39人，伤、残678人，保险公司赔付死亡赔偿金780万元，赔付医疗费及伤残金709.99万元。

第六节　农村税收与改革

财政部门征收的农业税税种有农业税、农业特产税、契税、耕地占用税，简称“农业四税”。

一、“农业四税”征收

（一）农业税

1978年，全县农业税征收执行国家“一定五年”不变的政策。从1980年起，按国务院批转财政部《关于执行农业税起征点办法的情况报告》，对县内长期低产缺粮的生产队实行起征点办法，达不到起征点的免征农业税，一定三年不变。至1982年，全县减免农业税原粮累计3555吨。

从1983年起，恢复原“一定五年”农业税征收任务。是年，农业税征收金额23.72万元，占原征收任务数的47.42%。

1985年后，对县内遭受较大旱灾、洪灾以及大面积水稻病虫害后造成减产5～8成的农户，实行先征后退减免政策，对绝收的农户农业税全免并按月发给救济粮。茂兰镇尧埃村、瑶庆的吉王组、洞塘木朝村等村组部分被煤水污染和水冲沙压的农田无法耕种，实行挂账免征农业税。瑶山、瑶麓两乡，茂兰镇的洞给，洞塘乡板寨的瑶寨，翁昂的洞常等地散居的瑶族群众，居住在极贫地区，长期享受社会性减免农业税政策，直至2002年才对瑶山、瑶麓及散居瑶族群众恢复征收农业税。

2002年，对历年农业税及附加采取征收实物粮食为主、折征代金为辅的征收方式进行调整，是年起，全县农业税及附加征收全部折征代金，执行到2004年年底。

2004年1月1日，全省农业税税率由7%调整为6%。调整后，全县是年依率计征税额（细粮）1878.6吨，折税金279.25万元（计征价格1.49元/公斤），应征附加43.47万元，合计322.72万元。全县直接减轻农民负担55.7万元。

从2005年1月1日起，执行国家免征农业税政策，对县内从事农业生产、有农业收入的单位和个人免征农业税。

1978—2004年农业税任务、减免、征收情况统计表

表17－5

年度	完成正税		农业税减免		加征地方附加（万元）
	稻谷数量（吨）	折合税金（万元）	稻谷数量（吨）	折合税金（万元）	
1978	1228.40	28.38	550.00	12.71	2.56
1979	2099.10	48.49	199.20	4.60	3.88
1980	758.50	17.52	1246.50	28.80	1.40
1981	417.70	9.65	174.72	40.36	0.77
1982	816.00	18.85	1357.50	31.36	1.51
1983	1814.80	41.92	750.70	17.34	3.34
1984	1772.30	40.94	4.30	0.10	3.28
1985	519.90	16.74	1485.70	47.84	1.46
1986	1207.50	38.88	1115.00	36.00	3.14
1987	1627.60	52.41	1254.90	40.41	4.20
1988	1061.90	54.90	500.00	17.84	4.39
1989	1730.20	78.76	307.40	13.99	7.41
1990	1838.80	83.70	219.60	9.99	10.92
1991	1890.50	86.06	131.90	6.00	6.89
1992	2032.60	104.59	19743	10.00	8.37
1993	1778.20	110.42	233.30	14.48	8.83
1994	1783.30	175.78	216.00	21.00	14.41
1995	1782.60	179.00	202.90	20.00	14.00
1996	1934.20	274.54	211.30	30.00	21.96
1997	2372.70	237.27	324.10	46.00	21.00
1998	2306.10	232.61	380.40	54.00	19.98
1999	1271.90	200.00	597.80	94.00	19.06
2000	992.10	156.00	362.50	57.00	14.87
2001	936.80	147.31	487.80	76.70	14.04
2002	2025.20	300.89	151.40	22.50	60.51
2003	1953.00	291.00	187.90	28.00	60.12
2004	1462.70	217.31	4162.50	61.94	43.47

（二）农业特产税

国务院于1983年11月12日颁发《关于对农林特产品征收农业税的若干规定》、贵州省政府于1984年5月17日颁发《贵州省征收农林特产税的实施办法》后，从1987年起在全县开征农林特产税。

1988年，由于县、乡（镇）政府重视，逐步理顺农林特产税的征收环节，征收农产品的品目逐步增多，征收网点逐渐增加，偷税、漏税现象减少。

1993年，对采矿生产所用坑木应交农林特产税额进行实地调查核定后，经县政府同意，将1992年年初起征的采矿坑木农林特产税吨矿0.10元调整为吨矿0.30元。

1994年，将农林特产税更名为农业特产税。是年6月，按《贵州省征收农业特产税办法》向全县从事农业特产生产，用应税未税的农业特产品连续加工，收购烟叶、毛茶、水产品、木、原竹、黑木耳、银耳、生漆、天然树脂、毛绒、牛羊皮产品的单位和个人，征收农业特产税。

从1995年起，每吨原煤征收农业特产税由0.30元调整为1.50元。

2002年10月，县政府根据省政府办公厅《关于调整农业特产税及附加征收管理有关规定的通知》，印发《关于调整农业特产税及附加征收管理有关规定的通知》，对县内农业特产税应税品目、税率进行调整，调整后的税目、税率为烟叶税率20%；毛茶税率8%；牲畜产品、牛皮和羊皮的税率5%，羊毛、兔毛的税率10%，暂停征收猪皮的农业特产税；果品税率8%；原木、原竹税率8%；水产品税率8%；生漆、天然树脂税率8%；食用菌税率8%；花卉（含盆景）税率8%；蚕茧税率8%；药材税率7%；经济林苗木税率5%；林产品税率7%。农业特产税附加比例，按全省统一的正税8%执行。

根据2004年4月5日省财政厅《关于降低农业税税率，取消除烟叶外的农业特产税和对农户直接补贴的通告》，荔波县从2004年1月1日起，除烟叶外，对农业特产税应税产品取消农业特产税。

1987—2003年全县农业特产税征收统计表

表17－6 单位：万元

年度	征收税金	其中		年度	征收税金	其中	
		正税额	8%附加			正税额	8%附加
1987	1.94	1.90	0.04	1996	157.68	146.00	11.68
1988	6.47	5.99	0.48	1997	197.52	182.89	14.63
1989	5.18	4.80	0.38	1998	270.00	250.00	20.00
1990	7.86	7.28	0.58	1999	289.83	268.36	21.47
1991	14.15	13.10	1.05	2000	271.11	251.03	20.08
1992	19.14	17.72	1.42	2001	232.26	215.06	17.20
1993	43.18	39.98	3.20	2002	249.71	231.21	18.50
1994	88.56	82.00	6.56	2003	432.00	400.00	32.00
1995	111.51	103.25	8.26				

（三）耕地占用税

1989年，县政府根据《中华人民共和国耕地占用税条例》，制定全县耕地占用税征税标准为：玉屏镇的繁荣、和平、建设3个村，立化镇的立化村，每平方米6元；玉屏镇的板吉、菜园、时来3个村，茂兰镇的场坝村，阳凤的新场村，朝阳的田洞、交朝2个村，王蒙的高桥村，甲良镇的甲良村，播尧乡的和平村，每平方米4元；洞塘乡的新街村，佳荣乡的威岩村，方村乡的双江村，每平方米3元。除上述规定以外，其余各村每平方米2元，农民减半征收。

从1990年1月1日起，贵州省公路建设用地的耕地占用税统一按每平方米1.5元征收。

2001年9月，根据《贵州省耕地占用税实施办法》，县政府将全县划分为4个类别，调整征收标准，调整后的新税额标准从2001年10月1日起执行，原耕地占用税征收标准同时废止。调整后的税额标准为：玉屏镇的繁荣、和平、建设、板吉、菜园、时来6个村，每平方米10元；玉屏镇的罗家寨、拉鱼、福利3个村，立化镇的立化村，茂兰镇的场坝村，甲良镇的甲良、新场2个村，朝阳镇的田洞、交朝、花高3个村，瑶山乡的高桥、红光2个村，播尧乡的和平村，佳荣镇的威岩村，水尧乡的水尧村，水利乡的水利村，驾欧乡的六林村，共17个村，每平方米8元；洞塘乡的新街村，方村乡的双江村，翁昂乡的拉内村，捞村乡的群力村，永康乡的太吉村，瑶麓乡的瑶麓村，共6个村，每平方米6元。其余各村每平方米4元，农民占地按所在村税额减半征收。

2005年，县农税局针对部分土地征用后未及时缴纳耕地占用税的情况，对耕地占用税欠税进行清理，建立财政与国土、城建等部门相互协作工作机制，根据税收征管规定，发出催缴税款通知书，督促纳税人主动补税。通过专项清理，至10月，全县耕地占用税尾欠款153.5万元全部清收入库。

（四）契税

1992年，恢复征收契税，县财政局委托县建设局房屋管理所代征。

1998年9月，按省政府发布的《贵州省契税实施办法》征收契税。

2004年11—12月，县农税局对应征收的契税进行调查摸底，发现委托代征契税工作中存在少收、漏收现象。从2005年1月1日起，取消委托代征，实行财政直接征收管理，即县级部分由县农税局直接征收，所属乡（镇）部分由财政所征收，建设部门在办理土地使用证、房产证时必须有财政部门开具的“契税完税证”，对应纳税户按照“先税后费再办证”的程序进行征收，对尾欠户上门催收。

2006年12月，县政府办印发《关于继续加强煤矿转让契税清收工作的通知》，规定：县内煤矿等矿场以买卖、出售、赠予等形式进行转让，凡涉及土地、房屋权属转移的，照章征收契税；尚未缴清契税的煤矿企业，县国土资源局一律不予受理“采矿许可证”延期申报工作。

1989—2008年全县耕地占用税、契税收入统计表

表17－7 单位：万元

年度	耕地占用税收入	契税收入	年度	耕地占用税收入	契税收入
1989	7.21	—	1999	24.10	12.08
1990	3.81	—	2000	41.02	10.00
1991	12.91	—	2001	35.29	15.00
1992	10.19	1.10	2002	50.47	30.10
1993	11.02	2.10	2003	50.00	30.00
1994	38.64	5.70	2004	63.10	30.00
1995	10.50	2.00	2005	161.10	135.18
1996	15.27	2.00	2006	14.00	63.00
1997	16.05	2.09	2007	26.00	84.00
1998	24.57	3.37	2008	30.00	128.09

二、农村税费改革

2002年，荔波县被列为全省扩大农村税费改革试点县，根据省委、省政府《关于认真做好全省扩大农村税费试点工作的意见》《贵州省2002年扩大农村税费改革试点方案》等有关文件精神，是

年7月，县政府印发《荔波县2002年扩大农村税费改革试点实施方案》。按照实施方案，全县农村税费改革的主要内容有：取消乡统筹费，取消在农村进行的教育集资，取消所有面向农民征收的行政性收费和政府性基金，取消屠宰税，逐步取消统一规定的劳动积累工和义务工，调整农业税政策，调整农业特产税政策，改革村提留征收和使用方法。到2003年2月，全县农村税费改革完成并通过州税改检查组检查验收。改革后，全县农民负担与改革前负担相比，总减负额1113.36万元，总减负率71.45%，人均总减负额40.32元，占原人均负担总额的75.66%。其中，合同内减负总额101.49万元，平均减免率20.65%，人均减负额7.44元；政策内减负额478.01万元，平均减负率51.80%，人均减负额32.88元。

推行农村税费改革后，省、州每年给荔波县中央财政转移支付资金719万元，主要用于农村义务教育、村级公用经费、村组干部报酬、村级公积公益金、村级办公用房补助、乡村道路建设、计划生育补助、农村优抚等，农村义务教育经费的安排占农村税费改革中央转移支付资金的50%。

第七节　煤炭税费征收

一、机构

1996年8月30日，在立化镇政府所在地设立荔波县站台煤炭税费征收管理所，并在更班新站台、平寨站台、肯甫站台原煤入口处分别设立荔波县更班煤炭税费征收管理站、荔波县平寨煤炭税费征收管理一站、荔波县平寨煤炭税费征收管理二站、荔波县肯甫站台煤炭税费征收管理站。所、站行政关系隶属县政府办公室，业务接受县财政局指导。其中，肯甫站台煤炭税费征收管理站行政受肯甫综合检查站管理，财务由县站台煤炭税费征收管理所领导。所、站人员总计54人。

1998年4月1日，肯甫公路综合检查站和铁路煤炭税费征收站合并，建立新的综合检查站，隶属县平寨煤炭税费征收管理所管理，行政上归县政府办公室领导。是月，时来煤炭税费征收管理站业务隶属荔波县平寨煤炭税费征收管理所管理，行政上归县政府办公室领导。9月，佳荣税费征收站划归平寨煤炭税费征收管理所管理，佳荣乡政府协助管理，行政上归县政府办公室领导。是年，荔波县站台煤炭税费征收管理所改名为荔波县平寨税费征收管理所。

1999年4月，设立荔波县平寨煤炭销售管理所。5月，荔波县平寨税费征收管理所改为荔波县税费征收管理所。

2003年3月，撤销县煤炭销售管理所，其职能划归荔波县税费征收管理所。是年12月18日，荔波县税费征收管理所升格为正科级事业单位，下设平寨一站、平寨二站、更班站、肯甫站、佳荣站、时来站和播尧站7个税费征收管理站。是年12月，在县税费征收管理所加挂县煤炭准运准销验票管理总站牌子，在各税费征收管理站加挂县煤炭准运准销验票管理分站牌子。县煤炭准运准销验票总站在县煤炭工业局设办公室。

至2008年年底，县税费征收管理所下设水尧税费征收站、佳荣税费征收站、更班税费征收站、平寨税费征收一站、平寨税费征收二站、甲良税费征收站、播尧税费征收站、界牌税费征收站、肯甫税费征收站、甲良桥头征收点、播尧中心村征收点、佳荣第二征收点等13个征收站点和流动税费稽查大队。

二、税费征收

在县内出境的主要交通要道设立的税费征收管理机构，按照税法及相关法规，接受国税、地税及相关部门委托，对全县应税费矿产品进行集中统一征收，即对过境应缴税费煤炭依率计征各种税费。过境运煤车辆，必须到就近税费站过磅，以实际吨位完税后，方能出境，实行一车一票制。征收的税费，由管理所分渠道分别上缴县财政局、地税局、国税局及各规费管理部门。煤炭税费征收中，根据国家税费征收政策及相关法规，结合不同时期煤炭及其他矿产品生产、经营情况，适时调整征收标准。

1996年，国税分别征收煤炭运输环节、销售环节增值税，地税征收营运个人所得税、外销环节应缴企业所得税、个人或承包人经营应缴纳的个人所得税、资源税、城建税和教育附加费，地方规费征收工商行政管理费、矿产开发管理费、乡镇企业管理费、育林费、环保治理基金、民族地区采矿补贴、维持煤炭简单再生产费（含矿山安全设备费）、农业特产税、煤炭生产发展基金。

1998年2月—1999年12月，聘请县人大办、纪委等县直有关部门12人为税费征收所、站监督员。

2000年6月后，国税征收购进环节、销售环节应税税目；地税征收购进环节、销售环节应税税目和资源税、城建税、教育费附加；地方规费征收工商管理费、出境归口管理费、乡镇企业管理费、育林费、资源补偿费、维简费、排污费、民族地区采矿补贴、生产发展基金、农业特产税。

2002年，投入专款39.5万元，在一站、二站、更班、佳荣、水尧、播尧6个站建立电脑监控和开票系统，管理所通过图像监控和数字监控两套软件，随时查看各种数据、制作报表，及时掌握各站工作动态，规范税费征收工作。

从2004年1月1日起，实行“煤炭产品准运准销凭证”（简称“运销凭证”），由税费征收管理所行使“运销凭证”验票工作。“运销凭证”作为合法煤矿煤炭产品进入流通领域的通行凭证，由煤炭管理部门统一印制，对无“运销凭证”的煤炭，一律由税费征收管理站按每吨15元处以罚款。

2004年7月—2008年12月，国税征收销售环节税目，地税征收购进环节（扣缴）个人所得税、销售环节个人所得税、资源税、城市维护建设税、教育费附加，地方规费征收维简费、排污费、水土保持补偿费、县乡公路维改费、矿产资源补偿费。

1996-2008年煤炭税费收入统计表

表17-8

年度	原煤数量（吨）	税费总收入（万元）
1996	124949.30	517.54
1997	834444.85	3482.46
1998	865977.30	3586.81
1999	906325.70	3754.00
2000	953140.34	3884.82
2001	1135835.57	5992.83
2002	1550571.80	7219.30
2003	1505878.17	8011.27
2004	1499398.63	8678.89
2005	1049787.80	8820.89
2006	970227.16	8836.31
2007	1024921.89	10084.61
2008	1041346.47	12404.32

第二章　税　务

第一节　税务体制改革

1978—1982年，县税务局为县政府工作机构，经费由县财政拨给，业务上受黔南州税务局指导。

1983年，中央对税务系统实行机构、人员、经费、业务四垂直管理，县税务局于是年10月底交接完毕。

是年，按中央税制改革的规定，进行税制改革，实施国营企业第一步利改税，对国营企业征收国营企业所得税。1984年10月，全面实行国营企业第二步利改税。

1993年，县税务局进行人事制度改革，实行干部聘任制。

1994年9月28日，按照中央实行分税制的要求，县税务局分设为荔波县国家税务局、荔波县地方税务局，人员、经费、财产等按照国税三分之二、地税三分之一、业务骨干配比适当的原则进行分配。

一、国税机构改革

1995年3月，按照黔南州国税局批准的《荔波县国家税务局内设机构、职能配置和人员编制方案的意见》，县国税局内设办公室、税政股、征管股、计划财务股、人事教育股、监察室、发票管理所，直属机构有稽查分局、征收一分局（由原玉屏区所、玉屏镇所、县国税局征收股组成）、征收二分局（原立化国税所），派出机构有朝阳、甲良、茂兰3个国税所。

1997年3月，根据全州推行的保留税务所牌子，组建征收分局的规定，县国税局撤销原征收一分局，组建玉屏征收分局（管理朝阳、甲良两个国税所）；撤销原征收二分局，组建立化征收分局；撤销茂兰国税所，组建茂兰征收分局。2000年1月，甲良国税所改为分局，撤销朝阳国税所，合并到玉屏国税分局。

2001年5月，州国税局批准《荔波县国家税务局机构改革实施方案》，县国税局内设办公室、计划财务股、综合业务股、人事教育股、监察室，直属机构有稽查局，派出机构有玉屏、立化、茂兰、甲良4个国税分局，下设县国税局信息中心（事业单位）。

2002年11月，甲良分局撤销并入玉屏分局；立化分局撤销并入茂兰分局。

2003年7月，县国税局进行机构改革和业务重组，内设办公室、人事教育股、监察室，直属机构为计划征收股、管理股、稽查局、玉屏分局、茂兰分局、财务股，信息中心仍为事业单位。

2005年1月，撤销茂兰分局、玉屏分局，在县城设立玉屏税务分局（副科级），基层税务所的房产全部处理，国税系统税务干部全部集中到县城，原各基层税务所人员进入新成立的玉屏税务分局，负责全县17个乡（镇）的税收征收和服务管理工作。

2005年，管理股改为综合业务股，增设税源管理股。

2008年年末，全县国税系统实有人员49人。

二、地方税务机构改革

1994年9月，成立荔波县地税局。内设人秘股、税政股、计会征收股、征管股、稽查队，延伸机构有玉屏、甲良、朝阳、茂兰、立化5个税务所。1995年9月，县政府批准设立水尧乡、佳荣乡、播尧乡3个税务所。

1996年4月，县编委批复县地方税务局内设机构9个，延伸机构2个分局和乡（镇）税务所13个（洞塘乡、瑶麓乡不设），实际设置玉屏、立化2个分局和甲良、朝阳、茂兰3个税务所。

1997年6月，县政府批转《荔波县地方税务系统深化征管改革实施方案》，保留原内设机构，按经济区域设置征收分局和中心税务所，有玉屏、茂兰、立化3个地税征收分局和朝阳、甲良、佳荣3个中心税务所。对未设分局和中心税务所的乡，设置征收点，配备征收人员。取消播尧乡、水尧水族乡税务所。同时，稽查队改称稽查分局。

1998年10月，按省编办《关于上划各级地方税务局机关人员编制及有关事项的通知》，县地税局划归省、州地税局垂直管理，县地税局机构编制15个，实际有内设机构6个、延伸机构5个。是年，稽查分局改为稽查局，配备专职稽查人员6人。

2001年10月，全县地税系统机构改革，县地税局内办公室、人教股、监察室、计会股、税政股、征管股，直属机构为稽查局、玉屏征收分局，基层税务所有甲良、茂兰、立化、朝阳4个税务所。

2004年，经州地税局批准，朝阳税务所合并到玉屏分局办公，在朝阳设征收点，保留朝阳税务所编制；茂兰分局合并到立化分局办公，在茂兰设征收点，保留茂兰分局编制。

2008年，县地税局实有人员41人。

第二节 国税征管

一、征收税种

1994年分税制后，县国税局征收的税种有增值税、消费税、企业所得税、车辆购置税、储蓄存款利息所得个人所得税。

（一）增值税

县内增值税税源主要是原煤，原煤税收占全县国税收入的70%。1996年前，对原煤产销行业的税收，仅凭企业自行申报数纳税，无法核实其真实性，税源流失严重。1996年，县政府成立煤炭税费征收管理机构，统一征收税费后，煤炭应缴增值税委托煤炭税费征收机构预征，控制税源流失。原煤税费征收分生产、销售两个环节依率计征，纳税人在征收期凭各税费站预征完税凭证到国税局办理税款清算抵缴手续。1996年税率6%，2002年6月调整为13%。计税价格根据市场价格变化情况适时调整。

从2006年5月19日起，各税费征收单位对过境铁矿石、铁矿粉、硫矿石预征增值税。

（二）消费税

县内从1994年起开征消费税。县内没有生产和加工型的工业企业，按“消费税税目税率（税额）表”所列，县内仅有几家粮食白酒生产小作坊。纳税户有樟江食品厂及金银首饰店2家。

（三）企业所得税

按照分税制税种管辖的征收范围，县国税局负责征收中央企业所得税和地方金融机构所得税，征收企业有20家。

从2002年1月1日起，按国家工商总局的规定，在县内工商部门办理登记的企业，其企业所得税由国税局征收；在其他行政管理部门新登记注册领取许可证的事业单位、社会团体、律师事务所、医院、学校等缴纳所得税的组织，其企业所得由国税局征收管理；2001年12月31日前已在工商部门和其他行政管理部门登记注册，但未进行税务登记的企事业单位及其他组织，在2001年1月1日后进行税务登记的，其企业所得税按原规定的征管范围，由国税局、地税局分别征收管理。征收范围调整后，到2005年年底，县国税局征收管理所得税企业45户。

原国税局办公大楼

从2006年11月30日起，县内新办煤炭企业所得税实行产品过站出境预缴税款办法，预征企业所得税。

（四）个人所得税

县国税局征收的个人所得税主要是储蓄存款利息所得税，1999年11月1日开征。对个人取得的教育储蓄存款利息所得以及国务院财政部门确定的其他专项储蓄存款或储蓄性专项基金存款的利息所得，免征个人所得税。储蓄存款利息所得税按20%税率计征，委托县内所有金融机构代征代扣、结算缴库。

（五）车辆购置税

2001年1月1日，县内开征车辆购置税，由征费稽查所代征，按月逐级上划缴库。征收的车辆购置税主要有二轮摩托车、三轮摩托车、轻便摩托车及农用运输车。汽车的车辆登记注册入户全部由都匀车管所办理，各种汽车的车辆购置税全部在都匀缴纳。车辆购置税从2005年1月1日起，由国税局征收，原征范围不变。2005—2008年，征收税款累计182.81万元。

1994—2008年全县国税收入统计表

表17－9 单位：万元

年度	税收合计	其中			
		增值税	消费税	企业所得税	个人所得税
1994	1837.75	1561.49	0.98	182.93	92.35
1995	1796.31	1706.59	0.39	1.84	87.49
1996	2136.12	2121.66	0.51	13.95	—
1997	2138.23	2132.01	0.67	5.55	—
1998	2138.94	2131.23	0.11	7.60	—
1999	1591.3	1589.34	0.13	1.67	0.16
2000	1788.11	1741.93	0.81	11.97	33.40

续表17－9

年度	税收合计	其中			
		增值税	消费税	企业所得税	个人所得税
2001	2092.38	2026.47	0.33	10.43	55.15
2002	2834.36	2722.95	1.34	53.04	57.03
2003	3786.89	3639.15	2.17	84.27	61.30
2004	4847.37	4664.04	0.92	110.40	72.01
2005	5838.84	5706.58	0.85	48.90	82.51
2006	6142.13	5741.33	—	285.74	115.06
2007	6614.82	6327.22	—	158.81	128.79
2008	8874.27	8719.08	—	81.34	73.85

说明：1.1994年9月国税、地税机构分设，企业所得税征收和管理，由县地税局负责，县国税局仅对县水泥厂、县酒厂等几个国有企业征收企业所得税，这些企业处于低利润或亏损状况，因此，应征企业所得税数额少。2.1994年、1995年的税收合计数包含城建税、车船使用税、房产税、屠宰税、资源税、土地使用税、印花税、固定资产投资方向调节税、税款滞纳金罚没收入；1997年税收合计数包含税款滞纳金罚没收入2.88万元；2005—2008年的税收合计数包含车辆购置税。

二、征收管理

1988年以前，税收征管实行税务人员“一人进厂（场）统管各税”的模式。1989年以后，实行管理、征收、稽查三个环节分离，相互制约、相互监督的管理机制，税务人员按照不同的环节和岗位各负其责。

1997年年初，根据国家税务总局提出的“以建立纳税申报和优化服务为基础，以计算机网络为依托，集中征收，重点稽查”税收征管模式，县国税局分别在管理两个片区以上的玉屏税务分局、茂兰税务分局建立征收大厅，集中征收。无论纳税人居住地距离征收点有多远，征收期必须主动上门申报缴税，改变征收期税务干部到各乡（镇）场点挨家挨户上门开票收税的方式。办税大厅实行“一站式”服务，企业纳税申报，随时接受税源管理纳税评估，如发现有偷逃税行为，将信息传送到稽查部门另案处理。

2002年3月，在全省率先实行“税收会计统一核算”管理模式，取消基层单位会计核算，由县集中统一核算。此项目在2003年被评为全省国税系统优秀创新项目。

2005年1月后，对所辖重点企业和重点税源进行纳税评估监控管理，通过税源信息、监管和纳税评估，发现有异常的偷（逃）税疑点，及时向稽查部门提供信息。

2006年1—3月，评估全县加油站10户，出现异常情况6户，属销售差异率小于5%的有4户，销售差异率大于5%的有1户，税收负担率小于县内加油站平均税收负担率的有1户。

2007年2月，在全县推行纳税信用等级评定管理，以综合征管软件的数据资源为基础，对纳税人信用等级进行分类动态管理，建立国税系统纳税信用等级评定管理工作网络体系，计算机软件自动评定。是年，县国税局制定《荔波县国家税务局纳税人电子数据申报、银税库一体化缴税方式工作规程（试行）》，对纳税人和县国税系统工作流程、岗位进行规范。

是年，对增值税零申报和申报情况异常的企业进行纳税评估，全年评估纳税企业24户。通过纳税评估，企业自行补税15万元。

2008年7月，制定《荔波县国家税务局纳税服务一体化联动工作实施办法》，规范各部门的纳税服务行为。是年，重点对纳税户的户籍进行跟踪管理和规范税务登记管理，各部门信息及时沟通，纳税人经营范围、经营方式的变化情况也及时掌握，对新办企业及时进行税务登记，防止漏征漏管。

三、国税稽查

1994年税务机构分设至2000年，国税稽查的对象，按征管户数确定一定比例，同时根据群众举报和协查情报确定。

2001年以后，开始应用增值税防伪税控系统，对虚假增值税发票和虚开增值税行为进行监控。案件稽查按照选案、稽查、审理、执行4个程序办理。县国税局设置督查岗，对税收各个环节事前、事中、事后进行日常督查，预防不规范执法行为发生。

2003年，检查煤炭企业，查补税58.93万元，罚款3.12万元，移送公安机关案件1件。2004年，补税20.14万元，罚款13.69万元，移送公安机关案件1件。

从2005年7月1日起，按州国税稽查局《稽查集中选案规程》，县国税稽查部门将案源资料登记上报州国税稽查局，由州国税稽查局进行日常稽查、专项稽查、专案稽查选案，县按照州确定的稽查对象和下达的税务稽查任务通知书开展稽查工作。2005年，补税43.4万元，罚款17.06万元。

1994—2006年，县国税稽查局共办结稽查案件（含被稽查户数）2526件，查补税款599.1万元，所办案件无申请行政复议，其中由县法院强制执行企业1户。

2002—2006年，对公民举报案件进行实地检查7户（私营企业2户、个体5户），补税罚款总计14.63万元。通过防伪税控稽核系统协助有关单位调查增值税发票案件25件，县内发出委托协查发票案1件。

2007年，重点开展房地产及建筑安装企业、食品药品市场企业、沙石行业、铅锌矿行业税收日常检查、专项检查、专案稽查和案件协查，全年检查上述行业纳税户30户，查结28户，查补金额总计32.14万元。其中，查补税款17.17万元，加收滞纳金4.17万元，罚款10.8万元。是年，审理重大案件3件，查补税款11.97万元，加收滞纳金3.28万元，罚款9万元。

2008年，开展房地产及建筑安装业、建材生产及销售业、金融保险业、汽车维修及配件经营、电力行业5个行业税收专项检查，重点检查13户，查结12户，查出问题8户，查实率66.67%，查处金额29.25万元。其中，查补税款19.29万元，加收滞纳金9.09万元，罚款0.87万元。入库金额29.15万元，入库率99.66%。

四、信息化建设

1996年，县国税局配置计算机2台，主要用于打印税务登记证。1998年，使用计算机综合征管软件，业务涵盖税务登记、申报征收、发票管理、税收会计等税收业务全过程。至2000年，各业务部门和征收分局业务全面实现计算机操作管理。

2001年4月，县国税局在全州率先推行银行卡申报纳税征管方式。5月，新建的县国税局信息中心为全县国税系统提供现代计算机技术服务。

2003年，建设“一个网络、四个系统”金税工程，即开通金税网络，运行综合征管信息系统CTAIS、税收执法管理系统、三大数据系统整合、工作流程系统四大软件，全县个体户1637户全部录入计算机定税系统，纳税信息即时查询、即时监控。

至2008年，建成从税务总局到省、州、县国税局四级广域网络，将税收业务、行政管理、公文处理等税收工作全面纳入计算机管理和监控。

五、税务代理

1996年8月，成立县税务代理机构，从事县内税务代理工作，机构未定名称，属过渡性临时机构，工作人员为临时人员，隶属县国税局管理，自谋代理业务。税务代理机构开展的代理业务主要有代办税务登记、代理纳税申报、代理建账、代办发票领购、代理申请补退税手续及减免税手续、受聘税务顾问、代理制作涉税文书等。

1999年8月，税务代理机构与税务部门脱钩，经清理整顿后，报省税务师管理中心，省税务师管理中心于2000年3月16日批复，成立荔波县宏达税务师事务所有限责任公司。2003年12月，该公司不具备代理业务资质，采取注册税务师资源共享办法，与独山、三都、平塘、都匀等县（市）联合，以都匀为总公司，成立都匀正诚税务师事务所有限责任公司，荔波县设分公司。2005年3月，荔波县分公司随总公司名称变更为都匀瑞成税务师事务所有限责任公司荔波分公司。

1999—2008年税务代理统计表

表17－10　　　　单位：户

年度	代理企业	代理个体	年度	代理企业	代理个体
1999	31	441	2004	42	237
2000	35	420	2005	58	236
2001	35	452	2006	59	212
2002	37	527	2007	62	219
2003	36	230	2008	67	223

第三节　地方税收征管

一、征收税种

（一）营业税

1984年开征营业税。营业税是县内地方税主要税源之一，全县每年营业税收入占地方税全部收入的30%左右，主要税源为交通运输业、建筑业、服务业等行业，其他行业如金融保险业、邮政电信业、娱乐业等的营业税收入占比重较少。

（二）个人所得税

1994年1月1日，开征个人所得税。由县地税机关征收的个人所得税有：工资薪金所得，个体工商户生产经营所得，以及对事业单位的承包经营、承租经营所得，稿酬所得，特许权使用费所得，利息、股息、红利所得，财产租赁所得，财产转让所得，偶然所得和其他所得。

（三）土地增值税

1994年1月，开征土地增值税。2002年7月31日，按省地税局的规定，县内土地增值税预征率统一按1%计征，清理结算土地增值额的办法和税率不变。对所有房地产开发商以及个人转让私宅统一按1%征收土地增值税。

（四）城市维护建设税

1985年，开征城市维护建设税，按增值税或营业税税额计征。

（五）车船使用税

1986年，恢复征收车船使用税。县内没有内河航道运输，车船使用税只对拥有车辆并且使用的单位和个人征收，对依法属于免征的车辆免征车船使用税。

（六）房产税

1986年10月，开征房产税。1987年起，只在县城所在地玉屏镇征收房产税。1996年1月1日后，县内建制镇全部征收房产税。

（七）屠宰税

1978年前已开征屠宰税。2002年9月10日停止征收。

（八）资源税

1984年，开征资源税。原煤、铅锌矿、铁矿等矿产品资源税，1996年前由检查站、1996年后由税费征收站按实际吨位对运输出境车辆统一收取，不直接对开采人征收。

（九）城镇土地使用税

1989年，开征城镇土地使用税。县政府颁布《荔波县城镇土地使用税征收管理办法》，在玉屏镇开征土地使用税，并划分地段、等级，确定每平方米征收税额。

从1996年1月1日起，对地段划分和税额标准作相应调整，即玉屏镇内，根据路段等级分别按每年每平方米3元、1元征收土地使用税；立化镇、茂兰镇、朝阳镇、甲良镇、佳荣镇所在地土地使用税，每年每平方米按1元征收。2002年1月，对全县土地使用税的计税等级又作调整，玉屏镇内街道路段土地等级分为县城、建制镇及工矿区二等和县城、建制镇及工矿区四等两个等级，二等路段土地每年每平方米税额3元，四等路段每年每平方米税额1元。立化、茂兰、朝阳、甲良、佳荣5镇及立化矿区内的平寨、更班两个矿区按每年每平方米税额1元征收土地使用税。

（十）固定资产投资方向调节税

1991年开征固定资产投资方向调节税，同时停征建筑税。荔波县属边远山区，国家投资建筑项目少，投资方向调节税所列项目基本没有，只有税目税率表中未列出的固定资产投资，如职工宿舍、办公楼、综合楼等。国家拨款（计划内）投资修建的职工宿舍适用5%税率，其他固定资产投资（不包括更新改造）适用15%税率。2000年1月1日起，根据财政部、国家税务总局的通知，暂停征收固定资产投资方向调节税，但对2000年1月1日前的实际完成额进行清理，对应纳税款进行结算，多退少补。至2001年，对停止征收的投资方向调节税清理补征完毕，共清补16.33万元。

（十一）地方企业所得税

1994年1月1日，开征地方企业所得税，同时废止原国营企业所得税、国营企业调节税、集体企业所得税、私营企业所得税。

2003年，根据省政府《关于西部大开发若干政策措施的实施意见》中“对在1994年税制改革后没有享受过任何减征或免征企业所得税优惠政策的，在2003—2010年可享受‘三免两减半’（企业所得税前三年免后两年减半征收）的优惠政策”的规定，全县享受“三免两减半”优惠政策的企业16户。

（十二）印花税

1978年前已开征印花税。1994年划归地方税征收，是年完成0.92万元。1994—2008年累计征收95.81万元。

（十三）教育费附加

1980年，开征教育费附加，以单位和个人实际缴纳产品税、增值税、营业税的税额为计税依据，按规定附加率1%一并征收教育基金。1990年，教育费附加率由1%调整为2%。1994年取消产品税后，只对缴纳增值税、营业税征收教育费附加。

（十四）煤炭价格调节基金

从2006年起，征收煤炭价格调节基金，全年征收2831.73万元。2007年征收3146.1万元，2008年征收6507.64万元。

1994—2008年全县地方税主要税种征收统计表

表17－11　单位：万元

年度	税收合计	营业税	个人所得税	土地增值税	城市维护建设税	车船使用税	房产税
1994	—	226.98	92.35	—	34.32	4.37	7.04
1995	793.34	280.12	96.71	0.65	8.91	3.63	7.99
1996	1141.43	414.25	310.94	11.69	55.45	4.70	12.55
1997	1502.76	358.96	696.66	—	145.63	8.51	26.12
1998	2080.00	565.99	848.83	5.12	106.33	9.95	22.24
1999	2222.60	738.11	886.92	2.94	106.99	8.26	45.26
2000	2456.03	822.72	1059.87	—	133.39	9.64	62.18
2001	2520.00	682.70	1403.64	—	117.98	9.06	43.39
2002	2895.73	808.04	1327.60	10.33	192.00	8.29	54.62
2003	3244.45	926.83	1641.12	4.21	190.64	9.37	57.97
2004	4264.76	1012.19	2203.77	22.99	262.54	9.61	66.90
2005	5058.68	1750.05	1909.79	4.52	326.49	9.50	67.99
2006	5456.20	1753.58	2132.93	12.25	308.07	6.37	94.67
2007	60307.71	1307.26	2558.34	27.73	390.73	16.13	96.92
2008	7914.63	1268.00	3323.08	8.26	535.29	50.47	141.66

年度	印花税	屠宰税	资源税	城镇土地使用税	固定资产投资方向调节税	地方企业所得税	教育费附加税
1994	0.92	16.46	62.92	3.05	4.70	—	—
1995	2.80	6.91	56.13	3.15	37.34	283.66	5.34
1996	1.01	12.63	78.84	8.97	18.34	160.09	51.97
1997	0.95	17.13	29.77	9.24	6.40	203.39	—
1998	2.54	25.72	65.60	16.25	91.99	254.70	64.76
1999	3.38	63.83	21.70	22.25	20.35	64.50	58.32
2000	2.22	83.47	51.87	39.58	15.15	92.28	79.17
2001	1.66	62.24	27.52	22.96	1.18	73.90	73.78
2002	3.62	40.49	84.42	27.08	—	215.83	123.43
2003	3.47	—	122.56	29.18	—	142.08	117.02

续表17－11

年度	印花税	屠宰税	资源税	城镇土地使用税	固定资产投资方向调节税	地方企业所得税	教育费附加税
2004	11.51	—	167.60	54.17	—	284.02	169.49
2005	11.49	—	164.66	41.56	—	567.80	193.46
2006	9.99	—	328.89	37.99	—	586.02	185.53
2007	13.70	—	321.23	93.34	—	969.71	235.74
2008	26.56	—	245.38	167.86	—	1832.12	315.95

说明：1994年9月国税、地税分设，税收数据不全。

二、征收管理

1978—1988年，全县税收按片区、行业、街道、国营、集体、个体等进行管理，实行税务干部包干负责制，征收、管理、稽查集于一身。

1989年，全县首次开展“整顿税收秩序、治理税收环境”工作，实行双人上岗制，将基层征收单位征收、管理、稽查三个环节分开。

1995年初，按照税种管辖范围，对应缴纳地方税的企业、个体工商户换发税务登记证，税务登记、纳税鉴定等资料重新建档，规范纳税管理。

1995—1997年，对全县个体户税收征管沿用分税制前的“征、管、查”分离模式，1998—2000年，实行稽查集中在县地税局，征收、管理在基层的两分离模式。

2005年后，实行片区管理制，每个片区设专管员2名，负责对片区内个体工商户开业、停复业、转非、注销等进行调查核实。所有个体户的纳税定额，张贴定额公示牌，接受纳税人监督。

是年，县地税局推行“银税一体化”，即所有的纳税户在指定的银行开设“税款预存专户”（一般预存两个月税款）并将存折账号报告税务机关，到纳税期由银行按税务机关的通知，将该户税款划入“税款专户”，确保税款及时足额缴入国库。

2006年，县地税局作为全州地方税系统征管改革试点县之一，建立纳税评估制度，运行新MIS征收管理系统，推进税收管理科学化、精细化。

2007年，对边远地区月税额在200元以下的纳税户推行“简并征期”征收方法，将定期定额个体工商户若干个纳税期的税款合并为一期申报缴纳，按季、半年或年度征收税款，定期检查。年内，对缴纳地税的单位和个人以及代扣代缴税款的单位和个人进行“五清五查”（清理漏管户，查户籍管理；清理漏征户，查税款征收；清理定期定额户，查定额核定；清理发票领用户，查申报缴税情况；清理纳税人档案资料，查资料是否真实、准确、完整）和专项检查，检查17个乡（镇）2469户，其中个体工商户2268户、企业201户。查出漏征户57户、漏管户46户、应办证未办证79户。

2008年，运用县地税局自行设置的电子监控软件作为辅助工具，对各类税收征管实施全程监控。

三、地税稽查

1994—1996年，地税稽查部门主要参与清理调查整顿纳税户及催缴漏欠税、所得税汇算清缴等工作。1998年后，稽查工作按照选案、稽查、审理、执行4个程序进行。

至2006年的13年间，全县地税系统从各种信息、举报、交办、协查等案源中选定案件，经批准立案查办累计145起。经过审理，查出主要事实不清、主要证据不足4件；适用法律、法规、规章有错误之处130件；违反法定程序4件；处理意见不当2件。所办案件无一件申请复议。在执行税务处理过程中，1997年纳税人被强制执行1户，移送司法机关追究刑事责任1户。其间，2006年开展房产税、城镇土地使用税、车辆营运营业税、个人住房销售营业税等专项检查。全年立案6件，结案6件，查补入库税款37.77万元，加收滞纳金44.85万元，罚款6.6万元。

2007年，开展企业所得税、房地产行业、个人所得税、煤炭生产及运销行业专项检查，全年检查纳税户10户，查结9户，移送司法机关1户，查补税款16.24万元，罚款8.09万元，加收滞纳金0.44万元，入库率100%，处罚率50%。

2008年，检查房地产及建筑安装行业纳税户3户，查出有问题2户，查结2户，查处金额共3.97万元，其中移送公安机关立案侦查1户；检查矿产品及矿产品加工行业纳税户1户，查处金额24.85万元；检查金融保险业纳税户1户，查处金额22.43万元；检查其他行业纳税户3户，查出有问题2户，查处金额共9.62万元。

是年，根据州国税局、州地税局《关于加强税务稽查协作配合的实施意见》，县地税局、县国税局稽查部门检查企业3户，减少重复检查。与公安部门联合检查黔南天力房地产开发有限公司荔波分公司2007年纳税情况，经检查，定性偷税数额39.42万元，应补税额59.23万元，依法移送县公安经济侦查部门立案侦查。

1994—2008年全县地税稽查情况统计表

表17－12　　单位：万元

年度	稽查案件	结案	查补税款
1994	0	0	0
1995	0	0	0
1996	0	0	0
1997	23	—	29.21
1998	7	7	1296.05
1999	18	18	152.83
2000	10	10	217.13
2001	9	9	82.67
2002	22	22	149.35
2003	29	29	127.28
2004	11	11	96.44
2005	10	10	145.76
2006	6	6	44.85
2007	10	9	81.31
2008	8	6	60.87

四、信息化建设

1998年，县地税局配置计算机5台，单机运行，使用软盘交换数据。1999年，开始建设县地税局内部局域网，通过电信部门的电话线路，与各征收单位通过调制调解器拨号联网。2002年，建立县地税局局域网和内部办公信息网。

2003年，对基层征收单位网络进行改造，租用电信2兆光纤与县地税局进行联网。至此，全县地税系统计算机联网，实现县级数据集中。是年11月，县地税局MIS系统上线运行。2004年2月，县地税局OA系统上线运行。2006年年底，县地税局配有计算机30台。至2008年年末，全县地税系统信息化建设投入经费累计40万元。

第三章 金 融

第一节 银行业

一、人民银行

（一）机构

1991年，设综合计划股、人秘股、稽核金管股、货币发行股、保卫股、会计国库股、监察室。1994年，会计国库股分设为会计股、国库股。1996年，进行内设机构改革，设办公室、营业部、金融监管股、监察室、保卫股。1997年7月，设农村合作金融管理股。

1998年年底，人行跨省区建立分行，荔波支行隶属成都分行。

2004年1月，设在县人行的中国银行业监督管理委员会黔南监管分局荔波监管组正式分出，人行荔波县支行的部分监管职能随之划出。2006年7月，增设纪检监察室。

2008年，内设机构改革为综合业务股、基础业务股、发行股3个股，全行实有人员15人。

（二）信贷业务

1.临时贷款 1990年前，人行荔波县支行无零时性贷款业务。1991年后，对各商业银行在短期内资金营运发生困难时发放贷款，贷款期限不超过3个月，到期收回，不跨年度。至1997年，临时贷款发放总计550万元，收回550万元，每年的贷款都按期收回。其中，1994年为贷款最高年140万元，1998年后没有再办临时性贷款。

2.专项贷款 1986年，根据《中国人民银行专项贷款管理暂行办法》的规定，开始向县内煤炭、能源、水电、旅游、交通等方面的重大项目发放专项贷款。是年，发放贷款43万元。1991年后，资金发放重点支持项目有：县地方国营水尧巴合煤矿，朝阳、城关两地区在樟江沿河两岸栽种果树（沙田柚），17个乡（镇）实施温饱工程等。1986—1994年，发放贷款累计849.7万元。1995年后只办理贷款收回业务。1997年、1999年，先后将180万元、192万元专项贷款划转中国农业发展银行荔波信贷组。1999年，人行荔波县支行停办专项贷款。

3.支农再贷款 支农再待款主要为县内农村信用合作社提供充足信贷资金，解决支农资金不足。2004年，县人行首次争取到再贷款限额3000万元。至2008年年末，支农再贷款余额为零。

（三）征信管理

从2000年起，根据《银行信贷登记咨询管理办法》，县内金融机构建立银行信贷登记咨询系统，实行向贷款单位发放贷款卡、贷款卡年审制度。至2008年，发放贷款卡行政许可53户，年审贷款卡25户。

（四）货币发行与流通

1.现金发行与回笼 2000年3月底前，人行荔波县支行货币发行会计核算全部为手工操作。2000

年4月1日起，建立货币发行管理电子信息系统，启用电子会计核算凭证，取消手工操作。2005年5月，申报二级发行库，是年10月获准成为贵阳中支二级发行库。

1978—2008年现金发行和回笼统计表

表17－13 单位：万元

年度	发行	回笼	年度	发行	回笼
1978	254.5	246.2	1994	2481.5	4278.0
1979	282.8	273.6	1995	3776.5	4054.8
1980	314.3	304.1	1996	6871.9	7104.1
1981	349.2	337.9	1997	8342.9	7852.6
1982	387.9	375.5	1998	9592.0	10331.4
1983	408.4	508.1	1999	10838.7	11153.5
1984	453.8	725.9	2000	13150.0	15618.5
1985	477.7	907.4	2001	15408.5	13207.7
1986	530.8	1008.3	2002	14742.8	8936.9
1987	475.4	477.6	2003	18875.4	1205.0
1988	685.4	678.6	2004	12672.9	14450.4
1989	575.8	842.9	2005	13628.7	15807.2
1990	941.0	675.1	2006	13344.7	17483.6
1991	1314.8	974.0	2007	19740.0	28520.8
1992	1875.6	1784.1	2008	27196.1	36429.5
1993	2683.6	2062.2			

2.金银收兑　人行荔波县支行历年未收兑黄金。1986年，开始收兑白银。1998年，金银市场放开，人行荔波县支行停办此项业务。

1986—1997年人行荔波县支行白银收兑统计表

表17－14

年度	收兑白银数量总计（克）	单价（元/克）	收兑支付杂银总计（元）
1986	62725	0.75	47044
1987	8.7	0.75	6.5
1988	1615	0.75	1211
1989	8917	0.75	6688
1990	83.8	0.75	62.9
1991	109872	0.85	93391
1992	83336	0.85	70836
1993	59136	0.85	50266

续表17-14

年度	收兑白银数量总计（克）	单价（元/克）	收兑支付杂银总计（元）
1994	16905	0.85	14369
1995	10514	1.25	13143
1996	33303	1.17	38965
1997	17023	1.17	19917

3.损伤币复点 1978—2004年，残币复点工作由发行股负责，集中复点，上缴州中心支行抽查复点。人行荔波县支行挑剔复点损伤人民币累计23662.85万元。2005年以后，损伤人民币复点由人行黔南州中心支行负责，人行荔波县支行停办此项业务。

4.新版人民币发行 1978—1986年，县内发行使用第三套人民币。1987年，开始发行第四套人民币。1999年10月1日后，发行第五套人民币。

（五）经理国库

1985年起，按《中华人民共和国国家金库条例》的规定，人行荔波县支行组织管理国库工作，履行国库职责，保证财政资金及时划拨。

2003年8月，县农村信用联社申请，经黔南中心支库批准，县农村信用联社在17个乡（镇）设立15个国库经收处，办理国库经收业务。

2008年7月，荔波国库集中支付与州级国库集中支付正式联网运行。

（六）稽核检查

从1989年5月起，人行荔波县支行按中国人民银行、监察部颁布的《金融稽核检查处罚规定》，每年对各类银行、保险公司、其他金融机构进行联行和同城票据结算、托收承付结算稽核，对专业银行乱收费、乱罚息进行稽核，对全县邮政储蓄利率执行、公款私存情况进行稽核，对部分农村信用社进行稽核，对专业银行部分信贷资产稽核，对各专业银行结算纪律执行情况进行检查。在稽核检查中，查出不严格按照贷款章程制度办理贷款、无担保单位发放贷款总计28户，金额11万元，积压单位汇款31万元。根据金融法规，对积压汇款的机构，处罚息697.50元，对托收承户、逾期罚滞纳金80元。

2007年，中国人民银行总行、监察部废止《金融稽核处罚规定》，金融稽核工作停止。

（七）反假币

2003年7月，人民银行总行颁布《中国人民银行假币收缴、鉴定管理办法》后，人行荔波县支行采取摆摊设点、媒体、海报、发宣传资料等方式，每年开展反假人民币宣传月和反假人民币宣传进社区、进学校、进农村等活动，提高人民群众识别假币能力。2005年后，警民联手，加大打击假币犯罪活动。

2001—2008年，收缴假人民币9.54万元。

（八）安全保卫

1978—1997年，人行荔波县支行实行24小时值班制度，安装有电铃报警器。1998年，开始安装电子监控系统进行录像监控，全行安装摄像头4个，主要对发行库进行监控。2002年，摄像头增加到16个。2004—2008年，有值守人员8名，实行24小时双人武装守卫。

1978—2008年全县金融机构存款、贷款年末余额统计表

表17－15 单位：万元

年度	年末存款余额总计	年末贷款余额总计	年度	年末存款余额总计	年末贷款余额总计
1978	259	263	1994	11961	8360
1979	287	292	1995	13898	12185
1980	319	308	1996	13079	15032
1981	355	342	1997	16176	20043
1982	394	360	1998	20973	27578
1983	415	400	1999	23112	34247
1984	1121	1206	2000	29434	39609
1985	1192	1331	2001	32780	40465
1986	1270	1333	2002	38207	44178
1987	2260	2298	2003	48508	31639
1988	2426	2830	2004	59370	34283
1989	3169	3172	2005	73611	35676
1990	3687	3072	2006	81089	42362
1991	4850	3520	2007	106275	45695
1992	6638	4099	2008	137305	47014
1993	9829	5877			

二、建设银行

（一）机构

1979年2月1日，成立中国人民建设银行荔波县支行，有干部4人，劳动、人事、工资由县政府管理，业务由州建行管理。1984年1月，根据省组织、计划、人事、劳动、建设银行5个部门联合下发的《关于贵州省建设银行系统干部实行统一管理有关问题的联合通知》，建行荔波县支行受建设银行和地方党委双重领导，以建设银行领导为主（即以垂直管理为主）。

1987年，设会计出纳股、业务股、储蓄股、支行储蓄专柜。1989年4月，设迎宾储蓄所。1992年6月，增设房地产信贷部。

1993年，建行荔波县支行推行干部人事制度改革，对副股级以上中层干部实行聘任制，股级干部由县支行聘任，副行长以上干部由州中心支行聘任。

1996年3月，名称变更为中国建设银行荔波县支行，内设办公室、会计出纳股、业务股、支行储蓄专柜、迎宾储蓄所。2000年，内设机构改为科，设会计出纳科、业务科、保卫科、办公室。

2004年9月，中国建设银行荔波县支行改称中国建设银行股份有限公司荔波支行。

2008年，内设机构改革为营业室、客户部，实有人员15人。

（二）存贷业务

1.储蓄 1989年4月，建行荔波县支行开始办理现金业务，设储蓄专柜、迎宾储蓄所，办理各种个人储蓄业务，到12月，有储户217户。

1990年，开始运用点钞机，全行有点钞机3台。

1996年，对个人储蓄业务开办龙卡、生肖卡、理财卡、活期储蓄卡等，持卡人在全国各地设有建行服务机构的地方，均可支取现金。是年10月，建行荔波县支行系统开始运用计算机开展汇兑结算业务。

2004年5月，设置自动取款机，提供24小时服务，方便客户取款和个人账户查询。

2.贷款 1980年，国家将部分基建项目拨款改为贷款（简称“拨改贷”）之后，按照省、州安排，将部分基建拨款改为贷款，实行拨贷分开，除原属于县财政局管理的基建项目外，所有省属、州属单位基建项目投资均由县建行负责拨款和对建设资金进行监督管理，同时开办建筑施工企业的存、贷业务。对建筑企业流动资金贷款，按照“控制总量，调整结构，支持重点，扶优限劣，存贷并举，讲究效益”的原则发放。是年，完成计划项目基建拨款32万元、贷款102万元。自实行“拨改贷”后，建行荔波县支行发放贷款支持的重大项目有物资公司、烟草公司等企业的基建项目以及荔小公路（荔波至小七孔）、荔大公路（荔波至大沙坡）建设项目。

1999年9月，向荔波交通建设开发公司发放贷款800万元，改造小七孔油路。是年，开办个人住房贷款。

1993年10月—2001年3月，先后向黔南州大七孔水电开发公司总发放贷款8700万元，用于大七孔水电站建设。2003年11月，向荔波迎西开发有限公司发放贷款1500万元，建三力大酒店。

2004年，开办个人消费贷款业务，开始办理信用卡业务。

2007年8月，向荔波县国有资本营运公司发放贷款1100万元，用于土地储备项目。9月，向县鑫懋源房地产开发有限公司发放贷款2500万元。用于“樟江部落”项目建设。

2008年12月，向荔波风景名胜区贷款3300万元，用于县城路网改造项目建设。年末，建行荔波县支行有住房贷款户214户、个人消费贷款户265户欠贷，贷款余额8598万元，代发住房公积金贷款202户。

1980—2008年建行荔波县支行存贷情况统计表

表17－16 单位：万元

年度	存款余额	贷款余额	年度	存款余额	贷款余额
1980	—	102	1995	1035	1473
1981	—	78	1996	1346	4781
1982	—	120	1997	1580	5618
1983	—	65	1998	3508	5668
1984	—	8	1999	3771	8864
1985	—	9	2000	4705	9373
1986	—	4	2001	5663	10279
1987	—	14	2002	6854	10447
1988	—	35	2003	10306	1734
1989	59	41	2004	10894	2221
1990	126	59	2005	16509	3803
1991	194	33	2006	13153	4937
1992	365	195	2007	19575	7518
1993	522	1520	2008	26674	8598
1994	748	1237			

说明：1980—1992年的数据是专项基建项目贷款数；1993—2008年的数据为各项贷款余额。

（三）安全保卫

1989年，县建行设现金金库1个，配备手枪2支，用于支行的金库值班、守护、押运。先后制定完善各项安全防范制度，如重大突发事件、紧急处理预案，安全防范应急预案实施细则，水灾、火灾事故紧急处置预案等；组建义务消防队；每年同职工签订安全责任书。

2001年，实行现金守押社会化，撤销现金金库，委托县信用联社守库和现金押运。2005年8月，将手枪移交县公安局，另配置“97-1”式防爆枪2支。

三、农业银行

（一）机构

1979年10月，恢复中国农业银行荔波县支行，1980年4月正式开业，内设人秘股、会出股、农业资金管理股、信合股、企业拨款股，下设城关、甲良、朝阳、茂兰4个营业所。1981年7月，农业资金管理股更名为社队信贷股。1984年7月，成立计划信贷科。1985年1月，企业拨款股、社队信贷股分别更名为工商信贷股、农业信贷股。

1986年6—9月，先后成立资金组织股、支行储蓄专柜、支行办公室。1988年2—9月，先后成立企业管理办公室、审计稽核股、监察室、保卫股。1989年11月，成立思想政治工作办公室。1990年12月，成立纪检组和县人民检察院农行检察室（检察室受检察院和农行双重领导）。1991年1月，人事秘书股更名为人事教育股。1992年4月，撤销企业管理办公室，业务并入工商信贷股。是年12月，成立黔南州农业银行中心支行经济民警中队驻荔波县小分队。

1993年3月，农行荔波县支行机构改革，内设机构改为股级科（室），设人事秘书科、计划信贷科、财务会计科、监察稽核科、保卫科（下辖经济民警小分队）、电脑室，下设城关、甲良、朝阳、茂兰4个营业所和支行储蓄专柜。6月，成立县法院驻县农行经济庭金融审判法庭（受县法院和农行双重领导）。8月，建立综合档案室。1994年6月，恢复资金组织科。

1996年8月，内部机构重组，设办公室、计划财务部、资金组织部、监察稽核部，撤销县法院驻县农行经济庭金融审判法庭、保卫科、信合科，下设城关、甲良、朝阳、茂兰4个营业所和支行储蓄专柜。撤销保卫科下属经济民警小分队。9月，按国务院《关于农村金融体制改革的决定》，全县农村信用社与县农行脱钩。12月，撤销信合科。

1997年3月，增设立化储蓄所。1998年1月，将10个科（室）精简为计划财务部、资金组织部、信贷业务部、监察稽核部、保卫部、办公室；城关营业所改为玉屏储蓄所，迁址至玉屏镇市场路；立化储蓄所升格为立化营业所。

2001年5月，增设计算机中心。撤并立化、朝阳两个营业所。2003年，撤销信贷业务部，设置为业务发展部、风险资产经营部；撤销资金组织部、监察稽核部，设置监察保卫部；撤并甲良营业所和玉屏储蓄所。2008年年末，内设机构有计划财务部、风险资产经营部、业务发展部、监察保卫部、办公室，支行对外服务的营业机构有支行营业室、茂兰营业所，全行实有人员50人。

（二）存贷业务

1.存款 1980年4月，农行荔波县支行开办存款业务。存款业务主要有储蓄存款和对公存款两类。1995年9月，开通金穗卡业务，由支行储蓄专柜负责办理。

1980—2008年农行荔波县支行存款统计表

表17－17　　单位：万元

年度	年末存款余额	其 中	
		储蓄存款	对公存款
1980	105	32	73
1981	145	41	104
1982	192	53	139
1983	301	61	240
1984	423	72	351
1985	552	82	470
1986	649	113	536
1987	925	198	727
1988	1072	210	862
1989	1411	302	1109
1990	1648	357	1291
1991	2496	579	1917
1992	2886	763	2123
1993	3654	1053	2601
1994	2767	1396	1371
1995	3531	1816	1715
1996	5144	2318	2826
1997	6133	3277	2856
1998	7669	4569	3100
1999	10253	5861	4392
2000	11797	6598	5199
2001	13597	7798	5799
2002	15620	8680	6940
2003	17888	9612	8276
2004	19696	10544	9152
2005	21638	11267	10371
2006	30487	11304	19183
2007	25322	12874	12448
2008	30608	15310	15298

2.贷款 农行荔波县支行除发放国家政策性农业贷款外，对县内经济建设重大项目给予借贷支持，发放部分开发性项目贷款。1983年，试办开发性贷款，到1988年，累计发放34万元，投向荒山开发等各种耕地及生长周期在5年以上的林业、畜牧业、渔业等项目。1987年、1988年，分别发放贷款305万元、330万元，支持各乡（镇）农户购买生产资料、种子、树苗等。1986—1988年，向小七孔电站电力开发项目发放贷款340万元。1989年，发放县内营建造林基地、爆竹生产等项目借款50万元；巴合、水条、水庆3个骨干煤井生产建设，水庆煤井总借款184万元。1990年，向边远山区农户和县外贸公司改进桐油加工技术等发放借款394万元。1991年，向佳荣乡农贸市场建设发放借款51万元。1999—2001年，向大七孔电站建设项目发放借款3500万元。2002年，向黑山羊基地建设项目发放借款210万元，总购进黑山羊6700头；向温饱工程发放专项借款50万元，每年由粮食部门承借承还滚动流转，每年购进杂交水稻、玉米优良品种。2003年，向荔波民族中学发放贷款210万元，向黔南朝阳发电有限公司发放贷款5400万元。

2007年，根据农业银行总行《服务“三农”总体实施方案》《关于深化和扩大服务“三农”试点工作的意见》，农行荔波县支行拓展粮食主产区工程、农村基建民生工程、灾后重建项目和农业产业化龙头企业等融资项目，推出农户个人生产经营贷款、惠农信用卡等产品。同时，“三农”信贷重点支持农户、农村微型企业及个体户和小企业发展。是年11月，农行荔波县支行成为黔南州唯一获得贵州省分行确定开办乡村旅游小额信贷业务试点县，办理乡村旅游小额信贷业务22笔，金额总计106万元。

1980—2008年农行荔波县支行发放贷款统计表

表17－18 单位：万元

年度	发放贷款	收回贷款	贷款年末余额
1980	125.96	107.63	227.31
1981	133.00	17.00	343.30
1982	93.00	40.52	395.78
1983	100.00	114.33	381.45
1984	110.00	67.43	424.02
1985	175.63	168.03	431.62
1986	465.56	140.30	756.88
1987	641.19	308.32	845.72
1988	733.26	510.60	1068.38
1989	592.45	412.27	1228.56
1990	906.90	727.05	1365.41
1991	322.00	507.41	1102.00
1992	483.00	257.00	1328.00
1993	892.00	635.00	1585.00
1994	1356.00	1604.00	1337.00
1995	1067.00	865.00	1539.00
1996	2526.00	2181.00	1884.00
1997	2470.00	1150.00	3204.00

续表17－18

年度	发放贷款	收回贷款	贷款年末余额
1998	1477.00	1618.00	3063.00
1999	509.00	431.00	3141.00
2000	1121.40	213.00	4049.40
2001	3349.00	29.00	7369.40
2002	3793.40	299.00	9505.80
2003	3093.00	1136.80	11462.00
2004	2500.00	3057.93	10904.07
2005	1900.00	1268.14	11535.93
2006	411.00	833.62	11113.31
2007	737.40	2808.11	9042.60
2008	101.75	2932.20	6212.15

（三）代理业务

农行荔波县支行为太平洋保险公司代理太平盛世长寿养老保险、学有所成两全保险、家庭人身意外伤害保险，为新华保险公司代理养老金保险，为平安保险公司代理万能寿险，为中保、太保、平安保险公司代理财险业务。

四、工商银行

（一）机构

1986年8月，从人行荔波县支行分业成立工商银行荔波县支行，下设向阳路储蓄所，内设人秘股、计信股、会计股、出纳股、储蓄股。1992—1995年，将会计股、出纳股合并为会出股。1996年，增设西门储蓄所。1996—1997年，内设机构改革精简为办公室、业务部、营业部，将向阳路储蓄所、西门储蓄所合并成为樟江中路储蓄所。全行有职工34人。1998—1999年，将樟江中路储蓄所分设为西门储蓄所、向阳路储蓄所。2000—2001年，撤销向阳路储蓄所，其业务并入支行专柜。2002年，设办公室、营业部，将西门储蓄所迁到樟江中路并更名樟江中路分理处。到2008年，机构设置不变，实有人员23人。

（二）存贷业务

1.存款　工行荔波县支行存款业务主要有城镇储蓄、企业存款两类。

城镇储蓄存款业务采取增加储蓄种类、储蓄部门分片包干等措施组织存款，建立储蓄业务事后监督岗，避免各种差错发生。从1996年开始，全行储蓄窗口全面运用计算机操作处理各项业务。2000年4月1日起，按国务院《个人存款账户实名制规定》，严格执行实名制存款制度。是年，储蓄业务开办“牡丹卡”“灵通卡”，工行全国联通。企业存款业务由计划信贷部门负责办理，每年召开银企座谈会，促进企业存款余额逐年增长。

2.贷款　1993年前，工行荔波县支行贷款种类有工商企业流动资金贷款、集体工业设备贷款、小额设备贷款等，发放贷款对象为独立核算的工商企业、个体工商户。

1994年起，按中国人民银行下发的《信贷资金管理暂行办法》《对商业银行实行资产负债比例管理的通知》发放贷款。1996年6月，中国人民银行总行颁发《贷款通则》后，工行荔波县支行严格按照《贷款通则》办理贷款业务。

1998年后，按"区别对待、择优扶植"原则和国家的产业政策发放贷款，以企业的经济效益情况和产品发展前景确立贷款投向和数量。是年9月，开始办理个人住房贷款。

2000年后，贷款对象优先支持交通、能源、煤炭、电力、城建等行业，优先支持效益好的国有企业和出口创汇企业，支持商品销售快、效益好、产品适销对路企业。同时，信贷部门深入企业调查，了解企业经营的购、销、存以及盈、亏等情况，将企业划分为一级三等（3A、2A、1A）、二级三等（3B、2B、1B），区别对待，掌握贷款。1998—2002年，全行5年实现利润总额535万元，5年减亏损12万元，实际盈利523万元，平均每年盈余104万元。

2001年6月，开始办理个人消费贷款。

2003年，向黔南天力房地产开发有限公司"荔波金锣湾购物广场"项目发放贷款1200万元。2004年，向贵州省荔波旅游发展有限责任公司投入贷款290万元，用于宣传促销荔波县旅游业；向贵州明德实业有限责任公司投入贷款1200万元，用于修建二环西路、时来安置区、苗圃开发区和政务中心（按照县人大、县政府会议的决定，从县财政每月拿出30万元人民币存入工行荔波县支行，用于归还贵州明德实业有限责任公司的工程欠款约1200万元，直至还清为止）；向荔波县民族中学投放贷款110万元，用于校园扩建。

2005年，剥离不良资产3671万元。其中，县交通建设开发公司"荔大"公路贷款3487万元；县百货公司流动资金贷款86万元；县水泥厂流动资金贷款41万元；县医药公司流动资金贷款18万元；县乡企公司流动资金贷款12万元；县食品公司流动资金贷款10万元；私营业主梁开庆流动资金贷款20万元。

至2008年年末，个人住房贷款共办理1495笔，金额8811.25万元（包括还清的贷款户）；个人消费贷款共办理611笔，金额407.67万元（包括还清的贷款户）。各项贷款余额6033.74万元，比年初6471.25万元减少437.51万元。其中，企业贷款余额150万元；个人贷款1129笔，余额5883.74万元，个人贷款余额比年初6471.25万元减少587.5万元。

1986—2008年工行荔波县支行存款、贷款年末余额一览表

表17－19　　单位：万元

年度	存款	贷款	年度	存款	贷款
1986	352	251	1998	2281	4765
1987	556	357	1999	2283	4982
1988	697	478	2000	3354	6023
1989	768	539	2001	3803	5918
1990	865	567	2002	4790	6052
1991	980	659	2003	7167	8341
1992	1090	653	2004	9323	10321
1993	1659	693	2005	7827	5385
1994	2365	670	2006	10027	5419
1995	3148	812	2007	11910	6471
1996	3609	1409	2008	13657	6034
1997	4673	3402			

（三）新兴业务

1998年后，先后开办个人网上银行、企业网上银行、企业电话银行、个人电话银行、个人手机银行，代理业务有基金销售、保险销售等。

2008年，全年新增个人网上银行客户1630户、企业网上银行客户14户、个人电话银行客户964户、企业电话银行客户7户、个人手机银行客户215户，销售U盾280户，发行信用卡208张、灵通卡3007张，办理POS机商户6户、个人理财产品1860万元、对公理财新产品105万元，基金销售1620万元，代理人寿保险72万元、财产保险2.91万元。

（四）安全保卫

工行荔波县支行自建立起，安全保卫重点是值守业务库、各营业网点和早、晚护送现钞到储蓄所，同时保护工作人员人身安全及全行财产安全。保卫工作中，不断建立和完善全行安全保卫制度，进行防范设施改造，对保卫人员武器、弹药、保养、执勤是否到位进行不定期检查，对营业部执勤实行24小时监控，防范案件发生。到2008年，安全、案防、内控的案件控制20年无案件发生。

五、邮政储蓄银行

1987年，县邮电局开办邮政储蓄，相继建立县局邮政储蓄所、茂兰邮政储蓄所、立化邮政储蓄所、平寨邮政储蓄所、更班邮政储蓄所。至1998年年末，储蓄余额1997万元。是年收汇2000万元，兑付1200万元。

1999年8月，县邮政储蓄与全国联网，通存通取。2001年，率先在县内各金融机构中开通自动柜员机（ATM）取款业务。

2004年9月，将更班邮政储蓄网点调整至甲良镇。2005年4月，将平寨邮政储蓄网点调整到茂兰镇。是年，全县邮政储蓄余额7356万元。2006年，储蓄余额突破亿元，受省、州邮政局表彰。

2007年7月，县内邮政储蓄机构开办小额存单质押贷款业务，结束邮政储蓄只存不贷的历史。

2008年7月，进行邮政储蓄机构改革，全县3个邮政储蓄网点改为邮政储蓄银行二级支行，分别为樟江东路支行、甲良支行、立化支行，二级支行受中国邮政储蓄银行黔南州分行及荔波县邮政局双重领导。

1987—2008年全县邮政储蓄年末余额统计表

表17－20　　单位：万元

年度	储蓄余额	年度	储蓄余额
1987	9.01	1998	1997.00
1988	27.60	1999	2292.00
1989	36.00	2000	2543.00
1990	79.20	2001	2919.00
1991	227.00	2002	3456.00
1992	251.00	2003	3995.00
1993	753.00	2004	4592.00
1994	902.00	2005	7356.00
1995	1138.00	2006	11245.00
1996	1795.00	2007	15867.00
1997	1852.00	2008	19588.00

第二节　农村信用合作社

一、机构网点

1978年，在原有农村信用合作社中，将茂兰信用社与瑶庆信用社合并为茂兰信用社。年末，全县有农村信用社24个。

1985年6月，玉屏信用社与时来信用社合并为玉屏信用社。9月，建立茂兰信用社立化分社。

1986年7月，农行荔波县支行在玉屏镇开展信用合作社体制改革试点，将各乡信用社组建成一个中心社，实行统一核算，分级经营。试点完成后，于1987年全面推开，在区所在地分别建立玉屏、朝阳、甲良、茂兰4个中心社。玉屏中心社辖玉屏、水尧、水利、永康4个社，朝阳中心社辖朝阳、王蒙、瑶山、驾欧、捞村、翁昂6个社，甲良中心社辖甲良、甲站、阳凤、方村、播尧、觉巩、地莪7个社，茂兰中心社辖茂兰、洞塘、立化、佳荣、水维、岜鲜6个社。

1992年，农行荔波县支行将23个信用社撤并建为15个（不含中心社），即保留玉屏、水尧、永康、水利、朝阳、瑶山、翁昂、捞村、驾欧、甲良、方村、播尧、茂兰、洞塘、佳荣信用社，撤销甲站、阳凤、地莪、觉巩、王蒙、水维、岜鲜信用社，新建立化信用社。

1995年，建立县信用合作社联合社。撤销觉巩信用社并入播尧信用社。至年底，全县有玉屏、水尧、水利、永康、朝阳、瑶山、驾欧、捞村、翁昂、甲良、方村、播尧、茂兰、佳荣、立化、洞塘及县联社等法人机构17个，有联社营业部、地莪、阳凤、甲站4个非法人机构。

1999年6月，撤销茂兰中心社，分设茂兰、立化、佳荣3个独立法人社；洞塘信用社并入茂兰信用社，统一法人，降格为分社；撤销朝阳、甲良、玉屏3个中心社，其辖区各信用社改为独立法人社。至此，全县有法人社9个、非法人社13个，共22个信用社机构网点。

2000年4月，经人行荔波县支行批复，县联社在朝阳、瑶山、甲良、茂兰、佳荣、立化信用社和联社营业部建立国库经收处。6月，永康、水尧信用社并入玉屏信用社，更名荔波县玉屏信用社永康分社和荔波县玉屏信用社水尧分社；翁昂信用社并入朝阳信用社，更名荔波县朝阳信用社翁昂分社；洞塘信用社并入茂兰信用社，更名荔波县茂兰信用社洞塘分社；驾欧信用社并入瑶山信用社，更名荔波县瑶山信用社驾欧分社。

2001年7月，朝阳信用社翁昂分社更名为玉屏信用社翁昂分社；荔波县联社桥头分社由桥头迁至力达市场营业，更名荔波县联社力达分社。

2003年4月，玉屏信用社翁昂分社变更为朝阳信用社翁昂分社。6月，玉屏信用社大坪分社由原址迁到玉屏市场路50号，更名玉屏信用社农贸市场分社。

2005年4月，县联社迁址荔波县樟江园广场西侧综合大楼办公营业。7月，甲良农村信用社甲站分社迁址玉屏镇向阳中路4号，更名荔波县玉屏镇农村信用社十字街分社。

至2008年年末，全县信用社有职工120人，其中，获专业技术职称29人（经济师2人、助理经济师1人、助理会计师1人、经济员8人、会计员17人）。

二、管理体制

1978—1979年，农村信用社属人行荔波县支行管理。1980年，划归县农行管理。

1983年，恢复农村信用社股金分红付息制度，同时建立健全经营责任制，严格执行信用社的资金不准抽调，信用社的存贷款利率不能倒挂，贷款利率可以浮动等制度。

1984年，根据国务院批转《中国农业银行关于改革信用合作社管理体制的报告》，农行对全县荔波县支行信用社进行改革，恢复和加强信用合作社的“三性”（组织上的群众性、管理上的民主性、经营上的灵活性），实行自主经营、独立核算、自负盈亏。

1990年4月，推行中心社主任风险经营承包责任制，信用社的信贷计划、人员安排、财务收支、贷款审批等由中心社主任统筹安排。

1995年4月，县联社成立后，确定县联社的独立法人地位，统一管理全县信用社。

根据国务院《关于农村金融体制改革的决定》，1997年1月1日起，全县农村信用社与县农行脱离行政隶属关系，信用社的业务管理由县联社负责，金融监管由县人行负责。5月，县人行统一组织县联社机构网点申报金融许可证年检，玉屏、方村、播尧、阳凤、水尧、水利、永康、翁昂、捞村、瑶山、驾欧11个信用社年检合格。

1999年11月，按人行黔南中支《关于转发〈县级联社“三定”和信用社定员方案〉的通知》，人行荔波县支行对信用社实行等级制管理。

2003年12月，全县信用社从人行荔波县支行划归银监会黔南监管分局荔波监管组监管，直至2008年。

三、存贷业务

（一）存款

1978年后，各信用社逐步增加储蓄存款种类，组织各类存款，发展存款业务，年末存款余额逐年递增。

2003年，进行电子化建设，柜台业务使用计算机办理。8月8日，县联社营业网作为全省第三批开通储蓄通存通兑业务单位，与全省联网通存通兑。

2008年，全县信用社与全国信用合作社系统联网通存通兑并进行跨行电子汇兑。年末，全县21个网点平均存款余额1993万元。

（二）贷款

1978年后，全县农村信用社发放贷款，以承包户、专业户（重点户）为主，以农业生产为主和以流动资金为主，在保证农业贷款需要前提下，发放农村工商信贷。

1985年，信用社贷款实行期限管理，坚持贷款的期限性、偿还性，及时收回到逾期贷款，加速资金周转。是年发放贷款77万元，收回76万元。

1987年，建立贷款责任制，实行“包放、包收、包效益”管理，避免盲目贷款。

1995年，建立自有资金补充制度，在支持“三农”粮、棉、油、种、养、加农村经济发展的同时，走多业发展道路，扩大工商业、消费等领域贷款。

2000年，不良贷款余额2317.89万元，不良率72%。

2008年，开发“凤还巢”农民工创业贷款、“乡村游”旅游服务贷款、“居安乐”公务员消费贷款、“领头雁”大学生村干部创业贷款、“宅易贷”农民房产抵押贷款等十余项信贷产品，为“三农”、城乡居民、企业提供方便、快捷、灵活的金融服务。年末，不良贷款余额659.01万元，不良贷款率3%，8年减压不良贷款1658.8万元，年均下降207.4万元。

2001—2008年，全县信用社依法放贷、依法收贷，信贷业务快速增长。至2008年年末，发放各项贷款累计10363.3万元，余额26045.48万元，较1995年贷款余额1546万元增加24499.48万元。

1978—2008年全县农村信用社存款、贷款统计表

表17－21 单位：万元

年度	存款余额			贷款余额	
	合计	储蓄	对公存款	合计	其中农户贷款
1978	116.02	22.42	93.60	34.56	—
1979	134.26	29.00	105.26	45.99	—
1980	144.04	37.54	106.50	59.75	—
1981	142.63	55.70	86.93	57.78	—
1982	177.57	77.80	99.77	79.81	—
1983	197.88	85.73	112.15	146.32	—
1984	198.40	111.32	87.08	160.00	—
1985	220.38	150.36	70.02	160.99	—
1986	289.05	194.74	94.31	212.96	—
1987	411.23	279.74	131.49	332.50	—
1988	468.25	360.13	108.12	330.34	—
1989	420.51	243.97	176.54	314.49	—
1990	558.76	324.82	182.41	379.62	—
1991	860.11	470.33	389.78	444.53	—
1992	1322.56	989.82	332.74	545.44	—
1993	1742.82	1545.36	197.46	749.30	—
1994	2309.40	2038.20	271.20	1054.30	—
1995	2643.88	2272.15	371.73	1090.20	—
1996	3393.00	2859.30	533.70	1236.30	—
1997	3360.50	3032.20	328.30	1436.30	—
1998	3858.20	3434.10	424.10	2760.50	—
1999	4000.90	3422.00	578.90	2840.01	—
2000	4293.86	3963.06	330.80	3186.55	2606.53
2001	5103.59	4783.10	320.49	3575.01	2908.42
2002	6358.53	6019.00	339.53	7031.11	5143.08
2003	8491.21	8293.13	198.08	8164.05	5545.24
2004	12885.37	11809.16	1076.21	10836.11	6990.64
2005	18065.01	15632.64	2432.38	14982.86	8113.19
2006	24963.23	20951.52	4011.71	21163.35	10090.98
2007	30972.98	24856.31	6116.67	22557.86	10403.00
2008	41852.97	31176.67	10676.30	26045.48	17704.00

四、社员代表大会

1983年，县内各信用社分别召开第二届社员代表大会，建立理事会、监事会。

1995年4月，荔波县农村信用社联合社召开第一届社员代表大会，参加大会社员代表65人。大会通过《荔波县农村信用合作社章程》，选举产生理事会、监事会，选出理事9人、监事5人。大会宣布荔波县农村信用合作社联合社正式成立。

1998年7月，县联社召开第二届社员代表大会，民主选举产生第二届理事会、监事会，第二届理事会由11人组成，监事会由5人组成。

2004年10月18日，贵州银监局批复黔南银监分局，同意筹建荔波县农村信用合作社联合社统一法人治理首届社员代表会。11月9日，召开荔波县农村信用合作联社创立大会暨首届法人治理社员代表大会，出席大会社员代表53人。大会选举产生荔波县联社首届法人理事会、监事会，理事会由9人组成，监事会由5人组成。

第三节　金融监管

一、监管机构

1978—2003年，县内金融机构由县人行监督管理。

2003年12月，在县人行组建中国银行业监督管理委员会黔南监管分局荔波监管组，人员3人。2004年3月，改为银监会黔南监管分局荔波监管办事处，为正科级单位，编制3人，直至2008年。

二、监督管理

（一）银行业金融机构监管

在县人行监管时期，建立银行和非银行金融机构监管、货币发行、货币与利率、会计结算、账户管理等责任岗位，按照权限规定，对县内金融机构设置、撤并进行审批，重点对银行和非银行分支机构市场准入、退出和主要变更事项进行审查，提出审查意见并报州级人行审批。

1997年，县人行为全县36个金融、非金融机构换发“经营金融业务许可证”，换证率100%。

2004年1月，荔波银监办按照监管业务范围，对辖内银行业金融机构业务市场准入、机构准入进行监管。

到2008年年底，除县人行、荔波银监办2个管理机构外，经银监部门审批、核发“中华人民共和国金融许可证”的银行业金融机构33个，从业人员共243人。其中，工行机构1个，自动柜员机1台，人员14人；农行机构2个，自动柜员机2台，人员50人；建行机构1个，自动柜员机1台，人员17人；农村信用社机构22个，无自动柜员机，人员123人；邮政储蓄机构7个（业务由县邮政局代管），自动柜员机1台，人员35人；邮政储蓄银行二级支行3个，人员4人，其存款业务委托当地邮政储蓄机构代理，信贷业务自行开展。在全县17个乡（镇）中，除水利乡、瑶麓乡外，其他15个乡（镇）均设银行业金融机构网点。

（二）高级管理人员监管

2003年前，由县人行对高管人员任职资格进行审查，提出审查意见；对在任高管人员进行定期考核。

2004年后，荔波银监办根据《银行业金融机构高级管理人员监督管理暂行办法》，对辖内银行业金融机构高级管理人员任职资格进行初审并上报黔南银监分局，定期开展对高级管理人员的授权谈话工作。

2004—2008年，经黔南银监分局授权，荔波银监办对辖内银行业金融机构高管人员进行任前谈话32人，其中，工行3人、农行8人、建行3人、邮政储蓄银行3人、农村信用社15人。初审上报符合高管人员任职资格条件人员15人，其中，农行荔波支行1人、荔波农村信用社14人。

2008年年末，全县银行业金融机构符合审核制高级管理人员15人（工行1人、农行1人、建行1人、农村信用社12人）；符合备案制的高级管理人员共10人（工行1人、农行2人、建行1人、农村信用社3人、邮政储蓄银行3人）。

（三）现场检查和非现场监管

1978—2003年，由县人行对辖内金融机构业务活动进行现场检查和非现场监管。2004年后，由荔波银监办开展现场检查和非现场监管工作。

荔波银监办根据《中华人民共和国银行业监督管理法》的规定，经黔南银监分局授权，对辖内银行业金融机构业务开展现场检查。现场检查人员到被检查单位检查时，出示合法有效证件和授权检查通知书，检查结束时将“廉政回访卡”交被检查单位填写后直接邮寄黔南银监分局纪委，以监督现场检查人员是否存在违规违纪行为。

2004—2008年，通过非现场监督管理信息系统分析，由黔南银监分局授权荔波银监办自行开展或荔波银监办配合黔南银监分局开展的现场检查共23次。其中，对工行荔波县支行3次、农行荔波县支行7次、建行荔波县支行4次、农村信用社6次、邮政储蓄1次、农发行三都支行1次、农发行三都支行驻荔波信贷组1次。

非现场监管工作主要是按旬、月、季、年度，对农村信用社上报的报表进行审核、整理、分析、汇总、上报，并从中发现问题，督促整改，同时为是否开展相关专项现场检查提供依据。

2004—2008年现场检查项目一览表

表17－22

年度	现场检查项目	被检查单位	备注
2004	信贷资金流向钢铁、电解铝、水泥行业项目	县工行荔波县支行 农行荔波县支行	
	农业贷款、消费贷款、扶贫贷款项目和商业汇票业务	农行荔波县支行	
	商业汇票业务	建行荔波县支行	
	信贷、会计、计算机内控制度和所有10个法人社增资扩股合规性及贷款真实性	信用社	
2005	贷款分类偏离度、个人消费贷款	工行荔波县支行	
	贷款分类偏离度、个人消费贷款和商业汇票业务后续跟踪	农行荔波县支行	
	商业汇票业务后续跟踪	建行荔波县支行	
	信贷管理、贷款风险五级分类	农发行三都支行驻荔波信贷组	
	序时性	信用社	
2006	贷款分类偏离度后续跟踪	工行荔波县支行 农行荔波县支行	
	贷款分类偏离度	建行荔波县支行	
2007	商业性贷款检查	农发行三都支行	与三都银监办联合检查
	邮政储蓄的业务操作风险	邮政储蓄机构	
	贷款五级分类偏离度	农村信用社	
	安全防范设施达标进行检查	全辖银行业金融机构网点	与县公安局联合检查

续表17－22

年度	现场检查项目	被检查单位	备注
2008	销售农行汇理行业成长基金	农行荔波县支行	
	鑫懋源房地产开发有限公司2500万元贷款	建行荔波县支行	
	个人消费贷款、利润及拨备、案件防范进行检查	农村信用社	配合黔南银监分局检查

（四）专项检查

2005年，按照黔南银监分局的部署，在辖内银行业金融机构开展治理商业贿赂和案件防范专项治理。通过自查自纠，没有发现商业贿赂和金融案件。

荔波银监办每年督促、指导银行业金融机构按季召开案防工作分析会，在元旦、春节、“五一”、国庆等重要节假日进行专项安全检查，按季对银行业金融机构开展案防督查，重点检查案件防范和控制工作存在的问题。

2004—2008年，开展辖内银行业金融机构各类现场专项检查24次，发现问题66个。其中，工行5个、农行9个、建行9个、邮政储蓄10个、农村信用社33个。对检查项目写出专项检查报告，上报黔南银监分局，荔波银监办负责督促落实整改。5年间，辖内银行业金融机构未发生违法案件。

第四节　保险业

1980年下半年，恢复县保险代办处，开办企业财产保险、机动车辆及第三责任保险等险种。到1985年，累计保费10.7万元。1985年年底，筹建中国人民保险公司荔波县支公司，1986年1月开业，开办企业财产保险、机动车辆损失保险、机动车辆第三责任保险、货物运输保险、驾驶员及旅客座位保险、家庭财产保险、农村房屋保险、团体人身意外伤害保险、团体人身保险、子女婚嫁保险等险种。到1988年，保费收入62.7万元。1989年增至84.3万元，投保的国家、集体、个人的财产保额5546.3万元。1990年，开办有17个险种，服务范围由县城发展到农村，参加保险人数不断增加，保费收入增长到100.2万元。1995年，保费收入增长到431万元。

1996年，县保险公司进行机构改革，财险、寿险分业经营，分为中保人寿保险有限公司荔波县支公司和中国人民财产保险荔波县营业部。

一、人寿保险

（一）机构

1996年，成立人寿保险公司，内设营业部、业务股、财务股及茂兰保险服务所。1999年，更名为中国人寿保险公司荔波县分公司，2003年公司重组改制，更名为中国人寿保险股份有限公司荔波县支公司，内设团体业务部、银行保险部、营销部、客户服务中心、综合部及茂兰营销服务部。到2008年，内设机构不变，实有人员55人。

（二）保险销售

1980年，恢复保险业务，开办的人寿保险险种有团体人身意外伤害保险、团体人身保险、子女婚嫁保险等。1988年，广西红茂矿务局为更班、平寨、打油寨3个煤矿及医院、车队等总计3300人每人办理简易人身保险2份，为井下工人1600人办理保额1000元的团体意外伤害保险。至1989年，全县参加简易人身保险20137份。1990年，参加各种人身保险21906人。

1996年后，县人寿保险公司开展的险种有人身意外险、团体人身保险、养老保险、子女婚嫁教育保险、重大疾病保险、分红保险等。1998年，推出66鸿运、88鸿利、99鸿福、康宁定期、康宁终身等41种人寿保险产品。

从2003年起，县人寿保险公司先后与县工行、建行、农行、邮政储蓄、信用联社等金融机构合作，陆续开通“银保通”柜面销售系统，拓宽销售渠道。是年，为行政事业单位职工医疗保险配套推出职工补充医疗保险。2005年，全县煤炭行业进行统保，团险业务保费收入从1996年67万元增长到2008年731万元。

至2008年年末，个人保险销售业务从1996年的98万元增长到410万元；银保销售业务从2004年的30万元发展到318万元；团体保险销售业务从1998年的74万元增长到731万元。

1996—2008年人寿保险保费收入统计表

表17－23 单位：万元

年度	保费收入总计	其中			
		寿险	意外险	健康险	养老金险
1996	165.00	98.00	53.00	14.00	—
1997	247.60	166.00	63.00	18.60	—
1998	277.27	200.53	74.02	—	2.72
1999	314.94	227.29	87.65	—	—
2000	415.75	346.70	69.05	—	—
2001	286.06	175.60	98.57	3.89	8
2002	316.34	245.58	66.78	3.98	—
2003	358.07	236.49	82.61	38.97	—
2004	442.60	286.76	100.25	55.59	—
2005	625.90	341.69	176.44	107.77	—
2006	1062.28	448.87	334.30	279.11	—
2007	1140.81	490.35	468.61	181.85	—
2008	1450.00	718.48	529.42	202.10	—

（三）案件理赔

理赔工作坚持“主动、迅速、准确、合理”的理赔方针，以事实为依据，以条款为准绳，不惜赔、不乱赔，为客户提供优质、高效的服务，1996—2008年，发案累计5358件，给付保险金累计2310.11万元。

1996—2008年人身保险理赔统计表

表17-24

年度	理赔案件总数（件）	理赔金额合计（万元）	其 中	
			死亡、伤害给付金额（万元）	医疗给付金额（万元）
1996	412	47.10	25.00	22.10
1997	372	42.70	28.50	14.20
1998	371	41.49	41.49	—
1999	408	65.72	65.72	—
2000	625	102.75	97.07	5.68
2001	573	79.65	78.20	1.45
2002	498	104.44	103.86	0.58
2003	386	54.84	53.86	0.98
2004	412	97.39	97.39	—
2005	334	176.71	174.76	1.95
2006	327	287.91	287.91	—
2007	351	827.15	827.15	—
2008	289	382.26	382.26	—

二、财产保险

（一）机构

1996年6月，建立中国人民财产保险荔波县营业部。1998年，中国人民财产保险荔波县营业部更名中国人民财产保险股份有限公司荔波支公司，内设经理室、营销部、财务部、非车险部、理赔部、办公室6个部门，有工作人员7人。2008年年末，实有工作人员13人。

（二）保险销售

1980年，开办财产保险、机动车辆及第三责任保险。是年，县民政局拨出2.1万元，为全县烈属、复退军人及贫困户办理农房保险。至1985年，财产保险保费收入累计10.7万元（其中1985年5.1万元），投保的财产保额总计980万元。之后，开办的财产险种有企业财产保险、机动车辆损失保险、机动车辆第三责任保险、货物运输保险、驾驶员及游客座位保险、家庭财产保险、农村房屋保险。1987年，县民政局再次拨出2.07万元，为烈属、复退军人及贫困户房屋投保。1988年，广西红茂矿务局为更班、平寨、打油寨3个煤矿及医院、车队办理1500万元的企业财产保险。全县投保的国家、集体和个人财产保额5546.3万元。1990年，水尧乡和瑶庆乡农房均投保。

1998年，财产保险业务承保险种达36个，涵盖企财、家财、货运、农房、机动车交强、机动车商业、农业、畜牧、森林、旅游、学平险、人身意外伤害等方面。

2006年，新增机动车辆交通强制险。2007年11月，开展县内国家政策性能繁母猪承保工作，17个乡（镇）及4个规模养殖场统一投保，共签保单21份，承保能繁母猪4954头，收取保费29.72万元。

（三）案件理赔

参加保险的企业和个人，在遭受自然灾害和意外损失后，县财保公司按照“主动、迅速、合理”的原则，及时勘查，确认定损，在责任范围内予以补偿。

1998—2008年保险费收入、理赔统计表

表17－25

年度	保费总收入（万元）	上缴税金（万元）	理赔案件数（件）	赔款支出（万元）	赔付率（%）
1998	185.64	15.59	348	102.28	55.10
1999	220.83	18.32	356	124.32	56.30
2000	256.68	21.56	399	137.05	53.39
2001	263.46	19.63	449	135.40	51.39
2002	243.47	15.42	515	130.77	53.71
2003	305.89	16.52	526	174.40	57.02
2004	352.53	19.09	604	256.43	72.70
2005	438.93	23.29	623	257.39	58.64
2006	462.74	25.22	785	262.93	53.39
2007	606.05	31.91	909	366.45	60.46
2008	697.82	37.21	1017	419.16	60.06

第十八篇
交通运输　邮政　通信

1978—2008年，荔波县交通运输、邮政、通信快速发展。至2008年，全县公路里程1168公里，全县17个乡（镇）实现乡乡通油路，72%的村通油路或水泥硬化道路。境内有省道312、省道206，全长共109.4公里。同时1989—2008年，修建25条矿山公路，总里程180公里，投资总计900万元。全县机动车运输已普及，至2008年，机动车完成货运量223万吨，货物周转量19200万吨公里。公路管理不断加强，桥梁建设力度不断加大。实现了公路交通、铁路交通、水路交通、航空交通立体化。2007年9月29日，贵州航空有限公司对荔波机场进行试飞，确定荔波机场可以投入使用。2008年8月1日，深圳航空公司开通深圳—荔波往返航班，由南方航空公司执飞，此后，又逐步开通贵阳至荔波、成都至荔波、上海至荔波、南宁至荔波等航班。

1978年以来，邮政、通信业在体制改革中发展。1998年10月，邮政与电信分业经营，2008年，县邮政局下设甲良、茂兰、立化、平寨、更班、朝阳、佳荣7个支局。1998年，全县有邮路21条，单程总长825公里。2008年，乡邮邮路取消步班和自行车班，全部改为摩托车班。在通信上荔波县实现了普及电话，2008年，全县电话用户到达数23243户。其中，城市固定电话用户到达数7329户，农村电话用户到达数7343户，同时移动电话、宽带网逐步走向普及。从2004年起，中国移动实施“村村通移动电话”工程，至2007年年底，建成覆盖全县17个乡（镇）、94个行政村、各主要旅游景点、交通干道的移动通信网络。2008年年末，联通荔波分公司建成2G基站共54个，实现联通GSM网络“乡乡通”，村通网络覆盖率达80%，覆盖全县17个乡（镇）和部分景区景点。

第一章 公路交通运输

第一节 公路建设

1978年以后，不断修建和改造县、乡、村公路，到1990年，境内有县、区、乡公路20条（含简易公路），总里程422.2公里，4区1镇25个乡76个村通公路，另有村组公路及矿山公路102条总里程429.5公里。1995年，通乡公路总里程741公里。至2008年，全县公路里程1168公里，全县17个乡（镇）实现乡乡通油路，72%的村通油路或水泥硬化道路。

一、省道

境内有省道312、省道206，全长共109.4公里。

荔波—独山公路（S312） 起于荔波县城，终至独山县城南黔桂公路分岔处，荔波县境路段长41公里，于1957年建成通车。1998贵州省公路局投资1亿元对独荔公路进行改造，改造技术标准为山岭重丘区二、三、四级沥青混凝土路面，路基宽7.5米，路面宽6.5米，工程于2001年竣工通车。

荔波—三都公路（S206） 起于荔波县城北，经尧排、水江进入三都县境，与三都至九阡公路衔接，荔波县境路段长20.8公里。1974年起动工修建至1980年秋，毛路打通，可勉强通车。同年冬，省以国家分配地方发展资金投资10万元，按四级路标准进行第一次改造，由于资金不足，质量很差，1982年3月，投资64.5万元进行第二次改造，设计标准为4.5米泥结碎石路面，1983年12月竣工通车；2003年，投资1840万元对三都经荔波县城至界牌（全长46公里）公路进行三、四级油路改建，工程2004年5月竣工。

荔波—麻尾公路（S206） 该公路连接2省（区）3县（独山、南丹、荔波），在荔波县境内长47.6公里，按国家标准四级路修建，总投资144万元，1990年全线建成通车。1999年，对荔波至小七孔段进行改造，按四级公路技术标准实施，路基宽6.5米，路面宽5.5米，为沥青混凝土路面，工程于2000年12月竣工使用；2001年，投资1800万元对小七孔至麻尾段进行改造，按四级公路技术标准实施，路基宽6.5米，路面宽5.5米，为沥青混凝土路面，工程于2003年12月通过验收，交付使用。荔波经小七孔至麻尾路段改造后，成为县城至小七孔景区并连接至独山麻尾的交通要道。

二、县道

县境通往省内外邻县的公路干线有荔波—金城江、荔波—南丹、茂兰—佳荣—驯乐、甲良—麻尾公路、玉屏—播尧公路、尧棒—恒丰公路。

荔波—金城江公路 起于荔波县城，向东经水尧、茂兰、立化，延伸至环江及金城江等地，于1964年建成通车。这是荔波第一条出省公路干线。从1996年起，投资1500万元对荔波—大沙坡公路的县城至立化（全长37公里）路段进行改造，按山岭重丘三级公路标准修建，路面为砼路面，1998年全线改造完成；2004年2月，投资1076万元对荔波—大沙坡公路二期工程的立化至大沙坡（全长22.3公里）路段进行改造，按山岭重丘三级公路改建，为沥青表处路面，于2005年年底竣工投入使用。

荔波—南丹公路 从荔波县城起，经朝阳、王蒙、瑶山至广西南丹，是荔波第二条省际公路，全长82.5公里，1987年建成通车。2005—2006年，广西投资对南丹里湖至王蒙乡交界路段进行改造，荔波投资对王蒙至广西里湖乡交界地6.28公里路段进行改造，均按四级公路标准修建，为沥青表处路面。

茂兰—佳荣—驯乐公路 该公路在荔波县境内全长39公里，1990年建成。是荔波县通往广西的第三条公路，茂兰至佳荣段于2007年实施通乡油路改造，按四级公路技术标准实施，路基宽6.5米，路面宽5.5米，为沥青混凝土路面。佳荣至驯乐（何家寨）于2013年进行油路改造，按三级公路技术标准实施，路基宽7.5米，路面宽6.5米，为沥青混凝土路面。

甲良—麻尾公路 全长50公里，1959年建成通车。2001年5月，对该路段进行公路镶边改造建设，2001年10月竣工。2004年，投资708万元对该路段进行油路改建工程，按山岭重丘四级公路建设，工程于2005年6月完工投入使用。

玉屏—播尧公路 全长28.7公里，总投资421.24万元，1999年动工修建，按山岭重丘区四级公路建设，路基宽6.5米，路面宽5.5米，泥结碎石路面。2003年9月通过验收，交付使用。

尧棒—恒丰公路 荔波境内5公里，于2002年动工建设，同年竣工，按四级公路技术标准实施，路基宽6.5米，路面宽5.5米，泥结碎石路面。

三、乡道

1978年，县城至各区全部通公路。玉屏区有县城—永康公路；朝阳区有朝阳—驾欧公路；甲良区有甲良—阳凤、甲良—地莪拉强、播尧—觉巩、甲良—甲站公路；茂兰区有茂兰—立化、茂兰—佳荣、茂兰—洞塘、佳荣—水维、佳荣—岜鲜公路。1995—2000年，修建通往邻县的乡村公路有阳凤乡—独山麦寨、捞村乡巴公—南丹木伦公路。此后，不断加大公路建设投入，至2008年，县城至各乡（镇）全部通公路。全县有通乡公路67条，总里程787公里。

茂兰—佳荣公路 全长27公里，总投资51万元。1966年12月动工修建9.5公里至瑶麓，1971年12月动工修建瑶麓至拉滩段11公里，1977年由拉滩修至佳荣，当年12月竣工，全线通车；1986年10月至1987年10月，投资9万元修筑瑶麓至拉滩段铜鼓坳隧道，全长96米，高6米，宽5米；2007年，投资2000万元对茂兰至佳荣路段进行通乡油路改造。

朝阳—翁昂公路 全长30公里，1976年11月以民族机动金投资修建，1982年建成通车。

王蒙—捞村公路 全长25公里，1976年11月投资15万元开工修建，1982年9月竣工通车。1997年4月，投资68万元进行瑶山至捞村路段进行改造，1999年完成改造工程，交付使用。2007年改造为沥青路。

荔波—永康公路 全长12公里，1991—1995年修建，总投资84万元，按山岭重丘四级公路标准建设。1994年12月竣工，交付使用。于2003年扩宽为7.5米砂石路，2006年改造为沥青路。

阳凤——独山墨寨公路 是接通独山县境的县际断头公路，荔波境内2公里，1995年8月，投资18万元按山岭重丘四级路标准，泥结碎石路面新建，1996年9月竣工通车。

永康—翁昂公路 全长14.583公里，1997年12月投资162万元修建。1999年工程完工，交付使用。2008年改造为沥青路。

茂兰—洞塘公路 全长14.3公里，1998年年初以工代赈投资20万元，以省乡村公路技术标准进行改造，工程于1998年12月竣工验收，交付使用；2007年年初，总投资850万元，对茂兰至洞塘延伸至梅园公路进行改造、修建并沥青表处，2007年年底完工，投入使用。

洞塘—永康公路 全长9公里，2000年12月投资170万元开工建设，2001年9月25日竣工，交付使用。2004年，由茂兰保护区管理局改造为沥青路。

甲良—阳凤公路 全长9.46公里，总投资123.21万元，按山岭重丘区四级公路建设，2002年10月动工修建，2003年9月通过验收，交付使用。

驾欧—朝阳环景区旅游公路 全长26.12公里，以旅游国债项目总投资1798.12万元，按山岭重丘区四级油路新建，该工程于2005年6月开工，2008年1月底完成摊铺，全部开展碾压保养工作。

1978—2008年全县乡村公路修建、改造情况统计表

表18－1

公路名称	里程（公里）	新建或改造	建设标准	建设时间	总投资（万元）
水利至水岩	3.00	新建	等外	1978年	—
水利至拉应	2.00	新建	等外	1978年	—
板央至董港	6.00	新建	等外	1978年	—
太吉至尧古	5.00	新建	等外	1978年	—
母早至西竹	2.00	新建	等外	1978年	—
太吉至德门	3.00	新建	等外	1978年	—
田洞至花堤	4.00	新建	等外	1978年	—
田洞至寨平	1.00	新建	等外	1978年	—
拉欧至新街	4.00	新建	等外	1978年	—
界牌至红光	3.00	新建	等外	1978年	—
拉片至林场	3.00	新建	等外	1978年	—
播尧至尧花	10.00	新建	等外	1978年	—
架桥至几固	2.00	新建	等外	1978年	—
地蜡至台村拉榜	4.00	新建	等外	1978年	—
茂兰至甲介	8.00	新建	等外	1978年	—
立化至洞湖	6.00	新建	等外	1978年	—
立化至平寨新站台	1.50	新建	等外	1978年	—
平寨至平寨煤井	2.00	新建	等外	1978年	—
平寨至站台	1.00	新建	等外	1978年	—
佳荣至岜鲜	10.00	新建	等外	1978年	—
水功至拉柳	1.00	新建	等外	1979年	—
孟塘至拉转	3.00	新建	等外	1979年	—
洞流至王家寨	5.00	新建	等外	1979年	—
洞流至更朋	4.00	新建	等外	1979年	—

续表18－1

公路名称	里程（公里）	新建或改造	建设标准	建设时间	总投资（万元）
水利至水丰	6.00	新建	等外	1980年	—
孟塘至脚村	2.00	新建	等外	1980年	—
朝阳至翁昂	30.00	新建	等外	1982年	—
王蒙、瑶山至捞村	25.00	新建	等外	1982年	15.00
丰洞至罗布木	5.00	新建	等外	1982年	—
拉欧至拉圭	10.00	新建	等外	1982年	—
拉欧至板潭	2.00	新建	等外	1982年	—
立化至罗家寨煤厂	3.00	新建	等外	1982年	—
尧排至水春	7.00	新建	等外	1983年	—
水扒至董路	1.00	新建	等外	1983年	—
太吉至吉洞	2.00	新建	等外	1984年	—
太吉至董亥	8.00	新建	等外	1984年	—
立化至尧明	3.00	新建	等外	1984年	—
甲介至恒姑	4.00	新建	等外	1985年	—
洞流至水庆	7.00	新建	等外	1985年	—
立化至伍家	1.00	新建	等外	1985年	—
水维至拉潭	5.00	新建	等外	1985年	—
石灰坳至水架	4.00	新建	等外	1986年	—
翁昂至贬和	5.00	新建	等外	1986年	—
黄草坪至水条	6.00	新建	等外	1986年	—
打油寨至交土	3.00	新建	等外	1986年	—
岜鲜至拉先	4.00	新建	等外	1986年	—
拉片至纸厂	1.00	新建	等外	1987年	—
更班至岜项	5.00	新建	等外	1987年	—
拉片至拉项	3.00	新建	等外	1988年	—
水条至高里	5.00	新建	等外	1988年	—
巴格至洞塘煤厂	4.00	新建	等外	1988年	—
洞塘至板寨	3.00	新建	等外	1988年	—
拉滩至煤厂	4.00	新建	等外	1988年	—
幸福桥至莪洋	2.00	新建	等外	1988年	—
铅厂至巴灰	5.00	新建	等外	1988年	—
打里至坡顶	1.00	新建	等外	1989年	—

续表18－1

公路名称	里程（公里）	新建或改造	建设标准	建设时间	总投资（万元）
新场至麦寨	5.00	新建	等外	1989年	—
水扒至林场	5.00	新建	等外	1990年	—
立化至应昂	2.00	新建	等外	1990年	—
拉毛至拉埃	8.00	新建	等外	1990年	—
瑶山至捞村	18.00	改建	四级	1999年	—
洞塘至永康	9.00	新建	四级	1999年	—
尧排至水春	7.00	改建	四级	2001年	—
播尧至觉巩	7.50	改建	四级	2002年	—
甲良至阳凤	12.00	改建	四级	2003年	—
拉片至红光	8.30	改建	四级	2003年	33.20
长寨至比鸠	3.32	新建	等外	2003年	13.28
太吉至董亥	7.20	新建	等外	2003年	28.80
政府至打里	0.76	新建	等外	2003年	3.04
大枫树至寨近	12.84	新建	等外	2003年	51.36
甲新至中怀	8.50	新建	等外	2003年	34.00
寨平坳至寨平	2.70	新建	等外	2004年	8.10
抵瓦至水岩	12.31	新建	等外	2004年	36.93
拉祥至拉易	14.73	新建	等外	2004年	44.19
林场至瑶寨	8.00	新建	等外	2004年	24.00
寨索至寨票	6.00	新建	等外	2004年	18.00
拉仰至尧花	8.60	新建	等外	2004年	25.80
桥头至廖家湾	8.50	新建	等外	2004年	25.50
甲新至甲站	16.80	新建	等外	2004年	50.40
豆村至中心至架桥	13.70	新建	等外	2004年	41.10
群力至巴平	13.90	新建	等外	2004年	41.70
更班至洞湖	5.60	改建	等外	2005年	22.40
高桥至巴楼	5.20	新建	等外	2005年	20.80
拉祥至拉先	12.50	新建	等外	2005年	50.00
洪江至山江	8.00	新建	等外	2005年	32.00
新寨到岜马	8.80	新建	等外	2005年	35.20
甲岸至大利	6.40	新建	等外	2005年	25.60
拉强至梅桃	8.20	新建	等外	2005年	32.80

续表18－1

公路名称	里程（公里）	新建或改造	建设标准	建设时间	总投资（万元）
木朝至岜町	6.60	新建	等外	2005年	26.40
拉平至地莪	15.00	新建	等外	2006年	60.00
朝阳至八烂	8.20	新建	等外	2006年	32.80
幸福桥至高里	10.10	新建	等外	2006年	40.40
板央至抵朵	10.00	新建	等外	2006年	40.00
水维至甲料	14.70	新建	等外	2006年	58.80
桥边至板培	1.90	新建	等外	2006年	7.60
拉欧至板潭	5.70	新建	等外	2006年	22.80
洞流至王家寨	5.00	新建	等外	2006年	20.00
山脚至懂别	2.60	新建	等外	2006年	10.40
母早至西竹	2.83	新建	等外	2006年	11.32
回龙阁至板旺	2.70	新建	等外	2006年	10.80
星庞至拉美	9.00	新建	等外	2007年	58.50
播觉至黎明	5.90	新建	等外	2007年	38.35
麻桩至地莪	12.80	新建	等外	2007年	83.20
新街至董朋	6.60	新建	等外	2007年	42.90
把抹至尧并	2.70	新建	等外	2007年	17.55
平木至拉吾	3.90	新建	等外	2007年	25.35
拉毛至拉埃	7.40	新建	等外	2007年	48.10
板勇至丙花	2.30	新建	等标准	2007年	14.95
中学至金对	3.40	新建	等外	2007年	22.10
野河坡至朋宾	11.70	新建	等外	2007年	76.05
拉圭至新街	4.20	新建	等外	2007年	27.30
群力至平岩	2.70	新建	等外	2007年	17.55
水利至水丙	7.10	新建	等外	2007年	46.15
友谊桥至水功	9.90	新建	等外	2007年	64.35
肯甫至拉威堤	7.60	新建	等外	2007年	49.40
洞塘乡村	13.90	新建	等外	2007年	90.35
双江至拉街	7.40	新建	等外	2007年	48.10
小孔桥至四两寨至拉潭	3.60	新建	等外	2007年	23.40
水尧至水涝	3.40	新建	等外	2007年	22.10
花塔至洞常	7.70	新建	等外	2007年	50.05

续表18－1

公路名称	里程（公里）	新建或改造	建设标准	建设时间	总投资（万元）
拉片至英盘	5.30	新建	等外	2007年	34.45
石灰坳至罗卜木	9.80	新建	等外	2007年	63.70
苦李坳至石板	2.40	新建	等外	2007年	15.60
尧排至水架	5.40	新建	等外	2007年	35.10
岔路至罗家寨	17.46	新建	等外	2007年	113.49
寨莪至桥头至拉早	13.20	新建	等外	2007年	85.80
洞力至董刀至水扒	12.70	新建	等外	2007年	82.55
小河至益觉	10.10	新建	等外	2007年	65.65
茂佳至洞英	4.30	新建	等外	2007年	27.95
拉内至已陇	2.80	新建	等外	2007年	18.20
罗家寨至洞腊	6.40	新建	等外	2007年	41.60
拉学至拉先	0.60	新建	等外	2007年	3.90
水碰河至水碰	4.60	新建	等外	2007年	29.90
翁昂至尧桥	14.50	新建	等外	2008年	94.25
新街至三合	10.50	新建	等外	2008年	68.25
更益至洞多	6.70	新建	等外	2008年	43.55
三麻线至水甫	6.90	新建	等外	2008年	44.85
水维至大土	17.50	新建	等外	2008年	113.75
岜鲜至地牙	18.70	新建	等外	2008年	121.55
瑶麓至水庆	4.70	新建	等外	2008年	30.55
双江至交挠	5.70	新建	等外	2008年	37.05
干塘至丙外	2.80	新建	等外	2008年	18.20
野河坡至金华	3.00	新建	等外	2008年	19.50

说明：1978—2003年总投资无统计数据。

四、矿区公路

1978—1988年，由于煤炭生产的发展，运销量增加，先后修筑矿区简易公路18条，投资总计222.5万元，总里程80.5公里。

1989—2008年，修建25条矿山公路，总里程180公里，投资总计900万元。投资来源主要从政府掌握的煤炭调节基金、县财政资金以及煤矿投资人出资协调解决。

第二节　公路运输

一、人力车和畜力车运输

1978—1990年，县内民间短途运输货物仍使用人力车和畜力车（马车）。1990年，全县马车、人力车有5000多辆。1991—1995年，全县马车、人力车减少为3000多辆，年货运量15万吨。1995年以后，机动车逐渐增多。至2008年，全县马车、人力车只有1500余辆。

二、机动车运输

（一）客运

1978年后，先后开通荔波—麻尾、荔波—三都、荔波—金城江、县城—王蒙、县城—佳荣等客运班车，开通县城—茂兰、县城—小七孔的中巴车、旅游车、加班车。省、州、县线每日对开1班，区、乡线每日往返1班。

1985年，全县自有大客车2辆、小客车21辆进行旅客运输。汽车站（都匀运输公司正常客运班车）有客车4辆，全年客运量2.02万人次，旅客周转量67.89万人公里。

1988年，新增个体中巴车、小客车开往各区，每天1次。荔波—金城江、荔波—都匀（双班）、荔波—三都、荔波—独山、荔波—麻尾，每日对开客运班车1班。荔波汽车站每日发车16班。

1990年，县汽车站开通的客运班车线路有荔波—贵阳、荔波—都匀、荔波—金城江、荔波—独山、荔波—麻尾，县城—王蒙、佳荣、立化等。另有规定线路运营的中型客车（中巴车）和小客车发往独山、麻尾、立化、王蒙、小七孔、朝阳、茂兰、佳荣、洞塘、九阡、周覃等地，车次不定。是年，全县自有大客车6辆（个体）、中型客车10辆（其中个体7辆）、小客车4辆（集体），都匀汽运公司常驻荔波大客车11辆，红茂矿接送职工上下班大客车1辆。

随着小七孔、樟江风景名胜区的开发，游人逐渐增多，客运随之繁荣。1991年，全年客运量17.1万人次。1994年，全年客运量21.96万人次。

1997年，投资324万元新建了荔波汽车站。占地总面积7200.36平方米，建筑面积2393平方米。是年12月，经省运管局批准，荔波汽车站为二级客运站。该站日进站经营的客运车辆达180辆（次），客运班线30条，运行区间为黔桂两省（区）的贵阳、都匀、独山、三都、麻尾、凯里、南宁、柳州、金城江、南丹、环江等地以及县内各乡（镇）。1998年，全年客运量166.078万人次。

2000年，成立荔波县交通运输发展有限公司，部分个体客车转入该公司。是年，全年旅客周转量5355万人公里，日均投入100班次，日运送旅客3500人次。

2002年，成立黔南交运有限责任公司荔波分公司，客运车辆全部转入分公司，客运驾驶人员向分公司承包经营，分公司对承包经营者的经营、安全生产负责。至2004年，完成客运量226万人次，旅客周转量7153万人公里。

2007年，全县客运车辆发展至138辆，其中含旅游客车5辆，同年完成客运量143万人次，旅客周转量9123万人公里。

2008年，调整道路运输结构，按照“路、站、运、管、安”五位一体的发展思路，开辟农村客运市场，至12月，全县有农村客运班线18条，客运车辆158辆，全县乡（镇）农村客运覆盖率100%，行政村客运覆盖率79%，村村通车率87%。全年完成客运量290万人次，旅客周转量达9350万人公里。

（二）货运

1978年，县汽车队有职工13人，汽车7辆，年货运量0.76万吨，货物周转量56.47万吨公里。

1985年，全县有大货车119辆、小货车18辆，有拖拉机166辆。年货运量8.2万吨，货物周转量85万吨公里。

1987年，县运输社因经营效益差而解散，职工自谋职业。

1988年1月，按荔政〔1988〕1号文件撤销县汽车队。是年起，汽车站货运车辆实行个人承包经营。

1990年，全县自有大货车201辆（其中机关单位6辆，其余为个体车辆）、小货车56辆（机关单位和个体户各28辆），农忙耕田农闲运输的拖拉机178辆。年完成货运量10.16万吨，完成货物周转量529.56万吨公里。

1996年，全县自有大货车432辆、小货车82辆。全年完成货运量136万吨，完成货物周转量1246万吨公里。

1997年，全县自有大货车433辆完成货运量145万吨，货物周转量6950万吨公里。

2000年，全县自有大货车755辆，客运三轮车226辆，汽车维修89户，全年货运量160万吨，货物周转量14300万吨公里。

2003年，全县有营运货车740辆，全年完成货运量188万吨，完成货物周转量16100万吨公里。

2005年，完成货运量201.5万吨，货物周转量17745万吨公里。

2008年，完成货运量223万吨，货物周转量19200万吨公里。

（三）运输管理

1978—1983年，运输管理工作由荔波县交通局安排人员负责，业务属独山运管所负责和指导。1984年，成立荔波县交通监理站，行政属县交通局领导，业务由黔南州监理所负责。

1987年1月，全县城乡道路交通管理由公安机关负责统一管理，撤销交通监理站，建立交警队。群运工作也相应延伸到各区，形成交通运输管理网络。1989年11月，成立县运输管理所，属交通运输管理正股级事业单位。

1990年，根据县政府荔政〔1990〕31号文件《荔波县人民政府关于治理整顿道路水路运输市场的通告》开展荔波县治理整顿道路水路运输市场，由交通部门牵头进行一次认真的治理整顿，符合规定的允许继续营业，不符合规定的限期整改。清查“公挂私、私挂公”的营运车辆，共清查68辆，开展13家维修户的整治。

1991年，对全县222辆车进行治理整顿，完成整治率98.13%。根据省运管〔1991〕运字第16号文件《关于严格按报批程序申请和实行集体审批客运班次的通知》精神成立县客、货营运车辆新增审批领导小组，负责全县货车的审批及客运班次、线路的审批工作。

1992年，根据黔南州交通局黔南交办〔1992〕5号文件精神，开展全县1992年春运工作，每月5日晚和16日晚组织客、货车辆驾驶员开展安全学习。

1995年，按国家明确规定的道路运输职责范围，对客货运管理、汽车维修、客货运站场管理、运输相关辅助业、搬运装卸等开展治理整顿活动。

1997年，新公用型汽车站建成并投入使用，由贵州省都匀汽车运输公司经营，省运管局核准为二级客运站，同年，荔波县公路运输管理所新办公大楼建成。

1998年，重点对春运经营户的审核把关，同时对上车和出入车站物品的检查，严防和杜绝“三品”上车。全年检查各种营运车辆1450辆，纠正违章车辆的362辆，给予批评教育和警告410辆，给予适当罚款21辆，查扣欠费车辆13辆，依法拍卖一辆。

2001年春运期间，县交通运输管理部门开展客货运输秩序清理整顿活动，以车站为源头，查堵“三品”（毒品、易燃易爆物品、枪支刀具），严禁“三品”进站上车，印发宣传资料1500份，接待群众咨询400人次。全年检查各种营运车辆1110辆，给予警告363辆，罚款84辆，扣车27辆，追缴规费20万元。是年，办理城镇客运机动三轮车营运手续186辆，进行车辆技术等级评定742辆、二级维护2572辆（次）。

2002年，开展“公路运输管理年”活动，对客运车辆进行路检路查，制止超员超载，查处违章车辆。全年营运车辆换证859辆，占应换证的81%；检查维修业49户，换发维修业户许可证27户、检验员质检证18人，查处违章和安全隐患29起；检查各种营运车辆1609辆（次），纠正违章420辆；组织考核办理驾驶人员上岗资格证412人（客运178人、货运234人），车辆技术等级评定820辆、二级维护3720辆（次）。

2003年，开展营运客车挂靠清理和换证工作，换发新版“道路运输证”，全县各类营运车辆换证率达到99%。对维修业户58户进行清理登记、年审换证及客货机动三轮车年审办证；春运期间，加大客运车辆管理力度，强化路检路查的管理，制止超员超载，查处违章车辆，查堵“三品”进站上车。共检查各种营运车辆216辆，纠正违章36辆，拆除客运车私自增加座位4辆27座，现场制止超员6辆，不参加例检不准发班21辆。

2004年，检查营运车辆2490辆（次），纠正违章车辆736辆（次）。

2005年，营运车辆认证200辆，驾驶员从业资格认证176人。全年检查货车1033辆（次）、客运车辆641辆（次）、农用车500辆（次）、处罚违章车辆180辆（次）。

2007年，交通运输管理部门严查客运经营户的从业资格、营运证、二级维护及技术性能检测等手续，禁止无牌无证经营，对不符合要求的车辆，取消运营资格。路查路检以省、县、乡道为重点，向农村延伸，按照《超载超限运输车辆管理办法》，严厉查处超员、超限运输，坚决取缔“黑车”“黑户”“黑班”“黑线”，进一步规范市场秩序。

2008年，客运管理执行“三不进站、五不出站”（危险品不进站、无关人员不进站、无关车辆不进站；超载客车不出站、安全例检不合格客车不出站、驾驶员资格不符合要求不出站、客车证件不齐全不出站、出站登记表未经审核签字不出站）规定。运管所与县内客运企业、汽车站、二类维修企业签订安全生产责任书，各企业与安全生产岗位责任人签订安全生产责任状，层层落实运输安全责任。同时，开展安全生产百日督查活动、安全生产隐患排查活动、安全生产专项整治活动，对汽车站、客运企业、二类维修企业的基础档案、安全生产制度、规章落实情况进行检查，对企业存在的安全生产隐患下发整改通知书10份。全年检查货车753辆、客车665辆、其他车辆257辆，查出无经营证6起、无有效从业资格证1起、未按规定站点停靠2起、未按规定班线运行2起。

第三节　公路管理

一、公路养护

（一）道养公路

1978—1990年，境内省道荔波—独山公路的荔波大桥至甲良洞庭段，设有甲良、尧棒、鱼塘道班，养路48公里。1991—2004年，省道养护115.9公里。其中，独荔公路荔波段41.4公里，三麻公路荔波段74.5公里。2005年以后，三麻公路移交独山管理段管理养护。

（二）县养公路

1978—1990年，县养公路有县城至茂兰26公里，县城至朝阳10公里，县城至三都县边界20.8公里，茂兰至佳荣27公里，佳荣至广西驯乐12.2公里，甲良至麻尾（尧细）23.6公里，王蒙高桥至界牌6公里，新寨至阳凤9公里，朝阳田洞至小七孔19.9公里，茂兰至洞塘14.6公里，佳荣至水维7.4公里，播尧至觉巩6.5公里，共183公里，设有尧排、茂兰、水尧、黄草坪、花高、播尧、立化等处道班。

1991—1992年，全县管养县公路88.4公里、乡公路63.4公里，代养厂矿专用公路25公里。

1993年，管养县公路163.3公里、乡公路43.8公里，代养25公里，县公路好路率66%。

1996年，全县有管养县、乡公路里程219公里，因荔茂线路面改造减少养护26公里，实际养护县公路137.5公里、乡公路55.5公里。

1997年、1998年，公路好路率分别为76.9%、72.85%，连续两年获全州好路率第一名。1998年上半年，降雨持续时间长，公路毁坏严重，修复工程投入资金总计26.51万元。

2001年，道路养护部门抢修暴雨造成山体滑坡损毁的公路，全县管养县乡公路219公里，无差等路，晴雨畅通。

2002—2007年，管养县公路163.5公里、乡公路100.2公里。

2008年，县公路进行油路改造81.6公里，县公路养护里程减少为123.7公里，乡公路养护增加到160.19公里。抢修损毁严重的通村公路30公里。

（三）乡（镇）、村养公路

1978—2006年，乡（镇）、村养公路养护经费从征收养路费返还以及政府拨款解决。2007年后，执行《贵州省农村公路管理养护条例》，按照“县乡道县养，村道乡镇村共养”的原则和《荔波县农村公路管理养护体制改革工作实施方案》要求，为确保“修一条路，管一条路，养一条路，护一条路”，工程完工后，及时交付乡（镇）、村组织养护。至2008年年底，乡、村养护公路62条，共424.1公里。

二、公路绿化

境内道养、县养公路按要求在建成或扩建、改建时，植行道树。在公路界桩内的树木，禁止采伐、损坏。矿山、村级简易公路旁自然生长的树木，由村规民约议定保护措施加以保护。

1996—1998年，全县新植、补植公路绿化里程84公里，植树苗2.62万株。

2001年，投资2.3万元新植、补植42公里绿化树1.24万株。其中，荔大公路15公里0.47万株、荔何公路27公里0.77万株。

2002年，绿化麻小公路4公里，成活率90%，保存率95%。

2005—2006年，先后进行新阳公路绿化补植9公里，玉播公路绿化新植20公里，王蒙—瑶山—贵江公路绿化新植10公里。

2007年，水尧公路绿化新植和电视塔至洞塘旅游线花草种植26公里。

三、路政管理

1978—1983年，路政管理工作由荔波县交通局安排人员负责，业务属独山运管所负责和指导。1984年，成立县交通监理站，开展路政管理。

1986年，对县内107.5公里公路设施进行调查，发现被盗和毁坏的公里桩占14%、百米桩占40%、公路界桩占9.6%，公路行道树被偷砍，公路标志牌、地名牌、公路挡墙、桥梁栏杆被毁坏，养路材料被盗，公路两侧掘洞、挖煤17处，公里界内设置砖瓦、石灰窑12个，占用公路建房搭棚、挖沟渠、种植农作物等，由路政管理部门处理。

1989年11月，成立县运输管理所，属交通运输管理正股级事业单位。此后，交通运输管理、机械维修管理及稽查规费征收等道路运输管理工作按省、州工作要求正常开展。

1991年，在查处侵占路产路权人中，移送公安机关依法处理2人，收取占地赔偿费、车辆超限费、罚款等0.5万元。

1992—1993年，开展路政法规宣传，依法清除路障堆积物，查处砍伐行道树违法行为，取缔公路控制红线内各种窑洞、违章建筑物，恢复公路护栏、标志牌。

1994—1998年，每年上路开展法规宣传，印发宣传资料，书写标语。5年间，清除路障堆积物329处，依法拆除各种违章建筑14处，制止和拆除控制红线内违章建筑132处，取缔在公路自留地内修建的砖瓦窑、石灰窑、小煤窑、修车场、洗车场、加水站等125个，责令恢复被损坏的护栏23个、涵洞7座、公里桩22个以及修复被毁损路面，查处盗伐、砍伐、损坏行道树行为人，收取损坏公路补偿费总计3.47万元。

2001年，实施《贵州省公路路政管理条例》，开展路检、路查，收取超限运输费2.71万元、占用公路用地补偿费1.37万元、损害路产赔偿0.18万元。2001—2002年，查处路政案件21件。

2003年，依法开展超限运输、占用公路补偿、损害路产等专项治理，查处公路红线内违法建筑8处，制止红线内建筑3处，恢复路面3处，取缔非法采石场4个，警告批评违法人员58人。

2005年，开展过境公路超限运输治理，全年查处各类路政案件179件。

2006年，以省道206和县道918为重点，进行公路脏、乱、差整治，对公路沿线占道经营、路店不分、脏乱差现象、设置非公路标志等违章行为进行重点整治，查处各类路政案件13件。

2007年，定期对管辖范围内的路面进行巡查，对易出现交通堵塞和有安全隐患的路段采取安全防范措施，在交通事故多发地段增设相应的警示标志、标牌以及护桩、安全墩250个，设置防护钢丝栏1000多米。

2008年，对全县公路上设置的各类站点进行检查、抽查，依法拆除违规设置的收费站2个。省政府批准设置的2个超限运输检测站，设立规范，公示内容齐全，执法规范，无搭车检查和收费现象。全年查处各类路政案件32件。

四、规费征收

从1981年5月起，根据黔南州交通局《关于拖拉机、畜力车辆养路费征收问题的通知》，境内开始征收养路费。畜力车辆养路费由群运站（交管站、运管所）征收，机动车养路费由县监理所、养路费稽查站征收。1989年12月将原来的征费稽查站更名为贵州省交通厅荔波征费稽查所，属黔南州征费稽查处直管，副科级事业单位。负责汽车、摩托车、拖拉机养路费和车辆购置附加费征收。

第四节 桥 梁

一、公路桥

1978年，境内公路桥有樟江大桥、黄江桥、方村大桥、大七孔桥、幸福桥、瑶琼桥。其中，方村大桥、大七孔桥、瑶琼桥为连接公路的古桥。

1983年，在拉平村的方村河修建拉平桥，全长50米，一孔跨径35米，桥面净宽5米，设计为载重汽-15，挂-80，1983年建成通车。是甲良—地莪公路的中型石台石拱桥。

1987年6月，将位于梅桃和瑶琼村之间甲良河上的瑶琼石拱桥改建为混凝乱石拱桥，全桥长40.4米，一孔跨20米，桥面净宽7米，设计为载重汽-15，挂-80。是甲良至麻尾公路中型桥之一。

1984年11月，投资60万元在王蒙乡高桥村外孟塘和海利之间的樟江河段修建王蒙大桥，桥全长

130米，高18米，按四级公路标准修建。施工期间，于1986年1月19日夜10时左右，大拱及拱架全部垮塌。后重新拨款拆除重修，于1986年5月1日建成验收，交付使用。

1984年10月，县自筹资金51万元，州拨10万元补助，在县城南部㵲江比吉河段修建南门大桥（又称比吉大桥），全长148.8米，为三孔跨径40米，净宽7+2×0.25米，高16米的钢筋混凝土钢桁架拱桥，于1987年建成使用。是玉屏通往罗家寨、坡平、拉岜等村的公路大桥。

1991年9月，红茂矿务局投资5万元，县政府拨款3.02万元，重建茂兰—立化公路长寨桥。桥长26米，桥高4.8米，桥宽4米，按国家汽20-挂100设计，钢筋混凝土梁式桥，于1991年年底竣工并交付使用。

1980年，久安村民自筹资金，新建肯甫火车站至久安村横跨三岔河的甫安桥，全长60米，高12米，宽4.5米，为2礅3跨钢筋混凝土梁式桥。工程于1982年年初完工并投入使用。

1987年，以民办公助动工修建横跨方村河上游的纳核桥，全长50米，高7米，宽4米，有2礅3孔，设计为乡村大车道桥。后因资金不足停工，州交通局增拨款6万元后，于1990年年底建成使用。

1997年11月，投资68万元动工修建大七孔公路桥，1998年5月建成通车。桥全长67米，净跨45米，高15米、宽9米。

2007年2月，投资416.5万元，动工修建位于驾欧至朝阳公路K8+600处横跨方村河的联山大桥，全长68米，桥型设计为3～19.5米的钢筋混凝土小箱梁桥，工程于2009年4月竣工验收，投入使用。

二、钢丝绳便桥

1978年，在驾欧公社岜乃寨和简应寨之间的方村河段建成岜乃桥，桥长30米，宽1.5米，高9米。

1981年，将王蒙乡板麦—婆村的㵲江河渡口改建成钢丝绳便桥，称板麦桥，桥长80米，宽1.5米，高6米。

1986年，在时来乡水春村旁㵲江河上建成水春桥，桥长65米，高9.6米，宽2.6米。

1987年春，在朝阳乡花堤村寨平—花堤的㵲江河段上建成花堤桥，桥长95米，宽1.5米，高10米。

1988年，在朝阳乡拉良—拉香寨的㵲江河段建成拉香桥，桥长100米，宽1.5米，高8米。

1989年，在时来乡福利村旁㵲江河上建成福村桥，桥长70.25米，宽2.5米，高8.05米，属民办公助工程。

1991年10月，在玉屏镇坡平建成坡平钢丝桥，桥长48米，宽2米，高10米。1992—2008年，县境内未新建钢丝吊桥。

2000年8月，对因特大洪灾冲毁的㵲江沿河水春、福利、花堤三座吊桥进行重建，三座吊桥重建于2001年6月全部完工，投入使用。

三、漫水桥

至2008年，境内有寨马漫水桥、朝阳漫水桥、用平漫水桥、板麦漫水桥、坡平漫水桥、岜固漫水桥、脚村漫水桥等。漫水桥多为民办公助建成。

寨马漫水桥 位于朝阳镇寨马和寨莪之间的㵲江河段上，1990年12月国家补助8万元修建，1991年3月竣工。桥长83米，宽4米，高2.4米，按国家汽15-挂80设计。

朝阳漫水桥 位于朝阳乡交朝村和拉扶村之间的㵲江河段上，为朝阳至翁昂乡公路桥。1981年1月，总投资14.5万元修建，当年9月建成。由1号、2号两桥组成，1号桥为4孔跨径各8米的钢筋混凝土平板桥，礅台采用浅基铺底。2号桥为5孔跨径各8米的钢筋混凝土桥梁，礅台采用深基，挖至河底岩层。两桥共长91.5米，桥面净宽4.5米，引道500米，荷载汽-10、履-50设计。1982年雨季，两次洪水将2号桥江心洲岸的引道（过水路堤）冲毁，桥台八字翼墙倾斜（分离砌筑）河岸冲成大缺口，州拨款3万元，修复水毁桥段（含江心洲200米水泥过路面工程费）。1983年12月修复完成。

岜固漫水桥 位于驾欧乡小岜固和下岜固之间的方村河段上。1983年修建，1984年竣工，为9孔两台8礅混凝土漫水桥。全长64米，高2.5米，宽2米，可通行小型拖拉机。

脚村漫水桥 位于瑶山乡脚村寨脚的樟江河段上。1987年12月，群众自筹资金为主，国家适当给予补助修建，1989年2月竣工，全桥长85米，高1.6米，宽2.8米。为10礅9孔的钢筋混凝土漫水桥，系渡改桥。桥上可通行小型拖拉机和马车。

四、乡村石拱桥

全县乡村石拱桥有48座。其中，高寨桥、板孔桥、济美桥、板吉桥、继善桥、一心桥、万古桥、溪竹桥、尧古桥、洞英桥、裕后桥、小七孔桥、三多桥、和合桥、板潭石板桥、洪桥、界石桥（又名加寿桥）等建于清朝年间。位于王蒙乡高桥村跨响水河，建于清道光十年（1830）的小七孔桥最为著名，因桥有七孔而得名，小七孔风景名胜区名称由此而来，至2008年仍保存完好。

拉窝桥 位于茂兰拉窝村前，跨茂兰河的石拱桥。建于清代，现保护完好，为村民至乡、区、县必经之道。民国19年（1930）4月，红七军游击黔桂边由茂兰经此桥进军古州（今榕江县）。

洞英桥 位于茂兰乡洞英寨脚，跨茂兰河的三拱石桥，建于清代，现保护完好。民国19年（1930）4月，红七军进军古州曾从此桥通过。

第二章 铁路 水路 航空

第一节 铁路交通

一、铁路线

1978年前，广西为开发荔波茂兰片区煤矿，建成金城江—立化煤矿区铁路专用线，全长110公里。其中，荔波境内有27公里，经洞塘更甫、立化平寨，延伸3公里至更班矿井，为铁路终点。设有肯甫、平寨两个运煤专用站台，车站管理人员和站台设施等均按正规化要求配备齐全。这是境内唯一铁路线。

二、铁路运输

金茂铁路以运煤为主，主要是将广西红茂矿务局平寨、更班、打油寨3个矿井及荔波县各乡（镇）小煤窑生产的原煤运销广东、广西各地。

从1978年起，金茂铁路每日往返一次客货混合列车，日运载300—400人次。1988年以前，金茂

荔波境内唯一的铁路：立化—金城江线，主要运输煤炭

铁路每年货运量为运出原煤60万吨，以及一些零星木材和其他物资。1990年，运出原煤80万吨（红茂矿务局35万吨，荔波各乡小煤窑45万吨），运出木材2000立方米；运入化肥、水泥、农药、百货、矿区生活用品共18万吨。

1991—2001年，广西红茂矿务局的平寨、更班、打油寨3个矿井以及荔波县的国营煤矿、小煤窑产煤量多，金茂铁路专线运行正常。2002年，因荔波县境煤源枯竭，广西红茂矿宣布破产，金茂铁路运行列（次）逐年减少。

第二节　内河航运

一、航道及渡口

（一）航道

境内能通航的河流主要有樟江河、方村河、甲料河、三岔河4条。

樟江河在县境约150公里，流经之地多山岩峋嶙，形成陡峭的急流险滩，仅有水春附近5公里河段和时来至王蒙、瑶山30公里河段比较平缓，可通行载重1000公斤左右的木船和捕鱼的小舢板。源头的月亮山脚、岜鲜、水维等河段如遇春夏涨水季节，可放单漂原木至荔波县城，大木排行驶有困难。后由于在县城至王蒙、瑶山河段修筑水轮泵站、兴建拦河大坝，航道截为数段，航道隔断。

方村河流经地域在海拔750～850米山谷中，山岩峋嶙交错，形成急流险滩、伏流。下游地莪至驾欧20公里河段较为平缓，能通行小木船和小舢板，载重500公斤左右，仅为农活服务。20世纪70—80年代在地莪至驾欧河段修筑水轮泵站、兴建拦河大坝，航道截为数段，只能进行短距离农务运输。

甲料河在境内长30公里，河流上游地段系九万大山地区，河床陡窄，水量小，不能行船，数十公里河道仅能进行木材单漂运输。

三岔河在荔波境内河段35公里，流经地域属发育的喀斯特地区高山峻岭，谷深洞多，险滩急流，暗河、明河错综复杂，不能通船，只有几公里小段河流可行驶小舢板。

（二）渡口

1978年前，境内有渡口24个，后部分已经进行渡改桥。如1991年王蒙乡（今朝阳镇）寨马渡口进行渡改桥。至2008年，全县仍保留有民间渡口8个，即拉寨渡口、地莪渡口、寨票渡口、寨索渡口、拉干渡口、董雄渡口、拉崩渡口、洞腊渡口。这些渡口民办公助，渡船由县交通局补助资金购置，村民管理使用。

比吉渡口　位于县城南樟江比吉河段。为县城至永康、洞塘出黎明关或大哨坡出广西怀远等地主要渡口，也是时来乡罗家寨、拉岜等进城必经渡口。冬季枯水时行人由跳墩上过河，春夏水涨则渡船过河。旧时为私渡，各村民捐献粮款一年1次交给渡工。路人则每次都交渡船费。解放后，1953年县人民政府投资建成1座跨河石墩水飘桥，渡口废。1969年修东升水坝建水轮泵站后，水位升高，淹没桥面又恢复船渡。1986年建成南门大桥后，渡口废。

福村渡口　位于时来乡福村旁樟江河边。为村民耕作及客商入城之渡口。旧时为私渡，解放后，为民办公助，由县交通局补助造船资金，村民轮流管理使用，1989年11月建成钢丝索桥后，渡口废。

拉扶渡口　朝阳至翁昂乡必经的樟江河渡口。拉扶、板乐等村民至朝阳等地亦需经此渡船，冬季河水涸时过跳墩，旧时为私渡。1978年建成钢丝索桥后，渡口废。桥垮拆除后又恢复渡船。1981

年建成朝阳至翁昂公路漫水桥，渡口复废。

巴乃渡口 位于驾欧乡联山村巴乃寨旁方村河边，旧时为私渡。解放后，民办公助，县交通局拨款，修造船只，村民轮班义渡。1987年建成钢丝索桥，渡口废。

二、客货运输

（一）运输工具

县境内水上运输工具主要有木船、木舢板、机动船、渡船、游艇。

1.木船 长8～10米，宽1.5米，作运载货物用，也捎带少量乘客，沿河两岸农户自产自用。

2.木舢板 长3～4米，宽0.4～0.5米，是河道两岸农民自用运输货物、赶集的航运工具。

3.机动船 在樟江河水深河段行驶，以柴油机为动力，主要用于水春河旅游。1988年开发水春河风景区，始购置机动游船2艘。2004年，全县有机动船5艘。2008年，全县机动船发展到9艘。

4.渡船 境内渡船有木制渡船、铁制渡船。1991年，播尧乡董雄、寨票两渡口群众集资0.3万元，县政府补助0.8万元，州交通局补助0.7万元，增置铁制渡船2艘。1993年10月，群众集资0.2万元，县政府补助0.5万元，州交通局补助1.7万元，从思南造船厂购买15个座位铁制渡船2艘，配发播尧乡拉干、董雄两个渡口。1997年，有渡船13艘（其中工作船1艘）。2008年，全县有渡船9艘。

5.游艇 有手摇式游艇、机动游艇、竹筏式游艇及动物状游艇等，主要用于水上游乐。1997年，全县有橡皮漂流艇51艘、机动游艇3艘、手划铁质船28艘。2004年，有漂流艇217艘、游乐船61艘。2008年，全县有游艇65艘、漂流艇136艘。

6.竹筏 沿河两岸部分村民自制竹筏用于运输货物、摆渡。

（二）货物运输

在樟江河流县城—王蒙25公里河道，设有东门河码头、比吉码头、回龙阁码头、朝阳码头、寨马码头、王蒙码头，供船只靠岸，装卸货物。每个码头，每日舶大小木船5～10艘。春冬购销旺季，日运货量可达10余吨。木材从水上集运，每年有500～2000立方米。东风水坝至白岩、龙王洞2.5公里河段主要运输建筑用河沙，年运输量2000～3000吨。东风水坝以下也是在各水轮泵站之间行船。水春河风景区开发后，有机动游船2艘，从城北到三道浪往返输送游客。水春河段，比较平缓宽阔，农民可用船运货物或用木排运输。

方村河的地莪至驾欧20公里河道平缓，水流量大，沿河农民利用水路运送大宗货物粮食、肥料、柴草等。

三岔河水流量小，伏流、陡滩多，两岸农民用小舢板运送货物。

甲料河在县境内水小滩多，只能单漂原木至广西环江，每年运出木材300立方米。

三、运输管理

1987年县交通局内设局办公室、财务室、渡口管理港监站等2室1站。

1992年3月，港监站检查渡口10处，参加检查36人，发现安全隐患1处。是年，补发船员证书10人（渡口2人、湖区8人）。

1993年，港监站开展渡口船工、船只年检。全年检查船只98艘（次），查出违章6次。向船工和过渡行人进行安全宣传教育，受教育1.81万人次。

1994年，港监站检查渡口10个、旅游点3处。

1995年，渡口管理港监站更名为港监所。当年县港监所进行全县船只、渡口整顿，对渡口实行“五定”（定渡口、定渡工、定安全、定渡额、定制度）管理，在渡口岸边立“渡口守则”石碑，12个渡口定专人管理并签订安全监督管理工作责任书。

1996—1998年，县港监所每年与全县船舶管理单位签订水上交通安全目标管理责任书，与安委办、旅游局联合对渡口、景点游船进行安全大检查，对舢板船造册登记，对查出有安全隐患的船只进行限期整改或取缔。同时，在渡船上贴限载标志和安全标语。1998年，对全县船员、船只进行登记、船检，填写自用船舶证书300本。同时，通过电视、广播、发放宣传资料等方式进行水上安全宣传。

2003年4月，县港监所升格为正科级机构，更名为地方海事处，海事处每月定期和不定期对渡口、码头开展安全检查。

2005年，开展船舶年度检验和船员培训，共检验漂流艇152艘，清查退出营运市场船只26艘。全年制止无证驾驶1人，违规漂流操作15起，纠正游客不规范行为26次，抽查救护人员、水上安全员到位情况9次。

2006—2008年，每年开展机动船、漂流船、游乐船年度检验，开展水上安全大检查和例行检查，执法人员在“五一”、国庆等节假日期间到各渡口、码头进行现场监管。3年共举办船员培训班11期，培训船员1200人次。县地方海事处于2007年12月被省地方海事局评为全省海事系统先进单位。

第三节 航 空

1999年3月11日，省政府办公厅发出《关于加快支线机场建设前期工作的通知》，计划在独山（或荔波）修建支线机场。3月30日—4月1日，民航西南机场建设规划设计院对荔波机场场址进行踏勘，场址初步定在荔波水尧。5月18日，县政府向州政府请示新建荔波机场。10月，州政府向国家民航总局申请将荔波机场纳入国家民航机场建设计划。2000年1月，民航总局同意新建荔波机场。是年2月16日，广州军区空军与贵州省政府就新建荔波机场樟江民用机场达成协议，广州军区空军原则同意修建荔波民用机场。

2001年6月21日，国务院同意新建荔波民用机场。9月21日，黔南州政府同意组建荔波机场建设开发有限责任公司。27日，省发改委向国家发改委报送《贵州省黔南州荔波机场工程可行性研究报告》。11月8日，举行荔波机场工程建设奠基仪式。12月3日，民航总局在荔波主持召开荔波机场环境影响报告书预审会。2002年5月20日，国家环保总局审查通过荔波机场环境影响评价。12月11日，国家发改委批复同意荔波机场工程可行性研究报告。2003年7月，工程正式动工。

2007年11月，荔波机场通航庆典

2007年5月22日，荔波机场飞行区工程初步验收。6月19日—7月14日，民航总局校飞中心对荔波机场通信导航及目视助航飞行校验，完成所有校验科目。9月29日，贵州航空有限公司对荔波机场进行试飞，确定荔波机场可以投入使用。

荔波机场距县城12公里，机场占地面积场区内998.4亩、场区外1366.65亩，按4C级建设，跑道长2300米、宽45米，停机坪长100米、宽80米，设置停机位2个。航站楼建筑面积3400平方米，设计年旅客吞吐量22万人次、典型高峰每小时可接待150人次。机场总投资3.96亿元。

机场由荔波机场建设开发有限责任公司管理，设荔波机场公安分局、安全检查站、航务管理部、经营管理部、综合管理部、运行保障部、指挥中心等机构。

2008年8月1日，南方航空公司开通深圳—荔波往返航班。8月1日—11月23日，荔波机场航班起降90架次，进港人数3881人次，进港上座率67%；出港人数4010人次，出港上座率70%。

第三章　邮政　通信

第一节　邮　政

一、机构

1978—1998年，设县邮电局，经营邮政、电信业务。1998年10月，邮政与电信分业经营，设荔波县邮政局，下设甲良、朝阳、茂兰、立化、平寨、更班、佳荣、王蒙8个支局，在册人员总计73人、离退休职工45人。分营划归县邮政局的固定资产原值252万元。

2008年，县邮政局内设综合办公室、市场经营部、代理业务部、客户服务部、邮务服务部、营储班、护发班、护卫队，下设甲良、茂兰、立化、平寨、更班、朝阳、佳荣7个支局。全系统有人员82名，具有职业技能鉴定资格证书的占72%的，其中高级工占7%、中级工占58%、初级工占35%。

二、邮路及设施

1998年，全县有邮路21条，单程总长825公里。其中，委托办理汽车邮路3条，全长72公里；自行车班邮路、步班邮路18条，全长753公里（自行车邮路163公里、步班邮路590公里）。2008年，乡邮邮路取消步班和自行车班，全部改为摩托车班。

三、业务经营

1978—1997年间，县邮电局邮政业务主要有函件、包件、报刊发行三大类。1998年，县邮政局主营传统函件、包件、报刊发行业务。是年，收寄包件5万件，报刊业务流转额60万元，邮政业务收入处于亏损状态。分营后的第一个年度1999年亏损70万元。

2004年，在函件业务上，相继推出商业信函、DM广告、商务名片、贺卡等新型函件类业务；在包件业务上，发展轻小型、快递包裹为主；报刊发行向农村市场拓展，以党报党刊发行为主；机要业务承担传递政府部门通信机密任务，未发生丢失损毁事故。在巩固传统业务的同时，发展速递、物流、代收费等新业务，全县邮政系统的业务收入不断增加。是年，业务收入较1998年增长42.35万元，增幅33%，扭转亏损局面。

2005年，荔波县参加由中国地理杂志社主办的“中国最美丽的地方”评选活动，全县邮政网点推出评选荔波函件业务5万件。年末，县邮政局独立运营后第一次完成各项年度指标，业务收入246.55万元，完成全年计划245万元的100.63%。

2005—2006年，县邮政局相继印制20万枚景区门票明信片，专门刻制小七孔风景日戳。

2007年，又印制荔波风光明信片4万枚，开发荔波风光相关邮品，宣传荔波，提高荔波知名度。2008年提前2个月完成全年计划，年末业务收入为年计划的129.01%，超收129万元，增幅45.48%。

第二节 电 信

一、机构

1978—1998年，电信业务由县邮电局经营。1998年10月，设县电信局，隶属黔南州电信局。

1999年6月，县电信局改制重组，设贵州省电信公司荔波县电信局，隶属贵州省电信公司黔南州分公司，将移动业务分出，另设移动通信机构。

2000年8月，县电信局内设综合办公室、经营服务部，下设玉屏镇电信营业部和朝阳、甲良、茂兰、立化、佳荣5个镇电信支局。

2004年6月28日，县电信局改称贵州省电信有限公司荔波县分公司，县以下分支机构统一名称为营业部，即荔波县分公司玉屏镇营业部、朝阳镇营业部、甲良镇营业部、茂兰镇营业部、立化镇营业部、佳荣镇营业部、瑶山乡王蒙营业部、水尧乡营业部、播尧乡营业部。

2008年2月，贵州省电信有限公司荔波县分公司改称为中国电信股份有限公司荔波分公司，下属分支机构统一名称为：中国电信股份有限公司荔波分公司玉屏镇营业部、立化镇营业部、佳荣镇营业部、茂兰镇营业部、朝阳镇营业部、甲良镇营业部、瑶山乡王蒙营业部、水尧乡营业部、播尧乡营业部。

二、设施

1978年，建有无线电报电路1条，有荔波至都匀单路载波电路1套。1984年，开通双工电传电报电路1条、电传打字机3部。1987年，开通D4202中英文打字机2部。1988年开通4路插报机1部、机械电传机3部、15瓦收发机1部。1990年，置明线12路载波机1部。1991年，置500门磁石交换机。1995年11月，开通3000门程控电话。

1996年12月，开通无线126、127台寻呼业务（BP机）。1997年7月开通模拟移动通信。1998年，建成县城、茂兰、甲良、立化镇3个频点的寻呼直放站。

1998年，建成开通县城GSM数字移动电话及基站1个，开通会议电视系统和DDN数字数据网，建成“南宁—贵阳—昆明”地埋光缆工程荔波段、荔波—三都二干光缆工程。年内，进行市话4000门交换机和4800对市话电缆扩容，对瑶麓—佳荣、朝阳—瑶山光缆通信工程以及全县农话交换接入网设备进行改造，对茂兰、立化、甲良、佳荣集镇电缆进行扩容。是年，市话交换机容量达7000门，市话出局电缆8000对；农话装机容量1440门，农话出局电缆1500对，农话光缆总长137皮长公里。全县有8个乡（镇）通信实现“交换程控化和传输数字化”。

1999年，投资200万元进行用户线工程改造，建设开通东环SDH传输设备，保证出口传输电路畅通。

2000年，州电信局在水利乡高寨村建微波站，通过高寨微波塔，开通无线接入电话通信系统，甲良、方村、岜合煤矿、朝阳镇等边远地区能安装开通无线程控电话。建成贯通县城主要街道地下电缆管网工程，与7000门程控交换相匹配。10月，建设开通县城小灵通电话。

从2001年起，启动实施“乡乡通程控电话”工程。是年，新增洞塘乡256线、方村乡256线、驾欧乡128线、福利村256线、播尧乡512线、板麦村224线等农村交换点6个，农村交换机新扩容2976线，农村交换机总容量增至5760线。市话交换机新扩容2048线，总容量达到9216线。新架设光缆

57.87公里，全县有14个乡（镇）开通光缆通信。投资82.78万元，对立化、朝阳、佳荣、甲良、茂兰5个镇的市街电缆进行扩容，铺设电缆32.36公里，埋设管道0.62公里。投资19.54万元，建成佳荣、驾欧、方村、水利、甲良、阳凤、播尧、板麦、福利、水尧、板吉、拉鱼、廖家湾、白岩、瑶庆、洞英、拉伙等村寨电缆延伸工程，架设电缆共140.67公里。

2002年，投资113.39万元重点开展村通电话延伸建设工程。年底，全县有70个行政村开通程控电话，村通率41.66%。全年交换机扩容672门，市话交换机容量达9168门，实装率66.93%，农话交换机容量6368门，实装率79.05%。新建小灵通基站4个，全县基站达31个。建成开通宽带ADSL设备，全县宽带端口63端。2003年，建成水尧—飞机场架空电缆、瑶麓—水庆配线电缆、茂兰及朝阳镇配线电缆等工程，建成开通甲良、立化、茂兰、朝阳4镇小灵通基站。

2004年，因微波通信被光纤通信取代，黔南州电信公司将水利乡高寨村微波站撤除移交荔波电信局作电信移动基站用，基站面积301平方米。是年，新增电话交换机384门，新增小灵通基站信道数88个，新增宽带接入端口880个，建设开通茂兰、大七孔、水利高寨450兆无线程控电话。全县各乡（镇）均建有电信机房以及营业网点。

2005年，对县城及乡（镇）的基站、线路、网络等设施进行新建、延伸、改造、扩容、优化、升级。2006年，全县小灵通基站到达101个（其中县城69个、乡镇32个）；县城交换机容量9168门，实装用户7367部，交换机实装率80.36%；农话交换机容量10496门，实装8717部，交换机实装率83.05%；宽带设备容量3792端口，实装2440户，实装率64.35%；LAN共48端口，实装29端口，实装率60.41%。

2008年年初，荔波遭受持续20多天的冰冻灾害，全县通信光缆、电缆杆路倒杆断线，总计倒杆断杆50根、断线20公里，全县29个农村电话接入网点、5个ETS高山基站、94个小灵通基站相继中断通信服务，灾害造成损失350万元。灾害期间，县电信公司及时组织光电缆及下户线抢修，人工运送设备到各接入网点和450兆高山基站进行发电，确保通信畅通。冰灾过后，对佳荣、茂兰、翁昂、昔村450兆基站供电线路进行修复，对水尧、方村、甲良、播尧等地电缆和下户线进行整治，对福利、朝阳、王蒙、水尧、立化、洞塘基站电池进行更换，对县城小灵通基站、450兆基站和5个接入网机房进行整治，对全县宽带IP组网进行改造，对全县安全隐患较大的杆路进行整治。

是年11月，中国电信荔波分公司和联通荔波分公司决定成立CDMA网络过渡期工作组，重组过渡期的C网经营由双方工作组共同负责，交割前以联通为主导，交割后由电信为主导。

年末，县电信部门交换机容量9168门，实装用户7803部，交换机实装率85.11%；农话交换机容量10896门，实装8405部，交换机实装率77.14%；宽带设备容量4800端口，实装2998户，实装率62.46%；LAN共48端口，实装36端口，实装率75%。

三、业务经营

1978—1997年，电信业务主要有固定电话（市话、农话）、电报。1997年7月，开办移动电话业务。

1998年10月后，电信业务主营固定电话、移动电话。是年，市话放号276户，用户数2150户；农村电话放号138户，用户数596户；新增移动电话246户，用户数407户；新增无线寻呼317户，用户数1676户；新增公用电话8户，全年到达33户；新增数据用户3户，全年到达5户。

1999年，市话放号806部，用户数到达3112户；农话放号283部，用户数到达882户；公用电话新增32户，总数达91户；分组交换专线用户5户；DDN用户3户；互联网拨号上网用户28户。全县电话普及率达到2.5部/百人，县城电话普及率20.27部/百人。

2002年，市话用户到达6137户，农话用户到达5069户，全县电话普及率为7.04/百人，县城电话普及率31.16部/百人，农村电话普及率3.47部/百人。

2005年，通信市场竞争激烈，用户拆机数量大，县电信部门调整经营策略，完成固定电话放号3100部，小灵通减少270部，宽带业务ADSL用户新增550户，公用电话减少50户，无线程控电话装机放号1030部。

2006年，固定电话放号1000部；小灵通放号960部；宽带业务ADSL用户新增600户；公用电话新增200户，用户数到达1005户；“致富星”无线程控电话电话放号1500部，用户数到达2157部；办理个人通信助理转型业务278户。

2007年，全县电话（含市话、农话、小灵通、公用电话）累计净增2779户；“致富星”电话累计净增1364户，用户到达数3094户；公用电话累计净增115户，用户到达数1107户。全年宽带用户净增496户（含LAN）。

2008年，全县电话用户到达数23243户。其中，城市固定电话累计净增719户，用户到达数7329户；小灵通累计净增2890户，用户到达数4189户；农村电话累计减少712户，用户到达数7343户；“致富星”电话累计净增700户，用户到达数4382户；公用电话累计净增63户，用户到达数1153户。全年宽带用户净增780户（含LAN）。

1998—2008年全县电信基本业务统计表

表18－2

年度	固定电话用户（户）	小灵通用户（户）	宽带用户（户）	业务收入（万元）
1998	3545	—	—	465
1999	3994	—	—	458
2000	6373	108	—	524
2001	8860	210	—	640
2002	11206	599	128	710
2003	13052	2812	383	801
2004	11060	4790	812	952
2005	14166	4510	1352	930
2006	14903	5328	1890	1054
2007	12908	5536	2411	1121
2008	19054	4189	3054	1170

第三节 移动通信 联通通信

一、移动通信

1999年6月，从县电信局分出移动通信业务，建立中国移动通信集团贵州有限公司荔波分公司，资产分营307.50万元，有县城、立化、小七孔移动通信基站3个，有在职人员7人、退休5人。

2001年，在县城开发区广场东路投资60万元新建办公楼，占地1085平方米，建有传输中心机房，2003年竣工投入使用。是年，推出全球通、黔中游等多种通信服务品牌，开始建设荔波移动

“乡乡通”工程，新建移动通信基站和架设通信光缆，覆盖全县17个乡（镇）和部分景区景点。

2004年起，实施“村村通移动电话”工程，至2007年年底，建成覆盖全县17个乡（镇）、94个行政村、各主要旅游景点、交通干道的移动通信网络。

从2007年开始，逐步在乡（镇）建立营业网点，同时成立茂兰片区中心，实行属地化管理。至2008年，全县建成移动通信基站130个，设营业厅19个，在册员工和业务代理人员总计50人。

二、联通通信

2000年，中国联通公司进驻荔波，设立中国联通公司荔波营业厅，向社会招聘工作人员7名，新建2G通信基站和通信光缆。

2002年5月，成立中国联通公司荔波县营业部，新建CDMA2000网络通信基站并于年底开通。

2004年4月26日，成立中国联合通信股份有限公司荔波县分公司。

2005年年底，建成CDMA2000基站45个，实现CDMA网络“乡乡通”。

2008年8月，荔波CDMA2000网络划归荔波电信部门。至年末，荔波分公司建成2G基站共74个，实现联通GSM网络“乡乡通”，村通网络覆盖达80%，覆盖全县17个乡（镇）和部分景区景点。全县有营业厅7个（自建1个、合作6个）、专卖店4个，有代理及便利渠道商家70家，在册员工和业务代理人员总计45人。

第十九篇
城乡建设　环境保护

1978年以来，荔波县城建设经历了“量力而行、分期建设、流动发展，举债建设、卖地还贷，招商引资、以地换路”三个发展阶段。1990年以前荔波县还是贵州48个国家级贫困县之一，县城建成区面积不足0.5平方公里，人口不足1万人。东西南北四条小街宽不足10米，总长不到1.5公里，街道上晴天是“扬灰路”，雨天是“水泥路”，每逢赶场就无法通行。1990年后，荔波县城实现了“一年一个样，年年有变样”。荔波县城迅速扩大，城区面积从1990年的0.5平方公里发展到2008年的2.5平方公里。许多客商看到了荔波的发展前景，纷纷涌来开店兴业，富裕起来的农民也纷纷进城建房、买房，一个现代化的县城逐渐形成，被人们誉为贵州高原上的一颗明珠。荔波先后荣获贵州省“小城镇建设先进县”“园林绿化先进县”称号；连续六次在全省“黄果树杯”城镇综合治理竞赛中获县城组第二名；多次荣获全州建设目标考核一等奖；贵州第一个国家级“卫生县城”、第一个“世界自然遗产地”、国家级“科技示范县”“生态文明示范县”，还被《国家地理》杂志评为“中国最美的地方”，是人们心目中后发的旅游理想目的地，荔波跃入全省小城镇先进行列。

1978年以来，荔波县特别注重环境的保护，开展了一系列治理环境污染的工作。特别在煤炭开发，旅游业开发，世界自然遗产地申报的重大工程中，一直将环境保护、生态保护放在首要位置。2005年10月，荔波县创建国家级生态示范区建设工作通过国家环保总局复核验收。2006年3月23日，国家环保总局正式命名荔波县为第四批国家级生态示范区，县环保局被国家环保总局评为“全国生态示范区工作先进集体”。

第一章 城乡建设

第一节 县城建设

1978—1990年，县城建设发展缓慢，城内街道主要有以原十字街（即现在的小十字）为中心的东、南、西、北街和河街5条主街道及其他小巷共十余条，县城区面积不足1平方公里，其中向阳中路（北街）为商业街，河街（繁荣路）以路为市进行赶集交易活动。2001年，开始实施房地产开发后，先后对沙梨园片区、板吉片区、苗圃片区、时来坝片区进行开发建设。至2008年，城区面积扩展到3.8平方公里。

一、规划

1978年年初，县计委组织编制《荔波县城市功能局部规划示意图》。

1984年，县政府启动县城总体规划工作，到1985年10月完成《荔波县城1985—2000年总体规划》，1986年经省、州审查批准实施。

1991年，经县政府同意，对《荔波县城1985—2000年总体规划》中的道路网络进行局部修改设计。

1996—1997年，委托省城乡规划设计研究院对原县城总体规划进行修编，并通过省、州评审。修编后的总体规划期限为1996—2010年。修编后的规划范围为东起狮子口，西至回龙阁，北至登高坡，南至望城坡，包括已建城区和时来、官塘、板吉村寨、田坝，规划区面积为9.11平方公里，可供建设用地3平方公里。

1997年，成立县规划管理办公室，隶属县建设局领导，负责全县的房屋建设规划管理工作。是年，县政府制定《荔波县玉屏镇建设规划管理实施办法》，县城建设严格按照这一实施办法统一规划管理，任何单位和个人在规划区范围内建造房屋和构筑物都要通过规划管理部门审查，办理规划许可手续后实行放线施工。

2001年，委托重庆建筑大学规划设计院编制《樟江两岸及环城西路等重点地段控制性详细规划和园林建设规划》，并按照总体规划的建设要求，制定县城基础设施建设“十五”计划，将重点建设项目纳入“十五”计划中。

2007—2008年，编制《荔波县建设国际化专业旅游城市概念规划》《中国贵州荔波县旅游发展规划》《县城时来片区修建性详细规划》《荔波县樟江大街风貌规划及县城小街小巷整治规划》。

二、建设

（一）房屋建设

1990年以前，县城的房屋建设全部是砖瓦或木瓦结构，有代表性的建筑物是老电影院、邮电局大楼，县政府、农业局、县供销社、水电局、时来乡政府办公楼和人民大礼堂。

1990年以后，特别是县樟江大街、樟江北街、建设东路、建设西路、苗圃路、市场路、沙梨园路、民族路等开发后，县城房屋建设发生很大变化。县城居民从开发商手中购得土地开始建房，居民建房都是砖混结构，一般是3～4层，少部分是5层。邻街的房屋，一层是门面，二层以上住房。财政局、人社局、地矿局、汽车站、工矿贸易公司、县医院、烟酒糖公司、交通局等沿街单位新建砖混结构办公房，建成区面积不断扩大。2008年，县城的标志性高层建筑为三力酒店。

（二）公共设施建设

1.街道

1980—1987年，县政府投资共31.18万元，对县城东、南、西、北街与河街及政府大门通往马道6条主次街道进行整修，全部建成混凝土路面。

1990年12月，县委、县政府决定逐步改善县城街道等基础设施建设，成立大街建设指挥部，组织实施县城道路建设。1991年4月—1994年9月，总投资461.3万元，分三期建成樟江大街，街道长1344.1米、宽24米（两边人行道各6米）。

1992年9月—1993年8月，投资280万元，修建荔波至独山、三都、茂兰、朝阳4个方向的出城水泥路，1994年6月通过省验收，交付使用，由县城建局管护。4条出城路总长3601米，全部按宽30米水泥混凝土路面修建。

1994年4月，总投资92万元，开工建设樟江南路（即市场路），是年12月竣工投入使用，该路两端分别与综合市场和樟江大街相连，全长418米、宽16米（两边人行道各4米）。

1995年10月—1996年4月，总投资195万元，改造向阳路，全长670米。

1996年6月—1997年7月，总投资107.6万元，改造向阳北路，全长286米，宽20～24米。同时，总投资110万元，新建樟江北路，全长546米，宽16米，两边人行道各4米，该路两端分别与樟江大街和向阳北路连接。

2001年10月—2002年年底，投资195万元，对西门大街进行改造。

2002—2003年，分别完成民生路、建设西路、沙犁园站路、民族路、广场路、吉祥路、苗圃路、长征路的修建。

2006年2—3月，总投资142.56万元，对南门街进行改造。改造后的南门街道长792米、宽7.5米。

2007年，投资1000多万元，对风景管理处至信合宾馆1500米樟江大街实施综合改造，改造后机行道宽12米，两边绿化带和人行道分别为4.5米；投资900多万元，对樟江大街两则临街房屋进行立面改造；同时，实施恩铭大道、江滨路、阳光路、菜园路、板栽路、外环西路修建和北出口公路改造。其中，恩铭大道长1454米，宽35米，双向4车道，中间设有绿化隔离带，总投资3800多万元；江滨路长4964米，宽19米，总投资4700多万元；阳光路长745米，宽20米，总投资745多万元；菜园路长988米，宽20米，总投资1000多万元；板栽路长1170米，宽30米，总投资2650万元；外环西路长203米，宽20米，投资142.56万元；北出口公路长300米，宽30米，总投资800万元。

2008年，先后实施官塘大道一期、二期工程建设，其中一期工程长1240米，宽30米，总投资2790万元；二期工程长250米，宽15米，总投资450万元。2008年年末，县城街道主次干道总25条，总长18667米，其中主干次干道10条，支道15条，宽度8～35米不等，多数为20米。

在县城主要道路建设、改造的同时，还对小吃街及居民区小巷便道进行路面硬化，方便居民出行。

2.排水设施

县城污水管网建于20世纪80年代初期，设置地下排水管道，污水排放分两片运行。第一片包括樟江北街、农业局、财政局至汽车站、大榕树脚一带的污水，全部集中在金锣湾的地下排水道直接排入樟江河。第二片包括乡镇小区南街、苗圃街、樟江园广场、沙梨园片区、南门、马道、民中一带、农贸市场、西门的污水，通过地下排水道流入板吉排洪大沟，直接排入县城樟江河下游。在县城规划区内，樟江风景名胜区没有产生污染的厂矿，只有生活污水污染樟江河下游。

2007年，建县城污水处理厂，并列为重点建设项目，至2008年仍在建设中。

3.街道照明

1978年时，县城居民户户用上电灯，县城主要街道均安装路灯，为白炽灯泡。1990年，县城的4条主街道和樟江大桥路灯更换为新型光源汞灯和钠灯。

1991年，樟江大街改造第一期工程新安装路灯。至1995年年底，县城有路灯220盏，总装容量39千瓦，保证县城街道正常照明。其中，1994年投资10万元，在樟江大桥头广场中心安装20米高杆升降灯。

1998—1999年，实施街道路灯亮丽工程，至2005年，大小街道增至30余条，在原有路灯的基础上，主要大街新装路灯有宫廷灯64盏、中杆水银灯48盏、钠灯865盏、射灯6盏、空中玫瑰灯及七彩灯4盏、桥面射灯8盏、霓虹灯600米、大型广告牌灯15块，总装容量43.66千瓦。是年，包括主要大街亮丽工程在内，路灯总装容量增至21.62万千瓦。

2007年，进行樟江大街照明路灯改造，对樟江大街的所有管线实施地埋。改造工程完成后，县城街灯美观亮丽。

4.广场

1999年前，县城广场主要在县委、人民大礼堂、体育场、文化局后面一带，有球场，是县城群众活动的主要场所，1999年对该处大榕树进行保护，扩建改造后命名为榕园，2000年，将该广场改造成绿地，名为务政园。

2001年，将县司法局前面空地改造成绿地，建有鱼池，种有荷花，命名为荷花园。同时，对林业局对面的长廊改造成休闲长廊，命名为长廊休闲园。

从1999年开始在县城樟江大街西北部新建樟江园广场，至2002年交付使用，总建筑面积2.76万平方米，其中绿地面积1.45万平方米。园内建有音乐喷泉1组、旱地喷泉1组、大型电视屏幕1座，有专门的休闲运动区，配备系列休闲运动器材，设置花架、雕塑等。广场绿化种植热带、亚热带树种与境内原生树种，构成独特的植物景观。

2007年，为迎接贵州省第二届旅游产业发展大会在荔波召开，对县城实施大规模旧城改造和樟江沿岸景观改造，新建江滨公园，占地面积约3000平方米，总投资800多万元。

2008年，县城休闲广场有樟江园、荷花园、榕树园、长廊休闲园等，总建设面积4.47万平方米。其中，面积最大的休闲广场为樟江园。

（三）公用事业

1.城镇供水

县城用水以樟江河水为水源。1978年后，县城供水仍由城北自来水厂（黄泥坡清水池）供水。年供水量仅4万立方米。1988年，安装大小输水管长达4.1万米；1990年，日供水量达1250立方米，县城供水率为80%。

1995年，投入80万元扩建水厂，日供水量达5000立方米，水质综合合格率达90%，县城自来水普及率达98%。1999年，投入483万元对水厂进行技改扩建；2001—2006年，又先后投入927.06万元，再次对水厂进行技改扩建，日供水量突破10000立方米。至2008年，全城区供水主管网长达16公里，总管网长度为42公里，供水普及率达100%。

2.城区交通

1995年前，县城除有汽车站进行长途客运外，城内无公共交通工具及设施。1996年后，县城客运兴起，客运交通工具有人力三轮车及自制改装的机动边三轮车，其中自制改装机动边三轮车达80余辆。

1999年，全县取缔自制改装机动边三轮车，改换正规厂家生产的三轮车进行城区营运。是年，增加出租汽车10辆。因对机动三轮车缺乏有效监管，控制不严，导致数量猛增，至2006年达到255辆。机动三轮车大量增加后，争抢客源，且车况较差，安全隐患大，影响荔波旅游城市形象。从2007年8月1日起，禁止机动三轮车载客营运，城区客运车辆统一使用出租汽车从事客运。是年，共有出租汽车50辆。

3.民用燃料

县城居民长期使用燃煤作生活燃料。2001年，液化石油气开始在县城销售。由于具有使用方便、卫生等优势而逐渐得到普及，成为原煤的替代燃料。至2008年，县内有石油液化气储备供应站1家，气源由贵阳液化石油气供应总站用槽车运送至荔波县城，燃气用户也由最初的100多户发展到3000多户。

4.环境卫生

（1）环卫设施。1978年，县城清运垃圾工具只有人力车和手扶拖拉机各1辆。1981年添置130型汽车1辆，1987年购置131型密封式垃圾车1辆。1990年，环卫机具拥有手推车6部、130型货车1辆、131型密封式垃圾车1辆、垃圾桶84个、垃圾池6个。1991年后，县城不断增添公共卫生设施。1995年，购8吨洒水车1辆，晴天每天定时上街洒水2～3次。1996年，政府投资购买垃圾吊运车2辆，大型收运车2辆，小街小巷收运车2辆，做到垃圾日产日清，清收吊运率100%。至2005年，县城先后建成水冲式标准公厕8座，县城街道垃圾的清扫设施主要有吸尘车2辆、洒水车2辆，每天早、中、晚轮流对主要街道进行清扫和洒水。另外，在樟江大街安装有果皮箱60个，其他街道安装有可移动单、双桶果皮箱总计120个，居民小区和住户集中地段安装有10个铁合金底面积3平方米以上的小垃圾房。是年底，县财政投入环卫设施资金累计450万元。2006年，县政府出资购买吊臂车1辆。2007年，获省政府赠送1辆10吨洒水车、2辆小收运车、1辆越野车，建成水冲式标准公厕4座，安装果皮箱120个。2008年，政府出资购买清扫车1辆。

（2）街道清扫。从1979年开始，县城街道卫生由县卫生防疫站聘用临时工清扫。1984年7月，建立县环卫管理站，清洁工增至11人。1985年，辞退全部临时工，招收16名合同制清洁工，实行半日保洁制，清扫主要街道，清扫范围1.6万平方米，清扫保洁率70%。1991年，日清扫街道面积2.29万平方米。随着城区扩大，1995年后，日清扫面积4.87万平方米。2005年，环卫工人增至28人，日清扫面积26.5万平方米。2008年，县环卫站将县城分为28个服务区，实行承包清扫保洁制，承包人每天对承包路段进行大清扫2次，保洁时间至晚上9时。

（3）垃圾处理。1985年，为处理好垃圾问题，环卫部门投资0.68万元，在登高坡后面距县城3公里、原荔波至独山公路旁的董蒙山脚修建垃圾临时存放场，每天将城内生活垃圾清收吊运到该场倾倒，并及时消杀、填埋。2006年后，县政府向省、州申报县城生活垃圾填埋场项目，经省发改委批复，列入2007年省重点项目进行建设，2008年年底投入使用。县城公厕粪便通过三级化粪池排入污水管道，居民小区及县城所有的粪便和生活污水也通过2～3级化粪池处理后排入污水管道。

（4）卫生监管。1990年年初，成立县城建设管理监察队，受玉屏镇政府和县建设局双重领导。1991年，县政府发布《关于搞好玉屏镇市容环境卫生管理的布告》后，县建设局制定《玉屏镇市容环境卫生管理实施处罚细则》，环卫站及时制定县城环境卫生达标管理措施，将环卫工作分片包干，任务落实到人。1995年，制定《荔波县城镇市容环境卫生、城建监察管理办法》，加强县城“脏、乱、差”治理，并从城南、城北居委会聘请退休干部为县城市容卫生监督员。1996年4月，撤销县城建设管理监察队，成立县城镇建设管理监察中队，编制7人，归口县建设局管理。1998年4月为充实城建管理监察队伍，县劳动人事部门从复退军人中安置4名复退军人到城建管理监察中队，人员编制为事业。1999年，县公用事业局成立后，县城建管理监察中队划归公用事业局管理（事业编制）。城建管理监察中队先后制定《行政执法公示制度》《行政执法责任制度》《行政执法过错责任追究制度》《行政执法督查制度》等，对市政工程、公用事业、园林绿化、市容环境、卫生等实施监督、检查。至2008年，县环卫管理部门制定有环境卫生督察、清扫保洁管理、清收吊运车辆管理、垃圾场管理、环卫车辆、工具维修管理等制度，监督环卫工作正常开展，保持市容整洁。

（四）园林绿化

1978—1990年，县城总体绿化由县政府统一安排植树育树，各单位庭院绿化由单位自行安排种植花草树木。同时，号召城镇居民栽花种草，美化环境。

从1991年起，县城园林绿化工作由县环卫站负责。是年，樟江大街第一期工程竣工后，县政府投资2.7万元购置具有南国风光的南洋杉、假槟榔、小叶榕、鱼尾葵等4种树苗173株种植在大街两边绿化池内，县环卫站及时安排专人管理，成活率85%。樟江大街第二期、第三期工程竣工后，县环卫站购置桂花、夜合花、蒲葵、九里香等树种花苗对街道进行绿化，成活率90%，樟江大街形成独具特色的绿化带。

1993年，有环卫工人3名专门进行绿化管理。1994—1995年，完成樟江南路、出城公路及大桥头花坛绿化植物种植。

1996年，投入3万元在原有街道绿化池中补栽九里香3万株，其他树种40株，并将大榕树扇形花坛改建为草坪绿地。

至2005年，在县城主要街道种植鱼尾葵约370株、假槟榔560株、杧果树480株。在城市绿化中，除大量引进具有南国热带、亚热带特色的花草树木外，还选用县内树形优美、无害、根系不发达、易养护的原生树种，用于城市行道树、城市景观绿化，其中樟树400株、乐昌含笑180株、深山含笑260株，将荔波县城打造成为省内具有“南国”风光特点的城市。

2008年，县城区内公共绿地面积达到20多万平方米，绿地率22.51%，人均公共绿地面积7.46平方米，县城绿化覆盖率38%。

第二节　村镇建设

一、村镇规划与建设

1985年10月，开始村镇规划编制工作。1987年，省、州划拨规划经费近3万元，由县规划设计室和州规划设计室共同完成全县乡（镇）驻地规划编制工作。此后，乡（镇）驻地按规划进行建设。1990年后，各乡（镇）新建政府综合办公楼、邮电所、营业所、影院、文化娱乐场所，部分乡（镇）新建街道、农贸市场，场、路分开。1993年，完成驾欧乡、播尧乡、茂兰镇市场进行市场规划设计。

1994年，成立县村镇建设管理站，对乡（镇）的规划设计和建设进行管理。是年，茂兰镇、播尧乡、驾欧乡对原规划进行调整。

1995年，编制佳荣乡总体规划并通过审定，经县政府批准实施，成为县内第一个完成总体规划法定手续的乡。是年，省、州批准，将茂兰镇、佳荣乡列为县级小城镇建设试点乡（镇）。

2000年7月—2001年5月，州规划设计室编制甲良镇、立化镇、茂兰镇、佳荣镇、播尧乡总体规划。

1996—2006年，先后进行甲良、茂兰、'佳荣、立化、朝阳、翁昂、驾欧、方村、捞村、播尧、洞塘等乡（镇）所在地道路设计和施工建设，以及进行王蒙集镇、阳凤集镇农贸市场建设。其间，1999年，立化镇被省人民政府列为全省“双百”小城镇建设试点镇；2000年7月—2001年5月，州规划设计室完成甲良镇、立化镇、茂兰镇、佳荣镇、播尧乡的总体规划编制工作。

至2008年，荔波县先后获州“小城镇建设先进县”、省“小城镇建设先进县城”称号。

二、民族村寨建设与保护

瑶山乡董蒙村寨是荔波县具有代表性的瑶族村寨，有房屋42栋，其中瓦房39栋，人均住房9.7平方米。

瑶族住房原为“杈杈房”。随着生活逐渐改善，改建干栏式房屋。进入20世纪90年代，房屋大多为干栏式瓦房。

董蒙瑶族村寨具有代表性的建筑为禾仓，其结构类似吊脚楼，圆锥形，四柱脚，主体是篱笆包围的禾仓，尖顶是茅草屋顶。禾仓圆柱脚全部嵌镶倒扣瓦罐。这种禾仓防鼠、防虫、防霉变。

2000年，省建设厅、文化厅组织专家组到瑶山瑶族乡考察，选定董蒙和拉片两地作为全省20个重点民族保护建设村寨。此后，县政府按照省政府的要求，成立瑶山民族村寨保护建设领导小组，制定保护民族村寨措施，保护民族村寨建筑。

2001年，省建设厅拨款15万元，对董蒙、拉片民族村寨进行地形图测绘。2002年6月，荔波县委托省城乡规划设计研究院编制董蒙、拉片瑶族村寨保护建设规划。规划将保护范围划分为一级保护区和二级保护区两个层次。一级保护区为村寨中瑶族家居形态保存完好，历史及风貌遗存所在的范围；二级保护区为一级保护区的周围需控制协调的范围，包括核心一级保护区周围的完整山体、水体、林地、农田等距离在100米范围之内。保护内容包括自然生态、村寨聚居形态、历史文化、生活方式、民风民俗、特色景观。其中，董蒙瑶族民居建设因保存较为完好，作为重点保护对象；拉片在保护的基础上，可兴建民族文化博物馆、民族歌舞、节日活动表演场。规划通过省建设厅组织的专家评审，经全省重点民族村寨保护建设联席会议办公室批准实施。

从2003年起，县委、县政府筹措资金，按规划对拉片、董蒙两个民族村寨进行保护性建设，先后对民族村寨的道路进行硬化，对民房进行保护性改造，修建通往董蒙民族村寨旅游公路等。

至2008年，省、州、县投入民族村寨建设资金累计698.8万元，建成停车场、民族文化展演场、瑶族文化博物馆、接待站、旅游商品市场、寨内通车石板道、石板步道、公厕、排污沟、绿化、环卫设施、蓄水池、消防设施，并进行文物收集和保护。

三、新农村建设

从1997年起，首次对一类贫困村瑶山瑶族乡菇类村进行规划并实施改造。是年，投入资金36.9万元完成该村规划，将茅草屋改造为水泥砖房123户。

2002年，县财政投入49.5万元，改善瑶山瑶族乡拉片村瑶族群众住房，新建木质结构房屋33栋，每栋投入资金1.5万元。

2004年，中国人民解放军总参谋部捐资30万元，由群众投工投劳，对更粪民房进行改造建设，改造民房27栋，建成小水窖75口；“一池三改配套（养猪）”投入资金20万元（其中养猪10万元，一池三改10万元）。

2005年，瑶山乡菇类村被列为全省20个民族村寨保护之一，得到省州大力支持，完成对该组50户民房改造、人畜饮水、停车场、村寨路面硬化、进寨石板路、公厕等旅游基础设施建设。

2006年，投入100万元实施洞塘乡木朝村社会主义新农村建设项目，包括房屋改造、入户村道路修建等，该村基础设施改善后，具备了乡村旅游接待能力。是年9月，县政府投入49.5万元对洞塘乡板寨村民房和村寨环境进行改造。另外，省建设厅补助专项资金50万元，编制茂兰自然保护区内拉桥村整治规划，进行村寨环境整治。

2007年，洞塘乡板寨村列为省级“百村试点”社会主义新农村建设试点村，永康乡尧古村拉桥组（自然寨）列为省建设厅新农村建设试点村，县委、县政府按照“生产发展、生活宽裕、乡风文明、村容整洁、管理民主”的总要求，提出“试点村先行、以点带面、逐步推进”的思路，开展社会主义新农村建设。

是年，县建设局对板寨、拉桥两个村的民房、道路走向、给排水、绿化配置等进行规划设计。在规划设计时，结合板寨村、拉桥寨的历史、人文、地貌地形等因素，在房屋的立面改造上，依据板寨村、拉桥寨的传统民居模式，分别改造成仿木结构的小青瓦屋面，外立面改造成仿清水墙或实木墙，体现布依族、水族民居风格。项目实施后，投入资金总计90万元，解决板寨村群众饮水难问题；投入20万元实施“一池三改”（建沼气池、改厕、改圈、改厨）工程，建成沼气池200口，占全村总户数的52%；安装无线座机电话49部，电视覆盖率达80%；投入50万元对拉尤组移民新村房屋外立面进行改造；投资20万元对板寨村18户危房进行改造；投资21万元对板寨村1.1公里连户道路进行硬化；投资3万元建成200平方米的板寨村文艺表演场；投入10万元修建1个公厕；投入2万元修建停车场1个。同时，将板寨村、拉桥寨村庄整治列入申报世界自然遗产环境综合整治项目，省、州建设部门下拨资金43万元，用于拉桥民族村寨环境整治。县委、县政府组织资金进行村寨道路、停车场、供水、消防、牲畜棚、沼气池等基础设施建设。至此，板寨村、拉桥村成为道路硬化、村庄美化、卫生洁化、生产生活条件明显改善的社会主义新农村。

同时，县委、县政府将板寨、拉桥新农村建设与发展旅游业结合起来，争取到省投资1400万元，修建67公里乡村旅游公路，16个村民小组中有11个村民小组通柏油公路。依托板寨红七军会师旧址、黎明关等红色旅游景点和板寨瑶寨、拉桥水族寨民族风情景点以及喀斯特地貌景点，引导农户30户开展“农家乐”旅游接待服务。

是年，县财政投入320万元对玉屏镇拉鱼村、瑶山乡拉柳村进行村寨环境综合整治、房屋立面改造、道路硬化，新建停车场、公厕等。投入80万元对王蒙大街房屋立面进行改造。

2008年，实施瑶山乡拉片村和瑶麓乡大寨村环境整治。其中，投入121万元在拉片村新建水冲式公厕189平方米、垃圾收集点178平方米、休闲亭廊172平方米、绿化地700平方米、停车场960平方米、入村道路800米；投入114万元在大寨村建垃圾收集点138平方米、寨门1个、进村道路1060米、排水沟70米。

第三节 建筑业

一、建筑企业

1978年，县内属集体性质建筑企业有县建筑工程队、城关镇基建队（后改名城关镇建筑工程队）。1984年，县建筑工程队改为县建筑公司，城关镇建筑工程队改为玉屏镇建筑工程队。此后，建立甲良区建筑公司、方村建筑队。至1990年年末，全县建筑企业有4家，均属乡（镇）集体性质。

1993年9月，玉屏镇建筑工程队改为玉屏镇建筑公司。1998年6月，省建设厅核定玉屏镇建筑公司为四级施工企业。

1999年，将方村建筑队并入甲良区建筑工程公司，资质改为四级建筑企业。

2002年，按国家规定，具有三级以上资质的建筑企业才能承包建筑工程。为适应建筑市场要求，县建设局将县建筑公司、玉屏镇建筑公司、甲良区建筑公司、荔波县城乡开发公司合并，成立荔波县建设工程有限责任公司，资质为三级企业。

至2008年，县属建筑企业只有县建设工程有限责任公司1家。

此外，从1986年起，外来工程队先后进入荔波承接建筑工程，主要有柳州街道建筑队、广东电白工程队、广西陆川建筑队等。

二、建筑设计与监管

（一）建筑设计

1978—1980年，建筑设计工作由施工单位自行承担。

1985年，成立县建筑设计室（属集体所有制单位）。1987年，县建筑设计室经省建设主管部门批准，获得技术丁级证书。

1988年，县建筑设计室与县规划设计室合并，可进行木质结构、砖混结构、钢筋混凝土结构、高4～6层、局部7层等建筑项目设计。

2003年，县建筑设计室和县规划设计室实行职能分离，县建筑设计室不具备设计资质，挂靠黔南州建筑设计院，更名为黔南州建筑设计院荔波分院，实行企业管理，设计资质提升为乙级，主要承担县内工程设计和测量任务。到2008年，县内进行勘测设计单位仅黔南州建筑设计院荔波分院。

（二）违法建筑整治

1993年，开始对县城规划区内的违法建筑进行调查、整治。是年，整治违法建筑2户。1995—2003年，整治违法违规建筑34户。

2004—2006年，整治违法违规建筑55户，下达停工通知书28份（户），其中强制撤除1户。

从2007年起，对县内建设工程实行工程监理制度，在建工程由县国资监理公司进行监理。

2007—2008年，全县整治违法违规建筑117户，下达停工通知书83份（户）。

第二章 住房和房地产业

第一节 住房制度改革

1993年1月，成立县住房制度改革领导小组，根据《贵州省住房制度改革实施方案》的要求，拟定《荔波县实施〈贵州省住房制度改革实施方案〉办法》，在机关职工中进行广泛讨论后修订，经县委、县政府审定通过。同时，将《荔波县实施〈贵州省住房制度改革实施方案〉办法》《荔波县城镇公有住房出租租金标准实施细则》《荔波县城镇公有住房提租补贴实施细则》《荔波县公有住房出售实施细则》报省、州审批。3月，省、州房改领导小组批准县房改实施方案。9月，正式开展售房业务。到年底，有干部职工473人（户）向61个房屋产权单位预交购房款275.8万元，参加集资建房户63户，预交集资建房款31.5万元。1993年9月—1994年12月，县内出售公有住房新房按标准价每平方米180元计算购房款，旧房按重置价每平方米160元计算购房款，购房产权比例为71%。

1995年11月，县住房制度改革领导小组印发《关于执行住房公积金的通知》，从1996年开始建立全县住房公积金制度。1995年1月到1997年年底的新旧房屋（包括集资建房）均按每平方米304元计算购房款，购房产权比例为100%。

建立公积金制度后，在县建设局设县住房改革办公室，为住房公积金管理单位，负责住房公积金的归集、管理和使用审批工作，公积金使用和提取按县房改实施方案办理，具体业务由县建设银行信贷部统一办理，为缴交单位和职工建立明细账户，职工个人和单位均按工资总额计算，缴交比例最低为3%，县财政未匹配补贴住房公积金。

1998年，增加县工商银行及县农业银行为业务经办银行。

2000年，州房改领导小组批准《荔波县住房分配集市化改革实施细则》。到2003年10月，全县有42个单位855人缴存公积金，总计183.03万元。2004年6月，全县公积金缴存单位44个，缴存人数934人。

2004年6月，设立黔南州住房公积金管理中心荔波管理部，县房改办于是年7月30日将住房公积

县城居民居住小区之一

金管理职责移交黔南州住房公积金管理中心荔波县管理部，同时将其管理的公积金总额264.77万元全额划转县公积金管理部开设的专户，管理部为各缴存单位及职工设立总账及个人明细账，管理部从8月起正式办理业务。

2005年5月，荔波县开始办理个人住房公积金贷款业务，是年发放贷款130户，贷款年末金额844.1万元，收回贷款16.10万元。

至2007年，通过房改，全县有购买公有住房、集资建房户1285户。

2004—2008年全县公积金归集情况一览表

表19－1

年度	归集（万元）	支取（万元）	余额（万元）	缴交单位（个）	缴交人数（人）	缴交比例（%）
2004	286.26	46.95	497.08	122	5001	3
2005	830.55	110.17	1217.46	126	5110	5
2006	1091.32	169.58	2139.20	139	5499	5
2007	1203.12	284.92	3057.40	143	5695	5
2008	1467.70	464.87	4060.23	146	5744	5

说明：1996—2003年无公积金统计报表，住房公积金管理中心成立后，县公积金管理部门只移交累计金额、总单位数和总人数。

2005—2008年全县公积金贷款情况一览表

表19－2

年度	发放金额（万元）	发放户数（户）	收回本金（万元）	收回利息（万元）	收回罚息（元）	贷款余额（万元）
2005	844.10	130	16.10	9.03	16.94	828.01
2006	701.60	107	130.30	41.52	164.54	1399.30
2007	599.78	84	206.31	60.00	471.75	1792.78
2008	511.97	60	235.22	90.46	962.14	2069.52

第二节 房地产开发

1992年，成立县房地产开发公司，隶属县政府办。至1997年，县内仍未形成独立、规范的房地产市场，无商品楼房出售。

从1998年后，先后拍卖县城部分土地，开发建设沙梨园、教师新村、板吉新区、乡镇小区、苗圃新区、时来新区等住宅小区。在部分乡（镇）驻地，由开发商建成商铺、门面后对外出售。

在荔波县从事房地产开发的公司有黔南天力房地产开发有限公司荔波分公司、荔波县柳荔房地产开发有限责任公司。2004年，柳荔房地产开发有限公司开发的金荔大厦项目（骨科医院），总建筑面积9450.12平方米，项目总投资756.1万元。

2005年，成立县城乡房地产开发有限公司。是年，黔南天力房地产开发有限公司荔波分公司开发向阳中路金锣湾商场（步行街）和广场北路樟江园夜市项目，两个项目总用地面积7572.60平方米，总建筑面积1.08万平方米。县城乡房地产开发有限公司开发艺苑楼项目，总面积2635平方米，总投资144.2万元。

2006—2008年，县城乡房地产开发有限公司先后开发玉屏镇文明路建筑公司商住楼（总建筑面积2721.52平方米）、樟江北路金阁园小区（建筑总面积4200平方米）、荣西商住楼（建筑面积2404平方米）。

第三节 房屋管理与房产交易

1986年10月，成立县房产管理所，隶属建设局。1987年，开展城镇房屋产权清查，到1990年，县城私房产权清查、登记和户主变更手续全部完成。城镇公房管理仍由各单位自建、自用、自管。职工住宅公房按单位所定标准收取房租，作为维修费用。

1991—1993年，办理公、私房屋所有权证400户。

1995年，开始办理房屋产权过户业务。

1996年，县城房屋租赁管理工作开始起步，对县城310户房屋租赁情况进行调查，并整理建档。

1994—1997年，县房屋管理部门办理公、私房屋所有权证145户，处理房产纠纷5起，开展房产价值抵押评估99宗。

1998年，进行公有房屋产权登记并发产权证单位22个，勘丈房屋建筑面积1.81万平方米；私有房屋产权登记103户，勘丈房屋建筑面积约2.13万平方米，发证72户；房产抵押登记104宗，房产估价金额795.68万元。

2000—2001年，审核办理房屋所有权证233宗，办理房产证交易26宗，房产评估379宗，房产抵押登记1093宗，抵押金额5382.15万元。

2003—2005年，先后制定《荔波县县城房屋拆迁管理暂行办法》《荔波县城2004年房屋交易基准价公告》《荔波县县城房屋交易价指导意见》，并经县政府批准施行。3年共办理房屋产权登记661宗、房产抵押登记1425宗，抵押金额14800.12万元。同时，开始办理房改房（二手房）上市交易登记，2004—2005年两年共办理55宗，面积5008.31平方米。

2006—2008年，全县房屋登记3340宗，建筑面积总计28.02万平方米；二手房交易16680平方米，商品房交易17018.48平方米。

第三章 环境保护

第一节 环境污染

一、水污染

境内河流、湖泊、水库主要有樟江河、打狗河、方村河、伍家河、三岔河、水春河、大七孔河、鸳鸯湖、甲介水库、伍家河水库、洪江水库等，水污染源为生活废水污染和工业废水污染。

（一）生活废水污染

1993年10月，县地面水环境功能区划分工作领导小组对地面水污染情况进行实地调查，结果为：

樟江河水域的水质状况分为四段，水春河上段全长29.1公里，水质未受污染，水质较好，主要为居民生活饮用和灌溉；水春至杨家桥段全长9.4公里，水质受到水尧水功煤厂废水和生活污水轻微影响，2001年，水功片区煤矿关闭后，水质逐渐恢复，为城镇居民生活饮用水集中取水点；杨家桥至回龙角段全长4公里，水质受城镇生活污水污染；回龙角至王蒙段全长20公里，水质受城镇及沿途居民生活污水污染。

打狗河、方村河主要用于灌溉，水质主要受沿河居民生活污水污染。

三岔河全长20公里，为沿河居民生活饮用水源，水质受打油寨矿废水污染。

鸳鸯湖库容量52.5万立方米，为源头水，未受污染，水质清洁。

甲介水库主要用于灌溉，库容量82万立方米，受甲介煤厂废水污染严重，水质浑浊呈黄色，不符合农用水灌溉卫生标准。

非重点水域水春河、大七孔、洪江水库主要用于灌溉，水质未受污染，水质清洁。

（二）工业废水污染

境内工业废水源于煤矿、砖瓦厂排放的废水，集中在水尧、茂兰、立化、佳荣、方村、播尧等乡（镇）。

伍家河全长20公里，水质受平寨矿、更班矿及周围小煤窑废水污染，pH值、悬浮物、硫、铁严重超标。

1996年10月，县政府成立县工业污染源调查领导小组，在县地矿局设办公室，开展全县乡镇工业污染源调查。调查内容：有污染的工业企业基本情况；污染物排放情况，包括废水、废气、工业固体废物；污染损失和生态破坏情况；环境管理情况，包括环境管理现状和治理设施情况。调查煤矿40个，排放污染物为工业废水、工业固体废物，均无治理设施；调查砖瓦厂3个，排放污染物为工业废水、废气和工业固体废物，均无治理设施。

2007年9月—2008年11月，开展全县第一次污染源普查。经查，全县有污染源共222个。其中，工业污染源为51个（水力发电行业7个，畜禽屠宰行业5个，黏土砖瓦及建筑砖块制造行业9个，铁合金冶炼行业2个，石灰和石膏制造行业1个，铅锌矿采选业2个，烟煤和无烟煤开采洗选业25个）；生活污染源171个（住宿餐饮业105个，居民服务和其他服务业57个，医院3个，城镇居民生活污染源6个）。污染源普查数据显示，全县工业用水总量57.91万余吨。其中，新鲜用水量54.11万立方米，占用水总量的93.42%；重复用水量3万立方米，工业用水重复率6.58%。工业废水产生量212.51万立方米（由于以煤矿废水为主，故废水产生量大于工业用水量），排放量191.59万立方米。

二、噪声污染

境内噪声主要源于交通、建筑施工和生活噪声。2004年起，州环境监测站开展城区环境质量现状监测，监测频次1年2次。在1.68平方公里建成区内，按《城市区域环境噪声测量方法》测量，有效测点数32个，连续两天进行昼、夜间监测。全县昼间等效声级范围为43.7～71.7分贝，昼间平均等效声级为61.6分贝；夜间等效声级范围为31.3～65.4分贝，夜间平均等效声级为52.7分贝；全县昼夜等效声级为62.0分贝，声环境质量为中度污染。

三、大气污染

县内工业企业少，废气排放量较小，居民生活能源以液化气、煤、电为主。此外，境内森林茂密，植被较好，有利于污染物消散与净化，大气环境质量状况优，达到国家《环境空气质量标准》（GB3095-1996）二级标准。

从1998年起，创建国家级卫生县城，开展建设县城烟尘控制区工作。按照国家烟尘控制区有关技术标准，对县水泥厂进行治理，取缔1吨以下经营性燃煤锅炉，对1吨以上燃煤锅炉进行限期治理，长期坚持取缔县城经营性燃煤炉灶，基本达到国家烟控区控制指标，县城建成区内各种炉、窑、灶排放的烟气黑度为87%，达到国家排放标准，区内炉窑、工业生产排放的烟尘为79%，达到国家排放标准。2004年3月20日通过州环保局验收。

2008年，境内大气污染主要源于燃料（木柴、煤、液化气）燃烧和汽车尾气等。

四、电磁辐射污染

1997年12月—1998年3月，对全县电磁辐射污染源进行调查，全县电磁辐射污染源有邮电局无线电寻呼发射台、移动电话发射基站、广播电视发射机及调频发射机、林业局观音峰差转台、防汛指挥部单边带短波电台等。这些电磁辐射源位置比较分散，大都架设在野外或远离人群的地方，运行总功率仅为0.51千瓦，污染少。

第二节 污染治理

一、生活污染治理

（一）县城区环境污染治理

1998年以前，城区环境质量相对较好，未开展城区环境污染治理工作。

1998年10月，县环保局邀请重庆市荣昌环境净化工程公司的有关专家到荔波实地考察，提出城镇生活污水治理方案，即运用无能耗厌氧处理技术对生活污水进行净化处理。

是年，购置噪声监测仪器，对县城区域的建筑噪声、娱乐声进行监测管理，县环保局、公安局、文化局联合对县城噪声污染源进行监督检查，规范25家，取缔噪声严重超标卡拉OK厅4家及县城中心影响较大的噪声污染源。

2003年，整治县城经营性燃煤锅炉，控制大气中二氧化硫含量，限制使用燃煤炉具，促使饮食服务业主使用清洁能源。是年，县城饮食行业使用清洁能源占35%。年底，县城二氧化硫浓度为每立方米0.03毫克，比2002年每立方米0.14毫克有所下降；县城大气悬浮颗粒浓度为每立方米0.10毫克，比1999年每立方米0.21毫克明显降低。

2005年，重点开展城区油烟、噪声污染整治。全年办结群众污染投诉34件，县政府督办3件，人大、政协提案7件。

2006年，针对群众反映的环保热点难点问题，坚持整治城区主要街道经营性燃煤炉灶，对各宾馆、酒店、浴池燃煤锅炉，严格按照规定规范管理。规范建筑施工、建筑材料生产与销售、装潢、营业性娱乐场所噪声排放源的作业时间，重点保护医院、学校、居民小区等噪声敏感区域。

是年，荔波县大气污染物指标：大气总悬浮物颗粒物为0.07毫克/立方米，二氧化硫为0.07毫克/立方米，二氧化氮为0.12毫克/立方米，达国家空气质量二级标准，低于国家卫生县城允许浓度限值，空气质量优，达标率100%。地表水质方面，依照规范在县城地表水断面进行的监测中，氨氮、五日生化需氧量等主要污染物浓度均能按照功能区达国家排放标准，达标率100%。

2006年11月，荔波县“整脏治乱”专项行动动员大会

2007年，全面开展县城环境综合整治，集中式饮用水源地水质达标率100%，烟尘控制区覆盖率100%，噪声达标区覆盖率50%以上。大气污染指标中，大气总悬浮物颗粒物年均值为0.186毫克/立方米，二氧化硫为0.048毫克/立方米，二氧化氮为0.008毫克/立方米，空气污染综合指数P=1.085，达到国家空气质量二级标准，低于国家卫生县城允许浓度限定值，空气质量为良好。

2008年5月，开展县城沿街餐饮、服务行业经营性燃煤污染整治，整改店铺33家，取缔使用燃煤摊点15家，收缴燃煤炉灶40个。全年坚持环境现场监察执法检查。

（二）农村环境污染治理

从20世纪90年代起申报中央农村环保专项资金，为乡镇村寨修建污水和垃圾处理设施。

1991年，投入环保资金22.4万元，补助更班矿矿井废水治理工程。

1997年，投入环保资金40万元，修建瑶庆人饮工程，解决茂兰、瑶麓2个乡（镇）共5个村因污染造成的人畜饮水及农田灌溉问题。至1998年，投入环保资金96.9万元，实施环境治理工程16处。其中，洞流人饮工程投入资金总计40.43万元，解决该片区3个村22个自然村寨的人畜饮水问题。

2001年，投入资金19万元，为茂兰镇洞流村吉王组修建排污渠。

2006年，投资338.28万元，在佳荣镇拉滩片区实施“荔波县煤矿山生态恢复示范工程”。

2007—2008年，无农村环境治理项目。

二、工业污染治理

1996年，按照国务院《关于环境保护若干问题的决定》“一控双达标”（即到2000年，全国所有工业污染源排放污染物要达到国家或地方规定的标准；各省、自治区、直辖市要使本辖区主要污染物排放总量控制在国家规定的排放总量指标内；直辖市及省会城市、经济特区城市、沿海开放城市和重点旅游城市的环境空气、地面水环境质量，按功能分区分别达到国家规定的有关标准）及省、州的要求，开展“一控双达标”工作，制定《荔波县工业污染源达标工作方案》，推行排污许可证制度，对排放污染物实施定量化管理，即：对辖区内重点污染源（立化镇广西红茂矿务局更班矿、平寨矿、打油寨矿、水尧乡岜和煤矿、县水泥厂）下达首批限期治理通知；签订环境保护目标责任书，细化“城市环境目标考核”量化指标，将工业污染源达标工作纳入环境保护目标责任书重点考核内容。上述5个重点污染源治理项目经州监测站采样化验已达标排放。

是年起，执行《中华人民共和国环境影响评价法》和环保总局《建设项目环境影响评价文件分级审批规定》，在建设项目审批过程中，严格执行环境影响评价制度和“三同时”（即在进行新建、改建和扩建工程时，环保设施必须与主体工程同时设计、同时施工、同时投产）制度。

1997年，县环保部门补助县水泥厂环保资金2万元，治理该厂废水排放。

1999年11月，县政府下发首批污染源限期治理企业名单，列入名单的有更班矿、平寨矿、打油寨矿、巴合煤矿、县水泥厂。到2000年10月，更班矿、平寨矿、打油寨矿、巴合煤矿4家煤矿废水通过治理，经州环境保护监测站采样检测，pH值、悬浮物、化学耗氧量均符合国家排放标准；县水泥厂通过治理，二氧化硫浓度和排放量符合国家排放标准，烟（粉）尘浓度超标3.3倍，烟（粉）尘排放量超标1.44倍。

2003年，督促县医院完成医疗废水治理项目，并组织召开验收现场会，推广治理经验。

2006年，督促青利公司荔波分公司更班煤矿、兴茂煤矿和匀茂煤矿建成煤矿废水达标处理示范工程。

2007年，督促荔波县巴合煤矿、荔波县合茂煤矿投入治理经费60多万元，建设煤矿废水污染治理工程，建成日处理能力300吨的矿坑废水处理系统2套。督促青利公司更班矿完成省级限期治理项目中的工业矸场治理。

2008年，全县申报中央农村环保专项资金项目，建设污水处理站和垃圾收集站20个，项目总投资1326.85万元，在重点村寨和樟江沿岸村寨实施。

三、排污口整治

1998年5月—1999年5月，对排污口进行规范化整治，制定《荔波县排污口规范化管理规定（暂行）》《荔波县排污口规范化整治工作实施方案》《荔波县排污口规范化整治工作实施计划》《荔波县排污口规范化整治技术要求》，以整治污水排放口为主，兼顾整治废气、固体废物、噪声排放口（点、源）；以整治重点污染源及列入总量控制指标的几种污染物（烟尘、工业粉尘、二氧化硫、化学耗氧量、工业固体废物）的排污口为主，将责任、任务落实到相关部门。1999年6月，经州排污口规范化整治工作验收小组进行全面检查，通过验收。

四、主要污染物减排

2008年6月，县政府与州政府签订《荔波县2008年主要污染物总量减排目标责任书》后，印发《荔波县2008年主要污染物总量减排工作实施方案》《荔波县2008年主要污染物总量控制计划表》，将2008年二氧化硫排放量控制在3700吨、化学需氧量控制在600吨的两项指标分解落实到重点排污单位，同时与全县41个污染源单位分别签订《荔波县2008年主要污染物总量减排目标责任书》。污染物减排主要采取工程治理、调整结构、加强监管三大减排措施。在工程治理上，实施佳荣镇铅锌矿业公司、县铅锌矿业公司洗选废水治理工程，建成日处理能力300吨的铅锌废水处理系统2套并通过验收；新寨煤矿、匀茂煤矿、县巴合煤矿、宏茂煤矿投入治理经费总计80万元，对煤矿废水污染进行治理，建成矿坑废水处理系统4套，日处理能力300吨；开展城区综合治理，取缔经营性燃煤炉灶，推进清洁燃料工程建设，削减二氧化硫排放总量。在加大企业监管上，严肃查处违法排污行为。环境监察人员对限期治理企业现场执法达20多人次，对擅自停止运行污染治理设施等环境违法行为进行处罚。

第三节　环境监测

1997年11月，州环保局下发《关于对荔波城区进行环境背景值监测的通知》，1998年起，县环保部门每年投入资金4万元，请州环境监测站对荔波县城区进行环境质量背景值监测，监测项目有地面水、大气、噪声等。

从2004年起，根据州政府环境保护目标考核办公室《关于在全州各县市城区开展环境质量现状监测的通知》，将县城区环境背景值监测改为城区环境质量现状监测，监测费用仍为每年4万元，监测项目、监测时间和监测单位不变。

一、地面水监测

1998年，州环境保护监测站对荔波县地面水进行监测，设有自来水厂、洗布河、回龙角3个点对地面水进行监测，监测频次为夏天、冬天各1次，监测项目有水温、pH值、悬浮物、总硬度、总磷、化学耗氧量、石油类、非离子氨、亚硝酸盐氮、亚硝酸盐、挥发性酚、氰化物、砷、汞、六价铬、铅、镉、电导率18个指标。第一次监测结果为水质稳定，达到地面水二类标准；第二次监测15个指标，除细菌指标外，其余指标均未超标。

2005年，州环境监测站对境内樟江流域水质进行监测，监测结果为水质稳定，达到地面水一类标准；城区集中式饮用水源监测结果符合国家生活饮用水二级标准。

从2006年7月起，根据州政府环境保护目标考核办公室《关于开展城市集中饮用水源地水质月报工作的通知》，实施城区集中饮用水源地水质监测月报制度，每月监测1次，地表水源监测项目10个（水温、pH值、总磷、高锰酸盐指数、溶解氧、氟化物、挥发酚、石油类、氨氮、粪大肠菌群），地下水源监测项目8个（pH值、高锰酸盐指数、氟化物、硫酸盐、氯化物、氨氮、总大肠菌群、总硬度），县环保局采样、送样到州环境保护监测站进行水质分析，城区集中式饮用水源监测结果符合国家生活饮用水二级标准。同时，开展风景名胜区水质监测，结果均达国家二类水标准。

2006—2008年，县环保部门委托县疾病预防控制中心开展饮用水源水质监测，监测项目为常规10项，每年费用1万元。城区集中式饮用水源监测结果均符合国家生活饮用水二级标准。

二、大气、噪声监测

1998—2004年，州环境监测站对县内城区大气、噪声环境背景值监测，每年上半年、下半年各监测1次。大气质量监测点为狮子口、风景区保护处、县医院、时来坝，监测项目二氧化硫、氮氧化物、总悬浮颗粒物等均未超标。

2005—2008年，每年上半年（5月或6月）、下半年（10月或11月、12月）开展两次城市环境空气监测。在4年的8次监测中，空气质量为优5次、良好3次，特别是2008年的空气质量为优。

三、其他监测

从2003年起，县环保部门对有污染的企业进行监测。是年，全县检查工业污染企业54家，监测煤矿企业36家，重点工业污染监督性监测11家（水泥厂1家、铅锌选矿厂2家、煤矿8家）。监测后，对县水泥厂、青利公司更班煤矿等16家企业进行限期治理。

2004年，开展污染源单位排污申报登记监督性监测，全县监测煤矿36家、铅锌选矿厂2家、铁合金冶炼厂3家、酒店宾馆7家、水泥厂1家、医院1家。

从2005年起，按照省级重点工业污染源每季度监测1次，州级重点工业污染源半年监测1次，一般工业污染源每年监测1次的要求，对全县污染源单位进行排污申报登记监测。全县监测63家企业。其中，州级重点工业污染源3个（水泥厂1个、铅锌矿2个），一般工业污染源60个（铁合金冶炼4个、煤矿56个），县内无省级重点工业污染源。

2006年6月，投入3.5万元开展申报世界自然遗产地环境质量监测，在小七孔、大七孔、水上森林、板寨、卧龙坝、鸳鸯湖等地设置点位10个，监测项目20个。

2007年11月，投入3.5万元对樟江风景名胜区的大七孔、小七孔和茂兰自然保护区进行环境质量监测，监测水、气、声点位10个，监测项目30个。

2008年，州监测站对荔波县4个镇、3个乡、12个点进行土壤土质GPS定位及调查采样。

第四节 环境功能区划分

一、地面水环境功能区划分

1993年，根据《中华人民共和国水污染防治法》、《地表水环境质量标准》（GB3838-88）、《贵州省地面水域环境功能区划分初步方案》，完成《荔波县地面水域环境功能调查技术报告》（又称《水功能区划》）。

（一）河流水系功能区划

1.打狗河水系

（1）樟江

樟江上游支流农林区域：包括水维河、拉易河、兰淀山河、拉先河、水昔河等河流，流经水维、甴鲜、拉易、拉先、水庆、水春，现状最高功能为饮用，兼顾功能为农灌，主要环境问题为沿河少量水土流失。规划水体最高功能为生活饮用水一级保护区，划分类别为Ⅱ类。

樟江上游支流工矿区域：包括拉滩河、姑爽河、拉祥河等河流，现状最高功能为饮用，兼顾功能为农灌，主要环境问题为佳荣镇拉祥村铅锌矿采选，拉滩村、高里村煤炭开采排放的废水对水体造成的污染。规划水体最高功能为生活饮用水二级保护区，划分类别为Ⅲ类。

水春—杨家桥：流经水春、龙王洞、白岩村、板莪村，现状最高功能为饮用，兼顾功能为农灌，目前主要环境问题为荔波机场建设施工期开挖碳质泥层排放废水、沿途生活污水排放、一定程度的水土流失等。规划水体最高功能为生活饮用水一级保护区，划分类别为Ⅱ类。

杨家桥—回龙角：流经县城段，全长4公里，现状最高功能为饮用，兼顾功能为农灌，主要环境问题为县城生活污水对水体造成的污染。规划水体最高功能为生活饮用水二级保护区，划分类别为Ⅲ类。

回龙角—王蒙：流经福利、朝阳、拉香、寨马、王蒙，全长20公里，现状最高功能为饮用，兼顾功能为农灌，主要环境问题为沿途生活污水排放、一定程度的水土流失。规划水体最高功能为生活饮用水一级保护区，划分类别为Ⅱ类。

（2）方村河

甲站—方村（甲站河段）：现状最高功能为饮用，兼顾功能为农灌，主要环境问题为沿途生活污水排放、轻微水土流失。规划水体最高功能为生活饮用水一级保护区，划分类别为Ⅱ类。

甲良—方村：现状最高功能为工业用水，兼顾功能为农灌，主要环境问题为方村煤田矿坑水污染、沿途生活污水排放、一定程度的水土流失等。规划水体最高功能为生活饮用水二级保护区，划分类别为Ⅲ类。

方村—驾欧：现状最高功能为工业用水，兼顾功能为农灌，主要环境问题为煤田矿坑水污染、沿途生活污水排放、一定程度的水土流失等。规划水体最高功能为生活饮用水二级保护区，划分类别为Ⅲ类。

黄江：现状最高功能为工业用水，兼顾功能为农灌，主要环境问题为沿途生活污水排放、一定程度的水土流失等。规划水体最高功能为生活饮用水一级保护区，划分类别为Ⅱ类。

台村江（架桥河）：现状最高功能为饮用水，兼顾功能为工业用水，主要环境问题为水质受煤炭开采排放废水的轻微污染、沿途生活污水排放等。规划水体最高功能为生活饮用水二级保护区，划分类别为Ⅲ类。

清江、尧花河：现状最高功能为饮用水，兼顾功能为工业用水，主要环境问题为沿途生活污水排放、水土流失等。规划水体最高功能为生活饮用水二级保护区，划分类别为Ⅲ类。

小七孔河：现状最高功能为饮用水，兼顾功能为景观用水，未受污染等。规划水体最高功能为生活饮用水一级保护区，划分类别为Ⅱ类。

（3）打狗河

王蒙—捞村，流经王蒙、小七孔、瑶山、捞村。现状最高功能为饮用水，兼顾水力发电，主要环境问题为水土流失、沿途生活污水排放等。规划水体最高功能为生活饮用水一级保护区，划分类别为Ⅱ类。

2.三岔河水系

（1）茂兰河

甲介水库上游甲介河段：现状最高功能为工业用水，兼顾功能为农灌，主要环境问题为受片区煤炭开采污染，监测资料显示，现状水质为劣Ⅴ类。规划水体最高功能为工业用水，划分类别Ⅳ类。

甲介水库下游茂兰河段：现状最高功能为工业用水，兼顾功能为农灌，主要环境问题为受片区煤炭矿坑水污染。规划水体最高功能为工业用水，划分类别为Ⅳ类。

（2）瑶庆河

现状最高功能为工业用水，兼顾功能为农灌，目前主要环境问题为受水尧片区煤炭矿坑水污染。规划水体最高功能为工业用水，划分类别为Ⅳ类。

（3）伍家河

现状最高功能为工业用水，水质受平寨矿、更班矿及周围小煤窑废水污染严重。规划最高功能为饮用水二级保护区，划分类别Ⅳ类。

（4）三岔河

立化洞塘工矿段：现状最高功能为工业用水，环境问题主要是受煤炭矿坑水污染。规划水体最高功能为工业用水，划分类别为Ⅳ类。

三岔河洞塘段：现状最高功能为农灌，环境问题主要是上游水体受到污染。规划水体最高功能为饮用水二级保护区，划分类别为Ⅲ类。

（5）瑶麓河

现状最高功能为工业用水，兼顾功能为农灌，目前环境问题是受茂兰镇水庆村水条片煤炭企业污染。规划水体最高功能为饮用水二级保护区，划分类别为Ⅲ类。

3.甲料河水系

现状最高功能为饮用水，兼顾功能为农灌，目前环境问题主要是接纳沿途生活污水、少量水土流失等。规划水体最高功能为饮用水一级保护区，划分类别Ⅱ类。

（二）湖库水功能划分

1.鸳鸯湖

位于小七孔景区，库容量52.5万立方米。上游源头水，水质未受污染，水质清洁。主要功能为旅游、观光、划船，现状水质为Ⅰ类，划分类别为Ⅰ类。

2.打狗河水系水库

洪江水库：主要功能为饮用，兼顾功能为农灌、渔业等，水质受库区少量水土流失影响。规划主要功能为生活饮用水一级保护区，划分类别为Ⅱ类。

威刀水库：主要功能为农灌，兼顾功能为工业用水，受荔波机场建设开挖碳质泥层污水污染。规划功能为农灌，划分类别为Ⅲ类。

水江水库、芭芒水库、水维水库、董更水库、巴怀水库、内阁水库、鲁劳水库、朋宾水库、立新水库、水库向阳、夜寨水库：现状主要功能为农灌，兼顾功能为渔业养殖，规划功能为农灌，划分类别为Ⅲ类。

3.三岔河水系水库

水庆水库：现状主要功能为农灌，兼顾功能为工业用水，受煤矿废水污染。规划功能为农灌，划分类别为Ⅲ类。

甲介水库：受甲介片区煤炭开采矿坑水的严重污染，现状水质为劣Ⅴ类。规划功能为农灌，划分类别为Ⅳ类。

伍家河水库：受立化片区煤炭开采矿坑水的严重污染，现状水质为较差。规划功能为农灌，划分类别为Ⅳ类。

二、大气环境功能区划

从1998年起，按照国家烟尘控制区有关技术标准，对县水泥厂进行治理，取缔1吨以下经营性燃煤锅炉，对1吨以上燃煤锅炉进行限期治理，取缔县城经营性燃煤炉灶，县城区基本达到国家烟控区控制指标，县城区内各种炉、窑、灶排放的烟气黑度为87%，达到国家规定排放标准，区内炉窑、工业生产排放的烟尘为79%，达到国家规定排放标准，2004年3月通过州环保局验收。

三、噪声环境功能区划

通过布点监测、征求意见和会议讨论等程序，完成县城噪声功能区划分，2004年6月，经州环境保护局评审通过，由县政府批准实施。

四、水源地保护区

按照《荔波县地面水域环境功能区划》，水源地划为三类保护区：地表水源集中式生活饮用水水源地保护区；城镇集中式生活饮用水地下水源地保护区和城镇地下水源保护区；村镇集中饮用水源保护区。一级保护区水域长度为取水点上游1000米至下游100米，陆域宽度距河岸50米；二级保护区水域长度为取水点上游3000米至下游200米，陆域宽度距河岸2000米。2007年，根据省政府《关于划定黔南自治州福泉等9县（市）集中式饮用水源保护区的批复》、州政府环境保护目标考核办公室《关于做好饮用水源环境保护有关工作的通知》，按照饮用水源保护区界桩规范要求，县环保部门经过实地勘察后，在县城饮用水源一、二级保护区制作安装界碑6块、界桩30块。同时，制定集中式饮用水源污染防治应急预案，明确相关部门职责分工和应急措施，保障应急救援资金渠道。

2008年，对水源保护区内农户生活污水、人畜粪便污染源进行全面清理，共清理整治饮用水源保护区污染源和河岸生活污染源2家，确保饮用水源安全。

第五节　生态示范区创建

一、生态示范区建设

1998年10月，经国家环保总局批复同意，将荔波列为第三批全国生态示范区建设试点地区。之后，成立由县长任组长的荔波县创建国家级生态示范区领导小组，15个相关部门负责人为成员，在县环保局设领导小组办公室。委托省环境科学研究设计院编制《贵州省荔波县国家级生态示范区建设总体规划》，县政府于2001年12月29日批准实施。2002年6月5日，县政府与15个县直相关部门、17个乡（镇）政府签订《荔波县创建国家级生态示范区目标责任状》。

2002—2005年，全县先后投入资金8.56亿元，用于生态示范区建设。创建工作实施旅游扶贫开发、自然保护区建设、景区保护建设、生态移民、退耕还林、封山育林、农村能源改造、现代农业发展基地建设等项目，全县森林覆盖率比试点前增长9.79%，达到63.69%；自然保护区受保护地面积比试点前增长31.56%，达到48.06%；化肥施用强度比试点前下降12.08%，农药施用强度比试点前下降38.01%；城市人均绿地面积比试点前增长137.3%。生态示范区建设初步形成以生态保护为前提，以生态农业为基础，以生态旅游为龙头带动相关产业的发展模式。经随机抽样问卷调查，生态示范区建设公众知晓率98.7%，公众对生态环境质量满意率96%，公众对政府重视环境保护工作认可率97.3%。对照全国生态示范区建设试点验收标准，经验收组考核，荔波县创建国家级生态示范区各项条件及考核指标均达到全国生态示范区建设三类地区标准。2005年10月，荔波县创建国家级生态示范区建设工作通过国家环保总局复核验收。2006年3月23日，国家环保总局正式命名荔波县为第四批国家级生态示范区，县环保局被国家环保总局评为“全国生态示范区工作先进集体”。

二、绿色学校创建

2005年，县教育系统在全县开展创建绿色学校活动，成立创建绿色学校工作领导小组，在县教育局设领导小组办公室。是年11月，州环保局、州教育局批准瑶庆民族小学、荔波一小、荔波二小为黔南州绿色学校。

2006年10月，县职业高级中学、瑶山民族中学、瑶山民族小学、茂兰小学通过县级绿色学校验收。2007年11月，各校自查达到《绿色学校评估标准》后，向州环保局、州教育局申请验收。2008年12月26日，州环保局、州教育局批准县职业高级中学为黔南州绿色学校。

第六节 环保宣传 执法检查 排污费征收

一、环保宣传

1996年，在“6·5”世界环境日，县环保部门利用赶场天在城区主要街道向市民宣传环境保护知识，发放宣传资料2000份，群众咨询200多人次。

1998年，在世界环境日期间，开展以“为民荔波，保护樟江”为主题的环保宣传活动，在县城及部分乡（镇）设宣传点，接待咨询群众1000余人，发放宣传资料2685份。在城区主要街道和风景名胜区景点悬挂安装环保宣传标语106幅，与宣传、教育等部门联合举办“环保杯”中学生作文竞赛及中小学生环保知识讲座。

1999年以后，每年“6·5”世界环境日，县领导在电视台作电视讲话，举行县委、县政府、县人大常委会、县政协领导参加的全县大规模游行宣传活动，召开县领导、县相关部门主要领导和污染企业及群众代表参加的环保工作座谈会，举办中小学环保知识讲座、环保知识竞赛活动、环境法制培训班、环保演唱会，利用场天上街下乡设点开展环保咨询服务，悬挂制作环保宣传标语，群发环保宣传短信，增强全民环保意识。

2003年3月，举办“保护地球家园，再造秀美山川”中国环保之旅大型公益活动，全县机关干部职工参加植树造林。4月，在“小公民道德建设”宣传活动中，宣传环保知识。5月，在“法制宣传日”活动中，开展环境保护法律法规宣传。在“6·5”世界环境日，在县城、乡（镇）开展“水——20亿人生命之所系”世界环境日主题宣传活动。年内，环保宣传活动投入资金总计1.6万元，发放宣传资料1.55万份。

2005年，开展企业厂区美化、净化、绿化宣传，要求企业逐年增加绿化面积，绿化面积要保持占厂区面积的30%以上。对矿山企业采取到企业发放宣传资料、举办企业环保岗位人员培训班和环保知识讲座等形式，对企业员工进行现场宣传，发放宣传资料2000份。

2007年6月5日，在县有线电视台播出世界环境日“污染减排与环境友好型社会”环保主题及公布“12369”环保热线电话。开展环保知识咨询服务和环保污染投诉接待活动，解答现场咨询50人次，受理污染投诉案件1件。到甲良、佳荣、捞村等乡（镇）开展环保下乡宣传活动，发放宣传资料2000份，解答现场咨询30人次。

2008年，县环保局共投入资金16万元，开展环保宣传教育工作。

二、行政执法检查

从1996年起，开支环境保护专项检查。是年，县环保、矿管、煤炭、工商、安全生产等单位对违反《中华人民共和国环境保护法》《中华人民共和国水污染防治法》《中华人民共和国野生动物保护法》的单位、个人进行查处，对污染严重的小煤窑和未办理环保手续的煤厂进行炸封，对在市场上销售的蛇、青蛙等野生动物进行没收并放归自然。全年办理人大代表议案2件、群众来信来访12件，处理污染纠纷7件。

1998年，开展建设项目环境影响评价、“三同时”制度、环境与资源申报登记等执法检查。县环保、地矿、煤炭、公安等部门对水功片区煤厂废水直接排入樟江源头导致污染问题开展联合执法检查，责令23个煤井停止生产，对6个煤厂进行治理。年内，还对水尧、茂兰、立化、佳荣等乡（镇）煤炭生产企业严格执行有关环保制度的情况进行检查。

1999年，有关部门组成43人的联合执法工作组，取缔炸封水尧乡水功片区煤井和立化镇洞湖上寨后山片区煤井38个。根据群众举报，对樟江河道乱倒垃圾、排放油污及粪水情况进行调查，并对当事人进行警告和罚款。取缔县城燃煤锅炉5个，取缔樟江沿岸砖瓦窑2个。

2000—2001年，开展环保执法检查60次，对未执行环境影响评价及“三同时”制度的荔波铅锌选矿厂、佳荣铅锌矿业公司选厂、巴合矿第四采区、洞流村煤厂、巴格煤厂、匀茂煤厂、恒利煤厂、旺利煤厂及违法处置牲畜骨头业主2户依法下达环境执法通知文书，关闭樟江沿岸打煤场4个。

2002年，开展严查环境违法行为遏制污染反弹专项行动，共查处11家，分别下达行政执法文书。全年查处违法排污企业20家，下达行政执法书70份；进行矿山环境现状和污染现状调查160人次，调处污染纠纷25起。

2003年9月，整治违法排污企业保障群众健康环保专项行动以立化、茂兰、佳荣3个主要产矿乡（镇）为重点整治区域，整治流域为樟江、五家河和水功河。是年，执法人员进行环境现场监察执法检查200人次，下达整治通知20份。对重点污染源企业现场监察97人次；调处污染纠纷9起，查处环境违法事件7起。

2004年，重点检查县水泥厂等18户企业和县城集中式饮用水源地、樟江风景名胜区及茂兰喀斯特自然保护区，检查企业35户，立案查处7户，取缔影响集中式饮用水源2户。是年，开展《中华人民共和国大气污染防治法》执行情况专项执法检查，主要检查大气污染源企业的污染治理设施。开展“让百姓放心，清查放射性污染源”专项行动，对全县所有涉源单位进行全面排查，对县水泥厂放射源管理存在的问题下达整改通知。

2005年，执法人员现场检查企业50家，对长期未得到有效解决、群众反映强烈的环境污染问题，采取挂牌督办的方式，挂牌督办环境问题4个。其中，州级督办2个，县级督办2个；水污染3个，大气污染1个。对屠宰场、铅锌选矿厂2家州级督办企业的环境违法问题，分别下达限期整改通知。

2006年6月15日，重点检查县城集中式饮用水源地、樟江风景名胜区和茂兰喀斯特自然保护区可视范围污染企业环境违法行为，检查企业35户，立案查处7户，取缔影响集中式饮用水源的污染源。

2007年，全县整治违法排污企业、保障群众健康环保专项行动检查企业29家，下达现场执法通知书11份，查处违法单位5家。对污染企业16家进行现场监察共25次，其中，污染防治设施现场检查10次，建设项目现场检查4次，排污申报现场检查3次，水源保护区现场监察3次，其他环境监察5次。对辖区内产生尾矿的企业进行环境安全隐患排查，当场对佳荣铅锌矿业公司、县铅锌选矿厂和奴亚铁矿洗矿厂下达限期整改通知书。

2008年，现场检查企业36家，下达现场执法通知书8份。对污染企业32家进行现场监察共31次，其中，污染源现场监察12次，污染防治设施现场检查6次，限期治理项目现场检查2次，建设项目现场检查3次，排污申报现场检查6次，水源保护区现场监察2次。下达监察执法通知书5份，限期整改通知书2份，现场处理噪声污染事件1件。

三、排污费征收

县内从1986年起，按照国家《征收排污费暂行办法》，对污染企业征收排污费，主要征收项目为二氧化硫排污费。1986—2008年，全县征收排污费累计1119.56万元。每年征收的排污费，全额解缴财政，由财政统一管理，专款专项用于环境污染防治。

第二十篇
教育　科学技术

中共十一届三中全会后，荔波县委、县政府对教育投入不断加大，通过实施世界银行贷款项目、国家贫困地区义务教育工程、中小学危房改造工程、农村薄弱学校建设工程和港澳同胞、海外侨胞及社会各界爱心人士捐资助学工程等，县教育事业得到发展，教育程度不断普及，校舍逐渐改善，办学条件不断完善，文盲人口逐年减少，人口素质得到提高。2001年11月，“两基”工作通过省政府验收，2005年6月通过省政府的“两基”复查和普实验收，“两基”成果得到巩固，基础教育长足发展，2007年在全州教育综合考评中，荔波县荣获一等奖。普高教育成绩突出，2007年、2008年高考成绩位居全州第四位；职业教育蓬勃发展，在校学生突破1900人，黔南旅游学校在荔波挂牌，面向全州招生；县幼儿园投入280万元扩建，办学条件极大改善，并成立早期教育中心，省教育厅把荔波列为全省21个“双高普九”县之一。

随着教育事业的不断发展，县教育局出台一系列政策，鼓励教师“充电”，以实现小学教师大专化，中学教师本科化，力争高中教师有研究生学历的目标。制定和出台《荔波县关于实施“双高普九”进一步提高中小学教学质量的意见》《荔波县开展初中教师“三个一”综合考评工作方案》等文件，进一步创新教育工作思路。2006年荔波县教育局被省教育厅表彰为“贵州省农村中小学现代远程教育工作先进单位”。

1978年改革开放以来，县委、县政府高度重视提高全民科学素质，在群众实际的生产、生活中大力推广实用技术，开展多样性的科普活动。创建科普示范基地，带动一片农民致富。建立科普网站，创建全国科普示范县等，促进县域经济的发展。1994年12月，荔波县获得全州青少年科普活动“先进集体”和全省碘缺乏病宣传“先进集体”称号；1995年，又获联合国儿童基金会合作项目“先进集体”和全省科普宣传及健康教育的“先进集体”称号。荔波县科普事业不断发展，1997年至2002年荔波县科协多次被省、州评为“科协工作先进集体”。2002年12月荔波县科协被科学技术部、中共中央宣传部和中国科协评为“全国科普工作先进集体”，成为贵州省唯一上金牌榜的县。2004年，被中国科协命名为“全国科普示范县”。

第一章 教 育

第一节 基础教育

一、幼儿教育

1978年，县内有县幼儿园1所，设8个班，在园幼儿320人。1981年，城关区时来公社、城关镇菜园大队、茂兰区场坝、朝阳小学、甲良小学、永康小学、城关一小、城关二小先后办起学前班和幼儿班。

从1983年起，幼儿园教育实施《幼儿教育纲要》，采用统编幼儿教材，教学内容有语言、计算、美工、唱歌等，课外活动主要有游戏、郊游。同时针对小、中、大班的不同特点，教简单汉字和阿拉伯数字及20以内加减法。

1986年秋，县内办起第一所个体托儿园——小云星托儿园。在此之后，没有再开办新的民办托幼机构。

1988年，城关区时来公社幼儿班、茂兰场坝幼儿班、朝阳小学学前班、甲良小学学前班改建为幼儿园。是年，全县幼儿园（含学前班）入园幼儿1035人，教职工50人，专任教师42人。

1990年，国家颁布《幼儿园工作规程》《幼儿园管理条例》后，县教育主管部门开展全县幼儿园园长、小学学前班校长及教师培训、考试，提高幼儿教育质量和管理水平。是年举办师资培训班2期。年底，全县有幼儿园5所，入园幼儿764人；小学附设学前班共13个，入班幼儿1165人。入园（班）幼儿占全县适龄幼儿的10.22%。

1992年，按《贵州省幼儿园办园基本条件（试行）》《贵州省幼儿园（班）分类评定标准（试行）》，对全县在办幼儿园和学前班进行检查、评估。县幼儿园、朝阳幼儿园达贵州省三类幼儿园、县级示范园标准，茂兰幼儿园达贵州省三类幼儿园标准。

1994年，城关菜园幼儿班改建为幼儿园，全县幼儿园由5所增加到6所，入园幼儿837人；学前班25个，入班幼儿918人。适龄幼儿入园（班）率17%。

2002年，根据国家《幼儿园教育指导纲要（试行）》，对全县幼儿园、学前班的办学水平进行评估，县幼儿园达贵州省二类幼儿园标准，播尧幼儿园、时来幼儿园、立化幼儿园、六林幼儿园、拉欧幼儿园、地莪幼儿园和各小学附设的幼儿班均达贵州省办园基本条件。

2005年，撤销菜园幼儿园。2006年8月，立化小学、驾欧小学、六林小学、播尧小学、地莪小学5所小学学前班改建为幼儿园。2007年，时来幼儿园并入玉屏三小。

2008年，县投资280万元，按省级一类幼儿园标准建设县幼儿园，12月，通过省级一类幼儿园评估初评，全县有各类幼儿园、学前班62所（个）。其中，公办幼儿园10所，入园幼儿1217人；学前班52个，入班幼儿1730人。每个乡中心校及村校都设学前班，适龄幼儿入园（班）率51.5%。

二、小学教育

1978年，全县有完全小学102所、初级小学49所、办学点112个。1980年，黔南州确定瑶山小学为民族小学，为全州第一所寄宿制小学，对学生实行“三包”（包吃、包住、包穿）政策，免收书本费、学杂费。先后拨款修建教学楼、办公楼、宿舍，配备厨房、饭厅、生活用车等。是年，该校有在校生115人。

是年10月，县教育局投资5万元，新建瑶麓民族小学400平方米新教学楼。此后，国家每年拨款补助该校，学生减免学费、杂费、书本费，每人每年发给球鞋2双、衣服1套，家庭经济困难的学生享受人民助学金，特别困难的学生免交资料费、试卷费。

1986年9月，县政府将瑶麓民族小学列为县级文物保护单位（其前身为贵州省立荔波水庆乡初级小学）。

是年，针对水族女童入学难问题，在水利、水尧、永康、岜鲜4个水族乡中心校开办“水族女生班”，对水族女学生免收书本费、学杂费。

1986—1994年，水尧小学每年开办一个“水族女子班”。1987—2003年，永康小学每年开办一个“水族女子班”。1991—1996年，水利小学每年开办一个“水族女子班”。

2001年，按照省的规定，对规模小、生源少又与规模较大的学校距离在3公里左右的大部分校点进行调整，学校数由2000年的101所调整到99所，办学点由2000年的77个调整到47个。2002年后，根据学校生源情况，对小学校点作小调整，校点数逐年减少。

2008年，瑶山民族小学校园内发生地裂，国家地质灾害项目工程投入资金200多万元，贵州省财产保险公司捐赠35万元，帮助该校搬迁选址重建。瑶麓民族小学有班级6个，学生154人，瑶麓瑶族乡适龄儿童入学率达100%。水利、水尧、永康3个水族乡有小学16所，在校生2248人。

是年，全县有小学及教学点105所（个）、九年一贯制学校1所，在校生中少数民族学生16384人。小学适龄儿童入学率达99.6%，辍学率0.09%，15周岁完成率98.9%。

1978—2008年全县小学统计表

表20－1

年度	普通小学（所）	在校学生数（人）	学龄儿童入学率（%）
1978	263	18400	89.52
1979	242	16601	90.75
1980	209	15511	80.63
1981	195	15695	80.69
1982	196	16456	78.00
1983	174	18052	78.90
1984	140	18993	76.60
1985	137	19597	78.63
1986	139	20682	83.80
1987	119	21208	81.53
1988	128	21355	83.73

续表20－1

年度	普通小学（所）	在校学生数（人）	学龄儿童入学率（%）
1989	131	21922	83.44
1990	127	21734	86.30
1991	124	22345	89.60
1992	121	22744	89.12
1993	122	22921	96.00
1994	114	22334	96.10
1995	131	22502	96.52
1996	118	22377	97.10
1997	112	22216	97.20
1998	113	21782	97.52
1999	108	21070	98.30
2000	102	20283	98.92
2001	99	19746	99.29
2002	99	19095	99.30
2003	97	18506	99.37
2004	94	18175	99.50
2005	96	18044	99.29
2006	94	18681	99.50
2007	88	18202	99.70
2008	81	17488	99.60

三、中学教育

（一）初中

1978年，县内有荔波中学、甲良中学、朝阳中学、茂兰中学4所为完全中学。另有，播尧“五七”中学只办初中班；还有小学戴帽初中班30个。全县有初中在校生5331人。

1987年6月，荔波师范改为玉屏中学。

1992年秋，立化、方村、播尧、朝阳、驾欧、洞塘等乡（镇）中心完小恢复戴帽初中班。1993年秋，王蒙小学恢复戴帽初中班。

1995年底，经过调整，小学设置初中戴帽班和开办一贯制学校、完全中学，是在独立初中学校办学条件、教育教学设备、师资等条件不能满足初中学生入学需求的情况下设置的过渡度时期教育机构，按照省的有关规定，小学、初中、高中应独立办学。全县有独立初中6所、九年一贯制学校3所，在校初中学生4679人。学校实行“三制一管理”（校长负责制、教师聘任制、岗位责任制和教育教学目标管理）体制。

1996年8月，水尧乡政府投资50万元，创办水尧水族民族职业初中，解决水尧乡学生就近入学问题。该校行政由水尧乡政府领导，业务归县教育局管理，办学所需经费、师资、校舍建设、设施配备等3年内均由水尧乡政府负担，每年招收2个班，每班40～50人，课程按普通初中设置，学生参加全县普通初中统考。1999年8月，县教育局、水尧乡政府向县政府、州教委申请转为民办公助办学，学生学籍由教育局负责办理。协议规定水尧初中班统一使用国家规定的教学大纲教材、教学计划，并增设农村实用技术职业课，全县统考，成绩合格者，发给毕业证书，与其他初中班学生享受同等待遇。

1997年春，香港爱国人士邵逸夫捐资80万港币，省、州、县投入配套资金230万元，建瑶山民族中学，并将驾欧学校初中部和王蒙小学初中班原有师生并入，教学服务范围为瑶山、驾欧和捞村3个乡。

2002年6月，将荔波民族中学的初中部并入玉屏中学，玉屏中学升格更名为荔波县第二中学，成为县直属初级中学。2006年，在县城东北角望城坡脚下划拨土地102亩，重新修建荔波县第二中学，深圳盐田港集团捐资450万元修建“盐田港教学大楼”。

2008年，全县有初级中学8所（荔波二中、甲良中学、茂兰中学、朝阳中学、瑶山中学、方村中学、播尧中学、佳荣中学）、九年一贯制学校1所（洞塘学校），初中在校生9115人，校舍总面积63049平方米，生均图书18.9册。全县初中入学率100%，辍学率控制在2.5%以内。

（二）高中

1978年，除荔波中学设有高中部外，茂兰、朝阳、甲良中学办有高中班。全县有高中班10个，学制两年。

1980年，茂兰、朝阳中学高中部停止招生。全县仅有荔波民族中学和甲良中学招高中生。1983年，全县有高中班19个，在校生399人。1984年后，取消乡（镇）中学高中部，保留荔波民族中学高中部。是年，高中毕业生101人，高考录取34人，录取率33.7%。

从1997年起，用国家西部助学基金为考上重点大学的极贫家庭学生提供助学金补助，每学年5000元。1997—2006年，全县有10多名优秀学生得到此项补助。

2001年，扩大高中招生规模，全县高中招生701人，比扩招前增长300%。是年，贵州省实施高中“宏志班”助学工程，对应届初中升高中录取的品学兼优而家庭贫困的学生，提供高中三年助学经费6000元（每学年2000元），学校减免一半学费。全县有10余名优秀学生考入贵阳、遵义、凯里开办的高中“宏志班”就读。

2002年，荔波民中获州政府授予“黔南州办学水平优秀学校”称号。2003年，该校成为“贵州省示范性普通高中”。2008年12月，荔波民中被评为“贵州省第六次民族团结进步先进集体”，受省委、省政府表彰。

2008年年末，县内有高中学校1所，高中学校占地面积10万平方米，校舍建筑面积35000平方米，有教学班49个，在校生3068人，其中少数民族生占96%（荔波民中有班级47个，在校生2899人）。是年，高考录取率60%，名列全州第四，综合教育成绩获全州一等奖。

1978—2008年全县普通中学统计表

表20－2

年度	学校总数（所）	在校学生数（人）	年度	学校总数（所）	在校学生数（人）
1978	5	5992	1994	5	4845
1979	6	5410	1995	7	5088
1980	6	4153	1996	9	5881
1981	8	3211	1997	9	6418
1982	6	3374	1998	12	6683
1983	6	3268	1999	12	6956
1984	5	2995	2000	12	8830
1985	6	3064	2001	13	10180
1986	5	3235	2002	13	11708
1987	5	3663	2003	13	11990
1988	6	3379	2004	12	12189
1989	5	2801	2005	12	12253
1990	5	3005	2006	11	11868
1991	5	3247	2007	11	11513
1992	5	4051	2008	11	11674
1993	5	4392			

第二节 “两基”工作

1996年，荔波县“两基”工作（基本普及九年义务教育、基本扫除青壮年文盲）启动，县委、县政府会议专题研究，同年，成立“两基”工作领导小组，县委书记、县长作为第一责任人。实施《荔波县普及九年义务教育规划》和《荔波县普及九年义务教育和扫除青壮年文盲评估验收试行意见》，确定“以乡推进，整体实现”的办法。1996年，各乡镇也建立相应的责任制，签订《双线目标责任书》，推进“两基”工作协调发展。

一、基本普及九年义务教育

加大教育经费。1992年，全县教育经费财政预算内总支出为505万元，到1998年，财政预算内总支出为1293万元，比1997年增长16.91%；1999年，财政预算内总支出为1504万元，比上年增长16.32%；2000年，已增加到1735.6万元，比上年增长15.40%。提高师资水平。2000年，全县小学专任教师1161人，学历达标1137人，小学教师学历合格率97.93%。全县小学教师达任职要求998人，小学专任教师人职率96.71%。全县初中专任教师474人，取得大专以上学历460人，初中专人教师学历合格率97.26%。全县初中教师达任职要求369人，初中专任教师人职率94.74%。办学条件改善。至2000年，全县小学生均校舍面积4.58平方米，初中生均校舍面积4.50平方米，全县中小学危房率为

0.36%。校园设施完善，基本满足学校教育活动的需要。

在校初中生从1994年的4026人增加到2001年的8750人。初等教育阶段入学率达99.29%，初中入学率达103.17%。小学辍学率降至0.42%，初中辍学率降至2.41%。15周岁完成率达97.02%，17周岁完成率达82.63%。基本达到“两基”达标要求。

二、基本扫除青壮年文盲

1981—1988年，全县组织文盲、半文盲夜校，参加学习13623人，经考核验收，脱盲学员1825人。此间，玉屏镇和时来、茂兰、立化3个乡成为基本无盲单位。1988年2月，国务院颁布《扫除文盲工作条例》开展扫盲教育。

1989—1990年，全县参加文盲、半文盲扫盲学习8612人（其中女7590人），经考试验收，脱盲5889人（女4465人），朝阳、瑶麓、王蒙乡成为基本无文盲乡。

1991—1993年，对未完成扫除青壮年文盲的乡（镇），开展扫盲教育，除佳荣、瑶山两乡外，其余乡（镇）实现基本无文盲目标。1993年12月，经省政府评估验收，荔波县基本扫除青壮年文盲，成为无文盲县。

1997—2001年，全县扫除青壮年文盲1797人（其中女1348人），全县青壮年人口非盲率达97.71%。此期间，扫盲教育由识字为主向学技术带动学文化转变，全县参加各种农业技术短期培训148345人次。

2001年，“两基”工作通过省级评估验收。2005年，“两基”工作通过省级复查验收。

2002—2005年，将扫盲重点转移到脱盲后巩固提高培训上，防止新文盲产生。同时，结合农村产业结构调整和科技推广，适时开展各种实用技术培训，学文化与学科学相结合，扫盲与脱贫相结合。此阶段，全县扫除青壮年文盲610人（其中女483人），青壮年人口非盲率为98.75%；参加各种实用技术短期培训100776人次。2005年6月，全县通过省政府基本扫除文盲复查验收。

2006年后，全县开展“两个全覆盖”扫盲教育，即对15—24周岁有学习能力的文盲、半文盲，全覆盖参加当年扫盲教育，并达到脱盲标准；近三年脱盲人员全覆盖参加农业实用技术巩固提高班培训。

至2008年年底，全县15～50周岁人口剩余文盲、半文盲数1861人，青壮年非盲率97.9%。

第三节　职业教育　成人教育

一、职业教育

（一）职业中学

1984年9月，创办县职业高中，是年开设栽培专业班，招生50人。1985年9月，改称县职业中学，设5个班，学制三年。开设农学、林木、果树、畜牧兽医专业课程，学生191人。1988年，改称县民族职业中学。2005年9月，改为县职业高级中学。是年11月，确定为省级重点中等职业学校。2008年6月，该校创建校办企业荔波樟江驾驶培训学校。7月，加挂黔南旅游学校牌子。从该校创办到2008年年末，除进行普通中学课程教学外，开设的各种专业技能课程累计100余种，毕业生累计2215人。

1984—2008年荔波县职业高级中学情况统计表

表20－3　　单位：人

年度	招生数	在校生数	毕业生数	年度	招生数	在校生数	毕业生数
1984	50	50	—	1997	168	311	87
1985	55	105	—	1998	167	342	99
1986	100	205	—	1999	160	326	98
1987	102	200	40	2000	75	230	71
1988	112	260	42	2001	170	242	132
1989	102	230	33	2002	323	413	56
1990	1125	250	47	2003	415	803	59
1991	54	144	42	2004	184	873	156
1992	79	185	35	2005	710	1242	254
1993	83	189	50	2006	742	1352	268
1994	131	235	44	2007	826	1731	129
1995	110	261	48	2008	650	1942	371
1996	101	266	54				

（二）中等专业学校

1978年，县内中等专业学校有县师范学校、县卫生学校。

1985年，县师范学校改为县教师进修学校，进修对象为县内小学教师。1987年，撤销教师进修学校，改为玉屏中学。

1978—1991年，县卫生学校先后开办麻防医生培训班、赤脚医生培训班、护理员培训班、初级卫生人员提高班、乡村医生培训班，学制分别为3个月、6个月、1年等，学员累计295人。学校有专任教师1人，专业课程教师主要由县医疗卫生单位专业技术骨干兼职。1992—1993年，开办村医班、初级卫生人员提高班，学员分别为44人、39人，学习时间4个月。1994—1998年，开办村接生员培训班、村卫生员培训班各4期，学员74人、116人。其间，1997年，与三都县、州卫校合办社区医学函授中专班，学员58人，学习时间4年。1999年，与县民族职业中学合办农村医士中专班，学员21人，学习时间2年。2000年，办乡村医生中专水平培训班，学员13人，学习时间6个月。2002—2003年，办卫生法律法规知识培训4期，培训乡（镇）卫生员、计生员、校医、个体医生等283人。2004—2008年，办岗前培训班、传染病防治知识培训、基础医学知识培训、医疗机构麻醉药品和精神药品相关知识培训、急诊急救知识技能培训班、突发公共卫生事件知识培训、村卫生室人员培训班、乡镇卫生院管理人员培训班、母婴保健技术服务理论知识培训班等，培训对象为乡（镇）卫生、计生、村卫生室从业人员，5年累计培训1109人。

二、成人教育

（一）函授

中师函授　1985年，成立贵州省中师函授广播学校荔波工作站，设在县教师进修学校。符合条件的中小学教师30人报名参加学习，经统一考试，取得中函毕业证书11人。1988年7月，全县第二次招生30人，其中民办教师22人、社会青年8人。1985—1995年，累计招公办教师82人、民办教师59

人、代课教师58人，毕业100人。1999年，中师函授教育工作停止。

中华会计函授 1988年，建立荔波中华会计函授站，当年录取10人。采取自学、电教和面授方式进行学习，学制三年。首届毕业9人。1990年，录取35人。

农业函授大学辅导 1986年9月，县科协、团县委、县妇联成立县农业函授大学辅导站，在全县招生，每期学制1年，开设种植、养殖、加工和乡镇企业管理专业课。是年，招第一期新生36人。1987年，招第二期新生68人。1990年，招第三期新生55人。

（二）自学考试

从1984年上半年起，推行高等教育自学考试。1987年，开始中等教育自学考试。1987—2008年，全县有1231人参加各类自学考试，报考专业有汉语言文学、英语、法律、公安管理、会计等，取得毕业证书613人。

（三）成人高考

从1981年国家推行成人高考制度到2008年，全县参加考试1754人，录取854人，录取专业主要有教育类、医学类、财经类。

第四节 信息技术与远程教育

2003—2004年，实施“教育部·李嘉诚基金会现代远程教育项目学校”工程，全县有86所小学成为该项目接收播放点，甲良中学为农村信息站。2005年9月，县教育局设电教中心，负责全县信息技术与远程教育工作。次年，实施第二期农村中小学现代远程教育工程项目，此项目实施学校60所学校，解决了农村边远地区上课资源紧缺的问题，提高学校教学质量与教育服务。

2006年5月，建成远程教育资源库，各校依托县教育局的服务器建网站（页）。县民族中学和玉屏一小、玉屏二小等学校自筹资金在教室安装电视，接通远程教育接收机。

是年5月20日，举办全县首届中小学生信息技术创新与实践活动，中小学生300余人通过网络参加活动。6月，组织学生参加在深圳举行的第四届全国信息技术创新与实践活动，荣获二等奖1个、三等奖11个。

2007年1月，县教育局投资7万元购买网站服务器，建成荔波教育网（www.gzlbedu.cn）和荔波远程教育网（www.lbyc.cn）。同时开通OA办公自动化系统，通过OA平台进行办公。

2007年4月12日，举行第二届全县信息技术创新与实践活动，选出9名选手参加在重庆举行的全国NOC大赛，获一等奖2个、二等奖3个、三等奖4个。是年5月13—15日，由中央电教馆主办、贵州省电教馆承办的“教育部·李嘉诚基金会西部中小学现代远程教育项目”培训经验交流会在荔波举行。

2008年4月，组织学生12人参加全国第七届NOC作品类比赛，均获三等奖。是年，瑶山中学、茂兰中学、六林小学、玉屏三小成为贵州省农村中小学现代远程教育教学资源应用实验试点学校。

第五节 教师队伍

一、教师结构

1978年，全县有中小学教师1152人。1979年起，每年均有大中专毕业生分配到县内各中小学任教。1985年，全县中小学公办、民办教职工共1149人，其中专任教师967人、职工182人。1989年，全县民办教师118人全部转为公办教师。

1990年，全县专任教师1138人中，本科毕业34人，专科毕业114人，中师高中毕业800人，中师高中肄业及初师初中毕业149人，初师初中肄业以下41人。已评定职称1072人中，中学高级17人、一级49人、二级66人、三级53人，小学高级144人、一级465人、二级253人、三级25人；未评职称66人。

1990—1993年，为补充全县初中师资不足，从湖南、广西等省（区）聘请教师32人。同时，分配大专院校毕业生充实教师队伍。

从1994年起，代课教师通过考试、考核，逐步转为公办教师，对不符合转正条件的代课人员逐步清退。至1995年，小学教师队伍中，民办教师81人，占专任教师总数的8%；代课教师332人，占专任教师总数的38%。全县初中教职工372人中，本科学历19人，占专任教师总数的0.25%；代课教师30人，占专任教师总数的8%。全县高中学校专任教师46人中，本科学历17人。

1997年1月，全县民办教师全部转为公办教师（不符合的安排退养），荔波县成为全省第一个无民办教师县。

从2003年7月起，停止聘用代课教师，将原有代课教师全部清退。

2008年，全县幼儿专任教师6人，学历合格率100%；小学专任教师1040人，学历合格率100%；初中专任教师483人，学历合格率99.79%；高中专任教师208人，学历合格率75%。

1978—2008年全县教师统计表

表20－4　　单位：人

年度	教师总数	幼儿专任教师	小学专任教师	普通中学专任教师	职业中学专任教师
1978	1160	8	857	295	—
1979	994	8	737	249	—
1980	951	9	731	211	—
1981	975	24	770	181	—
1982	938	38	720	180	—
1983	909	43	692	174	—
1984	919	47	706	164	2
1985	947	43	723	158	23
1986	899	38	696	153	12
1987	1187	—	906	267	14
1988	1324	42	984	280	18
1989	1114	49	867	179	19
1990	1141	43	906	175	17
1991	1144	45	898	183	18
1992	1120	49	855	189	18
1993	1163	52	881	212	18
1994	1168	52	844	255	17

续表20－4

年度	教师总数	幼儿专任教师	小学专任教师	普通中学专任教师	职业中学专任教师
1995	1220	56	872	273	19
1996	1255	59	871	304	21
1997	1282	58	868	334	22
1998	1428	59	942	404	23
1999	1516	60	981	451	24
2000	1625	58	1040	504	23
2001	1788	62	1163	545	18
2002	1879	60	1182	592	12
2003	1871	52	1182	628	9
2004	1851	43	1133	634	41
2005	1902	47	1148	657	51
2006	1890	64	1100	673	53
2007	1890	67	1110	640	73
2008	1797	66	1040	617	74

二、师资培训

1978年后，采取离职和在职进修、短期轮训、办假期讲习班等形式进行教师培训。1983—1988年，全县教师参加省教育厅组织的“过教材关”考试，取得过教材关考试合格证书742人，合格率75.5%；选派或通过考试离职到外地学习的中小学教师123人。

1995年，县教育主管部门鼓励教师提高素质和学历，要求小学教师大专化，中学教师本科化，高中教师有研究生学历。

2000年以后，在选送教师赴外地学习的同时，邀请省内外教育专家到县内开办讲座，以组织教学公开课观摩和优质课评选等方式，提高教师教学水平。至2008年，参加讲座学习培训人数累计1100人次，组织教学公开讲课观摩活动20余次，开展优质课评选8次。全县参加学历学习并取得毕业文凭的教师799人。

第六节　校舍建设

1978年以后，县内学校基础设施建设以危房改造为主，经费来源于中央和省、州补助小学教育基建投资、支援不发达地区教育经费、危房改造和维修经费、国家发展资金、自筹基建投资资金、少数民族地区校舍建设补助等。1985年，立化镇尧明村群众集资3万元，地方财政补助2万元，修建尧明小学1栋2层6个教室的砖混结构教学楼，建筑面积437平方米。随后，立化中学、应昂小学、洞湖小学、久安小学等学校教学楼由群众和当地政府集资相继兴建。

1978—1992年，投入478.46万元，乡村群众集资45万元，改造全县中小学校203所，改造危房面积28020平方米，新建校舍面积39123平方米，并添置部分课桌凳。

1992—1997年，全县获世界银行中国贫困省教育发展项目贷款60.38万美元（折合人民币478.14万元），国内配套资金479.84万元，维修、重建64所学校教学用房总计26406平方米；配发教学仪器一类2套、二类24套、三类41套，价值37.04万元；配置图书77863册，价值31.04万元，分发95所学校；制作课桌凳500单人套，价值19.93万元。

1997—1999年，先后在岜鲜小学、拉平小学、坤地小学等6所学校实施国家扶贫项目教育工程，总投资94万元，新建教学用房2476平方米。

2000—2008年，投入省级财政扶贫资金165万元，义务教育工程资金467万元，省、州“普九”专项资金356万元，危房改造工程资金200万元，国家扶持青少年学生校外活动场所建设项目资金120万元，寄宿制工程资金573万元，义务教育阶段薄弱学校工程项目资金1114万元，中西部地区农村初中校舍改造工程项目资金1308万元，受地质灾害威胁搬迁工程项目资金1326万元，捐赠项目工程资金2126万元（1996年起），县、乡投入配套资金2995万元，征地200余亩，先后搬迁玉屏二小、洞麦小学、红泥小学、时来小学、荔波二中、肯甫小学、水尧小学、瑶山民族小学，扩建荔波民族中学、职业中学、佳荣中学、播尧中学、朝阳中学、茂兰中学、茂兰小学、梅桃小学。

至2008年年底，全县中小学校舍总面积175082平方米，小学生生均校舍面积6.4平方米，初中生生均校舍面积6.9平方米。

第七节 社会助学 勤工俭学

一、社会助学

县内社会助学活动主要是社会各界捐资修建“希望工程”学校，从1996年开始实施。到2008年，先后有国内外慈善机构及爱心人士捐资修建希望小学、“希望工程”教学楼等项目84个，总投资3406万元，建筑面积62266平方米；受助资金总额2227.6万元，主要用于“希望小学”项目土建工程；县政府配套投入1178.4万元，主要用于附属工程建设；受助学生累计11892人，受助金额总计289.25万元；获资助图书3万册、课桌300多双人套和一批办公用具、学习用品、衣物等。

2008年，深圳新兰德证券公司捐资修建肯甫小学

1997—2008年全县“希望工程”建设项目统计表

表20－5

序号	项目名称	工程规模（平方米）	总投资金额（万元）	捐资金额（万元）	捐资单位或捐资人	捐资人地址	竣工时间
1	瑶山逸夫中学逸夫楼	4495	218.25	80.00	邵逸夫	香港	1997年
2	志成瑶山小学教学楼	715	30.00	30.00	魏凤英	香港	1997年
3	播尧南航教学楼	783	36.58	10.00	南方航空公司	广州	1998年
4	一小可口可乐教学楼	1084	52.00	25.00	上海可口可乐公司	上海	1998年
5	上港水利小学教学楼	700	40.00	40.00	上海港务局	上海	1998年
6	佳荣希望小学大楼	714	32.31	30.00	深圳商贸控股有限公司	深圳	1998年
7	荔波民中深扶楼	5157	316.22	315.00	深圳商贸控股有限公司	深圳	1998年
8	甲中深扶学生宿舍楼	2012	95.39	95.00	深圳商贸控股有限公司	深圳	1998年
9	花堤希望小学深扶楼	714	30.00	30.00	深圳商贸控股有限公司	深圳	1998年
10	朝阳希望小学深扶楼	714	30.00	30.00	深圳商贸控股有限公司	深圳	1998年
11	波平希望小学深扶楼	714	30.00	30.00	深圳商贸控股有限公司	深圳	1998年
12	茂兰希望小学深扶楼	714	30.00	30.00	深圳商贸控股有限公司	深圳	1998年
13	金对希望小学深扶楼	714	30.82	30.00	深圳商贸控股有限公司	深圳	1998年
14	播中深扶多功能厅	934	64.13	60.00	深圳商贸控股有限公司	深圳	1998年
15	大土希望小学教学楼	330	18.08	17.00	黄佩球	香港	1999年
16	茂中双鸿楼	600	30.00	30.00	蔡双鸿	深圳	2000年
17	佳荣拉先小学教学楼	190	7.50	3.19	燃灯基金会	美国	2000年
18	佳荣拉学小学教学楼	210	6.40	3.00	燃灯基金会	美国	2000年
19	永康小学教学楼	340	12.00	12.00	青溪酒厂	贵阳	2000年
20	洞常小学教学楼	342	7.00	3.00	燃灯基金会	美国	2000年
21	水利水龙小学教学楼	150	4.00	2.49	爱德基金会	南京	2000年
22	方村拉街小学深扶楼	324	15.00	12.00	深圳商贸控股有限公司	深圳	2001年
23	玉屏石灰坳小学国民楼	209	11.00	10.00	汪国民	荔波	2001年
24	茂兰吉王小学教学楼	100	3.00	1.29	爱德基金会	南京	2001年
25	玉屏瑶寨小学教学楼	100	3.00	1.00	爱德基金会	南京	2001年
26	洞塘肯甫小学教学楼	150	4.60	1.99	爱德基金会	南京	2001年
27	玉屏尧排小学教学楼	80	1.00	1.00	爱德基金会	南京	2001年
28	董蒙小学教学楼	80	2.00	1.00	爱德基金会	南京	2001年
29	玉屏水扒小学教学楼	80	1.20	1.20	爱德基金会	南京	2001年
30	洞塘三合小学教学楼	80	1.82	1.82	爱德基金会	南京	2001年
31	永康尧古小学教学楼	320	11.50	3.00	燃灯基金会	美国	2001年

续表20－5

序号	项目名称	工程规模（平方米）	总投资金额（万元）	捐资金额（万元）	捐资单位或捐资人	捐资人地址	竣工时间
32	永康甲棒小学教学楼	120	4.00	3.00	爱德基金会	南京	2001年
33	佳荣拉毛小学教室	60	2.00	2.00	燃灯基金会	美国	2002年
34	觉巩小学教学楼	834	31.16	30.00	武汉凯迪公司	武汉	2002年
35	捞村力书小学教室	150	6.00	6.00	爱德基金会	南京	2003年
36	朝阳邑马小学教室	110	5.00	5.00	爱德基金会	南京	2003年
37	播尧拉美小学教室	110	5.00	5.00	爱德基金会	南京	2003年
38	佳荣甲料小学教学楼	180	4.00	4.00	爱德基金会	南京	2003年
39	荔波二小逸夫楼	2130	85.00	50.00	邵逸夫	香港	2003年
40	佳荣拉易小学教学楼	300	11.50	2.00	燃灯基金会	美国	2003年
41	洞塘木朝小学教学楼	290	10.00	2.00	燃灯基金会	美国	2003年
42	永康董亥小学教室	80	2.42	2.42	爱德基金会	南京	2003年
43	永康德门学教室	180	7.98	7.98	徐于亮	香港	2003年
44	朝阳洞麦小学君义楼	580	25.40	25.40	君义	丹麦	2003年
45	水利水岩小学教学楼	380	17.80	17.80	香港中商联合印刷公司	香港	2003年
46	甲站小学教学楼	555	19.63	10.00	贵阳新太乙房地产公司	贵阳	2003年
47	洞塘中学方军楼	818	29.33	10.00	杨方军	上海	2003年
48	荔波三小君义楼	1435	53.00	40.00	君义	丹麦	2004年
49	洞塘板寨八一小学教学楼	757	31.60	10.00	贵州省军区	贵阳	2004年
50	佳荣拉亮小学教室	168	6.14	6.00	航空港二建总队	徐州	2004年
51	方村红泥小学综合楼	210	8.00	3.00	燃灯基金会	美国	2004年
52	佳荣高里小学教室	117	4.52	2.00	燃灯基金会	美国	2004年
53	永康甲棒小学玉明楼	240	10.00	8.00	司玉明	荔波	2004年
54	甲良金华小学教学楼	431	16.60	10.00	香港惩教署教育基金	香港	2004年
55	播尧尧花小学教学楼	431	16.60	10.00	香港惩教署教育基金	香港	2004年
56	甲良甲岸小学教学楼	431	16.60	3.00	燃灯基金会	美国	2004年
57	佳荣拉吾小学教室	126	4.80	3.00	燃灯基金会	美国	2004年
58	佳荣水碰小学教室	113	4.30	2.00	燃灯基金会	美国	2004年
59	播尧曼井小学教学楼	470	20.00	20.00	澳海联李佳鸣	香港	2005年
60	茂兰水庆小学教学楼	642	25.00	15.00	邵逸夫	香港	2005年
61	水尧小学综合楼	750	30.15	25.00	丹麦苏恩深	丹麦	2006年
62	水尧育苗小学教学楼	547	21.96	10.00	兹恩基金吴新发	香港	2006年
63	甲良中怀小学教学楼	500	35.00	35.00	深圳经济合作发展基管会	深圳	2006年

续表20－5

序号	项目名称	工程规模（平方米）	总投资金额（万元）	捐资金额（万元）	捐资单位或捐资人	捐资人地址	竣工时间
64	甲良阳凤小学明德楼	1270	40.00	40.00	台湾台塑集团（王永庆）	台湾	2006年
65	洞塘尧所小学教学楼	240	13.00	10.00	深圳景深丽公司	深圳	2007年
66	瑶山小学学生宿舍楼	200	13.00	10.00	贵州天恒房地产公司（谢群）	贵阳	2007年
67	梅桃劲拓希望小学	533	60.00	40.00	深圳劲拓电子设备公司（吴限）	深圳	2007年
68	朝阳中学综合楼	1300	100.00	40.00	贵州银海房地产公司（冯晓丰）	贵阳	2007年
69	洪江小学综合楼	404	37.00	10.00	上海青基会（王伟陈俊）	上海	2007年
70	山江小学综合楼	404	30.00	20.00	加拿大（金兴国）	加拿大	2007年
71	水尧水扒圆梦小学	372	20.00	10.00	浙江医疗器械研究所刘弋青	浙江	2007年
72	县幼儿园明德综合楼	4025	350.00	50.00	贵州明德实业有限责任公司（赵明德）	荔波	2007年
73	架桥小学教学楼	445	38.00	25.00	深圳富士康集团	深圳	2007年
74	板吉小学教学楼	875	50.00	25.00	深圳富士康集团	深圳	2007年
75	水尧水捞小学教学楼	445	20.00	10.00	香港文娱会有限公司	香港	2007年
76	瑶庆小学学生宿舍及食堂	367	20.00	10.00	朱英龙	台湾	2008年
77	瑶山小学学生宿舍及食堂	324	18.00	10.00	朱英龙	台湾	2008年
78	洞塘肯甫小学教学楼	1221	80.00	52.00	深圳新兰德公司40万元，香港慈恩基金会12万元	深圳、香港	2008年
79	荔波二小教学综合楼	3296	200.00	45.00	台湾台塑集团	台湾	2008年
80	荔波二中教学楼	6808	458.00	450.00	深圳盐田港	深圳	2008年
81	民昂小学学生宿舍	305	18.20	10.00	朱英龙	台湾	2008年
82	洞塘学校综合楼	513	40.50	16.00	中国人权发展基金会	北京	2008年
83	水维小学学生宿舍	264	20.00	10.00	朱英龙	台湾	2008年
84	茂兰小学学生宿舍	561	35.00	10.00	朱英龙	台湾	2008年

二、勤工俭学

20世纪80年代中期，县内部分中小学开展一些适合本校实际、效益好、风险小的经营项目。朝阳小学开办学生学习用具小卖部，佳荣小学开荒建蔬菜基地，种植蔬菜补充食堂生活。

1992年，甲良中学兴建建材厂，采取借资、贷款方式建设经营。该校还承包林场2个，总面积7680亩，种植杉树20万株，并养殖黑山羊。在学校附近开辟苗圃场30亩，培植绿化树苗、花卉、草皮等。

1998年，荔波民中在当街校门外新建印刷厂（原荔中印刷厂建于1957年），实行承包经营责任制，当年扭转校办企业长期亏损的局面，之后勤工俭学效益逐年增长。该校利用县内旅游优势，在“五一”“十一”假期开放学生公寓，接待游客。同时组织学生担任导游，为游客服务，既让学生参加社会实践，又增长学生的社会知识。每学期为贫困生设置100多个勤工俭学岗位。

2002年，县教育局总结甲良中学、荔波民中等学校开展勤工俭学取得的经验，成立勤工俭学总公司。

2004年9月，勤工俭学总公司贷款、借资60万元，创办荔波家具城；筹集资金650万元，建成荔波县职业教育实训基地吉妮丽吉大酒店。该公司受县政府委托，接管国有企业荔波樟江天然食品厂。是年，瑶山中学建立苗圃、林场、经果园等学农基地，组织学生到基地为树苗打枝、嫁接、松土、浇水、施肥、喷药等，让学生掌握农村实用技术。

2005年后，甲良中学、荔波民中、县职业高中、瑶山中学、茂兰中学、播尧中学、县幼儿园等学校先后建立各类基地。全县学校有勤工俭学项目22个，较大型的项目有吉妮丽吉大酒店旅游服务实训基地、樟江驾校、荔波家具城、特种兔养殖场、甲良中学建材厂、甲良林场、水维林场、巴弓林场、梅桃黄连基地、益觉梨园基地、茂兰土鸡散养场、洞塘桑蚕基地、方村鱼塘、佳荣养猪场、瑶山经果园种植基地、县幼儿园竹园基地等。勤工俭学所得收入主要用于改善学校办学条件，补充办学经费的不足。

2008年，县委、县政府加大教育经费投入，满足学校运转，勤工俭学总公司由经营转向学校环境、学生宿舍、食堂等监督、规范管理。

第八节　教育管理

一、教育行政

1978年，全日制小学由县教育局管理，社队办的小学由社队管理。1984年，充实区、乡中心完小领导力量，首次基本配齐中心完小校长、副校长、教导主任，一些完小还配备总务主任。

1985年，按《中共中央关于教育体制改革的决定》，小学实行县、乡双重管理，中学实行县、区双重管理。校长实行任命制，教师由县教育局统一调配。

1988年，县教育局制定《荔波县中小学教师行为规范》《荔波县中学生行为规范》《荔波县中小学教研组活动制度》《荔波县中小学会考条例》《荔波县教职工调动的暂行规定》等规章制度，发到各校执行。

1995年7月，县教育局以玉屏中学、甲良中学、朝阳中学、茂兰中学教师聘任制。1997年7月又在总结四校经验的基础上，决定在玉屏一小、玉屏二小、朝阳小学、茂兰小学、甲良小学等五所大型小学实行学校内部管理体制改革，推行校长负责制和教师聘任制。1998年全县乡中心完小以上学校全部实施以校长负责制、教师聘任制为核心内容的“三制一管理”（校长负责制、教职工聘任制、岗位责任制、教育教学责任目标管理）和“四定”（即定编、定员、定岗位目标责任、定聘约）体制。至1999年，在全县中小学普遍实施《荔波县学校内部管理体制改革方案》《荔波县关于全县中小学内部管理体制改革工作的补充意见》《荔波县校长任期考核办法》《荔波县实施“三制一管理”学校教师考核办法（试行）》《荔波县实施内部管理体制改革学校教职工聘用合同制方案（试行）》《荔波县学校工作管理和教学常规管理实施意见》《荔波县初中阶段学籍管理办法（暂行）》等文件。

从2001年起，对义务教育阶段家庭经济困难学生免收书本费和杂费。从2005年起，对义务教育阶段家庭经济困难寄宿生给予生活补助费。

2006年，出台《荔波县教育系统党组关于对超编的中学、乡镇中心完小教师进行分流的意见》，规定超编学校教师到缺编学校支教的期限为三年，期满后，通过考核或竞争上岗方式返回原校，考核不合格者给予行文正式调动。是年，全县派出支教交流人员53人（中学38人）。

此后，县教育局相继发出《关于进一步加强中小学管理工作的意见》《关于进一步加强学校德育工作的指导意见》《关于规范学校办学行为全面实施素质教育的规定》《荔波县“十一五”中小学、幼儿园教师继续教育工作管理制度》《关于进一步加强师德师风建设的意见》《荔波县中小学、幼儿园骨干教师管理办法（试行）》《荔波县进城务工人员子女义务教育阶段就学暂行管理办法》《关于加强留守儿童教育管理工作的意见》《荔波县学校安全管理制度（试行）》《荔波县教育系统关于加强未成年人思想道德和法制教育的实施意见》《荔波县教育局关于加强义务教育阶段“控辍保学”工作的意见》《荔波县义务教育阶段学校学籍管理规定（试行）》《荔波县教育教学奖励办法（修订）》《关于进一步加强学校精细化管理的“八条要求”》14个管理文件，突出以教育教学为中心，加强教育教学管理，全县中小学教育教学管理工作制度化、规范化、精细化。

二、教育督导

1996年3月，成立县政府教育督导室，规格为副科级，事业编制3人，挂靠县教育局。

教育督导室建立后，参加教育局组织的开学工作检查，依法对全县各中小学贯彻落实教育方针、教育法律法规进行监督指导，组织对全县中小学办学水平进行督导评估。2001年，全县“两基”工作通过省级验收。2002年1月，教育部公布认定荔波县为全国第八批“两基”合格县。

“两基”验收合格后，按省关于“两基”工作年审要求，组织相关人员到乡（镇）、学校开展“两基”年审自查，及时填写年审表和“两基”自查情况报告报省督导室。2005年，全县“两基”工作通过省级复查和“普实”验收。同时，对乡（镇）政府及县涉教部门履行教育职责情况进行监督、检查。

2005—2008年，开展“两基”迎“国检”督导工作，针对全县“两基”迎“国检”工作存在的薄弱环节和突出问题，聘请特约专家组到乡（镇）学校进行调研，组织有关人员对各乡镇“两基”迎“国检”工作进行实战预演，对督查结果进行通报，并限期整改，迎接2009年“两基”工作国家检查。

三、招生考试

改革开放后，县内高中招生实行考试择优录取制度，考试科目为语文、数学、政治、英语、物理、化学等6科。从1992年起，历史、地理、生物等3科在初中二年级学科教学结束后参加全州会考，成绩合格方可参加高中升学考试。2003年，按照州教育局的规定，初中毕业升学考试科目调整为语文、数学、英语、物理、化学、政治和综合科（历史、地理、生物合卷）等7科。2005年，考试科目调整为语文、数学、英语、综合理科（物理、化学合卷）、综合文科（政治、历史合卷）。此外，体育科目考试为必考科目。高中毕业生按照国家规定参加全国统一考试。

在普及九年义务教育之前，初中招生也实行考试择优录取制度。实行义务教育后，小学毕业生全部免试就近升入初中。

小学招生按照入学年龄7周岁的规定，适龄儿童就近入学。

1987—2008年全县各学段招生情况一览表

表20－6　　　　单位：人

年度	学前教育	小学	初中	普高	职中
1987	—	3983	800	134	—
1988	1035	4127	1012	142	80
1989	1070	4183	608	129	60

续表20-6

年度	学前教育	小学	初中	普高	职中
1990	1227	3856	1084	207	66
1991	1231	4078	1128	152	54
1992	1517	4433	1636	138	79
1993	1636	3821	1547	138	83
1994	1786	3627	1759	132	131
1995	2175	2416	1882	190	110
1996	2262	3544	2355	180	101
1997	2158	3457	2468	138	168
1998	1981	3080	2555	216	100
1999	2028	2877	2608	238	100
2000	1681	2859	2889	578	75
2001	1537	2802	3464	701	20
2002	1904	2965	3456	851	40
2003	1884	3045	3304	770	135
2004	2330	2994	3204	1097	185
2005	2631	2840	2931	1246	645
2006	2616	2752	3078	838	742
2007	2130	2675	3018	862	826
2008	2256	2350	3257	942	650

1993—2008年全县普通高考录取情况一览表

表20-7　　单位：人

年度	报考人数	录取重点人数	录取本科人数	录取大专人数	录取率（%）
1993	142	1	5	18	16.90
1994	162	—	8	27	21.60
1995	155	—	5	25	19.35
1996	134	—	4	33	27.71
1997	151	—	7	34	27.15
1998	202	2	19	49	34.65
1999	210	1	32	75	51.43
2000	186	3	38	111	81.72
2001	238	25	73	82	75.63
2002	268	24	124	55	75.75

续表20－7

年度	报考人数	录取重点人数	录取本科人数	录取大专人数	录取率（%）
2003	576	29	190	192	71.35
2004	756	46	277	300	82.41
2005	923	43	228	314	63.38
2006	1022	36	165	299	48.92
2007	1210	92	232	417	61.24
2008	1290	77	278	427	60.62

四、教学设备

1978—1983年，投入20.34万元先后采购中学仪器230种、小学仪器24种，全县小学图书35370册、中学图书46780册。

1985年后，按教育部颁布的第二个《中学理科教学仪器配备目录》《小学数学自然教学仪器配备目录》配置中小学教学仪器。1984—1989年，投入资金33.24万元，配置的中学教学仪器增加到457种、小学教学仪器67种，小学图书增加到43240册、中学图书增加到52150册。

1990—2000年，全县投入230.35万元，采购文科、体育、音乐、美术、劳技、特教仪器。到2000年，全县《中学理科教学仪器配备目录》仪器品种增加到1103种，《小学数学自然教学仪器配备目录》为189种；全县图书小学达到103878册，初中达到128903册，高中达到168420册。

2001年，为通过省政府及教育部“普实”验收，将全县中小学实验室老化严重的仪器、老化的电线、松脱插座更换，排除存在的安全隐患，补充数量不足的实验器材。2008年，全县投入资金3249.59万元添置教学仪器和图书，其中《初中理科教学仪器配备标准》仪器品种达到1177种，《小学数学科学教学仪器配备标准》品种达到294种，《高中理科教学仪器配备标准》仪器品种达到1204种。全县图书小学达到173878册，初中达到198903册，高中达到268420册。

2007—2008年，县教育局投资2万元，建成荔波教育资源库，为全县中小学提供教育教学服务。

五、教研活动

1978年，县教育局设有教研室，组织各校开展教研活动。1979年12月，根据州教育局下发的《关于深入开展教学教研的意见》，各地中心校建立教研组。教研室组织全县初中、高中一些学科学期统考，并对统考质量进行分析。

从1980年起，全县小学全部恢复六年制。

1981年10—11月，全县分别召开各中心完小以上语文、数学教研组长会议，研讨全国统编教材。教研室人员还到各区、校放映教学影片，促进各校开展教学改革。

1983年，组织全县教师进行教材过关考试。是年，教研室恢复内刊《荔波教育》编辑工作，主要刊登交流学术论文、教学经验和教学动态等。

1986—1987年，召开小学语文、数学教学研讨会，教研人员到会指导，宣传教学大纲。1988年后，教研室每学年都要组织中小学各学科举行优质课评选活动。部分教师代表荔波县到省、州参加优质课评选。

1987年，县教育局制定“三级统考制度”，半期考试，由学校命题、制卷、评卷；学期考试由区组织，学年考试由县组织，并把统考情况编印成册，发至各中小学。

1990年4月，荔波与独山、平塘、三都四县联合举办第一届小学生“友谊杯”数学竞赛。

1991年4月，召开全县中小学“快速作文法”教学研讨会，在全县推广“快速作文法”。

1996年，在全县范围内推广“双语”复式教学实验。1998年8月，举办全县村完小以上教导主任培训班。是年，在全县普及“珠脑速算”教育。

1990—2000年，荔波、独山、三都、平塘4县连续10年联合进行小学一年级至六年级语文、数学联考，每次会考后，轮流在4县召开小学会考质量分析会。

2003年4月，选派中小学校长参加“教育部、李嘉诚基金会西部中小学现代远程教育项目”二期工程第二期项目学校校长培训。7月，组织教师到贵阳参加“中国著名教育改革家魏书生老师教育经验介绍暨学术报告会”。10月，组织76名中小学教师参加教育部特级讲师团赴都匀讲学活动。

2004年5月，开展全县中小学音乐专业教师音乐技能展演比赛。2005年，荔波县教育局确定县民族中学、职业中学、荔波二中等13所学校为“学生体质健康标准试点校”。是年，制定教师教育科研论文发表及评选获奖奖励方案。

2005年，县教育局组织编写《可爱的荔波》一书作为地方教材，在各校使用。

2007年3月，县教育局对全县初中专任教师进行课堂教学、专业知识、学生测评等“三个一”综合考试。7月，组织全县中小学英语教师参加“第三期美中友好志愿者英语教师培训”活动。

2008年，开办校长、教导主任论坛，主要交流成功办学和教育教学经验。

2003—2008年，坚持开展学校与学校之间的交流和教师与教师之间的结对帮扶活动，组织县城学校骨干教师“送教下乡”活动，支援师资力量薄弱的学校。

第二章　科学技术

第一节　科技队伍

一、科技人员构成

1978年7月，对全县从事自然科学技术工作的理学、工学、农学、医学等30个专业科技人员进行全面普查，全县有科技人员297名。其中，工程技术44人、农业技术83人、卫生技术140人、科研1人、教学29人；大专84人、中专152人、其他61人；属科技人员未从事科技工作的52人；闲散科技人员45人。

1980—1982年，经技术职称评定，全县从事农业技术工作的162人中，获工程师8人、助理工程师38人、技术员59人；全县医务人员评定和晋升技术职称57人。

1987年5月，对全县自然科学技术人员再次进行全面普查，全县有科技人员341人。其中，有技术职称253人，占74.19%；提拔到各级领导岗位任职85人，占24.93%。1988年10月，经事业单位职称改革，全县有12个系列专业技术人员1572人，其中，高级职称20人、中级职称255人、初级职称1297人。

1989年12月—1990年1月，开展全县专业人才普查，全县有卫生、农业、工程、中文、社会科学、会计、统计、经济、图书文博、档案资料、出版、播音、新闻、公证、律师、中小学16个职称系列，专业技术人员总计2582人（国家机关441人、企事业单位2141人）。其中，大学本科毕业80人、大专毕业192人、中专毕业1509人、其他学历801人；高级职称20人、中级职称288人、初级职称1833人；单位行政领导有技术职称178人。

1997年年底，全县企事业单位有各级各类专业技术人员1998人。其中，工程92人、农业130人、卫生332人、教学1430人、经济管理6人、会计师8人；在职专业技术人员1984人（高级24人、中级320人、初级1640人）。

2000年，全县有科技人员2545人，已评聘专业技术职务2411人。其中，高级26人、中级424人、初级1961人；教育1616人、农业346人、工程54人、医疗卫生395人。

2005年，全县有专业技术人员2906人（不含省、州垂管单位），已评聘专业技术2708人。已评聘人员中，高级41人、中级622人、初级2045人；教育1856人、农业198人、工程196人、医疗卫生394人、其他64人。

二、人才管理

1990年，县委、县政府建立科技进步奖励和举荐制度，制定科技进步奖励办法。

从2000年起，对符合县域经济发展需要的专业大学本科以上毕业生，直接招录到县内工作。

2001年，开始实行党政领导干部科技进步和人才目标管理考核制度。成立县科技教育工作领导小组，制定科技人才引进、培训、使用及建设规划的政策措施，建立科技副职选派制度，全县17个乡（镇）均配备有1名科技副乡（镇）长，170个村委会配备科技副主任。

是年，县委、县政府成立专家顾问组，聘请省、州科技专家担任科技顾问，参与重大事项论证。各部门、各乡（镇）制定吸纳人才优惠政策。

2002年，修订《荔波县科学技术进步奖励办法》及其《实施细则》，开展科技成果登记、科技人才评选推优工作，并将在工作中业务精、责任心强、政治素质好的科技人才安排到领导岗位。

至2003年，县内直接招录大学本科以上毕业生49人，其中，荔波籍25人、外地籍24人。

建立科技人才继续教育制度，有计划地输送科技人员外出学习，每年接受继续教育的科技人员不低于三分之一。同时，积极举荐先进科技工作者，对有突出贡献的优秀科技工作者，按规定享受政府特殊津贴，破格晋升职称。

第二节　科技培训与宣传

一、科技培训

1978—1990年，科技培训采取一课题、一事、一培训方法，不定期举办技术培训班，聘请科技人员讲授专业技术知识，并进行现场实习，学用结合。先后举办了双季稻、温室无土育秧、杂交稻优势利用、水稻宽窄行栽培、吨粮田、红麻高产技术开发、杂交稻旱作栽培、沼气制取与利用、西瓜引种高产示范、芭蕉商品生产技术开发等课题培训班124期，参加学习人员累计1.45万人次。

1991年，进行芭蕉“星火计划”专题技术培训3期，培训芭蕉种植人员300人。1992年，组织捞村乡、朝阳镇“星火带头人”技术培训班2期，培训100人。1993年，现场技术指导培训8期，培训250人。

1998—2000年，进行食用菌生产现场培训，利用“菌草技术”栽培香菇、平菇、金针菇试验项目，培训农村干部及农村青年骨干300余人，带动玉屏、瑶山、茂兰、立化等乡（镇）食用菌发展。2000年，在朝阳、瑶山、永康、水尧、水利、播尧等乡（镇）举办食用菌栽培技术培训班8期，培训430人，印发资料1400份。

2004年8—9月，开展“两山”青年农民科技培训，以培训捞村乡（一类贫困乡）、佳荣镇、瑶麓乡青年村干部及农村科技致富能手为主，同时对朝阳镇拉扶村、八烂村，甲良镇洞庭村、益觉村，驾欧乡新街村，水利乡水龙村的乡村干部、农村致富能手及项目覆盖农户进行培训，培训人数总计480人次。培训内容有二元杂交猪饲养及疫情防治、日本丰水梨的栽培技术、牛的饲养及管理、水稻病虫害防治、稻茬油菜无耕移栽技术、果菜类早熟丰产栽培技术、家禽饲养及疫病防治、速生松树移植及管理、麻竹育苗移栽技术、稻田养鱼技术、造林及管护、西瓜栽培技术等，培训课上播放各类农业实用技术影碟，发放各种技术资料3500份。

“十五”期间，科技培训以实施试验示范项目和非常规种养殖培训为主，办培训班总计55期，培训4500人次，发放技术资料1.5万册，播放光碟30张。每年有90%以上村干部接受普及性科技培训。

2006年3月，县委、县政府邀请贵州大学农学院果树和植保专家组到荔波作“贵州柑橘生产的现状、优势及发展方向”“脐橙的高接换种技术”“椪柑主要病虫害防治技术”“柚优质丰产栽培技术”等专题讲座。

是年，各单位、乡（镇）开展科技培训185期，培训5500人次，投入培训经费6.64万元。其中，种植业125期，培训3250人次，经费3.78万元；养殖业51期，培训1840人次，经费2.34万元；其他9期，培训410人次，经费0.52万元。

2006年“3・18”科技活动日，在立化镇尧明村，佳荣镇坤地村、威岩村开展农业适用技术培训。

2007年，建立科技特派员制度，拟聘的科技特派员11人次先后参加省、州培训3次。随后，组织科技特派员到捞村、佳荣、朝阳、洞塘等乡（镇）对农民急需的种桑养蚕、甘蔗种植及其他种植养殖技术进行培训、咨询和宣传，发放技术资料。是年，开展种桑养蚕、柑橘管理、铁皮石斛冻害减灾、火龙果冻灾恢复等技术培训班14期，培训1100人次，发放技术资料1.4万份。

2008年2—5月，冰冻灾害之后，聘请贵州大学农学院、省农科院等单位的专家和县内果蔬技术人员组成培训小组，针对种植面积较大的柑橘类果树受冻害情况，选择玉屏镇的拉岜、福利，朝阳镇的田洞、坪寨、鲁翁，瑶山乡的高桥等果园，作为灾后恢复技术现场教学点，组织发动周边群众到现场接受示范教学培训，带动柑橘冻害恢复1.3万亩。县内相关单位举办柑橘、铁皮石斛、火龙果、辣椒、早熟蔬菜、甘蔗、果梅、九阡李种植及冻害减灾技术培训班8期1.2万人次，发放技术资料2.12万份。

二、科技宣传

1978年，利用有线广播不定期举办科技知识讲座，聘请科技讲座通讯员45名。1979年9月，成立县科教电影放映队，定期到全县各区、社、大队巡回放映科教影片。

1980—1982年，县科技局定期和不定期编辑刊物《荔波科技》，同时，将本地、外地的经验与技术编印成通俗易懂的《农村科普资料》《科技情况与资料》《农业科学简讯》《科学动态》《科技信息》等刊物，发送县级机关单位、区（镇）、公社、大队、学校。在县城及各区（镇）开办“科普园地”“科技宣传栏”“科技橱窗”等科技宣传园地，普及科技知识。

从1993年起，每年的3月18日科技活动日，开展系列科技普及宣传活动。

是年，县科技局建立新技术服务部，开展科技下乡活动10次，发放各类科技资料、书籍15种678册，接受群众咨询1500人次，印发《科技进步法》100份，利用广播、电视和赶场天进行科技法规宣传。

1998—1999年，在农贸市场开办“科技服务窗口”，利用赶场天，进行科技知识宣传。

2002年，复制中央电视台《致富经》科技栏目光盘，分别在驾欧乡等地组织农户观看学习，县职业中学刻录为教学片。是年起，为各乡（镇）农业服务中心和174个村（居）委会订购《贵州科技报》《农村百事通》报刊，赠送科技光碟。

2003年“3・18”科技活动周期间，科技、科协、农业、气象局、环保、保护局等单位开展科技宣传、咨询服务、科技图片、邮展等活动，发放科技宣传资料23种9000份。是年5月“非典”期间，采取多种形式开展“依靠科学，战胜非典”系列科普宣传活动。

2004—2005年，开展文化、科技、卫生“三下乡”活动，发放各类科技宣传资料1.6万份，赠送《农村实用技术丛书》3000册。

2006年8月，在全县“法制宣传周”活动中，发放《专利法》《科技进步法》《防震减灾法》等科技相关法律法规宣传资料500份，解答群众咨询100人次。

2007—2008年，每年举办一次“科技活动周”宣传活动，在玉屏、播尧、佳荣、朝阳、瑶山、立化等乡（镇）开展农业技术服务和科技宣传活动，发放宣传资料3.6万份，群众咨询1.9万人次，展出挂图、展板30幅，展示新产品13个，送图书、科技新产品等。

第三节 科技应用推广

一、新品种引进推广

1978—1990年，先后引进新品种农作物类21种、畜牧鱼类24种、水果类11种到县内种植养殖。

1991年，从罗甸引进粉蕉4000株在王蒙、朝阳两乡（镇）的2个村、4个组共76户种植成功，向周边辐射发展。

1994年，向17个乡（镇）推广“叶面宝”3500瓶。

1997年，引进福建农业大学科技成果“菌草技术”，试种成功后，以樟江河谷为产业带，带动周边乡村发展。

1999年，从全国优质枇杷产区福建省莆田区引进优质枇杷品种长虹3号100株，在玉屏镇拉鱼村建立优质枇杷示范点，种植成活率达95%；在朝阳拉扶村、八烂村试种香稻8亩，获得成功；在朝阳、茂兰引种余晖彩糯玉米获得成功；引进“七彩山鸡引种育饲养研究”鸡苗饲喂成活率达90%，留种雌鸡年产蛋80～120枚，孵化率达70%，成活率达80%，料肉比为3.1∶1，已自繁两代，发展试点养殖10个。

2000年，引种玉米农大3138、农大108、黔2009组合3个，在茂兰镇种植310亩、甲良镇种植340亩、驾欧乡种植230亩、瑶麓乡种植350亩，均获成功。从福建引进高产优质高效荷兰豆种80公斤，在瑶山乡小七孔进行反季节栽培试验，种植面积20亩。

是年，在玉屏镇拉鱼村实施标准式稻鱼工程推广示范养殖，获得成功；在玉屏开始实施早熟蔬菜种植示范。实施的草莓大棚栽培试验示范项目，获得成功并推广。

2001年，县科技局从安徽引进2000株脱毒草莓，在朝阳镇八烂村试种成功并示范推广。在甲良镇实施星火计划项目辣椒残株二次结果栽培试验。

2002年，实施脱毒草莓引种及人工大棚栽培示范1亩；在玉屏实施山蒲三元杂交猪良种繁育示范。

2003年，投资200万元引进万头优质肉牛引种繁殖养殖；投资60万元引进千亩优质水果种植；投资120万元引进万头三元杂交猪养殖示范等农业科技项目；实施南板蓝根高产栽培示范120亩；在立化尧明实施人工种草养畜示范。

2004年，实施瑶山鸡品种选育及养殖示范。

2005年，发展中药材元胡种植，引进贵州万顺堂药业到荔波投资建设石斛种植基地。

至2005年年底，早熟蔬菜面积发展到1万亩；脱毒草莓引种及人工大棚栽培示范从3个大棚发展到187个大棚；南板蓝根高产栽培示范发展到600亩；立化尧明人工种草养畜示范有大型规模养殖场5个，引进优质良种肉牛500头；新增瑶山鸡养殖5万羽；新增三元杂生猪存栏1.5万头。

二、科技项目实施

科技项目立项和实施由各部门、乡（镇）申报，县科技局分类审核逐级申报。立项后，申报单位从各自的渠道解决资金，组织实施。

2002年，组织实施任豆树栽培和皇竹草栽培试验。组织实施脱毒草莓引种大棚栽培试验及辣椒批量快速烘干技术研究项目获得成功。

2002—2003年，瑶山乡“粮—猪—沼生态”农业建设示范列入贵州省星火计划项目，项目总投资15万元，其中，省星火计划专项资金10万元，自筹5万元。2002年4月，申报GEF荔波县生物多样性保护项目，通过专家实地考察，选择在3个点实施，即水尧乡瑶族移民新村，以山茱萸、白芨、仙茅为主的迁地共管保护地；永康乡尧古村，以水草、罗芙木、地棕、白芨、果子狸、穿山甲为主的栖息地共管保护地；永康乡尧兰村，以水草、罗芙木、地棕、白芨、果子狸、穿山甲为主的栖息地共管保护地。

2004年，获省列“板蓝根种植基地”建设项目、“酸梅系列产品开发研究”项目；获州列“荔波县干旱气象灾害及其防御对策研究”项目、“南板蓝根规范化种植技术培训”项目、“荔波县永康乡尧古村板蓝根规范化人工栽培试验示范”项目、“杨梅生态栽培及产业化技术体系研发与示范”项目、“黔南州数字化地震监测台站建设与防震减灾专项”项目。

2006年，申报立项并实施中药种植项目：水利乡元胡种植，面积98亩，总产量31500公斤，产值7万元；万顺堂药业在翁昂乡实施金钗石斛种植2万株，成活率50%；茂兰野生植物开发有限公司投资200万元，建设茂兰铁皮石斛基地，完成仿生地建设45亩，种植26万株，成活率50%。

2007年，按照县委、县政府提出的农业、农村“一桑、二畜、三果、四蔗、五辣”的发展思路，收集整理以桑蚕、辣椒、药材、甘蔗、蔬菜、酸梅、植物资源普查等攻关、示范、推广科技项目十余项，经申报批准立项7项，安排专项资金27万元。实施种桑养蚕试验示范、辣椒提纯复壮、铁皮石斛、生态旅游气候分析等科技项目4项，总投资14.9万元。

2008年，以桑蚕、辣椒、药材、甘蔗、蔬菜为重点，整理科技项目，获批准立项2个，安排专项资金12万元。实施的省、州专项科技项目有小蚕培育示范基地、本地线椒良种扩繁及高产示范栽培基地、瑶麓花生提纯保优及加工工艺改良、甘蔗种植示范基地等，项目总投资27万元。同时实施的县级科技项目有糖蔗种植试验示范、万寿菊种植试验示范、人参果引种种植试验、红皮大蒜种植试验项目4个，总投资8.39万元。

第四节　青少年科技活动

一、科技夏令营活动

1981年暑假，在桂林举办首届少数民族优秀学生科技夏令营，全县各学校的三好学生、优秀少先队员、优秀共青团员和优秀辅导员共35人参加。

1982年8月，在县内举办少数民族学生科技夏令营，有少数民族学生52人参加。夏令营学生由南京林学院教师和县林学会科技人员指导，制作国家级、省级保护的一、二、三级稀有珍贵树种马桂木、马尾树及发现新种荔波桑等生物标本100多件。

1983年8月，在桂林举办荔波县少数民族青少年科技夏令营，参加人员32人，主要开展弹射飞机模型比赛、标本采集、写生等活动。

1999年7月，组织荔波中学科技兴趣小组师生6人，到昆明参加世界园艺博览夏令营活动。

2000年，暑假期间，县城中小学生科技辅导员与茂兰喀斯特自然保护区管理处联合举办生态夏令营活动，参加人员36人。

二、科技实践活动

1980年5月，举办科技作品科普书画展览，展出作品120件，评出一、二、三等奖34件。1981年，荔波民族中学学生参加贵州省《科技幼苗》报举办的耳塞式收音机制作比赛，获一等奖2个。是年10月，举办科技作品、科普书画展览，收到作品284件，展出118件，评出一、二、三等奖9件。

1981年元旦，组织航模代表队参加黔南州第二届青少年航模比赛，获团体总分第一名，获5个单项第一名，2项比赛破州纪录。

1982年5月，举办小论文、小发明、科技作品展览，展示作品100件，评出一、二、三等奖6件，获奖作品选送参加全省第一届小发明、小论文比赛，获三等奖2件。是年，选送参加全州科技作品展览56件，获一等奖2件、二等奖3件、三等奖6件。

1984年，组织小论文、小发明作品参加全省第二届小论文、小发明竞赛，参赛作品19件，获二等奖5件、三等奖5件，县民族中学获集体奖。

1986年，全县选送科技作品18件参加全州第三届科技作品展览，获二等奖、三等奖各1件。选送参加全省第三届小发明、小论文竞赛作品14件，获二等奖、三等奖各1件，获二等奖的《带拉手的插销》被省推荐参加全国小发明、小论文竞赛，获三等奖；荔波民中被评为1986年省科技活动先进集体，荔波民中教师何小亚被评为1986年省优秀青少年科技辅导员。

1987年，参加全省第四届青少年科技小发明、小论文比赛作品18件，获一等奖1件、二等奖7件、三等奖2件，教师朱颖年获科技辅导员特等奖，朱吉光、徐国通、金胜芝获科技辅导员三等奖。

2005年3月，荔波青少年活动中心正式挂牌成立。

2006年5月，举办首届全县中小学生信息技术创新与实践活动，参加学生300余人，选出优秀选手12名参加7月在深圳举办的全国第三届信息技术与创新实践活动比赛，玉屏二小学生罗宇获小学组网络中文二等奖，其余学生分别获高中组网络中文、网络英文、初中组网络中文和小学组网络中文三等奖。

2007年，选送中小学生科幻画作品13件参加第四届全州青少年科技创新大赛、第二十二届全省青少年科技创新大赛，玉屏一小学生作品《我的梦想》《星球奥运会》分别获省、州两级二等奖，《太空城》获州级二等奖。是年，举办第二届全县中小学信息技术创新与实践活动，选出优秀选手9名到重庆参加全国比赛，获一等奖2名、二等奖3名、三等奖4名。

2008年，选送中小学生科幻画作品13件参加第五届全州青少年科技创新大赛，获三等奖3件。

第五节　科研成果

2002年4月、8月，县委、县政府颁布实施《荔波县科学技术进步奖励办法》及其《实施细则》，每两年开展一次全县科学技术进步奖励评选活动。2004年11月，全县科学技术进步奖励活动收到单位和个人申报2003—2004年度科技成果14项。

2005—2006年度，共收到申报县科技进步奖励项目10项。

1984—2008年全县获州以上科技成果奖项目一览表

表20－8

获奖单位或个人	获奖时间	获奖成果	授奖单位	奖别
许梦鲤、周新民、莫让中	1984年	500W－8单相电机水泵研制	州政府	二等奖
县科技局	1991年	荔波县香芭蕉商品生产技术开发成果	州政府	黔南布依族苗族自治州科学技术进步四等奖
县科技局	1993年	科技成果管理	州政府	黔南布依族苗族自治州科技成果管理奖

续表20－8

获奖单位或个人	获奖时间	获奖成果	授奖单位	奖别
县科技局	1994年	荔波县阻断丝虫病传播的现场应用研究	州政府	黔南布依族苗族自治州科学技术进步三等奖
县科委县气象局	1994年	荔波县樟江河谷芭蕉商品生产基地建设	州政府	黔南布依族苗族自治州科学技术进步四等奖
县区划办	1995年	非耕地资源调查	州政府	黔南布依族苗族自治州科学技术进步四等奖
县土管局环保站	1995年	地面水域环境功能区划分方案	州政府	黔南布依族苗族自治州科学技术进步四等奖
县林业局	1998年	地面水域环境功能区划分方案	州政府	黔南布依族苗族自治州科学技术进步二等奖
县农机推广站	1998年	水稻增产机械化综合技术	州政府	黔南布依族苗族自治州科学技术进步三等奖
贵州茂兰国家级自然保护区管理处	1998年	黔南州野生豹猫黑熊资源调查研究	州政府	黔南布依族苗族自治州科学技术进步四等奖
县医院夏配明等	1998年	烧伤膏的研究与临床运用	州政府	黔南布依族苗族自治州科学技术进步四等奖
畜牧局	1999年	畜牧传染病调查	州政府	黔南布依族苗族自治州科学技术进步三等奖

第六节　地震监测

1998年县境内发生4.9级地震后，荔波县于1999年向省地震局申请建设地震监测台。省地震局结合荔波地震资料史和国家重大工程机场建设及国家重点旅游区建设配套需要，于“十五”期间在荔波县建设地震监测台。项目经省政府向国家地震总局申报，获国家地震总局批准，荔波县正式成为贵州省13个数字地震监测点之一。

2004年6月，报经国家地震局审核批准，确定测震台点设在洞塘乡的木朝村。荔波县地震测震台位于北纬25° 17′、东经108° 01′，海拔高度556.77米，距茂兰—洞塘公路800米，距洞塘电话线路800米，可接通宽带线，通信有保障。2005年1月，国家地震局委派湖北地震设计院的专家到所选地点进行测震复核。之后，聘请武汉大学设计总院进行规划设计，2006年2月动工建设，2007年4月12日，各项监测设备安装完毕并投入运行。

专记：

创建全国科普示范县

从20世纪90年代初开始，县委、县政府贯彻落实《中华人民共和国科学技术普及法》，树立“科学技术是第一生产力”的思想，围绕全县经济建设，开展科技普及工作。1990—1993年，通过培训科技“二传手”和评定农民技术员职称，建立科普示范户，创建了拉扶、丙花两个科普示范村。示范村主要进行果树栽种、科学养殖和水稻温室两段育秧新技术推广，带动各乡（镇）建立科普示范户共500户。

1995年6月，县科协在瑶山租赁土地200亩，租期30年，创建“瑶山甜桃示范培训基地”，带动周围群众建立标准果园3000多亩。

1997年，县科协在瑶山乡拉片村瑶沙组建立酸梅示范基地140亩，科协供给苗木和肥料，按季节进行技术培训，农户出劳动力，分户经营、连片管理。

1998年1月—2001年12月，县科协租用县农业办公室的地下室自办竹鼠良种繁殖场，主要对野生竹鼠进行驯化、饲养、繁殖、疾病防治等技术研究。经过实践，野生竹鼠从55只繁殖到800只，成功掌握整套饲养和繁殖技术，在全省成为饲养繁殖成功的第一例。之后，由县林业高级工程师冉景丞主导编写出《竹鼠养殖基础技术》一书，印刷300册，用于技术培训，带动全县人工饲养竹鼠，满足旅游业餐饮需求。

樟江柚项目在1998—2001年间经不断培训和技术改进，到2002年，经品种选优，送果样参加全国第五次柚类科研评比，于是年11月25日获“金杯奖”。2003年11月1日，樟江柚果样参加重庆全国柑橘品种结构调整战略研讨暨优新品种展示会，获特优产品推荐证书。因樟江柚项目规模大，为使技术更加成熟，分别建坡平蜜柚高标准种植示范园、福利柚园低产改造示范，带动群众建立标准蜜柚果园近万亩。

2002年2月，县委、县政府向中国科协申报第二批创建“全国科普示范县（市、区）单位”获批准，创建时间为3年。

在开展“全国科普示范县”创建活动期间，形成以县委党校、职业技术学校、农业技术广播学校、中国农村致富技术函授大学为主，农民文化技术学校、职工夜校为辅的教育培训体系，每年对乡、村科技人员及干部培训达1.2万人次、劳动力技能培训10万人次。全县建立科普示范乡（镇）4个、科普示范村8个，均建有科普图书室；全县农村科普示范带头人占15%，科技示范户占16%；建成科技示范基地22个、科技服务实体6个。在创建活动经费投入上，除示范项目的援助、扶贫项目的实施、各乡（镇）及县直机关安排生产业务费外，2002—2004年县财政安排资金总计30.1万元。

2004年10月，荔波县的“全国科普示范县”创建工作经国家组织实地检查验收，中国科协于10月10日行文批准荔波为“全国科普示范县”。

2005—2007年，县财政投入科普经费总计17万元，巩固、完善、扩大科普示范县成果。至2008年，全县建成种植基地58个，建成荔波逸夫中学和荔波二小“青少年科技教育特色学校”；全县形成以捞村乡、洞塘乡为中心的17个乡（镇）4万亩甘蔗种植地，以洞塘乡、翁昂乡、永康乡为中心的2万亩酸梅种植基地，以朝阳镇、玉屏镇为中心的5000亩精品果蔬基地，以永康乡、水尧乡、甲良镇为中心的无公害肉牛养殖的大科普示范基地，真正形成“一乡多业、一村多品”发展格局。全县每年培育县级科技示范户100户，评选科技带头人20名。2008年3月，省科协代表中国科协到荔波开展“全国科普示范县”复查考核，通过验收。

第二十一篇
文化　传媒

1978年改革开放以来，荔波县在经济建设的同时，不断加快全县文化事业的发展，紧紧围绕打造文化荔波、建设旅游大县的理念和目标，狠抓文化基础设施建设、文化艺术人才的培养、文化传统资源的保护和文化艺术活动的开展等各项文化工作建设，使民族文化事业实现了长足进步，硕果累累。坚持文艺“两为”（为人民服务、为社会主义服务）方向和“双百”（百花齐放、百家争鸣）方针，围绕培养文艺人才，繁荣文艺创作，以“贴近实际、贴近生活、贴近群众”为宗旨，繁荣荔波县文艺事业。全县群众文化、图书馆、图书销售、文化遗产的挖掘与保护等文化工作不断加强。荔波县民族民间文化资源在全县17个乡（镇）均有分布，主要划分为布依族文化圈、水族文化圈、瑶族文化圈、苗族文化圈，各少数民族传统文化独具特色，民族风俗保存完好，民间文化艺术原始古朴、多姿多彩。1978—2008年，荔波组织力量对全县的民族文化资源进行全面的调查摸底，并制定措施，对面临失传的民间文化进行抢救，同时立足县情，围绕旅游产业抢救保护和合理利用民族民间文化资源，打造地域文化、生态文化，挖掘民族历史价值、凸现民族文化内涵。先后举办民族服饰展演、民间民歌赛、民族节日庆典、民族文化旅游月、“荔波荡漾”原生态歌舞大型实景演艺、多彩贵州系列大赛等大型活动，使民族文化得以从封闭的山寨、尘封的历史中走出来，步入艺术殿堂，大放异彩，在省内外引起极大轰动，彰显了荔波民族文化的独特魅力。

改革开放的三十年来，荔波广播电视事业建设和管理在改革发展开放中发生了巨大变化。从收听广播新闻到自办有线广播新闻节目播出，从有线广播到无线调频广播覆盖，从差转电视到卫星接收电视，从无线广播电视到有线网络电视多频道（47套）传输。1996年开通中央加密节目，2004年开通黔南州有线1～3套地方台电视节目，2008年开通贵州有线1～7套电视节目。2004—2005年，有线电缆电视网络升级为光纤电视网络传输，荔波广播电视节目传输质量有了很大提高。2008年8月，荔波有线电视宣传中心升级为荔波电视台，从事荔波新闻报道和外宣工作。1978—2008年，荔波拥有有线闭路电视站38座，大功率无线广播电视发射台1座，卫星接收地面站501座，卫星电视单收站10100座，广播电视覆盖率达93%。“村村通”广播电视从差转接收到卫星直播接收，高质量的卫星广播电视进了荔波千家万户。

第一章 文 化

第一节 群众文化

一、文化馆

1978年，设有县文化馆，开展群众文化活动。1980年，县文化馆扩建为600平方米，配置彩色电视机、放像机、康乐球机等文化设施，对外开展有偿服务。举办美术、书法、摄影展览、文艺调演、文艺晚会等文化活动。

进入20世纪90年代，随着群众文化需求的日益增长，县文化馆开办文化舞厅、录像放映室、台球室等公共有偿服务项目。1992年，开办录像带租赁部，出租影视录像带。

1993年，举办全县首届时装展演、首届花卉奇石盆景展。此后，每年举办春节迎春晚会和春节文化系列活动。

1999年，组建荔波少儿合唱团，有学员50人。

2002年5月，举办“云雾山杯”电视歌手大赛，全县报名参与竞赛的歌唱爱好者近千人，进入决赛100名，观众达3万人次。

2003年，举办“小灵通杯”电视歌手比赛。2004年，举办“铜锣弯楼盘开盘文化活动”。此外，在一些节庆活动中，辅导各机关企事业单位编排节目和进行文化活动策划。

2005年，建立“荔波县文化产业信息库”，列入信息库的文化产业项目152项。其中，荔波民族风情园、荔波民族旅游工艺品开发项目参加贵州省第二届深圳国际文化产业博览会招商活动。

从2007年开始，参与著名音乐人陈哲打造的《土风计划——水书表情》民族歌舞项目展演。2008年，启动“欢乐樟江园”广场群众文化活动，是年演出20场（次），观众累计10万人次。

二、文化站

1978年，各区、社有文化室。1979年后，区、社文化室逐渐改建为文化站。是年8月，建甲良民族文化中心站，为县内第一个公办农村文化站。1982年，建洞塘文化站、朝阳文化中心站。1983年3月，建茂兰文化中心站、方村文化站。1985年，建佳荣文化站、播尧文化站。各文化站配专职工作人员1名。至此，全县有公办文化站7个、集体文化站9个，部分村建有村文化室。各文化站、室根据自身条件，开展图书阅览、电影放映、体育竞赛、文艺晚会、广播宣传、黑板报等群众文化活动。后因人员、经费、场地等困难，大部分乡、村文化室未开展活动。

甲良民族文化中心站以文化工作为主，开展多种经营，逐步解决文化站经费短缺原因。先后修建电影院、水泥篮球场、旱冰场、露天戏台、招待所，添置电影放映机、彩色电视机、多功能收录机以及各类文娱用品，扩建文化站活动室，修建宣传橱窗。每逢传统节日，开展耍龙、舞狮、芦

荔波民间舞狮队

笙、花灯演出和篮球赛等活动。组织农村业余文艺队进行文艺交流演出。帮助辖区内7个乡建立文化站。1988年，甲良民族文化中心站被评为全国“以文补文”先进单位，1989年被评为贵州省“以文补文”先进文化站。

1990年，全县4个区、24个乡建有农村文化站14个、村级文化室3个，由县级文化管理部门统一管理。

1991年，全县行政区划“建并撤”后，文化站与广播电视站合并，17个乡（镇）设文化服务中心，行政属乡（镇）政府管理，业务归县文体广电部门指导。17个乡（镇）文化服务中心编制总计38人，实有在册人员30人，其中，专职19人、兼职11人。各文化广播电视站开展图书借阅、电影放映、民族节日文艺活动等群众文化活动。是年，甲良民族文化中心站获“省级达标文化站”称号，被州文化局评为“一级站”。1992年，该站获省精神文明委授予“农村精神文明建设先进集体”。

2002年3月，佳荣文化站开办佳荣镇芦笙队艺术培训班，组队参加荔波机场奠基仪式。8月，甲良民族文化中心站组织老年文艺队代表荔波县参加在独山举办的“中国独山首届花灯艺术节”。10月，举办贵州省第三届农民电影节，为开幕式分会场。

2005年7月，佳荣文化站承办贵州·荔波布依歌节暨佳（荣）驯（乐）精神文明联创活动。

三、民族文工队

1986年5月，成立县民族文工队，有队员20人，与县文化馆为馆队合一。1989年，按“队伍不散，保留骨干，人员轮换，面向基层，服务本县”的原则，进行队员调整，人员减至16人。是年，该队被评为全州群众文化工作先进单位。

1989年，先后参加全省首届民族民间艺术节、夜郎风采剧组演出、全州文工队调演，以及赴广州参加为期3个月的“羊城中华博览会”西南土风舞表演。1990年9月，赴北京参加“亚运会艺术节”演出。1991年，赴沈阳参加“国际秧歌节”“全国斗牛大赛”演出。

1992年，县民族文工队为县文化局直属事业单位，有队员20人，其中正式队员4人（合同工）、临时聘用队员16人，队员工资及工作经费由财政全额拨款。全年开展文艺下乡演出60场（次）。1993年10月，因县财政经费困难，县民族文工队解散，正式队员划归县文化馆，仍保留县民族文工队建制。1994—2006年，未开展活动。

2007年，恢复县民族文工队，人员20人，人员工资及工作经费由财政全额拨款。编创20多个新节目，于7月举办迎接香港回归祖国十周年文艺专场展演。全年开展文艺下乡宣传演出20多场，观众10万人次。

2008年，县民族文工队按“保留骨干、人员轮换”的原则，以及“推陈出新、创新发展”的办队理念，加强队伍建设，提高演出水平和质量。全年开展文艺下乡宣传演出活动60多场，观众20万人次。

第二节 民族民间文艺

一、民间文学收集整理

1982年，县民委、县文化馆整理编印《民族民间文学资料》，选辑布依族民歌67首、故事10则；苗族民歌1首；水族民歌6首、故事9则；瑶族民歌3首、故事3则。1989年，县民委编印瑶族民间故事选《射日月》，收录瑶族故事69则。

根据文化部、国家民委、中国民间文艺研究会关于编辑出版《中国民间故事集成》《中国民间歌谣集成》《中国民间谚语集成》的通知，1988—1990年，县文化部门全面收集整理民间故事、歌谣、谚语资料，精选出布依族、水族、苗族、瑶族、壮族、汉族等6个民族的民间故事300多则、歌谣5000余行、谚语1200余条，编辑出版《荔波县民间文学三套集成》。

2008年，文化馆编印民间文化旅游丛书《山乡之魂》《神话传说》《民间故事》《歌谣谚语》，共60万字。

二、民族民间艺术

（一）歌曲

县内民间歌曲，按内容有不同的表现形式，主要有浪哨歌、大歌和小歌、酒歌、叙事歌、礼俗歌等。

1.“浪哨”歌　“浪哨”歌是布依族青年男女社交活动中一种普遍的歌唱体裁。“浪哨”，布依族语意为与姑娘同坐之意，是布依族青年男女谈情说爱以歌传情的一种社交方式，俗称“赶表”或“玩表”。青年男女通过唱歌表达相识、相知、爱慕、盟誓、思念、送别等思想感情。歌者见物生情，遇见什么便以之作为素材即兴创作，以物喻事，以物喻人，表达自己内心情感。“浪哨”歌调式色彩丰富，曲调深邃委婉。

2.大歌、小歌　是布依族的重唱歌曲。它的和声以三度、二度音程连续重叠使用，颇具特色。和声、调式、结构都有其独特规律。

大歌和小歌是两种歌唱形式。它们的区别在于大歌有歌头（意为亲友们，听我唱）和歌尾（意为我唱完了）。歌唱内容一般以四句、六句为一首，情调较为庄重，多用在公开场合，一般用作酒歌和叙事歌，间作情歌。小歌无歌头有歌尾，需一人领唱一小节、一个乐句甚至一个乐段，第二声部即后和声，内容较为简练，一般四句为完整的一首，内在温情，常用做“浪哨”时成双对唱的情歌。

3.酒歌　在节日、喜庆、婚丧、建房、宴请宾客等宴会上演唱的民歌。在酒席上，主人和宾客之间互相祝福、问候、盘考、赞美村寨，感谢主人盛情款待等，均以歌代言。曲调较简单、平衡、开朗、热情，可随意填词，旋律可无限反复。其中水族酒歌仍是四声宫调式，一般由两个大段落组成，有与山歌迥然不同的歌头和歌尾。

4.叙事歌　演唱的主要内容有叙述古代各种传说、神话、故事（通常称“古歌”），叙述苦情（又称“苦歌”），风俗传统等。曲调较单一平衡，变化很小，演唱极易上口，很富人情味，因此很容易被听众接受，还常常催人泪下。县内世居民族都有叙事歌。

5.礼俗歌　是在婚、丧、建房以及各种庆贺、祭祀等活动中演唱的歌曲，内容广泛。礼俗歌的祭祀歌旋律平衡，似唱似吟，起伏不大，曲调口语化，一听便知念咒，但也有旋律性很强且优美的曲调。

（二）舞蹈

境内民间舞蹈多在丧葬、祭祀时表演。瑶族的《打猎舞》最具特色，包括打熊舞、打猎舞、打羊舞、打猴舞和生产舞5个相对独立部分，在丧葬祭祀中跳《打猎舞》用铜鼓伴奏，增加祭祀活动的庄严、肃穆气氛。布依族的《刷把舞》、白裤瑶的《猴鼓舞》、水族的《花架舞》等，既有祭祀内容又有娱乐成分。

（三）戏曲

境内民族民间戏曲主要有傩戏和花灯戏。

1.傩戏 县内傩戏有苗族傩戏和布依族傩戏之分。汉族傩戏主要流传于汉族聚居地区。布依族傩戏主要流传在布依族聚居的翁昂、觉巩、捞村、阳凤、播尧等乡村，在汉族、布依族杂居区的布依族也有流传。其共同点是表演时都戴木制面具。

布依族傩戏是布依族民间的无子求子、有子求福、还愿禳灾的活动，表演时无论唱、念或道白都用布依语，语言诙谐。一般演出活动最少要3天，最多可演13天。布依族傩戏仍是“傩夹戏”，是在求子、求福、还愿过程中表演一些节目，借以娱人。

汉族傩戏主要用于“还愿”表演。“还愿”是民间禳灾祈福、销愿（傩愿）的一种活动。“还愿”活动由掌坛师主持，一般要进行三天三夜，也有进行七天七夜的，根据主人的财力、物力和需要确定。

2.花灯 花灯遍布城乡，流传广泛。花灯分为台灯、地灯和愿灯，曲调丰富，传统剧目繁多。民间花灯艺人均口传心授，有剧本无曲谱。1987年进行花灯普查时，县内开展演出活动的业余灯班有10个，普查搜集到灯调250多个。

（四）民间乐器

境内民间乐器有打击乐器、弓弦乐器、弹拨乐器和竹管乐器等类。较为独特的有青瑶的独弦琴、布依族的姊妹箫、白裤瑶的木鼓，以及布依族、苗族的笔管，还有铜鼓和芦笙。这些乐器中，铜鼓、木鼓、芦笙等大多用于丧葬、祭祀活动，笔管、姊妹箫、独弦琴多用于娱乐活动。

1.弓弦乐器

民间弓弦乐器主要有青瑶特有的独弦琴，因它只有一根用马尾毛拧成的琴弦而得名。独弦琴共鸣筒的大小、形状和结构与京胡相似，演奏方法与京胡、二胡的演奏方法相似，但技巧较为简单，区别在于它的弓子只有约40厘米长（弓毛用马尾制成）。多用于青年男女谈情说爱时联络感情，传递信息和娱乐，不能作为伴奏乐器。

2.竹管乐器

民间竹管乐器有笔管、姊妹箫、芦笙3种。

笔管 是布依族、苗族、瑶族的一种竹管吹奏乐器。笔管用竹子制成，将竹管上端（留竹节、封口）的一面3厘米长削薄（紧靠竹节）制成发音簧片，在管身依次开3个音阶孔，可发4个音。笔管的下端安装一个锯开的小葫芦作为共鸣器。笔管可作为歌唱伴奏乐器，也可作为独奏乐器。

姊妹箫 是布依族一种特有的长管吹奏乐器，一个人同时吹奏两支，两支如同姊妹，故称姊妹箫。姊妹箫用小竹子制作，即在一节竹管的上端切掉一段3厘米，留下五分之一，留下部分再剖开，在破开的竹片两边各放进一片小篾片，用棉线缠紧，再在破开竹片的下方开一个方形发音孔，发音孔内夹一片薄竹片作分气簧片。音阶孔为圆形，开在管身的中下部。发音原理和哨子发音原理相同，音量较小，但音色特殊悠扬委婉。每支箫可发4个音，两支箫同时吹奏，青年男女之间谈情说爱时男吹女唱，表达情怀。

芦笙 是苗族、水族特有的六簧管乐器。小的长30厘米，大的长3米有余。民间按师传指法吹奏。多用于喜庆舞蹈伴奏，也用于丧葬、祭祀花灯。

3.打击乐器

民间打击乐器有铜鼓、木鼓。

铜鼓 是世居少数民族的一种乐器。铜鼓音色浑厚洪亮、庄重。演奏时，悬挂于木架上，如配以共鸣桶，即每敲打一次，可发出特殊的变音效果。

木鼓 是白裤瑶家族权力的象征，由专人保管，多在祭祀活动中使用。木鼓的共鸣箱用一段直径30厘米、高1米的原木，将中间掏空制成。共鸣筒的一头蒙上水牛皮便成木鼓。木鼓通常与铜鼓配套使用，木鼓已发展演变一种乐器，用于舞蹈伴奏。

（五）工艺美术

1.蜡染、叠染、印染 境内蜡染是苗族、瑶族妇女独特的手工工艺，图案有蕨菜纹、刺梨花、漩涡形、水波形、连锁纹等十余种。花纹鲜明、美观大方、古朴庄重、文静素雅、精巧细腻。

境内叠染是布依族妇女特有的传统工艺，做法近似蜡染，但不用蜡绘。制作方法是把自制白布按照所需花纹扎好或用粗麻线扎成花纹，然后放入染缸中浸染，拆线即得所需各种图案叠染制品，花纹粗放活泼、清净素雅，是布依族的床上制品。

印染在县内水族地区盛行，做工与蜡染相似。花纹绮丽工整，纱质均细，染工深透，经洗耐用，可制成服装及床上用品。

2.刺绣 是县内瑶族、苗族独特民间工艺。主要有挑花、绣花、补花、梭花等手法。常用于制作绑腿、腰带、帽圈、衣襟、袖筒、裙饰、背带等装饰。刺绣花纹独具特色的是背带花，所绣花卉草木、飞禽走兽以及各种吉祥文字，精致美观，朴素大方，主要有“十二块”“印心花背”“木瓜心”“水盆枪”等十余种图案、符号。

3.花布工艺 是县内布依族独特的工艺制品。用自纺自染的棉纱线于织布机上编织而成。用蓝、青、黑、白4色搭配织出柳条、格格、壁笆、辣花、梅花、鱼刺、桂花、花椒、兰尼等布纹近10种，花式150余个，以深色调为主，浅蓝相映，纹饰大方，装饰性强，纱线粗细均匀，布料厚实保暖，有“土呢子”之称。县内布依族花布曾远销日本、法国、东南亚等国家和地区。

4.竹编、藤编 是境内各民族常用的工艺制品，主要有提蓝、饭箩、斗笠、竹椅、凉席等，工艺细致精巧。

境内竹编制品以凉席较为有名，主要产于洞塘、翁昂等喀斯特山区，用茂兰喀斯特独有的泡竹篾条编制，工艺精良，具有地方民族特色，具有较高的实用价值和艺术价值，20世纪80年代曾远销日本、东南亚等国家和地区。

境内藤编制作做工精细，样式小巧，适用于家庭装饰。藤编制品主要用境内所产“狼鸡心”藤条编制。1982年，成立县民族工艺美术社，把美术融入民间工艺，年产10万件具有民族特色的藤编制品，畅销市场。小件藤编工艺品作为小七孔旅游纪念品，列为省科学技术开发重要项目。20世纪80年代末90年代初，藤编制品每年被省旅游产品领导小组评为旅游优秀产品。

5.剪纸 多流行于境内汉族、水族地区。剪纸图案由动植物向表达思想观念和颂扬社会主义制度发展，许多作品参加省、州各类艺术展览并获奖。

6.银饰 曾是境内水族、瑶族、苗族妇女的必备饰品，也是布依族喜爱的饰品。品种有头花、帽福、项圈、梳子、压领、手镯、帐钩，工艺有空心、实心、泡花、六方形等，浮雕花草龙凤、缀珠摇曳，为工艺珍品。

水族、苗族妇女还喜欢在项圈上套戒圈作装饰。水族青年以银饰为定情之物，素有“水家结婚定要银”之说。姑娘出嫁时必备一套银饰品项圈、头花、手镯等，重2公斤以上。佳节喜庆时，水族、苗族、瑶族姑娘佩戴银饰，银光闪闪、妩媚妍丽。小孩佩戴银饰以求吉祥。

7.雕刻 为境内瑶族、水族、布依族男子的一种手工艺。布依族雕刻主要有石雕、木雕两种，具有一定艺术价值，常在牌坊、墓碑、庙宇石磴雕有各式花纹图案。

水族的雕刻常见于墓碑和一些建筑物，所雕花鸟虫兽形象逼真、活灵活现。具有代表性的“水甫石板墓群”，雕刻的麒麟猛兽、凤凰鸳鸯、双龙戏珠、人物，造型逼真、精美壮观，堪称民间雕艺珍品，1982年已列为省级文物保护单位。

瑶族男子善牛角雕刻，常见的有“狩猎图”，形象生动，是精美动人的瑶族生活画面。

第三节 图书 新闻出版

一、图书馆

（一）图书借阅

1978年，县文化馆设有图书室，有藏书0.06万册。图书室对外办理借阅手续。

1982年3月，成立县图书馆，编制4人。图书馆利用文化馆办公楼160平方米场地开设报刊阅览室、儿童阅览室。书库总藏书量1万册，办理借书证600本、阅览证200本，年度书刊流通率3万册（次）。

1990年8月，图书馆更名为县民族图书馆，编制6人。是年，县财政拨给图书购置专项经费1万元，藏书量增至1.78万册，办理各类借阅证1000本，年接待读者2.03万人次。图书馆每月定期出黑板报介绍新书目2次。

1994年以后，县财政每年拨款1.5万元，用于征订报纸杂志和购买图书，图书馆年接待读者0.5万人次。同时，开展图书下乡活动，赠送图书0.3万册。是年，建成图书馆办公楼（2层楼），新馆占地面积230平方米，建筑面积700平方米，有各类图书1.9万册，发放各类借书证800余本，接待读者1万人次。

1998年，图书馆办公楼受地震影响，整体下陷，部分墙体断裂，县建设部门于2000年鉴定为危房后，划归县资本营运公司作为城建用地，图书馆暂无办公场所。

从2000年开始，县内实施农家书屋项目建设工程。

2004年11月，中央文明办拨款修建的荔波宣传文化活动中心投入使用后，图书馆搬到宣传文化活动中心办公，面积600平方米，藏书量增至3万册。

2008年，接受爱心人士捐赠图书5000册，自主购书500册，报纸杂志年藏入量76种，地方文献馆藏30余种。年底，馆藏图书总计3.6万册，全年接待读者0.5万人次。

（二）图书销售

1978年，县内设有新华书店，销售各种公开出版发行的图书及中小学课本。1987年，设立化矿区分销店。是年，书店扩建为396平方米。1989年，撤销立化矿区分销店。

20世纪80年代到90年代初，教科书、科普书、小说等图书需求量逐年递增，种类逐步丰富。1980年，图书经营仅1家书店，2008年发展到4家。全县有乡村农家书屋98个，总建筑面积2548平方米，总藏书量19.47万册。

1978—2008年荔波县新华书店发行情况统计表

表21－1　　单位：册、万元

年度	图书销售总量	营业额	其中销售课本		利润	费用
			数量	金额		
1978	8035	0.23	2678	0.07	0.19	0.20
1979	10430	0.26	4420	0.11	0.24	0.25
1980	21650	0.50	8920	0.26	0.27	0.31
1981	30110	0.88	16650	0.42	0.65	0.75
1982	357700	10.35	221400	5.59	1.03	0.79
1983	375200	10.50	248300	6.09	1.05	0.94
1984	374630	10.50	222133	5.80	0.61	0.94
1985	269008	14.12	166896	7.85	0.96	1.36
1986	782002	16.29	678689	8.94	0.75	2.04
1987	463641	17.64	381525	11.47	0.37	2.74
1988	328661	18.51	236969	12.53	0.70	2.56
1989	342360	24.17	303470	19.00	0.94	3.47
1990	499760	36.28	368210	29.27	1.25	5.51
1991	512200	45.75	40280	3.57	2.16	4.32
1992	601812	51.43	52765	4.73	3.25	5.21
1993	694300	60.42	58427	5.01	5.34	5.59
1994	701892	65.24	61148	5.43	6.15	7.10
1995	764582	69.46	64482	5.83	7.24	7.58
1996	798820	71.86	68018	6.02	7.51	8.00
1997	822514	72.99	70049	6.62	8.13	8.02
1998	864180	78.12	72180	7.06	8.62	8.25
1999	901982	82.45	75044	7.27	9.19	8.46
2000	912250	84.68	77128	7.72	9.67	8.86
2001	919877	86.64	77898	7.87	9.94	8.91
2002	925532	98.72	81460	9.11	12.48	9.54
2003	946870	107.64	82875	11.63	16.87	9.87
2004	957620	113.87	84026	14.63	18.37	9.93
2005	958266	114.44	86258	15.76	19.84	10.03
2006	961750	176.97	87149	21.19	20.88	10.46
2007	982640	208.36	87958	24.18	22.16	11.28
2008	1093686	215.77	88652	25.06	22.99	11.98

二、新闻出版

2005年之前，境内的新闻出版（版权）工作由县文体广播电视局文化稽查队管理。是年，全县有新闻出版业经营户41户。

2006年8月，成立县新闻出版（版权）局，隶属县文体广播电视局，工作人员由文化稽查队人员兼，主要负责县内印刷业、复印打印业、图书租赁零售业管理。是年，有新闻出版业经营户45户。至2008年，全县有小型印刷厂2家、图书书刊零售点7家、复印打印店11家及音像制品租赁、零售点7家。

第四节　文化遗产

一、文物

（一）文物保护单位

1979年，经中组部、中宣部批准，省委、省革委将邓恩铭烈士故居列为贵州省文物保护单位。

1981年4月，县政府公布第一批文物保护单位有荔泉书院、板寨会师旧址、洞英红军标语、坤地红军标语（一）、坤地红军标语（二）等5处。

1982年，省政府公布第一批文物保护单位，邓恩铭故居、水浦石板墓群入选。此后，1985年11月、1999年12月省政府公布的第二批、第三批文物保护单位中，荔波文物入选2处。

1986年9月，县政府公布第二批文物保护单位有永济泉、文庙启圣宫、文庙泮池、文庙棂星门基座、大七孔桥、小七孔桥、瑶麓小学校、北门榕树等8处。

2005年，向省推荐第四批省级文物保护单位6处，省政府于2006年6月公布第四批文物保护单位，荔波申报的项目除瑶山禾仓群外，其他5处入选。

荔波县文物保护单位一览表

表21－2

序号	名称	保护级别	确定时间	所在地点	类别
1	邓恩铭烈士故居	省级（第一批）	1982年2月	县城北街向阳路21号	革命遗址
2	水浦石板墓群	省级（第一批）	1982年2月	玉屏镇水浦村	古墓葬
3	瑶麓婚规碑	省级（第二批）	1985年11月	瑶麓乡瑶麓村	摩崖石刻
4	永济泉	省级（第三批）	1999年12月	玉屏镇繁荣路	古建筑
5	瑶麓岩洞葬	省级（第四批）	2006年6月	瑶麓乡瑶麓村	古墓葬
6	黎明关遗址	省级（第四批）	2006年6月	洞塘乡板寨村	革命遗址
7	水庆小学旧址	省级（第四批）	2006年6月	瑶麓乡瑶麓村	古建筑
8	板寨会师旧址	省级（第四批）	2006年6月	洞塘乡板寨村	革命遗址
9	水浦古建筑群	省级（第四批）	2006年6月	玉屏镇水浦村	古建筑
10	荔泉书院	县级	1981年4月	玉屏镇玉屏一小校园内	古建筑
11	洞英红军标语	县级	1981年4月	茂兰镇洞英村	革命遗址
12	坤地红军标语	县级	1981年4月	佳荣镇坤地村	革命遗址

续表21－2

序号	名称	保护级别	确定时间	所在地点	类别
13	大七孔桥	县级	1986年9月	瑶山乡	古建筑
14	小七孔桥	县级	1986年9月	瑶山乡	古建筑
15	文庙泮池	县级	1986年9月	玉屏镇建设西路	古建筑
16	北门榕树	县级	1986年9月	玉屏镇向阳中路	其他
17	文庙启圣宫	县级	1986年9月	玉屏镇向阳中路	古建筑
18	文庙棂星门基座	县级	1986年9月	玉屏镇向阳中路	古建筑
19	瑶麓小学校	县级	1986年9月	瑶麓乡瑶麓村	其他

（二）文物保护

1982年，国家文物局、省、州、县拨款维修邓恩铭故居，按故居原样放置物件，再现当年情景。1991年，用汉白玉雕塑邓恩铭半身像陈列于故居陈列室，设生平事迹展览室。

1984年，文化局内设文物管理所，编制3人，负责全县文物调查、管理、保护等工作。

2003—2004年，县委、县政府筹集资金820万元，对邓恩铭烈士故居、板寨会师旧址、黎明关等重点文物遗址进行维修。邓恩铭烈士故居修缮投入资金280万元，大修故居110平方米，新建陈列室230平方米，新布置展厅340平方米、展线160米（含故居），征集烈士遗物4件。板寨会师旧址修缮投入资金320万元，拆迁周边住宅14户，大修会师旧址1230平方米，新布置展厅600平方米、展线120米，征集红七军将士文物46件套，并于2004年7月1日正式开馆。黎明关修缮投入资金220万元，新布置反映抗战文化石碑16块、牌坊3座、烽火台1个、文化长廊40米，原样修复古道3公里，征集抗战文物4件。

2006年4月，启动邓恩铭烈士故居保护建设一期工程，对故居进行大修，在后院新建230平方米的资料图片辅助陈列室，并对复原陈列和辅助展览作调整、充实，重新布置“邓恩铭烈士生平革命事迹展览”展线长73米。是年，省政府公布邓恩铭烈士故居为省全民国防教育基地。

2006年，境内开展一次文物普查工作。

二、非物质文化遗产

2005年开始进行非物质文化遗产保护申报工作，至2008年，整理申报39项。其中，列为国家级保护名录3项，列为省级保护名录4项，列为县级保护名录32项。非物质文化遗产传承人中，获得高级职称4人、中级职称11人、初级职称12人。高级水书师欧海金、潘老平为国家级代表性传承人，谢朝海为省级代表性传承人，州级代表性传承人有12人。

全县非物质文化遗产名录一览表

表21－3

序号	项目名称	类别	民族	级别	时间
1	水书习俗	民俗	水族	国家级（第一批）	2006年6月
2	瑶族猴鼓舞	民间舞蹈	瑶族	国家级（第二批）	2008年6月
3	雯当姆	民间舞蹈	布依族	省级（第一批）	2005年12月
4	瑶族打猎舞	民间舞蹈	瑶族	省级（第一批）	2005年12月

续表21－3

序号	项目名称	类别	民族	级别	时间
5	瑶族陀螺竞技	竞技	瑶族	省级（第二批）	2005年12月
6	布依族笔管歌	传统音乐	布依族	县级	2005年8月13日
7	水族山歌	传统音乐	水族	县级	2007年9月17日
8	布依族山歌	传统音乐	布依族	县级	2007年9月17日
9	布依族竹竿舞	民间舞蹈	布依族	县级	2005年8月13日
10	苗族芦笙踩堂	民间舞蹈	苗族	县级	2005年8月13日
11	布依族刷把舞	民间舞蹈	布依族	县级	2005年8月13日
12	水族花架舞	民间舞蹈	水族	县级	2007年9月17日
13	瑶族铜鼓舞	民间舞蹈	瑶族	县级	2007年9月17日
14	布依族龙狮舞	民间舞蹈	布依族	县级	2007年9月17日
15	布依族上刀山下火海	杂技与竞技	布依族	县级	2007年9月17日
16	布依族古造纸技艺	传统手工技艺	布依族	县级	2005年8月13日
17	布依族酿造技艺	传统手工技艺	布依族	县级	2007年9月17日
18	苗族酿造技艺	传统手工技艺	苗族	县级	2007年9月17日
19	瑶族酿造技艺	传统手工技艺	瑶族	县级	2007年9月17日
20	苗族银制工艺	传统手工技艺	苗族	县级	2007年9月17日
21	布依族染制工艺	传统手工技艺	布依族	县级	2007年9月17日
22	水族染制工艺	传统手工技艺	水族	县级	2007年9月17日
23	瑶族染制工艺	传统手工技艺	瑶族	县级	2007年9月17日
24	苗族染制工艺	传统手工技艺	苗族	县级	2007年9月17日
25	布依族土法纺织工艺	传统手工技艺	布依族	县级	2007年9月17日
26	瑶族凿壁谈婚习俗	人生礼俗	瑶族	县级	2005年8月13日
27	布依族婚俗	人生礼俗	布依族	县级	2005年8月13日
28	水族婚俗	人生礼俗	水族	县级	2005年8月13日
29	苗族婚俗	人生礼俗	苗族	县级	2005年8月13日
30	白裤瑶二次洞葬（砍牛祭）	人生礼俗	瑶族	县级	2005年8月13日
31	青瑶岩洞葬	人生礼俗	瑶族	县级	2005年8月13日
32	苗族古藏	人生礼俗	苗族	县级	2005年8月13日
33	布依族六月六歌节	岁时节令	布依族	县级	2005年8月13日
34	布依族四月八斗牛节	岁时节令	布依族	县级	2005年8月13日
35	水族端节	岁时节令	水族	县级	2005年8月13日
36	水族卯节	岁时节令	水族	县级	2005年8月13日
37	苗族跳苗节	岁时节令	苗族	县级	2005年8月13日

第五节 文化市场管理

1978—1990年，县内文化市场种类由单一化逐渐向多元化发展，形成网吧、电子游戏、歌舞娱乐、艺术演出、音像制品租赁零售、印刷、打字复印、书刊租赁零售、艺术教育培训等的综合性市场。

1991年，成立县文化市场管理委员会，在县文化局下设办公室。

1991—1993年，全县文化经营项目有台球、录像放映、录像带租赁、录音带销售、图书租赁、卡拉OK、舞厅、娱乐室8种，有经营户81户。1994年，文化娱乐行业种类降至5种，经营户减少到51户。

1995年6月，成立县文化市场稽查队。

1995—1996年，全县文化经营户80户。1997年，文化经营户增至102户，涉及行业种类12种。

2003年，文化市场稽查出动检查95次，检查经营户和个体户100余家（次），开展专项行动5次。为执行好文化部提出的“一手抓繁荣、一手抓管理”的工作要求，县文化局加强文化市场经营户守法经营、文明经营、诚信经营的教育引导培训工作。至2004年，文化市场经营户90户。

2005年后，按照文化部新颁布的文化市场行政审批和行政执法等相关规定，县文化局与县公安、工商、消防、环保局等单位联合开展文化市场专项检查，查处文化市场非法行为，严禁未成年人进入网吧。

2007年7月，成立荔波县文化广播电视稽查队，为财政全额拨款股级事业单位，编制6人，对全县文化、新闻出版、广播电视市场进行稽查管理。

2005—2008年，查处收缴非法音像制品共2万盒（碟）、非法出版物10万余册，依法取缔无证网吧10家，办理行政处罚案件12件。2008年，全县有文化市场经营户42家，从业人员200多人。

第二章　广播　电视　电影

第一节　广　播

一、广播传输

（一）有线广播

1.农村广播　1978年，境内各区、公社建有广播站，空架明线，安装喇叭，传送有线广播信号，边远村寨购置收音机、扩音机，建立农村小片广播网点，形成以县广播站为中心，以片区广播站为基础，加上小片广播网点，连接千家万户的全县广播网。

20世纪80年代，各乡（镇）有线广播因缺乏维护经费，杆倒线断，先后停播。

1990年3月，按照贵州省广播电视厅3年内恢复农村有线广播网，实现50%的乡有广播站的要求，县广播电视局制定恢复县农村有线广播网的工作计划。1991—1993年，利用省、州配发的广播器材设备（有线广播扩大机17台、电力输出配电柜12台、播音控制桌8台、电源调压器5台、收录音机8台），县配套25瓦16欧号筒式高音喇叭40只，恢复17个乡（镇）广播。

1994年6月—1997年1月，全县各乡（镇）广播站改为文体广播电视站。1997年2月，乡（镇）广播工作从文体广播站分出，设广播电视站。

1999年，实施国家第一批农村广播电视“村村通”小片网建设，各乡（镇）获得国家配置的广播电视“村村通”小片网设备1套（50瓦扩音机1台、话筒1只、高音喇叭2只），收转贵州人民广播电台节目（1套）。节目收转由各乡（镇）文化服务中心维护和管理。

2.县城广播　1978年，县广播站在县城架设专线传输广播信号，县城户户有广播喇叭。1982年6月，在县城改用电灯零线传输广播信号到各户喇叭，由于串音，于1983年年底全部撤除电灯零线传输线路。1984年后，利用电力水泥杆架设广播专线5公里，改入户喇叭为户外街道组合音箱40只。至1987年，县城安装有组合音箱52只，广播专线7公里。

1990年4月，县城修建樟江大街，附挂在电力杆上的广播线路被拆除。有线广播只传送到南门、马道一带，有在用广播喇叭19只。1995年12月，县城向阳路进行扩建改造，电力杆重新规划建设，附挂在电力杆上的有线广播线路全部拆除，县城有线广播停播。

（二）无线广播

1986年，在县广播电视局办公楼顶安装输出功率50瓦92.3兆赫无线广播调频发射机1台，并正式发射信号，县城及朝阳区部分村寨可用有调频波段的收音机收听县广播站节目。由于调频信号对电视干扰严重，开播不久即停播。

1993年11月，购置TP-010-Ⅲ型10瓦调频广播发射机1台，安装发射调试成功，县城无线调频广播恢复。

1996年1月，在县城及时来、农场、板吉、南门等地架挂37只5瓦调频广播喇叭，使用到1996年年底，先后出现故障停用。

1997年5月，县广播站机房安装省给予价值2万元的100瓦调频广播发射机，是年11月，因该机无维修器材停止使用。

1998年4月，县内仅有30瓦105兆赫调频广播发射机1台正常发射信号，节目源为贵州卫星广播节目。

2007年，国家拨给专项资金100万元，用于官唐坡无线广播改建、扩建工程，2008年7月30日竣工并正式播出，县城由原30瓦105兆赫无线调频发射机转播贵州人民广播电台节目增加到4台／套，群众的调频收音机、车载调频收音机能清晰收到官唐坡发射台无线调频广播节目。

二、广播宣传

1978年，县广播站自办节目是《本县新闻和报刊摘要》，每天20时30分播报县内新闻，次日早晨、中午定时重播。

1979年，县广播站增加《科技广播》节目，选编新工艺新技术成果、科技养殖、日常生活等进行广播。

是年8月，举办全县广播通讯员业务培训班1期，各区、公社、机关单位、学校、厂矿、农村、部队的通讯员80人参加培训。新闻节目稿件由通讯员采写供稿。

1982年4月增办《本县文艺》节目，选编播出群众喜爱的国内外歌曲、戏剧、曲艺，录制播出县内布依族山歌、水族民歌、瑶族情歌、县文工队演出的文艺节目等。

1983—1987年，县委宣传部、县民委、广播局每年联合召开少数民族通信工作会议，表彰优秀通讯员。

从1987年起，县广播站与州内其他县（市）广播站交流自办节目，报道州内其他县（市）的重要新闻。

1990年，县广播站收到通讯员稿件1135篇，采用822篇。

1992年，全县有通讯员62人。此后，通讯员人数和投稿数量逐年减少。至1995年，县广播站有骨干通讯员22人，向县广播站投稿248篇，采用241篇。1998年，停办广播自办节目，通讯员队伍解散。

第二节　电　视

一、电视节目传输

（一）无线电视

1978年7月，县财政拨款1万元，购进输出功率10瓦发射6频道的黑白、彩色兼容电视差频转播机1台和相应器材，在松林坡建立临时电视差转台，是年11月30日晚试发电视信号，在县广播事业局的16英寸黑白电视接收机上收看广西电视台转播的中央电视台节目，这是全县第一次收到电视节目，但图像不清晰。

1979年10月，将松林坡差转机移到拉岜坡顶，建成荔波第一座电视差转台，发射成功，转播广西大明山2频道电视节目，收视图像清晰。是年，小七孔四级电站建立电视差转台，转播广西电视台节目。此后，广西红茂矿务局在荔波平寨、更班、打油寨及平寨火车站相继建小功率电视差转台。

自1981年6月贵州雷公山电视转播台正式用11频道转播贵州电视台节目后，荔波拉岜坡电视差转台转播贵州电视台节目。

1981—1982年，茂兰区、甲良区先后建电视差转台。之后，洞塘乡和久安村也先后建起电视差转台。

1983年10月，将拉岜坡电视差转台搬到罗家寨背后的望城坡，用10瓦机发射6频道转播贵州电视台节目。

1986年5月，投资22万元建设官塘卫星电视地面收转站，7月29日建成投入使用，转播中央电视台第一套节目。这是境内第一座卫星电视地面收转站，县城和朝阳部分村寨群众可以收看中央电视台第一套节目和贵州电视台节目。

1988年，永康乡获得州政府补助4万元，建起全县第一个乡级卫星电视收转站，转播中央电视台第一套节目。

是年，建成水尧、捞村、立化乡尧明村电视差转台3座。同时，在小七孔四级电站电视差转台原址、更班煤矿建成卫星电视收转站2个，在县教育局、小七孔一级电站建成卫星电视单收站2个。

1990年9月，茂兰区建成区级卫星电视收转站，转播中央电视台第一套、第二套节目。瑶庆乡、立化乡尧明村也建成卫星电视收转站。

1991年6月，投资10万元改造官塘坡卫星电视收转站，增强发射功能，官塘坡卫星电视收转站转播中央电视台第一套、第二套节目。至此，县城和朝阳部分村寨群众能收看3套电视节目。

从1992年起，按照省政府要求用4年时间在有稳定电源的乡（镇）逐步建立和完善卫星电视收转站，在播尧、方村、驾欧、翁昂、瑶麓5个乡（镇）建卫星电视收转站，省补助5个乡（镇）电视接收天线及设备各1套，州补助电视发射机和发射天线系统各1套，县政府补助每个乡（镇）建站经费7000元，建站乡（镇）自筹经费3000元，于年底完成建站工作。

1993年11月，县政府拨款3.5万元，补助佳荣、朝阳、捞村、水利、瑶山5个乡（镇）建站，其余7个乡（镇）自筹资金，解决建站的配套经费。至1997年12月，全县17个乡（镇）全部建成卫星电视收转站。

1992—1997年，全县有16个村、组先后建立村、组卫星电视收转站。

2006年，向国家申报的官塘坡无线广播电视发射台改建、扩建项目获批准。2007年，国家拨专项资金100万元，用于官塘坡无线广播电视发射台改建、扩建，2008年7月30日正式播出。县无线广播电视发射台设置发射中央电视台第一套电视节目、第七套电视节目、贵州卫星电视节目和黔南电视台新闻综合频道节目。

（二）有线电视

1992年9月，开始在县城实施有线电视网络建设，采用邻频传输系统，网络带宽220兆赫，下传12套电视节目。

1994年1月，茂兰镇建设有线电视网，网络传输16套电视节目，电视节目覆盖镇政府机关、长寨、拉伙、洞英等地住户。

1994年4月，朝阳镇建成有线电视卫星收转站，网络传输电视节目20套，电视节目覆盖镇政府机关、场坝、学校。是年，该镇的洪江村、山江村、拉香村、板麦村、洞莪村建成卫星电视小片网。

1996年，对县城有线电视网络进行第一次改造扩容，采用专业级邻频传输系统，开通中央电视台第三套、第五套、第六套、第八套加密电视，网络带宽550兆赫，改造后下传电视节目26套，县城有线电视网络用户增加到6500户。

1997年年底，全县有有线电视系统50个，其中，县、乡（镇）、村、组33个，厂矿、企事业单位17个。有终端用户6997户。其中，县、乡（镇）、村、组5775户，厂矿、企事业单位1222户。

1998—2002年，投入20万元对县城有线电视网络进行第二次机房设备升级改造扩容，增加开通电视频道，县城网络与黔南州有线电视网部分节目联网，电视节目由原22个频道增加到45个频道。

2005—2007年，投入70万元对网络进行第三次机房设备升级改造，机房设备采用1310毫米光纤传输设备、网络带宽860兆赫，下传电视节目47套，网络延伸至朝阳镇，广播电视覆盖朝阳镇4个村60%农户。

2008年，成立贵州省广播电视网络信息股份有限公司荔波县分公司。是年8月，县网络分公司投入480万元，将县城、朝阳镇、水利乡方村乡、甲良镇的网络电视用户以模拟接收方式升级为数字化电视信号接收模式，荔波县跨入标清数字电视接收时代。

二、电视宣传

1986年，官塘坡卫星电视地面收转站建成后，为创办县内电视新闻节目提供条件。1988年，开始适时播放自制电视宣传节目。1990年7月18日，县卫星电视收转站播放邓恩铭烈士故居开放的录像节目。

1993年，县政府拨款为县广播电视局购置摄像机、电视编辑机、播出设备、灯光设备等，县广播电视局自办《荔波新闻》和其他服务性节目。自办电视新闻节目每周一、三、五各播出1次。从1999年开始，星期一至星期五制作的县电视新闻节目，当天晚上在固定时间播出，第二天早晨和中午各重播1次，受到州表彰。1999—2003年，每年向州以上新闻单位报送电视新闻节目，年均70件。

2004年，向州以上新闻单位报送并被采用播出外宣新闻182条，获全州广播电视系统外宣工作二等奖。2005年，在州以上新闻单位采用播出的荔波新闻288条，获全州评比集体二等奖。

2006年，以外宣传工作为重点，向黔南电视台输送电视新闻450件，被采用420件，获外宣工作全州第一名；自办的电视新闻节目播出788件，比上年增加356件。

2007年7月，开办《一周要闻》《旅发大会特别报道》栏目。全年采制县内电视新闻在县广播电视台播出1645件，制作播出专题节目25部，重点报道申报中国南方喀斯特世界自然遗产地、举办第二届贵州省旅游产业发展大会、国际“人与生物圈”网络大会、全国第二届山地户外运动锦标赛和荔波飞机场建成通航等重大活动。向州以上新闻媒体报送的新闻稿件和电视新闻节目，被采用445件。其中，中央电视台采用7件，贵州电视台采用40件，黔南电视台采用398件。外宣工作列全州第一名。

2008年，广播电视工作开展有序，成绩优异。先后获得了全州“党的十七大安全播出先进单位”、全州“抗凝冻·促稳定”宣传报道工作先进集体和黔南州广播电视系统“抗凝冻·保民生”先进集体等荣誉称号。

三、广播电视“村村通”工程

2000年，国家实施“十五”计划项目农村广播电视“村村通”小片网工程建设。是年，全县第一批农村广播电视“村村通”小片网工程在17个乡（镇）98个行政村实施，获国家投资98万元。17个乡（镇）、98个行政村群众1万多户收看到网络电视节目，节目数量为8～24套不等。

2006—2007年，投入120万元实施全县第二批农村广播电视“村村通”工程建设，以整乡推进方式进行建设。2006年，瑶麓乡、茂兰镇、方村乡、驾欧乡、捞村乡实现全覆盖。2007年，玉屏镇等12个乡（镇）先后实现全覆盖，共用卫星天线“村村通”工程覆盖全县2.4万户。

2008年，投入79.73万元实施“十一五”第二批直播卫星广播电视“村村通”工程规划项目，全县17个乡（镇）共安装直播卫星广播电视“村村通”设备2278套，农户直接收听到中央、省级广播节目14套、电视节目48套。

第三节　电影放映

一、县城电影放映

1978年，县城有电影院1座，由电影管理站统管全县电影放映工作。1980年，电影管理站更名电影公司，与电影院实行两块牌子、一套人员。1981年8月，总投资44万元，在县城大榕树旁选址新建的荔波影剧院竣工开业，建筑面积1536平方米，有座位1002个。

20世纪80年代修建的荔波电影院

1982年，县电影公司行政归县文化局管理，业务属州电影公司直管。

1982—1989年，影剧院连年超额完成放映场次、观众人次、放映收入、发行收入四大指标，先后获电影发行放映工作全国先进集体1次、全省先进单位3次、全州先进单位2次。

1990年，县财政拨款10万元，省电影公司无息贷款10万元，县电影公司自筹5万元，为影剧院安装中央空调4台。

1998年，被评为全省“先进放映单位”，受省政府表彰。

2003年1月，根据县城规划建设，拆除影剧院，县城停止电影售票放映。

2003—2008年，电影公司按照中央提出的电影放映“2131”（即在21世纪农村要实现一个村一个月要看到一场电影）工程，主要在农村开展“2131”工程电影放映活动，解决农村群众看电影难问题，经费由中央拨60%，省、州、县拨40%。

二、农村电影放映

1978年，全县农村有水维、播尧、阳凤、王蒙、翁昂、捞村、佳荣、朝阳、地莪、方村、驾欧11个电影队，在村寨巡回放映。红茂煤矿赠送茂兰区电影放映机1台，在茂兰场坝露天放映电影。

1981年，甲良、茂兰、洞塘、水利先后建电影放映队，在会议室售票放映电影。

1982年，建朝阳电影院。1983年，建茂兰电影院及水尧、岜鲜、拉扶、坤地等4个放映队。

1984年，建甲良电影院。1986年，建立化乡、洞塘乡电影院。

1987年，建永康、瑶麓、福利、寨马、觉巩、甲站、拉圭、立化、瑶山、红光、巴乐、板江、板寨、花提、水尧煤厂等放映队。是年年底，全县有电影放映队35个，其中集体23个、个体11个、国营1个。

1988年，建佳荣乡电影院。

1994年，茂兰电影院停业。1995年，朝阳电影院停业。1997年，佳荣电影院停业。1998年，甲良电影院停业。

1978—2008年全县电影放映情况统计表

表21-4 单位：场、万人次

年度	放映场数总计	观众累计	其中农村放映	
			放映场数	观众累计
1978	2141	107.21	1610	75.35
1979	2135	102.09	1409	60.32
1980	2148	105.62	1340	60.9
1981	1546	94.42	813	47.92
1982	3714	200.48	2708	127.36
1983	3758	192.93	2870	129.91
1984	3721	154.03	2913	103.27
1985	4269	181.36	3429	127.85
1986	4335	194.44	3440	140.8
1987	4439	224.11	3535	176.55
1988	4657	206.33	3728	157.11
1989	4777	181.00	3730	130.33
1990	5613	210.35	4443	160.09
1991	8855	439.78	7084	212.52
1992	10201	547.73	8160	244.80
1993	950	285.00	760	228.00
1994	750	225.00	600	180.00
1995	700	210.00	560	168.00
1996	600	180.00	480	144.00
1997	450	135.00	360	108.00
1998	350	105.00	280	840.00
1999	1500	40.00	1500	40.00
2000	380	20.00	380	20.00
2001	319	34.00	319	34.00
2002	344	7.00	344	7.00
2003	150	1.00	150	1.00
2004	300	6.00	300	6.00
2005	20	0.90	20	0.90
2006	134	3.77	134	3.77
2007	416	6.20	416	6.20
2008	1130	39.65	1130	39.65

第二十二篇
卫生　体育

改革开放以来，荔波县各级政府把提高人民健康素质作为改善民生的重要目标，不断加大财政投入，县医疗卫生事业机构及人员逐年壮大，许多严重危害广大农村群众身体健康和生命安全的疾病得到有效控制，医疗服务水平发展迅速，1984年6月，县中医药事业起步发展，卫生基础建设不断完善，床位设置逐步增加。2008年，荔波已基本建立了以县级医疗卫生单位为龙头、以乡（镇）卫生院为枢纽、以村卫生室为网底的县乡（镇）、村三级公共卫生体系和医疗服务体系。2006年，新型农村合作医疗制度实施后，农民小病不出村、大病不出乡（镇）、重病才到县，“看病难”“看病贵”的问题有所缓解。1998年、2008年，荔波县两轮次初级卫生保健通过省、州政府组织的合格验收，卫生工作走在省、州前列，多次受到表彰和奖励。

荔波县在1997年获得贵州省级卫生县城基础上，县委、县政府以巩固成果、扩大范围、改善人居环境、提高生存、生活质量为目标，2002年又提出创建“国家卫生县城”的目标，经过三年的共同努力，2004年12月创建“国家卫生县城”工作顺利通过州、省、国家爱卫会的考核验收，荔波获得了贵州省唯一的“国家卫生县城”称号。

在体育事业方面，县体育设施不断完善，城镇、乡村、学校群众性体育运动广泛开展。民族民间传统体育项目得到继承，竞技体育游泳、田径、球类普及开展，为省、州培养体育人才。

第一章 医疗卫生

第一节 医疗卫生队伍

1978年，全县每千人拥有国家卫生技术人员1.27人。

2004年、2008年，从社会招聘卫生专业大中专毕业生共61名充实乡（镇）卫生院。2008年年末，全县卫生专业技术人员中，有中级以上职称62人（其中副高级以上职称7人），占卫生专业人员的18.78%；初级师（士）以下职称人员占卫生专业人员数的71.22%。全县每千人拥有国家卫生技术人员1.94人。

1978—2008年全县医疗卫生机构人员统计表

表22－1

年度	卫生机构（个）		卫生技术人员（人）		卫生机构病床位（张）	
	总计	其中医院	总计	其中医生	总计	其中医院
1978	36	31	232	62	80	75
1979	36	31	238	62	119	114
1980	36	31	253	66	107	102
1981	36	31	232	60	114	109
1982	36	31	247	64	157	152
1983	36	31	245	63	127	122
1984	37	32	235	60	135	130
1985	38	32	271	54	185	180
1986	39	32	332	60	191	186
1987	39	32	339	65	224	219
1988	39	32	350	60	215	210
1989	39	32	408	60	228	223
1990	39	32	394	61	249	244
1991	39	19	423	75	249	244
1992	26	19	429	105	211	206

续表22－1

年度	卫生机构（个）		卫生技术人员（人）		卫生机构病床位（张）	
	总计	其中医院	总计	其中医生	总计	其中医院
1993	26	19	309	114	211	206
1994	26	19	318	196	211	206
1995	26	19	370	204	211	206
1996	26	19	392	235	211	206
1997	27	19	378	234	211	206
1998	27	19	356	222	211	206
1999	27	19	350	213	211	206
2000	27	19	357	220	211	206
2001	27	19	329	197	211	206
2002	26	19	305	154	211	206
2003	26	19	312	160	211	206
2004	25	19	348	150	206	206
2005	24	18	307	150	204	204
2006	25	18	327	152	268	268
2007	25	18	320	149	318	318
2008	25	18	353	171	366	366

第二节　医　疗

一、西医

县内开展西医诊疗的医院主要有县人民医院、乡（镇）卫生院，进行常见病诊疗。个体诊所也用西医治疗常见病。

县医院是境内最大的西医综合医院，1996年被评为“二级乙等医院”“全球爱婴医院”。2008年，该院设内科、儿科、外科、妇产科、急诊科、五官科、口腔科、感染科、中医康复科、皮肤科10个临床科室和放射科、检验科、药剂科、病理科、B超心电科、麻醉科、胃镜室等医技科室，全院占地面积15000平方米，建筑总面积17535平方米，有业务用房面积8180平方米，拥有医疗技术人员160人，床位120张。

（一）设备配置

1978年后，县医院先后配置400毫安X光机、心电图机、B型超声诊断仪、麻醉机、膀胱镜、骨科器械、高频电刀、牙科治疗机、呼吸机、心电监护仪、液压万能手术床等，各类型器械设备基本配套。1998年2月，县医院与贵阳医学院附属医院合作，该院为县医院提供价值60万元的日立全身CT机（CT－W4）1台。2003年8月，县医院安装医院信息管理系统（HIS），对病房、药房、药库、收费室等实行HIS系统管理。在住院部大楼设立电脑查询机1台，供患者查询有关医疗情况。

2004年，设立出诊急救值班室，开通急救电话“96699”，实行24小时值班制度，配备救护车3

辆，随时出诊。

2005年，县医院购置价值275万元的GE螺旋CT机1台，年底投入使用。2006年3月，建立CT院外影像学远程会诊工作站，与贵阳医学院附属医院放射科进行CT远程会诊。

至2008年，县医院放射科配有螺旋CT机、500毫安X光机2台，并安装遥控及增加电视系统、CR；胃镜室配有奥林巴斯电子胃镜；B超心电科配有心电图机2台、黑白B超机2台。部分乡（镇）卫生院也先后配备X光机等医疗设备。

（二）诊疗技术

20世纪80年代至90年代初，县医院西医外科能做胆囊切除、胃大部分切除等部分上腹部手术，内科除治疗常见疾病外，能诊治一些疑难病症。1999年，县医院设皮肤科门诊。2004年4月，建立中心血库，为保障血液供应和用血安全，所有临床用血全部由州中心血站提供。

二、中医与中草药

（一）中医诊疗

1978—1983年，县内中医诊疗主要是民间中医利用中草药治疗常见疾病及部分疑难杂症。

1984年6月，成立县中医院，设中医内科和中药药房。1986年增设针灸科，1988年增设中医肛肠科（外伤）。中医内科诊疗采取中西医结合方式进行治疗；针灸科主要采用传统中医疗法，体针、耳针、头皮针、火针、新九针、灸法拔罐等，并辅以穴位注射、风湿治疗机、理疗等西医手段；肛肠科引进快速根治除痔术，以中药坐浴等配合治疗痔疮。1995年11月，中医院引进血液稀释生物平衡疗法新技术，加上中医药结合治疗老年中风，当年收治中风病人30多例，疗效好。后于2002年停用。

2005年9月，县中医院与水尧岜合水族医联合创办水族医骨伤科，挖掘水族民间草医治疗骨损伤，全部采用新鲜草药加工后外敷骨折处，不加任何辅助药物，疗效显著。

（二）中草药

县内出产中草药700多种。

1979年以后，甲良、朝阳、茂兰3个区卫生院制剂加工中药21个品种10万多支，县医院加工部分中草药针剂，供院内和各区卫生院使用。县中医院成立以后，加工炮制中药300多个品种，供院内治疗用。

1982年10月，成立县民族医药调查组，抽出4名中医中药人员，与省调查组进行为期1个月的民族医药调查，收集到民间秘验方265个，采集民间草药340种，制药物标本近千份，整理有效秘验方典型材料6份。

第三节　疾病预防控制

1978—2002年，县卫生防疫站负责开展传染病预防控制和计划免疫工作，县皮肤病防治站负责开展麻风病防治。2003年4月，县皮肤病防治站和县卫生防疫站合并建立县疾病预防控制中心。

一、防治

（一）传染病防治

结核病　肺结核是境内常见多发的慢性传染病。2003年以前，结核病没有进行统一管理，结核病人在医院就诊后就地治疗或转到上一级医院治疗，出院后没有进行随访和追踪管理。2004

年，实施FADLS结核病控制项目，主要有世行贷款、英国赠款结核病控制项目和全球基金结核病控制项目，设立结核病控制项目专科门诊，由县疾控中心归口管理。项目实施后，对辖区常住居民、暂住人口就诊或转诊的可疑性结核病人免费拍片、免费查痰，对发现的初治涂阳病病人、重症初治涂阳病病人、复治涂阳病病人，给予免费抗结核药物治疗。治疗方式以不住院化疗为主，全疗程6～8个月。2004—2008年，县结核病项目门诊共接诊可疑病人数1402人，共发现活动性肺结核病人427人。

麻风病 1978—1986年，对麻风病人进行隔离治疗，即送麻风村治疗。1986年以后，对新发现的麻风病人不再送麻风村隔离，采取不驻村、不隔离的社会治疗方式。1988年后，麻风病防治工作由县皮肤病防治站负责。2003年，县疾控中心开展麻风病防治工作。2007年7月，省皮肤病防治研究所在荔波举办麻风病线索调查培训班1期，对疾控中心业务人员和乡（镇）卫生人员进行麻风病线索调查方法培训。培训结束后，开展全县麻风病线索调查，当年发现新发麻风病11例，纳入系统管理，接受规范治疗。2008年，实施麻风病康复项目，对原已畸残的老麻风病病人进行手术矫正、外用药物和日常生活护理，部分畸残麻风病人病情得到缓解。

艾滋病 2005年，设立艾滋病初筛实验室，首次对81名娱乐场所从业人员和吸毒等高危人群开展HIV检测，发现艾滋病病毒携带者9例。2006年，县疾控中心设立艾滋自愿检测咨询门诊，同时成立艾滋病干预工作队，开展艾滋病防控工作。2006—2008年，对重点人群开展HIV监测2650人次，经州、省艾滋病监测中心确认阳性者28例，检出率1.06%；对各宾馆、酒店、发廊等公共场所发放安全套4.2万只、宣传塑料牌3000个、宣传挂历1500套、张贴宣传画2000张；开展娱乐场所管理人员、服务人员艾滋病防治知识培训3次，培训180人次。

非典型性肺炎 2003年年初，国内部分地区发生非典型性肺炎流行传染，县内及时成立荔波县非典防治工作领导小组，在县疾病预防控制中心设办公室。“非典”期间，各医疗机构（含16家乡镇卫生院）设立发热门诊，建立“非典”监测点，开通24小时疫情电话报告、工作值班电话及咨询专线电话。疫情报告专人负责，实行每日零报告制度，按“早发现、早报告、早隔离、早治疗”的原则，建立完善县、乡（镇）和村（居）委会三级疫情监测网络。在水甫、甲良、播尧、驾欧、界排、肯甫、佳荣等县域7个主要进出路口设立发热病人检疫检查站，重点检查外地入境车辆1.5万辆次，消毒车辆1500余辆，对4.5万人次进行体温检查和健康登记，全县登记外出人员4500人、返乡人员1950人。同时，对车站、宾馆、酒店等外流人口密集场所每天进行消毒，对从重点疫区返乡的重点人群进行流行病学调查20人，未发现预警病例及疑似病例。

乙型肝炎 20世纪80年代，县内乙型肝炎较为流行，调查显示人群感染率超过25%以上。1994年，开始在全县以有偿服务方式推广使用乙肝疫苗。从2003年起，将乙肝疫苗列入儿童免疫规划，对新生儿普种乙肝疫苗，并强调乙肝首针接种及时率。同时，每年加大乙肝防治宣传，提高群众自我防护意识，乙肝发病率明显下降。2008年，全县乙型肝炎感染率已下降至6%以下。

（二）寄生虫病防治

疟疾 1979年、1982年、1984年，时来乡水甫村、瑶庆乡的水庆村以及阳凤乡的部分村寨曾经出现恶性疟传染流行。1982—1983年，省寄生虫病研究所和县防疫站在瑶庆乡水庆村开展恶性疟对氯奎敏感性监测，显示县内恶性疟对氯奎已产生1级抗性。1984年，在阳凤乡开展间日疟虫株研究，证实县内间日疟原虫为短潜伏期株（速发型）。是年6—9月，调查蚊相地面32个点，发现雷嗜按蚊21个点，除樟江沿岸村寨未发现雷嗜按蚊外，其余各点均有发现，雷嗜按蚊发病高峰在8月、9月，因此认定雷嗜按蚊为荔波传疟的优势媒介，其次为中华按蚊。

20世纪80年代中期，疟疾病例主要为间日疟，集中在水尧、茂兰、佳荣、立化、洞塘等人口流动频繁的产煤乡（镇）。

1988年后，疟疾防治主要采取“查源、追踪、拔灶”的综合防治措施，每年落实血检任务，对诊断为疟疾、疑似疟疾、感冒和发热原因不明的“四热”（疟疾、疑似疟疾、感冒和发热原因不明）病人进行采血镜检，排查传染源。

1995—1997年，针对小煤窑疟疾疫情的反复性，在水尧、茂兰、佳荣和立化4个乡（镇）建立煤矿区灭疟专业队，人员从卫生、煤炭和乡（镇）各部门抽调。各专业队在每年5—10月到矿区，对流动人口开展血检普查和服药预防，3年间开展矿区流动人口血检1.2万人次，检出疟原虫阳性126例，阳性率1.05%，完成预防性服药3.2万人次。

1996年，水尧乡水捞村发生疟疾传染流行，全寨总人口130人，发病21例，患病率16.1%。1998年，佳荣镇移民新村疟疾传染流行，全寨87人，疟疾发病12人，患病率13.7%，通过及时抗疟处理，疫情迅速得到控制。

1988—2008年，全县常住人口发热血检204969人次，检出疟原虫阳性1656例，阳性率0.81%。其中，常住人口普查血检2346人，检出阳性33例，阳性率1.41%；外来流动人口发热血检6245人，检出阳性702例，阳性率11.24%。对外来人口普查4016人，检出阳性149例，阳性率4.71%。对发现的阳性病人进行追踪治疗和管理，同时对病灶点周围人群进行休止期抗复发治疗和疟疾发病高峰期服药预防。

丝虫病 境内曾是丝虫病高发区。1978—1979年，全县丝虫病控制处于反复防治阶段。1980—1984年为考核验收阶段。1982—1984年，经省、州考核，防治达卫生部规定标准。1984年，经卫生部考核，确认荔波县基本消灭丝虫病。1984年发现丝虫病人1例，1985年后无病例发生。全县基本消灭丝虫病后，开展丝虫病后期监测工作。1990年，对阳凤部分村寨的居民进行病原学检测584人和血清学检测230人，均为阴性。1991年，在水尧乡水尧村和玉屏镇时来村开展蚊虫调查，捕捉解剖库蚊2050只，未发现幼丝虫阳性蚊。1994年，卫生部丝虫病评审专家组对荔波县丝虫病后期监测工作进行考核，通过查看资料、现场核查，确定达到消灭丝虫病标准。

肠道寄生虫病 县内常见的肠道寄生虫病主要有蛔虫、蛲虫、鞭虫和钩虫。1993年，在县城玉屏一小、玉屏二小和民族中学3所学校开展肠道寄生虫病普查，抽查学生460名，肠道寄生虫感染率分别为蛔虫26.8%、蛲虫18.4%、鞭虫16.2%、钩虫8.7%。1994年、1997年，在17个乡（镇）部分小学开展普服药物（阿苯达唑）驱虫2次，服药人数分别为8500人、10800人。2008年6月，中国疾控中心、中华医学会、贵州省疾控中心在荔波联合举办新长征朝阳工程全国基层寄生虫病防治教育培训班，县直各医院和乡（镇）卫生院医生，各中心学校校长、校医以及从事健康教育工作人员等共120人参加学习。

（三）碘缺乏病防治

境内也是碘缺乏病流行区之一。1978年，县内甲状腺肿患病率22.54%，儿童甲肿率37.22%。1978—1987年，每年将碘缺乏病列为重要卫生防疫项目进行预防。至1987年，居民甲状腺肿患病率降至4.15%，儿童甲肿率降至8.31%，克丁病患病率为零，人群尿碘升至135.7微克/升，居民食用盐碘含量均值为2.35。1988—1995年，采取口服碘油丸措施预防碘缺乏病。1996年以后，以食盐加碘方式预防碘缺乏病，每年开展碘盐监测和尿碘监测。每年“5・15”碘缺乏病防治宣传日和其他卫生宣传日，在县城和各乡（镇）开展碘缺乏病防治宣传，采取发放宣传资料、播放影像光碟等形式，向群众普及碘缺乏病防治知识。

经过长期综合防治，至2008年，全县碘盐覆盖率达98.61%，碘盐合格率98.94%，合格碘盐食用率达97.57%；儿童尿碘含量中位数303微克/升，育龄妇女尿碘含量中位数259.5微克/升，尿碘水平基本达到世界卫生组织推荐的适宜水平；儿童智商均值升至106.12，达中等水平；儿童甲肿率降至5.12%。

二、计划免疫

1981年，县内开始实施计划免疫，在县城附近村寨进行疫苗预防接种。1982年，按省、州下达的指标，在城镇和交通方便、人口较密集的村寨进行接种。1984年，计划免疫工作按规划全面铺开，实行儿童计划免疫保偿制度，计划免疫儿童缴纳保偿费，保期3—5年。1988年，脊髓灰质炎疫苗、麻疹疫苗列入儿童基础免疫项目，以接种卡介苗、麻苗、脊灰苗和百白破疫苗为基础免疫，每年冷链运转6次。

1988—1990年，开展乙肝疫苗预防接种，接种人数累计6162人。

1992年，在完成基础免疫后，于是年12月和次年1月对0—4岁龄儿童开展两轮次脊灰疫苗强化免疫，接种率均达90％以上，全县保持无脊灰状态成果。1993年，规定每年12月5日和次年1月5日为脊灰强化免疫日，对5岁以下儿童脊灰苗强化免疫。

2002年，全县麻疹发病率已降至5/万以下。

从2003年起，取消儿童计划免疫保偿制度，对所有适龄儿童免费接种疫苗。

是年，荔波县作为全省实施麻疹控制项目试点，对全县8个月至15岁所有儿童进行麻疹疫苗普种，应种儿童38292人，实际接种38028人，接种率99.3％，当年的全县麻疹发病为零。此后，每年在适龄儿童中开展麻疹疫苗强化免疫活动。

从2005年起，对入托、入学儿童实施查验预防接种证管理制度，未接种国家免疫规划疫苗和未完成国家免疫规划免疫程序规定剂次的儿童，按照相关免疫程序补种相应疫苗。同时，乙肝疫苗列入免疫规划。2004—2008年，乙肝疫苗接种9457人。

从2008年起，增加流脑疫苗、乙脑疫苗和麻腮疫苗列为儿童免疫规划疫苗。是年，流脑疫苗接种1891人，接种率95.4%；乙脑疫苗接种1836人，接种率95.7%；麻疹发病率降至0.5/万以下。

1978—2008年全县常规免疫接种统计表

表22－2

年度	麻苗		百白破		脊灰苗		卡介苗	
	接种（人）	接种率（%）	接种（人）	接种率（%）	接种（人）	接种率（%）	接种（人）	接种率（%）
1978	20177	87.92	21815	75.84	—	—	—	—
1979	—	—	—	—	10052	92.29	—	—
1980	4308	87.75	8270	68.92	12066	61.12	45749	93.46
1981	2315	32.82	—	—	12079	84.10	—	—
1982	3087	96.47	3425	53.55	24935	53.22	—	—
1983	2948	76.71	—	—	9541	79.50	—	—
1984	3009	95.25	9652	95.55	11330	96.22	—	—
1985	17402	98.99	9434	98.22	9996	98.76	810	92.56
1986	2928	99.09	9265	97.91	9894	98.34	377	91.50
1987	28192	96.96	10339	97.67	11615	98.52	6310	98.27
1988	4337	89.11	3873	95.70	13476	9375	2423	95.99
1989	4022	97.72	5107	96.52	19386	98.85	4567	98.58

续表22－2

年度	麻苗		百白破		脊灰苗		卡介苗	
	接种（人）	接种率（%）	接种（人）	接种率（%）	接种（人）	接种率（%）	接种（人）	接种率（%）
1990	5801	98.63	7353	98.63	8729	98.93	7139	98.16
1991	2931	96.90	3007	97.80	3018	97.90	2986	98.10
1992	2519	99.00	2513	98.70	2513	98.70	2513	98.70
1993	2460	95.40	2441	94.70	2449	95.00	2445	94.80
1994	2416	94.30	2395	93.50	2419	94.50	2460	96.10
1995	2583	98.10	2580	98.00	2610	99.10	2583	98.10
1996	2746	96.70	2739	96.40	2802	98.60	2756	97.00
1997	2852	93.90	2846	93.70	2895	95.30	2878	94.70
1998	2435	92.30	2433	92.30	2478	94.00	2451	92.90
1999	2378	95.80	2386	96.20	2392	96.40	2364	95.30
2000	2183	96.80	2164	95.90	2185	96.90	2170	96.20
2001	2192	97.30	2193	97.30	2205	97.90	2196	97.50
2002	2063	97.90	2035	96.60	2082	98.80	2024	96.10
2003	2056	96.90	2024	95.40	2067	97.50	2042	96.30
2004	1985	97.30	1990	97.50	1995	97.70	1991	97.60
2005	1932	97.00	1945	97.60	1938	97.30	1913	96.00
2006	1856	96.10	1867	96.70	1874	97.00	1885	97.60
2007	1835	97.60	1850	98.40	1848	98.30	1852	98.50
2008	1886	98.30	1893	98.70	1878	97.90	1892	98.60

1993—2008年全县脊灰疫苗强化免疫统计表

表22－3 单位：人次

年度	应接种数	实接种数				
		合计	＜1岁	1岁	2岁	3岁
1993	21416	21338	4452	5078	5346	6462
1994	20412	20336	4434	5228	5262	5412
1995	19770	19528	4298	4946	5116	5168
1996	21570	21458	5124	5694	5356	5284
1997	23380	23162	5740	6026	5898	5498
1998	24614	24398	5511	6221	6394	6272
1999	23457	23213	4856	5858	6177	6322

续表22－3

年度	应接种数	实接种数				
		合计	＜1岁	1岁	2岁	3岁
2000	6626	4043	334	1155	1274	1280
2001	21122	20914	4710	4908	5406	5890
2002	19163	18788	4015	4746	4803	5224
2003	17405	17156	3012	4048	4596	5500
2004	22182	16170	3052	3966	4260	4892
2005	0	0	0	0	0	0
2006	2997	2915	1650	513	390	362
2007	18668	14508	3233	3784	3749	3742
2008	14779	14481	3434	3663	3750	3634

说明：实种儿童数合计中，2000年包括4岁1259人、5岁1273人，2004年包括4岁5298人，2007年包括4岁3836人。

第四节　妇幼保健

1978—2003年，县妇幼保健站负责开展全县妇幼保健工作。乡（镇）从1991年起在卫生院配妇幼专干1人。2004年，县妇幼保健站并入县计生服务站。

一、妇女保健

1978—1979年，因业务技术人员少，仅在部分公社开展妇女“两病”（妇女子宫脱垂、尿瘘）查治工作，培训部分农村接生员。从1980年起，对区卫生院的助产士和公社卫生院卫生员进行妇女子宫脱垂、尿瘘查治和新法接生业务知识培训。1985年，在玉屏区、朝阳区、甲良区、茂兰区所在地开展新法接生试点，并对这几个区所在地每个村培训村级接生员1名，当年的新法接生率为28.5%。1986—1987年，王蒙乡、瑶庆乡、永康乡、方村乡、水利乡、水尧乡也开展新法接生试点，开展新法接生试点乡11个，发有简易接生包。

1989年，新法接生开始纳入常规工作，对孕产妇进行系统规范管理，开展产前检查、产后访视、妇女常见病诊疗。

1991年后，部分村级配有接生员，负责对孕产妇进行产前检查和产后新生儿访视。1998年，全县普及新法接生，接生率为95%以上。

1978—2008年全县妇幼保健情况统计表

表22-4 单位：人

年度	产妇总人数	新法接生人数	住院分娩人数	产检人数	访产情况	系统管理	孕产妇死亡	
							总数	死亡率（/10万）
1978	2840	260	—	—	—	—	—	—
1988	2539	311	—	—	—	—	—	—
1989	2714	512	—	—	—	—	—	—
1990	2618	555	—	—	—	—	—	—
1991	2698	1200	207	961	955	47	8	296.5
1992	2693	1145	232	790	815	41	3	111.4
1993	2244	1513	213	1309	1034	54	9	401.1
1994	2469	1548	287	1489	1464	67	8	324.0
1995	2772	2217	263	1664	1648	62	4	144.3
1996	2796	2029	617	2133	1947	81	7	250.4
1997	2787	2180	322	2058	1917	69	5	179.4
1998	2863	2653	400	2694	2667	366	1	34.3
1999	2281	2134	401	2156	2130	412	1	43.8
2000	2344	2232	522	2067	2218	60	2	85.3
2001	2301	2194	570	2116	2106	631	4	173.8
2002	2188	2076	673	2034	2016	527	6	274.2
2003	2021	1951	705	1957	1949	601	2	98.9
2004	1911	1823	664	1831	1815	410	3	156.9
2005	1808	1713	686	1657	1677	671	1	55.3
2006	1823	1792	854	1747	1723	788	1	54.8
2007	1832	1791	987	1694	1110	1129	0	—
2008	1794	1748	1214	1609	1604	1261	2	111.4

说明：1978—1990年的住院人数、产检人数、产访情况、系统管理、孕产妇死亡等情况资料遗失。

二、儿童保健

1978—1987年，儿童保健工作只对县城的儿童进行一般体格检查。1988年以后，对学龄前儿童、县城区4所托幼机构以及散居儿童进行体格发育检查和健康评价。1988年8—10月，在甲良、方村、玉屏、时来、永康、水尧、瑶庆、茂兰、立化、瑶麓、岜鲜、水维、朝阳、王蒙、瑶山15个乡（镇）开展1985—1987年婴儿死因3年回顾性调查，3年内婴儿死亡552人，3年的死亡率分别为80.23‰、108.04‰、167.25‰。

1989年，对0～3岁儿童进行“421”系统管理，即1岁检查4次（42天、180天、270天、360天各检查1次），2岁检查2次（1岁半和两岁各1次），3岁检查1次，发现体格发育异常时，及时给予矫正和诊疗建议。

1991年以后，按常规开展儿童肺炎、腹泻、营养不良防治及5岁以下儿童死亡监测。

1978—2008年全县儿童保健情况统计表

表22－5　　单位：例

年度	活产婴儿数	0～7岁儿童数	0～3岁儿童系统管理		肺炎防治情况	腹泻防治情况	营养不良防治情况	0～4岁儿童死亡监测情况			
			总数	占比（%）				婴儿	占比（%）	新生儿	1～4岁儿童
1978	2640	—	—	—	—	—	—	—	—	—	—
1988	2539	624	—	—	—	—	—	—	—	—	—
1989	2714	645	—	—	—	—	—	—	—	—	—
1990	2618	451	—	—	—	—	—	—	—	—	—
1991	1880	625	58	3.08	214	317	117	174	96.66	128	22
1992	2024	666	41	2.03	198	283	129	84	41.50	40	9
1993	2244	541	58	2.58	178	215	132	116	51.69	67	19
1994	2469	557	93	3.78	127	289	98	166	67.23	75	12
1995	2772	687	102	3.68	172	198	121	140	50.50	84	17
1996	2081	2068	131	6.30	253	274	103	195	93.70	117	37
1997	2777	752	154	5.55	283	292	646	127	45.73	40	7
1998	2876	679	264	9.18	55	130	134	119	41.37	59	7
1999	2287	958	284	12.40	296	567	206	142	62.09	60	5
2000	2341	1309	582	24.90	405	708	315	101	43.14	27	4
2001	2295	918	533	23.20	270	311	194	115	50.10	44	8
2002	2199	898	432	19.70	213	271	195	95	43.20	53	5
2003	2029	567	277	13.70	320	110	144	98	48.29	23	8
2004	1920	690	297	15.50	212	367	115	65	33.85	44	13
2005	1803	643	671	37.20	95	122	48	65	36.05	39	3
2006	1815	587	792	43.60	342	374	81	72	39.66	45	7
2007	1839	759	828	45.00	344	364	76	111	60.35	84	14
2008	1803	1155	991	54.90	394	315	2	84	46.58	66	7

说明："—"表示此项工作尚未开展，空白格为数据资料遗失

三、国家"降消"项目

从2000年起，国家在12个省的贫困县实施"降低孕产妇死亡率和消除新生儿破伤风"项目，简称"降消"项目，项目实施期限至2009年。荔波县被列为"降消"项目县之一实施此项目。至2008年，省、州下拨经费107.79万元，县配套8.36万元，到位资金总计116.15万元。项目执行中，农村孕产妇住院贫困救助支付83.82万元，项目管理支付1.39万元，项目培训支付18.83万元，健康教育宣传

支付5.93万元，设备购置支付4.12万元，支出总计114.09万元。县卫生局在县核算中心设立专用账户，资金专款专用。

2000—2008年，共发放救助农村孕产妇救助金83.82万元（其中转诊误工补助4.86万元），受益产妇2504人（其中转诊误工1870人），平产救助2065人，剖宫产、难产救助439人。

2000—2009年荔波县“降消”项目指标执行情况统计表

表22－6

项目指标类别	项目目标控制标准		项目目标实现率	
	2000年	2009年	2000年	2009年
孕产妇死亡率	＜127.98/10万	60/10万	127.98/10万	0
新生儿破伤风发病率	＜1‰	＜1‰	0.85‰	0
住院分娩率	＞20%	≥75%	22.27%	76.16%
产前检查覆盖率	＞90%	≥85%	88.18%	83.59%
5岁以下儿童死亡率	＞95%	30‰以内	0	34.05‰
农村孕产妇住院分娩补助受益率	＞95%	90%以上	60%	100%
县乡医疗保健机构产科“三基”考核合格率	＞80%	≥90%	80%	100%
高危孕产妇住院分娩率	＞95%	≥90%	77.42%	98.89%
新法接生率	＞95%	≥98%	96.07%	98.61%
县乡医疗保健机构助产人员持证上岗率	95%	100%	0	100%

第五节　公共卫生

一、爱国卫生运动

（一）除“四害”

1978—1982年，县爱国卫生运动委员会办公室每年组织群众开展除“四害”（鼠、蚊、蝇、蟑螂）活动。

1983—1985年，每年开展群众性大规模灭鼠及消毒杀虫活动，蚊、蝇密度下降。1986年，在县城区及城乡接合部于春节前和9月进行两次大规模灭鼠。1988年3月，开展春季大规模灭鼠活动。

1994年7月，县爱卫办对鼠密度进行监测统计，全县鼠密度控制在国家允许范围内。

2002年7月，县创卫办组织玉屏镇所辖村进行除“四害”培训，在县城开展统一灭鼠行动，发放鼠药3500袋。是年，县防疫站、公用事业局联合对县城区垃圾收运站、垃圾处置场的蚊、蝇、蟑螂进行定期消杀。2003年4月、8月，在县城进行两次大规模统一时间、统一行动、统一投药的除“四害”活动，发放各类灭鼠、灭蚊、灭蝇、灭蟑螂药物43302袋（瓶、包）。

2004年4月20—21日，举办除“四害”培训班，参加人员100人，并在县城区及城乡接合部开展灭鼠活动，投鼠药5000包。

2005年9月，发放各种除“四害”药物42157（瓶、包、盒），“四害”密度控制和达到国家规定。

2006年，结合全县“整脏治乱”活动，向县城住户、机关单位、特殊行业业主发放除“四害”

药物，进行统一除“四害”活动。全年发放各种药物29557包（瓶）。

2007年8月，在县城和旅游区开展除“四害”活动，发放各类药物6500袋（瓶、包）。

2008年5月，在居民区、公共绿地、农贸市场、宾馆、饭店、农家接待点、民族村寨投放各类除“四害”药物共41200袋（瓶、包）。

（二）农村改水改厕

1984年3月，从县、区、乡三级卫生部门抽调136人组成饮水水源普查组，开展饮水卫生普查，全县有饮水水源2073个（地下水源585个、地面水源1488个），平均每个村寨有水源1.96个。其中，远离村寨的沟水、泉水、溶洞水源无污染175个，受不同程度污染水源1898个，污染水源占水源总数的91.56%，县城自来水由于没有坚持经常性沉淀与消毒，水质也不稳定。

1985年5月，县政府根据普查情况，制定农村改水方案，成立县农村改水办公室，设在县爱卫办，各区（镇）也成立相应机构开展农村改水工作。是年，实施水尧乡水扒村、岜莫改水工程。1986年，获州改水资金2.21万元，县民委拨款0.32万元，群众自筹0.54万元，受益群众投工投劳，对时来乡拉岜村、水尧乡董见村和瑶麓乡人畜饮水点进行改良，受益人口671人，大牲畜420头（匹）。1987年，获省、州改水资金30.5万元，动工兴修瑶山乡、播尧乡、玉屏镇板吉村、甲良乡七星村、洞塘乡木槽村、朝阳乡田洞村、时来乡拉岜村的廖家湾村民组的改水工程。同时，对县城自来水和西门大井进行定期水质化验监测，对朝阳乡鱼胆山、时来乡拉岜村的水质进行监测化验。

1994年，建成11个乡（镇）农村改水工程，其中集中式改水点9个、分散式改水点2个，受益群众570户3219人、大牲畜1410头（匹）。

1995年，获省、州改水资金11.1万元，建成播尧乡曼井村、玉屏镇石灰坳村、水尧乡水功村、方村乡交进村、红泥村、甲良镇吊井村、朝阳镇花堤村、翁昂乡拉内村、驾欧乡联山等村寨的改水工程，受益人口2085人、大牲畜3100头（匹）。此外，各居民点还自筹资金投工投劳新修和改建一批水井。

是年，在方村乡双江村拉岜组、甲良镇甲良村马道组、佳荣镇大土村进行农村改厕试点，41户建成双瓮式厕所。

1997年以后，农村改水工程项目由县水电局负责承担，县爱卫办协调县防疫站等单位做好水质监测资料收集工作。是年，朝阳镇板麦村46户农户中建成双瓮式卫生厕所，并在全县各村寨宣传普及卫生厕所的重要意义，动员群众自筹资金修建卫生厕所。

2004年12月，县政府成立以分管领导为组长的县农村改厕工作领导小组，下设办公室在县爱卫办。2005年，获中央补助资金7.5万元（250元/座），县配套资金2万元，分别在驾欧乡绿林村、新街村进行农村无害化卫生厕所改造试点，建成三格式无害化卫生厕所300座，完成全年农村改厕任务。

2007年，获中央补助资金245万元（350元/座）、省补助资金27.16万元（38.8元/座）、县拨经费3万元，实施“2008年农村改厕项目暨2007年中央补助地方公共卫生资金农村改厕项目”7000座。2008年8月，县政府与各乡（镇）签订《荔波县农村改厕目标管理责任书》，对全县农村无害化卫生厕所7000座建设任务实施目标管理。

二、职业卫生

1978年以后，县卫生防疫站先后组织对县农机厂、甲良煤厂、县水泥厂、县饲料公司、粮油加工厂、电石厂、木材加工厂等厂矿作业工人进行普查登记、健康体检，职工体检总计2460人次。开展职业卫生防护知识培训20余次，接受培训3500余人次，对患职业病患者，提出调离或调整工作岗位意见，并对他们建立健康档案。对生产环境不符合劳动卫生要求的厂矿企业，提出改善生产环境和增加职业病防护措施的建议。

1985年8月，成立防尘、防毒安全办公室，加强劳动卫生工作。1985—1990年，选定9个监测点，先后对职工体检471人次。至2008年各企业都贯彻《中华人民共和国劳动法》，不断改善生产环境，坚持监测，增强职工防病治病的措施。

三、学校卫生

1978年起，县防疫站每年对县城中小学校开展学生健康检查，建立学生健康档案，对学生的生长发育、营养、体质、常见疾病分别进行统计分析，存入学校卫生工作档案，对学生在校学习期间健康状况进行动态管理。1979年，对县城中小学生及幼儿园儿童进行沙眼普查2155人，发现沙眼患者1588人，占检查人数的73.68%。

1986—1990年，为学生体检8493人次。

1993年，对荔波民中学生进行寄生虫病调查460名，肠道寄生虫感染率分别为蛔虫26.8%、蛲虫18.4%、鞭虫16.2%、钩虫8.7%。1994年、1997年，在17个乡（镇）部分小学开展普遍服药物驱虫，两个年度服药驱虫人数分别为8500人、10800人。

1998年，在玉屏一小、玉屏二小和荔波职业中学开展学生贫血调查，调查1800人，血色素低于正常值人数占23%。到2008年，坚持采取一系列措施，保障学生健康安全。

第六节　新型农村合作医疗

2005年，全县开始实施新型农村合作医疗制度。12月，成立县新型农村合作医疗管理委员会、县新型农村合作医疗监督委员会、县新型农村合作医疗督查领导小组，同时成立县新型农村合作医疗管理委员会办公室，全面开展新农合工作。

同月，在玉屏镇的水甫村、福利村、时来村，茂兰镇的洞流村、瑶埃村、尧朝村，方村乡的红泥村、双江村、拉街村开展基线调查。每个村抽100户作为调查对象，重点对乡（镇）、村的经济发展水平、医疗卫生机构服务现状、农民疾病发生状况、就医用药及费用情况、农民对参加新农合的意愿等进行抽样调查，根据基线调查情况，制定《荔波县新型农村合作医疗实施细则》《荔波县新型农村合作医疗补偿暂行办法》，规范县、乡（镇）、村定点医疗机构基本用药目录、新农合管理程序，定制全县统一的“荔波县新型农村合作医疗证”“参合人员缴费登记册”等。同时，建立由县财政和民政部门代农村独生子女户、二女结扎户、特困户、五保户、现役军人家属、老复退军人、伤残军人、20世纪60年代精简下岗职工、烈属、孤儿缴纳参合基金的稳定筹资机制。是月16日，召开全县新农合工作动员大会，并与各乡（镇）签订责任书。根据开展工作要求，在县农村信用合作联社设立新农合专户，对新农合资金实行专户储存，专账管理，保障新农合资金安全运行。

县新型农村合作医疗管逛委员会办公室制定相关管理制度，每年与各定点医疗机构签订《荔波县新型农村合作医疗服务协议书》，规范工作运行：要求各定点医疗机构按月将减免补偿情况进行张贴公示，接受社会监督，确保新农合资金公开、公平、公正使用。同时，采取定期或不定期方式对各定点医疗机构进行督查，对定点医疗机构的准入、退出实行动态管理，严格执行《黔南州新型农村合作医疗责任追究办法（试行）》。

2006年，全县参合人数103485人，参合率73.17%。其中，为计生对象4958人、民政对象6443人代缴金额总计11.40万元；减免补偿29924人次，减免补偿金额总计163.59万元。2007年，全县参合率上升到81.28%。

2008年，全县参合人数134290人，参合率94.75%。其中，为计生对象4748人、民政对象11575人代缴金额总计16.32万元；减免补偿98812人次，减免补偿金额总计815.96万元。年内，参合患者住院费用获第一次减免后，自负费用在4000元以上的给予二次补偿，办理二次补偿448人，补偿金额总计108.5万元。向省新农合专户上交风险基金117.12万元。全县认定县、乡（镇）、村三级定点医疗机构60所（县级4所、乡镇级16所、村级40所）。

第七节　世界卫生项目

一、世界银行贷款“农村卫生人力开发项目”

1993—1999年，荔波县实施世界银行贷款“农村卫生人力开发项目”为世界银行对华贷款的第四个卫生发展人力开发支持项目，简称“卫生Ⅳ项目”，包括卫生人力规划、卫生人力培训、卫生服务与项目管理。项目计划总投资106.91万元，其中贷款60.43万元、配套46.48万元。

项目实施完成后，实际投入95.76万元，其中贷款74.06万元、配套资金21.7万元。县、乡、村三级卫生技术人员接受不同类别培训354人，其中学历培训8人、短期培训267人、临床进修49人、其他形式培训30人。乡村两级卫生技术人员有中专以上学历人数由1993年的124人、占卫生人员总数的23.9%，增至1999年中专以上学历207人、占卫生人员总数的37.1%，医师以上职称由1993年的27人增至1999年的63人。乡级卫生院配置部分医疗设备后，能开展三大常规检查有6所，能开展X光检查3所，能开展B超检查2所，能开展心电图检查4所。卫生院年平均诊疗人数由1993年的5476人增至1999年的7551人，年平均住院人数由1993年的123人增至1999年的206人。全县法定传染病发病率、婴儿死亡率、孕产妇死亡率分别由1993年的429.13/10万人、98.54/千人、49.02/万人下降为1999年的330.10/10万人、55.42/千人和零。

二、世界银行贷款“卫Ⅶ项目计划免疫子项目”

1996—2003年，荔波县实施世界银行对华贷款的第七个卫生发展计划免疫支持项目，简称“卫Ⅶ项目”。项目申请世行贷款26.40万元，利用国内配套资金5.2万元。其中，用于培训2.12万元，用于各种项目活动8.24万元，购置项目设备21.24万元。

项目实施后，经省、州各年度审评，计免接种率由项目实施前期基线调查的73%到中期上升为85%，终期达95%以上，标准卡痕率也由中前期的50%以下上升到70%左右。建立起县、乡、村三级疫情报告网，建立应急处理和快速反应机制。脊灰、白喉、破伤风、百日咳发病率为零；麻疹发病率由73.24/10万人下降为11.87/10万人，控制在30/10万以下，＜5岁组儿童麻疹发病率由24.08‰逐年下降为1.27‰；＜1岁婴儿死亡率由67.97‰下降为36.29‰；＜5岁儿童死亡率由47‰下降为29.05‰。安全接种点数达到56.9%。冷链运转接种频率≥6次接种点数达17个乡（镇）、169个村、193个点，17个乡（镇）均实行门诊接种和定点接种，基本实现完全门诊接种的乡（镇）8个。通过对特殊人群儿童采取针对措施，使他们与普通人群儿童一样同等享受免疫服务，减少漏卡、漏种和易患病儿童积累，实现最佳免疫屏障。

三、世界银行贷款“卫Ⅸ项目妇幼卫生子项目”

2000—2007年，荔波县实施世界银行对华贷款第九个卫生发展妇幼卫生支持项目，简称“卫Ⅸ

项目”。项目土建、设备、培训等各项费用计划投入259.38万元，到2007年年底，实际支出210.73万元（不包括价格不可预见费38.91万元，实物不可预见费12.97万元）。

项目实施后，在孕产妇保健方面，新法接生每年达95%以上，住院率逐步提高，孕产妇系统管理逐年上升；经过培训，高危识别能力得到加强，筛出率逐年提高，高危住院分娩达98%以上；产前检查覆盖率和检查≥5次以上，产后访视≥2次以上和覆盖率都相应升高；孕产妇死亡率逐年下降。在儿童保健方面，在17个乡（镇）的乡所在地，都开展儿童系统管理，县城由妇幼保健站承担儿童系统管理和入托、入园保健体检。全县各乡（镇）卫生院均开展5岁以下儿童肺炎、腹泻、营养不良等疾病监测。全县监测小儿肺炎2426例、小儿腹泻3141例、营养不良879例，死亡总计390例，死因主要是小儿肺炎大多合并心衰抢救不及时，腹泻中度、重度脱水并酸中毒，中度、重度营养不良各种并发症等。孕产妇和5岁以下儿童死亡监测中，孕产妇死因主要是产科出血、妊娠内科并发症未及时转院或在人工抬送转院途中，5岁以下儿童死亡主要是部分儿童家长因迷信延误治疗时机。死亡人数顺位是小儿肺炎、腹泻，其他为早产儿、出生窒息。2000年，发生新生儿破伤风2例、抢救无效死亡1例，2002年后无新生儿破伤风病例发生。

项目设备配置方面，乡、村级配备新法接生产包，卫生院配置制氧机、多功能产床和抢救台、婴儿培养箱、B超和胎儿心电监护仪、蓝光治疗仪、新生儿复苏台等。2002年以后，卫生院年平均抢救小儿重症肺炎成功200例以上，小儿腹泻及中度、重度脱水250例以上，胎儿宫内窒息和出生窒息抢救成功率有不同程度提高。

宣传、咨询等活动方面，通过宣传，提高群众自我保健意识，改变了一些陈规陋习，部分即将结婚的青年男女及时咨询，怀孕后及时产检，有病及时住院转诊。1997年与2007年孕产妇死亡之比下降率为83.01%；按1997年递减到2007年，减少44例孕产妇死亡；5岁以下儿童死亡1997年与2007年之比下降率为20.91%；按历年与1997年递减到2007年约500例婴儿免于死亡。2008年世行项目停止实施。

1997—2007年荔波县IX项目妇女综合服务情况表

表22－7

年度	孕产妇总数（例）	孕产妇系统管理（例）	孕产妇保健（例）	非住院新法接生（例）	住院分娩（例）	新法接生数（例）	高危孕产妇（例）	高危住院分娩（例）	孕产妇死亡（例）
1997	2787	68	2058	1898	306	2204	68	49	5
2000	2344	56	2067	1710	522	2232	155	120	2
2001	2301	76	2116	1624	570	2194	315	239	4
2002	2188	101	2016	1403	673	2076	266	223	6
2003	2024	601	1957	1246	705	1951	277	268	2
2004	1923	416	1786	1172	653	1836	154	154	3
2005	1769	671	1677	1032	680	1713	147	147	1
2006	1822	788	1747	936	854	1790	142	142	1
2007	1832	1129	1694	804	987	1791	160	160	0

说明：1997年数为项目开展前的基数。

1997—2007年荔波县Ⅸ项目儿童综合服务情况统计表

表22－8 单位：例

年度	活产数	3岁以下儿童数	3岁以下儿童系统管理	5岁以下儿童数	5岁以下儿童营养监测	5岁以下儿童中重度营养不良	7岁以下儿童监测	7岁以下儿童保健管理	5岁以下儿童死亡		
									新生儿	28天～1岁以内	1～4岁
1997	2777	7900	154	12331	849	464	17175	849	93	95	74
2000	2493	7694	582	13270	1309	271	17779	1891	54	100	4
2001	2295	7163	543	12764	1523	34	17889	795	44	71	8
2002	2181	6969	432	12170	797	29	17746	915	53	42	6
2003	2029	6505	277	11373	609	44	16974	2567	23	67	8
2004	1931	6141	791	10929	1731	115	16130	1969	44	21	13
2005	1803	5763	671	10239	1140	43	15407	3051	47	14	3
2006	1815	5549	1192	9759	2048	20	14547	2666	45	27	7
2007	1836	5434	2431	9394	2942	26	13870	5441	55	70	12

说明：1997年数为项目开展前的基数；2001年前的项目报表只统计1—10月。

四、世界银行贷款、英国赠款中国结核病控制项目

2004—2008年，荔波县实施世界银行贷款第十个卫生发展结核病控制项目，简称“卫X项目”。项目计划投资59.29万元。至2008年12月31日，项目投资累计18.85万元，完成计划31.79%。其中，世行贷款8.88万元，占计划23.72万元的37.44%；中央、省级配套资金到位5.1万元，占计划11.17万元的45.66%；国际赠款4.87万元，占计划9.96万元的48.90%。

项目实施后，以乡（镇）为单位，DOTS覆盖率为100%，接诊可疑肺结核病人1402例，初诊查痰1091例，发现病人427例。其中，初治涂阳208例、复治涂阳26例、涂阴193例。初诊病人就诊率835/10万，初诊病人查痰率78%，初治涂阳病人任务指标完成率102%。

2004—2008年肺结核病人发现及治疗情况统计表

表22－9 单位：人

年度	肺结核可疑者就诊人数	痰涂片检查人数	涂阳病人				初治涂阴病人数	
			新涂阳	全程治疗	复治	全程治疗	总数	全程治疗
2004	195	156	46	32	8	3	35	31
2005	221	177	47	43	7	5	30	23
2006	256	202	28	26	2	1	42	26
2007	384	281	41	27	4	2	44	34
2008	346	275	46	28	5	4	42	30

专记：

国家卫生县城创建

在1983年元旦、春节、“五一”期间，荔波县结合全国第二个文明礼貌月活动，组织开展以治脏为重点内容的卫生突击活动，清理垃圾、废料、污物200多吨，治理多处死角死面，疏通阴沟、阳沟共500多米，填平坑洼20多处；对办公区域、生活区域及室内外卫生、厕所等进行卫生检查。9月，县政府办公室下发《关于转发县爱卫会、安委会〈关于在我县城乡积极开展爱国卫生大扫除活动的意见〉的通知》，开展大扫除活动。1984年5月，成立环境卫生管理站，有管理人员2人、工人16人，负责城镇街道卫生清扫。在各街道设果皮箱和垃圾池，配备垃圾车2辆。同时，贯彻执行《贵州省环境卫生管理条例》《黔南州县以上卫生达标竞赛方案》和县政府下发的《加强城镇清洁卫生管理的暂行办法》《关于在城镇建立卫生制度的通知》《关于加强城镇清洁卫生管理，治理“三废”，维护交通秩序，改变县城脏乱差状况的通知》，各单位制定卫生公约，街道设卫生监督员，制定“门前三包”（包卫生、包绿化、包秩序）管理办法，县城分为4个片区，每片区设1个卫生小组，除督促片区内进行经常性卫生扫除外，片区之间每月进行交叉检查1次。10月，县政府发布公告，要求认真贯彻城镇卫生清洁管理制度，对侵占公共用地进行清理。1985年2月，在全县机关、事业单位和工矿企业中开展卫生竞赛活动。全年接受州环境卫生检查2次，每次检查30个单位。在第二次检查中，荔波县居全州第四名。

1986年3月，根据国务院办公厅转发城乡建设环境保护部、中央爱国卫生运动委员会《关于处理城市垃圾改善环境卫生面貌的报告》，对县城区生活的垃圾进行彻底清理，在全县机关、企事业单位中开展卫生定期大检查。在3月、10月进行的两次卫生大检查中，第一次检查单位达标12个，第二次检查达标单位28个。1987年，城区和甲良乡在全州卫生竞赛中获一等奖。1988年9月，州环境卫生检查小组对荔波县城区进行卫生考核，经检查考核，荔波县与瓮安县并列全州第一名。

1989年，全县机关、企事业单位开展一日一小扫、周末大扫除等卫生活动，治理脏乱差。7月，开展治理城镇环境卫生专项行动。10月，州爱卫会对机关单位、食品卫生、公共场所、街道消灭鼠害进行目标考核，全县达标单位23个。1994年，组织开展6次大规模的卫生大扫除。1995年，对县爱卫会成员单位进行具体分工，明确部门的责任。1996年，县政府召开3次专题会议，研究部署创“省级卫生县城”工作。采取印发宣传资料，有线电视每晚播放宣传标语，组建群众卫生监督队伍，举办“我为创建卫生县城做贡献”签名仪式等方式，开展创“省级卫生县城”活动。1997年，经省爱卫会组织“省级卫生县城”检查，通过验收。12月27日，在“省级卫生县城”命名表彰大会上，荔波县获“省级卫生县城”称号。

1998年，县爱卫会制定并实施《荔波县创建国家卫生县城规划（1998—2003年）》，巩固和提高省级卫生县城成果，开展创建“国家卫生县城”活动。1998—2001年，投入资金总计21563.68万元，用于县城基础设施和环卫设施建设，县城的道路硬化率达100%，绿化覆盖率36.8%，绿地总面积12.49万平方米，人均绿地面积6.38平方米。

2002年3月，成立以县委书记为组长的创建“国家卫生县城”工作领导小组，下设办公室，分管副县长任办公室主任，从卫生、城建、工商、教育、环保、玉屏镇政府等部门抽调7名工作人员专职开展工作。年内，县委、县政府发出《关于开展创建“国家卫生县城”活动的决定》《关于创建卫生村镇的决定》《荔波县关于整顿城镇交通秩序的通告》等文件；县政府与17个乡（镇）、县直103个单位签订《创建国家卫生县城目标管理责任书》；玉屏镇政府、各机关单位成立相应的工作领导小组，制定卫生制度或卫生公约；在县直机关开展卫生评比活动，实行“红黄绿牌制度”，对不达标单位进行全县通报批评和电视通报；建立卫生监督岗，聘请20名以离退休老干部为主的群众卫生监督队；玉屏镇与临街房主签订“门前三包”责任书，凡是评为红牌的予以批评或电视通报；县城内的4个居委会在住户中开展“卫生户”评比活动，并将评比结果张榜公布。9月10日，在县人民大会场召开创建“国家卫生县城”“卫生镇、村万人动员大会”，会后进行创建“国家卫生县城”游行和万人签名活动；向群众分发《致县城居民的一封信》《荔波县城七不行为》等宣传资料1万份。玉屏镇在开展创建“国家卫生县城”的同时，开展创建“省级卫生村寨”活动，到2004年4月，全镇有板旺、和平、建设、板吉、拉鱼5个村通过省爱卫会检查验收，获得“省级卫生村寨”称号。

2004年8月，荔波县“国家卫生县城”创建工作经省、州评审团专家评审，通过验收，并由省爱卫会向国家爱卫会申报国家级卫生县城。12月，国家爱卫会组织专家对荔波县创建“国家卫生县城”进行评审，获“国家卫生县城”称号。

2005年，为巩固“国家卫生县城”成果，成立以县委书记为组长的巩固“国家卫生县城”创建成果领导小组，下发《关于进一步加强爱国卫生工作，巩固“国家卫生县城”创建成果的通知》，提出爱卫工作要“在巩固中发展、在创新中提高、在提高中延伸”的工作思路，要求把巩固工作与“整脏治乱”工作相结合，大力开展健康教育工作，建立健全健康教育工作网络，全县中小学校健康教育开课率保持100%，行政、企事业单位职工健康教育普及率达95%以上，各级医疗部门开展多种形式健康教育宣传活动。11月9日，国家爱卫会委托省爱卫会授予荔波县“国家卫生县城”称号，授牌仪式在县城举行。2006年，县爱卫办结合“整脏治乱”专项行动，坚持每周两次的卫生督查制度，对不达标的单位下发整改通知书及电视通报；在全国“爱国卫生月”（4月）、节假日前组织各单位开展爱国卫生运动。是年，县爱卫办开展卫生督查96次，下发整改通知书79份；接待参观、学习的省内外县（市）11批（次）共82人次。

2007年，县委、县政府以申报世界自然遗产地和筹备贵州省第二届旅游产业发展大会为契机，提出“整脏治乱”与巩固“国家卫生县城”相结合，开展环境整治，加强环卫基础设施建设。全年清除违章建筑36处，拆除占道经营、乱搭乱建38家，清洗和覆盖乱贴乱画280处。12月，通过省级专家组“国家卫生县城”复查验收。

2008年，在全县推进、巩固“国家卫生县城”工作和“整脏治乱”专项行动中，县委下发《关于进一步加强“整脏治乱”城乡清洁工程建设工作的决定》，实行缴纳风险抵押金制度，严格执行督查制度和季度考核制度，即每周开展卫生督查2次，每季度对113个机关单位、17个乡（镇）进行巩固“国家卫生县城”“整脏治乱”考核评比。全年下发《限期整改通知书》63份、《扣罚责任风险抵押金通知书》85份，在县有线电视台进行电视通报35次。是年12月13—14日，国家爱卫会委托省爱卫会组织专家组对荔波县“国家卫生县城”进行复查验收，再次通过验收。

第二章　体　育

第一节　场地设施

1978年，县城有可容纳观众1050人的水泥地灯光篮球场1个，茂兰区建有水泥地篮球场1个。1982年，甲良文化站建水泥地篮球场1个。

1985年7月，在老杨家桥牌坊处修建长50米、宽25米、深水区1.8米、浅水区1.4米的室外游泳池，占地960平方米，有观众席位2000个，设有更衣室2间及器材储藏室。

1986年，朝阳区建朝阳体育场，设田径场、篮球场。朝阳、甲良、玉屏、茂兰区中学都建有水泥篮球场，并配备单杠、双杠、秋千、铁管、爬竿等体育器材，全县24个乡有水泥或简易篮球场。

1987年，在县城建标准门球场2个，可承接州级门球比赛。

至1990年，全县有篮球场58个、灯光球场7个、排球场3个、足球场1个。小运动场2个、游泳池1个、门球场2个。

2002年，县城建设第一条全民健身路径工程，有健身器材15件，分别安装于樟江园广场和荔波民族中学。

2005年，洞塘乡懂朋村投资3万元，实施全县第一个村级农民体育健身工程。

是年，开展全国第五次体育场地普查，全县有体育场地316个，标准体育场地164个（标准足球场3个、小运动场7个、篮球场152个、排球场1个、门球场1个），非标准体育场地152个，体育场地面积17.36万平方米。

2007年，在县城建设第二条全民健身路径工程，在樟江大桥旁安装健身器材15件。2008年，建成水埔村、水维村、平岩村、板寨村等全县第二批农民体育健身工程11个。

第二节　群众体育

一、城镇体育活动

1978年后，城镇体育活动除开展早锻炼、工间操外，还举办各种运动会，组队参加省、州及邻县举办的各种比赛、联谊体育活动等。

1980年，县体委举办太极拳和广播操骨干培训班2期，推广太极拳、广播体操运动。此后，广大群众参加长跑锻炼、打太极拳、做广播体操人数不断增加。

1981—1984年，县体育部门在元旦、春节等节日期间，组织群众性体育活动，如老年人中长跑比赛、太极拳表演赛等。1984年，县工会开办工人俱乐部，设康乐球、象棋、围棋、乒乓球，供群众娱乐、锻炼。

1986—1987年，先后举办两次全县职工游泳比赛。

1987年，成立县老年人体育协会。

1988年“五一”劳动节，县总工会主办荔波县职工迪斯科、健美操表演赛。

1990年6—9月，为迎接亚洲运动会在中国举行，县体委、总工会联合开展职工体育达标竞赛、职工工间操、职工篮球赛、普及迪斯科等活动，各机关单位、学校、企业职工积极参与。

20世纪90年代以后，各行业、系统的各种职工体育赛事增多。一些单位、系统在节假日开展各类职工体育活动。

1991—2008年城镇体育活动情况统计表

表22－10

年度	比赛项目	备注
1991	庆元旦系列文体活动	游泳、拔河、象棋、万人长跑等
1992	首届周末篮球赛	
1993	荔波县少年儿童运动会	共12支参赛队
1994	全县陀螺赛	
1995	儿童游泳比赛	
1996	教育系统举办第一届教职工运动会	之后每两年举办一次
1997	在荔波举办全州税务系统职工篮球赛	
1998	在荔波举办全省建设系统“建设杯”职工篮球赛黔南分赛	
2000	在县城举办“跨世纪千人迎春越野跑”活动	
	组队参加全州第三届钓鱼比赛	
2001	全县“移动杯”职工篮球赛	
	“云雾山杯”男子篮球赛	
2002	全县“农行杯”足球赛	
2003	迎新年长跑活动	
	保护樟江河万人长跑活动	
	全县“农行杯”足球赛	
	全县首届“信合杯”男子篮球赛	
	全县象棋、围棋赛	
2004	全县“信合杯”足球赛	
	全县第二届“信合杯”男子篮球赛	
2005	全县第三届“信合杯”男子篮球赛	
	全县第一届“丽吉杯”足球赛	
	全县“党员先锋杯”篮球赛	

续表22-10

年度	比赛项目	备注
2006	梅花节邀请聂卫平与县内围棋手对弈活动	
	第四届“信合杯”篮球赛	
	第二届“丽吉杯”足球赛	
	首届“中国移动杯”男子篮球赛	
	全县“计生杯”篮球赛	
	老年代表队参加全州第三届老年人运动会	参加象棋、门球、乒乓球、健身球操、太极拳、剑组5个项目比赛
2007	梅花节邀请聂卫平与县内围棋手对弈活动	
2008	全县首届政法系统体育运动会	篮球、象棋、围棋3项比赛
	妇联、文体广电局联合举办庆“三八”齐心协力活动	37支队伍参赛
	全县庆“五一”拔河比赛	36支队伍参赛
	县太极拳、剑协会参加在贵阳市举行的贵州省第七届太极拳健身展示会	获32式拳、剑组一等奖

二、乡村体育活动

1978年以后，农村广大群众的生活水平不断提高，农民群众体育健身活动日趋活跃，区、乡举办各种运动会，比赛项目有篮球、象棋、乒乓球、拔河、登山等。播尧乡在民族节日开展民族传统武术、耍狮、耍龙表演等。朝阳区乡乡有球队、有场地、有活动，每年举办一次全区群众性体育比赛。

1982年6月，县举办农民篮球运动会，拉扶村、瑶山、瑶麓、城关镇、方村等共10支代表队参赛。是年8月，县体委、民委、武装部结合民兵训练，联合举办首届农村各族青年民兵运动会，甲良、茂兰、朝阳、城关4个区的112名男、女青年和基干民兵参加篮球、登山、游泳、射击、投弹、环城跑6个项目比赛。

1983年春节，瑶麓女子篮球队应邀参加县机关篮球赛。是年8月，举办第二届青年民兵运动会。1985—1986年，全县举办农民体育比赛13次。

1986年，朝阳乡朝阳体育场每天有青少年、老年人到体育场进行篮球、打拳、体操等体育锻炼。朝阳乡拉扶村组织有男、女篮球队，在节假日期间到各区、乡或县城参加篮球比赛。1986年国庆节，朝阳乡拉扶村成立农民体育协会，是全州成立较早的农民体育协会，拉扶村的体育活动曾在中央电视台体育新闻节目播出。

1988年4月，在朝阳田径场举办全县首届农民田径运动会。

2008年，玉屏镇板旺村农民运动队代表荔波县参加在贵定举行的黔南州第二届农村运动会，参加项目有运粮接力（4×50米、4×100米）、颗粒归仓、滚轮胎等。

第三节　学校体育

1978年后，县内各学校正常开展体育课教学，抓好体育课、课间操、课外活动。

从1979年起，施行国家体委颁布的《国家体育锻炼标准》，实行达标制，县、区、公社各中小学开展达标教学活动。是年7月，举办全县少年体育运动会，各学校组织代表队参赛。

1981年，县民族中学学生达标23人、甲良中学学生达标4人。

1982年、1983年“六一”儿童节，先后举办两次全县少年田径运动会，各中小学选拔优秀田径运动员参加比赛。1983年，全县学生体育达标78人。

1984年，县内中小学应配备专职体育教师28人，实际配备2人。

1981—1987年，县体委和教育局联合举办各类少年体育运动会13次。

1990年，全县学校有体育教师28人，其中专职9人、兼职19人。全县小学生体育达标649人、中学生体育达标314人。是年，县教育系统举办运动会6次，其中县级3次、乡（镇）级3次，参加的中小学生2860人。

每年的秋季，各中小学都举行秋季田径运动会，在荔波民中和二中等学校还成立田径运动训练队，每天下午举行训练并组队参加各类田径比赛，取得多项优异成绩。

2007年8月，黔南州小学生传统体育项目田径运动会在荔波二小举行，比赛设短跑、长跑、跳远等大项17个、小项38个，全州12个县（市）组队参加，荔波县获团体总分第一名。是月，荔波民族中学足球队参加贵州省第一届示范性普通高中足球赛。

第四节　民族民间传统体育项目

境内民族民间体育活动历史悠久，主要项目有打陀螺、斗牛、武术、踢毽子、打猎操、耍狮、舞龙、踩高跷、木棍舞、游泳、赛马、划龙舟、射箭、荡秋千、扳手劲、跷跷板、跳绳、拔河等，这些都是农村各族青少年喜爱的传统项目。这些项目不受时间、场地的限制，规模可大可小，人数多少不限，简便易行，小型多样。

一、打陀螺

县内各族少年常以打陀螺比赛为娱乐项目，以旋转时间长者为胜。在瑶山，这项活动扩展到青年人。县内在“四月八”或春节举行打陀螺比赛。打陀螺为县内在外影响最大的民族民间传统体育项目。2004年11月，省体育局、省民委、省教育厅将瑶山乡民族中学定为陀螺训练基地并举行挂牌仪式。

荔波瑶族传统体育项目——打陀螺运动

2005年11月，县陀螺队参加在贵州民族学院举行的全省少数民族传统体育竞赛项目比赛，夺得男子团体第一名，男子单打第一名、第四名、第五名，女子团体第四名、女子单打第六名。是年12月21日，代表贵州省参加在云南举行的“云景村派杯”全国少数民族传统体育项目打陀螺邀请赛，夺得男子团体第三名。

2006年1月，荔波县举办黔桂两省（区）打陀螺邀请赛，县陀螺队夺得男子团体第一名，男子单打第一、第二名，女子团体第二名、女子单打第三名。12月，代表贵州省参加在云南景谷举行的景谷国际陀螺节打陀螺邀请赛，夺得男子团体第三名、混双第三名、男子单打第五名。

1986—2007年，县陀螺队代表黔南州参加全省第一届、第二届、第四届、第五届、第六届少数民族运动会，获男子团体第一名5次及男子单打第一名3次、第二名2次、第三名1次，获女子团体第一名3次、第二名1次、第四名1次及女子单打第一名1次、第二名1次；代表贵州省参加全国第五、第六、第七、第八届少数民族运动会，获男子团体第一名（第八届）、第三名（第七届）、第五名（第六届）、第六名（第五届）各1次及男子单打第三名1次（第七届），获女子团体第四名（第五届）、女子单打第五名（第八届）各1次。

2008年11月，县陀螺队代表贵州省参加在云南景谷举行的全国打陀螺邀请赛，夺得男子团体第三名、女子团体第五名、女子单打第三名。

二、划龙舟

划龙舟是县内乡村群众在端午节开展的活动。每年端午节，制作青、黄两只龙船进行比赛。每只龙船13人，由1人掌舵。项目有400米、800米往返。1980年恢复龙舟竞赛活动。自1987年举办第一届龙舟赛以后，每年举办一次。1990年，参赛队达37个518人，两岸观众达万人。1996年8月，组织龙舟队参加黔南建州40周年庆典，获龙舟竞赛第一名。2002年6月，举办第十五届龙舟赛，机关组有参赛队18支，农村组有参赛队26支。2007年6月，举办庆“申遗”迎旅发大会荔波县“6·10”活动周暨第二十届“信合杯”少数民族龙舟赛，机关组队15支、农村组队28支参加比赛。至2008年，已连续举办21届龙舟赛。

三、踢毽子

在农村各族青少年中普遍开展。毽子用公鸡毛和铜钱缝制，用脚踢或手打，可双人连踢，也可单人独踢，获得次数多者为胜。无比赛，只在民间青少年中开展娱乐健身。

四、武术

境内驾欧、播尧一带有习武的习惯，每年春节当地都开展表演活动。

五、舞龙耍狮

播尧、驾欧及玉屏镇组建有青年龙狮队，在春节表演，以示贺年。

六、踩高跷

踩高跷是农村青少年喜欢的一项活动。农村青少年在闲时以此娱乐、比赛。高跷用2.5米左右的木棍2根，各在下端离地20～40厘米处装上10厘米长的横木，比赛时手扶木棍，脚踩在横木上行走。横木装得离地越高，走时难度越大，走得快的取胜。

七、赛马

是县内各族人民喜爱的体育活动。每到春节，由县组织在时来坝或河沙坝进行赛马。驾欧、觉巩、播尧等地亦于春节期间组织赛马活动。1985年县政府拨款整修河沙坝作为赛马场。1986年，荔波骑手应邀参加三都县赛马比赛，获第二名。

第五节 体育比赛 人才培养

一、体育比赛

（一）游泳

1981年7月，县少年儿童游泳代表队参加在罗甸举行的全州少年儿童游泳运动会，队员获5项第一名、5项第二名。

1982年，在全州进行省第五届运动会运动员选拔赛上，荔波游泳队获6项第一名。在省第五届运动会上，荔波游泳运动员获第五名、第六名各1项。

1984—1985年，在全州少年儿童游泳选拔赛上，荔波游泳队获团体第一名和13项个人单项第一名；在全州第二届工人运动会上获2项第一名；在全省少年儿童游泳比赛中，获2项第二名、1项第三名、2项第四名；在全省第二届工人运动会上，获1项第四名、1项第六名。

1988—1989年，在全省游泳比赛中，获个人全能第一名、1项第二名、1项第四名。

1991年，荔波运动员杜凯参加全省少年组游泳比赛，获50米自由泳金牌，并打破2项省纪录3次。

1993年7月，在荔波举行全省少年游泳赛，荔波队获团体第二名。

2006年7月，县内残疾人覃建红代表贵州省参加在哈尔滨举行的全国第四届特殊奥林匹克运动会，夺得50米蛙泳金牌、100米蛙泳铜牌。

（二）田径

1982—1986年，荔波田径运动员在州级比赛中获4项第一名、4项第二名、1项第六名；在省级比赛中获3项第一名、1项第三名，打破1项省纪录；在全国协作区田径比赛上获1项第五名。

1989年，在全省少年田径比赛中，获全能第三名和1项第三名。

1990年3月，在黔南州中学生田径运动会上，荔波县代表队获1项第一名、1项第二名。是年，组织代表队参加在上海举行的“长江杯”全国传统体校田径比赛，获1项第六名。

1994年、2000年、2006年，参加三次全州传统体育项目田径运动会。

2007年8月，黔南州小学生传统体育项目田径运动会在荔波举行，荔波县代表队获团体第一名。

（三）球类

1986年，参加州财政、邮电、供销、税务系统篮球赛，荔波县邮政局代表队获第一名、税务代表队获第二名。

从1987年起，贵州、广西两省（区）河池、环江、天峨、南丹、三都、荔波、平塘、都匀、独山9个县（市）开展体育运动联赛，每年春、秋两季各举办门球联赛一次，轮流在9个县（市）举行。

1988年10月，参加在广西环江举行的两省（区）五县联防第二届“团结杯”篮球赛，荔波县代表队获男子组第二名、女子组第三名。

1989年10月，县篮球队参加在河池地区举办的黔南、河池两州（地）“振兴经济协作杯”篮球友谊赛。

1990年2月，县篮球队参加在独山举行的全州“税务杯”篮球运动会，获冠军。

1992年、1995年，先后组队参加在都匀市举行的“三好杯”篮球赛和足球赛。

1996年，县老年门球队参加黔桂两地10个县（市）老年门球赛，获第二名；参加全州老年门球选拔赛，获第五名。

2006年，举办黔桂两省（区）六县“友谊杯”门球邀请赛，获第二名；县男子篮球队参加三都“团结杯”篮球邀请赛及独山“东峰杯”篮球邀请赛，在“东峰杯”篮球邀请赛中获第二名。

（四）其他

1981—1984年，先后组队参加黔南州象棋、围棋比赛，获两项第六名；参加黔南州航模比赛，获团体第一名、两项第一名并创新纪录1项。

1986年11月，贵州、广西两省（区）五县象棋比赛在南丹举行，获团体第三名、1项第二名。

1989年11月，县老年人体育协会组队参加州老年人体育协会举办的中国象棋比赛。

1991年，县业余体校10名运动员参加国家级别比赛，获1项第六名；参加省级比赛，获3枚金牌、3项第二名、4项第三名、2项全能第四名。

1992年，全县有17名运动员参加省第八届运动会，分别获金牌1枚、银牌3枚、铜牌4枚。

2008年，荔波拳击运动员覃荣岑成为州拳击队集训队员，参加省2008年度拳击锦标赛，夺得48公斤级冠军。

二、人才培养

1978年以后，县内主要通过办少年体育学校、项目集训等方式培养体育运动员。1979年，县体委在荔波民族中学开办少体校篮球训练班，训练29人。1980年，少体校开展篮球、游泳两个项目训练，训练学生58人。

1982年，荔波县列为全省游泳项目布局点，重点开展游泳培训。1982—1985年，少体校培训游泳运动员111人。

1986年，县体委选送到镇远和州体委集训运动员9人，到广西百色地区集训8人。至1987年，向各类体育学校输送合格学生共10人，为黔南州输送航模运动员2人。

1988年，选送游泳运动员到省游泳队训练2人，县内培训游泳运动员10人、田径运动员6人。

1989年暑假期间，县体委举办5～11岁少年儿童游泳训练班2期，参加训练104人，从中选拔12人进行长期训练。

1990年10月，成立荔波县少年儿童业余体育运动学校，开设游泳、短跑、中长跑、投掷、女子篮球、象棋、围棋7个班，有正式学员22人、预备学员22人，短期集训20人。是年，县体委确定城关一小、城关二小、朝阳小学为传统体育学校，项目为游泳、田径，每所学校组建游泳队、田径队，开展长期训练。荔波民中为省定传统体育项目学校，有游泳、田径运动员48人。全县向各类业余体校输送学生33人。

1991—1997年，向黔南州输送运动员31人。其中，游泳12人、拳击9人、乒乓球10人。

第二十三篇
社会生活

1978年中共十一届三中全会以后，随着荔波县经济社会的不断发展，老百姓社会生活发生了翻天覆地的变化。荔波县是农业县，又是国家级贫困县，城镇居民、农村农民经济收入低，增长缓慢。县委、县政府采取一系列增产增收举措，逐步改善城乡人民的收入和生活条件。2008年全县农村人均纯收入达到2618.22元，人均生活消费支出达到2385.04元，城乡居民的消费结构支出及消费水平逐渐发生变化，在解决温饱的基础上，向精神文化和时尚消费品转变，老百姓的衣食住行发生了极大的变化。同时，全县精神文明建设活动开展，评比出一大批县级、州级文明单位、文明乡（镇）、文明示范窗口、精神文明先进工作者、文明公民等。特别是荔波创建国家卫生县城以来，全县社会新风、好人好事不断涌现。

第一章 城乡居民收入

第一节 城镇居民收入

1978年，城镇居民家庭收入以工资为主，当时全县行政、企业、事业等单位职工人均年工资520元。20世纪80年代后，随着改革开放不断深入，市场逐渐放开，部分居民从事商业经营，城镇居民收入渠道呈现多元化，收入构成相应发生变化，城镇居民家庭收入中，除工资性收入外，经营性收入、财产性收入等占一定比例，但仍以工资性收入为主。随着国家工资制度改革，经过十多次工资调整和晋升，职工工资收入逐步增长，到2008年，县内职工人均年工资19962元。

第二节 农民收入

荔波县系农业县，同时又是国家级贫困县，受生产条件制约，劳动方式相对滞后，生产力水平低，农民收入水平不高，增长缓慢。

改革开放后，县委、县政府采取一系列增产增收举措，逐步改善农民收入状况和生活条件。自农村实行家庭联产承包责任制后，提高了农民的生产积极性，生产力水平逐渐提高。1985年后，逐步调整农业产业结构，推广杂交稻良种、科学种田、多种经营，拓宽农村商品生产空间，发展第三产业，农民收入逐渐增加。

20世纪90年代以后，针对农民负担过重问题，县委、县政府出台《关于减轻农民负担的实施意见》，提出15条减轻农民负担的具体规定，涉及农村经济、农民生活的各个方面。特别是实施“八七”扶贫攻坚及对极贫村的重点扶贫开发，贫困人口先后越过温饱线，部分贫困家庭脱贫致富。但瑶山地区农民收入水平仍低于全县平均水平。

在稳定以家庭承包经营为基础、统分结合的双层经营体制下，将剩余农村劳动力逐步有序地向非农产业转移和向外输出劳务，以增加农民收入，并实施农村贫困人口异地移民开发，建移民新村等。

20世纪90年代末，为实现主要农产品总量需求平衡和农民收入稳定增长，实施“三增”（粮食增产、农民增收、发展后劲增强）、“两降”（降低人口自然增长率、降低贫困人口数）计划，采取以工代赈、移民项目及产业结构调整等措施，助农增产增收，农户种植的反季节蔬菜、酸梅、麻竹、樟江蜜柚、板栗、茶叶等生产项目初步产生效益，农业产业化经营初具规模，农民收入增加。

2005年后，全县取消农业税，减轻农户负担。2006—2008年，农村发展劳务经济，引导农民进入城镇，从事餐饮、商贸、旅游等第三产业。同时，在已脱贫地区加大产业结构调整，实行“四统三分”（统一技术、统一供种苗、统一管理水平、统一加工；分户种植、分户经营、分户加工）管理，形成“工厂+基地+农户”模式，农民增收渠道逐步多元化。

1978—2008年全县农村人均纯收入和支出统计表

表23－1 单位：元

年度	人均纯收入	人均生活消费支出	人均食品消费支出
1978	99.30	90.70	72.20
1979	118.09	98.60	82.40
1980	145.56	131.65	93.35
1981	186.12	158.14	102.44
1982	251.76	203.81	140.10
1983	237.38	190.76	138.31
1984	265.77	226.99	163.81
1985	247.00	242.28	171.86
1986	257.30	245.27	175.16
1987	298.65	261.05	187.41
1988	366.46	290.37	202.55
1989	371.00	315.50	215.50
1990	415.31	351.07	229.47
1991	376.82	326.58	205.09
1992	390.27	363.36	238.72
1993	701.00	691.30	495.50
1994	697.89	684.03	482.16
1995	983.14	935.70	666.97
1996	1086.00	1037.12	718.79
1997	1229.92	1200.24	806.15
1998	1254.23	1083.67	730.25
1999	1152.13	1132.80	742.52
2000	1196.63	987.49	591.60
2001	1199.96	941.50	602.12
2002	1175.71	1001.35	608.73
2003	1283.61	1036.49	644.71
2004	1494.55	1264.55	675.31
2005	1654.70	1537.57	836.98
2006	1751.38	1778.98	847.38
2007	2158.78	1972.63	971.58
2008	2618.22	2385.04	1108.06

1978—2008年全县金融机构存款与城乡居民存款一览表

表23－2 单位：万元

年度	金融机构存款余额	城乡居民存款余额	年度	金融机构存款余额	城乡居民存款余额
1978	335	108	1994	11960	4357
1979	387	136	1995	13879	5721
1980	377	145	1996	13079	5094
1981	552	204	1997	16176	6365
1982	623	383	1998	20973	11669
1983	1122	372	1999	23112	12954
1984	1073	370	2000	29443	17682
1985	1238	511	2001	32780	20966
1986	1763	594	2002	38207	25223
1987	2269	931	2003	48508	30743
1988	2426	948	2004	59370	37499
1989	3168	891	2005	73611	45393
1990	3686	1147	2006	81089	54995
1991	4849	1552	2007	106275	66857
1992	6637	2307	2008	137305	79199
1993	6450	2396			

第三节　衣食住行及其他

1978年改革开放以后，城乡居民的消费结构支出及消费水平逐渐发生变化，在解决温饱的基础上，向精神文化和时尚消费品转变。

一、饮食

20世纪80年代初期到中期，居民购买食品凭票证供应，饮食支出在消费支出中占有较大比例，传统饮食结构为米、面为原料制成的简单食品。80年代末到90年代，随着物资供应的丰富及收入的提高，取消各种供应票证，城镇居民的饮食传统和饮食习惯逐渐发生变化，从“有什么吃什么”到“想吃什么就吃什么”、从“吃得饱”到“吃得好”转变，各种副食加工品、精加工食品等丰富了城镇居民的饮食生活，肉类、禽类、蛋类、水产类等成为居民平常消费品。

20世纪80年代，农户的一日三餐所需粮食大多能自给自足，在边远深山地区及瑶山区尚有欠缺。农户之间的消费水平差别不大，粮食、蔬菜等自产自食，食物品种较为单一，副食品消费不多，逢节庆或逢婚丧嫁娶才杀猪宰羊款待亲朋，平日则半月以上消费一次肉食。随着农村经济体制改革的不断深入，农民收入水平的逐渐提高，农村居民的消费结构逐渐产生变化。进入20世纪90年代，农户餐桌上的禽蛋鱼肉逐步增加，同时消费观念和生活方式发生转变，不再局限自产自食的食物品种，常利用赶场天等时间到市场购买副食品丰富餐桌。21世纪后，部分农户走上富裕路，其饮食结构和习惯与城镇居民家庭基本相同。饮食开支占人均总支出的比例由1978年的78.12%下降到2008年的46.46%。但全县农村整体发展不平衡，尚有部分村民刚刚越过温饱线，存在返贫可能性的部分群体。

二、衣服

20世纪80年代初期，服装式样单调，颜色以灰、蓝、白、黑为主。80年代中后期，随着改革开放的不断深入，外地时尚服饰逐渐在境内流行，服装式样、品种、色彩逐渐丰富，毛料及各种时尚服装逐步成为居民衣着追求。20世纪90年代到2008年，居民衣着服饰讲究穿出个性、面料优质、做工考究的服装成为衣着首选，皮革服饰、羽绒服饰进入千家万户，衣着支出相应提高，尤其是年轻人的衣着，追求品牌，追赶时尚潮流。

在农村各少数民族着装长期以本民族传统服装为主。改革开放后，随着村民与外界交往的日益频繁，农村青年外出打工接受新观念，城乡物资流通迅速，农村居民服饰向多样化转变。到2008年，除老年人和一些较为边远贫困山区村民着传统服装外，一般农村居民穿着流行服装。

三、居住

在20世纪80年代初，县城居民多住木质结构瓦房。随着市场的逐渐放开，人们收入有所提高，一些率先富裕起来的城镇居民开始在老屋的基础上翻盖砖混结构新房，二三层、四五层不等。部分单位建职工宿舍，以福利形式分给职工。20世纪90年代初期，机关单位、企业、事业单位实行职工集资建房，进行住房制度改革后，住房逐渐货币化、商品化，城镇居民的居住条件得到较大改善，不仅房屋质量提高，面积也大幅增加。进入21世纪后，商品房消费成为住房的主要渠道，消费支出比例增大，许多城镇居民购房者为获得一套理想的商品房住宅，花掉所有积蓄或者贷款购买。部分城镇居民多次改造装修原有住房，室内装饰讲究时尚舒适。高层建筑增多，楼层由20世纪80年代的三四层、90年代的七八层，到21世纪的安装有电梯的十几层高楼。

20世纪80年代，农村居民大多居住木板草房、土坯房，砖木结构的平房极少。到90年代中后期，一些先富裕起来的农户开始翻建住房，或在原址建砖木结构住房。平房居多，亦有二三层楼房。21世纪初，家庭住宅条件改善的农村居民房子越建越好，按照城镇居民住房装修装饰，贴墙瓷砖、铺瓷砖地板。随着县内旅游业的发展，旅游区农户将自家住宅改建成具有经商功能的商铺，开旅社、饭店，办起“农家乐”。但在边远山区，仍有部分简陋且不再适宜居住的危房需要改造。

四、出行

在20世纪80年代，人们的出行工具多为自行车，县城内无公共交通设施。至20世纪90年代中期，拥有摩托车的居民家庭逐渐增多，县城内开始有服务营运的人力、电动三轮车，改变了人们的出行方式。21世纪后，部分富裕家庭购置家庭轿车，县城有出租车。此外，随着高速公路、航空、铁路的开通和改善，出行更加快捷方便，外出旅游成为家庭消费支出的一项内容。

荔波系山区，1978年时农民的出行十分不便，出行大多靠步行或赶马车等。20世纪80年代后，道路等基础设施不断修建，部分农户购置摩托车。90年代后期至21世纪初，一些农户开始购置小货车从事经营活动，城乡汽车客运业逐渐发展，农民到县城或赶集交易，大多乘坐客运汽车。

五、其他消费

通信方面，20世纪80年代，居民通信以信件为主，急事、要事通过邮电局电报、电话联系。至20世纪90年代，部分城镇居民家庭安装固定电话，电话费成为消费支出的一个部分。20世纪90年代中期以后，移动电话进入居民生活并逐渐普及，手机成为城镇居民常用、不可或缺的通信工具。

家用电器消费方面，20世纪80年代，部分居民家庭拥有洗衣机、收录机、电冰箱、电视机。到90年代，电冰箱、电视机、全自动洗衣机等家用电器成为城镇居民家庭的必备生活用品。21世纪后，空调、电热水器、计算机等高档耐用消费品在城镇居民中普及。

20世纪90年代后期以后，部分村民开始拥有收音机、电视机等家用电器，固定电话也逐步进入农民家庭。到2008年，部分农民拥有手机，移动电话消费成为村民的日常支出，条件较好的农民家庭拥有的耐用消费品与城镇居民已基本相同。同时，农村居民在文化、卫生、教育方面的消费逐年上升。

第二章　精神文明建设活动

第一节　创建文明单位

1996年，全县开展创建文明单位、乡（镇）窗口活动，每两年进行一次检查评比，通过民意调查、测评打分、实际效果等综合评比，评出县级、州级文明单位、文明乡（镇）、文明示范窗口、精神文明先进工作者、文明公民等，由县委、县政府和州文明办予以命名表彰。1998—1999年，开展创建文明单位、文明行业和争做文明公民活动。2003—2005年，荔波县被省文明委评为全省创建文明县城工作先进县。至2008年，全县共评选出州级文明单位12个、州级文明乡（镇）7个、州级文明示范窗口3个。

第二节　创建文明村寨和“十星级”文明户

从1995年起，全县开展文明村寨和“十星级”（爱国星、教育星、科技星、法制星、和睦星、婚育星、新风星、勤俭星、公德星、环卫星）文明户创建活动。

文明村寨创建以道路硬化、饮水设施、建池改厕、村文化活动室建设等农村基础设施建设为主，改善群众生产生活条件，引导和组织农民群众在房前屋后栽花种树，绿化、美化、香化、亮化家园。活动以对各农户房前屋后和相应公共场所卫生状况进行评比亮分方式，对落后的农户加强卫生督促检查。在“十星级文明户”创评活动中，制定村规民约，加强农民群众思想道德建设，引导农民群众革除陋习、破除迷信、移风易俗，发扬孝敬老人、与人为善等传统美德，组织群众开展拔河、象棋、篮球、唱歌等文体活动。通过文明村寨创建活动，全县18个示范点实现道路硬化，群众全部用上自来水，电视普及率达80%以上，农户改厕改灶70%以上；村级图书阅览室、宣传栏、文体活动场地等基础设施完善，农民群众科技意识、法律意识和市场经济意识明显提高，农户、村道清洁卫生，物放有序，村容寨貌得到改善。

1995—2003年，先后有水尧乡水捞村（1995年）、佳荣镇大土村（1997年12月）、水尧乡瑶族新村（1999年）、佳荣镇甲料村（2000—2001）、朝阳镇朝阳村（2002—2003）等5个村获州级命名“文明村寨”称号。有4星级农户6510户、5星级农户5247户、6星级农户4422户、7星级农户3630户、8星级农户3241户、9星级农户2840户、10星级农户2429户，合计28319户。2004年，全县星级农户总数上升为34782户，创建文明新村20个、文明生态村20个。

2004—2006年，有玉屏镇板旺村（2004—2005）、朝阳镇八烂村（2004—2005）、茂兰镇尧朝村（2004—2005）、甲良镇洞庭村（2004—2005年）、玉屏镇水春村（2005—2006）5个村获州级命名“文明村寨”称号。

第三节 创建文明新村示范点

2003年，开展“四引”（引导农民勤劳致富奔小康，引导农民学习科技知识，引导农民开展文体活动，引导农民建设美化家园）工程文明新村创建活动，选定17个乡（镇）的18个村（组）实施“四引”工程。创建活动以提高农民素质、劳动致富奔小康和建设富裕、文明、民主的现代化新农村为指导思想，以经济建设为中心，以发展农村经济和农民致富为主要内容，做到物质文明和精神文明融为一体，相互促进，达到社会主义新农村建设的目标要求。为18个村（组）送文化、卫生、科技、法律“四下乡”活动，进行村寨道路硬化，修建沼气池，改圈改厕，建立图书室和体育场所，设立科普宣传栏，进行人畜饮水改良，绿化村寨，建立治安联防机制，开展“十星级”文明村寨创建等。至2005年，18个示范村（组）均达标合格。

第四节 社会新风

一、弘扬正气，见义勇为先进事迹

莫秀强是甲良镇派出所治安队员。1994年1月8日晚12时许，刚巡逻回家的莫秀强听到“有人抢劫……”的呼喊声，便立即赶到出事地点。看到三名歹徒在抢劫一名学生，他立马上前制止歹徒的不法行为，并抓住一名歹徒不放。歹徒挣脱逃跑，莫秀强一人在黑夜中奋力追赶，又将歹徒抓住。这时，另一名歹徒用刀向他猛砍过来，他头部受了重伤，血流不止，歹徒再次挣脱逃跑。此刻他忘记了个人的安危，咬紧牙关，忍着剧痛，猛追60多米后与歹徒在稻田搏斗，最后终于将歹徒制服擒住。另外2名歹徒见势不妙，仓皇逃跑。

蒙黔俊是荔波县民族中学初二（四）班学生，13岁，1993年9月11日，放学回家途经樟江河回龙角处，听到有人呼喊“救命”，随即看见河中有一女孩挣扎，他便马上划船去救。因船在急流中难行，他不顾汹涌的水势，弃船跳入水中，奋力游向落水女孩，将女孩救上岸。这时岸上的几个女孩说还有一名女孩在水中，蒙黔俊又迅速游向河中，反复潜入水里救人。后因另一女孩落水时间过长，救上岸已溺死。

1994年3月18日，县委、县政府发出《关于表彰见义勇为青年莫秀强、少年蒙黔俊的通报》，授予莫秀强“见义勇为青年”、蒙黔俊“见义勇为少年”称号，并号召全县人民、广大青少年向他们学习。

二、“感动中国”候选人张雁泉事迹

张雁泉是荔波县茂兰国家级自然保护区工作人员，因工作性质使他有机会深入到茂兰保护区的每一个角落，接触到很多贫困家庭，看到那些因贫困而读不起书的孩子，产生了帮助他们的念头，由于自己的能力有限，张雁泉就想到了网络。2004年，在各大网络社区里出现了名为“这个故事不外传”的帖子，用图片和文字把茂兰保护区里这些贫困的孩子介绍给大家，并在帖子的最后出现了“254135948”这个用于联系的QQ号。一传十，十传百，茂兰国家级自然保护区里有一群贫困孩子的故事被大家知晓，很多有爱心的网友都闻讯把这个QQ号加为好友，希望帮助这些孩子。

此后，张雁泉工作之余的时间都通过QQ与想要帮助贫困孩子的网友联系，有时候为了建立信任，介绍情况，得和网友聊上一个月才能实现捐助，长时间的QQ聊天，别人还以为他在网恋。通

过他牵线，辍学的孩子在好心人的帮助下重新回到课堂，好心人捐助的衣物被送到孩子们手上。很快，这些误会解除了，妻子承担家务支持他，而他所在的保护区管理局则拿出一间会议室给他存放捐助来的衣物。通过QQ网友的资助，茂兰保护区里因贫困辍学的孩子已经有238人重返课堂。有1.5万多名网友伸出援助之手，收到近70万元的钱物，张雁泉利用捐助的18500多册课本图书建起了12个图书室、2个环境教育中心，并使保护区内一位身患先天性淋巴肿瘤的小覃得到了救治。较早受到QQ网友资助的荔波县翁昂乡拉类村的何慧朗，考上了贵州大学，对于那些通过QQ资助她的叔叔、阿姨念念不忘。

2004—2007年，有越来越多的人知道了这个QQ号，并把它加为好友，把贫困学生的信息向外传递。为了便于在QQ上更清楚地传递贫困孩子的信息，他给每位需要帮助的孩子在电脑上建立了一个文件夹，除了孩子的一些基本情况外，还详细罗列了孩子家里的房屋、屋内陈设、家庭收入、开支情况等，并且还不断更新。受助学生每学期的成绩，获得的每个奖励，以及为每位受助孩子建立的“爱心存折”的每次支取，都被他用文字和图片的形式记录下来，再通过QQ传给捐助的网友。

2007年11月26日《贵州日报》对其事迹予以详细报道后，在社会上引起强烈反响，来自海内外的众多热心读者及网友纷纷将爱心投向大山里。同年12月14日，《贵州日报》将张雁泉作为贵州选区推荐的2007年度中央电视台评选的“感动中国”候选人。

人　　物

一、人物传

赵尔和（1916—2001）　1916年5月生，山西寿阳人。1937年1月参加革命工作，1939年4月加入中国共产党，小学文化。参加八路军，当战士，任班长、管理员。后任二野五兵团五十一师153团司务长、管理员。进军贵州后转业，任荔波县粮食局副局长、中共荔波县机关党总支书记等职。抗日战争中曾立团体二等功。离休后享受地级待遇。2001年2月4日在荔波逝世。

杜介厘（1916—2007）　1916年9月1日生，男，汉族，山东省郓城县人。1935年参加西北军，1939年参加八路军，1940年加入中国共产党。其间，先后任区队长、连长、军分区司令部侦察参谋、情报科长、独立团营长、师部军政科长。1941年进入抗日军政大学冀鲁豫分校军事队学习，1942年返回军分区继续参加抗战直到日军投降。在解放战争期间，先后参加淮海战役、渡江战役及解放大西南战役。

1950年2月3日，杜介厘率部队下地方工作和军大五分校人员共计17人到达荔波县城。2月4日，荔波县人民政府宣布成立，杜介厘奉命任县长后，张贴荔波县人民政府成立的布告。同时，根据荔波县人民政府各区的地理位置、社会和干部情况等，开展一系列工作。为应付突然事变的发生，决定以第4兵团过境留下的十多人为基础，从荔波游击队和县公安局中抽调部分人员，组建50多人的县大队。

1950年4月23日、24日，股匪袭扰周覃和基长区狮山乡等地，杀死农民余和贵等人，杜介厘率领政府工作人员，冒雨奔袭周覃塘党寨韦光辉和方村区杨鸣皋匪部，毙匪分队长杨龙声于交进河边，匪第二中队司令郑臻华逃窜。1950年7月18日，本寨、拉芒、开寨、筹洞、七里冲、尧连、星朗和老罗洞等处匪徒围攻荔波县人民政府驻地——基长。下午4时，杜介厘命令七连和政府工作人员分成几个小组，吹冲锋号，从多路向土匪出击，毙伤土匪多名，土匪溃退，县大队乘胜追击，俘获土匪20多人，缴获步枪30余支。1950年11月19日，匪首都堪、莫廷毅纠合两千余人，分三路侵扰基长区。当时，驻守基长的部队只有4个排和1个警卫班，加上政府工作人员不足200人。杜介厘率一个排和警卫班到基长背后坡顶指挥，派一个排的兵力在北端街口坡上阻击，防止土匪进入街上。另组织若干个战斗小组分散在基长周围，固守各要道，机动灵活近距离袭击土匪。战斗两个小时，打退由狮山、地坝方向逼近街口的土匪。驻上道的一个排几次打退从新民方向进犯的股匪。

1953年调到重庆工作，先后担任江北煤矿矿长、永川煤矿矿长，永荣矿务局局长、党委书记，煤炭部重庆设计研究院院长、党委副书记。1982年离休，2007年11月25日在重庆逝世。

潘文兴（1919—2005） 男，水族，三都水族自治县九阡镇板南村人（九阡镇原为荔波县九阡乡，1957年建立三都水族自治县时划归三都管辖）。潘文兴曾就读于荔波县城关小学，高小毕业后考进都匀师范初中部，后又考入都匀省立中学高中部，1944年考入贵州大学法律系，1949年夏毕业，获法学学士学位。

潘文兴的伯父和胞兄被国民党反动派贪官诬陷杀害，因此，潘文兴从小就对国民党反动派十分仇恨。在贵州大学读书期间，经常阅读中共党组织散发的革命传单、进步刊物，逐步认识了国民党反动派的反动本质，积极参加中共党组织领导的反迫害、反内战、反饥饿的学潮运动。

1949年7月，他从贵州大学毕业回到家乡九阡后，在中国人民解放军进军大西南的胜利鼓舞下，与贵大同乡同学覃杰、韦永培等秘密联系，发动周覃、九阡、荔波一带的人民群众起来反抗国民党反动派的统治，并密商组建反蒋武装——荔波人民游击队。同时，潘文兴还与从江人民游击队的莫御取得联系，协商联合开展组建人民武装游击队的工作。1949年8月初，莫御派赖蓉茂到九阡，当得知在广西从事秘密工作的中共党员文纵等在莫御处时，潘文兴即星夜赶往，与他们取得联系。返回九阡后，根据中共党组织的指示，立即分片负责发动群众，筹集枪支弹药及粮秣。随后，莫御又派刘放前往协助工作。经过广泛的宣传、发动群众，各乡青年踊跃参加，顺利地组建成立了荔波人民游击队。游击队下设4个大队，推举潘文兴为司令员、覃杰为政治委员。1949年11月，都匀、独山等地相继解放，潘文兴、覃杰立即派刘放、潘文歧、潘文举、韦凯儒等到独山，向人民解放军一五一团领导和中共独山地委、独山军分区负责人汇报，要求解放军派部队与荔波人民游击队解放荔波。鉴于解放大军要西进川滇，分不出兵力，一五一团首长指示：“如游击队有力量可先行解放荔波县城。”根据这一指示，1949年11月8日，游击队在周覃乡板光寨召开会议，宣布成立“黔桂边区临时人民自治委员会荔波分会”及“黔桂边区游击队直属第一支队”（即荔波人民游击队）。12月13日，游击队各大队会聚周覃，15日在下拉院寨脚田坝召开誓师大会，宣读中国人民解放军《三大纪律八项注意》《中国人民解放军宣言》，部署解放荔波县城的战斗任务。当天下午5时许，游击队开抵城郊，占领登高坡、螺蛳坡高地，控制了县城西北角，与城内国民党保警队激战两小时，国民党荔波末任县长文厚均眼看大势已去，半夜弃城而逃。16日凌晨，潘文兴、覃杰率领游击队解放荔波县城，随即成立由17人组成的荔波县解放委员会，暂时行使地方权力，维护地方秩序。

1950年2月4日，荔波县人民政府成立，潘文兴任第三区区长。1950年3月，国民党残匪陈与参围攻县城，潘文兴又率领游击队投入剿匪斗争，至1951年1月，全歼盘踞在荔波境内的陈与参“反共救国军”残匪。

1951年2月，潘文兴被中共党组织选送到中央民族学院军政训练班学习。1952年，先后任荔波县民政科科长、副县长。1955年，调贵州省民族事务委员会，先后任副科长、副处长、第五届贵州省政协委员。1984年，潘文兴退休，2005年2月因病去世，终年84岁。

艾福田（1936—1995） 男，汉族，中共党员，四川省天全县新业乡瓦子坪村人。

1958年8月，艾福田毕业于地质部重庆地质学校，当年9月担任广西429地质队技术员，1959年11月担任广西地质专科学校老师，1961年4月担任贵州地质局地质队技术员，1962年8月担任荔波县城关供销社业务员，1964年3月担任荔波县水电局水利勘测员、队长。1984年至1990年3月，先后担任政协荔波县第一、二、三届副主席。1991年2月兼任荔波县旅游局局长，1993年4月再次当选第四届荔波县政协副主席（正县级）、党组副书记。

艾福田是荔波水电事业的开发者和建设者，担任水电局水利勘测队队长20余年，走遍荔波山山水水。作为佳荣坤地引水渠、地莪小河电站、县城自来水厂、捞村洞考引水渠、驾欧引水渠、朝阳洪江水库、飞虎山电站及灌溉工程、小七孔一级电站、觉巩迎春水坝等县级重点工程的技术主管，亲自规划、勘测、设计、施工、管理，对每个技术环节进行把关，对每个工程严密设计、精心概算、筛选最优方案，为国家节约经费，为百姓解决农田灌溉和人畜饮水困难。他脚踏实地，一心扑在工程上，每月只回县城家里一两天，大家形容他“大禹治水三过家门而不入”。

艾福田是荔波樟江国家级风景名胜区的开拓者和奠基人，在其担任县政协副主席兼任县旅游局局长期间，于1984年自费考察九寨沟，认为荔波小七孔景色堪比九寨沟，坚定了他开发的决心。他爬陡壁，攀悬崖，探溶洞，穿密林，涉河水，识草木，辨禽兽，掌握资料，设计景点，规划线路，筹集资金，组织建设。从小七孔到大七孔，从地我宫到水春河，倾注了他全部心血与汗水，他为创建荔波樟江国家级风景名胜区做出重大贡献，被人们誉为“荔波旅游事业的开创者”。

艾福田担任县政协驻会副主席，经常关注农村和农业，邀请县直部门和技术专家座谈，为乡镇寻找发展经济脱贫致富的门路，他不顾年高体病，以他具有地质技术的优势，为边远贫困乡村勘测煤炭资源，制定开发计划。他充分发挥智力支边作用，邀请省、州有关专家，组织农民开展技术培训，让百姓掌握致富的一技之长。

艾福田扎根在群众当中，跟老百姓交朋友，没有官架子；他解民忧、助民富，与人民群众结下深厚的鱼水之情。他先后4次被推选为县人大代表，担任一届县人大常委会委员。1983年12月获“贵州省劳动模范”称号，1988年7月国家民委、劳动人事部、中国科协授予“少数民族地区先进科技工作者”纪念章，1990年10月国家民委授予“全国民族团结先进个人”称号，1991年省旅游局授予“全省旅游行业先进工作者”称号，1993年3月获“黔南州科教兴州奖”，享受州政府特殊津贴。1995年10月18日逝世，享年60岁。

二、人物简介

张聚国　1924年2月生，河南滑县人，1947年6月参加革命工作，1947年6月加入中国共产党，中专文化。参加工作后历任冀鲁豫军区补充六团四连文化干事、团政工队分队长、冀鲁豫军区军事训练队文书、十七军补训师二团参谋。1951年2月至1973年4月先后任中共惠水县一区区委委员，中共惠水县七区、一区区委委员，县委宣传部部长（县委委员），县人民政府副县长，县委副书记、书记、第一书记，中共黔南州委政策研究室负责人。1973年4月至1978年2月任中共荔波县委第一书记、县革委会主任。在荔波主持县委工作期间，动员和带领全县党员和人民群众，艰苦努力，集中力量把农业搞上去，加快调整好荔波的经济建设，及时贯彻落实党的民族政策、经济政策、干部政策、知识分子政策、统战政策，联系全县各条战线工作实际，及时拨乱反正，使各项工作逐年好转。1978年2月后调到省文教办公室任秘书处处长（党组成员），中共贵阳医学院党委副书记等。1984年3月离休，享受正厅级待遇。

姚福孔、姚建儒　姚福孔，男，水族，1925年生，水尧乡水捞村人，1958年参加工作（教师），1985年8月退休。姚建儒，男，水族，1938年生，水尧乡水捞村人。两人祖上世代都精通中医，尤其以接骨术见长，年幼时各自跟随父辈学习医术，之后成长为家传医术的第六代传人，经常到广西和独山、三都、九阡、三洞、荔波县城等地行医。1985年8月，为改善就医条件，方便治疗病人，更好地为乡亲和患者服务，两人共同投资1万元，在水尧乡水捞村岜合组公路旁修建了占地面积1200平方米的荔波县第一家私人诊所——岜合利民医院。

2005年10月，姚福孔、姚建儒两位老人在继续经营“岜合利民医院”的前提下，与县中医院合作开办水族骨伤专科门诊。奇特的水族接骨术引起了上级卫生部门的重视，县中医院将“水族骨伤医术”作为科技项目申报，获“国家重点科技建设水族医药骨伤”项目资金，用来开发水族骨伤医术。在行医的同时，两位老人也非常重视对后人的培养，在他们的悉心传授下，目前各自分别有了3位传人。

自开办利民医院和与县中医院合作开办水族骨伤专科门诊以后，由于其医德正、医术高、用药奇、疗效好，很多患者慕名前往就医，先后治愈了5000多名骨伤患者，成为远近闻名的骨伤科神医。

韦国仁　男，水族，1928年农历三月二十八日生于贵州省荔波县城南门街一个水族家庭，九三学社成员，中共党员。1953年，韦国仁毕业于贵阳医学院，后留校任教。历任中华医学会皮肤科学会第五届、第六届副主委，第三届、第四届主委；中国麻风防治协会第二、三届理事；贵州省麻风防治协会第一、二届副理事长；《中国皮肤性病学》杂志、《贵州医药》杂志及全国协编教材《皮肤性病学》编委；九三学社贵州省第二、三届委员，第六、七、八届全国政协委员。韦国仁教授从事医学教研42年，积累了大量的医学实践经验，具有较高专业理论知识和技术水平。在英语方面，他能读、能译、能写，日语也可借助工具书阅读专业书刊。结合贵州省情在十多年从事麻风病社会防治研究方面，取得了突出的成绩，1998年应邀出席在荷兰海牙召开的国际第十三届麻风学术大会。为了指导搞好麻防和皮防工作，韦教授编写了《麻风病防治问答》和《常见皮肤病防治常识》专著，参与编写教材《皮肤性病学》，在国家和省级医学杂志发表论文20余篇。韦国仁教授在工作中埋头苦干，刻苦钻研，工作成绩突出，赢得了一系列荣誉。1983年被评为贵阳医学院附属医院先进工作者，1984年被评为贵州省首届民族团结进步先进工作者，1986年被评为贵州省四化建设标兵，获“五一劳动奖章”，1987年获卫生部授予的全国卫生文明建设先进个人，1988年获国务院授予的全国民族团结进步先进个人荣誉证书及奖章。

蒙明儒　男，布依族，1929年5月出生，荔波县玉屏镇人。中共党员，第三届全国人大代表。

1952年11月参加革命工作，先后任玉屏镇财粮干事、玉屏镇镇长、荔波县第六区（玉屏区）副区长。1956年12月，当选为荔波县副县长。1957年4月，随贵州省民族参观团赴北京参加“五一”观礼，受到毛泽东、刘少奇、周恩来、朱德等党和国家领导人的亲切接见。

1958年3月，当选为荔波县副县长。1960年12月，当选为独山县副县长，政协独山县委员会第副主席，黔南州第三届人民代表大会代表，黔南州政协第二届委员会委员。1961年8月，恢复荔波县建制，调回荔波县工作，任副县长。1962年1月当选为荔波县副县长，黔南州第四届人民代表大会代表，黔南州政协第三届委员会委员。同年10月当选为贵州省第三届人民代表大会代表。1963年9月当选为荔波县副县长。

1964年11月，当选为第三届全国人民代表大会代表，赴北京出席代表大会，受到毛泽东、刘少奇、周恩来等的亲切接见。1965年12月，当选为荔波县副县长。其间，参加中共黔南州委组建的“四清”工作团到都匀县牛场公社、长顺县摆所公社进行“四清”工作。1966年5月至1967年3月，任荔波县人民委员会副县长。1978年12月当选为贵州省第五届人民代表大会代表。1980年当选为荔波县人民政府副县长。1984年当选为政协荔波县第一届委员会主席。贵州省水家学会顾问，贵州省历史文献研究会会员，1992年年底退休。

欧海金　男，水族，1934年7月生，荔波县水尧乡水捞村人，中专文化。1948年10月，跟随伯父学习水书，1953年出师后从事水书习俗活动。1956年1月，被组织选送到黔南卫校学习，毕业回乡后从医。后任乡青年干事、乡党委秘书。1963年5月，因病休假回家疗养。康复后一直开展水书习俗研究及运用工作。1981年参加黔南民研所水书习俗交流座谈会；1985年4月至1988年6月，与水书专家姚福祥先生合译家传水书《亥子卷》；1986年3月，与贵州民族学院研究员陈宝国研究水书习俗；1991年10月，给贵州民族学院教授潘朝霖传承水书；1996年2月至3月，给水书大师王品魁讲解水书《正七卷》并翻译该书。2003年8月至2008年3月，先后接受中央电视台、贵州电视台、南开大学、中山大学、清华大学、《中国民族报》《人与生物圈》等专家学者和媒体的采访。2002年7月，被县人民政府聘为“荔波县水书研究员”；2005年1月，被黔南州人民政府聘为“黔南州水书征集抢救专家”；2007年10月，被评聘为“贵州省级非物质文化遗产代表性传承人”；2008年6月，被聘为“黔南州级非物质文化遗产代表性传承人”；2008年12月，被贵州省人事厅评为“高级水书师”。

潘老平　男，水族，1936年3月27日生，贵州省荔波县佳荣镇拉易村人，小学文化。自幼攻读祖传水书古籍，受长辈传教，精通水书的诵读和运用。2002年被县人民政府聘请为“水书研究员”。是年7月，第一次带头公开水书秘籍，表示愿意无偿捐献给国家，成为水族历史上首个公开水书秘籍的水书先生。2003—2004年，参加县水书办共同破译夏陶符号碎片上24个符号及宋代八莲瓣碗上10个神秘符号。2005年8月，被黔南州水书办聘请为黔南州水书专家组成员。2004年至2008年7月参加县水书办公室注录、翻译水书。2006年至2008年7月，参加县水书办组织的水书《泐金·纪日卷》《金银》及清华大学十册馆藏水书的翻译工作。2003年至2008年7月，参加县水书办组织的水书习俗祭祀活动9次，均为主祭师、主祭人之一。2007年10月，被评聘为“贵州省非物质文化遗产代表作水书习俗传承人”。2008年6月，被评聘为“黔南州非物质文化贵州首批代表作传承人”。曾多次受到国内外专家学者、新闻媒体的采访和受邀参加水书习俗的表演活动。2008年12月，被贵州省人事厅评为“高级水书师”。

蒋荣生　男，汉族，1940年11月生，荔波县玉屏镇人，曾任县美协主席。2008年12月，被评为贵州省高级工艺师。一生喜好工艺、美术、书法，特别是工艺方面较为突出。1984年，组建成立“荔波工艺美术社”，生产的工艺产品除在本县销售外，还销往黔桂两省区的周边县。1988年，由其引领的荔波工艺美术社被列入全国少数民族用品生产企业名录。1991年3月，随贵州代表团参加全国旅游工艺品内销交易会。同年，被确定为全国轻工系统民族用品定点生产企业。其编织的工艺品一度成为荔波旅游产品畅销。1998年，开始潜心钻研花木盆景奇石工艺。2001年，成立“荔波花木盆景奇石协会”，任主席。随后，协会应邀参加柳州国际奇石展，12件作品入围，5件获优秀作品奖。2000年着手《樟江胜景》构思、创作，历经数年，几易画稿，完成了长60米的“荔波胜景图”，展现51个景点，将荔波名胜风景全部收入画卷，为其晚年力作。

蒙熙能　男，水族，1941年12月生，永康乡德门村人，大专文化。1957年读初中时与父亲学习水书，1963年父亲去世后又师从水书先生姚继安继续学习水书。1968年4月，荔波师范速成班毕业，先后在永康小学、县教育局供职。1985年4月离职回家，从事水书习俗传承。2002年11月，参加县抢救水书经验交流暨水书捐赠仪式，向国家捐赠5册家传水书。2003年12月，参加县水书办组织的夏陶符号破译工作，并接受中央电视台“走近科学”栏目采访和拍摄《水书之秘》专题片。2003年至2006年，翻译水书4册，书写水文条幅52条。2004年、2006年分别参加贵州省水书家学会学术研讨会和黔南州首届国际水书学术研讨会。2006年4月参加贵州电视台拍摄的5集水书专题片；6月，参加中央电视台教育频道“文明中华行”栏目拍摄的《神秘的水书》专题片。2007年、2008年分别参加水书《泐金·纪日卷》和《金银》卷的翻译工作。2008年12月，被贵州省人事厅评为“高级水书师”。

罗世槐 男，汉族，1946年3月生，江西省上犹县人。1970年毕业于武汉大学历史系。先后任中共荔波县委宣传部副部长、荔波县文体广电局局长兼党组书记、荔波县文联主席（兼）、荔波县文体局局长兼党组书记。贵州省作家协会会员。罗世槐积极从事文学创作，先后在省内外报刊上发表近200篇小说、小小说、散文、歌词、古体诗。先后出版《喀斯特森林的璞玉——荔波》《不言集》《丘壑集》著作。其中，小小说《留院察看》获《贵州党风》1991年度优秀文章奖。由其作词、崔文玉作曲的《村野水女》参加1993年全省“广播新歌”征评，获第一名，参与全国“广播新歌”征评，获优秀奖。2003年参加黔南州“关爱女孩行动”文艺调演，小品《一个被遗弃女孩的早晨》获原创一等奖，散文《十六岁的花季是什么》获原创三等奖。2004年，小小说《她知道》发表在《微型小说选刊》，参加新世纪推理微型小说全国征文大奖赛获三等奖，收录在《中国推理侦破微型小说》一书。小小说《炊烟》获嘉诚化工杯《散文.诗歌组》三等奖，歌词《人生就是一条河》获首届“千重山杯中华当代、精美短文短歌大赛”优秀奖，手机小说《笨女》参加“关爱女孩手机文学大赛”获一等奖。2007年散文《炊烟呵炊烟》获“妙手杯”散文大赛入围奖，并收入文集，诗歌《自由洞腔》获第二届“星光杯”全国诗歌散文大赛优秀奖，并入选《2009年度诗歌散文精选》一书。

龙贵雄 男，苗族，1963年6月生，初中文化，荔波县佳荣镇大土村人。1989年至1995年任大土村民组组长期间，带领本组群众上山植树造林达23460多亩，使荒山变成了大土村家家户户的“绿色银行”，带领村民开山造田达750多亩，解决了粮食自给问题。从1994年起，他又带领几百名乡亲开始了艰难的开山修路征程。1995年，担任大土村党支部书记后，对修路的信心更足，在全体村民的共同努力下，1997年修通了水维至大土村11公里的山村公路。公路修通后，大土村速生杉木林经济价值倍增，据专家评估，户均林木价值达30万元以上，实现了其提出的“造林起步、造田饱肚、修路致富”的大土村发展“三部曲”，2000年5月，被评选为全国劳动模范。

冉景丞 男，土家族，1968年12月生，贵州省思南县人。1985年考入东北林业大学野生动物系，1989年7月毕业，获农学学士学位。1989年7月至1993年9月，在贵州茂兰国家级自然保护区永康、翁昂片区从事管理工作；1993—2008年，先后担任贵州茂兰国家级自然保护区管理处科研科副科长、科长、助理工程师、工程师、高级工程师、主任工程师、局长、研究员。其间，被贵州大学、贵州师范大学聘为硕士研究生导师。分别当选为中国共产党贵州省第十次代表大会代表，中国人民政治协商会议贵州省第十届、十一届委员会委员，中国人民政治协商会议黔南布依族苗族自治州第九届、十届委员会委员，中国人民政治协商会议第六届荔波县委员会委员，荔波县第十五届人大代表。先后主持“亚热带喀斯特森林区岩溶作用与碳循环研究”（岩溶动力学重点实验室课题）“荔波洞穴研究”“少数民族地区参与喀斯特森林湿地资源管理”（IUCN荷兰委员会湿地保护项目）、“喀斯斯森林水土保持与生物成土作用研究”（贵州省省长基金）等8项科研项目。其中“亚热带喀斯特森林区岩溶作用与碳循环研究”获2004年黔南州科技进步二等奖。参与IUCN物种保护项目、IGCP299、IGCP379、IGCP448、IGCP513等国际对比研究项目及“茂兰喀斯特林区几种猛禽繁殖生态观察”“贵州野生猫科动物资源调查”“民族传统文化与生存方式对茂兰保护区的影响”等多项相关国家基金、省重点项目、国家生态基础研究项目及调查。其中“茂兰景观昆虫研究”获2003年贵州省科技进步三等奖。

在从事“荔波洞穴研究”时，对荔波县境内的喀斯特洞穴成因、发育和地下生态系统都有较系统的研究，并撰写出版了《荔波洞穴研究》《自然保护区管理手册》等，参与编辑了《喀斯特森林生态研究》（一、二、三集）、《茂兰景观昆虫》《贵州朱家山自然保护区科学考察集》等20余部著作。30余万字的《荔波洞穴研究》，是国内第一本针对某一区域的洞穴研究专著，而且作为申报世界自然遗产的重要内容之一。先后在《动物分类学报》《中国岩溶》《地球科学》《世界林业研究》等20多种国内外学术期刊独立或合作发表了110余篇研究论文。

多次参加国际、国家、省级学术研讨会。2000年参加中国鸟类研究——第四届海峡两岸鸟类学术研讨会，2002年参加加入WTO和中国科技与可持续发展——挑战与机遇、责任和对策会议，2005年参加全国第十一届洞穴大会，2007年参加人与生物圈国际会议等。1992年获林业部科学技术进步三等奖。1998年撰写的研究论文《亚热带森林岩溶区土壤CO_2迁移动态初步研究》获全国优秀学术成果一等奖、新世纪中国西部研究成果特等奖、黔南州优秀论文二等奖。2001年获黔南州科教兴州奖。2002年获“贵州青年五四奖章”、第三届“黔南州十大杰出青年”。2003年获贵州科技进步三等奖一项、黔南州科技进步二等奖两项、中国林业青年科技奖。2004年获全国野生动物资源调查先进个人、全国百佳模范新闻人物。2005年获黔南州州管专家、黔南州优秀论文一等奖。2006年获贵州省绿化奖章、黔南州第一届青年科技奖、全国自然保护区管理先进个人、贵州省省管专家。2007年国务院特殊津贴专家。2008年获黔南州科教兴州奖、荔波县突出贡献奖。

三、人物表

（一）烈士名录

姓　名	性别	籍贯	民族	年龄（岁）	工作单位及职务	牺牲时间及地点	授予称号	批准单位	批准时间
覃建华	男	贵州荔波	布依族	21	解放军53570部队78分队战士	1979年2月17日，在中越边界自卫还击战中牺牲	烈士	解放军总政治部	1979年3月25日
罗光余	男	贵州荔波	布依族	19	解放军53572部队73分队战士	1979年2月28日上午，在中越边境自卫还击战中牺牲	烈士	解放军总政治部	1979年3月25日

（二）获省部级以上表彰劳动模范、先进个人名录

姓　名	性别	民族	获奖时所在单位	获奖称号	授奖单位	获奖时间
韦荣芝	女	布依族	荔波县中医院	少数民族地区长期科技工作者	国家民委、人事部、中国科协	1983年7月
覃爱银	女	布依族	板吉村	“三八红旗手”	全国妇联	1983年
邓碧林	男	水族	茂兰保护区管理局	1983—1985年度全国森林防火先进个人	林业部	1983年、1985年
吴光美	女	苗族	荔波县朝阳镇政府	长期从事妇女工作，先进工作者	全国妇联	1989年3月
蒙熙林	男	水族	荔波县军休干部	全国民兵预备役先进工作者	国防部	1989年11月
韦国菊	女	布依族	荔波县档案局	档案工作先进工作者	贵州省人民政府	1989年12月

续表

姓 名	性别	民族	获奖时所在单位	获奖称号	授奖单位	获奖时间
杨志明	女	汉族	荔波县科协	全国科协先进工作者	中国科协	1990年4月 1991年4月 1995年8月
高 琳	女	汉族	荔波县体委	全国优秀体育裁判员	国家体育总局	1990年
玉振强	男	布依族	都匀陆军预备役师	贯彻条令先进个人	贵州省军区	1991年5月
石平举	男	水族	荔波县公安局	先进工作者	公安部	1991年10月
韦茂隆	男	布依族	荔波县人民检察院	先进工作者	最高人民检察院	1991年11月
吴孟春	男	水族	荔波县水利局	省科技兴农人才奖	省人民政府	1992年2月
曾武生	男	汉族	荔波县水利局	农田基本建设先进个人	省人民政府	1995年10月
李德森	男	汉族	荔波县人事劳动局	1995年度安全生产先进个人	省人民政府	1996年10月
杨爱仙	女	布依族	—	先进工作者	全国妇联	1996年8月
杨智英	男	侗族	荔波县水利局	全省农田水利基本建设先进工作者	省人民政府	1996年10月
				1997—1998年全省冬春农田水利基本建设先进工作者	省人民政府	1998年11月
谭光顺	男	布依族	荔波县建设村民兵连连长	民兵预备役部队基层建设先进个人	省人民政府、省军区	1997年7月
姚显文	男	壮族	荔波县农业局	科技兴农人才奖	省人民政府	1997年6月
蒙若旭	男	布依族	荔波县水利局	全省农田水利基本建设先进个人	省人民政府	1997年10月
覃正魁	男	布依族	荔波县水利局	全省农田水利基本建设先进个人	省人民政府	1997年10月
				农村水利电力初级电气化建设先进个人	水利部	2001年11月
莫锦高	男	布依族	荔波县玉屏镇武装部	扶贫工作先进个人	省人民政府、省军区	1998年9月
覃祖林	男	布依族	荔波县水利局	全省农田水利基本建设先进个人	省人民政府	1998年11月
王远扬	男	汉族	荔波县水利局	全省农田水利基本建设先进个人	省人民政府	1998年11月
覃利恒	男	布依族	荔波县国土局	先进个人	省人民政府	1998年12月
覃仲怀	男	布依族	荔波县教育局	全国教育督导先进个人	教育部、中国教育奖励基金会	1998年12月
何艳举	男	布依族	永康乡供电所	全国青年星火带头人	中国共产主义青年团中央委员会、科技部	1998年
蔡国芬	女	汉族	荔波县农业局	科技兴农人才奖	省人民政府	1999年9月
陈 军	男	汉族	荔波县水利局	科技兴农人才奖，农村水利电力初级电气化建设先进个人	省人民政府、水利部	1999年9月 2001年11月
莫炳雄	男	布依族	荔波县金对小学	烛光奖	教育部、中华慈善总会	1999年9月
孟品立	男	布依族	荔波县教育局	中华扫盲奖	教育部	1999年12月
陆兴华	男	布依族	荔波县建设局	先进个人	建设部	2000年1月
龙贵雄	男	苗族	佳荣镇大土村	全国劳动模范	国务院	2000年4月
				先进工作者	国务院	2005年5月

续表

姓　名	性别	民族	获奖时所在单位	获奖称号	授奖单位	获奖时间
莫灿轩	男	布依族	荔波县科协	扶贫工作先进个人	科学技术部、中国科学院、中国科协	2000年12月
覃志明	男	布依族	荔波县志明钢材门市	优秀个体工商户	省人民政府	2000年12月
冯关芳	男	汉族	荔波樟江风景名胜区管理处	全国风景名胜区先进个人	建设部	2000年12月
				全国国家重点风景名胜区综合整治先进个人	建设部	2002年12月
陈培生	男	汉族	荔波县水利局	农田水利基本建设先进个人	省人民政府	2001年10月
徐自余	男	布依族	荔波县农业局	农业科技先进工作者	省人民政府	2001年11月
覃应周	男	布依族	荔波县畜牧局	第五届科技兴农人才奖	省人民政府	2001年11月
吴荣祥	男	布依族	荔波县水利局	农村水利电力初级电气化建设先进个人	水利部	2001年11月
何瑞武	男	布依族	荔波县水利局	农村水利电力初级电气化建设先进个人	水利部	2001年11月
江兴龙	男	苗族	荔波县林业局	科技兴农人才奖	省人民政府	2003年12月
谭晓辉	女	布依族	荔波县食品厂	科技兴农人才奖	省人民政府	2003年12月
何继恩	男	瑶族	荔波县瑶麓瑶族乡人民政府	民族团结先进个人	省委、省人民政府	2003年
欧晓猛	男	布依族	玉屏镇计生委	计划生育工作荣誉奖	国家计生委	2004年12月
冉景丞	男	土家族	茂兰自然保护区管理局	全国野生动物、野生植物、湿地和大熊猫调查先进个人	国家林业局	2004年12月
覃红建	男	布依族	荔波县水尧水族乡水尧新村	贵州省绿化先进工作者	省人民政府	2006年3月
蒙应平	男	布依族	荔波县瑶山乡	全国自然保护区管理先进个人	国家环境保护总局、国家林业局等	2006年10月
				劳动模范	贵州省人民政府	2005年4月
罗光毅	男	布依族	甲良镇甲良村	全国劳动模范、先进工作者	国务院	2005年5月
				复员退伍先进个人	省军区	2005年7月
董豫黔	男	汉族	荔波县人民政府	2001—2005年农村税费改革试点工作先进工作者	省委	2005年8月
卢世勇	男	苗族	荔波县玉屏二小	中国青少年社会教育“银杏奖”	教育部等十部委	2005年9月
李文茂	男	汉族	荔波县科协	全国农村科普工作先进个人科普先进个人	中国科协	2005年10月 2006年2月
胡晓陆	男	汉族	荔波县人事劳动和社会保障局	全国人事系统先进个人	人事部	2005年12月
彭能富	男	布依族	荔波县甲良镇人民政府	全省绿化先进工作者	省人民政府	2006年3月
余祖刚	男	布依族	荔波县教育局	全省“两基”先进个人	省委、省人民政府	2006年6月
莫远景	男	布依族	荔波县文广局	广播电视“村村通”工作先进个人	国家广电总局、国家发改委、财政部	2006年9月
吴树凡	男	水族	荔波县水利水族乡武装部	抗凝冻保民生	省人民政府	2008年

说明：前志已记载的，本志不再收录；未报送者未收录。

（三）高级专业技术人员名录

姓　名	性别	籍贯	民族	工作单位及职务	技术职称	获得职称时间
周芳芹	女	安徽	汉族	荔波县农村工作局	高级农艺师	1984年11月
覃仲怀	男	贵州荔波	布依族	荔波县教育局	中学高级教师	1988年7月
龙佳鸾	男	贵州福泉	汉族	荔波县教育局	中学高级教师	1988年7月
柯新光	男	贵州贵阳	汉族	荔波县民族中学	中学高级教师	1993年12月
覃真理	男	广西上林	壮族	荔波县民族中学	中学高级教师	1995年9月
玉克熹	男	贵州荔波	布依族	荔波县教育局	中学高级教师	1995年9月
徐庭煜	男	贵州荔波	汉族	贵州茂兰国家级自然保护区管理处	高级工程师	1995年12月
梁宇兴	男	贵州独山	布依族	荔波县水利局	高级工程师	1995年12月
史大茂	男	贵州荔波	汉族	荔波县教育局	中学高级教师	1996年11月
姚文贞	男	贵州荔波	布依族	荔波县中医院	副主任医师	1996年9月
蒙若红	女	贵州荔波	布依族	荔波县人民医院	副主任医师	1997年12月
蒙秉忠	男	贵州荔波	水族	荔波二中	中学高级教师	1997年12月
饶永宝	男	贵州荔波	布依族	荔波县教育局	中学高级教师	1999年11月
全修彪	男	贵州荔波	水族	荔波中等职业技术学校	中学高级教师	2000年11月
周　明	男	贵州荔波	布依族	荔波二中	中学高级教师	2000年12月
陆金鹏	男	广西来宾	壮族	荔波县植保植检站	高级农艺师	2000年12月
肖匀波	男	贵州荔波	布依族	荔波县人民医院	副主任医师	2000年12月
何利铭	男	贵州荔波	汉族	荔波二中	中学高级教师	2001年3月
吴泽伟	男	贵州荔波	水族	荔波二中	中学高级教师	2001年12月
冯关芳	男	湖北武汉	汉族	荔波樟江风景名胜区管理处处长	高级工程师	2001年12月
韦仁勋	男	贵州荔波	布依族	荔波甲良中学	中学高级教师	2002年3月
史琼珍	女	贵州荔波	汉族	荔波二中	中学高级教师	2002年12月
覃剑华	男	贵州荔波	布依族	荔波二中	中学高级教师	2002年12月
全心明	男	贵州荔波	苗族	荔波二中	中学高级教师	2002年12月
陈宝宇	男	贵州荔波	汉族	荔波县教育局	中学高级教师	2002年12月
王家胜	男	贵州荔波	布依族	荔波甲良中学	中学高级教师	2002年12月
何瑞武	男	贵州荔波	布依族	荔波县水利局	高级工程师	2002年12月
周永祥	男	贵州都匀	汉族	荔波县交通运输局	高级工程师	2002年12月
童秀明	男	贵州荔波	汉族	荔波二中	中学高级教师	2004年4月
柏作常	男	贵州荔波	布依族	荔波甲良中学	中学高级教师	2004年12月
覃德平	男	贵州荔波	布依族	荔波二中	中学高级教师	2004年12月

续表

姓　名	性别	籍贯	民族	工作单位及职务	技术职称	获得职称时间
覃家远	男	贵州荔波	布依族	荔波二中	中学高级教师	2004年12月
刘文英	女	贵州荔波	汉族	荔波二中	中学高级教师	2005年12月
莫祖远	男	贵州荔波	布依族	荔波中等职业技术学校	中学高级教师	2005年12月
覃锦旭	女	贵州荔波	布依族	荔波中等职业技术学校	中学高级教师	2005年12月
李典金	女	贵州荔波	布依族	荔波甲良中学	中学高级教师	2005年12月
冉景丞	男	贵州思南	土家族	贵州茂兰国家级自然保护区管理局局长	研究员	2005年12月
莫秋炯	女	贵州荔波	布依族	荔波中等职业中学教师	中学高级教师	2006年12月
玉　胸	男	贵州荔波	布依族	荔波县教育局	中学高级教师	2006年12月
韦正教	男	贵州荔波	布依族	荔波佳荣中学	中学高级教师	2006年12月
杨　耄	女	贵州荔波	布依族	荔波中等职业技术学校	中学高级教师	2006年12月
汪秀权	男	贵州罗甸	汉族	荔波中等职业技术学校	中学高级教师	2006年12月
岳青成	男	贵州荔波	汉族	荔波二中	中学高级教师	2006年12月
陈荔琼	女	贵州荔波	布依族	荔波二中	中学高级教师	2006年12月
罗仁贵	男	贵州荔波	汉族	荔波二中	中学高级教师	2006年12月
曾宪民	男	贵州荔波	汉族	荔波二中	中学高级教师	2006年12月
熊志斌	男	贵州黎平	苗族	贵州茂兰国家级自然保护区管理局	高级工程师	2006年12月
欧佳玲	女	贵州荔波	布依族	荔波二中	中学高级教师	2007年12月
莫伯凯	男	贵州荔波	布依族	荔波县教育局	中学高级教师	2007年12月
熊莲敏	女	贵州荔波	布依族	荔波中等职业技术学	中学高级教师	2007年12月
周兴民	男	贵州荔波	布依族	荔波县人民医院	副主任医师	2007年12月
周仕涛	女	贵州荔波	布依族	荔波县人民医院	副主任医师	2007年12月
玉　卓	男	贵州荔波	布依族	荔波二中	中学高级教师	2008年12月
罗庆显	女	贵州荔波	布依族	荔波二中	中学高级教师	2008年12月
覃建飞	男	贵州荔波	布依族	荔波甲良中学	中学高级教师	2008年12月
韦正应	男	贵州荔波	布依族	荔波佳荣中学	中学高级教师	2008年12月
江兴龙	男	贵州福泉	苗族	县林业局	高级工程师	2008年12月

（四）省级以上中共党代会代表、人大代表、政协委员名录

姓　名	性别	籍贯	民族	工作单位及职务（职称）	类别	备注
何正光	男	贵州荔波	瑶族	荔波县瑶山瑶族乡乡长	省第十一次党代会代表	第十一届
韦荣芬	女	贵州荔波	瑶族	荔波县瑶麓瑶族乡瑶麓村卢家一组	省人大代表	第七届
何吉勇	男	贵州荔波	瑶族	荔波县瑶山瑶族乡乡长	省人大代表	第八届
韦国旗	男	贵州荔波	布依族	荔波县公安局干警	省人大代表	第八届
吴爱仙	女	贵州荔波	水族	荔波县中医院主管护师	省人大代表	第九届
何学稳	男	贵州荔波	布依族	荔波县翁昂乡纪委书记	省人大代表	第九届
陆兴华	男	贵州独山	布依族	荔波县人大常委会主任	省人大代表	第十届、第十一届
何继恩	男	贵州荔波	瑶族	荔波县科技局副局长	省人大代表	第十届
黄艳鹏	女	贵州荔波	水族	非公经济人士	省人大代表	第十届
王国平	男	贵州荔波	瑶族	荔波县玉屏镇镇长	省人大代表	第十一届
潘秀莲	女	贵州荔波	水族	荔波县佳荣镇卫生院医师	省人大代表	第十一届
覃福义	男	贵州荔波	瑶族	瑶麓乡干部	省政协委员	第五届
覃伙高	男	贵州荔波	瑶族	瑶麓乡干部	省政协委员	第七届
冉景丞	男	贵州思南	土家族	贵州茂兰国家级自然保护区管理局局长、研究员	省政协委员	第九届、第十届

四、前志补遗

（一）传记

韦汉超（1901—1938）　男，壮族，生于1901年，原名韦展书，广西东兰人。1925年参加韦拔群领导的东兰农民协会和农民自卫军，曾入东兰农民运动讲习所学习。1926年9月带领都邑家军参加攻占县城，驱逐反动县知事的战斗。1927年任东兰家军瑶族马刀队队长，参加韦拔群领导的武装暴动，进攻凤山县城，后坚持农村游击斗争，反击国民党新桂系的“清党”屠杀。1929年10月参加攻占东兰县武篆、三石和县城等战斗，12月参加百色起义，任东兰县苏维埃政府土地委员会主席和县农民赤卫军常务连长，同年加入中国共产党。1930年11月红七军主力北上中央苏区后，他担任红七军二十一师（后为右江独立师）六十三团三营营长、独立营营长、都邑瑶族独立营营长，率部转战东兰、凤山、南丹、河池和贵州荔波等县，参加了创建右江革命根据地和第一、二、三次反“围剿”作战。他在弄肖、板坡、弄棒垌、九顿圩、戈棉峒等战斗中屡建战功。1932年秋冬，韦拔群、陈洪涛牺牲后，他率领红军游击队从东兰突围到南丹、河池和贵州荔波等县坚持游击斗争。1935年建立中共荔波支部，韦汉超任书记，1936年韦汉超等又在翁昂建中共翁昂支部，谭耀机任支部书记。荔波、翁昂支部建立后，立即开辟了一条由捞村经广西南丹拉索、长老、河九坪、大同、东山板兰、中山到东兰中心县委驻地西山的秘密地下交通线。这条地下交通线不但加强了两支部与东兰中心县委的联系，也加强了黔桂边境县与东兰中心县的联系。东兰中心县委的指示和右江上游革命委员会的重要文件、文告源源不断地传到荔波，并在两个支部各自的活动范围内很快散发和宣传到贫苦群众中去。两个支部的建立与工作的开展，使中国共产党的主张在黔桂边境得到传播，对唤醒贫苦人民群众认清国民党军阀的反动本质、自觉起来进行抗争起了积极作用，许多人都参加了黔桂边委领导的秘密外围群众组织——黔桂边区革命同盟会，并由此走上革命的道路。1937年8月，根据右江上游革命委员会的指示，领导成立南丹、河池革命委员会并任主席，负责开展南丹、河池、荔波等地的斗争。1938年在宜北县被叛徒杀害。

蒙九龄（1904—1928）　男，布依族，荔波县城南门街人。1922年，滇军张开儒奉命前往广东讨伐陈炯明叛军，途经荔波县城时，18岁的蒙九龄投笔从戎，从军报国，加入滇军开赴广东。平叛战争胜利后，1925年1月，蒙九龄考入黄埔军校第三期步兵科学习，1926年1月17日毕业，随即参加北伐。1927年8月1日，参加了党领导的南昌起义，为创建党的军队做出了贡献。

南昌起义后，根据中共中央的指示，起义部队撤离南昌，开赴广州。此间，蒙九龄任朱德部属教导大队副大队长。10月，朱德、陈毅率领的起义军第三师、第二十一师各一部约800余人，转战至江西大庾（今大余）县境，将部队改编为国民革命军第五纵队。1927年11月，部队取得国民党第十六军四十七师第一四O团番号，进行隐蔽斗争。1928年1月，蒙九龄随朱德、陈毅率部脱离十六军，转战至湘南，并在朱德、陈毅的领导下发起了湘南起义，蒙九龄被任为起义军第七师三团团长。4月，他在湖南资兴为掩护大部队转移上井冈山会师，率三团阻敌断后，在资兴城外老虎山上英勇牺牲，时年仅24岁。2011年12月，贵州省政府追认蒙九龄为革命烈士。

（二）明至民国时期荔波县历任知县（知事、县事）、县长一览表

姓　名	职别	籍贯	出身	到任时间	备　考
尹东表	知县	—	—	明嘉靖年间（1522—1566）	时荔波县隶广西庆远府
刘邦征	知县	—	—	明万历末年（1620）	时荔波隶属广西庆远府
叶有声	知县	—	—	明万历二十六年（1598）	时荔波隶属广西庆远府
何天衢	知县	—	—	明万历三十年（1602）	时荔波隶属广西庆远府
申　翀	知县	湖广祁阳	进士	明崇祯年间（1628—1644）	时荔波隶属广西庆远府
王家珍	知县	江南山阳	进士	清顺治中期（约1652）	在任20余年
胡启睿	县令	辽东	—	清康熙元年（1662）	赴任被害
张　瑛	县令	江西安福	进士	清康熙年间（1662—1722）	
李元贞	知县	奉天	—	清康熙七年（1668）	
刘　棻	知县	永新	贡生	清康熙十九年（1680）	
傅鸿业	知县	奉天	—	清康熙二十三年（1684）	主纂修旧志
尹维旆	知县	阆中	进士	清康熙二十七年（1688）	
韦圣揆	知县	芜湖	贡生	清康熙二十八年（1689）	
李瑞征	知县	容城	进士	清康熙三十年（1691）	
陈金斗	知县	鄞县	荫生	清康熙三十二年（1693）	
陈　延	知县	吴江	监生	清康熙三十七年（1698）	
陈芳夏	知县	富平	监生	清康熙四十二年（1703）	
岳　维	知县	四川南江	进士	清康熙四十五年（1706）	
曹秉谷	知县	正向旗人	—	清康熙四十九年（1710）	
田　淹	知县	阳城	举人	清康熙五十年（1711）	
查　溥	知县	海盐	贡生	清康熙五十五年（1716）	
任天宿	知县	福建顺昌	进士	清康熙五十八年（1719）	
苏　潮	知县	长泰	举人	清雍正二年（1724）	
沈志荣	知县	德清	进士	清雍正七年（1729）	
吕　瑛	知县	云南昆明	监生	清雍正十年（1732）	雍正九年（1731）前县隶广西庆远府，雍正十年（1732）改隶贵州都匀府，时以方村县治。后创始改建县城于蒙石里
金明基	知县	—	—	清乾隆三年（1738）	
陈于中	知县	—	—	清乾隆四年（1739）	
赵世纶	知县	—	—	清乾隆四年（1739）	
李怀春	知县	—	—	清乾隆中期（约1765）	
吴明馨	知县	—	—	清乾隆中期（约1765）	

续表

姓　名	职别	籍贯	出身	到任时间	备　考
吴基龙	知县	—	—	清乾隆四十六年（1781）	
鲁寿松	知县	—	—	清乾隆末年（1795）	
杨　约	知县	—	—	清乾隆末年（1795）	
蔡元陵	知县	—	—	清嘉庆十七年（1812）	
武占熊	知县	—	—	清嘉庆二十二年（1817）	嘉庆二十四年（1819）复任
杨以增	知县	山东	进士	清道光初年（1821）	
于成保	知县	浙江	太医院吏目	清道光初年（1821）	
刘树棠	知县	四川	进士	清道光初年（1821）	
冯绍彭	知县	—	—	清道光初年（1821）	
覃武保	知县	广西容县	举人	清道光中期（约1835）	
稀松龄	知县	旗人	—	清道光中期（约1835）	
周　虞	知县	—	—	清道光中期（约1835）	
舒　文	知县	旗人	—	清道光中期（约1835）	
蒋时淳	知县	湖南	—	清道光中期（约1835）	署两任
何　珽	知县	—	—	清道光十九年（1839）	
谢人龙	知县	四川	—	清道光末年（1850）	
潘渭春	知县	福建	—	清道光末年（1850）	
叶华春	知县	福建	—	清道光末年（1850）	
吉尔通阿	知县	旗人	—	清道光末年（1850）	
严鉷	知县	浙江	—	清道光三十年（1850）	
毕楚珍	知县	江南	—	清咸丰元年（1851）	
魏承祝	知县	湖南衡阳	举人大挑知县	清咸丰三年（1853）	
李　珍	知县	直隶	—	清咸丰四年（1854）	
蒋嘉穀	知县	浙江绍兴	幕僚	清咸丰五年（1855）	亲率兵勇讨贼师溃阵殁
赵　煦	知县	—	—	清咸丰六年（1856）	
吴德容	知县	湖南宜章	—	清咸丰七年（1857）	在任8年
彭培垣	知县	湖南	—	清同治四年（1865）	
胡永春	知县	—	—	清同治五年（1866）	
王子林	知县	云南	—	清同治五年（1866）	
高　荃	县丞县事	云南	—	清同治五年（1866）	清同治五年（1866）任方村县丞，旋署县事
钟毓材	知县	广西	—	清同治六年（1867）	
谷应贤	知县	—	—	清同治六年（1867）	

续表

姓　名	职别	籍贯	出身	到任时间	备　考
钱　壥	知县	云南昆明	—	清同治八年（1869）	在任5年。同治十年（1871）征派民工修月城及永济泉（东门大井）
苏忠廷	知县	四川纳溪	拔贡	清同治十二年（1873）	
刘树勋	知县	四川	举人	清光绪初年（1875）	
罗卿云	知县	云南	—	清光绪初年（1875）	
张学渠	知县	四川	—	清光绪初年（1875）	
万舞庭	知县	四川	—	清光绪初年（1875）	
方人钰	知县	四川	—	清光绪初年（1875）	
刘树培	知县	广西临桂	军功	清光绪八年（1882）	光绪二十七年（1901）复任
崇　俊	知县	旗人	进士	清光绪九年（1883）	
郑寅亮	知县	河南	解元	清光绪十一年（1885）	
唐则璲	知县	广西临桂	进士	清光绪十三年（1887）	在任3年，卒于任
曾世隆	知县	四川江安	拔贡	清光绪十四年（1888）	
宋泽春	知县	湖南湘潭	监生	清光绪十五年（1889）	
梁宗辉	知县	广西玉林	举人	清光绪十七年（1891）	
汤炳巩	知县	湖南长沙	监生	清光绪二十年（1894）	
白建鋆	知县	四川	军功	清光绪二十二年（1896）	在任3年
张济辉	知县	四川綦江	优贡	清光绪二十四年（1898）	
黄增益	知县	浙江	监生	清光绪二十五年（1899）	
杨　煜	知县	四川酉阳	监生	清光绪二十八年（1902）	
陈介白	知县	四川巴县	举人	清光绪三十年（1904）	
谢锡铭	知县	福建诏安	拔贡	清光绪三十二年（1906）	
黄凤祥	知县	云南昆明	举人	清光绪三十三年（1907）	
石作栋	知县	甘肃兰州	进士	清光绪三十四年（1908）	在任4年
陈敏章	知县	贵州遵义	副榜	民国元年（1912）	在任4年
喻　竹	知县	贵定	附生	民国5年（1916）	
廖葆真	知县	黎平	附生	民国6年（1917）	
傅良弼	知县	贞丰	附生留学日本	民国7年（1918）	
杨　健	知县	四川酉阳	讲武生	民国8年（1919）	
蒋　峻	知县	三穗	警察毕业	民国10年（1921）	
刘　琅	知事	郎岱	附生	民国11年（1922）	
龙焕章	知事	独山	附生	民国12年（2923）	

续表

姓 名	职别	籍贯	出身	到任时间	备 考
景士清	知事	云南	附生	民国12年（1923）	
马秉升	知事	云南	附生	民国13年（1924）	
蓝继武	知事	贵阳	廪生	民国14年（1925）	
李退谷	知事	贵阳	廪生	民国14年（1925）	
李炜新	县长	独山	廪生	民国15年（1926）	荔波县行政公署改为县政府，县知事改称县长。民国18年（1929）复任
徐致和	县长	铜仁	崇武生	民国16年（1927）	
罗运钧	县长	德江	讲武生	民国17年（1928）	
廖家谟	县长	贵定	附生	民国18年（1929）	在任未满1月
韩知重	县长	四川	中学毕业生	民国19年（1930）	民国23年（1934）复任
拓泽忠	县长	贵阳	日本留学生	民国19年（1930）	
王公威	县长	贵定	中学毕业生	民国20年（1931）	
何干群	县长	兴义	中学毕业生	民国21年（1932）	
徐孟坚	县长	绥阳	中学毕业生	民国22年（1933）	
云	县长	湖北襄阳	讲武生	民国24年（1935）	
宋 植	县长	安徽	附生	民国25年（1936）	
汪 汉	县长	安徽	江淮法政大学毕业	民国25年（1936）	
陈世宇	县长	正安	厦门大学毕业	民国28年（1939）	
段叔瑜	县长	贵阳	日本留学生	民国30年（1941）	
刘仰方	县长	江苏	大夏大学毕业	民国31年（1942）	
陈企崇	县长	山西临县	山西省立法学院毕业	民国32年（1943）	
刘 琦	县长	黎平	曾任上校军职、台江县长	民国34年（1945）	
张 曜	县长	榕江	贵州法政专门学校、中央军校军官高等教育班及中央训练团毕业。历任少将军职	民国34年（1945）	
周绍伊	县长	四川兴文	私立大夏大学文学士，中央军校高等教育班毕业，陆军第一六四师副师长兼政治部少将主任	民国37年（1948）	
文厚均	县长	—	—	民国38年（1949）	民国末任县长

附　　录

一、重要文献辑录

（一）县级文献

中共荔波县委　荔波县人民政府
关于建立旅游开发区的决定

荔发〔1992〕24号

为加速樟江风景名胜区旅游事业的发展，促进我县经济振兴，经县委、县人民政府研究决定建立旅游经济开发区。

一、旅游开发区定名为樟江风景名胜旅游开发区。其范围包括：小七孔、大七孔、水春河三个风景区及其缓冲地带的生活服务区，玉屏镇服务中心，王蒙服务中心，以及拉片、水春、水扒、罗家寨四个民族旅游村寨。

二、凡在旅游开发区的指定范围内投资兴建接待服务设施，其投资方调节税可按5%征收。从营业日起免征十年所得税，免征三年的产品税、增值税。免征五年的房产税、奖金税、个人收入调节税。

三、凡在旅游开发区的指定范围内征地进行建设性投资的，只交征地费用，耕地占用税只收三分之一，免征十年土地使用税。

四、在旅游开发区内兴办文化娱乐设施可享受二、三条的优惠待遇。

五、鼓励全民、集体和个人到风景区管理处指定的景区内设立临时摊点经营饮食和照相，出售旅游商品。

六、在景区的总体规划指导下，投资开发大七孔、水春河的景点建设或交通建设的单位和个人，投资用于景点建设额在300万元以上的，可按景区总投资的比例分成二十年的门票收入，并免收同期的所得税和个人收入调节税。

中共荔波县委

荔波县人民政府

1992年7月16日

中共荔波县委关于进一步加强社会主义精神文明建设的决议

（1997年6月7日中共荔波县八届二次全委会议通过）

荔发〔1997〕12号

中共中央《关于加强社会主义精神文明建设若干重要问题的决议》，是指导我国社会主义精神文明建设的纲领性文件。全县各级党委、政府和广大党员、干部、群众，必须认真贯彻执行。现就加强思想道德、文化建设、精神文明创建活动等方面的问题，作出如下决议。

一、正确认识我县精神文明建设的形势

（1）党的十一届三中全会以来，我县各级党委、政府认真贯彻两个文明一起抓的战略方针，在大力发展经济、推进物质文明建设的同时，社会主义精神文明建设也取得了显著成绩，呈现出积极、健康、向上的发展态势。主要表现在：一是坚持党的基本路线不动摇；二是邓小平建设有中国特色社会主义理论已经成为全县各级党政领导、广大干部和各族群众的行动指南和精神支柱；三是实施“科教兴县”战略促进科技和教育事业的发展；四是广泛深入地开展思想道德建设，涌现出一批先进模范人物；五是坚持正确的舆论导向，为全县的改革开放和现代化建设营造良好的舆论环境；六是文化建设与时代精神相结合，弘扬主旋律，初步呈现文化繁荣的景象；七是群众性精神文明创建活动得到了广泛的开展；八是广泛深入地开展了民族平等、民族团结的教育，大力发展民族经济和民族文化，增进各民族之间的平等互助和团结合作；九是加强民主与法制教育，加大了反腐倡廉、扫除黄、赌、毒等社会丑恶现象和打击刑事犯罪斗争力度，社会治安综合治理得到进一步加强。所有这些，对促进我县的改革、发展、稳定起到了重要作用。

（2）在肯定我县精神文明建设成绩的同时，必须清醒地看到存在的差距与问题。我们对怎样切实加强精神文明建设还缺乏深入的研究；“一手比较硬，一手比较软”的问题还没有真正得到解决；精神文明建设还缺乏长远、全面的规划；道德失范、黄、赌、毒等丑恶现象和封建迷信活动时有发生。

（3）加强社会主义精神文明建设既是“九五”计划和2010年远景目标的重要任务，又是实现和完成这个计划目标的重要保证。我们要从坚持党的基本路线、建设有中国特色社会主义的高度，从加强民族团结、促进全县各民族的全面进步和共同繁荣的需要，从富民兴县、加快经济发展的实际出发，进一步认识加强社会主义精神文明建设的重要性和紧迫性，正确处理物质文明和精神文明的关系，增强责任感和使命感，努力开创全县精神文明建设的新局面。

二、我县社会主义精神文明建设的指导思想和奋斗目标

（1）总的指导思想是：坚持以马列主义、毛泽东思想和邓小平建设有中国特色社会主义理论为指导，坚持党的基本路线和基本方针，紧密联系荔波实际，加强思想道德建设，发展教育科学文化，以科学的理论武装人，以正确的舆论引导人，以高尚的精神塑造人，以优秀的作品鼓舞人，培育有理想、有道德、有文化、有纪律的社会主义公民，提高干部群众的思想道德素质和科学文化素质，团结和动员全县各族人民解放思想，实事求是，振奋精神，艰苦创业，为富民兴县而努力奋斗。

（2）今后14年全县精神文明建设的奋斗目标是：牢固树立建设有中国特色社会主义的共同理想，牢固树立坚持党的基本路线不动摇的坚定信念；以思想道德修养、科学教育水平、民主法制观

念为主要内容，实现公民素质的显著提高；以积极健康、丰富多彩、服务人民为主要要求，实现文化生活质量的显著提高；以社会风气、公共秩序、生活环境为主要标志，实现城乡文明程度的显著提高；形成物质文明建设和精神文明建设协调发展的良好局面，促进和保证全县“九五”计划的完成和2010年远景目标的实现。

（3）“九五”期间，我县要在围绕完成“九五”计划，打好扶贫攻坚战、积极实施科教兴县战略的同时，大力加强思想道德建设与文化建设。坚持精神文明重在建设的方针，把长远目标同阶段性任务结合起来，从战略高度认真研究和解决精神文明建设中干部群众普遍关心的重要问题。坚决制止党政机关和干部队伍中存在的消极、腐败现象，进一步树立密切联系群众，勤政务实、廉洁奉公的党风政风；坚决纠正损害群众利益的行业不正之风，大力培育良好的职业道德和敬业精神；坚决扫除黄、赌、毒等社会丑恶现象；坚决禁止制造和传播文化垃圾的行为，造就繁荣有序的文化市场；坚决治理一些地方社会治安不好和环境脏、乱、差的状况，创建更多的文明村镇、文明单位和文明户；广泛深入地开展科普活动和文化科技下乡活动，反对封建迷信，形成文明、健康、崇尚科学的社会风尚。

三、进一步加强思想道德建设

（1）我县思想道德建设的任务是：实现富民兴县，建设有中国特色的社会主义；坚持爱国主义、集体主义、社会主义教育；加强社会公德、职业道德、家庭美德建设；弘扬长征精神，引导人们树立正确的世界观、人生观和价值观，培育有理想、有道德、有文化、有纪律的社会主义“四有”新人，不断提高全县各族人民的思想道德素质。

（2）坚持理论联系实际，加强对马列主义、毛泽东思想，特别是邓小平建设有中国特色社会主义理论的学习、宣传和研究。以县委中心学习组为依托，重点抓好县以上领导干部和科局级领导干部的理论学习，提高各级领导班子的思想政治素质，增强把握全局和解决实际问题的能力。以县委党校为基地，重点抓好骨干培训，以此带动党员和群众的理论学习。在干部群众中坚持不懈地进行党的基本理论、基本路线、基本方针的教育，进一步解放思想、更新观念，使干部群众坚定实现富民兴县、建设有中国特色社会主义的信念。

（3）深入持久地开展爱国主义、集体主义、社会主义教育。全面贯彻落实《爱国主义教育实施纲要》。以邓恩铭烈士故居作为爱国主义和青少年德育教育基地，进一步加强和完善这一基地的建设，充分发挥其教育示范作用。以现代化建设的伟大成就和宏伟目标，中国近现代史、中共党史和基本国情、省情、州情、县情，优秀的民族传统和革命传统，民族团结和祖国统一，国家安全和全国国防教育，作为新时期爱国主义教育的主要内容。运用大众传媒、文艺作品、课堂教育、唱国歌、升国旗及各种宣誓仪式等形式，抓好爱国主义教育。

（4）要以为人民服务为核心，以集体主义为原则，以爱祖国、爱人民、爱劳动、爱科学、爱社会主义为基本要求，深入开展社会公德、职业道德、家庭美德教育。提倡尊重人、关心人、热爱集体、扶贫帮困、见义勇为、为社会多做贡献，反对和抑制拜金主义、享乐主义和个人主义。严禁把经济活动的商品交换原则引入党的政治生活和国家机关的政务活动。大力倡导文明礼貌、助人为乐、爱护公物、崇尚科学、保护环境、遵纪守法的社会公德。大力倡导爱岗敬业、诚实守信、办事公道的职业道德，纠正行业不正之风。大力倡导尊老爱幼、男女平等、夫妻和睦、邻里团结的家庭美德。

（5）弘扬“坚定信念、艰苦创业、无私奉献、依靠群众、团结奋进”的长征精神。我县正处于扶贫攻坚、艰苦创业时期，要在全省学习大关精神的同时，结合我县实际，学习和发扬佳荣乡大土村自力更生、扎实苦干、排难奋进、艰苦创业的精神，打好扶贫攻坚战，鞭策和促进我县樟江园林风光带建设区、小康建设区、旅游开发区、两高一优农业示范区的建设和综合开发。

（6）各级机关、单位的党员干部和国家公务员，要加强自身思想品德修养，牢固树立公仆意识，勤政务实，公正廉洁，依法行政，增强群众观念，积极主动为基层、为群众服务。各级各部门要依据行业特点制订文明单位量化和物化指标，深入持久地开展创建文明单位活动。

（7）切实抓好"三五"普法教育，加强依法治理工作。坚持法制宣传与依法治理相结合，进一步增强干部群众的法律意识和法制观念，不断提高各级干部依法办事、依法管理的水平和能力，促进依法治县、依法治乡（镇）、依法治村和依法管理各项事业，推动我县法制建设的进程。综合运用教育、法制、行政、经济、舆论等手段，约束和制止不文明行为，形成扶正祛邪、扬善惩恶的良好氛围。

（8）认真做好青少年的思想道德教育工作。全县各级各类学校要全面贯彻党的教育方针，加强和改进思想政治工作和德育工作，加强教师队伍建设，逐步完善教育设施；积极组织学生参加生产劳动和社会实践，搞好学风、校风建设，充分发挥共青团、少先队员团结引导广大青少年进步的重要作用；深入开展"希望工程""青年志愿者""希望书库"和"手拉手"等活动；全面实施我县九年义务教育规划。充分发挥各级"关心下一代工作委员会"等组织和老同志的积极作用。学校、家庭、社会要紧密配合，为青少年的健康成长创造良好环境。

（9）努力抓好先进典型的宣传工作，使先进典型的高尚精神和工作经验真正成为大家学习的榜样，变成人们的精神风貌和工作方式，在全社会形成树正气、立新风、学先进的良好氛围。

（10）思想道德建设要落实到基层。农村要抓到村组，城镇要抓到居委会和居民小组，学校要抓到班级，机关单位要抓到科室，厂矿要抓到车间班组。各级各部门都要加大工作力度，逐步做到基层单位的思想道德建设有人管事，有章理事。

（11）加强对中国茂兰喀斯特森林自然保护区和中国樟江风景名胜区保护意识的教育。中国茂兰喀斯特森林自然保护区和中国樟江风景名胜区是前人留下来的宝贵遗产。樟江是我们的母亲河，各级党委、政府和各机关单位要采取各种形式，加大宣传和教育的力度，提高全民高度自觉的保护意识，留下青山碧水，造福子孙万代。

四、努力推进文化事业的发展

（1）文化事业要坚持为人民服务，为社会主义服务的方向和百花齐放、百家争鸣的方针，努力创建一个良好的文化环境。进一步繁荣我县文学艺术、新闻舆论、广播电视、体育、社会科学文化事业，繁荣社会文化市场和群众性文化活动。结合我县特点，努力发掘少数民族优秀文化内涵，繁荣少数民族文艺，弘扬主旋律，为全县人民提供内容健康、形式多样的精神产品。

（2）树立精品意识，发挥民族文化优势，以地方和民族特色文化为基础，以"五个一工程"为龙头，抓好优秀文艺作品的生产。大力培养文艺人才，支持鼓励文艺工作者深入生活，力争创作出一批反映现实生活、具有时代气息的优秀作品。要制作、出版一套反映荔波全貌的录像片、画册、投资指南，鼓舞和教育全县人民并借以宣传荔波，提高荔波知名度。

（3）抓好城乡群众文化工作。要围绕全省"南下通道经济"抓好我县旅游、经贸、通道、生态科学四个文化带建设工程；切实抓好"艺术之乡""先进文化乡（镇）""先进文化企业""先进文化街道""农村儿童文化园""争创先进文化县"的创建活动。未建立文化站的乡（镇），"九五"期间要全部建立。逐步完善县图书馆、文化馆、文物管理所的配套设施建设，努力发掘、管理和保护我县文物。切实抓好文化下乡进厂进校活动，把文艺表演、书刊、音像制品、电影等精神产品送到基层。

（4）努力发展广播电视事业，提高全县广播电视覆盖率。加强广播电视的软件和硬件建设，不断完善县、乡（镇）卫星电视收转站和闭路电视系统，增设调频广播系统；力争到2000年，通电的乡（镇）和村，广播电视覆盖率达到百分之八十。逐步完善县有线电视中心和县广播站的设施，制作出高质量的广播电视节目。

（5）大力开展全民健身活动，创造条件完善体育设施，逐步达到体育先进县的硬件标准；坚持开展具有民族传统的体育活动；乡（镇）要建有和完善体育活动设施。

（6）深入贯彻《中共中央关于进一步做好文艺工作的若干意见》，加快全县艺术表演团体、群众文化体制改革的步伐，不断增强县文工队及群众文化活动的活力。积极开展“以文补文”“多业助文”活动，大力发展文化产业。倡导和鼓舞社会力量兴办文化，拓宽文化事业发展的路子。要创造条件建立县文联。

（7）依法加强文化市场的管理工作，促进全县文化市场的健康发展。坚持：“一手抓繁荣，一手抓管理”，大力扶持健康的文化产品和有益的文化娱乐活动，决不允许腐朽的思想文化和低级庸俗的文化娱乐活动滋长蔓延。完善文化市场执法机构及其管理规章制度，加大执法力度，规范经营和管理行为，坚持不懈地开展“扫黄打非”斗争。反对和制止封建迷信活动，严禁以发展文化、旅游为名乱建寺庙、滥塑佛像和建造宣传封建迷信的场所。

（8）新闻宣传工作必须坚持党性原则，坚持实事求是，坚持团结稳定鼓劲、正面宣传为主，牢牢把握正确的舆论导向。宣传、文艺、广播、电视等新闻媒体要充分发挥主导作用，发挥各自的优势，讲求宣传艺术，提高引导水平，注意宣传质量，严肃新闻纪律，讲求职业道德，努力做好新闻宣传工作。

（9）认真搞好理论研究工作。抓好社会主义市场经济理论与实践的研究和精神文明建设的研究，积极为我县实施“九五”计划和跨越世纪宏伟目标献计献策，提供科学的决策依据。

五、深入持久地开展群众性精神文明创建活动

（1）精神文明创建活动要开展到基层，吸引广大群众参与。在全县深入持久地开展文明城镇、文明单位、文明行业、文明村寨、文明家庭和军民共建、警民共建等精神文明创建活动；建设健康的社区文化、村镇文化、企业文化、校园文化、机关文化。坚持开展“双拥”活动和民族团结进步活动。

（2）开展创建文明城镇活动，要以提高市民素质和城镇文明程度为目标；创建文明单位要围绕实现优美环境，优良秩序，优质服务为目的；创建文明行业要以服务人民、奉献社会为宗旨。依据各自的行业特点，制定量化和物化标准，规范行业行为，树立行业新风。

玉屏镇作为全县政治经济文化中心，要认真实施县人民政府《关于批转创建卫生县城规划的通知》，着力加强对市民的“县城意识”教育和文明市民教育，净化社会环境，整治市容市貌，提高服务质量，维护社会稳定。在创建卫生县城上，要加大绿化、美化、净化的力度，力争在20世纪末将县城建成旅游服务一条龙的花园城市。县内沿交通干线的乡镇，要率先搞好创建活动，充分发挥引导、示范、辐射作用。

党政部门和机关单位，要带头搞好创建活动，要大力倡导实事求是，勤政廉政，公道正派为主要内容的从政道德规范，广泛开展“便民、利民、为民”活动，积极组织干部、职工参加兴办各类公益事业的义务劳动，提高干部整体素质，提高工作效率。

国有、集体、个体私营等各类企业尤其是国有企业的精神文明创建活动，要着眼于加强和改进思想政治工作，培育“四有”职工队伍。要全心全意依靠工人阶级，进一步搞好企业文化建设，增强职工的主人翁责任感，提高干部职工的政治思想素质和业务素质，塑造良好的企业形象，树立艰苦奋斗、开拓进取的企业精神，增强企业凝聚力，促进企业管理水平和经济效益的不断提高。

农村要以提高农民素质，稳定脱贫奔小康和建设社会主义新农村为目标，开展多形式、多层次创建活动。文明村镇建设要将农村经济发展、基层组织建设、党员“双学双带”活动、扶贫攻坚、社会治安综合治理、计划生育落实、村级卫生室建设、文化教育工作、实施“百村书库”工程、村容村貌改变等作为创建内容，每年进行检查、评比、表彰。文明村镇称号不搞终身制。广泛开展以“遵纪守法户”“科技示范户”“五好家庭户”“双文明户”等创建活动。深入开展以管理水平、产品质量、经济效益、环境保护、领导职工素质为内容的创建文明乡镇企业活动。继续抓好乡镇农村精神文明活动中心的建设。

继续抓好文化科技卫生下乡扶贫工作，抓好农民技术培训和实施，提高农民现代文明素质的“绿色证书工程”。继续抓好村规民约建设，反对封建宗教活动，反对大操大办婚丧嫁娶，逐步改变农村不良卫生习惯，倡导文明健康的生活方式。

（3）抓好规划，建立健全制度，以城镇为龙头，以农村为重点，广泛深入地开展创建活动。全县每年至少建一个文明集镇和一批文明村寨。对开展创建活动成绩突出的，要给予表彰和奖励。县精神文明办依据县情制定实施细则和各种创建活动的量化、物化标准，各级各部门要坚持标准，严格评选，防止形式主义，务求取得实效，努力在全县形成全党动手、全民参与、各方配合，共建文明、共促繁荣的局面。

六、加大对全县精神文明建设的投入

要增加对精神文明建设事业的投入，形成多渠道投入的机制。要认真落实国务院《关于进一步完善文化经济政策的若干规定》以及有关的配套文件，切实解决目前宣传文化事业投入较少、比例偏低、硬件设施比较落后等问题。对精神文明的硬件建设，要予以重视和安排。对县文化馆、图书馆、邓恩铭烈士故居、县有线电视中心、体育场以及乡镇卫星广播电视收转站和精神文明活动中心等，要给予必要的经费保证；对代表地方和民族特色的艺术团体和重点文物保护单位，要积极给予扶持。要努力改善文化管理部门的工作条件。要建立多渠道投入的筹资机制，力争在20世纪末修建成县老年、青少年活动中心。

各级财政对宣传文化事业的投入，要随着经济的发展逐年增加。要创造条件建立精神文明建设的专项基金，进一步完善落实宣传文化事业的优惠政策。积极争取中央、省、州对我县宣传文化事业更多投入。对贫困乡镇兴办文化事业和兴建文化设施，要给予积极扶持，勤俭办好宣传文化广播电视事业，提高资金使用效益。

七、加强和改善党对精神文明建设的领导

（1）全县各级党委和政府要始终坚持“两手抓、两手都要硬”的方针，把两个文明作为统一的奋斗目标，同部署、同落实、同检查、同表彰。考核、评价党政领导班子和主要领导干部，不仅要看领导物质文明建设的实绩，而且要看领导精神文明建设特别是思想道德、文化建设、创建精神文明活动的实绩，并以此作为干部考核使用和奖惩的基本依据。

（2）坚持统一领导齐抓共管的领导体制。在党委统一领导下，人大、政府、政协以及党政各部门和工会、共青团、妇联等人民团体齐抓共管、形成合力。要着力统筹解决好精神文明建设的政策、投入、队伍等问题。要充实、加强、健全县精神文明指导委员会及其办公室，对每个成员单位明确分工、赋予实责，防止和克服只挂名不理事现象，形成权威性强、功能健全的领导机构。精神文明办归口同级党委宣传部管理。乡镇、街道、机关学校、企业单位要配备负责精神文明建设的专职或兼职人员。

（3）加强精神文明建设首先要从严治党，抓好党风建设。在发展社会主义市场经济和对外开

放条件下，全县共产党员领导干部必须坚定共产主义信念，全心全意为人民服务，大公无私，清正廉洁，服从大局，艰苦奋斗，关心群众疾苦，在两个文明建设中发挥模范带头作用。

要广泛开展对股级以上领导干部以讲学习、讲政治、讲正气为主要内容的党性党风教育，加强对党员特别是领导干部的严格要求、严格管理、严格监督。

（4）进一步加强宣传文化广播电视部门的领导班子建设和队伍建设。要选调一批政治强、业务精、作风正的同志充实宣传思想文化教育队伍，以保证精神文明建设持续健康发展。

（5）各级党委要切实加强对宣传思想文化工作部门的领导。县委宣传部要加强对宣传思想文化工作的管理，进一步发挥职能作用。宣传思想文化战线的共产党员，要在精神文明建设中自觉发挥表率作用和骨干作用。

全县共产党员和各族人民，要紧密团结在以江泽民同志为核心的党中央周围，高举建设有中国特色社会主义的伟大旗帜，认真贯彻落实党的十四届六中全会精神，努力建设高度的物质文明和社会主义精神文明，为实现富民兴县的宏伟目标而奋斗！

中共荔波县委

1997年7月8日

中共荔波县委　荔波县人民政府
关于创建生态县、公园县的决定

荔发〔1999〕5号

各乡镇党委、人民政府，县直机关各级党组织、各工作部门：

1998年我县先后被林业部、全国绿委会和国家环保总局授予全国绿化造林“百佳县”和全国生态示范建设试点县。这充分体现了我县在合理开发利用资源、环境生态保护与建设方面所做出的艰辛努力和取得的可喜成就。但我们还必须清醒地看到樟江河上游流域植被破坏、天然林的砍伐、水资源污染还比较严重；现有残次林更新和改造任务还相当繁重和艰巨；县城和乡镇“四化”达标还远远跟不上；公路道旁、村前寨后绿化还十分薄弱。为此，切实加强对环境生态的保护与建设，创建生态县、公园县具有极其重要和深远的意义。现根据县委常委会研究，就创建生态县、公园县作出以下决定：

一、指导思想

以邓小平理论和党的十五大及十五届三中全会精神为指导，紧紧围绕省委、省政府“可持续发展”战略和省政府《关于十年基本绿化贵州的决定》精神，结合荔波实际，以“严格保护、统一规划、统一管理、合理开发、永续利用”为出发点，以实现环境、生态、经济效益同步发展，加快富民兴县进程为宗旨，努力创建生态县、公园县。

二、目的意义

创建生态县、公园县是两个文明建设的重要组成部分，是保护人类赖以生存和发展的物质基础，是走生态效益、环境效益、经济效益协调发展的道路，是实现环境脱贫、生态致富的有效途径，是一项功在当代、利在千秋的综合性系统工程。创建生态县、公园县是以富民强县为目的，是推动我县旅游业发展，经济腾飞的重大举措。

三、总体目标

自1999—2008年完成生态县、公园县创建工程。逐步形成生态、环境、经济协调发展的新格局。具体分两步走，第一步是1999—2003年，实现城乡绿化，玉屏、朝阳、茂兰、立化、佳荣、驾欧等乡镇政府所在地和景区基本实现“四化”达标。第二步是2004—2008年全县所有乡镇基本实现“四化”达标，完成农村文明卫生创建工作。

四、具体工作措施

（一）建立健全机制，切实加强领导

为确保创建生态县、公园县工程有组织、有计划、有步骤地实施，如期实现整体目标，成立由县主要领导为指挥长，分管领导为副指挥长，涉及部门负责人为成员的创建工程指挥部，指挥部下设创建生态县办公室和创建公园县办公室。由办公室制定总体实施方案和年度实施计划，并具体负责抓好创建工作的实施。各乡镇要成立相应的领导机构，明确专人负责。县乡分别成立创建工作督查组，定期或不定期对工程实施进展情况进行督促检查，发现问题及时研究解决。对工作不力的单位和负责人给予通报批评，对因工作失职而影响整个创建工作进度的责任人给予就地行政撤职处分。

（二）加强天然林的保护与管理

拥有世界上唯一保护完好的喀斯特森林生态，是我县创建生态县和公园县的优越条件，继续保护好天然林对创建生态县、公园县具有极大的推动作用。因此，县委、县政府要制定出台关于天然林保护措施。县人民政府要发布关于创建公园县、生态县保护森林资源的有关通知，禁止采伐天然林，禁止火烧山，禁止采伐樟江河流域、方村河流域、甲料河流域上的涵养林，禁止采伐独荔公路、荔大公路、三荔公路、荔界公路以及茂兰至佳荣、甲良至麻尾、小七孔至麻尾、界牌至捞村等主要公路两旁各50米以内的森林，并在2000年前将25度以上的坡耕地全部退耕还林；禁止砍伐寨旁、路旁、屋旁、江河旁的名木古树。要关闭天然林木材市场，取消乡镇林工商公司，统一由县林工商公司经营人工造林木材。县林业局要设立天然林保护管理办公室，增设一名副局长专抓天然林保护工作，重点抓好樟江源头天然林的保护。天然林保护办公室要根据我县天然林的分布情况、分布特点制定管理与保护规划及图表，分片实施，条块管理，责任到人。各乡（镇）党委、党政府要明确一名领导专抓天然林保护工作。同时，林业部门和各乡（镇）要加大对天然林保护的宣传力度。新闻媒体要配合林业部门和各乡（镇）做好天然林保护的宣传工作，不断提高干部群众对天然林的保护意识，并以实际行动投入到天然林的保护行列。各乡（镇）要发动群众使用节柴灶和煤炭燃料，兴建沼气池，使用沼气燃料，减少群众生活用柴，避免天然林的砍伐。

（三）加大城乡绿化工作力度

城乡绿化好坏是我们创建生态县、公园县成败的关键。因此，各级干部特别是领导干部要提高对城乡绿化工作重要性的认识，积极行动起来，切实抓好城乡绿化、美化工作。各级党委、政府要把城乡绿化工程列入重要议事日程，党政领导要亲自抓负总责，分管领导要具体抓。要建立绿化工作目标考核责任制，严格奖惩制度，变压力为动力，推动城乡绿化工作的稳步实施。

城乡绿化工程要从实际出发，因地制宜，突出重点，先易后难，分步实施。要切实搞好规划设计，既要有整体效应和超前意识，又要体现地方特色。在选择绿化品种上要考察、认真研究，不搞盲目性和一刀切。城区要以常绿树种为主，公路沿线以常绿灌木树为主，农村则以经济林和用材林为主。做到宜林则林，宜果则果，宜茶则茶，宜药则药，宜竹则竹。在投入上要集社会力量，多渠道筹集绿化资金。实行政府、部门、社会共同投入，重点以社会投入为主。计划、林业、城建、环保、效能等部门要把造林绿化工作作为生态建设、环境保护项目上报，争取上级部门的支持。同时，抓住珠防工程建设契机，加快全县绿化工作步伐。县级财政每年专项安排一定的绿化工作经费，保证绿化工作的正常运转，确保创建生态县、公园县如期圆满实现。

城乡绿化可划分为城镇绿化、农村绿化、交通干线绿化三大块。具体绿化方案和措施由城镇绿化办公室、农村绿化办公室、交通绿化办公室研究制定，报县委常委会议讨论通过。城镇绿化主要抓好县城和镇政府所在地及城镇郊外2公里范围内的荒山荒坡绿化。同时抓好河道、景区的绿化工作。具体由城建部门和风管处负责。农村绿化要始终围绕植树造林、封山育林、天然林的保护而进行，执行造、封、管一体化。重点抓好退耕还林工作。凡25度以上的坡耕地要全部退耕还林。同时抓好寨旁、屋旁、河旁的绿化工作。农村绿化工作还要结合“四区一控”提出的六大绿色基地建设一并抓好，既要达到绿化、美化环境的目的，又要增加农民收入。农村绿化工作具体由县林业局负责。交通干线绿化要在巩固现有成果的基础上，积极向外引进优质树种，对出县外的几大主要公路干线进行绿化，重点抓好独荔公路、荔大公路、麻小公路等主要干线的绿化工作。新建或扩建公路要在工程设计中一并确定绿化线，做到公路建设与绿化工程同步实施，同时验收。具体由县交通局负责。

（四）进一步开展城乡“四化”达标活动

县城要结合创建国家级卫生县城实施，抓好“绿化、美化、香化、净化”工程。一是兴建樟江大街东、南、西、北四个垃圾站，撤掉影响市容市貌的建筑物和垃圾箱，规范市政建设。二是实施樟江之滨雕塑、楼阁、望江长廊建设项目。三是实施亮丽工程，在所有沿街建筑物和高楼大厦制作广告灯箱或霓虹灯，形成夜市风景，塑造荔波新形象。四是对城区街道、院落阳台全部实施绿化，做到街街有景、院院有绿、户户有花。

景区内要以还大自然本质为目的，努力实施绿化、美化、香化、净化。要不惜一切代价征用景区内公路沿途两侧田土和荒山荒坡进行植树造林，消灭空白点，使景区形成一片，连成一体，提高旅游品位，增加旅游收入。

农村要围绕创建卫生文明村寨这个中心开展“四化”达标活动，既要尊重地方民族风情和民族特色，又要符合现代发展需要，塑造优美、良好的新型农村。逐步形成乡乡镇镇是景区，村村寨寨是景点新格局。

创建生态县、公园县是一项长期而艰巨的任务，是跨世纪宏伟工程，各级各部门要引起高度重视，以求真务实的态度，扎扎实实按照县委、县政府的决定要求抓好此项工作。

本决定自通过之日起执行。

中共荔波县委
荔波县人民政府
1999年3月5日

中共荔波县委　荔波县人民政府
关于进一步加强农业和农村工作的决定

（1999年3月7日中共荔波县八届五次全委会议通过）

荔发〔1999〕17号

党的十五届三中全会和省委八届二次全会分别通过的《中共中央关于农业和农村工作若干重大问题的决定》和《中共贵州省委关于进一步加强农业和农村工作的决定》，以及中共黔南州委、州政府《关于进一步加强农业和农村工作的意见》，回顾总结了我国、我省、我州农村二十年改革和发展的巨大成就和主要经验，明确提出了农业和农村工作跨世纪的发展目标和基本方针，对我国、我省、我州农村经济、政治、文化建设作出了全面部署，制定了推进农业和农村工作的重大政策措施，是指导我们建设社会主义新农村的行动纲领。认真贯彻执行中央和省委的《决定》及州委的《意见》，是当前和今后全县各级党委和政府的重要工作。

一、认真领会两个《决定》和一个《意见》精神，把握重点，统一思想，提高认识

联系荔波实际，抓好两个《决定》和一个《意见》精神的贯彻落实，对于进一步深化我县农村改革及其他各项改革，进一步推进全县农业和农村政治、经济、文化及精神文明建设等工作向前发展，有着十分重要的意义。深刻领会两个《决定》和一个《意见》的精神实质，必须把握重点，着重在以下几个方面统一思想，提高认识。

一是始终坚持党的农村基本政策不动摇，最重要的是稳定家庭承包经营为基础、统分结合的双层经营体制。

二是要始终坚持把发展农村经济，提高农民收入作为整个农村工作的中心不动摇，农村各项工作，都要服从和服务于发展农村经济，提高农民收入这个中心。

三是要始终坚持党对农村工作的领导不动摇，最重要的是坚持用邓小平理论和党的基本路线指导农村改革和发展，认真贯彻落实党在农村的各项政策，充分调动和发挥广大干部群众的积极性，建设好农村基层组织，发挥党员的“双带”作用，加强基层干部队伍建设，做到两个文明一起抓。

四是要进一步加强农业的基础地位，保持农业和农村经济的持续发展，保持农民收入的稳定增长，保持农村社会稳定。

五是要坚持以市场为导向，突出抓好调整和优化农业产业结构，大力推进农业产业化经营，大力实施科教兴农战略，加大农业基础设施建设投入，大力推进扶贫攻坚进程。

二、全县农村改革二十年的成就和主要经验

党的十一届三中全会以来，全县农村改革和发展取得了巨大的成就。1998年全县农业总产值达到14697万元（90价，下同），比1978年的5425万元增长170.91%；粮食总产量稳定增加，1998年实现51890吨，比1978年的37757吨增长37.43%；乡镇企业持续发展，1998年完成产值33353万元，为1978年的4.6倍，翻2.14番，年均递增7.94%。农民人均纯收入1998年达到1254元，比1978年增加955元翻2.05番；1998年有1万贫困人口解决温饱，全县贫困人口总数由1993年的84320人下降到15810人。

回顾二十年的农村改革和发展，我们积累了丰富而宝贵的经验，主要是：

1. 切实加强了对农业和农村工作的领导。各级党委、政府始终把农业放在国民经济发展首位，切实做到了各级主要领导亲自抓，分管领导具体抓，班子成员一起抓，各部门积极支持配合，全县上下形成重视农业，关心农业，支持农业，加强农业的良好氛围。

2. 坚持党在农村的基本政策不动摇。党的十一届三中全会以后，全县全面推行家庭联产承包责任制，不断深化农村经济体制改革。尤其是党的十四大以后，全县上下进一步坚持改革开放，以市场为导向，大力发展多种经营和乡镇企业，调整农村所有制结构，提高农产品商品率，使农村逐步形成了以公有制为主体、多种所有制经济共同发展的格局。

3. 大力加强农业基础设施建设，不断改善农业生产条件。全县农田有效灌溉面积由1978年的39658亩，增加到1998年的55695亩，保灌面积由1978年的32744亩增加到1998年的51645亩。结合荔波实际，认真组织实施了以工代赈坡改梯工程。认真抓好以植树造林为主要内容的生态建设。

4. 坚持科技兴农。大力推广先进的农业实用技术，实施以良种良法为龙头的农业科技示范项目，取得良好的效果。

5. 加大扶贫攻坚力度。坚持扶贫工作领导责任制，发扬动感情、动脑筋、动真格的“三动”精神，加大人力、物力、财力投入，狠抓落实，于1996年全县面上越过温饱线。

6. 大力发展农村教育科技文化等各项社会事业。加强民族团结教育，各族干部群众团结和睦，共同发展。农民的整体素质，包括科学文化水平、市场经济意识、民主法制观念有了明显提高。二十年的改革开放，全面促进了荔波农村的社会主义物质文明和精神文明建设的发展，推动了全县农村经济和社会的协调发展。

二十年改革开放的实践，也使全县上下充分认识到，荔波的农村生产力发展水平还处于社会主义初级阶段的较低层次，同先进地区相比，还有诸多问题和困难，主要有：

1. 全县农业的基础还十分脆弱，人均保灌面仅0.32亩，低于全国0.81亩的人均水平，生产条件仍比较差，劳动方式依旧，劳动强度较大，抵御自然灾害的能力还比较弱。

2. 农村经济结构还不够合理，农村二、三产业比重过小，第一产业中，粮食比重过大，经济作物种植比例小。

3. 农产品商品化程度还比较低，商品率不到40%，并且流通渠道还不很畅通；农民现金收入低，农业投入不足。

4. 科技文化教育还比较落后，有的地方文盲半文盲还占相当大的比例，农业劳动者的素质还比较低。

5. 大多数农民的生活离小康还有较大差距，其中一部分还比较贫困，巩固越线成果和抑制返贫的任务还十分艰巨，扶贫攻坚难度还很大。进一步加强农业和农村工作，对保持全县经济持续、快速、健康发展和社会稳定具有极为重要的意义。

三、当前及今后全县农业和农村工作的总体要求和重点

当前及今后的一段时间，全县农业和农村工作总的要求是：高举邓小平理论伟大旗帜，以党的十五大和十五届三中全会精神和州委、州政府《意见》为指导，认真贯彻落实省委八届二次全会《决定》和州委、州政府《意见》，坚持把农业放在国民经济发展的首位，全面贯彻执行党在农村的各项方针政策，加强法制宣传教育工作，深化农村经济体制改革，增加农业投入，加强农业基础设施建设，大力实施科教兴农战略，推进农业产业化经营，以非耕地资源开发为重点，加大扶贫攻坚力度，确保实现主要农产品总量需求平衡和农民收入稳定增长，努力实现“三增”“两降”“一稳”（粮食增产、农民增收、发展后劲增强、降低人口自然增长率，降低贫困人口数、稳定农村社会秩序）奔小康，推动农村经济加快发展和社会全面进步。

工作重点主要是：

第一，全面贯彻落实党在农村的基本政策，进一步深化农村改革。

1. 稳定以家庭承包经营为基础、统分结合的双层经营体制，稳定土地承包关系。认真贯彻执行从1994年起，耕地承包期再延长50年，非耕地资源开发承包期再延长60年的政策。在稳定家庭承包经营的基础上，培育、发展和壮大集体经济实力。

2. 大力发展农村非公有制经济，继续完善我县农村所有制结构。要采取更灵活、更有效的政策措施，进一步创造良好的环境，在国家法律和政策允许的范围内，对非公有制经济发展实行“五不限”，即不限发展比例，不限发展速度，不限经营方式，不限经营规模，不限经营范围。积极扶持农民兴办各种经济实体，发展股份合作制经济，发展混合所有制经济。

3. 采取有力措施，切实减轻农民负担。进一步建立健全农民负担监督卡制度、预决算制度和专

项审计制度，严肃查处加重农民负担的违纪、违法行为。根据中央有关税制改革的精神，做好费改税试点工作，全面推进农村费改税工作。

4. 加大依法治县的宣传教育力度，保持农村的社会稳定，正确处理新形势下的农村内部矛盾，运用法律、行政、经济和思想等手段，用说服教育、示范引导、效益驱动和提高服务水平的方法处理与农民的关系，妥善解决、化解矛盾。

5. 积极开展劳务输出，充分发挥农村剩余劳动力的作用。通过产业结构调整，加快非耕地资源开发和二、三产业的发展，积极鼓励和引导农村剩余劳动力逐步有序地向非农产业转移和向外输出劳务，有效解决农村劳动力剩余问题。

6. 有重点、有计划地积极实施农村贫困人口的异地移民开发工作。

7. 推行农村合作医疗，切实保障广大农村群众的身体健康。

第二，积极调整和优化农村经济结构。发展农业产业化经营，努力提高农村经济效益。

1. 调整优化产业结构和产品结构，在决不放松粮食生产的前提下，全面发展农林牧副渔各业。在确保粮食总量稳定增加的同时，高度重视粮食的品种质量，并采取措施逐步增加优质稻米的比重，满足人民群众生活的需要。结合小城镇、街道或集贸市场建设，大力发展农村二、三产业。

2. 大力发展畜牧水产养殖业，提高畜牧水产养殖业在农业总产值中的比重。重点是加快牛的品种改良步伐，实施稻鱼工程，把发展草地畜牧业和渔业生产作为我县新的经济增长点来抓，力争实现畜牧业产值点农业产值50%以上的目标。

3. 大力发展乡镇企业。各级党委和政府要进一步加强对乡镇企业的领导，大力扶持、合理规划、分类指导、依法管理，把乡镇企业真正办成“一把手经济”，把乡镇企业作为农民增收和财政创收的主要支柱来抓。重点抓好甲良、茂兰、立化、佳荣等乡镇工业小区建设，建立和完善乡镇企业管理机构。

4. 以市场为导向，积极推进农业产业化经营。结合本地区自然资源优势，根据市场需要，把发展粮食、油料、烤烟、茶叶、蔬菜、药材、竹类、水（干）果和畜牧等作为支柱产业来抓。创造条件，兴办一个农业生态园区，一个农业经济园区和一个现代农业示范区，逐步形成全县农业产业化新格局，提高农业资源产出率和农产品商品率。大力培育各种类型的农村“企业”，引导“龙头企业”同农民形成合理的利益关系，增加农民货币收入，实现共同发展。重点抓好樟江蜜柚项目的开发，力争三年内实施标准化、规范化种植3万亩。

第三，大力实施科教兴农战略，努力提高农业科技含量。

1. 大力推广农牧业实用技术。要充分认识优良品种对农牧业增产的关键性作用，大力抓好“种子工程”和种养殖业的“六普及三提高”“四良四改三提高”及适合我县农村机械综合技术的推广，切实提高科技进步对农业和农村经济增长的贡献率。

2. 加强农业科研和科技推广队伍的建设。农业科研机构要面向农业，面向农村，着重解决发展大农业和农村经济中亟须的、重要的关键技术问题。切实加强乡（镇）、村农技推广体系建设。支持创办民营科技攻关机构和发展民营科技企业、民办专业技术服务组织。切实采取措施，加强和稳定农业科技队伍，努力改善其工作和生活条件，充分调动和发挥农技人员的积极性和创造性。

3. 切实加大农民技术培训的力度。按照“实际、实用、实效”的原则，紧紧围绕发展农业产业化经营和发展生产的需求，多渠道、多形式、多层次、多学科地大力开展农民技术培训工作，继续加强农村劳务输出和农村扫盲工作，通过劳务输出，实现异地“培训”，通过加强农民扫盲工作，提高农村特别是贫困石山区、深山区农民的综合素质。

第四，大力加强农业基础设施建设，切实改善农业生态环境，提高农业综合生产能力。

1. 坚持高质量、高标准，扎扎实实地抓好以工代赈坡改梯工程建设，同时利用以工代赈等资金分步骤、有重点地加固河堤防护，确保河两岸良田被水冲毁降到最低限度，逐步实现坡改梯1年1万亩的目标。

2. 大力加强农田水利基本建设。坚持“以小为主，大、中、小相结合，以蓄为主，蓄引提排相结合；以管为主，建管并重；以配套为主，配套改造与适当新建相结合”的方针，重点抓好小水池、小山塘、小水窖和机提灌站的“三小一提灌”配套建设。2000年前建设小水池3000个、小水窖2000个、小山塘200个、机提灌站100个，使粮食生产在旱涝保收的基础上实现稳产高产。

3. 认真抓好城乡绿化工作，调整林业发展思路和经营方式，依法保护森林资源。对天然林的采伐，坚决实施“两禁止、三关闭、一保护”的措施。抓好退耕还林工作，以封山育林为主，结合人工造林、飞播造林、人工促进更新、低产林改造等方式恢复和发展森林植被，努力提高森林和绿地覆盖率，改善生态环境，实现创建生物多样性、生态农业旅游示范县的规划目标。

4. 认真抓好农业综合开发和粮食自给工程项目的实施、督促、检查、指导和管理工作。以增粮、增钱、增后劲为中心，以改造中低产田土和造林为重点，工程改造与生物改造相结合，提高耕地质量，增加稳产高产基本农田。

5. 为减少农民的劳动强度，提高劳动效益，保护生态资源环境，在农村开展节能灶、沼气池等技改项目。

第五，切实加大扶贫攻坚力度，推进农村小康建设。

1. 切实抓好小额信贷扶贫到户工作，以稳定解决温饱为中心，进一步打好扶贫攻坚战。继续发扬“三动”精神，弘扬大关精神和大土精神，采取各种切实有效措施，在巩固脱贫成果的基础上，确保在2000年内使全县农村人口百分之三十的农户生活达到小康，百分之三十五的农户生活接近小康，百分之三十五的农户全面解决温饱的目标。

2. 切实加快农村小康村建设步伐。以加快樟江河谷“四区一控”建设为重点，切实抓好分级负责、建立健全农村小康村建设领导机构，要将小康村建设任务层层分解到乡（镇），采取切实措施因地制宜、分类指导、梯次推进，确保小康村建设任务的顺利完成。

3. 要以法律的形式落实农民合理负担定项限额，抓好农村税费改革试点。严禁乱收费、乱集资、乱罚款和乱摊派。加强对农民负担检查和监察的力度。

4. 加快小城镇建设步伐。切实抓好县城建设和重点乡（镇）建设，坚持“突出重点，以点带面，逐步推开、层层推进”的原则，实施重点带动战略，高质量、高水平地完成全县小城镇建设的规划建设任务。

第六，抓好千里农村经济示范带建设。

重点主要是驾欧经小七孔至瑶山、朝阳到玉屏公路，甲良、方村、水利到玉屏公路，玉屏至水尧、茂兰、立化公路等三条公路主干线沿线地带和时来、茂兰、方村、洞阳、南门等五坝地带。主要内容包括五个方面：农业科技、林业生态、农田水利、乡镇企业、小城镇建设。

四、1999年农业和农村工作的目标和主要任务

1. 按照全县当前和今后农业和农村工作总体要求，1999年全县农业和农村工作的目标和主要任务是：实现农业总产值增长4.08%；粮食总产量52000吨，比上年增长2.1%；畜牧业总产值4000万元，比上年增长2.3%；乡镇企业总产值41400万元，比上年增长25.08%；农业人均纯收入1400元，比上年增长5.26%，解决1万个农村贫困人口温饱，年度返贫率控制在12%以内。

2. 围绕上述目标，1999年要着重抓好几个工作重点。

一是抓好科技兴农项目实施，逐步完善对科技人才的管理，对科技人员实行有偿服务，促进农业快速发展，早日进入市场经济。

二是抓好农田水利建设。完成坡改梯1.25万亩，完成“三小一提”工程（小水池、小水窖95个，小山塘13口和机提灌站4个）。

三是抓好农业产业化的起步。即樟江柚产业化、林业产业化、畜牧产业化、茶叶产业化、蔬菜产业化。

四是抓好城乡绿化，要求11250亩35度以上的坡地全部退耕还林，25度以上坡地逐步还林退耕，全县城乡绿化和干线公路绿化全面启动，人工造林46488万亩，其中封山育林15870亩。

五是抓好乡镇企业。挖潜注新，全面提高现有乡镇企业、特别是骨干企业的经济质量，加快招商引资，扩大乡镇企业的数量，集中力量抓好甲良、茂兰工业小区建设。

五、切实加强党对农村工作的领导，全面完成农业和农村工作的各项任务

1. 加强领导，统一思想。各乡（镇）党委、政府和县直各部门要用党的十五大、十五届三中全会和省委八届二次全会精神统一思想，始终坚持把农业和农村工作摆在重要位置，把主要精力和工作重心放在农业和农村工作上，要充分发挥县农业和农村工作领导小组及涉农部门的作用。主要领导对农业和农村工作要亲自抓，分管领导要具体抓，各级各部门尤其是党政领导机关都要大力支持农业、服务农业、保护农业，继续做好计划生育“4321工程”和县直机关包村扶贫工作，进一步形成全社会重视和加强农业的强大合力。各级领导要切实改进领导方法和工作作风，深入基层，深入生产实际，加强调查研究，总结和推广农民在实践中创造的经验，帮助基层解决困难和突出问题，多为基层办好事、办实事。

2. 努力增加对农业的投入。按照《中华人民共和国农业法》中的有关规定，切实加大对农业的投入。对农业的投入，原则上按经常性财政收入的增长比例增加。建立和完善以财政资金为导向，以农户投资为主体，以利用社会资金和外资为补充的多元化、多层次、多渠道的农业资金投入机制，保证各项财政支农资金和协调督促专项支农资金足额及时到位，专款专用，不得挪作他用。要坚持审计制度，用审计法规来监督资金到位及使用情况。

3. 加强农村基层民主法制建设，推动农民依法治县的全面开展。进一步扩大农村基层民主，坚持公平、公正、公开原则，逐步建立健全村民委员会民主选举制度、民主决策制度和民主监督制度。

4. 加强村级组织建设，开展群众性精神文明创建活动。以“五个好”为目标，继续抓好以党支部为核心的村级组织建设“四个一工程”，巩固和发展三年集中整顿的成果；按照中央提出的“六个好”的要求，切实加强乡（镇）党委建设；充分发挥共青团、妇联、民兵等群众组织的作用，提高农村基层组织的整体水平。要抓好农村计划生育工作，切实把全县农村人口自然增长率控制在13‰以内。坚持“两手抓，两手都要硬”方针，以全面提高农民的思想道德素质和科学文化素质为目标，以邓小平理论为指导，把农村精神文明建设同农村经济工作、基层民主政治建设和社会治安综合治理结合起来，深入开展创建“文明家庭”“文明村寨”“文明乡镇”活动；对农村进行爱国主义、集体主义、社会主义教育，进行党的基本路线和方针政策教育，进行社会公德、职业道德、家庭美德教育，培养“四有”新型农民。引导农民移风易俗、革除陋习，反对封建迷信和封建宗族势力活动，坚决打击各种违法犯罪活动，确保农村社会稳定。

1999年4月5日

中共荔波县委　荔波县人民政府关于创建科技先进县的决定

荔发〔1999〕6号

各乡（镇）党委、人民政府、县直机关各级党组织、各工作部门：

为认真贯彻党中央、国务院《关于加速科学技术进步的决定》和省委、省政府《关于实施科技兴黔战略的决定》，进一步落实“依靠、面向”方针，使我县经济发展转移到依靠科技进步和提高劳动者素质的轨道上来，加快我县经济建设和社会发展步伐。根据《省人民政府转发省科委关于我省创建科技先进县的意见通知》精神，结合荔波实际，把我县建成省级科技先进县。为此，特作出如下决定：

一、牢固树立“科学技术是第一生产力”思想

邓小平同志提出了“科学技术是第一生产力”的伟大理论；“科技兴国”是江泽民总书记三大治国方略之一；国务院总理朱镕基在全国人大九届一次会议记者招待会上正式向中外宣布“实施科教兴国战略是本届政府最大的任务”。充分体现了党和国家领导人根据国际、国内形势的发展和变化，对科教工作的高度重视。为此，全县各级党委、政府、广大干部、职工和人民群众要进一步牢固树立“科学技术是第一生产力”“经济是中心、科技是关键、教育是基础”的思想，不断增强科技意识，真正把经济发展转移到依靠科技进步和提高劳动者素质的轨道上来。实现我县“九五”计划和2010年远景规划目标，必须坚定不移地贯彻“依靠、面向”的方针，围绕确定的科技进步目标，在全县范围内掀起科技创先活动的高潮，充分发挥我县优势，以改革开放为动力，培养人才为根本，以增大科技投入为保障，坚持科技进步与经济发展相结合，科技发展的近期目标与长远规划相结合，力争在两年左右的创先活动中，使全县科技发展有一个大的飞跃，科技进步对经济增长的比例从“八五”期末的27.6%提高到48.5%以上。

二、创建科技先进县的主要任务和目标

1. 大力推进农业和农村科技进步。农业和农村经济发展的根本出路在于依靠科技进步。要把加强和改进农业科技工作摆在农村工作的突出位置，运用先进的实用技术和科技成果，促进传统农业向“三高”现代化转化，大幅度提高土地利用率、农业劳动生产率。到2000年年末，力争科技对农业增长的贡献率从“八五”期末的32.4%提高到46%，彻底解决我县1万多人的温饱问题，全县农民人均纯收入1500元以上，使农村生活基本上接近小康水平。

在创先活动中推广“两高一优”农业生产模式，提高农业综合开发水平和农产品科技含量，加速农业生产步入良性循环的轨道。

实施以推广良种良法及配套先进农艺为中心的高效农业，大面积推广粮、烟、茶、果、蔬菜等优良新品种和节本省工的高效低耗的种养技术和成果。农业生产先进适用技术覆盖率达90%以上，增产效果高达17%以上，四大粮经作物（水稻、玉米、烤烟、油菜）良种覆盖率要从85%上升到95%以上，农作物病虫害损失率控制在5%以下，粮食单产比1998年增加28公斤以上。

大力推广畜禽、水产新品种及养殖综合技术的推广应用，使主要家畜良种覆盖率达80%以上。大力推广青贮氨化、驱虫及疫病综合防治等科学技术。使广大农户在创先工作开展的两年时间中，通过发展养殖业，年收入增加的比重有了较大幅度的增长。

要继续推进农科教结合，普及农科知识、完善科技推广培训和社会服务体系，稳定农业科技队

伍，建立和完善县农业办公室综合性培训基地和县民族职业培训学校、村级科技干部培训学校，加大对农村科技力量和农村科技二传手的农村适用技术的培训。力争在创先活动中，全县村村建有农民文化技术学习班或夜校，每年要有90%以上的农村基层干部和80%以上的农村劳动力接受1次以上的农业适用技术培训，3%以上的青壮年劳动力接受绿色证书培训，并取得合格证书；获得农民技术职称的人数占农村劳动力的1%以上；技术人员的知识，适用技术更新培训要达到20%以上。

突破危害农业、制约农业的技术难点，采取综合技术措施，增强防灾抗灾能力。重视和跟踪生物技术、信息技术等现代高新技术在农业上的应用，加强农业应用基础研究，为建设现代化农业奠定坚实的理论基础和提供技术保障。

2. 广泛开展科技兴县、兴厂、兴企活动，创建科技型工业企业。加速工业科技进步，提高工业增长的质量和效益，根本途径在于依靠科技进步。搞好国有企业的深化改革，建立现代企业制度，大力发展乡镇企业，调整产品结构、提高劳动生产率和经济效益，加快产品的更新换代，提高产品质量和市场竞争力。

建立健全企业技术创新组织和促进科技进步的运行机制，把增加企业技术创新能力作为创先活动的重要内容。加强企业职工培训，使每年职工培训面达职工总数的20%以上。加大企业技术改造力度，在创先活动中，使工矿企业和主要行业技术装备和工艺接近或达到省内先进水平，新技术产品有所突破，力争每年开发2个以上的州级产品投放市场。科技进步对工业经济增长的贡献率提高到2000年的38%以上。加强支柱产业的重点建设，发挥煤炭、铅锌、铁石、白云石为主的矿产资源优势，瞄准市场行情，发展一批科技骨干工业企业，加大水力资源的利用力度，对现有的水泥厂、金属镁厂进行技术改造，提高生产能力和产品的科技含量。力争创先活动期末，使我县国民生产总值达到2.5亿元，年均递增12.3%，比“八五”期间增加3.84个百分点，工业产值达到2.5亿元，年均递增16.73%。

3. 组织实施好科技扶贫工作，打好扶贫攻坚战。帮助贫困乡（镇）、村、组选准脱贫致富开发项目，推广先进适用技术和科技成果，组织科技培训，支持贫困乡（镇）、村发展科技和教育。帮助每个贫困户确定脱贫出路，掌握几门能形成稳定收入的种、养、加技能，并形成能够开发利用当地资源，带动区域经济发展的科技型支柱产业，切实依靠科技解决温饱，脱贫致富奔小康。力争在创先活动期间使瑶山、佳荣等贫困乡（镇）提前越过温饱线。

4. 继续抓好各类示范工程，逐渐向高效农业转化。高产示范工程是实现行政、资金、物资技术推广相结合，发展生产，提高农村经济效益的较好形式。在创先活动中，县、乡（镇）村都要办好各自的高产示范工程，县每个示范工程面积不得少于400亩，乡（镇）不得少于300亩，村组不得少于100亩。同时加强农业高产、高效示范基地建设，启动我县“四区一控”项目。在樟江沿岸的玉屏、朝阳、瑶山、捞村和甲良、茂兰、佳荣等地建立水稻丰产坝，在甲良、方村、播尧、玉屏、建立优质蛋白玉米丰产基地，并组织实施粮、猪、沼良性循环项目。使其形成1.74万吨规模的商品粮基地；玉屏、朝阳、茂兰建立蔬菜基地，在时来、板吉等地建早熟蔬菜基地；甲良片区开发1万亩茶叶基地；利用秸秆氨化、青贮等先进技术，增加牲畜存栏和出栏头数，稳定生猪生产，建好瘦肉型猪基地，在玉屏、朝阳、方村、甲良等地建立快育肥商品牛基地，并适度发展高产网箱养鱼工程、高产稻田养鱼工程、山塘水库养鱼工程和樟江青虾养殖工程，在甲良、驾欧、播尧建设好优质烟高产示范基地，在樟江河谷沿岸的玉屏、朝阳、瑶山、捞村建立3万亩樟江蜜柚基地和0.5万亩的荔波早桃基地；在洞塘、水尧、永康、水利等地建立2万亩的酸梅基地。在佳荣建8万亩用材林基地，并逐步形成我县的早熟蔬菜、水果、药材等集团产业优势。

5. 大力推动社会发展领域的科技进步。围绕控制人口数量、提高人口素质，保护环境资源，搞好医药、卫生城乡建设、劳动安全，减灾防灾以及文体领域的建设发展，解决一批与社会发展相关的科技问题。

坚持科技与计划生育工作相结合，利用先进科学节育技术，使我县人口自然增长率控制在12‰以内。组织、落实好荒山、荒地综合开发治理，综合开发利用，生物资源持续利用示范工程及小河流域治理，生态农业示范工程，搞好中低产田土改良，贯彻以营林为基础的方针，利用先进科学技术和成果提高造林成活率和保存率，使全县森林覆盖率到2000年年末达55%以上。抓好旅游资源的开发利用，充分利用国家级樟江风景名胜区、茂兰国家级喀斯特森林保护区的品牌优势和中共一大代表邓恩铭故居这一爱国主义教育阵地，努力形成革命历史和山水风光旅游互相辉映的旅游格局，坚持经济、社会、生态、科技相统一，坚持社会效益和经济效益的统一，实现环境保护和生物资源的持续利用。提高常见病、多发病、传染病等预防和治疗水平，重视营养品的技术研究与开发。改善饮水条件，净化生态环境，提高人民身体素质。

三、深化改革，建立科技新体制

1. 深化科技改革的重点是调整结构，分流人才，建立适应社会主义市场经济体制和科技自身发展规律的科技新体制。科技新体制有利于解放和发展第一生产力，有利于调动广大科技人员的积极性，有利于促进科技经济一体化，有利于加快我县经济发展和社会进步。

2. 认真贯彻“稳住一头、放开一片”的方针，在巩固和发展县、乡（镇）专业技术推广机构和专业技术推广队伍的同时，大力发展各类民营科技企业和民间农村技术经济服务组织，发展公司加农户，技、农、工、留一体化，产、供、销一条龙的产业集团。

3. 加强科技管理体系建设，为全县各乡（镇）村配备科技副乡（镇）长、科技副村委会主任。成立乡（镇）科技工作领导小组，协调管理乡（镇）科技工作，在村级成立科技经济组织，形成国家农业技术推广机构与群众性农村科普组织及农民专业技术服务相结合的农技推广网络，以疏通科技流向千家万户和各生产环节的渠道。建立市场、科研、开发、生产一体化的企业技术开发体系，企业要实行厂长（经理）科技进步责任制，并有明确的职责和考核办法。县属各企业要加强同行业的联系与合作，增强技术开发能力。

四、加强科技队伍建设，提高全民科技文化素质

1. 科技人才是第一生产力的开拓者，是创先活动和科教兴县的骨干。要充分发挥现有科技人员的作用。全县科技人员在创先活动中、要垂范在先、加强自身建设、提高自身的素质。同时加强培训科技人才及各类专业技术能手，加快急需人才的引进，为科技工作提供后备力量。

2. 在创先活动中，要围绕科教兴县，教育是基础，教育要先行的方针，努力发展各类职业技术教育和成人教育，通过教育主渠道、培养科技后备力量。采取各种形式，加强对科技人员的继续教育，不断地更新知识。要在全县形成尊重知识，尊重人才的社会风气，稳定和壮大科技队伍。

五、增加科技投入

加大科技投入的力度，充分发挥第一生产力的作用。科技投入是科技进步的必要条件，也是开展创先活动的必要保证。从1999年起全县科技投入要占全县财政总支出的1.5%。把科技事业费和科技三项经费纳入县财政年度预算科目，科技三项费要达到财政当年预算支出的0.5%以上，并每年递增0.2%，到2001年达到1%。要逐步建立30万元以上的科技发展基金，并制定好使用办法，提高经费使用效益。要引导和鼓励企业增加科技投入。县办工业企业和乡（镇）骨干工业、企业每年按不低于销售总额的1%提取发展基金，作为科技研究开发和技术引进费用。同时加大力度搞好“三跑”“三引”工作，使引入用于科学技术开发的资金达到本县科技投入的30%以上。全县各事业单

位相应成立科技管理机构并明确一名副职负责此项工作，应从事业费和自身创收中拨出一定比例的经费用于科技投入，促进本单位的科技进步。乡（镇）人民政府也要逐步增加科技投入，切实搞好创建科技先进乡（镇）活动。

六、加强党委和政府对创先活动的领导

1. 创先活动是科技兴国、科技兴黔、科技兴县的有效措施，各级党委和政府责无旁贷。加强党委和政府对创先活动的领导，是顺利实施科技兴县的根本保证。因此，各级党委和政府要认真解决创先活动中的实际问题。

建立创先领导责任制，县乡党政、县直各部门、各企事业单位的一把手要亲自抓“第一生产力”，并把科技工作列入目标管理内容，建立考核奖励制度，自觉抓好科技工作。各级领导要对创先活动的实际情况经常进行督促检查，党政主要领导每年至少听取四次科技管理部门的科技工作汇报，并组织召开一次全县科技工作会议。

2. 成立“创先活动”领导小组（另行文），加强对创先工作的宏观决策和管理，负责该项工作的领导、组织和协调。同时要发挥县乡（镇）科技管理和推广机构以及村科普组织的作用，搞好服务，当好参谋、行使好职权，为创先活动做出贡献。

3. 创建科技先进县，加快科技进步、加速荔波经济和社会发展，是全县各级党政领导、共产党员、干部职工和人民群众的一项艰巨任务。各部门、各单位、各乡（镇）要团结协作，通力合作，动员和组织干部职工和广大人民群众投入到创先活动中，为把我县建成科技工作先进县而努力奋斗。

中共荔波县委关于荔波县跨世纪发展思路的决定

荔发〔1999〕28号

1997年，中共荔波县八届三次全委扩大会议，认真贯彻党的十五大精神，运用邓小平建设有中国特色社会主义理论，围绕经济建设这个中心，在历届县委、县政府工作的基础上，从荔波的县情出发，提出要利用一切反映社会化生产规律的经营方式和组织形式，远谋近思，科学地把我县县域经济定位为以旅游为龙头的及其相关产业发展的经济体系；以煤炭为龙头的及其矿产品开发和粗加工的经济体系；以绿色产业为龙头的及其非耕地资源开发和绿色产品深加工的经济体系；以粮食为龙头的及其农林牧副产品深加工的经济体系，并快速健康地实施农业产业化，壮大和充实县域经济，增强县域经济实力，同时以强化四大基础、调整四大结构，打好两个攻坚，实施三大战略，抓住一个关键位具体目标和措施，运用超常规思维，采取超常规手段，实现超常规跳跃式发展。经过两年的实践和探索，这一战略性思路不断得到充实和完善，现已形成了荔波县跨世纪发展思路，它包括制定“思路”的县情基础，指导思想和原则，未来荔波经济社会的发展方向和具体任务，不仅目标明确、措施有力，而且还有项目载体和效益分析，是指导荔波县社会经济持续、快速、健康发展的纲领性文件，为此，经县委研究，决定用《荔波县跨世纪发展思路》替代《荔波县国民经济和社会发展“十五”计划和2015年远景目标纲要》。围绕荔波县跨世纪发展思路，荔波县人大常委会要及时组织讨论，并形成相关决议，荔波县人民政府要在县委《决定》和人大《决议》的基础上，制定切实可行的实施方案。使我县资源优势迅速转化为经济优势，抓住我县的基本矛盾，努力提高人民群众的物质文化生活水平，把我们贫穷落后的荔波有力地推向朝气蓬勃、欣欣向荣、美丽富饶的21世纪。

中共荔波县委

1999年12月1日

附：《荔波县跨世纪发展思路》全文

荔波县跨世纪发展思路

荔波县跨世纪发展思路是："444231"思路。即县城经济的基本框架定位为四大经济体系和围绕四大经济体系实施强化四个基础，调整四个结构，打好两个攻坚，实施三大战略，抓住一个关键。

四大经济体系 一是以旅游为龙头及相关产业协调发展的经济体系。大力发展交通运输业、饮食酒店业、文化娱乐业、雕刻绘画业、花卉盆景业和绿色产品加工业，走旅游扶贫，旅游致富，旅游强县，旅游奔小康的路子。二是以煤炭为龙头及其矿产品开发和粗加工的经济体系。抓大放小，搞好骨干煤井及其他矿产品的规划和开发建设。三是以绿色产业为龙头及其非耕地资源开发和绿色产品深加工的经济体系。扩大樟江柚、酸梅、麻竹和茶叶基地的生产规模，大力实施商品牛改良，走绿色产品加工升值的路子，提高农产品的商品比率，增加农民的货币化收入。四是以粮食生产为龙头及其农副产品深加工的经济体系。

强化四个基础 一是强化以农田水利基础建设为重点的农业基础为突破口，形成农业产业化、农产品商品化，以增加农民收入为目的，搞好农业和农村工作。2002年前彻底解决80%稻田的人为灌溉（要达到小水窖3000个、小水池200个、小山塘200个、机提灌溉100个），确保粮食生产在旱涝保收的基础上实现稳产高产。二是强化以交通为重点的交通通信能源基础设施建设。到2002年前要完成一纵（独山到荔波至广西环江县）一横（麻尾至小七孔至水春河）的干线公路建设，同时要逐步完成乡际间公路和村级公路建设，使村村通"县标"砾石四级路面，形成以干线公路为主体，以乡级公路为框架，以村级公路为网络的四通八达的公路网。要按省委、省政府的要求，积极争取在2003年动工兴建荔波水功机场，构筑立体交通网，促进资源开发和经济发展。要开发荔波县丰富的水能资源，使之尽快变为经济优势，小水电要实现产业化。2000年前要进入国家电网，架设完毕麻尾—荔波—茂兰110千伏输电线路，对全县农网进行改造，解决农村95%的农户用电问题，村村组组通电，全面实现初级电气化县。三是强化以人才为重点的教育教学基础设施建设。在2002年前要消灭所有学校的危房，要完善60所村级小学、27所乡中心小学、11所初级中学及党校和职业农民技术学校的教育基础设施建设，新建县城第三小学，使所有适龄儿童都能入学，要深化教育体制改革，推选素质教育，提高教育教学质量，发展普教、农教、职教，实施党校、职校体制改革，提高全县各民族受教育水平，提高劳动者素质。四是强化以乡镇、集镇建设为重点改善投资环境的基础设施建设，进一步加强以县城为核心，以乡镇为重点，以村寨为基础的城乡集镇建设，彻底改善投资环境。1. 做好乡镇集镇建设的总体规划，体现民族文化特色，提高民族文化含量，保护有特色的民居民宅，设想建设具有民族文化特色的建筑群体。2. 加大一日城改造力度，到2003年县城的所有一日城改造必须实施完毕，所有的乡镇集镇建设必须围绕旅游定位，把县城建设成为全国最佳优秀旅游县城。3. 2000年实施时来新城开发建设，建成江滨大道和恩铭大道，开成高档次，独具规模的旅游服务中心。4. 对县城、乡镇集镇建设进行硬化、绿化、净化、亮化、香化、美化"六化"达标，县城2001年达村，乡镇除翁昂、捞村、播尧、方村、洞塘外2002年达标，2004年全县30%的村进入文明村寨行列，改善民居民宅，扩大农民住房面积，实现人畜分开，彻底改变农村脏、乱、差的现状。5. 利用各种政策手段加快城镇、乡村集镇建设，2005年实现县城现代化、乡镇城市化、城乡一体化的目标，使县城达到国家最佳优秀旅游县城、国家级文明卫生县城。

调整四个结构　一是调整所有制结构。贯彻党的十五大精神大力发展非公有制经济，把它作为新经济增长点，这是荔波客观实际的需要，也是荔波经济发展的需要，是荔波未来经济发展的主导形式，要使非公有制经济对财政贡献（除煤炭外）达到50%以上，且居决定地位。1. 制定更加优惠的政策，创造更加优越的条件，发挥政府在市场经济中的职能作用，大力发展民营科技企业，发展私营科技企业。使我县非公有制经济在现有基础上更加发展壮大，力求上规模、上档次、上市场。2. 创造符合国家经济制度的经济形式，不断改革经济体制，保护和实现多种经济形式并存，达到蓬勃发展的格局。3. 县委、县政府要积极鼓励全县机关、干部职工开发非耕地，办企业、办产业、财政适当给予贴息，增加干部收入和财政收入。4. 为个体私营经济、民营企业和投资者全方位地搞好投资服务，并创建适合非公有制经济蓬勃发展的、良性运行的、快速持续健康发展的经济组织机构。5. 加快农村经济体制改革，优化农村经济组织形式，鼓励和积极引导农村私有经济的发展，鼓励有能力的农民以合法的方式相对集中地对耕地和荒山进行所有权的开发，同时发展农村第三产业，全面启动农村市场。6. 加强对非公有制经济及私有民营个体企业的领导，行政执法部门必须无条件地保护非公有制经济和私有民营企业，适当时候由县人民政府颁布保护规定，保护它们合法利益，在非公有制经济领域里要健全和发展它们的组织，使其在政治上有地位，组织上有依靠。二是调整农业产业化结构，在抓好粮食生产的同时把重点转向实施农业产业化的开发，从重抓常规性农业向农业产业化转变，从传统农业向现代化农业改变，从狭义农业向广义农业转变，从粮食农业向创税农业转变，在1999年初步启动农业产业化的实施，逐步解决农村农民经济结构单一的问题，提高农产品的科技含量，提高农产品的商品率，扩展农产品市场占有份额，增加农民的货币化收入比例，在项目区内种植10万亩速生丰产杉木林、5万～8万亩经济林竹、3万～4万亩荔波樟江柚、2万亩酸梅、2万亩大板栗、1万亩茶叶、1万亩果银杏、5000亩魔芋、5000亩白板蓝根、5000亩黄草，采取公司+农户、农户+基地、公司+市场的经营组织形式，建立健全农村服务体系，大力开发农产品加工，走加工升值的路子，增加农民的货币化收入，使农民早日脱贫奔小康。三是调整县域经济下的区域经济结构。县域经济以旅游、矿产品开发、绿色产业、粮食生产的四大经济体系为框架，在自然条件较为优越的樟江河谷地带实施“四区一控”工程，即小康带建设区，到2001年玉屏、朝阳、瑶山、捞村等乡（镇）80%农户达到小康，两高一优农业示范区，到2002年实现蔬菜种植5000亩、水稻制种5000亩、蜜柚2万亩，樟江园林风光带建设区，到2000年河岸全部种上竹子，绿化荒山8万亩，河道开发30公里，旅游开发区，控制污染和毁损，加强对县城排污工作的治理，樟江沿岸生活垃圾不能倒到河里，加强对河道、河堤的整治工作，沿河25度坡退耕还林，达到山上带帽子、山腰挂果子、田坝种谷子、河岸种竹子、路旁建无污染的厂子、水上行船子，走集约经营和可持续发展的路子，人民群众口袋里有票子的目标，以茂兰为中心，重点开发煤炭、铅锌矿、金矿等资源为重点的项目，大力吸引资金，建立茂兰、立化南下工业小区，开发矿产资源。以甲良为中心，在甲良片区发展建材业，茶叶加工业及其他农产品加工，使县域经济和区域经济互相促进，蓬勃发展。四是调整财源结构，加快财源建设。一手抓即期财源，二手抓潜在财源，努力把部分潜在财源变为预期财源，在几年内彻底改变财政收入70%靠煤炭的这一畸形经济形式，充分利用矿产、土地、水能、旅游等资源优势，采取多手段的开发方式，使资源优势尽快转化为经济优势，形成二元以上经济结构，达到快速、持续、健康发展的县域经济结构格局。1. 抓好现有煤炭产业的健康发展，利用一厂一策，一井一策的手段，加大煤炭开发力度，上档次，以规模建设年产3万吨以上的骨干煤矿20个以上，以黑促绿，以地下促地上，积累经济发展的资本。2. 抓好煤炭以外的矿产品开发和加工企业，大力发展生产型乡镇企业。3. 抓好以绿色产业为优势的农业产业化企业。增大地方性财源比例。4. 依靠特色资源围绕旅游最大可能地发展个体私营经济和第三产业，使个体私营经济和第三产业对财政的贡献率达到最佳状态。

打好两个攻坚 一是扶贫攻坚。尽管我县已于1996年年底越过温饱线，但我县农民生活水平还不高，农村贫困人口还有一定比例，农村贫困面还相当大，15%的农民还处在温饱线以下，他们大部分是“一族三山”（即瑶族、瑶山、深山区、石山区）人口，加之全县60%的农田是靠天吃饭，农田水利基础设施较差，部分农民素质低，稳定地解决温饱的根基不牢，一遇自然灾害大有返贫可能，从这一实际出发，扶贫仍然是我们的攻坚任务。因此，要继续扎实执行好扶贫攻坚“三部曲”的有效措施和政策。第一步，有效地解决贫困群众的吃、穿、住，以解决温饱。第二步，有效地解决贫困群众的水、电、路，以巩固扶贫成果。第三步，加快实施贫困地区农业产业化，利用国家扶贫政策和资金，上项目、上产品、上市场，使农民具有固定的、长期的、具有一定市场份额的商品货币化收入，奠定向小康迈进的基础。二是小康攻坚，作为农村经济发展的阶段性目标，就是增加农民收入，达到小康生活标准，全县实施“八七”扶贫攻坚计划以来，尽管已取得可喜的成绩，但小康建设难度仍十分大，无疑也是一个攻坚。根据全县实际情况，经过艰苦努力，一部分乡（镇）、村、组可以优先进入省定小康村镇的行列，首先要抓好“四区一控”项目区内近5万人的小康建设问题，使他们在2001年基本进入小康；其次要抓好有条件乡镇的小康建设问题，立化、瑶麓争取在2001年全面奔小康；再次抓好除上述地区以外其他乡镇的小康建设问题，2001年要抓出1～2个小康村。各级党委和政府要切实抓好农业和农村工作，稳定增加农民收入，把农业产业化作为农民增加收入的主要途径，始终抓住扶贫攻坚和小康建设攻坚这一农村工作的“牛鼻子”，以小康工作总揽农业农村工作的全局。

实施三大战略一是科教兴县战略。为迎接知识经济时代的到来，采取多种形式，加快人才培养步伐，加大农业适用技术的培训力度。到2002年全县农村要实现60%的科技示范户，贫困地区、深山区要求达到40%，其他地区科技示范户要求达到70%以上。实现两个科技示范乡。二是开放带动战略。要解放思想，打破陈旧观念，实施全方位开放，夯实各方面基础，营造良好的行政环境，改善投资条件，实施优惠政策，大力引进县外资金，只要原则上不违背国家法律、法规、政策规定，一切优惠政策都可以实施，你帮我发展，我助你发财；只要能发展，微利也干，让利也干，一时无利也要干。三是可持续发展战略。严格执行计划生育政策，控制人口数量，提高人口素质，使人口增长与经济发展相适应；加快卫生体制改革，有效推动农村合作医疗，逐步形成医疗保险产业化，完善国家和社会养老保障机制；保护生态环境，重点以实施“两禁止、三关闭、两保护、建四区、严治理”，即禁止砍伐天然林、禁止放火烧山；关闭乡镇林工商公司、关闭杂木市场、关闭木炭市场；保护喀斯特森林、保护水源涵养林；建立除国家级茂兰喀斯特原始森林保护区外的四个县级自然生态环境保护区，即建立佳荣—瑶麓—水尧樟江上游自然生态保护区、甲良—方村—水利—玉屏自然生态保护区、永康—翁昂—捞村自然生态保护区、朝阳—瑶山—驾欧—播尧自然生态保护区，洞塘、立化原则上划归茂兰喀斯特原始森林保护处进行保护，扩大保护的业务范围；严格治理水土流失，要十分珍惜土地资源，合理开发和利用每寸土地，保持耕地的动态平衡。以创建全国喀斯特生态旅游公园县为目标、争取实施生态旅游农业示范县项目，实施全方位的各行各业的可持续发展战略。

抓住一个关键从经济学的观点看，无论是哪个地区环境再优越，资源再丰富，如果没有一支好的干部队伍，如果没有一个好的思想观念和思维方式，没有一个懂经济、懂政治、懂社会的领导班子，再好的资源都不能得到很好开发，再好的机遇也会失去。因此，一个地区的发展快与否，经济强与弱，人的因素是主要的。所以，抓好干部队伍和领导班子建设是我县跨世纪发展思路的关键。2000年前每年自筹资金25万元用于农村村级干部的培养，主要采取四种形式。一是招收村干班，学制两年，毕业后回原村任村委会科技副主任，已招收了150人就读，1999年继续招生100人。二是对现职45岁以下村干部利用农函大教材、县设总站、片设分站、乡镇设教学点，用严格的教学计划对现职村干部进行培训。三是举办短期村干部培训班，每年农闲都要进行一期四班。四是县里出钱给工资，选派村干部到发达县，先进县去挂职，全方位培养村干部和村级后备干部，提高村级干部群体素质。五是全力培养农村经济管理、农业科技人才二传手，每个村民组都要有5～10人不等的农业科技乡土人才。六是培养一支乡镇企业、经济管理、旅游开发等方面的科技、经营管理人才队伍，同时鼓励全县干部参加在职进修函授学习，到2002年年底前要求全县副科级以上领导干部必须达到大专以上文化学历。

跨世纪发展思路，是荔波县今后几年乃至十几年发展的总体战略，荔波的经济发展，万变不离其宗，超不出这规划，超不出这个基本框架，超不出县域经济的这个格局，这是荔波县情所决定的，这是发展市场经济的需要，是产业结构调整和产业升级政策的需要，是国家大政方针的需要，是荔波经济持续、快速、健康地向前发展的实际需要。

具有挑战性的21世纪稍纵即到，时间对于我们来说就是生命，对于我县来说就是命运，21世纪的建设，21世纪的经济，需要的是高含金量的速度，速度慢了等于坐以待毙，这就要求我们各级党委政府和全体干部职工要具有强烈的责任感，必须顾全大局，苦干实干，必须团结务实，开拓创新，继续贯彻执行党的十五大精神，高举邓小平理论的伟大旗帜，我们的目标一定会实现，我们的目标一定能够实现，荔波的明天一定更加美好。

中共荔波县委关于荔波县保护母亲河行动方案的决定

荔发〔2000〕26号

《荔波县保护母亲河行动方案》已经八届县委第六十次常委（扩大）会议研究通过，现予以印发执行。

围绕荔波县保护母亲河行动方案，县人大常委会要进一步组织讨论，并形成相关决议；县人民政府要在县委《决定》和县人大《决议》的基础上，制定相关的一系列政策措施和切实可行的实施方案，并组织实施。最终使荔波樟江河变得更加美丽，风姿多彩，青山常在，绿水长流，人民幸福安居乐业。

附：荔波县保护母亲河行动方案

中共荔波县委

2000年7月10日

荔波县保护母亲河行动方案

樟江河是国家级樟江风景名胜区的重要组成部分。近年来，县委、县政府对保护樟江采取了一系列有效措施，取缔了污染樟江河的厂矿，治理了污水，恢复了植被。樟江河污染问题得到初步遏制，樟江河环境日趋向好。但是，今年6月的两次特大洪水灾害，樟江河遭受严重创伤，沿河山体滑坡，树木植被损毁，河面增宽，河床变浅。为保护好人类共有共享的樟江河，保护好国家旅游资源，保护好荔波的母亲河，根据荔波县跨世纪发展思路和2000年6月30日“保护母亲河行动”第一次会议精神，特制定保护母亲河行动方案。

一、任务目标

保护母亲河行动是一项社会系统工程，工作内容多，涉及面广，必须动员全社会的积极支持和参与，因此，要采取统一规划，分步实施的方式进行。

（一）第一阶段（2000年6月30日—2001年6月30日）

1. 大造声势，广泛宣传。①举行保护母亲河行动万人签名活动；②印发关于保护母亲河行动给全县人民的一封信；③广播电视报道保护母亲河行动工作进展；④悬挂保护母亲河相关的标语或制作永久性标语；⑤举办保护母亲河知识竞赛。

2. 清理樟江河白色污染。由于6月两次洪水暴发，樟江河被塑料袋、垃圾等严重污染，为恢复樟江河的原貌，7月10日前组织县机关干部职工和沿河村组群众义务清理樟江河白色污染，重塑樟江河形象。

3. 划定保护樟江河的范围。组织调研小组，专题调查研究，8月10日前完成樟江河保护范围和界定方案，报县委、县政府研究决定，并以文件的形式固定下来。

4. 编制保护母亲河行动规划，根据樟江河保护范围，结合樟江两岸的地形、气候、水文地质的实际，规划沿河两岸绿化树种，草种以及种植方式。

5. 任务责任到位，第一阶段完成樟江河保护范围绿化面积的30%。因此，2000年11月30日前必须做好三件事，即任务分解、苗木准备、明确责任。

①任务分解。根据樟江沿河两岸绿化工作易难程度，先易后难，先实施交通方便的河段，先河坎后山腰山顶逐步实施绿化，并将任务分解或发包到机关单位和沿河村组，定桩插牌划界。

②苗木准备。按照规划要求和各类苗木实际需要，备足苗木，确保苗木供应。

③明确责任。把樟江河绿化工作纳入沿河乡镇及各机关单位的年度考核内容，制定统一的技术管理措施，明确实施单位的责任，并签订保护母亲河行动绿化工作责任状。

（二）第二阶段（2001年7月1日—2002年12月底）

1. 保护母亲河行动绿化实施单位对所承包绿化地段，进行科学管护，绿化未成活的树种要补栽补种。

2. 按规划对尚有50%的绿化面积进行分解落实，准备所需苗木，按技术要求及时栽种，强化管理。

3. 2002年12月对各单位完成的绿化面积进行检查验收，绿化树成活率达到95%以上的可以移交保护母亲河行动专门工作机构管护，未达到要求的继续补救完善。经验收达到要求后方可移交。

（三）第三阶段（2003年1月以后）

1. 完善保护母亲河行动各项工作制度和管理措施。

2. 总结经验，表彰保护母亲河行动中涌现出来的先进单位和先进个人。

二、政策措施

保护母亲河行动是一项功在当代、利在千秋的伟大事业，是一项长期性的工作，完成这一艰巨的工作任务，必须有一系列的政策措施作保障。因此，在行动第一阶段中要制定出台以下几个方面的配套政策。

1. 关于樟江河河坎禁止建房的决定。

2. 关于樟江沿岸边禁止堆放杂物、倾倒生活垃圾和建筑垃圾的决定。

3. 关于樟江沿河两岸禁止取砂（土、石）的决定。
4. 关于樟江沿河两岸禁止办厂（场）的决定。
5. 关于樟江河禁止电、毒、炸鱼和猎鸟的决定。
6. 关于樟江沿河两岸25度以上坡耕地退耕还林（草）的决定。
7. 关于樟江沿河两岸土地及河道开发的决定。
8. 关于樟江沿河两岸工业、生活污水排放与治理的有关规定。

三、组织机构

动员、组织全民投入保护母亲河行动。尽快实现樟江河绿化、美化、净化工作目标，领导是关键。因此，必须健全组织，划定职能，落实编制，安排人员，使保护母亲河行动有人抓、有人管。

1. 建立荔波县保护母亲河行动工作领导小组，下设办公室，樟江沿河乡镇也要建立相应的工作领导小组。
2. 扩增县环保局编制，充实人员，组建荔波县保护樟江母亲河执法大队。
3. 建立荔波县公安局樟江河道治安管理派出所。
4. 建立荔波县樟江河开发有限责任公司。

四、经费安排

从环境治理基金中每年安排20万元作为开发启动和配套资金，一定三年不变。

中共荔波县委　荔波县人民政府
关于创建“全国科普示范县”的决定

荔党发〔2002〕11号

各乡镇党委、人民政府，县直机关各级党组织、县直各工作部门：

根据中国科协科协办普字〔2002〕10号文件，《关于全国科普示范县（市、区）创建单位的复函》，正式批准我县参加全国科普示范县（市、区）创建活动。

为深入贯彻落实党的十五届五中、六中全会精神，按照县委、县人民政府提出的“以邓小平理论为指导”，进一步贯彻落实“七一”重要讲话，按照“三个代表”的要求，坚持“三个有利于”的根本标准，把发展作为主题，把结构调整作为主线，把改革开放和科技进步作为动力，努力加强四大基础（交通、农业、能源、教育基础设施），实施三大战略（科技兴县、开放带动、可持续发展），调整三大结构（产业、所有制、区域经济），开发三大资源（旅游、矿产、能源），以经济建设为中心，以增加城乡居民收入为根本，促进两个文明协调发展，加快富民兴县步伐的全县社会经济发展总体思路，紧紧围绕经济建设这个中心，组织全县各级干部和广大科技工作者，农村科技骨干，积极开展丰富多彩的科技活动，大力宣传科学思想，普及科技知识，倡导科学方法，弘扬科学精神，充分发挥科普工作在提高劳动者素质，促进县域经济发展、社会进步中的基础作用。始终坚持以市场为导向，实行农、科、教结合，推进产业结构调整和农业产业化进程，推动科技成果向现实生产力转化，促进我县经济社会全面发展。

县委、县政府决定2002年至2004年参加“全国科普示范县”创建活动，各级党委、人民政府，县直机关各级党组织、各工作部门要结合工作职责，积极配合参与创建活动。各单位在保障科普经费的前提下，适当安排创建活动经费。

中共荔波县委
荔波县人民政府
2002年5月8日

中共荔波县委　荔波县人民政府
关于开展创建国家卫生县城活动的决定

（2002年9月9日）

荔党发〔2002〕15号

各乡镇党委、人民政府，县直机关各级党组织、工作部门、社会团体：

为进一步扩大对外开放，深化改革，不断改善人民群众工作、生活环境，创造优质的环境迎接更多的中外来宾到我县旅游观光、投资、开发建设，促进全县两个文明建设的快速发展，实现旅游强具的目标。根据中共中央、国务院《关于卫生改革与发展的决定》《关于加强卫生工作的决定》和全国爱卫会《关于开展创建国家卫生城市活动的通知》精神，县委、县人民政府决定在进一步巩固省级卫生县城的基础上，开展创建国家卫生县城的活动。

一、创建国家卫生县城的指导思想

以江泽民同志的“三个代表”为指导，以改善广大群众工作和生活环境，提高生活质量，加速两个文明建设为根本目的，坚持“政府组织、职能部门负责、全民动员、科学治理、社会监督”的创建方针，按照经济建设、城市建设、卫生建设健康发展的原则，标本兼治，使创建卫生县城和爱国卫生工作经常化、制度化、规范化，努力提高县城整体功能水平，带动全县经济健康发展。

二、创建国家卫生县城的总体目标

开展健康教育，提高居民的大卫生意识，形成良好的社会卫生风气；全面整治市容环境，完善县城卫生基础设施，改善县城卫生面貌；全面加强防害防病，提高行业卫生水平、增强人民健康素质。通过创建卫生县城活动，力争2004年达到国家卫生县城标准。

三、创建国家卫生县城的具体内容

（一）制定好县城爱国卫生活动年度计划和长远规划，并积极组织各单位开展除四害、爱国卫生月、六化评比、创建文明卫生单位等活动，确保取得实效。

（二）利用多种形式开展健康教育，抓好一个特殊人群和特殊行业健康教育试点。中小学校全面开展健康教育课。

（三）车站等公共场所开辟卫生专栏，设置数量足够的环卫设施。旅店、理发店等经营场所配备消毒设施，从业人员全面进行健康检查，有传染病的，严禁从事公共服务行业。饮水水质100%达到卫生标准，供水部门建立严格的卫生管理制度。

（四）从事食品生产、经营的单位卫生许可发证率达100%，建立严格的卫生、消毒管理制度。畜产品必须定点屠宰、定点销售，检疫上市。严禁传染病患者从事食品生产、经营工作，从业人员体检率、培训率达到100%，严禁销售变质食品。

（五）制定防治“四害”规划，年内开展4次灭“四害”活动，保证县城鼠密度大大低于无鼠害标准。切实加强传染病防治工作，不发生任何传染病流行现象，计划免疫接种率达到100%。

（六）全面治理工业污染，“三废”基本达标排放，不发生任何污染环境事故。严格执行县人民政府关于严禁燃放烟花爆竹的规定，在城区内行驶的车辆严禁鸣放高音喇叭，任何车辆不得在夜间鸣喇叭。

（七）严格学校卫生管理，配备必需卫生器材和环卫设施，教育学生养成良好的卫生习惯，建立学生健康档案。

（八）市容整齐、美观。突出抓好“六化”（即净化、绿化、美化、香化、亮化、硬化）。

1. 抓净化。集中力量、集中精力继续开展四大整顿；一是整顿交通，二轮摩托车驾驶员行车必戴头盔，加大无证行车的查处力度；严禁在城区人行道及严管街停靠、停放任何车辆；县城各单位货车一律在各自院内装卸货物。二是整顿市场、划行规市、严禁占道经营；取缔所有车道、人行道上的摊位、夜宵摊点；消除所有门店前的棚、架和堆放在人行道上的货物；拆除一切不规范的广告牌、指示牌、招牌；严禁在非指定地段从事任何经营活动。三是整顿建筑工地。县城内所有建筑工程，一律实行封闭施工，严禁占道堆放物料和占道作业，装运泥、砂、砖、瓦等车辆一律实行封闭式，按规定时间行驶线路进行装运。四是整顿环卫秩序。全面推广家庭生活垃圾袋装法；禁止在公共场所随地吐痰、乱扔纸屑、果皮、烟头等；禁止在临街阳台、雨棚、门窗上悬挂物品；禁止擅自进城淘粪；禁止城区的单位院内饲养家禽家畜；单位院内的简易厕所全部改为水冲式厕所，达到卫生标准要求；禁止损坏、侵占、盗窃市政公用设施；禁止在公共场所吸烟；全面推行“三制”，即门前三包责任制、环卫工人路段责任制、定期检查责任制。

2. 抓绿化。全面推行以草地和风景树交错相间，美观大方的绿化格局。对风景树定枝定型；按照多树种、多形状的要求，移植和培育一些观赏风景林；严禁占用公共绿地，严禁损坏县城花草树木和擅自修剪或砍伐绿化树木。

3. 抓美化。一是全面推行临街店面、公共场所、办公场所、生活场所用盆景等进行布局美化；二是街面实施一街一树一花一灯一景的规划建设，逐步实现县城园林化、公园化；三是县城主要街道临街门面要统一规划，限期装修；四是所有街道临街的门店要装霓虹灯，重点装饰樟江大街。

4. 抓香化。一是机关单位办公场所的阳台、办公室必须摆放鲜花盆景；二是机关院落必须按规划进行栽花种草；三是居民住户大力培植和摆放盆景；四是公共场所空地种植或摆放鲜花。

5. 抓亮化。各机关单位、住户临街门面，房屋必须进行彩灯装饰，大街小巷的路灯、彩灯必须按时开启，照亮率达到98%以上。

6. 抓硬化。县城主街、支街和居民生活区道路硬化率达100%，完好率保存在98%以上，人行道、下水道进行全面建设整修，达到标准要求，各单位完成交办的建设任务达100%。完善县城规划区内时来、板吉村的道路硬化。

（九）加强县城治安管理。认真抓好普法教育，不断提高市民法律意识，增强法制观念。认真搞好社会治安综合治理，建立健全机关、学校、企事业单位的安全保卫责任制；公安部门设置“110”报警台，成立防暴大队，24小时值班，加强治安监管；严格禁止和坚决查处嫖娼卖淫、吸毒贩毒、赌博等违法犯罪活动。

四、创建国家卫生县城的主要措施

1. 加强对创建工作的组织领导。成立荔波县创建国家卫生县城领导小组，组建创建办公室，全面负责创建国家卫生县城的组织工作。各部门要切实把创建工作纳入议事日程，相应成立创建卫生县城领导小组，实行一把手负总责，制定工作方案、工作计划。进一步加强创卫办的建设，做到领导、机构、编制、人员、经费、办公地点“六落实”，确保创建工作顺利完成。

2. 加大宣传力度，营造创建工作的浓厚氛围。创建国家卫生县城是全县人民的共同事业，必须充分搞好宣传，发动群众，形成创建卫生县城的共识，县委宣传部要把第九个“爱国卫生运动宣传月”（4月）定为“创建国家卫生县城宣传月”，县广播电视局要开辟“创建卫生县城”和“九亿农民健康教育行动”专栏，各中小学要开设健康教育课，全县市民要积极主动参与创卫活动。

3. 建立健全市容卫生管理队伍。一是环卫专业队伍。城区环卫工人按不低于常住人口2‰的比例配备，负责城区主要道路的清扫保洁、垃圾粪便的清运和无害化处理，公共厕所等场所的卫生管理工作。二是“门前三包”管理队伍，成立群众卫生监督队。三是城市管理监督队伍，行使城市管理执法职能。四是公安、交通、工商、环保、卫生、建设、交警等部门各司其职，抓好创卫的各项工作。

4. 落实创建工作责任制。根据卫生县城的创建方针，坚持条块结合、以块为重、条条落实、块块检查的工作方法，把创建卫生县城的各项任务分解到有关单位、部门和玉屏镇，并层层签订目标管理责任状。创建卫生县城要纳入双文明目标管理的重要内容。凡是小孩违禁追究家长或监护人的责任，单位、职工违禁追究单位负责人、主管单位负责人直到县级分管领导责任，一级对一级负责。县委、县政府抓各单位及玉屏镇，各单位及玉屏镇抓好下属单位、居（村）委员会。要实行四家班子领导包路段包片区责任制，将有关责任区分别安排到四大班子，由四大班子确定专人负责，认真抓好监督。

5. 加大依法管理的力度，严管重罚到位。凡违背创建卫生县城有关规定的，必须从严从重处罚，决不姑息迁就，对侮辱、殴打或阻挠城镇管理人员执行公务的，坚持依法从严查处。

6. 强化督查力度，做到奖惩到位。督查工作的主要内容是领导力度是否到位，责任明确是否到人，硬件建设是否落实，工作任务是否按照完成。县创建办、爱卫办将定期不定期地进行督查和抽查，督查结果通报全县，该表扬的要大力表扬，该批评的要坚决批评并限期改正，问题严重的单位负责人该处分的要处分。创建工作成绩突出的单位或个人予以奖励，对创建工作毫无起色的或未达标的，该处罚的要处罚，该换岗的要换岗。对有令不行、有禁不止、不按时完成任务的要坚决予以撤职。以确保创建工作的顺利进行。

中共荔波县委
荔波县人民政府
2002年9月9日

中共荔波县委　荔波县人民政府关于加快旅游业发展的决定

〔2003年5月29日中共荔波县九届四次全委（扩大）会通过〕

荔党发（2003）15号

我县是中共一大唯一的少数民族代表邓恩铭烈士的故乡，拥有世界级的中国贵州茂兰自然保护区和荔波樟江国家重点风景名胜区，少数民族风情浓郁，自然历史文化遗产丰富，旅游综合开发优势突出，发展潜力巨大。经过全县干部职工和各族群众的长期努力，旅游业有了较大的发展，成为县域经济新的增长点，旅游业大发展的格局已经初步形成。但是，我县旅游业发展总体水平与全国先进旅游区相比还有很大差距，主要表现为品牌知名度低，基础设施薄弱，旅游建设资金投入不足，融资和吸引外来投资能力弱，旅游从业人员文化素质偏低，服务质量不高，接待能力还很低，旅游宣传促销力度不够，缺乏人文景观、文化氛围，旅游商品开发力度还不够等。为充分发挥我县旅游资源优势，改善旅游环境，把旅游业培育成为我县新的支柱产业，使荔波尽快成为贵州旅游重点区和中国优秀旅游县，根据《中共贵州省委、贵州省人民政府关于加快旅游业发展的意见》（黔党发〔2002〕20号）精神，结合我县实际，作出加快旅游业发展的决定。

一、加快旅游业发展的指导思想、基本构架和总体目标

（一）**指导思想**：进一步加快荔波旅游开发建设步伐，突出重点，立足长远，实施精品旅游战略，把荔波建设成为全省旅游重点区、中国优秀旅游县，打造成为贵州乃至全国的旅游精品，使旅游产业成为荔波县域经济的支柱产业。

要做到四个结合：旅游开发与资源保护相结合；自然景观开发与民族文化开发相结合；景观建设与科普建设相结合；旅游发展与扶贫开发相结合。挖掘旅游文化底蕴和内涵，实现自然景观和文化、科技的有机组合，走可持续发展道路。

要运用好政府和市场两种手段，以政府的宏观规划管理和市场机制运作方式，营造良好氛围，吸纳社会资金有序参与开发建设。

要通过旅游开发，促进产业结构的战略性调整，带动扶贫开发和小康社会建设。

（二）**基本构架**：荔波旅游发展基本构架为“打好一张牌、发展两个区、建设三条线、拓展四个点、建成一个中心”的“一二三四一”发展格局。“打好一张牌”，就是顺应现代旅游发展趋势，以创品牌为目标，进一步研究、升华和提炼荔波旅游的内涵和特色，尽快推出荔波旅游特色品牌，充分发挥品牌效应，扩大影响，提高品位，增强吸引力。“发展两个区”，就是以荔波樟江国家重点风景名胜区和国家级茂兰自然保护区为重点实施重点突破，用三年至五年的时间，通过完善基础设施，充分挖掘旅游资源，开发新的景点，把“两区”建设成为全国知名旅游精品，支撑带动全县旅游经济快速发展。“建设三条线”，就是建设生态旅游线、民族风情旅游线、红色文化旅游线。在交通条件不断改善、景区景点质量不断提高的基础上，串联大七孔、小七孔、樟江河、水春河和茂兰自然保护区，形成一条环线生态旅游精品线；充分挖掘县内瑶族、苗族、水族、布依族等少数民族文化内涵，建成甲良拉干、拉料，水利大寨，玉屏水扒、水春，永康拉桥、尧古，洞塘瑶寨，瑶山菇类、内孟塘，朝阳寨马，瑶麓，佳荣大土等一批少数民族村寨，建成一条环线民族风情旅游精品线；多方吸纳资金，把邓恩铭故居建设成为集革命思想教育和民族风情展示为一体的精品旅游景点，与板寨红七军会师旧址相辉映，构成一条贯穿东西的红色旅游精品线。“拓展四个点”，就是进一步拓展月亮山、甲良片区、捞村河和佳荣坤地4个景点，扩大荔波旅游景区规模，使荔波成为名副其实的旅游县、公园县。“建成一个中心”，就是以建设贵州旅游快速发展区为载体，力争用三年至五年时间，把荔波建设成为贵州南线旅游中心。

（三）**发展目标**：力争用三年左右时间使荔波初步成为功能齐全、设施配套、在全国具有较高知名度、具有较好经济社会效益的旅游目的地。

具体目标是：2003—2005年，力争使旅游人数以每年35%的速度递增，旅游总收入年均增长35%左右；到2005年，接待游客50万人次，社会总收入2.5亿元，直接收入3000万元，间接收入2.2亿元，旅游业成为荔波的支柱产业，带动效应明显增强；到2010年，生态旅游、民族风情文化旅游、红色文化旅游、科考探险旅游及休闲度假旅游全面建成，全县旅游产品系列组合特色明显增强，旅

游基础设施和服务设施进一步完善，旅游规模进一步扩大，档次有较大提高，旅游发展由规模型向效益型转变，旅游客源由省内和两广扩大到全国，并逐步打开国际旅游市场，实现年接待游客135万人，社会总收入8.1亿元，直接收入1.1亿元，间接收入7亿元，使荔波成为我国西部的重要旅游目的地和旅游热点地区，成为全国旅游精品。

二、加快旅游业发展的工作重点

（一）搞好荔波县旅游发展详细规划，切实加大旅游业的开发。遵循“保护第一，开发第二，先规划，后建设”的原则，加快旅游开发。为突出荔波旅游特色，将自然生态景观、民族风情、历史文化等相互融合，在制定《荔波县旅游发展总体规划》的基础上，聘请具有较高资质的规划设计单位科学制定《荔波县旅游发展详细规划》，经法定程序通过后，实行公示，接受社会监督，全县相关基础设施建设要在旅游发展总体规划和详规框架内开展。在旅游规划区内，凡不符合规划的建筑物或其他设施，要限期改造或拆除，对违反规划的有关责任单位和责任人进行严肃查处。

实施旅游精品战略，在不断完善现有景区、景点设施，提高品位的基础上，统一规划，努力在较短的时间内建成和推出一批交通便捷、环境优美、安全舒适、服务优良，在全省、全国有一定竞争实力的旅游线路。积极发展以生态旅游、民族风情文化旅游、红色文化旅游、科考探险旅游及休闲度假旅游，以满足不同消费群体的需求。深入挖掘民族文化、历史文化，加大生态科普知识宣传力度，加快邓恩铭故居和板寨红七军会师旧址建设，建设民俗文化博物馆、革命历史博物馆和喀斯特生态博物馆。积极支持和鼓励创办旅游娱乐公司、旅游文化演出团队和生态休闲疗养度假中心等。将旅游发展与农村经济结构调整、扶贫开发和生态保护结合起来，积极发展乡村旅游和旅游观光农业。在旅游公路沿线保护建设一批民族村寨，开辟民族风情旅游项目。积极将樟江风景名胜区申报为世界自然遗产地，提升名胜区档次。争取把天然林集中的水甫一带建成县级喀斯特森林自然保护区，把甲料建成县级桫椤自然保护区，把台村建成县级湿地森林保护区，并积极申报建设国家地质公园。

（二）加大基础设施建设力度，抓好配套服务工作。进一步加大以旅游公路及市政设施建设为主的基础设施建设力度。独荔公路、麻小公路已经开通，三都经荔波至南丹、立化至大沙坡公路及茂兰保护区旅游公路即将完成改造，飞机场已经开工建设，三年后，荔波将形成一个以陆空为主的立体化交通格局。今后要着重抓好景区内部道路网络的建设和改造，修建景区内的游览步道。争取驾欧拉圭经朝阳洪江至县城，县城通往各景区、景点，县城通往佳荣、播尧、捞村等旅游资源富集区以及捞村至翁昂的旅游公路尽早立项开工，逐步形成以县城为中心，辐射各旅游景区的道路网络，切实改善交通不畅的境况。在景区内部结合各景点的特点，建设与人文、生态环境相协调，畅通、安全的人行步道和汽车通道，使用景区内部专用交通工具，一些景区和景点要在通过科学论证和规划的前提下，建设安全快捷的索道或扶梯。

积极向铁路主管部门申请，争取开通荔波立化、独山麻尾的旅游专列。加快樟江航运建设步伐，建成一批有较高档次的码头，提高船舶档次，开辟舒适、安全的水上旅游项目。合理安排和调整县内旅游交通运输线路，增加通往贵阳和广西南丹、环江、柳州等地的旅游客车。搞好通信、供水、供电和垃圾、污水处理等设施建设，建成一批清洁卫生的公共厕所。在全县所有乡镇旅游公路沿线、景区内开通程控电话和移动通信，建立旅游信息网络查询系统，民族村寨和各景区、景点都有较为完备的配套设施。建设一批上档次的星级饭店和宾馆，规划和发展一批安全、舒适、具有民族特色的家庭旅馆。加大旅游商品开发力度，对旅游商品开发和旅游商品销售市场进行统一规划，开发具有瑶族、苗族、水族、布依族等少数民族特色的服饰、食品、乐器以及花卉、盆景、奇石等旅游商品，以优惠政策吸引外地旅游工艺品公司到县内经营销售，激活旅游商品市场。培育和扶持一批县内旅游商品开发公司，使旅游购物在三年内达到占整个旅游消费的20%左右。

（三）进一步加强生态建设和环境保护整治工作。加大生态保护执法力度和景区保护条例执行力度，继续实施“两禁止、三关闭、两保护、建四区、严治理”的生态环境保护政策，积极争创全国生态旅游示范县。关闭取缔公路沿线可视范围内开山取石取土等各种污染环境、破坏生态的作业场，凡因建设需要经有关部门批准建立的，必须按规定在事前做好水土保持规划和按规定落实好保护生态措施。逐步关闭小七孔景区内4个梯级水电站，提升景区质量档次。对生活在景区、保护区、核心区的群众实行易地移民搬迁，保护景区、保护区的生态环境。以旅游公路沿线、景区周围为重点，实施沼气工程建设，解决群众生活燃料问题，有效保护天然林，实现农业生态良性循环。坚决打击各种非法捕杀、出售、食用野生保护动物行为，加强对水春至县城至小七孔及各主要河道的管护，在全县水域内禁止电鱼、炸鱼、毒鱼、网鱼，保护鱼类正常繁殖。用足用好国家退耕还林政策，对25度以上坡耕地、宜林荒山实施退耕还林或荒山造林，努力实现实施一个退耕还林项目就是打造一个旅游景点的目标，突出抓好荔波至小七孔樟江沿河、独荔公路沿线、麻小公路以及荔大公路和景区内的环境绿化，新建的旅游公路要同步建设绿化带，到2005年，全县森林覆盖率达到60%以上。抓好城镇和旅游沿线环境综合整治工作，加大对城镇和景区、景点、公路沿线垃圾、污水处理，保证县内各主要河道、水域水质达到国家环保标准。结合创建全国卫生县城，广泛开展爱国卫生运动，扩大城区绿化面积，对县水泥厂进行搬迁，彻底解决城镇中存在的“脏、乱、差”现象。凡通往景区公路两侧不符合旅游发展规划的地面建筑物，要坚决进行拆除，坟墓要进行迁葬或通过植树遮盖，景区公路沿线的村寨，其建设必须经县级有关部门严格审批。

（四）整顿和规范旅游市场秩序，提高旅游业服务质量。建立政府统一领导、部门相互配合的综合协调机制，按照标本兼治的原则，加强对旅游市场的监管，严肃查处和打击各种形式的欺客、宰客以及制售假冒伪劣商品、提供虚假服务承诺等损害游客合法权益的违法行为。

大力推进旅游景区、旅游商品、旅游设施、旅游服务、旅游管理的标准化体系建设。强化对旅行社和导游人员的管理，规范导游解说词和团队运作，提高服务质量。积极申报星级宾馆、饭店，加强管理、复核。加强旅游从业人才的培养，建立旅游教育培训基地，对全县所有从事涉及旅游服务的人员进行业务培训，统一持证上岗。有计划地培养和引进旅游专业人才到县内就业，提高旅游业管理水平。

建立健全旅游活动各个环节安全制度，落实责任制，强化旅游安全管理，防止各类安全事故的发生。旅游、卫生和安全管理部门要协调制定好旅游安全事故紧急处理预案，公安部门要加强社会治安管理力度，以110、120为中心建立社会联动系统，依法严厉打击各种违法犯罪行为，及时处置旅游安全突发事件，确保广大游客的生命财产安全。

（五）进一步加大旅游宣传力度，扩大荔波旅游知名度。聘请省内外知名专家担任荔波旅游发展和宣传顾问，为荔波旅游形象进行准确定位，对全县旅游的对外宣传进行总体策划，使荔波旅游开发目标更加明确，措施更加科学具体、有操作性。充分利用各种传媒，并通过创办荔波旅游网站，申办全国性有一定影响的会议以及展览、文化和体育活动，分年度办好具有较大影响、独具荔波特色的旅游节等多种形式加大旅游宣传推介力度。邀请知名艺术家到荔波创作，谱写能在全国唱响荔波的通俗歌曲，编排能充分展示荔波风土人情的文艺节目，注册上市反映荔波奇山秀水的声相影碟，摄制具有影响力的影视剧，制作一批高质量的民族歌曲和地方乐器演奏的乐曲声相制品，编写一本融荔波民族风情、土特产品、传说故事、地方趣事等为一体的旅游宣传图书和一本为游客提供吃、住、行、游、娱、购全方位服务的旅游指南。加强与县境周边省市、地州、县份旅游机构团体的沟通与交流合作，联合开发跨地域旅游线路，巩固和扩大客源市场。

三、加快旅游业发展的工作措施

（一）成立机构，加强领导。及时调整充实旅游发展委员会，确保决策机构工作的连续性，委员会作为常设工作机构，负责研究、贯彻关于旅游开发的有关政策，制定全县旅游发展规划，实施行业管理、环境整治执法、民族文化及旅游商品开发、宣传策划促销、协调和考核涉及旅游各单位的工作。旅游工作由县委、县政府主要领导亲自抓，作为县委、县政府的“一把手”经济，安排一名副县级领导专抓旅游开发工作，委员会成员由县涉及旅游的工作部门负责人组成，委员会办公室下设5个科，为正科级事业机构，机构工作人员从县内各部门中选调。明确各科室的工作目标任务，分段实施，稳步推进。

各涉及旅游的工作部门要围绕旅游开发做好相关工作，计划部门要指导和协调做好旅游业发展规划的编制和实施工作，把支持旅游业发展，特别是旅游基础设施和旅游重点项目建设纳入国民经济和社会中长期计划和年度计划；经贸、财政、税务、交通、建设、林业、水利、国土、文化、环保等部门要制定支持旅游业发展的配套政策措施；教育、人事等部门要制定旅游人才的培养和引进计划；公安、工商、物价、卫生、质量技术监督等部门要加强旅游运输、安全、价格、市场秩序、食品卫生、社会治安等方面的监督管理工作。

（二）进一步深化旅游投资经营体制改革，广泛吸引社会资金参与旅游开发。实施政府主导，社会参与的多元投资经营体制，既要充分发挥政府主导、规划和市场监管的主导作用，又要广泛吸纳社会资金参与旅游开发，引进现代企业经营管理体制经营景区景点，努力改变政企不分，经营管理不顺的现状。在积极向上争取国家资金投入的同时，争取金融机构加大对旅游基础设施建设的信贷投入和延长贷款期限。按照《中共贵州省委、贵州省人民政府关于加快旅游业发展的意见》（黔党发〔2002〕20号）文件规定的土地使用、税费等优惠政策措施执行外，结合本县实际制定更加优惠和宽松的旅游投资政策，为参与旅游开发的个人和企业提供优质便捷的服务。加强荔波旅游资源开发潜力宣传，吸引北京、上海及沿海发达地区和港澳台以及国外企业财团参与荔波旅游开发。积极探索旅游景区、景点转让、拍卖、合作、租赁经营权等形式开发旅游资源和进行旅游基础设施建设。

（三）进一步加大民族风情、民族文化挖掘力度，培育独具地方特色的旅游品牌。加大民族村寨保护和建设力度，聘请专家对县城建筑风格进行定位，对现有建筑进行改造包装，对新开发的城区按民族风格进行规划建设；对旅游公路沿线民族村寨进行保护，严格公路两旁居民建房用地审批，今后房屋设计必须统一规范，使其更具瑶族、苗族、水族、布依族等少数民族传统风格；对水族水书、瑶山瑶族等民族文化以及邓恩铭故居、板寨红七军会师旧址文化内涵进行挖掘，结合邓恩铭故居保护性建设工程的开工建设，引资修建集民族风情表演、民族婚俗、民族服饰展示、民族旅游工艺品展销为一体的民族一条街；引进市场机制经营民族村寨，保护民族文化，把发展民族文化旅游与带动少数民族脱贫致富结合起来。县内的各宾馆饭店要突出地方民族特点，统一着民族服装，使用民族特色的食谱、餐具、酒具用于旅游接待。

2003年6月5日

中共荔波县委　荔波县人民政府
关于进一步加快新阶段扶贫开发与小康建设的决定

（2003年6月20日）

荔党发〔2003〕25号

党的十六大明确提出了全面建设小康社会的奋斗目标。我县经过“八七”扶贫攻坚和新阶段近三年的扶贫开发，农村贫困人口总体上基本解决温饱问题，同时，我县自实施小康建设以来，已有部分乡镇和村组基本达到小康标准。但是，目前我县尚有未解决温饱贫困人口19088人，已解决温饱的人口越线水平低，极易返贫，小康建设虽然已经起步，但小康村数量少，总体水平不高，我县实现全面脱贫致富奔小康的目标任务还十分艰巨。全县各级各部门要认真学习和贯彻《中国农村扶贫开发纲要（2001—2010）》《中共贵州省委、贵州省人民政府关于切实做好新阶段扶贫开发工作的决定》和中央、省、州党委、政府关于扶贫开发与小康建设的有关工作部署和要求，扎实地做好新阶段扶贫开发与小康建设工作。

一、新阶段扶贫开发与小康建设的初步成果和基本经验

在中央国家机关和省、州有关部门，深圳对口帮扶单位和社会各界的大力支持帮助下，全县干部职工和人民群众团结一致、求真务实、与时俱进、奋力拼搏，使我县新阶段扶贫开发与小康建设工作取得了初步成效。农村各项基础设施不断完善，群众思想观念和精神面貌发生明显转变，人口与计划生育工作取得明显成效，生态环境建设步伐进一步加快，科技、文化、教育、卫生等社会事业有了较大发展，群众生产生活条件有了较大改善。三年来，共解决9712人的温饱问题，贫困人口由2000年年底的28800人降到2002年的19088人，全县农民人均纯收入由2000年的1196元增加到1255元；至2002年我县已经被省州批准命名的小康村有15个，共涉及5个乡（镇）、91个村民小组、2760户11155人，小康村农民人均占有粮食360公斤以上，人均纯收入达2500元。

在新阶段扶贫开发与小康建设实践中，全县广大干部群众把中央、省、州的各项方针政策与荔波县实际相结合，创造性地开展工作，积累了许多宝贵的经验。主要是：始终坚持把新阶段扶贫开发与小康建设作为推动全县经济发展的全局性工作，实行政府主导，动员和组织社会各界参与；始终坚持从解决贫困人口温饱这个最迫切的问题入手，把极贫村、特困户作为重点扶持对象，把农业产业结构调整，拓宽农民增收渠道作为主要措施，动感情、动脑筋、动真格，把扶贫开发与小康建设政策落实到村到户；始终坚持以经济建设为中心，以发展种养业和改善基本生产生活条件为重点，坚持走开发式扶贫和开放式扶贫的道路；始终坚持一手抓扶贫开发，一手抓小康建设不放松，扶贫开发与小康建设互相促进，相得益彰；始终紧紧抓住提高人口素质这个关键，积极发展科技、教育、文化、卫生事业，加强计划生育工作，促进农村经济、社会全面发展；始终注重充分发挥农村基层组织的积极作用，调动广大干部群众的积极性和创造性，认真开展“三级联创”活动，努力实践“三个代表”重要思想，大力开展“学大关”“学大土”活动，激励贫困乡村干部群众自力更生，艰苦奋斗，坚韧不拔，苦干实干，自我发展。

二、新阶段扶贫开发与小康建设目标

扶贫开发目标：到2005年基本解决19088贫困人口的温饱问题，使全县农民人均纯收入达到1500～1700元，基本解决农村通路、通电及农村饮水困难，全县贫困乡镇由10个降到2个以下，贫

困村由现在的94个降到16个以下；到2010年，全县农民人均纯收入达到1900～2000元，全面解决农村通路、通电和人畜用水问题，实现乡乡通油路、村村通电话，农户拥有电话率在40%以上，全部消除贫困乡镇和贫困村。

小康建设目标：全县国民生产总值年均增长速度在10%以上，高于全省及全州平均水平，经济总量和自我发展、自我积累能力明显增强，城乡居民生活水平进一步提高，基础设施建设得到进一步加强，特色经济和优势产业进一步发展，生态环境建设取得明显成效，各项社会事业较快发展。全县在樟江河谷“小康带”建成小康村27个，面上建成小康村50个，建成小康乡镇5个。建成的小康村农民人均纯收入达2500元以上，小康村人民群众生活水平、科技、文化、教育、卫生、通信等各项指标均达到或超过国家农村小康建设指标，全县农村群众生产生活条件有较大改善和提高。

三、扶贫开发与小康建设的指导思想

高举邓小平理论伟大旗帜，以党的十六大精神为指导，努力实践“三个代表”重要思想，继续贯彻落实中央、省、州关于新阶段扶贫开发与小康建设的各项方针政策；坚持以经济建设为中心，深化县情认识，以扶贫开发为先导，以小康建设为目标，一手抓扶贫，一手抓导富，全面加快小康社会建设步伐；坚持发展才是硬道理，通过发展推动扶贫开发与小康建设，通过发展解决前进中遇到的困难和问题；坚持改革开放，抢抓西部大开发机遇，不断加强基础设施建设，广泛动员社会力量，加快资源综合开发与合理利用，促进县域经济全面发展；坚持自力更生，不等不靠，充分发挥主观能动性，苦干实干，抢抓争快，全面推动新阶段扶贫开发与小康建设跃上新台阶。

四、加快新阶段扶贫开发与小康建设工作重点

（一）进一步加大产业结构调整力度，积极推进农业产业化经营。在稳定粮食安全的前提下，面向市场，依靠科技进步，大力发展优质、高产、高效和特色农业为重点，优化种植结构，以农业综合开发为契机，建设一批高产示范基地、农业综合开发基地，对农业产业化经营起到带动作用。进一步调整畜禽结构，以高代杂交优质肉牛和三元杂交猪的养殖和推广为主，因地制宜发展种养业，并鼓励和支持发展家禽规模养殖。利用我县丰富的非耕地优势，大力发展经果林、速生用材林和中药材等种植。结合我县加快旅游业发展，积极引导进行旅游商品的生产和加工。按照“公司+农户”的模式，扶持有市场开拓能力的企业到我县为农户提供资金、技术和农产品加工、储藏、运销服务，形成产、供、销一条龙的产业化经营，同时，培育农村各类市场中介组织，鼓励农民经纪人参与搞活流通。

（二）进一步加强基础设施和生态环境建设。

（1）加强农田水利基础设施建设。规划建设一批水利骨干工程，抓好“三小”水利工程建设。大力推广集雨节水灌溉技术，不断增加有效灌溉面积。加大实施“渴望工程”力度，着力改善饮水条件，到2005年，基本解决农村饮水困难，实现大多数村寨用上自来水。贯彻保护耕地的基本国策，在做好小城镇开发规划的同时，要严格控制基本农田保护区建设用地，继续实施“坡改梯”工程，增加单位面积投入，按照“稳、平、厚”的要求，配套完善灌溉设施和培肥地力措施，集中力量建设基本农田。积极推进农业综合开发项目实施，集中连片进行“山、水、林、田、路”综合治理。

（2）加强交通、通信、广播电视等基础设施建设。加快以公路为重点的交通建设，进一步加强全县交通网络建设，提高公路等级和通车里程，到2005年达到全县村村通公路，条件好的村组通油路。努力确保荔波机场2005年建成通航。积极规划争取建设通往县城的铁路，建立适应我县经济社会发展的综合运输体系。加强通信建设，提高农村电话普及率，到2005年实现80%的行政村通电

话；到2010年农村农户拥有电话率在40%以上。加大邮政网点建设力度，提高邮政通达深度和邮件传递及时率。推进广播电视“村村通”工程，进一步提高广播电视覆盖率。

（3）加快农村电网改造和水电站建设步伐。抓好农网改造工程建设，提高全县用电户覆盖率和用电质量。大力开发我县丰富的水力资源，积极争取建设大七孔二期工程，建设浪详和平林等骨干水电站，到2005年，使全县达到全国农村中级电气化县标准。

（4）加强生态环境建设。把保护治理生态环境与帮助群众增加收入结合起来，以实施退耕还林还草、珠防工程及小流域治理、天然林保护为重点，加强生态建设，进一步加大控制污染工作力度，建立适应经济社会可持续发展的良好生态系统。制定和完善我县天然林保护措施和相关政策，通过扶持发展其他产业帮助林区群众脱贫致富，在水土流失地区坚决实施封山育林育草，切实保护植被，努力提高森林覆盖率，2005年使我县森林覆盖率达60%。在重点旅游景区、无煤区、石漠化地区、退耕还林区和天然林保护区，有计划地实施沼气建设工程，逐步改变当地群众的生活能源结构，形成“养殖—沼气—种植”的生态循环体系。

（三）进一步加强科技推广工作，提高科技对经济增长的贡献率。要从增加人民群众经济收入出发，加大科技推广力度，要利用我县全国科普示范县的优势，加快科技知识推广和科技成果转化，促进经济的发展。农业生产上，加强农作物良种选育、引进、推广，研究高产、高效的种植模式和耕作方式，提高农业综合生产能力。要通过科技推广，实现农业栽培技术配套化、规范化、模式化，健全农业科技推广体系，建立激励机制，鼓励科技人员深入乡村，普及和传授科技知识，推广实用技术，培训乡土人才。要结合我县大力发展旅游业和矿产等资源丰富的实际，进一步提高各开发企业的科技水平、创新能力，以节能降耗、提高质量和效益为出发点，走技术引进、技术创新的道路，增强产品的市场竞争力。要建立和完善科技培训体系，建立县级科技培训中心，建立科技兴县激励机制，充分调动和发挥科技人员的积极性。

（四）进一步扩大就业渠道，积极稳妥推进劳务输出。扩大就业是促进经济发展，增加人民群众经济收入和推进城镇化的重要渠道，要大力发展市场前景良好的劳动密集型产业，努力增加就业岗位，以加强职业教育和就业培训改善农村劳动力就业结构。积极做好劳务输出工作，引导农村劳动人口向非农产业转移，要帮助劳务输出人员提高效益，化解风险，不断加大对劳务输出的组织领导和协调服务力度，通过加强劳动力资源管理，劳务输出信息收集，多方面为务工人员做好服务。要通过劳务输出，使务工人员增长见识，更新观念，学到技术和管理经验，今后成为当地经济发展的骨干，开拓市场的先锋。

（五）进一步大力发展教育事业。巩固、扩大“两基”成果，实现基础教育与职业教育协调发展目标。进一步完善基础教育办学条件，建立和完善贫困学生入学的保障措施：进一步扩大九年义务教育的人口覆盖率，积极发展学前教育，重视发展儿童早期教育，扩大高中阶段教育规模，大力发展职业教育。到2005年，全县初中毕业生升学率达到45%，高中在校生达3000人以上，职业教育高中在校生达300人。到2010年，普及九年义务教育的人口覆盖率进一步提高，初中阶段纯入学率超过90%，全县初中毕业生升学率达到70%，高中在校生达6000人左右，基本普及高中教育，村级以上学校基本实现卫星远程教育。

（六）进一步积极改善卫生医疗条件。坚持预防为主的方针，把预防保健作为出发点和着力点，坚持预防为主、防治结合，提高处理重大疫情和公共卫生突发事件的能力，大力宣传和开展爱国卫生运动，以改水、改厕为重点，加强卫生环境整治，普及疾病预防和卫生保健知识，帮助农民养成良好的卫生习惯和科学、文明、健康的生活方式。加快卫生基础设施建设进度，保证开展公共卫生和基本医疗服务所需的基础设施和条件，加强农村卫生医疗队伍建设，鼓励医学院校毕业生到我县服务，加强卫生技术人员业务知识和技能培训，鼓励有条件的农村医生接受医学学历教育。建立和完善新型农村合作医疗制度，医疗救助制度。到2010年，在全县基本建立起适应社会主义市场经济体制要求和农村经济社会发展水平的农村卫生服务体系和农村合作医疗制度。

（七）进一步加大人口与计划生育工作力度，促进人口与资源协调发展。进一步巩固和提高“村为主”，在已基本实现“村为主”的地方，要继续巩固和提高，积极向村（居）民自治迈进，不断提高“三为主”工作水平。建立“属地管理、单位负责、居民自治、社区服务”的城镇人口与计生管理机制，不断增强社区计生服务能力和自治能力，推进企事业单位的属地管理，实行企事业单位人口与计生法定代表人责任制，切实把流动人口等特殊人口群体纳入管理和服务范围。积极推进人口与计生综合改革和优质服务工作。要紧紧围绕“依法管理、优质服务、村（居）民自治、政策推动、综合治理”的方针把人口与计生综合改革抓好抓实。

（八）进一步抓好异地搬迁移民扶贫工作。对目前生活在自然环境恶劣地方的部分贫困户，要逐步把他们搬到适宜发展经济林木和粮食作物的地方居住；结合小城镇建设和旅游业的发展，引导有一定条件的农民到城镇从事二、三产业。在移民过程中，要将旅游开发移民与搬迁扶贫移民结合起来，妥善安排，稳步推进，要做好搬迁后续工作，帮助移民群众改善生产条件和提高生活质量。确保搬得出来，稳得下来，富得起来。

五、新阶段扶贫开发与小康建设工作措施

（一）调整充实领导机构，继续加强帮乡驻村活动，充分发挥基层组织的积极作用。

及时调整充实县扶贫开发与小康建设领导小组，党政一把手亲自挂帅，对扶贫与小康建设工作负总责、亲自抓，分管领导具体抓，各级、各部门共同参与，充分发挥各部门在扶贫开发与小康建设中的积极作用；进一步加强县四家班子和县部门帮乡驻村联系点开展扶贫工作制度，制定领导干部深入基层制度，包村干部长期驻村，实现工作重心下移，加强对部门、对联系村工作的考核，实行领导干部与各部门包村工作目标责任制，领导干部和部门要对联系村一包到底，直至达到帮扶的预定目标。

进一步加强农村基层组织建设。村组是扶贫开发与小康建设最基本的单位，要把扶贫开发与小康建设和农村党建工作紧密结合起来，扎实开展农村“三个代表”重要思想学习教育活动，按照创建“五个好”村党支部、“六个好”乡镇党委和“三级联创”的建设要求，建立健全农村基层组织建设常抓不懈的工作机制。党委要采取举办培训班、组织外出参观学习、选派干部挂职等多种形式，加强以党支部为核心的村级组织建设，提高村干部带领群众脱贫致富的能力，特别要选配好村党支部书记。关心村组干部生活，逐步提高村组干部待遇。积极稳妥地做好农村党员发展工作，充分发挥共产党员的先锋模范作用。

（二）加大资金投入和管理工作力度，以优惠的政策引资参与扶贫开发与小康建设。

努力增加财政投入。在积极向上争取各项建设资金及省、州财政转移支付的同时，要把农业扶贫开发与小康建设投入列入年度财政预算，调整支出结构，努力增加投入，逐年增加对扶贫开发与小康建设的投入。统筹安排各类建设资金，加强资金的管理使用。县扶贫开发和小康建设领导小组要加强对财政扶贫资金、以工代赈、民族发展、信贷扶贫等各项资金的统筹安排，协调其他可用于农村建设的各类资金投入扶贫开发与小康建设，保证资金及时足额到位，并加强对资金进行全面严格的审计和监督检查。

以优惠的政策措施，加大招商引资工作力度。凡是帮助我县增加农业收入的企业，在项目申报和办理各类手续上，要简化和减少行政审批程序，除特殊规定的重大项目外，都应实行“一站式”办理。兑现省委、省政府有关扶贫开发投资优惠政策，并根据本县实际制定更加优惠的政策。

（三）结合本县实际，抢抓历史机遇，突出优势，加快地方经济发展。

1. 抓住西部大开发的历史机遇。中央实施西部大开发战略，是为加快中西部贫困地区经济发

展，我们必须抓住西部大开发的历史机遇，积极争取和引进各类资金及项目，加大我县基础设施建设和生态建设力度，从根本上解决贫困地区农民生产生活及生存条件，以推进我县新阶段扶贫开发进程。用好用足中央对西部大开发的优惠政策，积极引进和争取各类扶持资金，以发展种养业为重点，大力调整农业和农村经济结构，加快农业产业化经营步伐，不断增加农民收入，尽快解决温饱，稳步迈入小康，尽快实现我县新阶段扶贫开发与小康建设的预定目标。

2. 大力发展旅游业，促进扶贫开发与小康建设。荔波已被省政府明确为贵州南线重点旅游区和《贵州省旅游发展总体规划》确定的全省12个综合旅游区和特色旅游区之一。我们要通过发展旅游业，争取和引进扶持资金，加快我县旅游区建设，加强旅游商品生产开发和建设，挖掘县内具有少数民族特色的服饰、食品、乐器以及花卉、盆景、奇石等旅游商品，开发系列具有民族的、传统的旅游工艺品、特色食品，充分挖掘和展示民族文化，建设瑶族、苗族、水族、布依族等少数民族村寨，拓宽农民的致富门路，充分利用旅游开发带动第三产业的发展，使群众在旅游开发中得到实惠，不断增加群众的货币收入，加快广大人民群众脱贫致富奔小康的步伐。

3. 要搞好扶贫攻坚与小康建设相结合。扶贫攻坚的目的是为从根本上改善贫困地区农民生存及生产生活条件，尽快解决温饱问题，最终迈入小康。实施扶贫攻坚，是小康村建设的基础，是贫困地区农民进入小康社会的必由之路。为此，在新阶段的扶贫开发中，对至今仍生活在深山区、石山区的“瑶山”“月亮山”尚未解决温饱问题的贫困农户，继续实施扶贫攻坚计划，作为新阶段扶贫开发的重点来抓，使这部分贫困户尽快解决温饱，为小康村建设打好基础，达到加快我县小康村建设的目的。

4. 大力实施农业综合开发项目建设。实施农业综合开发，是为加快农业产业化调整和农业现代化进程的一项富民工程，对小康村的建设起到积极推动作用。通过实施农业综合开发，加快项目区山、水、林、田、路的综合治理，加快项目区水利、电力、交通、通信及生态建设，加快项目区种养业发展和生态农业、观光农业的发展，不断增加项目区农民的收入，加快我县扶贫开发与小康村建设步伐。

5. 鼓励非公有制经济人士进行包村帮扶，参与扶贫开发与小康建设。我县贫困面大、贫困程度深，仅靠政府进行扶贫，难以满足我县新阶段扶贫与小康建设的需要。因此积极动员全社会各界积极参与，特别是非公有制企业参与包村帮扶，将是促进扶贫开发与小康建设取得显著成果的有效途径之一。鼓励和引导非公有制人士参与到扶贫开发与小康建设活动中，利用他们在资金、技术、信息、提供就业方面的优势，参与扶贫开发与小康建设，为群众脱贫致富奔小康做出积极贡献，同时也要维护好非公有制经济人士合法利益，促进他们的发展，壮大他们的经济实力，提高投入扶贫开发与小康建设的积极性，从而推动我县扶贫开发与小康建设的顺利开展。

2003年7月5日

中共荔波县委　荔波县人民政府
关于加强农业基础建设促进农业发展农民增收的意见

荔党发〔2008〕1号

为贯彻落实中央、省委和州委农村工作会议精神，切实加快农业农村经济发展，有力促进农业增效、农民增收，扎实推进我县社会主义新农村建设，结合我县实际，特提出以下意见。

2008年，全县农业和农村工作的总体要求是：全面贯彻党的十七大精神，以邓小平理论和

“三个代表”重要思想为指导，深入贯彻落实科学发展观，统筹城乡经济社会发展，把灾后恢复重建贯彻到“三农”工作的始终，落实好各项支农惠农政策，突出加强农业基础建设，积极促进农业稳定发展、农民持续增收。牢固树立用工业化的理念谋划农业，着力发展糖蔗、畜牧、桑蚕、林果、蔬菜、茶叶六大特色产业。积极推进现代农业建设，强化农村公共服务，推进农村土地流转，启动实施农民专业合作社，稳定粮食生产，全面推进糖蔗产业发展，千方百计推动乡村旅游业快速发展，拓宽农民增收渠道，切实解决农村民生问题，确保全县农业农村经济稳步健康发展。

2008年，全县农业农村工作的主要奋斗目标是：农业总产值24580万元，比上年增长10%（其中糖蔗产业总产值6250万元，比上年增长332.37%）。粮食总产量5.83万吨，与上年持平。农民人均纯收入2359元，比上年增长200元。减少农村贫困人口0.36万人，继续抓好11个新农村试点建设，启动建设乡村旅游示范村。

一、突出抓好农业基础设施建设，努力改善农业生产条件

1. 加强农村基础设施建设。着力提高乡村公路通行能力，认真做好规划，加大资金筹措力度，力争完成35公里通乡油路，完成20公里通村油路和91公里通村公路建设。积极实施蔗路配套工程，着力改善农村人居环境，加快农村商品集市建设，大力发展农村公共交通，加大农村通信畅通，加强小城镇基础设施建设。

2. 切实保护好现有耕地和实施高标准基本农田建设。实行最严格的耕地保护制度，切实保护基本农田。对符合征地条件的，要足额支付对农民的补偿，并积极探索防止被征地农民失地又失业的长效机制。实施高标准基本农田建设，综合治理山、水、田、林、路。为农业机械耕作和发展现代农业打好基础。

3. 狠抓农田水利工程建设。坚持以水库新建工程、病险水库治理工程、蔗水配套工程、饮水解困渴望工程、农田灌溉工程为重点，确保完成新增有效灌面770亩，新增节水灌面300亩，改善灌面250亩，恢复灌田4420亩，解决农村人饮2.2万人，新增水土流失综合治理2.7平方公里。今年要完成3000亩蔗水配套工程建设，完成330口蔗水配套小水池，安排蔗水配套项目资金100万元。

4. 搞好生态建设，建设绿色荔波。全面推进集体林权制度改革，实施分类经营；加大依法保护森林资源的力度，巩固生态建设成果；积极调整林种、树种和产业结构，结合荔波旅游产业发展形势，进一步抓好退耕还林工程、天保工程、珠防工程等，扎实抓好森林和林地管理、森林防火、森林有害生物防治工作，切实保护好生态建设成果。建设农村沼气池3000口、配套抓好改水、改厨、改圈、改厕工作。

5. 加快农业机械化发展。积极抢抓国家购机补贴政策机遇，努力增加全县农机具拥有量，提高全县农机装备水平。围绕糖蔗、畜牧、桑蚕、林果、蔬菜、茶叶六大特色产业建设，将新型农机具推广应用于产前、产中、产后各个环节。安排蔗机配套资金100万元，新增农业机械300台套。继续推进基层农机服务组织建设，重点培育农机大户和农机专业合作社，每年全县要组建1～2个农机专业合作社，加快农机服务市场化和产业化进程。

6. 加大农业综合开发工作力度，发挥项目区示范带动作用。坚持“统筹规划、突出重点，选优扶持、强化科技，注重效益、富裕农民”的工作思路，以提高综合生产能力和农业综合效益为出发点，以农业增效和农民增收为目标，以中低产田土改造和产业结构调整为重点，加大土地治理和产业化项目建设，把茂兰项目区建成农业基地和现代农业示范点。

二、围绕六大优势产业发展目标，建立以糖蔗产业为主导的特色产业经济发展基础

1. 深化对农业结构调整和农业产业化经营重要性的认识。全县各级各部门要紧紧围绕加快农业产业化发展尤其是全力推动糖蔗产业发展的目标，树立“围绕旅游办农业，办好农业推旅游”的联动意识，进一步加大对优质米基地建设和龙头企业的扶持力度，提升农产品精深加工能力，搞好农业品牌建设，努力把糖蔗、畜牧、桑蚕、林果、蔬菜、茶叶发展成为支撑荔波农业的产业品牌。

2. 明确目标和任务。当前和今后一定时期，全县农村经济发展，以建设高产高糖甘蔗达到13万亩、年产原料蔗65万吨，实现年产值达到1.6亿元为重点奋斗目标。在全县各乡镇耕地相对集中的地方优先规划发展甘蔗种植，培育公路沿线甘蔗产业经济带，建立十乡百村、百村千寨甘蔗种植区，扩大“一村一品”的内涵，重点扶持甘蔗种植大户，通过全县一盘棋整合产业发展资源，努力把荔波建成全省糖蔗产业大县，实现农业增效、农民增收和财政增长的产业发展多赢格局。今年，全县糖蔗种植要在现有1万亩的基础上扩大种植4万亩。年产原料蔗25万吨，实现产值6250万元，加快糖厂建设步伐，建立龙头企业带动产业发展的运作机制。

蚕桑产业重点加强现有桑园管护，确保稳定桑园面积1.2万亩，实现产值3600万元，建成优质蚕种繁殖场。畜牧产业主攻猪禽，坚持规模养殖、大户圈养和农户散养相结合，年内力争建成3个万头养猪场，4个千头猪场，20个百头养猪场（小区）。建成种草养羊规模场（小区）10个，10个万羽瑶山鸡养殖场（小区）。加快培育果蔬产业，发展商品蔬菜3.5万亩，新增果园0.2万亩。加大毛尖茶基地建设步伐，新增和改造茶园面积0.2万亩以上。

为全面推动六大产业稳步健康发展，全县各级各部门要将农业产业化、农田水利建设、基本农田建设、农业综合开发、扶贫开发、农村沼气、水土保持、退耕还林、乡村道路建设等适合农业产业化发展的项目资金捆绑使用，优先考虑六大产业布局，确保产业建设出效益。同时，围绕六大产业发展做好农业项目库建设，搞好农业招商工作，通过招商引进大型龙头企业带动农业产业化经营取得突破性进展。

3. 突出农村人力资源优势，加快劳动力转移输出步伐。充分开发利用农村人力资源优势，以实施“雨露计划”和“阳光工程”为契机，促进我县农村劳动力转移从数量型向质量型转变，提高输出成效，建设职业教学基地和输出培训教学点，大力培养农村实用人才，扎实推进农村劳动力转移培训，提高转移输出的组织化程度，着力打造劳动力输出品牌，切实做好跟踪服务工作。

4. 健全机构，加强领导，按照“一个产业，一个班子，一套人马”的原则，分别健全和完善六大优势产业领导机构，具体领导、协调、管理主导产业发展，农办、发改、经贸、科技、财政、水利、农业、林业、粮食、乡企、供销、畜牧、农机等部门要切实发挥职能作用，根据产业布局和发展重点，制定出具体实施方案和措施，切实抓好落实，进一步加快我县农业产业化经营，实现农村经济跨越式发展。

三、加快农村社会事业发展，不断改善农村生活条件

1. 大力发展农村教育事业。在巩固全县免除农村义务教育阶段学杂费，对贫困家庭学生免费提供课本的基础上，不断扩大家庭经济困难寄宿生提高生活补贴的覆盖面和适当提高补助标准。切实加大农村教育投入，加快农村义务教育校舍等基础设施建设，不断改善农村办学条件。推进落实我县高中阶段、义务教育阶段在校困难学生资助政策和优秀学生奖励制度，加大对职业高中的投入，根据农村经济发展需要设置相关技术技能专业。

2. 扩大新型农村合作医疗政策覆盖面，提高补助标准。进一步加强县、乡、村三级卫生服务网

络体系建设，加快覆盖全县乡村公共卫生服务体系，医疗服务体系、医疗保障体系和药品供应保障体系建设步伐，不断满足人民群众对卫生服务的需求，重点扩大新型农村合作医疗政策覆盖面，提高补助标准。2008年，落实好新型农村合作医疗制度参合标准由50元提高到100元，力争全县新型农村合作医疗参合率达到90%以上，对特殊困难群众实施医疗救助，切实解决农民群众“看病难、看病贵”的问题。

3. 扩大农村低保范围，更加关注民生。对因家庭人均纯收入低于当地低保标准的贫困居民，重点对那些因疾病、残疾、年老体弱、丧失劳动能力和生存条件恶劣等原因造成家庭生活常年困难的农村居民，实施农村低保制度，给予资金补助，是国家为保障收入难以维持最基本生活的农村贫困人口而建立的一种社会救济制度，一定要吃透政策，领会精神，切实加大农村最低生活保障补助力度，将符合条件的农村贫困家庭纳入低保范围，让困难农村居民感受到党和政府的温暖。

4. 加快发展农村文化体育事业。加强乡镇文化站和村文化活动室等文化基础设施建设，实施好“农民文化家园”百村推进计划，发挥好文化基础设施的作用。继续实施好广播电视“村村通”工程，完善管理制度，提高运行质量。加大农村优秀民族民间文化资源的发掘、整理和保护力度，加强农村文化市场管理，打击“黄赌毒”，实施农民体育健身工程，提高农民身体素质。

四、坚持扶贫导富两手抓，促进农村和谐发展

1. 总结经验、创新工作方法，注重扶贫效果。一是继续坚持主攻解决贫困乡村“三基本”的突出困难和问题，全面完成年度减贫任务。二是加大各类资源整合力度，集中投入，着力提高整村推进、综合扶贫开发的成效。三是坚持瞄准贫困农户和低收入农户，扎实抓好“雨露计划”的实施，进一步提高农村富余劳动力转移培训和农民实用技术培训工作质量。四是切实加大产业化扶持工作力度，做大做强做优特色优势产业，按照龙头企业+基地+农户的动作模式，推进农业产业化经营实现大跨越、大发展。五是与时俱进，着眼实效，大胆探索和创新扶贫开发新机制，着力提高扶贫开发水平。六是抢抓机遇，继续主动做好省、州有关部门帮扶以及社会帮扶的协调服务工作。

2. 全面推进社会主义新农村建设试点工作。紧紧围绕“三建三改五提高”“五好五推进”建设新农村试点工作的总体要求，加大工作力度，充分发挥广大农民群众的主体作用，特别是在产业发展、村容村貌建设上既要出成绩、出经验，又要有特色、能推广，确保新农村建设试点工作取得明显成效，新农村建设全面推进。

3. 启动发展乡村旅游产业试点工作，围绕荔波县打造国际化专业旅游城市的目标要求，结合建设社会主义新农村的实际，把乡村旅游作为一项重要内容抓实抓好，抓住荔波县作为全省发放乡村旅游贷款试点县的有利契机，积极搞好服务工作，出台相关鼓励政策，发动群众参与，引导社会支持，加快农村环境整治和乡村休闲旅游开发步伐，让广大农民群众分享乡村旅游发展的成果。力争在靠近风景区和保护区的乡（镇）打造出2～3个有特色的乡村旅游示范点。

五、强化农业科技和人才支撑，大力发展社会化服务

1. 切实加强农业科技服务体系建设。加大农业科技投入，围绕全县确立的主导产业，组织开展品种选育、优质无公害生产、标准化建设、病虫害防治等技术的研究、应用和推广。深入实施农业科技入户工程。充分调动农村基层技术人员的积极性、主动性和创造性，切实做到住得下、守得住、吃得苦、干得好，充分发挥好农村科技主力军的作用。积极引导建立各种农村专业合作经济组织，努力提高农民进入市场的组织化程度。

2. 建立健全动植物疫病防控体系。加快构建网络健全、队伍稳定、保障有力、处置高效的动

植物防疫病防控体系，全面推行重大动物疫病免费强制免疫，建立动物产地检疫、屠宰检疫、出县境检疫、畜禽标识和养殖档案管理制度。加强疫情监测，抓好重大动物疫病及人畜共患重大动物疫病的防控工作。完善重大动物疫病扑杀补偿机制。加大动物疫病体系建设投入力度，建成5个乡（镇）兽医站工作用房和36个村级兽医室，加强农村信息化建设，健全村级动植物防疫员队伍。

3. 完善农村市场体系。根据“万村千乡市场”“双百市场”“新农村现代网络”等工程目标要求，积极兴建村级综合服务站（农家店），优化市场结构和布局，加快发展农产品收储运和农资配送、连锁经营服务。加快发展各类流通中介组织，培育一批涉农商贸龙头企业。加大农产品综合市场、专业批发市场特别是产地批发市场的建设力度，完善农副产品流通体系。加大市场监管，维护市场秩序。

4. 加强农村信息服务体系建设。充分利用好“农村综合经济信息网”指导农业生产，解决农村经济信息直通车最后“一公里”的问题，实施“信息化村示范工程”，加快“村村通电话”“乡乡能上网”“广播电视村村通”工程建设，推进“三电合一”，扩大农村地区信息网络覆盖面。按照求实效、重服务、广覆盖、多模式的要求，整合资源，共建平台，健全农村信息服务体系，提供多种终端和接入方式，开展声讯和短信服务，积极探索信息服务进村入户的有效途径和方法。

5. 建立健全农村人才培养体系。着眼于推进农村劳动力转移就业和培育新型农民建设新农村的双重要求，统筹培训资源，整合培训资金，创新培训方式，确保完成农业适用技术培训2万—3万人次任务，提高农民的生产技能。加大“雨露计划”和“阳光工程”等农村劳动力转移就业培训支持力度，做好农民工就业公共服务和保障工作。鼓励支持外出务工农民带技术、带资金回乡创业，鼓励和扶持当地农民自主创业。

6. 加强农产品质量安全体系建设，实施名牌战略。一是建立健全我县农产品质量安全检测体系。二是按市场准入要求，积极推进农产品标准化生产，加快农产品产地认定和产品认证工作。三是加大名特优农产品的申报、认证、推广、保护和宣传工作，提高我县农产品的知名度，提高农产品生产的比较效益。

六、落实好各项支农惠农政策，调动农民生产积极性

1. 落实好对农业投入“三个明显高于”的政策。要把基础设施建设和社会事业发展的重点转向农村，新增教育、卫生、文化、乡村旅游等事业费和固定资产增量主要用于农村，逐步加大政府土地出让金用于农村的比重，建立“三农”投入稳定增长机制。确保财政支农投入的增量明显高于上年，固定资产投资用于农村的增量要明显高于上年，土地出让金收入用于农村的增量要明显高于上年，建设用地税费提高后新增收人主要用于“三农”，确保财政增加对农业农村投入落到实处。

2. 落实好农业补贴政策。不折不扣地执行和落实好各种农业补贴制度，千方百计扩大补贴范围，调动农民生产的积极性。一是落实好糖蔗种植补贴政策，包括县级财政补贴和龙头企业的补贴扶持政策以及各种奖励政策。二是落实好直接调动种粮积极性的“四补贴”政策，加大对种粮补贴、良种补贴、种粮农资综合补贴和购机补贴力度。三是落实好直接调动农民种植油菜积极性的种油补贴政策。四是落实好直接调动畜牧业生产的各种畜牧业补贴政策，加大对标准化规模养猪场、能繁母猪养殖及保险补贴和良种猪改良等的补贴力度，确保全县畜牧业稳定发展。

3. 落实好金融机构对“三农”的扶持力度政策。积极探索融资体制改革的思路，搭建“三农”融资平台。充分发挥农村信用社、农行、农发行在农村金融中的骨干作用，简化贷款担保和发放手续，扩大农村小额信贷投放，加大对农村基础设施建设、农户生产发展、农产品加工龙头企业的扶持力度，通过建立担保基金和担保机构等办法，切实解决好农户和涉农企业贷款难的问

题，缓解农业发展投入不足的现状。开展农业保险试点工作，提高农业抗御自然风险和市场风险的能力。

七、切实加强党对农村工作的领导

1. 坚持把“三农”工作作为全县工作的重中之重。全县各级各部门必须站在全局的高度，把社会主义新农村建设作为现代化建设进程中的一项重要历史使命，始终重视维护农民的利益，把增加农民收入作为事关全局的大事，放在更加突出的位置，把主要精力放在抓农业和农村工作上，形成党政一把手亲自抓、分管领导具体抓、部门配合抓的格局。

2. 转变作风，求真务实抓发展。全县各级党员干部一定要树立责任意识、机遇意识、服务意识和群众观念，经常深入一线，真抓实干，切实做到领导一线指挥，干部一线锻炼，工作一线推动，典型一线树立，情感一线加深。要身体力行，做给群众看，带着大家干，尤其是今年要带头抓好糖蔗产业。在切实转变农村工作思路，把农村工作重点转移到发展现代农业上来，把工作重心从常规农业转向休闲农业、特色农业和现代农业上来。

3. 推行农业农村工作的综合考核。各乡（镇）党委、政府要全面落实科学发展观和政绩观，保证支农惠农的各项政策措施落实到位。县委、县政府将对各乡（镇）党委、政府抓“三农”工作实行综合考核，把糖蔗产业发展作为考核领导班子特别是党政一把手执政能力和领导水平的重要内容，继续开展农业农村工作的督促检查，由县委督查室、县政府督查室牵头，组织涉农部门对全县农业农村工作进行督查指导，并把督查调研的情况列入综合考核的重要内容之一。

2008年3月25日

中共荔波县委　荔波县人民政府
关于进一步加强“整脏治乱”城乡清洁工程工作的决定

荔委〔2008〕16号

为进一步加大县城区、景区（景点）、乡镇街道及主要区域卫生与秩序的管理，以开展“公民道德建设工程——满意在荔波”“创建省级文明县城”为载体，深入推进“整脏治乱”专项行动“巩固提高”年工作，实现“整脏治乱”精细化管理，切实提升公民道德和文明行为，提高各单位各部门的工作责任感和管理执行力，从根本上解决不道德、不文明行为和“五脏五乱”的问题，确保“满意在荔波”和“整脏治乱”五年总体目标的实现，根据《贵州省城市市容和环境卫生管理条例》和《黔南州关于进一步加强“整脏治乱”工作意见》的通知精神决定如下：

一、总体要求

（一）**指导思想**：以广大市民群众满意为宗旨，以增强各单位各部门的工作责任心和管理执行力为重点，以提高广大市民群众的文明素质为目标，紧紧围绕《荔波县2008年度“整脏治乱”实施方案》中“五个延伸”“四个巩固”“三个提高”“两个确保”的工作思路；认真贯彻落实《黔南州关于进一步加强“整脏治乱”工作意见》的通知精神，坚持以人为本、求真务实的工作指导思想；坚持精细化管理、规范管理的服务理念；坚持管罚结合、建管并重的工作措施，加速提高县城的文明程度和居民生活的环境质量，促进我县经济社会又好又快地发展。

（二）**工作原则**：本着“标本兼治、管罚并举”的方针和“谁主管、谁负责”的原则，实行主管部门、院落部门和区域管理部门领导负责制，以注重细节、注重过程、注重具体、注重落实、注重质量、注重效果、注重经常性和长期性等“精细化管理”为工作内容，加强公众、舆论、不文明行为、责任意识和文明执法的监督，规范目标责任管理，做到大街小巷、集贸市场、小区院落、办公区域和景区景点无果皮、纸屑、烟头、蛛网；无车辆乱停乱放、广告乱贴乱画、犬禽乱窜乱跑；无摊点乱摆乱放、店铺占道经营，真正使城区、景区、小区、街道和乡镇驻地、机关部门院落达到干净整洁和规范有序。

二、工作措施

（一）加强领导、明确责任

1. 县整治办、县爱卫办在县文明办的领导下开展“整脏治乱”的卫生与秩序督促检查工作。由文明办牵头组织整治办、爱卫办负责定期和不定期地对城区街道、乡镇街道、景区（景点）、单位院落、社区小区要和主要公路沿线的“卫生与秩序”情况开展督促检查，并负责“整脏治乱”“卫生与秩序”责任抵押金罚扣款项的报支审定工作。

2. 县风景管理处、旅游局负责大七孔、小七孔、水春河、观音峰等景区及县城星级厕所、漂流码头、星级宾馆、望城坡观望点和相关景区景点河道湖面清洁的卫生和秩序管理工作。

3. 县公用事业局负责城区农贸市场外围交易经营场所、力达市场（场棚外围部分）、大街小巷、大小广场、公共绿化场地、公共厕所环境卫生的管理工作。

4. 玉屏镇党委、政府负责临街住户“门前三包”（门面和住户以屋檐滴水为线）、城郊接合部、小区社区环境卫生的管理工作。

5. 玉屏镇党委、政府、县工商局负责临街店铺的环境卫生管理工作。

6. 县资本营运公司负责畜禽市场、力达市场（场棚内）、集贸市场内（场棚内）环境卫生的管理工作。

7. 卫生局、食品卫生监督所负责饮食店铺、饮食摊点、旅社、饭店的环境卫生和食品安全的管理工作。

8. 环保局负责县城区沿街饮食店铺、摊点燃煤污染的治理工作。

9. 县建设局、县城管队负责城区乱搭乱建的清理、大街小巷施工场地、建设施工占道手续办理和大街小巷、经营摊点、街面店铺、公共环境、公共场所的乱贴乱画、乱摆乱放、犬禽乱串、占道经营等（含集贸市场内外）的管理工作。

10. 县公安局、县交警大队负责景区、城区车辆乱停乱行、行人不走斑马线、横穿公路闯红灯的管理工作。

11. 县公安局、派出所负责县城区主要街道占道或临街门面打麻将、玩扑克、摇筒等赌博行为及占道测字算命等迷信行为的治理工作。

12. 县运管所、县城管队负责客运车辆、的士的整洁卫生和占用人行道及公共活动场地的规范管理工作。

13. 县财政局负责执法部门“整脏治乱”卫生与秩序的罚款票据、罚款资金的管理；负责责任风险抵押金的收缴、抵扣入账、建账建册和款项支付的管理工作。严格实行收支两条线管理。

14. 县交通局、路管所负责荔波县境内主要公路沿线的收费站、公路路面和边沟的卫生与秩序管理工作。

15. 县民政局负责乞讨人员、流浪人员的管理和街巷的命名立牌建设管理工作。

16. 茂兰自然保护区管理局负责茂兰片区景区景点（永康穿洞、尧古村寨、拉桥村寨、打卦岩、梅园、板寨会师旧址除外）厕所和环境卫生（包括尧古村寨外围的环境和厕所）的管理工作。

17. 永康乡负责穿洞、尧古村寨、拉桥村寨；洞塘乡负责打卦岩、梅园、板寨会师旧址等景点的厕所和环境卫生管理工作。

18. 县畜牧局、水产站负责樟江河流的渔业管理工作。

19. 各乡（镇）负责辖区内主要公路沿线的村庄、驻地加油站、街道市场和所属站（所）、办公场所卫生与秩序的管理工作。

20. 各单位部门负责本单位部门住宿小区、办公院落、办公区域卫生与秩序的管理工作。

21. 县新闻中心、县广播电视台、县移动公司、县联通公司负责利用各自的媒体平台定期的加强舆论宣传和不文明行为的报道工作。

22. 各乡（镇）和各单位部门负责本乡镇全体村民、本居委会全体居民、本单位全体干部职工、本行业全体从业人员、本学校全体师生的文明素质教育工作。

（二）加强配合、通力协作。各部门和各行各业都要各司其职、各负其责，全力配合、通力协作，充分发挥各部门的职能和作用，结合本部门本行业的实际，加强干部职工、相关从业人员和服务对象的教育和管理，加强对本单位和本行业驾驶员的教育管理，督促和引导干部职工、相关从业人员和服务对象提高文明素质，从而提高公众满意度。

（三）加强宣传、营造氛围。充分利用报纸、广播、电视、网络、宣传栏、灯箱牌、手机短信、公益广告、宣传资料、宣讲会、培训会等多种载体和形式，广泛宣传，加大对不文明行为和脏、乱、差现象的报道，要敢于曝光、敢于揭丑、敢于披露，充分发挥舆论的监督作用。

（四）健全制度、务求实效。一是建立举报制度。县文明办将在主要景区、城区公共场所设置举报箱，公布举报电话，对举报的问题，认真做好登记，并将举报反映情况及时上报“整脏治乱”领导小组。二是建立督查通报制度。县四家班子主要领导每人每月至少督查一次并对发现的问题进行一次处罚；县四家班子负责“整脏治乱”工作的领导，每人每旬至少督查一次并对所发现的问题进行一次处罚；县整治办、县爱卫办工作人员每周至少检查三次并发现的问题进行相应次数的处罚。三是建立奖惩激励制度。对做得好的乡（镇）、部门和个人，由县文明办报请县委、县政府、县“整脏治乱”领导小组研究给予通报表彰和奖励，对做得差的乡镇、部门和个人进行通报批评。四是实行“整脏治乱”城乡清洁工程综合管理责任风险抵押金制度。①县四家班子主要领导和四家班子负责“整脏治乱”工作的领导，每人交纳责任风险抵押金2000元。②县四家班子其他领导和负责“整脏治乱”工作的主要部门的主要领导（承担“整脏治乱”工作的主要部门名单附后）及17个乡（镇）的党委、政府主要领导，每人交纳责任风险抵押金1500元。③其他各部门的主要领导（名单附后）和负责“整脏治乱”工作的主要部门的副职领导每人交纳风险抵押金1000元。④其他各部门的副职领导和负责“整脏治乱”，工作主要部门的所有领财政工资的干部职工每人交纳责任风险抵押金500元。

三、处罚规定

（一）县委、县人大、县政府、县政协四家班子的主要领导和负责“整脏治乱”工作的领导在大七孔、小七孔、水春河等主要景区；县城区的大街小巷和集贸市场、大小广场和车站码头、公共厕所和绿化场地、沿街住户和门面店铺、小区社区和单位院落、饮食摊点和宾馆饭店；乡（镇）的街道市场和办公场所、主要村庄和主要公路，发现烟头、纸屑、果皮、废弃物、乱停乱放（在城区指严管街路段）、乱堆乱放、乱搭乱建、乱排乱倒、卫生脏乱、燃煤污染、占道经营、畅放犬禽、不规范有序等问题（下同），每次从相关责任部门交纳的风险抵押金中扣除20元。

县四家班子主要领导和分管负责“整脏治乱”工作的领导在每月、每旬、每次的督查中必须至少要发现一个以上“整脏治乱”上述方面的问题，并且当时当场对相关责任部门进行教育和处罚。

县四家班子主要领导和分管负责“整脏治乱”工作的领导、整治办和爱卫办的工作人员在每月、每旬、每周的每次督查、巡查、检查中如有某个部门被处罚，四家班子分管该部门的领导应负连带责任分别受相应等额的处罚。

县四家班子主要领导和分管负责“整脏治乱”工作的领导，未在每月、每旬按时开展“整脏治乱”的督查并未发现上述问题，或者发现上述问题未当时当场对相关部门作出处罚的，每次扣其责任风险抵押金50元（以当日的《“整脏治乱”责任风险抵押金扣款通知单》为准）。

整治办和爱卫办的工作人员未在每周开展的三次“整脏治乱”检查中发现上述问题，或者发现上述问题未对相关部门当日作出处罚的，每次扣其所交责任风险抵押金50元（以当日的《“整脏治乱”责任风险抵押金扣款通知单》为准）。

（二）县整治办、县爱卫办每周每次对以下地点进行“整脏治乱”明察暗访中，发现问题的，分别从责任部门中扣除相应额度的责任风险抵押金：

（1）在大七孔、小七孔、水春河等主要景区、漂流码头、星级宾馆、县城区星级厕所、望城坡观望点，发现烟头、纸屑、果皮、蛛网、废弃物、车辆乱停乱放、厕所脏臭、河面（湖面）垃圾漂浮物等，每次从风景管理处、旅游局责任风险抵押金中扣除20元。

（2）在大街小巷、公共场所、公共厕所（星级厕所除外）发现烟头、纸屑、果皮、其他废弃物、公厕脏臭等，每次从公用事业局责任风险抵押金中扣除20元。

（3）在临街住户、小区社区发现烟头、纸屑、果皮、蛛网、废弃物、堆放杂物、垃圾、街面店铺或临街住户“门前三包”卫生不达标等，城乡接合部有暴露堆放垃圾等，每次从玉屏镇党委、党政府的责任风险抵押金中扣除20元。

（4）在临街店铺店内发现物品堆放凌乱，店内地面有烟头、纸屑、果皮或在门前堆放有垃圾的，每次从玉屏镇党委、政府、县工商局的责任风险抵押金中扣除20元。

（5）在畜禽市场、力达市场、集贸市场场棚内发现一个摊点、一个地方的卫生不达标，每次从资本营运公司责任风险抵押金中扣除20元。

（6）在县城区的饮食店铺、饮食摊点、饭店，发现主要从业人员没有配穿整洁的衣帽、没有“三防”设施、没有配备专用销售食品的工具、没有配备整洁规范的垃圾桶、没有把生熟食分开，每次从县卫生局、食品卫生监督所的责任风险抵押金中扣除20元。

（7）在县城区发现沿街饮食店铺、摊点有一户燃煤污染的，从县环保局的责任风险抵押金中扣除20元。

（8）在县城区的大街小巷、公共场所发现有乱贴乱画、犬禽乱窜、乱搭乱建、经营摊点有乱摆乱放（指没有按规划地点或指定地点摆摊设点）、街面店铺（含农贸市场和力达市场）有占道经营（含跨门经营）、人行道上有车辆乱停、建设工地杂乱和没有及时清运建筑垃圾、建设工地没有封闭和安全施工以及占道施工等，从县建设局、城管队的责任风险抵押金中扣除20元。

（9）在城区主要街道（严管路段）发现车辆乱停乱放、在划有停泊位的街道发现车辆不按指定地点停放、车辆闯红灯、人员不走斑马线闯红灯，每次从县公安局、县交警大队的责任风险抵押金中扣除20元。对外地到荔波旅游的车辆，公安交警人员重在及时进行疏导和批评教育。

（10）在县城城区主要街道发现占道或临街门面打麻将、玩扑克、摇筒等赌博行为及占道测字算命等迷信行为，每次从县公安局、玉屏镇派出所责任风险抵押金中各扣除20元。

（11）在主要公路沿线发现路面和路道边沟有暴露垃圾或成堆垃圾，每次从县交通局、路管所的责任风险抵押金中扣除20元。

（12）在车站发现有烟头、纸屑、果皮、蛛网、其他废弃物，有乱停乱放、乱搭乱建、乱摆摊设点等，每次从县运管所责任风险抵押金中扣除20元。

（13）在茂兰风景区的沿线、尧古村寨外围、凉水井、三岔河，发现烟头、纸屑、果皮、蛛网、废弃物、厕所脏臭等，每次从茂兰自然保护区管理局责任风险抵押金中扣除20元。

（14）在永康的穿洞、尧古村寨、拉桥村寨，洞塘乡的打卦岩、梅园、板寨会师旧址等景点，发现有纸屑、果皮、蛛网、其他废弃物和厕所脏臭等，每次分别从永康乡和洞塘乡党委政府的责任风险抵押金中各扣除20元。

（15）在樟江河道（玉屏镇的白岩至瑶山乡的界牌河段）发现有电鱼、炸鱼、毒鱼的每次从县畜牧局、水产站的责任风险抵押金中扣除20元。

（16）在部门发现住宿小区、办公院落、办公区域有果皮、纸屑、烟头、蛛网、废弃物、成堆暴露垃圾、敞放家犬家禽、乱搭乱建、院落楼道乱堆杂物、院落车辆乱停乱放等，每次从相关部门责任风险抵押金中扣除20元。如果多个部门共同拥有的院落和楼道，分别从每个部门责任风险抵押金中扣除20元。

（17）在乡（镇）发现主要公路沿线的村庄有暴露堆放垃圾；辖区驻地加油站厕所脏臭、环境卫生差，市场街道有暴露垃圾或垃圾没有及时清理保洁，办公场所、楼道、过道有蛛网纸屑果皮、有杂物乱堆乱放，有车辆乱停乱放和有明显的脏、乱、差现象的，每次从该乡（镇）党委、党政府的责任风险抵押金中扣除20元。

（18）各乡（镇）和各单位部门在每季度的“整脏治乱”检查考核中，通过抽查询问，发现有单位部门和乡（镇）对本乡（镇）的村民、居民、干部职工、教师学生、从业人员没有开展文明素质教育、宣传培训的，每季度从相关乡（镇）和单位部门的责任风险抵押金中扣除20元。

（三）县新闻中心每周不能完成一篇“整脏治乱”工作、“文明县城”创建和“满意在荔波”主题活动等方面的报道，县广播电视台每周不能完成一篇“整脏治乱”工作、“文明县城”创建和“满意在荔波”主题活动方面的正面报道以及一篇“不文明行为”或“整脏治乱”工作不力的舆论监督报道，每周从县新闻中心县电视台和县文体广电局主要负责人风险抵押金中扣除50元（以每周报县整治办的稿件纪录为准）。

（四）因执行本《决定》不力，导致在省、州“整脏治乱”工作检查考核和明察暗访中造成严重负面影响的，将对相关责任人作组织处理。

四、奖励规定

（一）在当年“整脏治乱”的年终专项考核测评中，荔波县获全州前三名或全省前二十名，对所交纳责任风险抵押金的领导和干部职工进行同等额度的奖励。无论全县是否获得上述名次，未被扣除的责任风险抵押金都予以退回相关单位和责任人。

（二）县交警队、县城管队、县卫生监督所、县环保局和其他获得执法授权委托书的部门、乡镇，在进行“整脏治乱”行政执法中所缴得的罚款，实行收支两条线，金额返还有关单位做工作经费和奖励经费。

（三）县文明办组织县整治办、县爱卫办在“整脏治乱”检查抽查和执行该项《决定》中，从责任风险抵押金中扣获的款额，金额返还县文明办，做“整脏治乱”和“文明县城”创建工作经费和奖励经费。

（四）实行“整脏治乱”民众参与的激励机制。鼓励广大市民群众积极参与到“整脏治乱”城乡清洁工程的监督管理中来。对积极谏言献策，真名实姓投诉反映影响公共卫生和公共秩序问题，积极参与“整脏治乱”监督管理的市民给予一定的奖励。

五、督查处罚执行程序

（一）县四家班子主要领导、负责“整脏治乱”工作的领导在督查检查中发现有问题，凭加盖有县文明办公章、有检查领导和随行检查人员签字的荔波县“整脏治乱”责任风险抵押金扣款通知单、当场当时对有关部门和乡（镇）的负责人进行处罚，并将荔波县“整脏治乱”责任风险抵押金扣款通知单交县文明办做好登记，县文明办负责将一式三份的荔波县“整脏治乱”风险抵押金扣款通知单分别交送县财政局、被处罚部门和乡（镇）。

（二）县文明办在组织县整治办、县爱卫办的“整脏治乱”明察暗访工作中，如发现上述问题，凭加盖有县文明办公章、有全体检查人员签字的荔波县“整脏治乱”风险抵押金扣款通知单、当场当时对有关部门和乡（镇）进行处罚，并将一式三份的“整脏治乱”风险抵押金扣款通知单分别交送县财政局、被处罚的部门和乡镇。

（三）被处罚的部门和乡（镇）在接到处罚通知单后要及时地组织整改，查找管理工作中的不足。县财政局接到处罚通知单后要及时从相关部门和乡镇的领导干部职工责任风险抵押金中扣除应扣的款额入账建册。

（四）县交警队、县城管队、县卫生监督所、县环保局和其他获得执法授权委托书的部门、乡（镇），在进行“整脏治乱”行政执法中，必须统一使用有财政局印章的票据，县财政局要加强票据管理，做好票据的登记核查和清收结算工作。

（五）县文明办要负责对所有具有“整脏治乱”行政执法权的部门的文明执法行为进行监督，对投诉、举报、反映和发现不文明执法行为的，及时向“整脏治乱”领导小组和文明委领导汇报，对核查属实的不文明执法工作人员及时地给予批评和教育，督促提高执法水平和素质。

六、工作要求

（一）本《决定》从2008年5月1日起执行，由县文明办负责解释。每个月进行一次检查通报。在每次的考核检查和明察暗访中，各乡（镇）和部门必须大力支持和配合。

（二）本《决定》出台后，各乡（镇）和部门及相关领导和干部职工必须在一周内，将应交纳的“整脏治乱”责任风险抵押金统一交到县财政局，财政局进行专人专户管理。县财政局如不能按时清收“整脏治乱”责任风险抵押金，不能从风险抵押金中将应受扣罚的金额按时如数扣除，追究县财政局主要负责人的责任，并从财政局的责任风险抵押金中等额扣抵。

（三）各乡（镇）、各部门的领导要对县委、县政府出台的该《决定》给予高度的重视。处罚不是目的，是教育广大市民群众提高文明素质、促进文明行为、促进城乡文明形象建设、推动部门搞好工作、增强领导干部责任心的手段，各乡（镇）、各部门要认真地按照县委、县政府和“整脏治乱”领导小组的有关工作方案和工作要求，结合本部门的工作实际，按照“精细化管理”的要求，做出精密细致的工作安排，及时成立相应的工作领导小组，制定相应的工作措施和办法，明确每个干部职工应尽的职责，确保“事事有人管、时时有人管”“样样有人抓、个个有责任”、力求达到“想得全、做得细、抓得实、办得好、稳得住、不被罚”。

（四）各乡（镇）、各部门要认真制定《市民文明素质教育培训工作方案》，认真贯彻落实《公民道德建设工程实施纲要》，组织开展“与文明同行、满意在荔波”的系列宣传教育活动，切实建立起文明素质教育培训的工作机制，要结合开展“十二包”（即领导包单位、单位包职工、职工包家属、家属包子女、教育包学校、学校包学生、学生包家长、乡镇包村民、社区包居民、司机包乘客、住户包客户、业主包工人）的教育包保措施，全力推进市民群众、干部职工、广大师生和从业人员的文明素质教育工作，真正把文明素质教育培训到每一个市民群众。

（五）县交警队、县城管队、县卫生监督所、县环保局和其他获得执法授权委托书的部门、乡（镇），在进行行政执法处罚中，必须要着装上岗或持证上岗，要本着奖惩促教育、促提高和“以人为本”的思想，严格遵循法律法规的规定，实行人性化管理，注意执法形象，开展文明执法，在尊重当事人合法权利的前提下，按照正当的程序进行非歧视的、理性化的执法活动。要公正、公平、公开、公心地开展执法行为，做到法律法规面前人人平等、相同对待、一视同仁。

（六）执法部门要加强执法的宣传和教育，要加强内部干部职工的执法培训和法律法规的学习，努力提高执法干部队伍的素质和水平。要让广大市民群众充分的了解和支持，真正让不文明的行为在我县逐步得到根除，做到群众心悦诚服、明理错误。

（七）各乡（镇）应及时招聘卫生保洁人员。各乡镇（除玉屏镇外）卫生保洁人员的定员是：甲良镇3人、播尧乡3人、方村乡1人、水利乡1人、朝阳镇3人、瑶山乡3人（其中王蒙2人）、佳荣镇3人、茂兰镇3人、立化镇3人、洞塘乡2人、驾欧乡2人、瑶麓乡1人、水尧乡2人、永康乡1人、翁昂乡2人、捞村乡2人。各乡镇保洁人员的工资，由县乡财政各承担一半，工资每月暂按600元计算。

（八）实行层层督查制。即四家班子领导进行定期不定期抽查，人大代表、政协委员进行不定期视察，文明办组织整治办和爱卫办进行定期不定期检查，职能部门安排专人进行巡查，各部门时时开展自查，确保该《决定》落到实处，取得实效。

（九）各乡（镇）、各部门在执行《决定》、推行“精细化管理”中，要注意在实践中总结创新，积极探索部门行业管理的新方法和新措施，及时反映工作中出现的新情况和新问题。

（十）各乡（镇）、各部门在执行该《决定》中，要将如何做好落实、搞好内部管理、明确工作责任和推动各项工作的方案、措施和相关文字资料于5月10日前报县整治办。

（十一）县财政局每月5日前应将上一个月风险抵押的处罚扣除情况及时送县文明办，县文明办在每月10日前将上一个月的“整脏治乱”督查检查处罚情况进行通报。

2008年4月21日

中共荔波县委关于实施全域旅游发展战略的决定

（2015年7月30日中国共产党荔波县委第十一届委员会第五次全体会议通过）

为全面贯彻落实习近平总书记视察贵州时的重要讲话精神，紧扣全省“两加一推”主基调主战略和黔南州“一圈两翼”总体部署，依托良好的生态资源和全域处处是景的自然优势，充分发挥“世界遗产地”和“世界生物圈保护区”两张世界级名片作用，以全域旅游发展战略推动县域经济社会发展，作出以下决定。

一、实施全域旅游发展战略的指导思想和基本内涵

（一）指导思想

全面贯彻党的十八大和十八届三中、四中全会精神，以邓小平理论、“三个代表”重要思想和科学发展观为指导，深入贯彻习近平总书记系列重要讲话精神，协调推进“四个全面”战略布局，积极适应经济发展新常态，守住生态和发展两条底线，大力实施全域旅游发展战略，推动新型工业化、新型城镇化、农业现代化、旅游产业化四个轮子一起转，奋力走出一条有别于东部、不同于西部其他省份县市的发展新路，推动全域经济社会快速、持续、健康发展，与全国同步建成小康社会，最终把荔波打造成世界知名、国内一流的旅游目的地和休闲度假胜地。

（二）基本内涵

以旅游业为核心，发展生态经济和文化经济，把一、二、三产业和城镇化导入可持续发展的轨道，实现相关产业与旅游业相生相融。实施全域旅游发展战略，不仅是县域内众多景区景点处处开花的内在要求，也是应对旅游井喷式发展的必然选择，更是通过旅游这个“核心”推动全域经济社会快速、持续、健康发展，把产业带动起来，让环境优美起来，使人民生活水平和幸福感提高起来，与全国同步建成小康社会的有效途径。

二、全域旅游发展战略的基本原则和工作目标

（一）基本原则

坚持解放思想、改革创新，破除旅游业发展体制机制障碍。

坚持守住底线、协调发展，实现生态保护与旅游发展相互协调、相互促进。

坚持规划引领、政策推动，加快旅游业发展方式转变。

坚持科学发展、生态优先，以旅游业促进经济社会协调发展。

坚持统筹兼顾、互促联动，带动旅游业与相关行业融合发展。

坚持扩大开放、合作交流，不断增强旅游业发展动力和活力。

坚持市场驱动、共赢发展，发挥市场配置资源的基础性作用。

坚持以人为本、民生优先，始终把游客满意和富民增收作为加快旅游业跨越发展的出发点和落脚点。

（二）工作目标

2017年把荔波打造成为贵州南部旅游中心和游客集散中心，带动周边县市旅游产业发展，切实担负起黔南旅游龙头的重任。

2020年把荔波打造成为贵州第一旅游名片，全县旅游接待人数达到2000万人次，旅游年综合收入达200亿元。

2025年实现境内AAAAA级景区2个，AAAA级景区4个，AAA级景区20个以上，逐步实现乡乡有景区，村村有景点，寨寨有景物，产业园区化、园区景点化的旅游发展格局，将荔波打造成黔桂旅游中心城市和游客集散地，最终实现世界知名、国内一流的旅游目的地和休闲度假胜地的奋斗目标。

三、全域旅游发展战略的工作重点

（一）谋篇布局，推进全域旅游总体规划，合理构建空间布局

深度对接国家、省、州区域经济社会发展规划战略，科学编制《荔波县“十三五”发展规划》《荔波县旅游发展总体规划（修编）》，做好《县城总体规划修编》、土地综合利用规划、产业功能布局规划、交通体系建设规划、生态环境保护建设规划“五规合一”的修编工作，要以《荔波县旅游发展总体规划（修编）》为依据，相互衔接、相互促进。全县各类规划应与旅游发展规划相适应，充分考虑相关旅游项目、设施的空间布局和建设用地要求。在空间布局上，立足发展生态经济和文化经济，依据各区域各乡镇地理位置、资源环境，民风民俗、气候特点规划打造景区景点，谋划特色突出的产业布局，按照荔波四大主体民族分布，科学布局旅游线路和旅游景点，进一步规划和开发民族村寨建设，形成“点在线上”，让游客深度体验荔波四大主体民族文化。紧紧依托丰富的乡村旅游资源和多彩的民族文化风情，彰显旅游元素，借助品牌景区提质扩容效应，带动全域众多景区景点和相关产业融合发展。

（二）围绕旅游产业，把一、二、三产业和城镇化导入可持续发展的轨道

围绕旅游这个“核心”，抓好一、二、三产业和城镇化建设，深度延伸旅游产业链，拓宽旅游

产业面，研发旅游新产品，培育新业态，最终构建以旅游产业为龙头，关联带动其他产业和城镇化可持续发展，实现百姓参与旅游受益。

1.围绕旅游抓一产。围绕“农旅结合，提供安全食品”的思路，大力发展现代山地特色高效农业，着力推进农业结构调整和产业升级，规划建设以瑶山（捞村）为核心的国家农业公园，加快推进荔波精品水果及休闲观光农业示范园区、万亩梅园观光农业示范园区、农耕文化示范园区等生态农业园区建设，发展壮大哈密瓜、枇杷、蜜柚、血桃、青梅等精品水果及花卉、盆景、中药材等特色产业。因地制宜地推进旅游扶贫，依托我县富集的乡村旅游资源，帮助贫困地区和贫困群体发展带动性强、参与度高的特色产业，积极鼓励群众发展农家乐、民族手工艺品等旅游相关产业，让群众吃上“旅游饭”，走上致富路。围绕打造“全国安全食品示范生产基地”，发展一批无公害绿色放心的农特产品，积极申报产地商品注册认证，提高遗产地农产品品牌影响力，培育发展家庭农场、农民合作社、农业产业化龙头企业等新型农业经营主体，把龙头企业与农民和农业合作社有机结合，让农业发展市场化、商业化。

2.围绕旅游抓二产。牢固树立“工业强县”战略不动摇，抢抓“互联网+”“工业4.0”“创客时代”等机遇，坚持高位嫁接、高端切入理念谋划工业发展，拒绝污染，走与生态环境相适应、与旅游相生相融的绿色、低碳、环保新型工业化道路，谋划发展一批绿色轻工、农特产品加工、旅游产品加工，民族医药大健康产业等工业项目，打造产业集群，形成产业支柱，做大“绿色GDP”，促进旅游业和工业同步发展，壮大县域经济总量。支持和培育民营企业、个体工商户发展，鼓励万众创新、大众创业，每个乡（镇、街道）创办一个以上返乡创业园进行孵化，引导各类能人和返乡农民创业，工到园区创业，围绕旅游服务产业，大力发展民族工艺品、旅游纪念品、特色食品加工等产业。

3.围绕旅游抓三产。一是在县级层面从县城东部至月亮湖区域打造现代服务业聚集区，重点发展电商大数据动漫产业、创意研发产业等。二是依托“高铁时代”优势，在加快核心景区的纵深开发，抓好景区扩容提质及服务设施建设的同时，优化县域宾馆酒店、餐饮服务、农家乐接待布局和规范化管理，提高旅游从业人员整体素质，提升旅游服务能力和水平。三是传承和发展世居主体民族文化，积极谋划和开发一批独具民族文化、生态文化和红色文化特色，文旅融合的旅游景点和精品旅游线路，在为全域旅游发展战略注入强大的文化内涵的同时，缓解核心景区管理压力。四是大力开发新产品新业态，推进索道、小火车、低空飞行、温泉等旅游项目建设，大力发展康体水疗、野外拓展、户外露营、山地运动等一批高山康体休闲度假旅游产品，推动旅游产品结构向观光、休闲、度假、养生复合发展转变。

4.围绕旅游抓城镇化。一是按照“做精县城”的思路，科学优化和精心修编县城总体规划、荔波现代服务业集聚区规划及四大主体民族建筑规划设计，优化空间布局，将县城规划区拓展至朝阳高铁站，面积达20平方公里以上。围绕国际化专业旅游城市的定位，做足亲水文章，完善城镇交通路网、垃圾污水处理、城市公交公厕等功能配套设施及小区公共服务设施建设。着力培育一批规范化、标准化的星级酒店、精品客栈和一批高档次的影视娱乐场所、购物中心，不断提升旅游城市品位和群众幸福感。加大城市绿化、美化力度，强化城市管理，提高城市管理水平和文明形象，建设宜居宜业宜游的山水园林城市。二是按照“做优乡镇”的思路，统筹推进城乡一体化建设，抢抓易地扶贫生态移民工程、“一事一议”奖补项目等政策机遇，加快推进小城镇建设，在城镇风格打造上呈现个性化、差异化和特色化。每个乡（镇、街道）都要结合新农村建设，引导经济基础好、群众意愿强、能够集中成片改造或建设的地方建设新型农村社区，社区内养老中心、幼儿园、文体活动中心、社区卫生室、农家超市、警务室等公共基础服务设施配套齐全，引导人口向城镇和新型农村社区转移。三是坚持开发与保护并重原则，按照“做美村寨”的思路，充分利用“美丽乡村·四在农家”、小康示范寨等项目，整合资源，打造一批看得见山、望得见水、记得住乡愁的旅游示范村寨，承接旅游观光，农家接待和民俗体验，同时加强对民族自然村寨的保护，防止民族村寨的不断消失。

（三）夯实全域旅游的基础支撑，促进旅游产业跨越式发展

夯实交通、金融、大项目和人才支撑，与互联网+深度融合，实现旅游业与相关产业齐头并进，跨越发展。

1.启动交通三年行动计划。加快贵南高铁、三都至荔波、荔波至榕江、荔波至南丹、荔波至环江“一纵一横”高速公路建设，推进荔波机场改扩建项目进程，有针对性地开辟和加密航班航线，做优外联交通体系建设。同时，加快打通各景区景点的联络线、断头线，形成全域旅游的大环线、小环线、网络线，努力构建“陆空并进，内优外快”的立体旅游交通体系。加强交通服务软环境建设，围绕“微笑服务”“温馨驿站”“情满樟江”“舒心旅途”目标，打造一流的交通旅行服务，向全社会传递荔波的正能量，树立良好的城市形象和旅游形象。

2.加强与金融领域的深度合作。整合资源搭建做大融资平台，将全县景区资源进行整体包装策划，加强银政企合作力度，推行政府和社会资本合作（PPP）模式，借助省州融资平台合作发行基金、债券等，巧借外力着力破解资金瓶颈，推动荔波旅游上市挂牌。同时，创新旅游投融资机制，探索建立多元化旅游投融资渠道，通过股权转让、特许经营权出让等方式，鼓励和引进社会资本参与全域旅游发展战略，结合荔波农村“三权”抵押改革试点，让村、寨群众通过“三权”抵押参与到全域旅游开发当中，助推全县大旅游发展。

3.坚持“走出去，引进来”的方式招商引资。建立县、乡（镇、街道）、村旅游招商引资三级联动工作机制，形成招商引资工作合力。依托荔波自身资源优势，招大商，寻求大项目支撑，以大项目促进旅游大发展。抓住广州奇码科技、云南敏大集团、陕旅集团、华谊健康等企业先后落户荔波投资兴业的契机，加快推进奇码电商、世界蜜月之都、三叠纪国际动漫乐园、月亮湖湿地公园、老荔波旧城改造、樟江河景观化治理与旅游航道开发、荔波现代服务业集聚区、城市综合商业区开发等一批大项目、好项目的实施建设，真正把荔波打造成为全球婚纱摄影基地和游客最向往的地方。

4.牢固树立人才是第一资源的思想。培养造就一支高素质的旅游人才队伍，制定人才培训规划，根据市场需求和旅游产业实际，确立一批旅游实践基地和旅游人才培养院校，定期组织旅游产业从业人员进行业务培训。重视高层次人才的引进和培养，重点加大对策划创意人才、经营管理人才、市场营销人才的引进和培养，允许有特殊才能的专业人才和管理人才以各种方式参与收益分配，逐步构建起有利于优秀人才成长的选人用人体制。

5.促进互联网+与旅游的深度融合。充分运用大数据、BAT、微信、APP等信息技术，加快智慧旅游网络平台建设，利用最先进的云计算、物联网、互联网与移动互联网、高性能信息处理、智能数据分析挖掘等信息技术，融入一、二、三产业和新型城镇化各个领域，形成智慧旅游引领旅游发展新格局。

（四）深化旅游体制改革，推进旅游转型升级

按照“全域旅游、融合发展”思路，进一步深化改革，构建适应新常态的旅游体制机制。一要建立旅游发展一体化管理体制，建立旅游管理委员会，搭建旅游综合发展平台，整合涉旅资源，统筹旅游行政管理职能，实现旅游行政管理与资源管理、资源保护与开发有机统一。二要创新景区经营管理模式，成立旅游发展集团公司，推行股权、管理权、营权分离的景区发展机制，通过合资、独资、租赁、拍卖、承包等多种方式经营景区，并适当放开乡（镇、街道）景点和景区的经营权。三要加强政府旅游服务职能，建立健全旅游信息咨询服务系统、旅游安全监测和预警预报系统、旅游应急服务体系、游客投诉处理机制和旅游高峰时段游客分流等机制，推进政府职能由管理为主向管理与服务并重转变，打造一个良性竞争和诚信经营的旅游服务市场环境。

四、全域旅游发展战略的保障措施

（一）**加强领导，精心组织**。成立由县委书记任组长，县长任常务副组长，相关县领导任副组长，有关部门负责人为成员的荔波县全域旅游工作领导小组，负责统筹、协调、组织各项工作。建立全域旅游工作联席会议制度，对全县旅游资源进行大普查、大盘查、大规划，并分步实施。定期研究推进工作，及时破解工作推进中的困难和问题。各乡（镇、街道）、县各部门要成立相应的组织体系，将发展旅游摆上重要议事日程并纳入年终目标管理考核，主要负责同志亲自抓，切实加强统一领导和组织协调工作的推进和落实。

（二）**明确责任，通力合作**。县各部门要高度重视、通力合作，真抓实干，采取有力措施，推进全域旅游发展战略顺利实施。要结合自身实际，制定促进旅游产业发展的具体措施，如研究制定鼓励性政策措施、建立全域旅游发展基金、策划生成旅游重点项目、加大向上争取旅游产业基础设施和重点项目资金补助力度、加大人才引进和培养力度等。各乡（镇、街道）要积极参与旅游产业发展，结合“四在农家·美丽乡村”建设，加大生态保护和环境整治力度，大力发展乡村旅游，农业观光旅游。

（三）**广泛宣传、营造氛围**。各乡（镇、街道）、县各部门要充分认识实施全域旅游发展战略的重要意义，不断创新宣传方式，拓宽宣传渠道，在宣传上统一使用“世界遗产地·地球绿宝石——荔波”及其LOGO，并充分运用到景区标志标牌、办公用品、员工服饰、户外广告、报纸杂志、广播电视广告、旅游商品以及旅游宣传折页中。通过做好媒体好声音、高端论坛、节会风采、策划事件营销等，加大宣传和营销力度，全方位、有步骤地宣传推广荔波旅游品牌，提升全民兴旅意识，使全社会进一步了解全域旅游的意义、目的、任务和进程，提高全社会的关注度和参与度，推动全域旅游的深入开展，形成全县上下齐心协力共促发展的良好氛围。

（二）国家、省、州级文献

国务院关于公布第二批国家级森林和野生动物类型自然保护区的通知

国发〔1988〕30号

各省、自治区、直辖市人民政府，国务院各部委、各直属机构：

国务院同意林业部提出的第二批国家级森林和野生动物类型自然保护区（共计25处），现予公布。望各地根据《中华人民共和国森林法》及国务院批准的《森林和野生动物类型自然保护区管理办法》规定，落实保护范围和保护对象，采取各种有效措施，防止乱砍滥伐森林，制止乱捕滥猎珍贵稀有野生动物，做好保护区的管理和建设工作。有关保护区的机构、人员编制和经费由地方政府解决。

1988年5月9日

第二批国家级森林和野生动物类型自然保护区名单

（国务院1988年5月9日公布）

一、雾灵山自然保护区

（略）

二、历山自然保护区

（略）

三、大青沟自然保护区

（略）

四、白石砬子自然保护区

（略）

五、双台河口自然保护区

（略）

六、丰林自然保护区

（略）

七、呼中自然保护区

（略）

八、古牛绛自然保护区

（略）

九、梅花山自然保护区

（略）

十、鄱阳湖候鸟自然保护区

（略）

十一、长岛自然保护区

（略）

十二、鸡公山自然保护区

（略）

十三、宝天曼自然保护区

（略）

十四、坝王岭自然保护区

（略）

十五、内伶仃岛—福田自然保护区

（略）

十六、车八岭自然保护区

（略）

十七、茂兰自然保护区

位于贵州省荔波县东南面的茂兰区，面积两万多公顷。1987年省政府批准建立。区内的喀斯特森林，气势壮观，是世界上同纬度地带所独有的珍贵森林资源，对于喀斯特地貌的以育理论、水文地质效应和森林群落的研究，有重要价值。

十八、白马雪山自然保护区

（略）

十九、哀牢山自然保护区

（略）

二十、周至自然保护区

（略）

二十一、牛背梁自然保护区

（略）

二十二、兴隆山自然保护区

（略）

二十三、祁连山自然保护区

（略）

二十四、贺兰山自然保护区

（略）

二十五、六盘山自然保护区

（略）

国务院关于发布第三批国家重点风景名胜区名单的通知

国函〔1994〕4号

各省、自治区、直辖市人民政府，国务院有关部门：

第三批国家重点风景名胜区名单已经国务院审起，现予发布。

风景名胜资源是不可再生的自然和文化遗产，保护工作是第一位的，只有在保护好资源的前提下，才能永续利用。地方各级人民政府要加强对风景名胜区内各单位的业务渠道不变，维护其合法权益。国务院各有关部门要密切配合，加强协作，促进风景名胜区各项工作的发展。

附：第三批国家重点风景名胜区名单（共35处）

1994年1月10日

第三批国家重点风景名胜区名单

（共35处）

天津市

盘山风景名胜区

河北省

嶂石岩风景名胜区

山西省

北武当山风景名胜区

五老峰风景名胜区

辽宁省
　　凤凰山风景名胜区
　　本溪水洞风景名胜区
浙江省
　　莫干山风景名胜区
　　雪窦山风景名胜区
　　双龙风景名胜区
　　仙都风景名胜区
安徽省
　　齐云山风景名胜区
福建省
　　桃源洞—鳞隐石林风景名胜区
　　金湖风景名胜区
　　鸳鸯溪风景名胜区
　　海坛风景名胜区
　　冠军豸山风景名胜区
河南省
　　王屋山—云台山风景名胜区
湖北省
　　隆中风景名胜区
　　九宫山风景名胜区
湖南省
　　韶山风景名胜区
海南省
　　三亚热带海滨风景名胜区
四川省
　　西岭雪山风景名胜区
　　四面山风景名胜区
　　四姑娘山风景名胜区
贵州省
　　荔波樟江风景名胜区
　　赤水风景名胜区
　　马岭河峡谷风景名胜区
云南省
　　腾冲地热火山风景名胜区
　　瑞丽江—大盈江风景名胜区
　　九乡风景名胜区
　　建水风景名胜区
陕西省
　　宝鸡天台山风景名胜区

甘肃省

崆峒山风景名胜区

鸣沙山月牙泉风景名胜区

青海省

青海湖风景名胜区

黔南布依族苗族自治州荔波樟江风景名胜区管理条例

（2001年4月29日黔南布依族苗族自治州第十一届人民代表大会第一次会议通过　2001年7月21日贵州省第九届人民代表大会常务委员会第二十三次会议批准　2001年8月24日黔南布依族苗族自治州人民代表大会常务委员会公告公布施行）

第一条　为加强荔波樟江风景名胜区管理，有效地保护、利用和开发风景名胜资源，促进本州经济社会持续发展，根据《中华人民共和国宪法》《中华人民共和国民族区域自治法》及有关法律、法规的规定，制定本条例。

第二条　在樟江风景名胜区进行保护、建设、旅游和管理等活动的单位和个人，应当遵守本条例。

第三条　樟江风景名胜区是以喀斯特原始森林和水文为特征，集山、水、林、湖、瀑、洞、石为一体的国家重点风景名胜区。由水春河景区、大七孔景区、小七孔景区、樟江风光带组成，总面积273.1平方公里。

根据《荔波樟江风景名胜区总体规划》，樟江风景名胜区划定为特级、一级、二级、三级保护区和外围保护区。

第四条　樟江风景名胜区的保护和建设应当坚持严格保护、科学规划、统一管理、合理开发、永续利用的原则，使生态效益、经济效益和社会效益协调发展。

第五条　樟江风景名胜区管理机构，由荔波县人民政府领导，主持风景名胜区管理工作，行使下列职权：

（一）贯彻执行有关法律、法规、规章和本条例；

（二）按照总体规划制定详细规划，报经批准后组织实施；

（三）制定风景名胜区管理制度，对风景名胜区实行统一保护和管理；

（四）会同有关部门对经营活动、交通安全、社会治安等进行管理；

（五）人民政府或者有关行政管理部门委托行使的其他职权。

樟江风景名胜区接受建设行政主管部门和相关行政管理部门的业务指导和监督。

乡（镇）人民政府、村（居）民委员会应当支持、协助做好风景名胜区的管理工作。

第六条　樟江风景名胜区内的所有单位，除各自业务受上级主管部门领导外，应当服从樟江风景名胜区管理机构对风景名胜区的统一规划和管理。

第七条　在樟江风景名胜区内禁止下列行为：

（一）砍伐、损毁古树名木、风景林木花草。

（二）毁林开垦、擅自砍伐林木。

（三）擅自开山、开矿、采石、挖砂、取土。

（四）围填堵塞河流、溪流、湖泊、山泉、瀑布。

（五）堆积、装贮、排放污染环境的废渣、废水和有毒有害气体。

（六）由水体环境倾倒垃圾和其他固体废弃物，在水中洗涤有毒、有污染的物品。

（七）猎、捕、炸、毒或者以其他方式伤害野生动物。

（八）其他危害风景名胜资源的行为。

第八条　在特级和一级保护区内禁止下列行为：

（一）建设宾馆、饭店、娱乐场所等。本条例公布施行前已建成的，应当逐步拆除。

（二）擅自采集动植物标本。

（三）移植风景林木。

（四）建造坟墓。已建而有损自然景观的，应当逐步迁出或者深埋，不留坟头。

第九条　樟江风景名胜区的水质以及樟江支流的水质按国家地表水环境质量Ⅰ类至Ⅲ类水标准执行。

第十条　在樟江风景名胜区内已建成的、有污染的建设项目应当限期治理，达不到环境质量标准的，由荔波县人民政府责令其关、停、转、迁。

第十一条　禁止侵占、破坏樟江风景名胜区内的河道、河滩、河堤及其设施。

第十二条　禁止违法占用、转让风景名胜资源及景区土地，擅自改变风景名胜资源性质及景区土地使用性质。

第十三条　在樟江风景名胜区内根据规划建设的项目，由樟江风景名胜区管理机构编制计划，经荔波县人民政府同意，报自治州人民政府批准后，方可依法办理报批手续。其建设工程选址意见书、建设用地规划许可证和建设工程规划许可证，由自治州人民政府建设行政主管部门核发。

建设项目的布局、高度、体量、造型和色彩等，应当与周围景观和环境相协调。

第十四条　荔波县人民政府应当做好樟江风景名胜区内的封山育林、植树绿化和25度以上坡地退耕还林还草工作，保护植被和野生动植物繁殖生长、栖息环境。

在樟江风景名胜区内推广沼气等适用技术，采取节柴措施、保护生态。

第十五条　荔波县人民政府应当加强樟江风景名胜区森林病虫害的防治和防洪工作，落实防范措施。

使用农药应当符合国家《农药安全使用标准》的规定。

第十六条　荔波县人民政府应当加强樟江风景名胜区护林防火工作，建立健全护林防火组织和制度，配备相应的防火设施和设备，规定特别防火期，设置禁火标志。

第十七条　鼓励和支持国内外经济组织和个人到樟江风景名胜区投资开发和建设。投资者的合法权益受法律保护。

第十八条　开发建设旅游设施项目，应当符合总体规划，进行科学论证，避免盲目建设。不得兴建有害旅游者身心健康的项目。

第十九条　樟江风景名胜区内民族村寨的规划、建设和改造应当有民族风格和地方特色。

保护和开发民族工艺品、民间艺术和民族文化，发展具有民族特色的旅游项目。

第二十条　进入樟江风景名胜区内的游人和其他人员，应当遵守法律、法规和规章制度，爱护风景名胜资源和公共设施，维护环境卫生和公共秩序。

第二十一条　樟江风景名胜区管理机构应当建立安全管理责任制，在景区内设置安全设施和安全标志。禁止在没有安全保障的区域开展旅游活动。

第二十二条　任何单位和个人符合下列条件之一的，由荔波县人民政府或者樟江风景名胜区管理机构给予表彰和奖励：

（一）在保护、建设、管理、治理工作中成绩显著的。

（二）在科研工作中成绩显著的。

（三）引进资金、技术、人才有贡献的。

（四）维护法律、法规的实施，同破坏风景名胜资源的行为作斗争做出贡献的。

第二十三条 违反本条例规定的，按以下规定给予处罚：

（一）违反第七条第（一）项、第（二）项和第八条第（二）项、第（三）项、第（四）项规定的，责令停止违法行为，限期恢复原状，没收违法所得，可并处100元以上2000元以下罚款。不能恢复原状的，依法赔偿损失，可并处5000元以上30000元以下罚款。

（二）违反第七条第（三）项、第（四）项、第（七）项规定的，责令停止违法行为，限期恢复原状，没收违法所得，可并处20元以上1000元以下罚款。不能恢复原状的，依法赔偿损失，可并处1000元以上30000元以下罚款。

（三）违反第七条第（五）项、第（六）项和第十一条规定的，责令停止违法行为，限期恢复原状，可并处300元以上5000元以下罚款。不能恢复原状的，可并处5000元以上30000元以下罚款。

（四）违反第八条第（一）项规定的，责令停止违法行为，限期拆除违法建筑，恢复原状，按占地面积，可并处每平方米30元以下罚款。不能恢复原状的，经上一级建设行政主管部门批准，可并处每平方米100元以上200元以下罚款，但最高不得超过100000元。

（五）违反第十二条规定的，责令停止违法行为，退出违法占用、转让的风景名胜资源或者恢复风景名胜资源及土地使用性质，没收违法所得，可并处2000元以上30000元以下罚款。

（六）违反第十三条规定，无权批准而批准、越权批准或者违反法定程序批准在樟江风景名胜区内进行建设的，其批准文件无效，对直接负责的主管人员和其他直接责任人员，依法给予行政处分。

第二十四条 本条例第二十三条规定的行政处罚，由荔波县人民政府有关行政管理部门依法委托樟江风景名胜区管理机构按照委托权限实施，或者由有关行政管理部门按照规定权限实施。

第二十五条 本条例未作处罚规定的违法行为，法律、法规规定处罚的，从其规定。

第二十六条 罚款必须使用省财政部门统一制发的罚款收据，全额上缴国库。

第二十七条 国家工作人员在樟江风景名胜区管理工作中玩忽职守、滥用职权、徇私舞弊的，由所在单位或者上级主管部门给予行政处分，造成损失的，依法予以赔偿。

第二十八条 本条例自公布之日起施行。

二、获省部级以上表彰先进单位名录

获奖单位名称	获奖称号	颁奖部门	获奖时间
荔波民族中学	“1986年班班有歌声活动”优秀奖	中共贵州省委	1988年1月
	2003—2005年度全省精神文明建设工作先进单位	中共贵州省委、贵州省人民政府	2006年12月
	贵州省第六次民族团结进步表彰大会先进集体	中共贵州省委、贵州省人民政府	2008年1月
荔波县审计局	全国审计系统先进集体	国家审计局、人事局、中国财贸工会	1990年6月
荔波县税务局	全国个体工商税户税法宣传及普法活动最佳组织奖	税务总局	1990年
荔波县卫生防疫站	《伯氨喹小剂量对间日疟和恶性疟的效果观察》获贵州省科学技术进步三等奖	贵州省人民政府	1990年12月
	全国消灭脊髓灰质炎工作先进集体	卫生部	2001年10月
	全国丝虫病防治先进集体	卫生部	2008年6月
荔波县人民政府	贵州省“八五”期间扶贫开发先进县三等奖	中共贵州省委、贵州省人民政府	1995年12月
	扶贫开发先进县	中共贵州省委、贵州省人民政府	1995年
	全国率先解决温饱先进县	中共贵州省委、贵州省人民政府	1996年
	提前完成造林十年规划指标	贵州省人民政府	1996年1月
	1995—1996年度冬春农田水利建设先进单位	贵州省人民政府	1996年2月
	1996年度粮食生产先进县	贵州省人民政府	1997年11月
	省级卫生县城	贵州省人民政府	1997年12月
	1997年度粮食生产先进县	贵州省人民政府	1998年10月
	2000年全省3000公里公路改造组织实施奖	贵州省人民政府	2001年2月
	2002年度征兵工作先进单位	贵州省人民政府	2003年12月
	全国科普示范县	中国科学技术协会	2004年
	国家级卫生县城	全国爱卫会	2004年
荔波县农机局	全国农牧渔业丰收奖二等奖	农业部	1997年11月
荔波县人民检察院	全国检察机关“文明接待室”	最高人民检察院	1997年11月 2000年11月 2004年3月 2008年2月
玉屏镇城北居委会	模范人民调解组织	司法部	1999年5月
荔波县科学技术协会	全国科普工作先进集体	科学技术部、中共中央宣传部、科学技术协会	2002年12月

续表

获奖单位名称	获奖称号	颁奖部门	获奖时间
贵州省茂兰国家级自然保护区管理局	全国自然保护区管理先进集体	环保部、农业部、国土资源部	1999年12月
	全国自然保护区示范单位	国家林业局	2006年5月
	贵州省第二届旅游产业发展大会先进单位	贵州省人民政府	2008年4月
荔波县立化镇资源开发公司	非共有制经济先进企业	贵州省人民政府	2000年12月
荔波县佳荣镇大土村党支部	先进基层党组织	中共贵州省委	2001年7月
荔波县国家税务局	1999—2002年文明单位	中共贵州省委、贵州省人民政府	2002年8月
	2003—2005年度全省文明单位	中共贵州省委、贵州省人民政府	2006年12月
	巾帼文明岗	全国妇女联合会	2007年2月
共青团荔波县委员会	全国未成年人保护工作先进集体	中共中央宣传部、全国人大内务司法委员会、共青团中央、教育部、司法部	2002年10月
荔波县中心法律事务所	残疾人维权示范岗	司法部、中国残联	2003年
荔波县扶贫办	民族团结先进集体	中共贵州省委贵州省人民政府	2003年12月
荔波樟江风景名胜区管理处	贵州省文明风景旅游区	贵州省人民政府	2004年
荔波县教育局	贵州省校务公开先进单位	教育部	2004年12月 2006年11月 2007年11月
	贵州省“两基”攻坚先进集体	中共贵州省委、贵州省人民政府	2006年6月
荔波县水尧乡水族乡农村税费改革领导小组办公室	2001—2005年农村税费改革试点工作先进集体	中共贵州省委	2005年8月
荔波县气象局	气象部门局务公开先进单位	中国气象局	2005年
	精神文明建设工作先进单位	中共贵州省委贵州省人民政府	2006年4月 2008年12月
荔波县环境保护局	国家级生态示范区建设优秀组织	国家环境保护总局	2006年10月
荔波县财政局	2003—2005年度全省精神文明建设工作先进单位	中共贵州省委、贵州省人民政府	2006年12月
荔波县人力资源和社会保障局	全国农村青年转移就业先进单位	共青团中央、农业部、教育部、科技部、劳动和社会保障部、国务院扶贫办、中国民主促进会中央委员会	2006年
	全国农村青年转移就业先进单位	劳动和社会保障部	2007年
荔波中等职业技术学校	全国中等职业教育德育工作实验基地	教育部	2007年5月
	全国教育系统先进集体	人事部、教育部	2007年9月

说明：此表仅收录报送的获得表彰单位，未报送的没有收录。

三、荔波县2009—2015年经济社会发展资料

2009年

2009年，荔波县主要经济指标稳步增长，实现了质量、速度和效益相统一。完成生产总值130365万元，增长16.4%；农业总产值达58343万元，增长8.8%；规模以上工业增加值达40014万元，增长16.8%。全社会固定资产投资实现大幅增长，完成投资103262万元，增长51.06%；社会消费品零售总额完成39811万元，增长23.19%；农民人均纯收入3009元，增长14.94%，以上三项指标均提前一年实现“十一五”规划目标。金融运行态势良好，完成财政总收入22669万元，增长24.45%，提前40天完成全年预期目标。金融机构各项存款余额16.5亿元，增长20.18%，各项贷款余额7.49亿元，增长59.28%。

2009年全县加大对“三农”的投入力度，全年财政投入达8660万元，增长33.5%。落实粮食综合直补、农机具购置补贴、退耕还林补贴等各项惠农政策，共兑现补贴资金3370万元。粮食生产抗灾夺丰收，总产量达6.2万吨，增长3.48%，再创历史新高。创建了“185”工程示范面积达6360亩，完成特色水果种植7500亩、辣椒1万亩、商品蔬菜6.2万亩，新增茶园3100亩，种桑养蚕效益稳步回升。农业产业化经营实现新突破，获州级龙头企业5个，新增农民专业合作社10个，完成土地流转2.7万亩。畜牧业方面新增万头养猪场1个、百头养牛场2个，大牲畜存栏6.38万头，肉类总产量达8789吨。农业综合生产基础条件，完成朝阳八烂1000亩节水灌溉工程，投入3690万元修建各类水利工程43处，瑶麓排洪渠、梅桃提灌站、东升橡胶坝已建成投入使用，治理小（2）型病险水库2座，建成“三小”工程330口，新增渠道23.5公里，新增灌溉面积1312亩，有效解决了5.61万人的饮水安全问题。木朝、福利等新农村示范点和拉片民族团结进步示范村建设取得新成效；全面完成11个一类、二类贫困村的整村推进，解决贫困人口3621人。

2009年，荔波县争取到新增中央投资项目73个，总投资13630万元，并完成投资9900万元，完工率达89.04%。建设了乡镇文化站、农村沼气和饮水工程，县中医院扩建、垃圾填埋场、污水处理管网等项目推进顺利。在城镇规划和建设上，完成了《老城区控制性详细规划》《县城风貌规划》《王蒙修建性规划》《驾欧旅游次中心概念性规划》《公路沿线可视范围村庄整治规划》以及6镇7乡的总体规划编制，县城规划控制已基本实现全覆盖。完成时来新区路灯工程和樟江大街夜景亮丽工程。驾麻高速公路全线开工建设，荔波段已完成投资1.3亿元，投资1780万元实施荔大公路大修工程，驾朝公路验收交付使用，茂兰大街改造和17条通村公路建设基本完成，寨票大桥建设进展顺利。电网改造完成投资3945万元，电力保障水平不断提升。

2009年，荔波县加快推进核心景区配套建设，建成景区门禁系统和监控系统，投资2860万元实施完成遗产地保护性基础设施项目，其中小七孔湿地景区亮点突出，成为喀斯特地区湿地建设的示范性样板。促成荔波至广州旅游包机，正式开通荔波至贵阳航线，航班达180架次，进出港8363人次。进一步理顺景区经营和旅游管理关系，旅游行业监管逐步强化，旅游市场实现健康发展。成功举办第四届“梅花节”主题活动。与北京市平谷区缔结友好区县，在世界旅游精英博鳌峰会上，荔波被评为“国际旅游王牌目的地”。旅游收入实现稳定增长，全年累计接待游客264.1万人次，增长20.96%，拉动了商贸、餐饮、宾馆酒店、交通运输、文化娱乐等第三产业繁荣发展。

在生态建设和环境保护中，完成了《荔波世界自然遗产地保护专项规划》及《遗产地人口外迁规划》，争取到省政府每年1000万元的遗产地保护专项资金补助。促成建立了“中国南方喀斯特”

研究院荔波教学科研基地，并与美国猛犸洞国家公园建立“友好公园”，争取到奔驰公司150万元援助资金。同时，开展遗产地社区群众的教育与培训，遗产地资源管理和保护等方面得到加强。落实退耕还林政策，大力实施珠江防护、封山育林、水土保持等生态建设工程，完成营造林3.1万亩；集体林权制度改革有序推进，完成勘界确权面积231.2万亩，发证率达97%。严格控制樟江沿岸开山采石、挖砂、建房等行为，重点治理乱倒垃圾、违法捕杀野生动物等现象，维护樟江生态平衡、优美和谐。

2009年，县内企业改革稳步推进，县饮食服务公司并购实现重组，供销企业体制改革进一步深化，林工商公司已完成改制方案，荔波供电局整体划转贵州电网公司。推进财政体制改革，全面推行部门预算和乡财县管，严格非税收入收支管理；完成规范公务员津补贴和义务教育绩效工资改革。全年偿还各类债务本息共7827万元。招商引资取得新进展，引进在建项目20个，实际到位资金40980万元，比上年增长29.73%。优化提升煤炭支柱产业，建立“一对一”煤矿帮扶制度，稳步推进和谐矿区建设，加快煤矿技改扩能，办矿规模和水平进一步提升，累计完成原煤产销量127万吨。促进商贸流通，开展产品质量和食品安全专项整治行动，严厉打击制售假冒伪劣商品的违法行为，较好地维护了人民群众的合法权利。

2009年，全县各项社会事业取得可喜成绩。“两基”工作代表贵州省顺利通过国家督导检查。全面化解“普九”债务，教育教学质量稳步提升。全县村级卫生室实现全覆盖，完成了7000座农村卫生改厕项目；新型农村合作医疗参合率达94.28%，城镇居民基本医疗保险参保率99.06%。继续稳定低生育水平，人口自然增长率为6.06‰。精神文明建设取得新成效，县城荣获“全国文明县城”称号。成功举办“全国陀螺邀请赛”“周末篮球赛”等赛事，参加全州首届运动会取得较好成绩；成功推出“土风计划”荔波《水书表情》剧目。投资390万元完成10个乡（镇）文化站、28个农家书屋、85个村级文化资源共享工程；完成县城数字电视整体转换；恢复组建县民族艺术团，积极挖掘民族文化，馆藏六部水书和四部布依族傩书被列为第二批国家珍贵古籍名录；水族民间酿酒工艺、布依族傩戏入选第三批国家级非物质文化遗产候选名录。启动编修第二部《荔波县志》，档案事业发展综合评估顺利通过国家检查验收。

2009年在保障和改善民生、涉及群众切身利益的问题得到进一步解决。建成的84套廉租住房、72套拆迁安置房已分配入住，完成1334户农村危房改造，困难群众住房难问题逐步得到解决。出台《荔波县被征地农民社会保障暂行办法》，探索扶持失地农民生活转型保障措施。落实“家电下乡”等惠民政策，共兑现补贴资金250万元。安排资金设立了12个避雷塔。全县参保人数达25862人，净增763人，征收基金1929.4万元，净增420.3万元，支付社会保障资金1268.6万元。促进就业再就业，通过公开招考安排了77名大中专毕业生就业，新增城镇就业人员574人，基本消除城镇“零就业”家庭。健全和完善城乡低保制度，农村低保进行了“一次扩面两次提标”，人数从最初的10954人扩大到24000人，保障标准从700元提高到785元，年人均补助水平从460元提高到580元，共发放农村低保金2343万元；发放城市低保金351万元，保障困难居民16000人，基本实现了应保尽保。发放五保供养金62万元，安排救灾救济资金411万元，启动实施居家养老试点，优抚安置、社会福利事业取得新的发展。加大社会治安综合治理力度，严厉打击各类违法犯罪活动，完善城区监控系统建设，“平安荔波”深入推进，安定团结的社会局面得到较好维护。

2010年

2010年，是荔波县面临困难最多，逆势奋进的一年，及时协调解决经济运行中的困难和问题，保持了加快发展的势头，全县生产总值完成17.69亿元，增长13.6%；全社会固定资产投资17.72亿元，增长71.59%；财政总收入完成2.8亿元，增长23.59%；社会消费品零售总额完成4.77亿元，增长20.75%；农民人均纯收入为3528元，增长17.3%。全县生产总值从2005年的81076万元增加到176880万元，年均递增12.87%，是2005年的2.18倍。财政总收入从11897万元增加到28016万元，年均递增18.68%，是2005年的2.35倍；财政一般预算收入从5556万元增加到13533万元，年均递增19.50%，是2005年的2.44倍。全社会固定资产投资从35442万元增加到177186万元，年均递增37.97%，“十一五”期间累计投资是“十五”期间的4.04倍。社会消费品零售总额从19113万元增加到47719.8万元，年均递增20.08%，是2005年的2.5倍。2010年年末金融机构存贷款余额分别达19.3亿元和9.2亿元，是2005年的2.62倍和2.58倍。

2010年，全县产业结构调整实现新进展，三次产业结构由2005年的24.9：37.3：37.8调整为2010年的18.9：36.6：44.5。“十一五”累计投入“三农”资金达4.72亿元，是“十五”的4.5倍。国家一系列强农惠农政策兑现到位，彻底取消农业税和各种收费，结束了农民种田缴税的历史。粮食产量连续六年创新高，2010年达到63510吨。农民专业合作经济组织达38个，有序推进土地流转3万亩以上，农业产业化步伐明显加快。创建“185工程”面积3.4万亩，重点实施的“十万亩经果林基地”已达6.8万亩，蔬菜、甘蔗、茶叶分别稳定在6.6万亩、1.8万亩和8100亩，建成规模养殖场35个，涌现出省级龙头企业1个和州级龙头企业5个，基本形成了“果蔬、畜牧、甘蔗、桑蚕、辣椒、茶叶”六大特色产业，荔波血桃、荔波蜜柚、“碧华园”无公害生鲜肉食品和“天然牧咯”虫草鸡逐步形成品牌优势。工业经济发展质量和效益明显提升，煤矿整合技改取得实质性进展，煤炭产销量累计达600万吨；完成水泥厂易地改造扩能达产，新建中小水电站5个，水电装机总量新增3.6万千瓦，全县规模工业企业由18家增加到28家。旅游业加速崛起，成功承办第二届贵州旅游产业发展大会，樟江风景名胜区顺利完成了国家AAAA级景区创建。启动了茂兰保护区游线建设，“四区一带”生态旅游格局基本形成。推出了洞塘木朝、板寨、瑶山拉片、拉柳、玉屏下白岩等一批乡村与民族文化旅游村寨，打造了“梅花节”旅游品牌，填补了贵州冬季旅游的空白，被评为“国际王牌旅游目的地”，荔波的知名度和影响力明显提升。旅游人数从2005年的55万人次增加到334.7万人次。商贸、酒店、餐饮、娱乐等服务业蓬勃发展，星级酒店已达34家，新增农家接待点239个。

“十一五”以来，城乡面貌呈现新变化，特别是加快交通、水利、城镇基础设施建设，累计实施各类基础设施项目273个、投资9.2亿元，其中争取到中央新增投资项目和中央预算内投资项目123个、投资1.88亿元，争取中央新增投资在全州名列前茅。交通发展实现历史性突破，荔波机场建成通航，麻驾高速公路全线贯通，荔波人民的两大期盼终得实现；新建乡镇客车站9个，新建、改（扩）建县乡公路727.3公里，率先在全州实现了乡乡通油路、村村通公路目标，初步形成了“内优外快”的立体交通格局。累计投入8658万元实施水利工程，重点完成了2座水库建设，3个小（2）型病险水库除险加固，建成“三小”工程3250口，新增有效灌溉面积8200亩，实施了54个农村饮水项目，解决了6.74万人的饮水安全问题。大力实施“景城互动”战略，突出科学规划引领建设，累计投入1600多万元完成了城区、景区及土地等27项规划，县城规划管理基本实现全覆盖。抓住“旅发大会”契机，实施新、老城区联动开发，集中力量推进城市建设“十大工程”，时来新区官塘大道、阳光路等5条道路如期建成，污水处理厂建成投入运行，官塘大桥建设完成82%工程量，县城区面积由2.5平方公里扩展到4.2平方公里。驾欧、瑶山、朝阳、甲良、茂兰、佳荣、瑶麓、翁昂等集镇建设启动推进，拉片民族团结进步示范村建设成为全省示范样板，以房屋立面改造为切入点的县城至小七孔景区沿线村寨整治展现出新的风景线。城镇化率已达35.48%。

2010年，推进土地承包经营权流转，集体林权制度改革基本完成。国有企业改革全面实施，水泥厂、樟江食品厂、粮油购销公司和饮食服务公司等一批国企改制并购工作顺利完成。财政改革全面推行部门预算和国库集中支付改革，加大了对乡镇的财政扶持，进一步理顺了“乡财县管”财政体制。新一轮政府部门机构改革基本完成，实施行政审批制度改革，组建成立县行政服务中心，推进“一站式”服务建设。全面放宽非公经济市场准入领域，实行政府领导重点帮扶民营企业制度，非公有制企业从2005年的96家增加到344家，成为县域经济发展的中坚力量。对外经济合作不断拓展，与北京市平谷区缔结友好区县，与深圳盐田港集团、光明新区结成了帮扶对子。招商引资累计到位资金18.86亿元，是“十五”的6.8倍。

荔波县始终坚持把保住青山绿水作为立县之本，《荔波世界自然遗产地保护项目专项规划》经省政府批复，先期实施的遗产地175户人口外迁试点工程已完工。拓展生态保护工作的国际交流与合作，承办“人与生物圈保护区网络”国际会议，会上形成的《荔波共识》受到国际社会的普遍认同。与奔驰公司开展了两期遗产地保护资助项目合作，成功与美国猛犸洞国家公园缔结“友好公园”，初步建立了国际组织框架下的生态保护新机制。推进退耕还林、珠江防护、九万大山等生态工程，结合经果林种植实施石漠化综合治理，新增有林地8.6万亩；积极实施天然林保护工程，争取国家重点公益林补偿资金3000万元。强化森林防火基础性工作，在全州首个组建森林消防专业队。集中开展打击非法盗采矿产资源行动，全力维护矿产资源开发秩序。强化樟江源头非煤矿山整治，持续推进樟江两岸补植、补造绿化工程，“秀美樟江”打造初现成效。深入开展整治企业违法排污专项行动，基本实现了“十一五”节能减排目标任务。

在人民生活方面，县级财政用于民生的投入逐年增加，累计投入6.7亿元，是“十五”的6.5倍，政府公开承诺办理的30件惠民实事基本落实。扶贫攻坚完成了40个贫困村“整村推进”，成功实施1468户移民搬迁，减少农村贫困人口34229人。建成198套廉租住房和72户安置房，完成2561户农村危房改造，困难群众住房难的问题逐步得到解决。建立村干部绩效工资奖励机制，提高了村干部待遇标准。结合新农村和基层组织建设，累计投入2012万元集中实施村级公益事业“一事一议”财政奖补项目，惠及4.9万人，实现了“一事一议”与党的建设双促进。全面实施城乡低保制度，农村低保进行了“一次扩面两次提标”，年保障标准从820元提高到1200元；城镇低保月保障标准从160元提高到220元，累计发放城乡低保金6120万元，惠及4.07万人。投入救灾救济资金1521.5万元，发放优待抚恤金1038万元。成立慈善总会，筹集慈善资金120万元。建立了城镇居民基本医疗保险制度和城乡医疗救助制度，基本养老、失业、工伤和生育保险覆盖面进一步扩大。新型农村合作医疗参合率已达96.52%。出台《荔波县被征地农民社会保障暂行办法》，加大农业产业基地和创业平台的扶持力度，努力帮助失地农民转型发展。积极拓展就业渠道，累计招考录用383名大中专毕业生，城镇新增就业2726人，帮助975名下岗人员实现再就业，动态消除“零就业”家庭。农民人均纯收入由1654元增加到3528元，年均增长17.25%，人民群众生活质量不断改善、幸福感得到增强。

“十一五”以来，县财政对教育、文化、卫生、体育事业的投入达到7.3亿元，是“十五”的3.5倍。全面实施城乡免费义务教育，高考升学率连续五年位居全州前列，2010年高考实现上线率达99.9%。县职中晋升为国家重点中等职业学校。实施完成116所学校新（改）建工程，全面化解农村“普九”债务，实现了“小县办大教育”的目标。县中医院易地扩建竣工，新（改）建乡镇卫生院16个、村级卫生室102个，覆盖城乡的公共卫生和医疗服务体系基本建立。继续稳定低生育水平，创建全国计划生育优质服务先进县工作通过评估检查。建成乡（镇）综合文化站10个、农家书屋62个、乡村体育场27个、文化信息资源共享工程86个，电视覆盖率达到95%以上。成功举办全国山地户外运动锦标赛。恢复组建县民族艺术团，荣获“中国民族器乐大赛”原生态类芦笙表演团体金奖，荔波原生态歌舞走进中央电视台“民歌·中国”演播大厅。民族古籍抢救工作中20部精品水书和10部布依族傩书列为国家珍贵古籍名录。瑶族猴鼓舞、水书习俗、布依族傩戏列入国家级非物质文化遗产名录，佳荣、瑶麓荣获“中国民族民间文化艺术之乡”。县档案馆被国务院列入首批“全国古籍重点保护单位”，档案事业通过国家综合评估验收。巩固国家卫生县城成果，荣获“全国文明县城”称号。安全生产工作，亿元GDP生产安全事故死亡率从2005年的7.1人降到2010年的0.91人，煤矿百万吨死亡率从17.89人下降到7.56人。2010年公共突发事件应急工作机制不断强化，提升公安、武警、消防队伍装备建设，“平安荔波”创建取得新成效，人民群众安全感不断增强。

2011年

2011年，荔波县生产总值从2006年的9.07亿元增加到21.6亿元，年均增长19.16%；财政总收入从1.29亿元增加到3亿元，年均增长18.39%；全社会固定资产投资从4.6亿元增加到22.7亿元，年均增长37.61%；社会消费品零售总额从2.7亿元增加到6亿元，年均增长17.32%；金融机构存贷款余额分别达21.46亿元和10.67亿元，是2006年的2.65倍和2.52倍；农民人均纯收入从2006年的1808元增加到4752元，年均增长21.32%。三次产业结构由21.28：36.48：42.24调整为18.49：33.58：47.93。主要经济指标均保持两位数增长，是历史上发展最快的时期。

2007—2011年，全县累计投入“三农”资金8.2亿元，发放各类惠农补贴资金2.8亿元。在稳定粮食产量的前提下，积极推进土地流转，共创建“185工程”面积7.1万亩，实施“10万亩经果林工程”面积7.5万亩，种植糖蔗面积1.35万亩、蔬菜6.6万亩，农机总动力达22万千瓦。建成万头养猪场3个，千头养猪场15个，建立农民专业合作经济组织47个，新增农业产业化龙头企业6个。扶贫攻坚取得明显成效，完成了48个贫困村“整村推进”、1618户移民搬迁工作，贫困人口累计减少34229人。投入1.6亿元实施退耕还林、珠江防护、九万大山等生态工程，新增营造林面积31.74万亩，森林覆盖率达63%。完成石漠化治理面积20平方公里。新农村建设积极推进，拉岜村列入全国“一村一品”示范村，拉片民族团结进步示范村成为全省示范样板村。成功申报国家重点生态功能区，被评为省级“绿化模范县”“绿化先进集体”。

实施旅游“加速开发”，成功开通重庆、贵阳、湛江旅游专列，推出了小七孔湿地、万亩梅原等一批新景点。探索开发了茂兰保护区游线建设，“四区一带”生态旅游格局基本形成。建成了木朝、板寨、拉柳、白岩等一批民族文化旅游村寨，旅游逐步从生态观光游向民族风情游、民俗体验游、休闲度假游转变。全县商贸、酒店、餐饮、娱乐等服务业蓬勃发展，星级酒店（商务）达41家，新增农家接待点100余家，签约并即将开工建设的五星级酒店4家、四星级酒店5家。2011年，县域内旅游人数达537万人次、旅游综合收入32.9亿元。

2007—2011年，全县煤炭产销量累计达570万吨。成功组建3家煤业集团，有序推进31家煤炭企业兼并重组。完成了水泥厂易地扩能改造，投资3.2亿元的南华糖厂顺利建成并将于今天投产开榨。新建小水电站3个，水电装机总量达8.64万千瓦。全县规模工业企业从18家增加到28家。工业园区建设全面铺开，“一区两园”规划、驾播园区进场道路路基工程全面推进。组建了工业园区投资开发有限责任公司，融资平台建设得到加强。2011年，全县规模以上工业增加值达5.11亿元。

基础设施逐步完善，累计投资9.2亿元实施各类基础设施项目273个，其中，中央新增投资项目和中央预算内投资项目131个、投资1.89亿元。麻驾高速公路全线贯通，新建乡镇客车站13个，新（改）建县乡村公路1278公里，率先在全州实现乡乡通油路、村村通公路目标。新一轮农村电网改造实现城乡全覆盖。累计投入4950万元实施“一事一议”财政奖补项目，投入1.3亿元完成了巴怀、内阁、鲁劳水库除险加固，完成县城防洪堤、樟江、驾欧河道治理和董榕水库建设。建成“三小”工程3250口、农村饮水项目94个、农田灌溉项目8个，新增有效灌溉面积9200亩，全县有效灌溉面积达7.5万亩，解决了农村9.84万人的饮水安全问题。

城镇建设步伐加快，2007—2011年，累计投入1600万元完成了城区、景区等27项规划。筹资近

2亿元完成了樟江大街综合景观改造、江滨公园、恩铭大道、县城北出口、时来路网一期工程等项目建设。新区路网框架基本形成，官塘大桥主体工程基本完工。泰龙西苑、盛世广场、樟江印象、今典华庭、荔波·中央城等一批房地产开发项目相继建成或开工建设，开发面积达80万平方米，城区面积由2.5平方公里扩展到5平方公里，城镇化率由23.8%提高到38%。村庄面貌明显改观，投入1500万元实施了县城至驾欧公路沿线村庄整治和景观打造工程，完成房屋立面改造1123栋。板寨、福利、拉鱼、拉柳等一批民族村寨展现了荔波民居特色新形象、新面貌。

开展以商招商、项目招商、节会招商，先后引进广西南华糖业集团有限公司、北京亮马港湾置业有限公司等一批知名企业进驻荔波发展。五年累计引进招商项目114个，其中上亿元重大项目21个，千万元项目45个，合同引资64.98亿元，到位资金42.24亿元。

实施民生工程，累计投入资金20亿元，支持民生事业加快发展。高考升学率连续5年位居全州前列，成为全省首批普及高中阶段教育试点县，县职业中学晋升为国家级重点中等职业学校。新扩（改）建幼儿园5所，荔波二中异地扩建顺利完成。完成了县中医院易地搬迁和县计幼服务中心大楼建设，成功创建“全国计划生育优质服务先进县”。体育比赛，参加全国、全省、全州民运会及有关赛事共荣获27金13银16铜的好成绩。为全民健身运动开展，建成乡村体育场27个。全面实施城乡低保制度，社会保障体系进一步健全。累计发放城乡低保金8506.43万元，惠及21.7万人次。投入救灾救济资金2238.45万元，发放优待抚恤金1248.22万元。建成了9个城乡社区居家养老服务中心和甲良敬老院。拓展就业再就业渠道，累计新增城镇就业人员2698人，城镇登记失业率控制在4.2%以内。保障性住房建设，完成了254套廉租房、72套安置房、76套公租房和4310户农村危房改造建设工作。

2011年深入开展“平安荔波”创建活动，严厉打击各类违法犯罪行为，确保了全县社会治安大局稳定。

2012年

2012年，全县地区生产总值完成27.2亿元，同比增长23.4%；全社会固定资产投资完成37亿元，增长68.1%；全部工业增加值完成8.35亿元，增长21.3%，其中，规模工业增加值完成7.6亿元，增长28.8%；社会消费品零售总额完成7.6亿元，增长31%；财政总收入完成3.04亿元，较上年略有增长，公共财政预算支出突破10亿元；农民人均纯收入完成5252元，增长20%。三次产业结构调整为17.2∶35.4∶47.4。金融机构存款余额28.13亿元、贷款余额14.16亿元，分别增长24.2%、34.8%。

2012年，全县投资1000万元以上的51个项目及29个中央预算内投资项目累计完成投资20.3亿元。深入落实国发2号文件，完成561个项目编制，主动对接并争取项目174个，落地76个，到位资金4.22亿元。加大基础设施建设力度，全县在建或建成通村油路里程145.5公里，建成冬修水利项目51个、农村饮水安全工程50个。成功列为全国生态文明示范工程试点县、中央财政小型农田水利设施建设重点县、省级统筹城乡综合配套改革试点县、省级文化旅游集聚区试点县、省级乡镇财政标准化建设试点县。邀请财政部科研所实地调研并组织编撰的《荔波世界自然遗产地保护与利用专题调研报告》已通过专家评审。

2012年，城乡面貌发生新变化，全县30个市政基础设施建设项目完成投资5.3亿元，县城供水改（扩）建工程主体完工，荔波古镇、民族体育活动中心等项目已开工建设；樟江印象、中央城等10个在建房开项目完成投资4.8亿元，新增住房858套，销售面积6.4万平方米。县城区域面积扩展到5.2平方公里，城镇化率达41.5%，城市公交车开通运行。

旅游产业方面，《樟江风光带景区详细规划》通过住建部审批，与澳青旅、北京德安杰、广东南湖国旅等知名旅游企业的合作，先后组团赴日本及中国香港、澳门、台湾、上海、重庆、安徽等新老客源地开展旅游宣传促销，促成35家省内外旅行社参与组团营销。成功举办了第七届梅花报春节、首届中国·荔波喀斯特山谷音乐节、申遗成功五周年庆典、“爱在荔波”“绿动全球·荔波启航”等系列活动；成功推出《水韵樟江》实景演艺文化产品，“地球之花·山水荔波”品牌效应日渐彰显。全年共接待游客790万人次，实现旅游综合收入105亿元，同比分别增长47.2%、218.4%，樟江景区门票收入5785万元，比2011年净增1372万元，增长31.09%，游客人数的增加有效拉动了商贸、餐饮、交通运输、文化娱乐等第三产业加速发展。

“三农”工作方面，累计发放强农惠农政策补贴资金3377万元，实施“185工程”15.6万亩，创办产业示范点45个，示范面积4.46万亩，建设新农村示范点10个，实现粮食总产量5.1万吨，同比增长30.4%。扎实推进“双十工程”，糖蔗、经果林、蔬菜种植分别达4.36万亩、8.3万亩、15万亩。完成土地流转4.3万亩，农业产业化经营组织发展到57家，州级以上龙头企业12家。全县规模养猪场48个、规模养鸡场168个、特种养殖场31个。投资7517.5万元完成了农田水利、河道治理、水库除险加固及人饮灌溉工程，有效解决农田灌溉面积1.5万亩、人畜饮水4.9万人、1.3万头。实施九万大山、珠防工程等生态建设，完成石漠化综合治理达18平方公里，水土治理23平方公里，绿化造林6.3万亩。

工业经济方面，“一区两园”基础设施建设累计完成投资6228万元，投资3.2亿元的荔波南华糖厂建成并投产开榨，投资4500万元的家具制造项目进入生产试运行。建成4个小型水电站，新增装机容量9870千瓦。建立煤矿安全生产包保责任制，组建了矿产品交易中心，全县“六证”齐全煤矿从年初的2家增加到8家，原煤产销量达61.6万吨，同比增长35.98%。新增规模工业企业4家，全县规模工业企业已达25家。

深化国有企业改制，完成林工商公司改制，食品公司、医药公司、外贸公司、物资公司等企业改制工作稳步推进。积极探索银政合作机制，成功向金融机构融资4亿元，用于城景基础设施建设。荔波农村金融网点覆盖面不断扩大，驾欧乡、水尧乡被省信用联社评为信用乡（镇）。启动殡葬改革工作，县城平稳实现集中治丧。创新招商方式，全县招商签约项目54个，合同引资54.7亿元，到位资金42亿元，同比分别增长47.8%、98%。用活“3个15万元”政策，支持民营经济加速发展，新增民营企业119户、个体工商户740户，全县民营企业、个体工商户分别达到495户、4042户。

2012年，全县85个“十大民生工程”完成投资3亿元，81个“一事一议”财政奖补项目完成投资2660万元，投资2657万元完成294户1402人扶贫生态移民工程。加快保障性住房建设，完成96套廉租房、198套公租房和1683户农村危房改造建设。新增城镇就业1376人，失业人员再就业316人，有组织劳务输出5170人，城镇登记失业率控制在3.6%以内。启动城乡居民养老保险试点工作，完成参保52770人。实施教育、卫生事业“双百工程”，荔波高级中学一期项目和县中等职业技术学校实验楼建成投入使用，高考实现历史性突破，录取率分别高于全国、全省17个百分点和22个百分点，义务教育均衡发展成效明显；成功创建县人民医院为“二级甲等医院”。健全和完善城乡低保标准稳定增长机制，全年累计发放低保金4268.7万元，救助金477.2万元，救助粮1406吨，救助人数达28173人，建成3个村级居家养老服务站点，新农合参合率达98.4%。加大扶贫攻坚工作，专项扶贫资金到位4540万元，信贷贴息扶贫资金3700万元，减少贫困人口9857人，方村乡实现“减贫摘帽”。人口出生率、自然增长率实现“双降”目标。“整脏治乱”排名实现全省前十名、全州第一名的目标，“国家卫生县城”通过复核验收。推动文化、体育、广电事业发展，投资2150万元完成23248户广播电视网络覆盖工程，成功举办各类文体赛事活动。积极推进撤乡建镇、撤镇设办工作，驾欧乡、播尧乡撤乡建镇，玉屏镇改办事处获省批准。继续推动“平安荔波”创建活动，严厉打击各类违法犯罪活动，组建特巡警防暴大队，建成“阳光工程”集中安置点。深入开展“大接访”“三访”活动，建立重大信访案件领导包案和县级领导定期接访制度，切实做好人民调解、矛盾纠纷和积案化解工作。建立健全突发事件应急处置机制，有效预防和避免了突发公共事件的发生，维护了社会和谐稳定。

2013年

2013年，荔波县地区生产总值完成32.6亿元，同比增长16.7%；固定资产投资完成43.32亿元，增长40.6%；规模以上工业增加值完成9.5亿元，增长21.3%；社会消费品零售总额实现8.1亿元，增长18%。全县财政总收入完成4.18亿元，增长33.34%；地方公共财政收入完成2.09亿元，增长34.86%；农村居民人均可支配收入6252元，增长15.95%，城镇居民人均可支配收入19515元；金融机构存贷款余额分别达38.34亿元、22.98亿元，增长33.74%、50.12%。增比进位在全省综合测评排名48位，比2012年上升了36位。

全县在建、新建、拟建项目达269个，总投资198.8亿元，开工率91.82%，累计完成项目实物投资76.54亿元（其中，投资1000万元以上的89个县级领导包保项目完成投资51.82亿元）；引资在建项目121个，到位资金61.74亿元，增长75.89%；争取中央预算内投资项目52个，总投资2.44亿元，争取上级补助专项资金10.1亿元，同比净增1.45亿元，增长18%；事关荔波经济社会快发展的驾荔高速公路、省道206环大小七孔景区公路有序推进，省道312荔波至甲良、省道206三洞至荔波二级公路改造工程启动建设，群众关注度极高的玉播公路建成通车，佳荣至何家寨、佳荣至水维、播尧至觉巩等县、乡道得到立项改造建设，全县60%的建制村通油路；玉屏、茂兰、朝阳、甲良、小七孔、水尧、永康、瑶麓、瑶山9个乡（镇、办事处）实现100%的建制村通油路（水泥路）；县城一级客运站异地搬迁开工建设；5座水库除险加固工程主体完工，投资2.4亿元的尧柳水库如期开工，三荔、大土水库等水利工程前期工作进展顺利，争取水利开发项目获批资金1.1亿元，到位资金7160万元；全面完成冬修水利、小型农田水利重点县等水利基础设施项目建设，新增灌溉面1500亩，改善灌溉面1688亩，恢复灌溉面2430亩，有效解决农村饮水安全1.9万人。

在改善人居环境，荔波县樟江市民休闲公园规划基本完成，列入全省100个城市综合体的樟江国际城及泊林城市综合体规划编制通过专家评审。县公共服务大楼、县城供水改扩建项目建成投入使用，环城西路、环城南路、环城北路、玉屏至朝阳（8.6公里）城市主干道一期工程、时来110千伏变电站正有序建设；4个旧城改造项目及6家星级酒店项目建设有力推进，荔波古镇、财富广场、嘉和中央城等16个房开项目完成投资7.06亿元，房地产销售面积达20.24万平方米；城镇基础设施建设完成投资25.94亿元，同比增加7.9亿元；甲良、翁昂等重点小城镇建设取得明显成效，全县城镇化率达43.66%，比上年提高了2.1个百分点。

2013年，三次产业结构调整为15：32：53。以旅游业为龙头的第三产业已成为全县国民经济第二支柱产业。荔波樟江景区创建国家AAAAA级旅游景区通过国家旅游局专家组景观质量评审，景区建设在全省100个旅游景区2013年度考核中排名前列。成功向金融机构融资6.3亿元实施大七孔、小七孔、水春河等核心景区及城镇基础设施的升级改造，新开发了小七孔景区八大水景和九个瀑布的湿地景观、卧龙河峡谷浪漫漂游观光带、枫树弯景观农业旅游文化度假中心、樟江经典文化游等项目。与48家省内外旅行社建立长期合作关系，与黄果树、西江苗寨等景区建立营销联盟，组团旅游推介；成功与澳青旅合作开展荔波至广州航线包机，全年上座率达63%；云南英安航空入驻荔波机场，开创了省内支线机场与民营航空企业合作新模式。全年接待游客521.9万人次，实现旅游收入44.73亿元，同比分别增长26.6%和30%，樟江景区门票收入6518万元，比2012年净增733万元，旅游业对GDP的贡献率达到26%。县域内“一园两区”基础设施建设完成投资6315万元、产业项目投资1亿元，入驻园区内9家生产企业实现产值4亿元。重视煤矿安全生产工作，全县“六证”齐全的9家煤矿企业生产正常，全年原煤产销量完成70.2万吨，同比增长14%；海南中和集团万吨青梅酒厂动工建设，甲良有机肥厂投入生产，全县规模企业达25家；充分运用“3个15万元”政策激活小微企业，全县民营企业、个体工商户发展到428家4549户，注册资金达14.45亿元；全面启动民贸民品企业信贷优惠政策扶持工作，全县民贸民品企业达37家，优惠贷款额突破1亿元。深入实施“双十工程”，全县糖蔗总面积达3.36万亩、产量近10万吨，经果林面积9.5万亩，产值2.73亿元；粮食总产量达4.56万吨，全面完成“1122”生态畜牧业工程，农产品加工业产值达7357万元，农民专业合作经济组织达123个，规模养殖场达450个，州级以上龙头企业8家；列为全省100个高效农业示范园区的荔波樟江精品水果及休闲观光农业示范园区规划通过州级评审，并完成投资2.16亿元；组建贵州荔波生态农业投资有限公司，搭建了园区融资平台；建成农资配送中心1个、二级配送站3个、村级经营网点41个。加大科技投入，强化科技在各行业的支撑和引领作用。

2013年，促成生态文明贵阳国际论坛分论坛在荔波县举办，荔波遗产地保护与利用模式得到国内外专家的认可和推崇，催生了生态保护与利用新的《荔波共识》。成功争取扶贫生态移民省级政策配套试点，在4个乡（镇）实施扶贫生态移民工程811户3648人，荔波“搬得出、留得住、能致富、管得好”的做法得到国家发改委、财政部、国土资源部、住建部、国务院扶贫办等五部委高度评价，翁昂乡生态移民安置点经验在全省工作现场会上得到充分肯定。2013年，荔波县分别获国家有关部委和省有关部门命名为“国家重点生态功能区补偿县、国家生态旅游示范区、美丽中国十佳旅游县、省级生态保护红线试点县”，瑶山拉片村、水利村获得省级生态村称号。坚守加快发展与保护生态两条底线，积极实施生态保护、生态工程性修复、产业培育等工程，新增营造林面积7.48万亩，完成石漠化综合治理13.46平方公里，水土流失治理37.64平方公里，全县森林覆盖率同期上升1个百分点。

推进乡镇行政区划调整，现有17个乡（镇）拟调整为8个乡（镇、街道办事处）；县医药公司、外贸公司改制工作有序推进，县食品公司、县物资贸易公司和巴合煤矿改制全面完成；深化行政审批制度改革，县级行政许可审批事项由172项精减为70项，压缩59%；非行政许可审批事项由134项精减为58项，压缩56%；便民服务事项由51项精减为39项，压缩24%。组建荔波县公共资源交易中心，整合部门职能及资源，规范建设工程招投标、土地使用权出让、政府采购等交易行为，有效解决部门效能不高等问题。2013年，荔波县经济发展软环境位列全州前茅；用活有关“试点”政策，有效解决小城镇建设用地指标、项目资金不足等问题；出台《关于繁荣房地产持续健康发展的意见》，有效缓解有房无市、有房无价问题；探索区域合作共建“飞地”产业园区，着力突破环境敏感和开发限制等问题；优化以资源换资本招商引资方式，借助外力加快发展，促成中鸿控股集团、广东乐其集团、广西欧艺集团等企业投资开发荔波旅游资源，初步与中信产业基金投资公司等企业集团达成投资开发协议，拟在未来3～5年由企业投资近80亿元参与荔波旅游资源的开发。

2013年，“十件民生实事”完成既定目标，荔波三中、荔波二幼、民族体育活动中心全面启动建设；县人民医院异地建设实现局部进驻；县城中心福利院主体完工、茂兰敬老院完成室内外装修工程，佳荣敬老院、长宁山公墓开工建设；建成通村油路135公里；1566户农村危房改造，72套廉租房、527套公租房、222户棚户区改造全面完工；12个村级组织活动场所、1个乡镇计生服务站、5个村级服务室、6个村级体育健身工程、5个农民文化家园及10000户“户户通”工程全面完成；市民广场绿化、硬化景观工程有序推进。总投资5.89亿元的40个民生工程、民生项目如期完工；大力实施教育“9+3”计划，荔波一小建成投入使用。县中医院通过“二甲”评审；新农合参合率达98.45%，惠及27万人次，同比增加9万人次。“水韵樟江”“瑶之韵”民族文化会演实现常态化，乡镇文化展演圆满落幕。全面推进人口计生“双诚信、双承诺”工作，人口计生“双降”目标继续保持。有组织转移农村劳动力就地就近就业5432人，城镇新增就业2476人；利用“一事一议”财政奖补资金实施公益事业项目81个，村级公益事业“一事一议”连续三年获省级优秀县；健全和完善城乡低保标准稳定增长机制，累计发放低保金4651万元，救助金709万元，救助人数达3.9万人；佳荣镇和翁昂乡实现“减贫摘帽”，佳荣拉祥、玉屏时来、甲良益觉、瑶山菇类、拉片5个村整村推进全面完成，有效减少贫困人口1.35万人，小康实现程度达81.5%，荔波县被评为全省同步小康创建“资源环境示范县”，玉屏拉岜村被评为全省同步小康创建“30佳示范村”；县域内各民族的团结进步，民族经济、民族文化等均有大的发展变化，深入开展“多彩贵州文明行动”，年终考核跃居全省一类县第六名、全州第二名。

2013年，坚持重大信访案件政府领导包案和定期接访制度，建立健全突发事件应急反应机制，有效化解矛盾纠纷、积案，避免公共突发事件发生。坚持“严打与专项整治”不动摇，加强“天网工程”建设，完善社会治安防控体系，严厉打击各类违法犯罪，有效维护了社会和谐稳定。在2013年全省安全感满意度测评中，全县得分98.04分，排名全省第六位、全州第三位，公安机关满意度均排全省、全州第二位，铲毒禁毒工作获国家禁毒委表彰。

2014年

2014年，全县克服经济下行和百年难遇的洪涝灾害等不利影响，经济社会保持健康平稳持续发展，增比进位综合测评85.66分，位列全省10个国家扶贫开发工作重点县第一名。全年完成地区生产总值41.49亿元，增长15.5%；全社会固定资产投资66亿元，增长32%，其中，固定资产投资55.05亿元，增长31.26%；500万元以上规模工业增加值12.2亿元，增长19.1%；社会消费品零售总额8.81亿元，增长13.4%；财政总收入5.23亿元，增长25.27%，其中地方财政收入2.71亿元，增长29.61%；城镇居民人均可支配收入21057元，增长10.7%，农村居民人均可支配收入6916元，增长12.2%；金融机构存、贷款余额分别为43.16亿元、31.27亿元，增长12.56%、36.47%；三次产业比重为20.31：29.28：50.41；小康实现程度预计达91.6%。

推进省“5个100工程”、州“5个20重点项目”，全年实施159个新建项目、64个续建项目，完成投资67.89亿元；招商引资签约项目47个，签约资金190亿元，到位59.85亿元，增长11.9%；争取中央预算内投资项目49个，总投资4.01亿元；争取上级补助资金11.93亿元，增长19.86%。驾荔高速公路、省道206三洞至荔波公路改扩建工程、环大小七孔景区公路、佳荣至何家寨、佳荣至水维公路建成通车；省道312荔波至甲良和国道243朝阳至脚村坳改扩建工程、小七孔大道、玉朝大道加快推进；争取到三都至荔波高速公路、贵阳至南宁高铁过境荔波，并初步完成前期工作；建成通村油路110公里，目前全县93%的建制村实现通村油路。洪江、伍家河等13座水库完成除险加固，尧柳水库建设及樟江河流域罗家寨段、瑶山段、打狗河捞村段河道治理加速推进，大土水库即将开工，三荔水库、拉寨水库、拉毛水库前期工作顺利推进，弄力电站基本建成，冬修水利、小型农田水利重点县等水利基础设施项目及30个农村饮水安全项目全面建成，新增、改善灌溉面积2.76万亩，有效解决3.51万人的饮水安全。

坚持规划先行，加快城乡一体化进程。《荔波县城市总体规划实施评估报告》获省政府批准，调整后的乡（镇）总体规划全面启动，完成县城风貌设计方案编制。环城西路、环城南路、环城北路、樟江北桥、坡平大桥建成通车，环城东路、环城西路二期、县城北出口拓宽、樟江大桥拆旧建新、罗家寨大桥、民族路二期等项目积极推进。县城“五大”环境文化全面实施，市政燃气管道铺设完成13公里，时来110千伏变电站建设有序推进，军警营房、樟江部落大酒店建成投入使用。荔波大剧院、四季花园酒店、天泰酒店、嘉和国际大酒店进入装修阶段。县城一级客运站、县城南北停车场、汽车4S店、党校片区开发等项目全面启动，旧城改造加快建设。荔波古镇、嘉和中央城二期、翰林苑等16个房开项目完成投资10.06亿元，房地产销售面积达20.37万平方米，吸引了全国24个省（市、区）和省内33个县（市）业主到荔波购房置业。“两违”现象得到有效遏制，甲良、瑶山、黎明关等小城镇示范建设成效显著。县城建成区面积扩大到7.8平方公里，城区人口达4.8万人，城镇化率预计达45.65%。

打造荔波旅游升级版，加快景区扩容，16个文化旅游升级版项目、旅游“十大工程”“五大项目”按时间节点完成既定目标。樟江景区观光栈道、休息亭廊、候车停靠站点等基础设施持续完善，小七孔景区实现封闭管理，景区精细化管理水平不断提高，容量大幅提升，争创国家AAAAA级旅游景区工作取得阶段性成果。瑶山景区、茂兰景区加快建设，成功打造全省首个生态汽车露营基地，甲良思凡谷、兰鼎山森林公园等10个新景区（点）开发有序推进，乡村旅游蓬勃发展。加强与旅行社合作，促成贵州省精品景区联盟，实现区域联动营销市场化，代表贵州参加中国国际服务贸易交易会。举办第九届梅花节和首届中国荔波蜜柚文化节，开通荔波至贵阳、荔波至重庆航线，全年起降航班1084架（次），乘客吞吐量46682人，分别增长225%、164%。全年累计接待游客636万人次，增长24.2%，樟江景区接待人数首次突破100万人大关，实现门票收入7147万元，增长9.66%，旅游综合收入达56.88亿元，增长27.1%。

工业方面推进“百千万”工程，有效刺激工业经济新增长。开展煤矿采掘机械化试点建设，全年实现原煤产销量55万吨。“一园两区”基础设施完成投资1亿元，产业项目完成投资1.2亿元，入驻园区10家企业实现产值8.58亿元；播尧返乡农民工创业园建成标准化厂房13000平方米，已入驻企业7家，意向落户18家。荔波水泥厂60万吨水泥粉磨站技改项目按期完成，茂兰甲醇汽油调配站、茂兰万吨青梅酒厂、甲良有机肥厂二期项目建设积极推进，茂兰绿宝石缫丝厂投入运营，霖华、隆鑫商混产销量达16万立方米，增长44%。充分发挥“3个15万元”和民贸民品等政策作用，实现新增微企120户、民贸民品企业40家，享受优惠利率贷款1.62亿元，个体工商户和民营企业分别发展到7402户、750家，注册资金达33.44亿元，全县规模企业23家。

优化农业产业结构，强化科技支撑作用，粮经作物实现双增，粮食种植面积达18.12万亩，总产量达4.74万吨，增长3.78%，经果林种植面积达10.51万亩，实现产值5.18亿元，新增土地流转面积15.6万亩。樟江农业示范园区基础设施建设完成投资4.8亿元，农耕文化园、十里花海农业休闲观光项目顺利推进，蜜柚、枇杷、血桃等主导产业种植规模达8.3万亩，园区内农民人均可支配收入达11350元。完成畜牧“3个6工程”建设，全县规模养殖场达450个，肉类产品产量达1.45万吨。培育农业产业化经营企业28个、专业大户198户，农民专业合作组织158个，县级以上龙头企业累计达30个。着力“三品一标”创建，“荔波蜜柚”获国家地理标志证明商标，全县通过“三品一标”认证的农特产品达9个，探索推出全省首个县级淘宝荔波馆，实现旅游农特产品网上购销；建成县级农资配送中心1个，二级配送站8个，村级经营网点50个。

2014年荔波纳入《左右江革命老区振兴发展规划》《贵州南部生态补偿示范区建设规划》《贵州省创建全国生态文明先行区规划》《建设黔南生态文明示范州规划》《黔南州生态保护与建设示范区建设方案》等规划。完成营造林面积7.2万亩，石漠化综合治理14.07平方公里，水土流失治理37.64平方公里，全县森林覆盖率达62.05%；成功申报黄江河国家级湿地公园。严厉查处生态环境破坏违法违规行为，加强饮用水源地常态监管，水质达标率100%；狠抓节能减排，朝阳和甲良污水处理厂建成并投入运行；建成空气质量自动监测站和机动车尾气检测站，加强对工地扬尘、餐饮油烟、机动车尾气排放等进行整治，县城环境空气优良率达100%。整合扶贫生态移民、一事一议等项目资金，实施黎明关、小七孔、瑶山等乡（镇）928户3694人生态移民搬迁，荔波生态移民“六动模式”和“八步工作法”成为全国推广样板。

以改革增动力促发展，向改革要红利惠民生，完成全县27个专题组66项改革；县直部门机构改革和乡镇行政区划调整顺利完成，推进实施“区镇合一”“镇园合一”，政府职能进一步转变；探索财税金融体制改革，先后成立荔波县国有担保公司和水利、交通、城建投资等7家融资平台公司，化解融资难题，启动“营改增”试点，完成56户“营改增”申报工作；深化行政审批制度改革，率先在全省推行企业登记“三证一章”制度。创新开展《电视问政》，打造“公众参与、媒体监督、干群互动”的问政平台；率先在全州出台《荔波县投资准入特别管理措施（负面清单）》，做到“非禁即允”；探索农村集体土地改革试点，推广运用“三权抵押”“统筹城乡试点”“集体产权房”等改革成果。

县委、县政府扎实做好民生实事，基本完成“十件实事”，有效应对“6・4”特大洪灾，妥善处置H5N1亚型高致病性禽流感疫情。实施教育卫生“双百工程”，推进“双轨并行，两单并举，立体教育全覆盖”教育改革，荔波“小县办大教育”模式得到省、州肯定。完成县医院及乡镇卫生院周转房建设180套，新农合参合率达97.63%，惠及34.52万人次，全县医疗保障能力得到较大提升。完成县民族体育活动中心主体工程及5个乡镇、10个村级农民体育健身场所和2794套“村村通”建设。全面完成2330户农村危房改造，84套廉租房、1178套公租房、317套棚户区改造，118栋小康房建设；茂兰敬老院投入使用，荔波县社会中心福利院及佳荣、播尧、小七孔敬老院项目有序推进。全县基本社会保险参保人数达13.88万人，基本养老保险、基本医疗保险综合覆盖率达86.2%，城镇新增就业2596人，城镇登记失业率为3%；累计发放城乡低保金4068.49万元、救灾救济款（物）858.82万元、医疗救助金764.98万元。推进精准扶贫工作，完成10个村整村推进，原水利乡、瑶山乡实现“减贫摘帽”，有效减少贫困人口1.35万人，贫困发生率下降到23.09%。整合资金2亿元实施“四在农家・美丽乡村”15个村寨建设，加快推进“六大工程”“七小工程”及2个示范乡（镇、街道）21个示范村小康创建工作，实施“一事一议”公益事业项目123个，完成投资4361万元，惠及群众5万余人。

严打与专项整治相结合，有效维护社会和谐稳定，荔波“十无村社”治理模式列入“2014中国十大社会治理创新”。完善“天网工程”和城市报警系统建设，提高公共场所巡防覆盖面和见警率，配齐“一村一警务助理”，强化防控力度和密度，健全社会治安防控体系，严厉打击各类违法犯罪活动，刑事案件发案率全州最低，2014年群众安全感测评位列全省第七位、全州第二位；巩固禁毒工作成果，非法种植毒品连续三年实现“零种植”目标。

2015年

2015年，全县生产总值达45.3亿元，是2010年的2.56倍；规模以上工业增加值达13.01亿元，是2010年的3.37倍；固定资产投资达68.37亿元，是2010年的4.05倍；社会消费品零售总额达9.88亿元，是2010年的2.07倍；财政总收入达5.55亿元，是2010年的1.99倍；金融机构存贷款余额分别达53.26亿元、35.99亿元，是2010年的2.77倍、3.91倍。自2014年以来，连续两年在全省10个国家扶贫开发工作重点县增比进位综合测评中排名第一位。

在扩（投）资强基础方面。全年实施项目307个，完成投资68.37亿元，增长24.21%。招商引资签约项目111个，签约资金226.55亿元，到位资金86.2亿元，增长44.03%。驾荔高速、小七孔大道、环景区公路、国道243朝阳至脚村坳、省道312石灰坳至甲良等公路建成通车，贵南高铁客运专线前期工作有序推进，交通领域完成投资14.95亿元。尧柳水库、大土水库、平林电站加快建设，三荔、拉寨水库前期工作有序推进，水利建设完成投资2.7亿元。全面完成环城路、老城区道路“白改黑”、樟江大桥、坡平大桥等项目建设，县城游客信息中心、大剧院、红船广场投入使用，樟江沿河景观打造、梦柳布依风情小寨和力书、巴平移民搬迁等工程有序推进，中央城等15个房开项目完成投资10.02亿元，销售面积达20.84万平方米，城镇项目完成投资22.16亿元。

加快农业结构调整，新增省级农业示范园区2个，园区总产值达27.81亿元。坚持稳粮扩经，经果林、茶叶、桑园分别新增0.5万亩、0.55万亩、0.12万亩，农业增加值完成8.48亿元。驾播、瑶庆、小七孔返乡创业园等园区进驻企业15家，产值达11.1亿元。全县9家“六证”齐全煤矿完成产销量37.56万吨。扶持微型企业400户，民营企业、个体工商户分别达1242家、8393户。规模企业达19家，规模工业增加值完成13.01亿元，增长12.7%。成功承办黔南州第七届旅游产业发展大会等12个大型旅游文化系列活动。先后推出水葩、赛娥、四季花海、甲乙汽车露营基地、甲良思凡谷等一批特色旅游精品景点。月亮湖湿地公园、三叠纪动漫主题乐园等项目开工建设，精心策划《跟着贝尔去冒险》节目在荔波县取景拍摄并在全国热播。成功加入中国世界遗产旅游推广联盟，积极组团赴韩国和港澳台、珠三角、长三角、京津冀、成渝等地进行宣传推介，旅游市场呈现井喷态势。

围绕全域旅游战略部署，启动实施“绿色荔波”建设三年行动计划，“六大工程”建设取得明显成效。成功举办第三届“水生态文明·黔南（荔波）论坛”。完成营造林7.42万亩，饮用水源地水质达标率和空气优良率均达100%。

深化旅游综合改革，组建旅游发展委员会，争取获得茂兰自然保护区旅游规划和开发权，有序推进旅游“三权”分离改革。率先在全省开展旅游景区明码实价试点，着力打造全国无价格欺诈旅游县。成功组建樟江实业有限责任公司，稳步推进投融资体制改革。建立政府与社会资本合作（PPP）项目库，设立（PPP）项目财政支出基金，累计融资到位7.91亿元。加快农村土地承包经营权确权登记颁证试点工作，启动实施公立医院、公务用车改革，有序推进教育、户籍、养老等社会事业改革。

促增收惠民生方面。城镇、农村居民人均可支配收入分别达23247元、7670元，分别增长10.4%、10.9%。教育、科技、卫计、文体等社会事业加快发展。启动实施“1+9”扶贫攻坚行动计划和月亮山三年扶贫决战行动，完成扶贫生态移民搬迁任务，全面实施农村环境综合整治工程，完成改圈8978个、改厕11404座。城乡社会保障、社会救助基本实现应保尽保、应助尽助。消防安全形势持续稳定，安全生产事故起数和死亡人数继续保持“双降”目标。

2015年完成“十件实事”情况：一是启动实施《樟江河流域综合治理三年行动计划》，樟江两岸江滨景观及主题公园打造项目完成投资1500万元，县城污水处理厂投入试运营，小七孔污水处理厂基本建成，大七孔污水处理厂开工建设。二是全县减贫人口1.15万人，14个贫困村出列，基本消除村级集体经济“空壳村”。三是完成保障性住房建设2520套、农村危房改造3118户、小康房118户。四是建成通村油（水泥）路265公里，94%的建制村通客运车辆。五是农产品物流中心因规划调整正在重新选址，南、北出口停车场完成场地平整，4个县级旅游星级公厕完成选址并启动建设。六是县域义务教育均衡发展通过国家级验收，基本普及十五年教育通过省级验收，一幼完成建设，三幼投入使用。七是启动烈士陵园规划设计工作，县城规划区内殡葬改革实现“三位一体”工作目标，火化场馆、长宁山公墓建成投入使用。八是完成邓恩铭故居（水甫）重建及修缮工作。九是全面完成城乡低保减量提标工作，城市低保标准由每人每月345元提高到每人每月440元，农村低保标准由每人每年1960元提高到每人每年2580元，全县基本社会养老保险、基本医疗保险综合参保覆盖率分别达85.83%、95.71%。十是组建城西社区、城北社区、水葩、拉欧、联山、板麦6个农民文艺队，完成水葩、赛娥民族示范村寨打造。

2010—2015年，荔波县成功申报贵南高铁客运专线过境荔波；三荔高速开工在即；机场改扩建工程有序推进；争取到省政府将荔波县创建全域旅游示范县；列入国家主体功能区建设试点示范县、国家生态示范县、国家生态旅游示范区、中国世界遗产旅游推广联盟、全省扶贫攻坚示范县、贵州省服务业聚集区；全县全域旅游模式获选2015年民生示范工程；荣登中国旅游风云榜；荣获全国首批民生改善十佳典范城市、全国首批创建生态文明典范城市、全国平安农机示范县、全国“六五”普法中期先进县、全国禁种铲毒优秀单位、国家重点生态功能区县域生态环境质量变好县、中欧绿色和智慧城市创新奖、中国最具投资潜力的旅游目的地奖、中国森林氧吧、中国最美休闲小城、中国最美丽县、省级小康寨行动计划重点示范县、全省信访工作“三无县”、贵州十大旅游微博奖等荣誉；获全国文明村1个、全省文明单位4个、全省文明街道1个、全省文明村1个、全省生态乡镇1个和全省生态村4个；尧古、太吉、董蒙、水甫、石磊等村寨列入中国传统村落保护名录，拉片村被命名为首批中国少数民族特色村寨。

机构名称、专业词汇全称与简称对照表

（按志中出现的先后排列）

全 称	简 称
中国共产党荔波县委员会	县委
常务委员会	常委
荔波县人民政府	县政府
中国工农红军	红军
爱国卫生运动委员会	爱卫会
科学技术	科技
县革命委员会	县革委
申报世界自然遗产地	申遗
贵州茂兰国家级自然保护区管理处（局）	茂兰管理处（局）
荔波樟江风景名胜区管理处	樟江管理处
荔波世界自然遗产管理办公室	遗产办
计划生育	计生
计划生育委员会（局）	计生委（局）
民族宗教事务局	民宗局
远程教育办公室	远教办
经济开发促进会	经促会
关心下一代工作委员会	关工委
关心下一代协会	关协
人民代表大会	人代会
人民代表大会常务委员会	人大常委会
中国人民政治协商会议荔波县委员会	县政协
精神文明建设委员会办公室	文明办
智力支编联系小组办公室	支边办
中国共产主义青年团荔波县委员会	团县委
少儿工作委员会	少工委
妇女联合会	妇联
妇女代表大会	妇代会
工商业联合会	工商联
非公有制经济	非公经济

续表

全 称	简 称
科协技术协会	科协
少年先锋队	少先队
文学艺术界联合会	文联
非典型性肺炎	非典
残疾人联合会	残联
个体劳动者协会	个协
严厉打击刑事犯罪分子	严打
交通警察	交警
人民检察院	检察院
人民法院	法院
法律法规普及	普法
人民武装委员会	武委会
人民武装部	人武部
农业机械	农机
安全生产监督管理局	安监局
经济贸易委员会（局）	经贸委（局）
民族贸易公司	民贸公司
供销合作社	供销社
工商行政管理局	工商局
食品药品监督管理局	食药监局
安全生产委员会	安委会
安全生产监督管理局	安监局
内部审计	内审
国有资本营运有限责任公司	资本营运公司
国家税务局	国税局
地方税务局	地税局
中国人民银行	人行
中国建设银行	建行
中国农业银行	农行
中国工商银行	工行
邮政储蓄银行	邮储行
中国银行业监督管理委员会	银监会

续表

全　称	简　称
农村信用合作社	信用社
中国人寿保险	寿险
中国人民财产保险	财保
房屋改革领导小组办公室	房改办
环境保护局	环保局
城乡建设局	城建局
乙型肝炎	乙肝
疾病预防控制	疾控
妇女儿童保健	妇幼保健
少年体育运动学校	少体校
村（居）民委员会	村（居）委会
最低生活保障	低保
建镇并乡撤区	建并撤

P

Q

R

S

T

W

X

Y

Z

非音序

编纂始末

《荔波县志（1978—2008）》，共23篇89章360节，近160万字，较为全面地记述了区域内政治、经济、文化和各项社会事业的发展历史与现状，充分展示荔波改革开放30年取得的辉煌成就，着意突出人文、生态、旅游、煤炭等得天独厚的资源禀赋。编修工作历时七载有余，历经召开推动大会、资料征集补充、编纂审校把关、聘请专家锤炼等过程。

召开推动大会 自2002年全省二轮修志工作部署后，我县于2004年7月召开了动员培训大会，由于种种原因工作停滞不前，县志续修启而未动。2009年7月8日，县委、县政府召开了第二部《荔波县志》工作推动会，会上印发《荔波县志（1978—2008）编修方案》组织学习，向与会部门乡镇赠送第一部《荔波县志》《荔波县情》《荔波革命老区史料汇编》等相关资料供参考借鉴，并进行了资料收集、断限分篇、体例规范、内容甄选等业务培训，帮助和指导乡镇、县直部门撰写志稿资料。会后，县委、县政府组成四个督查组，分别由县四家班子分管领导带队进行了为期一周的专项督查，并以《荔波督查》形式通报贯彻落实推动会情况：各乡镇、各部门成立编纂领导机构，落实资料员和执笔人，标志着二轮县志续修工作全面启动。县委、县政府始终十分关心关注县志续修工作，根据工作进展和需要调整领导班子，及时充实编纂人员，并给予人力、物力、财力强有力的保障。

资料征集补充 俗话说“巧妇难为无米之炊”，资料是修志的基础，是志书的生命。资料征集更是一项艰辛烦琐的工作，是续修县志的关键环节，资料的优劣决定志稿质量的高低。在二轮修志工作中，把资料征集补充工作贯穿始终。推动大会后，县志资料征集工作如火如荼，为乘势而上，2010年5月，县委、县政府专门组织承编单位领导及业务人员在玉屏镇召开现场会，学习《玉屏镇志》编修经验，激励先进、鞭策后进，促使资料征集工作的整体推进。推进会确定资料上交截止时间为2010年年底，但如期上交资料的单位和部门仅为70%，且资料参差不齐，合乎要求的不足半数。针对这一情况，2011年5月，县委、县政府组织了第二次专项督查，对未交资料或资料质量不合格的乡镇和县部门的分管领导、资料员和执笔人进行座谈并给予严厉批评，责令限时完成资料上交任务。其间，业务部门两次邀请州史志办陆兴和、陆春凡、王素琴、白映泉等领导、专家对未完成资料上交任务的部门和乡镇分管领导及执笔人作面对面的业务指导，复印省内已经出版的二轮志书相关章节作为参照范本，从技术层面给予指导帮助。在完成总纂后，由于部分单位和乡镇提供的资料横分纵述不到位，再次发回原单位进行资料补充。州级复审认为，仍有20多个县部门资料不够翔实，存在有因无果、有果无因或资料断限的情况，县委、县政府采取组织手段进行集体约谈，要求一把手亲自过问，执笔人员和资料员再次查阅档案限时保质完成资料补充任务。省级终审后，按照终审组领导和专家提出的把《荔波县志》打造成为贵州一流的、面向世界的精品佳志目标要求，确定旅游和遗产地申报章节内容延至出版前，增加“两瑶”扶贫和红茂矿务局进驻荔波开采煤矿资源章节，为此，分别召开了旅游、遗产地、扶贫、煤炭四个专题座谈会，邀请县内部分老领导和参与上述工作的有关同志60余人参加座谈共同商议，出谋献策，收集补充文字或口述资料，会后组织人员分赴广西环江和省、州相关部门征集补充专篇内容。为弥补下限至出版前全县社会综合发展情况，收集增加了2009年至2015年经济社会发展资料作为附录材料之一。直到出版前，志稿资料补充和完善工作仍在持续进行。

编纂审校把关 在编纂过程中采取资料征集和资料长篇并驾齐驱方式，一边对上交资料审查把关进行筛选，同时按篇章分解到编辑部人员，各司其职各负其责，根据资料征集进展完成资料长篇进度，定期召开会议通报存在的问题，集体研究解决方案；组织交叉审稿，发现问题及时消化处理。完成初稿后，编辑部门制作“总纂志稿审阅进度表”“第二部《荔波县志》自审进度表”“资料补充跟踪问效表”“《荔波县志》构成要件查缺补漏表”等表册，将任务分解落实到人，定量、定责、定质、定时完成审稿任务，进一步审校完善志稿。州级复审前，县政府聘请了李德余、黄玉成、冉孟华、姚锦超、程志安、蒙熙林、陈建军、黄吉林、徐明镃、廖其章、江兴龙11位阅历丰富、熟悉县情、热心修志工作的老领导、老同志为特约编审，定期碰头讨论听取意见，对《荔波县志》进行通审把关，特别对人名、地名、领导任职时间、事件经过、发展结果等史实确认核实，根据特约编审的意见修改之后，用半年时间，每周组织编纂人员进行阅读审稿，按志稿顺序逐篇、逐章、逐节通读，发现内容缺失断限、表述不到位、逻辑关系矛盾等问题，当场及时集体纠正，对志稿作全身“体检”，直至2015年11月3日顺利通过省级终审。

聘请专家锤炼 复审后，聘请州地方志办专家王素琴进行二次总纂，按照复审意见逐条逐款落实，同时继续征集资料作补充完善。在省级终审会上，省地方志办公室领导专家归然、钟莉、周声浩、车秀琴等对志稿又提出了修改意见和建议。终审后，聘请省修志专家周声浩和伍启林为《荔波县志》编修顾问，将县志作深度策划，对框架结构及部分内容进行梳理、调整、雕琢，强化一些薄弱环节，全面提升志稿质量。2015年12月，中国地方志指导小组常务副组长李培林莅临荔波调研考察，对荔波修志工作予以悉心指导；《荔波县志》成功申报获西部经济欠发达地区志书出版资助项目，得到中国地方志指导小组和方志出版社为其按照国家标准进行质量把关。志书的质量和影响力大幅提升。2016年10月中国社会科学院院长、中国地方志指导小组组长王伟光为本志作序。中国地方志指导小组办公室主任冀祥德对本志评价说：“《荔波县志（1978—2008）》体统记载了荔波县的社会发展状况，客观反映了1978年以来荔波县的政治、经济、文化、教育科技等方面的发展情况，具有浓厚的地方特色和重要的历史价值。本志指导思想正确，结构体例完备，记述方法得当，对社会各界人士认识和研究荔波县20世纪90年代至今的社会生活的发展提供了较翔实的资料，具有较高的出版价值。”国家方志馆馆藏部主任、方志出版社常务副社长于伟平对本志评价说：“该志资料翔实，体例完备，记述完整，内容丰富，坚持实事求是，客观真实反映出该地自然、政治、经济、文化、社会的全貌。此书稿具有出版价值。”

凸显资源禀赋 首先是突出“人杰”，该志收录了韦汉超、蒙九龄、赵尔和、杜介厘、潘文兴、艾福田等人物传记，增加了张聚国、姚福孔、姚建儒、韦国仁、蒙明儒、欧海金、潘老平、蒋荣生、蒙熙能、罗世槐、龙贵雄、冉景丞等人物简介；补录了明朝至民国时期荔波县历任知县（知事、县事）、县长名录；收集插入珍贵红军图片及精美随文图片。再就是凸显“地灵”，翔实记述了世界自然遗产地申报保护、旅游业繁荣发展以及曾是荔波经济支柱的煤炭业的兴衰历程，设“革命老区县——荔波”为特记，展示荔波厚重的红色文化，“两瑶”扶贫工作专记为精准脱贫同步小康积累了宝贵经验。该志突出体现了“人杰地灵”“物产丰富”的地域特色。

县志续修工作是一项繁杂而庞大的文化系统工程，时间跨度长、内容涉及面广、知识领域宽，仅仅依靠地方志编纂委员会办公室是不可能完成的，还得力于中国社会科学院、中国地方志指导小组、方志出版社及省、州地方志编纂委员会办公室领导、专家的精心指导，县委、县政府的高度重视，各乡镇（办事处）及县直工作部门的大力支持。在此，谨向所有关心、支持、帮助《荔波县志（1978—2008）》编纂工作的领导、专家、同仁及社会各界人士表示衷心感谢，对为本志提供资料和图片的单位和个人表示诚挚谢意，同时，对所收集到的资料和图片部分未知作者而不能一一署名而未具名，深表歉意，恳请谅解。虽然我们已尽心竭力，精益求精，但由于本志时间纵跨30年，史料征集困难，有的资料断限缺项；加之编者水平有限，难免会存在错误和不当之处，敬请各位领导、专家及读者批评指正。

编　者

2016年5月3日

出版说明

根据国务院办公厅颁发的《全国地方志事业发展规划纲要（2015—2020 年）》规定，到 2020 年必须全面完成第二轮地方志书规划任务。为确保这一目标顺利实现，针对当前部分民族地区与贫困地区志书出版经费困难的情况，在中国地方志指导小组组长王伟光、常务副组长李培林的亲自倡议和领导下，自 2015 年 8 月起中国地方志指导小组办公室启动民族地区与贫困地区志书出版资助工程，对经国务院扶贫开发领导小组办公室认定的国家级贫困县（区、旗、县级市），中西部地区、少数民族边疆地区、经济欠发达地区存在出版经费困难的省市县三级综合志书进行出版资助。

民族地区与贫困地区志书出版资助工程既是地方志系统的政治工程，又是全国地方志事业协调发展的促进工程，对于推进第二轮地方志书规划任务按期完成，实现地方志事业区域发展平衡，促进民族地区与贫困地区基础文化建设，具有重要的政治意义和文化意义。2016 年 4 月，该工程入选国家新闻出版广电总局实施的“十三五”国家重点图书、音像、电子出版物出版规划项目。

本书经民族地区与贫困地区志书出版资助工程领导小组批准，入选民族地区与贫困地区志书出版资助工程。

民族地区与贫困地区志书出版

资助工程领导小组办公室

2015 年 9 月